EQ

EQ

Encyclopaedia of the Qurʾān

VOLUME TWO

E–I

Jane Dammen McAuliffe, *General Editor*

Brill, Leiden–Boston

2002

ISBN 90 04 12035 1

Printed in The Netherlands on acid-free paper.

ABBREVIATIONS

AI = *Annales islamologiques*
AIUON = *Annali dell' Istituto Universitario Orientale di Napoli*
AO = *Acta orientalia*
AO-H = *Acta orientalia (Academiae Scientiarum Hungaricae)*
Arabica = *Arabica. Revue d'études arabes*
ARW = *Archiv für Religionswissenschaft*
AUU = *Acta Universitatis Upsaliensis*
BASOR = *Bulletin of the American Schools of Oriental Research*
BEO = *Bulletin d'études orientales de l'Institut Français de Damas*
BGA = *Bibliotheca geographorum arabicorum*
BIFAO = *Bulletin de l'Institut Français d'Archéologie Orientale du Caire*
BO = *Bibliotheca orientalis*
BSA = *Budapest studies in Arabic*
BSOAS = *Bulletin of the School of Oriental and African Studies*
Der Islam = *Der Islam. Zeitschrift für Geschichte und Kultur des islamischen Orients*
EI[1] = *Encyclopaedia of Islam*, 1st ed., Leiden 1913-38
EI[2] = *Encyclopaedia of Islam*, new ed., Leiden 1954-
ER = *Encyclopedia of religion*, ed. M. Eliade, New York 1986
ERE = *Encyclopaedia of religions and ethics*
GMS = *Gibb memorial series*
HO = *Handbuch der Orientalistik*
IA = *Islâm ansiklopedisi*
IBLA = *Revue de l'Institut des Belles Lettres Arabes, Tunis*
IC = *Islamic culture*
IJMES = *International journal of Middle East studies*
IOS = *Israel oriental studies*
IQ = *The Islamic quarterly*
Iran = *Iran. Journal of the British Institute of Persian Studies*
JA = *Journal asiatique*
JAL = *Journal of Arabic literature*
JAOS = *Journal of the American Oriental Society*
JE = *Jewish encyclopaedia*
JESHO = *Journal of the economic and social history of the Orient*
JIS = *Journal of Islamic studies*
JNES = *Journal of Near Eastern studies*
JRAS = *Journal of the Royal Asiatic Society*
JSAI = *Jerusalem studies in Arabic and Islam*
JSS = *Journal of Semitic studies*
MFOB = *Mélanges de la Faculté Orientale de l'Université St. Joseph de Beyrouth*
MIDEO = *Mélanges de l'Institut Dominicain d'études orientales du Caire*
MO = *Le monde oriental*
MSOS = *Mitteilungen des Seminars für orientalische Sprachen, westasiatische Studien*
Muséon = *Le Muséon. Revue des études orientales*
MW = *The Muslim world*
OC = *Oriens christianus*

OLZ = *Orientalistische Literaturzeitung*
Orientalia = *Orientalia. Commentarii periodici Pontificii Instituti Biblici*
Qanṭara = *al-Qanṭara. Revista de estudios arabes*
QSA = *Quaderni de studi arabi*
RCEA = *Répertoire chronologique d'épigraphie arabe*
REI = *Revue des études islamiques*
REJ = *Revue des études juives*
REMMM = *Revue du monde musulman et de la Méditerranée*
RHR = *Revue de l'histoire des religions*
RIMA = *Revue de l'Institut des Manuscrits Arabes*
RMM = *Revue du monde musulman*
RO = *Rocznik Orientalistyczny*
ROC = *Revue de l'orient chrétien*
RSO = *Rivista degli studi orientali*
SIr = *Studia iranica*
SI = *Studia islamica*
WI = *Die Welt des Islams*
WKAS = *Wörterbuch der klassischen arabischen Sprache*
WO = *Welt des Orients*
WZKM = *Wiener Zeitschrift für die Kunde des Morgenlandes*
ZAL = *Zeitschrift für arabische Linguistik*
ZDMG = *Zeitschrift der Deutschen Morgenländischen Gesellschaft*
ZGAIW = *Zeitschrift für Geschichte der arabisch-islamischen Wissenschaften*
ZS = *Zeitschrift für Semitistik*

AUTHORS OF ARTICLES

VOLUME II

Ibrahim M. Abu-Rabiʿ, Hartford Seminary
Nasr Hamid Abu Zayd, University of Leiden
Camilla P. Adang, Tel-Aviv University
Asma Afsaruddin, University of Notre Dame
Scott C. Alexander, Catholic Theological Union, Chicago
Mohammad Ali Amir-Moezzi, École Pratique des Hautes Études, Paris
Mohammed Arkoun, Sorbonne University
Ali S.A. Asani, Harvard University
Margot Badran, Georgetown University
Meir M. Bar-Asher, Hebrew University, Jerusalem
Shahzad Bashir, Carleton College
Thomas Bauer, University of Münster
Doris Behrens-Abouseif, University of London
Donna Lee Bowen, Brigham Young University
Gerhard Böwering, Yale University
William M. Brinner, University of California, Berkeley
Amila Buturovic, York University, Canada
Juan Eduardo Campo, University of California, Santa Barbara
Paul M. Cobb, University of Notre Dame
Frederick Mathewson Denny, University of Colorado, Boulder
Herbert Eisenstein, University of Vienna
Nadia Maria El Cheikh, American University of Beirut
Jamal Elias, Amherst College
Yoram Erder, Tel-Aviv University
Toufic Fahd, University of Strasbourg
Rizwi Faizer, Independent Scholar
Muhammad al-Faruque, Stanford University
Reuven Firestone, Hebrew Union College, Los Angeles
Dmitry V. Frolov, Moscow University
Patrick D. Gaffney, University of Notre Dame
Geert Jan H. van Gelder, University of Oxford
Avner Giladi, University of Haifa
Claude Gilliot, University of Aix-en-Provence
Alan Godlas, University of Georgia
William A. Graham, Harvard University
Sidney H. Griffith, The Catholic University of America
Sebastian Günther, University of Toronto
Li Guo, University of Notre Dame
Rosalind W. Gwynne, University of Tennessee
Wael B. Hallaq, McGill University
Timothy P. Harrison, University of Toronto
Isaac Hasson, Hebrew University, Jerusalem

Gerald R. Hawting, University of London
Valerie J. Hoffman, University of Illinois
Robert Hoyland, University of Oxford
Johannes J.G. Jansen, University of Leiden
Maher Jarrar, American University of Beirut
Anthony Hearle Johns, Australian National University
Gautier H.A. Juynboll, Leiden
Ahmet T. Karamustafa, Washington University, St. Louis
Enes Karic, Sarajevo University
Navid Kermani, Wissenschaftskolleg zu Berlin
Ruqayya Khan, University of California, Santa Barbara
Leah Kinberg, Tel-Aviv University
Frederik Leemhuis, University of Groningen
Keith Lewinstein, Smith College
James E. Lindsay, Colorado State University
Louise Marlow, Wellesley College
Richard C. Martin, Emory University
Ulrich Marzolph, Enzyklopädie des Märchens, Göttingen
Ingrid Mattson, Hartford Seminary
Jane Dammen McAuliffe, Georgetown University
Sheila McDonough, Concordia University, Montreal
Mustansir Mir, Youngstown State University
John A. Nawas, Catholic University, Leuven
Angelika Neuwirth, Free University of Berlin
Gordon Darnell Newby, Emory University
Daniel C. Peterson, Brigham Young University
Venetia Porter, The British Museum
David Stephan Powers, Cornell University
A. Kevin Reinhart, Dartmouth College
Andrew Rippin, University of Victoria
Franz Rosenthal, Yale University
Everett K. Rowson, University of Pennsylvania
Uri Rubin, Tel-Aviv University
Abdullah Saeed, University of Melbourne
Daniel J. Sahas, University of Waterloo
Lamin Sanneh, Yale University
Irene Schneider, Martin Luther University, Halle-Wittenberg
Hannelore Schönig, Martin Luther University, Halle-Wittenberg
William E. Shepard, University of Canterbury, New Zealand
Mona Siddiqui, Glasgow University
Jane I. Smith, Hartford Seminary
Devin J. Stewart, Emory University
Rafael Talmon, University of Haifa
Heidi Toelle, Sorbonne University
Roberto Tottoli, University of Turin
Kees Wagtendonk, University of Amsterdam (emeritus)
David Waines, Lancaster University
Paul E. Walker, University of Chicago
Earle H. Waugh, University of Alberta
Gisela Webb, Seton Hall University
Brannon M. Wheeler, University of Washington
Rotraud Wielandt, University of Bamberg
Timothy Winter, University of Cambridge
Robert Wisnovsky, Harvard University
Imtiyaz Yusuf, Assumption University, Bangkok, Thailand
A.H. Mathias Zahniser, Asbury Theological Seminary

SHORT TITLES

Abbott, *Studies II*
N. Abbott, *Studies in Arabic literary papyri. II. Qurʾānic commentary and tradition,* Chicago 1967

ʿAbd al-Bāqī
Muḥammad Fuʾād ʿAbd al-Bāqī, *al-Muʿjam al-mufahras li-alfāẓ al-Qurʾān al-karīm,* Cairo 1945

ʿAbd al-Jabbār, *Mutashābih*
ʿAbd al-Jabbār b. Aḥmad al-Asadābādī al-Qāḍī al-Hamadhānī, *Mutashābih al-Qurʾān,* ed. ʿAdnān M. Zarzūr, 2 vols., Cairo 1969

ʿAbd al-Jabbār, *Tanzīh*
ʿAbd al-Jabbār b. Aḥmad al-Asadābādī al-Qāḍī al-Hamadhānī, *Tanzīh al-Qurʾān ʿan al-maṭāʿin,* Beirut 1966

ʿAbd al-Raḥmān, *Tafsīr*
ʿĀʾisha ʿAbd al-Raḥmān, *al-Tafsīr al-bayānī lil-Qurʾān al-karīm,* 3rd ed., Cairo 1968

ʿAbd al-Raḥmān, *ʿAṣrī*
ʿĀʾisha ʿAbd al-Raḥmān, *al-Qurʾān wa-l-tafsīr al-ʿaṣrī,* Cairo 1970

ʿAbd al-Razzāq, *Muṣannaf*
ʿAbd al-Razzāq b. Hammām al-Ṣanʿānī, *al-Muṣannaf,* ed. Ḥabīb al-Raḥmān al-Aʿẓamī, 11 vols., Beirut 1390/1970; 2nd ed. Johannesburg 1983; ed. Muḥammad Sālim Samāra, 4 vols. (with indices of ḥadīth), Beirut 1408/1988

ʿAbd al-Razzāq, *Tafsīr*
ʿAbd al-Razzāq b. Hammām al-Ṣanʿānī, *al-Tafsīr,* ed. Muṣṭafā Muslim Muḥammad, 3 vols. in 4, Riyadh 1410/1989; ed. ʿAbd al-Muʿṭī Amīn Qalʿajī, 2 vols., Beirut 1411/1991; ed. Maḥmūd Muḥammad ʿAbduh, 3 vols., Beirut 1419/1999.

Abū Dāwūd
Abū Dāwūd Sulaymān b. al-Ashʿath al-Sijistānī, *Sunan,* ed. Muḥammad Muḥyī l-Dīn ʿAbd al-Ḥamīd, 4 vols., Cairo 1339/1920; ed. Kamāl Yūsuf al-Ḥūt, 2 vols., Beirut 1988

Abū l-Futūḥ Rāzī, *Rawḥ*
Abū l-Futūḥ Ḥusayn b. ʿAlī Rāzī, *Rawḥ al-jinān wa-rūḥ al-janān,* 12 vols., Tehran 1282-7/ 1962-5; 5 vols., Qumm n.d.

Abū Ḥayyān, *Baḥr*
Abū Ḥayyān al-Gharnāṭī, *Tafsīr al-baḥr al-muḥīṭ,* 8 vols., Cairo 1328-9/1911; repr. Beirut 1983; ed. ʿĀdil Aḥmad ʿAbd al-Mawjūd and ʿAlī Muḥammad Muʿawwaḍ, 8 vols., Beirut 1993

Abū l-Layth al-Samarqandī, *Tafsīr*
Abū l-Layth Naṣr b. Muḥammad b. Aḥmad al-Samarqandī, *Baḥr al-ʿulūm,* ed. ʿAbd al-Raḥīm Aḥmad al-Zaqqa, 3 vols., Baghdad 1985-6; ed. ʿAlī Muḥammad Muʿawwaḍ et al., 3 vols., Beirut 1413/1993

Abū Shāma, *Murshid*
ʿAbd al-Raḥmān b. Ismāʿīl Abū Shāma, *Kitāb al-Murshid al-wajīz ilā ʿulūm tataʿallaq bi-l-kitāb al-ʿazīz,* ed. Ṭayyar Altikulaç, Istanbul 1968
Abū ʿUbayd, *Faḍāʾil*
Abū ʿUbayd al-Qāsim b. Sallām, *Faḍāʾil al-Qurʾān,* ed. Wahbī Sulaymān Khāwajī, Beirut 1411/1991
Abū ʿUbayd, *Gharīb*
Abū ʿUbayd al-Qāsim b. Sallām, *Gharīb al-ḥadīth,* ed. Muḥammad ʿAbd al-Muʿīd Khān, 4 vols., Hyderabad 1384-7/1964-7; 2 vols., Beirut 1406/1986; ed. Ḥusayn Muḥammad M. Sharaf et al., 4 vols., Cairo 1404-15/1984-94; ed. Masʿūd Ḥijāzī et al., Cairo 1419/1999
Abū ʿUbayd, *Nāsikh*
Abū ʿUbayd al-Qāsim b. Sallām, *Kitāb al-Nāsikh wa-l-mansūkh,* ed. J. Burton, Cambridge 1987
Abū ʿUbayda, *Majāz*
Abū ʿUbayda Maʿmar b. al-Muthannā al-Taymī, *Majāz al-Qurʾān,* ed. F. Sezgin, 2 vols., Cairo 1954-62
Akhfash, *Maʿānī*
Abū l-Ḥasan Saʿīd b. Masʿada al-Akhfash al-Awsaṭ, *Maʿānī l-Qurʾān,* ed. Fāʾiz Fāris al-Ḥamad, 2nd ed., 2 vols., Kuwait 1981; ed. ʿAbd al-Amīr Muḥammad Amīn al-Ward, Beirut 1405/1985; ed. Hudā Maḥmūd Qurrāʿa, Cairo 1990
Allard, *Analyse*
M. Allard, *Analyse conceptuelle du Coran sur cartes perforées,* Paris 1963
Ālūsī, *Rūḥ*
Maḥmūd b. ʿAbdallāh al-Ālūsī, *Rūḥ al-maʿānī fī tafsīr al-Qurʾān al-ʿaẓīm wa-l-sabʿ al-mathānī,* 30 vols. in 15, Cairo 1345/1926; repr. Beirut n.d.
ʿĀmilī, *Aʿyān*
Muḥsin al-Amīn al-ʿĀmilī, *Aʿyān al-shīʿa,* 56 parts, Damascus 1935-63; 11 vols., Beirut 1986
Anbārī, *Bayān*
Abū l-Barakāt ʿAbd al-Raḥmān b. Muḥammad b. al-Anbārī, *al-Bayān fī gharīb iʿrāb al-Qurʾān,* ed. Ṭāhā ʿAbd al-Ḥamīd and Muṣṭafā al-Saqqā, 2 vols., Cairo 1969-70
Anbārī, *Nuzha*
Abū l-Barakāt ʿAbd al-Raḥmān b. Muḥammad al-Anbārī, *Nuzhat al-alibbāʾ fī ṭabaqāt al-udabāʾ,* Cairo 1294; Stockholm 1963; ed. Ibrāhīm al-Sāmarrāʾī, Baghdad 1970
Arberry
A.J. Arberry, *The Koran interpreted,* London 1955
Arkoun, *Lectures*
M. Arkoun, *Lectures du Coran,* Paris 1982
ʿAyyāshī, *Tafsīr*
Muḥammad b. Masʿūd al-ʿAyyāshī, *Tafsīr,* 2 vols., Tehran 1380/1961
Baghawī, *Maʿālim*
al-Ḥusayn b. Masʿūd al-Shāfiʿī al-Baghawī, *Tafsīr al-Baghawī al-musammā bi-Maʿālim al-tanzīl,* ed. Khālid ʿAbd al-Raḥmān al-ʿAkk and Marwān Sawār, 4 vols., Beirut 1983
Baghdādī, *Farq*
Abū Manṣūr ʿAbd al-Qāhir b. Tāhir al-Baghdādī, *al-Farq bayna l-firāq,* ed. Muḥammad Badr, Cairo 1328/1910; ed. Muḥammad Muḥyī l-Dīn ʿAbd al-Ḥamīd, Cairo n.d.
Baghdādī, *Taʾrīkh Baghdād*
Abū Bakr Aḥmad b. ʿAlī al-Khaṭīb al-Baghdādī, *Taʾrīkh Baghdād,* 14 vols., Cairo 1349/1931
Baḥrānī, *Burhān*
Hāshim b. Sulaymān al-Baḥrānī, *Kitāb al-Burhān fī tafsīr al-Qurʾān,* ed. Maḥmūd b. Jaʿfar al-Mūsawī al-Zarandī et al., 4 vols., Tehran 1375/1995; repr. Beirut 1403/1983
Baljon, *Modern*
I.M.S. Baljon, *Modern Muslim Koran interpretation (1880-1960),* Leiden 1961, 1968
Bāqillānī, *Iʿjāz*
al-Qāḍī Abū Bakr Muḥammad b. al-Ṭayyib al-Bāqillānī, *Iʿjāz al-Qurʾān,* ed. al-Sayyid Aḥmad Ṣaqr, Cairo 1954

Bāqillānī, *Intiṣār*
al-Qāḍī Abū Bakr Muḥammad b. al-Ṭayyib al-Bāqillānī, *Nukat al-intiṣār li-naql al-Qurʾān,* ed. Muḥammad Zaghlūl Salām, Alexandria 1971

Bayḍāwī, *Anwār*
ʿAbdallāh b. ʿUmar al-Bayḍāwī, *Anwār al-tanzīl wa-asrār al-taʾwīl,* ed. H.O. Fleischer, 2 vols., Leipzig 1846; Beirut 1988

Beeston, *CHAL*
A.F.L. Beeston et al., eds., *The Cambridge history of Arabic literature,* 4 vols. to date, Cambridge 1983-

Bell, *Commentary*
R. Bell, *A commentary on the Qurʾān,* ed. C.E. Bosworth and M.E.J. Richardson, 2 vols., Manchester 1991

Bell, *Qurʾān*
R. Bell, *The Qurʾān. Translated, with a critical re-arrangement of the sūras,* 2 vols., Edinburgh 1939; repr. 1960

Beltz, *Mythen*
W. Beltz, *Die Mythen des Koran. Der Schlüssel zum Islam,* Düsseldorf 1980

Bergsträsser, *Verneinungs*
G. Bergsträsser, *Verneinungs- und Fragepartikeln und Verwandtes im Ḳurʾān,* Leipzig 1914

Biqāʿī, *Naẓm*
Burhān al-Dīn Ibrāhīm b. ʿUmar al-Biqāʿī, *Naẓm al-durar fī tanāsub al-āyāt wa-l-suwar,* 22 vols., Hyderabad 1969-84; repr. Cairo 1992

Birkeland, *Lord*
H. Birkeland, *The Lord guideth. Studies on primitive Islam,* Oslo 1956

Birkeland, *Opposition*
H. Birkeland, *Old Muslim opposition against interpretation of the Koran,* Oslo 1955

Blachère
R. Blachère, *Le Coran. Traduit de l'arabe,* Paris 1966

Blachère, *Introduction*
R. Blachère, *Introduction au Coran,* Paris 1947

Bobzin, *Koran*
H. Bobzin, *Der Koran. Eine Einführung,* Munich 1999

Bobzin, *Reformation*
H. Bobzin, *Der Koran im Zeitalter der Reformation. Studien zur Frühgeschichte der Arabistik und Islamkunde in Europa,* Beirut/Stuttgart 1995

Bouman, *Conflit*
J. Bouman, *Le conflit autour du Coran et la solution d'al-Bāqillānī,* Amsterdam 1959

Bouman, *Gott und Mensch*
J. Bouman, *Gott und Mensch im Koran. Eine Strukturform religiöser Anthropologie anhand des Beispiels Allāh und Muḥammad,* Darmstadt 1977

Böwering, *Mystical*
G. Böwering, *The mystical vision of existence in classical Islam. The qurʾānic hermeneutics of the Ṣūfī Sahl at-Tustarī (d. 283/896),* Berlin 1980

Brockelmann, *GAL*
C. Brockelmann, *Geschichte der arabischen Litteratur,* 2nd ed., 2 vols. and 3 vols. suppl., Leiden 1943-9; with new introduction, Leiden 1996

Buhl, *Das Leben*
F. Buhl, *Das Leben Muhammeds,* trans. H.H. Schaeder, Leipzig 1930; 1931 (3rd ed.)

Bukhārī, *Ṣaḥīḥ*
Abū ʿAbdallāh Muḥammad b. Ismāʿīl al-Bukhārī, *Kitāb al-Jāmiʿ al-ṣaḥīḥ,* ed. L. Krehl and T.W. Juynboll, 4 vols., Leiden 1862-1908; 9 vols., Cairo 1958

Burton, *Collection*
J. Burton, *The collection of the Qurʾān,* Cambridge 1977

Chabbi, *Seigneur*
J. Chabbi, *Le seigneur des tribus. L'islam de Mahomet,* Paris 1997

Creswell, *EMA*
K.A.C. Creswell, *Early Muslim architecture,* 2 vols., Oxford 1932-40; 2nd ed., London 1969

Dāmaghānī, *Wujūh*
al-Ḥusayn b. Muḥammad al-Dāmaghānī, *al-Wujūh wa-l-naẓāʾir li-alfāẓ Kitāb Allāh al-ʿazīz,* ed. Muḥammad Ḥasan Abū l-ʿAẓm al-Zafītī, 3 vols., Cairo 1412-16/

1992-5; ed. ʿAbd al-ʿAzīz Sayyid al-Ahl (as *Qāmūs al-Qurʾān*), Beirut 1970

Damīrī, *Ḥayāt*
Muḥammad b. Mūsā al-Damīrī, *Ḥayāt al-ḥayawān al-kubrā*, 2 vols., Cairo 1956

Dānī, *Muqniʿ*
Abū ʿAmr ʿUthmān b. Saʿīd al-Dānī, *al-Muqniʿ fī rasm maṣāḥif al-amṣār maʿa Kitāb al-Naqṭ = Orthographie und Punktierung des Koran*, ed. O. Pretzl, Leipzig/Istanbul 1932; ed. Muḥammad al-Ṣadīq Qamḥawī, Cairo n.d.

Dānī, *Naqṭ*
Abū ʿAmr ʿUthmān b. Saʿīd al-Dānī, *al-Muḥkam fī naqṭ al-maṣāḥif*, ed. ʿIzzat Ḥasan, Damascus 1379/1960

Dānī, *Taysīr*
Abū ʿAmr ʿUthmān b. Saʿīd al-Dānī, *Kitāb al-Taysīr fī l-qirāʾāt al-sabʿ = Das Lehrbuch der sieben Koranlesungen*, ed. O. Pretzl, Leipzig/Istanbul 1930

Dāraquṭnī, *Muʾtalif*
Abū l-Ḥasan ʿAlī b. ʿUmar al-Dāraquṭnī, *al-Muʾtalif wa-l-mukhtalif*, ed. Muwaffaq b. ʿAbdallāh b. ʿAbd al-Qādir, 5 vols., Beirut 1986

Dārimī, *Sunan*
ʿAbdallāh b. ʿAbd al-Rāḥmān al-Dārimī, *Sunan*, Cairo 1966

Darwaza, *Tafsīr*
Muḥammad ʿIzzat Darwaza, *al-Tafsir al-ḥadīth*, 12 vols., Cairo 1381-3/1962-4

Dāwūdī, *Ṭabaqāt*
Muḥammad b. ʿAlī al-Dāwūdī, *Ṭabaqāt al-mufassirīn*, ed. ʿAlī Muḥammad ʿUmar, 2 vols., Beirut 1983

Dhahabī, *Mufassirūn*
Muḥammad Ḥusayn al-Dhahabī, *al-Tafsīr wa-l-mufassirūn*, 2 vols., Cairo 1976

Dhahabī, *Qurrāʾ*
Shams al-Dīn Muḥammad b. Aḥmad al-Dhahabī, *Maʿrifat al-qurrāʾ al-kibār ʿalā l-ṭabaqāt wa-l-aʿṣār*, ed. Sayyid Jad al-Ḥaqq, n.p. 1969

Dhahabī, *Siyar*
Shams al-Dīn Muḥammad b. Aḥmad al-Dhahabī, *Siyar aʿlām al-nubalāʾ*, ed. Shuʿayb al-Arnaʾūṭ et al., 25 vols., Beirut 1981-8

Dhahabī, *Tadhkira*
Shams al-Dīn Muḥammad b. Aḥmad al-Dhahabī, *Tadhkirat al-ḥuffāẓ*, 4 vols., Hyderabad 1375/1955

Dhahabī, *Taʾrīkh*
Shams al-Dīn Muḥammad b. Aḥmad al-Dhahabī, *Taʾrīkh al-Islām*, ed. ʿUmar ʿAbd al-Salām Tadmurī, 52 vols. to date, Beirut 1989-; 4 vols. (years 601-640), ed. Bashshār ʿAwwād Maʿrūf et al., Beirut 1408/1988

van Ess, *TG*
J. van Ess, *Theologie und Gesellschaft im 2. und 3. Jahrhundert Hidschra. Eine Geschichte des religiösen Denkens im frühen Islam*, 6 vols., Berlin/New York 1991-7

Fārisī, *Ḥujja*
Abū ʿAlī al-Ḥasan b. ʿAlī al-Fārisī, *al-Ḥujja lil-qurrāʾ al-sabʿa*, ed. Badr al-Dīn al-Qahwajī et al., 4 vols., Damascus 1985-91

Farrāʾ, *Maʿānī*
Abū Zakariyyāʾ Yaḥyā b. Ziyād al-Farrāʾ, *Maʿānī l-Qurʾān*, ed. Aḥmad Yūsuf Najātī and Muḥammad ʿAlī al-Najjār, 3 vols., Cairo 1955-72

Fīrūzābādī, *Baṣāʾir*
Majd al-Dīn Muḥammad b. Yaʿqūb al-Fīrūzābādī *Baṣāʾir dhawī l-tamyīz fī laṭāʾif al-kitāb al-ʿazīz*, ed. Muḥammad ʿAlī l-Najjār, 4 vols., Cairo 1964; repr. Beirut n.d.

GAP
W. Fischer and H. Gätje, eds., *Grundriss der arabischen Philologie*, 3 vols., Wiesbaden 1982-92

Gardet and Anawati, *Introduction*
L. Gardet and M.M. Anawati, *Introduction à la théologie musulmane*, Paris 1948, 3rd ed., 1981

Gilliot, *Elt*
C. Gilliot, *Exégèse, langue, et théologie en Islam. L'exégèse coranique de Ṭabarī (m. 310/923)*, Paris 1990

Gimaret, *Jubbāʾī*
D. Gimaret, *Une lecture muʿtazilite du Coran. Le tafsīr d'Abū ʿAlī al-Djubbāʾī (m. 303/915) partiellement reconstitué à partir de ses citateurs,* Louvain/Paris 1994
Goldziher, *GS*
I. Goldziher, *Gesammelte Schriften,* ed. J. Desomogyi, 6 vols., Hildesheim 1967-73
Goldziher, *MS*
I. Goldziher, *Muhammedanische Studien,* 2 vols., Halle 1888-90; trans., C.R. Barber and S.M. Stern, *Muslim studies,* London 1967-72
Goldziher, *Richtungen*
I. Goldziher, *Die Richtungen der islamischen Koranauslegung,* Leiden 1920; repr. 1970
Graham, *Beyond*
W.A. Graham, *Beyond the written word. Oral aspects of scripture in the history of religion,* Cambridge and New York 1989
Grimme, *Mohammed, I-II*
H. Grimme, *Mohammed. I, Das Leben nach den Quellen. II, Einleitung in den Koran. System der koranischen Theologie,* Münster 1892-5
Grünbaum, *Beiträge*
M. Grünbaum, *Beiträge zur semitischen Sagenkunde,* Leiden 1893
Ḥājjī Khalīfa, *Kashf*
Muṣṭafā ʿAbdallāh Ḥājjī Khalīfa, *Kashf al-ẓunūn,* ed. and trans. G. Flügel, 7 vols., Leipzig 1835-58; ed. Şerefettin Yaltkaya and Kilisli Rifat Bilge, 2 vols., Istanbul 1941-3; repr. Beirut 1992-3
Hawting and Shareef, *Approaches*
G.R. Hawting and A.A. Shareef (eds.), *Approaches to the Qurʾān,* London 1993
Hawting, *Idolatry*
G.R. Hawting, *The idea of idolatry and the emergence of Islam. From polemic to history,* Cambridge 1999
Ḥawwā, *Tafsīr*
Saʿīd Ḥawwā, *al-Asās fī l-tafsīr,* 11 vols., Cairo 1405/1985
Horovitz, *KU*
J. Horovitz, *Koranische Untersuchungen,* Berlin/Leipzig 1926
Hūd b. Muḥakkam, *Tafsīr*
Hūd b. Muḥakkam/Muḥkim al-Huwwārī, *Tafsīr,* ed. Balḥājj Saʿīd Sharīfī, 4 vols., Beirut 1990
Ibn ʿAbbās, *Gharīb*
ʿAbdallāh b. ʿAbbās (attributed to), *Gharīb al-Qurʾān,* ed. Muḥammad ʿAbd al-Raḥīm, Beirut 1993
Ibn Abī l-Iṣbaʿ, *Badīʿ*
Ibn Abī l-Iṣbaʿ al-Miṣrī, *Badīʿ al-Qurʾān,* ed. Ḥifnī Muḥammad Sharaf, Cairo n.d.
Ibn Abī Uṣaybiʿa, *ʿUyūn*
Aḥmad b. al-Qāsim b. Abī Uṣaybiʿa, *ʿUyūn al-anbāʾ fī ṭabaqāt al-aṭibbāʾ,* ed. A. Müller, 2 vols., Cairo 1299/1882; 3 vols., Beirut 1957
Ibn al-Anbārī, *Īḍāḥ*
Abū Bakr Muḥammad b. al-Qāsim b. al-Anbārī, *Īḍāḥ al-waqf wa-l-ibtidāʾ fī Kitāb Allāh,* ed. Muḥyī l-Dīn ʿAbd al-Raḥmān Ramaḍān, 2 vols., Damascus 1391/1971
Ibn al-ʿArabī, *Aḥkām*
Muḥammad b. ʿAbdallāh Abū Bakr b. al-ʿArabī, *Aḥkām al-Qurʾān,* 2nd ed., Cairo 1392/1972
Ibn al-ʿArabī, *Tafsīr*
Muḥammad b. ʿAbdallāh Abū Bakr b. al-ʿArabī, *Tafsīr al-Qurʾān,* 2 vols., Beirut 1968 (see Qāshānī)
Ibn ʿAsākir, *Taʾrīkh*
ʿAlī b. al-Ḥasan b. ʿAsākir, *Taʾrīkh madīnat Dimashq,* abridged ed. ʿAbd al-Qādir Bardān and Aḥmad ʿUbayd, 7 vols., Damascus 1329-51/1911-31; facsimile ed., 19 vols., Amman n.d.; 29 vols., Damascus 1404-8/1984-8; ed. Muḥyī l-Dīn ʿUmar b. Gharāma al-Amrāwī, 70 vols. to date, Beirut 1995-98
Ibn ʿĀshūr, *Tafsīr*
Muḥammad al-Ṭāhir b. ʿĀshūr, *al-Tafsīr al-taḥrīrī wa-l-tanwīrī,* 30 vols., Tunis 1984
Ibn ʿAskar, *Takmīl*
Muḥammad b. ʿAlī al-Ghassānī b. ʿAskar, *al-Takmīl wa-l-itmām li-Kitāb al-Taʿrīf wa-l-iʿlām,* ed. Ḥasan Ismāʿīl Marwa, Beirut/Damascus 1418/1997 (see Suhaylī)

Ibn al-Athīr, *Kāmil*
'Izz al-Dīn 'Alī b. al-Athīr, *al-Kāmil fī l-ta'rīkh*, ed. C.J. Tornberg, 14 vols., Leiden 1851-76; corrected repr. 13 vols., Beirut 1385-7/1965-7

Ibn al-Athīr, *Nihāya*
Majd al-Dīn al-Mubārak b. al-Athīr, *al-Nihāya fī gharīb al-ḥadīth wa-l-athar*, ed. Ṭāhir Aḥmad al-Zāwī and Maḥmūd al-Ṭanāḥī, 5 vols., Cairo 1963-6

Ibn 'Aṭiyya, *Muḥarrar*
Abū Muḥammad 'Abd al-Ḥaqq b. Ghālib b. 'Aṭiyya al-Gharnāṭī, *al-Muḥarrar al-wajīz*, ed. 'Abd al-Salām 'Abd al-Shāfī Muḥammad, 5 vols., Beirut 1413/1993

Ibn Ḍurays, *Faḍā'il*
Muḥammad b. Ayyūb b. Ḍurays, *Faḍā'il al-Qur'ān*, ed. Ghazwa Budayr, Damascus 1988

Ibn Ḥajar, *Tahdhīb*
Ibn Ḥajar al-'Asqalānī, *Tahdhīb al-tahdhīb*, 12 vols., Hyderabad 1325-7/1907-9; Beirut 1968

Ibn Ḥanbal, *Musnad*
Aḥmad b. Ḥanbal, *Musnad*, ed. Muḥammad al-Zuhrī al-Ghamrāwī, 6 vols., Cairo 1313/1895; repr. Beirut 1978; ed. Aḥmad Muḥammad Shākir et al., 20 vols., Cairo 1416/1995

Ibn Ḥazm, *Milal*
'Alī b. Aḥmad b. Sa'īd b. Ḥazm, *al-Fiṣal fī l-milal wa-l-ahwā' wa-l-niḥal*, ed. Muḥammad Ibrāhīm Naṣr and 'Abd al-Raḥmān 'Umayra, 5 vols., Beirut 1995

Ibn al-'Imād, *Shadharāt*
'Abd al-Ḥayy b. Aḥmad b. al-'Imād, *Shadharāt al-dhahab fī akhbār man dhahab*, 8 vols., Cairo 1350-1/1931-2; repr. Beirut n.d.

Ibn Isḥāq, *Sīra*
Muḥammad b. Isḥāq, *Sīrat rasūl Allāh* (recension of 'Abd al-Malik b. Hishām), ed. F. Wüstenfeld, Göttingen 1858-60; repr. Beirut n.d.; ed. Muṣṭafā al-Ṣaqqā et al., 4 vols. in 2, 2nd ed., Cairo 1955

Ibn Isḥāq-Guillaume
The life of Muhammad. A translation of Ibn Isḥāq's Sīrat rasūl Allāh, trans. A. Guillaume, Oxford 1955; repr. Karachi 1967

Ibn al-Jawzī, *Funūn*
Abū l-Faraj 'Abd al-Raḥmān b. 'Alī b. al-Jawzī, *Funūn al-afnān fī 'ajā'ib 'ulūm al-Qur'ān*, ed. Rashīd 'Abd al-Raḥmān al-'Ubaydī, Baghdad 1408/1988

Ibn al-Jawzī, *Muntaẓam*
Abū l-Faraj 'Abd al-Raḥmān b. 'Alī b. al-Jawzī, *al-Muntaẓam fī ta'rīkh al-mulūk wa-l-umam*, ed. Muḥammad and Muṣṭafā 'Abd al-Qādir 'Aṭā, 19 vols., Beirut 1412/1922; ed. Suhayl Zakkār, 11 vols. in 13, Beirut 1995-6

Ibn al-Jawzī, *Nuzha*
Abū l-Faraj 'Abd al-Raḥmān b. 'Alī b. al-Jawzī, *Nuzhat al-a'yun al-nawāẓir fī 'ilm al-wujūh wa-l-naẓā'ir*, ed. Muḥammad 'Abd al-Karīm Kāẓim al-Rāḍī, Beirut 1404/1984

Ibn al-Jawzī, *Zād*
Abū l-Faraj 'Abd al-Raḥmān b. Alī b. al-Jawzī, *Zād al-masīr fī 'ilm al-tafsīr*, intr. Muḥammad Zuhayr al-Shāwīsh, 9 vols., Damascus 1384-5/1964-5; annot. Aḥmad Shams al-Dīn, 8 vols., Beirut 1414/1994

Ibn al-Jazarī, *Ghāya*
Shams al-Dīn Abū l-Khayr Muḥammad b. Muḥammad b. al-Jazarī, *Ghāyat al-nihāya fī ṭabaqāt al-qurrā' = Das biographische Lexikon der Koranleser*, 3 vols. in 2, ed. G. Bergsträsser and O. Pretzl, Leipzig/Cairo 1933-5

Ibn al-Jazarī, *Munjid*
Shams al-Dīn Abū l-Khayr Muḥammad b. Muḥammad b. al-Jazarī, *Munjid al-muqri'īn wa-murshid al-ṭālibīn*, ed. Muḥammad Ḥabīb Allāh al-Shanqīṭī et al., Cairo 1350/1931; Beirut 1980

Ibn al-Jazarī, *Nashr*
Shams al-Dīn Abū l-Khayr Muḥammad b. Muḥammad b. al-Jazarī, *Kitāb al-Nashr fī l-qirā'āt al-'ashr*, ed. 'Alī Muḥammad al-Ḍabbā', 2 vols., Cairo 1940; repr. Beirut n.d.

Ibn Jinnī, *Muḥtasab*
Abū l-Fatḥ 'Uthmān b. Jinnī, *al-Muḥtasab fī*

tabyīn wujūh shawādhdh al-qirāʾāt wa-l-īḍāḥ ʿanhā, 2 vols., ed. ʿAlī al-Najdī Nāṣif et al., Cairo 1386-9/1966-9; repr. 1994

Ibn Kathīr, *Bidāya*
ʿImād al-Dīn Ismāʿīl b. ʿUmar b. Kathīr, *al-Bidāya wa-l-nihāya,* 14 vols., Beirut/Riyadh 1966; repr. Beirut 1988

Ibn Kathīr, *Faḍāʾil*
ʿImād al-Dīn Ismāʿīl b. ʿUmar b. Kathīr, *Faḍāʾil al-Qurʾān,* Beirut 1979

Ibn Kathīr, *Tafsīr*
ʿImād al-Dīn Ismāʿīl b. ʿUmar b. Kathīr, *Tafsīr al-Qurʾān al-ʿaẓīm,* ed. ʿAbd al-ʿAzīz Ghunaym et al., 8 vols., Cairo 1390/1971; 4 vols., Cairo n.d.; repr. Beirut 1980

Ibn Khālawayh, *Ḥujja*
Abū ʿAbdallāh al-Ḥusayn b. Aḥmad b. Khālawayh, *al-Ḥujja fī l-qirāʾāt al-sabʿ,* ed. ʿAbd al-ʿĀl Salīm Mukarram, Beirut 1971

Ibn Khālawayh, *Iʿrāb*
Abū ʿAbdallāh al-Ḥusayn b. Aḥmad b. Khālawayh, *Iʿrāb thalāthīn sūra min al-Qurʾān al-karīm,* Baghdad 1967

Ibn Khālawayh, *Iʿrāb al-qirāʾāt*
Abū ʿAbdallāh al-Ḥusayn b. Aḥmad b. Khālawayh, *Iʿrāb al-qirāʾāt al-sabʿ wa-ʿilaluhā,* ed. ʿAbd al-Raḥmān b. Sulaymān al-Uthaymīn, 2 vols., Cairo 1413/1992

Ibn Khaldūn, *ʿIbar*
ʿAbd al-Raḥmān b. Khaldūn, *Kitāb al-ʿIbar,* ed. Naṣr al-Ḥūrīnī, 7 vols., Būlāq 1284/1867

Ibn Khaldūn-Rosenthal
ʿAbd al-Raḥmān b. Khaldūn, *The Muqaddimah,* trans. F. Rosenthal, 3 vols., New York 1958; 2nd rev. ed., Princeton 1967

Ibn Khallikān, *Wafayāt*
Shams al-Dīn b. Khallikān, *Wafayāt al-aʿyān wa-anbāʾ abnāʾ al-zamān,* ed. F. Wüstenfeld, 4 vols., Göttingen 1835-50; ed. Iḥsān ʿAbbās, 8 vols., Beirut 1968-72; trans. M. De Slane, *Ibn Khallikān's biographical dictionary,* 4 vols., Paris 1842-71; repr. New York 1961

Ibn Māja
Muḥammad b. Yazīd b. Māja, *Sunan,* ed. Muḥammad Fuʾād ʿAbd al-Bāqī, 2 vols., Cairo 1952-3

Ibn Mujāhid, *Sabʿa*
Abū Bakr Aḥmad b. Mūsā b. Mujāhid, *Kitāb al-Sabʿa fī l-qirāʾāt,* ed. Shawqī Ḍayf, Cairo 1979

Ibn al-Nadīm, *Fihrist*
Muḥammad b. Isḥāq b. al-Nadīm, *Kitāb al-Fihrist,* ed. G. Flügel, 2 vols., Leipzig 1871-2; ed. Riḍā Tajaddud, Tehran 1971; 2nd ed., Beirut 1988

Ibn al-Nadīm-Dodge
Muḥammad b. Isḥāq b. al-Nadīm, *The Fihrist of al-Nadīm,* trans. B. Dodge, 2 vols., New York/London 1970

Ibn al-Naqīb, *Muqaddima*
Abū ʿAbdallāh Muḥammad b. Sulaymān al-Naqīb, *Muqaddimat al-tafsīr fī ʿulūm al-bayān wa-l-maʿānī wa-l-badīʿ wa-iʿjāz al-Qurʾān,* ed. Zakariyyāʾ Saʿīd ʿAlī, Cairo 1415/1995

Ibn Qayyim al-Jawziyya, *Tibyān*
Muḥammad b. Abī Bakr b. Qayyim al-Jawziyya, *al-Tibyān fī aqsām al-Qurʾān,* Beirut 1982

Ibn al-Qifṭī, *Ḥukamāʾ*
Abū l-Ḥasan ʿAlī b. Yūsuf b. al-Qifṭī, *Taʾrīkh al-ḥukamāʾ,* ed. J. Lippert, Leipzig 1903; repr. Baghdad 1967

Ibn Qutayba, *Gharīb*
Abū Muḥammad ʿAbdallāh b. Muslim al-Dīnawarī b. Qutayba, *Tafsīr gharīb al-Qurʾān,* ed. al-Sayyid Aḥmad Ṣaqr, Cairo 1958; Beirut 1978

Ibn Qutayba, *al-Shiʿr*
Abū Muḥammad ʿAbdallāh b. Muslim al-Dīnawarī b. Qutayba, *Kitāb al-Shiʿr wa-l-shuʿarāʾ,* ed. M.J. de Goeje, Leiden 1900

Ibn Qutayba, *Taʾwīl*
Abū Muḥammad ʿAbdallāh b. Muslim al-Dīnawarī b. Qutayba, *Taʾwīl mushkil al-Qurʾān,* ed. al-Sayyid Aḥmad Ṣaqr, Cairo 1954; Cairo 1973; Medina 1981

Ibn Qutayba-Lecomte
G. Lecomte, *Le traité des divergences du hadīt d'Ibn Qutayba,* Damascus 1962

Ibn Saʿd, *Ṭabaqāt*
Muḥammad b. Saʿd, *al-Ṭabaqāt al-kubrā*, ed. H. Sachau et al., 9 vols., Leiden 1905-40; ed. Iḥsān ʿAbbās, 9 vols., Beirut 1957-8

Ibn Taymiyya, *Daqāʾiq*
Taqī l-Dīn Aḥmad b. ʿAbd al-Ḥalīm b. Taymiyya, *Daqāʾiq al-tafsīr. al-Jāmiʿ li-tafsīr al-Imām Ibn Taymiyya*, ed. Muḥammad al-Sayyid al-Julaynid, 6 vols. in 3, Jedda/Beirut/Damascus 1986

Ibn Taymiyya, *Muqaddima*
Taqī l-Dīn Aḥmad b. ʿAbd al-Ḥalīm b. Taymiyya, *Muqaddima fī uṣūl al-tafsīr*, Beirut 1392/1972; Riyadh 1382/1962

Ibn Wahb, *al-Jāmiʿ*
ʿAbdallāh b. Wahb, *al-Ǧāmiʿ. Die Koranswissenschaften*, ed. M. Muranyi, Wiesbaden 1992

Ibyārī, *Mawsūʿa*
Ibrāhīm al-Ibyārī and ʿAbd al-Ṣabūr Marzūq, *al-Mawsūʿa al-qurʾāniyya*, 6 vols., Cairo 1388/1969; 11 vols., Cairo 1405/1984

Ihsanoglu, *Translations*
E. İhsanoğlu, ed., *World bibliography of translations of the meanings of the holy Qurʾān. Printed translations* 1515-1980, Istanbul 1406/1986

Iṣfahānī, *Aghānī*
Abū l-Faraj al-Iṣfahānī, *Kitāb al-Aghānī*, 21 vols. in 7, Cairo 1323/1905; 25 vols., Beirut 1955-62

Iṣfahānī, *Muqaddima*
Abū l-Ḥasan al-ʿĀmilī al-Iṣfahānī, *Muqaddimat tafsīr mirʾāt al-anwār wa-mishkāt al-asrār*, ed. Maḥmūd b. Jaʿfar al-Mūsawī al-Zarandī, Tehran 1374/1954

Iṣlāḥī, *Tadabbur*
Amīn Aḥsan Iṣlāḥī, *Tadabbur-i Qurʾān*, 8 vols., Lahore 1967-80

ʿIyāḍ b. Mūsā, *Shifāʾ*
al-Qāḍī Abū l-Faḍl ʿIyāḍ b. Mūsā, *al-Shifāʾ bi-taʿrīf ḥuqūq al-muṣṭafā*, 2 vols. in 1, Damascus 1978; ed. Muḥammad Amīn Qara et al., Amman 1407/1986

Izutsu, *Concepts*
Toshihiko Izutsu, *Ethico-religious concepts in the Qurʾān*, Montreal 1966

Izutsu, *God*
Toshihiko Izutsu, *God and man in the Koran*, New York 1964; repr. 1980

Jāḥiẓ, *Bayān*
ʿAmr b. Baḥr al-Jāḥiẓ, *al-Bayān wa-l-tabyīn*, ed. ʿAbd al-Salām Muḥammad Hārūn, 4 vols., Cairo 1948-50; repr. Beirut n.d.

Jalālayn
Jalāl al-Dīn Muḥammad b. Aḥmad al-Maḥallī and Jalāl al-Dīn al-Suyūṭī, *Tafsīr al-Jalālayn*, Damascus 1385/1965

Jansen, *Egypt*
J.J.G. Jansen, *The interpretation of the Koran in modern Egypt*, Leiden 1974, 1980

Jaṣṣāṣ, *Aḥkām*
Abū Bakr Aḥmad b. ʿAbdallāh al-Jaṣṣās al-Rāzī, *Aḥkām al-Qurʾān*, 3 vols., Istanbul 1335-8/1916-19

Jawālīqī, *Muʿarrab*
Abū Manṣūr Mawhūb b. Aḥmad al-Jawālīqī, *al-Muʿarrab min al-kalām al-ʿajamī ʿalā ḥurūf al-muʿjam*, ed. Aḥmad Muḥammad Shākir, Cairo 1361/1942

Jeffery, *For. vocab.*
A. Jeffery, *Foreign vocabulary of the Qurʾān*, Baroda 1938

Jeffery, *Materials*
A. Jeffery, *Materials for the history of the text of the Qurʾān. The Kitāb al-Maṣāḥif of Ibn Abī Dāwūd together with a collection of the variant readings from the codices of Ibn Masʿūd, etc.*, Leiden 1937

Jeffery, *Muqaddimas*
A. Jeffery, *Two muqaddimas to the Qurʾānic sciences. The muqaddima to the* Kitab al-Mabani *and the muqaddima of Ibn ʿAṭiyya to his* Tafsir, Cairo 1954

Jurjānī, *Asrār*
ʿAbd al-Qāhir al-Jurjāni, *Asrār al-balāgha*, ed. H. Ritter, Istanbul 1954

Jurjānī, *Dalāʾil*
ʿAbd al-Qāhir al-Jurjānī, *Dalāʾil iʿjāz al-*

Qur'ān, Cairo 1372; ed. Maḥmūd Muḥammad Shākir, Cairo 1404/1984

Justi, *Namenbuch*
F. Justi, *Iranisches Namenbuch*, Marburg 1895

Kaḥḥāla, *Muʿjam*
ʿUmar Riḍā Kaḥḥāla, *Muʿjam al-mu'allifīn*, 15 vols. in 8, Beirut n.d.; Damascus 1957-61

Kaḥḥāla, *Nisā'*
ʿUmar Riḍā Kaḥḥāla, *Aʿlām al-nisā' fī ʿālamay al-ʿArab wa-l-Islām*, 5 vols., Damascus 1379/1959

Kāshānī, *Minhaj*
Mullā Fatḥ Allāh Kāshānī, *Minhaj al-ṣādiqīn fī ilzām al-mukhālifīn*, 10 vols., Tehran 1347[solar]/1969

Kāshānī, *Ṣāfī*
Mullā Muḥsin Fayd Kāshānī, *al-Ṣāfī fī tafsīr kalām Allāh al-wāfī*, ed. Ḥusayn al-Aʿlamī, 5 vols., Beirut 1399/1979

Khāzin, *Lubāb*
ʿAlā' al-Dīn al-Khāzin, *Lubāb al-ta'wīl fī maʿānī l-tanzīl*, Cairo 1381/1961

Khwānsārī, *Rawḍāt*
Muḥammad Bāqir al-Mūsawī al-Khwānsārī, *Rawḍāt al-jannāt*, ed. Asad Allāh Ismāʿīlīyān, 8 vols., Tehran 1392/1972

Kisā'ī, *Mutashābih*
ʿAlī b. Ḥamza al-Kisā'ī, *Kitāb Mutashābih al-Qur'ān*, ed. Ṣabīḥ al-Tamīmī, Tripoli 1994

Kisā'ī, *Qiṣaṣ*
Muḥammad b. ʿAbdallāh al-Kisā'ī, *Vita prophetarum auctore Muḥammed ben ʿAbdallāh al-Kisā'ī*, ed. I. Eisenberg, 2 vols., Leiden 1922-3

Kulaynī, *Kāfī*
Abū Jaʿfar Muḥammad b. Yaʿqūb al-Kulayn, *Rawḍat al-kāfī*, ed. ʿAlī Akbar al-Ghifārī, Najaf 1395/1966; repr. Beirut n.d.

Kutubī, *Fawāt*
Ibn Shākir al-Kutubī, *Fawāt al-wafayāt*, 2 vols., Cairo 1299/1882; ed. Iḥsān ʿAbbās, 5 vols., Beirut 1973-4

Lane
E.W. Lane, *An Arabic-English lexicon*, 1 vol. in 8 parts., London 1863-93; New York 1955-6; repr. 2 vols., Cambridge 1984

Lecker, *Muslims*
M. Lecker, *Muslims, Jews and pagans. Studies on early Islamic Medina*, Leiden 1995

Le Strange, *Lands*
G. Le Strange, *The lands of the eastern caliphate*, 2nd ed., Cambridge 1930

Lisān al-ʿArab
Muḥammad b. al-Mukarram b. Manẓūr, *Lisān al-ʿArab*, 15 vols., Beirut 1955-6; ed. ʿAlī Shīrī, 18 vols., Beirut 1988

Lüling, *Ur-Qur'ān*
G. Lüling, *Über den Ur-Qur'ān. Ansätze zur Rekonstruktion der vorislamisch-christlicher Strophenlieder im Qur'ān*, Erlangen 1972; 2nd ed. 1993

Makkī, *Ibāna*
Makkī b. Abī Ṭālib al-Qaysī, *Kitāb al-Ibāna ʿan maʿānī l-qirā'āt*, ed. Muḥyī l-Dīn Ramaḍān, Damascus 1979

Makkī, *Kashf*
Makkī b. Abī Ṭālib al-Qaysī, *al-Kashf ʿan wujūh al-qirā'āt al-sabʿ wa-ʿilalihā wa-ḥujajihā*, ed. Muḥyī l-Dīn Ramaḍān, 2 vols., Damascus 1974

Makkī, *Mushkil*
Makkī b. Abī Ṭālib al-Qaysī, *Mushkil iʿrāb al-Qur'ān*, ed. Yāsīn M. al-Sawwās, Damascus 1974

Mālik, *Muwaṭṭa'*
Mālik b. Anas, *al-Muwaṭṭa'*, ed. Muḥammad Fu'ād ʿAbd al-Bāqī, Cairo 1952-3; Beirut 1985; ed. ʿAbd al-Majīd Turkī, Beirut 1994

Masʿūdī, *Murūj*
Abū ʿAlī b. al-Ḥusayn al-Masʿūdī, *Murūj al-dhahab*, ed. C. Barbier de Meynard and Pavet de Courteille, 9 vols., Paris 1861-77; ed. and trans. Ch. Pellat, *Les prairies d'or*, 7 vols. text and 4 vols. translation, Paris-Beirut 1962-89; ed. Qāsim al-Shamāʿī al-Rifāʿī, 4 vols., Beirut 1989

Māturīdī, *Taʾwīlāt*
Abū Manṣūr Muḥammad b. Muḥammad al-Māturīdī, *Taʾwīlāt ahl al-sunna*, ed. Ibrāhīm and al-Sayyid ʿAwadayn, Cairo 1391/1971; ed. Jāsim Muḥammad al-Jubūrī, Baghdad 1404/1983
Māwardī, *Nukat*
ʿAlī b. Muḥammad al-Māwardī, *al-Nukat wa-l-ʿuyūn fī l-tafsīr*, ed. al-Sayyid b. ʿAbd al-Maqṣūd b. ʿAbd al-Raḥīm, 6 vols., Beirut 1412/1992
McAuliffe, *Qurʾānic*
J.D. McAuliffe, *Qurʾānic Christians. An analysis of classical and modern exegesis*, Cambridge 1991
Mir, *Dictionary*
M. Mir, *Dictionary of Qurʾānic terms and concepts*, New York 1987
Mir, *Verbal*
M. Mir, *Verbal idioms of the Qurʾān*, Ann Arbor, MI 1989
Mufaḍḍaliyyāt
al-Mufaḍḍal b. Muḥammad al-Ḍabbī, *al-Mufaḍḍaliyyāt*, ed. Aḥmad Muḥammad Shākir and ʿAbd al-Salām Muḥammad Hārūn, Cairo 1942
Muir, *Mahomet*
W. Muir, *The life of Mahomet. With introductory chapters on the original sources of the biography of Mahomet, I-IV*, London 1858-61
Mujāhid, *Tafsīr*
Abū l-Ḥajjāj Mujāhid b. Jabr, *al-Tafsīr*, ed. ʿAbd al-Raḥmān b. Ṭāhir b. Muḥammad al-Suwartī, Qatar 1976; ed. Muḥammad ʿAbd al-Salām Abū l-Nīl, Cairo 1989
Mukarram, *Muʿjam al-qirāʾāt*
ʿAbd al-Āl Salīm Mukarram, *Muʿjam al-qirāʾāt al-qurʾāniyya*, 8 vols. to date, Kuwait 1982-
Muqātil, *Ashbāh*
Abū l-Ḥasan Muqātil b. Sulaymān al-Balkhī, *al-Ashbāh wa-l-naẓāʾir fī l-Qurʾān al-karīm*, ed. ʿAbdallāh Maḥmūd Shiḥāta, Cairo 1975
Muqātil, *Khams miʾa*
Abū l-Ḥasan Muqātil b. Sulaymān al-Balkhī, *Tafsīr al-khams miʾat āya min al-Qurʾān*, ed. I. Goldfeld, Shfaram 1980
Muqātil, *Tafsīr*
Abū l-Ḥasan Muqātil b. Sulaymān al-Balkhī, *al-Tafsīr*, ed. ʿAbdallāh Maḥmūd Shiḥāta, 5 vols., Cairo 1980-7
Muslim, *Ṣaḥīḥ*
Muslim b. al-Ḥajjāj, *Ṣaḥīḥ*, ed. Muḥammad Fuʾād ʿAbd al-Bāqī, 5 vols., Cairo 1955-6
Nāfiʿ, *Masāʾil*
Masāʾil al-Imām ʿan asʾilat Nafiʿ b. al-Azraq wa-ajwibat ʿAbd Allāh b. ʿAbbas, ed. ʿAbd al-Raḥmān ʿUmayra, Cairo 1413/1994
Nagel, *Einschübe*
T. Nagel, *Medinensische Einschübe in mekkanischen Suren*, Göttingen 1995
Nagel, *Koran*
T. Nagel, *Der Koran. Einführung-Texte-Erläuterungen*, Munich 1983
Naḥḥās, *Iʿrāb*
Abū Jaʿfar Aḥmad b. Muḥammad al-Naḥḥās, *Iʿrāb al-Qurʾān*, ed. Zuhayr Ghāzī Zāhid, 2nd ed., 5 vols., Beirut 1985, 1988
Nasafī, *Tafsīr*
ʿAbdallāh b. Aḥmad b. Maḥmūd al-Nasafī, *Madārik al-tanzil wa-ḥaqāʾiq al-taʾwīl*, ed. Zakariyyāʾ ʿUmayrāt, 2 vols. Beirut 1415/1995
Nasāʾī, *Faḍāʾil*
Aḥmad b. Shuʿayb al-Nasāʾī, *Faḍāʾil al-Qurʾān*, ed. Samīr al-Khūlī, Beirut 1985
Nasāʾī, *Sunan*
Aḥmad b. Shuʿayb al-Nasāʾī, *al-Sunan al-kubrā*, ed. ʿAbd al-Ghaffār Sulaymān al-Bundārī and al-Sayyid Kisrawī Ḥasan, 6 vols., Beirut 1411/1991
Nawawī, *Sharḥ*
Abū Zakariyyāʾ Yaḥyā b. Sharaf al-Nawawī, *Sharḥ Ṣaḥīḥ Muslim*, 18 vols. in 9, Cairo 1349/1929-30; ed. Khalīl Muḥammad Shīḥā, 19 vols. in 10, Beirut 1995
Neuwirth, *Studien*
A. Neuwirth, *Studien zur Komposition der mekkanischen Suren*, Berlin 1981
Nīsābūrī, *Tafsīr*
Abū l-Qāsim al-Ḥasan b. Muḥammad b.

Ḥabīb al-Nīsābūrī, *Tafsīr gharāʾib al-Qurʾān wa-raghāʾib al-furqān,* on the margin of Ṭabarī, *Jāmiʿ al-bayān,* 30 vols., Cairo 1323-9/1905-11; repr. Beirut 1392/1972; ed. Ibrāhīm ʿAṭwa ʿAwaḍ, 13 vols., Cairo 1962-4

Nöldeke, *GQ*
T. Nöldeke, *Geschichte des Qorāns,* new edition by F. Schwally, G. Bergsträsser and O. Pretzl, 3 vols., Leipzig 1909-38

Nwyia, *Exégèse*
P. Nwyia, *Exégèse coranique et langage mystique. Nouvel essai sur le lexique technique des mystiques musulmans,* Beirut 1970

Paret, *Kommentar*
R. Paret, *Der Koran. Kommentar und Konkordanz,* Stuttgart 1971; 1977; Kohlhammer 1980

Paret, *Koran*
R. Paret, *Der Koran. Übersetzung,* Stuttgart 1962

Paret (ed.), *Koran*
R. Paret (ed.) *Der Koran,* Darmstadt 1975

Penrice, *Dictionary*
J. Penrice, *A dictionary and glossary of the Koran,* London 1873; repr. 1971

Pickthall, *Koran*
M.M. Pickthall, *The meaning of the glorious Koran,* London 1930; New York 1976

Qāshāni, *Taʾwīl*
ʿAbd al-Razzāq al-Qāshānī, *Taʾwīl al-Qurʾān,* 2 vols., Beirut 1968. See Ibn al-ʿArabī

Qāsimī, *Tafsīr*
Muḥammad Jamāl al-Dīn al-Qāsimī, *Maḥāsin al-taʾwīl,* 18 vols., Cairo 1957-70

Qasṭallānī, *Laṭāʾif*
Aḥmad b. Muḥammad b. Abī Bakr al-Qasṭallānī, *Laṭāʾif al-ishārāt li-funūn al-qirāʾāt,* ed. ʿĀmir al-Sayyid ʿUthmān and ʿAbd al-Ṣabūr Shāhīn, Cairo 1972

Qasṭallānī, *Mawāhib*
Aḥmad b. Muḥammad b. Abī Bakr al-Qasṭallānī, *al-Mawāhib al-laduniyya bi-l-minaḥ al-muḥammadiyya,* ed. Ṣāliḥ Aḥmad al-Shāmī, 4 vols., Beirut/Damascus/Amman 1412/1991

Qummī, *Tafsīr*
Abū l-Ḥasan ʿAlī b. Ibrāhīm al-Qummī, *Tafsīr,* ed. Ṭayyib al-Mūsāwī al-Jazāʾirī, 2 vols., Najaf 1387/1967; Beirut 1991

Qurṭubī, *Jāmiʿ*
Abū ʿAbdallāh Muḥammad b. Aḥmad al-Qurṭubī, *al-Jāmiʿ li-aḥkām al-Qurʾān,* ed. Aḥmad ʿAbd al-ʿAlīm al-Bardūnī et al., 20 vols., Cairo 1952-67; Beirut 1965-7

Qushayrī, *Laṭāʾif*
Abū l-Qāsim ʿAbd al-Karīm b. Hawāzin al-Qushayrī, *Laṭāʾif al-ishārāt,* ed. Ibrāḥim Basyūnī, 6 vols., Cairo 1968-71

Quṭb, *Ẓilāl*
Sayyid Quṭb Ibrāhīm Ḥusayn Shādhilī, *Fī ẓilāl al-Qurʾān,* 6 vols., Beirut 1393-4/1973-4; rev. 11th ed., Cairo 1993

al-Rāghib al-Iṣfahānī, *Mufradāt*
Abū l-Qāsim al-Ḥusayn al-Rāghib al-Iṣfahānī, *Muʿjam mufradāt alfāẓ al-Qurʾān,* Beirut 1392/1972

Rashīd Riḍā, *Manār*
Muḥammad Rashīd Riḍā and Muḥammad ʿAbduh, *Tafsīr al-Qurʾān al-ḥakīm al-shahīr bi-Tafsīr al-Manār,* 12 vols., Beirut n.d.

Rāzī, *Tafsīr*
Fakhr al-Dīn al-Rāzī, *al-Tafsīr al-kabīr (Mafātīḥ al-ghayb),* ed. Muḥammad Muḥyī l-Dīn Abd al-Ḥamīd, 32 vols. in 16, Cairo 1352/1933; Tehran n.d.; Beirut 1981

Rippin, *Approaches*
Andrew Rippin (ed.), *Approaches to the history of the interpretation of the Qurʾān,* Oxford 1988

Rummānī et al., *Rasāʾil*
ʿAlī b. ʿĪsā al-Rummānī, Ḥamd b. Muḥammad al-Khaṭṭābī and ʿAbd al-Qāhir al-Jurjānī, *Thalāth rasāʾil fī iʿjāz al-Qurʾān,* ed. Muḥammad Khalaf Allāh Aḥmad and Muḥammad Zaghlūl Sallām, Cairo 1976

Rūzbihān al-Baqlī, *ʿArāʾis*
Rūzbihān b. Abī Naṣr al-Baqlī, *ʿArāʾis al-bayān fī ḥaqāʾiq al-Qurʾān,* 2 vols., Cawnpore 1301/1884

Ṣābūnī, *Tafsīr*
Muḥammad ʿAlī Ṣābūnī, *Ṣafwat al-tafāsīr. Tafsīr lil-Qurʾān al-karīm,* 3 vols., Beirut 1981

Ṣafadī, *Wāfī*
Khalīl b. Aybak al-Ṣafadī, *al-Wāfī bi-l-wafayāt. Das biographische Lexikon des Ṣalāḥaddīn Ḫalīl ibn Aibak aṣ-Ṣafadī,* ed. H. Ritter et al., 24 vols. to date, Wiesbaden-Beirut-Damascus 1962-

Sakhāwī, *Jamāl*
ʿAlam al-Dīn ʿAlī b. Muḥammad al-Sakhāwi, *Jamāl al-qurrāʾ wa-kamāl al-iqrāʾ,* ed. ʿAlī Ḥusayn al-Bawwāb, 2 vols., Mecca 1408/1987

Ṣaliḥī, *Subul*
Shams al-Dīn Muḥammad b. Yūsuf al-Ṣāliḥī, *Subul al-hudā wa-l-rashād,* ed. ʿĀdil Aḥmad ʿAbd al-Mawjūd and ʿAlī Muḥammad Muʿawwad, 12 vols., Beirut 1414/1993

Samʿānī, *Ansāb*
ʿAbd al-Karīm b. Muḥammad al-Samʿānī, *Kitāb al-Ansāb,* facsimile ed., D.S. Margoliouth, Leiden 1912; ed. Muḥammad ʿAbd al-Muʿīd Khān et al., 13 vols., Hyderabad 1382-1402/1962-82

Schawāhid-Indices
A. Fischer and E. Bräunlich, eds., *Indices der Reimwörter und der Dichter der in den arabischen Schawāhid-Kommentaren und in verwandten Werken erläuterten Belegverse,* Leipzig 1934-45

Schwarzbaum, *Legends*
H. Schwarzbaum, *Biblical and extra-biblical legends in Islamic folk-literature,* Wallford-Hessen 1982

Sezgin, *GAS*
F. Sezgin, *Geschichte des arabischen Schrifttums,* 9 vols., Leiden 1967-84

Shāfiʿī, *Aḥkām*
Muḥammad b. Idrīs al-Shāfiʿī, *Aḥkām al-Qurʾān,* 2 vols. in 1, Beirut 1980

Shāfiʿī, *Mufassirān*
Muḥammad Shāfiʿī, *Mufassirān-i shīʿah,* Shiraz 1349[solar]/1970

Shahrastānī, *Milal*
Abū l-Fatḥ Muḥammad al-Shahrastānī, *al-Milal wa-l-niḥal,* ed. W. Cureton, 2 vols., London 1846; ed. Muḥammad Fatḥ Allāh Badrān, 2 vols., Cairo 1947-55; ed. Fahmī Muḥammad, Beirut 1992

Shawkānī, *Tafsīr*
Abū ʿAbdallāh Muḥammad b. ʿAlī al-Shawkānī, *Fatḥ al-qadīr al-jāmiʿ bayna fannay l-riwāya wa-l-dirāya fī ʿilm al-tafsīr,* 5 vols., Cairo 1349/1930; repr. Beirut 1973

Sibṭ Ibn al-Jawzī, *Mirʾāt*
Shams al-Dīn Abū l-Muẓaffar Yūsuf b. Qizoğlu Sibṭ Ibn al-Jawzī, *Mirʾāt al-zamān fī taʾrīkh al-aʿyān,* ed. Iḥsān ʿAbbās, Beirut 1405/1985

Speyer, *Erzählungen*
Heinrich Speyer, *Die biblischen Erzählungen im Qoran,* Gräfenhainich 1931; repr. Hildesheim 1961

Sprenger, *Moḥammad*
A. Sprenger, *Das Leben und die Lehre des Moḥammad,* 3 vols., 2nd ed., Berlin 1869

Storey, *PL*
C.A. Storey, *Persian literature. A bio-bibliographical survey,* 2 vols. in 5, London 1927

Sufyān al-Thawrī, *Tafsīr*
Abū ʿAbdallāh Sufyān al-Thawrī, *al-Tafsīr,* ed. Imtiyāz ʿAlī ʿArshī, Beirut 1403/1983

Suhaylī, *Taʿrīf*
Abū l-Qāsim ʿAbd al-Raḥmān b. ʿAbdallāh al-Suhaylī, *al-Taʿrīf wa-l-iʿlām fī mā ubhima fī l-Qurʾān min al-asmāʾ wa-l-aʿlām,* ed. ʿAbdallāh Muḥammad ʿAlī al-Naqrāṭ, Tripoli 1401/1992

Sulamī, *Ziyādāt*
Abū ʿAbd al-Raḥmān Muḥammad b. al-Ḥusayn al-Sulamī, *Ziyādāt ḥaqāʾiq al-tafsīr,* ed. G. Böwering, Beirut 1995

Suyūṭī, *Durr*
Jalāl al-Dīn al-Suyūṭī, *al-Durr al-manthūr fī l-tafsīr bi-l-maʾthūr,* 6 vols., Beirut 1990

Suyūṭī, *Ḥuffāẓ*
Jalāl al-Dīn al-Suyūṭī, *Ṭabaqāt al-ḥuffāẓ,* ed. ʿAlī Muḥammad ʿUmar, Cairo 1973

Suyūṭī, *Itqān*
Jalāl al-Dīn al-Suyūṭī, *al-Itqān fī ʿulūm al-Qurʾān,* ed. Muḥammad Abū l-Faḍl Ibrāhīm, 4 vols. in 2, Cairo 1967
Suyūṭī, *Khaṣāʾiṣ*
Jalāl al-Dīn al-Suyūṭī, *al-Khaṣāʾiṣ al-kubrā,* Hyderabad 1320/1902; repr. Beirut n.d.
Suyūṭī, *Mufḥamāt*
Jalāl al-Dīn al-Suyūṭī, *al-Mufḥamāt al-aqrān fī mubhamāt al-Qurʾān,* ed. Muṣṭafā Dīb al-Bughā, Damascus and Beirut 1403/1982
Suyūṭī, *Muhadhdhab*
Jalāl al-Dīn al-Suyūṭī, *al-Muhadhdhab fī mā waqaʿa fī l-Qurʾān min al-muʿarrab,* ed. al-Tihāmī al-Rājī al-Hāshimī, Rabat n.d.; in *Rasāʾil fī l-fiqh wa-l-lugha,* ed. ʿAbdallāh al-Jubūrī, Beirut 1982, pp. 179-235
Suyūṭī, *Ṭabaqāt*
Jalāl al-Dīn al-Suyūṭī, *Ṭabaqāt al-mufassirīn,* ed. ʿAlī Muḥammad ʿUmar, Cairo 1976
Suyūṭī, *Taḥbīr*
Jalāl al-Dīn al-Suyūṭī, *al-Taḥbīr fī ʿilm al-tafsīr,* ed. Fatḥī ʿAbd al-Qādir Farīd, Cairo 1406/1986
Suyūṭī, *Tanāsuq*
Jalāl al-Dīn al-Suyūṭī, *Tanāsuq al-durar fī tanāsub al-suwar,* ed. ʿAbd al-Qādir Aḥmad ʿAṭā, Beirut 1406/1986
Ṭabarānī, *Awsaṭ*
Abū l-Qāsim Sulaymān b. Aḥmad al-Ṭabarānī, *al-Muʿjam al-awsaṭ,* ed. Ṭāriq b. ʿAwaḍ Allāh b. Muḥammad and ʿAbd al-Muḥsin Ibrāhīm al-Ḥusaynī, 10 vols., Cairo 1415/1995
Ṭabarānī, *Kabīr*
Abū l-Qāsim Sulaymān b. Aḥmad al-Ṭabarānī, *al-Muʿjam al-kabīr,* ed. Ḥamdī ʿAbd al-Majīd al-Salafī, vols. i-xii, xvii-xx and xxii-xxv, Baghdad 1398-1404/1977-83; Mosul 1401/1983
Ṭabarī, *Tafsīr*
Abū Jaʿfar Muḥammad b. Jarīr al-Ṭabarī, *Jāmiʿ al-bayān ʿan taʾwīl āy al-Qurʾān* [up to Q 14:27], ed. Maḥmūd Muḥammad Shākir and Aḥmad Muḥammad Shākir, 16 vols., Cairo 1954-68; 2nd ed. for some vols., Cairo 1969; ed. Aḥmad Sāʿīd ʿAlī et al., 30 vols., Cairo 1373-77/1954-7; repr. Beirut 1984
Ṭabarī, *Taʾrīkh*
Abū Jaʿfar Muḥammad b. Jarīr al-Ṭabarī, *Taʾrīkh al-rusul wa-l-mulūk,* ed. M.J. de Goeje et al., 15 vols., Leiden 1879-1901; ed. Muḥammad Abū l-Faḍl Ibrāhīm, 10 vols., Cairo 1960-9
Ṭabarsī, *Majmaʿ*
Abū ʿAlī l-Faḍl b. al-Ḥasan al-Ṭabarsī, *Majmaʿ al-bayān fī tafsīr al-Qurʾān,* intr. Muḥsin al-Amīn al-Ḥusaynī al-ʿĀmilī, 30 vols. in 6, Beirut 1380/1961
Ṭabāṭabāʾī, *Mīzān*
Muḥammad Ḥusayn Ṭabāṭabāʾī, *al-Mīzān fī tafsīr al-Qurʾān,* 20 vols., Beirut 1393-4/1973-4; vol. xxi, Beirut 1985
Tāj al-ʿarūs
Muḥibb al-Dīn al-Sayyid Muḥammad Murtaḍā al-Zabīdī, *Sharḥ al-qāmūs al-musammā Tāj al-ʿarūs min jawāhir al-Qāmūs,* 10 vols., Cairo 1306-7; ed. ʿAbd al-Sattār Aḥmad Faraj et al., 20 vols. to date, Kuwait 1965-
Thaʿālibī, *Iʿjāz*
ʿAbd al-Malik b. Muḥammad al-Thaʿālibī, *al-Iʿjāz wa-l-ījāz,* ed. Iskandar Āṣāt, Constantinople 1897; Beirut 1983
Thaʿālibī, *Iqtibās*
ʿAbd al-Malik b. Muḥammad al-Thaʿālibī, *al-Iqtibās min al-Qurʾān al-karīm,* ed. Ibtisām Marhūn al-Ṣaffār and Mujāhid Muṣṭafā Bahjat, 2 vols. in 1, Cairo 1412/1992
Thaʿālibī, *Yatīma*
ʿAbd al-Malik b. Muḥammad al-Thaʿālibī, *Yatīmāt al-dahr fī maḥāsin ahl al-ʿaṣr,* 4 vols., Damascus 1304/1886-7; ed. Muḥammad Muḥyī l-Dīn ʿAbd al-Ḥamīd, 4 vols., Cairo 1375-7/1956-8
Thaʿlabī, *Qiṣaṣ*
Aḥmad b. Muḥammad b. Ibrāhīm al-Thaʿlabī, *Qiṣaṣ al-anbiyāʾ al-musammā bi-ʿArāʾis al-majālis,* Cairo 1322; repr. Beirut 1980

Thaʿlabī-Goldfeld
I. Goldfeld, *Qurʾānic commentary in the eastern Islamic tradition of the first four centuries of the hijra. An annotated edition of the preface to al-Thaʿlabī's "Kitāb al-Kashf wa-l-bayān ʿan Tafsīr al-Qurʾān,"* Acre 1984

Tirmidhī, *Ṣaḥīḥ*
Abū ʿĪsā Muḥammad b. ʿĪsā al-Tirmidhī, *al-Jāmiʿ al-ṣaḥīḥ*, ed. Aḥmad Muḥammad Shākir et al., 5 vols., Cairo 1937-65

Ṭūsī, *Fihrist*
Muḥammad b. al-Ḥasan al-Ṭūsī, *al-Fihrist*, Najaf 1356/1937; Beirut 1983

Ṭūsī, *Tibyān*
Muḥammad b. al-Ḥasan al-Ṭūsī, *al-Tibyān fī tafsīr al-Qurʾān*, intr. Āghā Buzurk al-Ṭihrānī, 10 vols., Najaf 1376-83/1957-63

Tustarī, *Tafsīr*
Sahl b. ʿAbdallāh al-Tustarī, *Tafsīr al-Qurʾān al-ʿaẓīm*, Cairo 1329/1911

ʿUkbarī, *Tibyān*
Abū l-Baqāʾ ʿAbdallāh b. al-Ḥusayn al-ʿUkbarī, *al-Tibyān fī iʿrāb al-Qurʾān*, ed. ʿAlī Muḥammad al-Bajāwī, 2 vols., Cairo 1396/1976

Wagtendonk, *Fasting*
K. Wagtendonk, *Fasting in the Koran*, Leiden 1968

Wāḥidī, *Asbāb*
Abū l-Ḥasan ʿAlī b. Aḥmad al-Nīsābūrī al-Wāḥidī, *Asbāb al-nuzūl*, Cairo 1968

Wāḥidī, *Wasīṭ*
Abū l-Ḥasan ʿAlī b. Aḥmad al-Nīsābūrī al-Wāḥidī, *al-Wasīṭ fī tafsīr al-Qurʾān*, ed. ʿĀdil Aḥmad ʿAbd al-Mawjūd et al., 4 vols., Beirut 1415/1994

Wansbrough, *QS*
J. Wansbrough, *Quranic studies. Sources and methods of scriptural interpretation,* Oxford 1977

Wāqidī, *Maghāzī*
Muḥammad b. ʿUmar al-Wāqidī, *Kitāb al-Maghāzī*, ed. M. Jones, 3 vols., London 1966

Watt-Bell, *Introduction*
W.M. Watt, *Bell's introduction to the Qurʾān*, Edinburgh 1970, 1991

Wensinck, *Concordance*
A.J. Wensinck et al., *Concordance et indices de la tradition musulmane*, 8 vols., Leiden 1936-79; repr. 8 vols. in 4, 1992

Wensinck, *Handbook*
A.J. Wensinck, *A handbook of early Muhammadan tradition*, Leiden 1927

Wild, *Text*
S. Wild, ed., *The Qurʾān as text*, Leiden 1996

Yaḥyā b. Sallām, *Tafsīr*
Yaḥyā b. Sallām al-Baṣrī, *al-Taṣārīf. Tafsīr al-Qurʾān mimmā shtabahat asmāʾuhu wa-taṣarrafat maʿānīhi*, ed. Hind Shalabī, Tunis 1979

Yaʿqūbī, *Buldān*
Aḥmad b. Abī Yaʿqūb b. Wāḍiḍ al-Yaʿqūbī, *Kitāb al-Buldān*, ed. M.J. de Goeje, Leiden 1892, 1967

Yaʿqūbī, *Taʾrīkh*
Aḥmad b. Abī Yaʿqūb b. Wāḍiḥ al-Yaʿqūbī, *Ibn Wādhih qui dicitur al-Jaʿqubi historiae*, ed. M.T. Houtsma, 2 vols., Leiden 1883; repr. 1969

Yāqūt, *Buldān*
Yāqūt b. ʿAbdallāh al-Ḥamawī, *Muʿjam al-buldān*, ed. F. Wüstenfeld, 6 vols., Leipzig 1863-6; 5 vols., Beirut 1374-6/1955-7; ed. Farīd ʿAbd al-ʿAzīz al-Jundī, 7 vols., Beirut 1990

Yāqūt, *Irshād*
Yāqūt b. ʿAbdallāh al-Ḥamawī, *Irshād al-arīb ilā maʿrifat al-adīb. Muʿjam al-udabāʾ*, ed. D.S. Margoliouth, 7 vols., London and Leiden 1923-6; ed. Iḥsān ʿAbbās, 7 vols., Beirut 1993

Zajjāj, *Maʿānī*
Abū Isḥāq Ibrāhīm b. Muḥammad b. al-Sarī l-Zajjāj, *Maʿānī l-Qurʾān wa-iʿrābuhu*, ed. ʿAbd al-Jalīl ʿAbduh Shalabī, 5 vols., Beirut 1408/1988

Zamakhsharī, *Asās*
Maḥmūd b. ʿUmar al-Zamakhsharī, *Asās al-balāgha*, Beirut 1979

Zamakhsharī, *Kashshāf*
Maḥmūd b. ʿUmar al-Zamakhsharī, *al-*

Kashshāf ʿan ḥaqāʾiq ghawāmiḍ al-tanzīl wa-ʿuyūn al-aqāwīl fī wujūh al-taʾwīl, 4 vols., Beirut 1366/1947; ed. Muḥammad ʿAbd al-Salām Shāhīn, 4 vols., Beirut 1995

Zambaur, *Manuel*
E. de Zambaur, *Manuel de généalogie et de chronologie pour l'histoire de l'Islam*, Hanover 1927; repr. Bad Pyrmont 1955

Zarkashī, *Burhān*
Badr al-Dīn al-Zarkashī, *al-Burhān fī ʿulūm al-Qurʾān*, ed. Muḥammad Abū l-Faḍl Ibrāhīm, 4 vols., Cairo 1957; Beirut 1972; ed. Yūsuf ʿAbd al-Raḥmān al-Marʿashlī et al., 4 vols., Beirut 1994

Zayd b. ʿAlī, *Musnad*
Zayd b. ʿAlī Zayn al-ʿĀbidīn, *Musnad*, ed. Bakr b. Muḥammad ʿĀshūr, 1328/1910; Beirut 1983

Ziriklī, *Aʿlām*
Khayr al-Dīn al-Ziriklī, *al-Aʿlām. Qāmūs tarājim li-ashhar al-rijāl wa-l-nisāʾ min al-ʿArab wa-l-mustaʿribīn wa-l- mustashriqīn*, 10 vols., Damascus 1373-8/1954-9; 8 vols., Beirut 1979

Zubaydī, *Ṭabaqāt*
Abū Bakr Muḥammad b. al-Ḥasan al-Zubaydī, *Ṭabaqāt al-naḥwiyyīn wa-l-lughawiyyīn*, ed. Muḥammad Abū l-Faḍl Ibrāhīm, Cairo 1373/1954

Zubayrī, *Nasab*
Muṣʿab al-Zubayrī, *Nasab Quraysh*, ed. E. Lévi-Provençal, Cairo 1953

Zurqānī, *Sharḥ*
Muḥammad b. ʿAbd al-Bāqī al-Miṣrī al-Mālik, *Sharḥ al-mawāhib al-laduniyya*, ed. Muḥammad ʿAbd al-ʿAzīz al-Khālidī, 12 vols., Beirut 1417/1996

E

Ears

The organs of hearing. The Arabic term used in the Qurʾān for ear is *udhun* (pl. *ādhān*), occurring eighteen times in both Meccan and Medinan passages. The ear as anatomical object (see ANATOMY) is presented, for example, in Q 4:119, where Satan (see DEVIL) induces superstitious people to slit their cattle's ears; in Q 2:19, where fools (*sufahāʾ*, Q 2:13), upon sighting menacing storm clouds "press their fingers in their ears *(ādhān)* by reason of the thunderclap, fearing death"; in Q 18:11, where God sealed the ears *(fa-ḍarabnā ʿalā ādhānihim)* of the youths sleeping in the cave for a number of years (see MEN OF THE CAVE); and in Q 5:45, reflecting law in ancient Israel (see LAW AND THE QURʾĀN; TORAH; CHILDREN OF ISRAEL), "Life for life, eye for eye (see EYES), nose for nose, ear *(al-udhun)* for ear."

The sense of hearing is very important in the qurʾānic discourse, particularly when it is related to thoughtful awareness (see HEARING AND DEAFNESS; SEEING AND HEARING; KNOWLEDGE AND LEARNING). In one passage (Q 9:61), the prophet Muḥammad's antagonists (see OPPOSITION TO MUḤAMMAD) characterize him as being "an ear" *(udhun)* in the sense of one who listens to everyone. The Qurʾān retorts: "He is an ear of what is best for you" (Q 9:61). Hearing, whether in literal or spiritually/morally meaningful ways, is frequently mentioned in the Qurʾān, both with respect to human beings and God. God is almost exclusively characterized by the frequent noun and adjective derived from the main Arabic root for hearing and listening, *s-m-ʿ*, i.e. *samīʿ*, "one who hears" or "hearing" (e.g. Q 2:127, 137, 181; 4:58, 134; 21:4; 44:6; 58:1). *Samīʿ* often occurs with the definite article thus rendering a name, "the all-hearing," paired either with *ʿalīm*, "knowing," or *baṣīr*, "seeing," in forty-three of forty-seven occurrences (in Q 14:39 God is hearer of personal prayer [*duʿāʾ*, see PRAYER] and in Q 34:50 God "hears [all] and is [always] near" *[innahu samīʿun qarībun]*). God as "hearer/all-hearing" occurs in both Meccan and Medinan passages. Interestingly, the two occurrences where the word applies to humans (Q 11:24 and 76:2) are both Meccan. Q 76:2 tells of God's ordaining for humankind hearing *(samīʿ)* and sight *(baṣīr)*, two key divine attributes in the qurʾānic worldview (see GOD AND HIS ATTRIBUTES).

Active verbal words for hearing/listening, also derived from the frequently employed *s-m-ʿ* root, include the imperative *ismaʿ*, as in Q 5:108: "Fear (q.v.) God, and listen *(wa-smaʿū)*" and Q 36:25: "For my part, I believe in your lord; therefore hear me *(fa-smaʿūni)*"; the imperfect active in Q 7:179, concerning both humans and jinn (q.v.): "They have hearts (see HEART) wherewith they understand not, eyes wherewith they see not, and ears *(ādhān)* wherewith they hear not *(lā yasmaʿūna bihā)*"; and the arresting early Meccan passage Q 72:1: "Say: It has been revealed to me that a company of the jinn listened *(istamaʿa)* [to the Qurʾān recitation; see RECITATION OF THE QURʾĀN] and declared, 'We have truly heard *(ʾinnā samiʿnā)* a wondrous recital *(qurʾānan ʿajaban)!*'"

The frequent references to hearing and listening in the Qurʾān — of which there are far more than references to actual ears — bear witness to the strongly oral and auditory nature of the message (see ORALITY) and indeed to Muḥammad's prophetic vocation, which was spare in visionary episodes (see VISIONS) but rich in hearing and speaking (see REVELATION AND INSPIRATION; PROPHETS AND PROPHETHOOD). God's frequent command "Say!" *(qul)*, followed by what then is revealed to Muḥammad, occurs 332 times in the text, in addition to many hundreds of other words relating to saying/speaking (see SPEECH) derived from the same root (*q-w-l*, e.g. "He said *[qāla]*," with God often as subject, occurs 529 times; see LITERARY STRUCTURES OF THE QURʾĀN; LANGUAGE OF THE QURʾĀN). Since fatefully important utterances are continuously declared (see RHETORIC OF THE QURʾĀN), it is no wonder that ears and hearing are also prominent in the message that, when heard by the God-fearing, causes their skins to quiver, followed by softening of both skins and hearts (Q 39:23).

Frederick Mathewson Denny

Bibliography
Primary: ʿAbd al-Bāqī; A.Y. ʿAlī, *The holy Qurʾān*, Brentwood, MD 1989 (new rev. ed.).
Secondary: M. Allard et al., *Analyse conceptuelle du Coran par cartes perforées*, 2 vols., Paris 1963, i, 31 (physical morphology: the head and its parts); ii, 75; A.A. Ambrose, 'Höre, ohne zu hören' zu Koran 4,46 (48), in *ZDMG* 136 (1986), 15-22; H.E. Kassis, *A concordance of the Qurʾān*, Berkeley 1983; Penrice, *Dictionary*.

Earth

The land and land areas as distinguished from sea or air. In the Qurʾān, "earth" refers both to the terrestrial part of the universe, including the materials or elements of which it is composed, and, as will be seen below, the human body (see ANATOMY). In both cases, the Arabic *arḍ* is used (over 450 occurrences), although other words with such a signification may appear.

Primarily, *arḍ* denotes the earth in distinction from the heavenly sky (see HEAVEN AND SKY). This is the case in the many verses in which the paired couplet, "heaven and earth" *(al-samāʾ wa-l-arḍ)* or "heavens and earth" *(al-samāwāt wa-l-arḍ)*, occurs in a context referring to God as the creator, master or owner of the universe (see CREATION; LORD). Secondly, *arḍ* denotes the space assigned to humankind and earthly animals (see ANIMAL LIFE; LIFE). As such, it is said to be a carpet (*bisāṭ*, Q 71:19) or a bed (*firāsh*, Q 2:22; *mahd*, Q 20:53; 43:10; *mihād*, Q 78:6) spread by God (*daḥā*, Q 79:30; *madda*, Q 13:3; 15:19; 50:7; *farasha*, Q 51:48) for his creatures, with the implication that it is flat and floats on the surface of the sea. In order to prevent it from pitching (*māda*, Q 16:15; 21:31; 31:10), God has firmly anchored it to mountains, described as *rawāsin* (Q 13:3; 15:19; 16:15; 21:31; 27:61; 31:10; 50:7; 77:27) and, finally, has strewn it with pathways and rivers

(Q 13:3; 16:15; 20:53; 21:31; 43:10; 71:20). Sometimes this terrestrial space is designated as earth and sea, in which case *arḍ* is replaced by the couplet, *al-barr wa-l-baḥr* ("the dry land and the sea," Q 6:59, 63 and 97; 10:22; 17:70; 27:63; 29:65; 30:41; 31:31-2). Lastly, *arḍ* denotes the earth as the cosmic element from the depths of which terrestrial flora (see AGRICULTURE AND VEGETATION) arise in response to the fertilizing rain (Q 2:22, 126; 6:99; 7:58; 10:24; 13:4; 14:32; 16:10-1; 18:45; 20:53; 22:63; 23:18-20; 26:7; 27:60; 32:26-7; 35:27; 36:33-6; 39:21; 50:7, 9-11; 78:14-6; 80:24-32). In this last case, *balad* (Q 2:126; 7:57-8; 14:35; 35:9) and *balda* (Q 25:48-9; 43:11; 50:11) sometimes serve synecdochically for *arḍ*.

The earth is represented as dead one moment, alive the next, i.e. bare or covered with plants, as rain water — always referred to as *māʾ* ("water," "sperm") — restores it to life (Q 2:164; 7:57-8; 16:65; 23:18; 25:48-9; 29:63; 30:24; 35:9; 36:33; 43:11; 45:5; 50:9-11; 57:17; see WATER). Inasmuch as the Arabic word *māʾ* is masculine and *arḍ* feminine, together they form a genuine couple, the first one playing the part of the flora's father, the latter its mother. Although the verses describing the plants' conception, gestation and birth are scattered throughout several different sūras, there is no doubt about the process as a whole: God sends forth beneficent winds (see AIR AND WIND) that carry rain clouds to a dead and barren land. The rain then penetrates the earth, which quivers (*ihtazzat*, Q 22:5; 41:39) before swelling up (*rabat*, ibid.) like the belly of a pregnant woman, and it is only after the water has mingled with the dead plants, previously strewn by the winds (Q 18:45) and the earth is broken up by God (*shaqaqnā l-arḍa shaqqan*, Q 80:26) that flora sprout and grow (*akhraja*, 2:22, 267; 6:99; 7:57; 14:32; 20:53; 32:27; 35:27; 36:33; 39:21, 33; 78:14-6; 87:4; *anbata*, Q 2:61; 15:19; 16:10-1; 26:7; 27:60; 31:10; 50:9-11; 80:27; *anshaʾa*, 6:141; 23:19; 56:72). In this process, the female earth, elsewhere called "a receptacle for the living and the dead" (Q 77:25-6), appears to be a merely passive element whereas the male water is described as active, penetrating the earth, mixing it with dead plants so as to restore them to life, and thereby distinguishing itself, as elsewhere in the Qurʾān, by its life-giving power (see POWER AND IMPOTENCE).

If the earth's revival accompanies the new life of plants, its dying corresponds to the flora's fading away in the heat of the sun (q.v.). Under the influence of the sun, plants first wither and turn yellow, then gradually become hard and finally fall to pieces (*hashīm*, Q 18:45; *ḥuṭām*, Q 39:21; 56:63-5; 57:20) before being strewn by the winds, so that what the Qurʾān calls "dead land" *(balad mayyit)* is only land with no vegetation at all, a dead and barren ground (*arḍ hāmida*, Q 22:5), an arid and sterile soil (*ṣaʿīdan juzur*, Q 18:7-8; *ṣaʿīdan zalaq*, Q 18:40).

Consequently, the vegetation that covers the earth during what one may call its childhood and youth — its adornment or tinsel (*zīna*, Q 18:7; *zukhruf*, Q 10:24; see ORNAMENT AND ILLUMINATION) as the Qurʾān says — is a gift of fresh rain water (again, masculine in Arabic) which acts merely as the delegate here below of the springs and rivers of paradise (q.v.; see also WELLS AND SPRINGS). Moreover, an inventory of the species that, according to the Qurʾān, grow on earth shows that they are the same as those mentioned in reference to the gardens of Eden (see GARDEN), except for agricultural produce (*zarʿ*, Q 6:141; 13:4; 14:37; 16:11; 18:32; 32:27; 39:21; *zurūʿ*, Q 26:148; 44:26; *khaḍir*, Q 6:99; *al-ḥabbu dhū l-ʿaṣf*, Q 55:12; *ḥabb*, Q 6:99; 36:33; 78:15; 80:27; *ḥabba l-ḥaṣīd*, Q 50:9), olive-trees (*zaytūn*, Q 6:99, 141; 16:11; 80:29) and plants used for fodder (*qaḍb*, Q 80:28; *abb*, Q 80:31), all this referring to horticulture and husbandry, which are unnecessary and thus absent in paradise. The earth's and flora's decline and death are due, again, to the blazing sun (feminine in Arabic) which seems, in contrast to water, to represent the infernal fire (q.v.) in this world. This process, however, depends on other factors, such as the quality of the ground. The Qurʾān distinguishes more exactly between 1) good land *(balad ṭayyib)*, the plants of which sprout even in the absence of rain, since it is dampened by dew (Q 2:265), and 2) bad land, the plants of which hardly emerge at all (Q 7:58), together with a sterile, rocky soil that remains hard, dry and bare, even when watered by a downpour (*wābil*, Q 2:264). Moreover, the ground's composition is taken into account: It can be compact, dry and hard like stone (*ṣafwān*, Q 2:264; *ḥijāra*, Q 2:74 or *ḥajar*, Q 2:60; 7:160); easily separated like *turāb*, a matter composed of dry and hard grains of dust (numerous occurrences); compact, soft and humid like clay (q.v.; *ṭīn*, Q 3:49; 5:110; 6:2; 7:12; 17:61; 23:12; 32:7; 38:71, 76; *ṭīn lāzib*, Q 37:11) or discrete, soft and humid like *tharā* (Q 20:6).

If the earth, then, reveals itself as one of the cosmic elements from which the universe is composed, it also plays a role in the birth of humankind, since, as the Qurʾān indicates, it is the same matter from which the first human being was made (see BIOLOGY AS THE CREATION AND STAGES OF LIFE). In this context, the Qurʾān uses a rich and rather obscure vocabulary with no less than five words or expressions which describe the material employed by God to fashion Adam's body (see ADAM AND EVE): "clay as pottery" (*ṣalṣālin ka-l-fakhkhār*, Q 55:14), according to al-Ṭabarī (d. 310/923; *Tafsīr*, xi, 582) "a clay or mud that has not been baked, but only put out to dry"; "clay" (*ṭīn*, Q 6:2; 7:12; 17:61; 38:71, 76); "sticky clay" (*ṭīn lāzib*, Q 37:11); "clay from moulded mud" (*ṣalṣālin min ḥamaʾin masnūn*, Q 15:26-33), according to al-Ṭabarī (ibid., ad loc.) "a black, putrid and therefore stinking mud"; and finally "dusty earth" (*turāb*, Q 3:59; 30:20-1). It is worth noting that all these expressions, taken together, obviously refer to the different stages of the process of making pottery: The basic matter seems to be the dusty earth *(turāb)* which, once mixed with water, turns into a sticky, malleable mud *(ṭīn lāzib)* that is left for some time and changes into a rather putrid matter *(ṣalṣālin min ḥamaʾin masnūn)* which, when shaped, is put to dry and grows hard *(ṣalṣālin ka-l-fakhkhār)* before God gives it life.

Finally, it should be mentioned that dusty earth *(turāb)* is also the form to which the dead body returns after its decomposition, itself a process of withering: As in the case of plants, mortal remains first lose their humid part, i.e. the flesh. The bones (*ʿiẓām*, Q 17:49, 98; 23:35, 82; 36:78; 37:16, 53; 56:47; 79:11) then fall to little pieces (*rufāt*, Q 17:49, 98) as do dried out flora which ultimately turn to dust (*turāb*, Q 13:5; 23:35, 82; 27:67; 37:16, 53; 50:3; 56:47).

Heidi Toelle

Bibliography

Primary: Dīnawarī, Abū Ḥanīfa Aḥmad b. Dāwūd, *Kitāb al-Nabāt*, ed. and trans. M. Ḥamīd Allāh, *Le dictionnaire botanique d'Abū Ḥanīfa ad-Dīnawarī (Kitāb an-Nabāt, de sin à yāʾ). (Reconstitué d'après les citations et ouvrages postérieurs)*, Cairo 1973; *Lisān al-ʿArab;* Rashīd Riḍā, *Manār*, Cairo 1948-56; Ṭabarī, *Taʾrīkh;* id., *Tafsīr*, Beirut 1978.
Secondary: A.A. Ambros, Gestaltung und Funktionen der Biosphäre im Koran, in ZDMG 140 (1990), 290-325; G. Bachelard, *L'eau et les rêves*, Paris 1942; id., *La terre et les rêveries de la volonté*, Paris 1948; id., *La terre et les rêveries du repos*, Paris 1948; J. Bottero and S.N. Kramer, *Lorsque les dieux faisaient l'homme*, Paris 1989; W. Gabr, *Muʿjam al-nabātāt al-ṭibbiyya*, Beirut 1987; A. Hubaishi and K. Müller-Hohenstein, *An*

introduction to the vegetation of Yemen, Eschborn 1984; C. Lévi-Strauss, *Mythologiques*, 4 vols., Paris 1967-71; D. Masson, *L'eau, le feu, la lumière*, Paris 1985; M. Merleau-Ponty, *Phénoménologie de la perception*, Paris 1968; R. Nabielek, Biologische Kenntnisse und Überlieferangen im Mittelalter (4-15 Jh.), in I. Jahn (ed.), *Geschichte der Biologie*, Stuttgart 1998³, 113-5; D. Sidersky, *Les origines des légendes musulmanes dans le Coran*, Paris 1953; S. Subhi, *La vie future selon le Coran*, Paris 1971; H. Toelle, *Le Coran revisité. Le feu, l'eau, l'air et la terre*, Damascus 1999.

Earthquake see ESCHATOLOGY

East and West see GEOGRAPHY

Ecology see NATURAL WORLD AND THE QURʾĀN

Economics

The science investigating the production and distribution of a society's material resources. In the qurʾānic context, economics is a function of the injunctions, rules and guidelines of Islamic law (*al-sharīʿa*, see LAW AND THE QURʾĀN) that govern the behavior of the individual and society in the acquisition and disposal of material resources and wealth (q.v.). Though works treating taxation (q.v.), the economic role of the state, markets (q.v.), prices and household management were written by Muslim scholars in the pre-modern period (e.g. Abū Yūsuf [d. 182/798], *al-Kharāj;* Ibn Taymiyya [d. 728/1328], *Public duties;* Ibn Khaldūn [d. 809/1406], *Muqaddima*), economic matters on the whole were considered a part of Islamic legal literature (*fiqh*). Beginning in the late twentieth century, many Muslim scholars have sought to develop an Islamic system of economics as a discipline relying on both the guidelines found in canonical texts (i.e. Qurʾān and ḥadīth) and the fruit of Muslim historical experience.

The Qurʾān does not provide a blueprint for an economic system but rather a series of values, guidelines and rules which serve as the basis for developing appropriate economic systems and institutions for Muslim communities (Haq, *Economic doctrines*, 81-9; Naqvi, *Ethics*, 37-57). The many positive values include justice (see JUSTICE AND INJUSTICE), moderation (q.v.) and honesty as well as kindness to the disadvantaged, while the negative values are named as injustice, greed, extravagance, miserliness and hoarding. Similarly, the Qurʾān identifies prohibited economic activities such as usury (q.v.; *ribā*, considered by many Muslims to be equivalent to interest), misappropriation, and gambling (q.v.), as well as permitted ones such as trade. Five areas of economic behavior are prominently mentioned in the Qurʾān: justice and communal responsibility; the acquisition of wealth; the disposal of wealth; the protection of the disadvantaged and the regulation of transactions through contracts (see CONTRACTS AND ALLIANCES).

Justice and communal responsibility

Justice (*ʿadl*) is to be upheld in all aspects of life, including the economic (Q 4:58; 6:152; 11:84-7; 16:76; 42:15), and those who pursue economic affairs are exhorted to act fairly, truthfully, honestly and in a spirit of cooperation; to enter into transactions freely, without coercion, provide a fair description of the goods involved in a transaction and, when exchanging goods, ensure that proper standards of measure are used (Q 6:152; 7:85; 11:84-5; 12:59, 88; see WEIGHTS AND MEASURES). In contracts such as sale, purchase or lease, where there is a notion of exchange, justice is to be ensured by an equitable exchange between what is surrendered and what is received.

Practices considered to lead to gross injustice are prohibited or blameworthy (see LAWFUL AND UNLAWFUL; FORBIDDEN).

Injustice *(ẓulm)* and tyranny *(baghy, ṭughyān, ʿudwān)* are prominent themes in the Qurʾān and are forbidden in the strongest terms. Those who commit acts of injustice are required to repent (Q 5:39; see REPENTANCE AND PENANCE). They are warned that their punishment in the hereafter will be severe (Q 39:24) and that even in this world they will suffer (Q 29:31; see CHASTISEMENT AND PUNISHMENT; REWARD AND PUNISHMENT; WARNING). Many of the prohibited acts in commerce and finance are also described as unjust, such as dishonesty, cheating (q.v.), fraud, misrepresentation and theft (q.v.).

The community is called upon to ensure that justice is maintained and injustice avoided. Where qurʾānic norms and regulations are violated, the community, individually and collectively, is required to see that acceptable standards of practice are restored. This responsibility functions through the institution of "enjoining what is right and forbidding what is wrong" *(al-amr bi-l-maʿrūf wa-l-nahy ʿan al-munkar)* and is regarded by the Qurʾān as essential to social cohesion (Q 7:157; 9:71; cf. Ibn Taymiyya, *Public duties*, 73-82; see COMMUNITY AND SOCIETY IN THE QURʾĀN). For the Qurʾān, conditions most conducive to ensuring justice in the area of economic activity exist when the ethical, moral and legal injunctions provided in the Qurʾān are put into practice (see ETHICS IN THE QURʾĀN; GOOD AND EVIL; LAW AND THE QURʾĀN), together with those derived from the normative behavior of the Prophet (see ḤADĪTH AND THE QURʾĀN; SĪRA AND THE QURʾĀN; SUNNA).

Acquisition of wealth

The human being, as defined in the Qurʾān, naturally desires wealth and material gain. Regulation of this desire, however, in light of spiritual and moral values leads to socio-economic equilibrium. The desire for comfort and adornment (Q 18:46; 42:36) or for an easy livelihood is described as one of the pleasures of this world rather than an evil (see MATERIAL CULTURE AND THE QURʾĀN), and Muslims are encouraged to seek and earn such things, even during the pilgrimage (q.v.; *ḥajj*, Q 2:198; Qurṭubī, *Jāmiʿ*, ii, 274). The Qurʾān even allowed the Prophet to cut short the prayers lest economic activity be hampered (Q 73:20; see PRAYER).

The Qurʾān emphasizes repeatedly that all things in the universe belong to God, the creator (see CREATION); all human ownership is, therefore, custodial (Q 2:155, 247; 17:6). Wealth bestowed upon a person is a blessing (q.v.; *niʿma)* and is held in trust from God (Q 8:28; 24:33; see COVENANT). Although everything belongs to God, an individual is called to strive to share in this wealth; it is considered an acceptable and even beneficial activity provided that the qurʾānic rules and guidelines are followed. The resulting private ownership is seen as a right which is to be protected (Q 2:188; see PROPERTY). In turn, the community is allowed certain rights over the wealth of the individual: Unlimited private property would destroy the social obligations which go together with the possession of wealth, and balancing the interests, rights and obligations of the individual with the needs of the community is one of the key features of the qurʾānic economic outlook.

According to the Qurʾān, there are several methods by which wealth can be acquired but the most important appears to be labor or work *(ʿamal)* or earned acquisition *(kasb)*. These terms indicate that effort and a meaningful contribution are necessary for prosperity, including trade (Q 2:275) or even *jihād* (q.v.; Q 8:41, where booty, *ghanīma*, is considered a source of wealth; cf. Mālik, *Muwaṭṭaʾ*, 173-7; see

BOOTY). In contrast, idleness and reliance on others are contrary to the work ethic of the Qurʾān. Begging is discouraged except in the case of dire need. Certain industries and professions are prohibited, such as prostitution (Q 24:33), dancing and erotic arts in general (Q 17:32), the production of and trade in wine and intoxicants (q.v.; Q 2:219; 5:90; cf. Mālik, *Muwaṭṭāʾ*, 355-7) and gambling (Q 5:90-1). Any lawful work is not only considered good and permitted (*ḥalāl*, see PROHIBITED DEGREES) but also an expression of devotion (*ʿibāda*, see RITUAL AND THE QURʾĀN).

Distribution and disposal of wealth

Accumulation of wealth in the hands of a few is seen to cause societal imbalance, leading, in turn, to corruption (q.v.), misuse of economic power and injustice towards the weak or marginalized. One of the main features of the qurʾānic view of wealth distribution is the requirement of those in pursuit of prosperity to give a share of their wealth regularly, to specified categories of people, at specified times, according to certain conditions. The Qurʾān repeatedly commands the faithful to give to the poor and needy (Q 2:271; 9:60; 22:28; see POVERTY AND THE POOR), to one's parents (q.v.) and relatives (Q 2:83, 177; 4:36; see FAMILY). Further, it states that the reward for such giving is great (Q 92:5-7). It links this giving to belief (*īmān*, see BELIEF AND UNBELIEF) and warns of severe punishment for those who do not act generously (Q 74:42-4). The Qurʾān describes such distributive justice in terms of almsgiving (q.v.; *zakāt* or *ṣadaqāt*). Although the two terms were initially interchangeable in the Qurʾān, Islamic law later came to recognize *zakāt* as compulsory (and thus a right of the recipient) and *ṣadaqāt* as voluntary (and thus a sign of the generosity and good-heartedness of the donor; see GIFT-GIVING). The qurʾānic command to give is often coupled with the command to perform prayer *(ṣalāt)*.

Important in the distribution and thus also the acquisition of wealth are the specific formulae according to which property is bequeathed upon one's death (Q 4:11-2, 176; see INHERITANCE). This compulsory distribution of an estate among members of a family reinforces the distribution of a society's wealth and corresponds, again, to the qurʾānic idea of wealth as a trust. The owner is allowed some discretion and is permitted to bequeath up to one-third of his or her property according to preference, as established in the sunna, e.g. for charitable purposes. The owner, however, cannot control the distribution of the remaining two-thirds, which must be inherited by relatives according to qurʾānic regulations of division (Ibn Rushd, *Distinguished*, ii, 407). This is a further example of the qurʾānic objective of maintaining social cohesion by preventing the concentration of wealth in the hands of a few.

Acquisition of property does not mean that the owner has an exclusive right to own property and dispose of it at will. Rather, wealth must always remain in circulation and be fairly distributed (Q 59:7). Stinginess is criticized (Q 53:33-34; 59:9) while moderation (q.v.) is encouraged (Q 17:29). Hoarding wealth is prohibited and those who disobey are warned of hellfire (Q 9:34-35; see DISOBEDIENCE; FIRE). Similarly, squandering property is prohibited; in fact, the community must prevent individuals at risk to themselves *(sufahāʾ)* from wasting their own wealth (Q 4:5; Rāzī, *Tafsīr*, vii, 107). In another context, extravagant spending *(isrāf)* is linked to corruption (*fasād*, Q 2:60; 7:74; 11:85) with severe punishment to follow (Q 7:86; 13:25). In the same vein, individuals should not spend on prohibited goods or acts, such as illicit sex, alcohol or anything that leads to the corruption of society or injury to others.

Non-exploitation of the disadvantaged

According to the Qurʾān, wealth should be acquired by engaging in socially beneficial activities which take into account the needs of the weaker sections of the community. At the time of revelation, Mecca (q.v.) was a trading town and a substantial amount of money was used for lending at interest (considered to be equivalent to *ribā*). The prohibition of usury *(ribā)* is mentioned in four different contexts in the Qurʾān (Ṭabarī, *Tafsīr*, iii, 190). The first emphasizes that *ribā* strips wealth of God's blessing (Q 30:39). The second condemns *ribā*, equating it with wrongful appropriation of property (Q 4:161). The third asks Muslims to avoid *ribā* (Q 3:130). The fourth establishes a clear distinction between *ribā* and trade, urging the believers to take only the principal sum and to forgo even this if the borrower is unable to repay (Q 2:275-80; Ṭabarī, *Tafsīr*, iii, 108-14).

Increase of wealth by means of *ribā* is forbidden on the grounds that it is unjust and exploitative (*ẓulm*, Q 2:279). Given the deep-rooted nature of *ribā* in pre-Islamic and early Muslim society (see PRE-ISLAMIC ARABIA AND THE QURʾĀN), the Qurʾān had to be insistent, declaring that those who transgressed (see ENEMIES) should be prepared for "war (q.v.) against God and his Prophet" (Q 2:279). For the Qurʾān, the greatest injustice occurs when a rich person uses the wealth entrusted to him or her by God to exploit the weak and disadvantaged sections of the community. Since *ribā* occurs largely due to debts (q.v.), the creditor is commanded to give additional time to the debtor in financial difficulty without charging any interest (Q 2:280) and, if need be, to forgive the debt. It also declares that lending without *ribā*, i.e. "an admirable loan" *(qarḍ ḥasan)*, is a charitable activity (Q 2:245; 57:18; 64:17). Although the Qurʾān does not differentiate between rich and poor in dealing with the issue of *ribā*, there is some indication that its main concern was the impact of *ribā* on the poor and disadvantaged (Saeed, *Islamic banking*, 21-39). See also ORPHANS; WIDOW.

Regulation through fulfilling contracts

In order to regulate the economic activities of the community, the Qurʾān insists that transactions must be governed by rules, many of which the text itself supplies. To avoid misunderstanding or injustice, contracts should be in writing and witnesses used where appropriate (Q 2:282; Rāzī, *Tafsīr*, vii, 107; see WITNESSING AND TESTIFYING). The Qurʾān commands believers to fulfil promises (Q 6:152; 16:91; 17:34) and contracts (Q 5:1; 23:8) and emphasizes that this is a duty for which they will have to answer on the day of judgment (Q 17:34; see LAST JUDGMENT). Honoring obligations is not only an economic, moral and redemptive imperative but is also a hallmark of the believer (Q 2:177; Quṭb, *Ẓilāl*, i, 161). On the other hand, breaking one's word or commitment *(ʿahd)* is prohibited (Q 2:27; Qurṭubī, *Jāmiʿ*, i, 172; see BREAKING TRUSTS AND CONTRACTS). Believers are also commanded to pay their debts (Q 3:75), give full measure (Q 6:152; 7:85; 11:84-85; 17:35; 26:181), return what is entrusted to them (Q 2:283; 4:58), and avoid fraud and cheating (Q 26:181).

Such guidelines and regulations provide the basis for contract law in Islam. By regulating economic behavior, the Qurʾān appears to give a significant role to institutions such as the market and provide sufficient space for Muslims, collectively and individually, to develop economic institutions and systems within the framework of the qurʾānic outlook, values and norms. The overarching objective is to ensure that fairness and justice are maintained. It is these rights and obligations that, in theory, limit the absolute freedom available to members of a community in their pursuit of individual economic objectives.

Islamic economic principles in the modern period

In the twentieth century, Muslim scholars have sought to develop an Islamic economics in accordance with qurʾānic guidelines, the sunna and Islamic law, as well as historical experience. The following is a list of principles considered to be the basis of an Islamic economic system (Taleghani, *Society,* 25-9; Najjār, *Madkhal,* 45-87; Sadr, *Iqtiṣādunā,* i, pt. 2, 51-142):

1) Ownership of all things belongs to God alone, humans being entrusted with them as representative (*khalīfa,* see CALIPH) of God on earth (Khan, *Economic teachings,* 7).

2) Economic freedom and behavior is to be constrained by the categories of permitted and forbidden (*ḥalāl wa-ḥarām*) as well as ethical values.

3) Private ownership is recognized with minimal limitations meant to protect the public interest (Khan, *Economic teachings,* 7-14).

4) The role of the market is considered important, while state intervention is meant to protect the public interest and regulate standards of economic activity (Ibn Taymiyya, *Public duties,* 47-58).

5) Where the interests of the individual clash with those of the community, the interests of the community are given preference.

6) Fair compensation for one's labor and the prohibition of labor exploitation (Ibn Taymiyya, *Public duties,* 43-5).

7) One is free to dispose of or distribute one's wealth within the constraints specified by the Qurʾān and sunna.

8) The state (and community) should care for the disadvantaged through public spending programs (Siddiqi, *Role,* 5-30).

9) In trade and exchange, the performance of a socially beneficial and useful type of work should be the basis of profit.

10) Lending money at interest is *ribā;* transactions and economic activity should be free of interest (Saeed, *Islamic banking,* 49-50; Mawdudi, *Ribā,* 139-42).

11) Qurʾānic limitations on acquisition and disposal of wealth, income, consumption and spending are to be maintained.

A number of Islamic economic institutions are being developed to put these principles into practice, among the most important being Islamic financial institutions based on the prohibition of interest. Such an Islamization of economics appears to be increasingly well-received in the Muslim world.

Abdullah Saeed

Bibliography

Primary: Abū Yūsuf, *Kitāb al-Kharāj,* Cairo 1352/1932; Ibn ʿAbidīn, Muḥammad Amīn b. ʿUmar, *Radd al-muḥtār ʿalā al-durr al-mukhtār. Ḥāshiyyat Ibn ʿĀbidīn,* Beirut 1987; Ibn Khaldūn-Rosenthal; Ibn Rushd, *The distinguished jurist's primer. A translation of Bidāyat al-mujtahid,* trans. I.A. Khan Nyazee and M. Abdul Rauf, Reading 1996; Ibn Taymiyya, *Public duties in Islam. The institution of the hisba,* trans. M. Holland, Leicester 1982; ibid., *Fiqh al-muʿāmalāt,* Beirut 1995; Mālik, *Muwaṭṭaʾ,* trans. ʿĀ.ʿA.R. Bewley, Granada 1989; Qurṭubī, *Jāmiʿ;* Quṭb, *Ẓilāl;* Rāzī, *Tafsīr;* Sarakhsī, Muḥammad b. Aḥmad, *Kitāb al-Mabsūṭ,* Beirut 1409/1989; Ṭabarī, *Tafsīr;* Taleghani, Ayatullah Sayyid Mahmud, *Society and economics in Islam,* trans. R. Campbell, Berkeley 1982.
Secondary: M. Asad, *The message of the Qurʾān,* Gibraltar 1980; M.U. Chapra, *Islam and the economic challenge,* Herndon 1992; M.A. Choudhury, *The principles of Islamic political economics. A methodological enquiry,* New York 1992; Y. Essid, *A critique of the origins of Islamic economic thought,* Leiden 1995; I. Haq, *Economic doctrines of Islam,* Herndon 1996; S.W.A. Husaini, *Islamic environmental systems engineering,* London 1980; A.A. Islahi, *Economic concepts of Ibn Taimiyah,* Leicester 1988; M.F. Khan, *Economic teachings of Prophet Muhammad,* Islamabad 1989; S.A. Maududi, *Towards understanding the Qurʾān,* Leicester 1988; A.A. al-Najjār, *al-Madkhal ilā l-nazariyya al-iqtiṣādiyya fī-l-manhaj al-islāmī,* Cairo 1980;

S.N.H. Naqvi, *Ethics and economics. An Islamic synthesis,* Leicester 1981; M.B. al-Ṣadr, *Iqtiṣādunā. Our economics,* 2 vols., Tehran 1982; A. Saeed, *Islamic banking and interest. A study of the prohibition of riba and its contemporary interpretation,* Leiden 1996, 1999²; M.N. Siddiqi, *Role of the state in the economy. An Islamic perspective,* Leicester 1996.

Eden see PARADISE; GARDEN

Editions of the Qurʾān see PRINTING OF THE QURʾĀN; CODICES OF THE QURʾĀN; READINGS OF THE QURʾĀN

Education see KNOWLEDGE AND LEARNING

Egypt

Country in the north-east corner of Africa. Egypt or its capital, Miṣr, occurs by name five times in the Qurʾān, once in oblique form according to most readings (*qirāʾāt,* see READINGS OF THE QURʾĀN). The word Miṣr is mentioned in Q 2:61, 10:87, 12:21, 12:99 and 43:51. Egypt also appears in the Qurʾān as the kingdom of Pharaohs (Q 43:51; see PHARAOH); the country where Joseph (q.v.; Yūsuf) became viceroy, like his patron (*al-ʿazīz,* Q 12:78, 88), after having been a slave and then coming to prominence through his patron's wife (Q 12); the arena of the struggle of Moses (q.v.; Mūsā) and Aaron (q.v.; Hārūn) for their people, the Children of Israel (q.v.; Banū Isrāʾīl, especially sūras 2, 4, 7, 10, 20, 26, 27 and 28); and the refuge given to Jesus (q.v.) and his mother (Q 23:50; see MARY). There is a controversy about the reading of the word Miṣr (Q 2:61), and its significance. Most of the sources prefer the reading *miṣran,* "some country," whereas the rest read Miṣra, the surname of Egypt (al-Sijistānī, *Maṣāḥif,* 57; al-Farrāʾ, *Maʿānī,* i, 42-3).

It seems that, originally, Miṣr referred to the main city (q.v., *al-madīna*) of Egypt or a particular city *(madīna bi-ʿaynihā)* in that country (*Lisān al-ʿArab,* v, 176). Exegetes confirm this identification on the basis of some references in the Qurʾān (Q 7:123; 12:30; 28:15, 18, 20; Nasafī, *Tafsīr,* ii, 70, 219; iii, 229).

The origin of the name Miṣr is also dealt with by exegetes who generally attribute the name to its builder, Miṣr the son of Nūḥ (*Lisān al-ʿArab,* v, 176; see NOAH) or the grandson of Ḥām b. Nūḥ (Ibn al-Faqīh, *Buldān,* 115). His father's name is given in some sources as Miṣrayim, like the name of one of Ḥām's sons in Genesis 8:6, which is the Hebrew form of the word for Egypt. It is a dual form and therein is most likely a hint to the fact that ancient Egypt was regarded as two lands: Upper Egypt and Lower Egypt. The form Miṣr as used in Arabic after its conquest by the Muslims in 18-20/639-41 represents perhaps Lower Egypt only but was later applied to the entire country.

Egypt in qurʾānic exegesis and in sīra *and ḥadīth literature*

Even though Egypt is only cited by name five times, it is nonetheless the most frequently mentioned city or country in the Qurʾān (as is the case in the Bible). Some claim that the Qurʾān mentions Miṣr explicitly and indirectly 28 times in all (Ibn Ẓahīra, *Faḍāʾil,* 71; see GEOGRAPHY).

Exegetes suggest taking some words or expressions as allusions to Egypt or to a specific part of the country: "the land" (*al-arḍ,* Q 7:127, 129; 12:56, 80; 28:4, 6, 19), the Nile (*al-yamm,* Q 7:136; 20:39, 78, 97; 28:7, 40; 51:40), Alexandria (*iram dhāt al-ʿimād,* Q 89:7; cf. Ibn Ẓahīra, *Faḍāʾil,* 73), "a height, where there was a hollow and a spring" (*rabwatin dhāti qarārin wa-maʿīn,* Q 23:50; cf. Ṭabarī, *Taʾrīkh,* i, 597; Ibn

Ẓahīra, *Faḍāʾil,* 71; see WELLS AND SPRINGS). Other interpretations for this last expression — Jerusalem (q.v.), al-Ramla or Damascus — are suggested as well (ʿAbd al-Razzāq, *Tafsīr,* ii, 45-6; Nasafī, *Tafsīr,* iii, 121).

The Qurʾān does not mention Hagar (Hājar) and her Egyptian origin (see ABRAHAM). It also does not mention either the relations between Muḥammad (q.v.) and al-Muqawqis, the ruler of Egypt, or with Mary the Copt (Māriya al-Qibṭiyya; see WIVES OF THE PROPHET), the Prophet's concubine and mother of his son Ibrāhīm, who died in 8/630 (al-Zubayr b. Bakkār, *Muntakhab,* 55-62). But exegetes, ḥadīth and *sīra* traditionists and the so-called tales of the prophets *(qiṣaṣ al-anbiyāʾ)* provide a substantial addition to fill this gap. In the subsequent literature, Egypt became "the holy, good and blessed land" *(al-arḍ al-muqaddasa al-ṭayyiba al-mubāraka,* cf. Ibn Ẓahīra, *Faḍāʾil,* 6). See also EXEGESIS OF THE QURʾĀN; ḤADĪTH AND THE QURʾĀN; SĪRA AND THE QURʾĀN; PROPHETS AND PROPHETHOOD. The wealth (q.v.) of Egypt and its economic and political importance prompted an abundance of traditions in praise of the country (see POLITICS AND THE QURʾĀN). Most of these traditions were attributed to the Prophet, his Companions (see COMPANIONS OF THE PROPHET) or the Bible (q.v.) and eventually became incorporated into the exegesis of the relevant qurʾānic verses. See also SCRIPTURE AND THE QURʾĀN.

Isaac Hasson

Bibliography
ʿAbd al-Razzāq, *Tafsīr,* Beirut 1999; Farrāʾ, *Maʿānī,* Cairo 1980; Ibn al-Faqīh, *Kitāb al-Buldān,* ed. Y. al-Hādī, Beirut 1966; Ibn Ẓahīra, Jamāl al-Dīn Muḥammad b. Muḥammad Abū Ḥāmid, *al-Faḍāʾil al-bāhira fī maḥāsin Miṣr wa-l-Qāhira,* ed. M. al-Saqqā and K. al-Muhandis, Cairo 1969; *Lisān al-ʿArab;* Nasafī, *Tafsīr,* Beirut n.d.; al-Sijistānī, Ibn Abī Dāwūd, *Kitāb al-Maṣāḥif,* Cairo n.d.; Ṭabarī, *Taʾrīkh;* al-Zubayr b. Bakkār, Abū ʿAlī al-Qurashī, *Muntakhab min Kitāb Azwāj al-nabī,* ed. S. al-Shihābī, Beirut 1983.

Election

Choice or appointment by God of an individual or community, thereby designated to carry out or fulfill a task, assume a position of authority (q.v.) or pursue a mission or special purpose, especially that of conveying God's revelation. Related qurʾānic notions also include "choice" in the sense of the best and "divine will" in terms of God's will to choose. What is noteworthy is the connection of the qurʾānic concept of election to divine inspiration and revelation (see REVELATION AND INSPIRATION).

In the Qurʾān and in later literature, three different Arabic roots are used to render the sense of "choose" or "chosen." These roots, *kh-y-r* (whence *ikhtāra,* [Q 7:155; 20:13; 44:32], *yakhtāru* [Q 28:68], *ikhtiyār, khīra* [Q 28:68]), *ṣ-f-w* (whence *iṣṭafā* [Q 2:130, 132, 247; 3:33, 42; 7:144; 27:59; 35:32; 37:153; 39:4], *yaṣṭafī* [Q 22:75], *muṣṭafā* [Q 38:47], *ṣafwa*), and *j-b-y* (whence *ijtabā* [Q 6:87; 7:203; 16:121; 19:58; 20:122; 22:78; 68:50] and *yajtabī* [Q 3:179; 12:6; 42:13]) have essentially the same meaning when used in the Qurʾān. Different English translations of the Qurʾān tend to render these words as chose, choose, choice, prefer, taken and elected. Among the several citations, the following are illustrative of the general import of election in the Qurʾān: 1) From the root *kh-y-r:* God says to Moses, "Know that I have chosen you *(ikhtartuka).* Listen then to the inspiration" *(limā yūḥā,* Q 20:13); to the Israelites (see CHILDREN OF ISRAEL), "Your lord creates what he will and chooses *(wa-yakhtāru)* freely, but they have no power of choice *(al-khīra)*. Blessed be God and exalted above what is associated with him" (Q 28:68). 2) From the root *ṣ-f-w:* God says to Moses, "... I have chosen you *(iṣṭafaytuka)* of all humankind for my message and my word..." (Q 7:144); and of his messengers *(rusul),* "God chooses *(yaṣṭafī)* his messengers from the angels and humans" (Q 22:75; see ANGEL; MESSENGER). 3) From the root *j-b-y:* speaking of various prophets God says, "... and each we preferred above all beings; ... and we elected them *(wa-ajtabaynāhum)* and guided them to a straight path (see PATH OR WAY)" (Q 6:86-7); Jacob (q.v.) speaking to Joseph (q.v.) says: "Your lord will choose you *(yajtabīka),* and teach you to interpret events (or tales)" (Q 12:6). Muḥammad (q.v.), the last of God's messengers, is chosen/elected to speak to humankind, and, in Islamic tradition, is therefore often called "the chosen one" *(al-muṣṭafā),* i.e. the elect (of God). He is also said to be "God's elect (or best) of his creatures" *(ṣafwat Allāh min khalqihi).*

Election or choice *(ikhtiyār)* may be used in quite different senses, in historical, theological and philosophical works (see HISTORY AND THE QURʾĀN; PHILOSOPHY OF THE QURʾĀN; THEOLOGY AND THE QURʾĀN), among others, to express the concept of human choice or free will (see FREEDOM AND PREDESTINATION). In a religio-political sense it is used, primarily by Sunnīs, to refer to the election of a caliph (q.v.; *khalīfa,* lit. "successor") of the prophet Muḥammad, in theory by the consensus of a council (*shūrā,* see CONSULTATION) of leading figures, following the precedent of the five Companions of Muḥammad who "elected" Abū Bakr (q.v.) or that of the later six-man *shūrā* designated by ʿUmar (q.v.) before his death. Succession to the Prophet being one of the dividing lines between Sunnīs and Shīʿīs (see SHĪʿISM AND THE QURʾĀN), Shīʿīs speak not of election, but "designation" (*naṣṣ,* lit. "text") interpreted as "divine ordinance," in reference to Muḥammad's designation of ʿAlī (see ʿALĪ B. ABĪ ṬĀLIB) and, by inference, his descendants, as imāms (i.e. leaders of the Muslim community; see IMĀM), each of whom is believed to have possessed an inherent divine light (q.v.). In Sunnī legal usage, *ikhtiyār* also refers to the process of selection among useful points of law in the four orthodox schools, including the opinions of individual jurists who do not adhere to any of them (see LAW AND THE QURʾĀN). Finally, in astrology *ikhtiyārāt* is used for "selecting" among auspicious and inauspicious omens (q.v.).

William M. Brinner

Bibliography
A.L. Delcambre, Khiyār, in *EI²*, v, 25; T. Fahd, Ikhtiyārāt, in *EI²*, iii, 1063-4; C.V. Findley, Mukhtār, in *EI²*, vii, 519; L. Gardet, Ikhtiyār, in *EI²*, iii, 1062-3; I. Goldziher, *Introduction to Islamic theology and law,* trans. A. and R. Hamori, Princeton 1981, 175, 181; Lane, London 1863-93; E.I.J. Rosenthal, *Political thought in medieval Islam,* Cambridge 1958, 30, 128, 130, 144, 150, 183; A.J. Wensinck, *The Muslim creed,* London 1965, 192; id./J. Burton, Naṣṣ, in *EI²*, vii, 1029.

Elements (the four) see NATURAL WORLD AND THE QURʾĀN

Elephant see ANIMAL LIFE

Elijah

A messenger (q.v.) and prophet who is mentioned three times in the Qurʾān. In the first instance the name of Elijah (Ilyās) is cited along with those of Zechariah (q.v.), John (see JOHN THE BAPTIST) and Jesus (q.v.) with the statement that "all were of the righteous" (Q 6:85). The name of Elijah is next mentioned at the beginning of a passage (Q 37:123-32) that recounts his vicissitudes in the manner of other qurʾānic punishment stories (q.v.) involving the prophets and their peoples (see PROPHETS AND PROPHETHOOD). There Elijah is identified as one of the messengers, the one who called upon his people not to worship an idol called Baʿl (see BAAL; IDOLS AND IMAGES; IDOLATRY AND IDOLATERS). His people refused to obey him (see DISOBEDIENCE) and so he pronounced God's punishment (see ANGER): Only those who followed him survived. In the end of the passage Elijah is described as one of the "believing servants" (Q 37:132). In a verse from this same passage (Q 37:130) the name Elijah appears a third time, but in the mysterious orthographic variation Ilyāsīn instead of the usual form Ilyās. A variant reading proposed by the classical exegetical tradition substitutes the names Ilyās/Ilyāsīn in the passage with those of Idrīs/Idrāsīn (Ṭabarī, *Tafsīr,* xxiii, 96).

The extra-canonical Muslim traditions follow the accounts of the Bible (*1 Kgs* 18 f.; see SCRIPTURE AND THE QURʾĀN), relating that Elijah was sent from God after the death of Ezekiel (q.v.) because the Israelites had begun worshipping idols such as Baʿl, who was revered by the people of Baalbek and, according to other reports, had the form of a woman. Elijah's mission, his choice of Elisha (q.v.) as his disciple, together with the rejection of his message by his people and the punishment inflicted upon them by God, which consisted of a three-year drought, are described in great detail. Other traditions, however, attest to the association of the figure of Elijah with the prophet Idrīs (q.v.) and the mysterious al-Khiḍr (see KHAḌIR/KHIḌR). According to certain exegetes (cf. Suyūṭī, *Durr,* vii, 117-8), the name Idrīs could not have been anything but another name for Elijah, while other reports and traditions claimed that Elijah and al-Khiḍr were the same person, or at least that they were relatives who used to meet annually. The close relationship between these last two is based upon a tradition stating that both of them attained the gift of eternal life (see ETERNITY) in this world and that they are still alive on earth whereas, in contrast, Jesus and Idrīs are alive in heaven (q.v.). Elijah, according to other reports, was turned into a semi-angelic being at the conclusion of his mission among his people. God had Elijah dressed in light (q.v.) and removed from him the desire for food and drink. God then made Elijah ascend to heaven on a horse of fire (ʿUmāra b. Wathīma, *Badʾ al-khalq,* 68).

Arab lexicographers have debated the origin of his name and have concluded that it was taken from the Hebrew, along with other names such as Ishmael (q.v.) and Isaac (q.v.). Yet the Arabic form of the name (Ilyās) bears more similarity to the Christian Greek, Syriac and Ethiopic versions, than to the Hebrew one (see FOREIGN VOCABULARY). In fact, according to Jeffery (*For. vocab.,* 68), the term entered into Arabic from Syriac, as was the case with the name of the idol Baʿl, quoted in the qurʾānic story of Elijah (Q 37:125).

Roberto Tottoli

Bibliography

Primary: Abū l-Layth al-Samarqandī, *Tafsīr,* ed. Beirut 1993, iii, 123; Farrāʾ, *Maʿānī,* ii, 391-3; Ibn ʿAsākir, *Taʾrīkh,* fac. ed., iii, 81-8; Kisāʾī, *Qiṣaṣ,* 244-50; Majlisī, Muḥammad Bāqir, *Biḥār al-anwār,* 25 vols. in 15, Beirut 1983, xiii, 392-403; Sibṭ Ibn al-Jawzī, *Mirʾāt,* i, 459-65; Suyūṭī, *Durr,* 8 vols, Beirut 1983, vii, 116-20; Ṭabarī, *Tafsīr,* ed. Cairo 1968, xxiii, 91-6; id., *Taʾrīkh,* ed. de Goeje, i, 540-4; Thaʿlabī, *Qiṣaṣ,* 223-30; ʿUmāra b. Wathīma, *Badʾ al-khalq wa-qiṣaṣ al-anbiyāʾ,* in R.G. Khoury (ed.), *Les légendes prophétiques dans l'Islam,* Wiesbaden 1978, 63-71.

Secondary: I. Friedlaender, *Die Chadhirlegende und der Alexanderroman,* Leipzig and Berlin 1913, see *Index;* Horovitz, *KU,* 99, 101; Jeffery, *Materials,* 80, 160, 300, 324; id., *For. vocab.,* 68; Nöldeke, *GQ,* iii, 73.

Elisha

A prophet who is mentioned in two verses in the Qurʾān. In the first (Q 6:86), Elisha (al-Yasaʿ) is cited together with Ishmael (q.v.), Jonah (q.v.) and Lot (q.v.), where it is said that they were elevated above the rest of creation *(wa-kullan faḍḍalnā ʿalā l-ʿālamīna)*. Elisha is mentioned in a second verse (Q 38:48), along with Ishmael and Dhū l-Kifl (q.v.), where it is said that "all are among the excellent" *(wa-kullun mina l-akhyāri)*. The Qurʾān does not contain any details about his life and limits itself to mentioning his name together with those of other prophets (see PROPHETS AND PROPHETHOOD). The Arabic version of the name is usually read by lexicographers and exegetes as al-Yasaʿ, but exegetical literature also attests to the variant reading al-Laysaʿ (Farrāʾ, *Maʿānī*, ii, 407-8).

Muslim tradition has added a few particulars about the figure of Elisha. The son of a woman who gave hospitality (see HOSPITALITY AND COURTESY) to Elijah (q.v.), Elisha became his disciple either when Elijah cured him from a serious illness or when Elijah gave him food while he was starving (cf. *1 Kgs* 17:9 f.). According to other traditions, Elijah and Elisha were cousins or, at the very least, had some blood relationship (Sibṭ Ibn al-Jawzī, *Mirʾāt*, i, 460). From that moment, Elisha followed Elijah wherever he went, and was with him when he invoked God's punishment against his people around the time of his death (see PUNISHMENT STORIES). When Elijah was taken to God in heaven (q.v.), Elisha succeeded him as prophet among his people until his death. Certain traditions maintain, however, that Elisha was another name for Dhū l-Kifl or for al-Khiḍr, and possibly Ezekiel (Maqdisī, *Badʾ*, iii, 100; see KHAḌIR/KHIḌR; EZEKIEL).

Roberto Tottoli

Bibliography
Primary: Farrāʾ, *Maʿānī*, ii, 407-8; Kisāʾī, *Qiṣaṣ*, 248-50; Maqdisī, al-Muṭahhar b. Ṭāhir, *al-Badʾ wa-l-taʾrīkh*, ed. C. Huart, 6 vols., Paris 1899-1919, iii, 100; Sibṭ Ibn al-Jawzī, *Mirʾāt*, i, 460, 466; Ṭabarī, *Tafsīr*, ed. Cairo 1968, vii, 261-2; Thaʿlabī, *Qiṣaṣ*, 229-31.
Secondary: Horovitz, *KU*, 152; Jeffery, *For. vocab.*, 68-9.

Embezzlement

see MONEY; BREAKING TRUSTS AND CONTRACTS; THEFT; ORPHANS; WEALTH

Embryo

see BIOLOGY AS THE CREATION AND STAGES OF LIFE; INFANTICIDE; ABORTION

Emigrants and Helpers

Those who emigrated from Mecca (q.v.) to Medina (q.v.) with the prophet Muḥammad (Emigrants, *muhājirūn*), and the residents of Medina who received and helped them (Helpers, *anṣār*). In a broader sense, those who forsake home and land, giving up evil deeds and renouncing personal desires for the sake of God are called emigrants by the Qurʾān (*muhājir*, Q 4:100; 29:26). In some classical sources the Medinans who came to Mecca and met Muḥammad at ʿAqaba were also characterized as emigrants because Medina was considered to be the abode of polytheism (see POLYTHEISM AND ATHEISM) and from there they had come to the Prophet (Nasāʾī, *Sunan*, *K. al-Bayʿa*, ch. 13). Ḥadīth literature offers a definition of emigrant *(muhājir)* as one who abstains from things forbidden (q.v.) by God (Bukhārī, *Ṣaḥīḥ*, *K. al-Īmān*). The term, which became *mhaggrāyē* in Syriac, *magaritai* in Greek, was also used by non-Muslim writers at the time of the Arab conquests when mentioning the Arabs, perhaps suggesting the self-designation of the conquerors at the time (Hoyland, *Seeing Islam,* 547-8). In the course of Islamic history, various Muslim groups have been identified as *muhājirūn,* such as those who emigrated from Russian and Balkan territories to Turkey during the early decades of the twentieth century and those who emigrated from British India to Afghanistan and from India to Pakistan after its creation in 1947.

Technically, however, the Emigrants *(muhājirūn)* were those early Companions of the Prophet (q.v.) who undertook to emigrate (*hijra,* see EMIGRATION) from Mecca to Medina (known before the *hijra* as Yathrib) and who settled in the latter place during the period between 1-8/622-30. The Helpers *(anṣār)* were those Medinans who accepted Islam, received the Emigrants, provided them with shelter and protection, and helped them to settle in their new abode. While the great majority of the *muhājirūn* were members of the Quraysh tribe, the *anṣār* were exclusively the members of two Arab tribes residing in Medina — the Aws and the Khazraj, collectively known as Banū Qayla (see ARABS; TRIBES AND CLANS).

Muhājir, the singular of *muhājirūn,* is used in the Qurʾān and other Arabic sources in this technical sense, but *naṣīr,* the singular of *anṣār,* is not used to designate individual Medinan Helpers. Reference to those who had emigrated for the sake of God appears nineteen times in the Qurʾān, seventeen of which the exegetical tradition has related, directly or indirectly, to the Meccan Emigrants. The word *anṣār* and its cognates *nāṣir* and *naṣīr* appear forty-six times in the Qurʾān, but references to the *anṣār* of Medina appear only five times — twice in the form of *anṣār* (Q 9:100, 117), twice as "those who gave shelter and help" (Q 8:72, 74) and once as "others" (Q 59:9).

According to classical accounts of the early days of Islam, it was following the second pledge of ʿAqaba that the Prophet instructed his Companions to emigrate to Yathrib and to do so in small groups to avoid the attention of the Quraysh (q.v.). Within a few months almost all Muslims had left Mecca and reached Medina. Some went alone, others with their families. As soon as the Quraysh realized the danger of this move, they tried, either by persuasion or by coercion, to prevent the escape of Muslims, but had little success. Ibn Isḥāq (d. 150/767), Ibn Saʿd (d. 230/845) and several other early sources report that in only two instances did the Quraysh succeed in inducing apostasy (q.v.) by use of excessive force. Both individuals, however, reportedly returned to Islam and left Mecca at an opportune moment (Ibn Isḥāq, *Sīra,* ii, 87-90; Ibn Saʿd, *Ṭabaqāt,* iii, 271-2; iv, 130-2). Many of those who left their Muslim wives and children in Mecca were reunited with them as more and more people slipped through the fingers of the Meccans. Those who had earlier emigrated to Abyssinia (q.v.) now came back and emigrated to Medina, gaining credit for making two *hijra*s.

It is difficult to know precisely the number of those who emigrated in the first wave to Medina. Based on the lists of names in early Arabic sources it can safely be estimated that the total number of adult male emigrants was not more than eighty. If the reports in Ibn Saʿd (*Ṭabaqāt,* i, 238) and al-Balādhurī (d. 279/892; *Ansāb,* i, 314-5) about the brotherhood (*muʾākhāt,* established in the first year of the *hijra;* see BROTHERS AND BROTHERHOOD) are taken at face value — that no Emigrant was left without a brotherhood established between him and a Helper — then the number of adult male Emigrants was substantially less. These two sources name only ninety men between whom a brotherhood was established, forty-five from the category of the Emigrants and forty-five from that of the Helpers. One report in these sources puts the number at fifty on each side, raising the total to one hundred. In the light of these reports, the figure of eighty as the total number of (male adult) Emigrants seems unrealistic. Nonetheless, as more and more people accepted Islam and joined the Prophet in Medina, their number gradually increased. A recent work devoted to the biographical notes of those who made their *hijra* to Medina lists 304 names, including women and children (Ward, *Aṣḥāb al-hijra*). The Prophet assigned the status of *muhājirūn* to a number of nomadic tribes who converted to Islam by giving the oath of allegiance (*bayʿa*, see OATHS; PLEDGE) and settled in Medina. A few other nomadic tribes, such as Muzayna and Khuzāʿa, who signed special treaties with the Prophet, also received the status of *muhājirūn* although not by settling in Medina (Ibn Saʿd, *Ṭabaqāt,* i, 291, 293; also 303 for Qushayr b. Kaʿb). This clearly indicates that a special status was attached to the designation *muhājirūn* and that people from the very earliest phase of Islamic history sought to acquire it in one way or another. In this regard, one should mention the later, non-qurʾānic concept of seats or centers of emigration *(dūr al-hijra),* in reference to early Muslim garrison cities. Settling in these cities was counted towards one's status as a Muslim. In a certain sense, the notion of emigration even plays into Islamic concepts of salvation (q.v.).

The *anṣār,* who had entered into an agreement with the Prophet, welcomed the newcomers to their city and, despite limited resources, shared with them whatever they had. Some of them went so far as to divide their entire wealth in two and offer one half to their guests. To create a lasting tie between the *anṣār* and the *muhājirūn,* the Prophet introduced the aforementioned system of brotherhood.

According to the early sources the *anṣār,* i.e. the Aws and the Khazraj, were descendants of the famous Yemenite tribe of Azd, through Ḥāritha, Thaʿlaba, ʿAmr, ʿĀmir, etc. (see YEMEN) who migrated to the oasis of Yathrib sometime around 500 B.C.E. and became clients of Jewish tribes already settled there (see JEWS AND JUDAISM). As a result of their increased numbers and wealth, they eventually gained the upper hand over the Jews and became masters of the political affairs of the oasis. This prosperity, however, also had adverse effects. The two tribes (now divided into several clans) engaged in internal feuds that erupted in violence on a number of occasions, the biggest being the battle of Buʿāth which took place one year before the *hijra.* Though the Khazraj had usually maintained their supremacy in these feuds, they were severely defeated by the Aws at Buʿāth. This may explain why the Khazraj showed greater interest in Islam than the Aws; the former outnumbererd the latter as representatives *(nuqabāʾ)* at the first and second gatherings with the Prophet at ʿAqaba (for a discussion of the events at ʿAqaba, see Mélamède, Meetings), at the battle of Badr (q.v.) and in the number of women converts, according to Ibn Saʿd (*Ṭabaqāt,* iii, 419-627; viii, 315-460). Moreover, while all clans of the Khazraj had embraced Islam (q.v.) by the time of the *hijra,* four clans of the Aws, collectively known as Aws Allāh (Aws al-Manāt before the *hijra*), refrained from such affiliation until after the battle of Khandaq (Battle of the Trench, 5/627; see PEOPLE OF THE DITCH; EXPEDITIONS AND BATTLES; Lecker, *Muslims,* 19-49). Thus, the Khazraj enjoyed a position in Islam — at least in its early phase — over that of the Aws. This preferred position was evident under ʿUmar's (r. 13-23/634-44) system of calculating the amount of one's pension *(ʿaṭāʾ)* on the basis of temporal precedence in accepting Islam (*sābiqa,* see CONQUESTS; TAXATION; ʿUMAR). The largest amount, after the wives of the Prophet (q.v.), was given to those who had accepted Islam before the battle of Badr and had participated in that battle. Many members of the Aws did not qualify for this category due to their late conversion. That the Khazraj rose to greater prominence than the Aws was also reflected in the fact that Saʿd b. ʿUbāda, who was almost selected caliph (q.v.) by the *anṣār* after the Prophet's death, was from the Khazraj (Ibn Saʿd, iii, 568; ʿAbd al-Razzāq, *Muṣannaf*, v, 442-5).

The difficulties faced by the *muhājirūn* in the wake of their emigration and the need to elevate their status from dependence to self-reliance prompted the Prophet to conclude a series of agreements among various factions in Medina which are now collectively known as the "Constitution of Medina" (for details, see Serjeant, Sunna Jāmiʿa; Hamidullah, *First written constitution*). According to these agreements, the *muhājirūn* were given the status of an independent tribe with the same rights and responsibilities as those of other Medinan tribes who were named one by one with their clients (*mawālī*, see CLIENTS AND CLIENTAGE) without distinguishing between those of their members who already had converted to Islam and those who had not. Several qurʾānic verses appear to allude to these agreements (e.g. Q 3:101-3) and to emphasize the unity of the *umma* (see COMMUNITY AND SOCIETY IN THE QURʾĀN), the nucleus of which was composed of the *anṣār* and *muhājirūn*.

The *muhājirūn* and *anṣār* maintained their separate identity for quite a long time: It is even reported that, while digging the Trench in 5/627 to protect Medina from Meccan-led incursions, they dug separate areas without intermingling. In all major battles during the lifetime of the Prophet, their contributions were separately enumerated, and inter-marriage between the two groups was not common. They did, however, live in a brotherly and neighborly fashion, save rare occasions when friction occurred, above all in the events surrounding the selection of a successor to the Prophet. The *muhājirūn* gradually gained higher status in Medinan society until, eventually, from roughly 125 years after the *hijra*, both they and the *anṣār* largely identified themselves with the members of the Quraysh.

The *muhājirūn* and the *anṣār* came to be viewed as model interpreters of the Qurʾān, since they had been close to the Prophet, whose life was the living example of qurʾānic norms (see EXEGESIS OF THE QURʾĀN: CLASSICAL AND MEDIEVAL; SUNNA). Several noted qurʾānic scholars emerged from among them: Most outstanding among the *muhājirūn* were ʿAbdallāh b. Masʿūd (d. 32/652-3), one of the earliest Qurʾān reciters (*qurrāʾ*, see RECITERS OF THE QURʾĀN) and an exegete; ʿAbdallāh b. ʿAbbās (d. 98/716-7), known as the father of Qurʾān commentaries; and ʿĀʾisha bint Abī Bakr (q.v.; d. 58/678-9), the widow of the Prophet and the most prominent female exegete (see also ḤADĪTH AND THE QURʾĀN). From the *anṣār* came such noted scholars as Ubayy b. Kaʿb (who died during the caliphate of ʿUmar), one of the Prophet's secretaries entrusted with the task of writing down the revelation and whose reading the Prophet preferred (Ibn Saʿd, iii, 498-9; see READINGS OF THE QURʾĀN); and Zayd b. Thābit (d. 45/665), another secretary of the Prophet who later served as the head of the group responsible for the codification of the Qurʾān (see CODICES OF THE QURʾĀN; COLLECTION OF THE QURʾĀN). Both Ubayy and Zayd were from the Khazraj branch of the *anṣār*. In the following generations (i.e. Successors and Successors of Successors), qurʾānic scholars relied heavily on the understanding and interpretation credited to the *muhājirūn* and *anṣār*. No written work has come down to us from this generation of scholars due to the largely oral nature (see ORALITY; ORALITY AND WRITINGS IN ARABIA) of scholarly activity at the time (see KNOWLEDGE AND LEARNING; TRADITION AND CUSTOM). Questions of authenticity also surround material attributed to these early scholars. For example, the authorship of *Tanwīr al-miqbās* as ascribed to Ibn ʿAbbās by its compiler Abū Ṭāhir Fīrūzābādī, is seriously doubted (cf. Sezgin, *GAS*, i, 27).

Muhammad al-Faruque

Bibliography
Primary: ʿAbd al-Razzāq, *Muṣannaf;* al-Balādhurī, Aḥmad b. Yaḥyā, *Ansāb al-ashrāf,* ed. M. al-Firdaws al-ʿAẓamī, 13 vols., Damascus 1996-; Bukhārī, *Ṣaḥīḥ;* Ibn Ḥazm, *Jawāmiʿ al-sīra wa-khams rasāʾil ukhrā,* ed. I. ʿAbbās and N. al-Asad, Cairo 1956, repr. Gujranwalah ca.1980; Ibn Isḥāq, *Sīra,* ed. M. al-Saqqā, Beirut 1994; Ibn Isḥāq-Guillaume; Ibn al-Jawzī, Abū l-Faraj ʿAbd al-Raḥmān b. ʿAlī, *al-Wafāʾ bi-aḥwāl al-Muṣṭafā,* ed. M.ʿA. ʿAṭā, Beirut 1988; Ibn Saʿd, *Ṭabaqāt,* ed. I. ʿAbbās; Nasāʾī, *Sunan;* al-Rāghib al-Iṣfahānī, Abū l-Qāsim al-Ḥusayn, *Mufradāt alfāẓ al-Qurʾān,* ed. Ṣ.ʿA. Dāwūdī, Damascus 1997²; Suyūṭī, *Itqān;* Ṭabarī, *Taʾrīkh,* ed. M. Abū l-Faḍl Ibrāhīm.
Secondary: M.R. Aḥmad, *al-Sīra al-nabawiyya fī ḍawʾ al-maṣādir al-aṣliyya. Dirāsa taḥlīliyya,* Riyadh 1992; M.Ḥ. al-Dhahabī, *al-Tafsīr wa-l-mufassirūn,* 2 vols., Cairo 1992; M. Hamidullah, *The first written constitution in the world,* Lahore 1968; R. Hoyland, *Seeing Islam as others saw it,* Princeton 1997, 547-8; ʿA.ʿA. b. Idrīs, *Mujtamaʿ al-Madīna fī ʿahd al-rasūl,* Riyadh 1982; M. Lecker, *Muslims, Jews and pagans. Studies on early Islamic Medina,* Leiden 1995; G. Mélamède, The meetings at al-ʿAḳaba, in *Le monde orientale* 28 (1934), 17-58, repr. in U. Rubin et al. (eds.), *The life of Muḥammad,* Brookfield, VT 1998, 104-50; R.B. Serjeant, The *sunna jāmiʿa,* pacts with the Yathrib Jews, and the *taḥrīm* of Yathrib. Analysis and translation of the documents in the so-called 'Constitution of Medina,' in *BSOAS* 41 (1978), 1-42; repr. in U. Rubin (ed.), *The life of Muḥammad,* Brookfield, VT 1998, 151-92; Sezgin, *GAS;* B.A. al-Ward, *Aṣḥāb al-hijra fī l-Islām,* Beirut 1986; W.M. Watt, *Muhammad at Mecca,* Oxford 1953; id., *Muhammad at Medina,* Oxford 1956, repr. Karachi 1981.

Emigration

Departure from a place or abode. The Arabic term for emigration (*hijra,* from the root, *h-j-r*) denotes cutting oneself off from friendly or sociable relations (see SOCIAL INTERACTIONS; SOCIAL RELATIONS), ceasing to speak to others, forsaking, abandoning, deserting, shunning or avoiding (Q 4:34; 25:30; 74:5). It also means departure from the desert to the town or villages and vice versa. Its most common meaning is to forsake one's own land and take up residence in another country. The Qurʾān frequently uses the variations of the root *kh-r-j* to convey this sense (Q 4:66; 8:30; 9:40; 60:1). It also has been interpreted to mean an emigration from the territory of unbelievers to the territory of believers for the sake of religion (Q 4:97; 29:26). Technically, the term *hijra* has been used to designate the emigration of the prophet Muḥammad (q.v.) and his early companions from Mecca (q.v.) to Medina (q.v.) in 622 C.E. (Lane, viii, 2879-81; see COMPANIONS OF THE PROPHET; EMIGRANTS AND HELPERS). Although the standard sources narrate an earlier emigration of a group of Muslims from Mecca to Abyssinia (q.v.), the term is primarily used in the sense of emigration from Mecca to Medina. Its various derivatives appear thirty-one times in the Qurʾān, sixteen of which refer to the emigration of Muslims from Mecca to Medina and to departure from home for the cause of God (see PATH OR WAY).

The first emigration of Muslims was to Abyssinia (al-Ḥabasha, modern Ethiopia). Early sources place this in the fifth year of the Qurʾān's revelation to Muḥammad. According to the various accounts, when the Meccan persecution of the Prophet's followers intensified and Muḥammad found himself unable to protect them, he instructed them to disperse in various directions. Upon their inquiry of where, exactly, to go, he advised them to set out for Abyssinia, the "land of truthfulness," whose ruling (Christian) king was a just person, and to stay there until God relieved them from their difficulties (Ibn Isḥāq, *Sīra,* i, 358). Several groups of Muslims, therefore, both with and without their families, emigrated there. The Abyssinian king, the Negus, received them favorably. He inquired about their new religion and inquired about their understanding of Jesus (q.v.), the son of Mary (q.v.). In reply, their leader, Jaʿfar, recited Q 19:16-21, which had been revealed shortly before their leaving Mecca. The king, satisfied with this response, allowed them to stay in his country, denying the request of the delegation of Quraysh (q.v.) who had followed them to Abyssinia in the hope of convincing the king to force their return. A total of eighty-two people, excluding the youth, emigrated to Abyssinia at different times (Ṭabarī, *Taʾrīkh,* ii, 330), though Ibn Saʿd, (*Ṭabaqāt,* i, 204, 207) gives a higher figure of one hundred sixteen. When rumor reached this group that leading Meccans had been followers of the Prophet (Ṭabarī, *Taʾrīkh,* ii, 330, 340), thirty-three of their number returned to Mecca where they remained until their second emigration, this time to Medina. Those Muslims who had elected to stay in Abyssinia eventually left to join the Prophet in Medina.

A summary narrative of the second but more consequential emigration can be drawn from the most commonly available sources of early Islamic history. According to these accounts soon after the end of the boycott of the Prophet's clan, Banū Hāshim, by the rest of the clans of Quraysh, probably in 619 C.E., two important figures in the life of the Prophet died: his uncle Abū Ṭālib (see FAMILY OF THE PROPHET) who had continuously provided him with protection (q.v.) and his wife Khadīja (q.v.; see WIVES OF THE PROPHET), who had been a source of both financial and moral support. As chief of the Banū Hāshim, Abū Ṭālib was succeeded by his brother Abū Lahab who, it is said, had initially promised to protect Muḥammad in the same way as Abū Ṭālib had done, but soon withdrew this protection on the grounds that Muḥammad had alleged that ʿAbd al-Muṭṭalib (their common ancestor) was in hell (q.v.). This loss of security caused great distress to the Prophet and his followers, since he could now be easily targeted for harsher treatment (see OPPOSITION TO MUḤAMMAD). Thus, both he and his supporters were no longer safe in Mecca. Moreover, the Prophet probably realized that he had already achieved what he could in Mecca. No dramatic change in the attitude of the Meccans could be expected and no important conversions could be foreseen. Faced with such circumstances, he changed his strategy and decided to convey his message to the nomadic tribes of Arabia (see ARABS; TRIBES AND CLANS), doing this during the last three years of his stay in Mecca. In his quest to continue his mission he went to Ṭāʾif, a neighboring city at a distance of some twenty-five miles (40 km) south of Mecca and dominated by the Thaqīf, a branch of the Hawāzin. Like Mecca, Ṭāʾif was a commercial city (see ECONOMICS) and the Thaqīf, who maintained close ties with Yemen (q.v.), were a natural rival of the Quraysh. What actually prompted the Prophet to choose Ṭāʾif in preference to other localities is not clear, but he certainly sought to utilize their rivalry with the Quraysh to his advantage. The people of Ṭāʾif, however, not only rejected his message but encouraged the town rabble to throw stones at him. He was physically injured and left Ṭāʾif without any immediate success. On his way back to Mecca, he realized that his re-entry into the city would be highly risky, given his lack of protection and his failed mission at Ṭāʾif. So, through an intermediary, he approached three clan chiefs for protection. One of them, al-Muʿṭim b. ʿAdī, chief of the Banū Nawfal and a relative of the Prophet on his mother's side, appears to have agreed and took him to the Kaʿba (q.v.), where the protection was recognized by the leaders of the Quraysh (Ibn Isḥāq, *Sīra,* i, 419).

The Prophet then re-entered Mecca and remained there, preaching to the various tribes that came to the city for pilgrimage and fairs. During the pilgrimage season of 620 C.E. he met at ʿAqaba with six members of the Khazraj tribe in Yathrib (see MEDINA) who accepted his message and promised to propagate it. These six were the first from Yathrib (the name of Medina before the *hijra*) to convert to Islam, although reports do claim that two members of the Aws, killed before the battle of Buʿāth (between the Aws and Khazraj one year before the *hijra*), died as Muslims (Balādhurī, *Ansāb,* i, 274-5). Five of these six came back during the pilgrimage the following year and brought seven others with them, three of whom were from the tribe of Aws. They met the Prophet again at ʿAqaba and made a solemn pledge (q.v.) to support and protect him. This was known as the Pledge of Women *(bayʿat al-nisāʾ)* as no fighting was involved (Ibn Iṣḥāq-Guillaume, 198-9; cf. Q 60:12). They went back to Yathrib, having promised to convey Muḥammad's message to their brethren. The Prophet also sent Muṣʿab b. ʿUmayr to Yathrib to teach the Qurʾān to the new converts and to invite others to Islam. Their work was apparently so effective that converts were made from every family of *anṣār* (i.e. the Helpers or residents of Yathrib who were to receive and help the Emigrants — *muhājirūn* — from Mecca) except the Aws Allāh, a group of the Aws known as Aws Manāt before Islam.

In the following pilgrimage season (622 C.E.), 72 men and three women met the Prophet at ʿAqaba and made a pledge not only to obey him but also to protect and fight for him. This pledge is known as the Pledge of War *(bayʿat al-ḥarb).* Traditional accounts stress that the Prophet's uncle ʿAbbās, though not yet a Muslim, was present at this Pledge in order to oversee the smooth transfer of responsibility for Muḥammad's protection from the Banū Hāshim to the people of Yathrib (Ibn Isḥāq, *Sīra,* ii, 54-5). The authenticity of this anecdote is, however, seriously questioned by modern scholarship and is ascribed to Abbāsid propaganda efforts — ʿAbbās was the eponymous ancestor of this dynasty — aimed at enhancing their image. Soon after this group went back to their city, the Prophet instructed his Companions to leave, in small groups, for Yathrib. All but two of his Companions gradually left Mecca and reached Yathrib. Of the remaining two, Abū Bakr was asked by the Prophet to delay his emigration and to be his travel companion as the Prophet was expecting divine permission to emigrate (see OCCASIONS OF REVELATION; REVELATION AND INSPIRATION). The other, ʿAlī (see ʿALĪ B. ABĪ ṬĀLIB), remained in Mecca at the Prophet's instruction and later joined the rest of the Muslims at Yathrib.

The standard accounts continue that after receiving divine permission, the Prophet left Mecca on the same night the Quraysh surrounded his house to attack and kill him (Q 8:30). He stayed the first three days after leaving Mecca at the Cave of Thawr (Q 9:40; see CAVE), south of Mecca, then moved to Yathrib following an unusual route. On the 12th of Rabīʿ I he reached Qubāʾ, in al-ʿĀliya of Yathrib (topographically, Medina was divided into Āliya and Sāfila — upper and lower — Medina, respectively; see Lecker,

Muslims, 1-18; see GEOGRAPHY), where he stayed for about two weeks and built the first mosque (q.v.). He then moved to the main part of the city, called Sāfila, and settled at the spot on which his famous mosque is now located. The city changed its name to commemorate the occasion, from Yathrib to Madīnat al-Nabī (lit. the city of the Prophet), commonly shortened to al-Madīna (Medina being the popular English transliteration).

The early sources differ in their interpretations of who was saved by the *hijra:* the Prophet from Meccan persecution, or the Medinans from self-destruction. One side stresses that it was Muḥammad who was rescued as he sought a safe haven to avoid the persecution of the Meccans and to continue his mission. With this understanding it is the Prophet who receives salvation, the Medinans who provide it by offering Muḥammad and his followers shelter and protection (Ibn Saʿd, *Ṭabaqāt*, i, 217; for qurʾānic reference to shelter and assistance, cf. Q 8:72, 74; for a detailed discussion on the salvation issue, see Rubin, *Eye*, 169-85). One allusion to the potential salvific role of the Medinans is the insistence of the uncle of the Prophet, ʿAbbās (said to have been present at the second pledge of ʿAqaba), that the Medinans be serious about their commitment to sheltering and protecting Muḥammad and not abandon him when he moved to their city. Evidence of the view that perhaps Muḥammad did not need 'salvation' is found in ʿAbbās' reported statement that if the Medinans had such an intention [i.e. to abandon Muḥammad], they should leave him immediately, for he already enjoyed protection and honor in his city and from his clan (Ibn Isḥāq, *Sīra*, ii, 54-5).

In the reports that emphasize the Medinans as the actual recipients of salvation and the Prophet as the provider, the Medinans are depicted as being on the verge of collapse due to their internal feuds (between the Aws and the Khazraj, which resulted in a long-lasting war). It was for assistance in the resolution of this crisis that they had invited the Prophet (Ibn Isḥāq, *Sīra*, ii, 42; iv, 152-3; Ṭabarī, *Tafsīr*, ad Q 3:103). Several commentators, such as al-Ṭabarī (d. 310/923), al-Rāzī (d. 606/1209) and al-Qurṭubī (d. 671/1272), as well as Sayyid Quṭb (d. 1966) in modern times, are of the opinion that Q 3:103 and 8:63 refer to the chaotic situation which prevailed in Medina before the Prophet brought peace, stability and order. This interpretation understands Muḥammad to be the rescuer, and the Medinans the rescued. Some sources indicate that Muḥammad himself insisted on this understanding during reconciliation with the unhappy Medinans after the Battle of Ḥunayn (q.v.; 8/630; Ibn Isḥāq, *Sīra*, iv, 152-3; see also EXPEDITIONS AND BATTLES). While the exegetical and historical sources express no unanimity on this issue, they uniformly contend that both parties greatly benefited from the *hijra*.

Classical Muslim historiography is also unanimous in understanding the emigration to Medina as an event of great importance for the development of Islam (q.v.). According to this literature, for the great majority of Meccans the Prophet was an unwanted reformer who had created tension and uneasiness in their society and hence was rejected by them. Their disdain was compounded by the Prophet's lack of either elite status or strong financial backing. In Medina, after the *hijra*, his position changed markedly. There, he was an invited and accepted leader with the responsibility of saving the Medinan community from self-destruction and leading them to prosperity. He eventually became the undisputed leader of all of Medina, to whom issues were referred for final resolution (Ibn Isḥāq, *Sīra*, ii, 117). There, the Muslim community *(umma)* was established as a polity (see COMMUNITY AND SOCIETY IN THE QURʾĀN) and the Muslims, freed from the fear of persecution, began to flourish as a supra-tribal community.

Viewed through the lens of the exegetical literature that it generated, the Qurʾān also attests to the importance of the *hijra*. Not only are sūras of the Qurʾān tagged as Meccan or Medinan (based on the place/period of revelation, though some are understood to contain both Meccan and Medinan portions; see CHRONOLOGY AND THE QURʾĀN), but their contents also reflect the changed position of the *umma* after the *hijra*. While the major emphases of Meccan verses appears to be on belief in the unity of God *(tawḥīd)*, in the prophetic office of Muḥammad *(risāla)* and in the life to come (*ākhira*, see ESCHATOLOGY), the emphases found in Medinan verses are related to the social, economic, legal and political affairs of the *umma*. The classification of sūras as Meccan and Medinan also takes account of changes in tone and terminology (see FORM AND STRUCTURE OF THE QURʾĀN). While the pre-*hijra* verses use the vocative phrase "O you people" *(yā ayyuhā l-nās)*, post-*hijra* verses are often addressed to "O you who believe" (*yā ayyuhā lladhīna āmanū*, see BELIEF AND UNBELIEF). Classical qurʾānic exegesis thus saw the *hijra* as the demarcation for major changes in the course of the *umma*'s development and for changing themes of the qurʾānic message. The Muslim calendar provides another indication of the decisive importance accorded to this event. When ʿUmar b. al-Khaṭṭāb, the second caliph, established the Muslim calendar (q.v.), its beginning was set on the first day of the lunar year in which the *hijra* had taken place.

Early authors differ on whether the door of *hijra*, i.e. the period in which emigration could be undertaken for religious reasons, was closed after the conquest of Mecca (in 8/630) or whether it remained open indefinitely (see CONQUESTS). The disagreement revolves around two sets of conflicting traditions. In one, the Prophet said, "There is no emigration after the conquest" (ʿAbd al-Razzāq, *Muṣannaf*, v, 309; Bukhārī, *Ṣaḥīḥ*, *K. al-Fatḥ*). In another, the Prophet is reported to have said, "The *hijra* will not come to an end as long as the infidels are fought," or in a variation, "The *hijra* will not come to end until the sun shall rise from its place of setting" (Nasāʾī, *Sunan*, *K. al-Bayʿa*, ch. 18, no. 7747-8; Ibn Ḥanbal, *Musnad*, i, 191; iv, 99). The issue was so hotly debated in scholarly circles that both Abū Dāwūd (d. 275/889) and al-Nasāʾī (d. 303/915) included separate chapters in their ḥadīth compilations entitled "On whether the *hijra* has ended" and "Mention of disagreements regarding the *hijra* on whether it has come to an end," respectively. Both of them record conflicting traditions in their chapters on this topic. Madelung (Has the *hijra* come to an end?) has lately shown that the set of traditions which understand *hijra* as not having ended with the conquest of Mecca originates primarily in Syria with Umayyad backing. It was the Umayyads who compelled Muslims to relocate to newly conquered territories, a process initiated by the second caliph ʿUmar (q.v.; r. 13-23/634-44). The heated debate notwithstanding, the *hijra* acquired new significance and meaning after the death of the Prophet. No longer was it considered necessary to emigrate to Medina but the duty to emigrate to a safer place remained in force for Muslims whenever their faith and practice were at risk in their own lands (Q 4:97). For example, some Khārijīs (q.v.) demanded that those adhering to their cause break off from other Muslims, considered by them to be unbelievers or monotheists at best, and depart for a place defined as a seat or center of emigration (*dār al-hijra*, see Watt, Khārijite thought). Even in modern times, many reformist leaders urge the emigration of their followers when they are oppressed in their own lands or unable to perform their religious obligations as they would wish.

Muhammad al-Faruque

Bibliography
Primary: ʿAbd al-Razzāq, *Muṣannaf;* al-Balādhurī, Aḥmad b. Yaḥyā, *Ansāb al-ashrāf,* ed. M. al-Fardūs al-ʿAẓm, 13 vols., Damascus 1996-; al-Bayhaqī, Abū Bakr Aḥmad b. al-Ḥusayn, *Dalāʾil al-nubuwwa wa-maʿrifat aḥwāl ṣāḥib al-sharīʿa,* ed. ʿA. Qilājī, 7 vols., Beirut 1985; Bukhārī, *Ṣaḥīḥ;* Ibn Ḥanbal, *Musnad;* Ibn Ḥazm, *Jawāmiʿ al-sīra wa-khams rasāʾil ukhrā,* ed. I. ʿAbbās and N. al-Asad, Cairo 1956, repr. Gujranwalah ca. 1980; Ibn Isḥāq, *Sīra,* ed. M. al-Saqqā, repr. Beirut 1994; Ibn Isḥāq-Guillaume; Ibn al-Jawzī, *al-Wafāʾ bi-aḥwāl al-Muṣṭafā,* ed. M.ʿA. ʿAṭā, Beirut 1988; Ibn Kathīr, *al-Fuṣūl fī sīrat al-rasūl,* ed. M. al-Khaṭrawī and M. Mastū, Damascus 1985; Ibn Rushd, Muḥammad *(al-jadd,* the grandfather), *Kitāb al-Jāmiʿ min al-muqaddimāt,* ed. al-Mukhtār b. al-Ṭāhir al-Talīlī, Amman 1985; Ibn Saʿd, *Ṭabaqāt,* ed. I. ʿAbbās, repr. Beirut n.d.; Nasāʾī, *Sunan;* Ṭabarī, *Taʾrīkh,* ed. Ibrāhīm.
Secondary: M.R. Aḥmad, *al-Sīra al-nabawiyya fī ḍawʾ al-maṣādir al-aṣliyya. Dirāsa tahlīliyya,* Riyadh 1992; P. Crone, The first-century concept of *hiğra,* in *Arabica* 41 (1994), 352-87; M. al-Ghazālī, *Fiqh al-sīra,* Beirut 1976⁷; M.J. Kister, Notes on the papyrus account of the ʿAqaba meeting, in *Muséon* 76 (1963), 403-17; F. Krenkow, The topography of the hijrah, in *IC* 3 (1929), 357-64; Lane; M. Lecker, *Muslims, Jews and pagans. Studies on early Islamic Medina,* Leiden 1995; W. Madelung, Has the *hijra* come to an end? in *REI* 54 (1986), 226-37; G. Mélamède, The meetings at al-Akaba, in *Le monde orientale* 28 (1934), 17-58, repr. in U. Rubin et al. (eds.), *The life of Muḥammad,* Brookfield, VT 1998, 104-50; U. Rubin, *The eye of the beholders. The life of Muḥammad as viewed by the early Muslims. A textual analysis,* Princeton 1995; W.M. Watt, Khārijite thought in the Umayyad period, in *Der Islam* 36 (1961), 215-31; id., *Muhammad at Mecca,* Oxford 1953; id., *Muhammad at Medina,* Oxford 1956, repr. Karachi 1981.

Enemies

A military foe or hostile force. The root of the common Arabic term for "enemy" *(ʿaduww,* pl. *aʿdāʾ), ʿ-d-w,* occurs frequently in the Qurʾān. Its essential meaning is to run or gallop swiftly or, in so doing, to pass by or beyond something. The root therefore took on the meaning of passing beyond boundaries or limits, i.e. to transgress, a meaning which occurs commonly in the Qurʾān in various forms (e.g. Q 2:229; see BOUNDARIES AND PRECEPTS). An enemy is thus one who has transgressed against another.

The term "enemy" is often applied in the Qurʾān specifically to Satan (Q 2:168, 208; 6:142; 7:22; 12:5; 17:53; 18:50; 35:6; 36:60; 43:62; see DEVIL; IBLĪS) or more generally to those in ancient days who did not listen to previous prophets (Q 6:112; 25:31; 61:14; see PROPHETS AND PROPHETHOOD), especially the Egyptians who were the enemies of Moses (q.v.; Q 7:129, 150; 20:39, 80; 28:8, 15, 19; see also EGYPT; PHARAOH; ISRAEL). "Enemy" is also applied to those who refuse to believe in God and/or God's angels (Q 2:97-8; 8:60; 41:19, 28; 60:1-2; see ANGEL; FAITH), those actively opposing Muḥammad and his followers (Q 4:45, 101; 9:83, 120; see OPPOSITION TO MUḤAMMAD) or who do so discretely (Q 63:4), the idolatrous relatives of the believers (Q 64:14; see IDOLATRY AND IDOLATERS) including the relatives of Abraham (q.v.; Q 9:114; 26:77) and kinship groups hostile to one another even among the believers (Q 4:92; see KINSHIP; TRIBES AND CLANS).

"Enemies" is also used to describe the natural state of humankind in conflict with one another as a result of Adam's and his unnamed wife's banishment from the garden (q.v.; Q 2:36; 7:24; 20:123; see ADAM AND EVE; COSMOLOGY; FALL OF MAN). God commands them, "Descend [from the garden, from now on being] enemies one to another" *(ihbiṭū baʿḍukum li-baʿḍin ʿaduww).* This state of affairs persisted naturally until God brought friendship and unity among the believers (Q 3:103; see COMMUNITY AND SOCIETY IN THE QURʾĀN; FRIENDS AND FRIENDSHIP), although as mentioned previously, the Qurʾān does note that kinship groups among believers may retain old hostilities (Q 4:92).

The term is often used in formulaic expressions in the Qurʾān, some of which exist in part for the sake of literary style and rhyme (see LANGUAGE OF THE QURʾĀN). Satan, for example, is "a clear enemy to you" *(innahu lakum [or lil-insān] ʿaduwwin mubīn)* in eight verses (Q 2:208; 6:142; 7:22; 12:5; 17:53; 28:15; 36:60; 43:26). So too does God tell Adam and his wife in three different contexts to "get down, enemies one to another" (Q 2:36; 7:24; 20:123).

It is clear from these references that the meaning of the term has a variety of nuances. The identity of those called enemies is to an extent influenced by whether the verses in question are Meccan or Medinan (see CHRONOLOGY AND THE QURʾĀN). The Meccan material identifies enemies in mythic terms, usually placing the word within a context that finds parallels with biblical narrative. Pharaoh is enemy to Moses and Israel and, therefore, God (see above for citations); Satan is enemy to Adam and his unnamed wife. Idols are enemies to Abraham or, in theological/apocalyptic terms, Satan is by definition enemy to humans. Unbelievers will be enemies on the day of judgment and, on that day, God's enemies will proceed to the fire (see LAST JUDGMENT; FIRE; HELL; APOCALYPSE). In the Medinan verses the term takes on a more direct political and worldly tone while the apocalyptic references drop out (there remain parallels to biblical narrative in the Medinan material; see SCRIPTURE AND THE QURʾĀN). What is new in the Medinan verses is that God is enemy to unbelievers *(kāfirūn,* Q 2:98), who are the enemy of believers (Q 4:101; see BELIEF AND UNBELIEF). Dissenters, often termed "hypocrites," *(munāfiqūn)* are the enemy who would entice believers away from true belief (Q 63:4; see HYPOCRITES AND HYPO-

CRISY). Believers must be willing to go to war (q.v.) against God's enemies, meaning opponents of the growing community of believers (Q 9:80-3, 120; see JIHĀD).

In subsequent centuries, the Qurʾān commentators (see EXEGESIS OF THE QURʾĀN: CLASSICAL AND MEDIEVAL) would elaborate upon the qurʾānic meaning of "enemy," and, based upon the ḥadīth and sīra materials (see ḤADĪTH AND THE QURʾĀN; SĪRA AND THE QURʾĀN), often attempted to apply it to reconstructed history. It may be added that the potency of such qurʾānic expressions as "enemies of God" *(aʿdāʾu llāh)* and "friends of Satan" *(awliyyāʾu l-shayṭān)* made them useful for citation in propaganda and ideology (see Qāḍī, Religious foundation).

Reuven Firestone

Bibliography
Lane, Beirut 1980; *Lisān al-ʿArab,* Beirut 1990; Penrice, *Dictionary;* W. Qāḍī, The religious foundation of late Umayyad ideology and practice, in *Sober religioso y poder político en el Islam,* Madrid 1994, 231-73, especially 251-6.

Enjoining the Good and Forbidding the Evil   see GOOD AND EVIL; ETHICS AND THE QURʾĀN

Enoch   see IDRĪS

Entering Houses from their Backs
see HOSPITALITY AND COURTESY; HOUSE, DOMESTIC AND DIVINE

Envy

Discontentment at another's good fortune. The qurʾānic term for envy *(ḥasad)* is mentioned four times in the Qurʾān, denoting a human emotion that begrudges others and wishes them ill for what they possess.

The most well-known example of this term in the Qurʾān is Q 113:5: "And from the evil of an envier when he envies" *(wa-min sharrin ḥāsidin idhā ḥasada)*. In this verse, divine protection (q.v.) is sought from "the envy of an envier." This envy is semantically and syntactically grouped with other kinds of evil such as the evil of "darkness" (*sharr ghāsiq*, see DARKNESS) and the evil of those "who blow upon knots" *(wa-min sharri l-naffāthāti fī l-ʿuqad)*. A polemical context (see DEBATE AND DISPUTATION; POLEMICS AND POLEMICAL LANGUAGE) which provides another instance of the use of the word envy *(ḥasad)* is Q 2:109. There it is mentioned that the People of the Book (q.v.) — out of envy *(ḥasad)* — wish to turn the believers back into disbelievers (see BELIEF AND UNBELIEF). The verb "to envy" *(ḥasada)* is also employed in Q 4:54 in reference to this same group who "were given a portion of the book (q.v.)," wherein it is rhetorically asked, "Do they envy people for what God has given to them out of his favor?" (*am yaḥsudūna l-nāsa ʿalā mā ātāhumu llāhu min faḍlihi*, see BLESSING; GIFT-GIVING). This is a theme especially developed in the life story of Muḥammad in his relations to the Jews of Medina, whose refusal to convert is portrayed as resulting from envy (see JEWS AND JUDAISM; SĪRA AND THE QURʾĀN). In Q 48:15, those not permitted to accompany Muḥammad (q.v.) and his followers when they set out to collect booty (q.v.; see also ECONOMICS; EXPEDITIONS AND BATTLES; WAR) present themselves as the targets of envy. Although the word *ḥasad* is not employed explicitly in Q 12:8, which describes how Joseph's (Yūsuf) brothers resent what they perceive as their father Jacob's (Yaʿqūb, see JACOB) preference for Joseph (q.v.) and his brother (see BENJAMIN), the verse nonetheless seems to imply the notion in the brothers' reaction (see BROTHERS AND BROTHERHOOD; VIRTUES AND VICES).

Ruqayya Khan

Bibliography
Lisān al-ʿArab; Paret, *Kommentar;* al-Rāghib al-Iṣfahānī, *Mufradāt.*

Epigraphy

Epigraphy is the study or science of inscriptions, i.e. texts traced upon some hard substance for the sake of durability, as on a monument, building, stone, tablet, medal, coin, vase, etc. The use of the Qurʾān in the corpus of Muslim inscriptions will be the focus of this article.

Background

The durability of inscriptions was observed by pre-Islamic Arab poets who compared them to the traces left by their own desert encampments, both of which seemed able to defy the ravaging effects of time. For that purpose inscriptions had long been used by Greco-Roman and Near Eastern peoples to record their deeds and resolutions, their hopes and aspirations, their prayers and supplications. Often a fine monumental script was developed in order to convey these messages, imparting dignity and authority both to the text and to the medium into which it was carved. For certain civilizations little else remains of their literary heritage but the epigraphic record. This is particularly true of the people of pre-Islamic Arabia, whether the spice traders of ancient Yemen or the pastoralist tribes of the desert regions, who scribbled on the rocks around them with alacrity. The visibility of inscriptions meant that they were all, to a greater or lesser degree, public texts. Many were officially so, a proclamation by a representative of the political or religious establishment on behalf of the whole community, expressing the principles by which it was governed and conducted itself. Others were deliberately so, a declaration by a wealthy patron vaunting his magnanimity and virtue. Still others (notably epitaphs and graffiti) were more subtly so, a personal statement by individuals seeking to demonstrate their credentials, thereby affirming their membership in a community and their adherence to its moral precepts and guiding tenets. Given this intention and the need for ease of comprehension, inscriptions tend to draw upon a common repertoire of phrases which, though each genre and cultural group has its own particular expressions, remain fairly limited and exhibit to a high degree the recurrence of set formulae.

Muslims not only continued but also expanded this tradition, and inscriptions are found on most kinds of objects created by Muslims wherever they lived, in all periods and in a number of different languages (chiefly Arabic, but also Persian and Turkish, as well as other languages). They are borne by the humblest of materials such as oil lamps and other unglazed ceramics as well as by the finest and most expensive, such as rock crystals and jade (see MATERIAL CULTURE AND THE QUR'ĀN; CALLIGRAPHY). This predilection for the written word in Islam is paralleled by the central role that the concept of writing plays in the Qur'ān. The verb "to write" (from the root letters *k-t-b*) occurs, in its various forms, 58 times, and the noun therefrom is attested some 260 times, most often in the sense of scripture (see BOOK). In what Muslim scholars have considered to be one of the earliest passages revealed by God is found the statement, "He who taught by the pen" (Q 96:4). Sūra 68 is entitled "The Pen" (Sūrat al-Qalam) and opens with the asseverative oath: "By the pen and that which they inscribe." Those who have received a revelation from God are referred to as People of the Book (q.v.). Humankind's every deed is said to be written down so that at the last judgment (q.v.) one will be given "his/her book," on the basis of which that individual's fate (q.v.) will be decided (Q 69:19-26). This predilection together with a pronounced preference for non-figurative expression, especially in the religious sphere, meant that in Islam inscriptions were not only a means of communication and of visual propaganda but also an art form.

The portrayal of the Qur'ān in inscriptions

Though cited directly or alluded to innumerable times, the Qur'ān is not specifically mentioned in inscriptions as a distinct entity until at least a century after Muḥammad's time. On a second/eighth century graffito from northern Arabia there appears the expression, "he believes... in every messenger he has dispatched and book he has sent down" (Muaikel, *Jawf,* no. 12). In the inscription of 135/752 commissioned by the caliph al-Saffāḥ (d. 136/754) for the refurbished mosque of Medina, believers are called upon to act in accordance with "the book of God" (Combe et al., *Répertoire chronologique,* no. 38). A more explicit statement is given on a tombstone from Egypt dated 195/810: "[The deceased] testifies that the book is truth, which God sent down with his knowledge. Falsehood does not come to it from before it nor from behind it, a revelation from [one who is] wise, praiseworthy. He believes in what is in it, the sure and the doubtful (see DIFFICULT PASSAGES), the abrogating and the abrogated (see ABROGATION), from its beginning to its end" (Combe et al., *Répertoire chronologique,* no. 89). The second sentence is Q 41:42, one of the comparatively few verses in which the

Qurʾān offers an insight into its own character and status. On another epitaph from a slightly later period, this time from Mosul, the owner bears witness that "the Qurʾān is the speech of God, sent down, uncreated" (Combe et al., *Répertoire chronologique,* no. 117). The last word alludes to the virulent early medieval debate over the nature of the Qurʾān, whether it was to be considered co-eternal with God and thus uncreated, or created by him at a fixed point in time (see CREATEDNESS OF THE QURʾĀN; INQUISITION). The former opinion won out and became part of the standard Muslim creed (see CREEDS). Evidently inscriptions reflected this creed and present us with the generally accepted view of the nature of the Qurʾān.

The citation of the Qurʾān in inscriptions

Given that Muslims considered the Qurʾān to be the "book of God" *(kitāb Allāh),* God's final and definitive revelation to humankind (see REVELATION AND INSPIRATION), it was natural that they should have turned for inspiration to this scripture when they came to write inscriptions. Qurʾānic phrases or passages added gravity and prestige to the medium onto which they were inscribed and underlined the piety and probity of the owner of the inscriptions in which they appeared. The Qurʾān's words imparted new meaning and significance both to the text incorporating its verses and to the building or object bearing its imprint. Qurʾānic inscriptions on buildings are sometimes situated too high to be read or in places poorly lit. In such instances a qurʾānic text's purpose might often be chiefly symbolic, bearing witness to the sacred nature of the building itself (see HOUSE, DOMESTIC AND DIVINE). The literal message of the text, however, was usually important, too. Some scholars have argued that many inscriptions were too ornate to be legible (see Ettinghausen, Communication), but a fair proportion of people knew the Qurʾān by heart, as its memorization was often the principal mode of primary education. They thus needed only to decipher a word or two in order to identify the verse being quoted, especially as the repertoire of verses (q.v.) used was very limited. Moreover, the frequency with which inscriptions conclude with a blessing (q.v.) for "the one who reads [this text]" and then "says amen" (e.g. Imbert, *Jordanie,* nos. 1, 5, 11, 22-3, 72, 82, 106, 151, 156; Moraekhi, *Medina,* B11, L4a, L17, R8; Baramki, al-Bādiya al-sūriyya, nos. 22, 33, 56, 65, 71, 77) conveys the impression that they were usually meant to be understood. Often it would seem that they were recited out loud as is suggested by such expressions as "Oh God, forgive… the one who reads [this text aloud] and the one who hears, then says amen" (Nevo, *Negev,* EL200C, GM389). Lastly, one should bear in mind that the lettering was generally highlighted by some bright substance so that, as Abū l-Raddād tell us in the account cited below, the text "could be read from a distance."

The authors of a thorough study of qurʾānic texts inscribed on buildings conclude that "the verses chosen to decorate Islamic monuments show the greatest possible variety and invention both in the selection of the verses and where they were placed in relation to the architecture of the building" (Dodd and Khairallah, *Image,* i, 61-3). The reason for this lack of conformity is that the choice of verses did not depend upon any one factor but rather might be determined by the type of material or object involved, the space available, the nature of the occasion, the personal intentions and tastes of the author/commissioner, the prevailing fashion or dominant tradition, religious and political considerations, the effect intended and so on (for magical protection see the section on "seals and amulets" below; see also AMULETS; MAGIC, PROHIBITION OF). But whatever the occasion, the choice was usually deliberate, as is illustrated by the following account:

When I [Abū l-Raddād, supervisor of the nilometer in Egypt] wanted to engrave texts on the nilometer, I consulted Yazīd b. ʿAbdallāh, Sulaymān b. Wahb and al-Ḥasan the eunuch as to what was most appropriate. I informed them that the most fitting, in my opinion, would be to inscribe verses of the Qurʾān and the name of the Commander of the Faithful (see CALIPH), al-Mutawakkil [r. 232-247/847-861], together with that of the governor al-Muntaṣir since he would be responsible for the work. The three disputed about that and Sulaymān b. Wahb, on his own initiative and without our knowing, sought out the opinion of the Commander of the Faithful. The latter then wrote that verses in conformity with the matter of the nilometer should be inscribed as well as his name. I therefore extracted from the Qurʾān the verses that best suited this subject and had them engraved wherever possible on the marble on the outside of the structure. The letters, the thickness of a finger, were firmly embedded in the body of the marble and tinted with lapis-lazuli and so could be read from a distance (Ibn Khallikān, *Wafayāt*, iii, 112-3).

Verses might be selected for their applicability to the function of the building or object. A good example is provided by the four pieces picked by Abū l-Raddād for the nilometer, all of which maintain that water (q.v.) is a boon of divine origin: "We sent down blessed water from the sky with which we bring forth gardens and the harvest grain" (Q 50:9); "you sometimes see the earth (q.v.) barren, but no sooner do we send down rain upon it than it begins to stir and swell, putting forth every kind of radiant bloom" (Q 22:5); "do you not see how God sends down water from the sky and covers the earth with vegetation" (Q 22:63; see AGRICULTURE AND VEGETATION); "it is he who sends down rain for them when they have lost all hope (q.v.), and spreads abroad his blessings" (Q 42:28). Regarded as particularly pertinent to mosques (q.v.) was Q 9:18: "none should visit the mosques of God except those who believe in God and the last day, attend to their prayers and pay the alms-tax and fear none but God. These shall be rightly guided" (see ALMSGIVING; PRAYER). For prayer niches Q 17:78 was a popular choice: "Recite your prayers at sunset until nightfall, and the recitation at dawn, indeed the recitation at dawn has its witnesses" (see DAY, TIMES OF; RECITATION OF THE QURʾĀN; WITNESSING AND TESTIFYING). And on tombstones humankind's common fate was deemed a suitable topic as touched upon in Q 2:156: "We belong to God and unto God we shall return"; Q 21:35: "Every soul will taste death"; and the like (see DEATH AND THE DEAD).

Apart from such considerations, the particular aims of the author/commissioner might direct the choice of verses. Quite common was the desire to make some sort of declaration of faith (q.v.) and affirmation of allegiance to the one true God. This might be a personal statement, as in graffiti and epitaphs, or a public proclamation, as in official texts on monuments, milestones, coins, seals, etc. The texts most often used to this end were Q 2:255 (known as the Throne Verse), of which it was often considered sufficient to cite just the first few words: "God, there is no God but he, the living, the everlasting," and Q 3:18: "God is witness that there is no god but he, as also are the angels (see ANGEL) and men of knowledge; he acts with justice, there is no god but he, the mighty, the wise" (see GOD AND HIS ATTRIBUTES; KNOWLEDGE

AND LEARNING). Almost as popular and of similar content, stressing God's unity and majesty, was Q 112: "Say: God is one, the eternal God. He does not beget, nor was he begotten. None is equal to him." With their emphasis on God's oneness, such verses betray a certain polemical thrust (see POLEMIC AND POLEMICAL LANGUAGE), an assertion of Islam's validity as against those who practice a corrupt form of monotheism, associating others with God, the chiefly intended object of such words being the Christians (see CHRISTIANS AND CHRISTIANITY; DEBATE AND DISPUTATION). This is much more blatant in another very frequently quoted verse, Q 9:33: "It is he who has sent his messenger (q.v.) with guidance and the religion of truth (q.v.) to make it prevail over all religion (q.v.), even if the associators are averse."

The personal whims and preferences of the author/commissioner could also play an important part in determining which verses might be favored. In most cases this cannot be detected. Very occasionally, however, it will come to light, as when a qurʾānic phrase is adopted as a play on the patron's name. Thus the coins of al-Ḥakam b. Abī l-ʿĀṣ, governor of Fars and Khuzistan in 56-58/676-78, mostly bear the legend, "God is the lord of judgment *(ḥukm)*," echoing numerous qurʾānic verses. ʿAbd al-ʿAzīz b. ʿAbdallāh, governor of Sistan in 66/685-86, liked to have the slogan, "in the name of God the all-mighty *(al-ʿazīz)*," a popular qurʾānic epithet for God, stamped on the coins of his province. Such puns on names were very popular, like officials with the name Maḥmūd opting for Q 17:79, "Your lord may exalt you to an honorable station *(maqām maḥmūd)*," and so on. They could often be worked in very subtly as in the text commemorating an addition to the congregational mosque at Isfahan in 480/1087, which cites Q 23:1-6, the concluding words of which ("what their right hands possess," *mā malakat aymānuhum*) allude to the name of the reigning Sultan (Malik Shāh) and his official title ("right hand of the caliph," *yamīn al-khalīfa*).

Individual discretion and creation are present to some degree in inscriptions but inevitably — as with dress, architecture and the like (see ART AND ARCHITECTURE AND THE QURʾĀN) — the influence of fashion would also make itself felt. What was in vogue in one generation might be regarded as outmoded by the next. On early Egyptian tombstones, for example, Q 22:7 was very popular: "The hour is coming, of that there is no doubt, and God will raise those who are in the graves," a verse which subsequently lost ground to Q 55:26-7: "All who live on earth are doomed to die, but the face of your lord will abide forever in all its majesty and glory (q.v.)." Trends were presumably often set by political elites. Certainly this seems to be borne out by the frequency with which the earliest dated occurrence of a phrase in graffiti follows, by a couple of decades, its earliest dated occurrence in an imperial inscription. And it is more frivolously confirmed by the following anecdote: "When people met in the time of al-Walīd [founder of many mosques and palaces] they would talk about nothing but building and construction; next (the debauched) Sulaymān came to power... and they would ask one another about copulation and slave girls; and then when [the pious] ʿUmar b. ʿAbd al-ʿAzīz held office, people would meet and discuss their night prayers, their memorization and recitation of the Qurʾān and their fasting (q.v.)" (Ṭabarī, *Taʾrīkh*, ii, 1272-3).

Religious and political conditions might also have a part to play (see POLITICS AND THE QURʾĀN). The devolution of the caliphate into discrete polities in the third-fourth/ninth-tenth centuries, many of them headed by Shīʿī dynasties (see SHĪʿISM

AND THE QUR'ĀN), meant that sectarian concerns assumed a greater role in the choice of qur'ānic verses (for Fāṭimid Egypt see Bierman, *Writing signs*). In Syria during the Crusades, "holy war" was championed in stone as well as in deed (Tabbaa, Monuments; Hillenbrand, Jihad; see JIHĀD). The use of Q 43:88-9 ("And his [i.e. the Prophet's] saying: 'Oh my lord, these are a people who do not believe'") in a graffito has been interpreted as a criticism of the notoriously dissolute ruler al-Walīd II, who had stayed in a palace in the immediate vicinity before his assassination in 126/744 (Imbert, Coran). And the blanket use of qur'ānic texts on monuments, coins, papyrus protocols, milestones, etc., by ʿAbd al-Malik from 72/691 onward was chiefly a response to the divisive effects of the second Arab civil war (65-72/684-91). In this he was not totally innovative, for certain of the participants in the civil war had already been testing this idea. One claimant to the caliphate, the Khārijī (see KHARAJĪS) leader Qaṭarī b. al-Fujā'a, minted coins bearing the rallying cry "judgment belongs to God alone" (cf. Q 6:57; 12:40, 67; 28:88; 40:12; 42:10). And coins bearing the legend "Muḥammad is the messenger of God," part of Q 48:29, were issued by a governor of Fars loyal to another contender, ʿAbdallāh b. al-Zubayr, of whom it was said that "he had come out of zeal for the house of God, and he was full of threats against the westerners (i.e. ʿAbd al-Malik's supporters), alleging that they were transgressors of the law" (see Hoyland, *Seeing Islam*, 550-4).

The manipulation of the Qur'ān in inscriptions

An inscription may simply cite one or more qur'ānic verses, whole or in part, without interfering with the wording or order in any way and with very little additional information save the name of the author/commissioner and a date. Onto a rock face near Mecca, for example, is etched Q 65:3: "God is all-sufficient for whoever puts his trust in him. He will surely bring about what he decrees. He has set a measure for all things. Umayya b. ʿAbd al-Malik wrote this in the year 98/716" (Rāshid, *Makka*, ʿAsila 2). And a tombstone from the region south of Mecca simply quotes the Throne Verse (Q 2:255) followed by the name of the deceased (Zaylaʿī, *Ḥamdāna*, no. 1). Sometimes the qur'ānic text is presented alone, unencumbered by any other data. Thus a first-second/seventh-eighth century basalt tombstone from southern Syria tells us nothing of the persons interred below except perhaps that they had stood by, or had done so in the eyes of their companions, the words of Q 37:61: "For the like of this [i.e. the joys of paradise] let all men strive" (Ory, *Hawran*, no. 1).

Very often a subtle amendment to the text is introduced for the sake of clarity. On ʿAbd al-Malik's coinage of 77/696 and on most inscriptions thereafter, Q 9:33 ("It is he who sent his messenger with guidance...") is slightly filled out (from Q 48:29) to read: "Muḥammad is the messenger of God whom he sent with guidance...." Alteration may also be made to personalize the quotation, in particular changing the subject of a verb from "they" to "I." Most of the discrepancies between the inscribed qur'ānic text and the official qur'ānic text, however, suggest that the inscriber, especially in the case of graffiti, would be working from memory. Subtle variants would, therefore, be likely to creep in. A graffito from the environs of Mecca slightly adjusts Q 38:26 from "Oh David, we have made you a deputy on the earth, so rule *(faḥkum)*...!" to the more straightforward "Oh David, we have made you a deputy on earth in order that you may rule *(litaḥkuma)*..." (Fahmī, *Makka*, no. 2). Another graffito from the same area (Rāshid,

Makka, no. 2) attempts to render Q 2:21: "Men, serve your lord *(uʿbudū rabbakum),* who has created you and those who have gone before you, so that you may guard yourselves against evil *(laʿallakum tattaqūn)*"; the graffito, however, introduces variants from Q 4:1 *(ittaqū rabbakum)* and Q 2:189, 3:130, 200 and 5:100 *(laʿallakum tufliḥūn).*

More commonly still, especially in the case of graffiti, an inscription will be an eclectic blend of phrases taken from different verses of the Qurʾān. The words may still be faithfully conveyed. Thus an Egyptian marriage contract inscribed on silk begins with snippets from Q 11:88 ("my success lies only with God and in him I trust") and Q 9:129 ("And he is lord of the mighty throne"), unchanged except for the insertion of an "and" (Ragib, Contrat, 32; see CONTRACTS AND ALLIANCES; MARRIAGE AND DIVORCE; TRUST AND PATIENCE). Very often the phrases will be slightly modified and/or supplemented as required or desired. For example, the text "My lord, lord of the heavens and earth and what is between them, there is no God but he, and so I adopt him as a protector" (Rāshid, *Medina,* no. 21) is assembled from Q 26:24 (or Q 37:5; 38:66; 44:7, 38) and Q 73:9, with a small amendment to personalize the quotation ("I adopt him" rather than "you adopt him!"). The text "My lord is God and my religion is Islam, in him I trust and unto him I turn, and all shall return to him" (ʿUshsh, Jabal Usays, no. 87, dated 119/737) borrows from Q 40:28, 11:88 (cf. Q 42:10) and 5:18 *(wa-ilayhi l-maṣīr,* cf. Q 40:3 and 64:3), and inserts the phrase "my religion is Islam" which, though not strictly qurʾānic, plays on Q 5:3 ("I have approved for you as a religion Islam") and Q 3:19 ("religion with God is Islam"). The text "I believe that there is no god except him in whom the Children of Israel (q.v.) believed, [believing as] a Muslim *ḥanīf,* nor am I among the associators" (Donner, Hanakiyya, W1) quotes verbatim part of Q 10:90, then adapts a statement about Abraham (Q 3:67) to suit the inscriber. Finally, the text "Provide for him from your bounty, and enter him into your mercy (q.v.), and perfect upon him your favor, and make him one of the prosperous" (Nevo, *Negev,* SC301) takes from Q 24:38 (paraphrased), 7:151, 48:2 (or 5:3), and adds the Qurʾān-like closing request to be made "one of the prosperous."

The media on which qurʾānic texts appear

Muslims have carved inscriptions onto most of the kinds of objects that they have produced, at all times since the death of their Prophet and in all the lands that they have inhabited (so not just the Muslim world, but also China, America, etc.), and a substantial proportion of these inscriptions incorporate qurʾānic verses, whole or in part, reported verbatim or paraphrased. Our task here is limited to noting some of the most common media onto which Qurʾān-bearing texts have been inscribed.

Buildings

Public edifices and grand residences would almost always be adorned with some sort of inscription. By far the most numerous are those recording the foundation or renovation of a structure. They might say no more than what was done, when and at whose command. The patron would, however, very likely take the opportunity, by including appropriate qurʾānic verses, to indulge in a little self-glorification by adding titles and eulogies and underlining the majesty and significance of his work. How much care sometimes went into this latter aspect can be observed from the example of the tomb and college of Sultan Ḥasan (757-64/1356-62) in Cairo. At the great entrance, which opens onto the sunlit streets and leads inside to where enlightenment may be found, the famous Light Verse

(Q 24:35) is encountered, which begins: "God is the light (q.v.) of the heavens and the earth; the likeness of his light is as a niche wherein is a lamp (q.v.), the lamp in a glass, the glass as it were a glittering star." The prayer niche, indicating the direction of Mecca (q.v.), is adorned with the highly relevant verse: "We have seen you turn your face towards heaven [for guidance, O Muḥammad]. Now we will make you turn in a direction that will please you. Turn towards the holy mosque; wherever you are, face towards it. Those to whom the scripture was given know this to be the truth from their lord" (Q 2:144). On the eastern walls, which are sacred by virtue of their alignment towards Mecca and paradise (q.v.), letters larger and more elaborate than elsewhere speak of victory (q.v.) and eternal reward (see REWARD AND PUNISHMENT): "We have given you a glorious victory so that God may forgive your past and future sins and perfect his goodness upon you... He has caused you to do as you have done that he may bring the believers, both men and women, into gardens watered by running streams, there to abide forever..." (Q 48:1-6). And in the adjoining tomb of the Sultan there is quoted the Throne Verse, a basic statement of the Islamic faith to which any Muslim could assent.

Less common than foundation inscriptions, though socially more important, are endowment (see INHERITANCE) texts and decrees. The latter record the assignment of buildings to a religious body, whether to be owned by it or to be used for its support (see MAINTENANACE AND UPKEEP; PROPERTY). The format of the inscription might be much the same as for a foundation (identification of the building, date, name and titles of the benefactor), but the choice of qurʾānic verses would generally be different, the most popular being the very apt Q 2:181: "Whoever alters a will after hearing it shall be accountable for his crime (see SIN AND CRIME). God hears all and knows all" (see BREAKING TRUSTS AND CONTRACTS). The text of a decree will, of course, chiefly be taken up with details of the issuing authority's resolutions, as also with the name and titles of that authority and the date of issue. The Qurʾān may well intrude, however, in the customary warning to potential violators of the decree, particularly Q 26:227 ("Wrong-doers will come to know by what a great reverse they will be overturned"), and in the concluding phrase, most often taken from Q 3:173: "God is sufficient for us and most excellent as a protector."

Tombstones and rocks

Inscriptions on tombstones (epitaphs) and on rocks (graffiti), though they are visible to passers-by, are, unlike texts on monuments and the objects of state, not so much concerned with addressing the public as making a personal statement. They begin by invoking God, starting with a simple exclamation *(Allāhumma)* or calling upon his name (*bi-smi llāh,* see BASMALA). Then some sort of petition will usually be made, most often for forgiveness, mercy, blessing or approval, concepts that form an important part of the qurʾānic worldview. It may also be asked that favor be conferred on other parties, such as relatives, the Muslim community, prophets (see PROPHETS AND PROPHETHOOD) and angels, and often, in conclusion, the reader of the inscription and/or somebody else says "amen, amen, lord of the worlds" or just "amen" (e.g. Abbott, Kasr Kharana, dated 92/710; Cantineau, *Palmyre,* no. 39, 110/728; Couroyer, Beit Gibrin, first/seventh-eighth century). For this purpose the phrase, "invoke a blessing upon" (*ṣalli ʿalā,* lit. "pray for"), will frequently be used, especially for the prophet Muḥammad, as in Q 33:56 (e.g. Kessler, Inscription; Miles, Taʾif, 241), but

FIGURES I–X

[I] Clockwise, from top.
Reverse of ʿUmayyad gold dinar, Damascus ca. 73/692-4. Center contains a modified form of the standard Byzantine cross-on-pediment symbol; margin is inscribed with "*bismi llāh lā ilāh illā llāh waḥda Muḥammad rasūl Allāh.*" The earliest gold issue that is surely Arab, and the first coinage to contain the *shahāda*.
Obverse of first-issue ʿAbbāsid dinar dated 132/[749-50]. Inscription is the same as that of the ʿUmayyad dinar of 77/696-7 (see below), whereas the reverse center (not pictured) is inscribed with *Muḥammad rasūl Allāh*.
Obverse of ʿUmayyad gold dinar dated 77/[696-7]. Margin is inscribed with *Muḥammad rasūl Allāh arsalahu bi-l-hudā wa-dīn al-ḥaqq li-yuẓhirahu ʿalā l-dīn kullihi* (cf. Q 48:29; 9:33); center is inscribed with "*lā ilāh illā llāh waḥda lā sharīk lahu*"; reverse center (not pictured) is inscribed with part of Q 112.
Obverse of al-Maʾmūn's anonymous coinage dated 207/[822]. The center is the same as that of the ʿUmayyad dinar of 77/696-7. Courtesy of the University of Pennsylvania Museum (Islamic Coins, S4-143980, S4-143981; coins were formerly on loan to the American Numismatic Society).

[II] 3rd/9th century Egyptian carved stone panel containing the *basmala* and Q 3:18: "In the name of God, the compassionate, the merciful. God is witness that there is no god save him. And the angels and the men of learning [are also witnesses]. Maintaining his creation in justice, there is no God save him, the almighty, the wise." No individual's name is inscribed on this panel. Courtesy of the Arthur M. Sackler Gallery, Smithsonian Institution, Washington, DC (S1993.8).

[III] Portion of stone-carved band with Q 9:18 on the south face of the southwest minaret of the Mosque of al-Ḥākim in Cairo, early 5th/11th century. The verse, which begins "the mosques of God shall be visited and maintained," is the most common inscription found on mosques throughout the Muslim world. Photograph courtesy of Jonathan Bloom and Sheila Blair.

[IV] Top row: Nishapur dinar, 450/1058-9 (under the Seljuk Tughril Beg). Obverse center is the same as that of the ʿUmayyad dinar of 77/696-7 (see plate I), with *ʿadl* inscribed above, and *al-qāʾim bi-amr Allāh* below; outer margin is inscribed with a passage from Q 30:4-5 ("*lillāhi l-amr min qabl wa-min baʿd wa-yawmaʾidh yafraḥu l-muʾminūn bi-naṣri llāhi*"). Reverse margin reads *Muḥammad rasūl Allāh arsalahu bi-l-hudā wa-dīn al-ḥaqq li-yuẓhirahu ʿalā l-dīn kullihi wa-law kariha al-mushrikūn* (cf. Q 48:29; 9:33); center is inscribed with *lillāh Muḥammad rasūl Allāh al-Sulṭān al-Aʿẓam Shāhānshāh Ajall Rukn al-Dīn Ṭughril Beg*. Bottom row: Mosul copper, 585/1189-90, under the Zengid prince of Mosul, Masʿūd, and his overlord, the Ayyubid Ṣalāḥ al-Dīn. Obverse contains an allegorical figure of the moon. Reverse center begins with the *shahāda*. Images courtesy of the Smithsonian Institution, National Numismatic Collection, Douglas Mudd. Identification and transcription courtesy of Michael Bates of the American Numismatic Society.

[v] The minaret of Jām (590/1193-4), built for the Ghūrid overlord Muḥammad b. Sām and located in central Afghanistan. The lower shaft is decorated with interlacing bands that contain all 98 verses of Q 19, Sūrat Maryam ("Mary"), certainly one of the most extensive qurʾānic inscriptions ever erected. The band at the top of the middle shaft contains Q 61:13 about God's present victory, while the band around the top of the upper shaft contains the profession of faith (*shahāda*). Photograph from a private collection.

[VI] Early 8th/14th century Iranian *miḥrāb*. The section shown here is inscribed with Q 59:22: "He is God, other than whom there is no other god. Knower of the invisible and the visible. He is the compassionate, the merciful." Courtesy of The Metropolitan Museum of Art, New York. H.O. Havermeyer Collection. Gift of Horace Havermeyer, 1940 (40.181.4).

[VII] Top row: Granada dirham. Anonymous and undated (ca. 596-853/1200-1450), under the Naṣrids. Obverse is inscribed with the *shahāda*. Reverse reads *lā ghālib illā llāh tʿ Gharnāṭa* (*tʿ* presumably abbreviates *taʿālā*, "exalted be he"). Bottom row: Lahore gold mohur, 1015/1606-7. First regnal year of Jahāngīr: Obverse is inscribed with "*Allāh lā ilāh illā Muḥammad rasūl Allāh hūr darb 1115 Lā*" (cf. Q 37:35; 48:29). Reverse reads *ghāzī Jahāngīr Bādishāh Muḥammad Nūr al-Dīn sana 1.* Images courtesy of the Smithsonian Institution, National Numismatic Collection, Douglas Mudd. Identification and transcription courtesy of Michael Bates of the American Numismatic Society.

[VIII] Beginning of the inscription in *thuluth* by the hand of Amānat Khān Shīrāzī that frames the south archway of the Taj Mahal, 1048/1636-7: "In the name of God, the compassionate, the merciful. Yā Sīn. By the wise Qur'ān. Lo! You are of those sent on a straight path. A revelation of the mighty, the merciful ..." (Q 36:1-5). The south archway contains the first 22 verses of Q 36 and continues on the west, north and east archways. Photograph courtesy of Jonathan Bloom and Sheila Blair.

[IX] Band with Q 9:108 inscribed vertically in *thuluth* by ʿAlī Riḍā-i ʿAbbāsī, 1025/1616-7 at the beginning of the inscription in tile mosaic framing the entrance portal to the Imām Mosque (formerly the Shāh Mosque) in Iṣfahān. The verse mentions a mosque whose foundation was laid the first day. The inscription continues with a Shīʿite ḥadīth quoted on the authority of Ibn ʿAbbās that ʿAlī b. Abī Ṭālib is the Prophet's successor. Photograph courtesy of Jonathan Bloom and Sheila Blair.

[x] Early 12th/18th century Persian silver battle standard with niello inlay. The little finger contains Q 61:13: "Help from God and near victory." The other fingers contain the Shīʿa invocation of ʿAlī b. Abī Ṭālib. The twelve round cartouches in the outer circle on the hand proper contain the names of the twelve Imāms in *nastaʿlīq* script. The other side of this standard (not displayed here) is inscribed with the Throne Verse (Q 2:256), believed to have very strong protective power, and a poem imploring divine aid. Courtesy of The Metropolitan Museum of Art, New York. Gift of Dr. Marilyn Jenkins, 1984 (1984.504.2).

also for others (e.g. Ory, ʿAyn al-Garr, no. 1: "May God bless all the Muslims").

Supplicants will also put forward many more elaborate entreaties. They wish to be admitted into paradise (q.v.), the terms here being *janna, jannāt al-naʿīm* (literally, gardens of bliss; see GARDEN) and *madkhal* (esp. Q 4:31; cf. Grohmann, *Arabic inscriptions,* Z11: *adkhilhā madkhalan karīman*), attested 137, ten and three times respectively in the Qurʾān. And they desire to be united with their Prophet (e.g. Hawary-Rached, *Steles,* nos. 3-4, 13; Imbert, Qastal al-Balqaʾ, nos. 2, 7-8, 14, 16), an idea not found in the Qurʾān, though the expression *alḥiqhu bi-nabiyyihi* is reminiscent of Q 26:83 (*alḥiqnī bi-l-ṣāliḥīn,* "unite me to the righteous"). They seek to be preserved from the torment of the day of reckoning, to be spared God's punishment, to be saved from hell (q.v.) and to receive succor on the day of resurrection, all concepts crucial to the qurʾānic theory of divine retribution (see RESURRECTION; RETALIATION; REWARD AND PUNISHMENT). They, or the deceased at least, beg to be instructed in his proof (q.v.; e.g. Hawary-Rached, *Steles,* nos. 3, 10, 13, etc.; Imbert, Qastal al-Balqaʾ, nos. 2, 6-8, 10), presumably a reference to Q 6:83 ("This is our proof which we bestowed upon Abraham") and Q 6:149 ("To God belongs the conclusive proof"). Finally, we find inscriptions where supplicants advance the more positive requests of being rewarded for the best of their deeds (see GOOD DEEDS; EVIL DEEDS), having their devotions and good actions accepted, receiving God's favor and guidance and being granted good health, virtue and prosperity, all again bristling with qurʾānic thinking and terminology.

The other major objective of inscribers of epitaphs and graffiti is to convey some of the essentials of their faith and to pronounce their adherence to it, to give a summary of the principles by which, as is so often written of the deceased, "he has lived, by which he has died and by which he will be raised alive, if God wills." Always in first place is some declaration about God. Very commonly various epithets and predicate phrases will be assigned to him, almost all corresponding to portions of qurʾānic verses: "the clement, the generous," "praiseworthy, glorious," "the forgiving, the compassionate," "the mighty, the wise," "the lord of the worlds," "the manifest truth," "to him belongs sovereignty and praise," "he gives life and brings death," "in his hand is the sovereignty and he is able to do all things" (Q 67:1; e.g. ʿAbd al-Tawab, *Nécropole,* no. 1). Very frequently his unity will be affirmed, both by simple assertions that he is one and by recourse to pertinent qurʾānic verses, especially Q 6:163 ("He has no associate"; used on Umayyad papyrus protocols), Q 72:3 ("He has taken no companion nor offspring"; e.g. Hawary-Rached, *Steles,* no. 18) and Q 2:255 and 3:18 as cited above. Next in line is the prophet Muḥammad (q.v.), whose importance to humankind is highlighted with the aid of such qurʾānic texts as the aforementioned Q 9:33 (first appearing on coinage from 77/696), Q 37:37 ("He brought the truth and confirmed those already sent"), Q 36:70 ("to warn whoever lives and that the word may be fulfilled against the unbelievers"), and Q 33:45 ("a summoner to God by his permission and a light-giving lamp"; Hawary-Rached, *Steles,* nos. 20, 28-9).

Objects and furnishings

This is a very broad category, comprising a vast range of artifacts and fittings fashioned out of many different materials: metal, glass, wood, clay, ivory, textiles, rock crystal and jade, to name but the most common. At the more basic end of the spectrum inscriptions might be rare or record no more than the place of manufacture, the name of the craftsman responsible, and perhaps a very brief blessing or prayer for the future owner. Items at the luxury end of the scale, by contrast, could bear quite effusive texts, containing praise for the commissioner, moral maxims, profane poems and qurʾānic quotations. The last-mentioned of these would most likely be featured on objects of a religious nature (e.g. wooden Qurʾān-stands, glass mosque lamps) or those found in a religious context (e.g. the cloth covering the Kaʿba [q.v.] in Mecca, carved wooden panels in mosques), and especially on those being donated to mosques and shrines. There would seem to have been considerable diversity in the choice of verses and only very occasionally was a particular text linked to a particular object (keys to the Kaʿba were usually inscribed with Q 3:96-7, which refers to Mecca and its sanctuary; mosque lamps often bore Q 24:35, the Light Verse; bronze water-cauldrons might bear Q 9:19, which alludes to giving drink to pilgrims; see PILGRIMAGE).

Coins

The qurʾānic legends that appear on the earliest purely epigraphic coins, the gold dinars and silver dirhams struck by the Umayyad caliph ʿAbd al-Malik in the 70s/690s, served as a statement of the essence of the Islamic message and the difference between Islam and the other monotheistic religions. The dinar of 77/696-7 is a conflation of three verses to this effect: 1) "There is no god but God alone. He has no associate" on the obverse center ("associate" [*sharīk*] occurs in Q 6:163; 18:111; 25:2); 2) "Muḥammad is the messenger of God, who sent him with guidance and the religion of truth to make it prevail over all religion, even if the associators are averse" (Q 48:29; 9:33) in the margin; and 3) "God is one, the eternal God. He begot none, nor was he begotten" (Q 112) in the margin. On dirhams is added the last phrase of Q 112: "None is equal to him."

These phrases remained unchanged on coins up to the end of the Umayyad caliphate in 132/750, and they stayed in use under the ʿAbbāsids (the main reverse inscription was changed to the simpler "Muḥammad is the messenger of God"). Yet while these basic phrases tended to predominate, certainly until the breakup of the caliphate, different qurʾānic verses were used at different times as slogans. To mention but two examples here: The leaders of the ʿAbbāsid revolution, wishing to emphasize their links to the clan of the Prophet, adopted Q 42:23: "Say, for this I ask of you no recompense other than love of kin" (Bates, *Islamic coins,* 18). The Almoravids, seeking to stress their zeal for holy war, used Q 3:85: "He who chooses a religion other than Islam, it will not be accepted from him and in the world to come he will be one of the lost" (Bates, *Islamic coins,* 28). Sectarian aspects are underlined by the addition of certain non-qurʾānic phrases to the standard profession of faith. For example, on coins of the Fāṭimids in Egypt and the Ṣulayḥids in Yemen (both Shīʿī dynasties) is found "ʿAlī is the friend of God" (Lowick, Dinars, 263); and on a coin of the Fāṭimid caliph al-Muʿizz (341-65/953-75) is inscribed the longer, more emphatic expression, "ʿAlī b. Abī Ṭālib (q.v.) is the nominee of the Prophet and the most excellent representative and husband of the radiant chaste one" (Bates, *Islamic coins,* 31; see FAMILY OF THE PROPHET).

A wide variety of qurʾānic texts appears on coins from across the empire, used by different rulers in different circumstances and at various times. On the whole these demonstrate certain basic themes: aspects of government and God's role in its execution (see POLITICS AND THE QURʾĀN), the victorious nature of Islam, its position in respect of unbelievers, and so on. Sometimes they will be brief snippets of generic pious import (see PIETY), such as "our sufficiency is in God" on Mongol coins of Abū Saʿīd, "the kingdom belongs to God" on coins of Ibrāhīm of Ghazna (Lane Poole, *Catalogue,* 6.219, 2.556), "might is God's" on a Fāṭimid coin of al-Muʿizz (Bates, *Islamic coins,* 31), and a host of others (see Codrington, *Musalman numismatics,* 23-30; Lane Poole, *Catalogue,* indices). At other times most or all of a verse will be used. On coins of the Naṣrid Yūsuf I in Spain and of the Mongol chief Hūlāgū, for instance, one finds Q 3:26: "Say: 'Lord, sovereign of all sovereignty, you bestow sovereignty on whom you will and take it away from whom you please; you exalt whomever you will and abase whomever you please. In your hand lies all that is good" (Lane Poole, *Catalogue,* 2.171, 6.8). The expression, "Victory comes only from God, the mighty, the wise" (Q 3:126), was popular and appears, for example, on the obverse of coins of the Mamlūk ruler Nāṣir Muḥammad, and on the reverse in a form adjusted to suit the sovereign: "There is no victory except with the Sultan al-Malik al-Nāṣir..." (Lane Poole, *Catalogue,* 4.499). Reference to the Qurʾān being "the words of God (see WORD OF GOD)" occurs on medieval North African gold coins from Fās (Lane-Poole, *Catalogue,* 5.211). And in a message against the unbelievers we find most of Q 48:29 cited on a Mongol coin of Uljaitū: "Muḥammad is the messenger of God. Those who are with him are hard on the unbelievers but merciful to one another. You see them adoring on their knees, seeking the grace of God and his good will. Their marks are on their faces, the traces of their prostration" (Lane Poole, *Catalogue,* 6.129; see BOWING AND PROSTRATION). A notable exception to this practice of using qurʾānic phrases is encountered on the coinage of the Ottoman sultans who, with the exception of a few examples inscribed with the standard profession of faith, favored ostentatious formulae highlighting their greatness and the perpetuation of their reign (Lane-Poole, *Catalogue,* 8.xlii, 427-8).

Seals and amulets

In private and public collections are found many thousands of Islamic seals and amulets from the early Islamic period up to the present day. These are made from a variety of stones or metals (see METALS AND MINERALS). This section discusses, first, early Islamic seals inscribed with qurʾānic verses or other pious phrases and, second, amulets that use qurʾānic phrases or make allusion in other ways to God and the Qurʾān. The terms amulet and talisman are often used interchangeably; in Arabic there is no single word, but a variety (*ḥirz, ṭilasm, ḥijāb,* etc.). The preferred term in the present context is "amulet," defined as an object "often worn on or close to the human body, and used for protective purposes" (Ruska and Carra de Vaux, Tilsam; see also Maddison and Savage-Smith, *Science,* 133, where amulets are additionally defined as "made out of lasting materials... apparently made to function over a long period"). Seals and amulets have certain basic differences: The seal is engraved in reverse and made with the intention of stamping onto something, such as a document, to validate it, whereas the amulet is generally engraved in positive and made for a variety of purposes: to bring good luck, to protect from the evil eye, and so on. As will be discussed, however, they both draw upon the same body of pious expressions of Islamic belief for the tone and content of their inscriptions.

The phenomenon of using pious phrases for sealing has its roots in the pre-Islamic tradition. There are close parallels with Sasanian seals which appeal to deities for protection. As has been argued, not only was the presence of the religious text an expression of a person's direct link with God, but it also provided a mark of authenticity for the object being sealed (Kalus and Gignoux, Les formules, 138). Where specific phrases from the Qurʾān are used on early Islamic seals, these generally consist of just a few words, sometimes supplemented by non-qurʾānic phrases. Particularly popular is the phrase "God is sufficient for me" from Q 9:129 and 39:38, which also appears on early Islamic coins and glass stamps (Walker, *Arab-Sasanian,* 102; Morton, *Glass stamps,* 156). Other popular phrases include "as God wills" (sometimes compounded with "there is no power except in God" from Q 18:39 and "I ask forgiveness of God"), "the kingdom belongs to God" from Q 40:16 (also as "glory" and "glory belongs to God" from Q 4:139 and elsewhere) and the standard profession of faith (Kalus, *Ashmolean,* I.1.1.1; see WITNESS TO FAITH). Longer qurʾānic phrases also feature, such as Q 9:127 (Kalus, *Bibliotheque Nationale,* I.1.1.22) and Q 112 (Kalus, *Ashmolean,* I.1.1.4). A commonly recurring theme is the inevitability of death: "Obey your Lord before that day arrives which none can defer against the will of God. For on that day there shall be no refuge for you, nor shall you be able to deny your sins" from Q 42:47 (Naqshabandi and Horri, *Iraq,* no. 61). A seal in the British Museum (Porter, *Catalogue,* Marsden collection 4) includes a mention of its owner having learned the *sabʿ al-mathānī,* thought to refer to the whole of the Qurʾān or to the seven verses of the first sūra (see FĀTIḤA).

Chroniclers and historians (see HISTORY AND THE QURʾĀN), in particular al-Masʿūdī (d. 345/956), Ibn al-ʿArabī (d. 638/1240) and al-Qalqashandī (d. 821/1418), document the use by the caliphs of the phrases, qurʾānic or otherwise, that they affixed on their seals in place of a signature (collected in Gignoux and Kalus, Les formules). The authors do not always agree, however, on which phrases were used by which caliphs. For example, al-Masʿūdī relates that the seal of Muʿāwiya b. Yazīd (64/683-84) was engraved with "In God is the trust of Muʿāwiya" (*Tanbīh,* 307), while according to al-Qalqashandī his seal bore "This world is a deception" (*al-dunyā ghurūr, Ṣubḥ,* vi, 354), an abbreviated form of Q 3:185 and 57:20. The pious phrases used on these caliphal seals correspond to those inscribed on documents, such as "Praise be to God, lord of creation" from Q 1:2, used by the Fāṭimid caliphs, and "The sovereignty belongs to God," used by their viziers. These phrases, both on documents and seals, served the same function as a modern signature, identifying and authenticating the author, and are known as an *ʿalāma* or motto (Stern, *Fatimid decrees,* 127-8).

The nature of these phrases, however, with their expressions of belief or trust in God, lends an added dimension which goes beyond the simple act of validation, especially in the case of seals which personalize the inscription, emphasizing that the owner "believes in God" (Kalus, *Bibliotheque Nationale,* 17). Hence the seal, because of both the words it bears and the stone types from which it is made, which are themselves believed to have protective powers and other beneficent properties, overlaps in function with the amulet. This is most clearly illustrated by the following observation of the ninth-century Muslim scholar al-Jāḥiẓ (d. 255/868): "When a believer takes off his signet ring to affix his seal upon some piece of business and the seal has on it 'God is sufficient for me' or 'I trust in God,' then he surely suspects that he has left the shelter of God, mighty is his name, until he returns the signet to its place" (al-Jāḥiẓ, *Book of Misers,* 42).

Another instance of this amuletic aspect

of Islamic seals is offered in a sardonyx seal of the Ḥimyarite period (ca. third-sixth century C.E.) in the British Museum (Walker, South Arabian gem). It was originally engraved with the name Nadīm in south Arabian script (see ARABIC SCRIPT) and an eagle grasping the tail of a serpent, then re-engraved probably in the eighth century with the qurʾānic verse Q 3:191: "Give us salvation from the punishment of the fire (q.v.)," the first word having been amended to "give me" in order to personalize the phrase. The seal may also have been believed by its Arab owner to have amuletic properties on account of the south Arabian script engraved upon it, which was regarded as one of a series of Kabbalistic alphabets by Ibn Waḥshiyya (fl. fourth/tenth cent, although concrete proof of his existence has yet to be found; Porter, Magical, 140). This seems to be corroborated by a seal inscribed in Arabic with the words "We have repented to God" set into a Carolingian cross brooch found in Ireland (Porter and Ager, Carolingian, 212-3), where again it is presumably the script that is chiefly responsible for the amuletic value of the seal.

The overlapping function of seal and amulet has its roots in the ancient Near Eastern tradition: "Early stamp seals probably derived from amulets and it is likely that seals, whether stamps or cylinders, never lost their amuletic meaning and were always invested with magical powers in the eyes of their owners" (Finkel, Magic, 7). In the Islamic world amulets are most commonly inscribed in positive, to be read straight off, though they can also be rendered in negative, like seals. In this case their power does not become active "until the inscription has been stamped onto a surface where it can be read in the correct sequence" (Maddison and Savage-Smith, *Science*, 133). On amulets there will also often be imprinted a symbol or motif, such as a zodiacal figure, drawn from a vast number of possibilities.

The use of a verse from the Qurʾān on amulets is seen as a powerful tool in magic (Hamès, Le Coran, 129-60), for "it is a guide and a healing to those who believe" (Q 41:44). Moreover, the Qurʾān as a whole was believed to be a source of protection, and the number of extant miniature Qurʾāns indicates that they were frequently carried for this purpose (Canaan, Decipherment, 72; Kalus, *Bibliotheque Nationale*, 71; Donaldson, Koran, 254-66). On amulets complete qurʾānic verses may be inscribed or just short extracts therefrom, such as appear on the early seals discussed above. By far the most popular verses for amulets are the Throne Verse (Q 2:255) and the short chapters at the end of the Qurʾān, especially Q 112 (Canaan, Decipherment, 71-6). These two were often combined with other popular verses (Kalus, *Bibliotheque Nationale*, III.1.1.8: Q 2:255 and 13:13). One example blends Q 112, 12:64 and 61:13 ("help from God and a speedy victory"), the last a common feature of talismanic shirts probably worn in battle (Porter, *Catalogue*, OA+1334; Maddison and Savage-Smith, *Science*, 118). The names of the seven sleepers of Ephesus (see MEN OF THE CAVE), whose story is told in Q 18:1-25, also appear on amulets (Reinaud, *Monumens*, ii, no. 25) as do "the most beautiful names of God" (drawn from or inspired by the Qurʾān), sometimes inscribed in their entirety (99) in tiny script (Kalus, *Bibliotheque Nationale*, III.1.4) or with just one or two added to qurʾānic quotations. The most frequently recurring "names" on amulets are "pardoner" and "preserver," the latter said by Redhouse (Names, no. 85) to be "often employed as a written preservative, spell or charm, on houses etc. against danger of every kind."

Such is the prevalence and multi-purpose nature of verses such as Q 2:255, the

Throne Verse, that only a very general impression of their function and significance on amulets now long separated from their owner can be garnered. Some verses, however, are more specific. For example, there are six, all containing words from the root "to cure," traditionally believed to be very efficacious against illness (Canaan, Decipherment, 75). Two of these verses — Q 10:57: "and a healing for the diseases of your hearts" and Q 16:69: "from its [the bee's] belly comes forth a fluid of many hues, a medicinal drink for mankind" — are engraved in reverse on an amulet in the British Museum (Porter, Magical, 144). Alongside the verses on this particular amulet are magical squares, known as *wafq* or *budūḥ*. This is a 3 x 3 square consisting of letters or their number equivalents, which is so named because in each corner are the letters which make up the artificial word *budūḥ* (Macdonald, Budūḥ; Maddison and Savage-Smith, *Science*, 106-7, and its bibliography for magical squares) and which was deemed to have a favorable influence on childbirth, stomach complaints, the expediting of letters and so on. Sometimes included are the "mysterious letters of the Qurʾān" (Schuster, Magische Quadrate, 20 fig. 2; see LETTERS AND MYSTERIOUS LETTERS), which appear singly or in groups at the beginning of twenty-nine sūras of the Qurʾān and which are widely used on amulets. The widespread use of these letters on amulets results from the belief that "they represent the heavenly language used by the Almighty from whom they derive their natural power… or that they are the names of the Almighty himself" (Canaan, Decipherment, 94).

Strong qurʾānic associations are also present in a group of esoteric symbols with an essentially protective function which as with the magic squares, frequently appear on amulets, bowls, mirrors, manuscripts and other media and are known as "the seven magical signs." They include the five- or six-pointed star called "Solomon's seal" (see SOLOMON), though sometimes the whole group of symbols are referred to as Solomon's seal. Al-Būnī (d. 622/1225), one of the most important Muslim writers on occult sciences, argued that the signs stood for the seven letters omitted from the first sūra of the Qurʾān and that "every letter contains one of the names of God" (Būnī, *Shams*, 93). It was also believed that the combination of signs stood for the greatest name of all (Anawati, Le nom supreme, 26-7). Al-Būnī's text, which principally contains prescriptions for a wide variety of conditions and ailments, includes magical squares, the "seven magical signs," "the most beautiful names of God," as well as the exhortation to recite qurʾānic verses, in particular the Throne Verse (see further Fodor, Notes, 269-71).

The Qurʾān hints at the existence of amulets made from perishable materials rather than stone: "If we sent down to you a writing inscribed on real parchment and the unbelievers touched it with their own hands, they would still say 'this is nothing but plain magic'" (Q 6:7). Still, in Islam pieces of papyrus or paper inscribed with qurʾānic verses, again particularly Q 2:255 and 112:1-4, did serve as amulets (Bilabel and Grohmann, *Texte*, 416; Fodor, Notes, 272). Early block-printed amulets on paper (ca. tenth-eleventh century C.E.) called *ṭarsh*, of which about fifty are known, have been found in Egypt (Kubiak and Scanlon, *Fustat*, 69; two are on parchment, see Schaeffer, Schneide tarsh, 408). After being stamped with qurʾānic verses, names of God and other texts deemed powerful, they are rolled up inside amulet holders ready to be worn about the person. In the case of the Schneide *ṭarsh* there are at least seven separate qurʾānic passages as well as invocations to jinn (q.v.) and angels

(Schaeffer, Schneide tarsh, 416). The stamps, which do not appear to have survived, are thought to have been made in the following way: the text was engraved onto a flattened, moist clay tablet and, after this tablet dried, either molten tin was poured onto the tablet or a thin sheet of malleable tin was pounded into it so that the grooves of the letters appeared on the metal (Bulliet, Tarsh, 435). Modern paper amulets, too, have qurʾānic verses as well as magic squares and other symbols (Fodor, Notes, 273).

In conclusion one might draw attention to an interesting group of amulets bearing qurʾānic texts that are made of strips of lead about six to ten cm (two to four inches) long. Found in Andalusia and dating to the early medieval period, they have inscriptions in angular script. One clear example has the whole of Q 112 (Ibrahim, Evidencia, 708-9). Some show evidence of having been rolled. The fashioning of lead amulets in strips which are in some cases used for exorcism, is an extension of an ancient Near Eastern tradition, examples being known from Mandaic, Hebrew and Greek contexts.

Epigraphy without the Qurʾān

Though the Qurʾān features in a fair proportion of Muslim inscriptions, it is by no means ubiquitous. Carving texts onto hard surfaces requires time and care, especially if it is to be clear, well-formed and even esthetically pleasing. In all cases, save simple graffiti, the services of a professional engraver would generally be called upon, but this could prove expensive, and so there would be reason to minimize the length of the text. A long qurʾānic citation in a well-executed inscription is, therefore, a sure indication of wealth or influence or fame. A study of cemeteries in a region of southern Syria provides some confirmation of this. Tombstones in the luxury material of marble are invariably inscribed, in fine style, with one or more qurʾānic verses. These would only rarely, however, grace tombstones in the cheap local stone of basalt, which would usually bear, in rough letters, just the *basmala* ("in the name of God"), the name of the deceased, and sometimes, though not always, a date (Ory, *Hawran*, 15-6).

Even when the author/commissioner could afford an extensive text, he might feel a qurʾānic quotation unnecessary. The Umayyad caliph al-Walīd b. ʿAbd al-Malik constructed many wondrous monuments bedecked with Qurʾān-laden inscriptions, but on his desert lodge in east Jordan, a place he frequented when heir apparent, he simply recorded that "he built these residences in the year 81" (Combe et al., *Répertoire chronologique*, no. 12). And the foundation inscriptions of roadside hostels, intended for housing and feeding travelers, were rarely deemed worthy of a qurʾānic citation (none in Sauvaget, Caravanserails; Mayer, Satura, mentions one in Palestine that cites Q 25:11). Water installations (drinking fountains, cisterns, etc.), on the other hand, were very often furnished with a qurʾānic text, probably because water (q.v.) was seen as a gift from God and described as such in the Qurʾān on a number of occasions.

Otherwise, a qurʾānic verse might be considered inappropriate to the context. The most blatant example is gold or silver drinking vessels (see CUPS AND VESSELS), the use of which was condemned by the prophet Muḥammad and for which poetry was felt to be a more suitable adornment. Thus a gold bowl belonging to a hoard discovered at Nihāwand and part of a wine service is embellished with some lines of the fourth/tenth-century Iraqi poet Ibn al-Tammār: "Wine is a sun in a garment of red Chinese silk. It flows, its source is the flask. Drink, then, in the pleasance of time, since our day is a day of delight which has brought dew" (Ward, *Metalwork,* no. 38). In poetic graffiti dedicated to the themes of being away from home and a victim of fate, a qurʾānic quotation would have been an anomaly; or at least that is what we are led to believe by a tenth-century collector, whose texts include the following lines: "The calamities of time (q.v.) have driven me from place to place, and shot me with arrows that never miss. They have separated me from those that I love, ah woe to my love-smitten and infatuated heart. Alas for the happy time that has passed as if it were a dream" (Iṣfahānī, *Strangers,* no. 8).

It would also appear that the use of the Qurʾān in inscriptions varied in popularity according to dynasty, region, era, and so on. The Mamlūks of Egypt and a number of other dynasties were very fond of honorific titles and these were often so numerous as to crowd out qurʾānic verses in the inscriptions of themselves and their agents. Iran saw itself not only as a Muslim country, but as a land possessing its own national culture. The Qurʾān therefore had to jostle for position with indigenous poetry, especially extracts from the Persian national epic, the *Shāhnāme.* Thus Kāshān in central Iran churned out ceramic tiles both with qurʾānic legends and with such lines as "Last night the moon came to your house. Filled with envy I thought of chasing him away. Who is the moon to sit in the same place as you?" (Porter, *Tiles,* no. 34). In Ottoman times there seems to have been a move away from the Qurʾān altogether, its verses disappearing from the coinage and building inscriptions and many epitaphs favoring poems composed specially for the occasion (though sometimes with qurʾānic allusions and snippets). The following is an unpublished example from the citadel of Maṣyāf in Syria: "This place derives its glory from its inhabitants, and the truth resides in total fidelity. A man created this blessed place who is called Muṣṭafā [i.e. the founder]. He hopes from the generous God pardon before the chosen Prophet, and for kindness out of God's beneficence, for protection and a just victory: and [he hopes too for] a good end of all things, by his grace, on the day of resurrection. The palace of Kisrā has vanished, and this gift of his [i.e. of the founder] must suffice (1268/1852)." Many conclude with a relevant phrase, which provides the date when the numerical values of its letters are added up (a chronogram). Thus on one of the walls of Qayrawān there is inscribed a poem which begins with "This rampart announces to us the days of felicity," and ends with "Its date is 'thanks to the seigneur felicity has come' [i.e. 1123/1712]" (Roy and Poinssot, *Kairouan,* no. 44).

Moreover, in addition to poetry, the Qurʾān had to compete with an amorphous body of oral material. Most important were prayers of supplication *(duʿā,* pl. *adʿiyya).* For example, a graffito dated 64/683 found near Karbalā in Iraq opens with one of the prayers said at the Festival of the ʿĪd (compare Sanduq, Hafnat, with Nawawī, *Adhkār,* 156; see FESTIVALS AND COMMEMORATIVE DAYS). Numerous epitaphs repeat the prayer to be spared the punishment in the grave (compare Hawary-Rached, *Steles,* no. 4, with Bukhārī, *Ṣaḥīḥ,* iv, 199). The graffito of an Umayyad official contains the prayer to be reunited with someone in the hereafter (compare Musil, Arabia Petraea, no. 1, with Ṭabarī, *Taʾrīkh,* ii, 353, uttered by Ḥusayn b. ʿAlī before his death in 61/680). Otherwise there are found pious sayings, such as "Any friend who is not [a friend] in God, then his friendship is aberrant, lifeless, empty, and his attachment ephemeral" (Sharon, Rehovoth, no. 1), and "in God is a consolation for every disaster and a compensation for every loss" (Hawary-Rached, *Steles,* no. 29). An additional category is wise maxims, such as that engraved on a bowl of the Ghaznawids beginning with "Keep your tongue by saying little, verily calamity is linked with discourse." And also popular sayings of Muḥammad, such as "The Prophet, may God bless him and give him peace, said that whoever builds a mosque, though it be only like the hollow of a sand grouse, God will build for him a house in paradise" (Da-sheng and Kalus, *Chine*, no. 10, on a mosque in Quan-Zhou).

Finally, one should note that, though the vast majority of Muslim inscriptions draw from a common pool of source texts and from a shared stock of expressions and phrases, one encounters texts that break out of this mould. In such cases the author/commissioner decides to drop the public façade so as to speak in a more personal vein, using his own words. A good example is the following: "This is the grave of the slave girl of Mūsā b. Yaʿqūb b. al-Maʾmūn, surnamed Umm Muḥammad. She died leaving behind twenty children and grandchildren. All of them and she herself were afraid of her death in a distant foreign land, anxious about it. And indeed she died while on her way to Jerusalem, in this place, and none of them was present with her except some stranger" (Elad, Epitaph; cf. Sharon, *Corpus inscriptionum*, ʿAqabah 4). See also ARCHAEOLOGY AND THE QURʾĀN.

Robert Hoyland with contributions from Venetia Porter (Coins; Seals and amulets)

Bibliography

Primary (including publications of inscriptions): N. Abbott, The Kasr Kharana inscription of 92 H. (710 A.D.). A new reading, in *Ars islamica* 11-12 (1946), 190-5; ʿA. ʿAbd al-Tawab, *Stèles islamiques de la Nécropole d'Assouan*, 3 vols., Cairo 1977-96, i; D. Baramki, al-Nuqūsh al-ʿarabiyya fī l-bādiya al-sūriyya, in *al-Abḥāth* 17 (1964), 317-46; M. Bates, *Islamic coins*, New York 1982; Bukhārī, *Ṣaḥīḥ*, ed. Krehl; Būnī, Abū l-Abbās Aḥmad b. ʿAlī, *Shams al-maʿārif al-kubrā*, 4 vols., Beirut n.d.; J. Cantineau, *Inventaire des inscriptions de Palmyre. Fasicule IX. Le sanctuaire de Bel*, Beirut 1933; O. Codrington, *A manual of Musalman numismatics*, London 1904; B. Couroyer, Inscription coufique de Beit Gibrin, in *Revue biblique* 71 (1964), 73-9; C. Da-sheng and L. Kalus, *Corpus d'inscriptions arabes et persanes en Chine*, Paris 1991-, i; F.M. Donner, Some early Arabic inscriptions from al-Hanakiyya, Saudi Arabia, in *JNES* 43 (1984), 181-208; A. Elad, An epitaph of the slave girl of the grandson of the ʿAbbasid caliph al-Maʾmun, in *Muséon* 111 (1998), 227-44; S.ʿA. Fahmī, Naqshān jadīdān min Makka al-mukarrama, in *al-Manhal* 48 (1407/1987), 346-61; A. Grohmann, *Arabic inscriptions. Expédition Philby-Ryckmans-Lippens en Arabie. IIe partie. Textes épigraphiques. Tome* 1, Louvain 1962; H. Hawary and H. Rached, *Catalogue général du Musée Arabe du Caire. Stèles funéraires*, 10 vols., Cairo 1932, i; Ibn Khallikān, *Wafayāt*, ed. Iḥsān ʿAbbās; F. Imbert, La nécropole islamique de Qastal al-Balqaʾ en Jordanie, in *Archéologie islamique* 3 (1992), 17-59; id., *Un corpus des inscriptions arabes de Jordanie du nord*, Ph.D. diss., Aix-en-Provence 1996; Iṣfahānī, Abū l-Faraj, *The book of strangers. Medieval Arabic graffiti on the theme of nostalgia*, trans. P. Crone and S. Moreh, Princeton 2000; al-Jāḥiẓ, *The Book of Misers. Al-Bukhalāʾ*, trans. R.B. Serjeant, Reading 1997; L. Kalus, *Ashmolean Museum Oxford. Catalogue of Islamic seals and talismans*, Oxford 1986; id., *Bibliothèque Nationale, Département des monnaies, médailles et antiquités. Catalogue des cachets, bulles et talismans islamiques*, Paris 1981; C. Kessler, ʿAbd al-Malik's inscription in the Dome of the Rock. A reconsideration, in *JRAS* 1970, 2-14; S. Lane Poole, *Catalogue of oriental coins in the British Museum*, 10 vols., London 1875-90; N. Lowick, Some unpublished dinars of the Sulayhids and Zurayʿids, in J. Cribb III, *Coinage and history of the Islamic world*, London 1990; al-Masʿūdī, *Kitāb al-Tanbīh wa-l-ishrāf*, ed. M. de Goeje, Leiden 1894; G.C. Miles, Early Islamic inscriptions near Taʾif in the Hijaz, in *JNES* 7 (1948), 236-42; M.K. al-Moraekhi, *A critical and analytical study of some early Islamic inscriptions from Medina in the Hijaz, Saudi Arabia*, Ph.D. diss., Manchester 1995; A.H. Morton, *A catalogue of early Islamic glass stamps in the British Museum*, London 1985; K.I. Muaikel, *A critical study of the archaeology of the Jawf region of Saudi Arabia*, Ph.D. diss., Durham 1988; A. Musil, Zwei arabische Inschriften aus Arabia Petraea, in *WZKM* 22 (1908), 81-5; U.N. Naqshabandi and H.A. al-Horri, *The Islamic seals in the Iraq Museum*, Baghad 1975 (in Arabic); Nawawī, *Kitāb al-Adhkhār*, Beirut and Damascus 1971; Y. Nevo, Z. Cohen, and D. Heftman, *Ancient Arabic inscriptions from the Negev*, 3 vols., Jerusalem 1993-, i; S. Ory, Les graffiti umayyades de ʿAyn al-Garr, in *Bulletin du Musée de Beyrouth* 20 (1967), 97-148; id., *Cimetières et inscriptions du Hawran et du*

Gabal al-Duruz, Paris 1989; V. Porter, *Catalogue of the Arabic seals and amulets in the British Museum*, forthcoming; id., *Islamic tiles*, London 1995; Qalqashandī, Shihāb al-Dīn Abū l-ʿAbbās Aḥmad b. ʿAlī, *Kitāb Ṣubḥ al-aʿshā*, 14 vols., ed. M.ʿA. Ibrahim, Cairo 1913-8; Y. Ragib, Un contrat de mariage sur soie d'Egypte Fatimide, in *AI* 16 (1980), 31-7; S.ʿA. al-Rāshid, *Kitābāt islāmiyya ghayr manshūra min 'Ruwāwa' al-Madīna al-munawwara*, Riyadh 1993; id., *Kitābāt islāmiyya min Makka al-mukarrama*, Riyadh 1995; M. Reinaud, *Monumens arabes, persans et turcs du cabinet de M. le Duc de Blacas et d'autres cabinets*, 2 vols., Paris 1828; B. Roy and P. Poinssot, *Inscriptions arabes de Kairouan I*, Paris 1950; ʿI. al-Sanduq, Ḥajar Ḥafnat al-Abyaḍ, in *Sumer* 11 (1955), 213-7; M. Sharon, *Corpus inscriptionum arabicarum Palaestinae*, Leiden 1997; id., Five Arabic inscriptions from Rehovoth and Sinai, in *Israel exploration journal* 43 (1993), 50-9; Ṭabarī, *Taʾrīkh;* M.A. al-ʿUshsh, Kitābāt ʿarabiyya ghayr manshūra fī jabal Usays, in *al-Abḥāth* 17 (1964), 227-316; J. Walker, *Catalogue of the Muhammadan coins in the British Museum. The Arab-Sasanian coins*, London 1941; R. Ward, *Islamic metalwork*, New York 1993; A.ʿU. al-Zaylaʿī, *Nuqūsh islāmiyya min Ḥamdāna bi-Wādī ʿUlayb*, Riyadh 1995.

Secondary (The number of secondary works on Muslim epigraphy is vast, so those listed here are limited to those which contribute something to the issue of the Qurʾān and epigraphy. For a broader reading list see the bibliographies in Blair, *Islamic inscriptions* and J. Sourdel-Thomine et al., Kitābāt.): I.A. Bierman, *Writing signs. The Fatimid public text*, Berkeley 1998; S. Blair, *Islamic inscriptions*, Edinburgh 1998 (an excellent handbook for beginners and experts alike, which was used for this article), esp. 210-6; J.M. Bloom, The mosque of the Qarafa in Cairo, in *Muqarnas* 4 (1987), 7-20; E. Combe, J. Sauvaget and G. Wiet, *Répertoire chronologique d'Épigraphie arabe*, Cairo 1931; E.C. Dodd and S. Khairallah, *The image of the word. A study of quranic verses in Islamic architecture*, 2 vols., Beirut 1981; R. Ettinghausen, Arabic epigraphy. Communication or symbolic affirmation, in D.K. Kouymjian (ed.), *Near Eastern numismatics, iconography and history. Studies in honor of G.C. Miles*, Beirut 1974, 297-317; C. Hillenbrand, Jihad propaganda in Syria from the time of the first Crusade until the death of Zengi. The evidence of monumental inscriptions, in K. Athamina and R. Heacock (eds.), *The Frankish wars and their influence in Palestine*, Jerusalem 1994, 60-9; R. Hillenbrand, Qurʾānic epigraphy in medieval Islamic architecture, in *REI* 54 (1986), 171-87; R.G. Hoyland, *Seeing Islam as others saw it*, Princeton 1997; id., The content and context of early Arabic inscriptions, in *JSAI* 21 (1997), esp. 86-9; F. Imbert, Le Coran dans les graffiti des deux premiers siècles de l'hégire, in *Arabica* 47 (2000), 381-90; L.A. Mayer, Satura epigraphica arabica I, in *Quarterly of the Department of the Antiquities of Palestine* 1 (1932), 37-43; A.S. Melikian-Chirvani, Iranian metal-work and the written word, in *Apollo* (1976), 286-91; J. Sauvaget, Caravanserails syriens du moyen-age, in *Ars islamica* 6 (1939), 48-55; 7 (1940), 1-19; J. Sourdel-Thomine, Clefs et serrures de la Kaʿba, in *REI* 39 (1971), 29-86; id. et al., Kitābāt, in *EI²*, v, 210-33; Y. Tabbaa, Monuments with a message. Propagation of *jihad* under Nur al-Din, in V.P. Goss and C.V. Bornstein (eds.), *The meeting of two worlds. Cultural exchange between East and West during the period of the Crusades*, Kalamazoo 1986, 223-41. *(Seals and amulets):* G. Anawati, Le nom supreme de Dieu, in Congresso di studi arabi e islamici, *Atti del terzo Congresso di studi arabi e islamici. Ravello 1-6 settembre*, Naples 1967, 7-58; F. Bilabel and A. Grohmann (eds.), *Grieschische, koptische und arabische Texte zur Religion und religiosen Literatur in Agyptens Spätzeit*, Heidelberg 1934; R. Bulliet, Medieval Arabic tarsh. A forgotten chapter in the history of printing, in *JAOS* 107 (1987), 427-38; T. Canaan, The decipherment of Arabic talismans, in *Berytus* 4 (1937), 69-110; 5 (1938), 369-97; B.A. Donaldson, The Koran as magic, in *MW* 27 (1937), 254-66; I. Finkel, Magic and jewellery, in D. Collon (ed.), *7000 years of seals*, London 1997, 19-20; A. Fodor, Notes on an Arabic amulet scroll, in *AO-H* 27 (1973), 268-9; P. Gignoux and L. Kalus, Les formules des sceaux sasanides et islamiques. Continuité ou mutation? in *SIr* 11 (1982), 123-53; C. Hamès, Le Coran talismanique, in A. de Surgy (ed.), *Religion et pratique de puissance*, Paris 1997, 129-60; T. Ibrahim, Evidencia de precintos y amuletos en al-Andalus, in *Arqueologia medieval española*, Madrid 1987, 706-10; W. Kubiak and G. Scanlon, *Fustat expedition final report*, Winona Lake, IN 1986; D.B. Macdonald, Budūḥ, in *EI¹*, i, 770-1; F. Maddison and E. Savage-Smith, *Science, tools and magic. vol. xii.1 of The Nasser D. Khalili collection of Islamic art*, London 1997; V. Porter, Islamic seals. Magical or practical? in A. Jones (ed.), *University lectures in Islamic studies 2*, London 1998, 135-51; id. and B. Ager, Islamic amuletic seals. The case of the Carolingian cross brooch from Ballycottin, in *Res orientales* 12 (1999), 211-9; J.W. Redhouse, The most comely names, in *JRAS* 12 (1880), 1-69; J. Ruska and B. Carra de Vaux/C.E. Bosworth, Tilsam, in *EI²*, x, 500-2; K.R. Schaeffer, The Schneide tarsh, in *Princeton University Library chronicle* 56 (1995), 401-9; H. Schuster, Magische Quadrate im islamischen Bereich, in *Der Islam* 49 (1972), 1-84; S. Stern, *Fatimid decrees. Original documents from Fatimid chanceries*, London 1964; J. Walker, A south Arabian gem with Sabean and Kufic legends, in *Muséon* 75 (1962), 455-8.

Error

Departure from truth or accuracy. The qurʾānic terms for error derive from the Arabic verb for "to err, go astray (q.v.), deviate from the right course" *(ḍalla)* and are attested at least sixty times in the Qurʾān. In qurʾānic usage the semantic field of *ḍalla* ranges from accidental mistakes to conscious transgressions in the realms of rightful belief and conduct (see BELIEF AND UNBELIEF; SIN, MAJOR AND MINOR). It is not clear, however, whether the concepts of deviance and mistake conveyed by this term are always regarded as something culpable or whether they could be considered, at times, excusable. The majority of instances in which *ḍalla, ḍalāl* and *ḍalāla* occur concern the relation between believers/unbelievers and God; in only a few cases are these words employed with regard to human relations (see SOCIAL INTERACTIONS; SOCIAL RELATIONS). Occasionally, the Qurʾān uses words derived from the verb "to be misguided or led astray, seduced" *(ghawā)* to express notions of error.

The connection between unbelief *(kufr)* and error *(ḍalāl)* is clear from Q 4:136 where it is stated that one who disbelieves in God, his angels (see ANGEL), his books (see BOOK), and his messengers (see MESSENGER; PROPHETS AND PROPHETHOOD) as well as in the last day (see LAST JUDGMENT) has wandered "far astray [i.e. is in serious error, *ḍalāl baʿīd*]." In Q 3:164, error denotes the state of pagan unbelievers before God "sent to [the believers] a messenger from among themselves...," while, in Q 4:44, error is a condition that those who have been given "a portion of the book" deliberately "purchase." Use of transactive verbs such as "to buy" *(ishtarā)* or "to exchange" *(tabaddala)* in connection with ideas of error or erring occurs elsewhere in the Qurʾān. Mention is made in Q 2:16 and Q 2:175 of those "who buy or trade error for guidance" *(ashtarawū l-ḍalāla bi-l-hudā)* and in Q 2:108 of those "who exchange disbelief for belief" *(man yatabaddali l-kufra bi-l-īmān)*. Understanding *shirk* (i.e. associating partners with God; see POLYTHEISM AND ATHEISM) as a form of *ḍalāl* is evident in Q 4:116, 13:14, 36:23-4 and 46:5. The prophet Abraham (q.v.) uses terms for error to describe his father's and forefathers' practice of worshipping images (*tamāthīl*, Q 21:54 and 26:86; see IDOLS AND IMAGES). On the other hand, in Q 54:24, the tribe of Thamūd (q.v.) — after rejecting God's messengers — declares that "we would indeed be in error *(ḍalāl)*..." in following "a mortal, one of us." Attribution of one's mistakes to error occurs at Q 26:20 where Moses (q.v.) says that he had been among the erring *(mina l-ḍāllīna)* when he had committed a certain unnamed act. The effect of this wording is to underscore the unintentionality of a grave action of his. Error is theologically associated with blindness (Q 27:81; 30:53), blinding darkness (q.v.; Q 2:17), blindness and deafness (Q 43:40), and a hardened heart (q.v.; Q 39:22). See HEARING AND DEAFNESS; SEEING AND HEARING; THEOLOGY AND THE QURʾĀN.

Excess as a form of error is invoked in Q 12:8 and 12:95 where the word *ḍalāl* is twice used by Joseph's (Yūsuf) brothers to describe what they consider to be their father Jacob's (Yaʿqūb, see JACOB) excessive fondness for Joseph (q.v.) and once by the "women in the city" who perceive Zulaykha as being in "manifest error" *(ḍalāl mubīn)* as a consequence of her intense passion for Joseph (Q 12:30). Likewise, in Q 7:146, excessive pride (q.v.; *yatakabbarūna fī l-arḍ bi-ghayri l-ḥaqq*) causes a rejection of divine signs (q.v.) which in turn leads to being on a "path of error." Finally, it should be said that error *(ḍalāl)* and guidance *(hudā)* are quite often paired in the Qurʾān, letting this couplet serve as a rhetorical device to impress upon listeners the significance of the choice they are called to make between the two as they are summoned to faith (q.v.).

Ruqayya Khan

Bibliography
Lisān al-ʿArab; Paret, *Kommentar;* al-Rāghib al-Iṣfahānī, *Mufradāt.*

Eschatology

Doctrine about the final things to come at the end of time. Two of the earliest and most important messages given to the prophet Muḥammad (q.v.), prominent in the Meccan revelations (see CHRONOLOGY AND THE QURʾĀN), were about the oneness of God and the accountability of human beings at the last day (*yawm al-qiyāma,* lit. the day of resurrection; see GOD AND HIS ATTRIBUTES; LAST JUDGMENT; RESURRECTION). These two message were so integrally linked that the Qurʾān in many places suggests that faith in God *is* faith in the *yawm al-qiyāma,* the time when all will be resurrected and held accountable. The recognition of God's unity or oneness, *tawḥīd,* also necessitates a response of moral and ethical uprightness (see ETHICS AND THE QURʾĀN), and it is on the basis of one's comportment in life that judgment (q.v.) is rendered and final reward or punishment is accorded (see REWARD AND PUNISHMENT). It is no coincidence that those who have earned a place in the gardens (see GARDEN) of paradise (q.v.) are often referred to as the people who affirm God's oneness *(ahl al-tawḥīd).*

The Qurʾān is very clear, in its articulation of eschatological realities, that the theme of ethical and human accountability in this world is paramount. There is, in other words, a direct relationship between the present world *(al-dunyā)* and the life to come *(al-ākhira).* While God has foreknowledge of every deed, it is people's freely chosen deeds in this world that determine their fate (q.v.) in the next (see EVIL DEEDS; GOOD DEEDS; FREEDOM AND PREDESTINATION). Q 7:172 insists that God has created humanity with the knowledge of his lordship (see LORD), making it inexcusable in the end not to have known the truth (q.v.). As *al-dunyā* and *al-ākhira* are linked by ethical responsibility (q.v.), the one the realm of action and the other the realm of recompense for that action, they are also clearly distinguished. The earthly realm is the place of vanity and false pleasures, as the Qurʾān affirms in many places, while the hereafter is the abode of permanence and true life (q.v.). "For what is the life of this world but play and amusement? Best is the home in the hereafter for those who are righteous" (Q 6:32). For most Qurʾān commentators the distinction between the pleasures of this world and the next is not that the former are physical and the latter are spiritual, but rather that the former lead to pain and suffering (q.v.) and the latter do not, the former are subject to change and the latter are constant, the former are temporary and the latter are eternal.

The message that human bodies will be resurrected and brought to judgment fell on unbelieving ears as Muḥammad tried to persuade his fellow Meccans of its reality and urgency (see OPPOSITION TO MUḤAMMAD). They scoffed at the possibility of life being breathed into dead bones (Q 17:98-9; see DEATH AND THE DEAD), much as they scoffed at the reality of only one deity. It is apparent from the verses of the Qurʾān, however, that the Prophet was talking about a very different concept from the one life/one death belief prevailing in the Arabia of his day (see PRE-ISLAMIC ARABIA AND THE QUR'ĀN). Many of the verses (q.v.) of the Qur'ān insist that all of life is a constant process of creation (q.v.) and recreation. Therefore as God brings life out of death at every moment, he can do it, albeit in a more dramatic way, at the day of resurrection. "Who will bring life to these bones when they have rotted away? Say: 'He will revive them who brought them into being'" (Q 36:78-9). "He brings out the living from the dead, and brings out the dead from the living, and he gives life to the earth (q.v.) after it is dead. And thus you shall be brought out [from the dead]" (Q 30:19).

Human life and death

The Qur'ān leaves no doubt that the individual life span from birth to death is understood as part of the overall structure of God's creation of the world and the events to come on the final day. Creation (q.v.) is both the bringing into being of the world and humankind as a generic whole, and the creation of every individual in the womb of his or her mother (see BIOLOGY AS THE CREATION AND STAGES OF LIFE). Individual time is set within the context of collective time (see COSMOLOGY). The Qur'ān affirms the idea that each human span is for a fixed term *(ajal)* both for individuals (Q 6:2; 7:34; 16:61; 20:129) and for nations (Q 10:49; 15:4-5). As God ascertains the life spans of persons and of communities, in his hands lies the fate (q.v.) of all that he has brought into being. Two Qur'ān references also state that God causes humans to die twice and to live twice (Q 2:28; 40:11). Commentators have suggested a number of possibilities for the meanings of those two lives and deaths; the most common interpretation is that they refer to death before life in this world (i.e. before we are first born we are in fact dead), life given to us at the time of our birth (q.v.) in this world (q.v.), a second death which is the termination of life on earth, and rebirth or second birth at the day of resurrection.

Although Islamic tradition has greatly expanded the descriptions of the process of death, the Qur'ān itself contains little mention of these matters. Q 56:83 describes the soul (q.v.) of the dying person coming up to the throat, and in Q 6:93 death is portrayed as a kind of flooding-in process *(ghamarāt al-mawt)* at which time angels (see ANGEL) stretch forth their hands and ask that the souls be given over to them. The question of the condition of persons in the grave before the coming of the resurrection has also been the subject of much speculation but little qur'ānic clarification. One of the only clues in the Qur'ān as to whether or not the dead have any degree of consciousness is the indication in Q 35:22 that the living and the dead are not alike, and that while God can accord hearing to whomever he wills, the living cannot make those in the graves hear them (see HEARING AND DEAFNESS).

Certain individuals, such as those martyred in the cause of Islam (see MARTYR; PATH OR WAY), are noted as living (Q 2:154; 3:169) and it is said that they will rejoice in God's bounty and blessing (q.v.; Q 22:58-9; 3:170-1). It also seems that some persons are already in the fire (q.v.; Q 40:46-9; 71:25), although it is not certain whether such references are to past, present or future punishment (see TIME). The qur'ānic scripture provides only brief and oblique references to what has been later referred to as the punishment of the grave, although the subject has been greatly elaborated in traditional eschatological manuals. Two verses speak of angels smiting the faces and backs of those who reject God's word *(kuffār)* upon taking their souls at death as a warning of the punishment of the fire (Q 8:50; cf. 46:27). (See also BELIEF AND UNBELIEF.)

From the evidence of the Qurʾān, then, it is difficult to say much with certainty about the period between death and resurrection. Matters become clearer in the descriptions of the events associated with the final day, although this is not to suggest that they are spelled out in chronological or systematic sequence in the Qurʾān. Some 56 Meccan and eleven Medinan sūras deal in some way with resurrection and judgment. All of the events, from the signs (q.v.) of the coming of the hour to the final assessment and determination, support two basic themes central to Islamic eschatology. The first is that bodies will be resurrected and joined with spirits in the reunion of whole and responsible individuals. The second is that there will be a final judgment of the deeds and actions of every individual while on earth (q.v.), and that the assessment will be in God's hands and through God's absolute justice (see JUSTICE AND INJUSTICE). The following elements, referred to in various places throughout the Qurʾān, make up the events that constitute the end of earthly time and the transition to eternity (q.v.; see also DEATH AND THE DEAD).

Signs/conditions of the hour (ashrāṭ al-sāʿa)
The narrative of the events to occur on the final day is graphically and dramatically sketched in the Qurʾān. This is a day when specific signs will be given indicating the reversal of the natural order and a disintegration of the structure of the natural universe (see NATURAL WORLD AND THE QURʾĀN). The story begins, in effect, with the startling descriptions of what are known as the signs of the hour, the cataclysmic events that will occur just preceding the actual resurrection *(baʿth)* and judgment (see APOCALYPSE). In seven different places the Qurʾān talks about the splitting of the heavens (see HEAVEN AND SKY) and, in two, the rolling up of heaven, indicating that the resurrection of the dead and the last judgment are about to occur. Sometimes in the descriptions of the cataclysmic events is included a vivid picture of eight angels carrying above them the throne of God (q.v.; Q 69:17). The Qurʾān uses many different terms for the day of resurrection, including "the sure reality," "the doom," "the reunion," "the gathering," "the resuscitation," "the day of meeting," "the day of judgment," "the day of sorting out" and some others. Of these many names, the single appellation suggested in Q 11:84 — "the all-encompassing day" *(yawm al-muḥīṭ)* — is one of the most telling. God brings all humanity back to life, i.e. back to himself, in the resurrection of bodies, the in-gathering and infusing of new life as the first step in the process of calling human beings to an accounting of their earthly deeds.

There is no indication in the Qurʾān when the last day will arrive, and it is apparent that such knowledge belongs only to God. "People ask you about the hour. Say: Truly such knowledge is with God… Perhaps the hour is near" (Q 33:63). Commentators have interpreted this to mean that the signs of the hour will appear with no warning and that they will signal a dramatic interruption, indeed, cessation, of the normal activities of life and the world. The Qurʾān is most graphic in describing the cataclysmic events upsetting the rhythms of the natural world. "When the sun (q.v.) is folded up, when the stars are thrown down, when the mountains are set moving… when the seas are made to boil, when the souls are reunited… when the scrolls are unrolled, when heavens are torn away, when hell (q.v.) is set ablaze, when the garden (q.v.) is brought near…

[then] shall a soul know what it has produced" (Q 81:1-4). This startling picture represents a reverse process of creation. The heavens, understood as seven layers, are stripped away, rolled up and destroyed. The stars, lamps set in the lowest part of the heavens, fall and are extinguished, and the sun and moon (q.v.) are covered. The earth itself shakes and rocks until it is finally split apart and ground to dust, its mountains first put in motion and then leveled. Even the seas mix together in a kind of primordial chaos.

The traditional eschatological manuals go on to describe a series of events which have only scant mention, or sometimes none at all, in the Qurʾān. One is the appearance of the beast of the earth, cited in Q 27:82: "And when the word is fulfilled against them, we shall bring forth to them a beast of the earth to speak to them. For humanity does not have faith in our signs (q.v.)." Tradition names the beast Dajjāl, and sometimes suggests that it will be defeated by Jesus (ʿĪsā). Jesus (q.v.) in this capacity is not specifically mentioned in the Qurʾān. In the traditions, however, he is often interpreted as assuming the role of the divinely guided one *(mahdī)* who will kill the Dajjāl (see ANTICHRIST), and do various other things prior to the actual coming of the hour. Others see Jesus and the *mahdī* as two distinct figures. The Qurʾān provides no clarification of this issue.

The trumpet, the resurrection (qiyāma) *and the gathering* (ḥashr)

The terrifying blast of the trumpet which will signal the actual moment of the resurrection is mentioned several times in the Qurʾān, referred to either as *al-ṣūr* or *al-nāqūr*. The qurʾānic imagery is stunning in these descriptions, as illustrated in Q 69:13-6: "When the trumpet is blown with a single blast, and the earth and the mountains are lifted up and crushed with a single blow, then, on that day, the happening will occur, and heaven will be split, for on that day it will be very frail...." The first sounding of the trumpet is followed by a second, which signals the dramatic final cataclysm in which all earthly affairs cease and everything animate and inanimate ceases to exist save God. Again the Qurʾān does not order these events as such but the impetus for developing this theme of absolute cessation *(fanāʾ)* comes from such verses as Q 28:88 and 55:26-7, which say that everything will perish except the countenance of God (see FACE OF GOD). Because of the repeated qurʾānic assurance that every soul will taste death, the commentators have assumed that there must be a point at which all creatures are annihilated before being brought back to life in the resurrection of bodies joined once again with souls. In order for God's oneness to be manifested, there must be death; in order for God's justice and mercy (q.v.) to be demonstrated, there must be life again, a re-investing of souls and bodies previously rendered lifeless with the living breath of God.

The Qurʾān spares little in describing the day of judgment as one during which even the most pious will be afraid (see FEAR; PIETY). The whole resurrection process culminates in what is often called the terror of the gathering *(ḥashr)*, when reunited souls and bodies assemble to await the judgment. The Qurʾān alludes to this terror in such verses as Q 21:103 and 37:20 f. and traditions supply the particulars. Some say that the waiting will last 50,000 years based on Q 70:4 ("The angels and the spirit [q.v.] ascend to him in a day whose measure is fifty thousand years") while others interpret it as only a thousand (see NUMBERS AND ENUMERATION). After all the waiting and torment, greatly elaborated in the traditions, comes the act interpreted by many to signal the moment of the judgment itself. Q 68:42 talks about "... the day when the thigh is exposed and they are called to fall down in prostration, but are not able to" (see BOWING AND PROSTRATION). Some commentators have interpreted this uncovering to mean that God himself exposes his leg as the signal for the beginning of the judgment process while others have seen it as a metaphor (q.v.) for the seriousness of the moment. Eschatological manuals have taken the various Qurʾān verses specific to that judgment and tried to put them into sequential order. Again it should be noted that such an order is absent in the Qurʾān itself.

The reckoning (al-ḥisāb)

That a time of reckoning will come is a constant theme in the Qurʾān. No doubt is left that each individual alone will be responsible for his or her past decisions and deeds, the sum of which is in some fashion recorded and presented as one's own "book" (q.v.): "Truly we give life to the dead, and we record what they send before, and their traces. And everything is kept in a clear register" (Q 36:12; see RECORD OF HUMAN ACTIONS). As is attested in Q 17:13, this completed book is fastened onto the neck of the deceased when the spirit departs his or her body at death. No passage, perhaps, is more explicit than Q 69:19-31: "As for the one who is given his book in his right hand, he will say, 'Take and read my book. I knew that I would be called to account.' And he will be in a blissful condition... But as for him who is given his book in his left hand, he will say, 'Would that my book had not been given to me and that I did not know my reckoning!'.... [And it will be said:] Seize him and bind him and expose him to the burning fire...."

The particular elements that make up the occasion of the reckoning have sometimes been categorized as the "modalities of judgment." Although most of these modalities are based on references from scripture, the Qurʾān contains no ordering or even grouping of them, and credal affirmation of them implies only that they are real (see CREEDS). The Qurʾān, for example, refers a number of times to the balance *(mīzān)*, one of the most important eschatological realities. In general, the balance refers to the expression of God's justice in this world. In the plural *(mawāzīn)* it has the clear eschatological reference of the scales by which deeds are weighed on the day of resurrection: "As for the one whose scales are heavy [with good works] he will live a pleasant life. But as for the one whose scales are light... [his fate will be] raging fire" (Q 101:6-11; see WEIGHTS AND MEASURES). Thus the balance is also the coordination of justice in this world with the measuring of human responsibility justly in the next. There is no hope of protest on the part of one who would wish for mitigating circumstances by which judgment should be postponed or lightened. Judgment is final and the direct consequence of one's deeds. Even one's own limbs will testify to the accuracy of the judgment rendered: "On that day we will seal their mouths, and their hands will speak to us and their feet will bear witness to what they have acquired" (Q 36:65; see WITNESSING AND TESTIFYING).

The Qurʾān has little more to say about the judgment process itself. The saved and the doomed are distinguished beyond any doubt (see SALVATION), and all that remains is their consignment to the garden and the fire, so graphically detailed in the scripture. Islamic tradition, however, builds on several other brief Qurʾān references as indicative of what else will happen before the final separation of the blessed and the damned.

The crossing of the bridge (ṣirāṭ), *the possibility of intercession* (shafāʿa) *and preparation for the final consignment*

The bridge is not specifically mentioned in the Qurʾān as a modality of the eschaton. The Qurʾān does, however, frequently use *ṣirāṭ* as meaning the path or way, especially in its references to the straight path, *al-ṣirāṭ al-mustaqīm,* first appearing in the Qurʾān's opening sūra (see FĀTIḤA). Of these references only two, Q 36:66 and 37:23-4, are usually cited to support the idea of a bridge to or over hell, and the first is rather indefinite. The latter refers to the *ṣirāṭ al-jaḥīm* and was adopted into Islamic tradition to signify the span over hell *(jahannam),* the top layer of the fire. The traditions take the term, used repeatedly in the Qurʾān, to represent the proper and prescribed mode of action for all the faithful, the straight path, and apply it in a much more specific sense as the last modality in the process assessing the degree to which every individual has followed that path. Eschatological manuals often affirm that those who have neither faith nor good deeds to their credit find that the bridge has become sharper than a sword and thinner than a hair, and that their fall from it signifies an inescapable descent into the fire. The faithful, however, are said to move easily and swiftly across a broad path, led by the members of the Muslim community and by the Prophet himself first of all.

The question of whether there can be any possibility of intercession (q.v.) in the judgment process has engaged commentators in a variety of ways. The several forms of the word for "intercession," *shafāʿa,* occur 29 times in the Qurʾān. On the whole the text holds out no hope for the last day: "Protect yourselves against a day when no soul will be able to avail another, and no intercession will be accepted..." (Q 2:48; see PROTECTION). The basic argument of the Qurʾān is that God is sovereign in arranging the relationship between himself and his creatures and that no human efforts at mediation are valid or effective. Every individual is responsible for his or her own deeds and acts of faith, and will be called to full account for them. Nevertheless, certain verses have been interpreted as leaving room for the possibility of some kind of intercession. Aside from God himself, those designated as possibly performing this function are angels (Q 53:26), true witnesses (Q 43:86), and those who have made a covenant (q.v.) with God (Q 19:87). A few verses describe intercession for those who are acceptable. Tradition has wanted to invest the prophet Muḥammad with an intercessory function, although none of the qurʾānic verses mentioning *shafāʿa* refer to him specifically. God did call upon Muḥammad to ask forgiveness (q.v.) for living believers (Q 47:19) and this has been taken by many to be the earthly precedent for intercession on the day of judgment. Despite the contrary evidence provided in the Qurʾān, popular belief has often chosen to see that all but the most sinful will be saved by Muḥammad's intercession and God's mercy at the final time (see SIN AND CRIME; SIN, MAJOR AND MINOR). The Qurʾān itself leaves no question whatsoever that divine justice will prevail on the day of judgment, that retribution will correspond in direct proportion to the degree of one's faith (q.v.; *īmān*) and the nature of one's religious acts *(ʿibāda).*

The torment of the fire (al-nār)

According to the consistent witness of the Qurʾān the alternatives for each individual at the day of judgment are two: the bliss of the garden or the torment of the fire. For the latter abode the Qurʾān offers a variety of designations, seven of which have been interpreted to be actual names or terms of specification: *hāwiya, jaḥīm, saʿīr, jahannam, laẓā, saqar* and *ḥuṭām*. Some scholars identify the use of *jaḥīm* as characteristic of the majority of Meccan references, with other terms, particularly *jahannam,* used in later verses. The overwhelming understanding of the abode of the damned, however, is as the fire, *al-nār,* just as what might be called heaven in other traditions is best rendered by its common qurʾānic designation as the garden(s). Many of the details of the fire, as of the garden, are reminiscent of the Bible (see SCRIPTURE AND THE QURʾĀN), while others occasionally reflect the tone of early Arabian poetry (see POETRY AND POETS). On the whole, however, the picture afforded by the Qurʾān is uniquely its own.

The Qurʾān does not offer a detailed plan of the realms of the fire. Q 15:43-4 describes *jahannam* as having seven gates, each gate with its layers, each descending one an abode of increased torment. *Jahannam* is sometimes used to refer to the totality of the fire and sometimes only to the topmost circle. Later traditions supplied each of the gates of the fire with innumerable guardians who torture the damned. On the bottom of the pit of the fire grows the dreadful tree Zaqqūm (Q 37:62-8) with the heads of devils for flowers, from which sinners must eat. The Qurʾān offers a number of rather specific indications of the tortures of the fire: Its flames crackle and roar (Q 25:12); it has fierce, boiling waters (Q 55:44), scorching wind, and black smoke (Q 56:42-3); it roars and boils as if it would burst with rage (Q 67:7-8). As those who are damned enter the fire a voice will cry out: "Seize him and drag him into the depths of the chastisement of *jahannam,* then pour out boiling water over his head" (Q 44:47-8). The people of the fire are sighing and wailing, wretched (Q 11:106); their scorched skins constantly exchanged for new ones so that they can taste the torment anew (Q 4:56); they drink festering water (q.v.) and though death appears on all sides they cannot die (Q 14:16-7); people are linked together in chains of 70 cubits (Q 69:30-2) wearing pitch for clothing and fire on their faces (Q 14:50); hooks of iron will drag them back should they try to escape (Q 22:19-21). In four verses the Qurʾān affirms that God intends to fill up the realm of the damned to capacity, as in Q 11:119: "Truly I shall fill *jahannam* with jinn (q.v.) and humankind together."

Torment is thus portrayed in physical rather than spiritual or psychological terms in the Qurʾān and regret, if expressed, is for the consequences of one's deeds rather than for the actual commission of them. The community of Islam, however, has offered a variety of interpretations as to whether or not the punishments, or indeed the rewards, of the life to come are to be understood in their most literal sense. While the predominant understanding has been of the corporeal nature of the ultimate recompense, this view has generally not insisted that the realities of the next world will be identical with those of this world. While definitely physical, recompense in the ultimate sense is generally understood to have a reality beyond what we are now able to comprehend. Contemporary Qurʾān commentators are especially insistent that the recompense of the hereafter, while sentient, is in some way different from the experiences that we now know and understand. See EXEGESIS OF THE QURʾĀN: EARLY MODERN AND CONTEMPORARY.

The bliss of the garden(s)

The Qurʾān provides some very specific categories of people for whom eternal habitation in felicity is assured: those who refrain from doing evil, keep their duty, have faith in God's revelations, do good works, are truthful, penitent (see REPENTANCE AND

PENANCE), heedful and contrite of heart, those who feed the needy and orphans (q.v.) and who are prisoners (q.v.) for God's sake. These form a close parallel to the acts of omission and commission that afford one a place in the fire. There are also very detailed descriptions of the nature of the reward and of the habitations to be enjoyed by the virtuous (see VIRTUES AND VICES).

Paradise in the Qurʾān is generally referred to as the garden *(al-janna),* although its descriptions are usually of gardens in the plural. The term *naʿīm,* delight, is used frequently in the early Meccan sūras in association with the garden or gardens. There are two references to the name *firdaws* (i.e. paradise; Q 18:107 and 23:11; see FOREIGN VOCABULARY) as the abode of the blessed. As was true of the descriptions of the fire, the Qurʾān does not provide an ordered picture of the structure of the garden. Roughly, however, it can be said to parallel the divisions of the fire. In Q 23:17 God says, "We created above you seven paths *(ṭarāʾiq)*...," which supports the conception of a seven-tiered heaven familiar to Near Eastern cosmogony. Some argue that *firdaws* is the most spacious and highest part of the garden, directly under the throne of God, from which the four rivers of paradise flow (see WATER OF PARADISE). Others argue that it is the second level from the top, and that the uppermost portion is either the garden of Eden or ʿIlliyūn (q.v.). Q 55:46 talks about two gardens: "As for him who fears standing before his lord (q.v.) there are two gardens *(jannatān).*" All descriptions following this verse are of things in pairs — two fountains flowing, fruit of every kind in pairs and two other gardens beside these with two springs (see WELLS AND SPRINGS). This has caused some commentators to speculate that there are actually four realms of the blessed, of which either *firdaws* or Eden is the top.

Within the garden(s) are certain specific features. Many verses speak of the rivers flowing underneath and Q 47:15 describes rivers of water, milk (q.v.), wine (see INTOXICANTS) and honey (q.v.) in the garden. In general, it can be said that there is neither too much heat in paradise nor bitter cold and that there is plentiful shade from spreading branches dark green with foliage. The early Meccan sūras put special emphasis on the shade to be found in paradise, e.g. Q 76:13-4: "Reclining therein on couches, they will find neither sun nor bitter cold. And next to them is shade...." References to rivers in paradise are especially common in the later Meccan and the Medinan sūras, appearing some 35 times. The *sidrat al-muntahā,* called the lote tree of the outermost limit, is described in Q 53:14-6 as being close to the garden of refuge; tradition soon located it specifically at the top of the garden(s) to parallel the tree of Zaqqūm at the pit of the fire. In Q 39:73 we read that people will be driven into the garden in troops until they reach it, whereupon the gates will be opened and they will be welcomed.

Scenes of the joys awaiting the dwellers in the garden are wonderfully rich in the Qurʾān (see JOY AND MISERY). The faithful are described as content, peaceful and secure; they hear no idle talk and experience only peace (q.v.); they do not taste death; they enjoy gentle speech (q.v.), pleasant shade and fruits neither forbidden nor out of reach, as well as cool drink and meat as they desire; they drink from a shining stream of delicious wine, from which they will suffer no after effects (Q 37:45-7); they sit on couches facing each other as brothers (see BROTHERS AND BROTHERHOOD), wearing armlets of gold (q.v.) and pearls, green and gold robes of the finest silk (q.v.) and embroidery, waited on by menservants (Q 52:24; 56:17; 74:19; see MATERIAL CULTURE AND THE QUR'ĀN). Among the joys afforded to the inhabitants of the garden, specifically to males, is the companionship of young virgins with lovely wide eyes (Q 44:54; 52:20; see HOURIS). These creatures, which the Qur'ān identifies as the *ḥūr*, have been the subject of a great deal of discussion on the part of traditionists (see ḤADĪTH AND THE QUR'ĀN) and commentators.

Despite the graphic terms in which the physical pleasures of the inhabitants of the garden are portrayed, there are clear references to a kind of joy that exceeds the pleasures of the flesh. Greater than the delights of the gardens, says Q 9:72, is satisfaction *(riḍwān)* from God. And in Q 6:127 the Qur'ān talks about the final meeting place of those who have heeded the straight path: "For them there will be an abode of peace *(dār al-salām)* in the presence of their lord. And he will be their friend (*walī*, see FRIENDS AND FRIENDSHIP) because of what they have done."

As we have seen, the post-judgment qur'ānic option is either the punishment of the fire or the bliss of the garden. The only possible exception comes in Q 7:46: "And between them is a partition *(ḥijāb)*, and on the heights *(al-a'rāf)* are men who know them all by their signs. And they call to the inhabitants of the garden, 'Peace be upon you.' They do not enter it, though they wish to." It is clear from the preceding verses that this partition separates the inhabitants of the garden from those of the fire and that the men on the heights can view persons in both circumstances. Considerable discussion has arisen about the meaning of this verse. Although it is doubtful that the qur'ānic reference is to an abode for those understood to be in an intermediate category, some exegetes have developed a kind of "limbo" theory on the supposition that there is a classification of people who do not automatically enter the garden or the fire (see BARZAKH; BARRIER).

The issue of whether the abodes of fire and garden are already in existence has been of great interest to exegetes and theologians (see THEOLOGY AND THE QUR'ĀN). The majority of the Mu'tazila (see MU'TAZILĪS), for example, rejected the notion that they have already been created on the grounds that the physical universe does not allow for their existence yet. The Ash'arīs disagreed, saying that location is not the issue and that it is not impossible to imagine another world or level of existence unattainable by our present faculties. Besides, they argued, the Qur'ān itself states that Adam and his wife (see ADAM AND EVE) were in the garden of Eden; it must thus already have been created. Most credal statements affirm that the garden and the fire are a reality and that they are already in existence.

Even more engaging has been the question whether the recompense of the two abodes will be for all eternity. The issue, of course, is more tantalizing when asked of punishment. Will the damned be damned forever? The intention of the Qur'ān itself is not entirely clear in this context. Q 32:14 talks of the punishment of eternity and Q 41:28 calls the fire the *dār al-khuld* (the house of eternity). The form *khālidūn* (eternally) is used numerous times to describe the stay of the wicked in the fire, as in Q 43:74: "The guilty ones are in the punishment of *jahannam* eternally." On the other hand, some verses seem to leave open the possibility that punishment will not necessarily be forever. Q 78:23, for example, states that sinners are in the fire for a long time and Q 10:107 says they are in it as long as the heavens and the earth endure. Q 6:128 may be the clearest statement that in this matter, as is true of all things, the affair is completely in the hands of God: "Then [God] will say, 'The fire is your resting place. [You will] abide there forever, except as God wills....'" This verse, related specifically in reference to the jinn or beings created of fire, assures that they too will be subject to the judgment of God on the final day. The unbelievers *(kuffār)* will be in the fire eternally, says the Qurʾān, yet many theologians have interpreted the reference to mean that as long as the fire lasts the wrongdoers will be in it — but that through God's mercy even the fire will be brought to an end.

The other matter of concern to Muslim theology in relation to the final consignment has been the question of the beatific vision of God. Q 75:22-3 provides what many have felt to be positive affirmation of that vision: "[On that day] faces will be radiant, looking toward their lord." The Qurʾān also speaks of the face of God (*wajh Allāh,* cf. Q 2:115; 30:38; 76:9) and the face of the lord (Q 13:22; 55:27; 92:20). Many in the early Islamic community, however, denied that such a vision is to be understood as a direct view of the actual visage of God. The Muʿtazila, for example, argued that since God is an immaterial substance devoid of accidents, he by definition is not visible. To say that he can actually be seen, they said, would be anthropomorphism (q.v.), citing as proof Q 6:103, "Vision cannot attain to him...." The majority opinion, however, followed the conclusion of the school of al-Ashʿarī (d. 324/935-6) that the vision of God in the next world is indeed a reality.

Classical Qurʾān commentaries on the verses dealing with eschatology tend to underscore fear of eternal punishment as an incentive to right conduct. Much modern commentary, in contrast, seems to have shifted in emphasis from reflections on the enormity and distaste of the purgation of the fire to the wonder and glory of God's beneficence in providing an ordered structure for this life and the next, and to human responsibility and accountability in relation to his constancy within the framework of that order.

Jane I. Smith

Bibliography
Primary: al-Qāḍī ʿAbd al-Raḥīm b. Aḥmad, *Aḥwāl al-qiyāma [*or *Daqāʾiq al-akhbār fī dhikr al-janna wa-l-nār],* ed. and trans. M. Wolff, *Muhammedanische Eschatologie,* Leipzig 1872; al-Ghazālī, Abū Ḥāmid Muḥammad, *Abu Hamid al-Ghazali. The remembrance of death and the afterlife. Book XL of the revival of the religious sciences,* trans. T.J. Winter, Cambridge 1989; Bayḍāwī, *Anwār,* Istanbul 1868; Ibn Kathīr, *Bidāya,* Cairo 1969; id., *Tafsīr,* Beirut 1966; Ibn Qayyim al-Jawziyya, *Hādī l-arwāḥ ilā bilād al-afrāḥ,* ed. M. al-Zaghlī, Riyadh 1997; Qurṭubī, *al-Tadhkira fī aḥwāl al-mawtā wa-aḥwāl al-ākhira,* Cairo 1969; S. Quṭb, *al-Yawm al-ākhir fī ẓilāl al-Qurʾān,* Cairo 1980; id., *Ẓilāl,* Cairo 1959; Suyūṭī, *al-Budūr al-sāfira fī umūr al-ākhira,* Beirut 1996; id., *Bushrā al-kaʾīb bi-liqāʾ al-ḥabīb,* Cairo 1969; Ṭabarī, *Tafsīr,* Cairo 1954-68; al-Taftāzānī, *A commentary on the creed of Islam. Saʿd al-Dīn al-Taftāzānī on the creed of Najm al-Dīn al-Nasafī,* trans. E.E. Elder, New York 1950; id., *Sharḥ al-ʿaqāʾid al-Nasafiyya,* ed. A.H. al-Saqqā, Cairo 1987.
Secondary: ʿA. ʿAbbūd, *al-Yawm al-ākhir wa-l-ḥayāt al-muʿāṣira,* Cairo 1978; Sh. ʿAbd al-Jabbār, *Mādhā baʿd al-mawt?* Baghdad 1984; M. Asín Palacios, *Islam and the Divine Comedy,* London 1926; J.M.S. Baljon, *Modern Muslim Qurʾān interpretation,* Leiden 1961; H. Corbin, *Terre celeste et corps de resurrection,* Paris 1960; R. Eklund, *Life between death and resurrection according to Islam,* Uppsala 1941; A. Fāʾiz, *al-Yawm al-ākhir fī ẓilāl al-Qurʾān,* Beirut 1975; M. Fakhry, *A history of Islamic philosophy,* New York 1970; L. Gardet, *Dieu et la destinée de l'homme,* Paris 1967; Ḥ.ʿI. al-Jamāl, *al-Mawt wa-l-ḥayāt,* Cairo 1973; A.M. Khouj, *The end of the journey. An Islamic perspective on death and the afterlife,* Washington, DC 1988; ʿA. Kishk, *Riḥla ilā l-dār al-ākhira,* Cairo 1980; S. Makino, *Creation and termination,* Tokyo 1970; ʿA. Nawfal, *al-Ḥayāt al-ukhrā,* Cairo 1965; id., *Yawm al-qiyāma,* Cairo 1969; T. O'Shaughnessy, *Eschatological themes in the Qurʾān,* Manila 1986; id., *Muḥammad's thoughts on death,* Leiden 1969; D. Rahbar, *God of justice,* Leiden 1960; ʿA. al-Raḥbāwī, *al-Yawm al-ākhir,* Aleppo 1973; M. Sadeddin, *Eschatology in Islam,* Istanbul 1960; I.M. al-Ṣaffār, *al-Taʿābīr*

al-qurʾāniyya wa-l-biʾa l-ʿarabiyya fī mashāhid al-qiyāma, Najaf 1966; S. el-Saleh, *La vie future selon le Coran,* Paris 1971; M.M. al-Ṣawwāf, *al-Qīyama. Raʾy al-ʿayn,* Mecca 1978; J. Smith and Y. Haddad, *The Islamic understanding of death and resurrection,* Albany 1981; A.J. Wensinck, *The Muslim creed,* New York 1965.

Eternity

The state of being in infinite time (q.v.) as contrasted with the ever-changing quality of earthly existence (see COSMOLOGY). In the Qurʾān, God is the only eternal being in both the past and the future, while created beings will dwell in states of bliss or damnation for eternity *(khulūd, abad)* only in the afterlife (see ESCHATOLOGY). In addition, the Qurʾān denounces a pre-Islamic Arab belief according to which existence and death are attributable to nothing more than time (*dahr,* see FATE; HISTORY AND THE QURʾĀN).

God's eternal existence is denoted in the affirmation that he was not begotten (*lam yūlad,* Q 112:3) and his titles "the first" and "the last" (*al-awwalu wa-l-ākhiru,* Q 57:3; see GOD AND HIS ATTRIBUTES). He is also called the everlasting refuge (*al-ṣamad,* Q 112:2) in the context of his relationship with the created world (see CREATION). These references, and the general qurʾānic notion of God as a limitless being, led exegetes to state explicitly that God is a being with neither a beginning nor an end (e.g. al-Rāzī, *Sharḥ asmāʾ Allāh,* 315-8, 323-32).

The greatest part of the qurʾānic discussion of eternity is concerned with human beliefs and destinies (see DESTINY). Although no human has ever been assigned the gift of escaping death (Q 21:34), human desire for such a state is exemplified in the fact that Satan (see DEVIL) was able to lure Adam (see ADAM AND EVE) to a forbidden deed by promising him an undecaying kingdom and the tree of eternity (*shajarat al-khuld,* Q 20:120; some Muʿtazilīs [q.v.] discussed whether or not the garden in which Adam dwelt [cf. Q 2:35] was the garden of eternity; cf. van Ess, *TG,* ii, 274-5). The inevitability of the cycle of life and death led pre-Islamic Arabs (see AGE OF IGNORANCE; PRE-ISLAMIC ARABIA AND THE QURʾĀN) to believe that humans exist only in their earthly states and, consequently, time *(dahr)* in the sense of fate is an all-powerful universal force (Q 45:24). The Qurʾān denies this doctrine due to its atheism (see POLYTHEISM AND ATHEISM), and a tradition from Muḥammad, reported in various versions (Bukhārī, Muslim, Ibn Ḥanbal, Abū Dāwūd, Mālik; see ḤADĪTH AND THE QURʾĀN), states that what is called time is nothing other than God exercising his powers (cf. al-ʿĀtī, *al-Zamān,* 66).

Against the materialistic fatalism of pre-Islamic Arabs (q.v.), the Qurʾān proclaims God's promise of an eternal reward or punishment (see REWARD AND PUNISHMENT) for humans in the afterlife as contingent upon their earthly actions (see LAST JUDGMENT; GOOD DEEDS; GOOD AND EVIL). On the day of eternity (*yawm al-khulūd,* Q 50:34), the righteous will be told of the pleasures they can enjoy in the garden (q.v.) of eternity (*jannat al-khuld,* Q 25:15) with its eternal *(dāʾim)* fruit and shade (Q 13:35). They shall live there forever (*abadan,* Q 4:122; 5:119; 9:22, 100; 18:2-3; 64:9; 65:11; 98:8) with their spouses (Q 4:57; see MARRIAGE AND DIVORCE). In contrast, those who were evildoers (see EVIL DEEDS) or unbelievers (see BELIEF AND UNBELIEF) will be put forever in a place of severe chastisement (Q 4:169; 10:52; 25:15; 33:65; 72:23; 98:6; see CHASTISEMENT AND PUNISHMENT). They are God's enemies since they denied his signs (Q 41:28), and God shall forget them in the fire (q.v.) on account of their acts (Q 32:14). The eternity of paradise (q.v.) and hell (q.v.) is made subject to God's will in one place in the Qurʾān where it is stated that the punishment and reward will continue so long as he sustains the existence of the heaven and the earth (Q 11:107-8).

It is noteworthy that the classical Islamic period witnessed extensive theological and philosophical controversies regarding the createdness or eternity of the cosmos. Authors of such discussions, however, for example al-Ghazālī (d. 505/1111) and Ibn Rushd (d. 595/1198), relied almost exclusively on rational arguments instead of the authority of the Qur'ān to substantiate their viewpoints. Finally, the created versus the eternal nature of the Qur'ān itself was the subject of extensive theological debates (see CREATEDNESS OF THE QUR'ĀN).

Shahzad Bashir

Bibliography
Primary: al-Ghazālī, Abū Ḥāmid Muḥammad, *Tahāfut al-falāsifa. A parallel English-Arabic text*, tr. M.E. Marmura, Provo, UT 1997; Ibn Rushd, Abū l-Walīd Muḥammad b. Aḥmad, *Tahāfut al-tahāfut*, ed. M. Bouyges, Beirut 1930; Rāzī, *Sharḥ asmā' allāh al-ḥusnā*, ed. Ṭ. ʿAbd al-Ra'ūf Saʿd, Cairo 1976.
Secondary: R. Arnaldez, Ḳidam, in *EI²*, v, 95-9; I. al-ʿĀtī, *al-Zamān fī l-fikr al-islāmī (Ibn Sīnā, al-Rāzī al-Ṭabīb, al-Maʿarrī)*, Beirut 1993; S. van den Bergh, Abad, in *EI²*, i, 2; G. Böwering, Ideas of time in Persian Sufism, in *Iran* 30 (1992), 77-89; van Ess, *TG*; I. Goldziher/A.M. Goichon, Dahriyya, in *EI²*, ii, 95-7; F. Meier, The ultimate origin and the hereafter in Islam, in G.L. Tikku (ed.), *Islam and its cultural divergence. Studies in honor of Gustave E. von Grunebaum*, Urbana, IL 1971, 96-112; H. Ringgren, *Studies in Arabian fatalism*, Uppsala 1955; W.M. Watt, Dahr, in *EI²*, ii, 94-5.

Ethics and the Qur'ān

The subject matter of this article is elusive, since the word "ethics" itself is used in various ways in English. If we take the definition of a standard reference work, we learn that "ethics" is "(1) a general pattern or way of life, (2) a set of rules of conduct or moral code, and (3) inquiry *about* life and rules of conduct..." (*Encyclopedia of philosophy*, iii, 81-2). This article's focus, then, will be qur'ānic ethics in senses (1) and (2) above; we might also use the word "morality," i.e. "beliefs about human nature, beliefs about ideals — what is good for its own sake, rules stipulating action, and motives (ibid., vii, 150). Both terms, ethics and morals, suggest the scope of our inquiry. The Qur'ān abounds with "rules of conduct," and, taken in its entirety, establishes much of a "way of life." While it has little by way of "inquiry about rules of conduct," that is, what philosophers call philosophical or meta-ethics, nonetheless it is possible to infer from the qur'ānic text certain meta-ethical presuppositions and methods.

It must be recognized from the start that the Qur'ān contains more exhortation than stipulation. Despite the plethora of rules that confronts the Qur'ān's reader in the first sūras (which, chronologically speaking, are actually from the latter part of the period of revelation), most of the Qur'ān rallies Muslims to act rightly, and reframes their moral knowledge in a context of retribution and reward in this world (see BLESSING; CHASTISEMENT AND PUNISHMENT), and judgment and subsequent punishment and reward in the next (see LAST JUDGMENT; REWARD AND PUNISHMENT).

Two general points about qur'ānic morality follow from recognizing the nature of the qur'ānic discourse. The Qur'ān assumes that (a) humans know the good and nonetheless often fail to follow it; (b) that since humans know the good, they know too that explanations of why the good is the good are beside the point; the good has the utility of guaranteeing success and reward, but nothing suggests that the good is good for some reason extrinsic to itself. These two moral facts are framed by two other important features of qur'ānic ethics: (a) that the Qur'ān takes for granted the vices, virtues and modes of human organization present at the time of revelation, and (b) that it has a jaundiced view of human capacity and goodwill (see COMMUNITY AND SOCIETY IN THE QUR'ĀN; PRE-ISLAMIC ARABIA AND THE QUR'ĀN).

Yet the Qur'ān's embeddedness in seventh-century Arabian society and those particular notions of virtue and vice should not cause us to lose sight of novel features of its ethical perspective: 1) an assertion of the ultimate meaningfulness of human acts and a variety of compelling theories of why humans should act virtuously; 2) an emphasis on individual but also collective responsibility for the ethical treatment of all persons, whether male or female, infant, wayfarer, neighbor, parent, or wife (see CHILDREN; FAMILY; WOMEN AND THE QUR'ĀN; KINSHIP). The Qur'ān should be seen as revolutionary not in its content, but rather in its justification. It did not so much provide new rules, as a new perspective — namely, that the claims of morality transcend mere human interest and are the very purpose of human existence.

While the distinction between "religion" and "ethics" so dear to philosophical ethicists is unnatural to the Qur'ān, nonetheless the focus here will be on passages discussing virtuous conduct toward human beings rather than those concerned with virtuous attitudes towards God, right beliefs about God, etc. (for discussion of this aspect of right conduct, see FAITH; BELIEF AND UNBELIEF). In addition, this essay will concentrate on passages important within the Qur'ān itself and not necessarily on those esteemed in later legal, theological, or mystical scholarship (see LAW AND THE QUR'ĀN; THEOLOGY AND THE QUR'ĀN; ṢŪFISM AND THE QUR'ĀN). Questions of the sequence of qur'ānic revelation — so important for choosing among apparently contradictory qur'ānic passages — will, for the most part, lie outside the scope of this article (on this, see ABROGATION; CHRONOLOGY AND THE QUR'ĀN).

Accordingly, these issues will be considered in what follows: (1) ethical knowledge (human capacity and human nature; motivations to moral action; the reality of moral choice), (2) terminology (classifying acts; classifying actors), (3) ethical knowledge and moral reasoning, (4) the nature of the Qur'ān's ethical stipulations (rules; principles; admonitions to virtue), and (5) ethical sociology (Muslims and non-Muslims; Muslims).

Ethical knowledge

Human capacity

Three grand ethical questions reveal the assumptions underlying the qur'ānic view of ethics: What is the innate moral nature of human beings? What motivates them to moral action? Are moral choices "real?"

Human nature

The description of human nature in the Qur'ān is not sanguine. It repeatedly complains that human beings are fickle: If harm touches a human he calls to his lord, inclining towards him; then if granted a favor from God he forgets that for which he pleaded before (cf. Q 39:49). They are attentive to God and upright in conduct when in jeopardy or when suffering, but heedless when secure (Q 17: 83; 41:51; 70:19-21). They seek evil as much as good (Q 17:11), they are prone to oppression and ingratitude (cf. Q 13:34; 22:26; see GRATITUDE AND INGRATITUDE), they are hasty (Q 17:11; 21:37), weak (Q 4:28), and they are oppressive and ignorant (Q 33:72; see IGNORANCE).

This bleak picture is modified in two ways. The same human nature that is inclined to err, can also, as we shall see below, recognize the good by reflection, reason, or instinct. In addition, innate human responses to evil and good show that human nature is not hopelessly corrupt, e.g. Q 49:7: "… God has made you love faith and has made it beautiful to your hearts and made hateful to you ingratitude *(kufr)*, wickedness *(fusūq)* and rebellion. These are the rightly guided!" Nothing in the Qur᾿ān's jaundiced view of human propensities suggests that humans cannot act ethically, and consequently there is no need for supernatural grace or a redemptive sacrifice (but see below on predestination). Indeed, the entire qur᾿ānic *kerygma* makes no sense if ethical and virtuous action is not possible. In its description of human nature, the Qur᾿ān maintains an artful tension between the possibility of human perfection and the reality of human moral deficiency.

Motivations to moral action

If human nature is pulled between inclinations to evil conduct and recognition of the good, what, then, motivates humankind to act virtuously? Here the Qur᾿ān offers some of its most distinctive and original arguments, which are incomprehensible without some knowledge of the Arab milieu in which the Qur᾿ān arose. There are three overlapping motives to human virtue — two are claims that God has on humankind, and the third, more common one, is what might be seen as a prudential motive.

The first motivation to moral action is the myth of the primordial covenant (q.v.). This is an overtly mythological story of a primordial commitment to obey God. It is, as al-Nīsābūrī (*Tafsīr,* ix, 85) says: "The establishment of compelling evidence against *(ḥujja ʿalā)* all who are responsible *(jamīʿat al-mukallafīn)* [to God, but would attempt to deny that obligation]." Its source is Q 7:172: "When your lord took from the children of Adam, from their loins *(ẓuhūrihim)* their seed and called them to testify of themselves: 'Am I not your lord?' They said, 'Indeed yes!' We testify; lest you should say on the day of resurrection, 'We were unaware of this!'" In this myth, all human beings *in potentia* acknowledged their obligation to obey God's dictates because of his status as their sovereign. The last sentence makes it clear that what is at issue here is whether humans are innately morally responsible. The answer is yes, they have committed themselves primordially to obedience (q.v.; *al-mīthāq al-awwal ʿalā l-fiṭra,* as al-Ṭabarī in *Tafsīr,* ix, 112 calls it), and so to morality.

The argument most central to the Qur᾿ān's view of human moral obligation is that of "thanking the benefactor." This understanding of human ethical motivation begins with God's status as the creator of humankind and the world (Q 19:67; 30:8; 50:16; 89:15; see CREATION). A clear statement of the argument is found in Q 39:5-7: "He created the heavens and the earth with truth *(bi-l-ḥaqqi),* and made night follow day and made day follow night; he subjected the sun (q.v.) and the moon (q.v.) to service, each running for a stipulated term. Is he not the mighty and forgiving? He created you from a single soul then made of it its mate and sent down to you eight couples of cattle. He created you in your mothers' bellies, creation after creation, in the three darknesses. This is your God, your lord; his is sovereignty, there is no god but he. How then did you depart? If you are ungrateful *(takfurū),* God is quit of you, nor is he content with ingratitude from his bondsmen. If you are thankful *(tashkurū),* it contents him with you…."

According to pre-Islamic norms, one who spared a life, that is, in effect, gave life, was owed something by the one who benefited from this generosity (see BLOODSHED). The benefactor was entitled both to reward and to public acknowledgement of the benefactor's generosity in sparing life. In the qur᾿ānic understanding, by giving life, by not taking life, as well as because of a whole series of other benefactions — rain, food, sustenance — God establishes a claim *(ḥaqq)* on humankind (see Bravmann, Ancient Arab background; Reinhart, *Before revelation*, chap. 6). This is clear in Q 14:32-4: "It is God who created the heavens and the earth and sent down from the sky water, then produced by it fruits as sustenance for you; and he made ships serviceable to you to run upon the sea for you by his command; and made rivers serviceable to you. And he makes serviceable to you the sun and the moon in their courses and made serviceable to you the night and the day. And he gives you of all you ask him; if you counted the benefactions of God you could not reckon them. Truly humankind are wrong-doers, ingrates!"

Consequently, like the warrior who spared a life, God is entitled to a proclamation *(shukr)* of his generosity and a gesture that would content *(raḍā)* him. The passage quoted at the beginning of this section says that it is the proclamation of his sovereignty that contents him, and further, that by being an obedient bondsman one expresses the gratitude that is owed: "Be a bondsman *(fa-ʿbud)* and be one of the thankers" (Q 39:66).

In the qur᾿ānic moral calculus, the obligation of humans to act morally arises from their obligation to acknowledge and repay their debt to the creator and benefactor. Since what God asks is obedience to his command — to perform the cultus (see PRAYER; ISLĀM; WORSHIP), to struggle (see JIHĀD), to act rightly — human beings are then obliged, though not compelled, to act in accord with his desires.

The third and most prominent claim to obedience and the religious and moral behavior the Qur᾿ān enjoins is fear (q.v.), or to put it more conventionally, a prudential concern for one's eternal fate. Perhaps *the* central theme of the qur᾿ānic revelation is the reality of the judgment that forms an inevitable part of the cosmic order: "… God has created the heavens and the earth and that which is between them only by right *(bi-l-ḥaqqi)* and for a stated term.… Have they not journeyed in the land and seen the consequence of those who were before them?… Their messengers (see MESSENGER) came to them with signs *(bi-l-bayyināti)*; for God did not wrong *(ẓ-l-m)* them, but they wronged themselves. Then the consequence for those who did evil was evil, for they denied *(k-dh-b)* the signs *(āyāt)* of God and mocked them. God originates creation then brings it back, then to him you return.… As for those who had faith and did good deeds *(ṣāliḥāt)*, they shall rejoice in a garden; as for those who rejected or denied our signs and the encounter with the next life, they will be in punishment" (Q 30:8-11, 15-6).

These themes are present on almost every qur᾿ānic page. Thus, while relations between humankind and God may be governed by a primordial covenant and by the claim of God on those whom he has benefacted in the here-and-now, also and overwhelmingly, the force of sanction for ill-deeds and reward for good deeds confronts the moral actor. Accordingly, in the long run humankind is given a clearly prudential motive to act virtuously. Virtue produces bliss (eventually) and vice leads to eternal chastisement.

These three factors — keeping a promise made primordially, paying back what is owed by acting well, and fear of punishment — all motivate the Qur᾿ān's audience to act ethically.

The reality of moral choice

One problem with the qur᾿ānic text — one that has received perhaps too much attention from Muslim theologians and Western polemicists — is the question of "predestination" in the Qur'ān. It is important to note that terms for "predestination" used in later disputes *(qadar, taqdīr, qaḍā')* do not, in the Qur'ān, necessarily suggest predetermination of human moral choice. Rather, there are a number of texts suggesting that rejection of the qur'ānic message or the Prophet (and similarly plotting against the Prophet, hypocrisy in commitment to him and to God, and the like; on the hypocrites, see, for example, Q 4:88; see OPPOSITION TO MUḤAMMAD; HYPOCRITES AND HYPOCRISY), are the results of God's "turning away" the hearts of the recalcitrant. Examples include Q 5:49: "Then if they turn away, know that God wishes to strike them for some of their sins," and Q 4:88: "Do you wish to guide whom God has led astray *(aḍalla)?* Whom God leads astray, you [Muḥammad] can find no road for him" (see also Q 30:29). Similarly, "... God leads astray whom he wishes and guides to himself those who turn to him [in repentance]" (Q 13:27; see also Q 6:35, 125; 7:178; 10:100; 11:34; 81:28-9); "The one whom God leads astray *(yuḍlil)* has no protecting friend *(walī)* after him" (Q 42:44); and "... So when they turned aside *(zāghū),* God caused their hearts to go astray *(azāgha llāhu qulūbahum)*. And God does not guide a corrupt people *(al-qawma l-fāsiqīna)*" (Q 61:5). These texts have been read, understandably, as suggesting that God causes the errant to err. If this is the case, moral choice is illusory and punishment for moral transgressions seems unjust.

On the other hand, the entire argument of the Qur'ān, that humans will be judged for their actions and that they ought to behave in such and such a manner, makes no sense if humans are not understood to be faced with real moral choices and with justified (in humanly comprehensible terms) consequences. Those who were concerned to assert the reality of human moral judgment also had a large number of texts to point to; for example, "... Who wishes, let him have faith; and who wishes, let him reject" (Q 18:29); or "God does not charge a soul beyond what it can encompass. He has for it only what it has earned and against it what it has earned" (Q 2:286). Similarly, the following passage assumes the efficacy of moral behavior and the consequentiality of those acts: "... Do not those who believe know that, had God wished, he would have guided the people altogether; and catastrophe does not cease to afflict those who reject according to what they do" (Q 13:31). In these texts, as well as in many other passages, the Qur'ān clearly states that human beings earn their fate and they are free to choose virtue or vice.

In sum, on the vexed question of predestination, predetermination and the like, the Qur'ān asserts the controlling authority of God, while also assuming the reality of human agency. For later systematizers, this contradiction had to be resolved in one direction or the other; but the religious sensibility of the Qur'ān can hold the two in tension and assert both limits to human capacity and the fact of human ethical responsibility (for further discussion on this, see ASTRAY; FREEDOM AND PREDESTINATION; FATE; DESTINY).

Terminology

The best index of ethics in the Qur'ān is the terms used in it to discuss moral and immoral behavior.

Classifying acts

The Arabic term most frequently translated as ethics, *akhlāq,* is not found in the Qur'ān and there are few words that suggest a technical terminology for "ethics" — i.e. terms like the English words "virtue (q.v.)" or "conduct." Rather, the terms used to describe virtue and vice are for the most part plain words like "good" and "bad," "right" and "wrong." A general feature of qur'ānic ethical terminology is that it typically commends the good far more than it stipulates what the good is; the Qur'ān assumes that much of the good and its opposite is known or recognizable *(ma'rūf)*. It is notable that the Qur'ān exhorts the Muslim to act virtuously but seldom specifies the exact form of that virtuous conduct. At most, the Qur'ān provides lists of good or bad acts that suggest the scope of morality, but do not define it (see also GOOD DEEDS; EVIL DEEDS; GOOD AND EVIL; SIN AND CRIME; SIN, MAJOR AND MINOR).

Virtuous acts

The most prominent word for virtuous conduct is *ṣāliḥ* or other words from the root which occur some 171 times in the Qur'ān. The root appears in verbal forms as in, "Who does right *(man ṣalaḥa)* from among their fathers, wives, and offspring [shall enter the garden of Eden]" (Q 40:8; also 13:23). Its most common form is a nominal in stereotype with *'amila* as "do good deeds," or "those who do virtuous acts" (*alladhīna 'amilū l-ṣāliḥāt,* e.g. Q 2:25 and numerous other instances). *'Amila l-ṣāliḥāt* is so common as to amount almost to a chorus in qur'ānic discourse. Very often *ṣāliḥ* is joined to other fundamental qur'ānic concepts, as in Q 5:93: "For those who have faith and do good deeds there shall be no transgression *(junāḥ)* concerning what they have eaten. Therefore — [be one of those who] fear God and have faith and do good deeds; then, fear God and have faith; then, fear God and do kindness *(aḥsanū);* God loves those who do kindness." (On *junāḥ* and *aḥsanū* see below.) *Ṣāliḥ*-acts explicitly earn the doer paradise (q.v.; Q 2:25; 5:93; 18:107) and this twinning of faith and good deeds led Izutsu (*Concepts,* 204) to speculate that *ṣāliḥ* is the outward expression of the faith enjoined by the Qur'ān. It certainly is the case that *ṣāliḥ* is sometimes found among the qualities listed in passages that read like catechisms of what it means to be a virtuous Muslim (see, for instance, Q 2:277; 5:69). Yet, for all its prominence, the *ṣāliḥ* is undefined and this it shares with the other important terms for virtue. The hearer of the Qur'ān knew or recognized a good deed and he or she will be rewarded for doing that good deed. The specifics in context, however, are left to the Muslims' faculties to recognize.

Another important qur'ānic term for virtue is *birr* and various derivatives of the root letters *b-r-r* (see Izutsu, *Concepts,* 207-11). *Birr* seems to be a general word connoting virtue or righteousness in the context of religious attitudes and acts, and can occur also in verbal form, as in Q 2:224: "... act well *(tabarrū),* fear God, and reconcile people," or Q 60:8: "... to be good to [your opponents] and be equitable toward them." From the same root comes *barr,* which seems to mean, literally, "pious," that is, filial toward parents (see Q 19:14, 32). The most common form, however, is the nominative, *al-birr,* which is used eight times in the Qur'ān (Q 2:44, 177 [twice], 189 [twice]; 3:92; 5:2; 58:9), mostly in passages coming from the later period of revelation. In three instances (Q 3:92; 5:2; 58:9) it is paired with *taqwā,* "piety" or "an awareness of God," or another derivative of the root letters *w-q-y;* in all cases it is overtly virtue in a religious context that is implied. There is some evidence that *birr* is a pre-Islamic religious term, since Q 2:189 addresses what seems to be a pre-Islamic taboo and re-defines the term not as a superstitious act, but as the fear of God: "it is not *birr* to go to houses from their backs but rather, pious is the one who fears God *(wa-lākinna l-birra mani ttaqā).*" The verse continues with an exhortation to enter houses by their doors *(abwāb)* and to fear God. *Birr* does refer also to ethical behavior, however: "You do not attain *birr* until you spend *(tunfiqū)* from that which you love; and whatever you spend, God is aware of it" (Q 3:92). More elaborately, at Q 2:177 *birr* is defined in one of the familiar "creeds" of the second and third sūras: "It is not *birr* that you turn your faces to the east and the west, but *birr* is one who has faith in God and the last day and the angels (see ANGEL) and the book (q.v.) and the prophets (see PROPHETS AND PROPHETHOOD), and [one who] gives wealth from love of him to kin and orphans (q.v.) and the unfortunate and *ibn al-sabīl* (probably those who have recently immigrated to Medina; see EMIGRATION) and to those who ask — and who frees slaves (see SLAVES AND SLAVERY) and undertakes worship and pays *zakāt* (see ALMSGIVING), and who fulfill their compact *(ʿahd),* when they make compacts (see BREAKING TRUSTS AND CONTRACTS), and the steadfast *(al-ṣābirīn)* in adversity, in stress and time of tribulation (see TRIAL); those who have integrity *(ṣadaqū)* — these are the ones who fear God *(al-muttaqūn).*"

Here, again, *birr* is contrasted with mere cultic practice, but is defined as faith and ethical behavior. It seems that toward the end of the period of revelation, a vocabulary defining virtuous membership in the community was in the process of development. *Birr* was among the terms that had significance in the pre-Islamic world but were being redefined to convey a new, qurʾānic ethical sense.

The common term *khayrāt* also refers to "good works" as in: "Vie with one another in good works" (Q 2:148; see also 3:114 where it is linked with enjoining the *maʿrūf;* see below for a discussion of this term). The term usually is stereotyped with "vie in" or "hasten to" (e.g. Q 23:56). *Khayr* itself means "good," and in certain contexts has an explicitly moral sense, as in Q 3:26: "In your hand (God) is the good *(al-khayr).*" Izutsu (*Concepts,* 217 f.) points out that this term usually refers to bounty and wealth, or to bounty and wealth properly used (but see also Q 5:48; 8:70). *Khayr,* then, is a natural good, but beyond that, not much more can be said.

Likewise, it is difficult to translate *ḥ-s-n* and its derivatives more precisely than with the word "good." Aside from aesthetic description and mere approval in a number of places, the root sometimes suggests ethical action: "Then we gave Moses (q.v.) the book complete for those who do good *(alladhī aḥsana)*..." (Q 6:154). More often, it is overtly a reference to religiously-approved behavior, especially when this form is used in the plural, e.g. Q 3:172: "Those who responded to God and the messenger after the wound befell them, for those among them who did well *(aḥsanū)* and feared God — a mighty reward!" Izutsu (*Concepts,* 224 f.) suggests that the root *ḥ-s-n* refers to pious acts and includes ethical acts informed by the pre-Islamic virtue of prudent forbearance *(ḥilm).* Of the first usage, a good example is the curious passage at the end of Q 5:93: "For those who have faith and do good deeds *(ṣāliḥāt),* there shall be no transgression *(junāḥ)* concerning what they have eaten. Therefore — [be one of those who] fear God and have faith and do good deeds, then fear God and have faith, then fear God and do kindness *(aḥsanū);* God loves those who do kindness."

The most obvious "ethics" usage of the root is with the form *iḥsān,* which occurs twelve times (Q 2:83, 178, 229; 4:36, 62; 6:151; 9:100; 16:90; 17:23; 46:15; 55:60 [twice]), e.g. "kindly treatment of parents" (Q 2:83, *bi-l-wālidayni iḥsānan*), or "Divorce twice, then take back with *maʿrūf* or release with *iḥsān*" (Q 2:229). The point of these passages is to incite the listener to what he/she knows to be proper behavior.

Indeed, among the most common terms

for virtuous acts, as a class, is *maʿrūf,* literally, "the known." It appears thirty-two times in the Qurʾān, but is so taken for granted as a concept that even the commentators do not feel a need to explain it (see the discussions on the first occurrence of the term, Q 2:178, in Ṭabarī, *Tafsīr;* Nīsābūrī, *Tafsīr;* Qurṭubī, *Jāmiʿ*). It is often paired with *iḥsān* and seems to mean nothing more specific than "good deed," or "virtuous conduct." It is worth noting that the implication of *maʿrūf,* as an ethical term, is that "the right thing" is known. One lexicographer suggests that the test of the *maʿrūf* is that "it is that in which the self finds ease *(sakinat ilayhi l-nafs)* and it deems it good, because of its goodness — intellectually, revelationally, and customarily" (Abū l-Baqāʾ, *Kulliyāt,* iv, 185). In other words, the Qurʾān assumes that some part of the good enjoined by the Qurʾān is known without revelational stipulation, perhaps being that which the Prophet's audience knew to be the good from earlier (pre-Islamic) times (see Hodgson, *Venture of Islam,* i, 163). The scope of the term may be suggested by Q 4:6: "[the guardian of orphans' wealth] who is poor: let him consume [of that wealth] what is appropriate *(fa-l-yaʾkul bi-l-maʿrūf)*" or Q 9:71: "And the faithful men and women are protégés of each other, commanding the good *(maʿrūf)* and forbidding the reprehensible *(munkar),* undertaking *ṣalāt* and paying *zakāt,* and obeying God and his messenger..." The phrase "commanding the good and forbidding the reprehensible *(al-amr bi-l-maʿrūf wa-l-nahy ʿan al-munkar)*" is one of the most common both in the Qurʾān and in later ethical and moral literature (for a recent discussion of this, see M. Cook, *Commanding right and forbidding wrong*). Here, the very word for "good" itself denotes a knowledge extrinsic to revelation.

None of these qurʾānic terms for virtue seems novel, though at least in the case of *birr* there is clear evidence of a term from pre-Islamic religious life being re-understood. For the most part, not only is the terminology of virtue familiar to the seventh century audience, but the very context of ethics is alluded to rather than specified. Although later Islamic ethical thought moved in the opposite direction (G. Hourani, *Reason and tradition,* 15-22; Reinhart, *Before revelation,* 62-76; 177-84), it is clear that the Qurʾān assumed its listeners knew the meaning of virtue, and could be assumed to recognize the virtuous course in a particular situation.

Vice

Vice, too is in large part assumed to be obvious in context. Perhaps it is here that the Qurʾān's appeal to prudence (see below) is most important. Vice is not defined, but the consequences of vicious behavior are set forth at length in the threats of judgment (q.v.) and punishment so prominent in all parts of the Qurʾān.

A common word for vice is *fasād,* and other words from the root. The root occurs forty-eight times in the Qurʾān, thirty-five times in stereotype with *fī l-arḍ,* "on (the) earth." Without the phrase "on (the) earth" it can mean "to ruin" (Q 27:34), and in other places it refers to *kufr,* rejection of or turning away from God (e.g. Q 3:63; 7:86; 16:88); in still other places *fasād* or *mufsid* is opposed to *ṣāliḥ* and so means "to do evil acts" (e.g. Q 2:220). In the cases where it is linked to the phrase "on (the) earth" it invites us to see the corruption of an otherwise benign state. It is the acts of humankind that corrupt the earth (see CORRUPTION): "Had not God repelled some of humankind by others the earth would have been corrupted" (*la-fasadati l-arḍu,* Q 2:251). The movement from literal ruin to metaphorical moral corruption can be seen in the glosses to the verse: "And when he (man) turns away he strives on the earth to corrupt it and to destroy tillage *(al-ḥarth)* and the generations (q.v.; *al-nasl*)" (Q 2:205). The commentators harmonize these two terms and understand them first as "cropland and livestock," but also as "women and children" (see Nīsābūrī, *Tafsīr*, ii, 98-200; Ṭabarī, *Tafsīr*, ii, 312-9). Humans can, then, by malice, corrupt an otherwise benign creation; and humans, like crops, can be ruined by the moral depravity of others. In the latter case, the need for moral intervention (by others) is clear: if the vicious are not "repelled," they will corrupt others.

F-ḥ-sh is found twenty-four times in the Qurʾān and is defined as a transgression of the boundary *(al-ḥadd;* cf. Ṭabarī, *Tafsīr*, ii, 64). There is good reason to think, from its citation in verses referring to transgressions by wives (e.g. Q 4:15, 25) and the so-called people of Lot (q.v.; Q 27:54-5), that the term refers particularly to sexual transgression, of which "adultery" (*zinā*, see ADULTERY AND FORNICATION) is one instance (Q 17:32; see BOUNDARIES AND PRECEPTS).

The root *kh-b-th* is found twenty-two times in the Qurʾān, fourteen of them in the form *khabīth*. Like *f-ḥ-sh*, it evokes the notion of disgust, as in Q 21:74: "We delivered [Lot] from the village that was wont to practice wickednesses *(al-khabāʾith).* Truly they were an evil people, depraved *(fāsiqīn)*." The term *khabīth* is frequently offered as the antinomy for the ordinary word *ṭayyib*, "good." These two are contrasted with each other and the attraction of the wicked is admitted: "Wickedness *(al-khabīth)* and good *(al-ṭayyib)* are not equivalent, though the plenitude of wickedness pleases you" (Q 5:100).

F-s-q is also sometimes a term of moral disapproval, indicating depravity of some sort. The root appears in the Qurʾān fifty-four times. Its semantic field includes cultic transgressions, such as swearing by divining arrows (Q 5:3; see FORETELLING; OATHS AND PROMISES) and betraying covenants (Q 3:81-2). For the most part, however, *f-s-q* is a term of theological opprobrium and Izutsu (*Concepts*, 157 f.) goes so far as to call it a species of *kufr*. Like other terms of ethical opprobrium, the term has little specific content — the Qurʾān's audience is to recognize it when they see it.

The meaning of the root *n-k-r* in the fourth form is "to disapprove," and so the passive participle *munkar* means "to be denied, be disavowed, disapproved of." It is regularly paired with *maʿrūf*, as a slogan, however, and so its meaning must also be "the wrong thing to do," "that which cannot be affirmed as right," "that which is known to be wrong." It occurs sixteen times in the Qurʾān, nearly always alongside *maʿrūf*, as in Q 3:113-4, where the most virtuous of the People of the Book (q.v.) are described as reciting the signs of God and prostrating themselves, having faith in God and the last day, commanding the *maʿrūf* and forbidding the *munkar*, competing in the doing of good deeds *(khayrāt):* "... they are among the virtuous *(al-ṣāliḥīn)*" (Q 3:114).

Ithm, *junāḥ*, *dhanb*, *khaṭaʾ*, and *jurm* are all terms for acts disapproved of, and each is frequently translated as "sin"; these five terms refer primarily to a violation of one of the legal or ritual norms instituted in Qurʾān. Although an illegality or ritual transgression is an ethical failure in the qurʾānic view, there does remain a sense in which these are formalistic failings that do not incite feelings of repulsion as do the other terms discussed above. *Ithm*, for instance, appears in Q 2:85 referring to a covenant *(mīthāq)* violated (cf. Q 2:84), and in Q 6:120 in reference to failure to recite the name of God over food; in Q 58:9 it refers to conspiring, after having been "forbidden conspiracy/confidential conversation" (*nuhū ʿan al-najwā*, Q 53:8). *Junāḥ* is connected to circumambulating Ṣafā and Marwa during *ḥajj* or *ʿumra* (see PILGRIMAGE) in Q 2:158, while in Q 4:24 the term refers to additional contractual stipulations in addition to the bride-portion. *Dhanb* is found in, for instance, Q 26:14 where it refers to murder as grounds for punishment; and in Q 81:9 the female infant asks what transgression of hers justifies her being killed (*bi-ayyi dhanbin qutilat*, see INFANTICIDE). *Khaṭaʾ* is equivalent to *junāḥ*, as in Q 33:5, which is concerned with the technicalities of lineage determination: "There is no technical transgression in mistakes you make." In Q 4:92, *khaṭaʾ* refers to mistaken killing, while Q 2:286 connects the word in its fourth verbal form to "forgetting."

It is harder to assign a precise scope to *jurm*. In Q 11:89 the term in its first verbal form refers to the failings of the people to whom the prophets Noah (q.v.), Hūd (q.v.), Ṣāliḥ (q.v.) and Lot were sent. Q 10:17 suggests that a *mujrim* is someone who declares God and his revelations to be false, and the *mujrimūn* about to fall into the fire (q.v.) in Q 18:53 seem to refer to those who associated gods with God (see Q 18:52); Q 25:31 states that the enemy who is appointed for every prophet comes "from the *mujrimīn*." A *mujrim* seems, then, to be one of those damned for what are theological, rather than strictly ethical, transgressions.

The three words *sayyiʾ/sawʾ/sūʾ* (all from the same root: *s-w-ʾ*) correspond well to the semantic scope of the English word "evil," both in its applicability to misfortunate acts, that is, natural evil, as in Q 16:58-9: "If one of them is given news of [the birth of] a female, his face darkens and he is silently angry; he retreats from people as a result of the evil news given him *(min sūʾi mā bushshira bihi)*...," and to morally reprehensible acts, i.e. theological or moral evil, as in Q 6:136, a verse that speaks of the tribal custom of giving tithes to "partners" of God: "Evil is their rule *(sāʾa mā yaḥkumūna)*." It may be that the root suggests evil to be an intrinsic feature of the act, as in Q 4:17-8 where "evil" deeds are done unwittingly: "... those who do evil in ignorance *(yaʿmalūna l-sūʾa bi-jahālatin)*..." Al-Nīsābūrī (*Tafsīr*, ii, 64) adds that *sūʾ* encompasses "all acts of disobedience, whether of the limbs or of the mind *(qalb)*."

Without doubt, words from the root *ẓ-l-m* are the most frequent terms for wrong-doing, appearing 310 times in the Qurʾān. The meaning of this term is complex and has engendered a relatively large body of discussion (e.g. Izutsu, *Concepts*, 164-77; Hourani, Injuring oneself; Husain, The meaning of zulm). In the broadest sense, the root means "wrong," or "wrongdoing," e.g. Q 40:17: "[On the day of judgment] each soul is requited according to what it has earned. No wrongdoing *(ẓulm)* on the day! God is swift at reckoning *(ḥisāb)*." This last word, the commercial term "reckoning, calculating, accounting," suggests that *ẓulm* is *unearned harm* — either in deed or in proportion. It is undeserved conduct vis-à-vis another that is denoted by *ẓulm* and its cognates.

The objects of *ẓulm* have occasioned much discussion. First, one human can do *ẓulm* to another by theft (cf. Q 12:75), by consuming an orphan's property (Q 4:10), or by preventing the faithful from going to worship (cf. Q 2:114). Second, one can wrong God: "Whoever transgresses God's limits, they are the *ẓālimūn*" (Q 2:229); also, "who does greater wrong than one who, reminded of the signs of his lord, turns away from them" (*wa-man aẓlamu mimman dhukkira bi-āyāti rabbihi fa-aʿraḍa ʿanhā*, Q 18:57). There can be no question of "harming" God — as an orphan is harmed by having his property consumed — but rather of "doing wrong by him," given the obligations that obtain in the relation between humankind and God (see above).

The third and most controversial object of *ẓulm* is the self *(ẓalama nafsahu)*. Thirty-six times the Qurʾān links the self/soul with *ẓulm*, e.g. Q 7:23: "They (Adam and Eve) said: 'Our lord! We have wronged ourselves *(ẓalamnā anfusanā)*. If you do not forgive us and show us mercy we shall be among the lost!'" The faithless, whose fate is the fire (of hell), are also described as people who have "wronged themselves:" "The likeness of what they (the faithless) spend in this worldly life is to a frosty wind which strikes the crops of a people who wronged themselves, then destroyed it: God did not wrong them but they wrong themselves *(wa-lākin anfusahum yaẓlimūn)*" (Q 3:117); "Then we gave the book as inheritance *(awrathnā)* to those whom we chose of our bondsmen — among them were those who wrong themselves *(minhum ẓālimun li-nafsihi)*, among them were those who are tepid, and among them are those who race ahead in good deeds by God's leave..." (Q 35:32).

Hourani (Injuring oneself, 49-51) points out that the concept of "wronging oneself," as a purely ethical concept, is problematic, especially from the point of view of the Aristotelian tradition that has dominated Western (and Islamic philosophical) ethical reflection. "Wronging," that is, acting in a way that evokes the judgment that an act is morally unjust, requires the object of the action to be non-consenting, and unless one is a dualist, the agent (the "wronger") of acts done to the self necessarily consents in actions done by the agent. Therefore, one cannot be "morally unjust to," i.e. "wrong," the self. Hourani suggests that implicit in the root meaning of *ẓ-l-m* is the notion of harm, as well as wrong. Consequently, *ẓālim li-nafsihi* is "harming oneself," inasmuch as a moral transgression has harmful consequences on the day of judgment. He concedes there may be in these qurʾānic passages some notion of the wrongdoer as having harmed himself because of some quality of the vicious acts done, although he thinks it likely that this is a later, philosophical reading into the qurʾānic text (Hourani, Injuring oneself, 56).

Acts, then, are categorized by the Qurʾān in terminology suggesting strongly that its message is to exhort Muslims to do the right act and eschew the wrong act, more than to define for them right and wrong. The same seems to be true of concepts for categorizing moral actors.

Classifying actors

Virtuous acts are signs of *ṭāʿa*, "obedience," "submissiveness," or "allegiance," on the part of humankind (Lane, 1890-1; see Q 3:100, where a Muslim obedient to People of the Book allies himself to their rejectionism, when the Muslim had previously been one of the faithful). One obeys God and his messenger and those given command: "And the faithful men and faithful women are protégés of each other, commanding the good *(al-maʿrūf)* and forbidding the reprehensible, undertaking *ṣalāt* and paying *zakāt*, and obeying God and his messenger — to these God will show mercy" (Q 9:7; cf. 3:32; 4:59, 8:1). Obedience is a public, not a private virtue (Q 24:53, Q 47:21). Those who are obedient and loyal not only ally with each other as "protecting friends," or protégés, as above, but ally themselves with God as well: "And the wrongdoers *(ẓālimūn)* have no protector *(walī)* nor ally. Or have they chosen protectors *(awliyāʾ)* other than him? But God [alone] is the *walī*" (Q 42:8-9). The virtuous then are protégés or clients (see CLIENTS AND CLIENTAGE; PROTECTION) of God and "no fear comes to the protégés of God nor do they grieve" (Q 10:62).

The opposite of the virtuous, the unrighteous, are those who "rebel against" *(ʿ-ṣ-y)* God. Adam's transgression was that he rebelled against his lord (Q 20:121), while Pharaoh (q.v.) also rebelled against the messenger that God sent (Q 73:16). Rebellion is listed as a failing which the faithful avoid: "[O you who are faithful]... God has made you love faith and has made it beautiful to your hearts and made hateful to you ingratitude *(kufr)*, wickedness *(fusūq)* and rebellion *('iṣyān)*. These are the rightly-guided!" (Q 49:7).

The wicked are not just moral failures but active "enemies of God." The notion of moral transgression as enmity gives a sharply affective edge to the notion of ethical failure. It is not, in qur'ānic discourse, that the vicious are merely misguided, but their moral failures make them active agents of corruption and opponents of God and his messenger: "... [The hypocrites] had faith, then rejected; their hearts are sealed up so they cannot understand... They are the enemy, so beware of them! May God fight them; what liars they are!" (Q 63:3-4). The nature of this enmity is emphasized by the numerous places in which Satan, too, is described as an enemy — of mankind and of God. (e.g. Q 7:22; 12:5; 35:6; 43:62). Enmity toward God is heartily reciprocated: "Who is an enemy of God and his angels and his messengers and Gabriel (q.v.) and Michael (q.v.), then God is an enemy to the ingrates *(kāfirīn)*" (Q 2:98).

Despite this emotional characterization of ethical transgressors, the most prominent description of those who believe or act wrongly, is that they are "astray" *(ḍ-l-l* or *gh-w-y)*: "Adam rebelled against his lord, and so went astray *(ghawā)*" (Q 20:121); "... who rebels against God and his messenger has manifestly gone far astray *(qad ḍalla ḍalālan mubīnan)*" (Q 33:36). The ethical implication of this terminology is that the errant can find, or be led to the correct path again. Repentance requires reform, however: "Who does evil out of ignorance *(bi-jahālatin)* then repents afterwards and does well *(aṣlaḥa)* [then God] is forgiving, merciful" (Q 6:54). Such a view is completely consonant with the qur'ānic emphasis on God as merciful, compassionate, and forgiving, themes found on nearly every page of the Qur'ān. Forgiveness (q.v.) is a human virtue as well: "And those who avoid the greatest sins and indecencies and when angry, they forgive" (Q 42:37; see also 42:40, 43).

Though there may be other terms with a scope that would place them under "ethics" (e.g. *fājir, i'tidā'*, etc.), this sample suffices to show the shape and content of qur'ānic ethical valuation. Acts have moral values, and morally aware humans, as humans, recognize these values. The lie (q.v.) is bad, an act of kindness toward one's parents is good. Acts are valued also because they affirm or deny theological truth or they signify obedience or disobedience to Islamic cultic norms. For the most part, however, the human capacity for moral knowledge suffices to provide judgment in particular cases. The details of moral conduct need not be specified. The qur'ānic contribution is less information that this act is good, that act bad, than it is the clarification of the stakes in choosing a particular ethical path. One may be God's protégé or God's enemy; a final judgment will recompense virtue and the oppressed and punish vice and the oppressors. The Qur'ān, in sum, does not so much inform as incite, it calls not so much for the correct assessment of acts, as for action.

Ethical knowledge and moral reasoning

From this discussion of ethical terminology, it should be obvious that the ethical epistemology of the Qur'ān differs from ethical epistemology as it developed within later Islamic theology and jurisprudence (see G. Hourani *Islamic rationalism*, passim; Reinhart, *Before revelation*, passim).

As we saw above, the ability of humankind to perceive values, and the assumption of already-existing Arab cultural norms play a role in the knowledge of right and wrong. As Hourani noticed, (Ethical presuppositions) the Qurʾān takes for granted that thinking, or reflecting, will guide one to right action. (Even later commentators, who otherwise rejected this epistemological theory, recognized that the Qurʾān refers to knowledge that is common to all humans, e.g. Qurṭubī, *Jāmiʿ*, v, 185, commenting on Q 4:36, says: "Scholars are utterly agreed that this *āya* is efficacious — nothing of it is abrogated. And it is [found] thus in all the scriptures. Even if this were not so, this would be known by means of the intellect, even if it were not revealed in scripture.")

Though the noun *ʿaql* (glossed variously as "intellect, reason, mind") is never referred to, the Qurʾān uses verbal forms of *ʿ-q-l* for the activity of thinking, reflecting, ratiocinating, 49 times. There are places where it seems to mean something like "using common sense," and others where it means, "reflect and draw the logical conclusions." Both aspects of using the *ʿaql* are relevant for qurʾānic epistemology, as when the Qurʾān suggests that to read scripture requires one to draw the conclusion that righteous behavior is enjoined on scriptuaries as on others: "Do you command that people be good *(birr)* and you forget yourselves, while you yourselves recite scripture? Have you not reflected? *(a-fa-lā taʿqilūn)*" (Q 2:44). It seems that the signs of God — which include but are not limited to scripture — must be reflected upon before action takes place; but when they are reflected upon one is led to moral truth: "Thus God makes clear his signs that perhaps you might reflect *(laʿallakum taʿqilūna)*" (Q 2:242). The Qurʾān repeatedly lists features of nature (see NATURAL WORLD AND THE QURʾĀN) — e.g. that man has eyes (q.v.), ears (q.v.), a heart; that God has metaphorically sown humans on the earth; that he has given life and death and distinguished night from day — and urges the hearer to draw the right conclusion: "Will you not reflect *(a-fa-lā taʿqilūn)?*" (cf. Q 23:78-80). Ignoring the knowledge the intellect provides leads one to perdition: "[The people of hell] say, 'Had we listened or reflected *(naʿqilu)* we would not have been among the dwellers in the flames'" (Q 67:10). Likewise, ethical reflection can prevent one from being led astray and into moral transgression: "[Satan] has led a large group of you astray; did you not reflect *(a-fa-lam takūnū taʿqilūn)?*" (Q 36:62). It would seem that an argument based on proof *(burhān)* is decisive — again a reference to thought as a source of religio-ethical knowledge: "And we extract from every nation a witness and we say, 'Bring your proof *(burhān)!*' Then they will know the truth is with God and what they invented has led them astray" (Q 28:75).

The same appears to be true for the root *f-k-r*, which is used 97 times. The root appears, as does *ʿaql*, in assertions that humans have been given the means to religio-moral knowledge if they reflect upon what they know: "They ask you about date-wine (*khamr*, see INTOXICANTS) and games of chance (*maysir*, see GAMBLING). Say: In both is great sin *(ithm)*, and utility for humankind, though their sin is greater than their utility. They ask you also what to spend. Say: What is superfluous. Thus God clarifies to you the signs, perhaps you will consider *(laʿallakum tatafakkarūn)*" (Q 2:219; cf. 2:242).

Despite the existence of epistemologically significant signs (q.v.), and the injunction to reflect upon them, there are still matters where the Qurʾān suggests that intuition and reflection are insufficient: the Qurʾān repeatedly says "prescribed *(kataba* or *kutiba)* for you/them is such and such," followed by a rule or an adjuration (e.g. 2:187; Q 2:216 for warfare). In many other cases, such a prescription is indicated by the simple imperative: "Give orphans their property" (Q 4:2); or "Call to witness against [adulterous women] four of you" (Q 4:15). The claim of God to make such prescriptions is rooted in several covenantal assumptions (see above), but the form of the command implies that this is a moral requirement whose justification is simple — it is God's command. Implicit in the command form, however, is also the epistemological assertion that this norm is not *definitively* known except by revelation — hence we may read for *kutiba ʿalaykum,* "it is [scripturally] ordained for you" (Q 2:216) and in the divine imperative "[God orders in this revelation that you] call to witness..." (Q 4:15). The intellect is not a sufficient guide; it may also not be an altogether reliable guide; some acts clearly may seem intuitionally to be repulsive, while they are nonetheless enjoined upon the faithful: "Battle is ordained for you though it is hateful to you; it may happen that you hate a thing, but it is good for you, and it may happen that you love a thing and it is evil for you; God knows and you do not" (Q 2:216). Because "God knows and you do not," revelation remains an indispensable part of the qurʾānic moral epistemology. Nonetheless, most medieval Muslim scholars underestimated the role assigned to ethical reflection by the Qurʾān in Islamic moral knowledge (see G. Hourani, *Reason and tradition;* Reinhart, *Before revelation*).

Nature of the Qurʾān's ethical stipulations

It is often suggested that the Qurʾān is full of rules, or, in more contemporary phraseology, that "the Qurʾān contains rules for every aspect of life." In fact, even the most liberal counting produces only 500 verses (albeit, many of these are very long — sometimes, as much as ten or twenty times the length of the shorter verses) of the roughly 6220 in the Qurʾān that are "rules" (al-Mahdī li-Dīn Allāh, *al-Baḥr,* i, 238-308), and these include many *āyāt* with important legal implications. Yet these could hardly be called 'rules" in the normal sense of the word: e.g. "He it is who created for you that which is on the earth" (Q 2:29); or "Woe to those worshiping heedless of their worship who make show [of worship] but refuse to give aid" (Q 107:4-7).

It is useful to recognize that the kinds of qurʾānic ethical stipulations can be sorted roughly into three classes, which we might call rules, principles, and admonitions to virtue.

Rules

"Rules" are decrees, which usually occur in the imperative. They are distinguished from principles and admonitions by the way in which their observance or neglect is assessed. Rules are either observed or not observed — the statement "Aḥmad observes the rule, 'Forbidden to you is carrion and blood and the meat of swine (Q 5:3)'," is true if he avoids those things, and false if he does not avoid them. There are rules aplenty in the first several sections of the Qurʾān (i.e. those revealed in the later periods of revelation), and these stipulate diet (e.g. Q 2:173), how to divorce (e.g. Q 2:227-32; see MARRIAGE AND DIVORCE), cultic practice (Q 3:57), etiquette (e.g. 24:27) contracting debt (2:282; see DEBTS), as well as many other matters (see LAWFUL AND UNLAWFUL).

Principles

Yet to characterize the ethical content of the Qurʾān as "rules" would be a mistake. A good deal of the qurʾānic ethical advice and command is not in the form of rules, but what Dworkin calls "principles:"

"Principles are standards to be observed... because it is a requirement of justice or fairness or some other dimension of morality..." (Is law a system of rules?, 43). "Principles are not applied, as rules are, in an 'all or nothing' fashion, but instead, a principle is something which [one] must take into account... as a consideration inclining in one direction or another" (ibid., 47). Principles have a dimension of "weight" or relative importance which one must take into account when two or more principles are in conflict — which, because of their generality, they often are (see PROHIBITED DEGREES).

Principles may look to a qurʾānic reader like rules, but a consideration of some will show their difference. For instance, there is the maxim "The good deed *(al-ḥasana)* and the evil deed *(al-sayyiʾa)* are not equivalent; repel [harm] by what is better..." (Q 41:34). This sort of Golden Rule, in its generality, can hardly be said to be observed or not observed in an 'all or nothing fashion,' as a rule is. To obey this injunction is not like avoiding swineflesh. One must judge that a given act in a given situation is better than other alternatives — all of which might also be good. The principle in Q 41:34 might be seen to conflict, in some situations, with other principles, such as "Warfare [in the sacred month] is a major [transgression] but blocking [one] from the way of God and rejecting him and expelling people from the sacred mosque is greater with God; tribulation *(al-fitna)* is greater than killing" (Q 2:217; see FIGHTING). So, if one is blocked from the sacred mosque during the sacred month, does one "return evil with good," or bear in mind that "tribulation is worse than warfare?" The Muslim must weigh these two principles, and make a decision based on how they are weighted. (This is not the same as resolving a conflict between two rules; both principles are invoked and in force.) There are many such principles — some obviously moral maxims, some less obviously so: "Do not be extravagant; God has no love for the extravagant" (Q 6:141); or, "Those who are steadfast in desiring the countenance of their lord and undertake the worship *(al-ṣalāt)* and spend of what we bestowed upon them covertly and overtly and overcome evil with good: It is they whose aftermath will be the home (*ʿuqbā l-dār,* i.e. paradise)" (Q 13:22). The Muslim is to weigh the value of spending versus the folly of extravagance, according to the situation. There is no rule in either of these texts, only principles. In fact, the majority of the Qurʾān's injunctions are of this sort — guidelines rather than stipulations.

Some of these maxims, too, are orientational rather than prescriptive. The Qurʾān elaborates upon Q 13:22 a few verses later: "God expands the provision of those whom he wishes, and contracts [it for those whom he wishes] while they rejoice in the life of the world — but what is the life of the world but [mere] pleasure compared to the afterlife? (Q 13:26). This passage, too, shapes the ethical perspective of the attentive Muslim, but it is certainly not a rule or a call to a specific action. It is, rather, a principle, a moral fact which, to differing degrees, according to the situation, will inform his or her moral judgment.

Ethicists who describe ethical knowledge and reflection as grounded in rules have recently come under criticism. And the critics of such analysis would find support in the style of qurʾānic ethical discourse. Some of these critics assert the relative importance of moral *reasoning* over moral rules, and, though the distinction is sometimes artificial, it is clear that these qurʾānic principles have more to do with judicious judgment after reflection than with mere obedience or following prescriptions. The importance of the intellect (q.v.; *ʿaql*) and reflecting upon *(fikr)* likewise suggest that the Qurʾān is less about prescription than about guidelines and comparative judgment.

Admonitions to virtue

There is another critical perspective, however, that also finds support in qurʾānic ethics, and this is the claim that ethics is about the *cultivation of virtues* more than it is about rules or reasoning. For such ethicists, it is emulation rather than obedience or reflection that shapes most ethical endeavors. From this perspective, ethical questions are not decided by reflection of the sort "What ought I to do?" but, rather, "What would the sort of person I want to be do in this case?" The domain of this ethical method is virtue — how to be courageous, what is courage in a given situation, what is generosity, and so on.

The Qurʾān has many references to virtues and to specific vices. Goldziher has argued (*MS* [Eng. tr.], i, 18-44) and Izutsu concurs (*Concepts*, 45-119) that the Qurʾān redefines and sometimes denigrates the tribal virtues summed up in the term "manliness" *(muruwwa)*, and moves the Muslim toward a new set of religious virtues. Izutsu suggests that, nonetheless, there is a religious re-appropriation of some of these tribal virtues by giving them "a consistent theoretical basis" (*Concepts*, 45). Here we can offer only a brief demonstration of qurʾānic virtues to show the importance of these themes in the Qurʾān's ethical discourse (for more detailed discussions of some of these virtues, see VIRTUES AND VICES; JUSTICE AND INJUSTICE; TRUST AND PATIENCE; PIETY).

Justice (*ʿadl*, literally, "equity" and *qisṭ*, "giving fair measure") is repeatedly enjoined throughout the Qurʾān. *ʿAdl* is used in quasi-legal contexts (cf. Q 2:282; 4:58), but elsewhere seems to mean simply "being fair" or "fairness" (cf. Q 4:3, 129; 16:76, 90). Almost as important as *ʿadl* is its near synonym *qisṭ*. The root letters *q-s-ṭ* appear in various forms, and with various glosses, often linked to judging in judicial matters (e.g. Q 2:282): sometimes as a mere synonym of *ʿadl* (e.g. Q 49:9); more generally, as the virtue "equity:" "Oh you who believe! Be upright in equity *(kūnū qawwāmīna bi-l-qisṭ)*, witnesses to God" (Q 4:135; cf. 5:8). God likewise will act with *qisṭ* (Q 21:47). As with the terms for "good" and "bad" discussed above, the exact scope of *qisṭ* is not spelled out in the Qurʾān; rather, the term appeals to the sense of virtue latent in its listeners, inculcated by moral education and moral exemplars — surely including the prophet Muḥammad.

Other virtues enjoined on Muslims include endurance *(ṣabr)* and integrity *(ṣidq)*. Endurance (*ṣ-b-r*, in various forms) is among the most commonly cited virtues in the Qurʾān. It seems to mean something like the ability to maintain commitment despite difficult circumstances (Q 2:177) and to persevere. One is to show fortitude, and do good deeds (*ṣāliḥāt*, Q 11:11); to be persistent and rely upon [the] lord (Q 16:42); to struggle and be steadfast (Q 16:110): "Endure *(ṣbirū)*, show fortitude toward others *(ṣābirū)*, be steadfast *(rābiṭū)*, fear God, that you might succeed" (Q 3:200; cf. 68:48, "wait steadfastly for your lord's decree *[fa-ṣbir li-ḥukmi rabbika]*"). *Ṣabr* is something prayed for (e.g. Q 2:250; 7:126) and the term is frequently paired with *ṣ-d-q*.

Though the root *ṣ-d-q* is often translated as "telling the truth," it is clear that the term means, rather, something like "integrity" or "being true to"; that is, it calls for a correspondence between reality and speech, behavior and public profession. It means fulfilling promises (*ṣādiqīn*, Q 34:29), and therefore *ṣidq* can be something characteristic of God whose threats and promises are not empty (*ṣadaqa llāhu*, Q 3:95; 33:22), and also of humankind who must act in accordance with their professions of faith (Q 33:23). In addition to acting out one's faith, the root also implies a public quality, a proclaiming of one's allegiance — the root concept of *ṣadīq*, "friend" (Q 26:101). The archetypes of this public integrity are prophets such as Abraham (q.v.) and Idrīs (q.v.), each of whom is an affirmer, a warner (q.v.; *ṣiddīqan nabiyyan*, Q 19:41, 56). The concept underlying these words is simply the public performance of commitments made in private.

The vices contrary to these virtues would be pretension, boasting (see BOAST), and hypocrisy; all three are the objects of qur'ānic obloquy. For example, the Qur'ān condemns acting pretentiously, i.e. without integrity between conduct and true moral commitment, in "those who spend their wealth in the sight of men" (Q 4:38), or, "Why do you say what you do not do? It is hateful to God that you say what you do not do" (Q 61:2-3). Hypocrites *(munāfiqūn)* are condemned because "they say with their mouths what is not in their hearts" (Q 3:167). The root *n-f-q* appears 34 times in this sense: "The hypocrites fool God; he fools them! If they rise to worship they stand up sluggishly to be seen *(yurā'ūn)* by the people nor do they mention God but a little" (Q 4:142).

There are many virtues and vices commanded and condemned in the Qur'ān — Donaldson (*Studies*, 16 f.) lists humility (see MODESTY), honesty, giving to the poor (see POVERTY AND THE POOR), kindness, and trustworthiness, and as vices he mentions boasting, blasphemy (q.v.), slander — and there are many more besides. Indeed, there are lists of virtues and vices at many points in the Qur'ān, for instance Q 17:23-39, which Donaldson (*Studies*, 25) compares to the Decalogue (though there are 11 points — 4 virtues and 7 vices listed). Q 25:63-72 is a series of injunctions to dignity and equipoise; Q 31:13-19 enjoins theological commitment and modest reserve (cf. Q 2:177; 4:36; for other discussions see Donaldson, *Studies*, 14-59; al-Shamma, *Ethical system*, passim).

Ethical sociology

In recent literature, ethics is discussed mostly as a series of problems that the individual faces as an individual. Universal ethics is assumed to require an interchangeability among persons, and it is only very recently that ethical "roles" have received the attention they require. In the Qur'ān, while the locus of moral responsibility is the individual, the nature of one's moral responsibilities is in large part shaped by the group to which one belongs: some roles entail behaviors, some roles (on the part of others) provoke behaviors. There is also a sense in which the community as a whole is viewed as a moral agent (a perspective articulated in later legal thought as the concept of *farḍ al-kifāya* (J. Esposito (ed.), *Oxford encyclopedia of the modern Islamic world*, s.v. *farḍ al-kifāyah*). The constantly-repeated refrain ordaining that Muslims "command the good and forbid the reprehensible" *(al-amr bi-l-ma'rūf wa-l-nahy 'an al-munkar)* assumes one party exhorting another. So it is necessary here to discuss "ethical sociology" — the groups recognized by the Qur'ān as incurring or provoking distinctive moral attitudes and behaviors. The corporate bodies recognized in qur'ānic ethics and discussed below are: Muslims (and *mu'mins*, "believers"), scriptuaries (i.e. Peoples of the Book), hypocrites, and rejectors.

The Qur'ān acknowledges the existence of what might be called "ethnicity" — that is, tribal and ethnic identities (see TRIBES AND CLANS), though it maintains that piety outweighs ethnic descent: "O people! We have created you male and female and have made you peoples *(shu'ūb)* and tribes *(qabā'il)* that you might know one another. But the noblest with God is the most god-fearing *(atqā)* among you" (Q 49:13). Yet though recognized, "tribe" seems to be a pejorative term since it is otherwise found to refer only to Satan's minions (Q 7:27). The other term for such social groups, *ḥizb* (pl. *aḥzāb*), is found more frequently, but it, too, suggests divisiveness (though there is a *ḥizb Allāh*, a "clan of God" [Q 5:56; 58:22], in opposition to the *ḥizb shayṭān*, the clan of Satan [Q 58:19]). None of these "political" categories has any ethical significance.

Muslims and non-Muslims

The Qurʾān uses the term nation *(umma)*, which seems to be the people who fall under the jurisdiction of a particular prophet's message (e.g. Q 10:47) and who share a particular "historical epoch *(ajal)*" (Q 7:34). Thus Christians and Jews form communities separate from Muslims. This distinction between nations is deliberate (Q 11:118; cf. 5:48; 10:19; 16:93; 42:8), and consequently the relations of Muslims to each other differ from their relations to other "nations," such as the Christians and the Jews (see CHRISTIANS AND CHRISTIANITY; JEWS AND JUDAISM).

This "Islamic *umma*" (a phrase not attested in the Qurʾān; rather, "a nation submissive to you," *ummatan muslimatan laka*, Q 2:128) is envisioned as a community of virtue: "Who call to the good *(al-khayr)* command the good *(al-maʿrūf)*, and forbid the reprehensible *(al-munkar)*: These are the successful" (Q 3:104). Muslims are urged to collaborate in virtue and not vice (cf. Q 5:2), and they are in law a single entity (cf. Q 5:48). Harmony among its members is enjoined: "Let not one group ridicule another group which might [in fact] be better than they *(khayran minhum)*; nor women [ridicule] other women who might be better than they; neither defame yourselves nor apply derisive nicknames; bad is the name depraved *(biʾsa l-ismu l-fusūqu)* after faith" (Q 49:11). Sūra 49 has the rules to construct the social solidarity of the Muslim *umma*. Some of the rules are rules of courtesy — lowered voices, not yelling at people who are indoors (Q 49:2-5; see Qurṭubī, *Jāmiʿ*, xvi, 303-10). Others are rules of law to deal with disorder within the community: support the correct side but make peace between the groups in conflict (Q 49:9). Suspicion (q.v.; *ẓann*), spying, and gossip (q.v.) are compared to eating the flesh of one's dead brother (Q 49:12). The faithful are given status as brethren (Q 49:10; see BROTHER AND BROTHERHOOD). In this sūra, too, is the distinction (not of much account elsewhere) between the faithful *(al-muʾminūn)* who have faith without uncertainty and strive *(jāhadū)* with their property and themselves in the path of God (*fī sabīli llāhi*, see PATH OR WAY), and are people of integrity *(al-ṣādiqūn)*, as opposed to the Bedouin (q.v.), who, instead of saying, "We have faith *(āmannā)*," ought to say "We submit *(aslamnā)*," for the faith has not entered their hearts (cf. Q 49:14-5).

The visible commitment to the Islamic summons and the willingness to sacrifice money, comfort and life to that end define the roles and responsibilities in qurʾānic social ethics. Those who have joined the Muslim community physically, and sacrificed their wealth, are protégés of each other (or the faithful in general; cf. Q 9:71; 8:72). Those who have not joined the community are not entitled to the same support unless they actually seek it "in religion" *(fī l-dīn)*; then Muslims are duty-bound to aid them — unless there be a treaty in force to the contrary (Q 8:72).

Since the Muslims are a single group, relations with non-Muslims are shaped by that fact. Yet, in the end, the claims of ethical behavior outweigh those of communal solidarity. The distinction between Muslims and non-Muslim Peoples of the Book is fundamental to qur'ānic behavioral norms, but a common ethical monotheism of the members of these traditions seems to underlie more superficial distinctions. For example, Q 3:84-5 lists in credal fashion the faith described as Muslim, in a way that is inclusive of more than just the *umma* of Muḥammad: "We have faith in God, in what has been sent down to us and what has been sent to Abraham, Ishmael (q.v.)... We do not distinguish any of them from the others. We are to him submitters. And who follows other than the submission *(al-islām)* as a religion *(dīnan)* — it will not be accepted from him; he will be, in the afterlife, a loser" (Q 3:84-5). Consequently the Qur'ān recognizes the existence of virtue and even religious virtue among Peoples of the Book: "... Of the People of the Book, there is an established people reciting the signs of God at the time of night prostrating themselves. They have faith in God and the last day and they command the good and forbid the reprehensible and hasten to good deeds *(al-khayrāt);* these are among the righteous *(al-ṣāliḥīn)*. And whatever good they do, they will not be rejected" (Q 3:113-4). In other words, the Qur'ān assumes a moral universe shared with the other Peoples of the Book.

Christians and Jews, then, are not a demonized Other, the anti-thesis of Muslims, but they belong to the same religious genus. Yet, because of their theological errors, and, more importantly, due to their animus against Islam (cf. Q 5:82 for the anti-Jewish and anti-"associator" polemic), the Muslims are enjoined not to take them as friends: "O you who are faithful! Do not take the Jews and Christians as friends. They are each other's protégés *(awliyā')*. Who has taken one of them as a protégé — he is one of them. God does not guide a wrong-doing people" (Q 5:51; the whole anti-People of the Book polemic can be found at Q 5:41-82; see also Q 3:118; 4:144; see POLEMIC AND POLEMICAL LANGUAGE). Furthermore, their theology leads them to moral error (Q 5:62-3).

Indeed, it is the claim of the scriptuaries that moral norms do not apply to other than their own moral communities that brings God's condemnation: "... And among [the People of the Book] are those who if you entrust them with a *dīnār,* do not return it to you unless you insist upon it; this is because they say 'We have no duty toward the gentiles *(al-ummiyyīn,* see ILLITERACY).' They say of God a falsehood, which they know" (Q 3:75). Only a single verse enjoins struggle against People of the Book (this, contrary to Vajda in *EI*², i, 264): "Fight those who do not believe in God nor the last day and do not forbid that which God and his messengers have forbidden and who are not religious with the religion of truth *(lā yadīnūna dīna l-ḥaqqi)* from among those given the scripture until they give a reward [for being spared] while they are ignominious" (Q 9:29; for this translation, see Bravmann, Ancient Arab background). In sum, the boundaries of religious identity are irreducible in the qur'ānic understanding and crucially shape the ethical conduct of Muslims toward one another and towards others. A norm of moral conduct that transcends communal boundaries is, however, equally a part of the qur'ānic message.

Of social groups other than the People of the Book, two groups remain. One is the *munāfiqs*. Whatever the original meaning of this term, the usage of the Qur'ān conforms to the traditional definition of the term as "hypocrites" (for a survey of the term and its interpretation, see Brockett, al-Munāfiḳūn). Though *munāfiqs* may be analyzed as a separate group in various ways, for the present purpose they may be viewed as insincere Muslims. Sincerity and pretension are discussed in this article both above and below.

The final social group that has ethical significance is the *kāfir* (ingrate, rejecter, unbeliever, pl. *kuffār*), who is equivalent to the *mushrik* (polytheist, synthetist, associationalist). Their theological errancy leads them also to commit morally aberrant acts and the qurʾānic instruction on their treatment is uncompromising — they are to be fought and subdued and compelled to acknowledge the single God and his messenger, save in the case of a compact (Q 9:4-6). So central is the animus against the non-faithful that qurʾānic citations could fill this article, but a few of the clear ones follow: "Will you not fight a folk who broke their oaths and sought to expel the messenger — they began it with you first!... Fight them! God will chastise them with your hands and then will abase them and give you victory over them..." (Q 9:13-4); "So do not obey the ingrates *(al-kāfirīn)* but struggle against them with a mighty struggle" (Q 25:52; see also Q 9:5); "So fight them until there is no disorder *(fitna)* and religion — all of it — is for God!" (Q 8:39). As with Christians and Jews, Muslim women may not be given up to *kuffār,* but while the scriptuary women may marry Muslim men, *kāfir* women may not. Thus, Muslims are a group distinct from other — Wagner suggests that Islam creates a spiritual endogamy (*La justice,* 37).

Yet even with the *kuffār,* there are places where a more generous response is enjoined: "It may be that God ordains affection between you and those of them who act with enmity toward you... God has not forbidden you — with respect to those who did not war against you in religion nor drove you from your houses — that you be good to them *(tabarrūhum)* and equitable with them..." (Q 60:7-8). It must also be said that identification with the *kuffār* is easily changed: "Yet if they cease, God sees what they do" (Q 8:39), and "Say to those who reject that if they cease, it will be forgiven them..." (Q 8:38), and even "If any of the polytheists seeks your protection, protect him that he might hear the word of God *(kalāma llāhi),* then convey him to his secure place; that is because they are a folk who do not know" (Q 9:6).

Muslims

The Islamic community contains only two categories of persons: Muslims, and the Prophet (who is "dearer to the faithful than themselves," Q 33:6) and his family (see FAMILY OF THE PROPHET; PEOPLE OF THE HOUSE). Muḥammad's wives (see WIVES OF THE PROPHET), called "mothers of the faithful" (Q 33:6) are not allowed to remarry (Q 33:53) and their punishment for immorality is double that of other women (Q 33:30). The Prophet is permitted different marriage practices (Q 33:50) and his acts are exemplary (Q 33:21). His decisions are not subject to appeal (cf. Q 33:36). Yet, he, too, is subject to rebuke for ethical failure (80:1-10; see IMPECCABILITY) and his judgment in earthly affairs is subject to error (Q 34:50). In all, his role as messenger is decisive and obedience to him is demanded as it is to God. To love the messenger is to love God (cf. Q 3:31, lit. "if you love God, follow me [i.e. Muḥammad]") and both should be obeyed (Q 3:32; 4:59; cf. 4:80). Otherwise, the Qurʾān levels the ranks of Muslims and makes them of the same status and responsibility.

This ethical corporatism holds within the Muslim community, as well. Islam creates a bond analogous to kinship, since the marriage rules make of Muslim women a group eligible for marriage only to Muslim men (Wagner, *La justice,* 37). In addition, the Qurʾān recognizes the natural bonds of family, and assigns moral duties to Muslims based on their roles within families. The reality of the claims made by familial affinity can be seen in the qurʾānic rejection of the pre-Islamic practice of permanent wife-repudiation by public declaration that the repudiated wife is as one's mother, as well its rejection of the practice of the adoption of children by public declaration of kinship. It is "natural," that is, "blood" ties that are affirmed: "God has not made for man two hearts in his breast, nor made your wives whom you repudiate (i.e. by saying that their backs are as your mothers' backs for you, *tuẓāhirūna minhunna*) your mothers, nor has he made those whom you claim [as sons], sons. That is just a saying of your mouths... Proclaim their real parentage. That will be more equitable in the sight of God..." (Q 33:4-5).

It follows that taking care of the family is especially enjoined — parents, orphans who are wards, wives, familial relations *(dhū l-qurbā)*, e.g. "They ask you what they shall spend. Say: You spend for good, then, on the two parents, and kin, and orphans and the unfortunate and wayfarers *(ibn al-sabīl)*, and what you do of good, then God knows it" (Q 2:215). Children are viewed, quite literally, as an asset (cf. Q 17:64) and, like other assets, they can be an occasion of discord: "Your wealth and your children are disturbances" (*fitna*, Q 8:28); but, unlike other forms of property or other disturbances, they may not be dispensed with, as tradition says had been the pre-Islamic custom among those who did not want to be burdened with a child. "Do not kill your children in fear of poverty; We shall provide for you. If you kill them, upon you is a great wrongdoing *(khiṭān kabīran)*" (Q 17:31; cf. 6:151).

One is obliged to treat parents kindly, and to leave part of one's wealth to parents and relatives (Q 2:180; 4:36). Oddly, the obligation to show kindness to parents is stereotyped with injunctions to refrain from false faith and worship, e.g. "Say: Come, I will recite to you that which your lord has sanctified for you: That you not associate anything with him, and show kindness *(iḥsānan)* to the two parents, do not kill your children from [fear of] poverty" (Q 6:151; cf. 2:83; 17:23). It seems clear that parents were at some psychological level associated with polytheism and the old ways (see POLYTHEISM AND ATHEISM; SOUTH ARABIA, RELIGION IN PRE-ISLAMIC); one is obliged to deal with them kindly despite their error (q.v.): "We have stipulated to humankind *(al-insān)* concerning his parents — his mother carried him, weakness on weakness, and his weaning is two years — thank me and your two parents. To me is the journeying. But if both make an effort to make you associate with me what is not known [to be true, *mā laysa laka bihi ʿilmun*], do not obey them but consort with them in the world kindly *(maʿrūfan)*..." (Q 31:14-5).

Orphans are identified with other unfortunates (Q 2:177; 89:17-8). Unlike many other ethical obligations, the concern with orphans dates from the earliest qurʾānic revelations, "you are not generous with orphans" (Q 89:17), and continues into the later sūras (e.g. Q 6:152). And, as with parents and other relations, one is enjoined to kindness towards them (Q 2:83, 220).

Women, with men, are part of the fundamental order of creation (Q 4:1). It has been understood — reasonably from a grammatical standpoint — that verses addressing the Muslims that use the grammatical masculine (*yā ayyuhā lladhīna āmanū*, and the like; see GENDER; GRAMMAR AND THE QURʾĀN) are addressed to women as well, unless there is contextual evidence to the contrary. So, women are included in all ethical stipulations addressed to Muslims. Moreover, men and women are described as each other's protector (Q 9:71) and in both the act of creation (Q 42:11) and the promise of final intercession (Q 47:19), women are explicitly included (see also Q 33:35). On the other hand, women are seen as the source or object of backbiting, gossip, and other social discord, and they are warned against such behaviors (Q 24:31; 33:59).

Relations between the sexes are grounded in the assumption that women are in a dependent relationship to men — as daughters, wards, wives, or slaves. Hence the designation of half shares in inheritance (q.v.) compared to their male counterparts (e.g. in Q 4:11, though the verse may also be read as a *requirement* that shares be given them, since these are also called *naṣīban mafrūḍan,* "mandated shares" as in Q 4:7; see also Q 4:19). Q 4:34 explicitly says: "Men are the custodians *(qawwāmūn)* of women by what *(bimā)* God favored some of them (masc.) over others (unmarked), and by what they spend of their (masc.) wealth. So virtuous women *(al-ṣāliḥāt)* are submissive *(qānitāt),* guarding for the hidden what God has guarded. Those from whom you fear uprising *(nushūzahunna),* exhort them, then banish them from the sleeping place *(fī l-maḍāji'i),* then strike them. Then if they obey you, do not seek a way against them. God is sublime, great" (cf. 2:228; for further discussion, see Wadud, *Qur'ān and woman,* 74-78).

Wives are the objects of qur'ānic ethical concern — they must be dealt with kindly (Q 65:2); must be given their marriage portion (Q 4:4); must be given what remains of their property (Q 4:20); even in divorce they must be treated kindly (Q 33:49; 65:2); they must be protected in marriage and divorce so as to be supported (Q 65:6); and the obligation of paternity must be acknowledged and enforced (Q 2:233). Divorce is discouraged (Q 4:35). Sexual relations between men and women married to each other are endorsed (Q 2:223 says that women are "tillage" for men), and while lusting after men instead of women is condemned (Q 27:55; 7:81; see HOMOSEXUALITY), the implication is that sexual desire between married men and women is legitimate.

The Qur'ān, then, recognizes that social roles determine many ethical obligations. Yet there remains also the notion that ethical obligations of fairness and justice transcend the boundaries of kinship or social group: "O you who are faithful! Be upright in justice *(qisṭ),* witnesses to God though it be against yourselves or the two parents or kin if he is rich or poor... (Q 4:135; cf. 31:15).

Given this corporatism in qur'ānic ethical thought, it is not surprising that in later times some believed Muslims were assured salvation by being Muslim. This was, however, a mistake — at least from the Qur'ān's perspective (see Madelung, Murdji'a). While roles and responsibilities are determined by membership in one group or another, ethical responsibility lies solely with individuals. It is individuals who are enjoined to act, and it is individuals who are promised requital according to how they have acted. In no place does the Qur'ān say Muslims will be in paradise, but those who are addressed by the Qur'ān's words — surely including Muslims — are promised hell for their ethical transgressions.

Conclusion

Qur'ānic ethics fit neatly no single Western philosophical category; it is likely this is true for any lived — as opposed to academic — system. Yet the qur'ānic approach to what is called ethics can be clarified by judicious reference to Western philosophical ethics. For example, it has seemed obvious to scholars that the Qur'ān and the Islamic law derived from it represent a classic, almost a maximal, case of deontological ethics — that is, an ethical system in which behaviors said to be ordained are deemed right because of their nature, and one acts virtuously because that is what one ought to do, apart from outcomes (Gk. *deon* = duty). In addition, qur'ānic ethics might seem — especially in light of later developments in Islamic theology — clearly to be a classic case of what ethicists call "divine command theory" (Frankena, *Ethics*, 28-9). This might take the form of *theological voluntarism* in which something is good solely because God commanded it (see G. Hourani, *Reason and tradition*, 17); or it might be seen as *naturalism* in which God commands the good because its nature is "good" (as in Ralph Cudsworth, in Raphael, *British moralists*, i, 106-12).

There is certainly evidence to support these initial impressions: for many qur᾽ānic imperatives, there is no attempt to persuade, no explication of useful social consequences, no appeal to values already agreed upon. Yet, as pointed out above, there are, to the contrary, many instances where the imperative is presented with an appeal to follow reason or reflection. "Here are the signs, here is the evidence," the Qur᾽ān proclaims; "now, acknowledge the claim that God has on you to act morally!" There is also a clear prudential argument for acting in accord with qur᾽ānic imperative, namely, the threat of punishment for transgression and the promise of eternal felicity for obedience to the command to act virtuously (though there is no argument that the good is defined by pleasant or desirable circumstances). Every virtuous act is promised a reward (Q 99:7) and, so, every good deed has a telos apart from itself. Yet there is nothing to suggest causation — that the good is good because it leads to reward. Rather, the good coincides with reward but the affect of the text — the wrath, anger (q.v.), and repugnance at vice — suggests that the good and bad are so, independently of the strategic considerations of a utilitarian Muslim.

It is helpful, too, to ask, what is the qur᾽ānic ethical epistemology? Here again, the answer is complex. Later Ashʿarī and Ḥanbalī theoreticians asserted that the only means to moral knowledge was revelational declaration, or methodologically sound inference from such declarations. Yet there is no doubt that the Qur᾽ān appeals to many sources of knowledge (see KNOWLEDGE AND LEARNING), and indeed that the qur᾽ānic stipulations are incomprehensible without appeal to other sources of knowledge.

First, it is undoubtedly the case that the Qur᾽ān assumes some moral facts to be known by human beings *qua* human beings. Second, there is some evidence that human beings can perceive moral truth when confronted with a particular situation. This latter feature conforms to what has been called "moral sense theory," that is, the belief that some faculty analogous to sense or taste provides moral information when presented with a circumstance which calls for moral action. Like the English moralist Hutcheson, the Qur᾽ān seems to suggest that humans are disposed to feel approval or condemnation when they consider persons of good character, and their actions. Like Hutcheson (Raphael, *British moralists*, i, 302), also, the Qur᾽ān believes that humans innately feel gratitude, and a sense of obligation that ensues from that perception. How else can the near total absence of definitions for ethical terms be construed? What is the meaning of "well" in "treat your parents well *(iḥsānan)*," or "kindly" in "give your wife her marriage-portion kindly" (*bi-l-maʿrūf*, literally, "according to the known") — what do these terms mean, exactly?

There may be many answers, but since the Qur᾽ān did not spell out the details, it obviously expected its audience to draw upon their own knowledge, sense of fairness, justice, and gratitude to fill in these many undefined terms. As with all ethics, however (Frankena, *Ethics*, 7), qur᾽ānic morality is not mere convention — it is critical of convention, and it also demands a self-consciousness and self-examination that is the very stuff of ethical deliberation. So, the Qurʾān is not purely a kind of moral sense theory, nor is it averse to moral reasoning and deliberation.

In our consideration of the nature of qurʾānic moral stipulation, we saw that the Qurʾān has both rules (which are sometimes deontic, sometimes teleological), but also principles and admonitions. These weighted rules, and exhortations to virtuous conduct, are what ethicists call *aretaic* judgments. These take us beyond basic principles of ethical behavior and moral obligation and into more complex statements of value, and appreciation, and beyond obedience and conformity to estimation and value judgments (Frankena, *Ethics*, 61). Here we can place the concerns of social solidarity and of fellow-feeling that are also so much a part of qurʾānic moral language. The Qurʾān urges one to act with *iḥsān*, with *maʿrūf*, to choose *khayr* and *ṭayyib*, and suggests that hearts (by which the Qurʾān refers both to affect and consciousness; see HEART) are drawn to the good and recoil from the bad.

The most important ethical feature of the Qurʾān is its recasting of moral conduct. As Brown has pointed out (*Apocalypse of Islam*, 80-1), the Qurʾān calls its audience to re-view the world, themselves, and their acts *sub specie aeternitatis*, to take a view that transcends the day-to-day perspective of petty utilitarianism and self-interest. Killing an infant daughter may make good economic sense in the quotidian, but, the Qurʾān says, viewed from a larger moral perspective, it is an abomination. To sacrifice property and lives for the qurʾānic kerygma may not be a good investment in worldly terms, but in meta-worldly terms it is a "can't lose" proposition.

Yet, to repeat, this recasting of moral perspective rested upon a foundation of moral knowledge shared by the first/seventh century Ḥijāzī Arabs who were its first audience. As Bravmann has shown with *"al-jizya ʿan yadin"* and in many more cases perhaps than we can recover, the Qurʾān appeals to, while redefining, contemporary moral norms. As Islam and the Qurʾān moved from this culturally coherent environment, through time and space, the shared foundation was lost and had gradually to be replaced — with local norms, with the codified Sunna (q.v.), and through reasoned inference of what was understood to be implicit in qurʾānic moral discourse. In some cases, this demonstrably took Islamic ethical reasoning in a direction different from its original orientation. Nonetheless, the Qurʾān has remained primary in theory, and crucial in moral practice for Muslims over the 1400 years of Islamic history.

A. Kevin Reinhart

Bibliography

Primary: Abū l-Baqāʾ al-Kaffawī, Ayyūb b. Mūsā, *al-Kulliyyāt. Muʿjam fī l-muṣṭalaḥāt wa-l-furūq al-lughawiyya*, ed. ʿAdnān Darwīsh and Muḥammad al-Miṣrī, 5 vols., Damascus 1974; al-Mahdī li-Dīn Allāh b. Aḥmad b. Yahyā b. al-Murtaḍā, *Kitāb al-Baḥr al-zakhkhār. al-Jāmiʿ li-madhāhib ʿulamāʾ al-amṣār*, ed. ʿAlī b. ʿAbd al-Karīm Sharfaddīn, 6 vols., Beirut 1394/1975; Nīsābūrī, *Tafsīr*, ed. Ibrāhīm ʿAṭwa ʿAwaḍ, 24 vols., Cairo 1962-4. Qurṭubī, *Jāmiʿ*, ed. Muḥammad Ibrāhīm al-Ḥifnāwī, 22 vols., Cairo 1414/1994. Ṭabarī, *Tafsīr*, 30 vols., Cairo 1388/1968.

Secondary: M. Bravmann, The ancient Arab background of the qurʾānic concept *al-ğizyatu ʿan yadin*, in id., *The spiritual background of early Islam. Studies in ancient Arab concepts*, Leiden 1972, 199-212 (originally published in *Arabica* 13 (1966), 307-14; 14 (1967), 90-1; 326-7; A. Brockett, al-Munfiḳūn, in *EI²*, vii, 561-2; D. Brown, Islamic ethics in comparative perspective, in *MW* Special issue: J. Brockopp (ed.), *Islamic ethics of killing and saving life* (1999), 181-92; N. Brown, The apocalypse of Islam, in id., *Apocalypse and/or metamorphosis*, Berkeley 1991, 69-94; M. Cook, *Commanding right and forbidding wrong in Islamic thought*, Cambridge 2000; D. Donaldson, *Studies in Muslim ethics*, London 1963; M. Draz, *Étude comparée de la morale théorique du Koran suivie d'une classification de versets choisis formant le code complet de la morale pratique,* Paris 1951; R. Dworkin, Is law a system of rules?, in id. (ed.), *The philosophy of law,* Oxford 1977, 38-65; *The encyclopedia of philosophy,* ed. P. Edwards, 8 vols. in 4, New York 1967; J. Esposito (ed.), *The Oxford encyclopedia of the modern Islamic world,* 4 vols., New York 1995; M. Fakhry, *Ethical theories in Islam,* Leiden 1991; W. Frankena, *Ethics,* Englewood Cliffs, NJ 1967, 1973² (rev. ed.); Goldziher, *MS,* Eng. tr. C.R. Barber and S.M. Stern; E. Gräf, Zur Klassifizierung der menschliche Handlungen nach Ṭūsī dem Šaiḫ al-Ṭāʾifa (gest. 460), und seinen Lehrern, in W. Voigt (ed.), *XIX Deutscher Orientalistentag* 1975 *in Freiburg im Breisgau,* Weisbaden 1977, 388-422; M. Hodgson, *The venture of Islam. Conscience and history in a world civilization,* 3 vols., Chicago 1974; G. Hourani, Ethical presuppositions of the Qurʾan, in id., *Reason and tradition in Islamic ethics,* Cambridge 1985, 23-48 (originally published as Ethical presuppositions of the Qurʾān, in *MW* 70 (1980), 1-28); id., 'Injuring oneself' in the Qurʾān, in the light of Aristotle, in id., *Reason and tradition in Islamic ethics,* Cambridge 1985, 49-56 (originally published as *Ẓulm an-nafs* in the Qurʾān, in the light of Aristotle, in G. Anawati and L. Gardet, *Recherches d'islamologie. Recuil d'articles offert à Georges C. Anawati et Louis Gardet par leurs collègues et amis,* Louvain 1978, 139-48); id., *Islamic rationalism. The ethics of ʿAbdaljabbār,* Oxford 1971; id., *Reason and tradition in Islamic ethics,* Cambridge 1985; M. Husain, The meaning of ẓulm in the Qurʾān, tr. with comments by Kenneth Cragg, in *Muslim world* 49 (1959), 196-212; Izutsu, *Concepts;* W. Madelung, Murdjia, in *EI²,* vii, 605-7; H. Motzki, Wal-muḥṣanātu mina n-nisāʾi illā mā malakat aimānukum (Koran 4:24) und die koranische Sexualethik, in *Der Islam* 63 (1986), 192-218; A. Nanji, Islamic ethics, in P. Singer (ed.), *A companion to ethics,* Oxford 1991, 106-18; A.-J. Paccard, *Étude sur l'Islam primitif. La morale de l'Islam d'après le Coran,* Thésis, Faculté libre de theologie protestante, Paris 1913; D. Rahbar, *God of justice. A study in the ethical doctrine of the Qurʾān,* Leiden 1960; F. Rahman, Law and ethics in Islam. Paper presented at the *Ethics in Islam. Ninth Giorgio Levi Della Vida Conference* 1983; D. Raphael (ed.), *British moralists* 1650-1800, Indianapolis 1991; A. Reinhart, *Before revelation. The boundaries of Muslim moral thought,* Albany 1995, chapter 6; J. Renard, Muslim ethics. Sources, interpretations and challenges, in *MW* 69 (1979), 163-77; S. al-Shamma, *The ethical system underlying the Qurʾān. A study of certain negative and positive notions,* Tübingen 1959; J.-C. Vadet, *Les idées morales dans l'islam,* Paris 1995; A. Wadud, *Qurʾān and woman. Rereading the sacred text from a woman's perspective,* New York 1992, 1999² (rev. ed.); G. Wagner, *La justice dans l'Ancien Testament et le Coran aux niveaux des marriages et des échanges de biens,* Neuchâtel 1977.

Ethiopia

Derived from the Greek term, *Aithiopes,* designating mythical or actual peoples defined as having dark skin and living south of Egypt (q.v.), and applied to roughly the area of ancient Axum or Abyssinia (q.v.) in northeast Africa, directly across the Red Sea from Arabia. As the opposition to Muḥammad (q.v.) increased, a group of his followers left Mecca (q.v.; see EMIGRATION), seeking the protection of the Christian king (see CHRISTIANS AND CHRISTIANITY) of the region. See GEOGRAPHY.

Reuven Firestone

Eulogy see LAUDATION

Eve see ADAM AND EVE

Evening

The latter part and close of the day, evening *(ʿishā, ʿashīy)* appears in the Qurʾān in both specific and semantically ambiguous ways. Its primary importance is related to worship (q.v.) since evening is specified as one of the obligatory prayer times (see DAY, TIMES OF; PRAYER). The qurʾānic text, however, shows a great deal of variance regarding the naming and timing of the evening prayer: It is mentioned as dusk (*ghasaq,* Q 17:78), evening twilight (*shafaq,* Q 84:16), times during the night (q.v., *zulafan mina l-layli,* Q 11:114) and so forth. In fact, the phrase canonized in Islamic law as evening prayer *(ṣalāt al-ʿishāʾ)* is mentioned only once in the Qurʾān (Q 24:58).

The compiler of prophetic traditions, al-Bukhārī (d. 256/870), cites a number of reports in which the evening worship is commonly referred to as darkness (q.v.; *ʿatma*). It also appears that some people did not make nominal distinctions between the evening and sunset prayers: One ḥadīth says that Muḥammad urged people to ignore the Bedouin habit of calling the prayer at sunset *(maghrib)* evening prayer (*ʿishāʾ*, Bukhārī, *Ṣaḥīḥ*, i, 10, no. 538; see ḤADĪTH AND THE QURʾĀN). A similar alteration exists in the Turkish language in which the sunset prayer *(maghrib)* is called evening prayer *(akşam namazı)* and the evening prayer *(ʿishāʾ)*, bed-time prayer *(yatsı namazı)*. What further reinforces this relative semantic imprecision is that Muḥammad himself was not very rigorous regarding its timing; on the contrary, many Companions (see COMPANIONS OF THE PROPHET) report that he delayed the evening prayer on many occasions and performed it early on many others. Any hour after sunset seems to have been acceptable (ibid., no. 536).

Equally ambiguous is the frequent adverbial usage of evening in conjunction with morning (q.v.) in the Qurʾān. That the lord (q.v.) should be praised morning and evening is mentioned in many places in the Qurʾān (*bi-l-ghadāti wa-l-ʿashī*, e.g. Q 6:52; 18:28; *bukratan wa-aṣīlan*, e.g. 76:25). In such instances the phrase functions as a powerful stylistic and didactic device (see RHETORIC OF THE QURʾĀN) and is informed by diurnal and nocturnal frames of reference (see DAY AND NIGHT). Nevertheless, even here the semantic ambiguity has elicited different interpretations. The phrase varies as *bukratan wa-ʿashiyyan* (Q 19:11, 62), *ghuduwwan wa-ʿashiyyan* (Q 40:46), *bukratan wa-aṣīlan* (Q 25:5; 33:42) and *bi-l-ghuduwwi wa-l-āṣāl* (Q 7:205; 13:15; 24:36). Although *aṣīl* is hardly synonymous with *ʿishāʾ*, most classical exegetes treat it as such (e.g. Ṭabarī, *Tafsīr;* Ṭūsī, *Tibyān; Jalālayn;* see EXEGESIS OF THE QURʾĀN: CLASSICAL AND MEDIEVAL). The more contemporary Usmānī (d. 1949; *Tafseer-e Usmānī*) is cautious in his interpretation, arguing that *aṣīl* is the space between mid-day and the next morning that includes all four prayers after the morning prayer. Ṭabāṭabāʾī (d. 1982; *Mīzān*) digresses even further in interpreting *aṣīl* as the afternoon (q.v.) prayer *(ʿaṣr)* only (see EXEGESIS OF THE QURʾĀN: EARLY MODERN AND CONTEMPORARY).

Most exegetes, however, seem particularly concerned not to overlook the metaphoric value of the conjunction of evening and morning (see METAPHOR) in the context of paradise (q.v.; Q 13:15; 19:62) or hell (q.v.; Q 40:46). Both places, they argue, lack the usual sunrise or sunset and thus cannot experience evening. In paradise, for example, the perpetual light (q.v.) is occasionally rearranged so as to give the impression of the passage of time. It is in that sense that the qurʾānic evening has only a linguistic and not an empirical reality.

Amila Buturovic

Bibliography
Primary: Abū Ḥayyān, *Baḥr;* Bukhārī, *Ṣaḥīḥ; Jalālayn;* Ṭabarī, *Tafsīr;* Tabarsī, *Majmaʿ;* Ṭabāṭabāʾī, *Mīzān;* Ṭūsī, *Tibyān;* Shabbīr A. Usmānī, *The noble Qurʾān. Tafseer-e-Usmānī*, trans. M.A. Ahmed, Lahore 1991.
Secondary: L.E. Goodman, Time in Islam, in *Asian philosophy 2* (1992), 3-19; D.A. King, Mīḳāt, in *EI*², vii, 26-32; R.B. Serjeant et al., Calendars, the time of day and mathematical astronomy, in id. and R. Lewcock (eds.), *Ṣanʿāʾ. An Arabian Islamic city*, London 1983, 32-5.

Everyday Life, Qurʾān In

Introduction

The topic of religion in everyday life has become a subject of increasing interest for historians and social scientists alike. The role of scripture, however, in everyday life has hardly been studied. "Everyday life" is not, it should be said, as obviously or immediately discernible as one might suppose, but entails a variety of complex activities of individuals as well as of communities within a specific cultural domain. The definition of 'everyday life' adopted here is "the routine non-ritual activities of ordinary people… who do not occupy positions of importance or celebrity in their society" (Beckford, Socialization, 140). The methodological problem of classifying or documenting these phenomena must face the difficulty that study of the abundant historical and religious sources provides little information about the Muslim populace at large or their general everyday life. Anthropological studies tend to be more interested in the form of those religious activities connected to social and communal structures, such as rituals, devotional practices, saints' festivals, sermons, ceremonies and the like, than in their contents. Very rarely do these studies pay attention to the role or function of the Qurʾān in such religious activities.

Mention must be made, however, of three important contributions of the latter half of the twentieth century that do examine the role that the Qurʾān plays in various aspects of daily life, and which one may consult for detailed analyses of the phenomenon. The first is the anthropological study of Sayyid ʿUways, "The shout of the silent" *(Hutāf al-ṣāmiṭīn),* which treats the phrases and expressions written on cars and trucks in Egypt. The author counted 55 qurʾānic quotations, which amounts to 27.5% of the religious expressions and 8.9% of all the written expression collected (ibid., 82, 135-42). The second is William Graham's *Beyond the written word.* It was during the author's first visit to Egypt, which coincided with the month of Ramaḍān (q.v.), that he sought to comprehend the significance of the recited Qurʾān (see RECITATION OF THE QURʾĀN), eventually devoting an entire chapter to 'The Recited Qurʾān in Everyday Piety and Practice" (ibid., chapter eight) where brief accounts are given of the role of Qurʾān recitation in worship (q.v.), Muslim education, communal life (see COMMUNITY AND SOCIETY IN THE QURʾĀN), and family and personal life (pp. 102-9). The third study worth mentioning is Padwick's *Muslim devotions,* where a great deal of attention is given to the Qurʾān quotations to be found in texts of devotion.

As studying the role of the Qurʾān in everyday life is a "work in progress," certain aspects have, at the time of the writing of this article, been more closely documented than others. For example, regional differences, as well as those that are observable between rural and urban contexts, have to be examined more fully. This article is correspondingly limited to the available data, supplemented by the personal observations of the author.

Insofar as the Qurʾān sought, from its inception, to re-shape and re-form the everyday life of the prophet Muḥammad and his followers, it is necessary to consider aspects of everyday life that the Qurʾān regulates on the basis of the Qurʾān itself. It is fair to say that, after the Prophet's death, the role of the Qurʾān in everyday life gradually increased. With the expansion of Islam (q.v.) into regions with different historical, religious and cultural traditions, the position occupied by the Qurʾān developed beyond that of its function in the early Muslim community at Medina (q.v.). The part that the Qurʾān played in shaping the lives of the early Muslims will thus be treated as a necessary background to understanding its similar function in more recent times.

Shaping everyday life

The first command issued to the Prophet in the process of the revelation of the Qurʾān was to "recite, *(iqraʾ)* in the name of your lord who created, created man from a clot" (Q 96:1-2; see BLOOD AND BLOOD

CLOT). As preparation for the heavy mission with which he was to be charged, he was subsequently commanded to keep awake during part of the night in prayer (q.v.), reciting the Qurʾān and repeating the name of his lord (q.v.; cf. Q 73:2-8). Recitation of the Qurʾān thus became the very heart of all kinds of prayers — whether invocation of God's blessing *(duʿāʾ)* or the obligatory ritual *(ṣalāt)*. For example, Q 17:78 speaks of the dawn prayer as (recitation of the) Qurʾān at daybreak (*qurʾān al-fajr,* Padwick, *Muslim devotion,* 108). The repetition of God's name *(dhikr)* was also identified with the recitation of the Qurʾān; it is repeatedly mentioned that the Qurʾān is for reminding (*dhikr,* e.g. Q 54:17, 22). The Qurʾān can itself be construed as a reminder, and the word *dhikr* thus became, like the word for book (q.v.; *kitāb*), one of the names of the Qurʾān (q.v.). Muslims are supposed to remember and mention the name of God (Allāh) at every moment, regardless of whether they are standing, sitting or lying down (Q 3:191). Only the unbelievers (see BELIEF AND UNBELIEF) and the hypocrites (see HYPOCRITES AND HYPOCRISY) are those who abstain from doing so (Q 4:142; 37:13).

Like *dhikr* and prayer, glorification of God (q.v.; *tasbīḥ*) is repeatedly demanded of the Prophet as well as of all believers. It is through *tasbīḥ* that the believers join the whole universe in a cosmological prayer, because everything and every being on earth (q.v.) and in heaven (q.v.), glorifies God (Q 13:13; 17:44; 24:41 etc.). This kind of cosmological prayer is to be performed day and night, early and late, before sunrise and before sunset (Q 3:41; 20:130; 33:42 etc.; see DAY TIMES OF; EVENING). Such forms of sacred utterance represent different dimensions of the essential relationship between the creator and his creatures, the continuous acts of praise (q.v.; *ḥamd*) through worship *(ʿibāda)*. Jinn (q.v.) and humans are created only to worship God (Q 51:56). Strongly related to *dhikr, tasbīḥ* and *ḥamd* is the magnification of God (*takbīr,* i.e. saying "God is the greater [or the greatest]," *Allāhu akbar*). While the Qurʾān speaks of God as "the great, the transcendant" (*al-kabīru l-mutaʿālī,* Q 13:9) and "the exalted, the great" (*al-ʿaliyyu al-kabīr,* Q 22:62; 31:30; 34:23; 40:12; cf. 4:34; see GOD AND HIS ATTRIBUTES), Muslims are ordered to exalt God over all other deities (see POLYTHEISM AND ATHEISM). The order was first directed to the Prophet as part of his prophetic mission to "get up and warn" (*qum fa-andhir,* i.e. his people; Q 74:2; see WARNER) and to "exalt his lord" (*wa-rabbaka fa-kabbir,* Q 74:3). The command to utter the *takbīr* is also directed to Muslims when fasting (q.v.; Q 2:185) and also while on pilgrimage (q.v.; Q 22:37).

There are five daily ritual prayers that are obligatory for a Muslim *(ṣalāt):* the dawn prayer of two units of prostration (*rakʿa;* see BOWING AND PROSTRATION); the noon prayer of four; the afternoon prayer also of four; the sunset prayer of three; and the evening prayer of four. A Muslim recites the first chapter of the Qurʾān, Sūrat al-Fātiḥā (see FĀTIḤA), and other qurʾānic verses at every unit of prayer, amounting to 17 daily recitations from the Qurʾān. This number would be much higher if the believer were to perform the non-obligatory prayers called *nawāfil.* As every *rakʿa* includes *takbīr, dhikr, ḥamd, tasbīḥ* and *duʿāʾ,* in addition to Qurʾān recitation, *ṣalāt* represents in itself a channel of communication between humans and God through the recitation of the Qurʾān. The importance of the five daily *ṣalāt* is thus related to this function. In this respect, Sūrat al-Fātiḥa, which is to be recited at every *rakʿa,* occupies a special position in the liturgical use of the Qurʾān. According to a well-known ḥadīth, God says, "I divided the prayer, i.e. al-Fātiḥa, in two [parts] between me and my servant" *(qasamtu l-ṣalāta baynī wa-bayna ʿabdī nisfayni):* When he says, "Praise be to God, the lord of the worlds" *(al-ḥamdu lillāhi rabbi l-ʿālamīna),* I say, "My servant has praised me" *(ḥamadanī ʿabdī);* When he says, "The merciful, the compassionate" *(al-raḥmāni l-raḥīm),* I say, "My servant has exalted me" *(athnā ʿalayya ʿabdī);* When he says, "Sovereign of the day of judgment" (*māliki yawmi l-dīni,* see LAST JUDGMENT), I say, "My servant has glorified me" *(majjadanī ʿabdī);* When he says, "It is you that we worship and you from whom we seek help" *(iyyāka naʿbudu wa-iyyāka nastaʿīnu),* I say, "This verse is between me and my servant, and all that my servant requests is his" *(fa-hādhihi l-āyatu baynī wa-bayna ʿabdī wa-li-ʿabdī mā saʾala);* When he says, "Guide us to the straight path, the path of those whom you have blessed, not the path of those who have provoked your anger upon them, nor the lost" *(ihdinā l-ṣirāṭa l-mustaqīma, ṣirāṭa lladhīna anʿamta ʿalayhim ghayri l-maghḍūbi ʿalayhim wa-lā l-ḍāllīna),* I say, "This is for my servant and all that my servant requests is his" *(hādhā li-ʿabdī wa-li-ʿabdī mā saʾala).*

In addition to its importance as the basic channel of communication between God and humans, the Fātiḥa contains in its seven short verses, according to al-Ghazālī (d. 505/1111), all the topics covered in detail throughout the entire Qurʾān: information about God's essence *(dhāt),* his attributes *(ṣifāt)* and his actions *(afʿāl),* which together constitute the doctrine of faith (q.v.); the after-life (*al-maʿād,* see ESCHATOLOGY), reward and punishment (q.v.; *al-thawāb wa-l-ʿiqāb*), and allusion to the qurʾānic narratives (q.v.), as well as to certain legal injunctions (*aḥkām,* Ghazālī, *Jawāhir,* 39-42; see LAW AND THE QURʾĀN). This interpretation, as elaborated by al-Ghazālī justifies the other name given to the sūra, "the essence (lit. mother) of the scripture (lit. book)" *(umm al-kitāb).* If prayer occupies the highest position in the religion, it is through recitation of Sūrat al-Fātiḥa *(umm al-kitāb)* that the Qurʾān becomes the heart of prayer. Seen in this light, the mandatory prayer cannot be reduced to a mere ritual devoid of personal meaning. Further, it can be fit to the pattern of a person's life since it can be performed anywhere, at any time, in privacy or with others, although it is highly recommended as sunna (q.v.), i.e. a prophetic precedent, to perform it in congregation *(jamāʿa)* at the mosque.

Formal ritualism in Islam should be understood in terms of congregational prayers, such as the Friday noon prayer *(ṣalāt al-jumuʿa/al-jumʿa)* and the prayer on the two feast days, (*ṣalāt al-ʿīdayn;* see FESTIVALS AND COMMEMORATIVE DAYS) of which a sermon *(khuṭba),* replete with qurʾānic rhetoric (cf. Gaffney, *Prophet's pulpit,* append.), is an essential part. The prayers of the two feast days are important, though non-obligatory, sunna. The first is to be performed after the end of the fasting month of Ramaḍān (q.v.), i.e. *ṣalāt ʿīd al-fiṭr,* while the second is to be performed on the final day of the annual pilgrimage rite at Mecca on the tenth of the month of Dhū l-Ḥijja, i.e. *ṣalāt ʿīd al-aḍḥā.* Prayer, the most important tenet of Islam after the confession of faith (*shahāda,* see WITNESS TO FAITH), is at the heart of all religious action (*ʿibādāt*) and thus is termed the essence of religion *(mukhkh al-ʿibāda),* as well as the pillar of religion (*ʿimād al-dīn*). Neglecting it is tantamount to neglecting Islam altogether (*man tarakahā fa-ka-annamā taraka l-dīn,* Ibn Māja, *K. Iqāmāt al-ṣalāt wa-sunnat fīhā,* nos. 1068, 1069, 1070).

Fasting *(ṣiyām)* was another way the Qurʾān regulated the life of the Prophet and the early Muslim community, both spiritually and physically. It is mentioned in the Qurʾān that the establishment of fasting was in accord with what had been prescribed (*kutiba,* lit. "written") for "those who had come before you" (cf. Q 2:183), suggesting that it is an essential part of any revealed religion and that the Muslim community stands in continuity with the history of such religions, a continuity that partially compensates for the inevitable dissociation of early Muslims from their immediate, pagan society. Obligatory fasting lasts one month, "the month of Ramaḍān in which the Qurʾān [understood to mean the first verses of the Qurʾān] was revealed" (Q 2:185). Associated with the day-long fast is a night-prayer, *(ṣalāt al-qiyām),* recommended as sunna to be performed collectively every night. During the last ten days of the month, it is a recommended practice to stay at the mosque day and night, completely committed to devotion *(iʿtikāf).* One night out of these last ten, the Night of Power (q.v.; *laylat al-qadr*), is considered the most important, because it was the night that witnessed the first episode in the revelation of the Qurʾān. It is "better than one thousand months" (Q 97:3), i.e. devotion on that specific night is evaluated, and will be rewarded, as equal to the devotion of one thousand months. "The angels (see ANGEL) and the holy spirit (q.v.) descend in it [i.e. the Night of Power] on every errand by the permission of their lord. Peace (q.v.) it is until the break of dawn" (Q 97:4-5). Although there is no consensus on the exact date of the Night of Power, Muslims generally believe it to be the twenty-seventh night of Ramaḍān. Scholars (q.v.; *ʿulamāʾ*) of the Qurʾān explain that the reason that the exact night is not specified is to encourage Muslims to undertake devotion during the entire time it is expected, i.e. the last ten nights of the month.

The practices associated with Ramaḍān are well suited to illustrate the extent to which the Qurʾān infuses the texture of everyday life for Muslims (for Ramaḍān and everyday life, see Jomier, *L'islam vécu en Égypte,* 33-74). It is Ramaḍān in particular, that has drawn attention to the importance of the oral dimension of the Qurʾān, so much so that Ramaḍān has been perceived as "the month of months in the Muslim calendar (q.v.)." The historian of religion W. Graham has written: "I was fortunate to be in Cairo during the month of Ramaḍān, which fell that year in December. It was there, walking the streets of the old city amidst the animated bustle of the nocturnal crowds of men, women and children, that I first heard at length the compelling chanting of the professional Qurʾān reciters. It seemed that wherever I wandered in the old city, from Bāb Zuwaylah to Bāb al-Futūḥ, the drawn-out, nuanced cadences of the sacred recitations gave the festive nights a magical air as the reciters' penetrating voices sounded over radios in small, open shops, or wafted into the street from the doorways of mosques and from under the canvas marquees set up specially for this month of months in the Muslim calendar. If it was only an impressionistic introduction to the living tradition of Qurʾān recitation, it was also an unforgettable one" (Graham, p. x.; see also Jomier, op. cit., 60-73).

After the *shahāda,* prayer, almsgiving (q.v.) and fasting, the fifth and final pillar of Islam is the pilgrimage *(ḥajj)* to the holy sanctuary at Mecca (q.v.), the Kaʿba (q.v.; cf. Q 2:197; 3:96-7; 9:3). A pre-Islamic ritual practice (see PRE-ISLAMIC ARABIA AND THE QURʾĀN), it was given Islamic orientation by the qurʾānic ascription of its origins to Abraham's (q.v.) cry to God (Q 2:125-7; cf. 22:26). Although it is obligatory to undertake it only once during one's life, and only for those who can afford it, Muslims are often eager to perform the pilgrimage more than once. With the technological advancements in transportation, the number of contemporary Muslims who want to go on pilgrimage has steadily increased to the extent that the Saudi authorities have been forced to set an annual quota for every Muslim country. To avoid huge crowds during the month of the pilgrimage itself, Muslims have increasingly opted for the 'lesser pilgrimage' (*ʿumra,* Q 2:196; cf. 2:158), which has traditionally been understood as a supererogatory act of personal devotion. In an article in the Egyptian newspaper *al-Ahrām,* an Islamist writer recently criticized the thousands of Egyptian Muslims heading to Mecca during the month of Ramaḍān to perform *ʿumra.* The aim of such criticism is to draw the attention of Muslims to the priority given in Islam to communal and social duties over the mentality of devotion for personal salvation. Yet the angry reaction to such criticism reflects the importance of both *ḥajj* and *ʿumra* for Muslims at large (see articles by Fahmī Huwaydī, in the January 12, 19 and 26, 1999 issues of *al-Ahrām*).

The role of the Qurʾān in both the *ḥajj* and the *ʿumra* is most clearly observed during the seven-fold circumambulation of the Kaʿba (the *ṭawāf*). The phrases that constitute the supplication *(duʿāʾ al-talbiya)* that is chanted in the course of this ritual, although not taken verbatim from particular sūras, are all taken from the language of the Qurʾān. The words of this supplication are as follows: I am here, come O God, I am here *(labbayka Allāhumma labbayka);* indeed all praise and grace and sovereignty are yours *(inna l-ḥamda wa-l-niʿmata wa-l-mulka laka);* You have no partner, I am here, I am here, come O God, I am here *(la sharīka laka, labbayka, labbayka Allāhumma labbayka).* Another formulaic derived from the Qurʾān, the *takbīr,* is as important a component of the ritualism of the *ḥajj* as the supplication (for more on the *ḥajj,* see Jomier, *L'islam vécu en Égypte,* 113-84).

It was not only through such rites as mentioned above that the Qurʾān regulated the early Muslims' everyday life. The piecemeal *(munajjam)* manner of the Qurʾān's revelation itself corresponded to the needs and demands of the community (see OCCASIONS OF REVELATION; REVELATION AND INSPIRATION). According to the exegetical tradition, demands made by early Muslims are reflected in the Qurʾān in the frequent occurrence of the phrase, "They ask you (*yasʾalūnaka,* i.e. Muḥammad)," attested 15 times. The questions to which the Qurʾān responds cover many different areas of religious and social interest. What is significant for our subject are those questions related to everyday life: expenditures for charity (*al-infāq,* cf. Q 2:215, 219), fighting during the prohibited month (Q 2:217); wine (see INTOXICANTS) and gambling (q.v.; al-khamr wa-l-maysir, Q 2:219), care of orphans (q.v.; *al-yatāmā,* Q 2:220), menstruation (q.v.; *al-maḥīḍ,* Q 2:222), permitted food (Q 5:4; see FOOD AND DRINK; LAWFUL AND UNLAWFUL) and the spoils of war (*al-anfāl,* Q 8:1; see BOOTY). In the qurʾānic response to such matters, it was important to dissociate Muslims from the traditions and practices related to pre-Islamic idol worship (see IDOLATRY AND IDOLATERS). For example, the mention of an idol's name while slaughtering an animal, whether for sacrifice (q.v.) or merely for consumption, was replaced with mention of the name of God (Q 6:119-21; see CONSECRATION OF ANIMALS).

Qurʾānic regulation of the everyday life of the individual as well as of the community developed with subsequent generations. The Qurʾān came to be understood as the repository of all kinds of knowledge alongside the prophetic tradition, sunna, for both the individual and the community. It was al-Shāfiʿī (d. 204/820) who definitively expressed the view that the Qurʾān entails everything and contains, explicitly or implicitly, solutions to all problems of human life, present or future (*Risāla,* 20 and *al-Umm,* 271). Although his central concern was jurisprudence, Muslim theologians and philosophers (in their rational inquiry for the bases of sound knowledge) also upheld the supreme position of the Qurʾān (see PHILOSOPHY OF THE QURʾĀN; THEOLOGY AND THE QURʾĀN). Their point of view is summed up in the principle that complete consistency exists between sound rationality and authentic revelation *(muwāfaqat ṣarīḥ al-maʿqūl li-ṣaḥīḥ al-manqūl).* The predominant view of Muslims worldwide, both past and present, is epitomized in the following statement: "As a word from God, the Koran is the foundation of the Muslim's life. It provides for him [sic.] the way to fulfilment in the world beyond and to happiness in the present one. There is for him no situation imaginable for which it does not afford guidance, no problem for which it does not have a solution. It is the ultimate source of all truth (q.v.), the final vindication of all right, the primary criterion (q.v.) of all values, and the original basis of all authority (q.v.). Both public and private affairs, religious and worldly, fall under its jurisdiction" (Labib, *Recited Koran,* 11). Beyond being the source of all sorts of knowledge (see KNOWLEDGE AND LEARNING; SCIENCE AND THE QURʾĀN), both religious and secular, the Qurʾān is a formative element of society and polity alike (see POLITICS AND THE QURʾĀN). It is "the basis not only of a faith and a religion; it is the basis also of a civilization, one which has phenomenalized itself in the clear light of the day. No one who has studied the civilization of Islam impartially can fail to appreciate the central role which the Koran has played both in its origin and in its development." (ibid., 12). For everyday life, however, the most prominent presence of the Qurʾān can be found in its recitation.

Recitation: Oral/aural communication

The continuing function of the Qurʾān in everyday life is mainly based on its essential characteristic as an orally recited text (see ORALITY). Though it was recorded in written form as early as the time of the Prophet (see CODIFICATION OF THE QURʾĀN), it has been always orally transmitted. Throughout the centuries, Muslims have learned the Qurʾān largely from the mouth of a teacher who has committed the text to memory *(ḥāfiẓ* or *qāriʾ).* The student also ordinarily combines study and memorization. This method of learning the Qurʾān entails both reciting and listening. In order to insure this method, Muslim scholars throughout history have forbidden reliance upon the written text alone in learning the Qurʾān. The same method was applied to learning the prophetic traditions *(aḥādīth),* so much so that reliance on a book was considered a "grievous mistake" (Ibn Jamāʿa, *Tadhkirat al-sāmiʿ,* 87, Ibn ʿAbd al-Barr, *Jāmiʿ,* i, 69). This oral/aural, or reciting/listening, dimension of the Qurʾān that lies at the root of its role in everyday life is an essential dimension of the structure of revelation *(waḥy)* itself, i.e. revelation as a pattern of communication (Izutsu, *Revelation,* 128). The report about the first encounter between Muḥammad and the archangel Gabriel (q.v.) is indicative of this oral/aural dimension. It is reported that in this first encounter, wherein the first five verses of what eventually came to be sūra 96 were revealed, the archangel Gabriel ordered Muḥammad to "recite" *(iqraʾ).* A terrified Muḥammad reacted by saying, "What shall I recite?" *(mā aqraʾ).* Apparently Gabriel's command was ambiguous to Muḥammad and it was not clear to him what he was supposed to recite. After three repetitions of the same command and response, Muḥammad (q.v.) understood that he was supposed to repeat what Gabriel recited. In a later revelation the Prophet was advised to follow the [angel's] recitation (*fa-idhā qaraʾnāhu fa-ttabiʿ qurʾānahu,* Q 75:18), which is understood to mean that he should not repeat hastily what was recited to him, but should first listen to the angel's recitation and then repeat it.

Listening attentively *(inṣāt)* to qurʾānic recitation is, according to the Qurʾān itself, an avenue for receiving God's mercy (q.v.; Q 7:204). Listening is not merely a passive action, but represents the internal act of comprehension. It was through listening to the Qurʾān recited by the Prophet that some of the jinn converted to Islam (Q 46:29-30; 72:1). Many are the reports of the influence that the Qurʾān's recitation has over people. Stories are preserved in Islamic literature which recognized that even the unbelievers were fascinated by the overwhelmingly poetic effect of the Qurʾān, an effect incomparable to that of poetry itself (see LANGUAGE AND STYLE OF THE QURʾĀN; POETRY AND POETS; RHETORIC OF THE QURʾĀN). Important in this context is the report about one of the scribal recorders of revelation who enjoyed what was dictated to him by the Prophet so much that he reached the point of spiritual unification with the text. Being able to anticipate the final wording of the verse under dictation, he thought he had attained the state of prophethood (see PROPHETS AND PROPHETHOOD). The full account is as follows: The prophet Muḥammad was dictating Q 23:12-14 to one of his scribes — verses which explain the gradual process of creating a human being out of a sperm (see BIOLOGY AS THE CREATION AND STAGES OF LIFE). When the Prophet finished the last sentence, the man was so deeply impressed that he exclaimed, "So blessed be God, the fairest of creators" — a sentence which fits the rhyming pattern of the verse and closes it. The Prophet was highly surprised, the story continues, because what the man said was exactly the last sentence revealed to the Prophet. Although the scribe in this story thought he could produce something like the Qurʾān (see INIMITABILITY; CREATEDNESS OF THE QURʾĀN), and accordingly claimed that the Qurʾān had been invented by Muḥammad, a deeper significance can be found in the story. It indicates the aesthetic dimensions which always affect those who encounter the Qurʾān. The language of the text could capture the scribe's imagination and could inspire him to anticipate what might follow because of its powerful structure and cadences (Ṭabarī, *Tafsīr,* i, 45 and xi, 533-5).

In order to resist the influence exerted by listening to the recitation of the Qurʾān the people of the Quraysh (q.v.) at Mecca used to make noise around the reciter (Q 41:26). Listening *(samāʿ)* was understood as inseparable from and as important as recitation itself. This intrinsic correlation of recitation *(qirāʾa)* and listening *(samāʿ)* led to the notion of the ethics of recitation *(ādāb al-tilāwa)* and the ethics of listening *(ādāb al-samāʿ)*. According to a prophetic ḥadīth, if the reciter is to recite the Qurʾān as if it were revealed into his heart (q.v.), the listener is to be aware of the fact that he or she is listening to the recitation of God's speech (Ibn Ḥanbal, *Musnad,* nos. 19635, 19649).

As the Qurʾān is essentially orally transmitted through recitation and memorization, the first step in the education of a Muslim child is the memorization of some of the short sūras such as Sūrat al-Fātiḥa (Q 1), Sūrat al-Ikhlāṣ (Q 112) and Sūrat al-Falaq (Q 113) and Sūrat al-Nās (Q 114), the last two being known as al-Muʿawwidhatān ("the two cries for refuge and protection").

This first step is followed by the memorization of other sūras until the child has memorized the whole Qur'ān by the age of ten or twelve. (This author memorized the entire Qur'ān by the age of eight.) The importance of this tradition for Muslims is perfectly expressed by Graham: "The very act of learning a text 'by heart' internalizes the text in a way that familiarity with even an often-read book does not. Memorization is a particularly intimate appropriation of a text, and the capacity to quote or recite a text from memory is a spiritual resource that is tapped automatically in every act of reflection, worship, prayer, or moral deliberation, as well as in times of personal and communal decision or crisis" (Graham, *Beyond,* 160).

Consequently, qur'ānic recitation *(qirā'at al-Qur'ān)* developed as an independent discipline with rules and methods of its own (see RECITATION, THE ART OF). A professional reciter *(qāri')* would recite the Qur'ān in a rather embellished way known as *tartīl,* a term used twice in the Qur'ān for "recitation" (Q 25:32; 73:4). It is reported that the Prophet said, "Embellish the Qur'ān with your voices." It is also reported that he said, "He who does not recite the Qur'ān melodiously is not one of us." To such precepts the Prophet added his personal example, that on the day of his victorious entry into Mecca (see CONQUESTS) he was seen on the back of his she-camel vibrantly chanting verses from Sūrat al-Fatḥ. The rules of recitation with embellishment *(tartīl)* became a discipline called *tajwīd,* rendered as "euphonious recitation." It is an art related to music. The study of qur'ānic recitation (including learning the science of *tajwīd* and practicing recitation of the Qur'ān) thus became a prerequisite for a Muslim aspiring to become a singer or a musician. Most of the very famous Arab singers (e.g. Sayyid Darwīsh, Umm Kalthūm and Zakariyyā' Aḥmad) in Egypt are known to have studied *tajwīd* and started their career as Qur'ān reciters.

With the progress of technology, especially in the field of audio and video taping, learning *tajwīd* rules has become more accessible for large numbers of Muslims. Now there is no need to attend the sessions of an expert *shaykh* or *qāri'* in order to learn *tajwīd.* Sets of cassettes produced by one reciter (e.g. *al-Muṣḥaf al-Murattal* by Shaykh Maḥmūd al-Ḥuṣarī which appeared for the first time in Egypt in 1960) encouraged other reciters to record their recitations (*qirā'āt,* see RECITERS OF THE QUR'ĀN). All of these *qirā'āt* are now available on CD-ROM, accompanied by *tajwīd*-teaching programs. Many of the encyclopaediac classical commentaries such as those of al-Ṭabarī (d. 310/923), al-Qurṭubī (d. 671/1272), Ibn Kathīr (d. 774/1373) and others are also now on CD-ROM (see EXEGESIS OF THE QUR'ĀN: CLASSICAL AND MEDIEVAL; COMPUTERS AND THE QUR'ĀN). With the spread of internet service thousands of web sites about Islam have emerged, many containing the Qur'ān in Arabic and its translation into the relevant language of the site (see TRANSLATION OF THE QUR'ĀN). Some sites even present video recordings of qur'ānic recitations.

A "correlation between highly oral use of scripture and religious reform movements" can be observed, and it has been noted that the "'internalizing' of important texts through memorization and recitation can serve as an effective educational or indoctrinational discipline" (cf. Graham, *Beyond,* 161). The recent radical Islamist movements, who introduce themselves as the best substitute for current political regimes, make very good use of the recitation of the Qur'ān, among other things, to spread their ideologies. Governments in Muslim countries, whose "religiosity" is often challenged by the Islamist movements, have not hesitated to encourage memorization and recitation of the Qurʾān by spending a great deal of money on recitation competitions and memorization competitions. In Egypt, for example, the highest competition for the recitation and memorization of the Qurʾān is sponsored by the Ministry of Religious Endowments *(wizārat al-awqāf),* with prizes presented to the winners by the President or the Prime Minister on the eve of the Night of Power *(laylat al-qadr),* i.e. the twenty-sixth of Ramaḍān, every year.

Thus, as an essential element of Muslim daily religious life, *tartīl al-Qurʾān* has become not only a profession but an institution. Recitation of verses of the Qurʾān is always performed at the opening of a project, a meeting, a celebration, etc. It is the first item to be broadcast on every radio or television station in almost every Muslim country and it is also the closing item (see MEDIA AND THE QURʾĀN). The Arabic MBC television station, for example, though broadcasting from London, follows the same tradition. Recitation of the Qurʾān is an equally essential part of all funeral ceremonies and processions (see DEATH AND THE DEAD), i.e. the body-washing ceremony *(ghusl),* the funeral-prayer *(ṣalāt al-janāza),* and the condolence-receiving session *(ʿazāʾ),* where two professional reciters are often hired to recite either at the house of the deceased or at the neighborhood mosque (for further discussion of the place of the Qurʾān in everyday life, see esp. J. Jomier, *L'islam vécu en Égypte,* 185-219).

Everyday language

It is worth noting that qurʾānic phrases, expressions, formulae and vocabulary have become an essential component of the Arabic language. Qurʾānic language, in capturing the imagination of Muslims and Arabs from the moment of its revelation, has affected almost every field of knowledge, namely theology, philosophy, mysticism, linguistics, literature, literary criticism and visual art.

The linguistic structure of the Qurʾān, although basically a "parole" in the pre-Islamic Arabic language, has been able to dominate this language by transforming the original signs of the language system so that they act as semiotic signs within its own system. In other words, qurʾānic language is trying to dominate the Arabic language (q.v.) by transferring its linguistic signs to the sphere of semiotics where they refer only to one absolute reality, which is God (see SEMANTICS OF THE QURʾĀN; SEMIOTICS AND NATURE IN THE QURʾĀN). The function of such a transformation is evasion of the seen reality in order to establish the unseen divine reality of God: that is why everything in the whole seen reality from top to bottom, according to the Qurʾān, is nothing but a sign that refers to God. Not only natural phenomena, whether ani-mate or inanimate, are semiotic signs but human history (see HISTORY AND THE QURʾĀN), presented in the Qurʾān to express the everlasting struggle between truth and non-truth, is also referred to as a series of signs (q.v.; *āyāt,* sing. *āya*). The Qurʾān itself is divided into chapters or sūras (q.v.), each of which is divided into verses (q.v.), also known as *āyāt* (sing. *āya*). The comprehensive employment of this word in the Qurʾān, in both the singular and the plural, solidly supports this semiotic interconnection.

By surrounding the activities of everyday life with its recitation, the qurʾānic language has successfully dominated the standard Arabic language *(al-fuṣḥā),* as well as the various local dialects. Although the role of education, religious as well as secular, cannot be overlooked, the oral/aural character of the Qurʾān constitutes the basic factor in its widespread and effective re-shaping of the Arabic language.

Illiterate people have been able, long before the age of mass education, to memorize and recite the Qurʾān. The same is true for blind persons who have been capable, long before the invention of the Braille system, of becoming professional reciters *(qurrāʾ)* of the Qurʾān. Even non-Arab Muslims are required to learn how to pray in Arabic. Every Muslim is expected to memorize at least Sūrat al-Fātiḥa and some short sūras in order to be able to perform the prayer in a legally acceptable fashion.

The possibility of non-Arab Muslims' reciting qurʾānic passages in translation during their prayer was first addressed by Abū Ḥanīfa (d. 150/775), founder of the Ḥanafī school of jurisprudence. From a Persian family himself, he did not find any religious objection to a Muslim who is unable to understand or to recite the Qurʾān in Arabic, performing the prayer in translation. He ruled it permissible even for those who had learned Arabic but still saw difficulties in reciting the Qurʾān in Arabic (Abū Zahra, *Abū Ḥanīfa,* 241). Al-Shāfiʿī, however, insisted that reciting a Persian translation of the Qurʾān prayer is not valid. Moreover, even recitation in Arabic, according to him, is not valid if the verse sequence is mistakenly altered. It is not enough to correct the mistake by returning to the proper sequence, rather the reciter must restart the entire sūra in its proper order (Shāfiʿī, *al-Umm,* i, 94). As the opinion of al-Shāfiʿī became the one accepted by later consensus *(ijmāʿ),* it became obligatory for non-Arab Muslims to recite the qurʾānic verses in Arabic in their prayer. As a result, languages like Persian, Turkish, Urdu, Malay and others spoken by Muslims became heavily influenced by the Qurʾān, or at least carry a qurʾānic imprint, because of its oral/aural character.

The traditional system of Islamic education (see TRADITIONAL DISCIPLINES OF QURʾĀNIC STUDY), whether in the classical school *(madrasa)* or in private tutoring, usually starts with study of the Qurʾān. Memorizing the whole Qurʾān was for a long time a pre-condition for a student to be admitted to higher education *(ʿālimiyya)* at al-Azhar University in Cairo. Even with the introduction of the modern secular educational system, the teaching of Islam continued as an essential part of the curriculum at all levels. This remains true for almost all Muslim countries. With the development of mass education in every Muslim country in the post-colonial era, learning the Qurʾān thus became even more widespread, a phenonemon which can be observed in any Muslim country. Even Muslim communities in the diaspora, whether living in western or non-western countries, seek to establish their own schools where they can teach Islam and the Qurʾān to their children.

The age of mass media made it much easier, as mentioned above, for an individual to have access to learning Qurʾān recitation properly without attending school or engaging a private teacher. Qurʾān recitation is broadcast every day from all radio and television channels in Muslim countries. It is heard at least twice a day, once at the beginning and again at the end of the daily broadcast. In some countries, such as Egypt, the broadcast of Qurʾān recitation is far more frequent, as it is heard both before and after each call to prayer *(adhān),* which occurs five times daily. Religious programs, where qurʾānic verses are quoted and explained, amount to about 25% of the total broadcasts every day. The Egyptian government established a special radio station in the sixties *(Idhāʿat al-Qurʾān al-karīm)* for the sole purpose of broadcasting Qurʾān recitation and related qurʾānic programs. The Friday prayer (q.v.) and the prayer during the two feasts are broadcast in their entirety, including the sermons, by both radio and television in almost every Muslim country. With the establishment of satellites, like Arab-sat and Nile-sat, the broadcast reaches Muslim communities in non-Muslim countries, making it possible for any Muslim to receive transmission of the entire pilgrimage procession from Mecca, thereby turning the previously ritualistic privilege of those with the necessary means into a publicly Islamic experience shared by all. The month of Ramaḍān, the "month of months" of the Muslim calendar, now enjoys widespread publicity in the satellite age. *Ṣalāt al-qiyām,* also known as *tarāwīḥ* or *tahajjud,* has also become an experience publicly shared with those who perform it at the Kaʿba in Mecca. *Laylat al-qadr* is a special occasion that some television stations broadcast from Mecca until the completion of the dawn prayer.

How much everyday language is influenced by the Qurʾān in such an all-pevasive context? It is impossible to provide an exact answer, but the phenomenon may be illustrated within the limits of this article by some examples. Qurʾānic phrases and verses spoken by Muslims in their ordinary language use include: the first part of the *shahāda, "lā ilāha illā llāh,"* translated as "There is no god but Allāh"; the phrase asking God's forgiveness (q.v.; *istighfār*), *"astaghfiru llāh,"* lit. "I ask the forgiveness of God"; the Islamic greeting, *"al-salāmu ʿalaykum,"* lit. "Peace be with you"; phrases with the name Allāh, e.g. *"lā ḥawla wa-lā quwwata illā bi-llāhi l-ʿāliyyi l-ʿaẓīm,"* rendered "All power and might are from God, the exalted, the great"; *"Allāhu akbar,"* lit. "God is greater/the greatest"; the invocation of God's protection against Satan *(al-istiʿādha)* and *al-basmala* (see BASMALA).

The first part of the *shahāda* has different connotations, depending on the situation: to express sadness upon hearing bad news about someone known to the person; reacting to news of somebody's death, when it is always followed by the qurʾānic expression *innā li-llāhi wa-innā ilayhi rājiʿūn,* "We surely belong to God, and surely we will return to him" (Q 2:156; cf. 3:83; 6:36; 19:4; 24:64; 28:39; 40:77 and 96:8). It also conveys a sense of anger or displeasure in certain contexts.

Istighfār, which is mentioned and recommended by the Qurʾān more than 50 times, is always present in everyday language and mostly associated with the *istiʿādha* (invocation of God's protection against Satan), either to express sorrow for anger or to persuade an angry person to calm down. The Islamic greeting *(salām)* also has its foundation in the Qurʾān as the greeting given by the angels to those who deserve paradise (cf. Q 6:54; 7:46; 10:10; 13:24; 14:23; 15:46; 19:62; 56:26). It is also the required greeting of the prophets (cf. Q 19:15, 33). As the word Islam itself is derived from the same root as *salām, s-l-m,* and as al-Salām is one of the most beautiful names of God *(asmāʾ Allāh al-ḥusnā),* it became an obvious choice as the greeting of Muslims. It is also part of a formula used to greet the souls of ancestors upon arrival at the graveyard, whether visiting or participating in a funeral. The formula is *al-salāmu ʿalaykum dāra qawmin muʾminīn, antum al-sābiqūn wa-naḥnu in shāʾa llāh bikum lāḥiqūn,* "Peace be upon you, residence of people of faith, you preceded us and we will join you, God willing." The qurʾānically derived Arabic phrase for "God willing" *(in shāʾa llāh)* is a very common expression among Muslims. Like the greeting *"al-salām ʿalaykum"* (also, *salām[un] ʿalaykum),* its usage in everyday language is not limited to Arab Muslims.

The name of God, Allāh, is present in almost every example offered here. In Arabic, especially in the Egyptian dialect, its frequency in everyday speech with multiple connotations is remarkable. It can express deep appreciation or admiration of a beautiful face, voice, song, poem, scent, sight, drink, meal, etc., if pronounced with a very long last syllable and closed at the end. It can express anger and dissatisfaction if pronounced with a higher tone stressing the double *lām* ending with the intonation of a rhetorical question. It can convey a connotation of teasing or mocking if it is repeated twice with an open ending. More will be said on this subject in the next section below.

The expression *lā ḥawla wa-lā quwwata illā bi-llāhi l-ʿāliyyi l-ʿaẓīm* contains three of God's names (Allāh, al-ʿĀlī and al-ʿAẓīm) in addition to reference to another of his names (al-Qawī, Q 11:66; 22:40, 74; 33:25; 40:22; 42:19; 57:25; 58:21). The expression is used in everyday language to express reaction to a situation where a sense of power or strong authority is displayed. The phrase *"Allāhu akbar"* has many functions: it is the marker of entry into the prayer context, in that sense it is called *takbīrat al-iḥrām*. It also indicates, within the context of prayer, movement from one praying position to another. It is always followed by *istiʿādha* and then *basmala* before reciting Sūrat al-Fātiḥa. The *istiʿādha* seeks God's protection against the devil (q.v.) by saying *aʿūdhu bi-llāhi mina l-shayṭāni l-rajīn,* especially when beginning Qurʾān recitation (cf. Q 16:98). Like the *istiʿādha,* the *basmala (bi-smi llāhi l-raḥmāni l-raḥīm),* "In the name of God, the compassionate, the merciful," is also to be recited before Sūrat al-Fātiḥa because, with the exception of the ninth sūra of the Qurʾān, it occurs at the opening of every sūra in the qurʾānic text (*muṣḥaf,* q.v.). It also appears in a verse within a sūra (Q 27:30).

Apart from their essential role in prayer, the *takbīr, istiʿādha, basmala* and Sūrat al-Fātiḥa play other important roles in the language and practice of everyday life. *Takbīr* is always used, for example, to express dissatisfaction in a situation where someone speaks or acts arrogantly. As for *istiʿādha,* besides its use in religious and devotional contexts (cf. Q 3:36; 7:200; 19:18; 23:97), it expresses, in everyday usage, the speaker's intention not to be involved in matters or affairs which he or she disapproves of or resents. The two sūras called al-Muʿawwidhatān (Q 113 and Q 114) are recited before sleeping, preceded as a matter of course by both *istiʿādha* and *basmala.* They are also recited by mothers to a crying baby. If *istiʿādha* is intended to seek protection against the devil (i.e. a negative dimension of life), *basmala* represents the positive dimension of seeking a blessing (q.v.; *baraka*).

By virtue of its positive connotation, *basmala* is frequently present in the diverse activities of everyday life. It is reported in a well-known ḥadīth that any action or behavior is incomplete if executed without having the *basmala* recited (*kullu shayʾin lā yudhkaru fīhi ismu llāh fa-huwa abtar,* Ibn Ḥanbal, *Musnad,* no. 8355). It should be recited upon entering a room or a house, opening a book, eating a meal, and it has become common behavior on television talk shows for a guest to start his or her answer with the *basmala,* regardless of the topic. It is very normal for students of all ages to whisper the *basmala* before exams, oral or written. It has recently been used by some airlines, e.g. Gulf Air, Saudi Air and others, on an audiotape played before takeoff. It is followed on the same tape by part of another verse of the Qurʾān, *subḥāna man sakhkhara lanā hādhā wa-mā kunnā lahu muqrinīn,* "Glory to God who tamed this [i.e. the sea and animals] for our use, for we are unable to control it" (cf. Q 43:13). The verse, meant to glorify God whose power makes it possible for people to travel on water and to ride on the backs of animals, is equally applied to modern technology. It has also been a general practice for many Muslims to recite the *basmala* followed by Q 43:13 when he or she starts his or her car. The *basmala* has a certain magical power according to some mystics who believe in the magical power of language in general and in the sacred power of Arabic, the language of the Qur᾿ān in particular (cf. Ibn al-ʿArabī, *Futūḥāt,* i, 58 f.; ii, 395 f.). It should be mentioned here that the literature about the magical power of language in Islamic culture is probably derived, at least partially, from the enigmatic letters at the beginning of some qur᾿ānic sūras, *al-ḥurūf al-muqaṭṭaʿa* (see LETTERS AND MYSTERIOUS LETTERS).

The recitation of Sūrat al-Fātiḥa *(qirāʾat al-fātiḥa)* expresses, in the broadest sense, the idea of donation, although the meaning varies with the context. If said in the context of condolences, at the graveyard or at mention of the name of the deceased, the recitation is a donation in return for God's mercy and a blessing for the soul of the deceased. If it is done while visiting or passing by a saint's shrine, its recitation is meant to gain a blessing *(baraka)* from the saint *(walī)*. It can also signal that someone has recently been or is about to be engaged. Betrothal is traditionally associated with the recitation of Sūrat al-Fātiḥa by some family members of the future groom and bride. It is also recited before the wedding contract session *(katb al-kitāb)* and on the wedding night and is meant to add a sacred nature to the marriage institution (see MARRIAGE AND DIVORCE).

The first verse of Sūrat al-Fātiḥa after the *basmala,* i.e. *al-ḥamdu lillāhi rabbi l-ʿālamīn,* is also part of everyday language. At the beginning of a meal, the *basmala* is recited, and at the end this first verse *(al-ḥamd)* is recited. But *al-ḥamd* is not limited to thanking God for blessings provided. Rather it should always be the reaction of the Muslim to whatever God bestows on him or her, hence the statement, "Thanks be to God who alone is to be thanked for unpleasant things" *(al-ḥamdu lillāhi lladhī lā yuḥmadu ʿalā makrūhin siwāh,* see GRATITUDE AND INGRATITUDE). This explains why the answer given by a Muslim to the casual question, "How are you?" is always answered by *al-ḥamd* regardless of how he or she really is.

Like *al-ḥamd,* the glorification *(al-tasbīḥ)* is also a part of everyday language, but conveys, like the recitation of Sūrat al-Fātiḥa, different senses according to context, e.g. different levels of excitement. An invocation *(duʿāʾ)* composed of most of the above elements is frequently recited as follows: "Glory to God, praise be to God; there is no other god besides God, God is great, and there is no power or strength other than in him, the exalted, the magnificent" (*subḥāna llāh, wa-l-ḥamdu lillāhi, wa-lā ilāha illā llāh, wa-Allāhu akbar wa-lā ḥawla wa-lā quwwata illā bi-llāhi l-ʿāliyyi l-ʿaẓīm;* for further discussion on the Qur᾿ān's influence on everyday language, see Jomier, *L'islam vécu en Égypte,* 221-40).

Artistic presentation, calligraphy and crafts

There is no need to elaborate on the artistic dimension of Qur᾿ān recitation, especially when performed by a professional *qāriʾ* endowed with a melodious voice. *Tartīl* based on mastering the rules of *tajwīd* is actually a musical performance. The use of different terminologies, such as *tartīl* instead of *ghināʾ* (singing), is meant to differentiate between melodious production as entertainment intended for amusement and that associated with serious religious activity. For the same reason, other forms of religious music, such as praise of the Prophet *(madāʾiḥ)* or religious folk poetry, are referred to as chant *(inshād)* and not singing *(ghināʾ)*. In daily life, however, Muslims react to Qur᾿ān recitation, whether listening to a reciter or a recording, in a manner similar to that prompted by a musical performance.

Offering condolences *(ta'ziya)* is an occasion to listen to Qur'ān recitation directly from a *qāri'*. In the Egyptian countryside, for example, people extoll the quality of a certain *qāri'* with a loud cry of "Allāh" after each pause between verses. They sometimes even ask the shaykh to repeat a verse or verses. It is expensive to hire a well-trained *qāri'* with a beautiful voice, such a *qāri'* being something of a star. The renown of the *qāri'* who is hired depends on the wealth of the deceased's family or the amount of inheritance (q.v.) he left behind. Thus paying condolences *(ta'āzī)* can offer a splendid opportunity for those who appreciate the art of Qur'ān recitation both to fulfil a religious duty and to experience exquisite recitation.

Again, in a fashion analogous to the enjoyment of music, qur'ānic recitation may be experienced through listening to a tape or compact disk. Like musical art, Qur'ān recitation can also be enjoyed through one's own practice of recitation. The division of the Qu'rān into 30 parts *(juz')* — each of which is further divided into two parts *(ḥizb)* which are themselves divided into four quarters *(rub')* — makes it feasible for a Muslim to enjoy daily recitation of at least one *rub'*, if not more. In a communal context, the recitation of the Qur'ān is performed weekly by a professionally trained shaykh in every mosque before the Friday prayer and sermon. At this weekly recitation, preference is given to the recitation of Q 18, Sūrat al-Kahf ("The Cave").

The ninety-nine most beautiful names of God *(asmā' Allāh al-ḥusnā)* — originally based on the Q 59:22-24 — are usually sung, accompanied by flute and drums, in Ṣūfī *dhikr* ceremonies. The singer, or *munshid*, melodically repeats over and over again the names of God while the participants sway back and forth to the right and to the left. Within the melody, the name of Allāh is uttered. The rhythm of the movement, as well as the utterance of the name of Allāh, gradually quickens in response to the melody. The end of the performance approaches when the name of Allāh alone is recited by repeating the first and the last letters *(alif, hā')*, thus indicating the attainment of the state of annihilation in God *(fanā')*. Apart from the ritual function of this musical presentation of the names of God, there is also the aesthetic side, interest in which is confirmed by the widespread distribution of these musical presentations in recorded form. The musical productions do not belong to an individual singer, but like folk songs are performed by anyone with a beautiful and strong voice capable of song. In such a fashion the musical presentation of God's names is not unlike their presentation in calligraphy (q.v.).

If the recitation of the Qur'ān has developed its own musical genre, its written form has developed two kinds of visual art, calligraphy and book decoration (see ORNAMENT AND ILLUMINATION). Manuscript decoration (see MANUSCRIPTS OF THE QUR'ĀN) was an art developed by Muslims through their efforts to invent markers or indicators for the early 'Uthmānic copies (*muṣḥaf*, see CODICES OF THE QUR'ĀN) of the Qur'ān, in order to facilitate recitation of the written text. First it was necessary to add diacritical points in order to differentiate between Arabic letters of similar written form; second, to establish signs indicating short vowels within and at the ends of words; and third, to create a system for the numbering of the verses and the demarcation of the beginning and end of each sūra. Different colorful artistic markers, still highly esteemed, were employed. The work of binding and covering the manuscript was considered a sacred craft to be performed only by those who were well-trained and had long experience. Many of these Qurʾān manuscripts, produced in the age before print (see PRINTING OF THE QURʾĀN), are now displayed in museums all over the world. In the wake of the revolutionary development of printing technology, the *muṣḥaf* decoration became an independent and technical art in the production of printed Qurʾāns.

It continues to be commonplace in any Muslim house, apartment or even a single room, to have a copy of the qurʾānic text placed in the highest possible position as a blessing *(baraka)*. It is also often seen behind the front or the rear window of a car. The golden *muṣḥaf* around the neck of a Muslim woman or girl is a beautiful piece of art. The production of such sacred art and jewellery is, it could be argued, one of the liveliest industries in the Muslim world.

The art of monumental calligraphy as connected to the Qurʾān consists of transforming the written text into visual tableaux. Letters and words are only elements that form the entire piece of art and are no longer meant to be read. In such elaborate calligraphy, the readability of the written text of the Qurʾān is less important than its artistically powerful presentation. According to the doctrine that the Qurʾān represents the eternal and uncreated utterance of God (*kalām Allāh al-azalī al-qadīm,* the Qurʾān is believed to have previous existence in heaven (see HEAVENLY BOOK) where it was, and still is, recorded on the preserved tablet (q.v.; *al-lawḥ al-maḥfūẓ*). It is written there in magnificent Arabic letters, each of which is as great as a mountain, specifically Mount Qāf, which is supposed to surround and encompass the entire earth (cf. al-Zarkashī, *al-Burhān,* i, 229). It has also been noted that the Islamic prohibition of any kind of figural representation of living figures (see ICONOCLASM) made the art of calligraphy prosper and flourish in various media (see ART AND ARCHITECTURE AND THE QURʾĀN).

As arabesque represents Islamic art in its abstract form, calligraphy represents a parallel form of artistic presentation of the word of God (q.v.). A variety of script forms *(khuṭūṭ)* are employed in qurʾānic calligraphy in both the Arab and non-Arab Muslim world (T. Fahd, Khaṭṭ). As might be expected, the verses and sūras most frequently presented in calligraphy correspond to those most often recited, underlining their particular significance in the everyday life of the Muslim. Commonly appearing in beautiful calligraphy are phrases such as "There is no god but Allāh" *(lā ilāha illā llāh)* and "Muḥammad is the messenger (q.v.) of God" *(Muḥammadun rasūlu llāh),* which together make up the testimony to faith *(shahāda);* the plea for God's forgiveness *(astaghfiru llāh);* and many other phrases that demonstrate the variety of ways in which the term Allāh is used. These include "There is no support or strength except in God, the exalted, the great" *(lā ḥawla wa-lā quwwata illā bi-llāhi l-ʿāliyyi l-ʿaẓīm);* the magnification of God *(Allāhu akbar);* the invocation of God to provide refuge from Satan *(al-istiʿādha);* the invocation of God's name *(basmala);* and, finally, the most beautiful names *(al-asmāʾ al-ḥusnā)*.

Since Allāh is the focal name that embraces all other names and attributes of God, it became, and still is, subject to much theosophical interpretation. A considerable portion of Ṣūfī literature is dedicated to explaining the multivalent significance of each letter of the name of Allāh. In calligraphy, the name is written either individually or at the center of the other names of God in many different forms and presentations: in the shape of a circle, square or triangle, each shape being an artistic expression of a particular Ṣūfī explanation of the divine reality. The circular shape, for example, is a visual mode of expressing the theory, elaborated by Ibn al-ʿArabī (d. 638/1240), of the relationship between the name Allāh and the rest of God's names. While the name Allāh occupies the center of the circle, which represents the universe, the other names of God, being countless, are represented as lines extending from the centre to every point of the circle. The artistic tableaux containing the calligraphic representations of the above-mentioned qurʾānic verses and words may be found everywhere in any Muslim community, on the walls of houses and offices, as bumper stickers or decals for car windows, as well as in mosques. The desk tops in many official buildings bear small plaques which display such verses as "On God I depend" (*tawakkaltu ʿalā llāh*, cf. Q 9:129; 10:71; 11:56, 88; 12:67; 13:30; 42:10, etc); "God is my lord" (*Allāh rabbī*, cf. Q 13:30; 18:38; 19:36; 40:28; 42:10; 43:64); "This is from God's grace" (*hādhā min faḍli llāh)*; and "Victory [comes] only from God" (*wa-mā l-naṣra illā min ʿindi llāh*). Tableaux containing particular verses like the Throne Verse (Q 2:255) and the Light Verse (Q 24:35) are best sellers, as are those inscribed with certain chapters such as Q 36 (Sūrat Yāsīn) and Q 112 (Sūrat al-Ikhlāṣ).

Such verses and sūras are also inscribed on small golden and silver pendants. The visual presentation of qurʾānic verses and phrases by metal inscription is not a modern phenomenon (see EPIGRAPHY). Inscribing copper, silver and gold (q.v.), as well as coins in general, is an ancient Islamic craft. Nowadays, it has become an industry, with almost every Muslim girl and woman wearing around her neck a pendant with a qurʾānic inscription, the most common being "What God wills" (*mā shāʾa llāh*), the *basmala*, "There is no god but Allāh" (*lā ilāha illā llāh*), and the Throne and Light verses.

The importance of both the Throne and the Light verses may have its roots in the mystical interpretation given to them, an interpretation that later became an essential aspect of folk Islamic beliefs (see POPULAR AND TALISMANIC USES OF THE QURʾĀN). The Light Verse exemplifies the rhetorical device of allegory (*tamthīl*), with the nature of God being compared to the nature of light. This light of God, however, is not the ordinary light known and enjoyed in daily life, but is rather an extraordinary kind of light which can only be perceived through similitudes. The similitude is expressed through extraordinary linguistic means in order to convey the extraordinary nature of God's light (see SIMILES). Al-Ghazālī (d. 505/1111) devoted a treatise (*Mishkāt al-anwār*) to explaining in detail the conception of the divine light in reference to the above-mentioned qurʾānic verse.

The Throne Verse, on the other hand, represents the master verse of the Qurʾān (*sayyidat al-Qurʾān*) for al-Ghazālī, since it contains the three major branches of the most important qurʾānic sciences, i.e. the science of knowing God (*ʿilm maʿrifat llāh*, cf. *Jawāhir*, 45-9). Compared with Sūrat al-Ikhlāṣ, which contains only one branch of the science of knowing God, i.e. knowing his essence, (*ʿilm maʿrifat al-dhāt*), the Throne Verse merits a higher position in al-Ghazālī's categorization. Both of these verses have generated an extensive theological and mystical literature and occupied the attention of many generations of Muslim scholars. Their popularity has also expressed itself, as has been noted, in manifold material representations of varying levels of artistic skill and craftsmanship.

Conclusion

In conclusion, it can be said that the Qurʾān was able to penetrate all aspects of daily life by re-forming and re-shaping the everyday life of the early Muslim community physically as well as spiritually. The spread of Islam in a very short period presented the Qurʾān to different socio-cultural environments, where it eventually enjoyed an exalted position. As it gradually infiltrated the texture of the Arabic language, including its proverbs (a topic touched upon here only tangentially; cf. M.B. Ismāʿīl, *al-Amthāl*), it succeeded in influencing all the languages spoken by non-Arab Muslims. It is at the level of language, the building block of thought and of community, whether the media of the language be material (see MATERIAL CULTURE AND THE QURʾĀN) or audio-visual, whether the form of conveyance be recitation or crafts, that the Qurʾān has had its most pervasive influence on all aspects of Muslim everyday life.

Nasr Hamid Abu Zayd

Bibliography

Primary: Abū Dāwūd; Bukhārī, *Ṣaḥīḥ;* Dārimī, *Sunan;* Ghazālī, Abū Ḥāmid, *Jawāhir al-Qurʾān,* Cairo n.d.; id., *Mishkāt al-anwār,* ed. Abū l-ʿUlā ʿAfīfī, Cairo 1966; Ibn ʿAbd al-Barr, Abū ʿUmar Yūsuf al-Qurṭubī, *Jāmiʿ bayān al-ʿilm wa-faḍlihi,* Cairo 1927; Ibn al-ʿArabī, Muḥyī al-Dīn, *Futūḥāt,* 4 vols., Cairo 1329 A.H.; Ibn Ḥanbal, *Musnad;* Ibn Jamāʿa, Muḥammad Ibrāhīm Saʿd Allāh al-Kindī, *Tadhkirat al-sāmiʿ wa-l-mutakallim fī adab al-ʿālim wa-l-mutaʿallim,* Hyderabad 1934; Ibn Khaldūn, *Muqaddima,* Beirut n.d.; Ibn Māja; Ibn Saʿd *Ṭabaqāt;* Mālik, *Muwaṭṭaʾ;* Muslim, *Ṣaḥīḥ;* Nasāʾī, *Faḍaʾil;* id., *Sunan;* Shāfiʿī, Muḥammad b. Idrīs, *al-Risāla,* ed. Aḥmad Muḥammad Shākir, Beirut n.d.; id., *Kitāb al-Umm,* Cairo n.d.; Ṭabarī, *Tafsīr;* Tirmidhī, *Ṣaḥīḥ;* Zarkashī, *Burhān,* Beirut 1972³.

Secondary: M. Abū Zahra, *Abū Ḥanīfa. Ḥayātuhu wa-ʿaṣruhu wa-ārāʾuhu al-fiqhiyya,* Cairo 1977³, 20; N. Abū Zayd, Al-Ghazālī's theory of interpretation, in *Journal of Osaka University of Foreign Studies* 72 (1986), 1-25; id., Divine attributes in the Qurʾān. Some poetic aspects, in John Cooper et al. (eds.), *Islam and modernity. Muslim intellectuals respond,* London 1998, 109-211; J. Art, Possibilities and difficulties in studying the place of religion in everyday life in the 19th and early 20th century, in L. Laeyenecker et al. (eds.), *Experience and explanations. Historical and sociological essays on religion in everyday life,* Frysky Academy-Ljouwert 1990, 103-16; Azhar Committee of Grand ʿUlamā, *Khuṭub al-jumʿa wa-l-ʿīdayn,* Cairo n.d.; J.A. Beckford, Socialization in small religions, in L. Laeyenecker et al. (eds.), *Experience and explanations. Historical and sociological essays on religion in everyday life,* Frysky Academy-Ljouwert 1990, 139-59; D. Bowen and E. Early (eds.), *Everyday life in the Muslim Middle East,* Indianapolis 1993; F. De Jong, Cairene ziyāra-days. A contribution to the study of saint veneration in Islam, in *WI (N.S.)* 17 (1976-7), 26-43; D. Eickelman, *Knowledge and power in Morocco. The education of a twentieth century notable,* Princeton 1985; id. and J.W. Anderson, Prints, Islam and prospects for civic pluralism. New religious writings and their audiences, in *JIS* 8 (1997), 43-62; id., *The Middle East and central Asia. An anthropological approach,* Upper Saddle River, NJ 1997³, esp. 165-9; A. El-Zein, Beyond ideology and theology. The search for the anthropology of Islam, in *Annual review of anthropology* 6 (1977), 227-54; T. Fahd, Khaṭṭ in *EI²,* iv, 1113-30; P.D. Gaffney, *The prophet's pulpit. Islamic preaching in contemporary Egypt,* London 1994; Graham, *Beyond;* C. Hirschkind, New technology of piety. Cassette-sermons and the ethics of listening. A paper presented at the IIAS Seminar: *Mass media and the transformation of Islamic discourse,* Leiden 24-6 March 1997; V.J. Hoffman-Laad, Devotion to the Prophet and his family in Egyptian Sufism, in *IJMES* 24 (1992), 615-37; M.B. Ismāʿīl, *al-Amthāl al-qurʾāniyya,* Cairo 1986; T. Izutsu, Revelation as a linguisic concept in Islam, in The Japanese Society of Medieval Philosophy, *Studies in Medieval thought* 5 (1962), 122-67; Abu Jafar, *Muslim festivals in Bangladesh,* Dacca 1980; A.H. Johns, On qurʾānic exegetes and exegesis. A case study in the transmission of Islamic learning, in P.G. Riddell and T. Street (eds.), *Islam. Essays on scripture, thought and society. A festschrift in honour of Anthony H. Johns,* Leiden 1997, 3-49; J. Jomier, *L'islam vécu en Égypte,* Paris 1994; id., La place du Coran dans la vie quotidienne en Egypte, in *IBLA* 15 (1952), 131-65; A. Labib, *The recited Koran. A history of the first recorded version,* trans. B. Weiss, M.A. Rauf and M. Berger, Princeton 1975; E. Lane, *The manners and the customs of the modern Egyptians,* London 1860⁵; A.L. Major, Whose voice is it anyway? Islam and television in Pakistan. A paper presented at the IIAS Seminar: *Mass media and the transformation of Islamic discourse,* Leiden 24-6 March 1997; L. Nabhan, *Das Fest des Fastenbrechens* (ʿīd al-fitr) *in Ägypten. Untersuchungen zur theologischen Grundlagen und praktischer Gestaltung,* Berlin 1991; K. Nelson, *Art of reciting the Qurʾān,* Austin 1985; C.E. Padwick, *Muslim devotion. A study of the prayer manuals in common use,* London 1961; Oxford 1996; N. Robinson, *Discovering the Qur'an.*

A contemporary approach to a veiled text, London 1996, esp. 17-24; Z. Sardar, Paper, printing and compact disks. The making and unmaking of Islamic culture. A paper presented at the IIAS Seminar: *Mass media and the transformation of Islamic discourse,* Leiden 24-6 March 1997; S. ʿUways, *Hutāf al-ṣāmiṭīn. Ẓāhrat al-kitāb ʿalā hayākil al-markabāt fī al-mujtamaʿ al-miṣrī al-muʿāṣir,* Cairo 1971; E. Westermarck, *Marriage ceremonies in Morocco,* London 1914; id., *Pagan survivals in Mohammedan civilization,* London 1933, repr. Amsterdam 1973; id., *Ritual and belief in Morocco,* 2 vols., London 1926, repr. New Hyde Park, NY 1968 (with foreword by Bronislaw Malinowski).

Evil see GOOD AND EVIL

Evil Deeds

Actions that are intended to harm others. The term normally understood as "evil deed" or "sin" *(sayyiʾa)* is mentioned in the Qurʾān 24 times in the singular, and 36 times in the plural. In many verses, the term is directly juxtaposed to "good deed(s)" (q.v.; *ḥasana,* pl. *ḥasanāt*) and is often interpreted by Muslim exegetes as denoting actions which are negative by means of their intentions and consequences. Other related terms include "sin" (*dhanb,* see SIN, MAJOR AND MINOR) mentioned in the Qurʾān 39 times in its various permutations, "wrong-doing," attested over 200 times in various derivatives of *ẓ-l-m,* and "disobedience" (q.v.; *maʿṣiya* [Q 58:8, 9] and *ʿiṣyān* [Q 49:7]). The first verbal form of the Arabic root for this last set of words, *ʿ-ṣ-y,* (*ʿaṣā, yaʿṣī*) is attested 27 times, whereas the adjective, *ʿaṣī,* occurs twice (Q 19:14, 44).

According to many Muslim exegetes, knowledge of good and evil, and specifically what constitutes good and evil actions, is evident to all people. This idea is found in Ibn al-ʿArabī's (d. 543/1148) exegesis of Q 7:172-3; 9:8; 23:111, 115; 91:7-10 and other passages (*Aḥkām,* ad loc.). Q 7:172-3 recounts how God took all humanity from the loins of Adam (see ADAM AND EVE) and made them testify to God as their creator. Insofar as good deeds (q.v.) are considered to be following God and his commandments (q.v.), evil deeds are disobeying God and rejecting his commandments. Q 28:59 implies that ignorance of God and his commandments cannot excuse evil actions since God never destroys a town (see PUNISHMENT STORIES) until he has sent a messenger (q.v.) reciting for them God's revelations (Qurʾān commentators have set forth the various "evil" characters who opposed the prophets; e.g. Ibn Kathīr, *Qiṣaṣ al-anbiyāʾ;* Thaʿlabī, *Qiṣaṣ;* Kisāʾī, *Qiṣaṣ;* see PROPHETS AND PROPHETHOOD). Q 7:38 is also interpreted to mean that people cannot account for their evil deeds with the claim that they were merely following the example of the generation (see GENERATIONS) before them. Further proof of this connection between faith (q.v.) and deeds is the fact that the acts of those who say that they believe in God while in their hearts they do not (see HYPOCRITES AND HYPOCRISY) are also considered as evil (or corrupt; see CORRUPTION), even if such people believe that they are doing good (Q 2:11-2).

Because the purpose of creation is the worship (q.v.) of God, all actions which are not in accord with this purpose are considered to be in vain *(bāṭil).* According to al-Ṭabarī's (d. 310/923) commentary on Q 18:102-8 (*Tafsīr,* ad loc.), those whose actions have been most unproductive and misleading in this world are those who thought that they were doing good by acquiring fame for themselves and their own works. A similar idea is expressed in Q 11:15-6. Earthly deeds, or actions oriented to this world and away from the worship of God, are inconsequential in the sense that things acquired on earth are ephemeral.

The notion of evil deeds as vanity is also

found in some of the Muslim exegesis of passages concerning the efficacy of other deities. Q 22:62, for example, contrasts God as the "truth" *(al-ḥaqq)* with the other things that people call upon for help as "vain falsehood" *(al-bāṭil)*. This relates to the idea that doing evil, like worshipping false gods, is a rejection of the truth. God as truth and rejection of God as falsehood *(al-bāṭil)* is also found in Q 47:3. Q 6:24 is interpreted by Fakhr al-Dīn al-Rāzī (d. 606/1210; *Tafsīr,* ad loc.) to mean that the false gods which people create for themselves will not intercede on their behalf on the day of judgment (see LAST JUDGMENT; INTERCESSION) as God will do on the behalf of his followers. This idea is found in such additional passages as Q 10:30, 11:21, 16:87 and 41:48. Muslim exegetes also point out that the many qurʾānic references to those who "associate" other things with God *(mushrikūn)* may refer not only to polytheists but also to those who put their own fame or wealth (q.v.) above the worship of God (see POLYTHEISM AND ATHEISM; IDOLATRY AND IDOLATORS).

It is in this sense that evil deeds are not only inconsequential but also misleading *(ḍalāl),* causing people to stray (see ASTRAY; ERROR) from the righteous path, which is the worship of God (see PATH OR WAY). Al-Ṭabarī, in his commentary on Q 7:53 (*Tafsīr,* ad loc.), reports on the authority of Ibn ʿAbbās that, on the day of judgment, those who did not worship God will not find their own creations able to intercede on their behalf before God. Q 50:16-29 describes how, on the day of judgment, the two angels who accompany each person on earth will appear and give an account of the evil and good deeds done by that person (see RECORD OF HUMAN ACTIONS). Some exegetes understand these "angels" not literally but as metaphors for the recording of each person's good and evil deeds. Q 50:22 stresses that, on this day, people will see the consequences of their actions, their evil deeds addressed as a waste of the time God had provided them for his worship. See also ETHICS AND THE QURʾĀN; GOOD AND EVIL.

Brannon M. Wheeler

Bibliography
Primary: Ibn al-ʿArabī, *Aḥkām;* Ibn Kathīr, *Qiṣaṣ al-anbiyāʾ,* Beirut 1991-2; Kisāʾī, *Qiṣaṣ;* Rāzī, *Tafsīr;* Ṭabarī, *Tafsīr;* Thaʿlabī, *Qiṣaṣ.*
Secondary: I. Goldziher, *Introduction to Islamic theology and law,* trans. A. and R. Hamori, Princeton 1981, esp. 16-20, 41-2 (on *shirk*); Izutsu, *Concepts;* Fazlur Rahman, *Major themes of the Qurʾān,* Minneapolis 1994[2].

Exegesis of the Qurʾān: Classical and Medieval

Interpretation of the Qurʾān in the premodern period. Qurʾānic exegesis *(tafsīr, taʾwīl)* is one of the most important branches of the qurʾānic sciences (*ʿulūm al-Qurʾān,* see TRADITIONAL DISCIPLINES OF QURʾĀNIC STUDY), but is only one part of the wider Islamic hermeneutics, which also comprises the legal hermeneutics operative in the arena of ḥadīth and law (see ḤADĪTH AND THE QURʾĀN; LAW AND THE QURʾĀN). This latter type of hermeneutics, however, plays a leading role in the qurʾānic commentaries.

Etymology and significance of the Arabic words tafsīr, taʾwīl, *and related terms*

The Arabic word *tafsīr* means the act of interpreting, interpretation, exegesis, explanation, but also connotes an actual commentary on the Qurʾān. The term is used for commentaries on scientific or philosophical works, being in this last case equivalent to *sharḥ,* "explanation," which is reserved primarily for profane purposes such as commentaries on poetry and on philological, grammatical and literary works, etc. (cf. Gilliot, Sharḥ; Rippin, Tafsīr [in *ER*, xiv], 236). Although *tafsīr* with no other qualification refers in most cases to a qurʾānic interpretation or commentary, its origin is not Arabic. The verb *fassara*, "to discover something hidden," is a borrowing from Aramaic, Syriac or Christian-Palestinian (*peshar, pashshar,* see FOREIGN VOCABULARY). The same verb is also found in Jewish-Aramaic. Accordingly, it cannot be determined whether Arabs (q.v.) or Muslims took the word over from the Jews or from the Christians (Fraenkel, *Die arämäischen Fremdwörter,* 28; Hebbo, *Fremdwörter,* 277-9; Horovitz, *Jewish proper names,* 74; Jeffery, *For. vocab.*, 92).

The emergence of the word *tafsīr* as a technical term is unclear. It occurs as a *hapax legomenon* in Q 25:33: "They do not bring to you any similitude, but what we bring to you [is] the truth, and better in exposition *(wa-aḥsana tafsīran)*." This unique attestation is in a polemical context (see POLEMIC AND POLEMICAL LANGUAGE), giving the assurance that any opposition to Muḥammad (q.v.) by the unbelievers (see BELIEF AND UNBELIEF) will be countered by divine assistance. Some of the qurʾānic commentators have proposed here an etymology by metathesis (*tafsīr/tasfīr,* "unveiling," or *takshīf,* "uncovering;" Suyūṭī, *Itqān,* iv, 192). It seems doubtful, however, to see in this verse the origin of *tafsīr* as a technical term (Wansbrough, *QS,* 154 f.).

The Arabic *taʾwīl*, "interpretation, exegesis," literally related to the notion of "returning to the beginning" (according to al-Ḥakīm al-Tirmidhī [d. 292/905 or 298/910]; Nwyia, *Exégèse,* 145-6), is the second technical term of the semantic field of interpretation. It occurs eighteen times in the Qurʾān, signifying the interpretation of narratives (q.v.) or of dreams (Q 12:36, 101; see DREAMS AND SLEEP), or a deeper interpretation (Q 3:7; Dāmaghānī, *Wujūh,* i, 197-8, where five meanings are given). It has recently been definitively shown that the verb *taʾawwala,* from which the term *taʾwīl* is formed, originally meant "to apply a verse to a given situation," before it came to mean allegorical interpretation (Versteegh, *Arabic grammar,* 63-4; Nwyia, ibid., meaning "reality," *ḥaqīqa*).

The antithesis *tafsīr/taʾwīl* has been attested since the first half of the second/eighth century, and probably before, in the earliest rudimentary attempts to classify exegesis. The Kūfan scholar Muḥammad b. al-Sāʾib Abū l-Naḍr al-Kalbī (d. 146/763) attributes to Ibn ʿAbbās (d. 69/688) the following classification: "The Qurʾān was [revealed] in four aspects *(wujūh): tafsīr* [the literal meaning?], which scholars know; Arabic with which the Arabs are acquainted; lawful and unlawful (q.v.; *ḥalāl wa-ḥarām*), of which it is not permissible for people to be unaware; [and] *taʾwīl* [the deeper meaning?] that only God knows" (see ARABIC LANGUAGE). When a further explanation of *taʾwīl* is demanded, it is described as "what will be" (*mā huwa kāʾin,* Muqātil, *Tafsīr,* i, 27). This categorization could have had its origin in the Jewish and patristic discussions on the four meanings of scripture (Heb. *peshat,* "literal translation"; *remez,* "implied meaning"; *derash,* "homiletic comprehension"; *sod,* "mystical, allegorical meaning"; Zimels, Bible; for patristic and medieval conceptions of the four meanings [literal/historical, allegorical/spiritual, tropological/moral and anagogical/eschatological], see De Lubac, *Exégèse;* Böwering, *Mystical,* 135-42).

Representative of this antithesis between *tafsīr* and *taʾwīl* is the opposition between the transmission *(riwāya)* of exegesis from early authorities, such as the Companions of the Prophet (q.v.), and an exegesis built upon critical reflection *(dirāya),* as a declaration of al-Māturīdī (d. 333/944) in his qur'ānic commentary indicates: "The *tafsīr* belongs to the Companions, the *ta'wīl* to the scholars *(fuqahā')*, because the companions saw the events and knew the circumstances of the revelation of the Qur'ān" (Māturīdī, *Ta'wīlāt*, 5; see OCCASIONS OF REVELATION; REVELATION AND INSPIRATION).

This opposition is not, however, always the same. In a tradition attributed to the Khurāsānī exegete Muqātil b. Sulaymān (d. 150/767), it is said: "He who recites the Qur'ān and does not know the *ta'wīl* of it is an *ummī*" (lit. "illiterate," but perhaps also a "pagan"; Muqātil, *Tafsīr*, i, 26-7; see ILLITERACY; RECITATION OF THE QUR'ĀN). Others have said that *tafsīr* is the explanation *(bayān)* of a term which has only one significance, whereas *ta'wīl* is the reduction of a plurivocal term to a single signification according to the context (Suyūṭī, *Itqān*, iv, 192), on the basis of which it could be argued that the distinction between the two terms remained a theoretical one. Abū 'Ubayd al-Qāsim b. Sallām (d. 224/838), whose interest in the text of the Qur'ān was primarily legal, had asserted that they were one and the same (Suyūṭī, *Itqān*, iv, 192; Wansbrough, *QS*, 155-6).

It could be said that the contradictions in the definition of both terms reflect not only differences in times, practices and individuals, but also the fact that the nascent Muslim exegesis was influenced by Jewish and Christian discussions about the four (or more; Muqātil, *Tafsīr*, i, 27, beginning with *"fī l-Qur'ān,"* lists 32 "literary genres" in the Qur'ān) meanings of scripture (see SCRIPTURE AND THE QUR'ĀN). The use of the term *wajh*, pl. *wujūh*, "aspect, face, significance," in these discussions may recall the Tannaitic *panim* of scripture, also connected with the Muslim debates on the seven "letters/aspects" *(al-aḥruf al-sab'a)* in which the Qur'ān is supposed to have been revealed (see READINGS OF THE QUR'ĀN).

Legitimation of qur'ānic exegesis

The nature of the early exegesis in Islam continues to be vigorously debated, as does the idea of opposition to this activity itself. No definitive explanation has yet been given for the supposed opposition to the practice of interpreting the Qur'ān, although three main solutions have been proposed (Leemhuis, Origins, 15-9; Gilliot, Débuts, 84-5). The first posits that the exegesis rejected by pious circles in early Islam was based on historical legends and eschatological narratives (*malāḥim*, Suyūṭī, *Itqān*, iv, 205, 207-8, quoting Ibn Ḥanbal; Goldziher, *Richtungen*, 55-61; see the names of the comparatively few scholars who objected to or refrained from *tafsīr* activity in Ṭabarī, *Tafsīr*, i, 84-9; id., *Commentary*, i, 17-9; Jeffery, *Muqaddimas*, 183-206 *[K. al-Mabānī]*; see ESCHATOLOGY). Birkeland (*Opposition*, 19 f.), however, sees no such aversion at all in the first Islamic century, e.g. among the disciples of Ibn 'Abbās, and believes strong opposition arose in the second/eighth century. Thereafter, exegesis gained general acceptance with the introduction of special rules for the transmission of reports (Birkeland, *Opposition*, 19 f.; id., *Lord*, 6-13, 133-7). The third solution was advanced by Abbott (*Studies*, ii, 106-12), who maintains that the opposition to *tafsīr* was limited to a special category of ambiguous or unclear *(mutashābih*, pl. *mutashābihāt)* verses (q.v.) of the Qur'ān (see AMBIGUOUS). Exegetes have never agreed, however, on which verses are unclear, or even what that qualification means precisely (Rippin, Tafsīr [in *ER*, xiv], 237-8). It can be thus concluded that opposition to exegesis was above all an opposition to the use of personal opinion (*ray'*, Birkeland, *Opposition*, 9-10), beginning from the end of the second/eighth century when the rules for the transmission of traditions mandated acceptable chains of authorities *(isnāds)*. Exegetical traditions without any origin *(aṣl)*, i.e. without authoritative chains — a category which included exegesis by personal opinion or that promulgated by popular preachers *(quṣṣāṣ)* — were rejected, even though their narratives were often the same as those of the traditions introduced by authoritative, sound chains of scholars.

In spite of the supposed aversion of some ancient scholars to qurʾānic exegesis and the fact that the Qurʾān itself does not explicitly state that it should be interpreted, commentators have been able to legitimate their exegetical practice over the centuries. One of the passages of the Qurʾān to which they refer for this legitimization is Q 3:7: "It is he who sent down upon you the book (q.v.), wherein are verses clear *(muḥkamāt)* that are the essence (lit. mother) of the book, and others ambiguous *(mutashābihāt)*. As for those whose hearts (see HEART) are perverse, they follow the ambiguous part, desiring dissension (q.v.), and desiring its interpretation *(taʾwīl)*; and none knows its interpretation, save God. And those firmly rooted in knowledge (see KNOWLEDGE AND LEARNING; INTELLECT) say, 'We believe in it; all is from our lord (q.v.)'; yet none remembers, save men possessed of minds." The first part of the last pericope ("and none knows its interpretation...) could be read in another way, since the Arabic text provides no indication of where stops and pauses should be taken: "And none knows its interpretation save only God and those firmly rooted in knowledge, who say...." With the latter reading, the interpretative task was open to unclear and ambigous verses, as well as to the clear ones (Wansborough, *QS*, 149-53; McAuliffe, Text).

The beginnings of qurʾānic exegesis

The beginnings of qurʾānic exegesis have also been the object of vigorous debate. At first glance, one is faced with two opposing versions, a traditional Muslim view and the Orientalist reading. According to the traditional Muslim version, the exegesis of the Prophet is the point of departure, then that of his Companions who transmitted and added to his exegesis, then that of the successors *(tābiʿūn)* who, in turn, transmitted and added to the previous interpretations. Finally, the following generations of exegetes took up the interpretations of the Prophet, the most revered Companions and successors, as established by the authoritative chains of transmission (*isnād*, Suyūṭī, *Itqān*, iv, 245-301; 207-8; 233-44; Leemhuis, Origins, 13-4; Gilliot, Débuts, 82-3).

Ten of the Companions are listed as exegetes: the four first caliphs (see CALIPH) — but above all ʿAlī (see ʿALĪ B. ABĪ ṬĀLIB) — then Ibn Masʿūd, Ibn ʿAbbās, Ubayy b. Kaʿb, Zayd b. Thābit, Abū Mūsā al-Ashʿarī and ʿAbdallāh b. al-Zubayr (Suyūṭī, *Itqān*, iv, 233). Others added to this list include Anas b. Mālik, Abū Hurayra, Jābir b. ʿAbdallāh and ʿAmr b. al-ʿĀṣ (Ḥājjī Khalīfa, *Kashf*, i, 428-30). Ibn al-Nadīm (fl. fourth/tenth century), who is only interested in written works in his "Index" of Arabic books, does not give such lists, but has only "the book of Ibn ʿAbbās transmitted by Mujāhid (b. Jabr)" (d. 104/722; *Fihrist*, 33).

Muslim tradition always counts the following figures among the successors *(tābiʿūn)*, those "who achieve celebrity for the science of exegesis *(tafsīr)*," said al-ʿAṣimī, a Khurāsānian Karrāmī (a theological current of Transoxiana; cf. Bosworth, Karrāmiyya) who wrote in 425/1034 (see Jeffery, *Muqaddimas*, 196 [*K. al-Mabānī*]): 1. Saʿīd b. Jubayr (d. 95/714; Gilliot, *Baqara*,

205-11); 2. ʿIkrima (d. 105/723), the client of Ibn ʿAbbās; 3. Abū Ṣāliḥ Bādhām, the client of Umm Hāniʾ (Bint Abī Ṭālib); 4. Mujāhid b. Jabr; 5. Abū l-ʿĀliya al-Riyāḥī (Rufayʿ b. Mihrān, d. 93/711); 6. al-Ḍaḥḥāk b. Muzāḥim (d. 105/723); 7. ʿAlī b. Abī Ṭalḥa (al-Hāshimī, d. 120/737); 8. Abū Mijlaz Lāḥiq b. Ḥumayd (al-Sadūsī al-Baṣrī, d. 106/724); 9. al-Ḥasan al-Baṣrī (d. 110/728); 10. Qatāda b. Diʿāma al-Sadūsī (d. 118/736; ibid.; for a traditional presentation of Qatāda as an exegete, see ʿA. Abū Suʾud Badr, *Tafsīr Qatāda;* Ḥājjī Khalīfa, *Kashf,* i, 430 has 1, 2 and 4 and includes Ṭāwūs b. Kaysān, ʿAṭāʾ b. Abī Rabāḥ, saying that all five were Meccans or died in Mecca [q.v.]; Nöldeke, *GQ*, ii, 167-8; for all these exegetes cf. Gilliot, *La sourate al-Baqara*). Our Karrāmī author remarks that all of them, save Qatāda, learned from Ibn ʿAbbās. It should be noted, however, that neither al-Ḍaḥḥāk nor al-Ḥasan al-Baṣrī were disciples of Ibn ʿAbbās.

Lastly, it is obvious that the two lists have a symbolic significance, since both enshrine ten figures. The fact that the majority of the figures on these lists of successors died in Mecca adds weight to the "soundness" of this being a transmission from the Prophet to the greatest Companions and successors. Confirming this vision of the religious propriety of exegesis is its multiple connections to the figure of Ibn ʿAbbās as the father of qurʾānic exegesis (Gilliot, Débuts, 85-8).

The early Orientalist point of view questioned the reliability of the authoritative chains of transmission as a means for reconstructing supposedly early *tafsīr* works. Actual reconstructions of the early history of exegesis in Islam are all based on one of several preliminary assumptions about the answer to following question: "Are the claims of the authors of the late second and third Islamic centuries, that they merely pass on the material of older authorities, historically correct?" (Leemhuis, Origins, 14-5). F. Sezgin responds affirmatively, going so far as to say that even Ibn ʿAbbās, the alleged father of qurʾānic exegesis, had a commentary (*GAS*, i, 19-24, 25-8); some early Muslim scholars have said that the transmitter of this supposed *Tafsīr,* ʿAlī b. Abī Ṭalḥa, did not hear the work from Ibn ʿAbbās himself (according to al-Khalīlī, d. 447/1055, in Suyūṭī, *Itqān,* iv, 237), but learned it from Mujāhid b. Jabr and Saʿīd b. Jubayr (ibid.). In contrast, J. Wansbrough believes "haggadic" or narrative exegesis to have begun rather late: "Extant recensions of exegetical writing here designated haggadic, despite biographical information on its putative author, are not earlier than the date proposed to mark the beginnings of Arabic literature, namely 200/815" (*QS,* 144, 179; see the use of Wansbrough's categorization by Berg, *Development,* 148-55, and additions to it, 155-7).

Certainly, the question cannot be answered by an unqualified "yes" or "no," and even if Sezgin had an express desire to prove the existence of early documents "in order to substantiate the claim for the validity of *ḥadīth* transmission and the *isnād* mechanism" (Rippin, Present status, 228), his work has prompted a reconsideration of the Orientalists' traditional critical view of the soundness of authoritative chains, especially in exegesis. One of the arguments of Wansbrough for rejecting the authenticity of the old *tafsīr*s was the intrusion of poetry, because poetry as an exegetical device is not present in the commentaries of Muqātil b. Sulaymān, al-Kalbī and Sufyān al-Thawrī al-Kūfī (d. 161/778). For Wansbrough, a virtual *terminus a quo* for this phenomenon may be elicited from Ibn Hishām's (d. 218/834) recension of the *Sīra* of Ibn Isḥāq (Wansbrough, *QS*, 142, 217; see SĪRA AND THE QUR'ĀN). But citations of poetry *(shawāhid)* to explain the qur'ānic text exist before this time, e.g. in Abū ʿUbayda (d. 210/885), and al-Farrā' (d. 207/822), and in the *Kitāb al-ʿAyn* of Khalīl b. Aḥmad (d. 175/791), or his redactor, al-Layth b. al-Muẓaffar (d. ca. 200/815; cf. Khan, *Exegetischen Teile*, 64-6; Talmon, *Arabic grammar*, 91-126). The analysis of the different versions of the *Masā'il Nāfiʿ b. al-Azraq ʿan Ibn ʿAbbās* (Gilliot, Textes [in *MIDEO* 23], no. 44), in addition to the poetic quotations in the *Majāz al-Qur'ān* of Abū ʿUbayda and in the *Kitāb al-ʿAyn*, demonstrates that the beginnings and development of *tafsīr* must be pushed back into the early second/eighth century and perhaps even earlier (Khan, *Die exegetischen Teile*, 67-82; Neuwirth, Die *Masā'il*). The same conclusion can be drawn from an analysis of the fragments of the summa, *al-Jāmiʿ*, of ʿAbdallāh b. Wahb (d. 197/812; Ibn Wahb, *Koranwissenschaften;* cf. Muranyi, Neue Materialien).

This does not mean, however, that the traditional Muslim representation of the genesis of qur'ānic exegesis can be accepted as a whole, as evinced by the example of the alleged *Tafsīr* of Ibn ʿAbbās. It has been shown that the three texts (to simplify and not speak of the confusion in the numerous manuscripts and their ascriptions, one example of which being the erroneous attribution of *Tanwīr al-miqbās min tafsīr Ibn ʿAbbās* to al-Fīrūzābādī, d. 817/1414, see Rippin, Criteria, 40-7; 56-9) circulating under the names of the *Tafsīr* of Ibn ʿAbbās, al-Dīnawarī (d. 308/920) or al-Kalbī, and which are supposed to transmit the exegesis of Ibn ʿAbbās, have their origin somewhere in the late third or early fourth century (Rippin, Criteria, 71). Even though it is likely that Ibn ʿAbbās did explain passages of the Qur'ān, it must not be forgotten that he was elevated to a kind of *heros eponymus* of qur'ānic exegesis *(turjumān al-Qur'ān)*, above all in ʿAbbāsid times (cf. Gilliot, Portrait; id., Débuts, 87-8). Moreover, al-Shāfiʿī remarks (Suyūṭī, *Itqān*, iv, 239) that, at most, a hundred reports of Ibn ʿAbbās on exegesis are reliable (meaning, perhaps, that they go back to the Prophet?).

It is clear from the foregoing that additional research is needed, including work on manuscripts, to elucidate more fully the problems of the beginnings and early development of qur'ānic exegesis. Such research should also take into consideration the problematic of the relation between orality (q.v.) and literacy (q.v.) in early Islam (cf. Schoeler, Writing; Berg, *Development*, 34-6 and passim).

The formative period

The formative period is understood to extend from the beginnings of written exegetical activity to the introduction of the philological and, above all, grammatical sciences in exegetical works (see GRAMMAR AND THE QUR'ĀN), the *terminus ad quem* being the commentary of Abū ʿUbayda (d. 207/825), entitled *Majāz al-Qur'ān*, or the *Maʿānī l-Qur'ān* of al-Farrā' (d. 207/822).

It is now certain that written works emerged at least by the early second/eighth century. It should not be concluded that such works were complete commentaries *ad litteram;* they might have amounted to a kind of notebook (*ṣaḥīfa*, see WRITING AND WRITING MATERIALS) and did not always follow the order of the qur'ānic text. The reason for using the Arabic word *tafsīr* for this period is because it is both a verbal noun, "to interpret," and a substantive, meaning a qur'ānic commentary: In this period, it is not always obvious if the exegete in question had ever produced a completed work or had only undertaken a kind of exegetical activity with some reliance on writing, as in the above-mentioned notebook. It is possible to distinguish three broad categories of *tafsīr* in this period: paraphrastic, narrative and legal.

Paraphrastic exegesis is represented, above all, by Mujāhid b. Jabr al-Makkī (d. 104/722), whose paraphrasis is mostly of a lexical nature, e.g. upon "Surely my lord" (Q 12:23), where Mujāhid comments "My lord, that is, my master." The commentary of Mujāhid has been published on the basis of a single manuscript, but it is not always identical to the source al-Ṭabarī (d. 310/923) used in citation of Mujāhid. It is, rather, the *Kitāb al-Tafsīr,* transmitted by Ādam b. Iyās (d. 220/835), from *(ʿan)* Warqā (d. 160/776), from Ibn Abī Najīh (d. 131/749), from Mujāhid. Comparison between the different versions shows that "the written fixation of the works that transmit *tafsīr* from *(ʿan)* Ibn Abī Najīh from Mujāhid must have taken place some time around the middle of the second century A.H." (Leemhuis, Origins, 21, in accordance with the study of G. Stauth, *Die Überlieferung des Korankommentars Muǧāhid b. Ǧabr,* cf. esp. 225-9). The same conclusion has been reached concerning Ibn Isḥāq's biography of the Prophet: "Whatever the role of writing in the transmission of *tafsīr* may have been before that time, such works, conceived as definitive and complete literary works, probably never existed. A living tradition precludes them" (Leemhuis, Origins, 22; Gilliot, Débuts, 88-9).

A *tafsīr* is also attributed to the celebrated proponent of free-will *(qadarī)* and model for the ascetics and mystics, al-Ḥasan al-Baṣrī (d. 110/728), but this was probably along the lines of the aforementioned notebooks, which were organized and compiled at a later date (van Ess, *TG,* ii, 45-6; Gilliot, Textes [in *MIDEO* 22], no. 36). The most important version of this commentary is that of the Baṣran Muʿtazilī ʿAmr b. ʿUbayd (d. 143/760 or 144/761), himself the author of a commentary (van Ess, *TG,* ii, 297-300; see MUʿTAZILĪS).

To the genre of Mujāhid's *tafsīr* belongs the *tafsīr* of Sufyān al-Thawrī al-Kūfī (d. 161/778), a traditionist, theologian, ascetic and jurist, whose exegetical traditions sometimes go back to Mujāhid. The small *tafsīr* which was edited under his name on the basis of a unique manuscript is not without its problems and should be compared with the traditions of Sufyān quoted by al-Ṭabarī or by Abū Isḥāq al-Thaʿlabī (d. 427/1035). One of his transmitters was Abū Ḥudhayfa (Mūsā b. Masʿūd al-Nahdī al-Baṣrī, d. 220/835), also an exegete and the author of a work called *Tafsīr al-Nahdī,* who appears in one chain of transmission of the *Tafsīr* of Mujāhid in al-Ṭabarī (Gilliot, Débuts, 89).

Another traditionist, exegete and jurist was Sufyān b. ʿUyayna (d. 196/811) who was born in Kūfa but lived and died in Mecca. The very small commentary published under his name is a purely speculative reconstruction based on exegetical traditions taken from later commentaries (Gilliot, Débuts, 89-90).

The second type of exegesis of the formative period, narrative exegesis, features edifying narratives, generally enhanced by folkore from the Near East, especially that of the Judeo-Christian milieu. (The narratives upon which this exegesis drew eventually gained the name *Isrāʾīliyyāt,* although it is also the heritage of Byzantium, Persia, Egypt, etc.) In narrative exegesis, it is the actual narrative that seems of prime importance; although the text of the Qurʾān itself underlies the story, it is often subordinated in order to construct a smoothly flowing narrative (Rippin, Tafsīr [in *ER,* xiv], 238).

To this genre belongs the *tafsīr* of al-Ḍaḥḥāk b. Muzāḥim (d. 105/723) who died in Balkh. The various chains of transmission concerning his exegesis go back to the

Prophet's companion Ibn ʿAbbās, although al-Ḍaḥḥāk probably never met him personally, but only heard the exegetical lessons given by a disciple of Ibn ʿAbbās, Saʿīd b. Jubayr, in Rayy (see TEACHING AND PREACHING THE QURʾĀN). Al-Ḍaḥḥāk's own qurʾānic interpretations are preserved in later recensions. Some of his exegetical traditions, one of which draws upon a midrash dealing with the creation (q.v.) of Adam (see ADAM AND EVE), show him to have been a narrator of the old-fashioned type, one who borrowed from Persian legendary lore circulating in Khurāsān. As with many older commentators, and notably Ibn ʿAbbās himself, it might be going somewhat too far to attribute to him an actual body of qurʾānic exegesis in the strict sense of the term. Instead, he should be regarded as one who imparted oral teachings on various passages of the Qurʾān and delivered moral lessons to the young warriors of Transoxiana, and this later came to be considered a commentary (van Ess, *TG*, ii, 508-9; Gilliot, Impossible censure, 65-70; id., EAC, 130).

Also belonging to this category are the two celebrated Kūfan exegetes, al-Suddī al-Kabīr (d. 127/746 or 128/747; Gilliot, *La sourate al-Baqara*, 216-21; id., Impossible censure, 72-5) and al-Kalbī, a genealogist and historian. Al-Kalbī's exegesis can be found not only in the problematic *tafsīr* attributed to him, but also in later Sunnī commentaries. Even though he was indeed a Shīʿī and believed in the doctrine of the "return" *(rajʿa)* of the Imāms (see IMĀM) after their occultation, his exegetical work was transmitted in Sunnī, not Shīʿī, circles (see SHĪʿISM AND THE QURʾĀN). In the fragments of his *tafsīr* compiled by the Shīʿī Ibn Ṭāwūs (d. 664/1266; cf. Kohlberg, *Ibn Ṭāwūs*, 343), it appears that he largely made use of historiographical materials (van Ess, *TG*, i, 298-301). In this connection, it should be borne in mind that the interpretations of al-Kalbī, although a Shīʿī, were appreciated especially in non-Shīʿī circles, notably among the Karrāmiyya, and were later considered, especially in Khurāsān, as sound and authentic, including their transmission of the exegetical traditions of Ibn ʿAbbās (van Ess, *TG*, i, 299).

Two Khurāsānian exegetes from Balkh of great note are Muqātil b. Ḥayyān (d. 135/753) and Muqātil b. Sulaymān (d. 150/767 or after), who both shared the experience of being warriors on behalf of the faith (*muqātil*, see FIGHTING). The former did not compose a complete commentary, but rather operated as a popular preacher *(qāṣṣ)*, imparting exegetical interpretations or narratives within the framework of edifying lessons. Interpretations of a midrashic type are to be found in his sermons, such exegesis later meeting a rather cold reception among adherents of the Iraqi rational school. Some of his exegetical traditions are quoted, for instance by al-Ṭabarī and by Abū l-Futūḥ al-Rāzī (d. after 525/1131; van Ess, *TG*, ii, 510-6; Gilliot, EAC, 131).

As for Muqātil b. Sulaymān, three of his works on qurʾānic exegesis are extant and published. These are the *Kitāb Wujūh al-Qurʾān*, "Aspects of the Qurʾān" (also named *al-Ashbāh wa-l-naẓāʾir*, "The interpretative constants of the Qurʾān"); a kind of rudimentary concordance entitled *Tafsīr khams miʾat āya*, "Commentary on five hundred verses"; and his *Tafsīr* ("Commentary") proper. Most Muslim jurist-theologians and traditionists later branded this Muqātil as a poor transmitter of traditions, although they almost all qualify him as a "great qurʾānic commentator." The criticism levelled at Muqātil actually betrays a discernible historical trend of backward projection, whereby ancient scholars come to be judged according to standards which only find widespread acceptance long after the scholar in question has died. Writers on heresy (q.v.) and theology have also depicted him as one given to anthropomorphism (q.v.). To be sure, Muqātil's recently published commentaries do show traces of anthropomorphic thinking, although not to the extent ascribed to him. The problem is that his commentary has been transmitted in two recensions, a Baghdadi and an Iranian one, only the first of which is extant. It is possible that later redactors of this text suppressed propositions which appeared shocking to them.

Muqātil's commentary poses yet another problem: the eventual mingling of his own material, in this eastern stretch of the Muslim world, with elements of the Kūfan tradition represented by al-Kalbī, who partly drew on interpretations offered by Ibn ʿAbbās or his pupils. Finally, the Baghdadi version — as published — includes interpolations probably by one of the transmitters of this material, al-Tawwazī (d. 308/920), himself a grammarian and a specialist in qurʾānic readings.

These qualifications notwithstanding, narrative exegesis does hold interest as an example of qurʾānic commentary belonging to the early period. It proceeds mainly by way of paraphrase and narratives, with very little use of ḥadīth, drawing instead on what would later be known as *Isrāʾīliyyāt*, "Tales from the Jews," and, more generally, on the legendary lore of the entire region. Moreover, since a number of theological points had not yet been entirely fixed at the time of its composition, certain positions are discernible in this commentary that must have shocked later orthodox sentiment (see THEOLOGY AND THE QURʾĀN), especially those that run counter to notions that came to prevail, such as the sinlessness of prophets and, above all, of the Prophet (van Ess, *TG*, ii, 516-32; Gilliot, Muqātil; id., EAC, 132-4; see PROPHETS AND PROPHETHOOD; IMPECCABILITY).

In the category of legal exegesis can be placed different types of commentary, for instance the first attempts to order the text of the Qurʾān and its interpretation according to legal topics. Whereas in narrative or textual interpretation "the order of scripture for the most part serves as a basic framework, for the legal material a topical arrangement is a definitive criterion" (Rippin, Tafsīr [in *ER*, xiv], 239). Another mode of legal exegesis addresses the abrogation (q.v.) of verses with prescriptive or proscriptive content for the purpose of determining legal positions.

Muqātil b. Sulaymān once again is a focal point in the development of legal interpretation. In his small legal commentary, *Khams miʾat āya* ("Commentary on five hundred verses"), which may have been derived from his great narrative commentary, he covers the following legal topics: faith (q.v.), prayer (q.v.), alms (see ALMSGIVING), fasting (q.v.), pilgrimage (q.v.), retaliation (q.v.), inheritance (q.v.), usury (q.v.), wine (see INTOXICANTS), marriage (see MARRIAGE AND DIVORCE), repudiation, adultery (see ADULTERY AND FORNICATION), theft (q.v.), debts (q.v.), contracts (see BREAKING TRUSTS AND CONTRACTS; CONTRACTS AND ALLIANCES) and holy war (*jihād*, q.v.). To this kind of exegesis also belong the fragments of Ibn Wahb's *Jāmiʿ*, although his material is not organized in a topical fashion: it is arranged according to primary sources, presenting us with a sort of *musnad*. He also includes material on the *qirāʾāt*, the readings of the Qurʾān (q.v.; Ibn Wahb, *Koranwissenschaften;* Muranyi, Neue Materialien).

Also under the heading of legal exegesis is Maʿmar b. Rāshid's (d. 154/770) *Tafsīr* in the recension of ʿAbd al-Razzāq al-Ṣanʿānī (d. 211/827): this recension is found both in the latter's *Tafsīr* and scattered throughout his compilation of prophetic traditions (entitled *al-Muṣannaf*). We find in them hundreds of examples of discussions about the qurʾānic text and its meaning, reflecting actual practice: "What should we do in such and such a case?" with recourse to ḥadīth (Versteegh, *Arabic grammar,* 65-7; Gilliot, Bilan, 158).

As for the topic of abrogation, a "book" *(kitāb)* on this subject is attributed to successors, such as Qatāda (d. 118/736), and to members of the early generations, such as Ibn Shihāb al-Zuhrī (d. 124/742), but comparisons with later material where these same names appear reveal great differences or different versions (Rippin, al-Zuhrī; Gilliot, Sémantique institutionnelle, 42-50; Muranyi, whose judgment is more optimistic concerning the antiquity of the texts attributed to the earlier scholars, in Ibn Wahb, *Koranwissenschaften,* i, 12-3, 51-2, from the *tafsīr* of Zayd b. Aslam, d. 136/753). With the edited work of Abū ʿUbayd (d. 224/838) on this subject, however, we can be certain of the authenticity of the attribution (cf. Abū ʿUbayd, *Nāsikh,* 174-90).

All of these genres of exegesis from the formative period have been integrated — to a greater or lesser degree, depending on the author — in the various commentaries from the next period.

An intermediary and decisive stage: the introduction of grammar and the linguistic sciences

The science of the readings of the Qurʾān *(qirāʾa)* developed in the ʿAbbāsid period, above all in Baṣra and Kūfa, while less so in the Ḥijāz. The specialists in this field were also grammarians and philologists who tried to explain the difficult or strange/rare *(gharāʾib)* words or expressions of the Qurʾān by appealing to the nascent science of grammar, the dialectical forms *(lughāt)* of the Arabs and ancient poetry (see DIALECTS; POETRY AND POETS; ORALITY AND WRITINGS IN ARABIA). The readings of the Qurʾān thus became a branch of the qurʾānic sciences and an integral part of exegesis. The great grammarian of Baṣra, Sībawayh (d. probably in 180/796 at the age of roughly forty years), had dealt with the Baṣran reading and was thus a precursor to the Baṣran philologist and grammarian of Jewish origin, Abū ʿUbayda Maʿmar b. al-Muthannā (d. ca. 210/825), who wrote a qurʾānic commentary entitled *Majāz al-Qurʾān,* "The literary expression of the Qurʾān" (see LANGUAGE AND STYLE OF THE QURʾĀN). *Majāz* here is used in a pre-rhetorical sense and cannot be translated as "figurative speech," its later meaning in stylistics. Rather, in this context, it means what is "usual/permitted" *(jāʾiz)* in the speech of the Arabs, even if it seems "unusual" *(gharīb).* For Abū ʿUbayda, God had spoken to the Arabs in their own language, making it natural to interpret the Qurʾān through recourse to the grammar and usage of the "profane" language of the Arabs, such as that found in poetry, a notion illustrated in his use of sixty poetic verses as witnesses (*shawāhid,* cf. Almagor, Early meaning, 307, 310-1; K. Abu-Deeb, Studies in the majāz and metaphorical language of the Qurʾān, 310-53, Wansbrough, *QS,* 219-6) to the usage of language in the qurʾānic text. His aim is not, however, purely literary but includes searches for literary evidence to demonstrate the then-nascent notion of the miraculous character of the Qurʾān, which became a full doctrine only in the fourth/tenth century (see INIMITABILITY). A work which occupies an intermediary position beween Abū ʿUbayda and the later treatises on the inimitability *(iʿjāz)* of the Qurʾān is the *Taʾwīl mushkil al-Qurʾān,* "The interpretation of the difficulties of the Qurʾān (see DIFFICULT PASSAGES)," of Ibn Qutayba (d. 276/889), which does not follow the text of the Qurʾān, but is divided into chapters (cf.

Rippin, Tafsīr [in *ER*, xiv], 239). It is worth mentioning that the author of a recent study (Versteegh, *Arabic grammar;* reviewed by Gilliot in *ZDMG* 146 [1996], 207-11) on the introduction of grammar into the exegetical enterprise has attempted to demonstrate that a segment of Arabic grammatical terminology could have its origins in the first qurʾānic commentaries, that is, those of the first half of the second/third century: Muqātil b. Sulaymān, al-Kalbī and others.

A closely related genre is that known under the title of *Maʿānī l-Qurʾān,* usually translated as "The significations of the Qurʾān," but better as "The qualities of the Qurʾān." *Maʿnā* means both signification and quality, and the purpose of the genre is not only to explain the qurʾānic text, but, above all, to enhance the allegedly "eminent qualities" in both its content and style. This type of commentary seeks to explain the lexicon of the Qurʾān, along with its grammar, variant readings and poetry, with lesser recourse to historiography and legends (see HISTORY AND THE QURʾĀN; MYTHIC AND LEGENDARY NARRATIVES). One of the earliest texts devoted to this type of analysis is the *Maʿānī l-Qurʾān* of al-Farrāʾ (d. 207/822), a Kūfan scholar with Muʿtazilī leanings (Beck, Dogmatisch-religiöse Einstellung; id., Die b. Masʿūdvarianten; Kinberg, *Lexicon,* 9-23), whose work was probably preceded by others with the same title written by such figures as his Kūfan teacher al-Kisāʾī (d. 189/805), considered one of the seven canonical readers of the Qurʾān (Beck, Kufischen Koranlesung), and the Baṣran al-Akhfash al-Awsaṭ (d. 215/830; Gilliot, Textes [in *MIDEO* 21], no. 81; al-Ward, *Manhaj al-Akhfash*). The genre continued into the following centuries, e.g. the works of al-Zajjāj (d. 311/923; *Maʿānī l-Qurʾān wa-iʿrābuhu,* "The qualities and the semantic grammar of the Qurʾān"), Abū Jaʿfar al-Naḥḥās (d. 338/950; *Iʿrāb al-Qurʾān,* "The semantic grammar of the Qurʾān"), Makkī b. Abī Ṭālib al-Qaysī (d. 437/1047; *Mushkil iʿrāb al-Qurʾān,* "The difficulties of the semantic grammar of the Qurʾān"; cf. A.H. Faraḥāt, *Makkī b. Abī Ṭālib;* Sh. ʿA. al-Rājiḥī, *Juhūd al-Imām Makkī b. Abī Ṭālib*), Abū l-Baqāʾ al-ʿUkbarī (d. 616/1219; *al-Tibyān fī iʿrāb al-Qurʾān,* "The elucidation of the semantic grammar of the Qurʾān"), and others (see SEMANTICS OF THE QURʾĀN). It should be noted that these prerhetorical and textual commentaries follow the text of the Qurʾān, but do not explain each verse, as would later be the case in the great classical commentaries such as that by al-Ṭabarī.

The role of grammar in the semantic, theological and juridical interpretation of the text of the Qurʾān also appears in the numerous books composed on the accepted variant readings *(al-qirāʾāt al-mutawātira),* and also on the "irregular" *(shādhdh)* readings, their grammatical analysis *(iʿrāb)* and their significations and qualities (*maʿānī,* Ḥājjī Khalīfa, *Kashf,* ii, 1317-23; Nöldeke, *GQ*, iii, 116-249; Pretzl, Wissenschaft, 1-47, 230-46; Gilliot, *Elt,* 135-64). Special books were also devoted to the pauses and beginnings of enunciation in the Qurʾān (Nöldeke, *GQ*, iii, 234-7), e.g. *Kitāb al-Waqf wa-l-ibtidāʾ,* "Elucidation of the pause and beginning in the Qurʾān," of the grammarian Abū Bakr al-Anbārī (d. 328/940). This branch has an obvious relationship to the discipline of the public recitation of the Qurʾān (*tajwīd,* Nöldeke, *GQ*, iii, 231-4).

Some later extended commentaries placed a special importance upon the variant readings and grammar, as did the philologist of Granada with Baṣran grammatical inclinations, Abū Ḥayyān al-Gharnāṭī (d. 754/1344), in his *Tafsīr al-baḥr al-muḥīṭ,*

"Commentary of the oceanic sea," which is actually an encyclopaedia of grammar and variant readings, although the author also treats other aspects of exegesis (al-Mashnī, *Madrasat al-tafsīr,* 104-9).

The introduction of grammar and the linguistic sciences was an important turning point in the history of qurʾānic exegesis (Gilliot, *Elt,* 165-203). Indeed, the integration of a positive discipline, like grammar, gave qurʾānic exegesis the appearance of a sure science, even if philology was a sort of *ancilla Corani,* serving apologetic purposes and adapting grammar in some cases, either to the peculiarities of the qurʾānic language or to its "weak style" (cf. Nöldeke, Zur Sprache). The jurists, theologians and exegetes, however, did not want the text of the Qurʾān to be subject to grammar, since, for them, the only sure science was one that derived from the ḥadīth or traditions of the Prophet. They did not abandon grammar, but showed marked preference for the "exegesis from tradition" *(al-tafsīr bi-l-maʾthūr)* which prevailed in the following centuries. Some, however, did find ways to counterbalance this exegesis from tradition with, for example, the introduction of dialectic theology *(kalām)* or Ṣūfī allegorical exegesis (see ṢŪFISM AND THE QURʾĀN).

Constitutive Sunnī corpora based upon traditions and later development

It is commonly said that the first Sunnī exegetical corpus based upon traditions is the commentary of al-Ṭabarī, but there were several others before him at the end of the second/eighth and the beginning of the third/ninth century, e.g. that of Yaḥyā b. Sallām al-Baṣrī (d. 200/815 in Egypt), who came from Iraq and established himself in Qayrawān. He interested himself in qurʾānic readings, along with the occasions of revelation, ḥadīth and the exegetical traditions of Iraq (q.v.), Mecca (q.v.) and Medina (q.v.), and is said to have shared the Murjiʾite conception of faith (Gilliot, Commentaire, 181-2, and passim; M. Muranyi, *Beiträge,* 16-20, 390-7; see DEFERRAL). Mention can also be made of ʿAbd b. Ḥamīd (or Ḥumayd, d. 249/863; see Gilliot, EAC, 134 n. 24) who was born in Kish in what is now Uzbekistan. While his qurʾānic commentary has not come down to us as such, abundant reference is made to it by later scholars such as the polymath al-Suyūṭī (d. 911/1505) in his exegetical compilation, itself based on traditions, *al-Durr al-manthūr fī l-tafsīr al-maʾthūr,* "The scattered pearls concerning exegesis of tradition," (Gilliot, EAC, 134). Another commentary, also quoted by al-Suyūṭī, that has not survived in full and which pertains to the same genre of exegesis based upon tradition, is that of the jurist and exegete of Khurāsān, Ibn al-Mundhir (Abū Bakr Muḥammad b. Ibrāhīm b. al-Mundhir al-Mundhirī al-Nīshābūrī, d. 318/930; *Tafsīr al-Qurʾān,* ms. Gotha 521 [from Q 2:272 to Q 4:91]; Sezgin, *GAS,* i, 496). It should be added that most of the canonical or sub-canonical collections of the prophetic traditions have a section on *tafsīr* or on the *faḍāʾil al-Qurʾān* ("the virtues/merits of the Qurʾān"), such as the collections of al-Bukhārī (d. 256/870), Muslim (d. 261/875), al-Nasāʾī (d. 303/916), etc. (cf. R.M. Speight, Function of ḥadīth). It has also been said that Ibn Ḥanbal (d. 241/855) had a *tafsīr* containing 120,000 traditions, probably an arrangement by his son ʿAbdallāh, if it ever existed at all (Gilliot, Abraham, 66). All these commentaries, however, were only compilations of traditions, with very limited intervention by the compilers themselves.

It can be said that the *Jāmiʿ al-bayān ʿan taʾwīl āy al-Qurʾan,* "The sum of clarity concerning the interpretation of the verses of the Qurʾān," of Abū Jaʿfar Muḥammad b. Jarīr b. Yazīd al-Ṭabarī (d. 310/923) is a landmark work, the first to combine fully the various formative stages or elements of Muslim exegesis described above. A central feature of the work is the attention given by the author to ensuring complete chains of authoritative transmission: 13,026 chains are thus offered in 35,400 cases (Gilliot, *Elt,* passim; Ṣ.Ḥ. Hallaq, *Rijāl al-Ṭabarī*), yielding a precious mine of information (30 volumes in the complete 1954 Cairo edition) for earlier sources of exegesis. Since so much related by al-Ṭabarī is tradition, he has often been regarded as essentially a compiler. Some have even balked at his transmission of numerous "legendary" traditions or *Isrāʾīliyyāt,* but such are to be found, already by his time, in nearly all commentaries and even the six canonical ḥadīth collection *(al-kutub al-sitta)* of Sunnism and the four canonical collections *(al-kutub al-arbaʿa)* of Shīʿism. The latter, while composed after al-Ṭabarī, contain reports and traditions which he would have had at his disposal that are earlier than the books themselves. Moreover, reducing al-Ṭabarī to the role of compiler alone would be to overlook the task which he set for himself, which involved nothing less than filtering most of the data he transmitted so as to ensure that it would meet the criteria of the Sunnite orthodoxy of his own day and environment. Indeed, he often took an outright theological stance, notably, but not only, against the Muʿtazilites. Additionally, there are places in his commentary where he actually speaks out in the tone of a dialectical theologian *(mutakallim),* something hardly agreeable to Ḥanbalite partisans, who occasionally made life difficult for him in Baghdad, even going so far as to accuse him of harboring Shīʿite tendencies.

Again, al-Ṭabarī's commentary amounts to something of a *summa,* with legal elements (he was a remarkable Shāfiʿite jurist, and he even founded his own school of law, which was a variation of the Shāfiʿite school), grammatical elements (he was an excellent grammarian, more attached to the Kūfan school without, however, neglecting the Baṣran), philological and rhetorical elements, and also references to the variant readings of the Qurʾān (to which he had devoted a separate work, see Gilliot, *Elt,* 135-64) and poetic material (M. al-Mālikī, *Juhūd al-Ṭabarī*). In short, al-Ṭabarī's commentary has been regarded as a key source of exegesis in Islam in subsequent centuries and even down to our own time.

A number of other commentaries mark this decisive stage of classical exegesis. The commentary of the collector of prophetic traditions, Ibn Abī Ḥātim al-Rāzī (d. 327/938; Dāwūdī, *Ṭabaqāt,* i, 285-7, no. 264), is composed of exegetical traditions of the classical commentators, together with chains of warrants for their validity, with very few interventions by the author (Ibn Abī Ḥātim al-Rāzī, *Tafsīr*).

The commentary of Abū l-Layth al-Samarqandī (d. 373/983), entitled *Baḥr al-ʿulūm,* "The ocean of sciences," is of average size and belongs to the genre of exegesis which relied largely on tradition, although its author was a Ḥanafite jurist and theologian (Gilliot, EAC, 138).

The Shāfiʿite of Nīshāpūr, Abū Isḥāq al-Thaʿlabī (d. 427/1035), the celebrated author of *Qiṣaṣ al-anbiyāʾ,* "Tales of the prophets," was a specialist on the readings of the Qurʾān, a traditionist, an exegete and a man of letters. Ibn al-Jawzī (d. 597/1200), while recognizing the importance of his qurʾānic commentary, faults him, as does Ibn Taymiyya (d. 728/1328), for integrating too many traditions which they consider unsound. Except for its introduction, al-Thaʿlabī's commentary, entitled *Kashf al-bayān ʿan tafsīr al-Qurʾān,* "Unveiling the elucidation of the exegesis of the Qurʾān," remains unpublished. This regrettable gap is perhaps due to the length of the commentary and the prevailing — mistaken — opinion that the essence of the qur'ānic exegesis embodying the interpretations of the Companions of the Prophet and of the early exegetes is sufficiently accessible in the great work of al-Ṭabarī. Also, al-Thaʿlabī did not hesitate to draw upon the exegesis of men like al-Kalbī and Muqātil b. Sulaymān, two commentators regarded with suspicion by the orthodox both in former times and especially today, regardless of the fact that traditions of similar or identical content are abundantly found in the commentaries of al-Ṭabarī and others (Gilliot, EAC, 139-40).

Abū l-Ḥasan al-Wāḥidī (d. 468/1076) is the author of a commentary praised by the partisans of tradition. He was one of the most noted disciples of al-Thaʿlabī and also of Abū ʿUthmān al-Ṣābūnī (d. 449/1057). Famous for his commentaries on the collected works of several poets as well as for his exegesis of the Qur'ān, he authored no less than three qur'ānic commentaries, called "Extended," "Abbreviated" and "Medium-sized" respectively, and also wrote *Kitāb Asbāb al-nuzūl*, "The occasions of revelation" (Gilliot, EAC, 141; id., Textes [in *MIDEO* 24], no. 66).

Al-Baghawī, also called Muḥyī l-Sunna (Revifier of the Sunna, d. 516/1122), composed, as a traditionist and exegete, a medium-sized commentary, most of the material for which he drew from the commentary of al-Thaʿlabī. One might, as a result, regard his commentary as a sort of abridgment of al-Thaʿlabī's work, duly purged of those traditions considered unacceptable by a strict traditionist like al-Baghawī. Indeed, this was probably the main reason for the praise given to al-Baghawī's work in certain circles. In contrast, criticism levelled against him faults him for drawing too much material from biblical and extra-biblical legend and lore (Gilliot, EAC, 143-4; M.I. Sharif, *al-Baghawī*).

The Karrāmīs of Nīshāpūr, and of Khurāsān and Transoxania in general, played a leading role in exegesis, qur'ānic readings and sciences, even if very little of their work is extant. Abū l-Ḥasan al-Ḥaysan b. Muḥammad (d. 467/1075), who belonged to a great family of scholars, taught exegesis and ḥadīth in Nīshāpūr. The only text of his to be preserved, *Qiṣaṣ al-anbiyā'*, "Tales of the prophets," is to be published (cf. C. Schöck, *Adam im Islam*). Another Karrāmī of Nīshāpūr, al-ʿAṣimī, was the author of the *Kitāb al-Mabānī*, which dealt with qur'ānic sciences and is the introduction to his commentary (Gilliot, EAC, 146; cf. id., Sciences coraniques).

The age of abridgment of the great commentaries of tradition material culminated in *al-Nukat wa l-ʿuyūn*, "The main points and essential features of exegesis," the six-volume commentary of the great Shāfiʿite jurist of Baghdad, Abū l-Ḥasan al-Māwardī (d. 450/1058); the six-volume *al-Muḥarrar al-wajīz*, "The accurate and brief commentary," by the Andalusian Ibn ʿAṭiyya (d. 541/1147; al-Mashnī, *Madrasat al-tafsīr*, 92-7); and the nine-volume *Zād al-masīr fī ʿilm al-tafsīr*, "Provisions for the journey concerning the science of exegesis," of the great Baghdadi Ḥanbalite traditionist, preacher and man of letters, Ibn al-Jawzī (d. 597/1200; McAuliffe, *Qur'ānic*, 57-63). In these three works, chains of transmission are generally reduced to the first figure (companion, successor or later exegete). In al-Māwardī's commentary, the various solutions of interpretation of a verse are summarized and numbered, while Ibn al-Jawzī's awards a prominent place to qur'ānic readings.

The Ḥanafite jurist and theologian Abū l-Barakāt al-Nasafī (d. 710/1310) wrote a medium sized commentary, *Madārik al-tanzīl wa ḥaqāʾiq al-taʾwīl*, "The reaches of revelation and the truths of interpretation," which amounts to a compendium of exegesis that might satisfy the most orthodox of Sunnis. This work may be considered in part as a kind of shortened version of those by al-Zamakhsharī (d. 538/1144; see below) and al-Bayḍāwī (d. 716/1316), while obviously refraining from repeating al-Zamakhsharī's Muʿtazilite positions (Gilliot, EAC, 144-5).

The *Gharāʾib al-Qurʾān wa-raghāʾib al-furqān*, "Wonders of the Qurʾān and desirable features of revelation," of Niẓām al-Dīn al-Nīsābūrī al-Aʿraj (d. after 730/1329), who studied with, among others, the astronomer Quṭb al-Dīn al-Shīrāzī, is a well-planned commentary which proceeds in four stages: variant readings; pauses (also the subject of his eight introductions); literal exegesis *(tafsīr)*, borrowing here from Fakhr al-Dīn al-Rāzī (see below) and al-Zamakhsharī; and spiritual exegesis (*taʾwīl*, G. Monnot, Exégèse coranique [in *EPHESS Annuaire* nos. 89-91, 98]; Gilliot, EAC, 142-3).

A much appreciated commentary today is the *tafsīr* of the Syrian Shāfiʿite traditionist, jurist and historiographer ʿImād al-Dīn Abū l-Fidāʾ Ibn Kathīr (d. 774/1373; eight vols., ed. A.A. Ghunaym et al.), who counted among his teachers the Ḥanbalite Ibn Taymiyya. His commentary is prefaced with an extended consideration of the principle of exegesis by tradition (McAuliffe, *Qurʾānic*, 71-6; for the relation between the different introductions to his commentary and his book *Faḍāʾil al-Qurʾān*, see Gilliot, Textes [in *MIDEO* 24], no. 63). He often quotes his predecessors, like al-Ṭabarī or Fakhr al-Dīn al-Rāzī, sifting and evaluating the exegetical traditions according to rather strict orthodox conceptions in the manner of his teacher Ibn Taymiyya. Comparison of this work to that of al-Ṭabarī or al-Rāzī shows that we are in a much less rich intellectual environment (cf. Calder, Tafsīr; on Ibn Kathīr, see also I.S. ʿAbd al-ʿAl ʿAbd al-ʿAl, *Ibn Kathīr wa-minhājuhu fī l-tafsīr;* Masʿūd al-Raḥmān Khan Nadwī, *al-Imām Ibn Kathīr. Sīratuhu wa-muʾallafātuhu wa-minhājuhu fī kitābāt al-taʾrīkh*).

Nearly contemporaneous with Ibn Kathīr was the exegete, grammarian and specialist in qurʾānic readings, al-Samīn al-Ḥalabī (Aḥmad b. Yūsuf, d. 756/1355 in Cairo; Brockelmann, *GAL*, ii, 111), who wrote the larger but less well-known qurʾānic commentary entitled *al-Durr al-maṣūn fī ʿulūm al-kitāb al-maknūn* ("The secret jewels. On the sciences of the hidden book"), which contains many grammatical explanations.

A very important later source for scholars of exegesis is *al-Durr al-manthūr* of the Egyptian Jalāl al-Dīn al-Suyūṭī (d. 911/1505), mentioned above. In this great compilation he draws upon several commentaries, some of which are now lost, and proceeds by compiling a series of exegetical traditions with few interventions. The same polymath also contributed to completing the small commentary of one of his teachers, Jalāl al-Dīn al-Maḥallī (d. 864/1459), which is thereby entitled *Tafsīr al-Jalālayn*, "Commentary of the two Jalāls." It is very popular today because of its very brief explanations of qurʾānic words and phrases.

The encyclopaedist exegesis in the tradition of al-Ṭabarī continued through the pre-modern period with commentaries such as that of the Zaydite jurist al-Shawkānī (d. 1250/1834), entitled *Fatḥ al-qadīr*, "Victory of the Powerful" (cf. al-Sharjī, *al-Imām al-Shawkānī;* M.H.A. Ghumārī, *al-Imām al-Shawkānī mufassiran*).

Special legal exegesis

While legal exegesis was operative at almost every stage of the history of exegesis, "the framework of legal analysis emerges quite clearly in some works, achieving a status reflected in titles" (Rippin, Tafsīr [in *EI²*], 84; McAuliffe, Legal exegesis) such as *Aḥkām al-Qurʾān*, "The legal rules of the Qurʾān" (Dhahabī, *Mufassirūn*, ii, 432-73), composed by the Ḥanafite al-Jaṣṣāṣ (d. 370/981), the Shāfiʿite Ilkiyā l-Harrāsī (d. 504/1110; Dhahabī, *Siyar*, xix, 350-2), the Mālikite Ibn al-ʿArabī (d. 543/1148; M.I. al-Mashnī, *Madrasat al-tafsīr*, 89-91; id., *Ibn al-ʿArabī al-Mālikī al-Ishbīlī wa-tafsīruhu Aḥkām al-Qurʾān*) and the Cordoban Mālikite al-Qurṭubī (d. 671/1272). The first three exhibit a particular interest in legal material and do not explain every verse of the Qurʾān. The third, a lengthy one, contains many legal "treatises" or developments of explanation, but is also a commentary *ad litteram* with many quotations from earlier commentaries or exegetes, like Muqātil b. Sulaymān and al-Kalbī, with grammatical analyses, etc. As such, it can be considered an exegetical encyclopaedia in the manner of al-Ṭabarī (al-Qaṣabī, *Qurṭubī*; al-Mashnī, *Madrasat al-tafsīr*, 98-101).

The exegesis of the dialectical/speculative theologians (mutakallimūn)

While here is not the place to discuss the early beginnings of dialectical theology *(kalām)* in Islam, it can be said to have been consolidated by the Muʿtazilites, even if they did not actually initiate it. Worthy of note are the Baṣran Muʿtazilite theologian and jurist ʿAmr b. ʿUbayd (see above) and Abū Bakr al-Aṣamm (d. 200/816) who was not, however, always accepted by the other Muʿtazilites. He composed a lost commentary containing not only Muʿtazilite views on the freedom of will and acts (see FREEDOM AND PREDESTINATION), but also historical, philological and legal matters (van Ess, *TG*, ii, 403-7). The great commentary of Abū ʿAlī al-Jubbāʾī (d. 303/915) has not been preserved, but important explanatory material from it has been recently reconstructed from quotations found in later works (cf. Gimaret, *Djubbāʾī*). The Ḥanafite jurist and Khurāsānian Muʿtazilite theologian Abū l-Qāsim al-Balkhī al-Kaʿbī (d. 319/931) wrote a 12-volume commentary on the Qurʾān which has not survived save for quotations found in later works, notably the *Ḥaqāʾiq al-taʾwīl fī mutashābih al-tanzīl*, "The realities of interpretation concerning the ambiguous passages of revelation," by al-Sharīf al-Raḍī (d. 406/1016; cf. Gimaret, *Djubbāʾī*, 28; Gilliot, EAC, 151).

Mention should also be made of the *Naẓm al-Qurʾān*, "The fine ordering of the Qurʾān," of Abū Zayd al-Balkhī (d. 322/934), also lost, passages of which can be found quoted in later sources. Several important philologists and grammarians, like al-Farrāʾ, Abū ʿAlī al-Fārisī and al-Rummānī, were Muʿtazilites. Moreover, the Muʿtazilites played a leading role in the elaboration of the doctrine of the inimitability of the Qurʾān and in the study of its stylistic aspects. From such beginnings, the genre of the *Naẓm al-Qurʾān* (the Muʿtazilite al-Jāḥiẓ [d. 255/868] composed a book so entitled) was later adopted by traditional Sunnite scholars, like the Shāfiʿite Syrian Burhān al-Dīn Biqāʿī (d. 885/1480) in his great commentary entitled *Naẓm al-durar fī tanāsub al-āyāt wa-l-suwar*, "The arrangement of the pearls regarding the correspondence of the verses and sūras," (Gilliot, Textes [in *MIDEO* 22], no. 39), or al-Suyūṭī in his small *Tanāsuq al-durar fī tanāsub al-suwar*, "The harmonious disposition of the pearls regarding the correspondence on the sūras."

Qāḍī ʿAbd al-Jabbār al-Hamadhānī (d. 415/1025) made important exegetical contributions, not only in his *Mutashābih al-Qurʾān*, "The ambiguous passages of the Qurʾān," where he explained those passages according to the Muʿtazilite doctrine, but also in several volumes of his great theological and juridical encyclopaedia, *al-*

Mughnī fī abwāb al-tawḥīd wa-l-ʿadl, "The sufficient [treatise] on the matters of unity and justice."

The nine-volume commentary of al-Ḥākim al-Jushamī (d. 494/1101; the correct vocalization is al-Jishumī, since he was born in Jishum in the district of Bayhaq), entitled *al-Tahdhīb fī l-tafsīr,* "Refinement in exegesis," survives in several manuscripts. One advantage of this commentary, compared with al-Zamakhsharī's *Kashshāf,* is the more solid support it shows for Muʿtazilite doctrine, notably the conception of the unity of God (Gimaret, *Djubbāʾī,* 25-6; Gilliot, EAC, 151-2).

Several Shīʿite exegetes, like Abū Jaʿfar al-Ṭūsī (d. 460/1067) and Abū ʿAlī al-Ṭabarsī (al-Ṭabrisī; d. 548/1153), were also Muʿtazilites; quotations of earlier Muʿtazilite commentators can thus be found in their works (Gimaret, *Djubbāʾī,* 23-5, 26).

As for Jār Allāh al-Zamakhsharī (d. 538/1144), the celebrated Muʿtazilite grammarian, exegete and man of letters from Khwārazm, his commentary, entitled *al-Kashshāf ʿan ḥaqāʾiq al-tanzīl wa ʿuyūn al-aqāwīl fī wujūh al-taʾwīl,* "The unveiler of the truths of revelation and of the essences of utterances concerning the aspects of exegesis," was long considered a model of Muʿtazilite exegesis. In point of fact, while Muʿtazilite standpoints are certainly to be found therein, many of its theological opinions often remained veiled, and its author is to be considered only a distant successor, one of only marginal importance (Madelung, Theology of al-Zamakhsharī, 485-95; Gimaret, *Djubbāʾī,* 11). His reputation for exegesis rests not so much on his Muʿtazilism as on his qualities as a grammarian, philologist, and master of rhetoric and literary criticism. For this reason he is still appreciated in Sunnite orthodox circles (Gilliot, EAC, 152-4).

The importance of the Muʿtazilite contribution can be illustrated through the example of the Zaydite Muʿtazilite scholar, Abū Yūsuf al-Qazwīnī (d. 488/1095), a disciple of the Qāḍī ʿAbd al-Jabbār, who wrote possibly the longest commentary ever composed: It is reported to have been 300, 600, or even 700 volumes. While the number is surely an exaggeration, there is no reason to doubt the testimony of Ibn ʿAqīl, who writes that al-Qazwīnī's commentary on Q 2:102 ("They followed what the Satans [see DEVIL] recited") took up an entire volume (Gilliot, EAC, 154).

The Sunnite reaction against the sectarian groups *(firaq)* and especially against Muʿtazilism is reflected in their qurʾānic exegesis, above all in the commentaries of the Sunnite dialectical theologians.

In the eastern part of the Islamic world, a Ḥanafite theologian who was later recognized as the founder of a school of dialectical theology, Abū Manṣūr al-Māturīdī (d. 333/944), wrote a commentary entitled *Taʾwīlāt al-Qurʾān,* "Exegeses of the Qurʾān," or *Taʾwīlāt ahl al-Sunna,* "Exegeses of the people of the sunna (q.v.)," of which only one volume has been published (the rest will be soon published). It is of major interest not only as representative of Māturīdite doctrine in Transoxiana, but also because it preserves much older exegetical material, including Muʿtazilite interpretations which the author rejects. It might also be added that, at times, he deals with subjects which are not to be found in other commentaries. While this work was glossed, notably in the gloss *(sharḥ)* of ʿAlāʾ al-Dīn al-Samarqandī (d. 539/1144), it has not left discernible traces in qurʾānic exegesis (Rudolph, *al-Māturīdī,* 201-8; Gilliot, EAC, 155).

The Shāfiʿite jurist and Ashʿarite theologian Fakhr al-Dīn al-Rāzī (d. 606/1210; cf. Anawati, Fakhr al-Dīn al-Rāzī) is also a significant representative of the exegesis of the dialectical theologians. His commentary, entitled *Mafātīḥ al-ghayb,* "Keys of the unseen," (also known as *al-Tafsīr al-kabīr,*

"The great commentary"), was a work of his mature years, begun in Khurāsān and pursued in various places. It is not clear that he finished the work himself, e.g. the commentary on Q 29-36 seems not to be his (cf. Jomier, Ensemble; id., Mafātiḥ al-ghayb). Certainly, the usual apparatus of qurʾānic commentary is found therein, as well as references to previous interpreters, including the Muʿtazilites. His exegesis not only follows that which relies on personal opinion *(raʾy)*, but is also very much a philosophical commentary, within the guideliness set by dialectical theology *(kalām)*. Where al-Rāzī considers it appropriate, he explains various issues in the form of scholastic *quaestiones* (Arabic *masʾala,* pl. *masāʾil*), to which he appends the opinions of different scholars with their lines of argument, before concluding with his own. Although his orientation was deliberately anti-Muʿtazilite, he did owe a considerable debt to their exegesis (McAuliffe, *Qurʾānic,* 63-71; Lagarde, *Index,* 1-15; Gilliot, EAC, 156-8).

For different aspects of the methodology and theology of Fakhr al-Dīn al-Rāzī as evidenced in his commentary, see M. ʿAbd al-Ḥamīd, *al-Rāzī mufassiran;* M.I. ʿAbd al-Raḥmān, *Minhāj Fakhr al-Dīn al-Rāzī;* M. Ḥusaynī Abū Saʿdah, *al-Nafs wa-khulūduhā;* ʿA.M. Ḥasan al-ʿAmmarī, *al-Imām Fakhr al-Dīn al-Rāzī;* M. al-ʿArabī Abū ʿAzīzī, *Naẓariyyāt al-maʿrifa ʿinda l-Rāzī;* M. Mahdī Hilāl, *Fakhr al-Dīn al-Rāzī balāghiyyan;* and ʿU. al-Turaykī, *al-Dhāt al-ilāhiyya* (full bibliographical information for these works is given in the bibliography of the article).

Another commentary should be mentioned here, even if it is not entirely matched to this section, the *Anwār al-tanzīl wa-asrār al-taʾwīl,* "The lights of revelation and the mysteries of interpretation," of the Shāfiʿite jurist and theologian Nāṣir al-Dīn al-Bayḍāwī (d. 716/1315-6, according to van Ess; cf. Gilliot, EAC, 160 n. 187). It depends a great deal upon al-Zamakhsharī's work, but while often regarded as a mere abridgment of the *Kashshāf,* it actually draws upon many other sources, which the author unfortunately fails to mention. Al-Bayḍāwī treats variant readings and issues of grammar more than al-Zamakhsharī, but also avoids repeating al-Zamakhsharī's theological views so far as possible. Some of these views, however, still lurk in his text, probably because he remained unaware of their implications. This commentary became one of the single most popular commentaries in the Muslim world. As such, it has been the subject of many glosses, and with that of al-Khaṭīb al-Kāzarūnī (d. 940/1553), now forms part of the curriculum of the University of al-Azhar in Cairo (Gilliot, EAC, 160-3).

Khārijite and Shīʿite exegesis

The oldest Khārijite commentary still exant is that of the Ibāḍite Hūd b. Muḥkim (or Muḥakkam) al-Hawwārī (d. ca. 280/893 or 290/902-3), of the Awres in today's Algeria. It has recently been edited in four volumes and actually forms a kind of abridgment of the commentary of Yaḥyā b. Sallām al-Baṣrī who lived for a period in Qayrawān. Naturally, a great part of the exegetical traditions contained in the work of Hūd are borrowed from Ibn Sallām, especially explanations given by al-Kalbī, Mujāhid and al-Ḥasan al-Baṣrī, and a large amount of exegetical material, especially Baṣran, is found in the work. This commentary is, above all, a valuable testimony to early Ibāḍite exegesis, notably on faith and works (see FAITH), — views which stand in opposition to the Murjiʾite views of Ibn Sallām — against the Sunnite conception of the intercession (q.v.) of the Prophet. Juridical matters in general, as well as those particular to the Ibāḍites are also to be found (cf. Gilliot, Commentaire).

The early Zaydite exegesis is represented

by the *Tafsīr* of Abū l-Jārūd (d. after 140/757-8) which exhibits predestinarian leanings and contains historical and midrashic passages. More than 200 quotations of his exegesis are preserved in the commentary of al-Qummī, hardly surprising since the Imāmī Shīʿites called the Jārūdites the "strong" Zaydites, with regard to their radical Shīʿite positions (Madelung, *Imam al-Qāsim*, 43-8; van Ess, *TG*, i, 253-61; Bar-Asher, *Scripture and exegesis*, 46-56; see SHĪʿISM AND THE QURʾĀN).

Imāmī Shīʿite exegesis can be divided into the Pre-Buwayhid school of exegesis and the Post-Buwayhid school, keeping in mind that the Buwayhid period (334-447/945-1055), known for its theological creativity and far-reaching internal innovations in Imāmite doctrine, constitutes a golden era for the Imāmī Shīʿites (Bar-Asher, *Scripture and exegesis*, 9-12).

Most of the commentaries of the first period were composed between the middle of the third/ninth and late fourth/tenth centuries, roughly the time between the Minor Occultation (which began 260/874 or 264/878) and the Major Occultation (329/941) of the twelfth Imām. The literature from the period of the fifth Imām, Muḥammad al-Bāqir (d. 113/731-2), and the sixth, his son Jaʿfar al-Ṣādiq (d. 148/765), "undoubtedly incorporates earlier exegetical material. However, early exegetical traditions seem to have been edited and modified" (Bar-Asher, *Exegesis*, 7-8). The commentators of this period are Furāt b. Furāt al-Kūfī (fl. second half of third/ninth and possibly fourth/tenth centuries), ʿAlī b. Ibrāhīm al-Qummī (alive in the days of al-Ḥasan al-ʿAskarī, d. 260/873; on the commentary ascribed to Ḥasan al-ʿAskarī, see Bar-Asher, Qurʾān commentary), al-ʿAyyāshī (fl. end of third/ninth and beginning of fourth/tenth centuries) and al-Nuʿmānī (d. ca. 360/971; Bar-Asher, *Scripture and exegesis*, 27-70). The main features of this Pre-Buwayhid school of exegesis are the following: commentary relying on ḥadīths of the Shīʿite tradition (cf. Bar-Asher, *Scripture and exegesis*, chap. 2); narrow and focused concern with the text of the Qurʾān, with special attention given to verses with potentially Shīʿite allusions; minimal interest in theological themes or specific issues bearing on the institution of the Imāma, such as those of the Imām's immunity from error and sin *(ʿiṣma)* or intercession *(shafāʿa)* on the day of judgment (Bar-Asher, *Scripture*, 159-189); an extreme anti-Sunnite tendency, expressed primarily by the hostile attitude to the Companions of the Prophet (Bar-Asher, *Scripture*, 71-86). The methods used by these commentators were interpretations of a textual nature, "seeking to harmonize between the text of the Qurʾān and the ideas they sought to derive from it," and also allegorical interpretation, "which grounds the basic concepts of the Imāmī-Shiʿite in the text" (Bar-Asher, *Scripture*, 87-124). Some of the recent editions of these texts have sometimes been censured, above all in the extreme anti-Sunnite declarations present in the manuscripts and lithograph editions.

Prominent among the tradition-based commentaries of the second period of the Imāmī Shīʿite exegesis (Monnot, Introduction, 314-7) are *Rawḥ al-jinān wa-rūḥ al-janān*, "The breeze of paradise and the spirit of the heart" (probably the first commentary written in Persian), of Abū l-Futūḥ al-Rāzī (fl. first half of the sixth/twelfth century; McAuliffe, *Qurʾānic*, 54-7; Gilliot, EAC, 149-50) and *al-Burhān fī tafsīr al-Qurʾān*, "The proof in interpreting the Qurʾān," of al-Baḥrānī (d. 1107/1696), which quotes almost exclusively exegetical traditions borrowed from previous exegetes and attributed to the Shīʿite Imāms.

The two greatest exegetes of this period, already mentioned above with the Muʿtazilites, are Abū Jaʿfar al-Ṭūsī (d. 460/1067), the author of *al-Tibyān fī tafsīr al-Qurʾān*, "Elucidation in interpreting the Qurʾān" (McAuliffe, *Qurʾānic*, 45-9), and Abū ʿAlī al-Ṭabarsī (d. 548/1153; cf. Abdul, Majma al-bayan; id., Unnoticed mufassir) who composed *Majmaʿ al-bayān li-ʿulūm al-Qurʾān*, "The confluence of elucidation in the sciences of the Qurʾān," a work which owes a considerable debt to al-Ṭūsī. These two commentaries exhibit a distinct kinship with accepted Sunnite exegetical writings, such as interest in the variant readings and grammatical or philogical explanations, and offer moderate points of view on passages of particular importance for the Shīʿites. One must, however, also take into account their Muʿtazilite outlook (cf. Gilliot, EAC, 148-9).

The Ismāʿīlites make a fundamental distinction in religion and knowledge between the exterior *(ẓāhir)* and the interior *(bāṭin)*, a distinction also reflected in their interpretation of the Qurʾān. The science of *tafsīr* (exoteric exegesis) is absent from their literature, since true meaning can be obtained only through *taʾwīl* (esoteric interpretation), which originates in the legitimate Imām. Hence, the Imām is often called "the speaking Qurʾān" *(Qurʾān-i nāṭiq)*, while the book itself is called "the silent Qurʾān" *(Qurʾān-i ṣāmit)*. This arrangement corresponds to the distinction between the hidden, spiritual meaning of scripture explained by the Imām *(taʾwīl)* and the divine message delivered by the Prophet in its literal form (*tanzīl*, descent). Even the physical objects mentioned by the Qurʾān are to receive an esoteric intepretation, often designating one of the Imāms or Fāṭima (q.v.) or one of the holy ancestors, like Abraham (q.v.; cf. Strothmann, *Ismailitischer Koran-Kommentar*, 15; Poonawala, Ismāʿīlī *taʾwīl;* A. Nanji, Hermeneutics). Numerous Ismāʿīlite interpretations of the Qurʾān go back to the letters of the Brethren of Purity (Goldziher, *Richtungen*, 186-207; Netton, *Muslim neoplatonists*, 78-89).

Important traces of the Ismāʿīlite way of interpreting the Qurʾān can be found in the commentary of al-Shahrastanī (d. 548/1153) entitled *Mafātīh al-asrār wa-maṣābīḥ al-abrār*, "Keys of the mysteries and beacons of the pious," with its twelve-chapter introduction, bearing on the first and second sūras of the Qurʾān. His exegesis fully belongs to the tradition of the great commentaries, in the light of the keen interest shown by the author in linguistic issues and exoteric exegesis. He does, however, turn, when necessary, to the "mysteries" *(asrār)*, i.e. esoteric exegesis, with Ismāʿīlite ideas, like the "accomplished" and "not yet accomplished" or the distinction between the "designated successor" *(waṣī)*, who is heir to the Prophet, and the Imām who comes after the *waṣī* (Monnot, Controverses théologiques, 281-96; id. Exégèse coranique [in *EPHESS Annuaire* nos. 93-7]; Gilliot, EAC, 158-60; cf. D. Steigerwald, *Pensée philosophique*).

Mystical exegesis

The important question to consider in the case of the mystical interpretation of the Qurʾān is, 'When did the introspective reading of the Qurʾān begin?' (Massignon, *Essai*, 118; Nwyia, *Exégèse*, 157). Certainly, al-Ḥasan al-Baṣrī, whose personality is so important for the history of spirituality in Islam, is a logical starting point, but his teaching has come to us only in the form of fragments. We are on much surer ground with Jaʿfar al-Ṣādiq (d. 148/765). Whatever the historical origin of the *Tafsīr* attributed to him, its entry into the mystical circles of the third/ninth century corresponds to attempts to consolidate Sunnite mystical doctrine (cf. Nwyia, Tafsīr mystique). Tustarī's (d. 283/896) method of qurʾānic interpretation, as exhibited in his *Tafsīr*, apparently follows the precedent set by al-Ṣādiq "who is on record with a statement concerning the four point pattern of qurʾānic exegesis; but actually, in his commentary of the Qurʾān applies two ways of interpretation, a literal *(ẓāhir)* and a spiritual *(bāṭin)* way, and stresses the hidden meanings *(bāṭin)* of qurʾānic verses" (Böwering, *Mystical,* 141).

The Tustarī tradition of Ṣūfism was very important in the following centuries (Böwering, *Mystical,* 18-42), particularly its influence on the mystical exegesis undertaken in Andalusia, e.g. that by the Cordoban Ibn al-Masarra (d. 319/931), who wrote *Kitāb Khawāṣṣ al-ḥurūf wa-ḥaqāʾiqihā wa-uṣūlihā,* "Particularities of the letters and their essences and their origins," on the isolated letters of the Qurʾān (under the influence of the *Risāla fī l-ḥurūf,* "Treatise on the letters," of al-Tustarī; see LETTERS AND MYSTERIOUS LETTERS), and Ibn Barrajān (born in Seville; d. 536/1142 in Marrakesh) who taught in Seville. Ibn Barrajān treated revelation as a whole as related to its principle, the divine names (see GOD AND HIS ATTRIBUTES), addressing his reader as a disciple and inviting him to follow a "whole and superior reading" (*al-tilāwa al-ʿulyā,* cf. Gril, Lecture supérieure) in his two commentaries: *Kitāb al-Irshād,* "Book of guidance," and *Iḍāḥ al-ḥikma,* "Illustration of wisdom." Ibn al-ʿArabī (d. 638/1240), who had read al-Tustarī, borrowed some of his expressions in his own commentary on Q 1 (chap. 5 of *al-Futūḥāt al-makkiyya*), and traces of his influence (Böwering, *Mystical,* 39-40) and of Ibn Masarra are to be found in his lost commentary *al-Jamʿ wa l-tafṣīl fī asrār maʿānī l-tanzīl,* "The general survey and detailing of the mysteries of revelation" (which had 66 volumes and stopped at Q 18:53; see K. ʿAwwād (ed.), Ibn al-ʿArabī. *Fihrist,* 356-7; Gilliot, Textes [in *MIDEO* 23], no. 111).

Ibn al-ʿArabī authored a large commentary which was in circulation until the ninth Islamic century; what we now possess is his small commentary, *Iʿjāz al-bayān fī tarjamat al-Qurʾān,* "The inimitability of clarity in the explanation of the Qurʾān," which stops at Q 2:252. The school of Ibn al-ʿArabī also had its exegetes, like Ṣadr al-Dīn al-Qūnawī (673/1274), who wrote a commentary on the Sūrat al-Fātiḥa, entitled *Iʿjāz al-bayān fī tafsīr umm al-Qurʾān,* "The inimitability of clarity regarding the exegesis of the essence [lit. mother] of the Qurʾān" (Chittick, Ṣadr al-Dīn Ḳūnawī); al-Qāshānī (d. 730/1329; cf. Lory, *Commentaires ésotériques*); and ʿAbd al-Karīm al-Jīlī (d. ca. 832/1428), who composed a commentary on the *basmala* (q.v.), "In the name of God, the merciful, the compassionate", entitled *al-Kahf wa-l-raqīm fī sharḥ bi-smi llāhi l-raḥmāni l-raḥīm,* "The cavern and the cave in the explanation of the *basmala.*"

Another great mystical exegete, al-Sulamī (d. 412/1021) of Nīshāpūr, had, like al-Tustarī, a major influence on mystical exegesis and thinking. One version of his major commentary, the *Ḥaqāʾiq al-tafsīr,* "The spiritual realities of exegesis" (which exists in two versions, a longer and a shorter), was published in 2001 (ms. Istanbul, Fātiḥ, 261). To this commentary is appended a separate addendum, entitled *Ziyādāt al-ḥaqāʾiq,* "Additions to the spiritual realities," which has recently been published. He was an original author, collecting most of his materials in the course of his journeys, particularly in Merv, Baghdad and Mecca. His approach is methodical and rigorous, shunning subjects of an edifying, anecdotal or biographical nature and avoiding those issues dealt with in legal commentary or in exegesis based upon tradition, as well as technical or philogical points, i.e. those materials pertaining to exoteric learning. He limits himself to interpretation which he considers material for a mystical exegesis of the Qurʾān, according to the principle stated in his introduction: "Understanding the book of God according to the language of the people of the truth." Such an esoteric approach to interpreting the Qurʾān inevitably aroused disapproval in orthodox circles, but his work also contributed to the establishment of mystical exegesis as an independent branch of qurʾānic hermeutics, coming to represent for the mystical interpretation of the Qurʾān what the commentary of al-Ṭabarī had been to traditional exegesis (cf. Böwering, Commentary; id., Sufi hermeneutics). The extracts of his commentary, originally published by L. Massignon and P. Nwyia, have been reprinted in *Majmūʿat-i āthār-i Abū ʿAbd al-Raḥmān al-Sulamī* (ed. N. Purjavādī, i, 5-292).

The celebrated author of *al-Risāla al-qushayriyya*, ʿAbd al-Karīm al-Qushyarī (d. 465/1072), also composed a six-volume commentary (cf. G.C. Anawati, Textes [in *MIDEO* 10, no. 47; 17, no. 35]), entitled *Laṭāʾif al-ishārāt*, "The subtle allusions," in which he notes qurʾānic allusions or indications of the spiritual state of those who recite the Qurʾān (cf. Halm, al-Ḳushayrī).

The commentary of Rūzbihān al-Baqlī al-Shīrāzī (d. 606/1209), entitled *ʿArāʾis al-bayān fī ḥaqāʾiq al-Qurʾān*, "The maidens of clarity regarding the realities of the Qurʾān," besides its high spiritual range, contains quotations from al-Sulamī and sometimes al-Qushayrī (*al-ustādh*, cf. Ernst, Rūzbihān). Rashīd al-Dīn al-Maybudī is the author of a large Persian commentary of mystical inspiration, entitled *Kashf al-asrār wa-ʿuddat al-abrār*, "The disclosure of the mysteries and the outfit of the pious," begun in 520/1126 (Storey, *PL*, i, 1190-1).

The Khwarazmite Najm al-Dīn Kubrā (d. 617/1220; cf. Algar, Kubrā) composed a commentary entitled *al-Taʾwīlāt al-najmiyya*, "The spiritual interpretations of al-Najm," also known as *Baḥr al-ḥaqāʾiq* or *ʿAyn al-ḥayāt*. This commentary was only begun by him, important contributions being made by his disciple Najm al-Dīn Rāzī Dāya (d. 654/1256; cf. Algar, Nadjm al-Dīn), and was finally completed by another Ṣūfī of the order of al-Kubrāwiyya, ʿAlāʾ al-Dawla Simnānī (d. 736/1336; F. Meier, ʿAlāʾ al-Dawla al-Simnānī; Landolt, La "double échelle"). This Ṣūfī of the Ilkhanid period rejected Ibn al-ʿArabī's ontology; his commentary, *Tafsīr najm al-Qurʾān*, contains the salient features of his thought (cf. Elias, *Throne carrier*).

The Moroccan Ṣūfī Ibn ʿAjība (d. 1224/1809) composed a four-volume commentary, entitled *al-Baḥr al-madīd fī tafsīr al-Qurʾān al-majīd*, "The outstretched sea regarding the exegesis of the glorious Qurʾān," in which he distinguishes between the classical textual intepretation *(ʿibāra)* and the allusions *(ishārāt)*, especially to the saints (Michon, Ibn ʿAdjība).

As for the Ottoman period, mention should be made of the allegorical commentary, *al-Fawātiḥ al-ilāhiyya wa l-mafātīḥ al-ghaybiyya*, "The divine openings and the secret keys," of al-Nakhjuwanī (d. 920/1514 in Āqshehir of today's Turkey; Brockelmann, *GAL*, S ii, 320-1). The most celebrated commentary of this period is the ten-volume *Rūḥ al-bayān*, "The spirit of clarity," composed by Ismāʿīl Ḥaqqī al-Brūsawī (d. 1137/1725), which is a classical commentary along with a mystical exegesis. He often quotes *al-Taʾwīlāt al-najmiyya* and Persian mystical poetry (Kut, Ismāʿīl Ḥaḳḳī). The thirty-volume *Rūḥ al-maʿānī*, "The spirit of the significations," begun by Maḥmūd al-Ālūsī (1270/1854) and finished by his son (cf. H. Péres, Ālūsī; Dhahabī, *Mufassirūn*, i, 352-62), is also a classical commentary, reserving at the same time considerable room for mystical interpretation.

Conclusion

The study of the Qurʾān gradually became divided into a profusion of sciences (i.e. disciplines; see TRADITIONAL DISCIPLINES OF QURʾĀNIC STUDY), each with its own handbooks, like *al-Burhān fī ʿulūm al-Qurʾān*, "The proof regarding the sciences of the

Qur'ān," of al-Zarkashī (d. 794/1391; Anawati, Textes [in *MIDEO* 4, no. 18; 6, no. 15]) or *al-Itqān fī 'ulūm al-Qur'ān*, "The mastery regarding the sciences of the Qur'ān," of al-Suyūṭī (d. 911/1505; Anawati, Textes [in *MIDEO* 10, no. 34]), which is itself based upon al-Zarkashī's work; or *Baṣā'ir dhawī l-tamyīz fī laṭā'if al-kitāb al-'azīz*, "The keen insights of those with discernment in the subtilities of the holy book," of the lexicographer al-Fīrūzābādī (d. 817/1414; Anawati, Textes [in *MIDEO* 8, no. 22]).

The vast exegetical tradition of the Qur'ān is a reminder that the Qur'ān has been the *magna carta* of Islamic societies throughout history; its exegesis is not limited to the various schools of qur'ānic commentators, but is found in almost every kind of literature, particularly belles-lettres (*adab;* cf. Gilliot, *Usages;* see LITERATURE AND THE QUR'ĀN).

Claude Gilliot

Bibliography
Primary: 'Abd al-Jabbār, *Mutashābih;* 'Abd al-Razzāq, *Muṣannaf;* id., *Tafsīr;* Abū l-Futūḥ Rāzī, *Rawḥ;* Abū Ḥayyān, *Baḥr;* Abū l-Layth al-Samarqandī, *Tafsīr;* Abū 'Ubayd, *Nāsikh;* Abū Ubayda, *Majāz;* Ālūsī, *Rūḥ;* 'Ayyāshī, *Tafsīr;* Baghawī, *Ma'ālim;* Baḥrānī, *Burhān;* Bayḍāwī, *Anwār;* Biqā'ī, *Naẓm;* Bukhārī, *Ṣaḥīḥ;* Dāmaghānī, *Wujūh;* Dāwūdī, *Ṭabaqāt;* Dhahabī, *Mufassirūn;* id., *Siyar;* Farrā', *Ma'ānī;* Fīrūzābādī, *Baṣā'ir;* Ḥājjī Khalīfa, *Kashf,* Istanbul; Hūd b. Muḥakkam, *Tafsīr;* Ibn Abī Ḥātim al-Rāzī, *Tafsīr al-Qur'ān al-'aẓīm,* ed. As'ad M. al-Tayyib, 10 vols., Mecca 1997; vols. 11-14 (Indices), 1999; Ibn al-'Arabī, *Aḥkām;* Ibn 'Aṭiyya, *Muḥarrar;* Ibn al-Jawzī, *Zād;* Ibn Kathīr, *Tafsīr;* Ibn al-Nadīm, *Fihrist,* ed. Flügel; Ibn Qutayba, *Ta'wīl;* Ibn Wahb, Abdallāh, *al-Ǧāmi'. Die Koranwissenschaft,* ed. M. Muranyi, Wiesbaden 1992; id., *al-Ǧāmi'. Tafsīr al-Qur'ān (Die Koranexegese),* ed. M. Muranyi, Wiesbaden 1993; id., *al-Ǧāmi'. Tafsīr al-Qur'ān (Die Koranexegese). Teil I,* ed. M. Muranyi, Weisbaden 1995; *Jalālayn;* Jaṣṣāṣ, *Aḥkām;* al-Kāfiyajī, *al-Taysīr fī qawā'id 'ilm al-tafsīr,* ed. N.b. M. Maṭrūdī, Damascus 1990; *K. al-Mabānī* (of al-'Aṣimī), in Jeffery, *Muqaddimas,* 183-206; Makkī, *Mushkil; Masā'il = Masā'il Nāfi' b. al-Azraq 'an Ibn 'Abbās,* ed. M.A. al-Dālī, Limassol 1993; Māturīdī, *Ta'wīlāt ahl al-sunna,* ed. J.M. al-Jubūrī, Baghdad 1983, i; Māwardī, *Nukat;* Mujāhid, *Tafsīr;* Muqātil, *Ashbāh;* id., *Khams mi'at;* id., *Tafsīr;* Muslim, *Ṣaḥīḥ;* Naḥḥās, *I'rāb;* Nasafī, *Tafsīr;* Nasā'ī, *Sunan;* Qāshānī, *Ta'wīl;* Qushayrī, *Laṭā'if;* id., *Das Sendschreiben al-Qušayrīs über das Sufitum,* trans. R. Gramlich, Wiesbaden 1989 (trans. of *al-Risāla al-Qushayriyya*); Qummī, *Tafsīr;* Rāzī, *Tafsīr;* Rūzbihān al-Baqlī, *'Arā'is;* al-Samīn al-Ḥalabī, Aḥmad b. Yūsuf, *al-Durr al-maṣūn fī 'ulūm al-kitāb al-maknūn,* ed. A.M. al-Kharrat, 11 vols., Damascus 1986; Shawkānī, *Tafsīr;* Sufyān al-Thawrī, *Tafsīr;* Sulamī, *Ḥaqā'iq al-tafsīr,* ed. N. Purjavādī, *Majmū'at-i āthār-i Abū 'Abd al-Raḥmān al-Sulamī,* 1 vol. to date, Tehran 1990-; id., *Tafsīr al-Sulamī (Ḥaqā'iq al-tafsīr),* ed. Sayyid 'Imrān, 2 vols., Beirut 2001; id., *Ziyadāt;* Suyūṭī, *Durr;* id., *Itqān,* Cairo 1974; id., *Tanāsub;* Ṭabarī, *The commentary on the Qur'ān,* trans. J. Cooper (abr. with notes and comm.), gen. eds. W.F. Madelung and A. Jones, 1 vol. to date, New York 1987-, i, 17-9; id., *Tafsīr,* ed. Shākir, i, 84-9; Ṭabarsī, *Majma';* Ṭūsī, *Tibyān;* Tustarī, *Tafsīr;* Ukbarī, *Tibyān;* Zajjāj, *Ma'ānī;* Zamakhsharī, *Kashshāf;* Zarkashī, *Burhān.*
Secondary: Abbott, *Studies II;* I.S. 'Abd al-'Al 'Abd al-'Al, *Ibn Kathīr wa-minhājuhu fī l-tafsīr,* Cairo 1984; M. 'Abd al-Ḥamīd, *al-Rāzī mufassiran,* Baghdad 1974; M. 'Abd al-Raḥmān, *Minhāj Fakhr al-Dīn al-Rāzī fī l-tafsīr bayna manāhīj mu'āṣirīhi,* Cairo 1989; M.O.A. Abdul, The majma al-bayan of Tabarsi, in *IQ* 15 (1971), 96-105; id., *Shaykh Tabarsi's commentary,* Lahore 1977; id., The unnoticed mufassir Shaykh Tabarsi, in *IQ* 15 (1971), 106-20; M. Abū 'Azīzī, *Naẓariyyāt al-ma'rifa 'inda l-Rāzī min khilāl tafsīrihi,* Beirut 1999; K. Abu-Deeb, Studies in the majāz and metaphorical language of the Qur'ān. Abū 'Ubayda and al-Sharīf al-Raḍī, in I.J. Boullata (ed.), *Literary structures of religious meanings in the Qur'ān,* Richmond, Surrey 2000, 310-53; M. Ḥusaynī Abū Sa'dah, *al-Nafs wa-khulūduhā 'inda Fakhr al-Dīn al-Rāzī,* Cairo 1989; H. Algar, Kubrā, in *EI²,* v, 300-1; id., Nadjm al-Dīn Rāzī Daya, in *EI²,* vii, 870-1; M.M.'A Āl Ja'far, *Āthār al-taṭawwur al-fikrī fī l-tafsīr fī l-'aṣr al-'abbāsī,* Beirut 1984; E. Almagor, The early meaning of majāz and the nature of Abū 'Ubayda's exegesis, in J. Blau (ed.), *Studia orientalia memoriae D.H. Baneth,* Jerusalem 1979, 307-26; M.A. Amir-Moezzi, *Le guide divin dans le shi'isme originel,* Lagrasse 1992; 'A.M. Ḥasan al-'Ammarī, *al-Imām Fakhr al-Dīn al-Rāzī. Ḥayātuhu wa-āthāruhu,* Cairo 1969; G. Anawati, Fakhr al-Dīn al-Rāzī, in *EI²,* ii, 751-5; id., Textes arabes anciens édités en Égypte, in *MIDEO* 1-18 (1954-88); S. Ateş, *Işârî*

tefsîr okulu, Ankara 1974; id., *Süelemî ve tasavvufî tefsîri,* Istanbul 1969; K. ʿAwwād (ed.), Ibn al-ʿArabī. *Fihrist,* in *Revue de l'Académie Arabe de Damas* 29-30 (1954-5), 356-7; ʿA. Abū Suʿūd Badr, *Tafsīr Qatāda,* Cairo 1979; M.M. Bar-Asher, The Qurʾān commentary ascribed to Imām Ḥasan al-ʿAskarī, in *JSAI* 24 (2000), 358-79; id., *Scripture and exegesis in early Imāmī Shīʿism,* Leiden 1999; E. Beck, Die dogmatisch-religiöse Einstellung des Grammatikers Yaḥyā b. Ziyād al-Farrāʾ, in *Museon* 94 (1951), 187-202; id., Die b. Masʿūd-varianten bei al-Farrāʾ (i, ii, iii), in *Orientalia* 25 (1956), 353-83; 28 (1959), 186-205, 230-56; id., Studien zur Geschichte der kufischen Koranlesung in den beiden ersten Jahrhunderten (i, ii, iii, iv), in *Orientalia* 17 (1948), 326-55; 19 (1950), 328-50; 20 (1951), 316-28; 22 (1953), 59-78; H. Berg, *The development of exegesis in early Islam. The authenticity of Muslim literature from the formative period,* Richmond, Surrey 2000; H. Birkeland, *The lord guideth. Studies on primitive Islam,* Oslo 1956; id., *Old Muslim opposition against interpretation of the Koran,* Oslo 1955; C.E. Bosworth, Karrāmiyya, in *EI²*, iv, 667-9; I.J. Boullata (ed.), *Literary structures of religious meanings in the Qurʾān,* Richmond, Surrey 2000; Böwering, *Mystical;* id., The Qurʾān commentary of al-Sulamī, in W.B. Hallaq and D.P. Little (eds.), *Islamic studies presented to Charles J. Adams,* Leiden 1991, 41-56; id., Sufi hermeneutics in medieval Islam, in *REI* 65-67 (1987-9), 255-70; Brockelmann, *GAL;* N. Calder, Tafsīr from Ṭabarī to Ibn Kathīr, in Hawting and Shareef, *Approaches,* 101-40; I. Cerrahoğlu, *Kuran tefsirinin doğusu ve buna hiz veren amiller,* Ankara 1968; id., *Tefsir tarihi,* 2 vols., Ankara 1988; W. Chittick, Ṣadr al-Dīn Ḳūnawī, in *EI²*, viii, 753-5; J.J. Elias, *The throne carrier of God. The life and thought of ʿAlāʾ ad-Dawla as-Simnānī,* Albany 1995; C. Ernst, Rūzbihān, in *EI²*, viii, 651-2; A.Ḥ. Faraḥāt, *Makkī b. Abī Ṭālib wa-tafsīr al-Qurʾān,* Amman 1404/1983; S. Fraenkel, *Die arämeischen Fremdwörter im Arabischen,* Leiden 1886; M.H.A. Ghumārī, *al-Imām al-Shawkānī mufassiran,* Jedda 1981; Cl. Gilliot, Abraham = Les trois mensonges d'Abraham dans la tradition interprétante musulmane. Repères sur la naissance et le développement de l'exégèse en Islam, in *JSAI* 17 (1997), 37-87; id., Bilan = L'exégèse coranique. Bilan partiel d'une décennie, in *SI* 85 (1997), 155-62; id., Commentaire = Le commentaire coranique de Hūd b. Muḥakkam/Muḥkim, in *Arabica* 44 (1997), 179-233; id., Les débuts de l'exégèse coranique, in *REMMM* 58 (1990), 82-100; id., EAC — L'exégèse du Coran en Asie centrale et au Khorasan, in *SI* 89 (1999), 129-64; (abridged Eng. tr.) Qurʾānic exegesis, in M.S. Asimov and C.E. Bosworth (ed.), *History of civilizations of central Asia. iv. The age of achievement (from A.D. 750 to the fifteenth century). Part two. The achievements,* Paris 2000, 97-116; id., *Elt,* esp. 135-64; id., De l'impossible censure du récit légendaire. *Adab* et *tafsīr.* Deux voies pour édifier l'*ethos* de l'*homo islamicus,* in *IOS* 19 (1999), 49-96; id., Muqātil. Grand exégète, traditionniste et théologien maudit, in *JA* 279 (1991), 39-92; id., Portrait "mythique" d'Ibn ʿAbbās, in *Arabica* 32 (1985), 127-84; id., Les sciences coraniques chez les Karrāmites du Khorasan. Le livre des fondations, in *JA* 288 (2000), 15-81; id., Sémantique institutionnelle = Exégèse et sémantique institutionnelle dans le commentaire de Tabari, in *SI* 77 (1993), 41-94; id., Sharḥ, in *EI²*, ix, 317-20; id., *La sourate al-Baqara dans le Commentaire de Ṭabarī,* Thèse de 3ème cycle, Université Paris III 1982; id., Textes = Textes arabes anciens édités en Égypte, in *MIDEO* 19-24 (1989-2000); id. and T. Nagel (eds.), *Les usages du Coran. Colloque, Aix-en-Provence, 5-7 novembre 1998,* in *Arabica* 47 Nos. 3-4 (2000), 315-562; D. Gimaret, *Une lecture muʿtazilite du Coran. Le Tafsīr d'Abū ʿAlī al-Djubbāʾī (m. 303/915) partiellement reconstitué à partir de ses citateurs,* Louvain/Paris 1994; A. Godlas, Ṣūfī Qurʾān commentary. Ṣūfī tafsīr, on http://www.arches.uga.edu/ ~godlas.suftaf/tafssufloc.html/; Goldziher, *Richtungen;* D. Gril, La 'lecture supérieure' du Coran selon Ibn Barraǧān, in C. Gilliot and T. Nagel (eds.), *Les usages du Coran,* in *Arabica* 47 (2000), 510-22; Ṣ.Ḥ. Hallaq, *Rijāl al-Ṭabarī jarḥan wa-taʿdīlan,* Beirut 1999; H. Halm, al-Ḳushayrī, in *EI²*, v, 526-7; ʿA.ʿA. Ḥāmid, *al-Baghawī wa-manhajuhu fī l-tafsīr,* Baghdad 1983; A. Hebbo, *Die Fremdwörter in der arabischen Prophetenbiographie des Ibn Hischām,* Frankfurt am Main/New York 1984; M. Mahdī Hilāl, *Fakhr al-Dīn al-Rāzī balāghiyyan,* Baghdad 1977; ʿA.R. Hītī, *Abū ʿAbdallāh al-Qurṭubī wa-juhūduhu fī l-naḥm wa-l-lugha fī kitābihi al-Jāmiʿ fī aḥkām al-Qurʾān,* Amman 1996; J. Horovitz, *Jewish proper names and derivatives in the Koran,* in *Hebrew Union College annual* 2 (1925), 144-277, repr. Hildesheim 1964; M.F. Ibn ʿAshūr, *al-Tafsīr wa-rijāluhu,* Cairo 1970, repr. in *Majmūʿat al-rasāʾil al-kamāliyya.* No. 1, Taif n.d., 307-495; Jeffery, *For. vocab.;* id., *Muqaddimas;* J. Jomier, Les mafātīḥ al-ghayb de l'imām Fakhr al-Dīn al-Rāzī. Quelques dates, lieux, manuscrits, in *MIDEO* 13 (1977), 253-90; id., Qui a commenté l'ensemble des sourates al al-ʿAnkabūt à Yāsīn (29-36) dans 'le tafsīr al-kabīr' de l'imām Fakhr al-Dīn al-Rāzī? in *IJMES* 11 (1980), 467-85; M.-N. Khan, *Die exegetischen Teile des Kitāb al-ʿAyn. Zur ältesten philologischen Koranexegese,* Berlin 1994; Kinberg, *Lexicon;* E. Kohlberg, *A medieval scholar at work. Ibn Ṭāwūs and his library,* Leiden 1992; G. Kut, Ismāʿīl Ḥaḳḳī, in *EI²*, iv, 191-2; M. Lagarde, *Index du Grand Commentaire de Faḫr al-Dīn al-Rāzī,* Leiden 1996; H. Landolt, La "double échelle" d'Ibn ʿArabī chez Simnānī, in M.A. Amir Moezzi [ed.], *Le voyage initiatique en terre d'Islam,* Louvain/Paris 1996, 251-64; F. Leemhuis, Origins and early development of the *tafsīr* tradition, in Rippin, *Approaches,* 13-30; O. Lory, *Les commentaires ésotériques du Coran d'après ʿAbd al-Razzâq al-Qâshânî,* Paris 1980, 1990[2]; H. de Lubac, *Exégèse médiévale. Les quatres sens de l'écriture,* 4 vols., Paris 1959-64; W. Madelung, *Der Imām al-Qāsim ibn Ibrāhīm und die Glaubenslehre der Zaiditen,* Berlin 1965; id., The theology of al-Zamakhsharī, in *Actas XII Congresso U.E.A.I.,* Madrid 1986, 485-95; J.M.M. Mahdī, *al-Wāḥidī wa-manhajuhu fī l-tafsīr,* Cairo 1979; A.S. Makram, *al-Shawāhid al-shiriyya fī tafsīr al-Qurṭubī,* 2 vols., Cairo 1998; M. al-Mālikī, *Juhūd al-Ṭabarī fī dirāsāt al-shawāhid al-shiʿriyya,* Fez 1994; M.I. al-Mashnī, *Ibn al-ʿArabī al-Mālikī al-Ishbīlī wa-tafsīruhu Aḥkām al-Qurʾān,* Amman 1990; id., *Madrasat al-tafsīr fī l-Andalus,* Beirut 1986; L. Massignon, *Essai sur les origines du lexique technique de la mystique musulmane,* Paris 1922; 1968[3] (rev. and enl. ed.); J.D. McAuliffe, Legal exegesis. Christians as a case study, in L. Ridgeon (ed.), *How Islam views Christianity,* London 2001, 54-77; id., *Qurʾānic;* id., Qurʾānic hermeneutics. The views of al-Ṭabarī and Ibn Kathīr, in Rippin, *Approaches,* 46-62; id., Text and textuality. Q 3:7 as a point of intersection, in I.J. Boullata (ed.), *Literary structures of religious meanings in the Qurʾān,* Richmond, Surrey 2000, 56-76; F. Meier, ʿAlā al-Dawla al-Simnānī, in *EI²,* i, 346-7; A. Merad, *L'exégèse coranique,* Paris 1998; J.-L. Michon, Ibn ʿAdjība, in *EI²,* iii, 696-7; G. Monnot, Les controverses théologiques dans l'œuvre de Shahrastani, in A. Le Bolluec (ed.), *La controverse religieuse et ses formes,* Paris 1995, 281-96; id., Islam. Exégèse coranique, in *École Pratique des Hautes Études. Ve section. Sciences Religieuses. Annuaire. Résumé des conférences et travaux* 89 (1980-1), 369-73; 91 (1982-3), 317-8; 98 (1989-90), 280-2; id., Islam. Exégèse coranique. Introduction à l'exégèse duodécimaine, in *École Pratique des Hautes Études. Ve section. Sciences Religieuses. Annuaire. Résumé des conférences et travaux* 91 (1982-3), 309-19; 92 (1983-4), 305-15; 93 (1984-5), 292-301; 94 (1985-6), 347-50; 95 (1986-7), 253-7; 96 (1987-8), 237-43; 97 (1988-9), 249-54; M. Muranyi, *Beiträge zur Geschichte der Ḥadīṯ und Rechtsgelehrsamkeit,* Wiesbaden 1997; id., Neue Materialien zur tafsīr-Forschung in der Moscheebibliothek von Qairawān, in Wild, *Text,* 225-55, esp. 252-3; Masūd al-Raḥmān Khan Nadwī, *al-Imām Ibn Kathīr. Sīratuhu wa-muʿallafātuhu wa-minhājuhu fī kitābāt al-taʾrīkh,* Damascus 1999; A. Nanji, Towards a hermeneutics of qurʾānic and other narratives in Ismaʿili thought, in R.C. Martin (ed.), *Approaches to Islam in religious studies,* Tucson 1985, 164-73; I.R. Netton, *Muslim neoplatonists,* London 1982; A. Neuwirth, Koran, in H. Gätje (ed.), *Grundriss der arabischen Philologie,* 3 vols., Wiesbaden 1987, ii, 96-135; id., Die *Masāʾil Nāfiʿ b. al-Azraq.* Élément des "Portrait mythique d'Ibn ʿAbbās" oder ein Stück realer Literatur? in *ZAL* 25 (1993), 233-50; Nöldeke, *GQ;* id., Zur Sprache des Korāns, in T. Nöldeke, *Neue Beiträge zur semitischen Sprachwissenschaft,* Strassburg 1910, 1-30 (trans. G.-H. Bousquet, *Remarques critiques sur le style et la syntaxe du Coran,* Paris 1953); Nwyia, *Exégèse;* id., Le Tafsīr mystique attribué à Ǧaʿfar al-Ṣādiq, in *Mélanges de l'Université Saint-Joseph* 43 (1968), 181-230; H. Péres, al-Ālūsī, in *EI²,* i, 425; I.K. Poonawala, Ismāʿīlī *taʾwīl* of the Qurʾān, in Rippin, *Approaches,* 199-222; O. Pretzl, Die Wissenschaft der Qoranlesung, in *Islamica* 6 (1934), 1-47, 230-246, 290-331; M. Ẓalaṭ al-Qaṣabī, *al-Qurṭubī wa-manhajuhu fī l-tafsīr,* Cairo 1979; Sh.ʿA. al-Rājiḥī, *Juhūd al-Imām Makkī b. Abī Ṭālib fī l-qirāʾāt al-qurʾāniyya wa-iʿrāb al-Qurʾān,* Alexandria 1994; A. Rippin, The present status of *tafsīr* studies, in *MW* 72 (1982), 224-38; id. (ed.), *The Qurʾān. Formative interpretation.* Aldershot 1999; id., Tafsīr, in *EI²,* x, 83-8; id., Tafsīr, in *ER,* xiv, 236-7; id., *Tafsīr Ibn ʿAbbās* and criteria for dating early *Tafsīr* texts, in *JSAI* 18 (1994), 38-83; id., al-Zuhrī. Naskh al-Qurʾān and the problem of early tafsīr texts, in *BSOAS* 47 (1984), 22-43; C. Roth and G. Wigoder (eds.), *Encyclopaedia Judaica,* Jerusalem 1971; U. Rudolph, *Al-Māturīdī und die sunnitische Theologie in Samarkand,* Leiden 1997; M.H.M. Salmān, *al-Imm al-Qurṭubī. Shaykh immat al-tafsīr,* Beirut 1993; id. and J.ʿA. al-Dasūqī, *Kashshāf taḥlīlī lil-masāʾil al-fiqhiyya fī tafsīr al-Qurṭubī,* Taif 1988; C. Schöck, *Adam im Islam,* Berlin 1993; G. Schoeler, Writing and publishing. On the use and function of writing in the first centuries of Islam, in *Arabica* 44 (1997), 423-35; Sezgin, *GAS;* M.I. Sharf, *al-Baghawī al-Farrāʾ wa-tafsīruhu lil-Qurʾān al-karīm,* Cairo 1986; A.Gh. al-Sharjī, *al-Imām al-Shawkānī,* Beirut 1988; R.M. Speight, The function of ḥadīth as commentary on the Qurʾān as seen in the six authoritative collections, in Rippin, *Approaches,* 63-81; G. Stauth, *Die Überlieferung des Korankommentars Muǧāhid b. Ǧabr,* Innaugural Dissertation, Giessen 1969, esp. 225-9; D. Steigerwald, *La pensée philosophique et théologique de Shahrastani (m. 548/1153),* Sainte-Foy, Québec 1997; Storey, *PL;* R. Strothmann (ed.), *Ismailitischer Koran-Kommentar,* 4 pts. in 1 vol., Göttingen 1944-8, pts. I-III; R. Talmon, *Arabic grammar in its formative age,* Leiden 1997; ʿU. al-Turaykī, *al-Dhāt al-ilāhiyya ʿinda Fakhr al-Dīn al-Rāzī,* Tunis 1988; C.H.M. Versteegh, *Arabic grammar and qurʾānic exegesis in early Islam,* Leiden 1993 (reviewed by Gilliot in *ZDMG* 146 [1996], 207-11); Wansbrough, *QS;* ʿA.M. al-Ward, *Manhaj al-Akhfash al-Awsaṭ fī l-dirāsat al-naḥwiyya,* Beirut/Baghdad 1975; A. Zimels, Bible. Exegesis and study. Talmudic literature, in *Encyclopaedia Judaica,* iv, 889-90.

Exegesis of the Qurʾān: Early Modern and Contemporary

This article deals with the exegetical efforts of Muslim scholars as well as with their views of exegetical methodology from the middle of the nineteenth century to the present.

Aspects and limits of modernity in the exegesis of the Qurʾān

Treating early modern and contemporary exegesis of the Qurʾān as a distinct subject implies that there are characteristics by which this exegesis differs noticeably from that of previous times. The assumption of such characteristics, however, is by no means equally correct for all attempts at interpreting passages of the Qurʾān in the books and articles of Muslim authors of the late nineteenth and twentieth centuries, and even where such an assumption holds true, those authors do not always deviate significantly from traditional patterns and approaches (see EXEGESIS OF THE QURʾĀN: CLASSICAL AND MEDIEVAL). Many Qurʾān commentaries of this time hardly differ from older ones in the methods applied and the kinds of explanations given. The majority of the authors of such commentaries made ample use of classical sources like al-Zamakhsharī (d. 538/1144), Fakhr al-Dīn al-Rāzī (d. 606/1210) and Ibn Kathīr (d. 774/1373) without necessarily adding anything substantially new to the already available interpretations. One should thus always bear in mind that in the exegesis of the Qurʾān there is a broad current of unbroken tradition continuing to this day. Still, in what follows attention will be directed mainly to innovative trends. The majority of the new approaches to exegesis has so far been developed in the Arab countries and particularly in Egypt. Therefore, this part of the Islamic world will be dealt with most extensively.

Elements of novelty include the content as well as the methods of interpretation. When mentioning content, it should be said, first of all, that new ideas about the meaning of the qurʾānic text emerged largely in answer to new questions which arose from the political, social and cultural changes brought about in Muslim societies by the impact of western civilization. Of particular importance among these were two problems: the compatibility of the qurʾānic world view with the findings of modern science (see SCIENCE AND THE QURʾĀN); and the question of an appropriate political and social order based on qurʾānic principles (see POLITICS AND THE QURʾĀN; COMMUNITY AND SOCIETY IN THE QURʾĀN) which would thus enable Muslims to throw off the yoke of western dominance. For this purpose the qurʾānic message had to be interpreted so as to allow Muslims either to assimilate western models successfully or to work out alternatives believed to be superior to them. One of the problems to be considered in this framework was the question of how qurʾānic provisions referring to the legal status of women could be understood in view of modern aspirations towards equal rights for both sexes (see FEMINISM; GENDER; WOMEN AND THE QURʾĀN). Hitherto unknown methodological approaches sprang partly from new developments in the field of literary studies and communication theory, partly from the need to find practical ways and theoretical justifications for discarding traditional interpretations in favor of new ones more easily acceptable to the contemporary intellect, but without at the same time denying the authority of the revealed text as such. These approaches were usually based on a new understanding of the nature of divine revelation and its mode of action in general.

Kinds of publications containing exegesis of the Qurʾān and discussing exegetical methods

The main place where exegesis of the Qurʾān can be found remains the commentaries. Most of them follow a verse-by-verse approach (*tafsīr musalsal,* i.e. "chained" or sequential commentary). In the majority of cases such commentaries start from the beginning of the first sūra (q.v.; see also FĀTIḤA) and continue — unless unfinished — without interruption until the last verse of the last sūra. An exception is *al-Tafsīr al-ḥadīth* by the Palestinian scholar Muḥammad ʿIzza Darwaza, which is based on a chronological arrangement of the sūras (cf. Sulaymān, *Darwaza*). Some *musalsal* commentaries are limited to larger portions of the text (known as *juzʾ*, pl. *ajāzʾ*) that were already in former times looked upon as units (e.g. Muḥammad ʿAbduh, *Tafsīr juzʾ ʿAmmā,* 1322/1904-5). Some are devoted to a single sūra (e.g. Muḥammad ʿAbduh, *Tafsīr al-Fātiḥa,* 1319/1901-2). In a few cases such commentaries deal only with a selection of sūras made by the author for demonstrating the usefulness of a new exegetical method (ʿĀʾisha ʿAbd al-Raḥmān, *al-Tafsīr al-bayānī,* see below) or the edifying purpose that the exegesis was originally meant to serve (e.g. Shawqī Ḍayf, *Sūrat al-Raḥmān wa-suwar qiṣār*). It should also be said that the traditional genre of commentaries which treat verses considered particularly difficult (see DIFFICULT PASSAGES) is still being pursued (e.g. Rāshid ʿAbdallāh Farḥān's *Tafsīr mushkil al-Qurʾān*). While it is true that most commentaries have been written for the consumption of religious scholars, some are explicitly designed to address the needs of a more general public. This is true, for example, in the case of Mawdūdī's (d. 1979) *Tafhīm al-Qurʾān* (see below), a commentary intended for Indian Muslims of a certain education who, however, do not possess knowledge of Arabic or expertise in the qurʾānic sciences.

The last decades of the twentieth century in particular witnessed the publication of an increasing number of commentaries which classified key passages of the qurʾānic text according to main subjects and treated verses related to the same subject synoptically. The ideas of exegesis underlying this "thematic interpretation" *(tafsīr mawḍūʿī)* and the pertinent theoretical statements proclaimed in them can vary greatly from one author to the next, as will be seen below; also, in such thematic commentaries, the procedures of determining the meaning of single verses sometimes differ hardly at all from those applied in commentaries of the *musalsal* kind. Therefore, this thematic interpretation can oscilate between mere rearrangement of textual material and a distinct method of exegesis with new results. Generally, however, thematic interpretation concentrates upon a limited number of qurʾānic concepts judged by the author to be particularly important. This effect has also been achieved by Maḥmūd Shaltūt in his *Tafsīr al-Qurʾān al-karīm. al-Ajzāʾ al-ʿashara al-ūlā,* who steers a middle course between the *musalsal* and thematic approaches in not commenting upon the text word by word, but focusing attention on key notions (see Jansen, *Egypt,* 14).

Where commentaries concentrate on a single, central qurʾānic theme or just a few (e.g. ʿAbd al-ʿAzīz b. al-Dardīr's *al-Tafsīr al-mawḍūʿī li-āyāt al-tawḥīd fī l-Qurʾān al-karīm*), this genre merges into that of treatises on basic questions of qurʾānic theology (see THEOLOGY AND THE QURʾĀN), such as Daud Rahbar's *God of Justice* or — on a less sophisticated level — ʿĀʾisha ʿAbd al-Raḥmān's *Maqāl fī l-insān. Dirāsa qurʾāniyya.*

In addition, books or articles written in the field of Islamic theology or law that argue from qurʾānic texts — which most of them do to a great extent — include an element of exegesis. Printed collections of sermons, on the other hand, are not as relevant for exegesis as one might expect, since Islamic sermons are nowadays primarily laid out thematically, not exegetically.

Discussions concerning the appropriate methods of exegesis are often located in introductions placed at the beginning of Qurʾān commentaries. A remarkable early modern case in point is Muḥammad ʿAbduh's introduction to his *Tafsīr al-Fātiḥa* (5-21, actually Muḥammad Rashīd Riḍā's account of one of Ābduh's lectures). A small separate treatise about the principles of exegesis, Sir Sayyid Ahmad Khan's *Taḥrīr fī uṣūl al-tafsīr,* was already printed in 1892 (Agra, in Urdu). Since that time quite a few books and articles entirely devoted to methodological problems of interpreting the Qurʾān have been published, most of them since the late 1960's.

Main trends in the exegetical methods and their protagonists

1. Interpreting the Qurʾān from the perspective of Enlightenment rationalism

The first significant innovation in the methods of exegesis, as they had been practised for many centuries, was introduced by two eminent protagonists of Islamic reform: the Indian Sayyid Ahmad Khan (1817-98) and the Egyptian Muḥammad ʿAbduh (1849-1905). Both of them, impressed by the political dominance and economic prosperity of modern Western civilization in the colonial age, ascribed the rise of this civilization to the scientific achievements of the Europeans and embraced a popularized version of the philosophy of the Enlightenment. On this basis they adopted an essentially rationalistic approach to the exegesis of the Qurʾān, working independently of each other and out of somewhat different points of departure and accentuations, but with similar results all the same. Both were inspired with the desire to enable their fellow Muslims in their own countries and elsewhere to share in the blessings of the powerful modern civilization.

For Sayyid Ahmad Khan, the traumatic experience of the Indian mutiny (1857), on the one hand, had roused in him the urge to prove that there is nothing in the Islamic religion which could prevent Indian Muslims from coexisting and cooperating peacefully with the British in a polity held together by a reasonable, morally advanced legal order and founded on scientific thinking. On the other hand, he had personally turned to a modern scientific conception of nature and the universe after many years of exposure to the impact of British intellectuals residing in India. These motives incited him to attempt to demonstrate that there could not be any contradiction between modern natural science and the holy scripture of the Muslims. (For a fundamental study of his principles of exegesis and the underlying ideas, see Troll, *Sayyid Ahmad Khan,* 144-170.)

Sayyid Ahmad Khan's basic notion for understanding qurʾānic revelation (see REVELATION AND INSPIRATION) is expounded in his above-mentioned treatise on the fundamentals of exegesis *(uṣūl al-tafsīr)* and put into practice in several other writings published by him: The law of nature is a practical covenant (q.v.) by which God has bound himself to humanity (see NATURAL WORLD AND THE QURʾĀN), while the promise and threat (see REWARD AND PUNISHMENT) contained in the revelation is a verbal one. There can be no contradiction between both covenants; otherwise God would have contradicted himself, which is unthinkable. His word, the revelation, cannot contradict his work, i.e.

nature (see CREATION). Sayyid Ahmad Khan complements this assumption with a second axiom: Any religion imposed by God — and hence also Islam, the religion meant to be the final one for all humankind — must necessarily be within the grasp of the human intellect, since it is possible to perceive the obligatory character of a religion only through the intellect (q.v.). Therefore it is impossible that the qurʾānic revelation could contain anything contradicting scientific reason.

If some contemporary Muslims believe the opposite, this does not stem, in Sayyid Ahmad Khan's opinion, from the qurʾānic text as such, but from an erroneous direction within the exegetical tradition: The holy book only seems to contradict modern science in certain places if one has not noticed that the passage in question must be understood metaphorically. According to Sayyid Ahmad Khan this metaphorical interpretation *(taʾwīl)* is, *nota bene,* not a secondary reinterpretation of an obvious meaning of the text, but a reconstruction of its original meaning: God himself had chosen to use certain metaphorical expressions in the text only on account of their currency as common metaphor (q.v.) in the Arabic usage of the Prophet's day, making them comprehensible to his contemporaries, the first audience for what had been revealed to him. Exegetes must, therefore, first try to understand the text as understood by the ancient Arabs to whom it was adressed in the time of the Prophet (see LANGUAGE AND STYLE OF THE QURʾĀN; PRE-ISLAMIC ARABIA AND THE QURʾĀN).

The practical result of Sayyid Ahmad Khan's exegetical endeavor on the basis of these principles is to eliminate miraculous events from his understanding of the qurʾānic text as much as possible, as well as all kinds of supranatural phenomena and other phenomena incompatible with his own scientific world view (see MIRACLE). In the case of doubt, the reasoning of modern science, not the meaning of the text which was most likely accessible to the ancient Arabs, is his criterion of truth (q.v.). He thus explains the prophet's night journey (see ASCENSION) as an event that took place only in a dream (see DREAMS AND SLEEP), while the jinn (q.v.) become, in his interpretation, some sort of primitive savages living in the jungle, etc.

Muḥammad ʿAbduh, taking over a well-known idea that can be traced back to the philosophy of the late phase of the European Enlightenment, conceived of the history of humankind as a process of development analogous to that of the individual and saw in the "heavenly religions" educational means by which God had directed this development towards its final stage of maturity, the age of science. According to him, Muslims are perfectly fit for sharing in the civilization of this age and can even play a leading part in it, since Islam is the religion of reason and progress. The Qurʾān was revealed in order to draw the minds of human beings to reasonable conceptions about their happiness in this world as well as in the hereafter. For ʿAbduh this means not only that the content of the Qurʾān conforms to the laws of nature, but also that it informs people about the laws that are effective in the historical development of nations and societies.

In this sense, the whole qurʾānic revelation seeks to bestow God's guidance *(hidāya)* upon humankind, and hence it has to be interpreted so as to make it easier for its audience to understand the goals God desires them to attain. Exegetes should devote themselves to the service of God's enlightening guidance and concentrate their efforts on searching the qurʾānic text to uncover God's signs (q.v.; *āyāt*) in nature and to discern the moral and legal norms of which the text speaks (see ETHICS AND THE QUR'ĀN). This is their proper task rather than digressing into complicated scholarly discussions about the possible sense of individual words and phrases or immersing themselves in a variety of levels of meaning — whether grammatical or mystical (see GRAMMAR AND THE QUR'ĀN; ṢŪFISM AND THE QUR'ĀN) — that might be discernible in the text, particularly since these various understandings were quite unfamiliar to the Arabs of the Prophet's time. In order to grasp that to which God intends to guide humankind, the text has to be understood — and here ʿAbduh agrees once more with Sayyid Ahmad Khan — according to the meaning its words had for the Prophet's contemporaries, the first audience to which the revelation was disclosed. Moreover, commentators must resist the temptation to make qur'ānic statements definite where they have been left indefinite *(mubham)* in the text itself — e.g., by identifying persons whose proper names have not been mentioned — as well as the temptation to fill gaps in qur'ānic narratives (q.v.) with Jewish traditions of biblical or apocryphal origin *(Isrā'īliyyāt)* since these were handed down by previous generations of scholars who never stripped them of what contradicted revelation and reason (*Tafsīr al-Fātiḥa*, 6, 7, 11-12, 15, 17).

The characteristic features of ʿAbduh's own exegetical practice are reflected most clearly in his voluminous commentary widely known as *Tafsīr al-Manār,* which has become a standard work quoted by many later authors alongside the classical commentaries. ʿAbduh's actual share in it consists of the record of a series of lectures that he gave at al-Azhar University around the year 1900 which covered the text of the Qur'ān from the beginning to Q 4:124. His pupil Muḥammad Rashīd Riḍā took notes of these lectures which he afterwards elaborated and showed to his teacher for approval or correction. In addition, he complemented the passages based on ʿAbduh's lectures by inserting explanations which he marked as his own — and in which he displayed a more traditionalist attitude than that of ʿAbduh (cf. Jomier, *Commentaire*). After ʿAbduh's death Riḍā continued the commentary on his own to Q 12:107.

ʿAbduh divides the qur'ānic text into groups of verses constituting logical units and treats the text of these paragraphs as a single entity. This corresponds to his view that single words or phrases are not the primary subject of interest for the commentator, but rather the didactic aim of the passage, and that the correct interpretation of an expression can often be grasped only by considering its context *(siyāq)*. His interpretations, which he often enriches with lengthy excursions, do not always consistently follow his own declared principles but show a general tendency towards stressing the rationality of Islam and its positive attitude towards science, while aiming at the same time to eradicate elements of popular belief and practice which he considers to be superstitious. For ʿAbduh, too, in the case of doubt, science is the decisive criterion for the meaning of qur'ānic wording.

Another Egyptian author, Muḥammad Abū Zayd, who published a commentary in 1930, can also be ranked among the exponents of a rationalistic exegesis inspired by a popular appropriation of the European Enlightenment. His book, *al-Hidāya wa-l-ʿirfān fī tafsīr al-Qur'ān bi-l-Qur'ān*, created a considerable stir and was finally confiscated by the authorities at the instigation of al-Azhar University, which condemned it in an official report (Jansen, *Egypt*, 88-9). The methodological device hinted at in its title — namely that of explaining particular qur'ānic passages by comparing them to parallel passages which address the same subject in a more detailed way or in similar, though not identical terms — was not completely novel even then, and has been taken up more than once by later commentators, so far without negative reactions on the part of the guardians of orthodoxy. What gave offence was apparently not the methodology so much as the ideas Muḥammad Abū Zayd tried to propagate by making a very selective use of it: He argues that a far-reaching *ijtihād* is permitted with respect to traditional norms of Islamic law, and he does his best to explain away any miracles and supranatural occurrences in the qurʾānic narratives concerning the prophets (see PROPHETS AND PROPHETHOOD).

Some commentaries contain elements of rationalistic exegesis in line with the insights of Sayyid Ahmad Khan or ʿAbduh, but use them only to a limited extent. Among these are *Tarjumān al-Qurʾān* (1930) by the Indian author Abū l-Kalām Āzād and *Majālis al-tadhkīr* (1929-39) by the Algerian reformist leader ʿAbd al-Ḥamīd Ibn Bādīs.

2. The so-called scientific exegesis of the Qurʾān

Scientific exegesis *(tafsīr ʿilmī)* is to be understood in light of the assumption that all sorts of findings of the modern natural sciences have been anticipated in the Qurʾān and that many unambiguous references to them can be discovered in its verses (q.v.). The scientific findings already confirmed in the Qurʾān range from Copernican cosmology (see COSMOLOGY) to the properties of electricity, from the regularities of chemical reactions to the agents of infectious diseases. The whole method amounts to reading into the text what normally would not ordinarily be seen there. Often trained in medicine, pharmacy or other natural sciences, even agricultural sciences, scientific exegetes are, for the most part, not professional theologians. This kind of exegesis has, however, gained entry into the Qurʾān commentaries of religious scholars as well.

It should be mentioned that Muḥammad ʿAbduh's commentaries are not themselves devoid of attempts to read discoveries of modern science into the text. As is well-known, he considered the possibility that the jinn mentioned in the Qurʾān could be equated to microbes. He also considered it legitimate to understand the flocks of birds which, according to Q 105, had thrown stones on the People of the Elephant (q.v.), to be swarms of flies which, by their polluted legs, had transmitted a disease to them (*Tafsīr juzʾ ʿAmmā*, 158). ʿAbduh's interest in such interpretations, however, did not parallel that of the supporters of scientific exegesis: He wanted to prove to his public that the qurʾānic passages in question were not contrary to reason by modern scientific standards, whereas proponents of scientific exegesis hope to prove that the Qurʾān is many centuries ahead of western scientists, since it mentions what they discovered only in modern times. Most enthusiasts of scientific exegesis regard this assumed chronological priority of the Qurʾān in the field of scientific knowledge as a particularly splendid instance of its *iʿjāz*, miraculous inimitability (q.v.), appreciating this aspect of *iʿjāz* all the more as a highly effective apologetical argument, in their view, to be directed against the West.

The basic pattern of scientific exegesis was not completely new: Several authors of classical Qurʾān commentaries, notably Fakhr al-Dīn al-Rāzī, had already expressed the idea that all the sciences were contained in the Qurʾān. Consequently, they had tried to detect in its text the astronomical knowledge of their times, then largely adopted from the Perso-Indian and Greco-Hellenistic heritage. Efforts of this kind were still carried on by Maḥmūd Shihāb al-Dīn al-Ālūsī (d. 1856) in his *Rūḥ al-maʿānī*, a commentary which, however, does not yet show any familiarity with modern western science.

The first author who attained some publicity by practicing scientific exegesis in the modern sense, i.e. by finding in the qurʾānic text references to modern scientific discoveries and advances, was the physician Muḥammad b. Aḥmad al-Iskandarānī; one of his two pertinent books printed around the year 1880 bears the promising title *Kashf al-asrār al-nūrāniyya al-qurʾāniyya fī-mā yataʿallaq bi-l-ajrām al-samāwiyya wa-l-arḍiyya wa-l-ḥayawānāt wa-l-nabāt wa-l-jawāhir al-maʿdiniyya* (i.e. "Uncovering the luminous qurʾānic secrets pertaining to the heavenly and terrestrial bodies, the animals, the plants and the metallic substances," 1297/1879-80).

The most prominent representative of this *tafsīr ʿilmī* in the early twentieth century was the Egyptian Shaykh Ṭanṭāwī Jawharī, author of *al-Jawāhir fī tafsīr al-Qurʾān al-karīm* (1341/1922-3). This work is not a commentary in the customary sense, but rather an encyclopaedic survey of the modern sciences or, more exactly, of what the author classes with them — including such disciplines as spiritism *(ʿilm taḥḍīr al-arwāḥ)*. Jawharī claims that these sciences were already mentioned in certain qurʾānic verses, passages upon which his lengthy didactic expositions of pertinent topics are based. All this is interspersed with tables, drawings and photographs. Unlike most other enthusiasts of scientific exegesis, Jawharī did not employ this method primarily for the apologetic purposes, mentioned above, of proving the *iʿjāz* of the Qurʾān. His main purpose was to convince his fellow Muslims that in modern times they should concern themselves much more with the sciences than with Islamic law; only in this way could they regain political independence and power. Other authors wrote books devoted to the scientific exegesis of qurʾānic verses mainly with apologetic intentions, among them ʿAbd al-ʿAzīz Ismāʿīl (*al-Islām wa-l-ṭibb al-ḥadīth*, Cairo 1938, reprint 1957), Ḥanafī Aḥmad (*Muʿjizat al-Qurʾān fī waṣf al-kāʾināt*, Cairo 1954, two reprints entitled *al-Tafsīr al-ʿilmī lil-āyāt al-kawniyya*, 1960 and 1968) and ʿAbd al-Razzāq Nawfal (*al-Qurʾān wa-l-ʿilm al-ḥadīth*, Cairo 1378/1959).

Some authors of well-known Qurʾān commentaries who do not rely exclusively on the method of scientific exegesis, but deal with the qurʾānic text as a whole (not only with verses lending themselves to this method), nevertheless practice scientific exegesis in the explanation of particular verses. Thus, elements of *tafsīr ʿilmī* occur, for example, in *Ṣafwat al-ʿirfān* (= *al-Muṣḥaf al-mufassar*, 1903) by Muḥammad Farīd Wajdī, in the *Majālis al-tadhkīr* (1929-39) by ʿAbd al-Ḥamīd Ibn Bādīs, and in *al-Mīzān* (1973-85) by the Imāmite scholar Muḥammad Ḥusayn Ṭabāṭabāʾī (d. 1982).

The scientific method of interpretation did not find general approval among Muslim authors who wrote Qurʾān commentaries or discussed exegetical methods. Quite a few of them rejected this method outright, like Muḥammad Rashīd Riḍā, Amīn al-Khūlī (whose detailed refutation of it [*Manāhij tajdīd*, 287-96] has often been referred to by later authors), Maḥmūd Shaltūt and Sayyid Quṭb (for these and other critics of the *tafsīr ʿilmī* and their arguments, see al-Muḥtasib, *Ittijāhāt al-tafsīr*, 302-13 and Abū Ḥajar, *al-Tafsīr al-ʿilmī*, 295-336). Their most important objections to scientific exegesis can be summarized as follows: (1) It is lexicographically untenable, since it falsely attributes modern meanings to the qurʾānic vocabulary; (2) it neglects the contexts of words or phrases within the qurʾānic text, and also the occasions of revelation (q.v.; *asbāb al-nuzūl*) where these are transmitted; (3) it ignores the fact that, for the Qurʾān to be comprehensible for its first audience, the words of the Qurʾān had to conform to the language and the intellectual horizon of the ancient Arabs at the Prophet's time — an argument already used by the Andalusian Mālikite scholar al-Shāṭibī (d. 790/1388) against the scientific exegesis of his time (*al-Muwāfaqāt fī uṣūl al-sharīʿa,* ii, 69-82); (4) it does not take notice of the fact that scientific knowledge and scientific theories are always incomplete and provisory by their very nature; therefore, the derivation of scientific knowledge and scientific theories in qurʾānic verses is actually tantamount to limiting the validity of these verses to the time for which the results of the science in question are accepted; (5) most importantly, it fails to comprehend that the Qurʾān is not a scientific book, but a religious one designed to guide human beings by imparting to them a creed and a set of moral values (or, as Islamists such as Sayyid Quṭb prefer to put it, the distinctive principles of the Islamic system; cf. below). Despite the weight of all these objections, some authors still believe that the *tafsīr ʿilmī* can and should be continued — at least as an additional method particularly useful for proving the *iʿjāz* of the Qurʾān to those who do not know Arabic and are thus unable to appreciate the miraculous style of the holy book (see Hind Shalabī, *al-Tafsīr al-ʿilmī,* esp. 63-69 and 149-164; Ibn ʿĀshūr, *Tafsīr al-taḥrīr,* i, 104, 128).

3. Interpreting the Qurʾān from the perspective of literary studies

The use of methods of literary studies for the exegesis of the Qurʾān was initiated mainly by Amīn al-Khūlī (d. 1967), a professor of Arabic language and literature at the Egyptian University (later King Fuʾād University, now University of Cairo). He did not write a Qurʾān commentary himself, but devoted a considerable part of his lectures to exegetical questions and also dealt with the history and current state of methodological requirements of exegesis in his post-1940's publications.

Already in 1933, his famous colleague Ṭāhā Ḥusayn had remarked in his booklet *Fī l-ṣayf* that the holy scriptures of the Jews, Christians and Muslims belong to the common literary heritage of humankind (see RELIGIOUS PLURALISM AND THE QURʾĀN; SCRIPTURE AND THE QURʾĀN) as much as the works of Homer, Shakespeare and Goethe, and that Muslims should begin to study the Qurʾān as a work of literary art and use methods of modern literary research for its analysis, just as some Jewish and Christian scholars had done with the Bible (*al-Majmūʿa al-kāmila li-muʾallafāt al-duktūr Ṭāhā Ḥusayn,* Beirut 1974², xiv, 215-9). He had added that such an approach was not to be expected from the clerics *(shuyūkh)* of al-Azhar, but that there was no reason to leave the study of holy scriptures to men of religion alone — why should people not be entitled to express their opinions about such books as objects of research in the field of literary art, "taking no account of their religious relevance *(bi-qaṭʿi l-naẓari ʿan makānatihā l-dīniyya)*" (ibid., 216)? He concluded, however, that it would still be dangerous in his country to embark publicly on an analysis of the Qurʾān as a literary text. Amīn al-Khūlī shared the basic idea contained in these remarks and developed them into a concrete program; several of his students, along with their own students, tried to carry it out, some of them not without bitter consequences, as foreseen by Ṭāhā Ḥusayn.

According to Amīn al-Khūlī, the Qurʾān is "the greatest book of the Arabic language and its most important literary work *(kitāb al-ʿarabiyya al-akbar wa-atharuhā l-adabī al-aʿẓam)*" (*Manāhij tajdīd,* 303; see LITERATURE AND THE QURʾĀN). In his view, the adequate methods for studying this book as a work of literary art do not differ from those that apply to any other works of literature. Two fundamental preliminary steps have to be taken: (1) The historical background and the circumstances of its genesis — or in the case of the Qurʾān, its entry into this world by revelation — must be explored. For this purpose, one has to study the religious and cultural traditions and the social situation of the ancient Arabs, to whom the prophetic message was first adressed, their language (see ARABIC LANGUAGE) and previous literary achievements, the chronology of the enunciation of the qurʾānic text by the Prophet (see CHRONOLOGY AND THE QURʾĀN), the occasions of revelation *(asbāb al-nuzūl),* etc. (2) Keeping in mind all relevant knowledge gathered in this way, one has to establish the exact meaning of the text word by word as it was understood by its first listeners (see FORM AND STRUCTURE OF THE QURʾĀN). In accordance with al-Shāṭibī, al-Khūlī assumes that God, in order to make his intention understood by the Arabs of the Prophet's time, had to use their language and to adapt his speech to their modes of comprehension, which were themselves determined by their traditional views and concepts. Hence, before the divine intention of the text can be determined, one has first to grasp its meaning as understood by the ancient Arabs — and this can be done, as al-Khūlī emphasizes, "regardless of any religious consideration *(dūna naẓarin ilā ayyi ʿtibārin dīnī)*" (*Manāhij tajdīd,* 304). It then becomes possible to study the artistic qualities of the Qurʾān, by using the same categories and by keeping to the same rules as are applied in the study of literary works. The style of the Qurʾān can thus be explored in given passages by studying the principles which determine the choice of words, the peculiarities of the construction of sentences, the figures of speech employed, etc. (see RHETORIC OF THE QURʾĀN; SEMANTICS OF THE QURʾĀN). Likewise, one can examine the typical structure of passages belonging to a particular literary genre. Since works of literary art are characterized by a specific relation between content or theme on the one hand and formal means of expression on the other, al-Khūlī attaches particular importance to the thematic units of the qurʾānic text and stresses that a correct explanation requires commentators to consider all verses and passages which speak to the same subject, instead of confining their attention to one single verse or passage (ibid., 304-6). At the same time, al-Khūlī's approach is based on a particular understanding of the nature of a literary text: For him, literature, like art in general, is primarily a way of appealing to the public's emotions, as a means of directing them and their decisions. He therefore argues that the interpreter should also try to explain the psychological effects which the artistic qualities of the qurʾānic text, in particular its language, had on its first audience.

Shukrī ʿAyyād, who wrote his M.A. thesis, *Min waṣf al-Qurʾān al-karīm li-yawm al-dīn wa-l-ḥisāb* (n.d., unpublished, although a critical summary exists in al-Sharqāwī, *Ittijāhāt,* 213-6) under al-Khūlī's supervision, is reputed to have been the first to carry out a research project based on these principles.

Also among al-Khūlī's students was ʿĀʾisha ʿAbd al-Raḥmān (pen name, Bint al-Shāṭiʾ), his wife. Her commentary, *al-Tafsīr al-bayānī lil-Qurʾān al-karīm,* is designed in conformity with the main features of al-Khūlī's methodological conception and in its preface explicitly refers to the suggestions received from him. ʿĀʾisha ʿAbd al-Raḥmān consciously selected a number of shorter sūras to show in a particularly impressive way the fruits to be gathered by the application of al-Khūlī's method. Each of them constitutes a thematic unit, and the author gives a rough indication of the place of the respective sūra in the chronology of the Prophet's enunciation of the qurʾānic text and expounds the significance of its theme during this time in comparison with other phases of the Prophet's activity. To illustrate this point, she hints at other relevant sūras (q.v.) or parts of them, and discusses questions of the occasions of revelation *(asbāb al-nuzūl)*. In doing so she attempts to give at least part of an outline of the historical background of the sūra under consideration (see HISTORY AND THE QURʾĀN). She highlights the most striking stylistic features of this sūra, e.g. relative length or shortness of sentences, accumulation of certain rhetorical figures, frequent occurrence of certain morphological or syntactical patterns, etc., and tries to demonstrate the specific relation of these features to the corresponding theme, citing a host of parallel verses from other sūras which treat the same subject or show the same stylistic features. She also considers the emotional effect these peculiarities are meant to have on the listeners and attends to such questions as the impact of qurʾānic rhymes (see RHYMED PROSE) on the choice of words and of the compository structure of the sūras. Additionally, she gives a careful verse-by-verse commentary in order to explain every single difficult word and phrase by comparing other qurʾānic verses which contain the same or similar expressions, quoting verses from ancient Arabic poetry, referring to classical Arabic dictionaries and discussing the opinions of the authors of — mostly classical — Qurʾān commentaries. In all this she displays a high degree of erudition. In general, ʿĀʾisha ʿAbd al-Raḥmān's commentary, as well as her other publications treating problems of the exegesis of the Qurʾān, have found a favorable reception even among conservative religious scholars, as she avoids broaching dogmatically sensitive points and apparently does not do anything but prove once more the stylistic *iʿjāz* of the Qurʾān, now on the level of advanced philological methods.

Another student of al-Khūlī, Muḥammad Aḥmad Khalaf Allāh, faced considerable difficulties in his use of al-Khūlī's approach and was exposed to the anger of leading religious scholars *(ʿulamāʾ)* at al-Azhar. In 1947 he submitted his doctoral thesis *al-Fann al-qaṣaṣī fī l-Qurʾān al-karīm* to the King Fuʾād University (now University of Cairo). On the basis of al-Khūlī's idea of literature as an instrument of appealing to emotions and directing them according to the author's intentions, Khalaf Allāh had set about studying the artistic means by which, according to his conviction, the qurʾānic narratives were so uniquely and effectively fashioned (Wielandt, *Offenbarung*, 139-52).

In order to be psychologically effective, narratives need not correspond absolutely to the historical facts. Khalaf Allāh even considers other requirements to be much more relevant for this purpose: They must refer to the listeners' customary language, previous conceptions and narrative traditions — in line with what al-Shāṭibī and al-Khūlī had already said about the importance of understanding the original reception of the message. They must be adapted to the listeners' feelings and mental condition. Finally, they must be well constructed. He thus arrives at the conclusion that the qurʾānic narratives about prophets of earlier times are, to a large extent, not historically true: Although Muḥammad's Arab contemporaries certainly believed them to be true reports about what actually happened, God used them in the Qurʾān not primarily as historical facts *(wāqiʿ taʾrīkhī)*, but as psychological facts *(wāqiʿ nafsī)*, i.e. as a means of influencing the listeners' emotions (*al-Fann*, Cairo 1965[3], 50, 111). In order to achieve this, God took the subject matter of these qurʾānic narratives from stories and ideas already familiar to the ancient Arabs. Moreover, for the purpose of supporting Muḥammad (q.v.) emotionally during the latter's often exhausting confrontation with the heathen Meccans (see OPPOSITION TO MUḤAMMAD), God reflected the Prophet's state of mind in the qurʾānic stories about earlier prophets by shaping these narratives according to Muḥammad's own experience.

Obviously, this interpretation implies that the content of the qurʾānic narratives about prophets corresponds for the most part to the content of the Prophet's consciousness as well as that of the original audience of the divine message. This makes it possible to trace important features of these narratives to what Muḥammad and his Arab contemporaries knew from local traditions or what Muḥammad could have said himself on the basis of his experience. According to Khalaf Allāh, however, this correspondence results from the fact that God, the only author of the holy book, had marvellously adapted the qurʾānic narratives to Muḥammad's situation and that of his audience. Khalaf Allāh never doubts that the entire text of the Qurʾān was inspired literally by God and that Muḥammad had no share whatsoever in its production.

Nevertheless Khalaf Allāh's thesis was rejected by the examining board of his own university, one of the arguments being that its results were religiously questionable. Moreover, a commission of leading scholars *(ʿulamāʾ)* of al-Azhar issued a memorandum classifying Khalaf Allāh as a criminal because he had denied that the qurʾānic narratives were historically true in their entirety. A short time later he was dismissed from his position at the university on another pretext.

Occasional attempts at studying the Qurʾān as a work of literary art were also made by authors not belonging to al-Khūlī's school, again, mainly Egyptians (for details up to the 1960's, see al-Bayyūmī, *Khuṭuwāt al-tafsīr al-bayānī*, 336-9). Sayyid Quṭb's *al-Taṣwīr al-fannī fī l-Qurʾān* bears witness to the aesthetic sensitivity of the author — who had previously made his name as a literary critic — and contains some cogent observations, but in contrast to the works of al-Khūlī's students it is not based on the systematic application of a method. The longest chapter of *al-Taṣwīr al-fannī* is devoted to the qurʾānic narratives; unlike Khalaf Allāh, Sayyid Quṭb does not voice any doubts about their historical truth. In short, it is possible to state that, since the 1970's, an increased interest in studying the qurʾānic narrative art has emerged (see e.g. ʿAbd al-Karīm Khaṭīb, *al-Qaṣaṣ al-qurʾānī fī manṭiqihi wa-mafhūmihi;* Iltihāmī Naqra, *Sīkūlūjiyyat al-qiṣṣa fī l-Qurʾān;* al-Qaṣabī Maḥmūd Zalaṭ, *Qaḍāyā l-tikrār fī l-qaṣaṣ al-qurʾānī;* Muḥammad Khayr Maḥmūd al-ʿAdawī, *Maʿālim al-qiṣṣa fī l-Qurʾān al-karīm*). Cognizant of Khallaf Allāh's fate, however, those authors who have addressed this topic in more recent times have tended to draw their conclusions rather cautiously.

4. Endeavors to develop a new theory of exegesis taking full account of the historicity of the Qurʾān

The school of al-Khūlī had already given much importance to the task of recovering the meaning of the Qurʾān as understood at the time of the Prophet and looked upon the Qurʾān as a literary text which had to be interpreted, as any other literary work, in its historical context. Since the late 1950's several scholars have come to the conviction that the qurʾānic text is related to history in a much more comprehensive way and that this fact necessitates a fundamental change of exegetical methods.

One such scholar is (Muhammad) Daud Rahbar, a Pakistani scholar who later taught in the United States. In a paper read at the International Islamic Colloquium in Lahore in January 1958, he emphasized that the eternal word of God contained in the Qurʾān — which is addressed to people today as much as to Muḥammad's contemporaries — "speaks with reference to human situations and events of the last 23 years of the Prophet's life in particular," as "no message can be sent to men except with reference to actual concrete situations" (Challenge, 279). Rahbar calls urgently on Muslim exegetes to consider what this means for the methods of dealing with the revealed text. In this framework, he attaches special significance to the question of the occasions of revelation *(asbāb al-nuzūl)* and to the phenomenon of the abrogation (q.v.) of earlier regulations by later ones *(al-nāsikh wa-l-mansūkh)* in the qurʾānic text. He expresses the expectation that exegetes react to the challenges of modern life more flexibly by taking notice of the fact that the divine word had to be adapted to historical circumstances from the very beginning, and that God even modified his word during the few years of Muḥammad's prophetic activity in accordance with the circumstances.

Fazlur Rahman, also of Pakistani origin and until 1988 professor of Islamic thought at the University of Chicago, proposed in his *Islam and Modernity: Transformation of an Intellectual Tradition* (1982) a solution for the hermeneutical problem of disentangling the eternal message of the Qurʾān from its adaptation to the historical circumstances of Muḥammad's mission and discovering its meaning for believers of today. According to him, the qurʾānic revelation primarily "consists of moral, religious, and social pronouncements that respond to specific problems in concrete historical situations," particularly the problems of Meccan commercial society at the Prophet's time (see MECCA); hence the process of interpretation nowadays requires "a double movement, from the present situation to qurʾānic times, then back to the present" (ibid., 5). This approach consists of three steps: First, "one has to understand the import or meaning of a given statement by studying the historical situation or problem to which it was the answer"; secondly, one has "to generalize those specific answers and enunciate them as statements of general moral-social objectives that can be 'distilled' from specific texts in the light of the socio-historical background and the... *ratio legis*"; and thirdly, "the general has to be embodied in the present concrete socio-historical context" (ibid., 6-7). A methodological conception coming close to this approach, although confined to the interpretation of qurʾānic legal norms, had already been evolved since the 1950's by ʿAllāl al-Fāsī, the famous Mālikite scholar and leader of the Moroccan independence movement (cf. *al-Naqd al-dhātī,* 125, 221; *Maqāṣid al-sharīʿa,* 190-3, 240-1).

A remarkable recent development in the arena of theoretical reflection on the appropriate methods of interpreting the Qurʾān is the plea of the Egyptian scholar Naṣr Ḥāmid Abū Zayd for a new exegetical paradigm, a plea made in several of his publications, particularly in his *Mafhūm al-naṣṣ* (1990). He submitted this book to the Faculty of Arts of the University of Cairo, where he was teaching in the Arabic Department, together with his application for promotion to the rank of full professor.

Abū Zayd's approach to the exegesis of the Qurʾān continues the tradition of al-Khūlī's school to a certain extent, but at the same time generalizes what had been the starting point of al-Khūlī's methodology, namely his idea about the form in which the Qurʾān can actually be subjected to interpretation. Whereas al-Khūlī had stressed that the Qurʾān is, above all else, a literary work and must be analyzed as such, Abū Zayd simply states that it is a text *(naṣṣ)* and must be understood according to the scientific principles which apply to the understanding of texts in general. His conception of what it means to understand a text is based on a model of the process of communication first introduced by the American mathematician and information theorist C.E. Shannon (in *The mathematical theory of information,* published in 1947 in co-authorship with W. Weaver) and widely accepted since the 1960's among experts of linguistic as well as literary text theory. The model can be presented in the following terms: The information contained in a message can be understood only if the sender transmits it in a code (i.e. a system of signs) known to the recipient. According to Abū Zayd this model is necessarily valid also for the process of revelation, in which a divine message is transmitted to human beings: The Prophet, the first recipient, would not have been able to understand the revealed text if it had not been fitted into a code understandable to him, and the same applies to his audience, the people to which it was sent. The code which is understandable to a prophet and to the target group of his message consists of their common language and the content of their consciousness, which is to a large extent determined by their social situation and their cultural tradition. Hence God must have adapted the qurʾānic revelation to the language, the social situation and the cultural tradition of the Arabs of Muḥammad's time. This has far-reaching consequences for the methods of exegesis: In order to be able to understand the divine message, the exegetes of today have, on the one hand, to familiarize themselves with the code tied to the specific historical situation of the Prophet and his Arab contemporaries, i.e. those peculiarities of language, society and culture that are not theirs any more; only in that way will they be able to identify in the qurʾānic text the elements belonging to this code and to distinguish them from the immutably valid substance of the revelation. On the other hand, they have to translate the code of the primary recipients, the Prophet and his Arab contemporaries, into a code understandable to themselves, i.e. into the language and the social and cultural situation of their own time. This also means that they cannot rely uncritically on the long exegetical tradition from the Prophet's time to their own: The commentators of past centuries, such as al-Zamakhsharī or Fakhr al-Dīn al-Rāzī, certainly did their best to translate the divine message into the codes of their respective times, but our time has a code of its own.

Obviously, this methodical paradigm makes it possible to interpret the qurʾānic text in such a way that conceptions corresponding to the social and cultural context of the Prophet's preaching, but not tenable for the interpreter of today, can be classed as belonging to a bygone historical situation and not obligatory anymore, without discarding the belief in the literal revelation of the Qurʾān and in the everlasting validity of its message. In fact, Abū Zayd has always declared unequivocally that he stays firm in this belief and that it is his conviction that the historical and cultural code in the text of the Qurʾān has been used by God himself, its sole author, and was not brought into it by Muḥammad.

Still, Shaykh ʿAbd al-Ṣabūr Shāhīn, a

member of the promotion board examining Abū Zayd's publications, voted against his advancement to the position of full professor, charging him, among other things, with a lack of orthodoxy. Several other supporters of traditionalist or Islamist views accused him of heresy *(ilḥād)* or unbelief *(kufr)*. At the instigation of a member of an Islamist organization, in 1995 a court in Cairo nullified his marriage on the grounds that he had abandoned the Islamic religion and thus could not be married to a Muslim woman. The Egyptian Court of Cassation failed to anull this verdict. As he was in danger of being "executed" as an apostate (see APOSTASY) by Islamist fanatics, he had to accept an appointment at a European university.

Mohammed Arkoun, a scholar of Algerian origin who taught in Paris for many years, arrived at methodological conclusions quite similar to those of Abū Zayd, but by a different theoretical approach. According to Arkoun, the *fait coranique*, i.e. the fact to which all attempts at understanding the Qurʾān have to refer in the final analysis, is the originally oral prophetic speech (see ORALITY; ISLĀM) which the Prophet himself and his audience believed to be God's revelation. This speech, which is attested in, but not identical with, the written text of the ʿUthmānic recension of the Qurʾān (see CODICES OF THE QURʾĀN; COLLECTION OF THE QURʾĀN), was performed in a language and in textual genres tied to a specific historical situation, and in mythical and symbolic modes of expression (see SEMIOTICS AND NATURE IN THE QURʾĀN; SYMBOLIC IMAGERY). It already contains a theological interpretation of its own nature and must be subjected to an analysis of its structure. The whole exegetical tradition is a process of appropriation of this *fait coranique* by the various factions of the Muslim community. The text as such is open to a potentially infinite range of ever new interpretations as long as history continues, although the advocates of orthodoxy insist on absolutizing the results of a particular interpretation established at an early stage of this process. Any scientific study of the Qurʾān and of the exegetical tradition referring to it has to keep in mind that religious truth, insofar as it can be understood by Muslims as well as by adherents of other "book religions," becomes effective provided it exists in a dialectical relation between the revealed text and history. Contemporary scholars must use the instruments of historical semiotics and sociolinguistics in order to distinguish particular traditional interpretations of the qurʾānic text from the normative meaning which this text might have for present-day readers.

5. Exegesis in search of a new immediacy to the Qurʾān

All exegetical trends outlined so far — including scientific exegesis, whose supporters claim that the Qurʾān is centuries ahead of modern science — are in one way or another characterized by a marked awareness of the cultural distance between the world in which the qurʾānic message was primarily communicated and the modern world. In contrast to these approaches, the Islamist exegesis tends to assume that it is possible for Muslims today to regain immediate access to the meaning of the qurʾānic text by returning to the belief of the first Muslims and actively struggling for the restoration of the pristine Islamic social order. It is in this later form of exegesis that the author's underlying conception of the revealed text often finds expression. For example, Sayyid Quṭb in his Qurʾān commentary, *Fī ẓilāl al-Qurʾān* (1952-65), insists that the Qurʾān in its entirety is God's message, and the instructions concerning the "Islamic system" or "method" *(niẓām islāmī* or *manhaj islāmī)* contained in it are valid forever. The Qur'ān is thus always contemporary, in any age. The task is not primarily that of translating the original meaning of the qur'ānic text into the language and world view of modern human beings, but that of putting it into practice, as done by the Prophet and his first followers, who took seriously God's claim to absolute sovereignty (*ḥākimiyya* in Abū l-Aʿlā' Mawdūdī's term) and set up the perfect "Islamic system."

One of the consequences of this goal — i.e. achieving the system of the first Muslims in the way they followed qur'ānic instructions — is the marked preference usually shown by Islamist commentators for ḥadīth materials in their references to the exegetic tradition (see ḤADĪTH AND THE QUR'ĀN; SĪRA AND THE QUR'ĀN). This can be seen in Sayyid Quṭb's commentary, in Mawdūdī's *Tafhīm al-Qur'ān* (1949-72) and also in Saʿīd Ḥawwā's *al-Asās fī l-tafsīr* (1405/1985), the (largely ill-structured and much less original) commentary of a leading Syrian Muslim Brother. Although these authors quote classical commentators such as al-Zamakhsharī, Fakhr al-Dīn al-Rāzī or al-Bayḍāwī (d. 716/1316) here and there, they suspect them of having succumbed to the corrupting influences of Greek philosophy and *Isrā'īliyyāt*. When relying on "sound" ḥadīth materials, however, they feel they are on the firm ground of the Prophet's own commentary and hence also of the intentions of the revealed text as understood by the first Muslims.

The Islamist ideal of subordinating oneself to the divine word as immediately as the first Muslims had done can produce positive as well as questionable exegetical results. This becomes clearly visible in Sayyid Quṭb's *Fī ẓilāl al-Qur'ān* where the author generally listens to the qur'ānic text with a great deal of personal attention and in relative independence of the exegetical tradition. On the one hand, this attitude of intense and direct listening sometimes enables him to grasp the original meaning and spirit of a given qur'ānic passage more adequately than many exegetes since the medieval period have been able to do. On the other hand, his presumed immediacy also tends to make him ignore or play down points in which the qur'ānic text cannot be easily harmonized with modern ideas.

6. Conceptions associated with the thematic interpretation of the Qur'ān

As stated above, the thematic interpretation *(tafsīr mawḍūʿī)* of the Qur'ān is not always equivalent to a complete break with the exegetical methods applied in traditional commentaries of the *musalsal* kind. Most authors, however, in reflecting on thematic interpretation, agree to a large extent about the advantages of concentrating one's exegetical endeavor on a limited number of themes dealt with in the Qur'ān. Two main arguments are put forward in favor of thematic interpretation: It enables exegetes to gain a comprehensive and well-balanced idea of what the divine book really says about the basic questions of belief, and thus reduces the danger of a merely selective and biased reading of the qur'ānic text; and commentaries based on such an interpretation are more suitable for practical purposes such as preparing Friday sermons or religious radio and television addresses (see EVERYDAY LIFE, THE QUR'ĀN IN), because these kinds of presentations usually have a thematic focus. An additional argument mentioned in support of thematic interpretation is that it allows exegetes to take a more active role in the process of interpretation, bringing their own modern perspective to bear in this process more effectively than the traditional verse-by-verse commentaries, since in the traditional commentaries the interpreter merely reacts to what is said in the text as it occurs, whereas in the *tafsīr mawḍūʿī* he can start from the application of his own questions to the text (Ṣadr, *Muqaddimāt*, 18-22).

Highly problematic and not representative of the prevailing views about *tafsīr mawḍūʿī* is the conception of thematic interpretation advocated in 1993 by the Egyptian philosopher Ḥasan Ḥanafī. According to Ḥanafī, revelation is neither affirmed nor denied by thematic interpretation, since this method deals with the qurʾānic text without any distinction between the divine and the human, the religious and the secular (Method, 202, 210). In contrast to the supporters of the thematic interpretation of the qurʾānic text, he considers the question of the divine origin of the Qurʾān to be largely irrelevant, but this is only partly true where Ḥanafī's own interest in the qurʾānic text is concerned. Irrespective of whether he personally attributes a religious character to the Qurʾān or not, his interest in interpreting this book and not any other text stems exclusively from the fact that many millions of Muslims believe the Qurʾān to be God's revealed word and can hence be most effectively influenced by its interpretation. Moreover, in Ḥanafī's opinion, it is one of the "rules" of thematic interpretation that the commentator should conduct exegesis on the basis of a socio-political commitment, with the added assumption that the interpreter is always a revolutionary (ibid., 203-4). While it is true that every interpretation comes with prior assumptions, there is no reason why they should only be revolutionary. Finally, according to Ḥanafī, thematic interpretation is based on the premise that "there is no true or false interpretation" (ibid., 203) and that "the validity of an interpretation lies in its power" (ibid., 210). By professing this principle, Ḥanafī actually abandons the notion of the hermeneutical circle as a model for interpretation, and, instead, looks upon this process as a one-way street whose only destination lies in influencing the audience according to the preconceived intentions of the interpreter. The notion of the hermeneutical circle, as analyzed in differing forms by Schleiermacher, Dilthey, Heidegger, Gadamer and others, implies an interaction between interpreter and text in which the interpreter puts questions to the text on the basis of his own prior conceptions, which are themselves reshaped by the text itself. As Gadamer stresses, the text must "break the spell" of the interpreter's presuppositions, and its subject matter effects the correction of his preliminary understanding. For Ḥanafī, in contrast, the text has no significance of its own: In his idea of thematical interpretation, the committed interpreter's prior understanding is absolute, and the text is considered to be relevant only in so far as its interpretation can serve the purpose of enhancing the power of the interpreter's revolutionary arguments, which are not subject to critical review.

Problems of gaining acceptance for new approaches to the exegesis of the Qurʾān

New methodological approaches such as those of Khalaf Allāh, Fazlur Rahman and Abū Zayd sprang from the widely felt need to extract the permanent tenets of the qurʾānic message from the historical forms in which they were communicated to the Prophet's contemporaries and to recast them in terms of a modern intellectual outlook. These approaches also showed that this need can be served without abandoning the belief in the divine origin of every single word of the qurʾānic text and the binding character of its basic precepts. Nevertheless, thus far, these approaches have not found wide acceptance among theologians and experts of religious law, and some of them have even provoked vehement reactions on the part of the religious élite. Some of the reasons for this phenomenon can be stated here.

The prevailing traditional exegetical paradigm has remained nearly unchallenged for centuries. It has thus become customary among religious scholars to confuse the permanence of their own way of interpreting the qurʾānic text with the everlasting truth of this text itself and, hence, to consider any attempt at promoting a new approach to exegesis as an assault on the authority of the divine book as such, but at the same time as an attack on their own interpretative authority. The latter is a particularly sensitive issue, as it concerns the social position of the *ʿulamāʾ*, who have lost much ground in the fields of jurisdiction, public administration, education and academic studies since the early 19th century due to the general secularization of political and cultural structures. Moreover, if one allows new exegetical paradigms based on the acknowledgment of the historicity of the qurʾānic text and all its subsequent interpretations, this leads inevitably to an increasing plurality of competing interpretations. Such a situation would not only be contrary to the interests of the *ʿulamāʾ*, for whom it would then become more difficult to defend their interpretative monopoly, but also to the intentions of the poorly legitimized present governments of most Muslim states. These governments are accustomed to appealing to the Islamic religion as a unifying ideology in order to mobilize the loyalty of the masses in their favor, and for this purpose a largely uniform understanding of Islam is most suitable. The relationship of mutual dependence of the religious establishment and the government which is nowadays typical of many Islamic countries makes the suppression of disagreeable innovations in the field of exegetical methodology relatively simple. Because of the above-mentioned presuppositions of their own exegesis, Islamists are strongly opposed to permitting a plurality of interpretations based on methods differing from their own. The present situation is additionally aggravated by the fact that methods which imply a more serious consideration of the historical dimension of the qurʾānic text and of the exegetical tradition referring to it are generally associated with the kind of research pursued by orientalists, who in their turn are accused of working for Western colonialism. This makes it very easy to start a massive campaign against any scholar advocating such methods. Under these circumstances, the fact that hardly any Muslim authors have appropriated the methods and results of modern non-Muslim qurʾānic studies is also quite understandable. Rare exceptions to this trend are Amīn al-Khūlī and Daud Rahbar, both of whom recognized the value of the preliminary chronology of the qurʾānic text established in Th. Nöldeke's *Geschichte des Qorāns (GQ)*. Still, on the basis of hermeneutical conceptions such as those of Abū Zayd and Fazlur Rahman, there will be continued attempts to enter into a far-reaching scientific exchange with non-Muslim scholars without questioning the literal revelation of the Qurʾān. See also CONTEMPORARY CRITICAL PRACTICES AND THE QURʾĀN.

Rotraud Wielandt

Bibliography
Primary: ʿĀʾisha ʿAbd al-Raḥmān (= Bint al-Shāṭiʾ), *Maqāl fī l-insān. Dirāsa qurʾāniyya*, Cairo 1969; id., *al-Tafsīr al-bayānī lil-Qurʾān al-karīm*, 2 vols., Cairo 1962-9; Muḥammad ʿAbduh, *Tafsīr al-Fātiḥa*, Cairo 1319/1901; id., *Tafsīr juzʾ ʿAmmā*, Cairo 1322/1904; id. and Muḥammad Rashīd Riḍā, *Tafsīr al-Qurʾān al-ḥakīm. al-Mushtahir bi-Tafsīr al-Manār*, 12 vols., Cairo 1324-53/1906-34 (1st printed vol.: iii 1324/1906; i: 1346/1927; xii: 1353/1934); Muḥammad Abū Zayd, *al-Hidāya wa-l-ʿirfān fī tafsīr al-Qurʾān bi-l-Qurʾān*, Cairo

1349/1930; Naṣr Ḥāmid Abū Zayd, *Mafhūm al-naṣṣ. Dirāsa fī ʿulūm al-Qurʾān,* Beirut/Casablanca 1990; Ḥanafī Aḥmad, *Muʿjizat al-Qurʾān fī waṣf al-kāʾināt,* Cairo 1954, repr. 1960 and 1968 *(al-Tafsīr al-ʿilmī lil-āyāt al-kawniyya);* Muhammad Akbar, *The meaning of the Qurʾān,* Lahore 1967-; Ālūsī, *Rūḥ;* Zafar Ishaq Ansari, *Towards understanding the Qurʾān,* London 1408-/1988-; Arkoun, *Lectures;* id., The notion of revelation. From Ahl al-Kitāb to the Societies of the Book, in *WI (N.S.)* 28 (1988), 62-89; Abū l-Kalām Āzād, *Tarjumān al-Qurʾān* (in Urdu), Calcutta 1930, Lahore 1947 (rev. ed.); Muḥammad ʿIzza Darwaza, *al-Tafsīr al-ḥadīth,* 12 vols., Cairo 1962; Shawqī Ḍayf, *Sūrat al-Raḥmān wa-suwar qiṣār,* Cairo 1980; Rāshid ʿAbdallāh Farḥān, *Tafsīr mushkil al-Qurʾān,* Tripoli, Libya 1984²; ʿAllāl al-Fāsī, *Maqāṣid al-sharīʿa al-islāmiyya wa-makārimuhā,* Casablanca 1963; id., *al-Naqd al-dhātī,* n.p. 1952, Tiṭwān n.d.²; H. Hanafi, Method of thematic interpretation of the Qurʾān, in Wild, *Text,* 195-211; Ḥawwā, *Tafsīr;* Ṭāhā Ḥusayn, Fī l-ṣayf, in *al-Majmūʿa al-kāmila li-muʾallafāt al-duktūr Ṭāhā Ḥusayn,* Beirut 1974², xiv, 215-9; Ibn ʿĀshūr, *Tafsīr;* ʿAbd al-Ḥamīd Ibn Bādīs, *Majālis al-tadhkīr min kalām al-ḥakīm al-khabīr,* (series of articles published in *al-Shihāb* 1929-39), partial ed. A. Bouchemal, Constantine 1944 (more complete, but unreliable: *Tafsīr Ibn Bādīs,* eds. Ṣāliḥ Ramaḍān and Tawfīq Muḥammad Shāhīn, Cairo n.d., ca. 1965); ʿAbd al-ʿAzīz Ibn al-Dardīr, *al-Tafsīr al-mawḍūʿī li-āyāt al-tawḥīd fī l-Qurʾān al-karīm,* Cairo 1990; Muḥammad b. Aḥmad al-Iskandarānī; *Kashf al-asrār al-nūrāniyya al-qurʾāniyya fī-mā yataʿallaq bi-l-ajrām al-samāwiyya wa-l-arḍiyya wa-l-ḥayawānāt wa-l-nabāt wa-l-jawāhir al-maʿdiniyya,* Cairo 1297/1879-80; ʿAbd al-ʿAzīz Ismāʿīl, *al-Islām wa-l-ṭibb al-ḥadīth,* Cairo 1938, repr. 1957; Ṭanṭāwī Jawharī, *al-Jawāhir fī tafsīr al-Qurʾān al-karīm al-mushtamil ʿalā ajāʾib badāʾiʿ al-mukawwanāt wa-gharāʾib al-āyāt al-bāhirāt,* 26 parts, Cairo 1341/1922, 1350/1931²; Muḥammad Aḥmad Khalaf Allāh, *al-Fann al-qaṣaṣī fī l-Qurʾān al-karīm,* Cairo 1953, 1965³; Sayyid Ahmad Khan, Sir Sayyid Ahmad Khan's Principles of Exegesis. Translated from his Taḥrīr fī uṣūl al-tafsīr, trans. D. Rahbar, in *MW* 46 1956, 104-12, 324-35; id., *Tafsīr al-Qurʾān,* vols. 1-6, Aligarh 1880-95, vol. 7, Agra 1904 (for other writings of this author containing Qurʾān commentary, see bibliography of C.W. Troll, *Sayyid Ahmad Khan. A reinterpretation of Muslim theology,* New Delhi 1978); id., *Taḥrīr fī uṣūl al-tafsīr,* Agra 1892; Amīn al-Khūlī, *Manāhij tajdīd fī l-naḥw wa-l-balāgha wa-l-tafsīr wa-l-adab,* Cairo 1961; id., *al-Tafsīr. Maʿālim ḥayātihi wa-manhajuhu l-yawm,* Cairo 1944; Abū l-Aʿlā Mawdūdī, *Tafhīm al-Qurʾān* (in Urdu), 6 vols., Lahore 1949-72, trans. S. Qutb, *Ẓilāl,* 30 parts, Cairo 1952-65; 13 parts, Cairo 1960-4 (inc. rev. ed.); 6 vols., Beirut and Cairo 1407/1987 (3rd legal edition); ʿAbd al-Razzāq Nawfal, *al-Qurʾān wa-l-ʿilm al-ḥadīth,* Cairo 1378/1959; S. Quṭb, *al-Taṣwīr al-fannī fī l-Qurʾān,* Cairo 1945; D. Rahbar, The challenge of modern ideas and social values to Muslim society. The approach to quranic exegesis, in *MW* 48 (1958), 274-85; id., *God of justice,* Leiden 1960; Fazlur Rahman, *Islam and modernity. Transformation of an intellectual tradition,* Chicago 1982; al-Sayyid Muḥammad Bāqir al-Ṣadr, *Muqaddimāt fī l-tafsīr al-mawḍūʿī lil-Qurʾān al-karīm,* Beirut 1400/1980; Hind Shalabī, *al-Tafsīr al-ʿilmī lil-Qurʾān al-karīm bayna l-naẓariyyāt wa-l-taṭbīq,* Tunis 1985, esp. 63-69 and 149-164; Maḥmūd Shaltūt, *Tafsīr al-Qurʾān al-karīm. al-Ajzāʾ al-ʿashara al-ūlā,* Cairo 1966⁴; al-Shāṭibī, Abū Isḥāq, *al-Muwāfaqāt fī uṣūl al-sharīʿa,* 4 vols. in 2, Cairo 1340/1922; Ṭabāṭabāʾī, *Mīzān;* M.F. Wajdī, *Ṣafwat al-ʿirfān fī tafsīr al-Qurʾān* (later reprints under the title *al-Muṣḥaf al-mufassar*), Cairo 1321/1903. For more comprehensive lists of Qurʾān commentaries of the 20th century, see Jansen, *Egypt,* 13 and bibliography, and Abū Ḥajar, *al-Tafsīr al-ʿilmī,* bibliography.
Secondary: Aḥmad ʿUmar Abū Ḥajar, *al-Tafsīr al-ʿilmī fī l-mīzān,* Beirut and Damascus 1411/1991; C.J. Adams, Abū l-Aʿlā Mawdūdī's *Tafhīm al-Qurʾān,* in Rippin, *Approaches,* 307-23; Muḥammad Khayr Maḥmūd al-ʿAdawī, *Maʿālim al-qiṣṣa fī l-Qurʾān al-karīm,* Amman 1408/1988; A. Ahmad and G.E. von Grunebaum, *Muslim self-statement in India and Pakistan* 1857-1968, Wiesbaden 1970, 25-42; J.M.S. Baljon, *Modern Muslim Koran interpretation* (1880-1960), Leiden 1961, 1968² (fundamental); id., A modern Urdu tafsīr, in *WI (N.S.)* 2 (1953), 95-107 (about Abū l-Kalām Āzād's *Tarjumān al-Qurʾān*); Muḥammad Rajab al-Bayyūmī, *Khuṭuwāt al-tafsīr al-bayānī lil-Qurʾān al-karīm,* Cairo 1391/1971; I.J. Boullata, Modern Qurʾān exegesis. A study of Bint al-Shāṭiʾs method, in *MW* 64 (1974), 103-14; O. Carré, *Mystique et politique. Lecture révolutionnaire du Coran par Sayyid Quṭb, frère musulman radical,* Paris 1984; M. Chartier, Muhammad Ahmad Khalaf Allâh et l'exégèse coranique, in *IBLA* 137 (1976), 1-31; I.A.H. Faruqi, *The Tarjuman al-Qurʾan. A critical analysis of Maulana Abu'l-Kalam Azad's approach to the understanding of the Qurʾan,* New Delhi 1982; ʿAbd al-ʿAẓīm Aḥmad al-Ghubāshī, *Taʾrīkh al-tafsīr wa-manāhij al-mufassirīn,* Cairo 1391/1971; J.J.G. Jansen, *The interpretation of the Koran in modern Egypt,* Leiden 1974 (fundamental); id., Polemics on Muṣṭafā Maḥmūd's Koran exegesis, in R. Peters (ed.), *Proceedings of the Ninth Congress of the U.E.A.I.,* Leiden 1981, 110-22; id., Šaykh Šaʿrāwī's interpretation of the Qurʾān, in R. Hillenbrand (ed.), *Proceedings of the*

Tenth Congress of the U.E.A.I., Edinburgh 1982, 22-8; A. Jeffery, Higher criticism of the Qurʾān. The confiscated Commentary of Muhammad Abu Zaid, in *MW* 22 (1932), 78-83; id., The suppressed Qurʾān commentary of Muhammad Abū Zaid, in *Der Islam* 20 (1932), 301-308; J. Jomier, Le Cheikh Tantâwî Jawharî (1862-1940) et son commentaire du Coran, in *MIDEO* 5 (1958), 115-74; id., *Le commentaire coranique du Manâr. Tendances actuelles de l'exégèse coranique en Égypt,* Paris 1954; P.J. Lewis, The Qurʾān and its contemporary interpretation, in *al-Mushir* 24 (1982), 133-44; A. Merad, *Ibn Bādīs. Commentateur du Coran,* Paris 1971; ʿAbd al-Majīd ʿAbd al-Salām al-Muḥtasib, *Ittijāhāt al-tafsīr fī l-ʿaṣr al-rāhin,* Amman 1400/1980² (rev. ed.); Iltihāmī Naqra, *Sīkūlūjiyyat al-qiṣṣa fī l-Qurʾān,* Tunis 1974, 1407/1987²; C. van Nispen tot Sevenaer, *Activité humaine et agir de Dieu. Le concept de "sunan de dieu" dans le commentaire coranique du* Manār, Beirut 1996; I.K. Poonawala, Muḥammad ʿIzzat Darwaza's principles of modern exegesis. A contribution toward qurʾānic hermeneutics, in Hawting and Shareef, *Approaches,* 225-46; Fahd b. ʿAbd al-Raḥmān al-Rūmī, *Manhaj al-madrasa al-ʿaqliyya al-ḥadītha fī l-tafsīr,* 3 vols., Riyadh 1986; L.J. Saldanha, *A critical approach to quranic exegesis by a contemporary Pakistani, Dr Daud Rahbar,* Ph.D. diss., Rome 1963; M. Ibrāhīm al-Sharīf, *Ittijāhāt al-tajdīd fī l-tafsīr al-Qurʾān al-karīm fī Miṣr,* n.p. 1982; ʿIffat Muḥammad al-Sharqāwī, *Ittijāhāt al-tafsīr fī Miṣr fī l-ʿaṣr al-ḥadīth,* Cairo 1972; ʿAbdallāh Maḥmūd Shiḥāta, *Manhaj al-imām Muḥammad ʿAbduh fī tafsīr al-Qurʾān al-karīm,* Cairo 1963; F.M. Sulaymān, *Muḥammad ʿIzzat Darwaza wa-tafsīr al-Qurʾān al-karīm,* Riyadh 1993; M. Muṣṭafā al-Ḥadīdi al-Ṭayr, *Ittijāh al-tafsīr fī l-ʿaṣr al-ḥadīth,* Cairo 1975; C.W. Troll, *Sayyid Ahmad Khan. A reinterpretation of Muslim theology,* New Delhi 1978, 144-70; R. Wielandt, *Offenbarung und Geschichte im Denken moderner Muslime,* Wiesbaden 1971; id., Wurzeln der Schwierigkeit innerislamischen Gesprächs über neue hermeneutische Zugänge zum Korantext, in Wild, *Text,* 257-82; S. Wild, Die andere Seite des Textes. Naṣr Ḥāmid Abū Zaid und der Koran, in *WI (N.S.)* 33 (1993), 256-61; id., *Mensch, Prophet und Gott im Koran. Muslimische Exegeten des 20 Jahrhundert und das Menschenbild der Moderne,* Muenster 2001; al-Qaṣabī Maḥmūd Zalaṭ, *Qaḍāyā l-tikrār fī l-qaṣaṣ al-qurʾānī,* Cairo 1398/1978; K. Zebiri, *Maḥmūd Shaltūt and Islamic modernism,* Oxford 1993.

Exhortations

Verbal incitements, usually in the imperative mood, encouraging action on the part of the addressee. "Exhortation" *(mawʿiẓa)* is attested numerous times in the Qurʾān (Q 2:275; 3:138; 5:46; 7:145; 10:57; 11:120; 16:125; 24:34); moreover, much of the qurʾānic rhetoric (see RHETORIC OF THE QURʾĀN; LANGUAGE OF THE QURʾĀN) may be understood as an "exhortation" to heed God's message as proclaimed by the prophet Muḥammad. It is explicitly recommended to the Prophet in Q 16:125, "Call unto the way of your lord (see PATH OR WAY) with wisdom (q.v.) and fair exhortation" *(udʿu ilā sabīli rabbika bi-l-ḥikmati wa-l-mawʿiẓati l-ḥasanati),* a verse that has served as a motto for al-Ghazālī's (d. 505/1111) famous attempt to introduce Aristotelian logic into religious apologetics (McAuliffe, "Debate"; Neuwirth, Ghazzali's Traktat). An earlier qurʾānic designation is *tadhkira,* literally "reminder" (Q 20:3; 56:73; 69:12, 48; 73:19; 74:49, 54; 76:29; 80:11), presented as the essence of the early recitations as such (see CHRONOLOGY AND THE QURʾĀN). The strong interest that Muslim Medieval theorists took in qurʾānic exhortations and modes of debate (McAuliffe, "Debate") — be they divine-human addresses (God admonishing and encouraging the Prophet and implicitly the community [see COMMUNITY AND SOCIETY IN THE QURʾĀN]) or interactions between humans (the Prophet being recommended to address the community or, more often, the unbelievers [see BELIEF AND UNBELIEF; DEBATE AND DISPUTATION]) — is easily explained by the predominance of address passages over all other kinds of qurʾānic expression (see LITERARY STRUCTURES OF THE QURʾĀN) such as narratives (q.v.), eschatological descriptions or legislative regulations (see LAW AND THE QURʾĀN).

The earliest manifestations of qurʾānic exhortations are short admonitions that recommend the fulfillment of ritual duties such as prostration before God (Q 53:62; 96:19; see BOWING AND PROSTRATION) and glorification of God (q.v.; Q 69:52; for other examples of early exhortations, see Q 86:17; 94:7-8; 108:2; cf. 106:3-4), or negative recommendations to avoid the unbelievers ("leave them *[fa-dharhum]* to chat and play until they meet their day which they are promised…," Q 70:42-4) or to remain patient with them (Q 52:48-9; 68:48-50; 86:15-7), always occurring as closures of sūras. Consoling words affirming the truth of the Qurʾān's revelation are also found in the final verses of some of the early sūras (Q 68:51-2; 74:54-5; 81:26-8; 85:21-2; 87:18-9). All these elements merge to form extended closing sections in the later tripartite sūras (see FORM AND STRUCTURE OF THE QURʾĀN), where affirmations of the revelation and encouragements of the Prophet (see OPPOSITION TO MUḤAMMAD) combine to create the standard closing section, sometimes extended to encompass polemics (Q 15:85-99; 17:82-111; 19:97-8; 20:130-5; 21:105-12; 37:149-82; 38:67-88; 43:84-9; 67:23-9; 72:20-8; 76:23-31; see POLEMIC AND POLEMICAL LANGUAGE). This frequently corresponds to an introductory section that is in the same tenor (Q 18:1-6, 109-10; 26:1-9, 192-227; 27:1-6, 76-93; 36:2-6, 69-83; 54:1-8, 58-9; 54:1-8, 43-55). These sections have been compared to the responsorial parts at the beginning and end of the "standard monotheist service" (Neuwirth, Referentiality). Even if in the Qurʾān the listener hears only the replica of a single actor, i.e. the sender, he or she will not fail to realize that it refers to or even quotes thoughts belonging to the addressees, thus leaving the impression of a dialogue (see DIALOGUES). Qurʾānic exhortations thus mirror, through the divine response to the unspoken pleas of the transmitter, the hardships and needs of the community (see TRIAL). Again, in a way similar to the monotheist service, in many sūras the dialogical parts frame a narrative account drawn from the store of knowledge of salvation history. In later Meccan texts this pattern becomes blurred, the closing section sometimes being doubled, exhortations forming the closure of both the second last and the last part (Q 23:72-7, 116-8; 25:55-60, 61-77); elsewhere the framing parts have grown into poly-thematic discourses dominated by, but not exclusively filled with, divine exhortations (Q 11:1-24, 103-11). In Medinan sūras, the sermon — sometimes filling the whole sūra — has replaced the exhortations of the earlier sūras.

Angelika Neuwirth

Bibliography

Th. Arnold, *The preaching of Islam,* Lahore 1956, 3-6; J. McAuliffe, "Debate with them in the better way." The construction of a qurʾānic commonplace, in A. Neuwirth, B. Embaló, S. Guenther and M. Jarrar (eds.), *Myths, historical archetypes and symbolic figures. Towards a new hermeneutic approach,* Beirut 1999, 163-88; A. Neuwirth, Al-Ghazzali's Traktat "al-Qisṭās al-mustaqīm" — Eine Ableitung der Logik aus dem Koran, in S.M. Stern, A. Hourani and V. Brown (eds.), *Islamic philosophy and the classical tradition. Essays presented by his friends and pupils to Richard Walzer,* London 1972, 159-87; id., Referentiality and textuality in Sūrat al-Ḥijr. Some observations on the qurʾānic "canonical process" and the emergence of a community, in I. Boullata (ed.), *Literary structures of religious meaning in the Qurʾān,* London 2000, 143-72; id., *Studien.*

Exile
see CHASTISEMENT AND PUNISHMENT

Exorcism
see POPULAR AND TALISMANIC USES OF THE QURʾĀN

Expeditions and Battles

Journeys undertaken for military purposes, including raids for the purpose of plunder and assassination, and single engagements of armed and/or mounted forces, each of which is intent upon decisive victory. The term "battle" may also be used in a figurative sense, and refers to a struggle with one's spiritual and psychological self, i.e. a battle against ego, greed, addiction, etc. Both senses are relevant to the use of this vocabulary in the Qurʾān.

There are several terms used in the Qurʾān to refer to acts of aggression, some of which make reference directly, and others indirectly, to expeditions and battles. The qurʾānic vocabulary for acts of aggression is as follows: 1) The root *f-t-ḥ* (attested thirty-eight times), which can simply mean "to open," has the sense of granting victory, deliverance. With reference to conquest (q.v.), it appears but five times (Q 48:1, 18, 27; 57:10; 61:13) though, even here, the reference to a physical battle is not clear; a spiritual victory could be intended. 2) The root *f-t-n* has a negative connotation and appears sixty times, with a range of meanings that extend from trial to sedition. As the feminine noun, *fitna*, twelve appearances seem pertinent, sometimes meaning persecution (cf. Q 2:191, 193, 217; 8:39), while at other times conveying the idea of sedition or tumult, and insinuating civil strife. 3) The root *gh-l-b* (attested thirty-one times) means to overcome, to prevail, to conquer. In the context of expeditions and battles it appears eight times; five times as an imperfect verb *(yaghlibu)*, twice as the perfect passive (*ghuliba*, Q 7:119; 30:2), and once as a verbal noun (*ghalab*, Q 30:3). 4) The active participle of the root *gh-w-r*, *mughīr*, meaning raider, appears only once (Q 100:3). 5) The root *gh-z-w* appears as an active participle, meaning raiders, once (Q 3:156). 6) The root *ḥ-r-b* provides a broad, direct reference to war (q.v.): It occurs four times as the verbal noun, *ḥarb*, meaning "war" (Q 2:279; 5:64; 8:57; 47:4); and twice in the third verbal form, as a perfect verb (*ḥāraba*, Q 9:107), "he fought," and in the imperfect (*yuḥāribu*, Q 5:33). 7. Words based on the root *j-h-d* appear forty times, and have the meaning of struggle for God or endeavor (*jahd*, meaning "most earnest," is not relevant here). This last-mentioned root is ambiguous in that it does not necessarily refer to the physical act of fighting. It appears in the third verbal form as the perfect verb *jāhada*, meaning "he struggled/fought, he strove," fifteen times. The imperfect *(yujāhidu)* occurs four times. It appears seven times as an imperative, *jāhid;* as a nominal verb, *jihād* (q.v.), meaning struggle/fight for God, four times; and as an active participle, *mujāhid*, four times. 8) The root *q-t-l* occurs 165 times with reference to fighting in general. As the perfect verb, "he killed" *(qatala)*, it appears 19 times; in the perfect passive, meaning "may he be slain or perish, may death seize him" *(qutila)*, seventeen times. As a nominal verb referring to the act of killing/slaying, it appears ten times; as an imperative *(qātil)*, ten times; as the passive verb *(yuqtalu)*, three times; and as a verbal noun meaning "fighting, battle" *(qitāl)*, thirteen times.

The presence of such aggressive vocabulary seems appropriate: according to Islam, Muḥammad, the recipient of the Qurʾān, was one of the many prophets encouraged by God to fight for his beliefs (see PROPHETS AND PROPHETHOOD; PATH OR WAY), and actually took up arms in defense of them. By telling us of battles fought by the prophets, the Qurʾān presents Islam as the climax to a trajectory of struggles through which monotheism (see POLYTHEISM AND ATHEISM) has evolved. Such qurʾānic episodes provide evidence of meaning in life, for, despite the numerous and terrible trials (see TRIAL) God puts one through, he is always on the side of those who do right.

The term *maghāzī* (from the root *gh-z-w*), which best translates the phrase "expeditions and battles," is not found in the Qurʾān, although a derivative occurs in Q 3:156. This is a significant comment on the disconnection that exists between the Qurʾān and traditions (*ḥadīth* and *akhbār*, see ḤADĪTH AND THE QURʾĀN). The Arab milieu into which the Qurʾān was introduced was characterized by constant raids (*ghazwā*, pl. *maghāzī*), whereby one tribe would seek to plunder the property of another, with minimum risk to life. Traditions of early Islam, ignoring this distinction, use the term freely to refer to the numerous expeditions and battles attributed to the Prophet. Indeed, the raid came to symbolize every achievement of the Prophet, so that the very genre of literature which tells of his expeditions, generally enumerated after his emigration to Medina (*hijra*, see EMIGRATION), is entitled *maghāzī*; the label *sīra-maghāzī* is applied to literature that tells of the entire life of the Prophet (see SĪRA AND THE QURʾĀN).

Muslims believe that the Qurʾān was revealed in portions from the moment Muḥammad was appointed Prophet until his death. Yet, the achronological and piecemeal nature of the collection of the Qurʾān (q.v.; see also CHRONOLOGY AND THE QURʾĀN) makes it difficult to place its verses — particularly those dealing with fighting — in the context of the Prophet's life. To a large extent, qurʾānic exegesis (*tafsīr*) constitutes the early Muslim community's use of traditions to introduce the realia of Islam and the life of the Prophet into the Qurʾān, so as to render an interpretation related to his teachings (see EXEGESIS OF THE QURʾĀN: CLASSICAL AND MEDIEVAL). At the same time in *maghāzī* literature significant passages of the Qurʾān are linked to the campaigns of the Prophet, creating corresponding material on the circumstances of revelation (see OCCASIONS OF REVELATION). Thus, *sīra-maghāzī* and *tafsīr* tend to overlap, although they do not always corroborate each other. In the compilations of Ibn Isḥāq (d. 150/767; in the recension of Ibn Hishām d. 218/834) and al-Wāqidī (d. 207/823), the only two examples of *sīra-maghāzī* literature extant in their entirety today, these events, which appear to act as a mnemonic device for the recollection of particular qurʾānic passages, are presented in a chronological sequence, inevitably indicating the progression of the verses concerned.

In view of this connection between the Qurʾān and traditions, this article will discuss not only the obvious qurʾānic passages which inform of expeditions and battles, but also those passages of the Qurʾān which are associated in the tradition literature with various campaigns. Accordingly, this essay is presented under the following sub-headings: Expeditions and battles of previous prophets; Historical battles; Expeditions and battles foretold; Expeditions and battles of the Prophet; Conclusion.

Expeditions and battles of previous prophets

The Qurʾān mentions numerous prophets whose struggles against idolatry (see IDOLATRY AND IDOLATORS) and sin were introduced as messages of encouragement to Muḥammad in his predicament. Noah (q.v.), Abraham (q.v.), Joseph (q.v.), Lot (q.v.), etc., may not have assumed the warrior proportions of the Prophet of Islam, but they battled, nonetheless, for the cause of monotheism.

There are a number of obvious references to battle: Samuel (q.v.) appoints Saul (q.v.; Ṭālūt) to lead the Israelites against the giant warrior and king of the Philistines, Goliath (q.v.; Jālūt); and David (q.v.), a youth, brings down the giant with a pebble from his sling (Q 2:247-51). David, who becomes poet, prophet and king, is skilled in the making of defensive armor: "We bestowed grace on David… And we made the iron soft for him. Make coats of mail… (Q 34:10-1; cf. 21:80). Neither was this the first time the Israelites were commanded to fight: Q 5:22-9 is essentially the biblical story of the spies narrated in Numbers 13-4. It tells of how the Israelites refused to obey Moses' (q.v.) command to capture their "promised land." As punishment, they were left to wander in the wilderness for forty years (see PUNISHMENT STORIES).

Historical battles

Four passages in particular, Q 17:4-8, 30:1-5, 85:4-9 and 105:1-5, are interpreted as referring to discernible historical events which occurred before or during the life of Muḥammad, though the references are minimal, and the precise occasions difficult to determine. They provide assurance to Muḥammad that God would stand by him. Each passage has its own set of problems that are resolved variously by different exegetes who may, and do, disagree as to the precise historical event to which reference is being made. It is the kerygma, brought to life by the story woven around the verse, which is relevant. The exegete's assessment of his own religious and socio-political milieu is thus a crucial aspect of what he brings to his interpretation. Moreover, there is a significant religious intent which guides the exegete as he shapes his rendition: to establish Muḥammad as the last and the best of prophets, and to make evident the miraculous nature or *iʿjāz* of the Qurʾān, which includes the ability to prophesy (see INIMITABILITY).

Q 17:4-8 states: "And we decreed for the Children of Israel (q.v.)... 'Twice you shall do mischief (see CORRUPTION)....' When the first of these came to pass, we sent against you our servants given to terrible warfare... but if you revert [to your sins], we shall revert [to our punishments]." In fact, there were several conquests and destructions of Jerusalem and many instances when the Jewish temple was defiled. The exegete chooses that moment of history which would render the message most meaningful; sometimes he even provides an alternative interpretation.

Muqātil b. Sulaymān (d. 150/767), who is believed to have studied exegesis with Jews and Christians and, therefore, to be well informed about their traditions, recognizes in Q 17:4-8 a reference to three destructions of Jerusalem, which he attributes to Nebuchadnezar, Antiochus and Titus, respectively. According to him, the Jews had lost their sanctuary in Jerusalem because they murdered the prophets, while Titus' destruction of Jerusalem was brought on by the murder of John the Baptist (q.v.). Asserting that it was the Muslims who eventually reclaimed and rebuilt the site, he emphasizes the Muslim claim to Jerusalem (*Tafsīr*, ii, 519-23).

Al-Ṭabarī (d. 310/923) recognizes two destructions, the first by Sanacharib and the second by Nebuchadnezar. It is through Ismāʿīl al-Suddī (d. 127/745), the Kufan exegete, that al-Ṭabarī learns why Nebuchadnezar had destroyed Jerusalem: John the Baptist, who had warned the Jewish king that he must not marry the woman he desired, had been beheaded. The tale has aroused comment because Nebuchadnezar lived several centuries before John the Baptist. Balʿamī, the Persian translator of al-Ṭabarī, explains the confusion using a kind of typological analysis, pointing out that the Israelites generally named bad kings "Nebuchadnezar" (Busse, Destruction of the Temple, 15). Significant, however, is the inevitable knitting together of the Hebrew Bible with the New Testament within the interpretation of a qurʾānic verse in a fashion that asserts the place of the Qurʾān in the series of God's revelations.

Busse informs us that, according to al-Zamakhsharī (d. 528/1144), Q 17:8 refers, however, to a third destruction of Jerusalem (by which he means its capture) which could relate to any of three possibilities, the last of which emphasizes Islam's claim to Jerusalem. They are: the conquest of Jerusalem by the Persians; Muḥammad's imposition of the poll tax (q.v.) on the Jews (of Medina and/or Khaybar); or the defeat of the Jews by a tribe of Arabs — probably a reference to the taking of Jerusalem by ʿUmar b. al-Khaṭṭāb, although ʿUmar neither took the city by force nor wrested it from the Jews (Zamakhsharī, *Kashshāf*, ii, 650, cited in Busse, Destruction of the Temple, 6). For the Shīʿite commentator ʿAlī b. Ibrāhīm al-Qummī (d. 328/939), however, Q 17:4-8 is an allegorical reference to the Umayyad persecution of the followers of ʿAlī, which climaxed in the massacre of al-Ḥusayn and his family at Karbalāʾ (Busse, Destruction of the Temple, 16; cf. Qummī, *Tafsīr*, i, 406).

According to El-Cheikh (Sūrat al-Rūm, 364), the exegeses of Q 30:1-5 (recognized as *al-āyāt al-bayyināt* because of their prophetic communication) indicate that the interpretations of these verses were affected by the relations of power between the caliphate and the Rūm (generally understood as Byzantium; see BYZANTINES). Three readings are available, depending upon how the text is vocalized. The recognized version on which the seven reciters (*qurrāʾ*, see RECITERS OF THE QURʾĀN) were agreed — "the Rūm have been defeated... but they... will soon be victorious," (*ghulibat al-Rūm... sa-yaghlibūn*) — is the version accepted by Mujāhid b. Jabr (d. 104/722), Muqātil b. Sulaymān, and al-Ṭabarī. The variant, "the Rūm were victorious [over the Persians]... they will be defeated [by the Muslims]" (*ghalabat al-Rūm... sa-yughlabūn*), was first asserted by Ibn ʿUmar, the son of ʿUmar al-Khaṭṭāb. A rarer variant was established by al-Qurṭubī (d. 671/1272), who reads: "the Rūm are victorious... they will conquer [again]" (*ghalabat al-Rūm... sa-yaghlibūn*).

With Mujāhid, Muqātil and al-Ṭabarī, the interpretations are similar: The qurʾānic words predict that, although the Persians defeated the Rūm, they (the Rūm) would soon be victorious over them; the believers can therefore rejoice in God's assistance to the People of the Book (q.v.). Muqātil provides a narrative framework for the passage with a tradition going back to ʿIkrima (d. 105/723), the client of Ibn ʿAbbās. Apparently, when the Prophet learned that God would soon grant the Rūm victory over the Persians, Abū Bakr went to the Meccans with the news, and Ubayy b. Khalaf, who was present, called Abū Bakr a liar. According to Muqātil, the news of the prediction that the Rūm would be victorious arrived on the day of Badr (q.v.), in which battle the Muslims defeated the Meccans; news of the actual victory of the Rūm arrived when the Muslims were at Ḥudaybiya (*Tafsīr*, iii, 403-5).

Al-Ṭabarī lists several traditions explaining Q 30:1-5. He portrays the Byzantine-Persian wars as a rehearsal for the wars between the Muslims and their Qurayshī opponents (*Tafsīr*, xxi, 10-4). Al-Qummī's interpretation, on the other hand, motivated by the Persians' rude rejection of the Prophet's invitation to Islam, maintains that it is the Persians who were victorious over the Rūm, but that they (the Persians) will in turn be defeated by the believers (*Tafsīr*, ii, 152-3). With the advent of the Crusades, however, the ideological affiliation that linked the Muslims and the Byzantines began to disintegrate. This may account for al-Zamakhsharī's preference for the variant reading — the Rūm were victorious, but soon they will be defeated by the Muslims (Zamakhsharī, *Kashshāf*, iii, 466-7, cited in El Cheikh, Sūrat al-Rūm, 361).

Q 85:4-9, "Killed were the makers of the pit of fire (see PEOPLE OF THE DITCH), of the fuel-fed fire (*qutila aṣḥābu l-ukhdūdi l-nāridhāti l-waqūdi*)... they ill-treated them (*naqamū minhum*) for... they believed in God," is variously explained, including a reference to the mistreatment of Muslims by the pagan Quraysh (q.v.). An alternate interpretation, however, is provided by Ibn Isḥāq (Ibn Isḥāq-Guillaume, 17), who holds that it refers to an expedition led by the Himyarite king of Yemen (q.v.), Dhū Nuwās, against the Christian settlement of Najrān (q.v.). When the latter refused to convert to Judaism, he had them burned.

Q 105:1-5 is believed to refer to the invasion of Mecca by the troops of Abraha (q.v.) the Abyssinian, an event which Ibn Isḥāq (Ibn Isḥāq-Guillaume, 26) asserts took place in the year of the Prophet's birth (570 C.E.). This conflicts with Muqātil's dating of Muḥammad's birth at forty years after the year of the Elephant — a traditional designation for the year of the Abyssinian invasion — and al-Kalbī's view that the Prophet was born fifteen years earlier (Conrad, Abraha, 234-5). The message, however, is that God alone was the savior of the Kaʿba (q.v.), which, as a sanctuary, must be protected from bloodshed. In a sense, the passage anticipates Sūrat al-Fatḥ's (Q 48) celebration of the truce of Ḥudaybiya which prevented fighting in Mecca.

Expeditions and battles foretold

The inimitable nature of the Qurʾān, as reflected in its ability to prophesy is indicated by al-Ṭabarī in his interpretation of Q 5:57 as a prediction and justification of Abū Bakr's victory over the people of apostasy (q.v.; *ridda*, Ṭabarī, *Tafsīr*, x, 411-4, cited in Kister, Illā bi-ḥaqqihi, 40), many of whom were defined by their refusal to pay the alms tax (*zakāt*, see ALMSGIVING), rather than by a rejection of God and his messenger. Shīʿīte exegetes, however, recognized a reference to ʿAlī's battles against those who had broken their vows of allegiance (Ṭalḥa and Zubayr), those who had strayed from the true faith (the Khawārij; see KHARAJĪS) and those who were unjust (Muʿāwiya; cf. Kister, Illā bi-ḥaqqihi, 40-1).

While there are no clear qurʾānic references to expeditions and battles in eschatological contexts, the thesis of a nineteenth-century scholar, P. Casanova, *(Mohammed)* is that the mission of Muḥammad was primarily to warn of the approaching end: that eschatology (q.v.), the subject of the earliest discourse reflected in both the Qurʾān and tradition, had given Islam an urgency and aggressiveness that enabled its several conquests. Indeed, numerous early Meccan passages warn of the approaching hour *(zalzalat al-sāʿa)* that would spearhead the end of time (Q 22:1; cf. 22:7; 33:63; 40:59; 42:16-7; 54:1; see APOCALYPSE; LAST JUDGMENT). Q 47:18 claims that the signs of the hour are manifest, while Q 21:1 warns that the reckoning is near. That Muḥammad saw himself as the harbinger of the hour is asserted by Abū l-Futūḥ Rāzī (d. 525/1131) who cites the tradition: "I am the resurrector *(ḥāshir)*... and I am the final one..." to explain the epithet "seal of the prophets" *(khātam al-nabiyyīn)* in Q 33:40 (*Tafsīr*, ix, 162, cited in Arjomand, Islamic apocalypticism, 246). According to tradition, ʿUmar b. al-Khaṭṭāb claimed that "the Prophet will not die until we conquer the cities [of Rome]..." (Arjomand, Islamic apocalypticism, 246-7). When the apocalypse did not arrive, verses such as Q 7:187 and 20:15 were emphasized instead, explaining that exact knowledge of the hour belongs to God alone.

Expeditions and battles of the Prophet

The most well-known expeditions and battles of the Prophet were fought against Arab non-Muslims at Badr, Uḥud, al-Khandaq ("the Trench"), Muʾta, Mecca, Ḥunayn (q.v.), and Tabūk, and against the Jews of the Qaynuqāʿ (q.v.), Naḍīr (q.v.), Qurayẓa (q.v.), Khaybar, and Fadak. Qurʾānic references to these events are brief and unclear — and only Badr, Mecca, Ḥunayn and Yathrib (or Medina) are named in the text. Nevertheless, a broad consensus regarding their occasions of revelation, which often signify socio-economic change, is reflected in *tafsīr* and *maghāzī* literature. Thus, it is believed that: Q 2:217, which justifies fighting during the sacred months, was revealed after the expedition to Nakhla (623 C.E.), a raid in which Muḥammad did not personally participate (Ibn Isḥāq-Guillaume, 288; Wāqidī, *Maghāzī,* 18). Q 8:41, which establishes that one fifth of the booty (q.v.) be set aside for God and his messenger, near relatives, orphans (q.v.), the needy, and the wayfarer, was revealed after the miraculous victory of the Muslims over the more numerous Quraysh at Badr (624 C.E.; Ibn Isḥāq-Guillaume, 321; Wāqidī, *Maghāzī,* 134); Q 16:127, which is understood to forbid the mutilation of the dead of one's foe, was revealed after the battle of Uḥud (625 C.E.), where Muḥammad was not only injured, but suffered the death of his uncle Ḥamza (see ḤAMZA B. ʿABD AL-MUṬṬALIB), whose body was mutilated by the enemy who had returned to avenge their recent defeat (Ibn Isḥāq-Guillaume, 387; Wāqidī, *Maghāzī,* 290). Q 59:6, which decrees that property taken without force *(fayʾ)* belongs entirely to the Prophet, was revealed during the raid on the Banū l-Naḍīr (625 C.E.) who surrendered without fighting when Muḥammad besieged them, on discovering their plot to kill him (Ibn Isḥāq-Guillaume, 438; Wāqidī, *Maghāzī,* 381). The more complex issues concerning verses from Q 33 (Sūrat al-Aḥzāb, "The Clans") associated with the battle of al-Khandaq, culminating in the execution of the Banū Qurayẓa (627 C.E.); and from Q 9 (Sūrat al-Tawba, "Repentance") associated with the raid on Tabūk (629 C.E.) and the repudiation of agreements with the polytheists, are discussed in greater detail below.

The expeditions of Muḥammad parallel the trials of many biblical prophets. They communicate to the believer that Muḥammad was indeed a prophet like any other, who struggled to maintain God's laws on earth. The reports that his small forces could overcome large, well-trained battalions of the enemy are understood by believers to indicate that, when he is willing, God will help them accomplish seemingly impossible feats.

Probably the most obvious assertion of victory found in the Qurʾān is at Q 48 (Sūrat al-Fatḥ, "Victory"): "Truly we have granted you a manifest victory" (Q 48:1), understood by both exegetes (Muqātil, *Tafsīr,* 4:65) and writers of *maghāzī,* i.e. Ibn Isḥāq (Ibn Isḥāq-Guillaume, 505) and al-Wāqidī (Wāqidī, *Maghāzī,* 614), as a reference to the culmination of hostilities which surfaced when the Prophet asserted his right to make a lesser pilgrimage (*ʿumra,* see PILGRIMAGE) to the Kaʿba. That the allusion is not to a typical battle fought and won, but rather, to the making of a truce at Ḥudaybiya resulting from the ordained respect for sanctuaries and a considerable self-control, is reflected in Q 48:24: "And it is he who has restrained their hands from you and your hands from them in the valley of Mecca...." Like many of the battles/victories alluded to in the Qurʾān, this passage may also be understood in a spiritual sense.

The vague nature of several qurʾānic statements leaves room for manipulation. Although the opponents of Muḥammad (see OPPOSITION TO MUḤAMMAD) fell into various groups — Jews *(yahūd)* and Christians (*naṣārā,* see CHRISTIANS AND CHRISTIANITY), as well as polytheists *(mushrikūn)* — they are often broadly referred to as disbelievers *(kāfirūn)*. Tradition, appreciating the sixth century Arabian context of the Prophet's life, has generally understood the "disbelievers" to refer to the Meccan Quraysh or polytheistic Arab tribes of the Ḥijāz, and to the Jews of the region, many of whom were settled in Yathrib (or

Medina, q.v.), Khaybar, Fadak, Wādī al-Qurāʾ, and Taymāʾ. Much of Muḥammad's prophetic career was, thus, one of confrontation with Arab pagans and Jews. This preponderance of aggression against Jews and Arabs is reflected in Q 5:82: "You will find the Jews and the polytheists the strongest among men in enmity to the believers...".

Moreover, since the Qurʾān does not specify any of the Jewish tribes of which tradition informs us (see JEWS AND JUDAISM), the exegete has a choice of traditions from which to explain the many qurʾānic references to disbelievers and People of the Book. Thus, while Ibn Isḥāq cites Q 3:10 and Q 5:56 as informing us of Muḥammad's raid on the Banū Qaynuqāʿ (Ibn Isḥāq-Guillaume, 363), and al-Wāqidī, Q 8:58 (*Maghāzī*, 177), al-Kalbī gives the impression that the Banū Qaynuqāʿ did not even exist (Schöller, Sīra and tafsīr, 25): Interestingly, the *maghāzī* traditions of ʿUrwa b. al-Zubayr (643-709) also do not inform us of the Banū Qaynuqāʿ (al-Aʿẓamī, *Maghāzī*). Time, the nature of oral tradition and the biblio-qurʾānic representation of the Jews as a people who repeatedly revoked their covenant (q.v.) with God (Faizer, Comparison, 469), had probably contributed to an exaggeration of the number of conflicts with the Jews. A slightly different account for the conflict with the Jews is given by both Crone and Cook (*Hagarism;* a hypothesis based on non-Islamic sources) and Wansbrough *(Sectarian milieu),* who, despite their very different approaches to the tradition of Islam, explain Muḥammad's religion as the expression of sectarian groups whose break with the community of Jews in Jerusalem resulted in a tradition of conflict with Jews.

The raid on the Banū Qurayẓa to which Q 33 apparently makes allusion is described vividly in the *sīra-maghāzī* of Ibn Isḥāq (Ibn Isḥāq-Guillaume, 461-9) and al-Wāqidī (*Maghāzī,* 496-529), who, significantly, do not substantiate the traditions concerning their execution per se with citations from the Qurʾān. This execution has resulted in a condemnation of the Prophet by modern historians such as W. Muir (*Mahomet,* 151) and F. Gabrieli (*Muhammad,* 73). Whereas Lings justifies this punishment as in keeping with Deuteronomy 20:12 (*Muhammad,* 232), W.N. Arafat rejects their execution as being "diametrically opposed to the spirit of Islam" (New light, 106). Kister repudiates Arafat's claims, protesting that these traditions are narrated in early *tafsīr* on Q 8:55-8 by such as Mujāhid b. Jabr and al-Ṭabarī, and that Muslim jurists, by deriving laws from the incident, have effectively acknowledged it (Massacre, 94-5).

Importantly, exegetes do not always agree on the significance of the verses they explain. Thus, al-Kalbī explains Q 59:11, not as a reference to the Banū l-Naḍīr alone, as is the usual practice, but to the Banū Qurayẓa as well, against both of whom, he claims, Muḥammad led a single expedition. Furthermore, al-Bayḍāwī (d. ca. 716/1316-7) interprets Q 17:8 as referring to the Banū l-Naḍīr and the Banū Qurayẓa who called the Prophet a liar and tried to kill him, at which Muḥammad subdued them and ordered them to pay the poll tax (*Tafsīr,* i, 534; cited in Busse, Destruction of the Temple, 7). Significantly, Crone, noticing the conflicting nature of the variant traditions, states: "We cannot even tell whether there was an original event: in the case of Muḥammad's encounter with the Jews there was not" (*Meccan trade,* 222).

Muslims have attempted to understand what the Qurʾān intends by treating its verses as a response to the experiences of the Prophet during his lifetime. Later decrees were believed to override earlier commands (see ABROGATION). Accordingly, Islamic law establishes that the People of the Book must be tolerated once they pay the poll tax, despite the fact that the Banū l-Naḍīr were exiled, and the Banū Qurayẓa, executed, because of the later revelation of Q 9:29, perhaps revealed during Muḥammad's final expedition against the Jews, the expedition of Khaybar: "Fight those (Jews of Khaybar)... until they pay the poll tax *'an yadin*," generally translated as "with willing submission." While traditions concerning the capture of Khaybar and Fadak tell us that the Prophet permitted the Jews to cultivate the land in exchange for half of their produce (Ibn Isḥāq-Guillaume, 515), early treaties drawn by Khālid b. al-Walīd (d. 21/642) show that *yad* probably meant property, the poll tax being imposed only on those who owned property (Rubin, Qur'ān and tafsīr, 138-42).

This raises the issue of Islam's aggression against the non-monotheist. Once again, the Qur'ān contains a variety of decrees which are seemingly contradictory (see RELIGIOUS PLURALISM): Thus, while Q 109:6 promotes tolerance, and Q 2:190 commands "Fight in the path of God . . . but do not transgress limits *(wa-lā ta'tadū)*," Q 2:216 insists that "fighting is commanded upon you even though it is hateful to you." Q 9:5, the "Sword Verse," commands: "when the sacred months are past, then slay *(fa-qtulū)* the polytheists *(al-mushrikīn)* wherever you find them and take them and besiege them...."

Rubin (Barā'a, 13-32) shows that the early Muslim exegetes preferred to interpret the sword verse in its context, that is, in relation to the situation of the Prophet when it was revealed and in association with the verses surrounding it. Q 9:1-5 are believed to have been revealed on the eve of the raid on Tabūk, when many of the pagans and hypocrites who had treaty obligations with the Prophet resisted joining him on the battlefield. Though al-Suddī explains the verses as a repudiation of Muḥammad's agreement with all pagans, al-Ṭabarī, al-Zamakhsharī, Fakhr al-Dīn al-Rāzī (d. 606/1209), and al-Bayḍāwī deny that the Qur'ān could decree such intolerance. They divide Muḥammad's non-monotheist allies into offensive and inoffensive groups and insist that the repudiation *(barā'a)* applied only to those non-monotheists who had violated their agreements. Al-Ṭabarī supports his interpretation with a tradition from Ibn 'Abbās: "... If they remained loyal to their treaty with the Prophet, ... [he] was ordered to respect their treaty and be loyal to it." Significantly, Muḥammad's treaty with the (pagan) Khuzā'a, who remained loyal to him, was for an unlimited period of time (Rubin, Barā'a, 24-30; see TREATIES AND ALLIANCES; BREAKING TRUSTS AND CONTRACTS).

Conclusion

The considerable consensus that has developed around the "expeditions and battles" of Muḥammad has led modern historians such as Watt *(Muhammad's Mecca)* and Welch (Muḥammad, 153) to claim that historical material concerning the Prophet may be obtained from the Qur'ān. At the same time, historians ranging from Caetani to Jones have commented on the chronological differences that characterize exegetical and biographical traditions (Jones, Chronology, 259). According to Crone, these traditions are tales inspired by the Qur'ān (*Meccan trade*, 204). Sachedina, examining the concept of *jihād*, expresses the dilemma somewhat differently: "... these exegetes and jurists were reponding to questions... as individuals... their writings reflect their individual and independent reasoning in an attempt to formulate an appropriate response to the socio-political realities of the Islamic public order" (Development of jihad, 36).

Such tenuous links between Qur'ān and tradition (biographical, exegetical and juridical) inevitably compel one who is seeking to understand its various decrees to attempt a more thorough investigation of the text. That there is a message seems clear: "My righteous servants shall inherit the earth" (Q 21:105). The Qur'ān condemns the unjustifiable shedding of blood (Q 17:4-8; see BLOODSHED). It establishes the right to strive, even fight, for a just and moral society: "And let not detestation for a people move you not to be equitable; be equitable. That is nearer to the consciousness of God *(taqwā)*" (Q 5:8). Free will is concretized in the declaration: "There is no compulsion in religion" (Q 2:256). In such a context, it seems probable that unbelief becomes problematic only when unbelievers take hostile action against believers: just war in such circumstances is what Islam condones.

There are problems: the equivocal nature of the terminology must be considered: the root letters *j-h-d* are usually glossed as "striving," but can mean "fighting"; *f-t-ḥ* is not merely "conquest" and "opening," but also "decision" and "outcome"; and *f-t-n* denotes either "dissension" or "unbelief." The various potential glosses of the Arabic root letters, combined with the existing lack of consensus regarding the chronology of the qurʾānic verses, permit varying interpretations of the issues concerned.

Rizwi Faizer

Bibliography
Primary: M.M. al-Aʿẓamī, *Maghāzī rasūl Allāh li-ʿUrwa b. al-Zubayr,* Riyadh 1981; Ibn Isḥāq, *Sīra,* trans. Ibn Isḥāq-Guillaume; Muqātil, *Tafsīr,* ed. Shiḥāta, 5 vols., 1979-89; Qummī, *Tafsīr,* Beirut 1991; Ismāʿīl al-Suddī, *Tafsīr al-Suddī al-kabīr,* al-Manṣūra 1993; Ṭabarī, *Tafsīr,* 30 vols. in 12, Beirut 1986-7 (repr. of Bulaq 1905-11); Wāqidī, *Maghāzī.*
Secondary: B. Ahmad, *Muhammad and the Jews,* New Delhi 1979; W.N. Arafat, New light on the story of the Banū Qurayẓa and the Jews of Medina, in *JRAS* (1976), 100-10; S.A. Arjomand, Islamic apocalypticism in the classic period, in B. McGinn (ed.), *The encyclopaedia of apocalypticism.* ii. *Apocalypticism in Western history and culture,* New York 1999, 238-83; M. Ayyoub, *The Qurʾān and its interpreters,* 2 vols., New York 1984-92; S. Bashear, Muslim apocalypses and the hour. A case study in traditional reinterpretation, in *IOS* 13 (1993), 76-99; A.F.L. Beeston, *Qahtan. Warfare in ancient South Arabia,* London 1976; R. Bell, Sūrat al-Ḥashr, in *MW* 38 (1948), 29-42; H. Busse, The destruction of the Temple and its reconstruction in the light of Muslim exegesis of *Sūra* 17:2-8, in *JSAI* 20 (1996), 1-17; C. Cahen, Djizya, in *EI²*, ii, 559-62; P. Casanova, *Mohammed et la fin du monde,* Paris 1911; L.I. Conrad, Abraha and Muḥammad. Some observations apropos of chronology and literary topoi in the early Arabic historical tradition, in *BSOAS* 50 (1987), 225-40; id., Seven and the *tasbīʿ*, in *JESHO* 31 (1988), 42-73; D. Cook, Muslim apocalyptic and *jihād,* in *JSAI* 20 (1996), 66-104; P. Crone, The first century concept of *hijra,* in *Arabica* 41 (1994), 352-87; id., *Meccan trade and the rise of Islam,* Oxford 1987; id., *Slaves on horses,* Oxford 1980; id. and M. Cook, *Hagarism. The making of the Islamic world,* Cambridge, UK 1977; F.M. Donner, *Narratives of Islamic origins. The beginnings of Islamic historical writing,* Princeton 1998; N.M. El-Cheikh, Sūrat al-Rūm. A study of the exegetical literature, in *JAOS* 118 (1998), 356-63; R.S. Faizer, Muhammad and the Medinan Jews. A comparison of the texts of Ibn Isḥāq's *Kitāb Sīrat rasūl Allāh* with al-Wāqidī's *Kitāb al-Maghāzī,* in *IJMES* 28 (1996), 463-89; R. Firestone, *Jihad. The origins of holy war in Islam,* Oxford 1999; F. Gabrieli, *Muhammad and the conquest of Islam,* London 1968; H. Gätje, *The Qurʾān and its exegesis,* trans. A.T. Welch, Oxford 1997; M. Gil, The constitution of Medina. A reconsideration, in *IOS* 4 (1974), 44-66; G.R. Hawting, Al-Ḥudaybiyya and the conquest of Mecca. A reconsideration of the tradition about the Muslim takeover of the sanctuary, in *JSAI* 8 (1986), 1-23; Hawting and Shareef, *Approaches;* M. Hinds, Maghāzī, in *EI²*, v, 1161-4; id., *Maghāzī* and *sīra* in early Islamic scholarship, in Université de Strasbourg. Centre de Recherches d'Histoire des Religions, *La vie du Prophète Mahomet. Colloque de Strasbourg. Octobre 1980,* Paris 1983; H. Hirschfeld, Essai sur l'histoire des Juifs de Médine, in *REJ* 7 (1883), 167-93; J.M.B. Jones, The chronology of the *maghāzī.* A textual survey, in *BSOAS* 19 (1957), 247-80; id., The *maghāzī* literature, in Beeston, *CHAL,* 344-51; M.J. Kister, A booth like the booth of Moses. A study of an early *ḥadīth,* in *BSOAS* 25 (1962), 150-5; id., The campaign of Ḥulubān, in *Muséon* 78 (1965), 425-36; id., *Illā bi-ḥaqqihi.* A study of an early ḥadīth, in *JSAI* 5 (1984), 33-52; id., Land property and *jihād,* in *JESHO* 34 (1989), 270-311; id., The

massacre of the Banū Qurayẓa. A re-examination of a tradition, in *JSAI* 8 (1986), 61-96; id., The *sīrah* literature, in Beeston, *CHAL*, 352-67; E. Kohlberg, The development of the Imāmī Shīʿī doctrine of *jihād*, in *ZDMG* 126 (1976), 64-86; M. Lecker, The death of the prophet Muḥammad's father. Did Wāqidī invent some of the evidence? in *ZDMG* 145 (1995), 9-27; id., Wāqidī's account on the status of the Jews of Medina. A study of a combined report, in *JNES* 54 (1995), 15-32; M. Lings, *Muhammad. His life based on the earliest sources*, Rochester, VT 1983; W. Muir, *Mahomet and Islam*, London 1895; D.S. Powers, The exegetical genre of *nāsikh al-Qurʾān wa mansūkhuhu*, in Rippin, *Approaches*, 117-38; A. Rippin, Introduction, in id., *Approaches*, 1-9; id., Muḥammad in the Qurʾān. Reading scripture in the 21st Century, in H. Motzki (ed.), *The biography of Muḥammad*, Leiden 2000, 298-309; id., The present status of *tafsīr* studies, in *MW* 72 (1982), 224-38; id., *Tafsīr*, in M. Eliade (ed.), *Encyclopedia of religion*, New York 1987, xiv, 236-44; U. Rubin, The assassination of Kaʿb b. al-Ashraf, in *Oriens* 32 (1990), 65-70; id., Barāʾa. A study of some qurʾānic passages, in *JSAI* 5 (1984), 13-32; id., Muḥammad's curse of Muḍar and the blockade of Mecca, in *JESHO* 31 (1988), 249-64; id., Qurʾān and *tafsīr*. The case of "an yadin", in *Der Islam* 70 (1993), 133-44; A.A. Sachedina, The development of jihad in Islamic revelation and history, in J.T. Johnson and J. Kelsay (eds.), *Cross, crescent, and sword*, Westport, CT 1990, 35-51; M. Schöller, *Sīra* and *tafsīr*. Muḥammad al-Kalbī on the Jews of Medina, in H. Motzki (ed.), *The biography of Muḥammad*, Leiden 2000, 298-311; V.H. Schützinger, Die arabische Legende von Nebuchadnezar und Johannes dem Täufer, in *Der Islam* 40 (1965), 113-41; E. Tyan, Djihād, in *EI*², ii, 538-40; J. Wansbrough, *The sectarian milieu. Content and composition of Islamic salvation history*, Oxford 1978; W.M. Watt, The condemnation of the Banū Qurayẓa, in *MW* 42 (1952), 160-71; id., *Muhammad's Mecca. History in the Quran*, Edinburgh 1988; id., The reliability of Ibn Isḥāq's sources, in Université de Strasbourg. Centre de Recherches d'Histoire des Religions, *La vie du Prophète Mahomet. Colloque de Strasbourg. Octobre 1980*, Paris 1983, 31-43; A.T. Welch, Al-Ḳurʾān, in *EI*², v, 400-29; id., Muḥammad. Life of the Prophet, in J. Esposito (ed.), *The Oxford encyclopedia of the modern Islamic world*, 4 vols., Oxford 1995, iii, 153-61; id., Muḥammad's understanding of himself. The qurʾānic data, in R.G. Hovannisian and S. Vryonis, Jr. (eds.), *Islam's understanding of itself*, Malibu 1983, 15-52; id./F. Buhl, Muḥammad, in *EI*², vii, 360-76.

Eyes

The organ of sight. The human eye, both as anatomical object and as capacity for physical sight or mental apprehension, is frequently encountered in the qurʾānic text, with examples from all chronological periods (see CHRONOLOGY AND THE QURʾĀN), most often with respect to human beings but occasionally, also, as anthropomorphic characterizations of divine capacity (see ANTHROPOMORPHISM). The most frequently used Arabic roots are *ʿ-y-n*, producing the forms *ʿayn*, pl. *ʿuyūn* and *aʿyun*, "eye(s)," and *ʿīn*, "wide-eyed female"; and *b-ṣ-r*, producing *baṣar*, pl. *abṣār*, "sight, eyesight, eyes," *baṣīr*, "seeing, understanding clearly," "[God as] all-seeing," and *abṣara*, "to see, seeing, having open eyes, to consider, be visible." Both groups denote actual ocular seeing in most instances but *b-ṣ-r* more often embraces mental apprehension as well (e.g. Q 7:201; see SEEING AND HEARING).

The ancient law of retaliation (q.v.) is recalled in Q 5:45, "Life for life, eye for eye *(wa-l-ʿayna bi-l-ʿayni)*," with God's charitable admonition to remit offenses committed against oneself as an act of atonement (q.v.). The emotional expression of eyes is captured in the vignette of Jacob (q.v.) mourning over his lost son Joseph (q.v.) until "his eyes *(ʿaynāhu)* became white with sorrow" (Q 12:84). Another example is the panicked rolling of the eyes of even the most covetous and unscrupulous sort of person from fear of the approach of death (*tadūru aʿyunuhum*, Q 33:19). An early Meccan passage (Q 68:51) concerning Muḥammad (q.v.) reports that "the unbelievers would almost trip you up with their [disapproving] glances *(yakādu… la-yuzliqūnaka bi-abṣārihim)* when they hear the message; and they say: 'Surely he is possessed.'" In Q 5:83 we read of the eyes of Christian listeners (see CHRISTIANS AND CHRISTIANITY) to the qur'ānic revelation "overflowing with tears" *(aʿyunahum tafīḍu min al-damʿ)* in recognition of the truth of the message. Those who reject faith (*kafarū*, see BELIEF AND UNBELIEF; FAITH; GRATITUDE AND INGRATITUDE) will have their eyes veiled *(wa-ʿalā abṣārihim ghishāwatun)* by God as part of their punishment (Q 2:7; see CHASTISEMENT AND PUNISHMENT).

Reference to God having eyes, in the sense of sight, is found in Q 23:27, where God commands Noah (q.v.) to "construct the ark (q.v.) under our eyes *(bi-aʿyuninā)*." There are numerous passages that tell of God's ability to see all things, e.g. Q 25:20: "Your lord is all-seeing" (*baṣīran*, cf. Q 17:1). God's seeing is not principally a passive activity but is rooted in his just and beneficent purposes for creation (q.v.; see also BLESSING; JUSTICE AND INJUSTICE), as in Q 67:19, where God asks whether birds can fly on their own: "None can uphold them except the most merciful, truly it is he that watches over all things" (*innahu bi-kulli shayʾin baṣīrun*, see GOD AND HIS ATTRIBUTES).

The human eye as romantic/sensuous fetish is linked with the houris (q.v.; *ḥūr*), beautiful, wide-eyed damsels who, according to several Meccan passages, will be wed to the righteous males in heaven (q.v.; Q 44:54; 52:20; 55:72; 56:22). The term *ḥūr*, pl. of *ḥawrāʾ*, refers to whiteness as in the large eye of the gazelle. The heavenly houris possess the ideal of feminine beauty with large, lustrous eyes that charm through a juxtaposition of white background — comprised of the eyeball and skin — and black pupil, lashes and eyebrows (see ANATOMY; COLORS). The houri's eye is not deployed so much for seeing as for being seen and enjoyed as a sign of affection, delight and bidding to blissful union (see PARADISE).

Despite its wide influence in ancient Arabia during the genesis of Islam (see PRE-ISLAMIC ARABIA AND THE QURʾĀN), the notion of the evil eye (e.g. *al-ʿayn*) does not occur in the Qurʾān, although believers are instructed (in Q 113:5) to fend off envy (q.v.; *ḥasad*) which is at the core of the concept of eye as malignant glance. Al-Ṭabarī (d. 310/923), in his exegesis of this passage, quotes the well-known prophetic ḥadīth which begins: "The evil eye is real" (*al-ʿayn ḥaqqun*, Ṭabarī, *Tafsīr*; see ḤADĪTH AND THE QURʾĀN).

Frederick Mathewson Denny

Bibliography
Primary: ʿAbd al-Bāqī; Ṭabarī, *Tafsīr*.
Secondary: S. van den Bergh, T. Sarnelli and Ph. Marcais, Ayn, in *EI²*, i, 784-6; J. Chelhod, *Les structures du sacré chez les Arabes*, Paris 1986, 155, 176; H.E. Kassis, *A concordance of the Qurʾān*, Berkeley 1983; Lane, s.v. *ʿ-y-n*; A.J. Wensinck/Ch. Pellat, Ḥūr, in *EI²*, iii, 581-2.

Ezekiel

Biblical prophet who figures in Islamic tradition. Ezekiel is not mentioned in the Qurʾān but exegetical literature claims a qurʾānic allusion to him at Q 2:243 as follows: "Have you not considered those who went forth from their homes in the thousands for fear of death (see DEATH AND THE DEAD)? God said to them, 'Die!' Then he gave them life (q.v.)."

Qurʾānic exegesis and extra-canonical traditions of various origins have given a vivid description of the events to which this verse alludes, in connection with the story of the vision of the dry bones (cf. *Ezek* 37:1-14). According to some reports (see, in particular, Ṭabarī, *Tafsīr*, ii, 585-91), a great many Israelites (see CHILDREN OF ISRAEL) — between three and ninety thousand — fled a plague out of fear of death and sought refuge outside their city, but God let them die. Other traditions state that these Israelites were so badly afflicted by a calamity that they sought the peace of death; or that death struck them when they disobeyed their king's order to fight against an enemy. Some sources also mention the name of their city, Dāwardān, and state that they died when they had already abandoned their homes. Ezekiel, passing by their corpses, called upon God to bring them back to life. God did so — after eight days according to some traditions — thus demonstrating his omnipotence to the Israelites. Other reports add that Ezekiel called on God when the corpses had already been dismembered and the bones had been scattered by beasts and birds and that they were prodigiously recomposed and restored to life.

The Muslim tradition contains a great many orthographical variations of Ezekiel's full name. Most sources, however, refer to him as Ḥizqīl b. Būzī/Būdhī/Būrī. Some sources add that he was also called Ibn al-ʿAjūz, "Son of the old woman," accounting for the origin of this name in various ways. Finally, a few exegetical traditions identify Ezekiel with Dhū l-Kifl (q.v.; Muqātil, *Tafsīr*, i, 202) and with Elisha (q.v.; Maqdisī, *al-Badʾ*, iii, 100).

Roberto Tottoli

Bibliography
Primary: Majlisī, *Biḥār al-anwār*, Beirut 1983, xiii, 381-7; Muqātil, *Tafsīr*, i, 202-3; al-Muṭahhar b. Ṭāhir al-Maqdisī, *al-Badʾ wa-l-taʾrīkh*, ed. C. Huart, 6 vols., Paris 1899-1919, iii, 100; Sibṭ Ibn al-Jawzī, *Mirʾāt*, i, 454-6; Ṭabarī, *Tafsīr*, ii, 585-91; id., *Taʾrīkh*, ed. de Goeje, i, 535-40; Thaʿlabī, *Qiṣaṣ*, 221-3; ʿUmāra b. Wathīma, *Badʾ al-khalq wa-qiṣaṣ al-anbiyāʾ*, in R.G. Khoury (ed.), *Les légendes prophétiques dans l'Islam*, Wiesbaden 1978, 59-63.
Secondary: J. Eisenberg/G. Vajda, *Ḥizqīl*, in *EI*², iii, 535; Speyer, *Erzählungen*, 412-3.

Ezra

Ezra (ʿUzayr) is identified in the Jewish sources as a high priest and scribe who helped to rebuild the Temple after returning from Babylonian exile with a number of Jewish families. He is seen as a highly pious and learned person who directed the religious life of the Jewish community, first in Babylon and then, later on, in Jerusalem (q.v.). Modern scholarly opinion considers Ezra a lettered man with spiritual tendencies who was a functionary of the Persian state which sent him to Palestine around the fourth century B.C.E. in order to promote the political authority of Persian rule.

Only once does the Qurʾān explicitly mention Ezra, in the course of disputing the claim, apparently made by some Jews in Medina, that Ezra was the son of God (see DEBATE AND DISPUTATION), a claim hard to verify in the Jewish sources. (According to Horovitz, *KU*, 128, Muḥammad could have heard about Jewish or Judeo-Christian sects that venerated Ezra in the way other sects venerated Melchizedek.) At any rate, one must understand the qurʾānic verse which mentions ʿUzayr in the context of Muslim-Jewish relations in Medina (q.v.) after the emigration (q.v.; *hijra*) made by the Prophet and the Meccan Muslim community to Medina in 622 C.E.: "The Jews call ʿUzayr son of God, and the Christians call Christ son of God. That is a saying from their mouth; in this they but imitate what the unbelievers of old used to say. God fights them *(qātalahumu llāhu)*: How they are deluded away from the truth!" (Q 9:30). The verse, which occurs in a Medinan sūra, was thus revealed in a context replete with theological arguments between the nascent Muslim community *(umma)* and the well-established Jewish community in Medina (see JEWS AND JUDAISM; OCCASIONS OF REVELATION).

The Qur'ān emphasizes the absolute divinity of God (see GOD AND HIS ATTRIBUTES) by pointing out that any act of association, however minute, would not be tolerated by the new Muslim community. In numerous verses, the Qur'ān warns against this divine association *(shirk)*. The Qur'ān takes the offensive against the contemporary Jewish and Christian leaders because, according to the Qur'ān, they deceived the masses into taking "their priests *(aḥbār)* and their anchorites (*ruhbān*, see MONASTICISM AND MONKS) to be their lords (see LORD) in derogation of God, and [they take as their lord] Christ (*al-masīḥ*, see JESUS), the son of Mary (q.v.); yet they were commanded to worship (q.v.) but one God. There is no God but he" (Q 9:31). In casting doubt on the divine claims attached to both 'Uzayr and Christ, the Qur'ān has in mind not just the Jewish and Christian communities in Arabia at the time (see CHRISTIANS AND CHRISTIANITY; POLEMIC AND POLEMICAL LANGUAGE), but the nascent Muslim community and its need to distinguish itself from those who claim 'Uzayr or Christ as the son of God. This process of religious formation initiated by the Qur'ān reflects a great deal of tension between the new Muslim *umma* and the more established Christian and Jewish *ummas* in Arabia (see COMMUNITY AND SOCIETY IN THE QUR'ĀN; ISLAM). Questions of prophetic identity being often linked to a community's notion of revelation, it remains to be asked why Ezra would be considered the son of God, why the qur'ānic text challenges this, and whether, in fact, 'Uzayr really is Ezra (see Wasserstrom, *Between Muslim and Jew*, 183-4).

In commenting on the qur'ānic verse that mentions 'Uzayr, al-Ṭabarī (d. 310/923) — the Muslim exegete *par excellence* — takes a cautious approach. He first asserts that, far from being a standard Jewish claim, this claim was made by a person called Pinhas, most probably a Medinan, who said, "God is poor and we are rich." Or, al-Ṭabarī continues, this claim may have been made by a number of Medinan Jews who visited the Prophet upon his arrival in Medina in 622 C.E. and asserted the divinity of 'Uzayr (Ṭabarī, *Tafsīr*, xv, 206 f.; Ibn Abī Ḥātim al-Rāzī, *Tafsīr*, vi, 1781-2). What is important to note, however, is that most Muslim exegetes glorify the important role played by 'Uzayr in renewing the faith of his people in the Bible after a period of decline in scriptural knowledge. Al-Ṭabarī, as well as other exegetes (see EXEGESIS OF THE QUR'ĀN: CLASSICAL AND MEDIEVAL), assert that 'Uzayr was one of the learned scholars *('ulamā')* of the people of Israel (see CHILDREN OF ISRAEL) who sought to revive the scriptures after the people of Israel forgot the importance of God's commands (see COMMANDMENTS; SCRIPTURE AND THE QUR'ĀN). While deeply meditating one day, God sent a light into his heart as a prelude to inspiring him with the entire biblical tradition, which 'Uzayr used in order to teach the people the forgotten laws of God. Finally, Muslim exegesis paints 'Uzayr as a spiritual seeker and a man of truth (q.v.) who refused to associate any being with God. On the other hand, "Muslim tradition says that God expunged 'Uzayr from the list of prophets because he refused to believe in qadar [divine decree] and inquired into it" (Rubin, *Between Bible and Qur'ān*, 197).

Ibrahim M. Abu-Rabi'

Bibliography
Primary: Ibn Abī Ḥātim al-Rāzī, *Tafsīr*, ed. A.M. al-Ṭayyib, 10 vols., Riyadh 1997; Ṭabarī, *Tafsīr*, ed. Shākir.
Secondary: G. Ahlstrom, *The history of ancient Palestine*, Minneapolis 1993; M. Ayoub, 'Uzayr in the Qur'ān and Muslim tradition, in W.M. Brinner and S.D. Ricks (eds.), *Studies in Islamic*

and Judaic traditions, Atlanta 1986; J. van Ess, *Zwischen Hadith und Theologie,* Berlin/New York 1975, 131-2; J. Finkel, Old Israelitish tradition in the Koran, in *MW* 22 (1932), 169-83; S.D. Goitein, *Jews and Arabs. Their contacts through the ages,* New York 1964; Horovitz, *KU;* D. Künstlinger, Uzair ist der Sohn Allāhs, in *Orientalistische Literatur-Zeitung* 35 (1932), 381-3; H. Lazarus-Yafeh, *Intertwined worlds. Medieval Islam and Bible criticism,* Princeton 1992, 50-74, especially 53, n. 10; U. Rubin, *Between Bible and Qurʾān,* Princeton 1999, 196-7; J. Walker, Who is Uzair? in *MW* 19 (1929), 303-6; S.M. Wasserstrom, *Between Muslim and Jew. The problem of symbiosis under early Islam,* Princeton 1995, 183-4 (for identifications of ʿUzayr).

F

Fables

see NARRATIVES; MYTHIC AND LEGENDARY NARRATIVES

Face

The front part of the head, including the eyes (q.v.), cheeks, nose, mouth, forehead and chin. The Arabic term for face *(wajh,* pl. *wujūh)* in the Qurʾān is generally applied to the face of human beings, seventy-two times across all chronological periods (see CHRONOLOGY AND THE QURʾĀN), but is also used less frequently to refer to the face of God (q.v.), eleven times in such constructions as "the face of God" *(wajh Allāh),* "his face" *(wajhuhu)* and "the face of your lord" *(wajh rabbika).* Depending on context and purpose, the term may also be rendered as countenance, essence, being, will, favor, honor (q.v.) or sake. For example, when used in relation to humans, *wajh* may mean being or essential/whole self as in Q 3:20: "I have surrendered my whole self to God" *(aslamtu wajhī lillāhi;* cf. Ṭabarī, *Tafsīr,* iii, 214, where this is explained through recollection that it is the face that is the noblest part of the human anatomy *[jawāriḥ]).* With respect to the physical human face, we find examples such as Q 4:43, where we learn that, when water (q.v.) is unavailable, pre-prayer ablution with clean sand is recommended (see RITUAL PURITY): "Rub your faces *(wujūh)* and your hands." On judgment day (see LAST JUDGMENT), the faces of those who lie (q.v.) regarding God will turn black (Q 39:60). Moreover, the unbelievers' faces will be turned upside down in the fire (q.v.) of hell (q.v.) as the ultimate humility, degradation and loss of the free agency enjoyed on earth (Q 33:66; see FREEDOM AND PREDESTINATION). The face bears the full brunt of the penalty of judgment day, according to Q 39:24 (see REWARD AND PUNISHMENT).

The Qurʾān favors the face as the focus of intention (q.v.) and purpose. The face represents the self in the person's faring well or being punished (see CHASTISEMENT AND PUNISHMENT). It is significant that both God and his human servants share, and in important ways meet, in the deeply personal symbolism of the face (see SYMBOLIC IMAGERY). Recipients of the revelation (see REVELATION AND INSPIRATION), when they realize its authenticity, fall down on their faces in prostration *(yakhirrūna lil-adhqāni sujjadan,* Q 17:107; cf. Q 17:109; see BOWING AND PROSTRATION) and tears. In several passages concerning proper ritual orientation (see RITUAL AND THE QURʾĀN), the human face is the searching probe that focuses the self on the appointed *qibla* (q.v.), literally "facing point," which for Muslims came to be the Kaʿba (q.v.) in Mecca (q.v.), the *axis mundi:* "We see the turning of your face *(qad narā taqalluba wajhika)* to heaven. Now shall we turn you to a *qibla* that will please you. Turn then your face in the direction of the sacred mosque (q.v.). Wherever you are, turn your faces in its direction" (Q 2:144).

The face serves as a relating coordinate for both worship (q.v.) in the direction of Mecca and God's guidance and blessing (q.v.) in general. Additionally, the concept of people facing each other openly is a significant ingredient in the personal nature of life in heaven (q.v.). All previous unpleasantness in interpersonal relations on earth will be banished: "We will remove from their hearts any hidden enmity: They will be brothers facing each other *(mutaqābilīn)* on raised couches" (Q 15:47; see BROTHER AND BROTHERHOOD; SOCIAL INTERACTIONS; SOCIAL RELATIONS).

The Ṣūfī tradition has always been particularly devoted to such passages as the following in their self-transcending search for union with God: "To God belong both the east and the west. Wherever you turn, there is the face of God" (Q 2:115); "Whatever of good you give benefits your own soul (q.v.), and you shall not do so except in seeking the face of God" (Q 2:272; see ṢŪFISM AND THE QURʾĀN). Two Meccan passages, one late and the other early, illustrate the ethical and spiritual power of the concept of the face of God in Muḥammad's prophetic career: "And do not call, besides God, on another deity. There is no deity but he. Everything perishes except his face" *(kullu shayʾin hālikun illā wajhahu,* Q 28:88); and, "He who spends his wealth (q.v.) for increase in goodness (see ECONOMICS; GOOD DEEDS), and has not in his mind expectation of a reward in return, but only desires the face of his lord *(illā btighāʾa wajhi rabbihi,* see LORD; ANTHROPOMORPHISM), the most high, will soon attain satisfaction" (Q 92:18-21).

Frederick Mathewson Denny

Bibliography
Primary: *Lisān al-ʿArab;* Ṭabarī, *Tafsīr.*
Secondary: J.M.S. Baljon, 'To seek the face of God' in Koran and hadith, in *AO* 21 (1953), 254-66; D.Z.H. Baneth, What did Muhammad mean when he called his religion 'Islam'? The original meaning of *aslama* and its derivatives, in *IOS* 1 (1971), 183-90 (on "submitting one's face"); M.M. Bravmann, Arabic *aslama (Islām)* and related terms, in M.M. Bravmann, *Studies in semitic philology,* Leiden 1977, 434-54; id., *The spiritual background of early Islam. Studies in ancient Arab concepts,* Leiden 1972, 22-3 (on "submitting one's face"); K. Cragg, *The mind of the Qurʾān,* London 1973, 165-6; M.A. Haleem, The face, divine and human, in the Qurʾān, in *IQ* 34 (1990), 164-79; Lane; H. Ringgren, *Islām, ʾaslama and Muslim,* Uppsala 1949, especially 22-4 (on "submitting one's face"); A. Rippen, 'Desiring the face of God.' The qurʾānic symbolism of personal responsibility, in I.J. Boullata (ed.), *Literary structures of religious meaning in the Qurʾān,* London 2000, 117-24.

Face of God

The visage of the creator, the sight of which the believer hopes to enjoy in the afterlife (see ESCHATOLOGY; BELIEF AND UNBELIEF; ANTHROPOMORPHISM). References to God's face appear frequently in the Qurʾān. In early Muslim theological debates the notion of God's face was an important, though not central, issue in discussions of theodicy. In mystical thought, God's face acquired a theophanic meaning as part of a complex understanding of how God relates to the created world (see GOD AND HIS ATTRIBUTES).

In the Qurʾān references to God's face or countenance *(wajh)* appear in the construction "the face of God" *(wajh Allāh),* "the face of their [or 'your']) lord" *(wajh rabbihim),* and "his face" *(wajhuhu).* Seeking the face of God is repeatedly presented as a desirable characteristic of virtuous human beings: "Whatever of good you give benefits your own souls, and you shall only do so seeking the face of Allah" (Q 2:272; see GOOD DEEDS); "Who spends his wealth for increase in self-purification, and has in his mind no favor from anyone for which a reward is expected in return, but only desires to seek after the face of his lord most high, soon will attain satisfaction" (Q 92:18-21).

Elsewhere, seeking the face of God is explicitly linked to other meritorious and ritually obligatory acts: "So give what is due to kinfolk, the needy, and the wayfarer. That is best for those who seek the face of God, and it is they who will prosper. That which you lay out for increase through the property of [other] people (see USURY) will have no increase with God: but that which you lay out for charity, seeking the face of God, [will increase]: it is these who will get a recompense multiplied" (Q 30:38-39; see ALMSGIVING; POVERTY AND THE POOR; KINSHIP); "Those who patiently persevere (see TRUST AND PATIENCE), seeking the face of their lord; establish regular prayers (see PRAYER); spend out of [what] we have bestowed for their sustenance, secretly and openly; and stave off evil with good (see GOOD AND EVIL); for such there is the final attainment of the [eternal] abode" (Q 13:22; see HOUSE, DOMESTIC AND DIVINE).

References to the face of God also appear in descriptions of his omnipresence; "To God belong the east and the west: wherever you turn, there is God's countenance, for God is all-embracing, all-knowing" (Q 2:115). References are more frequent in formulaic testaments to his eternality (see ETERNITY): "All that is on earth will perish, but the face of your lord will remain, full of majesty and honor" (Q 55:26-27); "And call not on another god besides God. There is no god but he. Everything that exists will perish except his face. To him belongs the command, and to him will you be brought back" (Q 28:88).

Belief that God possessed a visibly perceivable (though not earthly) body, and therefore a face, is reflected in early Islamic sources. The canonical collections of Sunnī tradition records a ḥadīth on the authority of Abū Hurayra (see ḤADĪTH AND THE QURʾĀN) in which, upon being questioned as to whether or not believers will see their lord on the day of resurrection (q.v.), the Prophet replies that God will be plainly visible at that time in the same way as the sun (q.v.) and moon (q.v.) are in this world (Muslim, *Ṣaḥīḥ*, i, 349).

In the early development of Islamic thought, God's face gets treated under two separate, yet related, rubrics, in neither of which it is a central issue of concern. The first is in the larger discussion of divine anthropomorphism and the second the eschatological concern over whether or not human beings can have a vision of God and, if so, what it would comprise. In the discussion of divine anthropomorphism, references to the face of God were subsumed in the wider discussion of 'the vision of God' *(ruʾyat Allāh)* which, together with the question of the divine word (see WORD OF GOD), was at the center of theological debates. Some early literalists maintained that qurʾānic references to God's body had to be taken at face value, but they were clearly outnumbered by their opponents who referred to them derrogatorily as corporealists *(mujassima* or *ḥashwiyya)*. Their opposition was most famously represented by the Muʿtazila (see MUʿTAZILĪS), who practised the concept of *tanzīh* (removal or withdrawal), consisting of the absolute denial of the possibility that any created quality could be attributed to God.

The attitude that eventually came to dominate Muslim belief was that of the Ashʿarīs who are famous for their theological principle of *bilā kayf wa lā tashbīh* ("without [asking] how and without comparison"). They acknowledged the literal truth of qurʾānic references to God's body, but simultaneously maintained that God was utterly transcendent and therefore his qualities could not be anthropomorphic. Thus God must have a face and the promise of a vision of God must be true, but God's face cannot be anything like a human face and vision of him cannot be the same as seeing anything in the created world (see SEEING AND HEARING; THEOLOGY AND THE QURʾĀN).

Ṣūfī thought, perhaps more than any other branch of the Islamic sciences, focused directly on the question of the precise nature of how human beings could perceive God (see ṢŪFISM AND THE QURʾĀN). From as early as the time of Junayd al-Baghdādī (d. 297/910), most Ṣūfīs had rejected the possibility that God could be seen visually. Instead, they emphasized two different notions of how he could be made visually manifest, through his theophanic manifestation in the created world *(tajallī)* and through the heart (q.v.; *qalb*) which functions as the most important mystical organ of perception.

Jamal Elias

Bibliography
Primary: al-Muḥāsibī, al-Ḥārith b. Asad, *al-ʿAql wa-fahm al-Qurʾān*, ed. Ḥ. al-Quwatlī, Cairo 1982³; Muslim, *Ṣaḥīḥ;* Zamakhsharī, *Kashshāf,* 4 vols., Beirut 1995.
Secondary: A.H. Abdel-Kader, *The life, personality and writings of al-Junayd*, London 1962; Böwering, *Mystical;* J.J. Elias, *The throne carrier of God. The life and thought of ʿAlāʾ ad-Dawla as-Simnānī*, Albany 1995; T. Izutsu, *God and man in the Koran. Semantics of the Koranic Weltanschauung*, Tokyo 1964; I.R. Netton, *Allāh transcendent. Studies in the structure and semiotics of Islamic philosophy, theology and cosmology*, London 1989; Nwyia, *Exégèse;* J.R.T.M. Peters, *God's created speech*, Leiden 1976.

Faction see PARTIES AND FACTIONS

Faḍīla see VIRTUE

Failure

A deficiency or inability to perform. In the Qurʾān, the God who is all-powerful (Q 8:41 etc.) cannot fail; nor can his messengers (Q 72:27-8; cf. Ṭabāṭabāʾī, *Qurʾān,* 80; see MESSENGER; POWER AND IMPOTENCE). The fact that their human audiences can and do fail constitutes the basis of the Qurʾān's account of God's dealings with humanity.

There is no qurʾānic term with the explicit meaning of failure. The root *kh-f-q* does not occur in the Qurʾān, while the root *f-sh-l* does appear four times (Q 3:122, 152; 8:43, 46), but in the sense of showing weakness or cowardice in battle (see COURAGE; EXPEDITIONS AND BATTLES). Eschatological failure (see ESCHATOLOGY) is sometimes expressed as the annulment of one's works (*ḥubūṭ al-ʿamal,* cf. Q 5:5; 6:88, 11:16; 39:65) as a result of lack of belief or faith (*īmān,* cf. Q 33:19; see BELIEF AND UNBELIEF; FAITH), a dislike of God's revelations (Q 47:9) or failure to follow what pleases God (Q 47:28). Failure is implicit in the root *kh-s-r,* one of the Qurʾān's commercial terms (see ECONOMICS), which connotes loss. Without *īmān* and good works, "man is in loss" (Q 103:2). What is lost is the self (*nafs,* Q 6:12; 7:9) and even one's family (Q 39:15; 42:45), either because the evildoer (see DEVIL) misleads them, thus sending them to hell (q.v.) or because he is parted from them when he himself is damned (Ibn Kathīr, *Tafsīr,* iv, 48). In other passages *kh-s-r* implies worldly failure: Joseph's (q.v.) brothers protest, "If the wolf eats him, we will be losers" (Q 12:14); and those who contemplate believing in Shuʿayb (q.v.) are warned by his enemies (q.v.) that they will be "the losers" (Q 7:90). The echo of this phrase at

Q 7:92 gives it religious meaning. Failure is also the consequence of the ruse *(kayd)* of miscreants (see CHEATING). Gravely astray (q.v.) is the *kayd* of the treacherous (Q 12:52), unbelievers (Q 40:25), Pharaoh (q.v.; Q 40:37) and the figure identified by exegetes as Abraha (q.v.; Q 105:2). The root *f-l-ḥ,* connoting success, governs passages that implicitly explain the nature of failure. Hence failure will be the lot of the unjust (Q 6:21; 12:23; see JUSTICE AND INJUSTICE), evildoers (Q 10:17; see EVIL DEEDS) and of sorcerers (Q 10:77; see MAGIC, PROHIBITION OF). Purifying the *nafs* brings success (Q 91:9), and one who "stunts it" *(dassāhā)* fails (*khāba,* Q 91:10). The latter term, associated with failure in pre-Islamic *maysir* games (Lane, 828), is the fate of "every stubborn tyrant" (Q 14:15; cf. 20:111) and of those who cry lies (Q 20:61; see FORETELLING; GAMBLING; LIE; PRE-ISLAMIC ARABIA AND THE QURʾĀN).

The collective failure of a community, as contrasted with personal eschatological failure, figures in the Medinan period (see CHRONOLOGY AND THE QURʾĀN). Hence the disbelievers in retreat are *khāʾibīn* (Q 3:127), and explanations are offered of the community's *(umma)* military setbacks (for Uḥud [q.v.] see Q 3:139-44; 152-5; 165-7), which are presented as tests or chastisements (see TRIAL; CHASTISEMENT AND PUNISHMENT). Shīʿī exegetes find references to the tragic future of Fāṭima (q.v.) and the Imāms (q.v.) in certain verses (cf. Ḥuwayzī, *Tafsīr,* iv, 186, 270-4; see SHĪʿISM AND THE QURʾĀN). From a Christian perspective, Kenneth Cragg has criticized the Qurʾān's insistence that God's purposes must not fail and that the prophet must therefore have recourse to arms (Cragg, *Event,* 132; id., *Mind,* 103-4, 194-7).

Timothy Winter

Bibliography
Primary: ʿA.ʿA. al-Ḥuwayzī, *Tafsīr nūr al-thaqalayn,* Qum n.d.; Ibn Kathīr, *Tafsīr.*
Secondary: M. Ayoub, *Redemptive suffering in Islam,* The Hague 1978; K. Cragg, *The event of the Qurʾān,* London 1971; id., *The mind of the Qurʾān,* London 1973; Lane; F. Rahman, *Major themes of the Qurʾān,* Minneapolis 1980, 17-36; M.H. Ṭabāṭabāʾī, *The Qurʾān in Islam. Its impact and influence on the life of Muslims,* London 1987.

Faith

Belief in God and a corresponding system of religious beliefs. No concept in the Qurʾān is more basic to the understanding of God's revelation through the prophet Muḥammad than faith. As the core of the truly good or moral life, faith is generally understood to encompass both affirmation and response.

According to the qurʾānic perspective, nothing of virtue (q.v.) is conceivable which does not arise directly from faith in the being and revelations of God (see REVELATION AND INSPIRATION). Such faith as it is articulated in the Qurʾān in its most basic sense means acknowledgment of the reality and oneness of God (see GOD AND HIS ATTRIBUTES) and of the fact that humans will be held accountable for their lives and deeds on the day of resurrection (q.v.). These two integrally related concepts frame the message of the Qurʾān and thus the religion of Islam itself. Faith in God is both trust in God's mercy (q.v.) and fear of the reality of the day of judgment (see LAST JUDGMENT). It also means that it is incumbent on those who acknowledge these realities to respond in some concrete way. The details of that response, and thus the relationship of faith and action, have been the subject of much debate in the history of Islamic thought.

The nature of faith

The Arabic noun rendered in English as either faith or belief is *īmān*. It is from the verb *amuna,* which in its several forms means to be faithful, to be reliable, to be safe and secure from fear. The fourth form of the verb, *āmana,* carries the meaning both of rendering secure and of putting trust in someone/something, the latter understood as having faith. The one who is faithful, therefore, the *muʾmin,* is he or she who understands and accepts the content of God's basic revelation and who thereby has entered a state of security and trust in God (see COVENANT). "The faithful *(al-muʾminūn)* are the ones whose hearts, when God is mentioned, are filled with awe. And when his revelations *(āyāt)* are recited to them, their faith is strengthened and they put their trust in their lord" (Q 8:2). The term *al-īmān* itself, used with the definite article, appears only 16 times in the text of the Qurʾān. Other derivatives of the fourth form of *amuna,* however, specifically *muʾmin* and *muʾminūn* (the singular and plural of the faithful) appear frequently in the Qurʾān. "O you who have faith" is a common refrain as God speaks to the members of his community through commandments (q.v.), admonitions, or words of counsel. Sometimes faith is expressed specifically as the remembrance (q.v.; *dhikr*) of God: "Those who have faith are those whose hearts find peace in the remembrance of God" (Q 13:28).

Implicit in the qurʾānic understanding of God is an unqualified difference between divine and human. The very recognition of God is often expressed by the term *tawḥīd,* meaning both God's oneness and human acknowledgment of it through the act of faith. It presupposes that there is no other being in any way similar to God (see POLYTHEISM AND ATHEISM), that God is utterly unique and that humans must not only testify to that uniqueness but embody their acknowledgment of it through their own lives and actions. As God alone is lord (q.v.) and creator of the universe (see CREATION), so the Muslim acknowledges that oneness by living a life of integrity and ethical and moral responsibility, in other words a life in which faith is reflected in all its dimensions (see ETHICS AND THE QURʾĀN). The greatest sin a human being can commit from the Islamic point of view is impugning the oneness of God (*shirk,* see SIN, MAJOR AND MINOR), i.e. to suggest by word or deed that anything else can in any way share in that divine unity.

The Qurʾān leaves no doubt that faith as a general category of human response did not begin with Muḥammad or those who heard the first messages he preached. Throughout the ages there were people who understood that there is only one God, and who responded with faith and submission. In the Qurʾān they are usually described not as *muʾminūn* but as *ḥanīf* (q.v.; pl. *ḥunafāʾ*), monotheists who lived a kind of pristine purity in the knowledge and recognition of God. The first of these to be acknowledged by name, and thus understood as an archetypal person of faith or submission *(islām),* was Abraham (q.v.). "Abraham was not a Jew, nor a Christian, but he was an upright man *(ḥanīfan),* one who submits *(musliman),* and he was not of those who practice *shirk (wa-mā kāna mina l-mushrikīna)*. The nearest of humankind to Abraham are those who follow him and this Prophet and those who have faith. God is the protector of the faithful" (Q 3:67-8). The Qurʾān contains numerous references to Abraham and his offspring as those who were the original *muslims,* those who acknowledged and surrendered to God. The faith of the *ḥanīf* served as a precursor of the *īmān* which was to emerge as the essential characteristic of those who became part of the religion of Islam. It is the faith of Abraham that was signaled in the Qurʾān as that which gave justification to Judaism and Christianity as religions of the book (q.v.; see also PEOPLE OF THE BOOK), not the manifestations of those religions in forms which did not acknowledge that they were precursors of the coming of Muḥammad. "They say: Become Jews or Christians, then you will be rightly guided. Say: No, [rather] the religion of Abraham, the upright *(ḥanīfan)*, and he was not one of those who practiced *shirk (wa-mā kāna mina l-mushrikīna)*" (Q 2:135).

Faith as gratitude, fear and responsibility

Many verses in the text of the Qurʾān attest that one of the primary ways in which faith is to be understood and expressed is by recognition that the world is the manifest gift of God (see GIFT-GIVING), and that its constituent elements are the signs (q.v.; *āyāt*) by which God makes evident his beneficent favors to humankind (see BLESSING). The person who has faith is the one who sees these signs and understands with his intelligence or intellect (q.v.; *ʿaql*) their nature as a gift from God. Those who are lacking in faith are the ones who fail to recognize and be grateful for these signs (see BELIEF AND UNBELIEF; GRATITUDE AND INGRATITUDE). Faith in its qurʾānic understanding, then, contains as an important ingredient the element of thankfulness to God for the bounties he has bestowed on humanity and praise (q.v.) of God as the only fitting response: "Only those have faith in our revelations *(āyātinā)* who, when they are reminded of them, fall down in prostration and give praise to their lord, and do not become arrogant" (Q 32:15; see ARROGANCE; BOWING AND PROSTRATION). Appreciation is expressed not only in the heart (q.v.) and by individual praise and prostration, but by active participation in helping support the faithful of the community (see COMMUNITY AND SOCIETY IN THE QURʾĀN): "Only those are faithful *(muʾminūn)* who have faith in God and his messenger (q.v.), then never doubt again (see UNCERTAINTY), but strive with their wealth (q.v.) and their lives for the cause of God (see PATH OR WAY). Such are the sincere" (Q 49:15). In listing some of the names of God, Q 59:23 identifies him as both *salām* (from *s-l-m,* the root letters of *muslim* and *islām*) and *muʾmin*. Rather than suggesting that God is a "believer," or one who possesses faith, as is said of a human person, the term *muʾmin* signifies that God witnesses to his own truthfulness or trustworthiness, that in effect he testifies to his own unicity, and that he is responsible for the signs that make humans *muʾminūn*.

It is important to underscore the importance of fear (q.v.) as a component of faith. The word generally rendered as piety (q.v.), godliness or devoutness is *taqwā,* derived from the root letters *w-q-y,* which, in their fifth and eighth verbal forms, mean to fear, especially God: "O you who believe," says Q 59:18, "fear God." Some have argued that to fear God *(ittaqa llāh)* is virtually synonymous with *āmana,* to have faith. Fear, however, is not a state in which the person of faith is terrorized or left in a pitiable condition bereft of consolation (q.v.). It is rather an attitude of trembling before the power and the majesty of God and the reality of the events to come at the end of time, including those signaling the coming of the "hour," the resurrection, the judgment and the final consignment (see ESCHATOLOGY). Fear as an element of faith is balanced in the Qurʾān by the very trust implied in the original definition of *īmān,* often rendered as *tawakkul,* with the implication of a kind of unshakable reliance on the fundamental goodness, justice and mercy of God (see JUSTICE AND INJUSTICE): "In God let those who are faithful put their trust" (Q 14:11). Such trust is not always easy to achieve, however, and so the Qur'ān assures the faithful that they must also have patience, especially when up against difficult circumstances (see TRUST AND PATIENCE). "O you who have faith! Seek help with steadfastness (*ṣabr*, lit. patience) and prayer (q.v.). God is with those who are steadfast *(al-ṣābirīn)*" (Q 2:153). Faith which is grounded in absolute trust expresses the certainty of conviction, and it is therefore the highest form of knowledge *('ilm)*. It is contrasted with other kinds of belief such as *ẓann* (supposition, opinion, assumption) and *khars*, which is close to guessing. The highest kind of faith is that generated by revelation. Many of the qualities which the Qur'ān affirms as an integral element of faith were part of the moral code that structured the lives of persons of conscience and honor (q.v.) in pre-Islamic Arabia (see PRE-ISLAMIC ARABIA AND THE QUR'ĀN).

The faithful are therefore described as those who are "protecting friends, one of another," as specified in Q 9:71. This verse continues by placing on male and female believers *(mu'minūn* and *mu'mināt)* the responsibility for carrying out what was to become one of the signal responsibilities for Muslims as developed in the schools of law and theology (see LAW AND THE QUR'ĀN; THEOLOGY AND THE QUR'ĀN), namely to enjoin what is right and forbid what is wrong. Thus doing good and avoiding evil (see GOOD AND EVIL), in the general qur'ānic understanding, is essential to an understanding and expression of faith. And the next verse again spells out clearly the reward for this discernment, namely the promise of God that the faithful men and women will abide in the blessed dwellings of the gardens of paradise (q.v.). In a number of references the Qur'ān affirms that those who have faith are regular and humble in their prayer, help and give asylum to the needy, pay the poor-tax (see ALMSGIVING; POVERTY AND THE POOR), guard their modesty (q.v.), love truth (q.v.) and honor their pledges (see CONTRACTS AND ALLIANCES), are not weary or faint-hearted, fight in the way of God (see JIHĀD), and always trust in the guidance of God regardless of the circumstances. Qur'ān commentators agree that while a person is still alive in this world there is always the possibility of his or her coming to a position of faith. But when the final hour arrives, and time as we know it comes to an end, then the opportunity to attain faith is gone forever and one must pay the consequences. Some interpreters insist that to fare well in that final judgment one must not have abdicated his or her faith at any time, that faith must continue unabated from the time at which one acknowledges oneself to be a *mu'min* to the last hour. Others allow that God in his mercy will accept the one who comes to the final judgment in a state of faith, regardless of earlier inconsistencies.

Faith and its qur'ānic opposites

The Qur'ān is replete with the kind of absolute dichotomy represented both by the choices of right and wrong, and by the ultimate consequences of those choices in the consignment to the garden (q.v.) or the fire (q.v.; see also REWARD AND PUNISHMENT). Faith becomes the ultimate criterion by which one is aligned either with the positive or the negative, and thus in many verses one sees the sharp contrast drawn between the person of faith and the one who lacks faith, who actively disbelieves, who thereby rejects the message and the promise of God. The quality that is set in opposition to faith is most often rendered as *kufr*, with its agent the *kāfir* contrasted with the *mu'min*. *Kufr* has two basic meanings in the Qur'ān, either the absence of faith, often rendered as disbelief, or ingratitude for God's signs *(āyāt)*. In one way these meanings connote somewhat different aspects of negative response to God, of lack of faith, and in another they are integrally related. Sometimes *kufr* is said to be the response of those whose intellectual reasoning does not enable them to believe and adopt a position of faith. One of the most obvious examples of this kind of *kufr* is that offered by those who cannot accept the reality of the resurrection and time of judgment: "... they rejected *(kafarū)* our signs, saying: "When we are bones and fragments, shall we be raised up as a new creation?... the wrongdoers reject all save disbelief *(kufr)*" (Q 17:98-9; see DEATH AND THE DEAD). The contrast of *kufr* with *īmān* is vivid, and serves to illustrate not only that there is a sharp difference between faith and rejection, but that acceptance of the resurrection and judgment is an essential element of faith.

The other dimension of *kufr* as it is contrasted with *īmān* relates to ingratitude. It was noted above that gratitude and corresponding attitudes of praise are fundamental to faith: "He gives you all that you ask for. If you count the favors of God you will not be able to number them. Man is truly a wrong-doer, an ingrate *(kāfir)*" (Q 14:34). As the person of faith allows the promises of God to assume reality, however difficult that may be for reason to accept, and to engender in him or her a grateful response, so the *kāfir* both rejects truth (Q 43:78) and is actively unaccepting of and ungrateful for the bounty of God's gifts to humankind: "Then remember me," says God, "[and] I will remember you. Give thanks to me, and do not reject [me] *(lā takfurna)*" (Q 2:152). In this striking negative parallelism, found throughout the Qurʾān between the concepts of faith and rejection/ingratitude, appears the definition of the qualities of the one in the negation of the qualities of the other. The original and in some senses prototypical *kāfir*, according to the Qurʾān, was the angel Iblīs (q.v.) who refused to obey God's command (see DISOBEDIENCE). "And when we said unto the angels, 'Bow down before Adam (see ADAM AND EVE),' they bowed down, all except Iblīs. He refused and was haughty, and so became a disbeliever *(wa-kāna mina l-kāfirīn)*" (Q 2:34).

Another qurʾānic term which stands in contrast to *īmān* is *nifāq*, generally rendered as hypocrisy (see HYPOCRITES AND HYPOCRISY) or dissimulation (q.v.). Unlike *kufr*, however, which is the mirror opposite of faith, *nifāq* is understood to be the act or condition of making a profession of faith verbally while inwardly not being a believer at all: "Have you not seen those who declare that they have faith in what is revealed to you and to those before you... When it is said to them, 'Come to what God has revealed and to the messenger,' you see the hypocrites *(al-munāfiqūn)* turn away from you with disgust" (Q 4:60-1). Some exegetes of the Qurʾān have posited that hypocrisy is sufficiently different from either faith or rejection that it should be categorized separately. The majority, however, have understood that *nifāq* is a kind of sub-set of *kufr*, both standing in essential opposition to *īmān*. Q 57:13-5 draws a dramatic picture of the great divide between the hypocrites and the faithful on the day of resurrection: Hypocrites (male and female, contrasting with the male and female believers of Q 57:12) will beg the believers to borrow from their light. But to the horror of the hypocrites, there will arise between them and the believers a gated wall, with mercy to be found on one side and doom on the other. The *munāfiqūn* will ask of the faithful, "Were we not with you?" But the answer is that while in one way they were, in another and more important way they led lives marked by temptation, hesitation and doubt, consumed with vain desires until it was too late. Now no ransom is possible (see INTERCESSION), and the lot of the hypocrites is the fire.

Faith and works; islām *and* īmān

In the Qurʾān, as we have seen, there is a close connection between having faith and doing good deeds (q.v.). The expression "those who believe and do good works" is repeated in many verses, and such people "are the inhabitants of the garden; they will abide there eternally" (Q 2:82). The Qurʾān closely links the term for good works *(ṣāliḥāt)* to *īmān*. The verb *ṣalaḥa* in Arabic means to be good, right, proper, pious and godly, and the *ṣāliḥāt* are the good deeds (q.v.) in which the faithful engage. The joining of faith and works is so integral to the Qurʾān that many have argued that the performance of works is implicit in the understanding of what it means to have faith. Faith is not so much believing in something or adhering to some kind of acceptance of the unseen (see HIDDEN AND THE HIDDEN) or what is not immediately evident to the senses or reason, as it is active testimony to what one holds unquestionably to be true. God acts on behalf of humankind, and men and women respond in the act of faith. But what is the content of that faith? What is the mix of mental discernment, verbal confession (see CREEDS) and the performance of good deeds that is really at the heart of *īmān?*

Despite their apparent qurʾānic association, the question arose early in the history of the Muslim community as to whether faith and works were to be understood as one and inseparable, or as two different though perhaps necessarily related concepts. The issue was directly related to the definition of who was a true Muslim, i.e. acceptable as a faithful member of the community, and who was not. Opinions differed widely, and in many cases depended on the understanding of two related matters pertaining to the question of faith: (1) What is the relationship of faith and works? (2) What is the relationship of *islām* (submission to God) to *īmān* (faith in God)? Several schools of interpretation, each with its own version of belief in the message of the Qurʾān, refused to separate faith and the accomplishment of good works *(aʿmāl)*. Others who were attempting to understand the meaning of *īmān,* however, found it important to distinguish between faith and works, including some who were willing to see the performance of good deeds as an overt means of achieving or actualizing faith. The question of the possibility of an increase or decrease of faith will be dealt with below.

The matter of faith and works for some was seen to be integrally related to the question of faith and submission. Islam is the only major religion whose very name suggests a bi-dimensional focus of faith. On the vertical axis it refers to the individual and personal human response to God's oneness, often described as the "faith" dimension, while on the horizontal axis it means the collectivity of all of those persons who together acknowledge and respond to God to form a community of religious faith. Muslims agree that the religious response of all those persons throughout the ages who have affirmed the oneness of God in faith can rightly be understood as personal *islām*. It was only with the official beginning of the community at the time of the emigration (q.v.; *hijra*) to Medina (q.v.), however, that there came to be a specific recognition that Muslims together form a group, a unity, an *umma,* although the term *islām* itself was not often used to refer to that group until considerably later. Nonetheless it was over the question of legitimate membership in the *umma* that some of the most serious controversies arose. Implicit in that discussion was the issue of whether there is a distinction between *islām* and *īmān* (see ISLAM).

In the Qurʾān there is no clear distinction between these two terms. Among the early traditions of the community, however, is one in which the Prophet is said to have defined *islām* specifically as distinct from *īmān*. The narrative is given in a variety of renditions in a large number of compilations. The most popular version tells the story of a man who comes to the Prophet of God while he is seated with some of his companions. This man, who is unknown to the assembled group, turns out later to be the angel Gabriel (q.v.). He asks the Prophet, "What is *islām?*" And the Prophet replies that it is the specific duties of witnessing that there is no God but God and Muḥammad is his messenger (see WITNESSING AND TESTIFYING), submitting to God with no association of anything else, performing the prayer *(ṣalāt),* paying the alms tax *(zakāt),* fasting (q.v.) during Ramaḍān (q.v.) and making the pilgrimage (q.v.; *ḥajj*) if possible. He then asks the Prophet, "What is *īmān?*" The answer given is that it is faith in God, his angels (see ANGEL), his books, his messengers, the last day and the resurrection and all of the particulars to attend the final judgment, and (in some versions) the decree *(al-qadr)* in its totality (cf. Bukhārī, *Ṣaḥīḥ,* i, 48; Ibn Ḥanbal, *Musnad,* i, 27, 51-2; ii, 107, 426; Muslim, *Ṣaḥīḥ,* i, 36-40).

In terminology developed in later Islamic theology a distinction was made between *īmān mujmal* (a brief summary of faith) and *īmān mufaṣṣal* (faith elaborated in detail). The former indicates that the essential content of faith is the affirmation that came to be known as the creed or *shahāda* (testimony) of Islam, that there is no God but God and that Muḥammad is the messenger of God. The details of that testimony *(īmān mufaṣṣal),* or the elements as found in the verses of the Qurʾān that came to comprise the content of faith, are those outlined above in the Prophet's answers to the question of the angel, "What is *īmān?*" Generally these are limited to the first five, sometimes said to parallel the five pillars *(arkān)* or responsibilities incumbent on the believing Muslim (these "pillars of Islam" are outlined in the Prophet's response to the angel's question, "What is *islām?*"). Sometimes, however, acceptance of *qadar* or the measure of divine foreordainment is also included in *īmān mufaṣṣal* (see FREEDOM AND PREDESTINATION).

In the several renditions of this tradition there seems to be a fairly distinct line drawn between *islām* and *īmān*. The former consists almost exclusively of the performance of the (five) specific duties prescribed by God through his Prophet for the Muslim; the latter is faith in (acceptance and affirmation of) the various elements proclaimed through the word of the Prophet as real and valid. The case could thus be made, as some did, that the Prophet himself distinguished between faith and works. Some traditions support this distinction by affirming that the Prophet asserted that *islām* is overt *(ʿalāniyya)* while *īmān* is in the heart, and that pointing to his breast he said, "Piety *(taqwā)* is here" (Ibn Ḥanbal, *Musnad,* iii, 134-5). Such a clear distinction was not always made, however, and in several traditions we see that while *islām* and *īmān* were generally given different emphases, they were definitely seen to be interrelated. In the Qurʾān commentaries (see EXEGESIS OF THE QURʾĀN), the traditions (see ḤADĪTH AND THE QURʾĀN) and the classical lexicons, three sets of relationships between faith and *islām* are proposed: different but separate; distinct but not separate; and synonymous. One frequently cited tradition reports the Prophet as having said that the most virtuous kind of *islām* is *īmān* (Ibn

Ḥanbal, *Musnad,* iv, 114) thus suggesting that faith is a sort of subdivision of *islām.* And in a number of narrations *islām* seems to consist of *īmān* plus works, as the Prophet, when asked to discuss *islām,* responded that the submitter should say, "I have faith," and should walk the straight path (*al-ṣirāṭ al-mustaqīm,* Ibn Ḥanbal, *Musnad,* iii, 413; iv, 385; Muslim, *Ṣaḥīḥ,* i, 65).

As the Qurʾān is not precise on the distinction between faith and submission, for the most part it also does not suggest that either is higher or of more value than the other. There is one verse, however, which does seem to suggest that there is, in fact, not only a distinction between *īmān* and *islām* but a quality judgment about them. Q 49:14 says, "The desert Arabs say, 'We have faith *(āmannā).*' Say [to them], 'You do not believe,' but [should] say, 'We submit *(aslamnā),*' for faith has not yet entered into your hearts...." For some commentators the verse has been taken to mean that the Arabs (q.v.) mentioned there came to follow the teachings of the Prophet only to obtain his bounty, and because they did not have true faith they should be classified as hypocrites, i.e. lying in their hearts (Bukhārī, *Ṣaḥīḥ,* i, 41-2). Others, seeing that the distinction apparently drawn in this verse does not represent the way in which the terms are used elsewhere in the Qurʾān, have been unwilling to say that *īmān* is superior to *islām* (i.e. that faith takes priority over works; cf. Bukhārī, *Ṣaḥīḥ,* i, 31). In general the exegetes and theologians define *īmān* as the specific act of faith most commonly understood as assent or attestation *(taṣdīq)* and affirmation or acknowledgment *(iqrār),* and make it clear that it has at least some areas of identification with *islām.*

The various elements of faith and faith-response are often associated with the parts of the body (see ANATOMY), such that the full acceptance of the content of faith lies in the heart, the public affirmation or profession comes through the lips, and the performance of the duties or responsibilities of the faith is done by the members. Some interpreters have wanted to say that only the matter of the heart is of primary significance, and that the affirmation and deeds are secondary. Only the latter constitute *islām,* they argue, and, while part of *īmān,* are not its crucial feature (see e.g. al-Ṭabarī, *Tafsīr,* vi, 564-5). Only a few Qurʾān commentators, notably Fakhr al-Dīn al-Rāzī (d. 606/1210), have argued for the essential identity of faith and submission (while different in generality, he says, they are one in existence, *Tafsīr,* ii, 628). Most agree with the giant of classical Qurʾān exegetes, Abū Jaʿfar Muḥammad al-Ṭabarī (d. 310/923), that on one level *islām* signifies the verbal submission by which one enters the community of *muslims,* and on the other it is coordinate with *īmān,* which involves the total surrender of the heart, mind and body (*Tafsīr,* ix, 518).

Early theological controversies over issues of faith

While the commentators argued with their pens over the centuries about the relationship of faith and *islām,* others in the early days of Islam were more vocal in their insistence that certain people must not be acknowledged as true members of the Muslim community and used what they saw as the distinction between the two terms to support their arguments. Who is truly a *muʾmin,* a member of the community of the faithful believers? The issue became one of genuine concern to the early Muslim community when a group of puritans called the Khārajites (*khawārij,* see KHĀRAJĪS; this group considered themselves to be the only "true Muslims") tried to draw the distinction by claiming that some *muslims,* especially claimants to the leadership of the Muslim community, such as ʿUthmān (q.v.) and ʿAlī (see ʿALĪ B. ABĪ ṬĀLIB), who had committed what they considered sinful acts and had failed to rule the community in the name of the Qurʾān, were in fact without *īmān* and thus should not be part of the *umma*. In the Qurʾān, as we have seen, the polarity is clear between those with faith, whether they are called *muʾminūn* or *muslimūn*, and those who do not have faith, the *kāfirūn*, the ungrateful rejectors of God's message. In their attempt to try to assure the absolute purity of Islam, to make sure that those who were Muslims were faithful in their hearts as well as submitters with their tongues and members, the Khārajites accused some members of the community of actually being infidels. For them the important distinction was not between Muslim believers and non-Muslim unbelievers, but rather between those within the body of Islam who had faith and those who did not, even if technically *muslimūn*. With these accusations came the first discussions of the nature of grave sin within Islam. Although the Khārajites were not themselves so much theologians as concerned Muslims who feared for the purity of the community once Islam had begun to spread rapidly beyond Arabia, they brought the issue of a definition of *īmān* and *muʾmin* to the fore for essentially the first time. The radical alternative of an essentially faithless Muslim was never adopted. Forced to resort to severe reprisals on those who disagreed with them, the Khārajites were relegated to an underground movement of political opposition.

Another group concerned with the matter of grave sin was called the Murjiʾites (see DEFERRAL). In distinction to the Khārajites, they held that even though a Muslim commits a grave sin, he may still remain a *muʾmin*, a person of faith. So long as one continues to profess *islām*, they said, it is not the responsibility of other Muslims to determine that he or she has given up all claims to true faith. The designation *murjiʾa* means those who postpone, and in this case indicates their belief that judgment about the presence or absence of faith in anyone must be left to God to decide on the last day. Nonetheless they were convinced that it is faith which provides for the ultimate salvation (q.v.) of humans, and that the essence of faith is not necessarily affected by one's deeds.

Other factions in the early history of Islam looked at what the Qurʾān has to say about matters of faith and works from a different perspective. For one of these groups, the Muʿtazilites, faith was said to be measured most accurately by the works that constitute it. Known as the "people of justice and unity *(ahl al-ʿadl wa-l-tawḥīd)*," they insisted on the absolute unicity of God, denying him any substantive attributes, and held that God is necessarily just, and wills and does only that which is good (cf. Gimaret, Muʿtazila, 787-91). In their view, humans are not predestined by God toward one condition or another, but make their own destiny by their deeds. For the Muʿtazilites, the primary issue was not whether the grave sinner is still a person of faith (indeed, they developed the notion of an "intermediate state" *[al-manzila bayna l-manzilatayn]*, refusing to classify a sinful Muslim as either a believer *[muʾmin]* or a disbeliever *[kāfir]*, but considering this individual a "malefactor" *[fāsiq]*; cf. Gimaret, Muʿtazila, 786-7), but that doing good works is an essential element of *islām/īmān*. Unlike those who wanted to identify the crucial component of *īmān* as heartfelt affirmation, with deeds a secondary result, the Muʿtazilites insisted that faith cannot exist without works. The necessity of putting faith into action is seen in one of the principles of Muʿtazilism: heeding the qurʾānic injunction (cf. e.g. Q 3:104, 110) of "ordering good and forbidding evil *(al-amr bi-l-maʿrūf wa-l-nahy ʿan al-munkar)*"; how frequently Muʿtazilites put this principle into practice, however, is a matter of debate (cf. Gimaret, Muʿtazila, 787; for a recent discussion of this principle in Islamic thought, see Cook, *Commanding the right*). The Muʿtazilites' stress on human reason as the way of understanding God's commands led them to the position that faith is actually the knowledge by which the revelation is manifested. *Īmān,* then, is both what the faithful one knows and the necessary deeds undertaken on the basis of that knowledge.

The testimony of faith

The position taken by various groups in the early history of Islam on the matter of faith as it is expressed in the verses of the Qurʾān, then, is obviously related to the larger issues they wished to press. While some chose to stress the importance of heartfelt acceptance, and others emphasized the importance of good deeds, still others looked to the matter of testimony by verbal pronouncement as the essential ingredient in faith. The Qurʾān affirms the importance of testimony in many places, none clearer than the passage which describes all humanity affirming God since the beginning of human creation: "When your lord took from the children of Adam, from their loins, their descendants, and made them testify concerning themselves, [saying], 'Am I not your lord?' they said, 'Yes! We testify *(shahidnā)*'" (Q 7:172).

Thus the testimony or *shahāda* is the content of *īmān mujmal,* faith summarized. One school that has clearly insisted on the importance of this kind of verbal testimony as essential to *īmān* is that of the Ḥanafites. For them, confession by the tongue is not merely a consequence of faith, but is the actual obligation of the person in whose heart *īmān* is to be found. Thus the very fact of God's having professed himself to be *muʾmin* (Q 59:23) means that *muʾmins* in turn are obligated to profess God as the essential act of faith. Many theologians who believe that the locus of faith is only to be found deep within the human heart consider the Ḥanafite position to place an overemphasis on the verbal nature of faith.

Abū Ḥanīfa (d. 150/767) raised an important issue in relation to faith, namely whether, once adopted, it is capable of increase or decrease. This (Murjiʾite) position was that *īmān* cannot be divided, and thereby cannot become more or less. It seems clear from the Qurʾān that it is possible for faith to grow or diminish, or even to disappear completely: "Whoever rejects God after his faith *(man kafara bi-llāhi min baʿdi īmānihi)*..." says Q 16:106. Most of the early doctors of Islam disagreed with the Ḥanafites on this matter, holding that faith can increase when one performs obedient acts, and likewise can diminish if one does unfaithful or disobedient deeds. Abū l-Ḥasan al-Ashʿarī (d. 324/936), once a Muʿtazilite but later devoting himself to a refutation of many of their views, is often said to have been the founder of what emerged as the orthodox or dominant school of theological reasoning in matters of divine justice and human responsibility. Al-Ashʿarī disputed Abū Ḥanīfa's doctrine that *īmān* cannot increase or decrease on the grounds that one's deeds and words have an indisputable effect on the quality and nature of one's faith (*Maqālāt,* 140-1).

Not all of those who affiliated themselves with the Ashʿarite school followed al-Ashʿarī in this affirmation, but in general it has become part of the understanding of most Muslims that what one says and does can have a significant effect on what is understood to be one's *īmān* or the content of faith. Whether or not faith actually increases or decreases remains a matter of conjecture. A popular twelfth-century credal formulation (see CREEDS) by the jurist and theologian Najm al-Dīn al-Nasafī (d. 537/1142) summarizes a number of the issues raised above and offers its own conclusions. It affirms that faith is assent by the heart to what God has revealed and verbal confession of it, that while works can increase or decrease the essence of faith cannot, and that while they may emphasize different aspects of the human response to God, *īmān* and *islām* are one.

Jane I. Smith

Bibliography
Primary: al-Ashʿarī, Abū l-Ḥasan, *Maqālāt al-islāmiyyīn wa-ikhtilāf al-muṣallīn*, ed. H. Ritter, Istanbul 1963²; Baghdādī, Ḍiyāʾ al-Dīn Khālid, *Belief and Islam. The annotated translation of Iʿtiqād-nama by Mawlānā Ḍiyāʾ al-Dīn Khālid Baghdādī (1778-1826)*, Istanbul 1993; Bayḍāwi, *Anwār;* Bukhārī, *Ṣaḥīḥ*, Cairo 1966; E.E. Elder, *A commentary on the creed of Islam. Saʿd al-Dīn al-Taftazānī on the creed of Najm al-Dīn al-Nasafī*, New York 1950; N. Faris (trans.), *The foundations of the articles of faith. Being a translation with notes of the Kitāb Qawāʿid al-aqāʾid of al-Ghazzālī's Iḥyāʾ ʿulūm al-dīn*, Lahore 1974; Ibn Ḥanbal, *Musnad*, 6 vols., Cairo 1895; Ibn Kathīr, *Tafsīr;* Ibn Taymiyya, *al-Īmān*, Cairo 1972; Muslim, *Ṣaḥīḥ;* Quṭb, *Ẓilāl;* Rashīd Riḍā, *Manār;* Rāzī, *Tafsīr*, 8 vols., Istanbul 1891; Ṭabarī, *Tafsīr*, Damascus 1959/60; Zamakhsharī, *Kashshāf*.
Secondary: M.R.Ḥ. ʿAbd al-Mutajallī, *al-Īmān fī l-Qurʾān al-karīm*, Cairo 1976; S. ʿAbd al-Raḥmān, *al-ʿAql wa-l-īmān fī l-islām*, Beirut 1979; M. Cook, *Commanding right and forbidding wrong in Islamic thought*, Cambridge, UK 2000; L. Gardet, *Dieu et la destinée de l'homme*, Paris 1967; id. and Anawati, *Introduction;* D. Gimaret, Muʿtazila, in *EI²*, vii, 783-93; M.ʿA.Q. Ḥanadī, *Arkān al-īmān fī ḍawʾ al-kitāb wa-l-sunna*, Jidda 1990; T. Izutsu, *The concept of belief in Islamic theology*, Tokyo 1965; id., *Concepts;* id., *The structure of the ethical terms in the Koran*, Tokyo 1957; ʿA.Ḥ. Maḥmūd, *al-Īmān*, Cairo 1967; M. Maḥmūd, *Riḥla min al-shakk ilā l-īmān*, Beirut 1971; G. Makdisi, Ashʿarī and the Ashaʿrites in Islamic religious history, in *SI* 17 (1962), 37-80; 18 (1963), 19-39; S. Makino, *Creation and termination*, Tokyo 1970; Nöldeke, *GQ;* F. Rahman, *Major themes of the Qurʾān*, Minneapolis 1980; H. Ringgren, The conception of faith in the Koran, in *Oriens* 4 (1951), 1-20; id., *Islam, aslama, and Muslim*, Upsalla 1949; J.I. Smith, *An historical and semantic study of the term Islam as seen in a sequence of Quran commentaries*, Missoula 1975; A. Wensinck, *The Muslim creed*, Cambridge 1932; M. Yazdī, *Uṣūl al-dīn wa-usus al-īmān fī l-Qurʾān*, Qum 1997.

Fall of Man

The primordial turning away from God by human beings, usually depicted in scripture in the persons of Adam and Eve (q.v.). The Qurʾān tells of the fall of humankind from a garden (q.v.) in which they enjoyed happiness — free from hunger, thirst and pain from the sun's heat (Q 20:118-9; Ṭabarī, *Tafsīr*, viii, 267-8) — to this present world (q.v.) in which they are subject to pain and, with it, moral and physical weakness (see FAILURE). This fall is an event in the drama that ensued when God announced to the angels (see ANGEL) that he was going to place on earth (q.v.) a vicegerent (Q 2:30; see CALIPH) fashioned from clay (q.v.; Q 15:26; 17:61). Satan (see DEVIL), when ordered to bow before Adam, refused (Q 2:34; 7:11; 15:31; 17:61; 18:50; 20:116; 38:74) and was expelled from heaven (Q 7:13; 17:63; see BOWING AND PROSTRATION). Motivated by anger (q.v.) and envy (q.v.), he swore to waylay Adam, his wife and their descendants, dragging them with him into hell (q.v.; Q 7:16-7; 15:39; 17:62).

The events of this drama are scattered over a number of sūras (q.v.), presented with varying emphases and from different perspectives. A synoptic overview is as follows. God set Adam and his wife in the garden where they were allowed to enjoy everything except the fruit of one tree (q.v.): "Do not approach this tree, for then you will be evil doers" (Q 2:35, 7:19; see EVIL DEEDS). He warned them that Satan was their enemy (see ENEMIES) and would try to deceive and mislead them (Q 20:117). Satan tempted them to eat from this forbidden tree, saying to Adam, "Shall I guide you to the tree of immortality and power? It does not wither" (Q 20:120); and "Your lord (q.v.) forbade you both this tree lest you become angels or [be numbered] among the immortals" (Q 7:20). They succumbed to his guile and ate its fruit. They realized they were naked, and tried to clothe themselves with leaves from trees of the garden (Q 20:12, cf. Ṭābarī, *Tafsīr*, viii, 468; Q 7:22). By eating of it they had sinned. God rebuked them: "Did I not forbid you that tree, and say to you 'Satan is a self-declared enemy to you!' " (Q 7:22). They asked forgiveness. God forgave them and offered them guidance, but expelled them from the garden (Q 20:122-3), as he had expelled Satan from heaven (see HEAVEN AND SKY), warning that they and their descendants would be foes one to another (Q 2:36; 7:24; 20:123), adding "On earth is for you a dwelling place and chattels for a time… on it you will live, on it you will die, and from it you will be brought forth" (Q 7:24-5). He also comforted them (see CONSOLATION): "When guidance comes to you from me, then whoever follows my guidance, no fear or grief shall come upon them" (Q 2:38; cf. 20:123), referring to the prophets he would send (see PROPHETS AND PROPHETHOOD).

Exegetes differ as to the nature and location of the garden (cf. Asad, *Message*, 590 n. 6). The name of Adam's wife, Ḥawwāʾ in Arabic, is not given in the Qurʾān, but the earliest commentators identify her by this name, a cognate of the Hebrew word for Eve (Eisenberg/Vajda, Ḥawwāʾ; see FOREIGN VOCABULARY).

The fall, then, is the result of Satan's first deception of humankind. It does not have the consequence of separation from God and need for a redeemer set out in the Christian doctrine of original sin (see SIN, MAJOR AND MINOR). Although the themes associated with the fall from the biblical tradition are found in the Qurʾān, the Qurʾān in no way associates the fall with original sin. Rather, the significance of the term is a function of the cosmological order of things: heaven is clearly "up there" in the Qurʾān, and one may "fall" from it (see COSMOLOGY IN THE QURʾĀN). Humankind, the qurʾānic word is *insān,* is forgetful, impulsive (Arnaldez, Insān) and in a sorry state, *fī khusrin* (Q 103:2; Ṭabarī, *Tafsīr*, xii, 684-5). One has to endure hardships from which one would otherwise have remained exempt. One needs guidance, however, not redemption (see CRITERION; FAITH; SALVATION), and the prophets, above all Muḥammad (q.v.), give this guidance. If a human being accepts this guidance, on the day of resurrection (q.v.) he or she will enter heaven. The fall has generated numerous popular stories concerning the way in which Adam and Eve were tempted, the different spots on earth to which they fell, and their eventual reunion to beget their children (q.v.) and cooperate in the building of the Kaʿba (q.v.; Kisāʾī, *Tales*, 55, 65-7 and other collections of *Qiṣaṣ*).

Anthony Hearle Johns

Bibliography
Primary: Ibn Kathīr, *Qiṣaṣ al-anbiyāʾ*, ed. S. al-Laḥḥām, Beirut 1988; Kisāʾī, *Qiṣaṣ;* id., *The tales of the prophets of al-Kisāʾī*, trans. W.M. Thackston, Boston 1978; Ṭabarī, *Tafsīr;* Thaʿlabī, *Qiṣaṣ*, ed. Beirut.
Secondary: R. Arnaldez, Insān, in *EI²*, iii, 1237-9; M. Asad, *The message of the Qurʾān*, London 1980; J. Eisenberg/G. Vajda, Ḥawwāʾ, in *EI²*, iii, 295; A.J. Wensinck/L. Gardet, Iblīs, in *EI²*, iii, 668-9.

Family

Those who live in one house or share a common lineage. While several qurʾānic terms can be understood as referring to family, it is impossible to distinguish, on the basis of terminology alone, between household and biological family, or between one type or another of the latter (e.g. core, compound, joint or extended family; cf. Smith, Family).

Āl (Lane, 127) at Q 15:59 and 61 (the family of Lot [q.v.]; Bell, i, 246); 3:11 and 8:54 (the family of Pharaoh [q.v.]; Bell, i, 45, 167) may mean either household or (in the case of Pharaoh) followers. *Āl Ibrāhīm* (the family of Abraham [q.v.]) at Q 4:54 may refer to the Arabs (q.v.) or Muḥammad (q.v.) as their representative (Bell, i, 77, n. 3).

Ahl also has several meanings (cf. al-Rāghib al-Iṣfahānī, *Mufradāt,* s.v. *a-h-l;* Lane 121). In many verses (q.v.) throughout the Qurʾān, it refers to the people of a house or dwelling (e.g. Q 28:29; 29:32; 38:43; 52:26); in others, more specifically to a family (e.g. Q 4:92; 12:93; 39:15 [pl.]; 83:31; 84:9, 13); but in quite a few of the aforementioned verses (as well as Q 11:45, 46, 81; 15:65; 20:10, 29; 66:6), these meanings are interchangeable. In some cases, *ahl* designates people, e.g. "the people of this town" of Q 29:34 (Bell, ii, 387; cf. Robertson-Smith, *Kinship,* 27).

Bayt, literally a tent or, in towns, a room (in a large family house) that houses a conjugal family (Bianquis, Family, 636; see also Robertson-Smith, *Kinship,* 202), is also used in a compound phrase, e.g. *ahl bayt* and *ahl al-bayt,* literally "people of a/the house," for instance, in Q 11:73 (Bell, i, 212) and Q 28:12 (Bell, ii, 375), and can designate either household *(jamāʿat al-bayt,* cf. al-Rāghib al-Iṣfahānī, *Mufradāt,* s.v. *b-y-t)* or family. In the Medinan verse Q 33:33 (Bell, ii, 414) it probably refers to the Prophet's family (*ahl bayt Muḥammad,* Ṭabarī, *Tafsīr,* ad loc.; see FAMILY OF THE PROPHET; PEOPLE OF THE HOUSE).

ʿAshīra, as a person's kinsfolk (see KINSHIP; PARENTS; TRIBES AND CLANS), his nearer or nearest relations, or next of kin by descent from the same father or ancestor (Lane, 2053; see also al-Rāghib al-Iṣfahānī, *Mufradāt,* s.v. *ʿ-sh-r;* cf. *Jalālayn*'s commentary on *rahṭ* in Q 11:91: *rahṭuka=ʿashīratuka;* according to al-Rāghib al-Iṣfahānī [*Mufradāt,* s.v. *f-ṣ-l*], *faṣīla* at Q 70:13 is also identified with *ʿashīra: wa-faṣīlat al-rajul=ʿashīratuhu al-munfaṣila ʿanhu*) appears in Q 9:24 (Bell, i, 176). *ʿAshīrataka al-aqrabīna* at Q 26:214 means a clan, the nearer ones (Bell, ii, 362).

Qurbā (Q 42:23; Bell, ii, 487) designates relationship, or relationship by the female side (Lane, 2508) whereas *aqrabūna* (cf. Q 2:180, 215; 4:135) and phrases such as *dhū l-qurbā* (cf. Q 2:83, 177; 4:36), *dhū maqraba* (cf. Q 90:15; Bell, ii, 658) and *ūlū l-qurbā* (e.g. Q 4:8) refer to kinsfolk, relatives. Relationship, i.e. nearness of kin, specifically relationship by the female side (?), is also expressed by *raḥim,* pl. *arḥām,* (lit. womb, Lane, 1056), as at Q 60:3 (*arḥāmukum=qarābatukum, Jalālayn,* ad loc.). See also *ūlū l-arḥām* (those who are related in blood, blood relations) in Q 8:75 (Bell, i, 170) and Q 33:6 (Bell, ii, 411).

Both types of familial relations, i.e. descent *(nasab)* and marriage *(ṣihr),* are mentioned in Q 25:54 (Bell, ii, 350). It has been suggested that at the time of the Prophet, the family structure within the Arabian tribal system went through a transition from matrilineal-matrilocal, which was common in central Arabia and influential, to a certain degree, during the early Islamic period, to patrilineal-patriarchal-patrilocal, a form dominant in Mecca even before the time of Muḥammad. The latter evolved when, due to their involvement with trade, nomad tribes became sedentary, which in turn led to growing individualism (Watt, *Muhammad at Medina,* 273; see PATRIARCHY; NOMADS).

The Qurʾān stresses the nuclear family and deemphasizes larger groupings like tribes and clans (Robertson-Smith, *Kinship,* e.g. 203 f.; Stern, *Marriage,* 81; Watt, *Muhammad at Medina,* 272-89, Excursus J, esp. 385, 387-8; Bianquis, Family, 614 f.; Al-Azhary-Sonbol, Adoption, 47-8). Muḥammad himself created a polygamous virilocal family (Watt, *Muhammad at Medina*, 277, 284). That the core, biological family, consisting of a man, his wife (or wives) and their offspring, is the natural, basic social unit finds its expression in many verses. Meccan and early Medinan verses (see CHRONOLOGY AND THE QUR'ĀN), such as Q 35:11; 39:6; 42:11; 53:45; 75:39; 78:8, understand God's creation (q.v.) of humans (and other creatures) as gendered to be a sign of his omnipotence (see Bouhdiba, *Sexuality*, Ch. 1; see POWER AND IMPOTENCE; SIGNS). In some verses (e.g. Q 30:21), the typical elements of human conjugal life, common dwelling, love and mercy, are also enumerated as such. A beautiful simile is used in Q 2:187 where husband and wife are depicted as raiment *(libās)* for each other (see CLOTHING). According to the Qur'ān, the conjugal framework existed for Adam and Eve (q.v.; e.g. Q 2:35; 7:19) and shall continue to exist in the hereafter (e.g. Q 2:25; 3:15; 43:70; see DEATH AND THE DEAD; ESCHATOLOGY). Offspring are presented as an indispensable element of the core family in this world (e.g. 3:61; 7:189; 13:38; 16:72; 25:74; see also BLESSING) as well as in the world to come (Q 52:21; Bell, ii, 535). Nevertheless, preoccupation with wife/wives and children is a danger for a Muslim (see Q 64:14; cf. 18:80-1; Bell, i, 281; on the motif of children as temptation, see CHILDREN), and family ties will be of no avail on the day of judgment (Q 31:33, cf. Bell, ii, 403; Q 35:18, cf. Bell, ii, 430; Q 60:3, cf. Bell, ii, 572; see LAST JUDGMENT).

Duties of the members of the core family towards one other, as defined by the Qur'ān, reflect a patrilineal-patriarchal family pattern modified by monotheist ethics and a special sensitivity towards women and children in a changing society and under new economic conditions (see ECONOMICS; PRE-ISLAMIC ARABIA AND THE QUR'ĀN; WOMEN AND THE QUR'ĀN). Muslims should respect their parents and be kind to them, because of the concern the latter showed while rearing them (e.g. Q 17:24), but they must disobey their parents in idolatry (e.g. Q 29:8; see DISOBEDIENCE; IDOLATRY AND IDOLATERS). A husband, sometimes referred to as *ba'l* (a lord, master, owner; Lane, 228; e.g. Q 4:128) or *sayyid* (a chief, lord or master; Lane, 1462; see Q 12:25), owns his wife/wives — limited polygamy is allowed (Q 4:3) — and female slaves, with whom sexual relations are allowed (Q 4:3). "Your women are to you [as] cultivated land; come then to your cultivated land as you wish" (Q 2:223; Bell, i, 31); men have a rank above women (Q 2:228) and serve as their overseers (Q 4:34). A father owns his biological children, who are attributed to him, not to their mother (e.g. Q 2:233; *al-mawlūd lahu*, "to whom the child is born," cf. Bell, i, 33; see Zamakhsharī's *Kashshāf* ad Q 2:233, … *al-awlād lil-ābā' wa-li-dhālika yunsabūna ilayhim;* on the issue of formal adoption, which is forbidden, see CHILDREN); and is responsible for the welfare of his wife/wives and offspring (Q 2:233; 65:6, both in the context of divorce). A wife should obey her husband (see OBEDIENCE), who is allowed to punish her physically for failing to do so (Q 4:34). This concept of patrilineal-patriarchal family is also reflected in the relatively detailed qur'ānic regulations concerning marriage and divorce (q.v.), including the waiting period *('idda)*, women's modesty (e.g. Q 24:31) and inheritance (q.v.). The Qur'ān, however, grants women a religious status which in principle is equal to that of men (e.g. Q 33:35) and economic rights, such as the right to own property (q.v.), to receive the bridewealth (q.v.) directly, to inherit and to bequeath, etc., which represent a considerable attempt to achieve social reform and protection for the oppressed (Bianquis, Family, 619).

In several verses, most of them Medinan, Muslims are ordered to support and show kindness to relatives (*dhū/dhawū al-qurbā,* for other similar phrases see above) — probably members of their extended families — alongside needy people such as those under their protection, orphans (q.v.), the poor, the wayfarer *(ibn al-sabīl),* etc. (e.g. Q 2:177; 4:36; 8:41; 16:90; see POVERTY AND THE POOR). In these Medinan verses, blood ties and the duties they entail are again emphasized, after having been denounced in Mecca (O'Shaughnessy, Youth, 37-8). Some ideas of the qur'ānic concept of the extended family and its dimensions can be inferred from verses dealing with inheritance, categories of people with whom marriage is prohibited, the regulation of the presence of women in public and familial environments (Q 24:31; 33:55) and those concerning eating in the houses of one's relations (Q 24:61).

Avner Giladi

Bibliography
Primary: Bell; *Jalālayn;* al-Rāghib al-Iṣfahānī, *Mufradāt,* Ṭabarī, *Tafsīr;* Zamakhsharī, *Kashshāf.*
Secondary: Kh. ʿAkk, *Bināʾ al-usra al-muslima fī ḍawʾ al-Qurʾān wa-l-sunna min buḥūth al-ʿulamāʾ,* Beirut 1998; A. al-Azhary-Sonbol, Adoption in Islamic society. A historical survey, in E. Warnock Fernea (ed.), *Children in the Muslim Middle East,* Austin 1995, 45-67; T. Bianquis, The family in Arab Islam, in André Burguière et al. (eds.), *A history of the family,* 2 vols., Cambridge 1996, i, 601-47; A. Bouhdiba, *Sexuality in Islam,* London 1985; N. Imāra, *al-Usra al-muthlā fī ḍawʾ al-Qurʾān wa-l-sunna,* Riyadh 1980; Lane; T.J. O'Shaughnessy, The qur'ānic view of youth and old age, in *ZDMG* 141 (1991), 33-51; W. Robertson-Smith, *Kinship and marriage in early Arabia,* London 1907; A.M. Salīm, *Bināʾ al-usra fī hudā l-Qurʾān,* Damascus 1996; R. al-Sayyid, *Mafāhīm al-jamāʿāt fī l-islām,* Beirut 1984; R.T. Smith, Family. Comparative structure, in *International encyclopedia of the social sciences,* 17 vols. in 8, New York 1972, v-vi, 301-12; G. Stern, *Marriage in early Islam,* London 1939; W.M. Watt, *Muhammad at Medina,* Oxford 1956.

Family of the Prophet

The extended family (q.v.) of the prophet Muḥammad (q.v.), to which the Qurʾān contains several references clearly intended to distinguish them from other Muslims. This is in accord with the general tendency in the Qurʾān of exalting the family and descendants of most prophets (see PROPHETS AND PROPHETHOOD), as is evidenced, for example, in Q 3 (Sūrat Āl ʿImrān), a sūra named after the family of ʿImrān (q.v.), the father of Moses (q.v.).

The specific contexts in which the Qurʾān refers to the prophet Muḥammad's family are diverse. Q 8:41 and 59:7 designate a portion of the booty (q.v.) and other property (q.v.) acquired from infidels (see WARFARE; EXPEDITIONS AND BATTLES; BELIEF AND UNBELIEF) that is to be distributed to the Prophet's kin (see KINSHIP), among others, apparently since they were not eligible to receive alms (*ṣadaqa, zakāt,* see ALMSGIVING; TAXATION). Again, Q 33 contains many verses that prescribe a code of conduct and of dress (see CLOTHING) to be followed by the wives of the Prophet (q.v.) in keeping with their superior status in the Muslim community (see COMMUNITY AND SOCIETY IN THE QURʾĀN). Moreover, Q 33:33 refers explicitly to the family of the prophet Muḥammad as the *ahl al-bayt,* "People of the House," and their distinctive state of purity: "God desires only to remove impurity from you, O People of the House, and to purify you completely." On the other hand, Q 111 severely curses renegades among the Prophet's relatives who opposed his mission, primarily his uncle Abū Lahab and his wife.

Muslim commentators on the Qurʾān differ in their definitions of the Prophet's kin. Some interpret the term broadly to include the Prophet's tribe (see TRIBES AND CLANS), that is, the Quraysh (q.v.). Others define it more narrowly by limiting it to his clan, the Banū Hāshim. The Shīʿa (q.v.), in consonance with their veneration of ʿAlī b. Abī Ṭālib (q.v.) and his descendants as the true heirs of the Prophet, generally restrict the definition of the term *ahl al-bayt* to the Prophet's immediate family, i.e. his daughter Fāṭima (q.v.), son-in-law ʿAlī, and their two sons, Ḥasan and Ḥusayn, and their descendants (see Bar-Asher, *Scripture*, 93-8; Sharon, People of the House; Madelung, Hāshimiyyāt). In support of such an interpretation, they cite reports in which the Prophet once gathered Fāṭima, ʿAlī, Ḥasan and Ḥusayn under his mantle *(kisāʾ)* and, referring to them as his family, prayed for their protection (q.v.). Hence they became known as the people of the cloak *(ahl al-kisāʾ)*. Popular and theological qurʾānic commentaries among the Shīʿa elevate the religious rank of the Prophet's immediate family *(ahl al-bayt)* by claiming that many verses in the Qurʾān which describe true believers refer first and foremost to them and only tangentially to the rest of the community (see THEOLOGY AND THE QURʾĀN). Thus, some Shīʿī commentators hold that Q 76 (Sūrat al-Insān, "The Human"), which extols those humans who choose to do good over evil (see GOOD AND EVIL), was revealed specifically to describe the virtues of the *ahl al-bayt*, whose lives and actions can actually be considered a form of true exegesis of the Qurʾān. See also PEOPLE OF THE HOUSE.

Ali S.A. Asani

Bibliography

Primary: Abū ʿUbayda, Maʿmar b. al-Muthannā al-Taymī, *Tasmiyāt azwāj al-nabī wa-awlādihi*, ed. Kamāl Yūsuf al-Ḥūt, Beirut 1985; M. ʿAmilī, *al-Majālis al-saniyya fī manāqib wa-maṣāʾib al-ʿitra al-nabawiyya*, 5 vols. in 2, Beirut 1978[6]; Ḥākim al-Haskanī, *Shawāhid al-tanzīl li-qawāʿid al-tafḍīl fī l-āyāt al-nāzila fī ahl al-bayt*, ed. M. Bāqir al-Maḥmūdī, 2 vols. in 1, Beirut 1974; Ibn Abī l-Dunyā, *al-Ishrāf fī manāzil al-ashrāf*, ed. Najm ʿAbd al-Raḥmān Khalaf, Riyadh 1990; Ibn al-Mibrad, Yūsuf b. Ḥasan, *K. al-Shajara al-nabawiyya fī nasab khayr al-bariyya*, ed. Muḥyī l-Dīn Ḍīb Mastū, Damascus 1994; al-Maqrizī, Tāqī al-Dīn Aḥmad b. ʿAlī, *Maʿrifat mā yajibu li-āl al-bayt al-nabawī min al-ḥaqq ʿalā man ʿadāhum*, ed. M.A. ʿAshur, Cairo 1973; Markāz al-Ghadīr lil-Dirāsāt al-Islāmiyya (ed.), *Muntakhab faḍāʾil al-nabī wa-ahl baytihi. Min al-siḥḥa al-sitta wa-ghayrihā min al-kutub al-muʿtabira ʿinda ahl al-sunna*, Beirut 1996; Suyūṭī, *Iḥyāʾ al-mayyit bi-faḍāʾil āl al-bayt*, ed. Kāẓim al-Fatlī, Beirut 1995; al-Ṭabarī, Muḥibb al-Dīn Aḥmad b. ʿAbdallāh, *Dhakhāʾir al-ʿuqbā fī manāqib dhawī l-qurbā*, Cairo 1937, repr. Beirut 1974.

Secondary: A. Abū Kaff, *Āl bayt al-nabī fī Miṣr*, Cairo 1977; M. Amir-Moezzi, *The divine guide in early Shīʿism*, trans. D. Streight, Albany 1994; M. Ayoub, *Redemptive suffering in Islam*, The Hague 1978; M.M. Bar-Asher, *Scripture and exegesis in early Imāmī Shiism*, Leiden 1999; I. Goldziher/C. van Arendonk/A. Tritton, Ahl al-bayt, in EI[2], i, 257-8; M.ʿU. Ḥajjī, *Faḍāʾil āl al-bayt fī mīzān al-sharīʿa al-islāmiyya*, Damascus 1999; S. Makkī, *Maẓālim āl al-bayt*, Beirut 1984; W. Madelung, The Hāshimiyyāt of al-Kumayt and Hāshimī Shīʿism, in SI 70 (1989), 5-26; id., *The succession to Muhammad*, Cambridge 1997; M. Sharon, *Ahl al-bayt* — People of the House, in JSAI 8 (1986), 169-84.

Famine

Extreme hunger, denoted in the Qurʾān by the synonymous terms, *makhmaṣa* and *masghaba*. *Makhmaṣa* occurs at Q 5:3 (cf. Ṭabarī, *Tafsīr*, iv, 424-5) and Q 9:120. The first instance is situated in the context of food taboos (see FOOD AND DRINK; FORBIDDEN) where it is stated, "Whoever is constrained by hunger (*makhmaṣa*, i.e. to eat of what is forbidden) not intending to commit transgression, will find God forgiving and merciful (see FORGIVENESS; MERCY)." The second instance suggests hunger suffered for the cause of God (*fī sabīli llāhi*, see PATH OR WAY). The full sense of the word in both passages, says al-Ṭabarī (d. 310/923; *Tafsīr*, ad loc.), describes the condition of a stomach emaciated from hunger or starvation (*shiddat al-saghab*, see SUFFERING). *Masghaba* is used at Q 90:14 in the sense of deprivation in reference to how the virtuous (see VIRTUE) should behave, feeding the needy "on a day of hunger [or famine]" (cf. Ṭabarī, *Tafsīr*, xii, 594-5).

More important is the well-known scene in the story of Joseph (q.v.), although neither of the above terms appear in it. The prophet Joseph had been summoned from his prison cell (see PRISONERS) to interpret the king's (i.e. Pharaoh, q.v.) dream (see DREAMS AND SLEEP) of seven fatted cows devoured by seven lean ones and of seven green ears of corn and seven dry ones (Q 12:43-8). Joseph's interpretation was that seven years of abundant crops would provide a surplus for storage in addition to a sufficiency for current consumption after which seven hungry years *(sabʿun shidādun)* would consume most of what had been set aside in earlier times. Al-Ṭabarī, citing several exegetical sources, understands the seven years of dearth to have resulted from severe and prolonged drought (*qaḥṭ* and *jadūb*, Ṭabarī, *Tafsīr*, vii, 227, ad Q 12:48). Following the period of scarcity, a year of abundant rain would allow various food plants to yield their pressed juices in plentiful quantity (Q 12:49). Al-Ṭabarī notes that commentators differ as to which specific food plants were meant, the suggestions including sesame, grapes, olives and other fruits (see AGRICULTURE AND VEGETATION); other commentators suggest that "pressed juices" referred to increased supplies of milk from domestic animals (Ṭabarī, *Tafsīr*, vii, 230-1, ad Q 12:49). Al-Ṭabarī adds that minor differences over the proper pronunciation of a word in this last verse do not hinder agreement as to its essential meaning.

The four passages, however brief, when considered together convey the clear impression that famine was not an unfamiliar foe among the Arabian populace and beyond. Yet unlike other "acts of God" mentioned in the Qurʾān (e.g. Q 11:67; Q 99; Q 101; see PUNISHMENT STORIES; APOCALYPSE) there is no hint in the text itself or in the commentaries that hunger and famine were counted among the divine punishments (see CHASTISEMENT AND PUNISHMENT).

David Waines

Bibliography
Primary: Ibn Abī l-Dunyā, *Kitāb al-Jawʿ*, ed. M. Khayr Ramaḍān Yūsuf, Beirut 1997; Ṭabarī, *Tafsīr*.
Secondary: F.M. Donner, Mecca's food supplies and Muhammad's boycott, in *JESHO* 29 (1977) 249-66.

Farewell Pilgrimage

The pilgrimage (q.v.) to the Kaʿba (q.v.) at Mecca (q.v.) led by the Prophet in year 10 of the *hijra* (see EMIGRATION), so called because it occurred just months before he died, 'taking leave' of the Muslim community (see COMMUNITY AND SOCIETY IN THE QURʾĀN). It is viewed as the primary occasion when the Prophet taught his followers the rites of the Islamic pilgrimage and thus figures prominently in subsequent discussions of its rituals and meaning. It was also the occasion of important announcements concerning the status of several pre-Islamic customs in Islam (see PRE-ISLAMIC ARABIA AND THE QURʾĀN). The Prophet's last pilgrimage represents for later Muslims the completion of divine revelation and the scripture and is thus understood as a time of special holiness. The phrase "farewell pilgrimage" *(ḥajjat al-wadāʿ)* does not occur in the Qurʾān itself; the related verb, *waddaʿa*, "to take leave, bid farewell," occurs once at Q 93:3, but with the figurative meaning of to forsake or abandon: "Your lord has not forsaken you, nor does he detest you."

The Prophet prepared to perform the pilgrimage *(ḥajj)* in Dhū l-Qaʿda 10/632 and set out with a group of his followers, including his wives (see WIVES OF THE PROPHET), from Medina (q.v.) toward the end of that month. He led the pilgrimage, teaching the customs of the pilgrimage to his followers and answering their questions about specific regulations. A large number of the oral traditions concerning the pilgrimage that are preserved in the standard compilations (see ḤADĪTH AND THE QURʾĀN) are set during the Farewell Pilgrimage and treat questions which arose on this occasion.

According to the majority of accounts, the Prophet performed both the *ʿumra* (lesser pilgrimage) and *ḥajj* (greater pilgrimage) rituals. While he allowed his followers to resume their profane state in between an initial *ʿumra* and the *ḥajj* itself, he maintained the sacred state of *iḥrām* (see RITUAL PURITY), he said, because he was leading animals to be sacrificed (see SACRIFICE; CONSECRATION OF ANIMALS). During the pilgrimage, the Muslims continually questioned the Prophet about their religious obligations. In his answers to them, he is reported to have cited qurʾānic verses such as Q 2:125, "Take as your place of worship (q.v.) the place where Abraham (q.v.) stood" and Q 2:158 "Al-Ṣafā and al-Marwa are among God's rites" They apparently crowded him so much that he performed the circumambulation of the Kaʿba and hurried between Ṣafā and Marwa (q.v.) mounted on a camel. As part of the ceremonies, the Prophet sacrificed a cow or several cows on behalf of his wives. Together with ʿAlī (see ʿALĪ B. ABĪ ṬĀLIB), who had come to perform the pilgrimage upon returning from a mission to Yemen (q.v.), the Prophet sacrificed one hundred camels. According to some traditions, he sacrificed sixty-three camels and ʿAlī the remaining thirty-seven; others have him sacrificing thirty, thirty-three, or thirty-four camels and ʿAlī the remainder (see the chapters on the rites of the pilgrimage in the various ḥadīth compliations: Abū Dāwūd, *Sunan,* ii, 139-219; Bukhārī, *Ṣaḥīḥ,* iii, 80-285; Ibn Māja, *Sunan,* 962-1055; Muslim, *Ṣaḥīḥ,* viii, 72-237; ix, 2-171; al-Nasāʾī, *Sunan,* vi, 110-277; Tirmidhī, *Jāmiʿ,* ii, 152-219).

After completing the rituals, the Prophet gave what is now known as the Farewell Speech (Ibn Isḥāq-Guillaume, 651-2; Ibn Ḥajar, *Fatḥ al-bārī,* viii, 103-10), in which he abolished a number of pre-Islamic customs. Chief among these was the *nasīʾ,* or intercalary month. From then on the Muslim community would operate on a strictly lunar calendar (q.v.) that would not be adjusted to bring it into alignment with the solar calendar. The Prophet abolished all old blood feuds, implying that the creation of the Islamic *umma* had made all disputes based on the former tribal system obsolete (see TRIBES AND CLANS; BROTHER AND BROTHERHOOD; BLOOD MONEY; KINSHIP). In addition, all old pledges were to be returned, another indication of this new beginning (see CONTRACTS AND ALLIANCES; OATHS AND PROMISES). The Prophet informed his followers that they were entitled to discipline their wives but should do so with kindness (see MARRIAGE AND DIVORCE; WOMEN AND THE QURʾĀN). He commanded that one could not leave one's wealth (q.v.) to a testamentary heir (see INHERITANCE); that one could not make false claims of paternity (see FAMILY; ILLEGITIMACY) or of a client relationship (see CLIENTS AND CLIENTAGE). The tradition of holding four months (q.v.) of the year, Dhū l-Qaʿda, Dhū l-Ḥijja, and Muḥarram (months 11, 12, and 1) and Rajab (month 7) sacred was upheld at this time. This measure seems related to the Islamic adoption of the pilgrimage itself, along with the understanding that the shrine at Mecca lies on holy ground.

Among the qurʾānic passages reportedly revealed during the Farewell Pilgrimage are Q 110, some verses in Q 9 (see Bell, Muhammad's pilgrimage), and some verses from the opening of Q 5. Several reports describe Q 110 as hinting at the approaching demise of the Prophet, and on these grounds the text is called Sūrat al-Tawdīʿ ("Leave-taking"; Zamakhsharī, *Kashshāf,* iv, 219; Ṭabarsī, *Majmaʿ,* v, 844). Nöldeke, however, holds that Q 110 was revealed earlier, probably even before the conquest of Mecca, when the Prophet first foresaw an eventual victory over the Meccans (Nöldeke, *GQ,* i, 219-20). The attribution to the Farewell Pilgrimage, he asserts, is based on an erroneous interpretation of the text related from Ibn ʿAbbās. While Q 9:36-7 do contain the regulations concerning the sacred months mentioned in the Farewell Speech, these verses may have been revealed earlier. Nöldeke accepts the dating of some sections of Q 5:1-10 to the Farewell Pilgrimage, including the well-known passage, commonly held to be the final revelation: "This day have I perfected your religion for you and completed my favor unto you, and have chosen for you as religion Islam" (Q 5:3; cf. Nöldeke, *GQ,* i, 227-9).

Devin J. Stewart

Bibliography

Primary: Abū Dāwūd, 4 vols., Mecca n.d.; Bukhārī, *Ṣaḥīḥ,* 7 vols., Cairo 1985; Ibn Ḥajar, *Fatḥ al-bārī,* ed. ʿA.b.ʿA. Bāz (with the numeration of ʿAbd al-Bāqī), Cairo 1970, repr. Beirut n.d.; Ibn Isḥāq, *Sīra;* Ibn Isḥāq-Guillaume; Ibn Māja; Muslim, *Ṣaḥīḥ,* 18 vols., Beirut 1972; Nasāʾī, *Sunan,* 8 vols., Beirut 1980; Ṭabarī, *Taʾrīkh;* Ṭabarsī, *Majmaʿ;* Tirmidhī, *Ṣaḥīḥ,* 4 vols., Beirut 1983; Zamakhsharī, *Kashshāf.*

Secondary: R. Bell, Muhammad's pilgrimage proclamation, in *JRAS* (1937), 233-44; Nöldeke, *GQ;* W.M. Watt, *Muhammad at Medina,* Oxford 1956; A.J. Wensinck/J. Jomier, Ḥadjdj, in *EI²,* iii, 32-7.

Fasting

Abstaining from food or, with ritual fasting, abstaining from food, drink and sexual activity. The Qurʾān recognizes three different kinds of fasting (*ṣiyām, ṣawm; ṣawm* is also interpreted as *ṣamt,* "silence," cf. Q 19:26): ritual fasting, fasting as compensation or repentance, and ascetic fasting. Ritual fasting is prescribed in Q 2:183-7 "as it was prescribed to those before you, ... on counted days... The month (q.v.) of Ramaḍān (q.v.), in which the Qurʾān was sent down... let him fast the month." This fast takes place during the daylight hours: Sex, except in the case of a voluntary retreat or withdrawal for prayer (*iʿtikāf,* see ABSTINENCE), is allowed during the night of the fast, as is eating and drinking until dawn (see DAY, TIMES OF; DAY AND NIGHT). Fasting as compensation or repentance is found in, for instance, Q 2:196 where, in the case of inability to observe certain pilgrimage (q.v.; *ḥajj*) rituals, fasting or almsgiving (q.v.) or sacrifice (q.v.) is prescribed. And for the insufficient fulfillment of the pilgrimage rules *(tamattuʿ),* a sacrifice or a fast of three plus seven days is required (also Q 2:196). As expiation for killing game during the pilgrimage (see HUNTING AND FISHING), a sacrifice, feeding the poor or fasting is required (Q 5:95). For unintentional manslaughter (see BLOODSHED) — apart from blood money (q.v.) — the manumission of a slave or a fast of two consecutive months (Q 4:92) is demanded. Perjury/breach of oath (see OATHS AND PROMISES) calls for feeding or clothing ten poor persons or the manumission of a slave or, if these measures are not possible, a fast of three days (Q 5:89). For breach of the oath of *ẓihār* (a specific form of divorce; see MARRIAGE AND DIVORCE), the feeding of sixty poor persons or a fast of two consecutive months is required (Q 58:3-4; see BREAKING TRUSTS AND CONTRACTS). Traces of some of these rules are found in pre-Islamic times — tariff rates and compensations resemble Christian practices (cf. Vogel, *Pécheur,* 17-71) — and further research may shed light on the nature and degree of Christian or other influences. The third kind of fasting, ascetic fasting, is found in Q 33:35: "humble men and humble women, men who give alms and women who give alms, men who fast and women who fast, ... for them God has prepared forgiveness...." Certain words whose base meaning is not "fasting" are taken to indicate the practice: *sāʾiḥāt* (Q 66:5) and *sāʾiḥūn* (Q 9:112), both from the Arabic root meaning "itinerant," are taken by commentators on the Qurʾān to mean, respectively "women who fast" and "men who fast"; and in Q 2:45,153, *ṣabr,* "patience," is interpreted as fasting.

Origin of the fast of Ramaḍān

The question of the origin of the fast of Ramaḍān (the abstension from food, drink and sexual activities during the daylight hours of the lunar month of Ramaḍān) is complicated and conclusive evidence is scarce. The Qurʾān is almost the only contemporary source. One of the puzzles is the question of what exactly is meant by "Ramaḍān in which the Qurʾān was sent down" (Q 2:185). Tradition has it that Muḥammad used to spend a month every year in a cave (q.v.) on Mt. Ḥirāʾ for "religious devotion" *(taḥannuth),* and at one time, during the month of Ramaḍān, the Prophet received his call (Ibn Isḥāq, *Sīra,* 151-2; Ibn Isḥāq-Guillaume, 105-6). The story is primarily based on qurʾānic material (Q 2:185; 53:1-11; 81:23; 96:1-5) with some additions like the notion of *taḥannuth,* which probably is an ancient form of worship (Kister, Al-taḥannuth, 232-6), although some (notably Calder, Ḥinth, 236-9) consider it a later custom (see SOUTH ARABIA, RELIGION IN PRE-ISLAMIC).

Two other verses of the Qurʾān speak about a night of revelation. Q 97:1: "We sent it down in the Night of Destiny (*laylat al-qadr,* see NIGHT OF POWER)" and Q 44:3: "in a blessed night *(layla mubāraka).*" The Night of Destiny is an ancient New Year's night in which God decides humankind's destiny in the coming year; it is commonly held to be the night of the 27th of Ramaḍān. The "blessed night" is either equated with it or it is held to be the night of 15 Shaʿbān, the starting point for popular voluntary fasting. According to A.J. Wensinck, these two nights distinguished an ancient New Year's period around the summer solstice which underlies the establishment of the Ramaḍān fast (Arabic, 5-8). But the notion of two New Year's nights within a period of forty days is improbable. The ancient Arabic calendar (q.v.), like others in the region, recognized a New Year, either in spring or in autumn. The observance of 15 Shaʿbān is more likely a product of Islam (Wagtendonk, *Fasting,* 102; Kister, Shaʿban, 34).

Muslim tradition is uncertain about what is meant by "sent down in Ramaḍān." Generally, it is thought to commemorate Muḥammad's first revelation (cf. Goitein, Ramadan, 101-9), although it is sometimes considered to indicate the "sending down" of the entire Qurʾān (to the lowest heaven). The desire of the exegetes to combine these two ideas, or to maintain them side by side, gives the impression of an effort to harmonize conflicting opinions (Wagtendonk, *Fasting,* 87; see ibid., 63-7, 118-20, for yet another reason for the fast of the month of Ramaḍān, namely as a commemoration of the month in which the battle of Badr [q.v.], the first major military victory of the Muslims, occurred).

The three phases of the qurʾānic establishment of fasting

Fasting was established in three phases, Ramaḍān being the third. The first phase is that which forms the background to the revelation of Q 2:183. Tradition reports that when Muḥammad arrived in Medina (q.v.) after the emigration (q.v.; *hijra*) from Mecca, he saw the Jews fasting. It happened to be ʿĀshūrāʾ, the Day of Atonement or Yom Kippur, in which Jews fasted from sunset to sunset . When asked, he learned that they were fasting because Moses (q.v.) and the Israelites (see CHILDREN OF ISRAEL) were delivered on that day from Pharaoh (q.v.) with God's help. The Prophet subsequently ordered the Muslims to fast because "We have a better right to Moses than they [the Jews] have," as he remarked (Ṭabarī, *Taʾrīkh*, iii, 1281; id., *History*, vii, 26). Clearly this tradition incorrectly renders the motive of the Jewish fast. On the other hand, it fits Muḥammad's notion of Moses as his predecessor who had a similar message to convey (cf. the attention to the story of Moses earlier in the sūra, Q 2:49-74). Goitein has convincingly demonstrated that the connection between fasting and revelation in Q 2:185 resembles one of the motives of the fast of Yom Kippur (ʿĀshūrāʾ). The second giving of the tablets of the Law to Moses as an element of the liturgy of Yom Kippur can explain why Muḥammad adopted this day of fasting for the Muslims.

The second phase is expressed in Q 2:183-4: "Fasting is prescribed for you as it was for those before you...," apparently for a fixed period, *ayyām maʿdūdāt*, "(on) counted days (or 'for counts of days,' i.e. 'fixed')," as compensatory provision must be made for days of illness or travel. The verses date from the period just before the change of the direction of prayer (*qibla*, q.v.) when relations with the Jews were already strained (see JEWS AND JUDAISM); a "new" fast was intended. The reference to "those before you" may contain an echo to the short-lived ʿĀshūrāʾ-fast, though the People of the Book (q.v.; *ahl al-kitāb*) or even humankind in general may have been meant. The rule which allows one to redeem the fast by simply paying a ransom *(fidya)* of feeding a poor person betrays the same uncertainty as that which accompanied the change of *qibla*. Commentators openly state that, originally, healthy persons who did not want to fast were not required to do so. Others, harmonizing the different tendencies in historical memory, associate this ruling with aged people who could only fast with hardship. But with that interpretation it is hard to see why this alleviation was not repeated in the next verse.

The character of the fast of the "counted days" still resembled somewhat the discontinued ʿĀshūrāʾ. Tradition relates that only once in twenty-four hours was it permitted to interrupt the fast. Indication that the fast was even more stringent is given in Q 2:187, however, where it is implied that people used to engage in *illicit* sexual relations during the night of the fast: "It is made lawful for you to go to your wives on the night of the fast... God is aware that you were deceiving yourselves in this respect and he has turned in mercy towards you and relieved you" (cf. Q 2:189 for a similar deceit). Sex (see SEX AND SEXUALITY) is henceforth allowed, like eating and drinking, during the whole night of the fast. If, however, an allusion to voluntary withdrawal to a mosque *(iʿtikāf)* is perceived in Q 2:187 *(wa-l tubāshirūhunna wa-antum ʿākifūna fī l-masājidi)*, a clearer idea about the period of the "counted days" of Q 2:184 may be achieved, for this could indicate a connection with an ancient religious period, similar, for instance, to the first ten days of the month Dhū l-Ḥijja. This period, which included the Night of Destiny *(laylat al-qadr)*, is unlikely, therefore, to have been part of Ramaḍān initially. Tradition, however, is understandably uncertain about the exact time of the fast of the "counted days," considering that Q 97 is devoted to the Night of Destiny and is therefore important for the explanation of Q 2:185.

A number of arguments strongly suggest locating the *iʿtikāf* and the *laylat al-qadr* in Rajab, which, unlike Ramaḍān, was a sacred month of celebrations. In early Islam, the "lesser pilgrimage" *(ʿumra)* continued to take place during Rajab (Wagtendonk, *Fasting,* 106); it was the month of the sacrifices of the sacrificial animals (*ʿatāʾir,* see CONSECRATION) and the first-born of the flocks and herds, and these in turn determined the state of ritual purity (q.v.; *iḥrām*) as well as the rites of *wuqūf* and *ʿukūf* with sexual abstinence and, as a result of vows, possibly also fasting. Some traditions, in fact, refer to Rajab as the month of the Prophet's *taḥannuth* (see Kister, Al-taḥannuth, 223-4), when Muḥammad received his revelation of the reward of fasting on the twenty-seventh day of the month, a day of *iʿtikāf* and recitation of Q 97 for ʿAbdallāh b. ʿAbbās (Kister, Rajab, 197, 200-1). Fasting was so popular in Rajab under Abū Bakr and ʿUmar that they reproached the *"rajabiyyūn"* for making Ramaḍān into Rajab and had them punished (Ṭurṭūshī, *Ḥawādith,* 129-30; Goitein, Ramadan, 93). Another (indirect) indication is the predilection for the *ʿumra* in the last ten days of Ramaḍān (Paret/Chaumont, ʿUmra). In Islam, the twenty-seventh of Rajab corresponds to the twenty-seventh of Ramaḍān, respectively the date of Muḥammad's ascension (q.v.; *miʿrāj*) to heaven, and the commonly accepted date of *laylat al-qadr*. The *miʿrāj* is in fact another call-vision, an initiation to prophethood, similar to the vision of *laylat al-qadr.*

In any case, the *iʿtikāf* period was chosen for the fast of the "counted days" because the Night of Destiny *(laylat al-qadr),* with which the revelation of the Qurʾān was connected, occurred during it. This night was not necessarily the time of Muḥammad's first revelation, but rather a symbolic date with which the entire revelation was associated just like, for instance, the association of the Torah with *Shavuot* in Judaism.

The third and last phase of the establishment of the fast is its extension into a whole month, the month of Ramaḍān. Q 2:185 abrogates 2:184; the healthy are no longer permitted to forgo the fast: the uncertainty has disappeared. The increase of fasting days is balanced by the alleviation concerning the nights. The motif of fasting as commemoration of the revelation to Muḥammad (see REVELATION AND INSPIRATION) has not changed. The main question concerns the immediate cause of the revelation of Q 2:185 (see OCCASIONS OF REVELATION). Goitein (Ramadan, 105) maintains that the fast of Ramaḍān is an extension of its last third (the counted days) when "the absolute certitude came" without any indication of what caused this certitude. The mention of Ramaḍān, however, in Q 2:185 sounds new and unexpected. Although the use of the word *furqān* (literally, the distinguishing, i.e. between good and evil; see CRITERION) here is not new, the complicated way in which it is used certainly is: the Qurʾān is "guidance for humankind and proofs of the guidance and of the *furqān.*" We see here the subordination of the *furqān* to the Qurʾān instead of the juxtaposition of book (q.v.) and *furqān* or the identification of both found elsewhere (see Watt-Bell, *Introduction,* 145-7). It is as if the notion of *furqān* was essential but, at the same time, the priority of the sending down of the revelation had to be maintained by all means. Tradition conflates the two concepts: the *furqān* came down on the 14th or the 17th of Ramaḍān (Ibn Isḥāq, *Sīra,* 150). This leads to the meaning of *furqān* in Q 8, which is about the victory at Badr on 17 Ramaḍān 2/623. *Furqān,* probably a Syriac/Aramaic loanword, in Q 8:29

(and 8:41) can mean "deliverance" (*najāh*, cf. Bayḍāwī, *Anwār*, ad Q 8:29). This notion — central to the Jewish Pesach-story, deliverance from Egypt's Pharaoh — was adopted by Muḥammad who, naturally, associated it with the Arabic root *f-r-q*, "to separate, discern," and applied it to the victory at Badr, which brought the separation of believers and unbelievers (Bell, *Introduction*, 136-8). The theme of the end of Pharaoh (Firʿawn) and the salvation *(najāh)* of the believers is important in the Qurʾān (cf. Q 7:141; 10:90; 20:78; 26:65; 44:30). Here, at Q 8:29, this salvation is expressly called *furqān*: "If you fear God, he will appoint for you a *furqān*" (cf. *Exod* 14:13, "Fear not and see the salvation of the lord"; see CRITERION). In Q 2:49-50, the root *f-r-q* appears for the first time in connection with the deliverance from Pharaoh and the forty nights of Moses on Mount Sinai: "We divided *(faraqnā)* the sea for you."

The victory at Badr brought at once a fundamental improvement in the situation of the Muslims, which was threatened both by the Meccans and by the confrontation with the Jews of Medina (see OPPOSITION TO MUḤAMMAD). The truth of the Qurʾān had been at stake (Q 8:20-32). The victory of Badr was for Muḥammad also the promised judgment over the unbelieving Meccans (Q 8:33), comparable to the end of Pharaoh (Q 8:54). This is the background of Q 2:185. The authority of Muḥammad was determined by what God had sent down to Muḥammad on the day of the *furqān*, the day of Badr (Q 8:41). The fast of Ramaḍān must have been established shortly after Badr or at least before the month of Rajab in the year 3/625. The reference to the victory of Moses over Pharaoh in the above-mentioned tradition is certainly rooted in fact, rather than being just "a fanciful accretion" (Goitein, Ramadan, 97). After all, Muḥammad must have witnessed in his early contacts with the Jews of Medina not only Yom Kippur but also Pesach and Shavuot which, (especially the latter) commemorate the revelation of the Law.

The length of the fast, an extension from ten to thirty days, must be seen against the background of the popularity of fasting, both by Jews and Christians, in the centuries preceding Islam (cf. also the two months of penitential fasting, Q 4:92; 58:3-4).

Kees Wagtendonk

Bibliography

Primary: Bayḍāwī, *Anwār;* Bukhārī, *Ṣaḥīḥ*, ed. L. Krehl and W. Juynboll; Ibn Isḥāq, *Sīra*, ed. F. Wüstenfeld; Ibn Isḥāq-Guillaume; Ṭabarī, *The history of al-Ṭabarī. vii. The foundation of the community*, trans. M.V. McDonald, Albany 1987; id., *Taʾrīkh*, ed. M.J. de Goeje; Ṭurṭūshī, Ibn Abī Randaqa Abū Bakr Muḥammad b. al-Walīd, *al-Ḥawādith wa-l-bidaʿ*, ed. M. al-Ṭālibī, Tunis 1959.
Secondary: R. Bell, *Introduction to the Qurʾān*, Edinburgh 1953 (note on al-Furqān, 136-8); C.C. Berg, Ṣawm, in *EI²*, ix, 94-5; N. Calder, Ḥinth, birr, tabarrur, taḥannuth. An inquiry into the Arabic vocabulary of vows, in *BSOAS* 51 (1988), 214-39; S.D. Goitein, Ramadan. The Muslim month of fasting, in S.D. Goitein, *Studies in Islamic history and institutions*, Leiden 1966, 90-110 (rev. ed. of the important study of F. Goitein, Zur Entstehung des Ramadān, in *Der Islam* 18 [1929], 189-96); G.R. Hawting, Taḥannuth, in *EI²*, x, 98-9; id., The tawwābūn, atonement and ʿĀshūrāʾ, in *JSAI* 17 (1995), 166-81 (important for the dating of 10 Muḥarram); D.A. King, Ḳibla, in *EI²*, v, 82-8; M.J. Kister, Al-taḥannuth. An inquiry into the meaning of a term, in *BSOAS* 31 (1968), 223-36 (repr. in Kister, *Studies in Jāhiliyya and early Islam*, London 1980); id., Rajab is the month of God, in *IOS* 1 (1971), 191-223 (repr. in Kister, *Society and religion from Jāhiliyya to Islam*, Aldershot 1990); id., "Shaʿbān is my month." A study of an early tradition, in J. Blau et al. (eds.), *Studia orientalia memoriae D.H. Baneth dedicata*, Jerusalem 1979, 15-37 (repr. in Kister, *Society and religion from Jāhiliyya to Islam*, Aldershot 1990); K. Lech, *Geschichte des islamischen Kultus. i. Das ramadān-Fasten*, Wiesbaden 1979; Ph. Marçais, ʿĀshūrāʾ, in *EI²*, i, 705; R. Paret, Furḳān, in *EI²*, ii, 949-50; R. Paret/E. Chaumont, ʿUmra, in *EI²*, x, 864-6; M. Plessner, Ramaḍān, in *EI²*, viii,

417-8; C. Vogel, *Le pécheur et la pénitence au moyen-age,* Paris 1969, 1. La pénitence tarifiée, 17-24; 2. Le pénitentiel de Finnian (milieu du VIe siècle), 52-62; 3. Le pénitentiel de saint Colomban (fin du VIe siècle), 62-71; K. Wagtendonk, *Fasting in the Koran,* Leiden 1968 (fundamental and still valuable); Watt-Bell, *Introduction;* A.J. Wensinck, Arabic new year and the feast of tabernacles, in *Verhandelingen der Koninklijke Nederlandse Akademie van Wetenschappen, Afdeling Letterkunde, Nieuwe Reeks* 25 (1925), 1-17.

Fate

The principle, or determining cause or will, through which things occur as they should. Although the pre-Islamic concept (see PRE-ISLAMIC ARABIA AND THE QUR'ĀN; SOUTH ARABIA, RELIGION IN PRE-ISLAMIC; AGE OF IGNORANCE) of an impersonal fate (*dahr,* see TIME) is attested in the Qur'ān (Q 45:24; 76:1; cf. "accident of time" *[rayb al-manūn],* Q 52:30), the qur'ānic message is that God, and not an impersonal agent, governs the world (cf. Böwering, Ideas, esp. 175-7). But are some, or even all events in history predetermined by God from eternity (q.v.)? This thorny question, which has generated involved debates and discussions among Muslims — particularly in theological *(kalām)* and philosophical *(falsafa)* circles — up until the present, does not receive a univocal answer in the Qur'ān. The predestination theme appears in the form of an uncompromising emphasis on the supreme agency and omnipotence of God, but it is counterbalanced by an equally strong assumption of human responsibility for human action (see FREEDOM AND PREDESTINATION).

Several qur'ānic terms in particular are associated with predestinarian ideas. Foremost among these are *qaḍā* (or *qaḍā'*) and *qadar,* which later become technical terms in *kalām* (see THEOLOGY AND THE QUR'ĀN). The verb *qaḍā,* "to decide, to determine, to judge," occurs sixty times in the text. Leaving aside the occurrences that are not relevant to this discussion, it is used principally to underline God's creative power (in verses of the type "When he decrees a thing, he says to it 'Be' and it is," as in Q 2:117; 3:47; 19:35; 40:68; also cf. 19:21; see CREATION), to emphasize his ultimate judgment (q.v.; Q 40:20; 10:93; 27:78; 45:17; etc.; see LAST JUDGMENT), or to declare him the master of death (Q 39:42 and 34:14; see DEATH AND THE DEAD). The verb seems to assume a deterministic tone in Q 17:4, however, where reference is made to God's decree that the Israelites (see CHILDREN OF ISRAEL) will twice cause corruption (q.v.) on the earth (though many commentators understand the verb to mean "to inform" here, as in Ṭabarī, *Tafsīr,* viii, 20), and in Q 12:41, where Joseph (q.v.) informs his two prison mates of their fates. It is, of course, possible to read these verses as confirmation of God's foreknowledge of events rather than as evidence of his predestination, but there is little doubt that God is portrayed here as shaping the destinies of at least some groups and individuals.

Words of the root *q-d-r* are equally abundant. The verbs *qadara* and *qaddara,* "to measure, to determine," are used primarily to convey the central idea that God measures and orders his creation, that while he is unbounded and infinite, everything else is limited and determinate (Ringgren, Studies, 97-103; Rahman, *Themes,* 12, 23, 67). All other words of this root (chief among them the noun *qadar* and the adjectives *qadīr* and *qādir,* "mighty," as an attribute of God in an expression like "God is powerful over all things") serve to underscore God's omnipotence. Of special significance is the expression *laylat al-qadr,* "the night of measure (or might)," in sūra 97 (Sūrat al-Qadr, "Power"; see NIGHT OF POWER). Commentators and theologians are united in identifying this night as the time of the revelation of the Qur'ān (cf.

Q 44:3-4) and, while some of them understand this event as the transference of God's eternal decree to the temporal-spatial plane and reach predestinarian conclusions, the Qurʾān itself gives us no clear pointers in this direction.

Another potent qurʾānic word is *ajal*, "term." It seems to be the temporal equivalent of *q-d-r*, words that evoke the idea of a "measured creation." Everything but God is limited and fixed, not only in space but also in time. Thus all humans are appointed a fixed term of life on earth: "It is he who created you from clay (q.v.) and assigned [you] a term" (Q 6:2; see BIOLOGY AS THE CREATION AND STAGES OF LIFE). Whether this term can be shortened (see CHASTISEMENT AND PUNISHMENT; REWARD AND PUNISHMENT) by sins (see SIN, MAJOR AND MINOR) or lengthened by good deeds (q.v.) is a question debated later by theologians, but the Qurʾān insists, instead, only on the limited nature of created beings as opposed to the absolute unboundedness of God.

Two other prominent qurʾānic concepts that relate to God's role in shaping human destiny are *amr*, "command, word," and *rizq*, "bounty, sustenance." The former, a complex concept, normally refers to God's creative command 'Be' or, parallel to the concept of *qadar*, expresses the qurʾānic view that the creation is subject to laws authored by God — hence the idea that nature is *muslim*, i.e. that it submits to God (see COSMOLOGY; NATURAL WORLD AND THE QURʾĀN; SEMIOTICS AND NATURE IN THE QURʾĀN). Some *amr* verses, however, seem to supply evidence of God intervening in human events on certain occasions (for instance, Q 11:73, on the conception of Isaac (q.v.) and Q 30:3-4, on a prediction of Byzantine victory [see BYZANTINES]), but the emphasis is clearly on God's supreme sovereignty, as suggested by Q 3:128, where the Prophet is told that he has no part in the divine command. The term *rizq*, too, is generally used to highlight God's agency since it conveys the idea that sustenance belongs to God alone, but it also connotes a "sense of specific allotment" (McAuliffe, Rizq), especially in verses where one's lot is said to be "straitened" or "made ample" (Q 89:16 or 13:26; see BLESSING).

Apart from the ones so far mentioned, there are other qurʾānic concepts that are frequently invoked in *kalām* discussions of predestination, such as *lawḥ*, "tablet" (Q 85:22; see PRESERVED TABLET), *qalam*, "pen" (Q 68:1), and *kitāb*, "book" (q.v.; 261 occurrences, including attestations in the plural and dual forms). The first two concepts remain undeveloped in the Qurʾān, while the last — the book, along with verses related to "writing" where God is the author — plays a central role as the manifestation of God's knowledge, will and wisdom (q.v.), as best exemplified in the verse "Nothing will happen to us except what God has written for us" (Q 9:51). From here, it is an easy step to the thoroughly predestinarian view that God has determined all events in pre-eternity. A closer scrutiny suggests, however, that the *kitāb* verses — like the *qadā* (or *qaḍāʾ*), *qadar*, *ajal*, *amr*, and *rizq* verses — are really about God's absolute, infinite sovereignty as opposed to the measured, limited, contingent nature of his creation. It is for this reason that the Qurʾān is adamant about God's supreme agency, as in the verse "You did not throw when you threw, but God threw" (Q 8:17, referring to the battle of Badr [q.v.], when the Prophet threw a handful of dust toward the Meccan forces).

Does God's omnipotence and omniscience leave any room for human agency? It is clear that human beings, who were not created in play (Q 23:115), have a special place in the creation in that God breathed his own spirit (q.v.) into them (Q 15:29; 38:72; 32:9), endowed them with the capacity to know (exemplified by God teaching Adam [see ADAM AND EVE] the names of things, Q 2:30f; see KNOWLEDGE AND LEARNING) and entrusted them with the unique trust (Q 33:72) of being his vicegerent on earth (Q 2:30; see CALIPH). It is a fundamental assumption of the Qurʾān that human beings, unlike angels (see ANGEL), do not fulfill this role, so to speak, automatically, and that they are as likely to fail in this endeavor as to succeed. Indeed, the Qurʾān itself is an invitation for them to assume this role, provided to them as guidance by God in his mercy (q.v.; many verses, e.g. Q 2:185). It is in this context that the final reckoning, *ḥisāb*, of human acts on the day of judgment is to be understood.

Human agency, therefore, is a reality. It is the responsibility of human beings to purify their souls (Q 91:7-10) and they have the initiative on this front since God only turns them in the direction they choose (Q 4:115) and does not change the condition of a people until they change it themselves (Q 13:11). Those who fail bring misfortune upon themselves by doing injustice to their own souls (numerous verses, e.g. Q 65:1). If they realize their error (q.v.) and repent (see REPENTANCE AND PENANCE), God forgives them (see FORGIVENESS) and guides them to the right path (e.g. Q 28:16; see PATH OR WAY) but, if they persevere in their injustice (see JUSTICE AND INJUSTICE), God entrenches them in this state by placing seals on their hearts (see HEART) and ears (q.v.) and veils on their eyes (q.v.; Q 2:7; see SEEING AND HEARING; HEARING AND DEAFNESS). The Qurʾān itself is best understood as God's guidance to humanity prompting them to help themselves by acknowledging God's sovereignty and serving him by committing good deeds.

In addition to the verses considered, there are numerous verses of the intriguing type "God guides to truth whom he wills and leads astray whom he wills" (e.g. Q 14:4), which would seem to deny any agency to humans in their salvation (q.v.). An examination of these "will-verses" suggests, however, that they are to be understood as expressions of God's absolute liberty of action, or better yet, as powerful reminders of his final authority and power. Simply put, nothing happens outside the orbit of his will. Perhaps the best way to reconcile the apparent discrepancy between this unflinching qurʾānic insistence on God's omnipotent, overpowering agency and its equally fundamental assumption of human accountability as demonstrated, among other things, by its highly developed eschatology (q.v.) is to argue as does the modern Muslim philosopher Fazlur Rahman (*Themes*, 22) that the Qurʾān is prescriptive, not descriptive. It is a document that is meant to bring about a change in human attitude and behavior in order to orient humanity towards God; it is not a cold, descriptive account of the scope and boundary of divine and human action. It is meant to reawaken and strengthen human capacity for moral action, not to stifle it by relentless reiteration of God's power (see ETHICS AND THE QURʾĀN). For Muslim scholars who hold this view, the numerous verses on God's omnipotence and supreme agency lose their predestinarian ring and assume the function of awakening in human beings the properly pious attitude of grateful patience and equanimity in the face of fortune and misfortune alike (as, for instance, in Q 22:35; see TRUST AND PATIENCE; GRATITUDE AND INGRATITUDE; TRIAL).

In summary, many would argue that the majority of the seemingly predestinarian verses in the Qurʾān are really expressive of God's supreme sovereignty, that the emphasis is clearly not on predetermination of events but on God's creative activity which continuously "measures out" his creation (God's control of life and death, for instance, would be understood in this sense) or on his all-encompassing knowledge and will. From this interpretive perspective, the qurʾānic insistence on God's absolute sovereignty is not a description of a deterministic universe dominated by God but an urgent reminder that invites humanity to moral action. In contrast to the pre-Islamic understanding of human destiny, the God of the Qurʾān is not an impersonal Fate but a personal God who invites human beings to dynamic involvement in the world and who himself responds dynamically to human action. See also HISTORY AND THE QURʾĀN.

Ahmet T. Karamustafa

Bibliography
Primary: Ṭabarī, *Tafsīr,* 12 vols., Beirut 1412/1992.
Secondary: G. Böwering, Ideas of time in Persian mysticism, in R.G. Hovannisian and G. Sabagh (eds.), *The Persian presence in the Islamic world,* Cambridge, UK 1998, 172-98; W. Caskel, *Das Schiksal in der altarabischen Poesie,* Leipzig 1926; van Ess, *TG;* I. Goldziher/W.M. Watt, Adjal, in *EI²*, i, 204; J. McAuliffe, Rizq. 2. In the Ḳurʾān, in *EI²*, viii, 568; F. Rahman, *Major themes of the Qurʾān,* Minneapolis 1989; H. Ringgren, *Studies in Arabian fatalism,* Uppsala 1955 (fundamental); W.M. Watt, *The formative period of Islamic thought,* Edinburgh 1973.

Father(s) see FAMILY; PARENTS; PATRIARCHY

Fātiḥa

The first sūra of the Qurʾān, "The Opener," more properly "The Opening of Scripture" (*fātiḥat al-kitāb,* see BOOK). It occupies a unique place formally and theologically in the ʿUthmānic text of the Qurʾān and in ritual prayer (*ṣalāt,* see CODICES OF THE QURʾĀN; RITUAL AND THE QURʾĀN; PRAYER). Its seven brief verses stand at the head of the qurʾānic text, the remaining 113 sūras being arranged roughly from longest to shortest. It is the one sūra that every Muslim must be able to recite by heart in order to perform the ritual prayer (full legal observance of which requires repeating the Fātiḥa seventeen times daily [Quṭb, *Ẓilāl,* i, 21]: twice for the dawn *ṣalāt,* three for the sunset, and four for each of the remaining three [see DAY, TIMES OF]. On the legally obligatory [except among the Ḥanafīs] Arabic recitation of the Fātiḥa in *ṣalāt,* see *al-Fiqh ʿalā l-madhāhib al-arbaʿa,* 186-8; Khoury, *Der Koran,* 140-1). Even apart from the *ṣalāt,* the Fātiḥa is easily the most-repeated sūra in Muslim use — as devotional prayer, hymn of praise (q.v.), supplication, invocation, social convention, protective or curative talisman (see AMULETS), or word of solace (see EVERYDAY LIFE, THE QURʾĀN IN). As the primary prayer and scriptural formula in Muslim communal and personal life, the Fātiḥa is comparable to the *Shema* in the Jewish tradition and the *Paternoster* in the Christian.

The text of the Fātiḥa (with standard verse numbering) runs as follows: (1) "In the name of God, the merciful compassionate one ["merciful Lord of mercy" — K. Cragg]. (2) Praise be to God, lord (q.v.) of all beings [or worlds], (3) the merciful compassionate one, (4) master of the day of reckoning. (5) You alone do we worship (q.v.), and upon you alone do we call for help. (6) Guide us on the straight path, (7) the path of those whom you have blessed, not of those upon whom your anger (q.v.) has fallen, nor of those who are astray (q.v.)." (See also PATH OR WAY; BLESSING; LAST JUDGMENT; MERCY.)

Muslims have many different names for the Fātiḥa. Fakhr al-Dīn al-Rāzī (d. 606/1210) cites twelve (*Tafsīr,* i, 179-83), the first ten of which are also given by Ṭabarsī

(d. 518/1153; *Majmaʿ*, i, 31-2), while the first four to seven are given by most commentators. The twelve, beginning with the more frequent, are: the aforementioned *fātiḥat al-kitāb; al-ḥamd,* "Praise"; *umm al-Qurʾān/al-kitāb,* "the Quintessence (lit. "Mother") of the Qurʾān/Scripture" (cf. Q 3:7; 13:39; 43:4); *al-sabʿ al-mathānī,* "the Seven Mathānī" (i.e. traditions or repeated verses; cf. Nöldeke, GQ, i, 114-6; Bell-Watt, *Introduction,* 134; cf. Q 15:87); *al-wāfiya,* "the Complete"; *al-kāfiya,* "the Sufficient"; *al-asās,* "the Foundation"; *al-shifāʾ* (or *al-shāfiya*), "Healing"; *al-ṣalāt,* "Worship"; *al-suʾāl,* "the Request"; and *al-duʿāʾ,* "Supplication." Abū Ḥayyān (d. 745/1344; *Baḥr,* i, 153) gives most of these and others, e.g. *al-rāqiya,* "the Charm/Enchantment"; *al-wāqiya,* "the Protector"; *al-kanz,* "the Treasure"; and *al-nūr,* "Light." Exegetes have discussed the many names given this sūra, each of which points to some role or understanding of the Fātiḥa in Islam (see Kandil, Surennamen, 44-50; cf. Suyūṭī, *Itqān,* i, 52-3).

The Fātiḥa takes the form of a first-person-plural prayer formula clearly intended for human utterance rather than a first- or third-person word of God, a point that has been noted since the earliest days of Islam. A testimony to this is the practice among Sunnī Muslims of ending their recitation of this sūra with *āmīn* ("amen"; see RECITATION, THE ART OF) — this being the only sūra so treated (Ibn Kathīr, *Tafsīr,* i, 31-2; Zamakhsharī, *Kashshāf,* i, 73-5). Shīʿīs reject this (see SHĪʿISM AND THE QURʾĀN): Al-Ṭūsī (d. 460/1067) says one should not seal the recitation of the Fātiḥa with *āmīn;* indeed, doing so voids the *ṣalāt* (*Tibyān,* i, 46; cf. Ṭabarsī, *Majmaʿ,* i, 65, who says one should say instead, "Praise be to God, lord of beings"). There are only three similar qurʾānic instances of prayers: Q 113 and Q 114 (known as "the two sūras of taking refuge [i.e. from evil]," *al-muʿawwidhatān*), both first-person-*singular* invocations of God against evil powers; and parts of the last two verses of Sūrat al-Baqara, Q 2:285-6 (known as the "seals of the Cow," *khawātīm al-Baqara*), which, like the Fātiḥa, contain first-person-plural prayer formulae. Muslim tradition has long recognized the link between the Fātiḥa and the *khawātīm,* the latter sharing the special blessing *(baraka)* of the former — e.g. Ibn ʿAbbās' (d. 68/686-7) report of an angel (q.v.) saying that Muḥammad (q.v.) was given two lights accorded no earlier prophet, namely the Fātiḥa and the *khawātīm,* the recitation of even one letter of which brings an answer to prayer (e.g. Muslim, *Ṣaḥīḥ. K. Ṣalāt al-musāfirīn,* 254; Nasāʾī, *Sunan,* xi, 25; Ibn Kathīr, *Tafsīr,* i, 342).

The Fātiḥa in Muslim and non-Muslim scholarship

Classical qurʾānic scholarship preserved several variant readings for the Fātiḥa which were ascribed to various pre-ʿUthmānic codices (see Jeffery, *Materials,* 25, 117, 185, 195, 220, 227, 232; Khoury, *Der Koran,* i, 146; cf. Ibn Kathīr, *Tafsīr,* i, 22, 24-8; Ibn Hishām al-Anṣārī, *Iʿrāb,* 1-4). Major examples are: for *mālik(i),* "master, possessor, lord," in Q 1:4, *malik(i),* "king, sovereign" (Ibn Masʿūd, Ubayy, ʿAlī, ʿĀʾisha et al., also preferred by Ṭabarī, *Tafsīr,* i, 148-54; cf. Jeffery, *Muqaddimas,* 134; Zamakhsharī, *Kashshāf,* i, 57 says *mālik* is preferred because it is the reading of the people of the *Ḥaramayn*, i.e. Mecca and Medina), or also *mālika, maliku, malīku, malīki, malku* (various authorities); in Ubayy's codex, *Allāhumma,* "O God!" precedes Q 1:5, and *iyyāka* is read *iyāka* (also meaning "you"); in Q 1:6, for *ihdinā,* "Guide us," three variants with the same or a similar sense are known, e.g. *arshidnā* (Ibn Masʿūd); also, *al-ṣirāṭ al-mustaqīm,* "the straight path," is given by Ibn ʿUmar

(d. 73/693), Ubayy (d. 21/642), and Jaʿfar al-Ṣādiq (d. 148/765) without the first *al-* ("the path of the straight"); al-Aʿmash and al-Rabīʿ spell *ṣirāṭ* as *zirāṭ* and Ibn ʿAbbās spells it *sirāṭ;* in Q 1:7, for *alladhīna,* "those who," *aladhīna* (Ubayy), or *man,* "whoever" (Ibn Masʿūd, ʿUmar, Ibn al-Zubayr); for *ghayri,* "not those," *ghīra* (Ibn Masʿūd, ʿAlī, ʿUmar et al.), *ghayra* (ʿAlī, Ubayy, ʿUmar et al.); for *wa-lā,* "and not/nor," *wa-ghayri, wa-ghayra* (Ubayy, ʿAlī et al.; cf. Ṭabarī, *Tafsīr,* i, 182-4).

The meaning of several words in the text has also been debated in the tradition, notably that of *ʿālamīn* in Q 1:2, "creatures, beings" (lit. "worlds"). Ṭabarī (d. 310/923; *Tafsīr,* i, 143-6) takes it as the different communities of men, jinn (q.v.), and all created species (see CREATION), each being an *ʿālam* ("cosmos, world"; see Ibn Kathīr, *Tafsīr,* i, 23-4; Zamakhsharī, *Kashshāf,* i, 53-5; Dāmaghānī, *Wujūh,* 331-2; cf. Jeffery, *For. vocab.,* 208-9; Nöldeke, *GQ,* i, 112 n.1; Paret, *Kommentar,* 12); some exegetes have limited *ʿālamīn* solely to rational beings (e.g. Ṭūsī, *Tibyān,* i, 32; cf. Ayoub, *Qurʾān,* i, 47); Rāzī says it refers to all things real, imagined or even unimaginable (*Tafsīr,* i, 234-5; cf. Ibn Kathīr, *Tafsīr,* i, 24). The final verse has also been a point of grammatical divergence for interpreters and translators. Some have read the verse (without change of meaning) as "The path of those whom you have blessed, [the path of] those on whom your wrath has not fallen, and [the path of] those who are not astray" (Ṭabarī, *Tafsīr,* i, 181-2).

Most Muslim scholars, following Ibn ʿAbbās and Qatāda (d. ca 117/735), have considered the Fātiḥa an early Meccan revelation (see CHRONOLOGY AND THE QURʾĀN), primarily because of its centrality to ritual prayer *(ṣalāt),* which began in Mecca (q.v.); Mujāhid (d. 104/722) alone among early authorities (see EXEGESIS OF THE QURʾĀN: CLASSICAL AND MEDIEVAL) held it to be Medinan. In an effort to reconcile the two positions, some say that it was revealed both in Mecca, when the *ṣalāt* was prescribed, and again in Medina (q.v.), when the *qibla* (q.v.) was changed (see ABROGATION). It is also said to have been the first sūra revealed in its entirety (M. ʿAbduh, *Tafsīr al-Fātiḥa,* 20-22; Ṭabarsī, *Majmaʿ,* i, 35). Muslim exegesis has largely focused on the following: (i) the meaning and implications of the text (including such questions as whether the latter portion refers to three specific communities: Muslims — *alladhīna anʿamta ʿalayhim,* Christians (see CHRISTIANS AND CHRISTIANITY) — *al-maghḍūbi ʿalayhim,* and Jews (see JEWS AND JUDAISM) — *al-ḍāllīn* (e.g. Ṭabarī, *Tafsīr,* i, 185-95; Ṭabarsī, *Majmaʿ,* i, 65; Zamakhsharī, *Kashshāf,* i, 71), or to previous peoples to whom the Qurʾān often refers elsewhere (see ʿAbduh, *Tafsīr al-Fātiḥa,* 46-8; Ṭabarsī, *Majmaʿ,* i, 59-66; see GEOGRAPHY; GENERATIONS); (ii) whether the *basmala* (q.v.) is a prefatory formula, as elsewhere, or the first verse of the Fātiḥa (Ṭabarī and some other exegetes deny this; others affirm it, as its inclusion as Q 1:1 in the Cairo text shows); (iii) the disagreement among the Companions (see COMPANIONS OF THE PROPHET) as to whether the Fātiḥa was originally intended to be included in the qurʾānic text at all (Ibn Masʿūd did not put the Fātiḥa [or *al-muʿawwidhatān*] in his recension, saying that if he had, he would have had to place it before every part of the Qurʾān; Shawkānī, *Tafsīr,* i, 14; see COLLECTION OF THE QURʾĀN); (iv) the bipartite structure of the sūra (the initial praise, or *ḥamd,* portion through *iyyāka nastaʿīn* [Q 1:2-5], and the ensuing supplication [Q 1:6-7]); (v) the aforementioned textual variants (*qirāʾāt,* see READINGS OF THE QURʾĀN); (vi) the identification of the Fātiḥa as the *sabʿan min al-mathānī,* "seven of the repeated [verses]/traditions," mentioned in Q 15:87; and (vii) the aforementioned tradition of closing every repetition of only this sūra with *āmīn.* Recently,

M. Arkoun (Lecture) has sought to analyze the dual function of the Fātiḥa as (i) something voiced by the Prophet in a liturgical context no longer accessible to us and (ii) a text within the composite qurʾānic text that has been the subject of exegetical interpretation as a meaningful whole (see FORM AND STRUCTURE OF THE QURʾĀN).

Non-Muslim, Western scholars, following Nöldeke (*GQ*, i, 110-5), have generally agreed that the Fātiḥa is Meccan, but not from the very earliest period, since they date the institution of *ṣalāt* later in the Meccan period. While R. Bell, R. Blachère, R. Paret, W. Watt and others have discussed the sūra, there has been little major change in the general picture presented by Nöldeke-Schwally. S. Goitein, however, emphasized in a 1966 article that the Fātiḥa is "a liturgical composition created deliberately" for use in "a fixed liturgy" and set before the actual qurʾānic text as a prefatory sūra, the provenance of which was the communal prayer rite (Prayer, 82-4). Still more emphatically, Neuwirth and Neuwirth (1991) argued that (i) the first substantive of the paired *sabʿan min al-mathānī wa-l-Qurʾān al-ʿaẓīm* of Q 15:87 refers to the Fātiḥa (minus the *basmala*, but with the final verse divided into two to keep seven verses [q.v.]) as a liturgical text received alongside the Qurʾān, and, correspondingly, (ii) the Fātiḥa is clearly a liturgical prayer, specifically an *introitus* to the *ṣalāt*, rather than a regular sūra, which has parallels in very similar formulae in contemporaneous Christian and Jewish liturgical use.

The Fātiḥa in Muslim life

The role of the Fatiḥa in piety (q.v.) and practice is immense and can only be adumbrated here. Above all, it is the anchor of the *ṣalāt*, in which, according to a prophetic ḥadīth (see ḤADĪTH AND THE QURʾĀN), it must be recited for the performance of the ritual to be valid (Bukhārī, *Ṣaḥīḥ* 10:94:2; Muslim, *Ṣaḥīḥ. K. al-Ṣalāt*, 38, 41; see also Jeffery, *Muqaddimas*, 135; Wensinck, *Concordance*, ii, 12). Its special quality is signaled in the *ḥadīth qudsī* (see ḤADĪTH AND THE QURʾĀN) that sometimes accompanies this prophetic ḥadīth, in which God says, "I have divided the *ṣalāt* between myself and my servant," then declares that he himself responds to each phrase of the Fātiḥa as it is uttered, in answer to the worshiper's prayer (Muslim, *Ṣaḥīḥ. K. al-Ṣalāt*, 38, 41; Ṭabāṭabāʾī, *Mīzān*, 39; further refs. in Graham, *Divine word*, 183-4; see also EVERYDAY LIFE). Tradition holds it to be unique among revelations, both pre-qurʾānic and qurʾānic (see REVELATION AND INSPIRATION), a special blessing given to Muḥammad (e.g. Ālūsī, *Rūḥ*, 97-8). As Ibn Māja (ix, 19) quotes the Prophet, "Every important matter one does not begin with 'al-Ḥamd' is void." Commentators of all ages have devoted significant attention to it; most major modern Muslim thinkers have commented on it either separately or within a full *tafsīr* (e.g. ʿAbduh, Rashīd Riḍā, Mawdūdī, Sayyid Quṭb, Ḥasan al-Bannā, Ṭabāṭabāʾī; see EXEGESIS OF THE QURʾĀN: EARLY MODERN AND CONTEMPORARY). In addition to being the most universally known and repeated part of the Qurʾān among Muslims, its repetition is, along with that of the *shahāda* ("testimony" by which one declares oneself to be a Muslim; see WITNESS TO FAITH), the most significant oral mark of Muslim faith. For example, J. Bowen in a recent unpublished paper (Imputations) points to its symbolic importance as a litmus test for the "true Muslim" in contemporary Indonesia. So much is the Fātiḥa the quintessential prayer that its dialect form, *fatḥa*, comes to be used in some North African Ṣūfī contexts for other prayers as well (Crapanzano, *Ḥamadsha*, 189, n. 4; see DIALECTS; ṢŪFISM AND THE QURʾĀN). The sacred power, or *baraka*, of the Fātiḥa is universally attested in all eras in popular practice:

as a talismanic healing aid (see MEDICINE AND THE QURʾĀN); as defense against evil spirits; as an intercessory prayer for the dead (see DEATH AND THE DEAD; INTERCESSORY PRAYER); in burial rituals and when approaching a cemetery or visiting a grave; on recovery from sickness; to avert danger; in naming and circumcision (q.v.) rituals; in thanksgiving for food and drink (q.v.); to "seal" a promise, treaty, marriage, or other contractual agreement (see CONTRACTS AND ALLIANCES; MARRIAGE AND DIVORCE); to bless a place, a time of plowing or harvest, or the admission of an apprentice to a guild; to give oneself courage (q.v.) in battle; as the quintessential superogatory prayer; as consolation (q.v.) to the bereaved after a funeral; as prayer upon visiting a saint's shrine; and in every *ʿĪd al-Fitr* and *ʿĪd al-Aḍḥā* celebration (Bukhārī, *Ṣaḥīḥ* 66:9, 76:34; Snouck Hurgronje, *Mekka*, 29, 43, 53, 129, 140, 143; Westermarck, *Ritual*, i, 113 and passim [see index for numerous examples]; Jomier, *Place du Coran*, 135-6, 141, 148-9; Piamenta, *Muslim conception of God*, 5, 24-6 [further refs.]; Khoury, *Der Koran*, 138-40; Lane, *Manners*, 61, 76, 236-7, 260, 458, 465, 480, 521; see FESTIVALS AND COMMEMORATIVE DAYS).

William A. Graham

Bibliography
Primary: M. ʿAbduh, *Tafsīr al-Fātiḥa*, Cairo 1319/1901-2, repr. 1382/1962-3; Abū Ḥayyān, *al-Baḥr al-muḥīt*, ed. ʿA. Mawjūd and ʿA. Muʿawwad, 8 vols., Beirut 1993; Ālūsī, *Rūḥ;* Ḥ. al-Bannā, *Muqaddimat tafsīr al-Qurʾān*, Beirut 1972; Bukhārī, *Ṣaḥīḥ;* Dāmaghānī, *Wujūh;* Ibn Hishām al-Anṣārī, *Iʿrāb fātiḥat al-kitāb wa-l-baqara*, ed. M. Mursī, Cairo 1407/1987; Ibn Kathīr, *Tafsīr;* Ibn Māja; Jeffery, *Muqaddimas;* Kāshānī, *Minhaj;* Muslim, *Ṣaḥīḥ;* Nasāʾī, *Sunan;* Quṭb, *Ẓilāl;* Rashīd Riḍā, *Manār;* Rāzī, *Tafsīr;* Shawkānī, *Tafsīr;* Suyūṭī, *Itqān;* Ṭabarī, *Tafsīr;* Ṭabarsī, *Majmaʿ;* Ṭabāṭabāʾī, *Mīzān;* M.S. Ṭanṭāwī, *Tafsīr sūratay al-fātiḥa wa-l-baqara [min al-Tafsīr al-wāsiṭ]*, Benghazi 1974; Ṭūsī, *Tibyān;* Zamakhsharī, *Kashshāf.*
Secondary: M. Arkoun, Lecture de la Fatiha, in *Mélanges d'islamologie dédiés à la mémoire d'A. Abel*, Leiden 1977, 18-44; M. Ayoub, *The Qurʾān and its interpreters*, 2 vols., Albany 1984; Blachère, *Introduction;* J.R. Bowen, Imputations of faith and allegiance. Islamic prayer and Indonesian politics outside the mosque (unpublished paper); K. Cragg (trans.), *Readings in the Qurʾān*, London 1988; V. Crapanzano, *The Hamadsha. A study in Moroccan ethnopsychiatry*, Berkeley 1973; W.S. Cuperus, *al-Fatiha dans la pratique religieuse musulmane du maroc. À partir du 19ème siècle*, Utrecht 1973; M. al-Gharawī, *al-Ism al-aʿẓam aw al-basmala wa-l-ḥamdala*, Beirut and Qum 1982; S.D. Goitein, Prayer in Islam, in *Studies in Islamic history and institutions*, Leiden 1966, 73-89; C. Snouck Hurgronje, *Mekka in the latter part of the 19th century* [1888], trans. J. Monahan, Leiden 1931, repr. 1970; Jeffery, *For. vocab.*; id., *Materials;* id., A variant text of the Fātiḥa, in *MW* 29 (1939), 158-62; J. Jomier, La place du Coran dans la vie quotidienne en Égypt, in *IBLA* 15 (1952), 131-65; L. Kandil, Die Surennamen in der offiziellen Kairiner Koranausgabe und ihre Varianten, in *Der Islam* 69 (1992), 44-60; A.Th. Khoury (trans. and comm.), *Der Koran*, 8 vols. to date, Gütersloh 1990-; E. Lane, *An account of the manners and customs of the modern Egyptians*, 1836; 1860[5], repr. New York 1973; Ministry of Endowments and Social Affairs, *Kitāb al-Fiqh ʿalā al-madhāhib al-arbaʿa. Qism al-ʿibādāt*, Cairo 1967; A. Neuwirth and K. Neuwirth, Sūrat al-Fātiḥa — "Eröffnung" des Text-Corpus Koran oder "Introitus" der Gebetsliturgie? in W. Gross, H. Irsigler, and T. Seidl (eds.), *Text, Methode und Grammatik. Wolfgang Richter zum 65. Geburtstag*, St. Ottilien 1991, 331-57; Nöldeke, *GQ;* R. Paret, Fātiḥa, in *EI*[2], ii, 184; id., *Kommentar;* M. Piamenta, *The Muslim conception of God and human welfare as reflected in everyday Arabic speech*, Leiden 1983; A. Spitaler, *Die Verszählung des Koran nach islamischer Überlieferung*, Munich 1935; Watt-Bell, *Introduction;* Wensinck, *Concordance;* E. Westermarck, *Ritual and belief in Morocco*, 2 vols., London 1926, repr. New York 1968; H. Winckler, Fātiḥa und Vaterunser, in *ZS* 6 (1928), 238-46.

Fāṭima

Only child of Muḥammad and his first wife, Khadīja (q.v.), to survive their deaths. Fāṭima is not mentioned by name in the Qurʾān but the classical exegetical tradition (see EXEGESIS OF THE QURʾĀN: CLASSICAL AND MEDIEVAL) has associated certain verses with her and with her hus-

FIGURES I–IX

[I] Sūrat al-Fātiḥa from a monumental manuscript written in *kūfī* and lavishly illuminated, found in the Great Mosque of Sanʿāʾ (Sanʿāʾ, Dār al-Makhṭūṭāt, inv. no. 20-33.1). Probably produced in Damascus at the end of the 1st/early 8th century. Courtesy of Hans-Caspar Graf von Bothmer, University of Saarbrücken.

بسم الله الرحمن الرحيم الحمد لله
رب العالمين الرحمن الرحيم ملك يوم الدين اياك نعبد
واياك نستعين اهدنا الصراط المستقيم صراط الذين
انعمت عليهم غير المغضوب عليهم ولا الضالين

بسم الله الرحمن الرحيم الم ذلك
الكتاب لا ريب فيه هدى للمتقين الذين يومنون بالغيب
ويقيمون الصلوة ومما رزقناهم ينفقون والذين يومنون
بما انزل اليك وما انزل من قبلك وبالاخرة هم يوقنون
اولئك على هدى من ربهم واولئك هم المفلحون ان
الذين كفروا سوا عليهم ءانذرتهم ام لم تنذرهم لا
يومنون ختم الله على قلوبهم وعلى سمعهم وعلى
ابصارهم غشاوة ولهم عذاب عظيم ومن الناس من

[II] Sūrat al-Fātiḥa in *naskh* on a manuscript from the eastern Islamic world dating from 428/1037. Reproduced by kind permission of the Trustees of the Chester Beatty Library, Dublin (Is.1430, f. 1b).

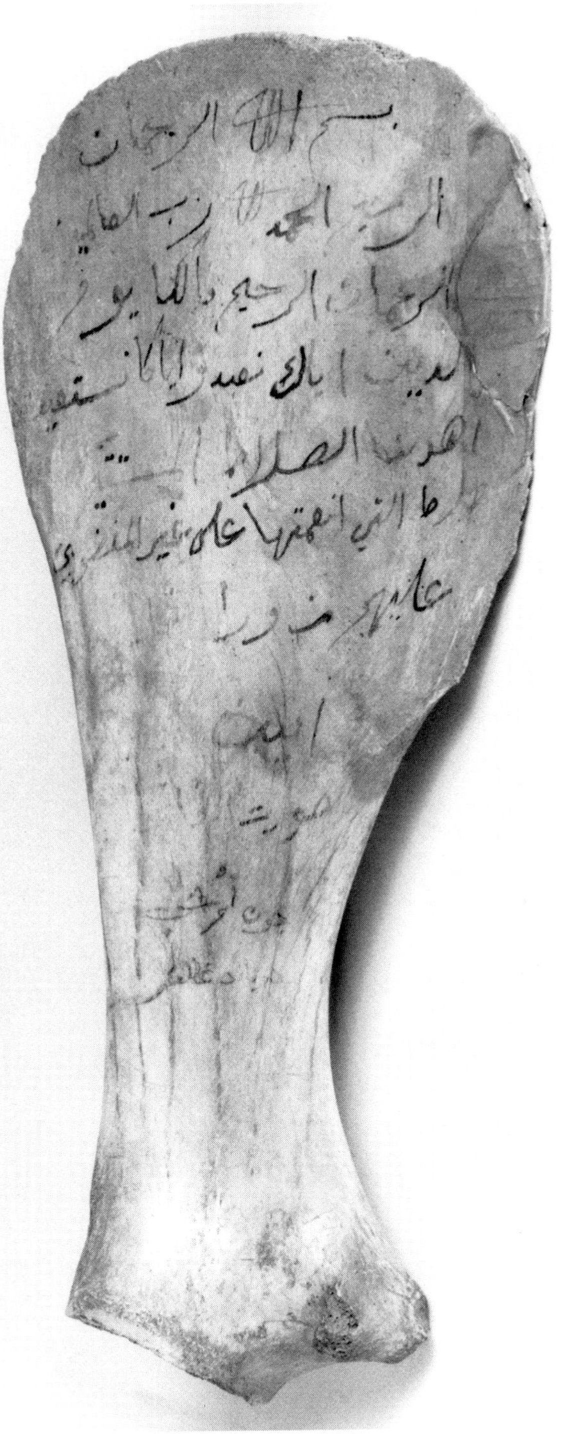

[III] Sūrat al-Fātiḥa inscribed upon the shoulder blade of a camel, undated. Courtesy of Princeton University Library, Department of Rare Books and Special Collections (Manuscripts Division, Islamic Third Series, no. 295).

[IV A] Second half of Sūrat al-Fātiḥa in *rīḥān* from a 9th/15th century Persian manuscript of the Tīmūrid period by the hand of Ibrāhīm b. Shāh Rukh (grandson of Tamerlane). Courtesy of The Metropolitan Museum of Art, New York. Gift of Alexander Smith Cochran, 1913 (13.228.2).

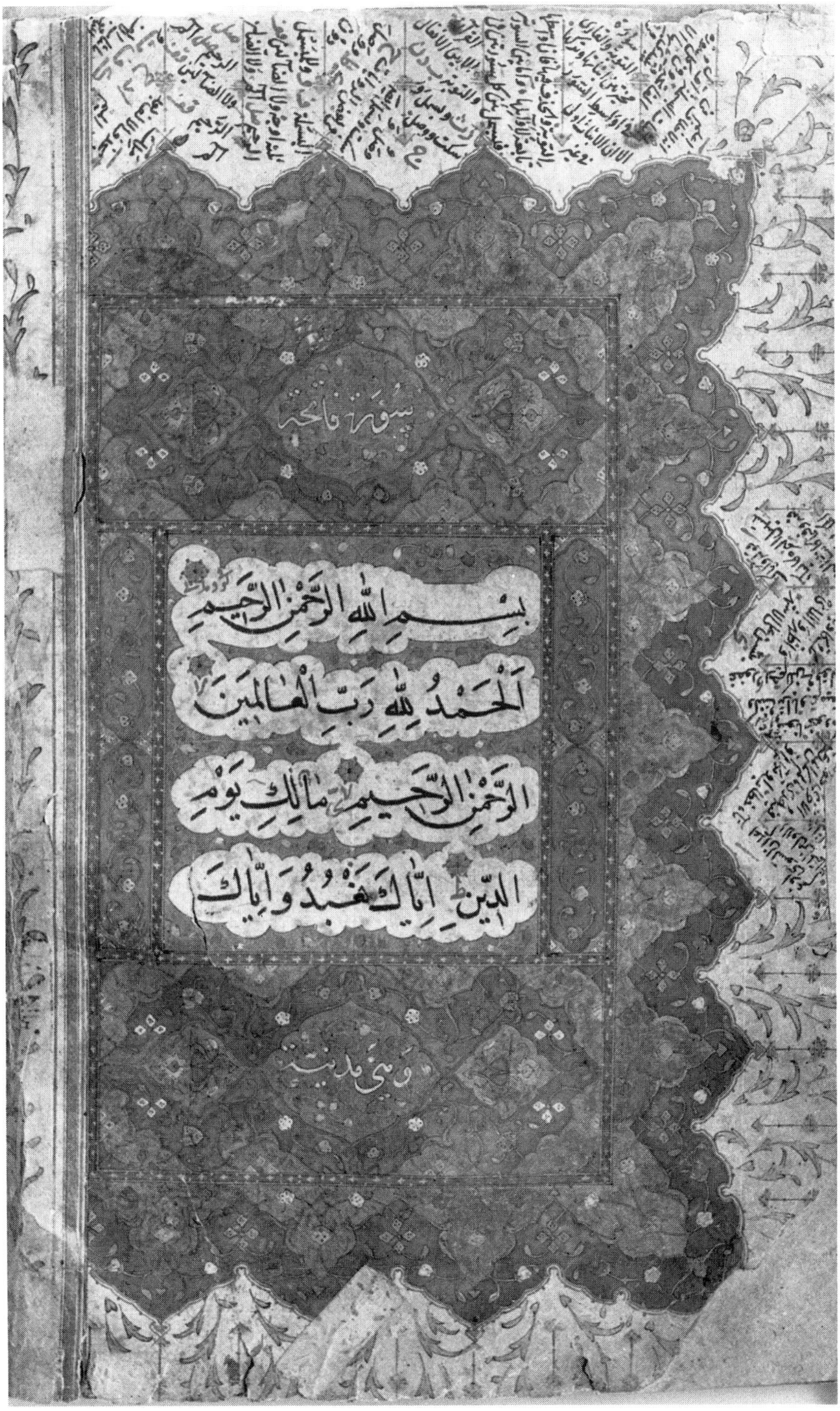

[IV B] First half of Sūrat al-Fātiḥa in *rīḥān* from a 9th/15th century Persian manuscript of the Tīmūrid period by the hand of Ibrāhīm b. Shāh Rukh (grandson of Tamerlane). Courtesy of The Metropolitan Museum of Art, New York. Gift of Alexander Smith Cochran, 1913 (13.228.2).

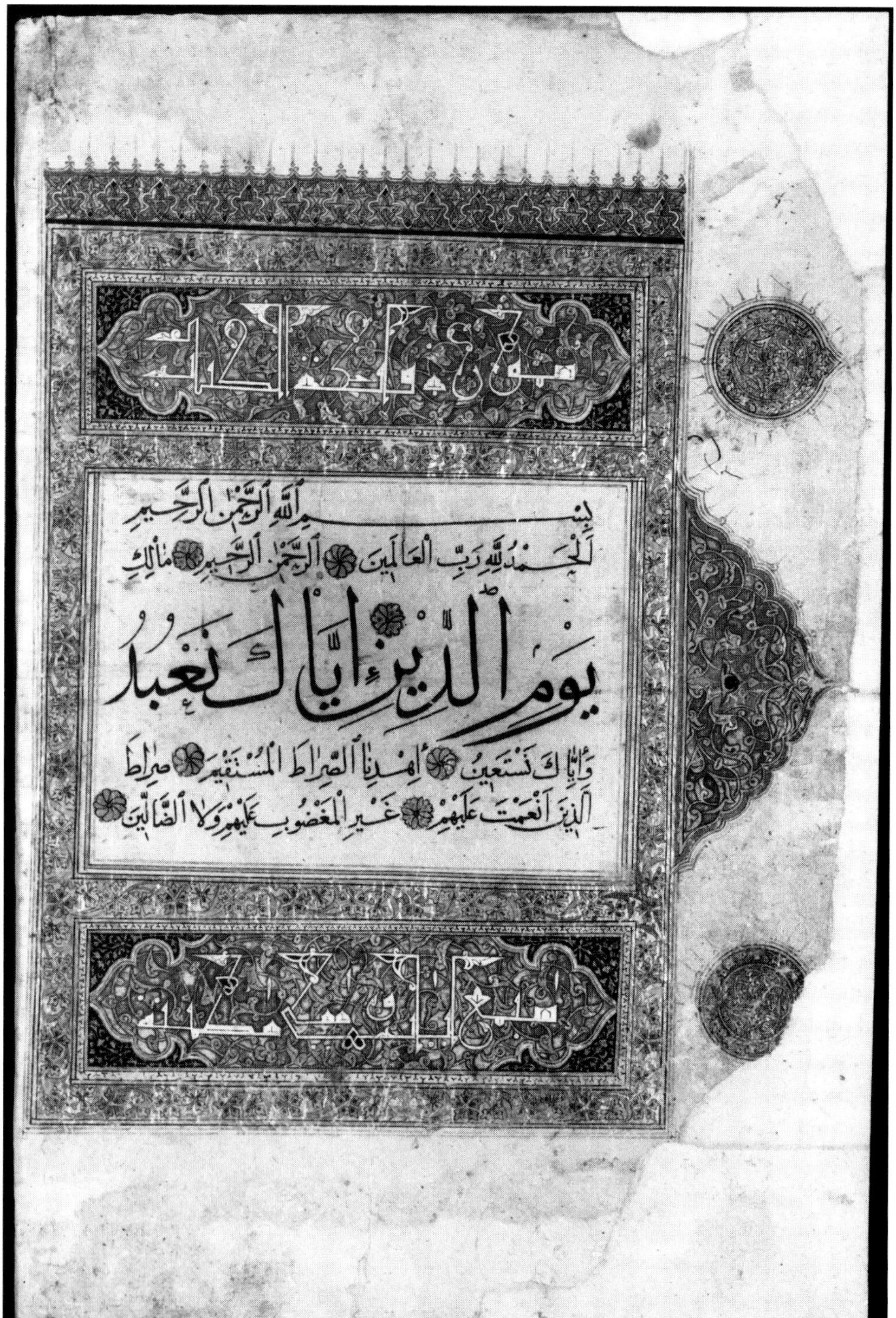

[v] Sūrat al-Fātiḥa in *thuluth* from a Turkish manuscript dating from 868/1454. Courtesy of The Metropolitan Museum of Art, New York. Rogers Fund, 1968 (68.179, folio 1).

[vi] Sūrat al-Fātiḥa in *naskh* from an Iranian manuscript, ca. middle 10th/16th century. Courtesy of the Arthur M. Sackler Gallery, Smithsonian Institution, Washington, DC (S1986.82.1b & 2a).

[vii] The first half of Sūrat al-Fātiḥa (Q 1:1-5) in *naskh* from a double-page Turkish frontispiece (second half of the 10th/16th century). Courtesy of the Arthur M. Sackler Gallery, Smithsonian Institution, Washington, DC (S1986.77.1b).

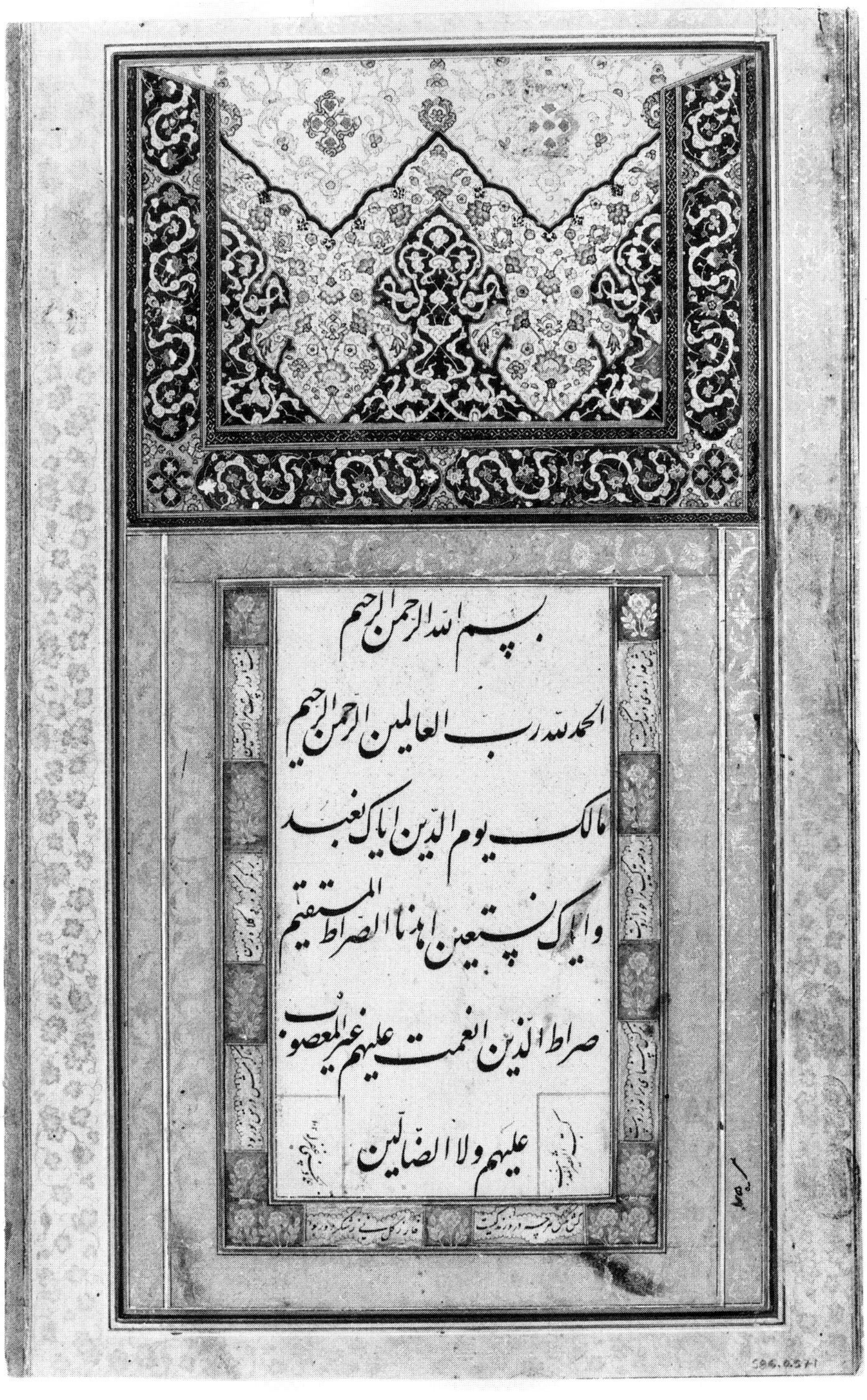

[VIII] Sūrat al-Fātiḥa in *nastaʿlīq* from a Persian manuscript, 1020/1611, by the hand of ʿImād al-Ḥasanī. Courtesy of the Arthur M. Sackler Gallery, Smithsonian Institution, Washington, DC (S1986.371).

[IX] Sūrat al-Fātiḥa in *naskh* from a double page Iranian frontispiece, 1206/1791-2. Courtesy of the Arthur M. Sackler Gallery, Smithsonian Institution, Washington, DC (S1986.87.1).

band and children. Particularly in Shīʿī Islam, the figure of Fāṭima as the closest blood link (see BLOOD AND BLOOD CLOT; KINSHIP) to the Prophet himself, generated a hagiographical literature as well as practices of devotion and supplication (see SHĪʿISM AND THE QURʾĀN).

Of the qurʾānic verses that commentators have linked to Fāṭima, the most important are Q 33:33 and 3:61. The first of these makes reference to the "people of the house" (q.v.; *ahl al-bayt*), which has ordinarily been understood in the more specific sense of "the family of the Prophet" (q.v.), namely, Muḥammad, Fāṭima, her husband ʿAlī b. Abī Ṭālib (q.v.), and their sons al-Ḥasan and al-Ḥusayn (Ṭabarī, *Tafsīr,* xxii, 6-8 who also includes a tradition attributed to ʿIkrima that interprets *ahl al-bayt* as the Prophet's wives [see WIVES OF THE PROPHET]; Ibn al-Jawzī, *Zād,* vi, 381, reverses the order of these options.) Traditions which depict the Prophet sheltering his family, actually or symbolically, under the expanse of his cloak (see CLOTHING) have provided another title for this group of five: "the people of the cloak" (*ahl al-kisāʾ,* Ṭabarī, *Tafsīr,* xxii, 7-8; cf. Spellberg, *Politics,* 34-7, for the relation of Fāṭima and the Prophet's wife ʿĀʾisha; see also ʿĀʾISHA BINT ABĪ BAKR). Q 3:61 contains the challenge: "Come, let us call our sons and your sons, our women and your women, ourselves and yourselves; then let us invoke God's curse (q.v.) on those who are lying *(thumma nabtahil fa-najʿal laʿnata llāhi ʿalā l-kādhibīna).* Muslim exegetes have depicted as the "occasion for the revelation" (*sabab al-nuzūl,* see OCCASIONS OF REVELATION) of this verse an episode in which the Prophet proposed to a delegation of Christians (see CHRISTIANS AND CHRISTIANITY) from Najrān (q.v.) an ordeal of mutual adjuration *(mubāhala).* To underscore the veracity of his theological claims, Muḥammad offered his family, including Fāṭima, as witnesses and guarantors. The exegetical tradition on Q 3:42, "Then the angels (see ANGEL) said: 'O Mary (q.v.), truly God has chosen you and purified you and chosen you over the women of the world *(al-ʿālamīna)*'," has linked this qurʾānic praise of Mary, the mother of Jesus (q.v.), with the Muslim veneration of Fāṭima (McAuliffe, Chosen, 19-24). Key to this linkage is one or another variant of the ḥadīth (see ḤADĪTH AND THE QURʾĀN) in which Muḥammad lists the outstanding women of all time as: Mary, Āsiya (the wife of Pharaoh [q.v.]), Khadīja and Fāṭima (Ṭabarī, *Tafsīr,* iii, 263; Rāzī, *Tafsīr,* viii, 46; but cf. such Shīʿī commentaries as those of Abū l-Futūḥ Rāzī, *Rawḥ,* iii, 36-7 and Mawlā Fatḥ Allāh Kāshānī, *Minhaj,* ii, 224, who insist upon the absolute superiority of Fāṭima). Shīʿī literature elaborates the connection of Mary with Fāṭima, viewing both as women of suffering (q.v.). Fāṭima endured the death of her father and both mothers experienced, actually or proleptically, the violence inflicted upon their sons. So entwined is their hagiographical connection that one of the epithets born by Fāṭima is *Maryam al-kubrā,* Mary the Greater (McAuliffe, Chosen, 27; Stowasser, *Women,* 80).

This connection between Fāṭima and Mary has been given a spiritually esoteric interpretation by the modern French Islamicist Louis Massignon. Other appropriations of the figure of Fāṭima can be found in such diverse sources as contemporary devotional writings (Biographie de Fâtima az-Zahrâʾ, 109-18; Rahim, Fatima, 16-8), the corpus of traditional Malay literature (Wieringa, Does traditional) and the revolutionary writings of the Iranian ideologue Ali Shariʿati (d. 1977).

Jane Dammen McAuliffe

Bibliography

Primary: Abū l-Futūḥ Rāzī, *Rawḥ;* Ibn al-Jawzī, *Zād;* Kāshānī, *Minhaj;* Rāzī, *Tafsīr,* Ṭabarī, *Tafsīr.*

Secondary: M.A. Amir-Moezzi and J. Calmard, Fâṭema. Daughter of the Prophet Moḥammad, in *Encyclopaedia Iranica*, ix, 400-4; Biographie de Fāṭima az-Zahrâʾ, in *Aux sources de la sagesse* 5 (1998), 109-18; M. Hermansen, Fatimeh as a role model in the works of Ali Shariʿati, in G. Nashat (ed.), *Women and revolution in Iran*, Boulder 1983, 87-96; H. Lammens, *Fāṭima et les filles de Mahomet. Notes critiques pour l'étude de la Sīra*, Rome 1912; L. Massignon, L'expérience musulmane de la compassion, ordonnée à l'universal. A propos de Fâtima, et de Hallâj, in *Eranos Jahrbuch* 24 (1955), 119-32; id., Der gnostische Kultus der Fâṭima im schiitischen Islam, in *Eranos Jahrbuch* 5 (1938), 161-93; id., *La mubāhala de Medine et l'hyperdulie de Fâṭima*, Paris 1955; id., La notion du voeu et la dévotion musulmane à Fatima, in *Studi orientalistici in onore di Giorgio Levi della Vida*, 2 vols., Rome 1956, ii, 102-126; id., L'oratoire de Marie à l'Aqça. Vu sous le voile de deuil de Fatima, in *Les Mardis de Dar El-Salam. 1952. Les fouilles archéologiques d'Ephese et leur importance religieuse pour la chrétienté de l'Islam*, Cairo 1954, 5-37; id., Les origines de la méditation shiʿite sur Salmân et Fâtima, in *Mélanges d'orientalisme offerts à Henri Massé à l'occasion de son 75ème anniversaire*, Tehran 1963, 264-268; J.D. McAuliffe, Chosen of all women. Mary and Fāṭima in qurʾānic exegesis, in *Islamochristiana* 7 (1981), 19-28; id., Fāṭimah bint Muḥammad, in *ER*, v, 298-9; H.A. Rahim, Fatima al-Zahraʾ, in *Alseerat* 11 (1976), 16-8; W. Schmucker, Mubāhala, in *EI²*, vii, 276-7; Ali Shariʿati, *Fatima is Fatima*, trans. Laleh Bakhtiar, Tehran, n.d.; D. Spellberg, *Politics, gender and the Islamic past. The legacy of ʿAʾisha bint Abi Bakr*, New York 1994; B. Stowasser, *Women in the Qurʾān, traditions, and interpretation*, New York 1994; L. Veccia Vaglieri, Fāṭima, in *EI²*, ii, 841-50; E. Wieringa, Does traditional Islamic Malay literature contain Shiʿitic elements? ʿAlî and Fâtimah in Malay *Hikayat* literature, in *Studia Islamika* 3 (1996), 93-111.

Fealty see OATHS AND PROMISES

Fear

Emotion marked by alarm; dread; reverence or awe. Three principal qurʾānic concepts are usually translated by the English word "fear." In their most common nominal forms these concepts are: (a) *taqwā* and related derivatives, probably from the triliteral Arabic root *w-q-y* (or *t-q-w* or *t-q-y*; see below for a brief discussion of the possible root letters) attested 239 times; (b) *khawf* and related derivatives from *kh-w-f*, attested 123 times; and (c) *khashya* and related derivatives from *kh-sh-y*, attested forty-eight times. There are six additional concepts regularly translated into English as either denoting or connoting some kind of fear, anxiety, or cautiousness: (d) *ḥidhr* and related derivates from *ḥ-dh-r*, attested twenty-one times; (e) *ishfāq*, not appearing as a noun, but only in participial and verbal forms derived from *sh-f-q*, attested ten times; (f) *rahab* and related derivatives from *r-h-b*, attested eight times; (g) *fazaʿ* and related derivatives from *f-z-ʿ*, attested six times; (h) *ruʿb*, derived from *r-ʿ-b*, attested five times; and (i) the various derivatives of the root *w-j-l*, attested five times.

Taqwā, khawf, *and* khashya

Taqwā is one of the central concepts in qurʾānic theology and ethics. Izutsu (*Concepts*, 195-200) describes *taqwā* as "the very heart and pivot" of qurʾānic teaching, and even goes so far as to equate *taqwā* with *īmān* itself, the qurʾānic term most often translated as "faith" (q.v.) or "belief" (see BELIEF AND UNBELIEF). Although certain English versions of the Qurʾān employ the notion of "fear" in their renderings of *taqwā*, it is crucial to note that these versions identify *taqwā* as a very specific kind of fear, namely the "fear of God" (e.g. Arberry, Pickthall, Y. ʿAlī). In fact, this rendering of *taqwā* directly parallels the biblical concept of "fear of the Lord" (Heb *yirʾāh yhwh*, Gk *phobos theou* — e.g. *Ps* 19:10; *Prov* 7:1; *Isa* 11:2-3) and thus should not be confused with the ordinary sense of "fear" as a negative and usually disturbing emotional reaction to impending harm. Although it does include a distinct awareness of the potential danger of incurring divine wrath (see ANGER), *taqwā* as "fear of God" describes the psychic state of an individual who is reverent, devout, and solicitous in his or her service to God (see PIETY), rather than one who is afflicted by distressing or debilitating anxiety. Indeed, this is the only sense in which verses such as Q 47:17, which identifies *taqwā* as God's reward for those who are open to divine guidance, are at all intelligible.

Taqwā is an abstract noun expressing action (i.e. a *maṣdar*) which is generally taken to be a morphologically altered substantive (originally either *taqyā/taqyan* or *waqyā/waqyan*), as opposed to an adjective *(ṣifa),* of either the first or eighth verbal form of the root *t-q-y* (or possibly *t-q-w*), or *w-q-y* (*Lisān al-ʿArab,* v, 15, 402; Bustānī, *Muḥīṭ,* 982; Lane, i, 310). In pre-Islamic poetry, the eighth verbal form, *ittaqā,* did not connote a religious attitude, but rather denoted an action of self-defense through the placement of a buffer between oneself and something that one feared (see Tibrīzī's commentary on Abū Tammām's *Dīwān al-ḥamāsa,* 254; see Izutsu, *God,* 234-6). Among some pre-Islamic Arab poets who evidence monotheistic influence, however, there are instances of *muttaqī* having the sense of "pious believer," and *taqwā* having a religious sense (Izutsu, *God,* 235).

The simplest literal meaning of either of the verb forms of either of the roots *(t-q-y/t-q-w,* or *w-q-y)* is basically the same: "to be on one's guard," "to be extremely cautious," and/or "to protect oneself from harm." In at least one instance, one English translation of the Qurʾān uses elements of the narrower literal sense by rendering *al-muttaqūn* ("those who practice *taqwā,*" — the plural active participle of the same root) as "those who ward off evil" (Pickthall, at Q 2:2; see GOOD AND EVIL). In other instances, however, this same translation contributes to the formulation of a broader theological concept of *al-muttaqūn* as "those who protect themselves from harm" specifically by "keeping their duty to God" (e.g. Pickthall, at Q 8:34) or, alternatively, by living "righteous" lives (e.g. Y. ʿAlī, at Q 8:34).

What is significant about these translations is that they reflect the link that can be found in the classical qurʾānic commentary literature between the narrower root meaning of *taqwā* as "protecting oneself from harm" and its broader construal as "piety," "righteousness," or "godfearing" (e.g. Q 2:237, Pickthall, Y. ʿAlī, and Arberry, respectively). Al-Ṭabarī (d. 310/923), for example, glosses the qurʾānic expression, "they practiced *taqwā (ittaqaw),*" in the following way: "they feared the punishment [of God] and thus obeyed him by fulfilling the obligatory duties [he imposes], and they eschewed acts of disobedience against him" *(khāfū ʿiqābahu fa-aṭāʿūhu bi-adāʾi farāʾiḍihi wa-tajannabū maʿāṣīhi;* Ṭabarī, *Tafsīr,* ad Q 2:103). Al-Bayḍāwī (d. prob. 716/1316-7) further articulates the link between "fear" and devotion in his enumeration of three different "degrees" *(marātib)* of *taqwā,* each degree presumably indicating the relative moral and spiritual state of the individual. He also locates the scriptural support for the existence of each of these three degrees in three specific qurʾānic proof-texts. Al-Bayḍāwī's first degree of *taqwā* consists of "guarding against eternal punishment (see REWARD AND PUNISHMENT) by ridding oneself of ascribing partners to God *(shirk),*" supported by Q 48:26. The second degree of *taqwā* entails "avoiding everything sinful, in deed or omission, even what would generally be considered minor offenses (see SIN, MAJOR AND MINOR)," supported by Q 7:96. Finally, the third degree of *taqwā* involves "being far removed from whatever would distract the innermost self from the real (i.e. God), and renouncing the world (q.v.), devoting one's entire life to him," supported by Q 3:102 (Bayḍāwī, *Anwār,* ad Q 2:2).

According to this tripartite scheme, the most basic understanding of *taqwā* does indeed center around the notion of a prudent "fear" of divine retribution, ideally resulting in a life of adherence to God's commands (see COMMANDMENTS). This basic understanding reflects the original qurʾānic usage (at Q 5:2, the first attestation based upon the chronological ordering of the sūras; see CHRONOLOGY AND THE QURʾĀN), namely of *taqwā* as "eschatological fear of Divine chastisement" (cf. Izutsu, *God,* 234-8). It is noteworthy that the lexicographical tradition basically echoes the commentary literature in this regard by defining *taqwā* as "taking precautions *(al-iḥtirāz)* against God's punishments by obedience (q.v.) to him," and as "the imitation *(al-iqtidāʾ)* of the Prophet in word and deed" (Bustānī, *Muḥīṭ,* 982). As both this reference to prophetic emulation and al-Bayḍāwī's third degree suggest, however, if developed to its fullest extent, *taqwā* becomes the ideal and all-encompassing posture of the human being before God. In terms of the dominant qurʾānic paradigm for the human-divine relationship, the individual who cultivates *taqwā* is the human "servant" (q.v.; *ʿabd*) who perfectly "fears" his or her divine "master" *(rabb),* not by cowering in terror at the prospect of punishment for dereliction of duty, but rather by remaining ever watchful and steadfast in his or her respect for and devotion to the master. Within this context one can better appreciate Izutsu's assertion (e.g. *Concepts,* 196) that, in qurʾānic discourse, *taqwā* ("fear of God") and *muttaqūn* ("godfearing") function almost as synonyms for *īmān* ("faith") and *muʾminūn* ("believers"). In order to evoke more effectively this important sense of the concept as well as to avoid English readers' misinterpreting *taqwā* as an ordinary type of "fear," one recent English translation of the Qurʾān deftly renders *taqwā* as "God-consciousness" (Asad, passim).

Along with *taqwā,* two additional concepts, *khawf* and *khashya,* account for almost 90% of all references to "fear" in English-language translations of the Qurʾān. Although these concepts are largely synonymous with each other, they are only partially synonymous with *taqwā.* Unlike *taqwā,* which has an almost exclusively positive connotation as a foundational qurʾānic virtue (see VIRTUES AND VICES), *khawf* and *khashya* have both the positive connotation of a virtue to be embraced and cultivated as well as the negative connotation of those unwelcome states of anxiety or dread typically associated with "fear."

The standard that separates the positive and negative connotations of *khawf* and *khashya* appears simply to be whether the object of the fear is God and his chastisements (see CHASTISEMENT AND PUNISHMENT) or some other phenomenon. When God and his chastisements are their object, *khawf* (e.g. Q 5:94; 7:205; 13:13; 14:14; 55:46) and *khashya* (e.g. Q 9:13; 21:49; 24:52; 36:11; 98:8) are almost always synonymous with each other — and with *taqwā* — as states of piety. Even Satan (see DEVIL) is portrayed in a minimally sympathetic light when he declares, "I fear God!" *(akhāfu llāha)* as he hastily retreats from successful temptations so as not to share in the divine retribution his human dupes will surely incur (Q 8:48; 59:16). When, however, both *khawf* and *khashya* lack God and his chastisements as their object, they usually connote highly undesirable states.

It is interesting to note, however, that in this context there is a subtle but interesting difference between these two otherwise synonymous terms. Cases of *khawf* directed at a phenomenon other than God usually elicit divine compassion and seem to occasion overt divine consolation (q.v.; e.g. Q 2:38; 11:70; 20:46; 29:33; 43:68), whereas similar cases of *khashya* appear in certain instances to involve those who compete with God for human attention (sometimes even God's expressed enemies [q.v.]). Rather than occasion God's consolation, these cases seem to invite implied admonitions against the cardinal sin of ascribing partners to God (e.g. Q 5:3, 44; 9:13-8; 33:37-9; see POLYTHEISM AND ATHEISM).

On the basis of this difference between *khawf* and *khashya* one might conclude that, of the three principal qur'ānic terms for "fear," *taqwā* and *khashya* are specialized forms of religious or moral "fear" which take God and his chastisements as their only proper object, while *khawf* seems to refer to "fear" in the more generic sense of a morally neutral emotion which may take either God and his chastisements (in which case it is a desirable emotion), or any other phenomenon (in which case it is undesirable), as its legitimate object (cf. Izutsu, *Concepts*, 198). In the light of this distinction, it is arguable that Abraham's (q.v.) proclamation, "I do not fear anything you associate with [God], unless my lord so wills!" (*wa-lā akhāfu mā tushrikūna bihi illā an yashā'a rabbī shay'an*, Q 6:80), becomes an expression of the divinely inspired courage (q.v.) that can free God's servants from being victimized by fear. With such courage, Abraham, as the archetypal Muslim, is able to rise above the petty fears that ensnare the human soul, and fear only God and his will. The implication of the verse is that all Muslims are invited to follow in the footsteps of the Abrahamic archetype and enjoy the same freedom from victimizing fear (i.e. freedom from the grip of *khawf* directed at phenomena which may menace, but which ultimately cannot harm God's faithful servants).

Other qur'ānic concepts denoting "fear"

There are six remaining qur'ānic terms construed as referring to some kind of fear. *Ḥidhr* sometimes conveys a sense of "fear," but more often a sense of "wariness" and "caution." Some lexicographers have suggested *ḥidhr* as a synonym for *taqwā (*e.g. *Lisān al-ʿArab),* but the preponderance of qur'ānic discourse makes a sharp distinction between the two. Unlike *taqwā* and *khashya,* but similar to *khawf, ḥidhr* can be legitimately directed at both God and other phenomena. Unlike *khawf,* however, *ḥidhr* can have the positive connotation of a virtue (i.e. "awareness" or "caution") even when it is directed at the expressed enemies of God or God's people (Q 63:4; 64:14). In other words, to be "wary" *(ḥidhr)* of the impious is a virtue, while to "fear" *(khawf)* them is a vice.

The noun *ishfāq* is not attested in the Qur'ān. *Mushfiqūn,* however, a plural active participle (fourth verbal form) derived from *sh-f-q,* accounts for eight of ten attestations of a derivative from this root, while the verb *ashfaqa* (also form IV) accounts for the remaining two. In three instances, *mushfiqūn* appears together in the same verse with *khashya,* where the former is often translated as those who "tremble" (e.g. Arberry) or "quake" (e.g. Pickthall) in reverent fear — usually of judgment and divine chastisement (Q 21:28, 49; 23:57). It is noteworthy that, in one instance, *ashfaqa* denotes what might be interpreted as the profound "shudder" elicited from the largest and most majestic elements of creation — namely "the heavens and the earth and the mountains" — when they were offered the "trust" *(amāna)* of moral responsibility, but, according to the text, fearfully and wisely refused (Q 33:72).

In most of its eight attestations, *rahab* and the other nominal forms from the same root (i.e. *rahb, rahba, irhāb*) appear to describe a "reverent fear" or "awe" which seems to be, like *khashya,* appropriately directed at God alone (e.g. Q 2:40), though it too can be easily misdirected toward other phenomena (Q 59:13). *Fazaʿ* usually denotes "terror" or "fright." Of its six attestations, five are specifically eschatological (Q 21:103; 27:87, 89; 34:51; see ESCHATOLOGY; APOCALYPSE), and one is not (Q 38:22). All six, however, can be construed as having to do with being judged. *Ruʿb* usually indicates a paralyzing "terror" or "fright," and is roughly synonymous with *fazaʿ*. Of the five times it is attested, four (Q 3:151; 8:12; 33:26; 59:2) refer to instances when, as retribution for their perfidy, God has or will "cast terror" *(qadhafa, sa-ulqī,* or *sa-nulqī… ruʿb)* into the hearts of the unbelievers or oppressors of his faithful servants. The fifth attestation has to do with a description of how frightful the sleeping Men of the Cave (q.v.; *aṣḥāb al-kahf*) would look to someone who encountered them (Q 18:18). Finally, *w-j-l,* often translated as "quake," seems to have the two-fold connotation of many of the other words for "fear:" in three instances it represents the appropriate and natural response of the hearts of the believers to God (Q 8:2; 22:35; 23:60); but twice (Q 15:52, 53) it depicts Abraham's initial reaction to the messengers who come bearing the good news (q.v.) that he shall have a son, a reaction that appears unwarranted, for the messengers tell him not to be afraid.

Scott C. Alexander

Bibliography
Primary: ʿAbd al-Bāqī; Abū Tammām Ḥabīb b. Aws, *Dīwān al-ḥamāsa,* Cairo 1955 (Tibrīzī's recension); ʿA. Yūsuf ʿAlī, *The holy Qurʾān. Text, translation, and commentary,* New York 1946; Arberry; M. Asad, *The message of the Qurʾān,* London 1980; Bayḍāwī, *Anwār,* 2 vols., Beirut 1420/1999; B. al-Bustānī, *Muḥīṭ al-muḥīṭ,* Beirut 1867, repr. 1998; Dāmaghānī, *Wujūh,* i, 93-4 (for five meanings of *taqwā: khashyā, ʿibāda, tark al-ʿiṣyān, tawḥīd, ikhlāṣ*); al-Fākihānī, Tāj al-Dīn ʿUmar b. ʿAlī, *al-Ghāyat al-quṣwā fī l-kalām ʿalā āyāt al-taqwā,* ed. M.Y. Baydaq, Beirut 1995; al-Ghazālī, Abū Ḥāmid Muḥammad, *Iḥyāʾ ʿulūm al-dīn,* Bk. 33, trans. W. McKane, *Al-Ghazālī's book of fear and hope,* Leiden 1962; Ibn Abī l-Dunyā, *al-Wajal wa-l-tawaththuq bi-l-amal. Wa-maʿahu Ḥadīth Antunis al-Sāʾiḥ wa-mawāʿiẓuhu wa-amthāluhu,* ed. M. Yūsuf, Beirut 1997; *Lisān al-ʿArab,* Beirut 1956; Pickthall; Ṭabarī, *Tafsīr,* ed. Shākir.
Secondary: Izutsu, *Concepts;* id., *God,* Tokyo 1964, 234-8 (for *taqwā* and its root in pre-Islamic times, as well as its usage in the Qurʾān); H.E. Kassis, *A concordance of the Qurʾān,* Berkeley 1983; Lane; F. Rahman, *Major themes of the Qurʾān,* Minneapolis 1980; M. Ṣāliḥ, *al-Taqwā fī hady al-kitāb wa-l-sunna wa-sīrat al-ṣāliḥīn,* Damascus 1996; S. Terrien, Fear, in *The interpreter's dictionary of the Bible,* 4 vols., New York 1962, ii, 256-60.

Fear of God

see FEAR; PIETY

Feast Days

see FESTIVALS AND COMMEMORATIVE DAYS

Feet

The terminal parts of the legs. There are three Arabic terms for foot in the Qurʾān: 1) *qadam (*pl. *aqdām),* occurring eight times, 2) *rajil (*pl. *rijāl),* occurring three times, and 3) *rijl (*pl. *arjul),* with fifteen instances. Another term, *athar (*pl. *āthār),* occurring fourteen times, may mean "footstep" or "track," in the sense of a mark or impression left behind. References to the human foot in the Qurʾān are generally symbolic and metaphorical (see METAPHOR), usually in a positive sense of being on a firm footing when expressed by *qadam,* pl. *aqdām,* but most often in a negative sense when expressed by *rijl/arjul* (always in the plural). *Rajil* is used in its literal sense of "afoot" or "on foot" (Q 2:239; 22:27), "footsoldiers, infantry" (Q 17:64).

The first term, from the root *q-d-m,* most often means firm footing in the sense of security against danger, whether physical or spiritual/moral. In Q 2:250, David (q.v.) is depicted as leading Saul's (q.v.) force against Goliath (q.v.), with the Israelites (see CHILDREN OF ISRAEL) praying: "Our lord! Bestow on us endurance and make firm our steps *(thabbit aqdāmanā).*" In Q 10:2, the Qur᾽ān is characterized as "good tidings" (see GOOD NEWS) that provide a "sure-footing" *(qadama ṣidqin)* before God. Those who conclude fraudulent, deceitful covenants (*aymān,* see COVENANT; BREAKING TRUSTS AND CONTRACTS) will reap heavy punishment from God, both for the sin itself and for its possible consequence of causing another's foot to slip after it was firmly planted (*fa-tazilla qadamu ba'da thubūtihā,* Q 16:94). In Q 41:29, unbelievers call upon God to show them some evil people so that they might "crush them beneath our feet" *(taḥta aqdāminā).* In Q 55:41 sinners will on judgment day (see LAST JUDGMENT) be "seized by their forelocks and their feet *(aqdām).*"

The *r-j-l* root most often depicts feet in a baleful way, as in Q 26:49 (cf. Q 7:124), where Pharaoh (q.v.) threatens to cut off the hands and feet *(arjul)* of the Israelites and crucify them for believing in the "lord of Moses (q.v.) and Aaron (q.v.)" (Q 26:47-8; 7:121-2) without royal permission. The punishment of "those who wage war (q.v.) against God and his messenger, and strive for corruption (q.v.) throughout the land is execution, or crucifixion (q.v.), or the cutting off of hands and feet *(arjul),* or exile..." (Q 5:33; see CHASTISEMENT AND PUNISHMENT; LAW AND THE QUR᾽ĀN). The Qur᾽ān views feet, as it views hands (q.v.), eyes (q.v.), and ears (q.v.) as key factors of human agency and marks of "creatureliness" (see Q 7:195; see IDOLS AND IMAGES; ANTHROPOMORPHISM). Feet are not viewed negatively per se in the passages where *rijl/arjul* occur. Their sometimes symbolically negative cast relates to human will and motives, not to the anatomical appendages, which are created for good ends. The power of the human foot is seen in the dramatic passage in Q 38:42, when Job (q.v.), suffering from thirst and filthy sores, calls upon God for help and is commanded to "Stamp [on the ground] with your foot" *(urkuḍ bi-rijlika),* so as to bring forth cool, refreshing water for washing and drinking, as the passage concludes. The washing of the feet *(arjul)* in pre-worship ablutions is commanded in Q 5:6 (see CLEANLINESS AND ABLUTION; RITUAL PURITY).

Footsteps as traces or marks left behind by others are depicted in several passages, e.g. Q 43:22, where previous peoples followed their ancestors' (see GENERATIONS) footsteps *(āthār)* with respect to religion because of strong custom. God sent in the past messengers (see MESSENGER) such as Noah (q.v.) and Abraham (q.v.), and others, later, in their footsteps *('alā āthārihim),* such as Jesus (q.v.; Q 57:26-7). See also ANATOMY.

Frederick Mathewson Denny

Bibliography
Primary: 'Abd al-Bāqī; A.Y. 'Alī, *The holy Qur᾽ān,* Brentwood, MD 1989 (new rev. ed.).
Secondary: M. Allard et al., *Analyse conceptuelle du Coran par cartes perforées,* 2 vols., Paris 1963, i, 31 (physical morphology: limbs, skeleton, skin); ii, 75; H.E. Kassis, *A concordance of the Qur᾽ān,* Berkeley 1983; Penrice, *Dictionary.*

Feminism and the Qur᾽ān

Feminism is understood to be a mode of analysis that includes: (1) the recognition of gender equality and of women's rights that a particular religion, nation, society, or culture may affirm in its basic tenets but withhold in practice, and (2) identification of ways to secure the practice of such rights by women and men alike. The Qur᾽ān, the basic text of Islam, taken as the word of God (q.v.), enunciates the equality of all human beings within a system of social justice that grants the same fundamental rights to women and men (see COMMUNITY AND SOCIETY IN THE QUR᾽ĀN). Muslim women, however, have been denied the exercise of many of their rights within patriarchal societies that speak in the name of Islam (see PATRIARCHY). In developing their feminist discourses, women have looked to the Qurʾān as Islam's central and most sacred text, calling attention to its fundamental message of social justice and human equality and to the rights therein granted to women (see WOMEN AND THE QURʾĀN). While feminisms grounded in the Qurʾān are of most immediate concern to Muslims, they also make distinct contributions to theorizing gender possibilities and gender relations more generally. Drawing upon the Qurʾān, Muslim women have generated two basic feminist paradigms: 1) feminism with Islam (discussed in the first section of this article, *Qurʾān consciousness and women's rights*), and 2) Islamic feminism (discussed below in the second section, *Qurʾānic hermeneutics and gender equality*).

Qurʾān consciousness and women's rights

Feminism in Muslim countries and communities has from the start been formulated within religious parameters. The earliest paradigm, feminism with Islam, is a rights-centered feminism. Its beginnings are found in the late 19th century when some Muslim women in different parts of "the East," drawing upon their newly acquired literacy and expanding social exposure, brought their qurʾānic consciousness to bear as they grappled with issues related to their changing everyday lives in the face of encounters with modernity. Reflecting upon their own experience, and in the context of Islamic reformist movements calling for renewed *ijtihād* (individual investigation of the sacred texts) and of national liberation struggles against colonial rule, some Muslim women began to evolve what can be recognized as a "feminist consciousness" before the term itself existed. They pointed out that the Qurʾān accorded them rights that were being withheld from them in practice, often in the name of Islam, and drew attention to constraints imposed upon them in the name of religion, thereby beginning to articulate a "feminism" backed by religious argumentation.

Women in Egypt in the 1890's, for example, cited the Qurʾān to demonstrate that veiling the face was not a qurʾānic requirement as they had been made to believe (see VEIL; MODESTY). Women also argued against other practices and constraints imposed upon them, employing the holy book as their liberation text. One of the first Muslims to make a public demand for women's religiously-granted rights, such as access to mosque worship, education, and new work opportunities was Malak Ḥifnī Nāṣif, known also as Bāḥithat al-Bādiya, who presented her claims at a nationalist conference in Cairo in 1911 and who had two years earlier published her feminist views in her book *al-Nisāʾiyyāt*. She articulated and acted upon a "feminism" before the term existed in Egypt; before long, however, others cited her as a feminist forebear. In Beirut in the 1920's the Lebanese Nāẓira Zayn al-Dīn of Lebanon, a woman learned in religion, invoking the qurʾānic spirit of freedom, justice (see JUSTICE AND INJUSTICE), and equality, including equality between women and men, argued against such injustices as the face veil and polygamy (see MARRIAGE AND DIVORCE) in her book *Sufūr wa-ḥijāb* published in 1928. Although the term "feminism" had recently come into circulation, Nāẓira Zayn al-Dīn did not frame her call for the recuperation of women's qurʾānically granted rights in the language of feminism. Nevertheless, some of her Muslim contemporaries referred to her work as feminist.

Among the first Muslim women explicitly to link feminism and the Qurʾān were members of the Egyptian Feminist Union who demanded full and equal rights for women in the public sphere and a reduction of inequalities in the private or family sphere. They adopted a gradualist position in calling for controls on men's practice of divorce and polygamy, citing qur'ānic verses *(āyāt)* in support of their case. Egyptian feminist Iḥsān al-Qūsī referenced the Qur'ān in arguing for an end to the legalized institution of *bayt al-ṭāʿa* or the forced restitution of an estranged wife to the conjugal home.

Historically, the first Muslim women to declare publicly their feminism did so in the context of western colonial occupation. Secure in their Islamic identity and firm about a feminism of their own making, they refused to be silenced by detractors who misrepresented their feminism, attempting to delegitimize it as a western anti-Islamic foreign imposition. Muslim feminists stressed the Islamic notion of *maṣlaḥa* (well-being or prosperity) of the *umma* (community of Muslims) insisting that the exercise of women's rights would strengthen both the Muslim community and the nation as a whole, in its struggle to win and secure independence from foreign rule.

For most of the twentieth century, in different parts of the Muslim world, the paradigm of feminism with Islam that incorporated intersecting Islamic, nationalist, and humanitarian (later human rights), and democratic discourses remained paramount.

Qur'ānic hermeneutics and gender equality

Toward the end of the twentieth century, especially in the 1990's, it became evident that there was a major paradigm shift underway. This was a shift towards a feminism grounded exclusively in religious discourse with the Qur'ān as its central reference, or what is increasingly called Islamic feminism. The new Islamic feminism constitutes a move away from the earlier women's rights-based focus toward a wider focus on gender equality and social justice as basic and intersecting principles enshrined in the Qur'ān. Those who shaped the feminism with Islam discourse claimed an explicit feminist identity, while most of those who articulate Islamic feminism are reluctant to wear a feminist label.

The new Islamic feminism emerged in the context of Islamic religious resurgence (including the growth of a global *umma* of vast proportions), of the spread of Islamism or political Islam, and at a moment when Muslim women had gained access to higher education on an unprecedented scale (see POLITICS AND THE QUR'ĀN). Key formulators of the new Islamic feminist discourse are women who utilize their advanced training in the religious sciences (see TRADITIONAL DISCIPLINES OF QUR'ĀNIC STUDY) and other disciplines to reinterpret the Qur'ān. In making the Qur'ān the center of their attention, women are recuperating their right as Muslims to reflectively examine *(tadabbur)* sacred scripture, thus disputing the exclusive authority men have arrogated to themselves to define Islam. The female exegetes *(mufassirāt)* draw upon their own experience as women as they pose fresh questions. They proceed within an interpretive framework which maintains that the fundamental ideas of the Qur'ān cannot be contradicted by any of its parts. They perform skilled deconstructions of qur'ānic verses and enact fresh readings respectful of the spirit of the holy book while mindful of the letter of the text.

This new gender-sensitive, or what can be called feminist, hermeneutics renders compelling confirmation of gender equality in the Qur'ān that was typically obscured as male interpreters constructed a corpus of commentary (*tafsīr*, see EXEGESIS OF THE QUR'ĀN: CLASSICAL AND MEDIEVAL) promoting a classical doctrine of male superiority that reflected the mindset of the prevailing patriarchal cultures. Feminist hermeneutics distinguishes between the universal or timeless basic principles and the particular and contingent, which are understood as ephemeral. In the case of the latter, they have judged that certain practices were allowed in a limited and controlled fashion as a way of curtailing behaviors prevalent in the society into which the revelation (see REVELATION AND INSPIRATION) came, while encouraging believers on a path to fuller justice and equality in their human interactions. Feminist hermeneutics has taken three approaches: 1) revisiting verses *(āyāt)* of the Qur'ān to correct false narratives in common circulation, such as the accounts of creation (q.v.) and of events in the primordial garden that have shored up claims of male superiority (see ADAM AND EVE; FALL OF MAN); 2) citing verses that unequivocally enunciate the equality of women and men; and 3) deconstructing verses attentive to male and female difference that have been commonly interpreted in ways that justify male domination.

Exegetes such as Amina Wadud-Muhsin in her major work of exegesis *Qur'ān and woman,* and Riffat Hassan, in various articles and public lectures, have corrected the widely-circulated but erroneous narratives (traditionally repeated by the religiously trained and the wider populace alike) purporting to be qur'ānic. One such narrative insists that the woman was created out of the man (from a crooked rib of Adam) and thus woman was a secondary or derivative creature. Another concerns the events in the garden of Eden claiming that Eve tempted Adam, thus making woman responsible for the downfall of man and enforcing the stereotype of the female as seductress. Wadud-Muhsin and Hassan point to verses of the Qur'ān declaring that women and men were created at the same moment as two mates (each mate is referred to by the masculine noun *zawj*) out of a single self or soul *(nafs)*. For example, Q 4:1 states: "Oh mankind [humankind]! Reverence your guardian-lord, who created you from a single person, created, of like nature, his mate, and from the two scattered [like seeds] countless men and women." In the Qur'ān both Adam and Eve fell into temptation in the garden (q.v.), both were expelled, both repented (see REPENTANCE AND PENANCE) and both were equally forgiven.

The new interpreters stress that the Qur'ān makes clear the fundamental equality of women and men. Human beings, whatever their sex, are distinguished one above the other only in piety (q.v.; *taqwā*). "Oh mankind [humankind]! We have created you from a single (pair) of a male and a female... verily the most honored of you in the sight of God (is he [or she] who is) the most righteous of you [who possesses the most *taqwā*]" (Q 49:13). Aziza al-Hibri and other female exegetes point to the qur'ānic principle of *tawḥīd* as affirming the oneness of God as the supreme being and the equality of all human beings as his creatures. All Muslims are enjoined to fulfill the trusteeship or moral agency (*khilāfa,* see CALIPH) that is entrusted to them as human beings.

While fundamentally equal, humans have been created biologically different for the perpetuation of the species. Only in particular contexts and circumstances will males and females assume different contingent roles and functions. Woman alone can give birth (q.v.) and nurse, and thus in this particular circumstance a husband is enjoined by the Qur'ān to provide material support (see FAMILY) as indicated in Q 4:34, "Men are in charge of (or the managers of, *qawwāmūn ʿalā*) women because God has given the one more than the other *(bimā faḍḍala llāhu baʿḍahum ʿalā baʿḍin),* and because they support them from their means." Wadud-Muhsin, Hassan, and al-Hibri demonstrate that *qawwāmūn* conveys the notion of "providing for" and that the term is used prescriptively to signify that men ought to provide for women in the context of child-bearing and rearing but does not mean that women cannot necessarily provide for themselves in that circumstance. The term *qawwāmūn* does not signify that all men are unconditionally in charge of (or have authority over) all women all the time, as traditional male interpreters have claimed, nor does the term *faḍḍala* indicate male superiority over women, as is also commonly claimed. Such female exegetes thus show how common male interpretations have turned the specific and contingent into universals. In confronting the masculinist argument that men have authority over women, feminist Qurʾān commentary both deconstructs particular verses, such as those cited above, and draws attention to other verses that affirm mutuality of responsibilities: for example, Q 9:71, which says that "The believers, male and female, are protectors of one another" (i.e. they have mutual *awliyāʾ*; see FRIENDS AND FRIENDSHIP).

The rigorous scrutiny and contextualization of qurʾānic terms and phrases pursued by female commentators exposes the patriarchal inflections given to many qurʾānic passages in classical interpretations produced by men and demonstrates how such patriarchal interpretations contradict the basic qurʾānic message of gender equality. The project of Qurʾān-based Islamic feminism, while still in its foundational stage, continues to be meticulously elaborated and is fast gaining wider ground. See also GENDER; CONTEMPORARY CRITICAL PRACTICES; EXEGESIS OF THE QURʾĀN: EARLY MODERN AND CONTEMPORARY.

Margot Badran

Bibliography
L. Ahmed, *Women and gender in Islam,* New Haven, CT 1992; M. Badran, *Feminists, Islam and nation,* Princeton 1995; id., Towards Islamic feminism, in A. Afsaruddin (ed.), *Hermeneutics and honor,* Cambridge, MA 1999; Bāḥithat al-Bādiya (Malak Ḥifnī Nāṣif), *al-Nisāʾiyyāt,* Cairo 1909; F. Bennani, *Taqsīm al-ʿamal bayn al-zawjayn,* Marrakesh 1993; R. Hassan, Equal before Allah? in *Harvard Divinity School bulletin* 17 (January-May 1978), 2-4; id., The issue of woman-man equality in the Islamic tradition, in L. Grob, R. Hassan and H. Gordon (eds.), *Women's and men's liberation,* Westport, CT 1991, 650-82; A.Y. al-Hibri, An introduction to Muslim women's rights, in G. Webb (ed.), *Windows of faith,* Syracuse, NY 2000, 51-71; id., A study of Islamic herstory. Or how did we get into this mess? in A. al-Hibri (ed.), *Women and Islam,* New York 1982; F. Mernissi, *Beyond the veil. Male-female dynamics in modern Muslim society,* Bloomington, IN 1987 (rev. ed.); id., *Harem politique,* Paris 1987; id., *The veil and the male elite,* trans. M. Lakeland, Reading, MA 1991 (trans. of *Harem politique*); Z. Mir-Hosseini, Stretching the limits. A feminist reading of the sharīʿa in post-Khomeini Iran, in M. Yamani (ed.), *Feminism and Islam. Legal and literary perspectives,* New York 1991, 285-320; A. Najmabadi, Feminism in an Islamic republic. Years of hardship, years of growth, in Y. Haddad and J. Esposito (eds.), *Islam, gender and social change,* New York 1998, 59-84; A. Wadud (Wadud-Muhsin), Alternative qurʾānic interpretation and the status of women, in G. Webb (ed.), *Windows of faith,* Syracuse, NY 2000, 3-21; id., *Qurʾan and woman,* Kuala Lumpur 1992; New York 1999 (new ed.); M. Yamani (ed.), *Feminism and Islam,* New York 1996; N. Zayn al-Dīn, *al-Sufūr wa-l-ḥijāb,* Beirut 1928, Nicosia 1997.

Festivals and Commemorative Days

Periodic celebrations held either to honor the memory of particular individuals or to remember or mark events important in sacred history. The Qurʾān does not use the word holiday *(ʿīd),* but this word has come to be employed for two feast days: the breaking of the fast of Ramaḍān *(ʿīd al-fiṭr),* and the "great *ʿīd,*" the feast of sacrifice *(ʿīd al-aḍḥā)* at the end of the rites of the pilgrimage to Mecca (*ḥajj,* see

PILGRIMAGE). To these two feast days Muslims later added other celebrations and commemorative days, including the celebration of the Prophet's birthday, those commemorating the dates of death of various saints, and the Shīʿī (see SHĪʿISM AND THE QURʾĀN) commemoration of the passion and death of the Prophet's grandson, Ḥusayn.

The fast of Ramaḍān and ʿĪd al-fiṭr

The Qurʾān says in verse 2:183, "Fasting (q.v.) is prescribed for you as it was for those before you, that you may learn piety (or protect yourself, *laʿallakum tattaqūn*)." Ḥadīths tell us that before the institution of Ramaḍān (q.v.), Muslims observed the pre-Islamic fast of ʿĀshūrāʾ in the month of Muḥarram. After the emigration from Mecca to Medina (*hijra*, see EMIGRATION), according to ḥadīth (see ḤADĪTH AND THE QURʾĀN), the Prophet learned from the Jews that ʿĀshūrā was the day when Moses (q.v.) and the Israelites were rescued from the hand of Pharaoh (see CHILDREN OF ISRAEL). Muḥammad told the Jews, "We are closer to Moses than you," and ordered the Muslims to observe it. But when the fast of Ramaḍān was instituted, the fast of ʿĀshūrāʾ was made optional (Muslim, *Ṣaḥīḥ*, ii, 548-51). The excellence of fasting is such that the breath of a person who is fasting (which would normally not have a pleasant odor) would be sweeter than the fragrance of musk to God (ibid., 558-60). The Qurʾān tells us that Ramaḍān is the month in which the Qurʾān was revealed (Q 2:185; this is generally understood to mean that this is when the Qurʾān was first revealed). Ḥadīth tells us that Ramaḍān carries particular excellence because "the gates of mercy are opened, the gates of hell are locked, and the devils are chained" (Muslim, *Ṣaḥīḥ*, ii, 524). Of particular blessedness is the "night of power [or destiny]" (*laylat al-qadr*, see NIGHT OF POWER), described in the Qurʾān as "better than a thousand months; in it the angels and the spirit (q.v.) come down with the permission of their lord, concerning every matter; peace it is until the rise of dawn" (Q 97:3-5). Many ḥadīths tell us that this night is among the last ten days of the month of Ramaḍān, during which the Prophet would remain in the mosque in prayer *(iʿtikāf)*, a practice which is continued by pious Muslims today. Some ḥadīths specify that it is the night of the 27th of Ramaḍān (Muslim, *Ṣaḥīḥ*, ii, 573-4). The month of Ramaḍān is a time of extra prayers at night *(ṣalāt al-tarāwīḥ)* and often of added devotions and religious studies during the day, when Muslims (except the sick, old, travelers or menstruating women) should observe a total fast from all food, drink and sexual intercourse (see ABSTINENCE; PRAYER). All of these are allowed at nighttime, however, and in some countries the breaking of the fast at the time of the sunset prayer (often accompanied by giving of food to the poor) is a time of celebration and feasting. In urban areas, offices and businesses might alter their work hours to accommodate the fast, closing at noon and reopening in the evening, and families visit each other at night. In the "popular quarters" of Cairo, residents hang out colored lamps during Ramaḍān, and there are special displays of folkloric dances and Ṣūfī *dhikr* at nighttime. The feast that marks the end of Ramaḍān is a day when no fasting is allowed at all (Muslim, *Ṣaḥīḥ*, ii, 553), and it is customary for families to dress well on that day and visit each other (an important recent study of this fast is Nabhan, *Das Fest des Fastenbrechns*).

The pilgrimage to Mecca and ʿĪd al-aḍḥā

The *ḥajj* is an elaborate ritual that takes place once a year, involving a pilgrimage to Mecca, circumambulation of the Kaʿba (q.v.) seven times in a counterclockwise direction, praying at the place where Abraham (q.v.; Ibrāhīm) stood to pray, touching or kissing, if possible, the black stone that marks the commencement of circumambulation, running seven times between the hills of Ṣafā and Marwa (q.v.), stoning pillars representing Satan (see DEVIL), a vigil from noon to sunset on the plain of ʿArafa (q.v.) where pilgrims ask for forgiveness, and the sacrificial offering of an animal. All of these rituals contain special prescriptions and prohibitions regarding dress, bodily adornment or grooming, sexual activity, and hunting. The books of ḥadīth and *fiqh* are concerned with informing Muslims of the many details of the ritual and how to perform them. The rationale of the pilgrimage is clarified there mainly in terms of the provision of forgiveness (q.v.) of sins: "There is no day when God sets free more servants from hell than the day of ʿArafa. He draws near, then praises them to the angels, saying, 'What do these want?'" (Muslim, *Ṣaḥīḥ*, ii, 680). In this literature the commemorative functions of the rituals are not emphasized.

The Qurʾān tells us that the Kaʿba was built by Abraham and Ishmael (q.v.; Ismāʿīl) at God's command as a place of pilgrimage (Q 2:125, 127), and people are told to take the "station of Abraham" *(maqām Ibrāhīm)* as a place of prayer (Q 2:125), but the association of the rituals with events from the life of Abraham and his family may have come later. Most of the ritual elements were practiced in the pre-Islamic *ḥajj*, and were modified by the Prophet only in minor aspects. Later legends associated the well of Zamzam (see WELLS AND SPRINGS), located near the Kaʿba, with God's provision of water to Ishmael and his mother, Ḥajar, in the desert; the running between Ṣafā and Marwa with Ḥajar's frantic search for water; the stoning at Muzdalifa with Abraham and Ishmael's resistance of Iblīs's (q.v.) temptation to abandon God's command to Abraham to sacrifice his son; and the sacrifice of an animal as a commemoration of God's provision of an animal for Abraham to sacrifice in place of his son (Yāqūt, *Muʿjam*, ii, 943; Azraqī, *Akhbār*, i, 4-5, 31-2; Jeffery, *Islam*, 205-11; Denny, *Introduction*, 132-6). In this respect, the animal sacrifice is purely commemorative and has no redemptive significance. The language of the Qurʾān is less than explicit: the "gift" or "offering" is to be brought to its place (Q 2:196), and shared with the poor (Q 22:36; see also ALMSGIVING). "And for every nation *(umma)* we have appointed rites of devotion *(mansak)* that they may mention *(li-yadhkurū)* the name of God over the cattle that he has bestowed upon them *(ʿalā mā razaqahum min bahīmati l-anʿāmi)*" (Q 22:34). The feast of sacrifice is celebrated by all Muslims all over the world at the same time as it is celebrated by the pilgrims who are on the *ḥajj* (see also SACRIFICE; CONSECRATION OF ANIMALS).

The celebration of the two feast days is meant to be a time of rejoicing. Fasting on these days is not allowed. According to a ḥadīth, Abū Bakr entered the room of his daughter ʿĀʾisha (see ʿĀʾISHA BINT ABĪ BAKR), wife of the Prophet, and found girls singing about the battle of Buʿāth, a pre-Islamic custom. He was shocked and exclaimed, "Are the songs of Satan sung in the house of the Prophet, and this on a feast day?" The Prophet, however, told him to leave them alone: "Every people has its holiday, and this is ours" (Muslim, *Ṣaḥīḥ*, ii, 419-20; Bukhārī, *Ṣaḥīḥ*, 205-6). This text is interpreted as permitting songs and merry-making on the feast days, though many commentators hasten to caution against excess in this regard.

The visitation of tombs and celebration of saints' days

After the *ḥajj*, it is recommended that pilgrims visit the tomb of the Prophet in Medina (q.v.). The excellence of Medina over other places is well-attested in ḥadīth

(Muslim, *Ṣaḥīḥ,* ii, 686-99), and the space between the Prophet's tomb and his pulpit is described as "one of the gardens of paradise" (ibid., 696). There are ḥadīths prohibiting the visiting of graves, but this prohibition was lifted in later ḥadīths (Ghazālī, *Iḥyāʾ,* i, 320). In time, the tombs of people popularly recognized as saints *(awliyāʾ)* became the focus of pilgrimage because of the blessing *(baraka)* to be obtained from visiting them, especially during their anniversary celebrations, their *mawlid.* The devotees of some saints even claimed that the visitation of their tombs could replace the pilgrimage to Mecca.

The literal meaning of *mawlid* is "birthday," but in most cases the celebration takes place on the anniversary of the saint's death, which is seen as his or her rebirth into the presence of God or "wedding" with the divine presence. In fact, such celebrations in the Indian subcontinent are called *ʿurs,* "wedding." The celebration of *mawlids* might have begun with the (Shīʿite) Fāṭimid celebrations of the birthdays of the Prophet, ʿAlī (see ʿALĪ B. ABĪ ṬĀLIB), Fāṭima (q.v.), and the reigning Imām (q.v.; see also FAMILY OF THE PROPHET; PEOPLE OF THE HOUSE). N. Kaptein has demonstrated that the *mawlid al-nabī* was introduced in Egypt under the Fāṭimids, certainly by the 6th/12th century, but not before 415/1024, the date which is commonly attested being 517/1123 (*Muḥammad's birthday festival,* 9, 23). Although today's festivities differ in form from those of the Fāṭimids (the Fāṭimid celebrations were held in court during daylight hours, whereas the modern *mawlid* is a popular nocturnal carnival), we lack evidence as to how, exactly, Sunnī Islam adopted this Shīʿite tradition.

Sunnī historians and theologians trace the origin of the *mawlid* to a Prophet's birthday celebration in Ibril, southeast of Mosul, in 1207, arranged by Muẓaffar al-Dīn Kokböri Kokbürü, a brother-in-law of Saladin, and this celebration, influenced by Christian rites, bore many of the features of the modern-day *mawlid* (Ibn Khallikān, *Wafayāt al-aʿyān,* ii, 550 f.; von Grünebaum, *Muhammadan festivals,* 73-6). Von Grünebaum says that with the growth of Ṣūfism in Egypt under the Sunnī Ayyūbids (1171-1250), the *mawlid* took root there and spread from there throughout the Muslim world (*Muhammadan festivals,* 73). During the same period, in Muslim Spain and northern Morocco, the *mawlid* was introduced as a way of countering Christian influence. The Prophet's *mawlid,* in medieval times as well as today, was sponsored by the government and attended by prominent officials. The word *mawlid* is used not only for the day of celebration, but also for a poem celebrating the Prophet, and such poems may be found publicly recited throughout the Muslim world, in many different languages (Fuchs, Mawlid). We do not know when the anniversary celebrations of saints' days began, variously called *mawlid* or *ziyāra* or *ʿurs* in different countries, and their importance varies from one country to another. In Egypt, thousands of saints' days are celebrated annually, and some Ṣūfīs spend much of their lives traveling the circuit of *mawlid* celebrations (Hoffman, *Sufism, mystics and saints in modern Egypt,* 89-118; McPherson, *Moulids of Egypt*).

The sanctity of a saint's shrine is generated by the fact that it contains its own spiritual center, its own axis that reaches toward heaven, whereas the mosque directs prayers toward the spiritual center of the Kaʿba. To the saint's devotees, the pure body of the holy person buried in the tomb provides a center that constitutes a more direct link to heaven than may be found at a mosque. The degree of sanctity attributed to a saint's shrine depends on the holiness of the person, indicated especially through the degree of kinship to the Prophet. Saints' shrines exude a sense of power and tranquility, and people visit them to feel peace, seek refuge from their problems, and appeal to the intervention of the saint. Saints' shrines are perceived as places of mercy (q.v.) for the oppressed (see OPPRESSED ON EARTH) and places of power. Visitors cling to the *maqṣūra,* the barrier erected around the *tābūt,* a draped, box-shaped structure built over the burial place of the saint. They kiss and rub the *maqṣūra* and then rub their faces to transfer some of the saint's *baraka* to themselves. The holiness of the saint extends to the surrounding space and anything distributed there to visitors, such as water, candy or perfume. Visitors circumambulate the tomb in a counterclockwise direction, fervently murmuring prayers. Visitors might make a vow to sacrifice an animal and distribute the meat or some other food to the shrine visitors and the poor if their prayers are answered. Such sacrifices take place outside the shrine. *Dhikr,* the Ṣūfī ritual of repeated recitation of the names of God, accompanied by rhythmic breathing and particular body movements such as bowing forward or turning from side to side, often to the accompaniment of music and singing, may be performed within or outside a shrine during the *mawlid* or some other special visiting day. (In Cairo some of the major saints and members of the Prophet's family have weekly *dhikr*s on a particular day of the week.) Specific customs vary somewhat from one country to the next, but evince a remarkable similarity. Visitors also sometimes sing songs of praise to the Prophet and his family. Some visitors sit by the shrine, perhaps reading the Qurʾān. Others sit along the outside wall of the shrine to absorb the blessing of the saint.

During the *mawlid*s in Egypt, many people camp outside on the grounds surrounding the shrines for days or even weeks, offering food and drink to passers-by. The actual day of the *mawlid* is the last night of the celebration, the "great night," the culmination of the festivities' intensity. The festivities begin anywhere from two weeks to two nights before the great night, but build until they reach a feverish pitch on that night when the densest crowds are in attendance, and activities persist until the dawn prayer. Some *mawlid*s open with a procession of Ṣūfī orders, carrying banners and chanting praises. A few of them end with a procession as well. Secular activities, such as the selling of food and toys and attractions like shooting games for men and giant swing sets for children, also attract many people. Some *mawlid*s also feature stalls where barbers provide circumcisions. In the mosque of Sayyid Aḥmad al-Badawī on the "great night" of his *mawlid* in the Egyptian Delta town of Ṭanṭā, the vast floor of the mosque and shrine is covered with families packed tightly together, while they spend the night.

The celebration of *mawlid*s has been criticized by many modern Muslim reformers, especially because of the mixing of men and women and the prominence of secular activities, but also because praying at the tombs of saints is perceived by some Muslims as misguided or even idolatrous (see INTERCESSION). Defenders of the celebrations often point to the commemorative function of the *mawlid*s: They serve to educate people about the lives of the saints who are models of piety. The educational function of the *mawlid*s of the saints is not, however, very much in evidence. Only the *mawlid* of the Prophet appears to be accompanied by much oral recitation of his life. Visiting of the tombs of the Imāms in Shīʿī Islam is not as controversial as the visitation of the tombs of saints among Sunnī Muslims.

Commemorating Ḥusayn's martyrdom

Of all the Muslim festivals, the one that appears most directly commemorative is the Twelver Shīʿī commemoration of the death of the Prophet's grandson Ḥusayn at Karbalāʾ on the tenth day of the Islamic month of Muḥarram, the feast of ʿĀshūrā. Ḥusayn's death is not only perceived as a martyrdom or as a tragic victimization of the righteous members of the Prophet's family, it is also seen as having a redemptive effect for those who love Ḥusayn, grieve over his death, and are willing to share in the suffering of him and his family. "Just as Christ sacrificed himself on the altar of the cross to redeem humanity, so did Ḥusayn allow himself to be killed on the plains of Karbalāʾ to purify the Muslim community of sins" (Enayat, *Political thought*, 183). The customs of ritual grieving, involving oral recitations of the passion of Ḥusayn with public demonstrations of mourning, the "passion plays" (*taʿziya*, cf. Chelkowski, Taʿziya), and the processions of self-flagellation introduced by the Ṣafawids in the sixteenth century gave Shīʿism a distinct ritual complex that assumed great importance in the solidification of communal identity as well as emphasizing the distinctiveness of Shīʿism from Sunnism. In Egypt, an entirely Sunnī country, Ḥusayn's death is commemorated and love for Ḥusayn is celebrated, but the Shīʿī festival is distinctive for its identification with his suffering and the public display of mourning.

Valerie J. Hoffman

Bibliography

Primary: al-Azraqī, Abū l-Walīd Muḥammad b. ʿAbdallāh, *Kitāb Akhbār Makka*, in F. Wüstenfeld, *Die Chroniken der Stadt Mekka*, Leipzig 1858; Bukhārī, *Ṣaḥīḥ*, ed. M. Nizār Tamīm and H. Nizār Tamīm, Beirut 1995; al-Ghazālī, Abū Ḥāmid Muḥammad, *Iḥyāʾ ʿulūm al-dīn*, 4 vols., Cairo 1967; Muslim, *Ṣaḥīḥ*, trans. Abdul Hamid Siddiqi, 4 vols., New Delhi 1977; Yāqūt, *Buldān*, ed. Wüstenfeld.

Secondary: N. Abū Zahra, *The pure and the powerful. Studies in contemporary Muslim society*, Reading, UK (1997); P. Chelkowski, Taʿziya, in *EI²*, x, 406-8; F.M. Denny, *An introduction to Islam*, New York 1994²; H. Enayat, *Modern Islamic political thought*, Austin, TX 1982; H. Fuchs, Mawlid, in *EI¹*, iii, 419-22; I. Goldziher, *Muslim studies*, trans. C.R. Barber and S.M. Stern, London 1971; G.E. von Grünebaum, *Muhammadan festivals*, New York 1951; V.J. Hoffman, *Sufism, mystics and saints in modern Egypt*, Columbia, SC, 1995; A. Jeffery, *Islam. Muhammad and his religion*, New York 1958; N. Kaptein, *Muḥammad's birthday festival. Early history in the central Muslim lands and development in the Muslim west until the 10th/16th century*, Leiden 1993; J. McPherson, *The moulids of Egypt*, Cairo 1941; M. Momen, *An introduction to Shiʿi Islam. The history and doctrines of Twelver Shiʿism*, New Haven 1985; L. Nabhan, *Das Fest des Fastenbrechens* (ʿĪd al-fiṭr) *in Ägypten. Untersuchungen zur theologischen Grundlagen und praktischer Gestaltung*, Berlin 1991; V.J. Schubel, *Religious performance in contemporary Islam. Shiʿi devotional rituals in south Asia*, Columbia, SC 1993; C. Taylor, *In the vicinity of the righteous.* Ziyāra *and the veneration of Muslim saints in late medieval Egypt*, Leiden 1998.

Fetus see BIOLOGY AS THE CREATION AND STAGES OF LIFE

Fig see AGRICULTURE AND VEGETATION

Fighting

Violent physical struggle for victory. The Arabic term for fighting *(qitāl)* is a derived form of the root *q-t-l*, the essential meaning of which is to kill. Its third verbal form *(qātala)* suggests mutuality, i.e. to fight, and is the most common term for such combat in the Qurʾān. *Ḥāraba* in the Qurʾān likewise means to fight and is derived from the root *ḥ-r-b*, from which war *(ḥarb)* is derived, although it is sometimes used in reference to the activity of brigands who wage war against God by sowing corruption (q.v.) on earth (e.g. Q 5:33-4; cf. Abou El Fadl, Ahkam al-bughat). Attention here will be limited to fighting as derived from *qitāl* (see also EXPEDITIONS AND BATTLES; JIHĀD).

Competition and fighting between unrelated or distantly related kinship (q.v.) groups was a regular characteristic of pre-Islamic Arabian life (see CLANS AND TRIBES; PRE-ISLAMIC ARABIA AND THE QURʾĀN), and Jewish and Christian Arabs regularly engaged in such fighting along with non-monotheistic Arabs (q.v.; see CHRISTIANS AND CHRISTIANITY; JEWS AND JUDAISM). Common cultural norms in pre-Islamic Arabia regulated warfare and forbade fighting at certain sacred places (*ḥaram*, pl. *aḥrām;* see SACRED PRECINCTS) and during certain sacred periods known commonly as the sacred months *(al-ashhur al-ḥurum)*. Aspects of these pre-Islamic cultural characteristics are reflected in the Qurʾān, which, as the word of God, intended to replace the role of tribal culture in regulating much of Arabian social behavior (see Q 2:190-1, 194, 217; 9:5, 36; see COMMUNITY AND SOCIETY IN THE QURʾĀN; REVELATION AND INSPIRATION).

The Qurʾān refers to fighting between kinship groups, Muslims fighting non-Muslims or being attacked by them, Muslims fighting other Muslims, and fighting "in the path of God" (*fī sabīli llāhi,* see PATH OR WAY). The Qurʾān is not completely consistent insofar as some verses appear to discourage fighting (Q 15:94-5; 16:125) while others allow fighting for the purpose of defense (Q 2:190; 22:39-40), encourage fighting with certain restrictions (Q 2:191, 217) or command fighting without limitations (Q 2:216; cf. 9:5). Muslim exegetes have attempted to resolve the problem by suggesting that the qurʾānic doctrine on fighting evolved through stages during Muḥammad's prophetic mission from an early period of virtual pacifism to its final position of commanding believers to fight idolatry (see IDOLATRY AND IDOLATERS) and God's enemies (q.v.) without restriction (see CHRONOLOGY AND THE QURʾĀN; PROPHETS AND PROPHETHOOD). Modern scholars have begun to challenge this notion, suggesting that such an understanding may have been imposed on the Qurʾān by a later generation wishing to apply divine authority (q.v.) to the Islamic conquests (q.v.; cf. Sachedina, Justifications). The various qurʾānic statements on fighting may in fact reflect different layers of opinion about fighting among early Muslims (Firestone, *Jihad*).

Fighting "in the path of God" is commanded in the Qurʾān (Q 2:190, 244; 4:74-6, 84), as are other activities defined as pious (Q 2:195, 261-2; 4:89; 8:60, 72-4; 9:19-20, etc.; see PIETY). Those who engage in fighting in the path of God are admitted into the garden (q.v.; *al-janna*) or remain in some way alive after dying in battle (Q 2:154; 3:157-8, 169; 3:158, 169, 195; 4:74; 9: 89, 111; 47:4-6, 36; see LIFE), a view which has no parallel in pre-Islamic culture. God assists or even engages in the fighting on behalf of Muslim warriors (Q 3:123-5, 166-7; 8:17, 65-6; 9:14, 25-6; 48:23). Other verses also command fighting not defined specifically as in the path of God (Q 2:216; 4:76; 8:39; 9:123, etc.). The repetitive nature of the command along with the above and other evidence suggests that a significant faction of Muḥammad's followers opposed fighting religious wars, a view that seems to have lost out to a more militant faction (on qurʾānic evidence of resistance to religious warring, see WAR).

Reuven Firestone

Bibliography

Primary: M. Shaltūt, *al-Qurʾān wa-l-qitāl,* Cairo 1951; al-Taymī, Maʿmar b. al-Muthanna, *Kitāb ayyām al-ʿArab qabla l-Islām,* ed. ʿĀ.J. al-Bayyātī, Beirut 1987.
Secondary: Kh. Abou El Fadl, *Ahkam al-bughat.* Irregular warfare and the law of rebellion in Islam, in J.T. Johnson and J. Kelsay (eds.), *Cross, crescent and sword. The justification and limitation of*

war in western and Islamic traditions, Westport, CT 1990, 149-76; R. Firestone, Conceptions of holy war in the biblical and qurʾānic tradition, in *The journal of religious ethics* 24 (1996), 801-24; id., Disparity and resolution in the qurʾānic teachings on war. A re-evaluation of a traditional problem, in *JNES* 55 (1997), 1-19; id., *Jihad. The origin of holy war in Islam,* New York 1999; M. Khadduri, *War and peace in the law of Islam,* Baltimore 1955; A. Morabia, *La notion de Ǧihad dans l'Islam médiéval,* Paris 1974; R. Peters, *Jihad in classical and modern Islam,* Princeton 1996; A.A. Sachedina, Justifications for violence in Islam, in J. Patout Burns (ed.), *War and its discontents. Pacifism and quietism in the Abrahamic traditions,* Washington, DC 1996, 122-60.

Figurative Language see RHETORIC OF THE QURʾĀN; SIMILES; METAPHOR

Filth see CLEANLINESS AND ABLUTION

Fire

Combustion, manifested in light and heat, which was classified in the classical world as one of the four elements. Fire occurs in the Qurʾān both in the other world as well as in this world and it can assume different forms.

As far as the other world is concerned, it is the element that characterizes hell (q.v.) and therefore carries the charge of torment *(ʿadhāb)* for the damned. Within this context, the following terms, which in many cases merely denote hell, are used: *nār,* fire (sometimes specified by *jahannam: nār jahannam,* as in Q 9:35, 68; 35:36; 72:23; 98:6); *jaḥīm,* a term relating to the intenseness of fire; *saʿīr,* fire or flame; *laẓā,* flame (a single occurrence in Q 70:15); and *saqar* (only four occurrences, one in Q 54:48, the other three concentrated in Q 74:26, 27 and 42), a word originating in a root used to describe "a fire so hot that it melts bodies and spirits" *(Lisān al-ʿArab).* These last two terms are generally considered to be proper names for hell. Finally, there is *ḥuṭama* (two occurrences, both in Q 104:4 and 5) defined by the Qurʾān itself as "the fire lighted by God." Three other terms relating to the intensity of hell-fire and referring to the diverse figures it may assume can be found in connection with the word *ʿadhāb,* pain or punishment: *ʿadhāb al-ḥarīq,* "the torment of burning" (Q 3:181; 8:50; 22:9, 22; 85:10); *ʿadhāb al-ḥamīm,* "the torment of boiling water" (Q 44:48); and *ʿadhāb al-samūm,* "the torment of the blazing and stinking wind" (Q 52:27).

Fire fills up infernal space in its entirety, turning it into an igneous abyss from which there is no escape. The flames stretch out in horizontal columns (Q 104:8-9) and close around the damned who are additionally surrounded by the abyss's vertical burning walls (Q 18:29) and therefore unable "to repulse the fire neither from their faces, nor from their backs" (Q 21:39). These flames throw out sparks so heavy that the Qurʾān compares them, according to two different readings (see READINGS OF THE QURʾĀN) of the verse in question (Q 77:32), with either fortified castles *(qaṣr)* or logs *(qaṣar),* flying as fast as she-camels, the black color of which is tinged with yellow (Q 77:33). Such fire spares nothing and nobody: Its favorite combustible is stone and human flesh (Q 2:24; 66:6); part of its functions is to "roast" *(ṣallā, aṣlā)* the damned who are clad in igneous garments (Q 22:19) or in clothes made out of either boiling copper or pitch (Q 14:50, according to whether one reads *qiṭrin ānin,* as Ibn ʿAbbās does, or *qaṭirān,* as others do). Thus it spares nothing (Q 74:28-9) and burns away the skin, which, however, will be replaced by a new one every time that "it is done to a turn" (*naḍijat,* Q 4:56); "eager to roast" (Q 70:15-6), it is called *al-ḥuṭama* (Q 104:5-6) from a root meaning "to break," and is thought to shatter whatever enters it (cf. the discussion of *al-ḥuṭama* in Ṭabarī, *Tafsīr*, ad Q 104:5-9), penetrating even to their viscera (104:6-7). While doing so, it makes an awful noise (Q 25:12) that resembles the bray of an ass (Q 67:7), a sound generally considered to be very ugly (Q 31:19).

In this fiery furnace and in contrast with the numerous gushing springs (see WELLS AND SPRINGS) that characterize the qur'ānic paradise (q.v.), a single well spouts boiling water (Q 88:5), that is to say, liquid fire, with a putrid stuff called *ghassāq* (Q 38:57; 78:24-5) and pus (*mā' ṣadīd*, Q 14:16), the only beverage at the disposal of the damned (Q 6:70; 37:67; 38:57; 40:72; 47:15; 56:42, 54, 93; 78:25). They have to drink it straight out of the well, whether because it is poured on their heads or because they are immersed in it; this not only involves the burning up of their bowels but also of their skin (Q 18:29; 22:19-20; 40:72; 44:47-8; 56:42, 55, 93). Due to this igneous beverage that is incapable of quenching the thirst of the damned, they will roam in the midst of the flames and the boiling water (Q 55:44), and will drink it as if they were "lost and thirsty camels" (Q 56:55).

Hell-fire also brings about a specific vegetation, a bush and a tree, bearing fruits conceived to torture the damned, which together with *ghislīn* (Q 69:36) — like *ghassāq*, a putrid matter — are the only food of which their diet is composed: the *ḍarī'*, a well known dry bush that also grows in the Najd and the Tihāma (sometimes mentioned in ancient poetry as *the* exemplary bad pasture since it dries the she-camel's udders), bears blood-red, prickly fruit that has a bitter taste and "neither fattens, nor allays hunger" (Q 88:6-7). The *zaqqūm*, for its part, a tree mentioned thrice in the Qur'ān (Q 37:62; 44:43; 56:52) and corresponding, like the *ḍarī'*, to a terrestrial species which can be found in South Arabia, if one credits the remark made by the botanist Abū Ḥanīfa al-Dīnawārī (cf. *Lisān al-'Arab*), grows at the very bottom of the furnace. Its fruit looks like snakes' or demons' heads *(ru'ūs al-shayāṭīn)* that "seethe in the bellies like melted bronze, like boiling water" *(ka-l-muhli yaghlī fī l-buṭūn ka-ghalyi l-ḥamīm*, Q 44:45-6). These rather disgusting dishes, all derived from fire, are globally qualified as *ṭa'ām dhū ghuṣṣa*, "food that gets stuck in the throat" (Q 73:13).

In the end, the flames as well as the scanty infernal flora cast a smoky, sparing, dark shadow (Q 56:43-4) that, contrary to the beneficent shade spread by the luxuriant vegetation of paradise, does not at all refresh and, as such, is incapable of protecting the damned from the omnipresent fire.

The igneous element that invests the infernal space has its representatives in this world, all of them more or less connected with the other world. Fire is connoted in this world in connection with: the sun (q.v.); the cataclysms that have annihilated various non- or wrong-believing peoples (see PUNISHMENT STORIES), all of which — save perhaps the deluge — are connected with fire; the burning stakes set up for Abraham (q.v.) by his idolatrous kin who do not want to be turned from their unbelief (see BELIEF AND UNBELIEF; Q 21:68-9; 29:24; 37:97; Abraham, however, is able to walk unscathed through the flames, having been saved by God, who says 'O fire, be coolness and peace for Abraham' [Q 21:69]) and the People of the Ditch (q.v.; *aṣḥāb al-ukhdūd*, Q 85:4-8); the fire of war and the fire of sacrifice — each mentioned once (respectively at Q 5:64 and Q 3:183); the earthly fire of which humankind can take advantage (Q 36:79-80; 56:70-3); and, finally, the burning bush (Q 20:9-14; 27:7-9; 28:29-30). Although a very rich vocabulary is used to describe the above-mentioned cataclysms, the word generally used for terrestrial fire is *nār;* most of the terms employed with regard to hell-fire disappear, *jaḥīm* occurring only once in the context of the story of Abraham (Q 37:97).

As far as the qurʾānic sun *(shams)* is concerned, it clearly appears to be nothing other than hell-fire: it is said to set to the west of the earth in a well of black mud (or, according to another reading, in a boiling well: *fī ʿaynin ḥamiʾatin,* Q 18:86), and to rise the next day in the east, so that during the night, like the Mesopotamian sun-god Šamaš, it must pass through the subterranean hell where it takes in a supply of fire. Thus, the fiery Arabian sun's task consists in ripening and withering the earthly vegetation to which the spring rains have given rise (see EARTH). And in so far as *shams* is female, she forms a pair with life-giving-rain *(māʾ, ghayth),* sun's male homology in this world; the former represents the cosmic fire that characterizes hell, whereas the latter symbolizes the cosmic fresh water that characterizes paradise.

With respect to the terrestrial *ʿadhāb* of the annihilated peoples, the central igneous figure responsible for the death of four of them, Thamūd (q.v.), ʿĀd (q.v.), Midian (q.v.), Moses (q.v.) and his people — the annihilation of this last group, however, being only momentary, as they are restored to life shortly thereafter — is the thunderbolt to which the text refers with four different words. These are: *ṣāʿiqa,* "thunderbolt" (Q 41:13, 17; 51:43-5), *rajfa,* "a single shock" (Q 7:77-8), *ṣayḥa,* "a single cry" (Q 11:67, 15:80-3; 54:31), and *ṭāghiya,* "the excessive one" (Q 69:5), all used to describe the torment of the Thamūd, thus implying the same atmospheric phenomenon. *Ṣāʿiqa* is "a fire that falls off the heaven with a terrible thunder-clap" *(Lisān al-ʿArab)* as well as "the flash of lightning when it burns a human being" (ibid.), and one may therefore conclude that *rajfa* describes the shock actually felt by the struck victim, whereas *Ṣayḥa,* being at the same time a metaphor for God's anger (q.v.), expresses the audible apprehension of the phenomenon in question. Finally, *ṭāghiya* seems to refer to the fact that any excessive event, no matter what it is, is considered to be negative.

A second group of non- or wrong-believing people — the people of Lot (Q 7:84; 11:82-3; 15:74; 25:40; 26:173; 27:58; 51:33; 54:34) and the so-called "People of the Elephant" (q.v.; Q 105:1-5) — have been annihilated by stone rains, to which the *ṣayḥa* (Q 15:73) must be added, at least as far as the people of Lot are concerned. Solid rains in the Qurʾān are always bound to fire, because the stones are thought either to have been baked in it or at least branded (*musawwama,* Q 11:82-3) with it. They can also bring out a specific vegetation (see AGRICULTURE AND VEGETATION) — *ushar, ḥarmal* and *ḥanẓal* — that is, like the infernal flora, caustic and bitter, and therefore inedible even for animals, and capable of causing diseases like smallpox *(judarī)* and measles *(ḥaṣaba)* that are supposed to lead, like fire itself, to the putrescence of the entire body (see the legend of the People of the Elephant in Ṭabarī, *Taʾrīkh,* i, 942-5; id., *History,* 229-35; cf. id., *Tafsīr,* xxx, 303-4).

The last group of annihilated nations is composed of Pharaoh's (q.v.) troops and Noah's (q.v.) people, both apparently victims of water (q.v.): salt-water with regard to the first, fresh water for the latter. Yet some textual data point to the fact that seawater might have been considered a mixture of fresh water and fire: at first, the Qurʾān qualifies it as *milḥ ujāj* (Q 25:53; 35:12), the second of these epithets meaning not only "very bitter," but also "very hot," while the root it derives from refers to the blazing and burning of fire. Secondly, the narrative of Moses leading the Israelites out of Egypt (q.v.) is related in sixteen verses, scattered in ten different sūras (Q 2:50; 7:136, 138; 8:54; 10:90; 17:103, 20:77-8; 26:63-6; 28:40; 44:24-5; 51:40) in which the sea, when it is mentioned, is systematically designated by two different terms, *baḥr* and *yamm,* the first only occurring in connection with the successful crossing of the Israelites (see CHILDREN OF ISRAEL), the second, a foreign Semitic word with negative connotations, being assigned to the fatal crossing of Pharaoh's troops. These textual data seem to hint at the double nature of sea-water, composed of birth-giving, fresh water connoted by *baḥr,* and mortal fire designated by *yamm.* As for the qurʾānic deluge, it should be mentioned that it might have been considered a flood of hot water, in other words, of liquid fire, a conception that is also found in the Talmud and the Midrash, as well as in the apocryphal literature, which would explain why the qurʾānic flood is said to start when the *"tannūr"* — a round hole in the ground, used as an oven for baking bread — "will be coming to a boil" (Q 23:27; see Fraenkel, *Aramäischen Fremdwörter,* 26; Hebbo, *Fremdwörter,* 63-4). Thus, fire could also be responsible for the deluge.

While the references to fire as a destroying element are continuous and run throughout the entire text from beginning to end, the kind of fire of which human beings can make use is only mentioned twice (Q 36:78-80 and 56:71-3). It has been set by God in the "green trees" *(al-shajar al-akhḍar)* so that men can strike sparks from them. These passages obviously allude to the fact that the ancient Arabs used to produce fire by striking sparks either from different species of wood (e.g. *ʿafār, markh, sawwās, marj, manj, ʿushar*) or from flints. And since the "green trees" — where the fire is concealed and from which it only manages to escape when two pieces of wood are rubbed against each other — are among the figures that rain water is apt to assume, their watery nature reduces the fire's destroying violence and heat, thus making it serviceable for humankind.

The final situation in which fire is involved is that of the burning bush (Q 20:9-14; 27:7-9; 28:29-30) which catches Moses' eye one night while, on their way back to Egypt, he and his family are lost in the desert. At first, Moses takes it for a campfire where he hopes he may get a brand to warm them up and to light their way. But when the bush starts speaking, he suddenly realizes that it is God himself who appears to him in this form. And as trees and vegetation in general are, as just mentioned, of aqueous nature, the burning bush is a complex figure is which the vivifying water and the mortal fire are in balance. In other words, it appears as a perfect metaphor for "the one who gives life and death," that is to say, God.

Heidi Toelle

Bibliography

Primary: *Lisān al-ʿArab,* ed. Cairo 1979; Ṭabarī, *The history of al-Ṭabarī. v. The Sasanids, the Byzantines, the Lakhmids, and Yemen,* trans. C.E. Bosworth, Albany, NY 1999; id., *Tafsīr,* ed. A. Saʿīd ʿAlī, Cairo 1954; id., *Taʾrīkh,* ed. de Goeje.

Secondary: A.A. Ambros, Gestaltung und Funktionen der Biosphäre im Koran, in *ZDMG* 140 (1990), 290-325; G. Bachelard, *L'eau et les rêves,* Paris 1942; id., *La psychanalyse du feu,* Paris 1937; J. Bottéro, *Mésopotamie. L'écriture, la raison et les dieux,* Paris 1987; Dīnawārī, Abū Ḥanīfa, *Kitāb al-Nabāt* (volume ii, based on citations and later works by M. Ḥamīd Allāh), Cairo 1973; S. Fraenkel, *Die aramäischen Fremdwörter im Arabischen,* Leiden 1886; A. Hebbo, *Die Fremdwörter in der arabischen Biographie des Ibn Hischam,* Frankfurt am Main 1984; A. Hubaishi and K. Müller-Hohenstein, *An introduction to the vegetation of Yemen,* Eschborn 1984; W. Jabr, *Muʿjam al-nabātāt al-ṭibbiyya,* Beirut 1987; C. Lévi-Strauss, *Mythologiques. I à IV,* Paris 1964, 66, 68, 71; D. Masson,

L'eau, le feu, la lumière, Paris 1985; M. Merleau-Ponty, *Phénoménologie de la perception,* Paris 1968; Rashīd Riḍā, *Manār,* ed. Cairo 1948-56; D. Sidersky, *Les origines des légendes musulmanes dans le Coran,* Paris 1933; S. Subhi, *La vie future selon le Coran,* Paris 1971; H. Toelle, *Le Coran revisité. Le feu, l'eau, l'air et la terre,* Damascus 1999.

Firm Handle see RELIGION

Fish see ANIMAL LIFE; HUNTING AND FISHING

Fishing see HUNTING AND FISHING

Fitna see TRIAL

Fiṭra see CREATION

Flight see FLYING

Flogging

Beating with a rod or whip. Flogging *(jald)* is a common punishment in Islamic law (see CHASTISEMENT AND PUNISHMENT; LAW AND THE QURʾĀN), prescribed both as a *ḥadd* (i.e. divinely sanctioned) and as a *taʿzīr* penalty (i.e. at the judge's discretion; see PROHIBITED DEGREES). The Arabic term *jald* is from the root *j-l-d,* meaning to flog, whip or lash and it appears in the Qurʾān in the form of a command (q.v.) against the culprits (*ijlidū* at Q 24:2 and *ijlidūhum* at Q 24:4). Flogging is the *ḥadd* punishment prescribed in the Qurʾān for the crimes of fornication *(zināʾ)* and false accusation of fornication *(qadhf)*. As a *ḥadd* penalty, it is a claim of God *(ḥaqq Allāh)* which implies that it cannot be pardoned but rather must be implemented by the ruler (see KINGS AND RULERS). For the offence of *zināʾ,* the punishment according to Q 24:2 is one hundred lashes for the free, unmarried Muslim and fifty lashes for the slave (see SLAVES AND SLAVERY). This is considered to be the final verse to be revealed concerning the crime of *zināʾ,* after the earlier Q 4:15 which refers to the adulteress being confined in her family's house until her death (see DEATH AND THE DEAD) or until another piece of divine legislation came into force (see ADULTERY AND FORNICATION; ABROGATION). For the married person, the punishment of stoning (q.v.) as prescribed in the sunna (q.v.) of the Prophet became the majority opinion. Jurists, however, are divided as to whether the unmarried culprit is to be banished for one year after flogging and whether the married culprit is to be flogged before stoning (Tabrīzī, *Mischcat-ul-Masabih,* ii, 182-90).

False accusation of unchastity (see CHASTITY) or defamation is termed *qadhf* in the Qurʾān and incurs a penalty of eighty lashes for the free person and forty for the slave (Q 24:4-5). Furthermore, the future testimony of the *maqdhūf* should not be accepted (see WITNESSING AND TESTIFYING), although this too is the object of controversy due to the qurʾānic verses, "except those who afterwards repent" (Q 24:5; see REPENTANCE AND PENANCE). For the crime of drinking wine (*shurb al-khamr,* see INTOXICANTS), the *ḥadd* punishment is flogging or beating; according to the major collectors of ḥadīth this is what the Prophet prescribed without fixing a definite number of lashes and irrespective of whether the culprit was intoxicated or not (Tabrīzī, *Mischcat-ul-Masabih,* ii, 197-9; Ḥaṣarī, *al-Ḥudūd wa-l-ashriba*). The tradition of Anas b. Mālik (d. 91-93/709-711) reports that the Prophet gave a beating with palm branches and shoes forty times and that Abū Bakr (q.v.) gave forty lashes. When ʿUmar (q.v.) became caliph (q.v.), the number of drinkers had risen sharply and so he increased the punishment to eighty lashes (Bayhaqī, *Sunan,* viii, 320).

In the classical *fiqh* texts, flogging or lashing denoted a common *taʿzīr* penalty, i.e. a type of chastisement. When *taʿzīr* is inflicted in the form of flogging — except according to the Mālikī school — the number of lashes must not exceed that in the *ḥadd* punishment (Izzi Dien, Taʿzīr). Regarding the implementation of the lashes, the culprit is to be whipped either in the sitting or the standing posture at a time when it is neither too hot nor too cold. Mālik (d. 179/796) states that the flogging is to be applied to the back while Abū Ḥanīfa (d. 150/767) and al-Shāfiʿī (d. 204/820) claim that all parts are to be touched except for the sexual organs and the face (q.v.). Moreover, whipping as a form of punishment should not be so severe as to result in the death of the punished (Ibn Rushd, *Primer*). The ordinances in Muslim countries outline in great detail the circumstances and manner in which whipping is to be applied or excused (Waqar-ul-Haq, *Criminal laws*, 456-7).

Mona Siddiqui

Bibliography
Primary: Bayhaqī, Abū Bakr Aḥmad b. al-Ḥusayn b. ʿAlī, *al-Sunan al-kubrā*, 10 vols., Hyderabad 1926; Ibn Rushd, *The distinguished jurist's primer. A translation of Ibn Rushd's* Bidāyat al-Mujtahid, trans. I. Nyazee, Reading 1996; Tabrīzī [Tibrīzī], *Mischcat-ul-Masabih. Or a Collection of the "most authentic traditions" regarding the actions and sayings of Muhammed, exhibiting the origin of the manners and customs, the civil, religious and military policy of the Muslemans*, trans. Captain A.N. Matthews, Bengal Artillery, 2 vols., Calcutta 1823.
Secondary: ʿA. ʿAbd al-ʿAzīz, *al-Fiqh al-jināʾī fī l-Islām. Ḍurūb al-qatl, al-qiṣāṣ, al-diya, al-ḥudūd, al-taʿzīr. Amthila wa-taṭbīqāt naẓariyya*, Cairo 1997; M.S. el-Awa, *Punishment in Islamic law*, Indianapolis 1993; Burton, *Collection*, 71-5, 90-6; id., *The sources of Islamic law. The Islamic theories of abrogation*, Edinburgh 1990, 123-50; A. Ḥuṣarī, *al-Ḥudūd wa-l-ashriba fī l-fiqh al-islāmī*, Amman 1972; M.Y. Izzi Dien, Taʿzīr, in *EI²*, x, 406; M. Waqar-ul-Haq, *Islamic criminal laws. Hudood laws and rules. With up-to-date commentary*, Lahore 1994.

Flood see NOAH; PUNISHMENT STORIES

Flora and Fauna see AGRICULTURE AND VEGETATION

Flying

Moving in the air with or as with wings. The concept of flying appears in a variety of forms in the Qurʾān. Perhaps the closest reference to elevated motion through the air is associated with the flying mountain (cf. Q 2:63-93; 4:154) which rose up into the air and hovered over the heads of the Children of Israel (q.v.) to compel them to keep the covenant (q.v.). A related notion, that of propulsion through the air from one place to another, is associated with the *isrāʾ* and *miʿrāj* (Q 17:1), the journey (see ASCENSION) of the Prophet from Mecca (q.v.) to Jerusalem (q.v.) and thence to paradise (q.v.). The motif was picked up by Ṣūfīs and made an essential ingredient of their metaphysical understanding of inner space (see ṢŪFISM AND THE QURʾĀN; SPATIAL RELATIONS). A less direct reference to flying is more properly related to ideas of ascending and descending. For example, one finds a reference to ascending into the skies in Q 6:125, where the image is one of climbing stairs into the heavens (see HEAVEN AND SKY), and in Q 35:10, where the verb denotes the ascension of odors (see ODORS AND SMELLS) from words of purity (see PURITY AND IMPURITY), based on the same idea as the stench from evil words and deeds rising up into God's nostrils (see EVIL DEEDS). We also read of the descent of the table (q.v.; Q 5:114) as well as the "sending down" of manna (Q 2:57; 7:160; 20:80), a meaning with some affinity to that of God sending down manna to the Hebrew people in the wilderness and the "sending down" of the Qurʾān. The importance of descent is surely not the movement "down," but the affirmation of God's benevolence (see BLESSING) providing both spiritual and material food (see FOOD AND DRINK) for his people. The movement down is also fortified by references to the Night of Power (q.v.), the potent moment during Ramaḍān (q.v.) when the Prophet received the book (q.v.). Contemporary vigils during this holy night attract believers (see FESTIVALS AND COMMEMORATIVE DAYS), hopeful of catching a glimpse of the holy descent, the results of which will portend good omens (q.v.) for the year. Transport through the air is also implied in the verses affirming that God "raised" Jesus (q.v.; see RESURRECTION) as in Q 4:158, where God raised Jesus to him, or Q 3:55 where God comforts Jesus with "I will take you and raise you to myself...," as well as the fascinating story of the transportation of the throne of the Queen of Sheba (q.v.) to the court of Solomon (q.v.) as proof (q.v.) of God's true message (Q 27:22-43). There is also the dramatic case of Q 22:31 where those who associate anyone with God are said to fall from the sky and the birds or the wind will then toss them through the air into a distant place. Consequently flying in the Qurʾān is a constellation of meanings embracing movement across distances and through the air with a variety of religious metaphors and journeys (see METAPHOR; JOURNEY). Their ultimate purpose appears designed to express God's control of space and distance.

Earle H. Waugh

Bibliography
Primary: Ibn Isḥāq-Guillaume, 181-4; Vahidi, *The book of the master of the world and the offspring of the soul (Menaki-i hvoca-i cihan ve netice-i can)*, part. trans. A.T. Karamustafa, On the seven invocations and the seven journeys, in J. Renard (ed.), *Windows on the house of Islam*, Berkeley 1998, 311-7.
Secondary: A. Schimmel, *Mystical dimensions of Islam*, Chapel Hill, NC 1975; E.H. Waugh, *Religious levitation and the Muslim experience. A study of flight symbolism of intermediary figures and other images in medieval Islam*, Ph.D. diss., Chicago 1972.

Food and Drink

Nourishment, in solid and liquid form, that sustains life. This topic may be examined in contexts where the following verbal roots frequently occur in the Qurʾān: *ṭ-ʿ-m*, "to eat," (fourth form "to feed, nourish"), *ʾ-k-l*, "to eat," and *sh-r-b*, "to drink." (See AGRICULTURE AND VEGETATION for additional terms related to food and drink that deal with some of the major food resources available to the peoples of early Islam, and with vegetation in general.) The qurʾānic terms treated here are those that are related to food consumption. These key verbal roots occur more than two dozen times each, with *ʾ-k-l* and *sh-r-b* appearing together eight times. Of these latter phrases, the most famous is perhaps that in Q 7:31 where God beseeches the children of Adam to dress properly when attending the mosque (q.v.), and to "eat and drink, but avoid excess for he does not love the intemperate." A tradition transmitted by Aḥmad b. Ḥanbal and attributed to the Prophet stresses proper behavior in matters of food, dress and the giving of alms, since God loved to witness his servants enjoying his bounty (see BLESSING) without arrogance and extravagance. This expressed an essential Islamic ethical norm of moderation in all things. Another social norm associated with food is feeding the needy, either as a matter of one's daily routine (Q 74:44; 22:28; 89:18; 107:3) or as expiation for a ritual unfulfilled (Q 5:95; 58:4). The prophets of God are described as dependent upon food and drink just like all other human beings. In Q 25:20 it says, "We have sent no messengers (see MESSENGER) who did not eat and walk about the markets" (q.v.; see also Q 23:33; on Muḥammad, Q 25:7; Jesus [q.v.] and Mary [q.v.], Q 5:75), a signal of how basic these actions are to humanity.

Food and drink in the Qurʾān

General terms for food, nourishment and sustenance in the metaphorical sense of livelihood occur in but a few instances, almost exclusively connected with the divine creative power. For example, Q 41:10 reads "in four days he provided (the earth) with sustenance *(aqwāt,* sing. *qūt)* for all alike" and then, in Q 4:85, God is described as the *muqīt,* "nourisher" of everything (see also Q 26:79). A similar description of God is found in Q 6:14: "He gives nourishment [to all] and is nourished by none" *(huwa yuṭʿim wa-lā yuṭʿam),* a phrase structurally parallel to the description of God's oneness in sūra 112 *(lam yalid wa-lam yūlad,* Q 112:3). *Maʿīsha,* victuals, necessaries of life or livelihood, is found in the phrase "We deal out to them their livelihood in this world" (Q 43:32; see also 51:57). These expressions are precisely parallel to those discussed in the article AGRICULTURE AND VEGETATION, where a sign of God's benevolent, creative power is the water (q.v.) sent down from the skies bringing forth vegetation and crops from the earth (q.v.). In describing God's prophets, humankind's dependence upon food is expressed in Q 21:8 and for this divine bounty one is enjoined to "Eat of what your lord has given you *(kulū min rizqi rabbikum)* and render thanks to him" (Q 34:15).

There are more food terms of a specific nature, many only in unique references as, for example, the gourd *(yaqṭīn,* Q 37:146). In an interesting passage (Q 2:61) the Israelites, during their sojourn in the desert, plead with Moses to call upon his lord to provide a change in their monotonous diet *(ṭaʿām wāḥid),* to "... give us from that which the earth produces, green herbs *(baql),* cucumbers *(qiththāʾ),* garlic *(fūm),* lentils *(ʿadas)* and onions *(baṣal).*" According to al-Ṭabarī (d. 310/923), the Israelites were bored with eating nothing but quail meat and drinking "a honey sent down from the skies called *mann*" (*Tafsīr,* ii, 125-6, ad Q 2:61). The plants mentioned by way of contrast were common items in the diet of the Arabian populace, as each is found frequently in the extant Arabic culinary manuals of the medieval period. Al-Ṭabarī also notes that commentators differed as to the correct interpretation of *fūm,* invariably rendered in translations as garlic. Some commentators said *fūm* meant bread in general, others that it referred to wheat in the dialect of the Banū Hāshim. Oral tradition had it that one could say *fawwimū lanā* in the sense of "they prepare bread for us" *(ikhtabizū lanā).* But as al-Ṭabarī relates that the Israelites had neither bread nor anything else for variety, *fūm* might well have been intended to mean the bread they lacked (*Tafsīr,* ii, 127-30, ad Q 2:61). Fruits *(fawākih,* coll. sing. *fākiha)* are mentioned collectively several times (in contexts both terrestrial, Q 55:11, and eschatological, Q 23:19). Specific fruits are mentioned such as the pomegranate (*rummān,* Q 6:141), the fig *(tīn,* Q 95:1, cited along with the olive, *zaytūn),* a kind of black grape (*gharābīb,* Q 35:27), and grapes (*ʿinab,* Q 17:91; 80:28 etc.). These are often named in connection with the date palm (q.v.), the most important fruit-producing tree in the Middle East. Ibn Kathīr (d. 774/1373) notes that the reference to fruits and specifically to pomegranate and dates in Q 55:68 indicates that these two were superior in rank to all other fruits. Two spices commonly used in cooking, ginger (*zanjabīl,* Q 76:17) and mustard (*khardal,* Q 21:47), are both mentioned in eschatological contexts, while salt (*milḥ,* Q 25:53) only occurs in reference to salt and fresh sea water of the earth. Finally, several of the references to an ear or spike of grain (coll. *sunbul,* pl. *sanābil, sunbulāt*) appears in Joseph's interpretation of the Egyptian ruler's dream (Q 12:43, 46, 47); the word for bread (q.v.; *khubz*, Q 12:36) is mentioned only in the dream of Joseph's prison cell mate.

Rather more curious are the sparse references (in comparison, say, to the date palm) to milk (q.v.; *laban*) and honey (q.v.; *ʿasal*), common items of daily consumption. In Q 16:66, pure milk from cattle is noted as yet another sign of God's benevolence, but the only other reference to either is contained in a description of paradise (Q 47:15), the inhabitants of which will enjoy the delights of the rivers of water and wine and of milk and honey of biblical fame. In his commentary on the verse, Ibn Kathīr (*Tafsīr*, vii, 295-7) stresses the "unearthly" nature of these celestial sources of nourishment. Water and milk are of the purest quality imaginable, as is honey "which does not come from the bee's belly"; wine does not have the loathsome taste and smell associated with it because it was not made "from grape trodden upon by the feet of men." Several traditions attributed to the Prophet explain that in paradise there are seas of water, milk, wine and honey from which these rivers flow (Ibn Ḥanbal, *Musnad*, ii, 158; Tirmidhī, *Ṣaḥīḥ*, iv, 680-1, no. 2542). Another word, *raḥīq*, meaning pure wine tempered with the waters of the fountain Tasnīm (see SPRINGS AND FOUNTAINS) is also described as a heavenly reward for the righteous (Q 83:25).

There is a single reference to the sheep and goat (*ḍaʾn*, *maʿz*, Q 6:143), the former being the most commonly consumed animal flesh in the Middle East throughout the medieval period. Animal fat (*shaḥm*, pl. *shuḥūm*, Q 6:146), referring to either the cow or sheep, was the most widely used form of cooking fat; the other cooking medium, olive oil, appears only in the famous Light Verse (*zayt*, Q 24:35; Q 23:20 mentions a tree on Mount Sinai which yields an oil, *duhn*, and a condiment for the table; see also ANOINTING). The cow (*baqara*, and specifically, see Q 2:67; also *baqar*, Q 6:144 and *baqarāt*, Q 12:43) gives its name to the longest sūra of the Qurʾān, while the word for calf *(ʿijl)* occurs in several verses, most often associated with Israelite worship which incurred the anger of the lord (Q 2:51, 54, 93; 4:153; 7:152; see CALF OF GOLD). The prophet Abraham (q.v.) offered his guests roasted calf (*ʿijl ḥanīdh*, Q 11:69) in one verse and fatted calf (*ʿijl samīn*, Q 51:26) in another; these are the only passages in the Qurʾān where particular reference is made to food prepared in a domestic setting. Game (*ṣayd*, Q 5:1, 94, 95, 96) including fish (*ṣayd al-baḥr*, Q 5:96; *ḥūt*, Q 18:63 and see also Q 16:14; 35:12; see HUNTING AND FISHING) was consumed but was not permitted while on pilgrimage (q.v.); other food restrictions will be noted later. Fowl is mentioned only in connection with the delights of paradise (*laḥm ṭayr*, Q 56:21). A special case of food slaughtered for consumption is the camel sacrificed in Mecca (*budn*, sing. *badana*, Q 22:36-7; see also Q 22:28). The camel (q.v.) in general (*ibil*, Q 6:144) is mentioned as one of the "eight" kinds of livestock (i.e. the male and female of four species) permitted by God for human use.

In connection with the general food vocabulary brief mention may be made of certain verbs commonly found in the medieval Arabic culinary manuals, but which are used in a metaphorical or secondary sense in the Qurʾān. For example, two such verbs occur in Q 4:56 referring to punishment in hell (q.v.), "Those who deny our signs, we shall burn *(ṣalā)* in the fire (q.v.); just as their skins are thoroughly done *(naḍijat julduhum)* we shall exchange them for other skins..." The many occurrences of the verb *ṣalā,* conventionally meaning "to roast," all refer to punishment in the afterlife, in the sense of "to roast in hell." The single use of the verb *qalā(ū),* the primary meaning of which is "to fry" is used in the secondary sense (Q 93:3) of "to detest." Another, rather different observation may be made of two instances where nominal forms found in the Qurʾān are derived from verbal roots denoting processes for cooking meat; the verb *ḥanadha* (*ʿijl ḥanīdh,* Q 11:69, "roasted calf") means to roast meat in a hole in the ground covered by glowing embers or heated stones, while *ramaḍa* (Ramaḍān, Q 2:185) means to cook an animal in its skin in the same manner before skinning and eating it.

Finally, we may end this section noting the few terms for vessels or appliances used in the household (see CUPS AND VESSELS; INSTRUMENTS). A drinking cup is mentioned once (*ṣuwāʿ,* Q 12:72), while in Q 34:13 the terms *jifān,* large basins (sing. *jafna*) and *qudūr,* cauldrons (sing. *qidr*) are found. Other vessels include the cup (*kaʾs,* e.g. Q 56:18); glass bottles or goblets (*qawārīr,* sing. *qārūra,* e.g. Q 56:18); ewer, goblet (*abārīq,* sing. *ibrīq,* Q 56:18); dish, container, receptacle (*āniya,* sing. *ināʾ,* Q 76:15). Two occurrences of the term *tannūr* ("oven," Q 11:40; 23:27) both relate to the story of Noah (q.v.). The bee-hive-shaped oven of Babylonian origin became the most widely diffused appliance for domestic baking (as distinct from the larger communal oven, the *furn*) throughout the Middle East and can still be found in use to this day. The qurʾānic usage is metaphorical and Ibn Kathīr interprets Q 11:40 (following Ibn ʿAbbās and the majority of the pious ancestors), in the light of Q 54:11-2, which reads "We opened the gates of heaven with pouring rain and caused the earth to burst with gushing springs...." Hence, *tannūr* becomes a metaphor for the surface of the globe; the oven's orifices are the springs from which the divinely ordered deluge would burst forth to cover the earth.

Food taboos in scripture and tradition

The terms dealt with in the sections above have referred to qurʾānic contexts chiefly depicting the benevolent gifts of God to his creatures on earth or to his reward and punishment (q.v.) in the afterlife. The present section shall examine passages treating certain emblematic prohibitions of food and drink (see LAWFUL AND UNLAWFUL), the adherence to which were "markers" separating one religious community from another. According to the believer's perception, adherence to the food laws was also one determinant in the individual's path to salvation. In humankind's pristine state in paradise (q.v.), there was only one food prohibition when God said to Adam and his wife (see ADAM AND EVE) "eat of its fruits to your hearts' content wherever you will. But never approach this tree or you shall both become transgressors" (Q 2:35; cf. 7:19). The tree in question was the tree of immortality (*shajarat al-khuld,* Q 20:120). Seduced by their enemy Satan into defying their lord, Adam and his wife suffered banishment from paradise (see FALL OF MAN). The food prohibitions to Adam's descendants are offered in the same spirit, "Men, eat of what is lawful and wholesome on the earth and do not walk in Satan's footsteps, for he is your inveterate foe" (Q 2:168; cf. 6:142; see ENEMIES) and then "give thanks to God if it is him you worship" (Q 2:172). In the historical continuum from the Age of Ignorance (q.v.; *jāhiliyya*) to Islam, al-Ṭabarī (*Tafsīr,* iii, 317, ad Q 2:172) explains these verses to mean that whereas God himself had permitted what was lawful and wholesome, pre-Islamic food prohibitions followed obedience of the devil or the customs of the tribal fathers and ancestors (see SOUTH ARABIA, RELIGION IN PRE-ISLAMIC). For example, peoples of the *jāhiliyya* had prohibited the eating of certain camels, whereas Islamic prohibitions did not embrace these, as they were not enumerated by God in passages like Q 2:173, 6:142-5 and 5:3-4. Only the most interesting of these passages — namely, those found at the beginning of the sūra entitled *al-Māʾida,* "the Table" (Q 5) — shall be examined here, in conjunction with Ibn Kathīr's and al-Ṭabarī's commentaries on these verses.

The first four prohibited items are carrion *(mayta),* blood (*damm,* see BLOOD AND BLOOD CLOT), flesh of swine *(laḥm khinzīr),* and meat consecrated to anything other than God (see CONSECRATION OF ANIMALS). Carrion is dealt with in a separate article (see CARRION). Blood in this passage is interpreted to mean the "spilt blood" (*damm masfūḥ,* cf. Q 6:145) of a correctly-executed slaughter which then, according to a prophetic tradition, permitted the consumption of the animal's organs, the kidney and spleen. As for swine, the flesh of both domestic and wild species was prohibited; reading Q 5:3 again with Q 6:145, the commentators added that its flesh was an abomination and the prohibition extended to all parts of the animal, including its fat (Ṭabarī, *Tafsīr,* xii, 190 f.). Meat slaughtered without consecration to God alone meant flesh dedicated to created objects such as graven images. In his commentary to Q 6:118, al-Ṭabarī (*Tafsīr,* xii, 67) notes that this is addressed to those Peoples of the Book who believe in the unicity of God, namely Jews and Christians, but excludes idolaters and people like the Magians (q.v.; Majūs) who do not possess a scripture.

In connection with carrion *(mayta),* one should examine the next five items prohibited in Q 5:3, and which are essentially an extension of the preceding injunction: "You are forbidden the flesh of strangled animals *(munkhaniqa),* and of those beaten to death *(mawqūdha);* of those killed by a fall *(mutaraddiya)* or gored *(naṭīḥa)* to death; or mangled by beasts of prey *(mā akala l-sabuʿu).*" The phrase immediately following, "except what you have (lawfully) slaughtered yourselves," was interpreted to mean that if any of the preceding categories of animal were still alive, evidenced by the blinking of an eye or other movement, then its flesh was permitted if it were properly sacrificed. Some scholars among the Medinans, however, regarded all these categories as prohibited, the exceptive phrase applying only to what God had made legal for slaughter. In a story recounted by al-Ṭabarī, a group of idolaters asked the Prophet, "'When a sheep dies, who or what causes it to die?' The Prophet replied, 'God,' to which the idolaters retorted, 'So you claim that what you and your companions slaughter is permissible to eat, but what God kills is forbidden!'" This apparently prompted the revelation of the verse to eat only meat consecrated in God's name, for what he caused to die was understood to be carrion *(mayta).*

God, however, forgives the eating of prohibited meat when one is driven by hunger and where no sin is intended (Q 5:3). In two other passages that indicate God's forgiveness of violation of dietary laws (Q 2:173; 6:145), the condition of hunger is not mentioned explicitly. Commentators then explained that one could eat prohibited meat only from fear of dying of hunger (see FAMINE).

Running through the subject of food taboos is a matter of community distinction between believers and those who "walk in Satan's footsteps" (Q 6:142). This phrase and the pagans' habits mentioned in Q 6:138 are explained by al-Ṭabarī

(*Tafsīr*, xii, 139-46) to indicate that the idolaters' food customs were based upon their own judgment without heed to God's permission or, conversely, that they forbade themselves certain benefits granted by God to believers and therefore they obeyed the devil and defied the Compassionate One. In his commentary to Q 2:173, al-Ṭabarī (*Tafsīr*, ad loc.) notes that "intending neither to sin nor to transgress" when compelled to eat forbidden meat entails the intention neither to disassociate oneself from the way of God (see PATH OR WAY) nor to withdraw from the community of believers. In Q 5:5, another instance of intercommunity food customs, to which allusion has already been made, appears resolved: "The food of those who received the book (q.v.) is lawful to you, and yours to them." Al-Ṭabarī comments (*Tafsīr*, ix, 572-3) that the sacrificial meat and food of Jews and Christians who had received, respectively, the Torah and the Gospels was permitted; but forbidden for consumption were the sacrifices of those who possessed no scripture, who neither confessed the unity of God, nor adhered to the faith of the People of the Book (q.v.; see also Q 3:93). Al-Ṭabarī reports a tradition that points to a problem which possibly engaged some early Muslim scholars; by this account, the sacrificial meat of the Christian Arab tribe of Banū Taghlib was deemed forbidden owing to their persistent habit of drinking wine (*khamr*, see INTOXICANTS; Ṭabarī, *Tafsīr*, ix, 575; Ibn Kathīr, *Tafsīr*, iii, 57 [quoting the tradition from al-Ṭabarī]). This was another Muslim community "marker" to which we shall now turn.

"No blame shall be attached to those that have embraced the faith and done good works (see GOOD DEEDS; ETHICS AND THE QUR'ĀN) in regard to any food they may have eaten, so long as they fear (q.v.) God and believe in him and do good works" (Q 5:93). Al-Ṭabarī's comment on this passage (*Tafsīr*, xii, 139-46, ad Q 5:93) first relates it to a preceding verse (Q 5:90) that wine was among the abominations of Satan and therefore best avoided. Yet there were those in the nascent community, Companions of the Prophet (q.v.), who had died at the battle of Badr (q.v.) or at Uḥud, and who had been drinkers of wine before its prohibition expressed in Q 5:90; they were nevertheless forgiven owing to their belief in God and the good deeds they performed. Al-Ṭabarī defines wine as any beverage which "veils" *(khammara)* the mind in a metaphorical sense, the way a *khimār* "veils" or covers a woman's head (*Tafsīr*, iv, 320-1, ad Q 2:219). The sin resulting from this cloaked state of mind was that knowledge of the lord slipped into oblivion. Before the prohibition, wine and gambling were conceded to have some benefit, although their harm was greater than any good (Q 2:219). This, according to a report in al-Ṭabarī, prompted some to give up drinking until another verse was revealed which said, "And the fruits of the palm and the vine from which you derive intoxicants *(sakaran)* and wholesome food; verily in that is a sign for those who have sense" (Q 16:67) and those who had abstained resumed drinking. Another early verse had warned that believers should not attend their prayers in a state of inebriation (Q 4:43). When it was deemed appropriate and necessary, the prohibition found in Q 5:90, abrogating the earlier verses (see ABROGATION), was revealed (see OCCASIONS OF REVELATION) and wine drinking was made a sin in itself (see SIN, MAJOR AND MINOR; BOUNDARIES AND PRECEPTS).

The difference between wine and pork in qur'ānic food taboos was the progressive series of prescription against the former and the initial and absolute prohibition of the latter. In the present state of knowledge about early Islam it is difficult to determine whether this also reflected differing social attitudes during the formative period of the Islamic community. Possibly the prohibition of pork was more easily adopted than that of wine. For example, evidence suggests that whereas medical opinion accepted the curative properties of alcohol until at least the early fourth/tenth century, three centuries later even medical attitudes had hardened against its use. Of course, the pious, devout Muslim would have avoided alcoholic drink as a matter of religious principle from the beginning (see Waines, Medieval controversy).

One final observation to conclude this section concerns Mary Douglas' well known analysis of dietary rules in the Hebrew Bible and her conclusion that they could not be sustained in the Islamic context. For Douglas, the Jewish dietary laws were like signs which inspired meditation on the oneness, purity and completeness of God and by avoidance "holiness was given a physical expression in every encounter with the animal kingdom and at every meal" (Douglas, Abominations, 57). For Muslims, on the other hand, whose food taboos were far less exclusive in intent than the Jewish, the object of avoidance was more simply and directly piety (q.v.) towards and obedience (q.v.) of God.

Food and drink in early Islamic literature

Food and drink were topics of interest among the cultured urban public throughout the formative period of the Islamic community. That concern was both religious and secular. Apart from the relevant contents of scripture and the contribution recorded in the commentaries examined in this article, there had emerged by the third/ninth century the first compilations of traditions attributed to the prophet Muḥammad (see ḤADĪTH AND THE QURʾĀN). The ḥadīth collections of al-Bukhārī (d. 256/870) and Muslim (d. 261/875), for example, contained books on food and drink, and on matters related to hunting and butchery. Pious attention to the words and deeds of the Prophet extended to medicine as well; a book on this subject is found in both al-Bukhārī and Muslim (see also MEDICINE AND THE QURʾĀN). During a journey to eastern Islamic lands, the Andalusian scholar and jurist ʿAbd al-Malik b. Ḥabīb (d. 238/853) compiled a medical compendium which contains, along with data drawn anonymously from the Greek tradition, the earliest known collection of material from the Prophet and his Companions on medical themes in which he records the unattributed saying that "the best medicine is based on experience and its most important aspect is diet." Later, the qurʾānic verse "eat and drink but avoid excess" (Q 7:31) was interpreted as a scriptural foundation of Prophetic medicine since, according to Ibn Kathīr, some of the Prophet's Companions argued that God "had gathered together all of medicine in this half verse." This indicated the importance of diet in the preservation of health and its restoration in times of illness. Ibn Ḥabīb's work offers grounds to correct the view that Prophetic medicine *(al-ṭibb al-nabawī)* represented the "Islamic dethronement of Galen... in favour of Beduin quackery and superstition" (Burgel, Arabic medicine, 59). Rather, Prophetic medicine accepted the theoretical framework of humoral pathology but attempted to spiritualize its source of authority, reason, acknowledging only God as the creator and arbiter of body and soul.

Then, in what may be more properly called "secular literature" the food lore of the urban and urbane population was reflected in two encyclopaedic works, the *ʿUyūn al-akhbār* of Ibn Qutayba (d. 276/889) and the *ʿIqd al-farīd* of Ibn ʿAbd Rabbihi (d. 328/940). Earlier, the wine poems of Abū Nuwās (d. ca. 200/815) had crowned a long evolution of poets' involvement with the Bacchic theme; but it must be remembered, too, that it was Muslim mystics who put the erotic and Bacchic framework to use in their poetic expressions of drunken love for God. Finally, the earliest extant cookbook of the late fourth/tenth century by Ibn Sayyār al-Warrāq reflects culinary developments from the reigns of the first ʿAbbāsid caliphs; other cookbooks illustrate a rich and varied culinary tradition down to the eighth/fourteenth century, which spanned the regions from Iraq and Persia to al-Andalus. The cookbooks are also related to the medical interest in dietetics illustrated by the works of Abū Bakr al-Rāzī (d. 313/925) and his contemporary al-Isrāʾīlī (d. ca. 323/935).

Conclusion

In sum, food and drink touch the vital core of Islamic religious ethics, belonging in part to the worship *(ʿibādāt)* of God by the believers, following the explicit prohibitions of scripture, and in part also to the sphere of social relationships *(muʿāmalāt)* by the faithful adherence to injunctions such as feeding the needy and the weak. The necessity of bodily sustenance illustrates humankind's dependence upon its creator, but these signs of divine benevolence are a reminder of the believer's expected response of gratitude (see GRATITUDE AND INGRATITUDE).

David Waines

Bibliography

Primary: Ibn Ḥabīb, ʿAbd al-Malik, *Mukhtaṣar fī l-ṭibb* (Compendio de medicina), ed. C. Álvarez de Morales and F. Girón Irueste, Madrid 1992; Ibn Ḥanbal, *Musnad,* ed. Ghamrāwī; Ibn Kathīr, *Tafsīr;* Ibn Sayyār al-Warrāq, *Kitāb al-Ṭabīkh,* ed. K. Ohrnberg and S. Mroueh, Helsinki 1987; Ibn Zuhr, Abū Marwān ʿAbd al-Malik, *Kitāb al-Aghdhiya* (Tratado de los alimentos), ed. and trans. E. García Sánchez, Madrid 1992; M. Marin and D. Waines (eds.), *Kanz al-fawāʾid fī tanwīʿ al-mawāʾid,* Stuttgart/Beirut 1993; Ṭabarī, *Tafsīr,* ed. Shākir (up to Q 14:27); ed. A. Saʿīd ʿAlī; Tirmidhī, *Ṣaḥīḥ;* al-Turayqī, ʿAbdallāh b. Muḥammad b. Aḥmad, *Aḥkām al-aṭʿima fī l-sharīʿa al-islāmiyya,* Riyadh 1984.

Secondary: J.C. Burgel, Secular and religious features in medieval Islamic medicine, in C. Leslie (ed.), *Asian medical systems. A comparative approach,* Berkeley 1976, 44-62; M. Douglas, The abominations of Leviticus, in id., *Purity and danger,* London 1966, 1984; G.J. van Gelder, *God's banquet. Food in classical Arabic literature,* London 2000; Fazlur Rahman, *Health and medicine in the Islamic tradition,* New York 1989; S. Jayyusi, *The legacy of Muslim Spain,* Leiden 1992, 725-38; A. Manṣūr, *al-Nabatāt fī l-Qurʾān al-karīm,* Amman 1994; J.D. McAuliffe, Wines of earth and paradise. Qurʾānic proscriptions and promises, in R.M. Savory and D.A. Agius (eds.), *Logos Islamikos,* Toronto 1984, 159-74; I. Perho, *The Prophet's medicine,* Helsinki 1995; D. Waines, Abū Zayd al-Balkhī on the nature of forbidden drink. A medieval Islamic controversy, in M. Marin and D. Waines (eds.), *La alimentación en las culturas islamicas,* Madrid 1994, 111-27; id., *In a caliph's kitchen,* London 1989; id. and M. Marin, MUZAWWAR. Counterfeit food for fast and fever, in *Der Islam* 69 (1992), 289-301 (for the culinary culture of al-Andalus).

Foot see FEET

Forbidden

Excluded from acceptable behavior on legal and religious grounds. The Arabic terms *ḥarām* and *maḥẓūr* (the latter is not attested in the Qurʾān) refer to that which is impermissible, expressed in legal terminology as prohibited acts, the performance of which renders one liable to punishment (see CHASTISEMENT AND PUNISHMENT). Several derivatives of the root *ḥ-r-m,* which carries the notion of impermissibility or debarring, appear in the Qurʾān. Often, the verb *ḥarrama* — with God as the grammatical subject — is used to declare certain foods, acts or games of chance impermissible, e.g. the flesh of carrion (q.v.), blood, pork, usury (q.v.), homicide and numerous other things (Q 2:173, see BLOOD AND BLOOD CLOT; BLOODSHED; FOOD AND DRINK; GAMBLING; MURDER). The same verb is also used with a different shade of meaning, namely, to make untenable or bar from. The most notable of these uses occurs in Q 5:72: "He who associates anything with God, God will bar him *(ḥarrama llāhu ʿalayhi)* from the garden (q.v.), and his final rest shall be the fire (q.v.)." The verb is also often employed as the functional antonym of *aḥalla,* to render something *ḥalāl,* permissible, legitimate, tenable (cf. Q 4:160; 9:37). While the focus here will be limited to the root *ḥ-r-m,* it should be noted that the extensive use of *n-h-y* is also significant for the qurʾānic sense of the forbidden, e.g. Q 6:28 in reference to things forbidden to humans in this life and Q 7:20 in reference to God's forbidding Adam and Eve (q.v.) from eating from the tree (q.v.). Of course, this root is most well-known in the phrase "Commanding the right and forbidding the wrong" *(al-amr bi-l-maʿrūf wa-l-nahī ʿan al-munkar)* as the identifying character of the chosen community of God (e.g. Q 3:104; see COMMUNITY AND SOCIETY IN THE QURʾĀN; ETHICS AND THE QURʾĀN; GOOD AND EVIL).

Another derivative of *ḥ-r-m* is the word *ḥarām,* which has the meaning of a forbidden thing and, by extension, of a sacred space (see SPATIAL RELATIONS; SACRED PRECINCTS) or time (q.v.): "Turn your face (q.v.) toward the sacred mosque (q.v.; *al-masjid al-ḥarām*)," the Qurʾān declares in Q 2:149 (see also Q 2:150, 191; 5:97). In Q 5:97, the Kaʿba (q.v.) is also declared as *al-bayt al-ḥarām* or the sacred house (see HOUSE-DOMESTIC AND DIVINE). Similarly, sacrosanct status is given to a particular month or months (q.v.) during which no fighting (q.v.) or wars are to be conducted, known in pre-Islamic times as the sacred month *(al-shahr al-ḥarām),* an expression that appears on no less than six occasions in the Qurʾān, once in the plural form (see PRE-ISLAMIC ARABIA AND THE QURʾĀN; SOUTH ARABIA, RELIGION IN PRE-ISLAMIC). For reasons that are not entirely clear, but which may have been due to confusion over which month was in fact sacred, the Qurʾān at one point appears to change its position on the matter and implies that the persecution of believers is worse than fighting against unbelievers during this month (Q 2:217; cf. 2:194; compare with Q 5:2; see LAWFUL AND UNLAWFUL; WAR). The status of sanctuary in Islam, also known as *ḥarām* (cf. Q 28:57; 29:67) was bestowed upon three places of worship (q.v.): one in Mecca (q.v.), one in Medina (q.v.) and one in Jerusalem (q.v.). Mecca, in terms of overall physical space was the largest *ḥarām,* Jerusalem the smallest. Their precincts were defined in some detail and entry into them, especially those of Arabia, was subject to numerous conditions. Hunting wild game, uprooting any flora and killing humans were among the most notable prohibitions that applied within the boundaries of these sanctuaries (see HUNTING AND FISHING). Even the execution of murderers who had been legally sentenced to death was forbidden.

Sanctity extends also to people who are found in the sacred *(ḥarām)* areas, whether during the greater or the lesser pilgrimage (q.v.; see SANCTITY AND THE SACRED). This sanctified state is known as *iḥrām,* a state into which one enters physically, spiritually, geographically and temporally. Once a person enters this state, he or she should not, *inter alia,* engage in sexual intercourse (see SEX AND SEXUALITY), lie (q.v.), argue, hunt wild game (even speaking about or pointing to it is forbidden), kill any creatures (even fleas), use perfume, clip finger nails or trim or shave hair. Such matters as trimming hair or clipping finger nails should, of course, be done, but before entering the state of *iḥrām*. Hygienic practices, including taking baths, are permitted, even encouraged, at any time during the *iḥrām* period. Also highly recommended during this period is wearing a particular type of clothing (q.v.), preferably new, clean and white in color.

Another important derivative of *ḥ-r-m* that is not attested in the Qurʾān is *maḥram*, namely, a person who is within a prohibited degree of marriage. Blood relatives, relations arising out of marriage and suckling brothers and sisters are not permitted to marry (see FAMILY; MARRIAGE AND DIVORCE). Thus, a man cannot marry his mother, daughters, sisters, aunts, sisters-in-law or step-daughters, as well as any woman, however unrelated to him she may be, if both he and she had once been nursed by the same woman (cf. Q 4:23; see WET NURSING; FOSTERAGE; KINSHIP). The word *ḥarīm*, distorted into English as harem, refers to those parts of the house where women are not to associate with non-*maḥram* males (see WOMEN AND THE QURʾĀN). Thus, *maḥram* males, being excluded from the *ḥarīm* prohibition, can associate with females to whom they stand in such a relationship, both in the *ḥarīm* and elsewhere. *Ḥurma* is a term of general applicability, used to refer to things that have certain sanctity and are thus inviolate. In modern discourse on medicine and medical ethics (see MEDICINE AND THE QURʾĀN), the word has come to refer to the physical integrity of a person or the inviolability of the body.

Perhaps the most important of the uses of the word *ḥarām* is that found in law (see LAW AND THE QURʾĀN), where it is virtually synonymous with *maḥẓūr*, although this latter term is, relatively speaking, of far less frequent occurrence. Both terms mean forbidden or impermissible, a legal norm that has four counterparts (see PROHIBITED DEGREES): the obligatory *(wājib)*, the recommended *(mandūb)*, the permissible *(mubāḥ)*, and the repugnant *(makrūh)*. In the earlier, formative period, perhaps by the middle of the third/ninth century, these five legal norms had not yet been fully developed. Thus, al-Shāfiʿī (d. 204/820), for instance, often uses *makrūh*, especially in its verbal form *akrahu*, to denote prohibition. After the formative period, however, each of the five norms was distinctly represented by a separate word, though at times there was more than one word to denote a particular norm.

The value that is embedded in the forbidden is *ḥurma (*or *taḥrīm)*, which gives rise to punishment. Since the forbidden requires the relinquishing of particular acts *(ṭalab tark fiʿl)*, such as drinking wine (see INTOXICANTS) or gambling, it is distinguished from the recommended that enjoins the *performance* of certain acts. It is likewise distinguished from the permissible in that the latter equally allows the option of omission or commission. The forbidden stands in sharp contrast to the obligatory which requires the performance of particular acts. A question that arose in legal theory *(uṣūl al-fiqh)* was whether one and the same thing could be forbidden and obligatory. The answer was in the negative, but a differentiation was made concerning the nature of acts subject to this categorization. An act may be classified either as a number *(ʿadad)* or as a species *(nawʿ)*. As a number, an act, being one, unique individual, can in no way be both forbidden and obligatory. As a species, however, an act may be of various types, as is the case with prostration (see BOWING AND PROSTRATION) as an act of prayer (q.v.): it may be prostration before God, but it may also be before an idol (see IDOLATRY AND IDOLATERS; IDOLS AND IMAGES). The former is obligatory, the latter forbidden.

Nor is prohibition an indistinguishable entity. It may arise from a quality innate to the act itself or it may be external to that act, as if it were a contingent. For instance, consumption of the flesh of carrion or marrying a first-degree relation are prohibited because of the very nature of the acts involved. It is simply the case that carrion meat and mothers and sisters carry within themselves the value of prohibition. But undue enrichment and embezzlement are forbidden not on account of the nature of the object involved, i.e. money. Rather, they are deemed so because the proprietorship of the object (see POSSESSION; PROPERTY) belongs to someone else *(milk al-ghayr)*. See also BOUNDARIES AND PRECEPTS.

Wael B. Hallaq

Bibliography
Primary: al-Ghazālī, Abū Ḥāmid Muḥammad, *al-Mustaṣfā min ʿilm al-uṣūl*, 2 vols., Cairo 1906, i, 66-7, 72, 76-9; al-Ḥalabī, Ibrahīm b. Muḥammad, *Multaqā l-abḥur*, 2 vols., Beirut 1989, i, 208-32; al-Miṣrī, Aḥmad b. Naqīb, *ʿUmdat al-sālik wa-ʿuddat al-nāsik*, ed. and trans. N.H.M. Keller, *The reliance of the traveller*, Evanston, IL 1991, 311-22, 527-30, 608-9; al-Tahānawī, Muḥammad b. ʿAlī, *Kashshāf iṣṭilāḥāt al-funūn*, 2 vols., Calcutta 1862, i, 367-9; al-Ṭūfī, Najm al-Dīn b. Saʿīd, *Sharḥ mukhtaṣar al-rawḍa*, ed. ʿAbdallāh al-Turkī, 3 vols., Beirut 1987, i, 359-64.
Secondary: J. Chelhod, Les structures du sacré chez les Arabes, Paris 1955, 50-1; E. Gräf, *Jagdbeute und Schlachttier im islamischen Recht. Eine Untersuchung zur Entwicklung der islamischen Jurisprudenz*, Bonn 1959, 16-18; W.B. Hallaq, *A history of Islamic legal theories*, Cambridge 1997, 40, 175, 190 f., 194; Izutsu, *Concepts*, 237-41; B. Krawietz, *Die Ḥurma. Schariatrechtlicher Schutz vor Eingriffen in die körperliche Unversehrtheit nach arabischen Fatwas des 20. Jahrhunderts*, Berlin 1991; J.R. Lewis, Some aspects of sacred space and time in Islam, in *Studies in Islam* 19 (1982), 167-78; R.B. Serjeant, Haram and Hawtah. The sacred enclave in Arabia, in A.R. Badawi (ed.), *Mélanges Taha Husayn*, Cairo 1962, 41-58; S.H. al-Shamma, *The ethical system underlying the Qurʾān. A study of certain negative and positive notions*, Tübingen 1959.

Foreign Vocabulary

From the earliest period of Islam down to the present day, attentive readers have observed that there are words in the Qurʾān which appear to be of non-Arabic origin. Such observations, motivated by varying factors, have been the source of controversy, discussions and extensive study in traditional Muslim and Euro-American scholarship.

Why foreign words?

When the Qurʾān proclaimed itself to be written in "clear Arabic," the seeds of discussion, disagreement and analysis concerning the presence of "foreign words" within the text were sown. Not only is the point made a number of times that the Qurʾān is in Arabic (on occasion referred to as a *lisān*, "language") rather than some other language (Q 12:2; 13:37; 16:103; 20:113; 39:28; 41:3; 42:7; 43:3; 46:12), but this Arabic language is declared to be *mubīn*, "clear" (e.g. Q 26:195). Perhaps most significant in this regard is Q 41:44, "If we had made it an *aʿjamī* Qurʾān, they would have said, 'Why are its signs not distinguished *(fuṣṣilat)*? What, *aʿjamī* and Arab?' Say: 'To the believers it is a guidance and a healing; but those who believe not, in their ears is a heaviness, and to them it is a blindness (see SEEING AND HEARING; HEARING AND DEAFNESS); those — they are called from a far place.'" There is a contrast set up in this verse between what is Arab (i.e. Muḥammad) and/or Arabic and what is barbarous or simply foreign, *aʿjamī*. This latter word is to be understood both in terms of language and as a quality of a person, as reflected in Q 26:198-9, "If we had sent it down on an *aʿjamī* and he had recited it to them, they would not have believed it." This separation between Arab and foreign has dictated a good deal of the approach to the nature of the language of the Qurʾān. On occasion, the word *aʿjamī* is best understood in terms of the polemical motif of "informers" (those who told Muḥammad the stories which he claimed were revelation and who are understood to be foreign; see INFORMANTS) rather than as characterizing the language of the text itself; this is clear in Q 16:103, "And we know very well that they say, 'Only a mortal is teaching him.' The speech of him to whom they tend is *aʿjamī*; and this speech is Arabic, manifest." Be that as it may, this polemical perspective did not prove to be the dominant interpretative stance in Muslim thinking about these verses; glossing them as a matter of the actual language being used was more commonly applied.

A typical Muslim attitude towards this issue is illustrated by the following statement attributed to Ibn ʿAbbās (d. ca. 68/687) which is found at the beginning of an exegetical text dealing with Arabic dialects and foreign words in the Qurʾān. A number of variants to this statement exist, but the following translation presents the text in a widespread form. The text provides a common interpretation of the understanding of language in the Qurʾān and suggests, as well, a resolution to the problem of why it is that there are foreign words in the text at all, an issue which will be raised in the second section below:

From Ibn ʿAbbās concerning the words of God, "In a clear Arabic tongue." He said: that is, in the language of Quraysh (q.v.). If there had been other than Arabic in the Qurʾān, the Arabs would not have understood it. God has only revealed books in Arabic and Gabriel (q.v.) then translated them for each prophet into the language of his people. Therefore God said, "We do not send a prophet except in the language of his community" (Q 14:4). There is no language of a people more comprehensive than the language of the Arabs. The Qurʾān does not contain any language other than Arabic although that language may coincide with other languages; however, as for the origin and category of the languages used, it is Arabic and nothing is mixed in with it (Arabic text in Wansbrough, *QS*, 218; see Rippin, Ibn ʿAbbas, 20).

Underlying such a statement is an area of substantial concern and disagreement among Muslim scholars. Given the statements within the qurʾānic text as background, it may well be asked why Muslim exegetes would have ever considered the possibility of the existence of foreign words in the text at all. The qurʾānic text seems clear in its statement on the matter, which suggests that the exegetes created a problem not necessitated by their exegesis of the actual qurʾānic text. To arrive at a situation in which the presence of foreign words in the Qurʾān was seen as a problem that needed resolution, observations on the factual presence of foreign words in the Qurʾān must have arisen. Such observations would have been provoked in a number of ways.

It is certainly apparent that early Muslim authorities who are cited in ḥadīth reports had no qualms about considering some words to be "foreign" (see Ṭabarī, *Tafsīr*, i, 13-4; id., *The commentary*, 12-3). Abū Maysara (tradition no. 6) is quoted by al-Ṭabarī as stating, "There are expressions in the Qurʾān from every language." That statement was a datum of which all later exegetes had to take account. But, clearly, there was more to it than that.

Among the early exegetes, speakers of languages other than Arabic would certainly have noticed the similarity between words in the Qurʾān and their own languages. A number of Persian words were identified, often correctly in the judgment of contemporary scholarship, probably as a result of personal knowledge of the language (although the morphological structure of Persian words conveyed in Arabic also frequently makes them stand out as compared to words from neighboring Semitic languages). Another factor would be words that were known from other languages and whose meaning as used in the Qurʾān was such as to suggest a relationship between the qurʾānic usage and the foreign language. This may have occurred because the meaning of the Arabic root would not support such a usage: *dīn* as both "religion" and "day of reckoning" may be an example. Another example may be the way in which al-Zamakhsharī (d. 538/1144; *Kashshāf*, ad loc.) and following him al-Bayḍāwī (d. ca. 691/1291; *Anwār*, ad loc.) treat *ṣalawāt* in Q 22:40 as meaning a Jewish place of worship and judge this to be an Arabized version derived from *ṣalūtā*. These observations would have been derived from Muslim knowledge of Semitic languages other than Arabic.

This is a topic that has been studied in some detail by Ramzi Baalbaki in his "Early Arab lexicographers and the use of Semitic languages." Syriac — referred to as *suryānī* or *nabaṭī* (with the latter perhaps referring to a specific Eastern Aramaic dialect) — was well known as a spoken language according to anecdotes found in the works of Ibn Qutayba (d. 276/889) and Ibn Durayd (d. 321/933). The association of Syriac with Christianity is clear in the work of al-Bīrūnī (d. ca. 442/1050). The same may be said for Hebrew (*ʿibrī* or *ʿibrānī*) and Judaism, for which al-Bīrūnī is able to provide a reasonably accurate system of transliterating the language into Arabic. Baalbaki also suggests that there appears to have been an awareness of the relationship between these languages and Arabic. He claims, for example, that Ibn Ḥazm (d. 456/1064) makes his understanding of the relationship explicit, although whether it is possible to equate Ibn Ḥazm's observations with genuine linguistic reflection is still open to debate: Ibn Ḥazm speaks of the language of Abraham being Syriac; of Isaac, Hebrew; and of Ishmael, Arabic. It seems doubtful, however, that, in noting the genealogical relationship, Ibn Ḥazm is saying anything about the relationship of the languages as such.

It has frequently been noted that, among the classical Arab grammarians, lexicographers and exegetes, there were many who had a language other than Arabic, either as their mother tongue or as the language of their religious upbringing. It has always been suspected, therefore, that knowledge of this kind was brought to the study of "loan words" in Arabic, a topic of some interest both within the exegesis of the Qurʾān and in general lexicography. As a branch of Arabic lexicography, words which had been "Arabized," *muʿarrab* (see Fischer, Muʿarrab) were studied on the basis of the movement between languages in pre-Islamic and early Islamic times. The book by al-Jawālīqī (d. 539/1144), *Kitāb al-Muʿarrab min al-kalām al-aʿjamī ʿalā ḥurūf al-muʿjam* ("Arabized words coming from foreign languages organized alphabetically"), is the most renowned of its kind in the realm of general lexicography. He traced much of his material back to famous early exegetes and grammarians such as Abū ʿUbayd (d. 224/838), Abū Ḥātim al-Sijistānī (d. 255/869) and Ibn Durayd and, in a significant number of cases (although primarily non-qurʾānic ones), their opinions as to the source of words agrees with that of modern philologists, a fact which suggests a good measure of knowledge of the non-Arabic languages.

Another factor that prompted attention to foreign words was the rise of grammatical studies in Arabic because these led to understandings about the form of Arabic words which, in turn, then indicated the aberrance (by Arabic standards) of some words found in the Qurʾān. These would include examples of difficult morphological structures and irregular phonetic features as found in words such as *istabraq* (Persian for "silk brocade," Q 18:31; 44:53;

55:54; 76:21), *zanjabīl* ("ginger," Q 76:17), *barzakh* ("barrier," Q 23:100; 25:53; 55:20; see BARRIER; BARZAKH), *firdaws* ("paradise," Q 18:107; 23:11) and *namāriq* ("cushions," Q 88:15). Another form of these considerations would be identifying words from barren roots such as *tannūr* ("oven," Q 11:40; 23:27), *jibt* ("idol," Q 4:51) and *raḥīq* ("wine," Q 83:25). The isolation of these features as "aberrant" depended, of course, upon the establishment of a set of criteria which could act to define Arabic as such, criteria that were developed by early grammarians like Sībawayh (d. ca. 180/796) and al-Khalīl (d. ca. 160/776) in their fixation, for example, of the permissible morphological forms of Arabic words. Certain combinations of letters which could not occur in Arabic words were also determined and these acted as yet another criterion. Among the observations cited in al-Suyūṭī's (d. 911/1505) *al-Muzhir* (i, 270), the following examples are typical: a word cannot start with a *nūn* followed by a *rā*ʾ; a word cannot end in a *zā*ʾ preceded by a *dāl;* a *ṣād* and a *jīm* cannot occur in the same word; and a *jīm* and a *qāf* cannot be found in the same word. Words which violate these rules are deemed to be "foreign." Finally *hapax legomena* and other infrequently used words were also among the likely candidates for inclusion in lists of foreign words (even in some cases where the origin of the word does seem to be Arabic).

The theory of foreign words in the Qurʾān

Such observations about particular qurʾānic words must also be seen within the context of the controversies which surrounded the theoretical problem that Muslims, both past and present, clearly perceive to underlie the issue of foreign vocabulary in the Qurʾān: is it even possible that such vocabulary was included in the text when, by the testimony of the text itself, the Qurʾān is in Arabic which is clear and non-foreign?

To the early philologist Abū ʿUbayda (d. 208/824) is ascribed the statement, "Whoever suggests there is anything other than the Arabic language in the Qurʾān has made a serious charge against God" (Abū ʿUbayda, *Majāz,* i, 17-8; quoted in Jawālīqī, *Muʿarrab,* 4). This appears to have been a widespread sentiment in the formative centuries of Islam. Abū ʿUbayda clearly recognized the existence of a similarity between certain words in foreign languages and those in the Qurʾān. He states, "The form of a word [in one language] can correspond *(yuwāfiq)* to the form in another and its meaning [in one language] can approach that of another language, whether that be between Arabic and Persian or some other language" (*Majāz,* i, 17). Gilliot (*Elt,* 97) has pointed out that Abū ʿUbayda's argument insists upon the contemporary Arabic character of the qurʾānic language. That assumption, the basis of his hermeneutical approach to the text allows Abū ʿUbayda to support the use of secular language to help explain the Qurʾān. But, for Abū ʿUbayda, it excludes any sense of "foreignness" in the language. The "challenge," issued to the Arabs in the so-called *taḥaddī* verses, to imitate the Qurʾān would be meaningless if the Qurʾān depended upon foreign vocabulary. Al-Shāfiʿī (d. 204/820) suggested that no one knew (or knows) the entire stock of Arabic, so what might be thought of as "foreign" to one group of Arabs was, in fact, known to others:

Of all tongues, that of the Arabs is the richest and the most extensive in vocabulary. Do we know any man except a prophet who apprehended all of it? However, no portion of it escapes everyone, so that there is always someone who knows it. Knowledge [of this tongue] to the Arabs is like the knowledge of the *sunna* to the jurists *(fuqahāʾ)*: We know of no one who possesses a knowledge of all the *sunna* without missing a portion of it.... In like manner is the [knowledge concerning the] tongue of the Arabs by the scholars and the public: No part of it will be missed by them all, nor should it be sought from other [people]; for no one can learn [this tongue] save he who has learned it from [the Arabs]... (*Risāla*, 27-8; English trans. 88-9).

At the same time, al-Shāfiʿī admitted that there may be:

in foreign tongues certain words, whether acquired or transmitted, which may be similar *(yuwāfiq)* to those of the Arab tongue, just as some words in one foreign tongue may be similar to those in others, although these [tongues are spoken in] separate countries and are different and unrelated to one another despite the similarity of some of the words (*Risāla*, 28; English trans. 90).

Thus, while similarities may exist, they are there simply by coincidence and not because of a relationship between the words. Al-Shāfiʿī's position is one that concurs with his legal reasoning: the knowledge of the Arabs in language is a part of "tradition" which must form the basis of Muslim society. The study of language, like the use of reason in law, has its place, but it must always come second in significance and authority to traditional knowledge.

Abū ʿUbayd (d. 224/838), on the other hand, argued that words of foreign origin are to be found in the Qurʾān but they had been incorporated into Arabic well before the revelation of the Qurʾān and are thus to be considered Arabic. Furthermore, the nature of the Arabic usage of such words is superior to their usage as found in other languages (Gilliot, *Elt*, 98-9). Al-Ṭabarī (d. 311/923) provided another response to the problem, although the view may well not originate with him: words which appear to be foreign simply reflect a similarity between languages and that says nothing about the historical origins of the words. This idea is reflected in the above-quoted statement attributed to Ibn ʿAbbās (but which clearly originates at a later time): that words "coincide" (*ittafaqa* in Ṭabarī; *wāfaqa* in Ibn ʿAbbās) between languages. Al-Ṭabarī finally argues in favor of a position which suggests that certainty in these matters cannot be obtained; it can never be known for sure whether a word started in one language or another. Of the person who says, "[these words] were originally Arabic, and then spread and became current in Persian," or "they were originally Persian and then spread to the Arabs and were Arabized," al-Ṭabarī states:

[We should deem this person to be] unlearned, because the Arabs have no more right to claim that the origin of an expression lies with them rather than with the Persians than the Persians to claim the origin lies with them rather than the Arabs. [The only certain fact is that] the expression is employed with the same wording and the same meaning by two linguistic groups (Ṭabarī, *Tafsīr*, i, 15; id., *The commentary*, 14).

Such arguments were used in a variety of apologetic writings about the merits of the Qurʾān. Arguments to support the inimitability (q.v.) of the Qurʾān were reinforced by denying that any special words were introduced by Muḥammad. Ultimately, the point was a theological one tied to conceptions of the nature of Arabic as a language and Islam as divine revelation. To admit that there were foreign words in the Qurʾān that had been intentionally borrowed would undermine the meaning of the challenge put forth to the masters of Arabic speech to produce a chapter of text which was "like" the Qurʾān.

Still, for some people, especially in later centuries, the idea of "foreign" vocabulary was not denied. Al-Jawālīqī (*Muʿarrab*, 3), for example, speaks openly about "foreign words found in the speech of the ancient Arabs and employed in the Qurʾān" without any cautious restrictions. Al-Suyūṭī's works (discussed below in the next section) take the incorporation of foreign languages in the Qurʾān as a positive fact, the result, perhaps, of the increasing realization of the universal appeal of Islam and certainly taken as a part of the argument for the excellent qualities of the text. Contemporary writers — ranging from scholars such as Muḥammad Shākir (the editor of al-Jawālīqī's text) to Internet polemicists — have tended to return to the earlier positions, however, seeing the denial of foreign words as an important point in the "defense" of the Qurʾān.

Muslim treatises on foreign words in the Qurʾān

The observation that there are foreign words in the Qurʾān is found in the earliest texts of qurʾānic exegesis. In the *tafsīr* of Muqātil b. Sulaymān (d. 150/767), for example, the words *qisṭās* and *firdaws* are attributed to Greek, *istabraq* to Persian, *ḥūb* to Ethiopic, *yamm* to Hebrew, *maqālīd* to Nabataean, and *ṭāḥā* to Syriac. Proper names are also provided with foreign etymologies, Mūsā being Coptic and Nūḥ being Syriac. Similar observations may be made for the approach taken by other early works of *tafsīr* (see Versteegh, *Grammar and exegesis*, 89-90).

Various genres of early specialized exegetical works contain elements that contribute to the isolation of foreign vocabulary, building towards the construction of lists of such words. One example is found in dictionaries of the Qurʾān, the earliest form of which is essentially a compilation of lexical glosses to the text. Works devoted to *gharīb*, "difficult passages (q.v.)," manifest a conception of "difficulty" that is conceived in a variety of ways: foreign words, dialect words, bedouin words or lexical oddities are all included. Ibn Qutayba occasionally cites the foreign origins of words which he conceives to have become Arabized, as in the case of *istabraq* in Q 18:31 and *qisṭās* in Q 17:35 (*Gharīb*, 267, 254). The treatment by Abū Bakr al-Sijistānī (d. 330/942) of *istabraq* and *qisṭās* in his *Nuzhat al-qulūb fī gharīb al-Qurʾān* (p. 35 [for *istabraq*], 161 [for *qisṭās*, s.v. *qusṭās*]) is identical to that of Ibn Qutayba. Curiously, the same does not hold for the most famous book of its type, al-Rāghib al-Iṣfahānī's (d. 502/1108) *Muʿjam mufradāt alfāẓ al-Qurʾān*: it simply ignores any speculation about foreign words.

A work likely stemming from the fourth/tenth century but attributed to Ibn ʿAbbās, *al-Lughāt fī l-Qurʾān*, provides a listing not only of foreign words but also of Arab tribal dialects found in the Qurʾān. As Versteegh has commented, this list is designed to fulfil the exegetical function of connecting the language of scripture to the *ʿarabiyya* (Versteegh, *Grammar and exegesis*, 91; see ARABIC LANGUAGE). This work considers some twenty-four words (out of a total of over three hundred words treated in the text) to be related to foreign languages, including Aramaic/Nabataean, Syriac, Ethiopic, Persian, Hebrew, Coptic and Greek/Latin.

It is with Jalāl al-Dīn al-Suyūṭī, who died in 911/1505, that full lists of "foreign words in the Qurʾān" become significant. Al-Suyūṭī quotes (*Itqān*, ii, 119-20) two poems, one written by Ibn al-Subkī (d. 771/1369) and the other by Ibn Ḥajar (d. 852/1449) as representing previous efforts to compile all the foreign qurʾānic words together. But both of these works, al-Suyūṭī notes, did not reach the comprehensiveness of his own efforts. Al-Suyūṭī himself wrote at least two separate works and also incorporated the material into several other of his larger treatises (as well as treating the subject on a theoretical level in his *al-Muzhir fī ʿulūm al-lugha wa-anwāʿihā*). One work is called *al-Mutawakkilī fīmā warada fī l-Qurʾān bi-l-lughāt, mukhtaṣar fī muʿarrab al-Qurʾān,* a treatise named after the caliph al-Mutawakkil II ʿAbd al-ʿAzīz al-Mustaʿīn (d. 903/1497), who commanded that the learned author compile a list of qurʾānic words that are "to be found in the speech of the Ethiopians, the Persians or any people other than the Arabs." This list, al-Suyūṭī says, was extracted from his longer book *Masālik al-ḥunafāʾ fī wāliday al-Muṣṭafā.* Within the list, there are 108 words attributed to eleven languages and they are organized according to language and, within that organization, according to the textual order of the Qurʾān.

Al-Suyūṭī's second work, *al-Muhadhdhab fīmā waqaʿa fī l-Qurʾān min al-muʿarrab,* is arranged according to the alphabetical order of the words themselves. More variant opinions are given in the book than in the *Mutawakkilī* (that is, a given word is likely to be attributed to more than one language), although some words are termed simply "foreign" without a specific language from which they are thought to derive being specified. Al-Suyūṭī's *al-Itqān fī ʿulūm al-Qurʾān* also contains a chapter (number 38) on "foreign vocabulary." There, he makes reference to his *Muhadhdhab,* but not to *al-Mutawakkilī,* so it is likely that the former work, *al-Muhadhdhab,* was written first. While the lists in *al-Itqān* and *al-Muhadhdhab* are not identical, they are extremely close, both being arranged according to the alphabetical order of the words. 118 words are listed in *al-Itqān* and 124 in *al-Muhadhdhab,* but the content of the entries is clearly related and the overlap between the two works is almost complete.

Al-Suyūṭī is often viewed simply as a compiler of material. His re-use of material is certainly a notable characteristic which is observable within the large corpus of his works; the fact is also demonstrated by the existence of these three books that bring together similar material in slightly different organizational patterns. But al-Suyūṭī also participates fully within an attribute of the mature Muslim exegetical tradition which Norman Calder has termed "fundamentally acquisitive" by nature (Calder, Tafsīr, 133). The material which al-Suyūṭī presents in his lists of foreign words has been culled from many sources and, on numerous occasions, contains within itself in an unresolved manner substantial differences of opinion on many items. A considerable number of these words are cited as "foreign" within earlier exegetical works, and the act of collating all of these citations, as al-Suyūṭī has done, has produced a stock of vocabulary deemed to be "foreign" which remains relatively constant. Exegetes such as al-Suyūṭī frequently cite the foreignness of a given word with very little elaboration about why or how it should be considered so; the nature of the "acquisitive" tradition is such that the foreign status of a word is an element of exegesis which is accepted without necessarily any questioning. A major factor in this is the power of tradition. The acquisitive nature of the exegetical tradition has meant that nothing could be thrown away (at least, up to the time of Ibn Kathīr in the eighth/fourteenth century, as Calder has argued).

The exegetical conception of foreign languages

Of the words to be found in the lists of words Muslim scholars considered to be foreign, some appear to be common Arabic words. Trying to understand why these were deemed "foreign" sheds light on the entire category of foreign words and on how the designation itself has hermeneutical significance.

Arabic words which are classified as "foreign" make one immediately suspect that it must have been an exegetical problem which led to the suggestion of the foreignness of the word, as Arthur Jeffery argued in his work, *The foreign vocabulary of the Qurʾān.* The hermeneutical advantage is clear: if the word is foreign, then it is open to a far greater interpretational variation than if the word is to be taken as a common Arabic word.

The determination of the language to which a given "foreign" word belongs is also of particular interest. In specifying the non-Arabic language from which a given word might be thought to originate, Muslim exegetes seem to have incorporated two elements into their procedures: (1) some knowledge of foreign languages and (2) typical Muslim exegetical tools. At times, the combination of these two elements resulted in what must have appeared, even to the exegetes themselves, to be intuitively "wrong" designations.

It is also clear, however, that on occasion, the classical Muslim sources are at a loss in attempting to identify the source of a foreign word. This may be seen in two ways. First, one encounters the attribution of words to a language for which there are absolutely no historical or linguistic grounds on which to establish such a relationship. Secondly, apparent relationships are ignored even though this raises the questions of why, if the exegetes had a knowledge of the language in question (as Baalbaki's discussions make clear they did), they ignored the apparent source.

The explanation for these two situations, at least as they apply to the situation of qurʾānic vocabulary, lies in exegetical procedures and their importance, and in the development of *tafsīr* as an enterprise (see EXEGESIS OF THE QURʾĀN: CLASSICAL AND MEDIEVAL). Part of the explanation lies in the fact that the original suggestion that a certain word was foreign may have been made by those who did *not* know the language in question. When those who might have known better came along, it was not possible to reject the traditions which conveyed such opinions. It is worth pointing out, however, that the concept of the acquisitive tradition cannot simply be equated with the inherited stock of works of *tafsīr;* in a significant number of cases, no evidence of the traditions in earlier works of *tafsīr* can be found, even though such traditions are included in the lists of al-Suyūṭī, for example. The explanation for this may reside in the fact that earlier works which did contain these traditions have not come down to us, or it may be that these traditions were more a part of the living, popular Islam than of the recorded intellectual tradition and only become incorporated into "official" Islam at a late date.

Some specifics may help clarify this point. For example, while it appears to have been known that the Jewish Bible was written in Hebrew, the language of the biblical characters mentioned in the Qurʾān does not seem to have been connected to Hebrew very often. In al-Suyūṭī's *Mutawakkilī,* only nineteen words are cited as possibly being Hebrew and seven of those are cited in a manner which clearly indicates that al-Suyūṭī did not consider these claims to have much support. Other languages, such as Syriac and Coptic, seem to be more significant. This suggests that the ideas surrounding the languages from which "foreign" words were thought to originate were dictated to some extent by the *spoken* foreign languages known to the Arabs, suggesting a non-historical view of the world: that is, that the language spoken by a group of people in the present was the language they had always spoken.

There seem to be other factors at play as well. Certain common Arabic words (*taḥta* meaning "within" rather than "under" in Q 19:24; *baṭāʾin* referring to "outer" surfaces rather than "inner" ones in Q 55:54; *ūlā* meaning "last" instead of "first" in Q 33:33; *ākhira* meaning "former" instead of "latter" in Q 38:7) are attributed to Coptic when the words take on meanings that are contrary to their common Arabic designation. This may lead to the speculation that for Arabic speakers Coptic played a cultural role as a language of deception; there may well be a larger social picture behind this, namely of an image of Copts as deceptive in their dealings with Muslims and as twisting the Arabic language to their own advantage.

Likewise, the attribution of a number of words to Greek seems to convey certain cultural assumptions rather than specific linguistic knowledge. For example, the following words are commonly attributed to Greek: *qisṭ*, "justice"; *qisṭās*, "scales"; *ṣirāṭ*, "road"; and *qinṭār*, "hundred weight." It is noteworthy that while, in a number of instances, modern philology agrees with the judgments of early Muslim scholars about certain words being derived ultimately from Greek, that coincidence does not necessarily indicate linguistic knowledge. The idea that these words come from Greek does not, in fact, account historically for the presence of the words in Arabic. In no instance is it likely that the word passed directly into Arabic from Greek. It is far more likely that Aramaic or Syriac (possibly through Arabian or Syrian Christians; see CHRISTIANS AND CHRISTIANITY) was the conduit for the transmission of the Greek words. In a number of cases, Greek is not even the ultimate source; rather, the words are Latin and have moved into the Middle Eastern languages through their Hellenized forms during times of Greek administrative rule. The fact that Muslim exegetes decided that these words are Greek, therefore, is unlikely to be the result of observations of linguistic parallels or of linguistic knowledge. Such specification is more likely based upon observations of the non-Arabic nature of the words combined with speculations involving certain cultural assumptions about the nature of other societies in the past (and perhaps the present) — in this instance, the association of the Greek world with the marketplace (see Rippin, Designation of "foreign" languages, for further examples of this hypothesis).

Foreign vocabulary and the Qurʾān in modern scholarship

The Euro-American interest in the vocabulary of the Qurʾān has a long history and reflects a number of differing motivations. Ordinarily, the question of foreign vocabulary has been raised in an attempt to determine the sources of the Qurʾān. An assessment of the lineage of the Qurʾān in terms of its religious debt to its forerunners was approached through the question of vocabulary: if it could be demonstrated that the majority of technical terms within the Qurʾān were traceable to a particular source — be that Jewish, Christian, Jewish-Christian or Zoroastrian — then a likely context could be established for the overall development of the Qurʾān and Islam, at least in the opinion of some scholars. Such an approach would also allow for a determination of the unique elements of the Qurʾān by seeing where the shifts in vocabulary had occurred when words were compared to their etymological sources. The work of Abraham Geiger, which marks the beginning of the modern Euro-American study of the Qurʾān, bases an initial part of its argument on "the words which have passed from Rabbinical Hebrew into the Qurʾān, and so into the Arabic language" (Geiger, *Judaism and Islam*, 31), in order to respond to the question, as the German title of his book has it, "What did Muḥammad borrow from Judaism?" More contemporary studies differ very little from this original orientation because the task of understanding the Qurʾān must always revolve around trying to establish the historical and linguistic context within which the Qurʾān is to be read. The sense in which even some individual words are to be understood will differ depending on whether one conceives them as having been transmitted from Jewish or Christian sources. Overall, Arthur Jeffery's statement seems to sum up the fundamental impulse:

"This religion as he [Muḥammad] insists over and over again in the Qurʾān, is something new to the Arabs: it was not likely, therefore, that native Arabic vocabulary would be adequate to express all its new ideas, so the obvious policy was to borrow and adapt the necessary technical terms" (Jeffery, *For. vocab.*, 38).

An additional motivation for the study of foreign vocabulary has emerged from the study of Arabic as a source of comparative Semitic linguistic data. Many of the famous names of Islamic Studies from the nineteenth century — Nöldeke, Bergsträsser, Brockelmann — were also significant figures in comparative studies. The need was apparent from the beginning, therefore, to clarify the transmission of some terms into Arabic from other Semitic languages in order to avoid anachronistic use of the Arabic data in the attempt to deal with other languages (the continued influence of the Qurʾān on the Arabic lexicographical tradition, so ably demonstrated by the works of Lothar Kopf, indicates some of the potential pitfalls; on the general problem of Arabic as a source of meaning, see Barr, *Comparative philology*, and Kaltner, *Arabic in biblical Hebrew*). The role of Arabic as a language which could serve to clarify the meaning of obscure words in the Hebrew Bible, perhaps first evidenced in scholarship in the work of A. Schultens (1686-1750), has only recently been somewhat displaced by the more newly discovered material available in Akkadian and Ugaritic. Of course, there remains the problem of whether Arabic maintains a proto-Semitic meaning or has borrowed a sense from another language, thus accounting for similarities (see Margoliouth, Additions, 55-6).

This philological impulse has seen its flowering in the treatment of proper names in the Qurʾān; tracing the original language behind the form of the names of various biblical characters (see SCRIPTURE AND THE QURʾĀN) was thought to have established likely paths of transmission of stories into the Arab culture of pre-Islamic times. It is notable that the Muslim exegetes did not, for the most part, worry themselves about the "foreignness" of the names found in the Qurʾān, whether they be the names of people or the names of scriptures. This point makes clear that there are substantially different presuppositions and aims separating contemporary scholarship and medieval Muslim exegesis in their approaches to the topic. Commenting on Q 3:3, "He sent down the Torah (q.v.) and the Gospel (q.v.)," Fakhr al-Dīn al-Rāzī (d. 606/1209) sets forth various explanations which classical philologists have provided regarding the Arabic etymologies of *tawrāt* and *injīl*. Ultimately he dismisses the exercise as absurd:

"Torah" and "Gospel" are two foreign nouns, one of them from Hebrew, the other from Syriac. How is it appropriate for an intelligent person to study their adaptation to the patterns of the Arabic language? (Rāzī, *Tafsīr*, vii, 160).

Scholarship of the nineteenth and twentieth centuries, then, has established a fairly firm foundation for the study of qurʾānic vocabulary through the procedure of etymological derivation. Current contributions tend to focus on individual words, providing some refinement and clarification on smaller points. For the most part, however, the enterprise remains as contentious within modern scholarship as it was for medieval Muslims. The wide variety of postulated sources for the words considered to be of foreign origin has made it hazardous to suggest a single likely cultural focus for the background to the qurʾānic worldview. While many of the words studied have been shown to have a Jewish origin in terms of religious technical vocabulary, their vehicle of transmission more often seems to have been Christian Syriac (see LUXENBERG, *Die syro-aramäische Lesart des Koran*).

The scholarly work which has been completed on foreign vocabulary also lays a basis for the construction of a modern dictionary of the Qurʾān. Even there, however, much modern linguistic theory would doubt the relevance of etymological procedures that underlie the approach of scholars such as Arthur Jeffery. The contemporary emphasis on dictionaries which concentrate on word usage rather than word origin means that, while the material on foreign origins can continue to provide information for a diachronic examination of Semitic (and other) words, it will likely no longer be considered the basis from which specialized lexicographical work should start. See also GRAMMAR AND THE QURʾĀN; LANGUAGE OF THE QURʾĀN.

Andrew Rippin

Bibliography

Primary: Abū ʿUbayda, *Majāz;* Bayḍāwī, *Anwār;* Ibn Abbās, *al-Lughāt fī l-Qurʾān*, ed. Ṣ. al-Dīn al-Munajjad, Beirut 1978; Ibn Ḥazm, *al-Iḥkām fī uṣūl al-aḥkām*, Cairo 1978; Ibn Kathir, *Tafsīr*, 4 vols., Cairo n.d.; Ibn Qutayba, *Gharīb*, Beirut 1978; Jawālīqī, *Muʿarrab;* al-Rāghib al-Iṣfahānī, *Mufradāt;* Rāzī, *Tafsīr*, Teheran n.d.; Shāfiʿī, Muḥammad b. Idrīs, *Al-Imām Muḥammad ibn Idris al-Shāfiʿī's al-Risāla*, Eng. trans. M. Khadduri, Baltimore 1961; id., *al-Risāla*, ed. M. Sayyid Kaylānī, Cairo 1983; Sijistānī, Abū Bakr Muḥammad b. ʿUthmān, *Nuzhat al-qulūb fī gharīb al-Qurʾān*, Beirut 1982; Suyūṭī, *Itqān;* id., *Muhadhdhab;* id., *The Mutawakkili of as-Suyuti*, ed. and trans. William Y. Bell, Cairo [1926]; id., *al-Muzhir fī ʿulūm al-lugha wa-anwāʿihā*, Cairo 1958 (also ed. M. Abū l-Faḍl Ibrāhīm et al., 2 vols., Beirut 1987); Ṭabarī, *Tafsīr*, ed. Shākir, Cairo 1955; id., *The commentary on the Qurʾān by Abū Jaʿfar Muḥammad b. Jarīr al-Ṭabarī*, trans. J. Cooper et al., Oxford 1987; Zamakhsharī, *Kashshāf*, Beirut 1947; Zarkashī, *Burhān*, ed. Cairo 1957, i, 287-90.

Secondary *(general studies):* R. Baalbaki, Early Arab lexicographers and the use of Semitic languages, in *Berytus* 31 (1983), 117-27; J. Barr, *Comparative philology and the text of the Old Testament*, Oxford 1968; Winona Lake 1987²; N. Calder, *Tafsīr* from Ṭabarī to Ibn Kathīr. Problems in the description of a genre. Illustrated with reference to the story of Abraham, in Hawting and Shareef, *Approaches*, 101-40; Gilliot, *Elt*, 95-110 (excellent overview of the topic and bibliography); A. Hebbo, *Die Fremdwörter in der arabischen Prophetenbiographie des Ibn Hischam (gest. 218/834)*, Frankfurt 1984 (good general bibliography); J. Kaltner, *The use of Arabic in biblical Hebrew lexicography*, Washington 1996; L. Kopf, Religious influences on medieval Arabic philology, in *SI* 5 (1956), 33-59; repr. in id., *Studies in Arabic and Hebrew lexicography*, Jerusalem 1976, 19-45; id., The treatment of foreign words in medieval Arabic lexicology, in *Scripta Hierosolymitana* 9 (1961), 191-205; repr. in id., *Studies in Arabic and Hebrew lexicography*, Jerusalem 1976, 247-61; A. Rippin, The designation of "foreign" languages in the exegesis of the Qurʾān, in J.D. McAuliffe et al., *With reverence for the word. Medieval scriptural exegesis in Judaism, Christianity and Islam*, Oxford forthcoming; id., Ibn ʿAbbas's *al-Lughāt fī'l-Qurʾān*, in *BSOAS* 44 (1981), 15-25; id., Lexicographical texts, in Rippin, *Approaches*, 158-74; A. Schall, Geschichte des arabischen Wortschatzes, Lehn- und Fremdwörter im Klassichen Arabisch, in W. Fischer, *Grundriss der Arabischen Philologie. Band I. Sprachwissenschaft*, Wiesbaden 1982, 142-53; C.H.M. Versteegh, *Arabic grammar and Quranic exegesis*, Leiden 1993; Wansbrough, *QS*.

Secondary *(specific studies on qurʾānic foreign words):* R. Dvorák, *Ein Beitrag zur Frage über die Fremdwörter im Koran*, Munich 1884; id., *Über die Fremdwörter im Koran*, Vienna 1885; W. Fischer,

Muʿarrab, in EI^{2}, vii, 261-2; S. Fraenkel, *De Vocabulis in antiques Arabum carminibus et in Corano peregrines,* Leiden 1880; A. Geiger, *Judaism and Islam,* Madras 1898 (English trans. of *Was hat Mohammed aus dem Judenthume aufgenommen?*); id., *Was hat Mohammed aus dem Judenthume aufgenommen?* Baden 1833; H. Grimme, Über einige Klassen südarabischer Lehnwörter im Qoran, in *Zeitschrift für Assyriologie und verwandte Gebiete* 26 (1912), 158-68; J. Horovitz, Jewish proper names and derivatives in the Koran, in *Hebrew Union College annual* 2 (1925), 145-227; id., KU; Jeffery, *For. vocab.* (standard reference work with full bibliography); C. Luxenberg, *Die syro-aramäische Lesart des Koran. Ein Beitrag zur Entschlüsselung der Koransprache,* Berlin 2000; D.S. Margoliouth, Some additions to Professsor Jeffery's *Foreign vocabulary of the Qurʾān,* in JRAS (1939), 53-61; A. Mingana, Syriac influence on the style of the Ḳurʾān, in *Bulletin of the John Rylands Library* 11 (1927), 77-98; Th. Nöldeke, Willkürlich und missverständlich gebrauchte Fremdwörter im Korān, in id., *Neue Beiträge zur semitischen Sprachwissenschaft,* Strassburg 1910, 23-30; A. Siddiqi, *Studien über die persischen Fremdwörter im klassichen Arabisch,* Göttingen 1919; G. Widengren, Iranian elements in the ḳurʾānic vocabulary, in id., *Muhammad Apostle of God and his ascension,* Uppsala 1955, 178-98; M.R. Zammit, *A comparative lexical study of qurʾānic Arabic. Handbook of Oriental Studies. Section 1. The Near and Middle East. vol. 61,* Leiden 2002.

Foretelling in the Qurʾān

The interpretation of omens or inspired or mystic knowledge of what will occur. Leaving aside prophecy (*nubuwwa,* see PROPHETS AND PROPHETHOOD), which is clairvoyance of a different order and deserves to be treated separately, the Qurʾān and ḥadīth mention a great number of procedures used for penetrating the secrets of God and foreseeing the human fate (q.v.; see also HIDDEN AND THE HIDDEN). As in the case of divination (q.v.), foretelling connotes an association with pre-Islamic paganism (see PRE-ISLAMIC ARABIA AND THE QURʾĀN). A prayer is attributed to the Prophet which seems to legitimize recourse to such procedures: "My God," so he prays, "there is no ill omen *(ṭayr)* but the one that you allow *(illā ṭayruka),* there is no good omen *(khayr khayr)* but yours, there is no God but you and no might and power but in you" (Ibn Qutayba, *ʿUyūn,* ii, 146, who attributes it to Ibn ʿAbbās; Ibn Saʿd, *Ṭabaqāt,* iv, 2, 13, who attributes it to ʿAbdallāh b. ʿAmr b. al-ʿĀṣ; Ibn ʿAbd Rabbihi, *ʿIqd,* i, 397; Ibshīhī, *al-Mustaṭraf,* ii, 181 cited in Fahd, *Divination,* 437, n. 5).

The attention devoted to clairvoyance, foreseeing and foretelling in Islamic literature is considerable. In the second part of T. Fahd's *La divination arabe,* foretelling is classified according to the following procedures: 1) divination by lots (cleromancy, pp. 179-245), 2) divination by dreams (oneiromancy, pp. 247-367), 3) physiognomic (pp. 369-429), and 4) omens (pp. 431-519). The topic to be treated here is the possible appearance of such procedures in the Qurʾān and their explanation in ḥadīth and exegetical commentary (*tafsīr,* see ḤADĪTH AND THE QURʾĀN; EXEGESIS OF THE QURʾĀN: CLASSICAL AND MEDIEVAL).

Cleromantic procedures

Pre-Islamic Arabs used various cleromantic techniques to probe the will of the divinity, some of which are explicitly condemned in the Qurʾān on account of their pagan character: *al-istiqsām bi-l-azlām* (cf. Q 5:3, 90) and *maysir* (Q 2:219; 5:90-91). The Qurʾān is silent on two other procedures (although it is attested that the Prophet made use of them): *al-ḍarb bi-l-qidāḥ,* which indicates all other forms of lottery, and *al-qurʿa,* which designates drawing lots.

a) *al-istiqsām bi-l-azlām.* This qurʾānic expression indicates belomancy, i.e. "divining arrows," as practised in Arab sanctuaries. It designates more specifically the sacred arrows of Hubal in the Kaʿba (q.v.), those of Dhū-l-Khalaṣa in Tabāla (cf. Fahd, *Panthéon,* 95 f. and 61 f.), and those that the nomads (q.v.) took along with their holy stones in their migrations. They were sticks that were shaken in a sack or quiver and not arrows to be shot. They apparently were part of the cultic baggage for which the soothsayer (*kāhin*, see SOOTHSAYERS) of the nomadic tribes and the custodian *(sādin)* of the sanctuaries were responsible (cf. the Hebrew *qosēm*, *Num* 22:7; *Deut* 18: 10, 14; *Isa* 3:2; *Jer* 19:8-9). The sack that contained them had to be attached to the holy stone or somehow included with the priest's attire in the manner of the Urīm and Tumīm with the Hebrew nomads, which formed an integral part of the ephod (i.e. high priest's garment) at all stages of its evolution (cf. Fahd, *Divination*, 138 f.).

As with all cleromantic procedures, belomancy consists in leaving to chance the task of revealing the will or the thought of the divinity. The answer is obtained in two different ways: a) by asking the question explicitly, to which the divinity replies with "yes" or "no" and b) by successive elimination, as one singles out, for example, a culprit in a crowd. In such a manner Saul (q.v.) discovered that his son, Jonathan (q.v.), had violated a prohibition (*I Sam* 14:37 f.). A further example of belomancy is the collection of a set of symbolic signs, each of which corresponds to a group of ideas (adversity, woman, war, etc.), expressing more or less vaguely all possible eventualities in a given situation. Thus, an ideal world in miniature is constructed, a sort of microcosm in which the events correspond to those in the real world and which, consequently, enable these to be foreseen or divined (Février, *Histoire de l'écriture*, 509).

The development of belomancy among the Arabs (q.v.) finally led to ever more precise designations being ascribed to the arrows, so as to leave no doubts about the answer of the oracle. To the primitive arrows, which only bore mention of the words "yes" or "no," "good" or "bad," "do" or "don't," were added other arrows that bore precise announcements related to the circumstances, like "leave (for a journey)," "don't leave," "(act) immediately," "wait," "take one's turn at the water," "being of pure descent," "not being so," "pay off the blood price (see BLOOD MONEY)," etc. Blank arrows (without inscriptions) were given precise meanings according to the occasion, as explicitly agreed upon between the *sādin* and his consultants. Thus, every dispute could be resolved, thanks to the oracle of shaken arrows. It should be noted, however, that the abundance of designations given to the arrows of Hubal contrasts widely with the sobriety of the belomantic oracle of Dhū l-Khalaṣa, who only knew "imperative *(āmir)*," "prohibitive *(nāhī)*" and "expectative *(mutarabbiṣ)*." See Fahd's *La divination arabe* (185 f.) for the use of these oracles during the lifetime of the Prophet.

b) The *maysir* or game of chance (see GAMBLING) is a cleromantic procedure of pagan character, and the fact that it is condemned in the Qur᾿ān, along with *istiqsām* and *anṣāb* (Q 5:90), suggests its relation to idolatry (see IDOLATRY AND IDOLATERS). The *maysir* is, however, also prohibited twice along with wine (Q 2:219; 5:91; see INTOXICANTS), on the grounds that, though they have their advantages, they constitute a grave transgression (see BOUNDARIES AND PRECEPTS; PROHIBITED DEGREES) and are an instrument in the hands of the demon (see DEVIL) who can make use of them to sow enmity and hatred among the faithful, in order to keep them from praying and calling upon God.

The fact that *maysir* and wine are considered to be transgressions (sing. *ithm*, see SIN, MAJOR AND MINOR) of the divine law suggests that their sinful character comes only from their association with the pagan cult. In fact, *maysir* had to be used to divide the meat of the sacrifice (q.v.; see also CONSECRATION OF ANIMALS), and wine could be linked to a Dionysiac cult among the Nabateans, whose inscriptions make mention of a certain number of divinities who reject wine libations (E. Littmann, Deux inscriptions religieuses de Palmyre, in *JA* 9 t. 18 [1901], 386, cited in Fahd, *Divination,* 205, n. 3), which made Wellhausen (in *Göttingische Gelehrte Anzeigen* 164 [1902], 269) remark: "Eigentlich trinken arabische Götter überhaupt keinen Wein" (quoted in Dussaud, *Pénétration,* 146, n. 3). Dussaud adds, "Seule la diffusion du christianisme amena les poètes arabes antéislamiques à chanter le vin" (ibid.). From this, one can suppose that wine was taboo, as was pork, probably a heritage of the Syrian cults (cf. Fahd, *Divination,* 205, n. 3). One opinion, attributed to the Yemenite Ṭāwūs b. Kaysān (d. 106/724), affirms that drinking wine [constitutes part] of the [rituals for] concluding the pilgrimage (q.v.; *ḥajj*), the Prophet doing so during his last pilgrimage (Ibn Saʿd, *Ṭabaqāt,* ii, 1, 131). For the sake of conformity to qurʾānic legislation, Islam let this custom fall into disuse.

Thus, it appears, although without definitive proof, that the prohibition of wine in Islam is related to idolatry. The fact that the prohibition includes the game of *maysir,* which, according to Doutté (*Magie et religion,* 375), "a certainement la même origine que l'*istiqsām,*" leads one to believe that the latter had something to do with idolatry as well. It is not, however, out of the question that the game of *maysir* gave rise to drinking sessions and that their simultaneous condemnation was a mere consequence of this fact (for the modalities of the game, see Fahd, *Divination,* 207 f.).

In general, cleromantic procedures of ancient Arabia were limited to *istiqsām* and *maysir,* and Islam was able to supplant these pagan procedures with more refined methods better adapted to the cultures of the conquered peoples, giving rise to many cleromantic techniques, discussion of which will be limited to *ṭarq bi-l-ḥaṣā,* an ancestor of geomancy, and *qurʿa,* or the drawing of lots, procedures that were in use at the time of the Prophet.

c) *Ṭarq bi-l-ḥaṣā* is described by Ibn al-Aʿrābī (d. ca. 231/846) in the following terms: "The *ḥāzī* sits down and lets a young boy at his service draw lines in the sand or in the dust; he traces them nimbly and promptly so as to make it impossible to count them. Then, on the order of his master, he erases them two by two while saying, 'You two, eyewitnesses of God's will, let the evidence quickly appear!' If, at the end, only two lines remain, it is a sign of success; if there is only one left, it is a sign of failure and misfortune" (quoted after al-Ālūsī, *Bulūgh al-arab,* iii, 323; cf. *Tāj al-ʿarūs,* v, 129, 11.13 f., s.v. *khaṭṭ*). The term *khaṭṭ,* eventually replaced by *ṭarq,* designates geomancy in its varied forms, as an ancient science that, in Islam, underwent considerable development. There is an allusion to it at Q 46:4, explained by al-Ṭabarī (d. 310/923) as follows: "Bring me the proof that your gods have created anything from the earth (q.v.) and that they have any part in the [creation (q.v.) of] the heavens (q.v.), [even if only] from the lines that you draw in the sand *(athārātin min ʿilm);* for you, the Arabs, have become masters in *ʿirāfa, zajr* and *kihāna*" (*Tafsīr,* xxvi, 3).

It is, however, attested in the ḥadīth as licit. Muʿāwiya said to the Prophet: "But there are among us, O messenger of God, men who practice the *khaṭṭ.*" The Prophet is said to have replied to him: "It is said that there was one among the prophets who practiced the *khaṭṭ;* whoever will succeed in doing it according to his procedure will know what this prophet knew" (cf. Wensinck, *Concordance,* i, 40). It is perhaps here that one would have to look for the starting point of the phenomenal increase of geomantic procedures in the lands of Islam (see Fahd, *Divination*, 196 f.; id., Khaṭṭ).

d) *Qurʿa* or the drawing of lots. This is also a procedure that was widespread in Islam, particularly in its rhapsodomantic use, e.g. divination from isolated sentences taken haphazardly from inspired books like the Qurʾān and the ḥadīth in Islam, the Bible among the Christians, the poetry of Homer, Hesiod and Virgil among the Greeks and the Romans, or Ḥāfiẓ's *Dīwān* or Jalāl al-Dīn al-Rūmī's *Mathnāwī* with the Persians and the Turks.

The patronage of this practice is attributed to Jaʿfar b. Abī Ṭālib, who fell as a hero at the age of thirty-three in the battle of Muʾta in 8/629 (see EXPEDITIONS AND BATTLES). In the account of the departure for this battle, there is a rhapsodomantic foretelling that was not taken from him, but from one of his companions who had a premonition of his death at the moment of leaving, and mentioned a qurʾānic verse about hell (q.v.; cf. Q 19:71) that was pronounced by the Prophet (Ibn Isḥāq, *Sīra*, i, 791 f.; Ṭabarī, *Taʾrīkh*, i, 1610 f.; on this practice, see Fahd, *Divination*, 214 f.). Important here is that *qurʿa*, as the simple drawing of lots, was used by the Prophet to know which of his wives would accompany him on his incursions (Ṭabarī, *Taʾrīkh*, i, 1519; Ibn Saʿd, *Ṭabaqāt*, ii, 1, 78, 82, 83; see WIVES OF THE PROPHET).

It can thus be seen that there were two categories of cleromantic practice: one with an oracular character forbidden by the Qurʾān; and another that was fortuitious, which was tolerated.

Oneiromantic procedures

Oneiromancy, which occupies an important place in the civilizations of the ancient east, is well represented in the qurʾānic context. The sources have conserved numerous dreams of the Prophet himself, which marked out the great events that he experienced. The most important of these events was his ascension (q.v.; the *isrāʾ* and the *miʿrāj*). This was, according to Muʿāwiya b. Abī Sufyān, "a truthful dream that comes from God" (Ibn Isḥāq, *Sīra*, i, 265, l.16), an opinion confirmed by ʿĀʾisha (see ʿĀʾISHA BINT ABĪ BAKR), who said, "I have not noticed the absence of the Prophet's body, but God let his spirit travel during the night" (ibid., l.15).

This dream falls under the literary category of dreams of ascension out of and descent into hell, from which arose many writings relating to the ascensions of prophets (e.g. Abraham [q.v.], Moses [q.v.], Isaiah [q.v.], Baruch and Elijah [q.v.]; cf. Charles, *Apocrypha*, Index; Fahd, La visite de Mahomet aux enfers). Dreams of light (q.v.), announcing the birth of Muḥammad, also fit into a widespread tradition in the ancient East (see details in Fahd, *Divination*, 259 f.).

Before understanding the full light of the actual revelation, Muḥammad started with dreams that were qualified as truthful *(ruʾyā ṣādiqa)*. ʿĀʾisha reports that "the initiation of the messenger of God in prophecy [began] by truthful dreams. Every vision that he saw in his dreams was as clear as daybreak" (Ibn Isḥāq, *Sīra*, i, 151; Ibn Saʿd, *Ṭabaqāt*, ii, 2, 129). The Prophet himself said: "There is only one sign announcing prophecy and that is the dream; the Muslim sees it or it is seen for him" (Ibn Saʿd, loc. cit., 18); "it is, so it is rumored, one of the forty parts of prophecy" (Berakhōt, 57b, cited in Fahd, *Divination*, 267, n. 4).

Muḥammad's vocational awakening on Ḥirāʾ itself unites the triple call of Samuel's vocation and Ezekiel's inititation by absorption of the prophetic message (*Ezek* 2:8 f.; cf. *Jer* 5:10), and it goes through two stages: the first takes place during sleep, the second when awake. This is a typical example of the passage from dream to ecstatic trance (Ibn Isḥāq, *Sīra,* i, 152 f.; Fahd, *Divination,* 267-8).

The life of the Prophet (*sīra,* see SĪRA AND THE QURʾĀN) has retained a number of Muḥammad's dreams which reveal his thoughts. The typical example, which has evangelical reminiscences, is the Islamic form of the parable of the invited (cf. *Luke* 14:15-24; *Matt* 22:1-14) that the archangels Gabriel (q.v.) and Michael (q.v.) are said to have revealed to him in a dream (Ibn Saʿd, *Ṭabaqāt,* i, 1, 113); there the symbolic content and the interpretation are given conjointly, thus resembling the dreams of Joseph (q.v.; *Gen* 37: 5-8, 9-10; see also DREAMS AND SLEEP). The Babylonian Talmud compares these symbolic dreams to a sealed letter (Berakhōt, 55a).

The figure of Waraqa b. Nawfal can be likened, in relation to Muḥammad, to that of John the Baptist (q.v.) in relation to Jesus. His thankfulness to him is expressed in a dream (Ibn Isḥāq, *Sīra,* i, 153; Ibn Saʿd, *Ṭabaqāt,* i, 1, 130); his affection for ʿĀʾisha is revealed in another (Ibn Saʿd, *Ṭabaqāt,* 8, 44; Ibn Iṣḥāq, *Sīra,* i, 731-7); and his admiration for ʿUmar b. al-Khaṭṭāb (q.v.) in a third (Ibn Isḥāq, *Sīra,* i, 270; Ibn al-Athīr, *Usd,* iv, 62, 64).

Muḥammad's preoccupations as the founder of a religion and the chief of a community appear, for example, in the institution of the call to prayer (*adhān,* which was brought into being after a dream of ʿAbdallāh b. Zayd (Ibn Isḥāq, *Sīra,* i, 346-8; Ibn Saʿd, *Ṭabaqāt,* i, 2, 7). This dream fits into an ancient Semitic tradition admitting that the dreams of subjects can serve as a divine warning or as a message to their king or their chief (cf. A. Leo Oppenheim, *The interpretation of dreams,* 188, 199 f.; *I Sam* 3:1; a ḥadīth quoted by Ibn Saʿd [*Ṭabaqāt,* ii, 2, 18] makes it comprehensible). Many dreams seen by persons in the surroundings of the Prophet (e.g. his aunt, ʿĀtika, and Juhaym) and by himself announced the victory of Badr (q.v.) and the defeat of Uḥud (q.v.). At the beginning of his illness, he saw in a dream his impending end (see details in Fahd, *Divination,* 279 f.).

Is this oneiric climate, broadly attested in the *sīra,* also reflected in the Qurʾān? Q 12 (Sūrat Yūsuf) contains three dreams: the dream of Joseph (Q 12:4-5), that of his companions in prison (12:36) and that of Pharaoh (q.v.; 12:43). The order given to Abraham to sacrifice his son (Q 37:102, 105) was given to him in a dream. God brought Muḥammad's dream *(ruʾyā)* of his return to Mecca (Q 48:27) to fruition. His earlier dream, that of the *isrāʾ* and *miʿrāj,* had been given to him to test the faith of those that had followed him; it was in a way "the accursed tree" of the Qurʾān (Q 17:60). Other terminology for dreaming (*manām,* e.g. at Q 37:102) is indicative of a divine sign (Q 30:23), a summoning to God that is analogous to death (Q 39:42) and an instrument of divine supervision that was used by God to guide the steps of his Prophet and the believers (Q 8:43-4). The term *ḥulm* (pl. *aḥlām*) is used in the prophetic tradition to distinguish the true dream *(ruʾyā)* from the false, the latter being the result of passions or preoccupations of the soul (q.v.) or the inspiration of Satan, as in the following: "The *ruʾyā* comes from God and the *ḥulm* from Satan" (cf. Wensinck, *Concordance,* i, 504; Bukhārī, *Ṣaḥīḥ,* ii, 324 = *Khalq,* 11). This meaning could be suggested in Q 12:44 and 21:5, in which the plural, *aḥlām,* is preceded by the term *aḍghāth,* which denotes "incoherent dreams." At Q 12:44, one finds "the interpretation of dreams" *(taʾwīl al-aḥlām)* in the sense of dream *(ḥulm)* found in the Semitic languages, where it also refers to the prophetic dream (cf. Ehrlich, *Der Traum im alten Testament,* 1). One has to note that, also in Q 12:21, there is mention of "the interpretation of events" *(taʾwīl al-aḥādīth),* an expression which, if brought into relation with *anbāʾ al-ghayb,* would refer to the *ḥidthān,* a term later used to designate the *malāḥim* (cf. Fahd, *Divination,* 224-8; 272; 408; [ed.], Malāḥim in EI²). The gift of predicting coming events makes Joseph a prophet *avant la lettre* and makes the interpretation of dreams a means by which God makes his will known to humans.

Omens

Three qurʾānic verses (Q 7:131; 27:47; 36:18) allude to the *ṭāʾir/ṭīra,* which originally referred to the consultation of the flight of birds, and, later, to the bad tidings that this was considered to foreshadow. The contrary of *ṭīra* is *faʾl,* the good omen. This term is not qurʾānic, but can be found in the ḥadīth, where the capacity is attributed to the Prophet of distinguishing between *ṭīra* and *faʾl.* "He said: 'There is no *ṭīra, al-faʾl* is better.' He was asked, 'What is the *faʾl?*' He replied, 'It is the good word that every one of you can hear." (cf. Wensinck, *Concordance,* v, 40; see SEEING AND HEARING; HEARING AND DEAFNESS). Also attributed to the Prophet is the following: "The *faʾl* pleases me and I love a good *faʾl*" (Damīrī, *Ḥayāt,* 118). It is clear, then, that *ṭīra* is a bad *faʾl.* Elsewhere, he places the *ṭīra* alongside suspicion and jealousy, being three vices (see VIRTUES AND VICES) from which no one can escape. He counsels those stricken by them not to come back following a bad omen, not to act on the basis of suspicion (q.v.) and not to harm someone because of jealousy (Ibn Qutayba, *ʿUyūn,* ii, 8; Ibn ʿAbd Rabbihi, *ʿIqd,* i, 226). He is also imputed of having said the following: "The *ṭīra* is idolatry *(shirk)*" (Bukhārī-Qasṭallānī, viii, 442 f. *[ṭīra],* 444 *[faʾl]*).

A strange ḥadīth which made ʿĀʾisha shiver with indignation says: "The *ṭīra* is in the woman, in the dwelling and in the beast of burden" (Ibn Qutayba, *ʿUyūn,* 146-7). There is no question of ornithomancy here, but of domestic foretellings that a man draws from the gestures and words of his wife, of the inhabitants of his house and of the tools and animals that are at his service. This is the *ṭīra* in its broadest sense, and this is the meaning it has in the three qurʾānic verses that were quoted at the beginning of this section (for the onomatomantic *faʾl,* see Fahd, *Divination,* 452; id., Faʾl).

T. Fahd

Bibliography

Primary: *Berakhōt (Babylonian Talmud);* Bukhārī, *Ṣaḥīḥ;* R.H. Charles (ed.), *The apocrypha and pseudepigrapha of the Old Testament in English. With introductions and critical explanatory notes to the several books,* Oxford 1913; Damīrī, *Ḥayāt;* Ibn ʿAbd Rabbihi, *al-ʿIqd al-farīd,* 4 vols., Cairo 1928; Ibn al-Athīr, ʿIzz al-Dīn, *Usd al-ghāba fī maʿrifat al-ṣaḥāba,* 7 vols., Cairo 1970-3; Ibn Isḥāq, *Sīra,* ed. Wüstenfeld; Ibn Qutayba, *ʿUyūn al-akhbār,* 4 vols. in 2, Cairo 1973; Ibn Saʿd, *Ṭabaqāt;* Ibshīhī, Muḥammad b. Aḥmad, *Kitāb al-Mustaṭraf fī kull fann mustaẓraf,* 2 vols., Cairo 1902; Qasṭallānī, *Irshād al-sarī li-sharḥ Ṣaḥīḥ al-Bukhārī,* 8 vols., Baghdad 1971; Ṭabarī, *Tafsīr;* id., *Taʾrīkh; Tāj al-ʿarūs.*
Secondary: al-Ālūsī, Saʿīd Maḥmūd Shukrī, *Bulūgh al-arab fī maʿrifat aḥwāl al-ʿarab,* 3 vols., Cairo 1924; E. Doutté, *Magie et religion dans l'Afrique du Nord,* Paris 1909; R. Dussaud, *La pénétration des Arabes en Syrie avant l'Islam,* Paris 1955; [ed.], Malāḥim, in EI², vi, 216; E.L. Ehrlich, *Der Traum im alten Testament,* Berlin 1953 (Beihefte zur ZATW); T. Fahd, *La divination arabe. Études religieuses, sociologiques et folkloriques du milieu natif de l'Islam,* Leiden 1966, Paris 1987; id., Faʾl, in EI², ii, 758; id., Khaṭṭ, in EI², iv, 1128-30; id., *Le panthéon des l'Arabie centrale à la veille de l'hégire,* Paris 1968; id., La visite de Mahomet aux enfers, in Université des Sciences Humaines de Strasbourg. Centre de recherches d'histoire des religions, *Études d'histoire des religions. iii. L'apocalyptique.* Paris 1977, 181-210, repub. in T. Fahd, *Études d'histoire et de civilisation islamiques,* 2 vols., Istanbul 1997, ii, 225-50; J.G. Février, *L'histoire de l'écriture,* Paris 1942; A. Leo Oppenheim, The interpretation of dreams in the ancient Near East, in *Transactions of the American Philosophical Society* 46 (1956), 179-373; Wensinck, *Concordance.*

Forgery

Act of fabricating or producing falsely. Forgery is connoted in several qurʾānic concepts. Re-writing sacred scripture, either the Qurʾān or the scriptures of the Jews and Christians, is covered by two Arabic terms *(taḥrīf, tabdīl)*. These or their cognates convey the charge that Jews and Christians distorted revealed scripture before the Qurʾān (see SCRIPTURE AND THE QURʾĀN; JEWS AND JUDAISM; CHRISTIANS AND CHRISTIANITY). Also, within the Islamic tradition, various sectarian groups have charged that there were additions and deletions to the Qurʾān. Finally, the notion of forgery is connected with the concept of the inimitability (q.v.) of the Quran *(iʿjāz al-Qurʾān)*.

Forgery by the alteration of sacred text, either by letter substitution *(taḥrīf)*, mispronunciation *(taḥrīf)* or other forms of substitution *(tabdīl)*, contributes to some Muslims' understanding of the relationship of the Qurʾān to the scriptures of Jews and Christians. In Q 2:59 and 7:162 a group of Jews is said to have "exchanged the word that was told to them for another saying *(fa-baddala lladhīna ẓalamū qawlan ghayra lladhī qīla lahum)*," thereby falsifying scripture (cf. Q 2:75; 5:13, 41, *yuḥarrifūna*). In Q 4:46, the falsification is said to derive from deliberate mispronunciation of scripture, in which the words, "We hear and obey," were recast into "We hear and disobey." Forgery or falsification by omission was also charged (Q 2:146; 3:71), whereby parts of the original sacred text were purposely omitted. In qurʾānic usage, accusations of substitution *(taḥrīf* and *tabdīl)* seem to be a reaction to traditional modes of, chiefly, Jewish commentary on scripture that make use of substitution of words based on their numerical value (Hebrew *gematria*), on differences in meaning of homophones or homographs, and on differences in meanings of words with similar sounds and roots across cognate languages, in this instance Hebrew and Arabic. The word, "we disobeyed" *(ʿaṣaynā)* in Q 4:46 is a close homophone to the Hebrew word for "do" or "accomplish" *(ʿasah)* and the passage reflects a midrash on the disobedient Israelite worship of the calf of gold (q.v.) after having promised to obey God (see *Exod* 19:8 and following; see OBEDIENCE). Q 2:75 charges that a party of the People of the Book (q.v.) would change scripture even after they had understood it. From the qurʾānic evidence about *taḥrīf* and *tabdīl*, the Qurʾān rejects a common feature of the midrashic way of reading scripture, namely the toleration of multiple, simultaneous interpretations of the text (see READINGS OF THE QURʾĀN), which was, however, allowed for. Ḥadīth (i.e. prophetic reports), which sometimes were contradictory or diverse in their meaning, were accepted so long as their chain of transmission was deemed sound (see ḤADĪTH AND THE QURĀN). Post-qurʾānic commentators understood the Qurʾān to regard all scripture of Jews and Christians as corrupted and thereby to be either rejected or understood only through the filter of the Qurʾān itself.

Charges of forgery have been a feature of inter-Islamic polemics as well as of those between Muslims and the People of the Book. Q 12 was regarded by the Khārijīs (q.v.) as a forgery on the basis of its love themes (Ṭūsī, *Tibyān*, iv, 75; van Ess, *TG*, i, 75). Both Sunnīs and Shīʿīs (Bar-Asher, *Scripture*, 88-93; see SHĪʿISM AND THE QURʾĀN) have accused the other of substituting or repressing portions of the Qurʾān, including two complete chapters which appear in the codex of Ubayy b. Kaʿb, one of Muḥammad's secretaries (Nöldeke, *GQ*, ii, 33-8; Jeffery, *Materials*, 180-1; see COLLECTION OF THE QURʾĀN; CODICES OF THE QURʾĀN). All attempts at producing a definitive Shīʿī alternative Qurʾān have failed, and both Sunnīs and Shīʿīs use the same recension for liturgical purposes (see RITUAL AND THE QURʾĀN). Sunnī commentators have consistently held that the true Qurʾān defies all attempts at forgery and is inimitable. This is in keeping with Q 2:79, which condemns the falsification of scripture: "Woe to those who write the book (q.v.) with their own hands, then say 'This is from God,' in order that they might purchase a small gain therewith." See also REVISION AND ALTERATION.

Gordon Darnell Newby

Bibliography
Primary: Suyūṭī, *Itqān;* Ṭabarī, *Tafsīr,* ed. Shākir; Ṭūsī, *Tibyān;* Zamakhsharī, *Kashshāf.*
Secondary: C. Adang, *Muslim writers on Judaism and the Hebrew Bible. From Ibn Rabban to Ibn Ḥazm,* Leiden 1996; M.M. Bar-Asher, *Scripture and exegesis in early Imāmī Shiism,* Leiden 1999; van Ess, *TG;* J.M. Gaudeul and R. Caspar, Textes de la tradition musulmane concernant le taḥrīf (falsification) des écritures, in *Islamochristiana* 6 (1980), 61-104; Goldziher, *MS;* Jeffery, *Materials;* E. Kohlberg, Some notes on the Imami attitude to the Qurʾān, in S.M. Stern, A. Hourani, and Y. Brown (eds.), *Islamic philosophy and the classical tradition. Essays presented to R. Walzer,* Oxford 1972, 209-24; H. Lazarus-Yafeh, *Intertwined worlds. Medieval Islam and Bible criticism,* Princeton 1992; id., Taḥrīf, in *EI²,* x, 111-2 (contains a detailed bibliography); I.D. Matteo, Il taḥrīf od alterazione della Bibbia secondo i Musulmani, in *Bessarione* 26 (1992), 64-111; 223-260; G.D. Newby, The *Sīrah* as a source for Arabian Jewish history. Problems and perspectives, in *JSAI* 7 (1986), 121-38; Nöldeke, *GQ;* W. St. Clair Tisdall, Shiʿah additions to the Koran, in *MW* 3 (1913), 227-41.

Forgiveness

The act of pardoning or the quality of being merciful. All 114 sūras (q.v.) of the Qurʾān but one (Q 9) open with the formula "In the name of God, the merciful *(al-raḥmān),* the compassionate *(al-raḥīm)*" (see BASMALA) and the theme of divine forgiveness permeates throughout as in Q 2:286: "God does not burden any soul more than it can bear. It receives every good that it earns, and it receives every evil that it earns. 'Our lord! Do not condemn us if we forget or err… Our lord! Do not place upon us a burden greater than we have strength to bear, and pardon and forgive us, and have mercy (q.v.) upon us!'" (cf. Ṭabarī, *Tafsīr,* iii, 159).

God loves those who pardon others (Q 3:134; cf. Ṭabarī, *Tafsīr,* iii, 438) and the Qurʾān encourages believers to forgive their fellow human beings (cf. Q 15:85). In fact, although not as explicitly as in the New Testament (e.g. at *Matt* 5:7; 6:12, 14-5; 7:1-2), God's forgiveness of human beings seems to be at least potentially associated in the Qurʾān with their forgiveness of others (Q 24:22; 64:14). Ultimately, however, forgiveness of sins is a uniquely divine prerogative: "He is the one who accepts repentance from his servants and pardons evil deeds" (Q 42:25; cf. Q 3:135; 9:104). God is "the best of forgivers" (Q 7:155; cf. Ṭabarī, *Tafsīr,* vi, 78), the "forgiver of sin and accepter of repentance" (Q 40:3). The term *ghaffār* occurs ninety-six times as a divine name or attribute (see GOD AND HIS ATTRIBUTES), signifying, roughly, "the much forgiving." The essentially synonymous *tawwāb* and *ʿafūw* occur, counted together, fifteen times, and, as mentioned above, the *raḥmān/raḥīm* complex is widespread. (For the differences of connotation between *ʿafw, maghfira* and *raḥma,* see Rāzī, *Tafsīr,* vii, 150, ad Q 2:286.)

God's forgiveness, like his will, is sovereign and free (see FREEDOM AND PREDESTINATION; SOVEREIGNTY). He forgives whomever he will (Q 2:284; 3:129; 5:18, 40, 118; 9:15, 27; 48:14). "Your lord is a lord (q.v.) of forgiveness and of painful punishment" (Q 41:43; see CHASTISMENT AND PUNISHMENT). He will not forgive those who associate other gods with him in worship — believers should not seek pardon for idolaters (Q 9:113; see IDOLATRY AND IDOLATERS; POLYTHEISM AND ATHEISM) — but is ready to forgive anything else (Q 4:48, 116). And, in fact, he forgives "many things" (Q 42:30, 34). "Those who avoid major sins (see SIN, MAJOR AND MINOR) and abominations, all except petty wrongs — truly, your lord is ample in forgiveness" (Q 53:32). He forgives those who sin ignorantly but repent quickly (Q 4:17; see REPENTANCE AND PENANCE). He does not, however, forgive those who reject faith (q.v.; Q 4:168; 9:80; 63:5-6; see also GRATITUDE AND INGRATITUDE) and persist in evildoing (Q 4:18; see EVIL DEEDS), and he is unlikely to forgive repeated apostasy (q.v.; Q 4:137). To obtain his forgiveness, one must believe in him (cf. Q 8:38; 46:31; 47:34). Various individuals seek God's forgiveness in the qur'ānic narratives (q.v.) and believers are told to pray for it (e.g. Q 11:3, 52, 61, 90; 73:20; 110:3). Indeed, at God's command (Q 3:159), Muḥammad (q.v.) himself pleads for forgiveness on behalf of others (as at Q 4:64; cf. Ṭabarī, *Tafsīr*, iv, 160; see INTERCESSION). The imperative form of the verb *ghafara* occurs seventeen times in the Qur'ān, with speakers calling directly upon God to forgive them. The qur'ānic archetype of God's forgiveness of human beings is, of course, God's forgiveness of Adam (see ADAM AND EVE) after his disobedience (q.v.; see FALL OF MAN), the result being the absence in Islam of the concept of original sin (see COSMOLOGY).

Forgiveness from God is better than wealth (q.v.; Q 3:157). Indeed, it is among the great and oft-cited blessings of paradise (q.v.; Q 2:221, 268; 3:136; 4:96; 5:9; 8:4, 74; 11:11; 22:50; 24:26; 33:35; 34:4; 35:7; 36:11; 47:15; 48:29; 49:3; 57:20; 67:12; see REWARD AND PUNISHMENT). More than that, however, his gracious and unearned forgiveness offers humankind its only ultimate hope (q.v.; Q 7:23, 149; 11:47). See also MERCY.

Daniel C. Peterson

Bibliography
Primary: Ṭabarī, *Tafsīr*, 12 vols., Beirut 1992; Rāzī, *Tafsīr*.
Secondary: M. Allam, The concept of forgiveness in the Qur'ān, in *IC* 41 (1967), 139-53; D. Rahbar, God of justice. A study in the ethical doctrine of the Qur'ān, Leiden 1960, 141-75.

Form and Structure of the Qur'ān

Preliminary reflections about the redaction and canonization of the Qur'ān

Methodological dilemmas

Any assessment of qur'ānic form and structure depends on the position chosen by the researcher as to the redaction and the canonization of the qur'ānic corpus (see COLLECTION OF THE QUR'ĀN; CODICES OF THE QUR'ĀN; for a recent analysis of western views on the collection of the Qur'ān, see Motzki, Collection). Two apparently irreconcilable positions are currently infelicitously blocking each other in qur'ānic scholarship: on the one hand, there is the historico-critical approach which is oriented to older, more traditional biblical scholarship. It focuses on the development of the Qur'ān and views it as concomitant to that of its transmitter. It assumes the historicity of the basic Islamic traditions about the genesis of the Qur'ān, though sometimes tends to cling too closely to the reports contained in the biography of the Prophet (*sīra*, see SĪRA AND THE QUR'ĀN; ḤADĪTH AND THE QUR'ĀN) and thus unduly re-historicizes the Qur'ān. On the other hand, there is the counter-position of John Wansbrough's hyper-skeptical revisionist approach (see CONTEMPORARY CRITICAL PRACTICES AND THE QUR'ĀN) informed by a more modern trend in biblical scholarship, namely *Formgeschichte*, as well as semiological approaches that reject the traditional narrative altogether. This approach projects the role hitherto ascribed to the Prophet and the first caliphs in the redaction process onto an anonymous committee assumed to have assembled a century or more later. In A. Rippin's words: "Canonization and stabilization of the text of the Qurʾān goes hand in hand with the formation of the community (see COMMUNITY AND SOCIETY IN THE QURʾĀN). A final fixed text of the scripture was not required, nor was it totally feasible, before political power was firmly controlled (see POLITICS AND THE QURʾĀN); thus the end of the second/eighth century becomes a likely historical moment for the gathering together of oral tradition and liturgical elements leading to the emergence of the fixed canon of scripture" (Literary analysis, 161). This approach, which not only dismisses the *sūra* but also rigorously de-historicizes the Qurʾān, and, by confining itself to the macrostructure of the canonized final version, disregards the distinctive internal literary structures of the Qurʾān (q.v.), has been criticized for its mechanistic argument. Thus, J. van Ess comments: "Generally speaking I feel that the author [i.e. J. Wansbrough] has been overwhelmed by the parallel case of early Christianity. Islam comes into being at a time and in surroundings where religion is understood as religion of the Book (q.v.; see also PEOPLE OF THE BOOK). This understanding had been prepared by the developments in Judaism (see JEWS AND JUDAISM) and Christianity (see CHRISTIANS AND CHRISTIANITY), as well as in Manichaeism (see MAGIANS). Canonization was no longer something novel. It was expected to happen. This, in my view, suffices as a justification of the process in Islam taking place so rapidly" (Review of J. Wansbrough, 353). This article argues for a third way: a shift in focus from a "canon from above" to a "canon from below," and a reading of the Qurʾān which studies the sūra (q.v.) as a communication process and thus respects this redactionally-warranted unit as a genuine literary text.

Canonization and the problem of the "sūra" as a unit

Several recent studies on the Qurʾān have focused anew on the problem of its canonization, making this a central issue in qurʾānic research. What these studies have called into question is the traditional account of the redaction and publication of a unified and authorized final version of the Qurʾān through which the text came to occupy the status of a scripture bearing an intrinsic logic of its own. By focusing on this final phase and ranking it as the crucial event in qurʾānic genesis, an epistemological course has been set: The literary image of the Qurʾān as reflecting a text still in progress and thus displaying a unique micro-structural diversity due to its evolution out of an extended process of a liturgical communication, becomes blurred, being eclipsed by its macro-structural weight and the social importance of the henceforth normative corpus and its ideological implications for the construction of the community's identity.

According to the dominant Islamic tradition, the Qurʾān owes its authoritative final version to the redaction carried out by a committee summoned by the third caliph, ʿUthmān b. ʿAffān (r. 23-35/644-56). The creation of this codex does, it is admitted, impose on the sūras a sequence that, until then, had not been fixed. In many cases it also incorporates passages that had been transmitted in an isolated manner into completely new contexts. The committee clings faithfully, however, to the text material whose authenticity is warranted by reliable oral and/or written tradition (see ORALITY), taking into consideration the entire corpus of the qurʾānic revelations available at the time. The performance of the committee is, therefore, traditionally identified as an act of collection *(jamʿ)*, one accomplished in perfect accordance with the concept of its commissioner, ʿUthmān, who is reported to have imposed on the redactors — apart from observing some linguistic cautions — no further task than that of gathering all the extant parts of the Qurʾān. The traditional account of the collection of the Qurʾān accords with the evidence offered by the text itself, since the new codex, which does not claim any chronological or theological rationale for the sequence of the single units (sūras) — which appear to be arranged according to merely technical external criteria — does display inextinguishable traces of its compilation as a collection (see CHRONOLOGY AND THE QURʾĀN). On the surface, it presents itself as a corpus of unconnected texts of considerable structural diversity, not allowing for an immediate classification under one particular genre.

The traditional reports identify political constraints as the explanation of, and justification for, the admitted fact that the collection was carried out somewhat hastily and thus had to proceed in a rather mechanical fashion. Although other redactions had to be suppressed, the sequences of sūras in two of them (the codices *[maṣāḥif]* of Ibn Masʿūd [d. 32/653] and Ubayy b. Kaʿb [d. ca. 19/640 to 35/656]) are known to us. Both seem to have considered sūras 1, 113 and 114 to be not part of the corpus, but rather prayers to be uttered concomitant with the recitation of the Qurʾān (q.v.). The official redaction and publication of the standard text neither completely extinguished the memory of extant variants, later known as *qirāʾāt shādhdha,* nor precluded the emergence of further variants. Indeed, a number of reading traditions of the entire Qurʾān *(qirāʾāt mutawātira),* which, in many instances, diverge — although not substantially — from each other have come down to us. Seven of these (the so-called "seven readings," *al-qirāʾāt al-sabʿ*) even received canonical status through Ibn Mujāhid's (d. 324/936) scrutinizing selection of admissible qurʾānic text forms (see READINGS OF THE QURʾĀN). Although these have since enjoyed an equal status in the scholarly and the cultic tradition *(ʿilm al-qirāʾa, ʿilm al-tajwīd)* only two have survived and are still in use in modern times, namely the reading of Ḥafṣ *ʿan* ʿĀṣim (current in the Islamic east) and that of Warsh *ʿan* Nāfiʿ (current in the western Islamic world). Since modern audio media have further enhanced the status of the former, contemporary qurʾānic scholarship usually refers only to the Ḥafṣ text.

Yet, with the ʿUthmānic consonantal fixation of the text, a decisive course had been set with regards to its structure, which gave rise to a problematic development: namely, the joint codification of loosely composed passages and often unframed, conceptually isolated communications — so characteristic of the Medinan "long sūras" *(ṭiwāl al-suwar)* — together with the complex poly-thematic structures and mnemonic, technically sophisticated pieces that comprise the short and middle-sized sūras resulted in a most heterogeneous ensemble, a fact that did not remain without consequences. Once these elements melded to form a comprehensive and closed corpus, a codex (*muṣḥaf,* q.v.), they became neutralized as to their liturgical *Sitz-im-Leben* and their communicational context in the emergence of the community. Previously defined text-units distinguishable through reliable devices such as introductory formulas and markers of closure were, it is true, retained by the redaction process and labeled "sūra." They lost much of their significance, however, for, in the same codex there were now other units also labelled as "sūras," but whose constituent passages had not come to form a coherent literary structure and thus invalidated the structural claim raised by those sūras that were neatly composed. The neatly-composed sūras eventually ceased to be considered integral literary units conveying messages of their own and mirroring individual stages of a process of communication. On the contrary, once all parts had become equal in rank, arbitrarily selected texts could be extracted from their sūra context and used to explain other arbitrarily selected texts. Passages thus became virtually de-contextualized, stripped of the tension that had characterized them within their original units. Genuine text-units lost their literary integrity and could be mistaken for mere repetitions of each other.

Hence, with its final official canonization, the Qurʾān had become de-historicized. Not the process of its successive emergence as mirrored in the text, but the timeless, eternal quality of its message had become its brand. This made the understanding of the Qurʾān all the more dependent on the *sīra*, a corpus that, although transmitted and codified separately, had been grafted on the Qurʾān by its readers and listeners from early times. Prophetic tradition, in its development of haggadic meta-history, thus took the place that intra-qurʾānic history should legitimately have occupied, i.e. the history, however sparse the chronological evidence, of a liturgical and social communication process, that took on a distinctly textual shape in the Qurʾān and is reflected in the structure of the sūras. Further literary investigation into the micro-structure of the Qurʾān, which might reveal the still-traceable traits of that history, remains an urgent desideratum.

As M. Mir (The *sūra*) has stressed, Muslim exegetes have only recently rediscovered the most prominent micro-structure of the Qurʾān, namely the sūra as a unit containing meaning, a concept long neglected in Muslim circles and generally dismissed as irrelevant in western scholarship. Exceptions to this dismissal have more recently appeared (cf. M.A.S. Abdel Haleem, Context; A. Neuwirth, Zur Struktur; id., Symmetrie; id., Koran; id., Images; id., Erste Qibla; id., From the sacred mosque; id., Qurʾānic literary structure; A.H.M. Zahniser, Word of God; id., Sura as guidance; M. Sells, Sound, spirit and gender; id., Sound and meaning; A.H. Johns, Qurʾānic presentation; and S.M. Stern, Muhammad and Joseph).

Reflections of a canonical process

The older sūras in particular seem to mirror a development which in its essential traits reflects a canonization from below, as characterized by Aleida and Jan Assmann (Kanon und Zensur). These two scholars distinguish between a canon described as power-oriented and one that relies on a particular source of meaning, not least on the charisma of the transmitter of a message. According to the Assmanns' theory, "whenever the message is preserved to survive beyond the situation in which the original group was directly interacting, it will usually undergo a profound change in structure. The message gains a new appearance through scripturalization and moreover through institutionalization." In the case of the Qurʾān, then, a canon from below certainly precedes the canon from above. The latter comes about only with the authoritative final redaction, which became necessary to counteract the pressure of a reactionary tendency towards provincialization and fragmentization. The canon from below has thereby changed into a canon from above, a development comparable to that in early Christianity when the official Church contracted a pact with political power.

To discern the textual signs of a canon developing from below, we may draw on the new approaches developed in recent biblical studies, principally those of the American scholar Brevard S. Childs, who has proposed an understanding of the genesis of a canon as a process of growth. Canon in this context no longer covers the officially codified final form of a text, but rather signifies the "consciousness of a binding covenantal character deeply rooted in the texts" (C. Dohmen, *Biblischer Kanon*, 25) that is affirmed by the continuous references of later emerging text-units to a text nucleus and by the recurrent instances of intertextuality mirrored in the text-units developing around the nucleus. Even at the point where the genesis of a text conceived as a canonical process has come to a close with the end of the text's growth, its final form will not be a harmonious presentation but will leave the roughness caused by the organic growth unleveled. The final shape only re-locates interpretation, which, until then, had taken place in productive additions or changes within the text, and which henceforth takes place through exegesis and interpretation separate from the text.

Methodological conclusions

The following presentation of qurʾānic form and structure is based on these observations. At the same time it represents an attempt to comply with a provocative demand proffered by A. Rippin (Qurʾān as literature) that the Qurʾān should be studied by (a) situating it in its literary tradition and (b) situating it as the focal point of a readers' response study. But, diverging from Rippin's proposal, we will not go so far as to replace an immediately traceable intra-qurʾānic context with a speculative biblical or post-biblical one in order to provide the appropriate literary tradition. Nor will we embark on reconstructing a post-qurʾānic reader-response from the exegetical literature (see EXEGESIS OF THE QURʾĀN: CLASSICAL AND MEDIEVAL; EXEGESIS OF THE QURʾĀN: EARLY MODERN AND CONTEMPORARY). Rather, what we shall analyze — on the basis of individual sūras — is the qurʾānic communication process as taking place between speaker and listeners. The reader-response is thus replaced by a listener-response, the concept of the "implied reader" is modified into that of the "implied listener." Situating the Qurʾān in its literary tradition (see SCRIPTURE AND THE QURʾĀN; ORALITY) will be realized through the investigation of its peculiar referentiality, not stopping short at the notice of particular instances of a biblical background, but proceeding to examine the position of the sūra as a stage in an extended canonical process.

This article will discuss the language and style of the Qurʾān in general (see LANGUAGE OF THE QURʾĀN; GRAMMAR AND THE QURʾĀN; RHETORIC OF THE QURʾĀN) and on this basis the individual literary genres assembled in the Qurʾān will be surveyed in terms of form and content. To present such an inventory of the building blocks or *"enjeux"* (Ger. *"Gesätze"*) of the sūras is a useful propaedeutic step towards the literary assessment of the Qurʾān, although hardly any of the *enjeux* themselves appears as a self-sufficient communication, i.e. as a complete sūra. Rather, they are integrated in complex ensembles and thus, to be adequately understood, must be viewed in their wider context. The discussion will therefore survey the contextuality, i.e. the diverse combinations of individual *enjeux* displayed in individual sūras.

Now, the Qurʾān has never been conceptualized or intended as a primarily literary corpus whose purpose was to convey information to, or serve the re-education of, its readers (see HISTORY AND THE QURʾĀN). Rather, it has manifested itself — until its final publication — as a continuous hermeneutical process reflecting, and simultaneously conditioning, the attitudes of its listeners towards the message (see ETHICS AND THE QUR'ĀN; THEOLOGY AND THE QUR'ĀN). The literary ensembles — sūras — thus constitute essentially liturgical units that have developed not so much through the textual growth of the corpus as through a liturgical or communicational process that transpired within the emerging Islamic community. Their "history" can therefore be plumbed out only by closely considering the process of conveying the message, i.e. by surveying the subsequent changes in communication techniques and the hints at the performative framework, in terms of time, space and protagonists involved, as mirrored in the self-referential passages of the Qur'ān. Only such a synopsis of the literary and the communicational, i.e. liturgical development, will enable us to pursue the canonical process which finally produced the corpus as we have it today.

Linguistic, stylistic and literary character of the Qur'ān

Diversity of views

An early debate about the question of qur'ānic language — Meccan vernacular (Vollers, *Volkssprache*) or poetic koine (*'arabiyya*, Nöldeke, *Neue Beiträge;* Geyer, Zur Strophik) was decided in favor of the latter, though occasional linguistic interferences reflecting the Ḥijāzī vernacular are still discernible beneath the amendments later supplied by the classical philologists (see TRADITIONAL DISCIPLINES OF QUR'ĀNIC STUDY; INIMITABILITY). Still, the style and language of the Qur'ān have often been dismissed as defective, with verdicts ranging from Th. Nöldeke's "Sündenregister" (*Neue Beiträge*, 5-23) imposing upon the Qur'ān grammatical rules that were developed at a later date, to L. Kopf's (Religious influences, 48) denigration of the Prophet's stylistic talents, to R. Blachère's (*Histoire*, ii, 187-241, esp. 204-36) reaffirmation of Nöldeke's influential critique. Although recognizing the division of the text into three sections from the Meccan period and one from the Medinan period, based upon predominantly stylistic considerations, and thus admitting a poetic character for the earlier sūras as against a more prosaic one for the later sūras (Nöldeke, GQ, esp. i, 66-75; 143-4), Western qur'ānic scholarship has for a long time failed to draw due methodological conclusions and to analyze the qur'ānic texts in an accordingly complex manner. An attempt to broadly survey the literary qualities of the Meccan part of the corpus was undertaken by Neuwirth in several studies (see bibliography).

Qur'ānic composition fared even worse. Since the sensational hypothesis presented by D. Müller *(Die Propheten)* claiming a strophic composition for the sūras was dismissed without further scrutiny by subsequent scholarship (Nöldeke, GQ) the possibility that "a firm literary hand was in full control" of the composition and structure of individual sūras has been virtually excluded. Disclaimers (adduced by Rippin, Review of Neuwirth) range from Goldziher's (*Introduction*, 28, n. 37) statement, "Judgments of the Qur'ān's literary value may vary, but there is one thing even prejudice cannot deny. The people entrusted... with the redaction of the unordered parts of the book occasionally went about their work in a very clumsy fashion," to Wansbrough's (QS, 47) "... ellipsis and repetition [in the Qur'ān] are such as to suggest not the carefully executed project of one or of many men, but rather the product of an organic development from originally independent traditions during a long period of transmission." Although Nöldeke's work still built on the reality of the sūras (admitting, of course, subsequent modifications), the hypothesis of an artistically valuable composition — be it of the qur'ānic corpus or of the single sūras — has since been negated, and existing literary forms have been considered to be the result of a haphazard compilation.

The problem of periodization

As against the view just mentioned, through micro-structural analysis, structures do become clearly discernible beneath the surface. These structures mirror a historical development. Indeed, observations about style and structure complemented by thematic considerations have induced Western scholars (Weil, *Historisch-kritische Einleitung;* Nöldeke, GQ [repeated by Blachère, *Le Coran;* id., *Histoire*]) to declare a division of the text into three sub-sections from the Meccan period and one from the Medinan period, thus further developing the distinction between Meccan and Medinan text-units already made by Muslim traditional scholarship. Although the assumption (also held by Bell, *Qurʾān;* id., *Introduction*) of "a historical progression at work between the diverse sections, i.e. that stylistic and thematic considerations can be translated into historical conclusions" has been contested (Rippin, Review of Neuwirth), it should nonetheless be noted that stylistic developments in any literature, once attained, are not deemed reversible. Since Nöldeke's division still proves useful as a working hypothesis, it appears worthwhile to further scrutinize his observations. As a first step in that direction, Neuwirth *(Studien)* has tried to establish a critical basis for determining verse structures by scrutinizing the verse divisions of the "standard Ḥafṣ text" through consultation with other traditional schemes. The crucial procedures demanded in order to reach a valid periodization are, however, more complex, and they have to proceed from a thorough investigation of qurʾānic rhyme to that of verse and then to that of paragraph structure in relation to the diverse semantic units (see RHYMED PROSE).

Rhymes and verse structures as a criterion of relative chronology

The poetical structure of the Qurʾān is marked by rhyme endings of the verses. A description of these rhymes *in toto* is a necessary pre-requisite for the analysis of the composition of a sūra, since only a synopsis of all the rhymes figuring in the Qurʾān will allow us to isolate sequences of rhymes and to examine their relation to semantically coherent groups of verses. Such a classification has been undertaken for the Meccan parts of the Qurʾān by Neuwirth *(Studien)*. There, a significant difference was noted between those sūras classified as early Meccan (whose endings comprise some eighty types of rhyme), as middle Meccan (seventeen types of rhyme endings) and as late Meccan (five types of rhyme endings). The diversity of rhymes is, of course, related to the style at large: The sūras commonly considered the oldest, i.e. those that display *sajʿ*, rhymed prose in the strict sense — short units rhyming in frequently changing sound patterns reiterating the last consonant and based on a common rhythm — are made up of monopartite verses containing one colon each (see for the colometric structure, Neuwirth, Zur Struktur; id., *Studien*), e.g. Q 70:8-9, *yawma takūnu l-samāʾu ka-l-muhl/wa-takūnu l-jibālu ka-l-ʿihn*. Longer compositions, whose style is too complex to be pressed into short *sajʿ* phrases, usually display a bipartite (two cola) structure, e.g. Q 54:42, *kadhdhabū bi-āyātinā kullihā fa-akhadhnāhum akhdha ʿazīzin muqtadir*, or even pluripartite (more than two cola) verse, e.g. Q 37:102, *fa-lammā balagha maʿahu l-saʿya qāla yā bunayya innī arā fī l-manāmi annī adhbaḥuka fa-nẓur mādhā tarā qāla yā abati fʿal mā tuʾmaru sa-tajidunī in shāʾa llāhu mina l-ṣābirīn*. The relative length of the verses should not be dismissed as simply conditioned by a more or less complex content. Rather, the transition from *saj*ʿ speech to a more ordinarily flowing, though still poetically tinted, articulation attests to the transformation of an adherence to the standard pre-Islamic (*jāhilī*, see AGE OF IGNORANCE) tradition into a novel literary paradigm that may be considered as a genuine qurʾānic development marking a new stage in the history of the Arabic literary language.

Proportions between verse groups as a criterion

R. Bell (*Qurʾān*, 71) claimed that "many sūras of the Qurʾān fall into short sections or paragraphs. These are not of fixed length, however, nor do they seem to follow any pattern of length. Their length is determined not by any consideration of form but by the subject or incident treated in each." This claim is, however, no longer tenable. Bell's perception of the Qurʾān — not unlike that held by Nöldeke and many later scholars — relies heavily on the imagination of a written text and completely neglects the oral character of the majority of the Meccan compositions. The principally liturgical function of the qurʾānic texts, however, presupposes texts that are easily memorized and which, as long as writing is not involved, are dependent on mnemonic-technical devices. An analysis of the structure of the verses of the Qurʾān in terms of their division into segments and the relationship between the grammatical structure of each segment and the thematic contents carried out by A. Neuwirth *(Studien)* has resulted in a typology of sūra structures. Most Meccan sūras display fixed sequences of formally and thematically defined verse groups distinctly separated by a change of rhyme or other clearly discernible, sometimes formulaic markers of caesurae. A group of two verses may be adduced at Q 94:7-8, *fa-idhā faraghta fa-nṣab/wa-ilā rabbika fa-rghab* (new rhyme, strictly parallel structure); a group of three verses is Q 90:8-10, *a-lam najʿal lahu ʿaynayn/wa-lisānan wa-shafatayn/wa-hadaynāhu l-najdayn* (new rhyme, identical subject); a group of four verses is Q 90:1-4, *lā uqsimu bi-hādhā l-balad/wa-anta ḥillun bi-hādhā l-balad/wa-wālidin wa-mā walad/la-qad khalaqnā l-insāna fī kabad* (ensuing change of rhyme, oath cluster with assertion); a group of five verses is Q 99:1-5, *idhā zulzilati l-arḍu zilzālahā/wa-akhrajati l-arḍu athqālahā/wa-qāla l-insānu mā lahā/yawmaʾidhin tuḥaddithu akhbārahā/bi-anna rabbaka awḥā lahā* (ensuing change of rhyme, apocalyptical scenery succeeded by an eschatological process; see APOCALYPSE; ESCHATOLOGY); a group of six verses is Q 75:1-6, *lā uqsimu bi-yawmi l-qiyāma/wa-lā uqsimu bi-l-nafsi l-lawwāma/a-yaḥsabu l-insānu allan najmaʿa ʿiẓāmah/balā qādirīna ʿalā an nusawwiya banānah/bal yurīdu l-insānu li-yafjura amāmah/yasʾalu ayyāna yawmu l-qiyāma* (group made up by 2 + 2 + 2 verses, held together by concatenation; ensuing change of rhyme, the group is followed by two further groups of six verses: 2 + 4, 2 + 2 + 2); a group of seven verses is Q 56:81-7 (polemics against adversaries of the Qurʾān), followed by another group of seven verses (Q 56:88-94) presenting the eschatological retribution; a group of eight verses is Q 93:1-8, *wa-l-ḍuḥā/wa-l-layli idhā sajā/mā waddaʿaka rabbuka wa-mā qalā/wa-la-l-ākhiratu khayrun laka mina l-ūlā/wa-la-sawfa yuʿṭīka rabbuka fa-tarḍā* ... (ensuing change of rhyme, oath cluster with three assertions); groups of nine verses are Q 73:1-9, 10-18; for groups of ten verses and more cf. Neuwirth, *Studien*, 186 f.

These distinct verse groups often form part of clear-cut patterns of proportions. Thus, Q 75 is built on the following balanced verse groups: 6 + 6 + 6 + 6 + 5 + 5 + 5; Q 70 is made up of 6 + 7 + 7 + 7 + 7 + 9; Q 79 entails two groups of nine verses, its proportions being strikingly balanced: 5 + 9 / 6 + 6 + 6 / 9 + 5. Q 51 is made up of groups of 9 + 14 + 14 + 9 + 7 + 7 verses. Similar cases are found in many of those early Meccan sūras that exceed some ten verses, proportion being obviously a mnemonic device required in a situation where memorizing without written support was demanded from the listeners (see below for a further discussion).

The clausula phrase

Any similarity to *saj*ʿ is given up when verses exceed the bipartite structures. In these cases, the rhyming end of the verses follows the stereotypical *-ūn, -īn*-pattern that would hardly suffice to fulfill the listeners' anticipation of a resounding end to the verse. A new mnemonic-technical device is utilized, solving the problem. This device is the rhymed phrase, a syntactically stereotyped colon which is distinguished from its context insomuch as it does not partake in the main strain of the discourse, but presents a kind of moral comment on it, as "... give us full measure and be charitable with us. Truly God will repay the charitable" (*...fa-awfi lanā l-kayla wa-taṣaddaq ʿalaynā, inna llāha yajzī l-mutaṣaddiqīn,* Q 12:88), or else refers to divine omnipotence and providence, as "... that we might show him our signs. Truly he is the hearer, the seer" (*... li-nuriyahu min āyātinā, innahu huwa l-samīʿu l-baṣīr,* Q 17:1). An elaborate classification of the rhymed phrases has been provided by Neuwirth (Zur Struktur) on the basis of sūra 12, a text particularly rich in clausulae that, hardly by mere coincidence, display a large number of divine predicates (*al-asmāʾ al-ḥusnā,* see GOD AND HIS ATTRIBUTES). Although it is true that not all multipartite verses bear such formulaic endings, and occasionally do contain ordinary short sentences in the position of the last colon, still, clausula verses may be considered to be a characteristic developed in the late Meccan period, and present in later verses. The presence of clausulae should not be considered as a purely ornamental phenomenon due to the merely stylistic moods of the speaker and thus devoid of significance for periodization. On the contrary, their appearance marks a new and irreversible development: The clausula serves to turn the often-narrative discourse of the extended sūras into paraenetical appeals, thus immediately supporting their theological message. They therefore betray a novel narrative pact between the speaker and his audience, the consciousness that there is a basic consensus on human moral behavior as well as on the image of God as a powerful agent in human interaction, a consciousness that has of course been reached only after an extended process of the community's education (Neuwirth, Referentiality; id., Qurʾān, crisis and memory).

Orality, scripturality and the canonical process

In spite of the etymology of its earliest self-designation (*qurʾān* < Syriac *qeryānā,* i.e. recital, pericope to be recited in services), far too often the Qurʾān is implicitly considered to be a literary work, imagined as "authored by Muḥammad," as becomes apparent from all the critiques which blame the text for not fulfilling particular literary standards. Since the quest for an "Urtext" has long been prevalent in historical-critical studies, qurʾānic speech has usually been investigated according to the criteria of written compositions with no relation to oral performance. This view has been met with criticism in more recent scholarship, which has demanded that the quest for "original meaning" be replaced by a consideration of the Qurʾān's sociocultural context as necessary for its interpretation (Martin, Understanding the Qurʾān). Denny (Exegesis and recitation,

91) criticized the neglect of the "ritual-recitational dimensions of the Qurʾān" and Graham (*Beyond,* 80) stressed "the abiding and intrinsic orality of the Qurʾān as a scriptural book of revelation and authority." "Oral composition" such as has been claimed for ancient Arabic poetry by Zwettler *(Oral tradition)* and Monroe (Oral composition) on the basis of the thesis presented by M. Parry in 1930-2 *(The making of Homeric verse)* and followed by Lord (in *The singer of tales*), although not immediately applicable in the case of the Qurʾān, is still in need of debate. According to Parry and Lord, "oral poetry" is characterized by its composition during performance, a procedure which is supported by a thesaurus of formulaic phrases. In some cases this may apply to the Qurʾān (see below), but can hardly be proved for the bulk of its corpus. Many early sūras (e.g. Q 73 and 74) that surely were composed without the support of writing attest to their origin in nocturnal vigils (q.v.) rather than public performances. Later sūras (from the so-called Raḥmān period onward, see Watt-Bell, *Introduction;* Nöldeke, *GQ*), composed of multipartite verses with little poetic shaping and thus devoid of effective mnemonic-technical devices, strongly suggest an immediate fixation in writing if they were not initially written compositions.

To investigate the full scope of this development one has, however, to go beyond the mere technical aspects. It is noteworthy that, although the distinction between two decisive periods for the genesis of the Qurʾān (a *qurʾān* phase and a *kitāb* phase, the latter implying the use of writing as a mnemonic-technical device to preserve the text) has been accepted in historic-critical qurʾānic scholarship as a whole (Watt-Bell, *Introduction;* Nagel, Vom Koran zur Schrift; Robinson, Structure), the double self-representation of the qurʾānic text has never been explored under the perspective of its implications for the canonical process. One has to keep in mind, however, that the terms *qurʾān* and *kitāb* denote very different concepts. The first points to a communal event in progress involving a multiplicity of dramatis personae — a speaker reciting a message received from an "absent" commissioner that he is to communicate to a plurality of listeners. It thus stresses a horizontal human interaction. This dynamic, thanks to the striking phenomenon of qurʾānic self-referentiality, is mirrored clearly in the early sūras themselves, which have preserved lively scenarios of the reception of the qurʾānic revelation. The second concept focuses on the hierarchical quality of a transcendent message presupposing a vertical relationship between an "author" (or his spokesperson) and the "reader" (or the worshipper). Thus the notion of a *kitāb* in itself clearly implies a strong claim of canonicity. Indeed, it was realized as such by the early community who first observed *kitāb* as a transcendent scripture, on the one hand manifested in the texts held sacred by the adherents of the older religions (i.e. *tawrāt* [see TORAH], *injīl* [see GOSPEL], *zabūr* [see PSALMS]), and, on the other hand, being communicated to them in subsequent messages (*ḥadīth,* Q 51:24; 20:9; *nabaʾ*, Q 15:51; 26:69; 38:21) to form narrative pericopes (see NARRATIVES) within the more complex liturgical recitals *(qurʾān)*. They only later realized *kitāb* to be the entelechy of their own growing corpus of divine communications. What was *qurʾān* in the beginning, then, developed into *kitāb* in the end; so a similar claim of canonicity cannot, in principle, be excluded for the term *qurʾān* either, which in later usage comes very close to that of *kitāb*. In turn, the Muslim *kitāb* preserves much of its "*qurʾān*-ness" since throughout the process of revelation the presence of the listeners is maintained, the believers among whom, i.e. the community (see BELIEF AND

UNBELIEF), even step into the text, not only as protagonists in new scenarios of salvation (q.v.) history but as conscious voices in an ongoing debate. Thus the entirely vertical relationship between the sender and the recipients, which prevails at the close of the qurʾānic development, i.e. after the completion of the corpus, is not really relevant to the preceding stages. The direct or indirect reference to the notion of *kitāb* thus may serve as a reliable guide when tracing the ongoing process of canonization in the qurʾānic development.

The "enjeux" *or building blocks of the sūra* ("Gesätze," *structurally definable verse groups)*

Since the appearance of A. Welch's article (Ḳurʾān) in 1981, further attempts at a classification of the *"enjeux"* have been put forward. Contrary to Welch — who is skeptical of the intra-Meccan periodization and thus reluctant to discuss the forms according to their successive emergence —, Neuwirth *(Studien),* in an extensive study of the qurʾānic literary forms of Meccan sūras, does consider this periodization — i.e. the approximately chronological sequence of sūras *(Entwicklungsreihen)* presented by Nöldeke and accepted by Schwally and Blachère — as still valid and useful as a working hypothesis. Unlike Welch's article, which praises Bell's atomization of the sūra as an important step forward, Neuwirth's study insists on the significance of the sūra as a literary unit although conceding that many Meccan sūras have undergone developments *(Fortschreibungen)* during their liturgical use, and that Medinan sūras constitute a case of their own. It is, however, assumed that the Meccan sūra in its final composition is an intended unit that reflects a natural growth, not a haphazard combination of diverse elements. The acceptance of the sūra as an intended unit following verifiable compositional patterns that are important for the understanding of the ensemble of *"enjeux"* enables the perception of structural developments, which, again, make possible a rough periodization of the sūras as units as well as of their *"enjeux."*

The following list comprises only the main types of *"enjeux,"* focusing on the early manifestations of the particular elements. On the whole, Meccan and Medinan sūras consist of the same building blocks; a few elements that appear in Medinan sūras exclusively will be discussed at the end of the list (for a more exhaustive discussion, see Neuwirth, *Studien,* 187 f. and 238 f.).

Oaths and oath clusters (introductory and intra-textual sections)

From among the forty-three sūras ascribed by Nöldeke to the first Meccan period, seventeen are introduced by oaths. In eight instances, oaths appear within sūras. Two types of oath formulas can be distinguished: a group introduced by *wāw al-qasam* (fifteen times in introductory sections, three times within sūras) and another introduced by *lā uqsimu bi-* (twice in introductory sections, five times within sūras). The particular importance of the introductory sections of the qurʾānic sūras for the entire composition has not been discussed on any systematic level. Still, observations concerning the beginning of the sūras have led to quite far-reaching hypotheses about the special brand of Muḥammad's prophethood (see PROPHETS AND PROPHETHOOD): i.e. the early sūras betray a close relationship to the utterances of the pre-Islamic soothsayers (q.v.; *kuhhān,* sing. *kāhin*), and may even be considered the most reliable evidence for *kuhhān* speech itself (see also ORALITY AND WRITINGS IN ARABIA).

Now, the specimens of *kuhhān* sayings that have been transmitted in early Islamic literature are not always assuredly genuine, nor have they been studied regarding their literary form. Theories about their relation to qurʾānic speech, therefore, still lack a methodological foundation. Neuwirth (Der Horizont; id., Der historische Muhammad) has presented some preliminary observations about the relationship between *kāhin* expression and the early sūras. Whereas oaths still bearing traces of legally binding commitments (see OATHS AND PROMISES) are found sporadically in the Qurʾān — mostly in the context of solemn pronouncements invoking God as witness for the truth of a statement — the oaths appearing in the early Meccan sūras are completely devoid of any legal connotation, but form clusters that serve exclusively as a literary device. This is affirmed by several formal characteristics, the most striking of which is the multiplicity of the objects invoked. Unlike in the case of legally binding oaths, these are not of a superior order (God, the life of the speaker, etc.) but, rather, are objects chosen from the empirical realm. A second characteristic is the limitation of the oaths to the standard formula *wa*-X or *lā uqsimu bi*-X followed by an assertion, a "statement," usually worded *inna* Y *la*-Z, not implying any allusion to a legally binding commitment on the part of the speaker. The oath clusters may be classified as follows:

a) Oath clusters of the type *wa-l-fāʿilāt:* Q 37:1-3; 51:1-4; 77:1-4; 79:1-5, 6-14; 100:1-5. These oaths, which do not explicitly name the objects to which they refer, but only allude to them by qualifying them as being moved in different successive motions, have been considered the most intricate by both Muslim exegetes and Western scholars. Displaying a metaphorical language distinctly different from that of the rest of the corpus, they have come to be known as particularly enigmatic, not so much because of the few undeniable lexical and grammatical ambiguities, but because of a more fundamental difficulty: their pronouncedly profane imagery (horses on their way to a raid [*ghazwa,* see EXPEDITIONS AND BATTLES], clouds heavy with rain) which seems inconsistent with the overall purport of the sūras as documents of religious discourse.

b) Oath clusters alluding to sacred localities and the abundance of creation: Q 52:1-6; 90:1-3; 95:1-3. The localities mentioned refer to particular theophanies, thus functioning as symbols of divine instruction. The one locality constantly mentioned is Mecca (q.v.); it appears once alone (Q 90) and twice (Q 52 and 95) in combination with Mount Sinai (q.v.) as the second site. In all three oath clusters an immediately recognizable semantic coherence between the oath formulae and the following text passage is missing, thus delaying the anticipation of a solution to the enigma posed which is disclosed only at the end of the sūra: theophanies, i.e. divine communications, necessitate an account be rendered on the day of judgment.

c) Oath clusters relating to cosmic phenomena and liturgically significant time periods of the day and the night (see DAY, TIMES OF; DAY AND NIGHT) are found at the beginning of a number of sūras: Q 85:1-3; 86:1-3; 89:1-4; 91:1-7; 92:1-3; 93:1-2; they appear within sūras in: Q 51:7-9; 86:11-12.

What justifies the classification of sūras with introductory oath clusters as a type of their own is not so much the observation of such obvious traits as common topics or patterns of composition as it is the immanent dynamics dominating these sūras. With regards to form, this particular quality is due to the accumulation of parallel phrases in the introductory section creating a rhythm of its own. Structurally speaking, it is based on the anticipation of a solution to the enigma that is aroused in the listeners' minds by the amassed metaphorical elements, an enigma that is not immediately comprehensible or even plausible to them. It is this dynamization of the entire sūra created by the introductory oath clusters that is the main characteristic of this text group.

In the case of (a), the *fā'ilāt*-clusters, the anticipation of an explication of the ideas presented in the cluster in an oblique metaphorical way through their empirically known prototypes is fulfilled only at the end of the sūra (or the first main part). The metaphorically projected catastrophe is none other than the eschatological dissolution of creation. In the case of oaths referring to (b), symbols of creation and instruction, the anticipation of the ideas of judgment (q.v.; see also LAST JUDMENT) and account is suspended in a similar way and fulfilled only at the end of the sūra, or again, at the end of the first main part. Sūras introduced by oath clusters referring to (c), cosmic phenomena and liturgically significant day and night phases, respectively, betray a somewhat different structure of anticipation. They are characterized, it is true, by a hymnical (or polemical) *tonus rectus* that remains audible throughout the entire sūra. However, in both types it is the ever-stressed opposition between created beings in terms of moral behavior, structurally prefigured through the contrast of light (q.v.) and darkness (q.v.), that arouses the anticipation of a final affirmation of unity personified in the creator, a unity that alone gives meaning to the oppositions extant in the realm of created beings. Indeed, the concluding sections, in speaking of the believers' nearness to the divine speaker, lead back to the experience of divine unity felt in liturgy and Qur'ān recitation to which the images in the introductory section (liturgical time phases) allude.

In the later sūras, the anticipation aroused by the oaths is fulfilled immediately, without suspense, in the ensuing statement (Q 36:2, object: *al-qur'ān al-ḥakīm;* Q 38:1, *al-qur'ān dhī l-dhikr;* Q 43:2, *al-kitāb al-mubīn;* Q 44:2, *al-kitāb al-mubīn;* Q 50:1, *al-qur'ān al-majīd;* Q 68:1, *al-qalam wa-mā yasṭurūna*), all of which are followed by assertions related to revelation (see REVELATION AND INSPIRATION). The oath clusters have thus developed from functional units into merely ornamental devices. In these later and more extended sūras, where the primary function of the oaths, i.e. arousing tension toward the explication of the initial enigma, has become faint, the attention of the listener can thus concentrate on particular — structurally important — images bearing symbolic value. It is not by mere coincidence that the standard incipit characteristic of so many later sūras develops from one of the types of early oath clusters: In the end, the image of the book *(al-kitāb)* — which had constituted the object of most of the early Meccan intra-textual oaths (Q 56:75 f.; 81:15 f.; 84:16 f.; 86:11 f.) but appeared less frequently in the introductory part (Q 52:2-3) — alone remains in use, the most abstract of all the different symbols used, essentially no more than a mere sign. The book is thus the only relic that survives from among a complex ensemble of manifold accessories of revelation, originally comprising cosmic, vegetative, topographic, cultic and social elements. The book as the symbol of revelation par excellence successively acquires the dignity that it has preserved until the present day to represent the noblest emblem of Islamic religion.

Eschatological passages (introductory and intra-textual sections)

Clusters of *idhā*-phrases

Five sūras (Q 56:1-6; 81:1-13; 82:1-4; 84:1-5; 99:1-3) start with *idhā*-phrase-clusters, most of which have a distinct internal structure: Q 81:1-13: six pairs of verses; Q 82:1-4: two pairs; Q 56:1-6: two groups of three verses. *Idhā*-clusters are also encountered within sūras, e.g. Q 56:83 f.; 75:26 f.; 79:34-36; 100:9-11. They are typologically related to the oath clusters as they build up a pronouncedly rhythmical beginning to the sūra or part of the sūra; here, however, the tension is resolved immediately in the closely following apodosis. In their particularly concise and poetically tinted syntactical structure (*idhā* + noun + verb instead of the standard prose sequence of *idhā* + verb + noun), these clusters (ranging from two to twelve verses) present apocalyptic scenes depicting the dissolution of the created cosmos on the last day. It is noteworthy that the highly rhythmical *idhā*-phrases never exceed mono-partite verse structures and thus contribute to the pronounced *sajʿ* character of the early sūras. In some cases the *idhā*-phrases are not confined to natural and cosmic phenomena but proceed to depict the preparations for the final judgment (the blowing of trumpet, positioning of the throne, opening of the account books etc.). *Yawma* may also serve the function of the conjunction *idhā:* Q 52:9-10; 79:6-7.

Eschatological processes

In terms of grammar, the *idhā*-phrases constituting the protasis of a conditional period are followed by equally stereotyped apodoses referring to the foregoing with the adverb *yawmaʾidhin* (e.g. Q 69:15; 79:8; 99:4, 6). These "eschatological processes" depict the behavior of people in the apocalyptic setting and their separation into the groups of the blessed and the condemned (Q 56:7; see REWARD AND PUNISHMENT).

Diptycha: Descriptions of the hereafter

Continuing (in grammatical terms) the apodosis of the eschatological period, these descriptions of the hereafter are strictly divided into two counterparts. Introduced by *fa-ammā... wa-ammā* (Q 101:6-7, 8-9) or *wujūhun... wujūhun* (Q 80:38-9, 40-2), they juxtapose the situation of the believers in the paradisiacal garden (q.v.; *janna,* see also PARADISE) with that of the disbelievers *(kuffār)* or evildoers (*fāsiqūn* and the like; see EVIL DEEDS; HYPOCRITES AND HYPOCRISY) in the tribulations suffered in the fire (q.v.; *nār*) of hell (q.v.; *jahannam*). It is noteworthy that both depictions are particularly rich in imagery and together form a double image, consisting of either an equal number of verses (e.g. Q 51:10-4, 15-9: five verses each) or of two verse groups displaying a proportional relation to each other (e.g. the just of Q 69:19-24 as against the evildoers of 69:25-37, seven and fourteen verses, respectively). As such, they remind us of the closely juxtaposed pictorial representations of both sections of the hereafter depicted in Church iconography, thus suggesting the designation of "diptycha."

Flashbacks

Not infrequently, diptycha comprise recollections of the particular behavior of the inmates of the two abodes during their worldly life, serving to justify their eschatological fate. These are stereotypically introduced by *innahu kāna* (Q 69:33), and they are sometimes interspersed with direct speech, e.g. *yaqūlu yā laytanī* (Q 69:25). Some of them merge into a catalogue of virtues to be emulated (Q 32:15-7) or vices to be avoided (Q 83:29-33; see VIRTUES AND VICES). Independent flashback passages are Q 56:88-94; 75:31-5; 78:27-30; 84:13-5; subgroups of verses within passages are Q 52:26-8; 56:45-8; 69:33-4; 74:43-6; 83:29-32.

Signs *(āyāt)*

Signs implied in nature

Several descriptions of the "biosphere," of copious vegetation, fauna, an agreeable habitat for humans, the natural resources at their disposal, and the like, are incorporated into paraenetic appeals (see COSMO-

LOGY) to recognize divine providence and accept divine omnipotence, since all these benefits (see BLESSING; GRACE) are signs (q.v.; *āyāt*) bearing a coded message. If they are properly understood, they will evoke gratitude (see GRATITUDE AND INGRATITUDE) and submission to the divine will (Graham, The wind). The perception of nature, which, in pre-Islamic poetry, is a first step to the heroic defiance of its alien roughness (see GEOGRAPHY), has, by middle Meccan times, crystallized into the image of a meaningfully organized habitat ensuring human welfare and arousing the awareness of belonging (see NATURAL WORLD AND THE QUR'ĀN; SEMIOTICS AND NATURE IN THE QUR'ĀN). Extensive *āyāt* passages in the strict sense, with their explicit designation of "signs," do not occur before the second Meccan period; they are, however, preluded by enumerations of divine munificence, as in Q 76:6-16; 77:25-7; 79:27-32; 80:24-32; 82:6-8; 88:17-20; 90:8-10. Often recalling the imagery of the psalms, *āyāt* passages serve to express the progressive change in paradigm concerning the perception of nature. They soon become stock inventory: Q 15:16-25; 25:45-50; 36:33-47; 50:6-11; 14:32-4; 35:9-14, 27-8; 40:61-6; 41:37-40; 42:28-35; 45:12-5. Although signs do occur in polemical contexts (Q 21:30-33: *a-wa-lam yara...;* Q 78:6: *a-lam naj'al...;* Q 79:27-33: *a-antum ashaddu khalqan ami l-samā'u banāhā...;* Q 88:17: *a-fa-lā yanẓurūna...;* see POLEMIC AND POLEMICAL LANGUAGE), hymnical *āyāt* predominate.

Closely related to the hymnical *āyāt* is the hymn as such. Sections praising God's benevolence, omnipotence and his deeds in history occur predominantly in introductory sections (early: Q 87:1-5; 96:1-5; later: Q 67:1-4 introduced by a doxology [see GLORIFICATION OF GOD]; Q 35:1-2). They are also found distributed within the sūras (early: Q 53:43-9; later: Q 32:4-9; 25:61-2 introduced by a doxology *"tabāraka"*; Q 39:62-6). Loosely related to the hymn in a structural sense, but serving a different purpose — namely to present a moral example for the community — is the catalogue of virtues which appears already in early sūras and is frequent in later texts (Q 23:57-61; 25:63-76; 42:36-43). Its counterpart is the catalogue of vices which can be traced through the entire corpus (Q 104:1-2; 18:103-5; 53:33-7; 68:8-16).

Signs implied in history: retribution legends

Short narratives — the invasion of Mecca (Q 105; see ABRAHA; PEOPLE OF THE ELEPHANT); the Thamūd (q.v.) myth (Q 91:11-5); the story of Pharaoh (q.v.; Fir'awn) and Moses (q.v.; Mūsā, Q 79:15-26) — or ensembles of narratives like that in sūra 51 including: Abraham (q.v.; Ibrāhīm) and Lot (q.v.; Lūṭ, Q 51:34-7), Moses and Pharaoh (Q 51:38-40), the 'Ād (q.v.; Q 51:41-2), the Thamūd (Q 51:43-4), Noah (q.v.; Nūḥ, Q 51:46) — or evocations of stories (sūras 51, 53, 69, 73, 85, 89) — occur from the earliest sūras onward (see MYTHIC AND LEGENDARY NARRATIVES; PUNISHMENT STORIES). The latter sometimes form lists (sūras 51, 53, 69, 89). Longer narratives are introduced by the formula known from *āyāt* in nature: *a-lam tara...*, later by *wa-idh (fa'ala)...*, i.e. they are assumed to be known to the listeners. It is noteworthy that the longer narratives which occur in the first Meccan period are split into equal halves, thus producing proportionate structures (e.g. Q 79:15-26, six plus six verses; Q 51:24-37, seven plus seven verses; and 68:17-34, nine plus nine verses). This remains the rule in later narratives as well. Narratives successively develop into retribution legends or punishment stories (Horovitz, *KU*, *"Straflegenden"*), serving to prove that divine justice (see JUSTICE AND

INJUSTICE) is at work in history, the harassed just being rewarded with salvation (q.v.), the transgressors and the unbelievers punished by annihilation. At the same time, legends that are located in the Arabian peninsula may be read as reinterpretations of ancient notions of deserted space: sites lie in ruins no longer due to preordained natural processes, but to a fair equilibrium — maintained by divine providence — between human actions and human welfare (see GEOGRAPHY; GOOD DEEDS; FATE; DESTINY; TIME). Deserted sites acquire a meaning, voicing a divine message. The often-proffered view that it is the retribution legends that are signified with the qurʾānic phrase "the seven reiterated (utterings)," (*sabʿan mina l-mathānī,* Q 15:87) has been called into question by Neuwirth (Der Horizont). From Sūrat al-Ḥijr (Q 15) onward, retribution legends no longer focus predominantly on ancient Arabian lore but increasingly include biblical narratives (see SCRIPTURE AND THE QURʾĀN): Q 15:49-77 offers a detailed narrative about Abraham and Lot, followed by a shorter report about the People of the Thicket (q.v.; *aṣḥāb al-ayka*) and those of al-Ḥijr (*aṣḥāb al-ḥijr,* see ḤIJR).

A related genre in terms of function, which also serves paraenetic purposes, is the parable *(mathal)* — the owners of the blighted garden (*aṣḥāb al-janna,* Q 68:17-33); the good and corrupt trees (Q 14:24-7); the unbelieving town (Q 36:13-32; and cf. Welch, Ḳurʾān, 424). The particular relevance ascribed to parables is obvious from occasional introductory formulas such as *wa-ḍrib lahum mathalan* (Q 18:32; cf. 18:45). Parables are, however, less frequent than myths and historical narratives.

Salvation history narratives (occurring as complete sūras and central sections)

Although initially embedded in catalogues of narratives of partly extra-biblical tradition, stories about major biblical figures like Moses, Jesus (q.v.) and a number of patriarchs known from Genesis gain a function of their own: They become the stock inventory of the central part of longer Meccan sūras. Sūras from the second Meccan period onward may indeed be read as the enactment of a service (see below). The appearance of biblical stories in the center fulfills the expectation of monotheistic worshippers demanding that the central position of a service should be occupied by the reading of scriptural texts, as is customary in other monotheistic services. These stories are explicitly referred to as elements of *al-kitāb;* indeed, some sūras identify themselves as drawing on a pre-existing more extensive text, i.e. as excerpts from a transcendent scripture (see HEAVENLY BOOK; BOOK). Such a book, obviously imagined as being unchangeable and comprehensive, presupposes a stream of tradition that has come to a standstill and became frozen, constituting a store of warranted knowledge. Qurʾānic reference to scripture therefore presupposes a certain stock of narratives existing in a previously fixed form and dispatched by the sender in single portions to form neatly composed pericopes to be inserted into a more extensive recital that also contains less universal elements such as the debate about ephemeral issues of the community. This ceremonial function of the biblically inspired narrative is underlined by introductory formulas, e.g. *wa-dhkur fī l-kitābi* (Q 19:16, 41, 51, 54, 56). At a later stage, when the particular form of revelation communicated to the Muslim community is regarded as constituting a scripture of its own, i.e. when community matters are acknowledged as part of salvation history, whole sūras figure as manifestations of *al-kitāb*.

Although the central position of the narrative in the middle and late Meccan sūras is the rule, an exception is presented by Q 17:2-8. As has been argued by Neuwirth (Erste Qibla; id., From the sacred mosque), the particular composition of this sūra may be due to its unique rank as a testimony of a cult reform, the introduction of the Jerusalem direction of prayer (*qibla,* q.v.). Other outstanding cases are Q 18 and Q 12, the latter of which contains the expanded narrative of Joseph (q.v.; Yūsuf), which fills the entire sūra (cf. Mir, The story of Joseph; Neuwirth, Zur Struktur). The phenomenon of recurring narratives, retold in slightly diverging fashions, has often been interpreted as mere repetition, i.e. as a deficiency. These forms deserve, however, to be studied as testimonies of the consecutive emergence of a community and thus reflective of the process of canonization. Their divergences, then, point to a successively changing narrative pact, to a continuing education of the listeners and the development of a moral consensus that is reflected in the texts (cf. Neuwirth, Negotiating justice). In later Meccan and Medinan sūras, when a large number of narratives are presupposed as being well known to the listeners, the position acquired by salvation history narratives is occupied by mere evocations of narratives and debates about them (Neuwirth, Vom Rezitationstext).

Debate

Polemics

It has been argued that debate is one of the essential elements of the Qurʾān (McAuliffe, Debate; see DEBATE AND DISPUTATION). This is certainly true for the sūras from the middle Meccan period onward. In early Meccan texts, polemical utterances are more often than not directed against listeners who do not comply with the exigencies of the behavioral norms of the cult. These listeners are reprimanded by the speaker *in situ,* e.g. *a-fa-min hādhā l-ḥadīthi taʿjabūn/wa-taḍḥakūna wa-lā tabkūn* (Q 53:59 f.); *a-raʾayta lladhī yanhā/ʿabdan idhā ṣallā* (Q 96:9 f.). Sometimes curses (see CURSE) are uttered against absent persons: *tabbat yadā Abī Lahabin* (Q 111:1 f.) or against humankind in general: *qutila l-insānu mā akfarah* (Q 80:17); in other cases menaces are uttered against the ungrateful or pretentious: *waylun li-...* (Q 104:1; 107:4), and these may merge into a catalogue of vices (Q 104:1-2; 107:2-3, 5-7). Whereas in most of these early cases the adversaries are not granted an opportunity to reply: *mā li-lladhīna kafarū qibalaka muhṭiʿīn* (Q 70:36), later sūras present the voices of both sides. Lengthy polemics are put forward against the unbelievers, sometimes in the presence of the accused (*antum*-addresses), more often, however, in their absence. During the middle and late Meccan periods, when the community had to struggle against a stubborn opposition (see OPPOSITION TO MUḤAMMAD), they needed to be trained in dispute. Meccan sūras often begin and end with polemical debates, treating diverse points of dissent. In some cases, the absent adversaries are verbally quoted: *qālū...* (Q 15:6-7), while in other cases the simulation of a debate is presented, instructing the addressee and his listeners to react to a given statement of the adversaries with a particular response: *wa-yaqūlūna... fa-qul...* (Q 10:20). These instances — classified by Welch as "say-passages" — are to be regarded as virtual debates performed in the absence of one party of the discussants. As against these cases, there are *qul*-verses that do not refer to a debate, but serve to introduce prayers or religious mottos. Often polemics respond to the unbelievers' rejection of the Qurʾān, again figuring at the beginning of sūras (Q 15:1-3), the end of sūras (Q 21:105-12) or in the conclusions to main parts of sūras (Q 7:175-86).

Apologetics (closing sections, sometimes intra-textual)

Like polemics, apologetic sections frequently appear as framing parts of a sūra. From early Meccan texts onward they mostly serve to affirm the rank of the Qurʾān as divine revelation, usually constituting the nucleus of concluding sections (early: Q 73:19; 74:54-5; 85:21-2; 87:18-9; later: Q 26:192-227). In later sūras these concluding affirmations of the revelation tend to merge into exhortations of the Prophet (Q 11:109-23; 38:67-70; 76:23-31; see EXHORTATIONS). It is noteworthy that affirmations of the revelation finally become a standard incipit of sūras (Q 12:1-3; 13:1; 14:1-4; 28:1-3; 30:1-5; 32:1-3; 39:1-2; 40:1-4; 42:1-3; 45:1-6; 46:1-3), again often merging into exhortations (Q 41:1-8). In some cases, sūras are framed by two affirmations of revelation (Q 41:1-5 and Q 41:41-54). In later developments, introductory affirmations are reduced to mere evocations of the book. By far the majority of these sūras start with a pathetical evocation of the book, often introduced by a *"chiffre"* (Q 2:1; 3:1; etc.; see for the most plausible explanation of the initial "mysterious letters," Welch, Ḳurʾān, 412-4; see LETTERS AND MYSTERIOUS LETTERS). This incipit seems to hint at a newly achieved cultic function of the recited text which is no longer understood as the immediate communication of a divine message to the community, but as a recital from a sacred scripture assumed as pre-existing and only reproduced through recitation.

Additional *"enjeux"* to be found in Medinan sūras

Medinan sūras have not yet been studied thoroughly as to their form and structure. Summary analyses are presented by Nöldeke *(GQ)*, Bell *(Qurʾān)*, Welch (Ḳurʾān) and Robinson *(Discovering)*. Zahniser (The word of God; id., Sura as guidance) has discussed single sūras. A systematic investigation of their building blocks is still lacking. It may, however, be stated that with a few exceptions (oath clusters, *idhā*-phrase clusters), all the Meccan *"enjeux"* are met again in Medinan sūras; the eschatological sections and the *āyāt*, however, are no longer unfolded at length, but rather are summarily evoked. This should not be taken as a decisive shift in spiritual interest. Although new topics which occupy the focus of the community's attention do emerge, the earlier topics remain present, since it is the partial corpus of the early sūras (*qiṣār al-suwar*, later assembled in *juzʾ ʿammā*, Neuwirth, Koran) that is known by heart by the believers and serves as the textual basis for the emerging ritual prayers.

Regulations

Although occasional regulations — mostly concerning cultic matters — do occur in Meccan sūras (Q 73:1-3 addressed to the Prophet, revised for the community in Q 73:20), more elaborate regulations concerning not only cultic but also communal affairs figure in the Medinan context (see Welch, Ḳurʾān). Their binding force is sometimes underlined by a reference to the transcendent source (*kutiba ʿalaykum*, Q 2:183-7; *farīḍatan mina llāhi*, Q 9:60). Medinan regulations do not display any structured composition nor do they participate in neatly composed units; they suggest, rather, later insertions into loosely connected contexts.

Evocations of events experienced by the community

A new element appearing in Medinan sūras is the report of contemporary events experienced or enacted by the community, such as the battle of Badr (q.v.) in 2/624 (Q 3:123), the battle of Uḥud in 3/625 (Q 3:155-74), the expulsion of the Banū Naḍīr in 3/625 (Q 59:2-5; see NAḌĪR), the siege of Khaybar in 7/628 (Q 48:15), the expedition to Tabūk in 9/630 (Q 9:29-35) or the farewell (q.v.) sermon of the Prophet in 10/631 (Q 5:1-3; see FAREWELL PILGRIMAGE). It is noteworthy that these reports do not display a particularly artistic literary shaping. Nor do they betray any particular pathos. It does not come as a surprise, then, that, unlike the situation in Judaism and Christianity, where biblical history has been fused to form a mythical drama of salvation, no such "grand narrative" has arisen from the Qurʾān. A metahistorical blueprint of the genesis of Islam was constructed only later, through the *sīra* (cf. Sellheim, Prophet; see HISTORY AND THE QURʾĀN).

Contextuality: Synopsis of the literary and the communicational development

Types of early Meccan sūras

The spectrum of different ensembles is very broad in early Meccan times. Sūra types range from mono-partite pieces: pure *hijāʾ* (Q 111), pure exhortations through the Prophet (Q 94), pure eschatological discourse (Q 95; 100; 101) — to bipartite ones: oath cluster (Q 92:1-13), eschatological section (Q 92:14-21) — to the later standardized tripartite sūra: exhortations (Q 74:1-10), polemics (Q 74:11-48), affirmation of the Qurʾān (Q 74: 49-56). (See for their proportions, Neuwirth, *Studien*, 235-7.) Characteristic of this group as a whole is their striking self-referentiality. The sūras mirror a scenario locally situated in a Meccan public place, most probably close to the Kaʿba (q.v.), taking into account their pronouncedly articulate references to sacred space and human behavior therein, as well as sacred time. The rites at the Kaʿba seem to be the *Sitz-im-Leben* of many early sūras, the Kaʿba not only serving as the locale for the performance of their recitation, but its rites also marking particular times of the day respected by the community as ritually significant. Inasmuch as these sūras are memorized without any written support, their mostly distinct proportions are effective as mnemonic-technical devices.

Types of later Meccan sūras

Things change substantially in later Meccan times. We may localize the caesura with Q 15, where, for the first time, an allusion is made to the existence of a particular form of service in which scripture functions as the cardinal section (cf. Neuwirth, Vom Rezitationstext; id., Referentiality and textuality). In these sūras, the references to the Meccan *ḥaram* as the central warrant of the social coherence of the community have been replaced by new symbols. Instead of introductory allusions to liturgical times and sacred space we encounter an evocation of the book, be it clad in an oath (Q 36:2; 37:3; 38:1; 43:2; 44:2; 50:1) or through a deictic affirmation of its presence (Q 2:2; 10:1; 12:1; 13:1; etc.). Moreover, a new framework of the message in terms of space is realizable, and later Meccan sūras have broadened the scope for the listeners, who are led away from their local surroundings to a distant landscape, the holy land, which becomes familiar as the scenery where the history of the community's spiritual forebears has taken place. The introduction of the Jerusalem *qibla* is an unequivocal testimony to this change in orientation (Neuwirth, Erste Qibla; id. From the sacred mosque). In view of the increasing interest in the biblical heritage, it comes as no surprise that the bulk of the middle and late Meccan sūras (twenty-seven instances) seems to mirror a monotheistic service, starting with an initial discursive section (apologetic, polemic, paraenetic) and closing with a related section, most frequently an affirmation of the revelation. These framing sections have been compared to the ecclesiastic ecteniae (initial and concluding responsoria consisting of pleadings for divine support recited by the priest or deacon with the community complementing the single addresses through affirmative formulas). The center of the monotheistic service and, similarly, of the fully developed sūra of the middle and late Meccan period is occupied by a biblical reminiscence — in the case of the service, a lectio; in the case of the sūra, a narrative focusing on biblical protagonists (Neuwirth, Vom Rezitationstext). Ritual coherence has thus given way to scriptural coherence, the more complex later sūras referring to scripture both by their transmission through diverse processes of writing and by being themselves dependent on the mnemonic-technicalities of writing for their conservation. (For particular sequences of single *"enjeux"* and topics in these compositions, cf. the inventory in Neuwirth, *Studien,* 318-21.)

Types of Medinan sūras

It is true that, already in later Meccan sūras, the distinct tripartite composition often becomes blurred, with narratives gradually being replaced by discursive sections. Some compositions also display secondary expansions — a phenomenon that still needs further investigation. Yet, for the bulk of the middle and late Meccan sūras, the claim to a tripartite composition can be sustained. In Medina, however, sūras have not only given up their tripartite scheme, but they display much less sophistication in the patterns of their composition. One type may be summarily termed the "rhetorical sūra" or "sermon" (Q 22; 24; 33; 47; 48; 49; 57 until 66); they consist of an address to the community whose members are called upon directly by formulas such as *yā ayyuhā l-nāsu...* (Q 22:1). In these sūras, which in some cases (Q 59; 61; 62; 64) are stereotypically introduced by initial hymnal formulas strongly reminiscent of the biblical psalms, the Prophet (*al-nabī,* Q 33:6) appears no longer as a mere transmitter of the message but as personally addressed by God (*yā ayyuhā l-nabiyyu,* Q 33:45) or as an agent acting synergetically with the divine persona (*Allāhu wa-rasūluhu,* Q 33:22). As against these intended monolithic "addresses," the bulk of the Medinan sūras are the most complex. The so-called "long sūras" (Q 2-5; 8; 9) cease to be neatly structured compositions but appear to be the result of a process of collection that we can no longer reconstruct. As pointed out earlier, a systematic study of these sūras is still an urgent desideratum in the field.

Angelika Neuwirth

Bibliography

Primary: Ibn Qayyim al-Jawziyya, *Tibyān.*
Secondary: M.A.S. Abdel Haleem, Context and internal relationships. Keys to qurʾānic exegesis. A study of *Sūrat al-Raḥmān,* in Hawting and Shareef, *Approaches,* 71-98; A. Ambros, Die Analyse von Sura 112, in *Der Islam* 63 (1986), 219-47; A. and J. Assmann, Kanon und Zensur als kultursoziologische Kategorien, in ids. (eds.), *Kanon und Zensur. Archaeologie der literarischen Kommunikation II,* Munich 1987, 7-27; Bell; id., *Introduction to the Qurʾān,* Edinburgh 1953; H. Birkeland, *The lord guideth. Studies on primitive Islam,* Oslo 1958; R. Blachère, *Le Coran,* 3 vols. [i. *Introduction au Coran;* ii-iii. *Traduction nouvelle selon un essai de reclassement des sourates*], Paris 1947-50 (repr. 1957); id., *Histoire de la litérature arabe,* 3 vols., Paris 1952-66; P. Capron de Caprona, *Le Coran aux sources de la parole oraculaire. Structures rhythmiques des sourates mecquoises,* Paris 1981; F.M. Denny, Exegesis and recitation. Their development as classical forms of qurʾānic piety, in F. Reynolds and T. Ludwig (eds.), *Transitions and transformations in the history of religions. Essays in honor of Joseph M. Kitagawa,* Leiden 1980, 91-123; C. Dohmen and M. Oeming, *Biblischer Kanon — warum und wozu?* Freiburg 1992; J. van Ess, Review of J. Wansbrough, *Qurʾānic studies,* in BO 35 (1978), 353; T. Fahd, Kāhin, in *EI²*, iv, 420-2; R. Geyer, Zur Strophik des Korans, in WZKM 22 (1908), 256-86; id., Review of K. Vollers, *Volkssprache und Schriftsprache im alten Arabien,* in *Göttingische gelehrte Anzeigen* 171 (1909), 10-56; I. Goldziher, *Introduction to Islamic theology and law,* Princeton 1981 (trans. of his *Vorlesungen über den Islam);* Graham, *Beyond;* id., "The wind to herald his mercy" and other "Signs for those of certain faith." Nature as token of God's sovereignty and grace in the Qurʾān, in S.H. Lee et al. (eds.), *Faithful imagining. Essays in honor of Richard R. Niebuhr,* Atlanta 1995, 18-38; Horovitz, KU; A.H. Johns, The qurʾānic presentation of the Joseph story, in Hawting and Shareef, *Approaches,* 37-70; A. Kellermann, Die Mündlichkeit des Koran. Ein forschungsgeschichtliches Problem der Arabistik, in *Beiträge zur Geschichte der Sprachwissenschaft* 5 (1995), 1-33; L. Kandil, *Untersuchungen zu den Schwüren im Koran unter besonderer Berücksichtigung ihrer literarischen Relevanz für die*

Surenkomposition, Ph.D. diss., Bonn 1995; L. Kopf, Religious influences on medieval Arabic philology, in *SI* 5 (1956), 33-59; M.R.L. Lehmann, Biblical oaths, in *Zeitschrift für die alttestamentliche Wissenschaft* 81 (1969), 744-92; A. Lord, *The singer of tales,* Cambridge, MA 1960; R.C. Martin, Understanding the Qurʾān in text and context, in *History of religions* 21 (1982), 361-84; J.D. McAuliffe, 'Debate with them in a better way.' The construction of a qurʾānic commonplace, in A. Neuwirth et al. (eds.), *Myths, historical archetypes and symbolic figures in Arabic literature,* Beirut 1999, 163-88; M. Mir, The qurʾānic story of Joseph. Plot, themes, and characters, in *MW* 76 (1986), 1-15; id., The *sūra* as a unity. A twentieth century development in Qurʾān exegesis, in Hawting and Shareef, *Approaches,* 211-24; J.T. Monroe, Oral composition in pre-Islamic poetry, in *JAL* 3 (1972), 1-53; H. Motzki, The collection of the Qurʾān. A reconsideration of western views in light of recent methodological developments, in *Der Islam* 78 (2001), 1-34; D. Müller, *Die Propheten in ihrer ursprünglichen Form,* 2 vols., Vienna 1896; T. Nagel, Vom Koran zur Schrift. Bells Hypothese aus religionsgeschichtlicher Sicht, in *Der Islam* 60 (1983), 143-65; A. Neuwirth, Einige Bemerkungen zum besonderen sprachlichen und literarischen Charakter des Koran, in *ZDMG,* Suppl. iii, 1, 19. *Deutscher Orientalistentag in Freiburg* 1975, Wiesbaden 1977, 736-9; id., Erste Qibla — Fernstes Masgid? Jerusalem im Horizont des historischen Muhammad, in F. Hahn et al. (eds.), *Zion Ort der Begegnung. Festschrift für Laurentius Klein zur Vollendung des* 65. *Lebensjahres,* Hain 1993, 227-70; id., Der historische Muhammad im Spiegel des Koran — Prophetentypus zwischen Seher und Dichter?, in W. Zwickel (ed.), *Biblische Welten. Festschrift für Martin Metzger zu seinem* 65. *Geburtstag,* Göttingen 1993, 83-108; id., Der Horizont der Offenbarung. Zur Relevanz der einleitenden Schwurserien für die Suren der frühmekkanischen Zeit, in U. Tworuschka (ed.), *Gottes ist der Orient Gottes ist der Okzident. Festschrift für Abdoldjavad Falaturi zum* 65. *Geburtstag,* Cologne and Vienna 1991, 3-39; id., From the sacred mosque to the remote temple. Sūrat al-Isrāʾ between text and commentary, in J.D. McAuliffe et al. (eds.), *With reverence for the word. Medieval scriptural exegesis in Judaism, Christianity and Islam,* (forthcoming); id., Images and metaphors in the introductory sections of the Makkan suras, in Hawting and Shareef, *Approaches,* 3-36; id., Koran, in *GAP,* ii, 96-130; id., Negotiating justice. A pre-canonical reading of the qurʾānic creation accounts, in *Journal of qurʾānic studies* 1 (1999), 25-41; 2 (2000), 1-18; id., Qurʾān, crisis and memory. The qurʾānic path towards canonization as reflected in the anthropogonic accounts, in A. Neuwirth and A. Pflitsch (eds.), *Crisis and memory in Islamic societies,* Beirut 2001, 113-52; id., Qurʾānic literary structure revisited. Sūrat al-Raḥmān between mythic account and decodation of myth, in S. Leder, *Story-telling in the framework of non-fictional Arabic literature,* Wiesbaden 1998, 388-420; id., Referentiality and textuality in Sūrat al-Ḥijr. Some observations on the qurʾānic "canonical process" and the emergence of a community, in I. Boullata (ed.), *Literary structures of religious meaning in the Qurʾān,* London 2000, 143-72; id., Zur Struktur der Yūsuf-Sure, in W. Diem and S. Wild (eds.), *Studien aus Arabistik und Semitistik. Anton Spitaler zum siebzigsten Geburtstag von seinen Schülern überreicht,* Wiesbaden 1980, 123-52; id., *Studien;* id., Symmetrie und Paarbildung in der koranischen Eschatologie. Philologisch-Stilistisches zu Sūrat ar-Raḥmān, in L. Pouzet (ed.), *Mélanges de l'Université Saint-Joseph. Mélanges in memoriam. Michel Allard, S.J.* (1924-1976). *Paul Nwyia, S.J.* (1925-1980), Beirut 1984, 445-80; id., Vom Rezitationstext über die Liturgie zum Kanon. Zu Entstehung und Wiederauflösung der Surenkomposition im Verlauf der Entwicklung eines islamischen Kultus, in Wild, *Text,* 69-105; id. and K. Neuwirth, *Sūrat al-Fātiḥa.* "Eröffnung" des Text-Corpus Koran oder "Introitus" der Gebetsliturgie?, in W. Gross, H. Irsigler and T. Seidl (eds.), *Text, Methode und Grammatik. Wolfgang Richter zum* 65. *Geburtstag,* St. Ottilien 1991, 331-58; Nöldeke, *GQ;* id., *Neue Beiträge zur semitischen Sprachwissenschaft,* Strassburg 1910; M. Parry, *The making of Homeric verse. The collected papers of Milman Parry,* Oxford 1971; A. Rippin, Review of Neuwirth, *Studien,* in *BSOAS* 45 (1982), 149-50; id., The Qurʾān as literature. Perils, pitfalls and prospects, in *British Society for Middle Eastern Studies bulletin* 10 (1983), 38-47; id., Literary analysis of the Qurʾān, tafsīr and sīra. The methodologies of John Wansbrough, in R.C. Martin (ed.), *Approaches to Islam in religious studies,* Tucson 1985, 151-63; id., Muḥammad in the Qurʾān. Reading scripture in the 21st century, in H. Motzki (ed.), *The biography of Muhammad. The issue of the sources,* Leiden 2000; N. Robinson, *Discovering the Qurʾān. A contemporary approach to a veiled text,* London 1996; id., *Islam. A concise introduction,* Richmond (Surrey) 1999; id., The structure and interpretation of Sūrat al-Muʾminūn, in *Journal of qurʾānic studies* 2 (2000), 89-106; U. Rubin, Morning and evening prayers in early Islam, in *JSAI* 10 (1987), 40-64; G. Schoeler, Schreiben und Veröffentlichen. Zur Verwendung und Funktion der Schrift in den ersten islamischen Jahrhunderten, in *Der Islam* 69 (1992), 1-43; R. Sellheim, Prophet, Chalif und Geschichte. Die Muḥammad Biographie des Ibn

Isḥāq, in *Oriens* 18 (1965), 33-91; M. Sells, Sound, spirit, and gender in Sūrat al-Qadr, in *JAOS* 111 (1991), 239-59; id., Sound and meaning in Sūrat al-Qāriʿa, in *Arabica* 40 (1993), 403-30; G.R. Smith, Oaths in the Qurʾān, in *Semitics* 1 (1970), 126-56; S.M. Stern, Muhammad and Joseph. A study of koranic narrative, in *JNES* 44 (1985), 193-202; K. Vollers, *Volkssprache und Schriftsprache im alten Arabien*, Strasburg 1906, repr. Amsterdam 1981; Wansbrough, *QS*; Watt-Bell, *Introduction;* G. Weil, *Historisch-kritische Einleitung in den Koran*, Bielefeld 1844; A. Welch, Ḳurʾān, in *EI²*, v, 400-28; J. Wellhausen, *Reste arabischen Heidentums*, Berlin 1889, 1927, repr. Berlin 1961; A.H.M. Zahniser, The word of God and the apostleship of ʿĪsā. A narrative analysis of Āl ʿImrān (3:33-62), in *JSS* 37 (1991), 77-112; id., Sūra as guidance and exhortation. The composition of Sūratu n-Nisāʾ, in A. Afsaruddin and A.H.M. Zahniser (eds.), *Humanism, culture and language in the Near East. Studies in honor of Georg Krotkoff*, Winnona Lake 1997, 71-85; M. Zwettler, *The oral tradition of classical Arabic poetry. Its character and implications*, Columbus, OH 1978.

Fosterage

Entrusting a child to foster parents. There is no technical term in the Qurʾān for fosterage. As formal adoption of children (q.v.) is forbidden (Q 33:4-5; for dating see Bell, ii, 409, 411, 415), the qurʾānic discussion focuses exclusively on the prohibition for a man to marry women with whom he has foster relationships of a certain type (see FORBIDDEN; MARRIAGE AND DIVORCE).

According to Q 4:23 (from years 4-5 A.H., cf. Bell, i, 66, 71) a man is not allowed to marry his step-daughters (*rabāʾib*, sing. *rabība*, "a man's wife's daughter by another husband..." [Lane, 1005] whom the new husband rears as his own [see Bayḍāwī, *Anwār*, ad Q 4:23; Robertson-Smith, *Kinship*, 196-7, n. 3]) unless his marriage with their mother(s) has not been consummated. It is also forbidden, by the same verse, for a Muslim man to marry his foster (milk) mothers and foster (milk) sisters (see MILK; WET NURSING; LACTATION), i.e. females who were breast-fed by the same foster mother(s). These, as well as the prohibition of marriage with one's father's wife (Q 4:22), wife's mother, son's wife, and marriage with two sisters at the same time (Q 4:23), represent the negative qurʾānic attitude towards "incest du deuxieme type" (Héritier, *Les deux soeurs*, 87-91).

Muslim exegetes, commenting on Q 4:23, raise different legal questions (see LAW AND THE QURʾĀN) stemming from the qurʾānic prohibition of marriage with one's wife's daughter. For instance, whether *dakhaltum bihinna* ("[wives to whom] you have gone in") refers necessarily to full sexual relationships (see SEX AND SEXUALITY) or also to intimate contacts, not involving penetration (see, e.g. Ṭabarī, *Tafsīr;* Zamakhsharī, *Kashshāf*); or, in the light of the expression *fī ḥujūrikum* ("those who are under your care, protection," lit. "held in your bosom"), whether or not a Muslim man is allowed to marry his wife's daughter (by another man) who has not been under his care, living, for example, outside his own house (see, e.g. Ibn Kathīr, *Tafsīr;* see HOUSE, DOMESTIC AND DIVINE).

Although Q 4:23 explicitly mentions only foster (milk) mothers and foster (milk) sisters, Qurʾān commentators, relying on ḥadīth (see ḤADĪTH AND THE QURʾĀN), explain the verse as intended to duplicate for milk relationships the list of those blood relatives with whom a Muslim is forbidden to contract marriage (see, for instance, Rāzī, *Tafsīr*, ad Q 4:23). Thus the Qurʾān, and later on ḥadīth, add a unique element — which may have been rooted in pre-Islamic Arabic custom — to a long Semitic tradition of impediments to marriage, extending the range of incest beyond its parameters in Judaism and Christianity (see JEWS AND JUDAISM; CHRISTIANS AND CHRISTIANITY; PRE-ISLAMIC ARABIA AND THE QURʾĀN). Viewed in the light of Q 4:23, the ruling formulated by various ḥadīth reports in this regard (for instance, *inna llāha ḥarrama min al-riḍāʿi mā ḥarrama min al-nasab*) was understood to mean that to the list of women a man is forbidden to marry because of foster (milk) kinship are added his milk niece (maternal and paternal), milk aunt, milk daughter and the milk mother of his wife. It was also forbidden for a man to be married to, or to own, simultaneously two women who were milk sisters (see Giladi, *Infants*, 24-33). See also KINSHIP.

Avner Giladi

Bibliography
Primary: Bayḍāwī, *Anwār;* Ibn Kathīr, *Tafsīr;* Rāzī, *Tafsīr;* Ṭabarī, *Tafsīr;* Zamakhsharī, *Kashshāf.*
Secondary: Bell; A. Giladi, *Infants, parents and wet nurses. Medieval Islamic views on breastfeeding and their social implications,* Leiden 1999; F. Heritier, *Les deux soeurs et leur mere. Anthropologie de l'inceste,* Paris 1994; Lane; W. Robertson-Smith, *Kinship and marriage in early Arabia,* London 1907; J. Schacht/ J. Burton, Raḍāʿ, in *EI²*, viii, 361-2; G.H. Stern, *Marriage in early Islam,* London 1939.

Fountains see SPRINGS AND FOUNTAINS; WELLS AND SPRINGS; WATER

Freedom and Predestination

Unhampered or divinely controlled human activity. The question of free will and predestination, a question which accompanied the development of rational theology in all the religious systems of the Near East, was expressed in qurʾānic form as the issue of the extent of God's ability to determine events, including human acts. Muslim scholars refer to this issue as that of God's power and decree *(al-qadar wa-l-qaḍāʾ)*. The final Islamic answer, partially presupposed by pre-Islamic fatalism (see PRE-ISLAMIC ARABIA AND THE QURʾĀN), was, in contrast to that offered by Christianity, to assert the overwhelming force of God's predetermination at the expense of the individual's free will. Only during the second/eighth and third/ninth centuries was there heated discussion on the subject, initiated by a group of theologians, proponents of free will, who paradoxically received the name of Qadarites (*qadar* here refers to the possibility of human as opposed to divine power; see THEOLOGY AND THE QURʾĀN). Both parties, the Qadarites and their opponents, tried to support their respective doctrines by citations from the Qurʾān. While the general message of the Qurʾān seemed to downplay the role of the individual and to attribute to God complete and total power, particular qurʾānic passages provided fertile ground for arguments in support of and against human free will.

The pre-Islamic concept of the impersonal and irresistable fate (q.v.) or destiny (q.v.) identified as time (q.v.; *dahr* and *zamān*) was the point of departure for the qurʾānic message. In this pre-Islamic scheme, fate or destiny was an unfriendly and antagonistic force closely associated with the events of an individual's life, i.e. with the time of death *(ajal),* good and evil fortune, and even daily sustenance *(rizq)*. The outcome of one's acts or decisions, rather than the acts or decisions themselves, was thought to be predetermined. The individual person, far from being guided by, was in opposition to this "fate." It was perceived as distinct from this individual's actions, a predetermination that resulted in an inability to escape one's doom, regardless of what was decided or attempted. Of the two above-mentioned terms — power and decree — the first, power *(qadar),* better conveys the idea of impersonal fate, while the latter, decree *(qaḍāʾ),* which does appear in the pre-Islamic context, albeit much less frequently than *qadar,* could already mean God's decision (see Ringgren, *Studies in Arabian fatalism,* 5-61).

The qurʾānic point of view represented

a break with the previous conception of fatalism, though traces of the old belief did not disappear entirely, as in the variant of Q 103 ascribed to ʿAlī (see Jeffery, *Materials*, 192; cf. Q 52:30). Substituting impersonal fate with the personal God, known as creator, king and judge, omnipotent, and benevolent (see GOD AND HIS ATTRIBUTES) radically changed the situation. The transition to this new conceptual horizon was achieved in several steps, and a certain evolution of the qurʾānic views on predestination can be argued on the basis of the text, views which seem to have crystallized in the late Meccan sūras of the second and third periods (see CHRONOLOGY OF THE QURʾĀN). Over seventy percent of the qurʾānic citations used as theological arguments by both sides, starting from the famous letter on predestination of al-Ḥasan al-Baṣrī (d. 110/728) addressed to the Umayyad caliph ʿAbd al-Malik (r. 65-86/685-705), are taken from these periods. Only very occasional references are made to the early Meccan (poetic) sūras, though the beginning of the process of transition is already discernible in these earlier sūras.

Already in the early Meccan sūras God emerges as the lord (q.v.) of time who governs day and night (q.v.), e.g. Q 73:20. This idea later culminated in the direct juxtaposition of God, who governs the sun (q.v.) and moon (q.v.; Q 13:2; 31:29; 35:13; 39:5), with time, and a refutation of the latter's role in determining fate (Q 45:24, 26; cf. the famous ḥadīth: "I am *dahr;* in my hand are night and day," Bukhārī, *Ṣaḥīḥ*, ad Q 5:24 [cited in Watt, *Formative period*, 91]). Whereas previously time was thought to be the agent, it is now God who is understood to predetermine human sustenance (*rizq*, cf. Q 51:22, 58; 56:82; 89:15-6) and death (Q 56:60; see DEATH AND THE DEAD), as well as the fate of people after death (Q 70:38-42). The scope of predestination, however, also embraces birth, understood as the realization of the lord's decree (see, in addition to the citations for God's predetermination of death and sustenance, Q 77:20-3; 80:18-22). This notion of predetermination thus governs not only the results of human actions and the end of life, but also their beginning and initial cause (see BIOLOGY AS THE CREATION AND STAGES OF LIFE; BIRTH). The central term for determination in the early sūras is *qadar* and its derivatives, to which no form of the Arabic root letters *q-ḍ-y* (from which the noun *qaḍāʾ*) is ever adjoined. The new understanding of *qadar* as the manifestation of God's omnipotence eventually leads to the later utilization of the same root for conveying the idea of the lord's might, eventually embodied in two of his given attributes: the powerful (*al-qadīr*, 39 times) and the one who prevails (*al-muqtadir*, four times). This etymological connection with the notion of God's power set the term *qadar* in opposition to free will, eventually conceived by orthodox scholars as an infringement on God's omnipotence (see POWER AND IMPOTENCE). In comparison with God's might, helplessness over one's fate is emphasized (cf. Q 68:25). Q 97:1-3, which speaks of the Night of Power (q.v.; *laylat al-qadr*), so important in later dogma, seems to belong to a subsequent stage in the revelation, the Medinan period. Here, a link may be seen between the notion of the annual determination of everyone's fate for the coming year and parallels in the Jewish tradition, for exegetical literature *(tafsīr)* discussing the circumstances surrounding the revelation of this verse (see OCCASIONS OF REVELATION) indicates a context of dialogue with Judaism (see JEWS AND JUDAISM).

Starting from the Meccan sūras of the second period, the qurʾānic message takes a new direction. The reminiscences, motifs and ideas of the Hebrew Bible and the

New Testament are much more prominent (see SCRIPTURE AND THE QUR'ĀN): God's benevolence becomes equal in importance to his omnipotence (see BLESSING), the idea of the scripture as the book (q.v.) becomes dominant, and the history of the prophets (see PROPHETS AND PROPHETHOOD) and, later, the divine law (see LAW AND THE QUR'ĀN) are significantly developed. All this gave further impetus to the idea of predetermination. The fatalistic concept in its theistic variant unfolds further and incorporates old ideas, both those found in pre-Islamic poetry (see POETRY AND POETS) and in biblical sources.

The idea of a fixed term or life-span *(ajal),* while sometimes carrying a profane sense, is mostly used in reference to the terms set by God in his governance of the world (q.v.). The idea includes notions of death, an earthly punishment (see CHASTISEMENT AND PUNISHMENT) and the last judgment (q.v.). It also indicates an individual's life-span (cf. Q 11:3), fixed terms for communities and peoples (Q 7:34; 10:49), and even the whole of the universe (Q 30:8; 46:3). It is in the context of God as creator of the world that the concept of *qaḍā'* appears in the qur'ānic text. It is a divine decision that is prior to creation (q.v.; cf. Q 2:117; 3:47; 19:35; 40:68) and sets its fate (cf. Q 6:2; 10:11), thus becoming a term parallelled with *qadar*. This decree emerges as related to the lord's creative command *(amr)* that precedes the world and which initiates creation and rules everything in the world. The two concepts, *qaḍā'* and *amr,* are sometimes conjoined in one context (cf. Q 12:41), implying, as Muslim exegetes stress, the inseparability of creation from the establishment of its unchangeable fate. The Qur'ān also declares that what has been predestined for an individual or the universe has been recorded in a primordial book *(kitāb* or *kitāb mu'ajjal)* of fate: "No misfortune can happen on earth or in your souls but it is [recorded] in a book before we bring it about" (Q 57:22; cf. Q 3:145, 154; 6:38, 59; 9:51; 10:61; 20:52; 27:75; 35:11; see HEAVENLY BOOK). It should be stressed that the doctrine of predetermination gradually embraced not only the results of human acts but these acts themselves, considered to have been pre-conceived by the lord's wisdom: "With him are the keys of the unseen (see HIDDEN AND THE HIDDEN), no one knows it [or them] but he. He knows whatever is on land and in the sea; there falls not a leaf but he knows of it, nor a grain in the darkness of the earth, nor a thing either succulent or desiccated but is [inscribed] in a clear book" (Q 6:59). The introduction, during the Medinan period, of the idea of the annual renewal of the lord's decree concerning the fate of the individual and its connection with the Night of Power *(laylat al-qadr)* can be considered the logical culmination of the qur'ānic concept of predestination, informing the believer of its workings in history.

Later developments in Muslim thought uncovered a problem implicit in the qur'ānic concept of predestination as this related to the belief in God's benevolence towards his creatures. The Qur'ān understands heaven (q.v.) and hell (q.v.), respectively, to be the greatest fortune and misfortune to befall humankind. Whether one will enjoy the pleasures of the garden (q.v.) or suffer the torments of the fire (q.v.) is decided on the day of judgment in accord with the balance of good and evil deeds (see EVILS DEEDS; GOOD DEEDS) committed during one's lifetime and written down in a special book (see RECORD OF HUMAN ACTIONS; cf. Q 17:3-4, 71; 45:28-9; this is not to be confused with the primordial book, mentioned above, which contains the fate of the individual and the cosmos). One may logically conclude, then, that a human being is punished or rewarded for his acts since they are, indeed, of his making. It would seem that responsibility is presupposed by the idea of punishment and reward (see REWARD AND PUNISHMENT). Still, there is no decisive or unequivocal answer to the question of final reponsibility for these deeds: Are they the result of one's free choice or of God's predetermination of those acts and choices? A common qurʾānic statement is the following: "[God] leads astray (q.v.) whom he wills, and guides whom he wills" (Q 16:93; 74:31; cf. Q 6:125; 13:27). There are, however, verses in which divine guidance or misguidance are a function of previously committed good or bad acts (Q 2:26; 3:86; 16:104). Other contexts indicate that the choice between belief and unbelief (q.v.) is made by people themselves while God only gives them guidance *(hudā)* without forcing them to choose faith (q.v.; cf. Q 18:29; 41:17). The ambivalent treatment of the topic is clear in "This truly is a warning: Whosoever wills, let him take the [right] path (see PATH OR WAY) to his lord; but you cannot will, unless God wills it. God is all-knowing and wise" (Q 76:29-31). The qurʾānic message stops at this point, and never directly asks how God can punish those whom he himself has led astray, or how he can be the source of evil deeds, issues which already the first generations of Muslim rational theologians (*mutakallimūn*, see THEOLOGY AND THE QURʾĀN) began to debate. Similarly, the qurʾānic text mostly gives an overview of the crucial points in human life, dealing with topics such as belief and unbelief, life and death, good and evil acts without ever saying explicitly that every single act performed by a person, i.e. eating or abstaining from food, meeting with friends, etc., is preordained or predetermined.

It should be added that the second source of the Muslim tradition, the sunna (q.v.), also addresses the question. Chapters on *qadar* are found in four of the six canonical collections of traditions (see ḤADĪTH AND THE QURĀN), i.e. those of Bukhārī, Muslim, Tirmīdhī, and Abū Dāwūd, all of whom generally favored the predestinarian position, foreshadowing the final outcome of the debate on free will. Tradition has not preserved a single ḥadīth advocating free will (see Wensinck, *Muslim creed*, 51), and certain ones seem especially designed to refute the arguments of the Qadarites. That is why al-Ḥasan al-Baṣrī, who coined many arguments used by later generations of the proponents of free will, begins his letter with the statement that the predecessors *(salaf)* would not use any arguments but those of which God makes use in his scripture (Schwarz, Letter, 167; for the text itself see Ritter, Studien, 63).

The beginning of the debate is generally traced to the middle of the Umayyad rule (the first quarter of the eighth century C.E.) and is painted in terms of a dispute between theologians and traditionalists. The Muʿtazilis (q.v.), who take up the issue at a later date, are generally cast in the role of proponents of free will. Some scholars have argued that the origin of the Qadarite doctrine should be attributed to Christian influence, a position supported by historical data in the sources, but there is no unanimity on this point among the Western treatments of the topic (J. van Ess, Ḳadariyya). In any case the roots of the problem of free will in Islam lie in the domain of rational theodicy and the questions of God's justice (see JUSTICE AND INJUSTICE), the origin of evil in the world (see GOOD AND EVIL) and the justification of human punishment in this world and the next.

A comparison of the subtle exegetical passages in the letter *(risāla)* of al-Ḥasan al-Baṣrī (van Ess, *TG*, ii, 46-50) with the commentary on the relevant qurʾānic verses done by the last great theologian of the Muʿtazila, al-Zamakhsharī (d. 538/1144; cf. Nyberg, al-Muʿtazila, 791), in his *Kashshāf* highlights the continuity with the arguments used by the Qadarites. At the same time, the exegesis *(tafsīr)* of orthodox commentators, such as al-Ṭabarī (d. 310/923), al-Qurṭubī (d. 671/1272), Ibn Kathīr (d. 774/1373), and al-Suyūṭī (d. 911/1505) demonstrates that some verses were taken to speak explicitly against the Qadarite or Muʿtazilite position (Gilliot, *Elt*, 259-76; see EXEGESIS OF THE QURʾĀN: CLASSICAL AND MEDIEVAL). In other words, there is a wealth of traditional material, not yet properly studied, that can suggest how, and perhaps predictably so, the generations of Muslim scholars who lived after the early theological debates were concluded, came to view the qurʾānic rhetoric on free will and determinism as a message of divine omnipotence and predestination.

Dmitry V. Frolov

Bibliography
Primary: Abū Nuʿaym al-Iṣbahānī, *Ḥilyat al-awliyāʾ*, v, 346 f. (= the epistle on *qadar* by ʿUmar b. ʿAbd al-ʿAzīz); al-Ashʿarī, *Risāla ilā ahl al-thaghr*, Medina 1988, 240-66; al-Ḥasan al-Baṣrī, *Risāla*, in H. Ritter, Studien zur islamischen Frömmigkeit I. Ḥasan al-Baṣrī, in *Der Islām* 21 (1933), 1-83; also in J. Obermann, Political theology in early Islam. al-Ḥasan al-Baṣrī's treatise on *qadar*, in *JAOS* 55 (1935), 138-62; and in M. Schwarz, The letter of al-Ḥasan al-Baṣrī, in *Oriens* 20 (1967), 15-30; Ibn Ḥazm, *Milal*, Beirut n.d., iii, 33-8, 77-8; al-Jurjānī, Abū l-Ḥasan, *al-Taʿrīfāt*, Cairo 1938, 151-2, 155; *Lisān al-ʿArab*; Shahrastānī, *Milal*, Beirut 1990, i, 38-92.
Secondary: J. van Ess, *Anfänge muslimischer Theologie. Zwei antiqadaritische Traktate aus dem ersten Jahrhundert der Higra*, Wiesbaden 1977; id., Ḳadarriya, in *EI²*, iv, 368-72; id., *TG*; L. Gardet, al-Ḳaḍā wa-l-ḳadar, in *EI²*, iv, 365-7; id. and Anawati, *Introduction* (cf. index); Gilliot, *Elt*; H.S. Nyberg, al-Muʿtazila, in *EI¹*, vi, 787-93; D. Rahbar, *God of justice*, Leiden 1960; H. Räisänen, *The idea of divine hardening. A comparative study of the notion of divine hardening, leading astray and inciting to evil in the Bible and the Qurʾān*, Helsinki 1976; H. Ringgren, *Studies in Arabian fatalism*, Uppsala-Wiesbaden 1955, esp. 86-116; W.M. Watt, *The formative period of Islamic thought*, Edinburgh 1973, esp. 82-118; id., *Free will and predestination*, London 1948; A.J. Wensinck, *The Muslim creed*, London, 1932, 1965².

Free Will see FREEDOM AND PREDESTINATION

Freewoman see MARRIAGE AND DIVORCE

Friday Prayer

Weekly gathering of Muslims in the chief mosque (q.v.), at which they listen to a sermon *(khuṭba)* and perform ritual acts of worship (q.v.) at the time of the noon-day prayer. Direct reference to the Friday Prayer, *al-ṣalāt min yawm al-jumʿa*, occurs only once in the Qurʾān (at Q 62:9), where the expression denotes an occasion of ritual worship held on the "day of assembly" (the literal translation of the Arabic term for the sixth day of the week, *yawm al-jumʿa* or *yawm al-jumuʿa*) rather than a gathering for the express purpose of congregational prayer (q.v.). Whereas later developments — as reflected in ḥadīth literature, exegetical works and legal treatises — employ this term, usually abbreviated as *ṣalāt al-jumuʿa*, to designate the formal ceremony held in major mosques in the place of the noon *(ẓuhr)* prayer (one of the five daily prayers prescribed for Muslims; see PRAYER; NOON; DAY, TIMES OF) on Friday, the etymology of this qurʾānic phrase points to pre-Islamic usage (see PRE-ISLAMIC ARABIA AND THE QURʾĀN).

The Arabic name for this sixth day of the week, with close Hebrew and Aramaic parallels, derives largely from customs prevailing in Medina (q.v.) at the time of the Prophet, where Friday was identified as the "day of gathering" in that it served as the principal market day when Jews (see JEWS

AND JUDAISM; MARKETS) bought provisions in preparation for the Sabbath (q.v.; Jeffery, *Materials,* 170; Goitein, Djumʿa; see also SELLING AND BUYING). Hence, designating Friday as the day for congregational prayer among Muslims appears to originate in the juxtaposition of market activity and collective religious duty. Friday was not set apart as a day of rest, although the weekly conduct of this communal prayer defined a setting dedicated to devotion and instruction, to which an array of prescriptions was later attached (e.g. that the communal prayer was incumbent upon all male, adult, free, resident Muslims; that it should be held in only one mosque in each town; and various prescriptions for the number of attendants; cf. Goitein, Djumʿa). Although there is no evidence that the initiation or establishment of Friday as the day of communal prayer was of polemical intent, Friday has emerged as a 'symbol' of Islam as opposed, for example, to Saturday or Sunday. In modern times, many Muslim states have declared Friday an official day of rest (cf. Goitein, Djumʿa).

The summons to "hasten to the remembrance of God and put away your business" at the call to prayer and afterwards "to spread out in the land and look for the bounty of God" (Q 62:9-10), indicates the sacred ritual's occurrence in the proximity of commercial and social pursuits. The time of day also points to this conjuncture. Whereas midday may suggest an unsuitable hour for assembly in certain respects, historical observation of traditional periodic markets in Arabia has confirmed that, around noon, trading diminishes and people depart with their goods. Thus, it has been argued that the Prophet convoked this worship as those at market were preparing to disperse.

While abundant references to the practice of ritual prayer appear in the Qurʾān, including numerous verses that signal its establishment as a regular practice, such as Q 17:78, no clear precedent for the Friday Prayer in its familiar classical form occurs, a form which consists of an *adhān* and the *khuṭba,* followed (and sometimes also preceded) by a *ṣalāt* consisting of two *rakʿa*s (see BOWING AND PROSTRATION). Specifically, the sermon, *khuṭbat al-jumʿa,* that constitutes the distinctive feature of the Friday Prayer is not mentioned nor does the term *khuṭba* appear in the Qurʾān with this technical meaning. Nevertheless, commentators have discerned indirect allusions to preaching in the relevant verses. For instance, mention of *dhikr Allāh* with reference to Friday Prayer at Q 62:9 has been interpreted by al-Bayḍāwī (d. ca. 716/1316-7), *Jalālayn,* Mawdūdī (d. 1979), and others as referring to the sermon. Similarly, the lines "when they see some buying and selling, or some sport, they go for it, leaving you standing" (Q 62:11) have been read by Bukhārī (d. 256/870; *Ṣaḥīḥ,* bk. 11, no. 26) and others as leaving the Prophet standing "on the *minbar,*" that is, the ceremonial pulpit, an interpretation that indulges in anachronism since pulpits were only introduced under the Umayyads.

Patrick D. Gaffney

Bibliography
Primary: Bayḍāwī, *Anwār;* Bukhārī, *Ṣaḥīḥ; Jalālayn;* S.A.A. Mawdūdī, *Tafhīm al-Qurʾān,* 3 vols., Lahore 1954-65.
Secondary: C.H. Becker, Zur Geschichte des Islamischen Kultus, in id., *Islamstudien,* Leipzig 1924, 472-500; E.E. Calverley, *Worship in Islam,* Madras 1925; S.D. Goitein, Djumʿa, in *EI²,* ii, 592-4; id., The origin and nature of the Muslim Friday worship, in id., *Studies in Islamic history and institutions,* Leiden 1966, 111-25; Jeffery, *Materials;* F.E. Peters, *Muhammad and the origins of Islam,* Albany 1994; D. Sourdel, Appels et programmes politico-religieux durant les premiers siècles de l'islam, in G. Makdisi et al. (eds.), *Prédication et propagande au Moyen Âge,* Paris 1983, 111-31; J. Wensinck, Khuṭba, in *EI²,* v, 74-5; S.M. Zwemmer, The pulpit in Islam, in *MW* 23 (1933), 217-29.

Friends and Friendship

One attached to another by affection, loyalty or common experience. In the Qurʾān, the terms *walī*, *khalīl* and (in certain instances) *ṣadīq* all correspond in some sense to the English word "friend." Of these, the term *walī* (sometimes in the plural form *awliyāʾ*) appears most frequently, and it is often paired with *naṣīr*, "helper," or *shafīʿ*, "intercessor" (see INTERCESSION). Unless otherwise indicated, the term *walī* is used in all references cited below.

The Qurʾān envisages friendship primarily as an alliance (see COVENANT; LOYALTY; PROTECTION). It makes little distinction between alliances on the human plane and those between human beings and supernatural powers. For example, "Your friend is only God, his messenger (q.v.), and those who believe, those who perform prayer and give alms (see ALMSGIVING), while they are bowing down (see BOWING AND PROSTRATION); whoever takes as friend God, his messenger and those who believe, the party of God (see PARTIES AND FACTIONS) will prevail (see VICTORY)" (Q 5:55-6; the first of these verses is taken to refer to the imāmate of ʿAlī b. Abī Ṭālib [q.v.] in Shīʿī exegetical works; see Ṭūsī, *Tibyān*, iii, 549; see also IMĀM; SHĪʿISM AND THE QURʾĀN). The predominant qurʾānic concept of friendship thus presupposes the existence of a struggle in which individuals are called upon to take sides.

The Qurʾān repeatedly pronounces God, from whose will there is no escape (see FREEDOM AND PREDESTINATION), as the only friend and helper of the believers (Q 4:45; 9:116; 29:22; 33:17; 42:31; cf. 2:257; 3:68; 5:55-6; 6:127; 7:155; 18:26); according to most interpretations, these passages represent calls to communal solidarity and activism among the believers (e.g. Bayḍāwī, *Anwār*, i, 211 [ad Q 4:45]; see BELIEF AND UNBELIEF; COMMUNITY AND SOCIETY IN THE QURʾĀN). God's friendship with the believers manifests itself in divine aid and guidance (Māwardī, *Nukat*, i, 328 [ad Q 2:257]). The oppressed *(mustaḍʿafūn)* properly call on God to make for them a friend and helper (Q 4:75), while the unbelievers, oppressors and wrongdoers have no friend or helper (Q 4:123, 173; 9:74; 11:20; 18:102; 33:65; 42:8-9, 46; 48:22). No fear (q.v.) is upon the friends of God (Q 10:62), and God is humankind's only friend and intercessor (Q 6:51, 70; 32:4; cf. Q 42:9, 28; 45:19). On occasion, God has singled out prophets as his friends (see PROPHETS AND PROPHETHOOD), particularly in the case of Abraham (q.v.; Q 4:125, *wa-ttakhadha llāhu ibrāhīm khalīlan*); God is also the friend of the angels (Q 34:41; see ANGEL). Yet elsewhere, as an assertion of monotheism, the Qurʾān insists that God has no friend: "And say: Praise be to God, who took no son, has no partner in sovereignty (q.v.), and has no friend against baseness; magnify him greatly" (Q 17:111; cf. Bayḍāwī, *Anwār*, i, 554; see also Penrice, *Dictionary*, 52).

In a similar vein, the Qurʾān depicts polytheism (see POLYTHEISM AND ATHEISM) as a wrongful alliance, and stresses the impotence (see POWER AND IMPOTENCE) of false supernatural friends. Just as the believers are the friends of God, the unbelievers are the friends of the devils (Q 3:175; 6:121; 7:27, 30; see DEVIL; SPIRITUAL BEINGS; ENEMIES). Such false friends, however, will be of no value on the last day (see ESCHATOLOGY; LAST JUDGMENT), since they will be powerless to intercede with God (see INTERCESSION), the only true friend. Those led astray (q.v.) will thus find that they have no friends other than God (Q 17:97; 18:17; 42:44, 46; cf. 26:100-1 *[ṣadīq]*); those who take friends other than God will find no escape and will surely come to grief (Q 29:41; 39:3; 42:6, 9; 45:10; 46:32). More explicitly, those who take Satan as their friend will come undone (Q 4:76, where the believers are urged to fight against the friends of Satan, *fa-qātilū awliyāʾa l-shayṭān;* Q 4:119; 16:63; 19:45; cf. Q 18:50, with its warning against choosing Iblīs [q.v.] and his seed as friends).

The Qurʾān also places great emphasis on earthly alliances. The believers are enjoined not to take other than their own folk as intimates (*biṭāna,* Q 3:118; cf. Bayḍāwī, *Anwār,* i, 172, where the verse is explicated as a warning against trust and the sharing of secrets; see TRUST AND PATIENCE; SECRETS), nor to form friendships with members of other groups. This restriction of ties applies (see CONTRACTS AND ALLIANCES) to unbelievers (Q 3:28; 4:89, 139, 144) and to Jews and Christians (Q 5:51; cf. 5:57, 80-1, where some of the Children of Israel [q.v.] befriend the unbelievers; see also PEOPLE OF THE BOOK). Friendship is a manifestation of communal solidarity: The believers, male and female, are friends one of another, and this friendship is expressed through enjoining the good and forbidding the evil (see GOOD AND EVIL), performing prayer (q.v.) and giving alms (Q 9:71; see ALMSGIVING). Moreover, activism is the mark of friendship: "Those who believe, emigrate (see EMIGRATION), and strive with their wealth (q.v.) and themselves in the way of God (see PATH OR WAY); and those who give shelter and help, they are friends one of another" (Q 8:72; according to a widespread interpretation, this passage refers to the appointment by the *muhājirūn* and *anṣār* of one another, to the exclusion of their relatives, as heirs, e.g. Sufyān al-Thawrī, *Tafsīr,* 122; Bayḍāwī, *Anwār,* i, 375; cf. Ṭūsī, *Tibyān,* v, 189-90; see EMIGRANTS AND HELPERS. See also Q 5:55-6, cited above: according to one interpretation, the "friendship" referred to here constitutes obedience [q.v.] to God and his messenger, and assistance to the believers; according to another, it constitutes aiding God's religion [q.v.] and fidelity to it; cf. Ṭūsī, *Tibyān,* iii, 554. For a Ṣūfī interpretation, see Tustarī, *Tafsīr,* 50-1; see ṢŪFISM AND THE QURʾĀN). Similarly, the oppressors are friends one of another (Q 45:19); the believers should not take as friends those who prefer disbelief to belief (see BELIEF AND UNBELIEF), even if they are their own fathers and brothers (Q 9:23). "Those who choose unbelievers as friends, to the exclusion of believers: Do they aspire to power (*ʿizza*) through them? Power belongs entirely to God" (Q 4:139; cf. Bayḍāwī, *Anwār,* i, 236). Such people will also give God clear authority (q.v.) against themselves (Q 4:144; generally interpreted as a reference to the hypocrites, who take unbelievers as friends; cf. Bayḍāwī, *Anwār,* i, 238; see HYPOCRITES AND HYPOCRISY). As with every person who does not heed God, Muḥammad (q.v.) himself (for whom God is the only friend and helper, cf. Q 2:107; 7:196), will find himself with neither friend nor helper if, after receiving God's revelation, he heeds the wishes of the Jews and Christians (who desire that he adhere to their confession [*milla*], Q 2:120; cf. 13:37; see JEWS AND JUDAISM; CHRISTIANS AND CHRISTIANITY).

The Qurʾān thus portrays a friend primarily as a fellow member of a community, a person who can be trusted because he or she is presumed to share in and to be ready to fight (see FIGHTING) for the interests of the group; individuals who make friends with members of other groups will find their own trustworthiness called into question. In the classical period and later, the term *walī* was used for Ṣūfī saints (Böwering, *Mystical,* esp. 231-41), and in the Shīʿī tradition, of ʿAlī b. Abī Ṭālib and other imāms (Momen, *Introduction,* 17, 157), and these conceptions of friendship permeate the Ṣūfī and Shīʿī exegetical traditions respectively. The Qurʾān also uses the term *mawadda,* the meaning of which may include the bond of personal trust and affection primarily connoted in contemporary usage by the English word "friendship." (In this sense, see also the comments of al-Bayḍāwī on Q 3:118, referred to above.) Thus God may ordain *mawadda* where enmity now exists (Q 60:7; a reference, according to al-Bayḍāwī, *Anwār,* ii, 328, to joining the community of believers); Muḥammad asks for love among kin (*al-mawadda fī l-qurbā,* cf. Q 42:23); and God creates wives for men, so that they may share in mutual affection *(mawadda)* and compassion (*raḥma,* Q 30:21; see KINSHIP; LOVE AND AFFECTION; MERCY; MARRIAGE AND DIVORCE).

Louise Marlow

Bibliography
Primary: Bayḍāwī, *Anwār;* Ibn Abī al-Dunyā, *al-Ikhwān,* ed. M. ʿAbd al-Qadir ʿAṭā, Beirut 1988; Māwardī, *Nukat;* Sufyān al-Thawrī, *Tafsīr;* Ṭūsī, *Tibyān;* Tustarī, *Tafsīr.*
Secondary: Böwering, *Mystical;* Izutsu, *Concepts;* Mir, *Dictionary;* M. Momen, *An introduction to Shīʿī Islam,* New Haven and London 1985; Paret; Penrice, *Dictionary;* F. Rahman, *Major themes of the Qurʾān,* Minneapolis 1980, 1989.

Frog see ANIMAL LIFE; PLAGUE

Fruits and Vegetables see AGRICULTURE AND VEGETATION; FOOD AND DRINK

Fugitives see LAW AND THE QURʾĀN

Funeral see DEATH AND THE DEAD

Furniture and Furnishings

Movable articles and adornments within a house. Furniture and furnishings *(matāʿ* and *athāth)* in the Qurʾān are most commonly used as tropes for discussing the ephemeral nature of existence in the mundane world and for the pleasures and pains of life in the hereafter (see ESCHATOLOGY; REWARD AND PUNISHMENT). Two of the most widely esteemed passages in the Qurʾān, however, the Throne Verse (Q 2:255) and the Light Verse (Q 24:35), use terms for specific furnishings (*kursī,* "throne," and *miṣbāḥ,* "lamp") to help convey ideas about the majesty and mystery of the godhead (see GOD AND HIS ATTRIBUTES). In actual practice, Muslims often furnish mosques, traditional centers of Islamic education *(madrasas),* workplaces and their own homes with copies of the Qurʾān and objects upon which verses of sacred scripture have been inscribed (see EVERYDAY LIFE; EPIGRAPHY).

The most inclusive qurʾānic term for furnishings, *matāʿ* (pl. *amtiʿa*), occurs thirty-five times. In half of these instances it means "enjoyment" of worldly pleasures and their limitations, as in the following verse: "Say, 'The enjoyment of the world *(matāʿu l-dunyā)* is of little value; the hereafter is best for the godfearing'" (Q 4:77). Through such statements the Qurʾān seeks to direct the orientation of its audiences away from this world towards consciousness of their eternal fate in the afterlife. In a few instances, *matāʿ* denotes ordinary household comforts, as in Q 24:29: "It is not sinful for you to enter unoccupied houses — in these there are amenities *(matāʿ)* for you." Such comforts and furnishings *(matāʿ* and *athāth),* though temporary, are counted among the gifts God bestowed on humankind (see Q 16:80-3; see BLESSING; GRACE).

Specific furnishings are also mentioned in the Qurʾān, such as the throne *(kursī)* of God (Q 2:255; see THRONE OF GOD) and that of Solomon (q.v.; Q 38:34), the lantern *(sirāj)* as a metaphor (q.v.) for the Prophet (Q 33:46) and the sun (q.v.; Q 25:61; 71:16) or the lamp (q.v.; *miṣbāḥ*) as a metaphor for the source of divine light (q.v.; Q 24:35) and heavenly bodies (*maṣābīḥ*, Q 67:5). The vast plain of the earth (q.v.) is described as a ground cover (*firāsh*, Q 2:22) or carpet (*bisāṭ*, Q 71:19) created by God for people to travel upon. Other household furnishings mentioned include the beds (*maḍājiʿ*) to which disobedient women are confined (Q 4:34; see WOMEN AND THE QURʾĀN), the food table (q.v.; *māʾida*, Q 5:112, 114), the cradle from which Jesus (q.v.) spoke as a child (*mahd*, e.g. Q 3:46; 5:110) and the veil (q.v.; *ḥijāb*), which may refer to a partition in the home (Q 33:53) or a barrier (q.v.) between heaven and hell (Q 7:46), the Prophet and his audience (Q 41:5) or God and humanity (Q 42:51). More frequently, however, furnishings appear in qurʾānic discourses about the hereafter: the tomb is a sleeping place (*marqad*, Q 36:52) from which the dead are resurrected (see RESURRECTION; DEATH AND THE DEAD), the damned are consigned to a bed (*mihād*) of evil and misery (e.g. Q 3:12, 197; 7:41; see HELL), while the blessed recline on carpets (*ʿabqarī*, Q 55:76; *zarābī*, Q 88:16), elegant couches (for example, *surur*, Q 15:47; 56:15; 88:13; *arāʾik*, Q 18:31), silken cushions (*rafraf*, Q 55:76; *namāriq*, Q 88:15) and beds (*furush*, Q 55:54; 56:34). Immortal youths and beautiful houris (q.v.) offer the righteous food (see FOOD AND DRINK) from the paradisaical gardens (see PARADISE; GARDEN) in golden bowls (*ṣiḥāf*, Q 43:71) and invite them to drink from goblets (*akwāb*, for example, Q 43:71; 88:14), silver chalices (*āniya*, Q 76:15), wine cups (*kaʾs*, Q 56:18) and other drinking vessels (*abārīq*, Q 56:18; *qawārīr*, Q 76:16; see CUPS AND VESSELS).

The *muṣḥaf* (q.v.) of the Qurʾn is used as a furnishing for liturgical and educational purposes or as an instrument for obtaining God's blessing, to avert evil and misfortune, and for decoration. Since the early Islamic period, it has been prominently displayed in mosques, where it is usually placed on a stand (*kursī*) for use by the reciter (*qāriʾ*, see RECITERS OF THE QURʾĀN). It is also a common furnishing in Islamic primary schools (*kuttāb*s, *maktab*s). In modern times, with the advent of the printing press (see PRINTING OF THE QURʾĀN), Muslims normally purchase a *muṣḥaf* for display in their homes, workplaces, automobiles, trucks and buses.

Writing on manufactured furnishings owned by Muslims was practiced as early as the fourth/tenth century, but the use of qurʾānic texts on these objects is not very evident until the late twelfth century, especially among the elites. Thereafter, we find Qurʾān boxes skillfully crafted with inlaid texts such as the Throne Verse Q 3:18-9 (about God, Islam and scripture), Q 3:26-7 (about God's power), Q 56:76-80 (about the Qurʾān), and Q 59:23 (the names of God); and the distinctive Mamluk hanging lamps inscribed with phrases from the Light Verse. Pen boxes, ceramic plates, bowls, tiles and textiles also bore qurʾānic phrases and verses as did Persian and Turkish prayer rugs occasionally after the tenth/sixteenth century. Nowadays Muslims customarily acquire artfully framed verses of the Qurʾān, posters, calendars and other objects with qurʾānic writing on them for display at home, school, the workplace and, of course, mosques and shrines (see also MATERIAL CULTURE AND THE QURʾĀN; HOUSE, DOMESTIC AND DIVINE).

Juan Eduardo Campo

Bibliography

E. Atil, *The age of Sultan Suleyman the Magnificent*, Washington D.C. 1987; id. (ed.), *Islamic art and patronage. Treasures from Kuwait*, New York 1990; id., *Renaissance of Islam. Art of the Mamluks*, Washington D.C. 1981; I.A. Bierman, *Writing signs. The Fatimid public text*, Berkeley 1998; J.E. Campo, *The other sides of paradise. Explorations into the religious significance of domestic space in Islam*,

Columbia, SC 1991; *Descriptive catalogue of an exhibition of oriental rugs from the collection of James Franklin Ballard,* San Francisco 1923; Cl. Huart and J. Sadan, Kursī, in *EI²*, v, 509; J. Sadan, Mafrūshāt, in *EI²*, v, 1158-9; J. Sourdel-Thomine et al., Kitābāt, in *EI²*, v, 210-33.

Furqān

see CRITERION; NAMES OF THE QUR'ĀN

Future Life

see ESCHATOLOGY; RESURRECTION; PARADISE; HELL AND HELLFIRE; FIRE; GARDEN

G

Gabriel

The angelic being who "brings down" the qur'ānic revelation to the prophet Muḥammad's heart (q.v.; Q 2:97), Gabriel (Ar. Jibrīl, also Jabrāʾīl; Heb. Gabrīʾēl) is named three times in the Qurʾān, Q 2:97, 98 (where Michael [q.v.], too, is mentioned), and Q 66:4. Commentators on the Qurʾān such as al-Ṭabarī (d. 310/923), al-Zamakhsharī (d. 538/1144) and al-Bayḍāwī (d. ca. 716/1316-7) identify Gabriel as the messenger who brings the revelation to Muḥammad, and understand the two visions of Muḥammad recorded in Q 53:1-18 to be the Prophet's sighting of Gabriel (Pedersen, Djabrāʾīl, 636; see REVELATION AND INSPIRATION; ASCENSION). According to al-Ṭabarī, Gabriel (and Michael) are said to have purifed the belly and breast of Muḥammad; Gabriel is also reported by al-Ṭabarī to have taught Muḥammad to pray, to have guided Muḥammad on his ascension, and to have rebuked Muḥammad for his acknowledgment of al-Lāt, al-ʿUzza and Manāt (see SATANIC VERSES; see Pedersen, Djabrāʾīl, 363 for the references in al-Ṭabarī).

As the Qurʾān is also said to have been brought down by "the trustworthy spirit" (Q 26:193), Gabriel is identified by qurʾānic exegetes with the spirit, an identification also understood by them as evidenced in the qurʾānic discussion of Mary (q.v.), in which "our [God's] spirit" that is sent to her (Q 21:91) assumes the likeness of a perfect man (Q 19:17). Gabriel is further identified by the commentators with the spirit who, together with "the angels," descends and ascends to God (Q 16:2; 70:4; 97:4). As such, the figure of Gabriel becomes a rich source of theological reflection not only on the content of revelation — the duties and beliefs of the faithful — but on the nature of cognition itself, including distinctions between reason, prophetic revelation, and mystical knowledge (see ANGEL; HOLY SPIRIT).

Gabriel in ḥadīth and the "tales of the prophets"

The theme of Gabriel as transmitter of fundamental qurʾānic beliefs, duties and values appears in many ḥadīths used as teaching stories in Muslim community life. One such ḥadīth has the future caliph ʿUmar b. al-Khaṭṭāb reporting how "a [strange] man in white clothes and very black hair" came to Muḥammad and his Companions (see COMPANIONS OF THE PROPHET), sat down with his knees pressed against Muḥammad's, and questioned the Prophet on the meaning of Islam. In response, Muḥammad delineated the "pillars" of Islam. When the stranger left and Muḥammad was asked by his Companions to explain this odd event, he answered "He was Gabriel who came to… *teach you* your religion" (Bukhārī, *Ṣaḥīḥ*, i, 37; Tibrīzī, *Mishkāt*, i, 5; see FAITH).

Stories about Gabriel appear in those qurʾānic commentaries that include the folkloristic ("midrashic") interpretations of the Qurʾān as well as in the sense of classical literature known as the "tales of the prophets" *(qiṣaṣ al-anbiyāʾ)*. In one representative narrative, Gabriel offers Abraham (q.v.) aid when he is cast by Nimrod (q.v.) into a fire (q.v.). Abraham's refusal of even Gabriel's help becomes an example of trust in God *(tawakkul)* and of an interiorized understanding of the unity and transcendence of God *(tawḥīd)* from the theological perspective that it would be "hidden associationism" to rely upon or be afraid of any created being.

Gabriel in Islamic philosophy

The meaning of Gabriel as agent of revelation is taken up by medieval Muslim philosophers in their discussions about the generation of the universe (see CREATION) and about human knowledge (including prophetic knowledge; see KNOWLEDGE AND LEARNING; REVELATION AND INSPIRATION). Ibn Sīnā (d. 428/1037), utilizing certain elements of pre-Islamic, particularly neo-Platonic, philosophy in his reflection on the relationship of "being and beings," conceived of the generation of the universe as an eternal procession of "angel intellects" from a primordial divine unity (God). The tenth, or active intellect, is identified with Gabriel/Holy Spirit. Not only is "being" given by God through the active intellect, but the individual cognition process, including the prophet's knowledge (though in a complete form) is viewed as a bestowal of divine illumination on the human soul.

Gabriel in theosophical Ṣūfism

The "philosopher-mystics" of Islam, such as Muḥyī l-Dīn Ibn al-ʿArabī (d. 638/1240) and Shihāb al-Dīn Yaḥyā b. Ḥabash al-Suhrawardī (d. 578/1191) utilize the qurʾānic Gabriel-as-agency-of-revelation in their mystical theologies to identify particular stages and states in the path to integration of the self and unity with God. Ibn al-ʿArabī (as does Rūmī) uses Gabriel-narratives that emphasize the qurʾānic theme that human beings have the potential for knowledge — and hence ontological status — that the angels do not have. Suhrawardī, utilizing both pre-Islamic Greek and Iranian imagery in his school of "oriental wisdom," emphasizes the soteriological role of Gabriel as the one who illuminates the soul to its condition of forgetfulness and entanglement in the world of matter.

Gisela Webb

Bibliography

Primary: Bukhārī, *Ṣaḥīḥ;* Kisāʾī, *Qiṣaṣ;* Suhrawardī, Shihāb al-Dīn Yaḥyā b. Ḥabash, *Oeuvres et mystiques* (*Opera metaphysica et mystica* i, ii), ed. H. Corbin, Teheran-Paris 1976; id., *Oeuvres philosophiques et mystiques*, ed. H. Corbon, 3 vols., Teheran/Paris 1976 (note: vol. iii, ed. with [P] intro. by S.H. Nasr); Thaʿlabī, *Qiṣaṣ;* al-Tibrīzī, Muḥammad b. ʿAbd Allāh al-Khaṭīb, *Mishkāt al-maṣābīḥ* [an abridgment and augmentation of al-Baghawī's *Maṣābīḥ al-sunna*], trans. J. Robson, 4 vols., Lahore 1963-5.

Secondary: M.R. Bawa Muhaiyaddeen, Another hadisz qudsi, in id., *al-Asmāʾul-husnā. The 99 beautiful names of Allah*, Philadelphia 1979, 138-47; W. Chittick, *The Sufi path of knowledge*, New York 1989; H. Corbin, *Avicenna and the visionary recital*, Irving, TX 1980; id., *Creative imagination in the Sufism of Ibn ʿArabi*, Princeton 1969; P. Eichler, *Die Dschinn, Teufel und Engel im Koran*, Inaugural-Dissertation, Leipzig 1928, 123-7; 129-30;

A. Geiger, *Was hat Mohammed aus dem Judenthume aufgenommen,* Leipzig 1902, 12-5; A. Jeffery, Ibn ʿArabi's shajarat al-kawn (trans. and comm.), in *SI* 10 (1959), 43-77 and 11 (1959), 113-60; S. Murata and W. Chittick, *The vision of Islam,* New York 1994; S.H. Nasr, *An introduction to Islamic cosmological doctrines,* Boulder 1978; id., *Three Muslim sages,* Delmar, NY 1976; W. Niekrens, *Die Engel und Geistervorstellungen des Korans,* Inaugural-Dissertation, Rostock 1906, 38-42 (includes discussion of Michael); J. Pedersen, Djabrāʾīl, in *EI²*, ii, 362-4; F. Rahman, *Major themes in the Qurʾān,* Minneapolis 1980; id., *Prophecy in Islam,* Chicago 1979; J. Renard, *All the king's falcons. Rumi on prophets and revelation,* Albany 1994; A. Schimmel, *Mystical dimensions of Islam,* Chapel Hill, NC 1975; G. Webb, *The human/angelic relation in the philosophies of Suhrawardi and Ibn Arabi,* Ph.D. diss., Temple University, Philadelphia 1989; Wensinck, *Concordance.*

Gambling

Playing or gaming for money or other stake with the participants in such activity having no control over the outcome. Although related qurʾānic concepts (discussed below) include such terms as "playing, gaming" *(l-ʿ-b),* "betting" (associated with Q 30:1-4), and "the casting of lots" (*qurʿa,* in relation to Q 3:44; 37:141), the most precise qurʾānic example of gambling is *al-maysir.*

al-Maysir *and games of chance*

The term *al-maysir* is mentioned three times in the Qurʾān, always with the general connotation of gambling (games of chance). A first occurrence is in Q 2:219: "They question you about strong drink (see INTOXICANTS) and gambling/games of chance *(al-maysir).* Say: in both is great sin, and some utility for men; but the sin of them is greater than their usefulness...." The other two occurrences of *al-maysir* are in Q 5:90-1: "O you who believe! Strong drink and games of chance/gambling and idols (see IDOLS AND IMAGES) and divining arrows are only an infamy of Satan's handwork. Leave it aside in order that you may succeed. Satan seeks only to cast among you enmity and hatred by means of strong drink and gambling/games of chance, and turn you from remembrance of God and from (his) worship. Will you then have done?" Although it appears to be condemned primarily for being a diversion from prayer (q.v.) and a cause of divisiveness and hostility among the faithful, by being categorized together with idols (see IDOLS AND IMAGES) and divining arrows (see FORETELLING), it is seen as an "impure" practice (Fahd, al-Maysir, 924; see LAWFUL AND UNLAWFUL).

Commentators on the Qurʾān as well as Arabic linguists have debated at length the etymology of the term *al-maysir* (derived from the Arabic root *y-s-r,* meaning "to be easy" but from which also derives the term for the left hand, *al-yusrā;* for details on the pre-Islamic practice, see Fahd, al-Maysir, 923-4). The generally accepted glosses include: games of risk or chance, playing dice, a game with dice, gambling, as well as material or spiritual gain (e.g. titles) through bets or gambling. Al-Zamakhsharī (d. 538/1144; *Kashshāf,* i, 261) cites the word *al-maysir* as denoting the Arabic word *al-qimār,* i.e. gambling, namely "taking someone's property in an easy way, without effort and labor." In the same context, al-Zamakhsharī states that the word *al-maysir* is derived from the word *al-yasār,* denoting *al-ghinā,* "wealth," because, al-Zamakhsarī claims, "gambling [is] to grab someone's property" *(li-annahu salb yasārihi).* Al-Shawkānī (d. 1250/1832; *Tafsīr,* i, 220), on the other hand, lists the word *al-maysir* as meaning *al-jazūr,* a slaughtered animal the division of whose parts were subject to gambling among pre-Islamic Arabs *(al-jazūr alladhī kānū yataqāmarūna ʿalayhi).* This gloss of *al-maysir* is not completely divorced from al-Zamakhsharī's interpretation, for he also discusses meat acquired by means of gambling (*Kashshāf,* i, 262): he states that the arrow used by the pre-Islamic Arabs when gambling about how to distribute their prey is called *qidḥ* (pl. *aqdāḥ*), and he mentions that meat acquired by gambling was given away to the poor and never eaten by those who had actually won it *(wa-kānū yadfaʿūna tilka l-anṣiba ilā l-fuqarāʾ wa-lā yaʾkulūna minhā)*. For this purpose, the slaughtered animal was called *al-jazūr* (or *al-maysir*) because it was by gambling that its meat was shared, i.e. the winners received an easy gain in meat by gambling. The classical commentators of the Qurʾān record that the word *al-yāsir* denotes the person who supervises this specific ceremony of gambling over the meat of a slaughtered animal (see e.g. Ṣābūnī, *Tafsīr āyāt al-aḥkām,* i, 268).

Many commentators on the Qurʾān speak extensively about what could be subsumed under the headings of gambling and games of risk. Al-Zamakhsharī states, besides the above-mentioned, that *al-maysir* includes the games known as *nard,* "backgammon" ("trictrac" in Levantine dialect; also called *ṭāwila*) and *shaṭranj,* "chess." These games were allegedly banned by the Prophet because they were played by Persians *(min maysiri l-ʿajam)*. The same commentator mentions that the fourth caliph ʿAlī b. Abī Ṭālib (q.v.; r. 35-40/656-61) is once said to have declared that the games *nard* and *shaṭranj* are included in *al-maysir.* The Ṣūfī (see ṢŪFISM AND THE QURʾĀN) Qurʾān commentator Ismāʿīl Ḥaqqī l-Brūsawī (d. 1137/1725; *Tafsīr,* i, 338) includes in the category of *al-maysir* the child's game of dice and a game played with walnuts *(luʿb bi-l-jawz wa l-kiʿāb)*. This commentator quotes, in the same context, one of Islam's earliest authorities, Ibn Sīrīn (d. 110/728), who said "Everything that involves risk, everything that implies gambling is *al-maysir*" *(kullu shayʾin fīhi khaṭar fa-huwa min al-maysir)*. Mystical commentators of the Qurʾān claim that human destiny (q.v.) is too serious a matter to be interpreted and foretold by games of risk and gambling. Hence, Islam prohibits *al-maysir.*

The fact that the Qurʾān mentions *al-maysir* along with strong drink *(al-khamr),* idolatry *(al-anṣāb),* and fortune-telling, as well as divining arrows *(al-azlām)* is in itself reason enough for Muslim jurists to view all forms of *al-maysir* (through gambling, card games, dice, games that involve risk, etc.) that involve money or other valuables as strictly forbidden (q.v.; *ḥarām*). The reason for this is that gambling is a way to gain property from others that is easy and without labor.

The legitimacy of such leisure activities in Islamic thought is varied (see Rosenthal, *Gambling,* 9-26). Although recreation or play — designated by the root *l-ʿ-b* (which occurs twenty times in the Qurʾān) — is not condemned outright by Muslim jurists, it acquired judgments such as "an activity without a sound purpose" or "the activity of children resulting in tiredness without any profit." Consequently, the seriousness and usefulness of activities such as sports (regardless of whether or not they were used for gambling) had to be argued (see Rosenthal, *Gambling,* 13). The linkage of *al-maysir* with the notion of game or play *(al-luʿb)* is seen in the warning against "pigeon fancying and playing chess and *nard;* once a person gets accustomed to them, he finds it hard to stop and avoid their destructive consequences" (ibid., where al-Ghazālī's *Iḥyāʾ ʿulūm al-dīn* is cited). Indeed, there are legal pronouncements *(fatāwā)* claiming that the games of chess, backgammon, cards and dominoes, etc. are not *ḥarām* if the game itself is not played for money or any other material or spiritual gain, and if it does not imply excessive waste of time; i.e. if the game does not turn into sheer leisure.

Such legal pronouncements have been issued by the contemporary Sheikh Yūsuf al-Qaraḍāwī, who classifies the playing of chess under the category of things allowed. He considers playing chess as neither unclean *(karāha)* nor forbidden (*ḥarām*, see PROHIBITED DEGREES) but allowed *(mubāḥ)* under three conditions: (a) that the prayer at prescribed times is not neglected due to playing chess; (b) that chess is not played for money or material gain (i.e. that it does not turn into *qimār*); and (c) that chess players do not curse while playing, and abstain from rude words, from making false vows, etc. Many contemporary Muslim jurists consider card games, backgammon and other games allowable under the same conditions. Lottery and games that involve risk in any form are, however, unanimously treated by contemporary Muslim jurists as forms of *al-maysir*, i.e. forbidden things. They are considered to be *al-maysir* because they imply investing money or other substantive means in an action that could lead to gain for some and loss for others.

Betting and casting lots

The other qurʾānic allusions to activities in which the participants have no control over the outcome, but may lose or gain thereby, fall under the headings of "betting" and "casting of lots." In their commentaries on Q 30:1-4, which discusses the fortunes of the Byzantines (q.v.), qurʾānic exegetes relate that the polytheists made a bet with Abū Bakr (q.v.) that the Prophet's prediction of Byzantine victory and Persian defeat would not come true, and that Abū Bakr won the bet (see Rosenthal, *Gambling*, 26-31). One must note that the Qurʾān itself contains no allusion to "bet" in this passage, and the commentators use different Arabic words to describe the activity between Abū Bakr and the polytheists. Unspecified persons are said to have cast lots for the task of being Mary's (q.v.) guardian in Q 3:44. A more specific qurʾānic allusion to this practice *(sāhama)* is found in Q 37:141, in which Jonah (q.v.), as a result of losing the drawing of lots, is thrown into the sea (see Rosenthal, *Gambling*, 32-4).

Enes Karic

Bibliography

Primary: Ibn Qutayba, *al-Maysir wa-l-qidāḥ*, ed. Muḥibb al-Dīn al-Khaṭīb, Cairo 1923; Ismaʿīl Ḥaqqī al-Brūsawī, *Tafsīr rūḥ al-bayān*, 10 vols., Beirut 1405/1985; Nuwayrī, Aḥmad b. ʿAbd al-Wahhāb, *Nihāyat al-ʿarab fī funūn al-adab*, Cairo 1964-, iii, 118-20 (on *maysir*), trans. A. Huber, *Über das "meisir" genannte Spiel der heidnischen Araber* (Inaugural Dissertation), Leipzig 1883; Y. al-Qaraḍāwī, *al-Halāl wa-l-ḥarām fī l-Islām*, Beirut 1373/1973; id., *The lawful and the prohibited in Islam*, Indianapolis 1980 (trans. of *al-Ḥalāl wa-l-ḥarām fī l-Islām*); Ṣābūnī, *Tafsīr āyāt al-aḥkām*, 2 vols., Beirut 1391/1971; Shawkānī, *Tafsīr*, 5 vols., Beirut 1403/1983; Zamakhsharī, *Kashshāf*, ed. M.Ḥ. Aḥmad, 4 vols., Beirut 1407/1987.

Secondary: T. Fahd, *La divination arabe*, Leiden 1966, esp. pp. 204-13; id., Maysir, in *EI²*, vi, 923-4 (for additional bibliography); F. Rosenthal, *Gambling in Islam*, Leiden 1975; M.I. Siddiqi, *Why Islam forbids intoxicants and gambling*, Lahore 1981.

Garden

A fertile tract of land for the cultivation of flowers, herbs, vegetables or fruits. In Arabic, the term *janna* refers to "garden" in general; with the definite article *al-*, it refers particularly to paradise (q.v.), the celestial abode promised to the righteous in the next world (see REWARD AND PUNISHMENT).

As a single word *al-janna* is the most frequently used term in the Qurʾān to designate paradise (e.g. Q 2:214; 7:43; 19:63). It is also found in phrases such as *jannat* (or *jannāt*) *ʿadn*, "garden(s) of Eden" (Q 13:23; 16:31; 18:31; 61:12; etc.), *jannat al-khuld*, "garden of perpetuity" (Q 25:15), *jannat* (or *jannāt*) *al-naʿīm*, "garden(s) of bliss" (Q 10:9; 22:56; 26:85; 56:12; etc.) and *jannat al-maʾwā*, "garden of refuge" (Q 53:15). But this is not the only terminology for paradise. Several times it is called "the last abode" (*al-dār al-ākhira,* Q 2:94; 7:169; etc.), twice "the abode of peace" (*dār al-salām,* Q 6:127; 10:25), once "the abode of residence" (*dār al-muqāma,* Q 35:35), and "the abode of permanence" (*dār al-qarār,* Q 40:39; see HOUSE, DOMESTIC AND DIVINE). Further, the term *al-firdaws* (related to the Greek term *paradeisos,* traceable ultimately to the Avestan word *pairidaeza*), occurs twice (Q 23:11; 18:107), as does the term *ḥadāʾiq,* "gardens" (Q 27:60; 80:30). *Rawḍa* occurs once (Q 30:15), as does its plural, in the phrase *rawḍāt al-jannāt,* "meadows of the gardens" (Q 42:22). The Qurʾān also includes reference to garden in the dual (*jannatān,* e.g. Q 34:15; 55:46).

Earthly gardens find reference in the Qurʾān as well, mostly as manifestations of God's pleasure or displeasure with humans (see BLESSING; GRACE). For example, the Qurʾān mentions the two gardens of Sheba (q.v.; Sabaʾ) which, on account of the iniquitous behavior of the natives of the town, were turned into gardens that bore "bitter fruit, tamarisks and a few hawthorns" (Q 34:15-6; see AGRICULTURE AND VEGETATION). The earthly garden, which blooms when watered by rain from the heavens (see HEAVEN AND SKY) but whose verdure easily turns into stubble under arid conditions, also serves as a qurʾānic parable for the fleeting pleasures of this world (Q 18:32-5). The Qurʾān further invokes the earthly fruit orchard (specifically of date palms [see DATE PALM] and grapes, Q 17:91) as an analog to good deeds (q.v.) that reap countless benefits for the believer (Q 2:265-6).

Paradise *(al-janna)* is where God placed Adam and his wife after their creation (Q 2:35; 7:19). The Qurʾān provides broad reference to paradise as a physical place with specific geographical features. Water (q.v.) is a main component of the paradisaical garden(s); the believers are frequently promised the "garden(s) underneath which rivers flow," an expression that occurs more than thirty times (Q 9:100; 16:31; etc.). There are four rivers which flow through paradise, one of "fresh water," one of "milk (q.v.) that does not change in flavor," one of "wine (see INTOXICANTS) that is a delight to those who drink [from it]," and one of "pure honey" (q.v.; Q 47:15). Some paradisaical springs have specific names; one is called Kawthar (Q 108:1), implying abundance; another is called Salsabīl (Q 76:18); and a third is called Tasnīm (Q 83:27; see WELLS AND SPRINGS).

Paradise, the breadth of which is "as the breadth of heaven and earth" (Q 57:21), is described as an enclosed garden with gates, guarded by doorkeepers who admit the righteous (Q 39:73), along with their spouses (Q 43:70; see MARRIAGE AND DIVORCE), to happily dwell therein forever (Q 35:35; 43:71). Lush verdancy *(mudhāmmatān)* characterizes two heavenly gardens in particular (Q 55:64); there are references to "shady trees" (Q 56:28-30) and to "fruits and shade everlasting" (Q 13:35). Fountains (see SPRINGS AND FOUNTAINS) find plentiful mention (e.g. Q 15:45; 26:57, 134), and the phrase "shades and fountains" occurs in one verse (Q 77:41). Among paradisaical fruits are grapes (Q 23:19; 36:34) and pomegranates (Q 55:68). A mysterious tree called *sidrat al-muntahā,* "the lote-tree of the boundary" (Q 53:14-5), demarcates one extreme of the heavenly abode. The climate in paradise is described as temperate, devoid of intense heat or cold (Q 76:13).

The discourse of the inhabitants of paradise is one of peace (*salām,* Q 56:26) and praise of God (Q 35:34), unvitiated by idle talk (Q 88:11). The heavenly dwellers live together in fraternal companionship (Q 15:47; see BROTHER AND BROTHERHOOD), enveloped by peace (Q 50:34) and security (Q 44:51), their hearts emptied of rancor (Q 7:43; 15:47). They do not suffer from fatigue (Q 15:48; 35:35) and are free of all cares and labor (Q 35:34-5). They are reunited with the righteous members of their families, from among their parents, wives, and children (Q 13:23; 40:8; see FAMILY; KINSHIP). All that the heart desires and pleases is made available to them (Q 43:71). The paradise dwellers are thus satisfied with the heavenly reward they have earned (Q 52:18; 88:8-10) and with the physical circumstances of their existence (Q 7:43). According to the commentators, the Qurʾān (Q 6:103; 10:26; 50:35; 75:22-3) hints at the beatific vision of God in the after-life (Ṭabarī, *Tafsīr,* xv, 62-9; Rāzī, *Tafsīr,* xiii, 124-32; xvii, 77-8), a theme that became popular in later, particularly mystical, literature (see FACE OF GOD).

The pious believer (see BELIEF AND UNBELIEF; PIETY) accustomed to denial of certain material and physical pleasures or to modest indulgence in them on earth will be granted these pleasures manifold in paradise. Gastronomic delights (see FOOD AND DRINK) are promised in the form of "fruit and flesh as desired by them" (Q 52:22), nectar sealed with musk, blended with the water of Tasnīm (Q 83:25-7), and "pure wine" (*sharāban ṭahūran,* Q 76:21), which neither debilitates nor inebriates (Q 37:45-7). Dark-eyed maidens (*ḥūr,* Q 44:54; 52:20; 55:72; 56:22; see HOURIS), modest of glance (Q 55:56), and peerless of form (Q 56:34-5), are paired with the believers who are of the same age (Q 56:37). Handsome young men (*wildān,* Q 56:17; 76:19; *ghilmān,* Q 52:24) will circulate among the believers with "goblets, beakers and cups of refreshing drink" (Q 56:18; see CUPS AND VESSELS; INSTRUMENTS). The heavenly dwellers recline on couches (Q 56:15; 76:13; 83:23; 88:13), on green cushions and exquisite carpets (Q 55:76; see FURNITURE AND FURNISHINGS). They dress in robes of fine silk (q.v.; Q 22:23) and brocade (Q 76:21), and wear bracelets of gold (q.v.), pearls (Q 22:23) and silver (Q 76:21). Although these vivid descriptions invite comparison with earthly delights several times magnified (see MATERIAL CULTURE AND THE QURʾĀN), the Qurʾān also states that "no soul knows what joys are hidden from them in compensation for their deeds" (Q 32:17). In qurʾānic depiction, paradise is overwhelmingly a place of joyous repose, amiable companionship, physical, emotional, and spiritual well-being.

Ḥadīth and exegetical literature

The description of paradise and the heavenly compensations promised by the Qurʾān are further elaborated in the ḥadīth and exegetical literature *(tafsīr),* and in individual works on paradise. The following account, which is far from exhaustive, refers to some of the more common and distinctive topics contained in this extra-qurʾānic literature.

Paradise is described as a vast domain having eight gates and one hundred levels (*daraja;* Bukhārī, *Ṣaḥīḥ,* ix, 153). The distance between each level is as the distance between the sky (see HEAVEN AND SKY) and the earth (q.v.; ibid.; Tirmidhī, *Sunan,* iv, 82) or the length of a hundred years' journey (Tirmidhī, *Sunan,* iv, 81). The highest and most central level of paradise is occupied by Firdaws; directly above it is the throne *(al-ʿarsh)* of God (see THRONE OF GOD), and it is from this level that the rivers of paradise pour forth (Tirmidhī, *Sunan,* iv, 82; Abū Nuʿaym, *Ṣifat al-janna,* 115). Kawthar is described as a river whose two banks are piled with hollowed pearls (Bukhārī, *Ṣaḥīḥ,* xxiii, 66), and whose water is whiter than milk and sweeter than honey (Tirmidhī, *Sunan,* iv, 87; Ibn Ḥanbal, *Musnad,* viii, 202-3). The *ṭūbā,* "blessing, goodness," mentioned in Q 13:29, is understood by commentators to refer to a special tree in paradise, adorned with jewels, which stretches the distance of a hundred years' journey (Ṭabarī, *Tafsīr,* xvi, 443-4), as do other wondrous trees (Bukhārī, *Ṣaḥīḥ,* xxiii, 50).

The majority of the heavenly denizens will be drawn from the ranks of the poor and the weak (Bukhārī, *Ṣaḥīḥ,* xxiii, 48; Muslim, *Ṣaḥīḥ,* iv, 2186-7). One tradition states that the best of women will precede the best of men into heaven (Abū Nuʿaym, *Ṣifat al-janna,* 115). Since the ḥadīth literature mentions that each man will live with two wives (Muslim, *Ṣaḥīḥ,* iv, 2178-9; Tirmidhī, *Sunan,* iv, 84, 85), and each woman with her preferred husband (Shaʿrānī, *Mukhtaṣar,* 105; Rashīd Riḍā, *Manār,* xxxii, 91-2), most commentators are of the opinion that women will outnumber men in heaven (ʿAynī, *ʿUmda,* xii, 305; Wensinck/Pellat, Ḥūr, 582; to be contrasted to the tradition which states that there will be more women than men in hell on account of their disobedience toward their husbands, for which see Bukhārī, *Ṣaḥīḥ,* xxiii, 48; see WOMEN AND THE QURʾĀN). According to some accounts, paradise dwellers will visit one another on white camels resembling sapphire (Suyūṭī, *Jāmiʿ,* i, 469) and also have a winged horse, studded with pearls and sapphire (Qāḍī, *Daqāʾiq,* 42; id., *Eschatologie,* 198; Tirmidhi, *Sunan,* iv, 88), named Rafraf in some reports (El-Saleh, *La vie future,* 35-7).

The heavenly dwellers are eternally young; their bodies do not produce excretions (Muslim, *Ṣaḥīḥ,* iv, 2179, 2180; Tirmidhī, *Sunan,* iv, 85) and their clothes never wear out (Muslim, *Ṣaḥīḥ,* iv, 2182; Tirmidhī, *Sunan,* iv, 86). Each man will be as tall as Adam (see ADAM AND EVE), either sixty cubits (Muslim, *Ṣaḥīḥ,* i, 279) or ninety cubits (Ibn Abī Shayba, *Muṣannaf,* vii, 56), as old as Jesus (q.v.; thirty-three years), and as handsome as Joseph (q.v.; ʿAbd al-Razzāq, *Muṣannaf,* xi, 416). The earthly women are reborn as beautiful, young virgins (Rāzī, *Tafsīr,* xxxi, 166; Ṭabarānī, *Awsaṭ,* v, 357), whose optimal height is eighty cubits (Ibn Abī Shayba, *Muṣannaf,* vii, 56). The celestial houris sing in exquisite voices (Ṭabarānī, *Awsaṭ,* v, 49; Ibn Abī Shayba, *Muṣannaf,* vii, 57) and are said to be made of light or saffron (Suyūṭī, *Durar,* 43), musk, ambergris and camphor (Qāḍī, *Daqāʾiq,* 43; El-Saleh, *La vie future,* 38-43). The least blessed among the heavenly dwellers is described in some reports as having 70,000 or 80,000 servants, a thousand mansions made from pearls, chrysolite and sapphire (Ibn Abī Shayba, *Muṣannaf,* vii, 56), and seventy-two or seventy-three consorts (Tirmidhī, *Sunan,* iv, 98). The believers have but to desire a particular kind of food or a thing and it is instantly made available to them (Tirmidhī, *Sunan,* iv, 87).

The believers are assured of God's eternal satisfaction *(riḍwān)* with them (Bukhārī, *Ṣaḥīḥ,* xxiii, 48-9) and they praise and glorify him night and day (Muslim, *Ṣaḥīḥ,* iv, 2180; Tirmidhī, *Sunan,* iv, 85). According to some weak reports, Arabic will be the language of paradise (Abū Nuʿaym, *Ṣifat al-janna,* 100; Suyūṭī, *Jāmiʿ,* i, 59). The ultimate reward for the pious is described in some reports as the beatific vision of God, which will be as clear as the full moon on a cloudless night (Bukhārī, *Ṣaḥīḥ,* xxiii, 59-60); the most virtuous *(afḍal)* will be afforded this opportunity twice every day (Ibn Abī Shayba, *Muṣannaf,* vii, 58; Ibn Ḥanbal, *Musnad,* vi, 284). Against this backdrop of vivid, concrete description of paradise, one should also keep in mind the ḥadīth *qudsī* (see ḤADĪTH AND THE QURʾĀN) which states that God has prepared for the believer "what no eye has seen, no ear has ever heard, nor has ever occurred to the human mind [heart]" (Muslim, *Ṣaḥīḥ,* iv, 51; Rāzī, *Tafsīr,* xxxi, 58), underscoring the indescribable nature of the bliss that awaits the righteous in the hereafter.

The above is just a brief sampling of the more detailed descriptions of the heavenly abode occurring in the extra-qurʾānic literature which are couched in prophetic traditions of varying degrees of reliability (according to the categories developed by medieval traditionists). Individual works on paradise include many of these traditions indiscriminately, creating hyperbolic narratives that one modern author has described as "a textualization of the imagination" (Azmeh, Rhetoric, 218). To conclude this section, one may state that through their evocative imagery and bold metaphors these paradisaical accounts ultimately embody "an attempt to demonstrate the ineffability of the world to come" (Reinhart, Here and hereafter, 18). Further, by conceptualizing paradise both as a continuation and exaltation of worldly delights, they have "ennobled the Muslim view of this more ephemeral world" (Brookes, *Gardens of paradise*, 21).

Views of the Muʿtazilīs, philosophers, Ṣūfīs, and modern exegetes

Very briefly, the Muʿtazilīs (q.v.) in particular tended to downplay the exaggerated descriptions of paradisaical pleasures. They accepted literally the description of paradise as it occurs in the Qurʾān but rejected anthropomorphic attributions to God (see ANTHROPOMORPHISM) and thus the possibility of the beatific vision, arguing that the divine being cannot be comprehended by the human ocular faculty. The Ashʿarīs affirmed the reality of the divine attributes and the descriptions of paradise contained in the Qurʾān and canonical ḥadīth compilations, including the vision of God, but emphasize their other-worldly nature according to their principle of "without [asking] how *(bi-lā kayf)*." The early Ṣūfīs (see ṢŪFISM AND THE QURʾĀN), like Rabīʿa al-ʿAdawiyya and al-Ḥallāj, accepted these verses in their literal sense and emphasized above all the beatific vision as the ultimate reward for the believer (Gardet, Djanna, 450). The theosophical philosophers *(mutafalsifūn)* and the later Ṣūfīs *(ahl al-taṣawwuf)*, in contrast, stressed the allegorical interpretation of qurʾānic verses that describe paradise (ibid.).

Modern scholars such as Muḥammad ʿAbduh (d. 1905) and Mawlānā Muḥammad ʿAlī (d. 1951) have emphasized the other-worldly nature of the rewards promised to the righteous in the hereafter (Smith and Haddad, *Islamic understanding*, 166-8). This applies in particular to the beatific vision of God which cannot be explained in terms of this-worldly human perception (ʿAbduh, *Risāla*, 183-4). The reformist zeal of Muḥammad Rashīd Riḍā (d. 1935) was especially directed toward critical reevaluation of ḥadīths in general, including those that contain literalist and over-sensualized descriptions of heavenly pleasures (Rashīd Riḍā, *Manār*, x, 548; Gardet, Djanna, 451).

The Islamic garden as earthly paradise

Historians of Islamic art and architecture have generally assumed that the profuse, particularly royal, gardens in various Muslim countries developed as an attempt to replicate the heavenly garden on earth. One art historian summarizes this conventional view thus: "Indeed one can understand neither the Islamic garden nor the attitude of the Muslim toward his garden until one realizes that the terrestrial garden is considered a reflection or rather an anticipation of Paradise" (Dickie, Islamic garden, 90). Briefly, evidence adduced in favor of this view is as follows. Qurʾānic reference to the four main rivers of paradise is believed to be the origin of the quartered Islamic garden, divided by four water-channels that converge at a central point. This type of garden is typically enclosed within walls, again considered a reflection of the qurʾānic description of *janna* as a garden with gates (Q 39:73). In Persian, the quartered garden is known as "four gardens" *(chahar bagh)*, which is considered to be the prototype of the typical Islamic garden (see e.g. Lehrmann, *Earthly paradise*, 62). But it should be noted that the *chahar bagh* itself is pre-Islamic in origin, and the institution of royal pleasure gardens was already well-known in the ancient Near East in general (Denny, Reflections of paradise, 41). To draw an immediate and direct equation between the quartered garden in the Islamic world and the supposed heavenly "prototype" is, therefore, not without its problematic aspects.

In recent times, questions have been raised about this conventional view, primarily on the basis that no written evidence explicitly stating this equation between the earthly and celestial gardens exists from the pre-modern era in Arabic, Persian or Turkish. It has been argued that many modern scholars, both from within and outside the Islamic tradition, have assumed this implicit equation because of their need to reify Islam and thus to see religious symbolism in every artifact associated with Islamic civilization. Another possible influence on this conventional equation may have been the narrative genre indigenous to medieval Europe that speaks of an earthly paradise. Acquaintance with this genre could have prompted western scholars to transfer analogous assumptions to the study of the Islamic world (Allen, *Imagining paradise*, 6 f.). This recent revisionist position raises many interesting and pertinent questions; clearly the last word has not yet been spoken on this topic.

Asma Afsaruddin

Bibliography

Primary: ʿAbd al-Razzāq, *Muṣannaf;* Abū Nuʿaym, Aḥmad b. ʿAbdallāh al-Iṣfahānī, *Ṣifat al-janna*, Cairo 1409/1989; al-ʿAynī, Maḥmūd b. Aḥmad, *ʿUmdat al-qāriʾ*, Cairo 1983; Bukhārī, *Ṣaḥīḥ (bi-sharḥ al-Kirmānī)*, 25 vols., Cairo 1933-62; Ghazālī, Abū Ḥāmid Muḥammad, *Iḥyāʾ ʿulūm al-dīn* (Bk. 40. Kitāb Dhikr al-mawt wa-mā baʿdahu), Cairo 1933, iv, 455-67; id., *Dhikr al-mawt wa-mā baʿdahu. The remembrance of death and the afterlife. Book XL of The revival of the religious sciences. Iḥyāʾ ʿulūm al-dīn*, trans. T.J. Winter, Cambridge, U.K. 1989, 232-61; Ibn Abī l-Dunyā, *Ṣifat al-janna wa-mā aʿadda Allāh li-ahlihā min al-naʿīm*, rev. ed. N. ʿAbd al-Raḥmān Khalaf, Amman 1997; Ibn Abī Shayba, ʿAbdallāh b. Muḥammad, *al-Kitāb al-Muṣannaf fī l-aḥādīth wa-l-āthār*, Beirut 1409/1989; Ibn Ḥanbal, *Musnad*, ed. A.M. Shākir, Cairo 1366/1947; Muslim, *Ṣaḥīḥ;* al-Qāḍī, ʿAbd al-Raḥīm b. Aḥmad, *Daqāʾiq al-akhbār fī dhikr al-janna wa-l-nār*, Cairo 1343/1934; id., *Muhammedanische Eschatologie (Kitāb Aḥwāl al-qiyāma)*, trans. M. Wolff, Leipzig 1872, esp. 85-207 (Arabic text and German translation of the work, although under a different title); Eng. trans. *Islamic book of the dead. A collection of ḥadīths on the fire and the garden*, Norwich, UK 1977; Rashīd Riḍā, *Tafsīr al-Manār*, Cairo 1948-56; Rāzī, *Tafsīr*, Cairo 1357/1938; al-Shaʿrānī, Abū l-Mawāhib ʿAbd al-Wahhāb b. Aḥmad, *Mukhtaṣar tadhkirat al-Qurṭubī*, Cairo 1307/1889; Suyūṭī, *al-Jāmiʿ al-ṣaghīr*, ed. Ḥ. al-Dāmardāsh Muḥammad, Mecca and Riyadh 1419/1998; id., *al-Durar al-ḥisan*, in the margins of ʿAbd al-Raḥīm al-Qāḍī, *Daqāʾiq al-akhbār fī dhikr al-janna wa-l-nār*, Cairo 1343/1934; Ṭabarī, *Tafsīr*, Cairo 1374-/1954-; Ṭabarānī, *Awsaṭ;* Tirmidhī, *Sunan*, ed. ʿA.M. ʿUthmān, Cairo n.d.

Secondary: M. ʿAbduh, *Risālat al-tawḥīd*, Cairo 1963; T. Allen, *Imagining paradise in Islamic art*, Sebastopol, CA 1993, 1995 (electronic publication of Solipsist Press); A. al-Azmeh, Rhetoric for the senses. A consideration of Muslim paradise narratives, in *JAL* 26 (1995), 215-31; J. Brookes, *The gardens of paradise. The history and design of the great Islamic gardens*, New York 1987 (esp. 17-36, "The concept of the paradise garden"); W.B. Denny, Reflections of paradise in Islamic art, in S.S. Blair and J.M. Bloom (eds.), *Images of paradise in Islamic art*, Hanover, NH 1991, 33-43; J. Dickie, The Islamic garden in Spain, in E.B. MacDougall and R. Ettinghausen (eds.), *The Islamic garden*, Washington, D.C. 1976, 87-105; S. El-Saleh, *La vie future selon le Coran*, Paris 1971; L. Gardet, Djanna, in *EI*², ii, 47-52; J.B. Lehrman, *Earthly paradise. Garden and courtyard in Islam*, Berkeley 1980; K. Reinhart, The here and the hereafter in Islamic religious thought, in S.S. Blair and J.M. Bloom (eds.), *Images of paradise in Islamic art*, Hanover, NH 1991, 15-23; ʿA. ʿAbd al-ʿAzīz al-Shinnawī, *al-Janna wa-naʿīmuhu min al-Qurʾān wa-l-sunna*, Manṣūra, Egypt 1994; J. Smith and Y. Haddad, *The Islamic understanding of death and resurrection*, Albany 1981; A.J. Wensinck/C. Pellat, Ḥūr, in *EI*², iii, 581-2.

Garlic see FOOD AND DRINK

Gehenna see HELL AND HELLFIRE; FIRE

Gender

A religious and cultural construction, including prescribed, proscribed, and suggested behaviors and practices relating to women and/or men. Although there is no qurʾānic term for "gender" as such, both "gender-specific" and non-gendered (i.e. the enunciation of principles pertaining to all human beings) language pervade the qurʾānic text. (Another word that is absent from the Qurʾān is the biological term "sex" [see SEX AND SEXUALITY]. The common, contemporary term *al-jins* did not exist in Arabic at the time of the Qurʾān's origins but appeared later as a loanword in Arabic indicating genus and also a people, while its specific connotation as "sex" is a relatively recent usage.) To grasp how gender as a religio-cultural construct is conveyed in the Qurʾān it is important to observe how sex as a biological construct is employed. Gender as a religio-cultural construction is linked to biological sex though distinguished from it, yet occasionally in the Qurʾān the two seem to blur. This is indicated by a vast and complex repertoire of "gender terms" or "gendered vocabulary" in the Qurʾān. Moreover, Arabic, the language of the Qurʾān, is itself highly gendered in its grammatical structure (see ARABIC LANGUAGE; GRAMMAR AND THE QURʾĀN). The complex gendering of the language of the Qurʾān (including the presence and absence of personal nouns) and the textual and contextual embedding of words adumbrate the interpretive potential that this language exhibits.

Examination of the terms for gender and sex in the Qurʾān and how they are employed confirms the gendered-ness of the Qurʾān and indicates interpretive strategies for extracting deeper meanings that may clarify the message of the Qurʾān and serve as guidance. Five basic linguistic observations may be made. One, gender terms predominate over sex terms in the Qurʾān. Two, sometimes gender and sex terms are used inversely so that gender terms may indicate a biological condition or sex terms may make a religio-cultural statement. Three, the word "women" and other gender terms referring to female persons appear mainly in relation to men (see WOMEN AND THE QURʾĀN). Four, women are most frequently mentioned as wives. Five, the same word may be given similar or different inflections in the female and male forms.

When ascertaining meanings and messages in the use of gendered words it is crucial to contextualize them. Likewise, it is necessary to distinguish between what is specific and contingent from that which is universal and timeless. It is instructive to examine gendered vocabulary employed in the verses Muslim understand to have been revealed in Medina (q.v.), where specific instructions (taking into account prevailing conditions and practices) were given to the nascent community of believers and those revealed in Mecca (q.v.), which are believed to contain universal messages. The exegete Amina Wadud-Muhsin in *Qurʾān and woman* points out that verses revealed in Medina introduced reforms of existing practices and that most of them specifically benefited women. In the Meccan verses, woman is given as an exemplar for all humankind.

It is imperative to be attentive to the meaning words convey in qurʾānic Arabic, as distinct from post-qurʾānic Arabic, especially modern varieties of Arabic. There are also problems of translation into other languages. Rendering qurʾānic Arabic in 21st century English, for example, is highly demanding because of the different grammatical structures and the disparate range of vocabulary. From today's perspective, gender slippage may be observed in even the most highly respected translations such as translating *insān, nās* and *bashar* as either man or mankind instead of humankind or humans. Finally, the accepted standard translations of the Qurʾān into English were made in the early and middle decades of the twentieth century prior to increased gender sensitivity to language.

To gain an understanding of gender in the Qurʾān, it is instructive to observe that it conveys the intrinsic equality of human beings and their differences, both biological and functional. Believers (see BELIEF AND UNBELIEF), like all of God's creatures (see CREATION), are in essence equal before the creator; as males and females, however, these creatures are biologically different. Taking into account the fact of biological difference, the Qurʾān advances a religio-cultural construction of difference in what may be called a balancing system. A cultural balancing of difference, relating to the ways difference is performed, is linked to the childbearing capacity of females (see BIOLOGY AS THE CREATION AND STAGES OF LIFE; CHILDREN). Apart from the husband's duty to provide materially for his wife in the circumstance of childbearing and rearing, there is an absence of prescribed gender roles and functions (see MARRIAGE AND DIVORCE; FAMILY). There were certain disparate gender practices allowed in the Qurʾān as a means of reducing and controlling, and perhaps eventually eliminating, particular behaviors prevalent in Arabia at the time of the Qurʾān.

The biological or sex terms "male and female" are typically rendered by the nouns *al-dhakar* (pl. *dhukūr* and *dhukrān*) and *al-unthā* (pl. *ināth*), respectively. The terms male and female are used in the Qurʾān in two ways. One is in relation to procreation and to indicate biological difference or specificity. For example, Q 13:8 says: "God knows what every female (womb) bears..." and Q 42:49, "He bestows (children) male or female according to his will." The other way sex, or the biological terms male and female, are employed is to enunciate the principle of the fundamental equality of males and females before God so that there cannot be any doubt or confusion about the basic equality of biologically different human beings. For example, in Q 4:124, "Whoever does good deeds (q.v.), whether male or female, and believes — those will enter the garden (q.v.)." Another instance is Q 3:195, "And their lord has accepted of them and answered them 'Never will I suffer to be lost the work of any of you, be he male or female: you are members, one of another.'"

The culturally constructed categories man and woman are typically rendered by the nouns *rajul* (pl. *rijāl*) and *imraʾa* (pl. *nisāʾ, niswa*), respectively. Another word for man is *marʾ*, which appears only four times. *Rajul* is most often used to signify man, whereas *imraʾa* may also connote wife and indeed is used most frequently in this sense. Both *rajul* and *imraʾa* are found more frequently in the plural, while the plural for woman occurs about twice as often as the plural for men. Of the two plural forms for women, *nisāʾ* predominates (*niswa* appears only twice). Other gendered categories, more specific in meaning, are abundant in the Qurʾān, such as boy, girl, young man and young woman. The most numerous terms, however, are relational or familial categories such as mother, father, brother, sister, son and daughter.

The ways gender terms are used include, for example, "And in no way covet (see ENVY) those things in which God has bestowed his gifts more freely on some of you than on others: to men *(rijāl)* is allotted what they earn and to women *(nisāʾ)* what they earn but ask God of his bounty" (Q 4:32; see BLESSING; GRACE). Some interpreters have seen an allusion to the grudging acceptance of polygamy (q.v.) in the beginning of Q 33:4, "God did not make for any man *(rajul)* two hearts (see HEART) in one (body)." Another example relating to the possibility of dissolving a difficult marriage occurs in Q 4:128, "If a wife *(imraʾa)* fears cruelty or desertion on her husband's part there is no blame on them if they arrange an amicable settlement between themselves." The two previous examples have been less contested than Q 4:34, "Men are the protectors/maintainers *(qawwāmūn)* of women because God has given the one more than the other, and because they support them from their means." This verse has been interpreted in the classical exegesis (see EXEGESIS OF THE QURʾĀN: CLASSICAL AND MEDIEVAL) developed by male scholars as connoting male authority and superiority over women in general. Feminist hermeneutics points to the contingent prescription for husbands to support their wives materially in the specific context of childbearing and rearing and argues that, while this support is incumbent upon husbands, it may be obviated if the wife and mother so wishes. Thus, *qawwāmūn* should not be generalized and read to signify (and justify) male authority over women. The element of balancing and of equality in fathering and mothering are clearly enunciated in Q 2:233, "The mothers shall nurse their offspring for two whole years... but [the father] shall bear the cost of [the mothers'] food and clothing in a fair manner *(bi-l-maʿrūf)*... no mother shall be treated unfairly on account of her child. No father on account of his child... If they both decide on weaning by mutual consent and after due consultation there is no blame on them." Thus, man/men and woman/women appear in the Qurʾān in ways that lend themselves to interpretations of complementarity or a balancing of gender roles within the context of marriage and the family, that is, the duty and performance of complimentary roles, while leaving room for a woman during pregnancy and child-rearing to relinquish the support due her if she wishes. This is a zone lending itself to varying interpretations. Innovative or reformative interpreters argue that this is a strength of the holy text, which allows for contextual readings within changing environments and circumstances while preserving the principle of gender justice and equality.

Although *rajul* and *imraʾa* typically function as cultural constructs in the Qurʾān they sometimes seem to indicate biological sex. For example, "... Do you deny him who created you out of dust (see CLAY; EARTH), then out of a sperm-drop, then fashioned you into a man?" (*rajul*, Q 18:37) or "Oh humankind! Be careful of your duty to your lord, who created you from a single *nafs* (self, soul) and from it created its *zawj* (mate), and from them [that pair] spread [over the earth] a multitude of men and women" (Q 4:1). The occasional inversion of sex and gender terms allows interpretators to highlight the connection-cum-distinction between biology and cultural construction and serves to underscore the universal principles of equality and justice in the Qurʾān across the biological-cultural continuum.

Gender and sex, or cultural and biological identity, are also conveyed in the Qurʾān by proper nouns or names referring to specific individuals who may serve as role models and/or exceptional exemplars. These named persons are all men (most of whom are prophets, see PROPHETS AND PROPHETHOOD) with the sole exception of Mary (q.v.; Maryam), the mother of the prophet Jesus (q.v.; ʿĪsā) whom God has chosen "above the women of all the worlds" (Q 3:42). Not only is Mary cited in the Qurʾān by name, but "Maryam" is additionally given as a title to a sūra (Q 19; most other personal names given to sūras are those of prophets). She appears in numerous verses throughout the Qurʾān that detail the trajectory of her life and mission, and that imprint her religious and social importance. Although exceptional, Maryam, identified in Q 66:12 as among the "devout, or righteous" *(mina l-qānitīna)* in the masculine form, serves as an exemplar to all Muslims, men and women alike.

All other individual women appear in the Qurʾān unnamed but are known in two ways. First, by the mention of their link to a named male, including (1) the *zawj* or mate of Adam from whom all humankind descend (see ADAM AND EVE) and (2) the wife *(imraʾa)* or other female relative or intimate of a prophet (other than Muḥammad). The second way a specific woman may be known is through a telling description. For example, "a woman ruling over them and provided with everything; and she has a magnificent throne..." (Q 27:23) refers to Bilqīs (q.v.), the queen of Sheba (q.v). Moreover, this is a rare instance of a woman appearing in her own right and constitutes an example of a woman who is a supreme political leader.

The Qurʾān refers to a group of women by their relationship to the prophet Muḥammad (see WIVES OF THE PROPHET). The wives of Muḥammad are designated as *nisāʾ al-nabī,* "the women (i.e. wives) of the Prophet" as in Q 33:32, "O wives of the Prophet! You are not like any of the (other) women" and when a verse speaks directly to Muḥammad, as in Q 33:28, "O Prophet say to your wives *(qul li-azwājika).*" The daughters of Muḥammad are sometimes addressed, as in Q 33:59, "Tell your wives and daughters *(qul li-azwājika wa-banātika).*" Examination of references to the wives of the Prophet, as well as to his daughters, has given rise to varying interpretations about whether specific prescriptions were ordained only for such women or were meant to apply to all Muslim women (in instances where the specific mention of other women is absent). Modern women exegetes such as ʿĀʾisha ʿAbd al-Raḥmān (Bint al-Shāṭiʾ) and Zaynab al-Ghazzālī have found in the wives and daughters of the prophet Muḥammad models for active social roles for women lived in a combination that balances the importance of family roles.

There are some terms in the Qurʾān which exist grammatically in the masculine form but which refer to both women and men, such as *insān,* "human being," *nās,* "humankind," *bashar,* "human being" and *ahl,* "people." *Nās* and *ahl* operate as collective nouns while *insān* and *bashar* may also signify the singular. These terms have invariably been rendered in the standard English translations as mankind or man, giving the contemporary English speaker a skewed sense of the gender-inclusiveness of the original Arabic.

In the Qurʾān, because of the grammatical demands of the Arabic language, Arabic nouns appear in masculine or feminine form. "Believer," for example, must be rendered as male believer, *muʾmin,* or female believer, *muʾmina.* Nouns in the masculine dual or plural, however, may also include females. While terms such as *muʾmin* and *muʾmina* meaning believer (man believer and woman believer, respectively) are used in ways that appear self-evident (for one of the verses that explicitly enumerate male and female groups, see Q 33:35: *muslimīna wa-l-muslimāti wa-l-muʾminīna wa-l-muʾmināti wa-l-qānitīna wa-l-qānitāti wa-l-ṣādiqīna wa-l-ṣādiqāti...*), there are other nouns that have given rise to variant understandings when applied to men and women. For example, feminist hermeneutics would argue that *nushūz,* which connotes disobedience (q.v.)

or rebellion on the part of men and women to one another in the context of their marital responsibilities and obligations, and which in turn constitutes, in qurʾānic terms, an (equal) act of disobedience to God, has been incorrectly thought to appear in the Qurʾān only in relation to women. This has lead to the conviction in modern Arabic usage that only a woman is *nāshiza,* that is, a man cannot be *nāshiz. Nushūz* relative to women has been commonly rendered in English as denoting "disobedience, disloyalty, and rebellion" (relative to a husband) as in Q 4:34, yet when used in relation to men (relative to a wife or wives) it has been translated into English as "cruelty or desertion" as seen in Q 4:128. The male translators of the standard English versions of the Qurʾān have conducted an exegetical act in the very process of translating.

Pairing is an important concept in the Qurʾān. The Arabic language, which includes the dual form, facilitates the expression of this notion. All living things are created in pairs. While all creation is paired, God alone is one, "And of everything we have created pairs that you may bear in mind [that God is one]" (Q 51:49); "And God did create you from dust; then from a sperm-drop; then he made you in pairs..." (Q 35:11). The same word, *zawj* (in the masculine form), is used for each of the two parts, underscoring their absolute equality. Human beings were created from a single soul *(nafs)* to be the *zawj* (mate) of one another. In the creation story Adam and Eve, as noted above, are each the *zawj* of the other. While God created two *zawj*(s) (*zawjayn,* dual form) that are totally equal, he also created them different as *dhakar* and *unthā*. This equation of equality-with-difference is powerfully conveyed in Q 53:45, "That he did create in pairs *(zawjayn),* male *(dhakar)* and female *(unthā).*" As if to reaffirm this further there are instances when the term *zawj* is used on its own to indicate wife (rather than the more common term *imraʾa*). In direct qurʾānic address to Muḥammad, as seen above, the term *zawj* is used in the plural, *azwāj,* connoting his wives. There is also the rare example of a more general usage, as in Q 4:20. "But if you decide to take one wife in place of another *(zawjin makāna zawjin).*" In a departure from the use of a single term to designate one of the two in a pair *(zawj),* in modern Arabic, wife is rendered by *zawja,* the femine form of *zawj.*

The richness of gender vocabulary in the Qurʾān and its multiple contextualizations, along with the gendered suppleness of the structure and functioning of the Arabic language, assist exegesis attentive to the fundamental equality of all human beings, female and male, as well as to the reality of biological difference. Modern interpreters — mainly, but not only, females — are articulating new readings of the Qurʾān that draw upon the highly nuanced qurʾānic Arabic (see also FEMINISM).

Margot Badran

Bibliography
ʿĀʾisha ʿAbd al-Raḥmān (Bint al-Shāṭiʾ), *Nisāʾ al-nabī,* Cairo n.d. (1961?); id., *al-Tafsīr al-bayān lil-Qurʾān al-karīm,* 2 vols., Cairo 1962-9; Z. al-Ghazzālī, *Naẓarāt fī kitābi llāh,* 2 vols., Cairo 1994; R. Hassan, Feminist theology. The challenges for Muslim women, in *Critique* (Fall 1996), 53-65; A.Y. al-Hibri, An introduction to Muslim women's rights, in G. Webb (ed.), *Windows of faith,* Syracuse 2000, 51-71; J. McAuliffe, Chosen of all women: Mary and Fatima in qurʾānic exegesis, in *Islamochristiana* 7 (1981), 19-28; B. Freyer Stowasser, *Women in the Qurʾān, traditions and interpretation,* New York 1994; A. Wadud-Muhsin, *Qurʾān and woman,* Kuala Lumpur 1992, New York and Oxford 1999².

Generations

Stages in the succession of natural descent. Generations *(qarn,* pl. *qurūn)* is used some twenty times in the Qurʾān to refer to the groups of people (i.e. nations; cf. Ṭabarī, *Tafsīr,* xi, 26, ad Q 6:6) who had been destroyed by God for their disobedience (q.v.) and failure to heed his message (e.g. Q 6:6; 10:13; 11:116; 17:17; 19:74, 78; 23:31; 38:3; 50:36); the same word, *qarn,* also refers to the people who replace those generations. These destroyed peoples are cited as examples of wrongdoing and as warnings not to follow their doomed ways. The destroyed peoples are usually identified with a prophet named in the Qurʾān, such as Noah (q.v.), Lot (q.v.), Hūd (q.v.) for the people of ʿĀd (q.v.), Shūʿayb (q.v.; sometimes identified with the biblical Jethro) for the people of Midian (q.v.) and Ṣāliḥ (q.v.) for the Thamūd (q.v.). The traces of their existence, either in memory or artifacts, serve as a caution to humankind about the consequences of disobedience to God (see GEOGRAPHY).

The use of the category of generations in the Qurʾān is part of the larger qurʾānic argument that all of history can serve as a lesson for humankind, part of the total number of signs (q.v.) and portents God has sent down. Q 6:6, for example, states, "Do they not see how many generations before them we destroyed, which we had established on the earth, strengthening them as we have not strengthened you, for whom we sent down rain in abundance and made rivers flow beneath them. But we destroyed them because of their sins and brought forth another generation after them." The destroyed generations are described as having had great power and wealth (q.v.) that availed them nothing in the face of God's judgment (q.v.). Not all sinners are necessarily condemned without the possibility of redemption. The Qurʾān tells the story of the people of Jonah (q.v.; Yūnus or Dhū l-Nūn), who repented and were saved from destruction (Q 10:98; 37:139-48).

Post-qurʾānic commentators elaborate on details of the destroyed generations, making liberal use of materials derived from biblical commentaries and Arabian legends (see MYTHIC AND LEGENDARY NARRATIVES; SCRIPTURE AND THE QURʾĀN). In the story of Noah, for example, the number of people saved from destruction rises to seventy, including the giant Og (ʿŪj b. ʿAnaq; cf. Kisāʾī, *Tales,* 99, 251-3). Such elaboration became the locus for the narration of much fabulous lore. Scholarly critics of this genre point to quotations of verbatim speeches and poetry from the destroyed peoples as examples of the excesses of this material. See also PUNISHMENT STORIES.

Gordon Darnell Newby

Bibliography
Primary: Kisāʾī, *The tales of the prophets of al-Kisāʾī,* trans. W. Thackston, Boston 1978; Ṭabarī, *Annales,* ed. de Goeje, Leiden 1881; id., *Tafsīr,* Cairo 1954; Zamakhsharī, *Kashshāf.*
Secondary: M. Lidzbarski, *De propheticis, quae dicuntur, legendis Arabicis,* Leipzig 1893; E. Littman, *Thamūd and Safā,* Leipzig 1940; G.D. Newby, *The making of the last prophet. A reconstruction of the earliest biography of Muhammad,* Columbia, SC 1989; R. Mottahedeh, Some Islamic views of the pre-Islamic past, in *Harvard Middle Eastern and Islamic review* 1 (1994), 17-26.

Generosity see GOD AND HIS ATTRIBUTES; GIFT-GIVING; ALMSGIVING

Gentiles see JEWS AND JUDAISM; ILLITERACY

Geography

This entry starts with a short general overview of the geography *of* the Qurʾān, i.e. the geographical setting of the genesis of the text. It then proceeds to survey the geographical representations *in* the Qurʾān. As Kenneth Cragg *(Event)* has correctly pointed out, the events which are pivotal in the Qurʾān are located in a space shaped by pagan notions (see POLYTHEISM AND ATHEISM; SOUTH ARABIA, RELIGION IN PRE-ISLAMIC). Geography in the Qurʾān thus appears constructed against the pre-qurʾānic Bedouin (q.v.) views of space transmitted in ancient Arabic poetry (see AGE OF IGNORANCE; POETRY AND POETS). To make this background more intelligible, these pre-qurʾānic concepts need to be presented at least summarily. Subsequently, their de-mythicizing and re-coding in the qurʾānic urban context will be explored (see CITY). To this end, evidence about the developing "mental map" of the listeners will be collected, their changing perception of "local geography," and their acquisition of a new understanding of physical geographical phenomena will be investigated. Spatial self-orientation is, of course, not necessarily bound to "real," objective space, familiar from one's own experience; it may point to imagined space as well. Both the real home of the listeners on the one hand, and the community's imaginary home, i.e. the space of their spiritual yearning after the real home has turned into exile (see EMIGRATION), on the other, have to be given attention since the changing significance of particular sites and landscapes is apt to make the qurʾānic canonical process more transparent.

General overview: geography of the Qurʾān

The broader geographical framework of the Qurʾān is the Arabian peninsula. A specified historico-geographical map of the entire peninsula has been prepared in the framework of the *Tübinger Atlas zum Vorderen Orient* (TAVO) by Ulrich Rebstock: Islamic Arabia until the death of the Prophet. "This map presents the topographical setting of the nucleus of the Islamic empire that was emerging on the periphery of the Sasanian and Byzantine empires. It tries to reconstruct the process of the expansion of 'Islam,' i.e. the 'submission' to its claim, on the basis of early Islamic geography and historiography. The identification and localization of important places serves as a kind of framework into which the social, economic, and religious developments are fitted. The main focus is on the political and military actions with which the 'Muslims,' operating first from Medina and then from Mecca, tried to break the opposition of the urban and tribal Arabian aristocracy. The subtly differentiated contracts of the 'Muslims' with members of other religious communities, with traditional tribal confederations and with tribes allied to other powers give an insight into the precarious situation of the Islamic community at the death of their Prophet." (Rebstock, Islamic Arabia; see COMMUNITY AND SOCIETY IN THE QURʾĀN; ECONOMICS; MECCA; MEDINA; EXPEDITIONS AND BATTLES; TRIBES AND CLANS; OPPOSITION TO MUḤAMMAD.)

More precisely, however, the Ḥijāz is to be considered the Qurʾān's land of origin. The Ḥijāz is defined as the mountain barrier that runs through the western side of the peninsula. Although exact application of topographical conceptions can be problematic, it may be roughly described as bordering the Syrian provinces in the north and, in the southwest, the highlands of ʿAsīr that separate it from the Yemen. The Red Sea lowlands of Tihāma are situated to its west. In the east, the Ḥijāz merges into the Najd plateau, the elevated land above the coastal plain, which is primarily steppe and desert. Rainfall in the Ḥijāz is very scanty, and water is retained only in a few areas of clay soil, thus allowing rural cultures to emerge. In the Qurʾān al-Ṭāʾif and Yathrib are among the most prominent of these rural cultures. Several trade routes ran through the Ḥijāz; the main north-south route, which connected the area with the Byzantine province of Syria, ran parallel to the Red Sea, passing through a chain of oases such as al-Mudāwara, Tabūk, al-Aʿlā and Yathrib. Although the Ḥijāz was not directly on the sea, seafaring Ethiopia (Bilād al-Ḥabash; see ABYSSINIA), which was a commercial partner of pre-Islamic Mecca, and which, during Muḥammad's career, became a temporary asylum for a group of his followers, was easily accessible through the Red Sea harbors of Shuʿayba or Jidda. Much more difficult were travel and transport eastward across the *ḥarra* (basalt desert, covered with stones from lava flow), where the roads passed through one of the two main valleys (*wādīs*) of the Najd, the Wādī l-Dawāsir or the Wādī l-Rumma, which runs across the plateau until entering the Euphrates plain at Baṣra (see IRAQ).

Mecca: general

Among the cities of the peninsula, Mecca is certainly an exceptional case. It does not owe its importance to a vassal relationship with a mighty power as did al-Ḥīra, located on the border of Sasanian territory, nor is it a rural oasis city such as neighboring al-Ṭāʾif or the more distant Medīna. Situated in the Ḥijāz about seventy two kilometers inland from the Red Sea at 21°27' north latititude and 39°49' east longitude, Mecca is a barren place lying in a valley known as *wādī* or *baṭn Makka*, surrounded by steep, rocky mountain ranges. A number of side-valleys, known as *shiʿb*, converge at its lowest part, the Baṭḥāʾ, where settlement started and where the Kaʿba (q.v.) is located. Mecca's nearest neighboring city, at a distance of approximately fifty kilometers to the east, was the rural oasis al-Ṭāʾif, a place that seems to have been closely associated with Mecca since, according to the exegetical tradition, Q 43:31 refers to both with the joint eponym *al-qaryatāni*. The next important city was Yathrib, at 350 kilometers to the north of Mecca. Rainfall in the region of Mecca is scant and irregular. When occurring at all, the rains may be violent and cause torrents which pour down the valleys towards the *ḥaram*. The supply of water (q.v.) depended on wells and cisterns (see WELLS AND SPRINGS; SPRINGS AND FOUNTAINS).

Mecca's sanctuary must have existed from very ancient times; it is apparently the site intended by Ptolemy when he notes the existence of a place called Macoraba. The qurʾānic narrative that ascribes its foundation to Abraham (q.v.) and Ishmael (q.v.) may have already been promulgated in *ḥanīf* (q.v.) circles before Islam. The *ḥaram*, Mecca's *temenos*, was composed of a variety of holy objects and holy sites (see FORBIDDEN; SANCTITY AND THE SACRED; HOUSE, DOMESTIC AND DIVINE). The completely unadorned and roughly built structure of the Kaʿba is reported to have hosted a number of idols (see IDOLS AND IMAGES) that were later removed by Muḥammad. Embedded in the southeastern side of the Kaʿba was the black stone, *al-ḥajar*. Beside the building there was the Zamzam well. Loosely attached to the Kaʿba was the *ḥijr*, a low semicircular wall that extended from one of the faces of the building. In addition, there was the Station of Abraham, sometimes described as another stone, sometimes as a particular site, and even on occasion equated with the entire *ḥaram*. The pre-Islamic *ḥaram* known to Muḥammad at Mecca was not an imposing place; it was little more than a clearing, with the Kaʿba in its midst, the extent of which was marked off only by the exterior walls of the houses of Meccan merchants huddled closely around it.

Any effort to survey the modern academic analysis of the historical developments prior to or contemporary with the emergence of Islam is severely complicated by the controversy surrounding scholarly views of the value of the data presented by traditional Islamic sources. On one end of the spectrum stands W. Montgomery Watt's presentation *(Muhammad at Mecca, Muhammad at Medina)* which reconstructs the early developments from the data of the Islamic sources in an attempt to relate the material to the qurʾānic evidence itself. On the other end there is Patricia Crone's wholesale rejection *(Meccan trade and the rise of Islam)* of any such endeavor in view of the discrepancies between the secondary literature and the primary sources and of conflicting information within the sources. Although Crone has argued convincingly that Meccan trade was much more limited in extent than hitherto held hypotheses would admit, her more general conclusion is open to debate: "It is at all events the impact of Byzantium and Persia on Arabia that ought to be at the forefront of research on the rise of the new religion, not Meccan trade" (Crone, *Meccan trade,* 250). This statement, and the hypothesis that "Muḥammad mobilized the Jewish (see JEWS AND JUDAISM) version of monotheism against that of dominant Christianity (see CHRISTIANS AND CHRISTIANITY) and used it for the self-assertion, both ideological and military, of his own people" (ibid., 248), appear to neglect the development reflected in the self-referential parts of the Qurʾān itself. These self-referential texts relate the qurʾānic change in the paradigm of moral values (see ETHICS AND THE QURʾĀN) to a new perception of space in terms of urban structures; moreover they present the scenario of an ongoing argument between believers and pagans rather than between believers and Christians. These features corroborate much of the mainstream, traditional Islamic picture of the social and political developments in Arabia during the early seventh century rather than the revisionist reconstructions. The following survey of Mecca's situation contemporary with the emergence of the community closely follows the arguments of a non-partisan study that — very much in accordance with Albrecht Noth's research (Früher Islam) — seeks to associate qurʾānic references with the traditional Islamic reports, reviewing both from a modern sociological vantage point, namely Gottfried Müller's "Das Problem des integrativen Zusammenhangs periodisch stattfindender Märkte auf der Arabischen Halbinsel im Jahrhundert vor dem Islam."

Mecca's market networks

Traditional reports have been reconstructed by Müller to form the following picture: Mecca was founded as a city about 400 C.E. when the tribal coalition of Quraysh (q.v.) started to become more sedentary. In contrast to the Ghassānids, al-Ḥīra and the Ḥimyar, who had remained vassals to the great powers, i.e. the Persians, the Byzantines and the Abyssinians, Mecca had succeeded in creating independent forms of political and social organization after the Meccan clan of ʿAbd Manāf was privileged to act as an agent of those powers in long distance trade across the Arabian peninsula. The sedentarization of the clans of Quraysh implied that the formerly segmented administration of power which lay with rather autonomous family groups became centralized in the institution of the *malaʾ*, an urban assembly of notables that exercised leadership over the various family groupings. Mecca of the mid-sixth century presents itself as a society in which the political, economic and religious levels of organization were embodied in diverse institutions with individual functions complementing each other. Blood ties (see KINSHIP) as a common denominator thus lost significance and individual people were able to use their political and economic acumen to build networks of commercial partners. They could thus dominate the life of their community over a period of time, themselves embodying the common interests of the city. At the same time, in the realm of religious beliefs, the cults of family groups were marginalized in favor of that of a single deity who sacralized the order of the city-state entity. This process reduced interactions with the tribal gods — now down-graded to form part of a pantheon associated with the main deity — to merely marginal rituals practiced for pragmatic reasons. This development led to a sharpening of the antagonism that existed between Mecca and the local tribal groups outside Mecca and supported the integrative political, social and religious organization of its urban coherence.

On the cultic level, a parallel development took place. With the formation of an urban administration, the formerly tribal sanctuary of the Kaʿba gained a privileged status whereas the other sanctuaries increasingly lost their independent local signification, finally becoming subordinate to the exclusive *ḥaram* of Quraysh. The cultic invocation *(talbiya)* of Quraysh clearly expresses this state of affairs: *Labbayka Allāhumma labbayk/innanā laqāḥ/ḥumatunā ʿalā asinnati l-rimāḥ/yaḥsudūnanā l-nāsu ʿalā l-najāḥ* ("Here we are, O God, here we are/we are sperm/our sting is on the tips of our spears/people begrudge us our success," Ibn Ḥabīb, *al-Muḥabbar,* 315). According to this view, it is the exclusiveness of the cult at the Kaʿba that contrasts with the practices at the other sanctuaries which were integrated, as subordinate elements, into an encompassing cultic context.
The particular position of the *ḥaram* and the obligations pertaining to the cult of the Kaʿba (not to that at ʿArafa, pace Wellhausen, *Reste,* 85) constitute the "ferment" of the tribal confederation known under the common name of *ḥums* that was established in the mid-sixth century (see TREATIES AND ALLIANCES). It comprised the inhabitants of Mecca and individual tribes from different regions of the peninsula (Khuzāʿa, Kināna) who controlled the markets of their territories and who had acquired a kind of overarching identity. The counterpart of this alliance was the confederation of the *ḥilla* which subsumed those tribes that, although participating in the Meccan trade, constituted political and economic partners of only minor import for the prosperity of the city. These tribes addressed their deities with cultic invocations *(talbiya)* of their own and celebrated their rites at a site of their own, ʿArafa, located approximately ten kilometers east of Mecca. In contrast to Mecca, this space is considered *ḥill,* i.e. profane space. It is there that the *ḥilla* tribes performed their *ḥajj* before being allowed to enter the Meccan *ḥaram* (see PILGRIMAGE). The rites at ʿArafa are in stark contrast to those of the *ḥums* at the *ḥaram;* the *ḥums* distinguished themselves from the *ḥilla* through particular prohibitions to be respected during their ceremonies. These prohibitions rendered vital aspects of nomadic life taboo (see NOMADS), such as basic nomadic nourishment, dwelling in tents (see TENTS AND TENT PEGS), wearing particular clothes made of materials produced by cattle breeders (see HIDES AND FLEECE; CLOTHING) and performing the custom of the *ṭawāf* around the Kaʿba naked or without footwear. These and other prohibitions were not binding for the *ḥilla* tribes and thus were likely to separate the Meccan sedentary population from their nomadic past and to solidify, through recourse to cultic-cultural references, their adherence to urban life. With particular prohibitions of this kind the *ḥums* express their consciousness of being chosen, the offspring of Abraham: *naḥnu banū ibrāhīma wa-ahlu l-ḥurma wa-wulātu l-bayt wa-quṭṭānu makka wa-sukkānuhā fa-laysa li-aḥadin mina l-ʿarabi*

mithlu ḥaqqinā wa-lā mithlu manzilatinā ("We are the children of Abraham and the people of the *ḥurma* and the protectors of the house and the residents of Mecca and its inhabitants, and none of the Arabs have anything like our rights or our high rank," Ibn Ḥabīb, *al-Munammaq*, 143). The Meccan way of life has become an urban way of life.

Three major market sites — ʿUkāẓ, Majanna and Dhū l-Majāz, whose religious significance as tribal sanctuaries decreased when confronted with the commercial and centralizing functions of the Meccan *ḥaram* — were situated southeast of Mecca on the way to the oasis of al-Ṭāʾif. These sites were not populated except during market days (see MARKETS). Their precise dates, known as the *mawāsim al-ḥajj*, relied on the time of year and constituted the integral part of the *ḥajj* of the *ḥilla* tribes to ʿArafa during the three sacred months. Through the economic link with the long distance commerce of the Meccans, the *mawāsim al-ḥajj* constituted the most relevant regional commercial context of the peninsula. The sequence followed a strict plan culminating in the *ḥajj* of ʿArafa: Dhū l-Qaʿda 1-20: market at ʿUkāẓ, Dhū al-Qaʿda 21-29: Majanna; Dhū l-Ḥijja 1-8: Dhū l-Majāz, Dhū l-Ḥijja 9: *ḥajj* at ʿArafa, Dhū l-Ḥijja 10: *ijāza*, the ceremonial permission to enter the Meccan *ḥaram*, and Dhū l-Ḥijja 10-13: *ʿīd al-aḍḥā* in Minā, again outside the Meccan *ḥaram*. Although these markets were situated in districts belonging to particular tribes, they could become external stations for Meccan commerce since those tribes were integrated into the pro-Qurashī *ḥums* system.

According to Müller (Zum Problem), this Ḥijāzī market system, thanks to the reinterpretation of the ritual practices of the *ḥajj* as politico-economic activities and the construction of a *ḥums-ḥilla* antagonism, was subjected to Meccan control. This system did not exist in isolation from further market activities, but constituted the nucleus of a second more comprehensive market system, a sequence of regional markets which covered vast regions of the peninsula.

Yathrib/al-Madīna

Medina lies at 24°28' north latitude, 39°36' east longitude, about 160 kilometers from the Red Sea and some 350 kilometers north of Mecca. It developed from an oasis, surrounded on the southeast and west by *ḥarra* lands, i.e. lava flows. Several *wādīs*, whose fairly high water table warrants a number of wells and springs, cross the oasis from south to north. Medina, named Yathrib in Q 33:13, is attested by Ptolemy and Stephanus Byzantinus as Iathrippa, and appears as Yathrib in Minaean inscriptions. Al-Madīna, an Aramaic loan word, means "the town," or place of jurisdiction. Apart from ten qurʾānic occurrences as a common noun, it figures in four relatively late verses — Q 9:101, 120; 33:60, 63:8 — as referring to the oasis when it was inhabited mainly by Muslims. Medina emerged from a loose collection of scattered settlements, surrounded by groves of date palms (see DATE PALM) and cultivated fields. Characteristic features were a number of strongholds *(āṭām*, sing. *uṭum)* serving as a refuge in times of danger. In earlier times, the place had been primarily populated by Jewish clans, three of whom — Qurayẓa, al-Naḍīr and Qaynuqāʿ — still played a dominant role at the time of the emigration of Muḥammad and his followers from Mecca *(hijra)*. The first two cultivated particularly fertile land in the oasis, while the third, in addition to conducting a market, were armorers and goldsmiths. Some of them may have arrived in the course of the migrations caused by the defeat of Bar Kokhba, others might have been Arab converts. Though not politically united by their religion, in Q 2:47 f. they claim to be of Hebrew descent. The earlier Jewish domination of Medina came to an end when two large Arab groups, al-Aws and al-Khazraj, who are said to have left South Arabia after the bursting of the dam of Maʾrib, came to settle in Yathrib. Although they were initially under the protection of the Jewish groups, they later gained the upper hand; the Jewish groups, however, retained a measure of independence.

For at least fifty years before the emigration *(hijra)*, a series of blood-feuds had occurred between the Arab groups, behind which there may have been an economic factor. The disruption of social order in Medina was a decisive factor leading the Arabs of Medina to invite Muḥammad to join them. On two occasions, some early converts arranged for an agreement with Muḥammad; and, as a result of the last of these agreements, the *bayʿat al-ḥarb*, concluded in 622 C.E., some seventy of Muḥammad's Meccan followers, together with their dependents, emigrated to Medina in small groups. Muḥammad arrived last, reaching al-Qubāʾ in the south of the oasis on 12 Rabīʿ I (24 September 622).

Geography in the Qurʾān: the pagan background of qurʾānic geographical representation

It is noteworthy that the Qurʾān, in contrast to ancient Arabic poetry, avoids the explicit naming of topographical data. Only very few exceptions, mostly late, can be adduced. Mecca, for instance, is often evoked through its sanctuary (*al-bayt al-maʿmūr*, Q 52:4; *al-masjid al-ḥarām*, Q 2:144, 149, 150, 191, 196, 217; 5:2; 8:34; 9:7, 19, 28; 17:1; 22:25; 48:25, 28), or through its role as the hometown of the listener(s) (*qaryatuka* or *qaryatukum*, Q 47:13) or as the metropolis par excellence (*umm al-qurā*, Q 6:92), but is eventually explicitly named twice: at Q 48:24 *(Makka)* and Q 3:96 *(Bakka)*. Equally in Medinan times, the two places of pilgrimage, al-Ṣafā and al-Marwa, are named in Q 2:158, Yathrib is named in Q 33:13. Two battlefields (see EXPEDITIONS AND BATTLES) of early Islam, Badr (q.v.), a small place situated southwest of Medīna (Q 3:123) and Ḥunayn (q.v.), one day's journey from Mecca on the way to al-Ṭāʾif (Q 9:25), are recalled in a late text. Jerusalem (q.v.) is evoked through its sanctuary (*al-masjid al-aqṣā* in Q 17:1 and simply *al-masjid* in Q 17:7) or there is allusion to it through a location within its temple (*al-miḥrāb*, Q 3:37, 39; 19:11; 38:21). Sodom and Gomorra are evoked through *al-muʾtafikāt* (Q 9:70; 69:9; cf. *al-muʾtafika*, Q 53:53).

The striking scarcity of place names may be explained by the fact that real social space is perceived during the early Meccan periods less from an empirical viewpoint, as a stage for worldly human interaction, than from an eschatological perspective (see ESCHATOLOGY), as a multiply-staged forum of debate where divine truth should emerge victorious. It is only later, in Medinan times, that places turn into territories that need to be controlled and must thus be marked by unambiguous names. Changing notions of space, therefore, can be taken as milestones in the qurʾānic canonical process (see COLLECTION OF THE QURʾĀN; CODIFICATION OF THE QURʾĀN; FORM AND STRUCTURE OF THE QURʾĀN).

The Qurʾān *in statu nascendi* addresses a public that is accustomed to listening to recitals of texts which present the human condition in terms very different from the qurʾānic presentation, recitals which are preserved in the extensive corpus of pre-Islamic Arabic poetry. It must be assumed that this textual world of the ancient poets was familiar not only to the pre-Islamic listeners, but to later Arab converts as well. The ancient poets are thus in no way isolable from the Qurʾān. On the contrary, the

Qurʾān itself presents a response to them. Although far more interested in "the presence, the example and the provocation of the antecedent Semitic religions" (Cragg, *Event,* 15), Western scholarship has paid tribute to diverse aspects of this encounter (Farrukh, *Das Bild*), even claiming that ancient poetry provides the "spiritual background" for the Qurʾān (Bravmann, *Spiritual background*). Scholars have moreover acknowledged the achievement of the Qurʾān's re-coding (Izutsu, *God and man*) of the world imagined in poetry into a new paradigm of ethical values, stressing the dialectical relation (Montgomery, Poetry) that exists between the two realms of thinking. But although the qurʾānic construction of real and imaginary space is certainly one of the most important achievements in the context of the turn from paganism to Islam, no extensive study has been undertaken regarding the qurʾānic geographical representation of both the Arabian habitat and the biblical sites (see SCRIPTURE AND THE QURʾĀN).

Notions of space in pre-Islamic poetry

Deserted space

The pre-qurʾānic literary paradigm implies a perception of space as a challenge to humans, because it is not at their disposal. Not seldom does it present itself as "embattled space," demanding to be recovered by the Bedouin hero. Yet, even when space is not viewed in such a dynamic context but is presented in a more static way, it does not appear as an integral part of the poetical speaker's natural habitat; rather, it appears as an entity deprived of actual life and haunted by loss. Nonetheless, the role of topography in ancient poetry is striking, particularly when the poet in pre-Islamic (*jāhilī,* see AGE OF IGNORANCE) poetry's main genre, the *qaṣīda,* chooses to start his speech with an elegiac "*aṭlāl*-section" in which a broken-off love relation is remembered. He invests much diligence in describing the detailed features of the natural space where he finds himself, having come to a halt at a deserted campsite to recall a beloved of the past. The picture he designs to frame his first entrance does not, however, express enjoyment of nature or aesthetic delight in its extraordinary traits, but rather portrays the search for the reconstruction of the lost shape *("Gestalt")* of that space that was formerly replete with fulfilling social interaction but has meanwhile decayed and become disfigured through climatic influences. It is the poet who has to give space its distinctive features, to make it speak again — a situation which sometimes induces him to address the place, literally begging it to answer him. Some verses from the famous *nasīb* of Labīd's *Muʿallaqa* (vv. 1, 2, 10) serve well to illustrate this:

Effaced are the abodes, brief encampments and long-settled ones/at Minā the wilderness has claimed Mount Ghawl and Mount Rijām *(ʿafati l-diyāru maḥalluhā famuqāmuhā/bi-minan taʾabbada ghawluhā farijāmuhā).*

Dung-darkened patches over which, since they were peopled,/years elapsed. Their profane months and sacred ones have passed away *(dimanun tajarrama baʿda ʿahdi anīsihā/ḥijajun khalawna ḥalāluhā waḥarāmuhā).*

Then I stopped and questioned them, but how do we question/mute immortals whose speech is indistinct? (*fa-waqaftu asʾaluhā wa-kayfa suʾālunā/ṣumman khawālida mā yabīnu kalāmuhā,* trans. Stetkevych, Mute immortals, 9).

When scenes of idyllic group life are introduced, these are staged in the animal realm rather than the human, thus stressing the feeling of deprivation suffered by the poet who is in a state of loss regarding erotic and matrimonial fulfillment (see e.g. Labīd's *Muʿallaqa,* vv. 6-7).

Although space is presented as empty and desolate, the location tends to be very determinate. Place names abound (Thilo, *Die Ortsnamen*). Places are marked and are still recognizable as having been previously peopled, as *lieux de mémoire,* places of remembrance and yearning, though blurred and deserted at the time the poet speaks, and no longer *milieux* of human interaction. Geographical representation is thus in stark contrast to the physical absence of those for whom such representation is intended. It is further striking — as Hamori has noted (*The art,* 18) — that "in the *aṭlāl* scene, time present has no effective contents to speak of." The desertedness of space is not due to any historical event relevant to the present, but to the seasonal practices of the camel breeding tribes, who only in the winter and spring, when water resources were sufficient, would roam the desert freely with their camels, but with the beginning of the drought, would retreat to their own permanent sources of water. These exigencies thus limited longer-term encounters between members of different tribes to short periods and pre-determined the break-off of personal relations after short durations. Only rarely is the extinction of the traces of the encampment explained by phenomena which are beyond mere seasonally imposed needs, as in the verses of ʿAbīd (18.2-3; Caskel, *Das Schicksal,* 45).

Embattled space

Although the world of the pre-Islamic listeners to poetry appears well-mapped, place-names being adduced frequently and playing a prominent role in the initial part of the *qaṣīda,* and, although a sharp realization of physical-geographical phenomena can be attested, the relation of man to space appears to be tense. The pagan poet or more precisely his persona, the Bedouin hero, has to re-conquer space over and over again in order to meet the ideals of *muruwwa* and thus fulfill his role as an exemplary member of tribal society. Risky expeditions undertaken by the hero through most inhospitable areas and adventurous rides under extreme climatic conditions are among the stock topics of the closing part, the *fakhr,* of the ancient Arabian *qaṣīda.* One of the most famous testimonies of this poetical self- image — though in this case going back not to a tribally integrated poet, but rather to an outlaw — are certainly the triumphal final verses of al-Shanfarā's *Lāmiyyat al-ʿarab:*

I have crossed deserts bare as the back of a shield, where no traveler's beast sets foot *(wa-kharqin ka-ẓahri l-tursi qafrin qaṭāʿtuhu/ bi-ʿāmilatayni ẓahruhu laysa yuʿmalū).*

I tied one end of the waste to the other, squatting or standing on a peak *(wa-alḥaqtu ūlāhu bi-ukhrāhu mūfiyan/ʿalā qunnatin uqʿī marāran wa-amthulū).*

While the dark yellow mountain goats come and go about me like maidens in trailing garments *(tarūdu l-arāwī l-ṣuḥmu ḥawlī ka-annahā/ʿadhārin ʿalayhinna l-mulāʿu l-mudhayyalū),*

Until at dusk they stand about me, motionless, as if I were a white-legged, crookhorned one, with a twist in the legs, a scaler of summits (*wa-yarkudna bi-l-āṣāli ḥawlī ka-annanī/mina l-ʿuṣmi adfā yantaḥī l-kīḥa aʿqalū,* trans. Hamori, *The art,* 30).

Indeed, with only a slight exaggeration it might be held that space, being among those inimical elements that permanently threaten man is, in view of its momentum, one of the manifestations of fate (*al-manāyā, al-manūn, al-dahr,* see FATE; TIME; DESTINY) itself. The Bedouin hero, who does not find himself in a position of mastery over his habitat, but has to empower himself over and over again to defy his most threatening enemy, the all-consuming fate, does so in many instances by venturing into dangerous space. Space and fate are frequently viewed as closely related, such as a verse by ʿUrwa b. al-Ward (Caskel, *Das Schicksal,* 21) attests:

Many a gray (desert) where perishing is feared/where the traveler is threatened by the ropes of fate (I have crossed; *wa-ghabrāʾa makhshiyin radāhā makhūfatin/akhūhā bi-asbābi l-manāyā mugharrarū*).

Space, thus, is often presented as the site of a battlefield, a scene of human strife for self-assertion against threatening nature. Not least through his recollection of "special conquests," could the Bedouin hero counterbalance the resignation-inspiring view of man as an easy prey to the haphazard assaults of the anonymous powers of nature, and thus contribute vitally to the coherence of his tribal society.

"The old Arabic *qaṣīda* was both sensuous and logical as it faced *al-dahr,* time and mutability which unconcerned with human conduct and human reason govern the world. In a morally capricious universe, the heroic model allowed a view of the totality of experience as balanced and coherent. To achieve balance, the speaker of the *qaṣīda* offers himself to the voluntary experience of fullness as well as emptiness, of gain as well as loss" (Hamori, *The art,* 29).

Responses: the qurʾānic canonical process as reflected in the re-coding of the pagan notions of space

As against the heroic attitude of man towards space as displayed in poetry, the early qurʾānic revelations present earthly space as particularly inspiring of confidence. They present it as a locus of pleasure and enjoyment, as a venue for the reception of divine bounty and as a site of ethically-charged social interaction.

Aesthetically enjoyable space, symbolically significant space: the de-mythicizing of pagan heroic space

An early and dominant image is that of a well preserved tent, allowing man to repose, to enjoy matrimonial life, as well as to pursue his daily activities in a peaceful and self-confident way. Q 78:6-16 strongly reminds one of some psalms (q.v.) of praise which interpret worldly space as a secure housing for the created beings: "Have we not made the earth an expanse, and the mountains bulwarks? And created you in pairs (see CREATION)? And appointed your sleep as repose, and the night as a cloak (see CLOTHING; DAY AND NIGHT), and the day for livelihood? And built above you seven strong [heavens; see HEAVEN AND SKY]?" *(a-lam najʿali l-arḍa mihādā/wal-jibāla awtādā/wa-khalaqnākum azwājā/wa-jaʿalnā nawmakum subātā/wa-jaʿalnā l-layla libāsā/wa-jaʿalnā l-nahāra maʿāshā/wa-banaynā fawqakum sabʿan shidādā).* Worldly space, then, is a divine grace demanding gratitude (*shukr,* see GRATITUDE AND INGRATITUDE), a present that inspires forms of worship (q.v.) which, in turn, will enhance the coherence of the relationship between God and humankind. There is a whole qurʾānic genre of hymnic praises of divine omnipotence, the so-called *āyāt,* "signs" (q.v.; Neuwirth, *Studien;* Graham, "The winds") that rely on the very notion that the earth has been equipped with diverse means to make human life easy and pleasant (e.g. "God sent water down from the heavens and enlivened the earth with it after its death," Q 16:65: *wa-llāhu anzala mina l-samāʾi māʾan fa-aḥyā bihi l-arḍa baʿda mawtihā*). The revivification of the earth that seemed dead is a sign of divine providence: "Have you not seen God send water down from the heavens and the earth become green the next day?" (Q 22:63: *a-lam tara anna llāha anzala mina l-samāʾi māʾan fa-tuṣbiḥu l-arḍu mukhḍarratan*). The picture seems to reflect that of a rural oasis, such as al-Ṭāʾif or Yathrib: "We have showered down water, then split the earth in clefts, and made the grain to grow therein, and grapes and green fodder, and olive trees and date palms, and garden groves, and fruits and grasses, provision for you and your cattle" (Q 80:25-32: *annā ṣababnā l-māʾa ṣabbā/thumma shaqaqnā l-arḍa shaqqā fa-anbatnā fīhā ḥabbā/wa-ʿinaban wa-qaḍbā/wa-zaytūnan wa-nakhlā/wa-ḥadāʾiqa ghulbā/wa-fākihatan wa-abbā/matāʿan lakum wa-li-anʿāmikum*). These descriptions, of course, are not devoid of a symbolic dimension. The image of the dead land miraculously revived is evoked not least to provide an empirically evident antecedent for the divine power of reviving the dead that contradicts empirical verisimility. The idea is therefore central not only to the early sūras (see Q 79:27-33) but is reiterated over and over again in later phases (Q 22:5; 50:9-11; 57:17; 41:38-9).

Early Meccan descriptions like these do not solely convey the message of divine omnipotence, freeing a man from his burden to fight for his survival, a dominant theme of pre-Islamic poetry (see FREEDOM AND PREDESTINATION). Their objective is more far-reaching: the entire paradigm within which a man's self-respect was dependent on his achievements (which, in Meccan terms, might have been manifested in commercial success), was to be redefined. The focus shifts: from the human person being the sole agent in the process of restoring meaning to life, attention is turned towards created nature which displays divinely granted abundance (see BLESSING; GRACE). God appears as the decisive agent in the process of restoring meaning to life, communicating his message through aesthetically understandable phenomena. The addressee is — not unlike the situation of ancient Arabian poetry — the community. Be it the image of the firm land or the image of the sea (*baḥr*, cf. Q 16:4; 25:54-5; 35:12, *baḥrān;* cf. Barthold, Der Koran und das Meer), humankind is taught to rejoice in a divinely adorned cosmos which simultaneously manifests a new paradigm of social coherence.

Copiousness of vegetation as a divine gift

It is hardly astonishing that vegetation plays a significant role in conveying the image of the world as a hospitable realm of human life (see AGRICULTURE AND VEGETATION). The vegetation in the Qurʾān has been meticulously surveyed by Arne Ambros (Gestaltung und Funktionen). His presentation is very helpful for present purposes as it provides an insight to the listeners' perception of local, imagined and even transcendental landscapes; it will thus be summarized in the following. The Qurʾān offers no less than eleven detailed depictions of earthly vegetation. They are distributed over the entire corpus of the Qurʾān, figuring equally in the context of salvation (q.v.) history — located outside the peninsula — and in the reality of the listeners' present situation on the peninsula. Their frequency in relation to the scarcity of depictions of the fauna (for which only Q 16:5-8 could be adduced) points to the listeners' relationship towards the realm of plants as being basically different from that towards the realm of animals (see ANIMAL LIFE). An important element of this relationship is the delight in the beauty of plants; they are often viewed without regard to their usefulness.

One of the three main themes that

accommodate vegetation is the description of plants as a testimony to the bounty of God (no less than forty occurrences). The second theme is the perception of the permanent threat to which plants are subject in view of abrupt climatic changes and the scarcity of water supplies — an observation that often evokes the transitory nature of all beings. This theme unfolds thirteen times and in five of these both the first and the second themes are combined. The third theme is the diversity of vegetation in nature. This topic sometimes erupts in exclamations of admiration and delight never found in conjunction with descriptions of the animal world.

The most frequently mentioned locus of vegetation is certainly the garden (q.v.; *janna*), which also denotes an other-worldly garden. Particular plants that are grown in a garden are named, such as date palms and vines (Q 2:266; 17:91; 23:19; 36:34). *Janna* thus is not to be imagined as a merely ornamental garden, but rather as a plantation, a "garden from which one eats" (Q 25:8). The earthly garden is therefore a possession that permits a good living or even wealth (q.v.). Whereas *rawḍa* — a place with copious vegetation, a garden or a meadow — in the Qurʾān denotes only the paradisaical (see PARADISE) abode, *ḥadīqa* appears as a locale where copious plants, among them trees (q.v.), are to be found (Q 27:60; 80:30). In contradistinction, the qurʾānic *ḥarth* is a place where primarily cereals grow. It is presented in Q 3:14 as a possession desirable to humans. Associated with toil, *ḥarth* never appears in descriptions of paradise. It does serve, however, as a metaphor for the constraints that are demanded from humans as qualification for admission to the paradisaical afterlife: "Whoever desires the harvest *(ḥarth)* of the hereafter, we increase its harvest for him; but whoever desires the harvest of the world, we give it to him, but he has no part of the hereafter" (Q 42:20, *man kāna yurīdu ḥartha l-ākhirati nazid lahu fī ḥarthihi wa-man kāna yurīdu ḥartha l-dunyā nuʾtihi minhā wa-mā lahu fī l-ākhirati min naṣīb*). Remnants of mythical thinking are reflected in a *ḥarth* metaphor in Q 2:223: "Your wives are your *ḥarth,* so approach your *ḥarth* as you wish" *(nisāʾukum ḥarthun lakum fa-ʾtū ḥarthakum annā shiʾtum)*. The lexeme *zarʿ* (pl. *zurūʿ*) denotes sown plants. In view of its association with hard work, like *ḥarth* it is confined to worldly contexts; when it occurs in the singular form, *zarʿ,* it is synonymous with *nabāt,* the most frequent context being praise of divine care and providence (Q 6:141; 16:11; 32:27; 39:21). It is noteworthy that the region around Mecca is called in a prayer of Abraham the "valley with no existence of *zarʿ,*" (*wādi ghayr dhī zarʿ,* Q 14:37), or an uncultivable area, a wasteland.

The benefits to be made from vegetation are manifest in fruit. The least concrete notion seems to be *thamar,* "fruit." It is only once specified, in Q 16:67: "fruits of palms and vines" *(thamarāt al-nakhīl wa-l-aʿnāb)*. Used in the plural form, it encompasses all kinds of fruit — including those of the fields — and usually denotes the normal means of subsistence that is granted by God, but is liable to be taken away by him whenever he pleases (cf. Q 2:22; 14:32: "he sends water down from the sky and through it makes fruit spring up for you as a blessing *[rizqan],*" *anzala mina l-samāʾi māʾan fa-akhraja bihi mina l-thamarāti rizqan lakum*). A shortage of fruit (Q 7:130) figures among the punishments of the Egyptians (see EGYPT). A little more precise is *fākiha,* with the etymological connotation of enjoyable fruit (*f-k-h* denotes the sentiment of being cheerful), mostly appearing in paradisaical depictions.

After fruit, seeds figure prominently

among the parts of plants. The sprouting of seeds is viewed as a work of God (Q 6:95, *inna llāha fāliqu l-ḥabbi wa-l-nawā*). In most of the other instances, *ḥabb* or *ḥabba* serves as a symbol of the tiny thing that is yet not neglected by God: "Not a leaf falls but he knows it, nor a grain *(ḥabba)* in the darkness of the earth" (Q 6:59, *wa-mā tasquṭu min waraqatin illā yaʿlamuhā wa-lā ḥabbatin fī ẓulumāti l-ʿarḍi*). In Q 21:47 and 31:16 it is mentioned that God will reckon even the weight of one grain of a mustard-seed *(mithqāl ḥabbatin min khardalin)*.

In reference to individual plants there are, first of all, trees: the Arabic word *shajar* or *shajara* is also used to denote bushes and shrubs. Some contexts point to an Arabian habitat, Q 36:80 where the kindling of fire from *shajar* is considered to be a divine gift to humankind (also Q 56:71 f.). As a place where bees live, *shajar* appears in Q 16:68. A historical occurrence in Muḥammad's life is associated with a tree in Q 48:18: *idh yubāyiʿūnaka taḥta l-shajarati*. Other mentions of *shajar(a)* point to an extra-Arabian habitat, like the olive tree on Mount Sinai (q.v.; Q 23:20), the burning shrub of Moses (q.v.; Q 28:30; see FIRE), and the gourd shrub of Jonas (q.v.; Q 37:146). There is an otherworldly tree *(shajara mubāraka zaytūna)* in the famous Light Verse (Q 24:35). Otherwise, trees figure in paradise frequently, and are indeed characteristic of its landscape; but there is also an exotically shaped tree, *shajarat al-zaqqūm* or *shajar min zaqqūm*, in hell (q.v.; Q 37:62; 44:43; 56:52; cf. 17:60).

Very often the palm tree, a particularly important plant in Arabia, is mentioned: *nakhla* or, collectively, *nakhl* (pl. *nakhīl*). It is the only plant that is described in some detail in the Qurʾān (Q 6:99; 13:4; 26:148; 50:10; 55:11). In view of the importance of palms in the Arabian habitat, the metaphor of ruined palms provides a sufficiently shocking image to dramatize the theme of a people smitten with divine punishment, the ʿĀd (q.v.; Q 54:20; 69:7; see PUNISHMENT STORIES). *Nakhl* may appear in the same context as gardens. They also occur in extra-Arabian habitats, like Q 19:23, 25 (*nakhla* in the account of the birth of Jesus, q.v.) and Q 20:71 (Moses appearing before Pharaoh, q.v.), as well as in a description of paradise (Q 55:68). The fruit of the palm tree is mentioned rather seldom (Q 19:25, *ruṭab;* Q 16:67, *thamarāt al-nakhīl*).

Vines are mentioned eleven times *(ʿinab,* mostly *aʿnāb);* they appear in most cases (seven times) together with date palms (Q 18:32), perhaps due to a joint cultivation of both species. Vines also appear in descriptions of paradise (Q 78:32; the prohibition to consume intoxicating drinks is rather late [cf. Q 16:67]; see INTOXICANTS; CHRONOLOGY AND THE QURʾĀN). Besides date palms and vines, olive trees *(zaytūn)* occur five times, twice in the habitat of Mount Sinai.

Other plants named in the Qurʾān are tamarisk trees (*athl,* Q 34:16), onions (*baṣal,* Q 2:61), figs or fig trees (*tīn,* Q 95:1), mustard (*khardal,* Q 21:47; 31:16), lote tree (*sidr,* Q 34:16; 56:28; cf. 53:14, 16), ginger (*zanjabīl,* Q 76:17), pomegranates (*rummān,* Q 6:99, 141; 55:68), basil (*rayḥān,* Q 55:12), lentils (*ʿadas,* Q 2:61), garlic (*fūm,* Q 2:61) and the gourd shrub (*yaqṭīn,* Q 37:146). As against these, some generic names are difficult to identify: *khamṭ,* thorny shrubs (Q 34:16), *ḍarīʿ,* dried thorny shrubs (Q 88:6), *qaḍb,* fodder plants (Q 80:28; see GRASSES).

The empirical knowledge of these plants and moreover their places of cultivation clearly point to familiarity with and, indeed, the esteem of rural oases like al-Ṭāʾif as places of enjoyment and delight in the mental map of the listeners. Vegetation in paradise is not essentially different, but only more copious than earthly vegetation. It is noteworthy that only a few of the plants mentioned in the Qurʾān attest to the listeners' empirical knowledge of the vegetation of the desert.

Urban public space as a forum of meaningful social interaction

Ancient Bedouin poetry portrays the exemplary man, when appearing in public, as bound to burdensome constraints. He is expected to display extreme generosity, sometimes bordering on economic self-annihilation, so as to, through sacrifice, heroically defy the hardships imposed on weaker individuals by fate. Man in the Qurʾān is relieved of this burden. Moving in an urban space he orients himself to ethical values that are symbolically mirrored in the urban structures themselves. His "heroism" is not dependent on wealth and status, but piety (q.v.) and moral-ethical obedience (q.v.). Q 90 "The City" (Sūrat al-Balad) may serve as an example: "No, I swear by this city. And you are an inhabitant *(ḥillun)* of this city. And the begetter and that which he begat. We verily have created man in affliction *(kabadin)*. Does he think that nobody has power over him? And he says, 'I have destroyed vast wealth.' Does he think that nobody sees him? Did we not provide him with two eyes (q.v.) and a tongue and two lips, and guide him to the two mountain passes *(najdayn)*. But he has not attempted the ascent *(al-ʿaqaba)*. What will convey to you what the ascent is? [It is] the freeing of a slave, feeding in the day of hunger an orphan (q.v.) near of kin or a pauper in misery (see POVERTY AND THE POOR), and to be of those who believe (see BELIEF AND UNBELIEF) and exhort one another to perseverence (see TRUST AND PATIENCE) and mercy (q.v.). Their place will be on the right hand. But those who disbelieve our revelations, their place will be on the left hand. Fire will be an awning over them." The initial incantation evokes Mecca as the place of the origin of the addressee, joining it to the complex idea of procreation (see BIOLOGY AS THE CREATION AND STAGES OF LIFE). Mecca, as a city with a *temenos,* a *ḥaram,* i.e. a place where divine theophany has taken place, is thus a reference to the idea of divine interaction with humans. Allusions to both creation and divine communication at the beginning of history (see HISTORY AND THE QURʾĀN) have been identified as a stock introductory theme serving to arouse the listeners' expectation of an equally complex ending, of the fulfillment of both physical and spiritual time (Neuwirth, Images and metaphors; see FORM AND STRUCTURE OF THE QURʾĀN). Mecca, figuring from the beginning as a locus of divine self-manifestation, has attracted eschatological connotations similar to those of the biblical localities mentioned in comparable oath-introduced texts, namely Mount Sinai and Jerusalem, whose introduction at the beginnings of sūras serve as a prelude to eschatological discourses unfolded at the end of the texts.

What is particularly noteworthy in this sūra is the reflection of the urban structure in the image of a human being. The topographic features (the two paths, *al-najdān,* the steep path, *al-ʿaqaba*), recall features of the human body whose organs — some of which are dual as well — have been shaped to enable him to understand the proper ways of moral conduct. Both urban and bodily structures are thus divine tokens that have to be translated by the listeners into ethical imperatives. The topographic features of the difficult paths and the steep road which structure the public space of the city have to be read as moral tasks. To climb them means to restrain oneself in favor of others: to ease the burden of the slaves, the hungry and the poor. These "others" are presented as fellow creatures, whose bodily parts (*raqaba*, representing the social "class" of slaves), genetic relations (*maqraba*, representing the class of equals, or rich persons) or even whose ailments (*masghaba*, alluding to the class of the poor), through common rhyme patterns, evoke the aforementioned urban feature of *ʿaqaba*, thus including them in the morally demanding entity of urban public space. Mecca, indirectly introduced (vv. 1-2) as the scenario of this interaction, is obviously recognized as a body politic, suitable for implementing social activities in accordance with the divine will (cf. also Rippin, Commerce).

The pagan perception of man's ideal activity in the public space is exemplarily presented in this sūra ("I have destroyed vast wealth," Q 90:6, *ahlaktu mālan lubad*) by the words of the unbeliever himself. It is, however, not rejected with the arguments known from the counter-voice of the pagan poet, the often adduced "critic" who aims at the avoidance of exaggerated generosity and warns of extra-family-oriented overspending, which may lead to impoverishment. Whereas in pre-Islamic poetry visibility in public space meant wasting one's fortune by overspending to prove one's generosity, in the Qurʾān any insistence on such extreme practices are censured. Public appearance in the Qurʾān is rather governed by an ethical code which aims at a fair distribution of goods achieved in an un-heroic manner. It is the experience of the city as a structured space that in the Qurʾān provides the metaphors to communicate that code.

Restoring meaning to deserted space: the umam khāliya; *reconstruction of space in terms of salvation historical* lieux de mémoire

According to Kenneth Cragg, "Arabian history was awed by the recollection of whole prosperous communities which had disintegrated and passed away through the collapse, sudden or cumulative, of their earthworks and irrigation systems, most noteworthy of all the catastrophic end of the dam of Maʾrib and the irreparable loss of the precious oversoil by uncontrolled erosion" (*Event*, 88). This is certainly the factual background of the repeated evocations of bygone cultures, the *umam khāliya* or deserted localities in the Qurʾān. Yet, the frequent descriptions of deserted space as a marker of loneliness, of the search for meaning and never ending questions which figure so prominently in pagan poetry, also resound in the many allusions to deserted space in the Qurʾān. But in the Qurān — contrary to the situation in poetry — all the questions are answered. The desolate places are historical sites, evoked through the reports of events. Though seldom explicitly named, they still have become sites laden with symbolic significance, since their evocation marks the beginning of a conversion process: The believers are turned from a community rooted in a local collective memory (see e.g. Q 105:1 on the episode of the elephant; see ABRAHA), where reminiscences of local experience count (Q 106:1-2 on Mecca's past and present), into a community whose memory of imagined space is oriented towards an "other" tradition: that of salvation history. The development will reach its climax with the re-coding of significant geography as a whole, i.e. with its integration into a world that is scripturally informed. Before that stage is reached, allusions to deserted places that figure in Meccan texts are often related to the world of the listeners' experience, i.e. the Ḥijāz or the Arabian peninsula as a whole. These sites are, from the beginning, presented as collective *lieux de mémoire*, places replete with meaning, assuring the listeners of a divinely endorsed order, in which not capricious fate or cyclically occurring constraints dominate, but one in which an equilibrium of human action and welfare is achieved. For details about the local Arabian sites of *umam khāliya* we may simply refer to Josef Horovitz' seminal study, *Koranische Untersuchungen* (for Iram [q.v.] in Q 89:7, see Horovitz, *KU*, 89; for Thamūd [q.v.] in Q 11:61-8; 51:43 f.; 54:23-32; 69:5 f.; 89:8; 91:11 f., see Horovitz, *KU*, 11 f., 103 f. and also J. Stetkevych, *Muhammad;* for Madyan [see MIDIAN] in Q 7:85 f.; 9:70; 11:84 f.; 20:42; 22:43; 28:21; 29:35 f., see Horovitz, *KU*, 138; for Sabaʾ [see SHEBA] in Q 27:22, see Horovitz, *KU*, 115 f.; for Tubbaʿ [q.v.; or *qawm Tubbaʿ*] in Q 44:36 f., 50:13, see Horovitz, *KU*, 103; for Sodom and Gomorra [the qurʾānic *al-muʾtafikāt*] in Q 9:70; 69:9, see Horovitz, *KU*, 13 f.).

What is common to all of them, whether they are presented as known and visible to the first audience of the Qurʾān, or only adduced as mythical examples, is that they are spaces, imagined mostly as "cities" (*qurā*, sing. *qarya*, Q 47:14; cf. Q 30:9; 35:43; 40:22, 82), which, at the time of the Qurʾān, had become deserted. But what was, in pagan poetry, due to the seasonal cycle, i.e. the necessity of leaving campsites due to the lack of water, and successive devastation through natural decay, has been furnished in the Qurʾān with a historical reason. The devastation of the sites is caused by a divine retaliation, which the former inhabitants — the unbelievers — called upon themselves. That which in pagan poetry would arouse resignation: a temptation to allow oneself to succumb to the overwhelming power of fate from which the poet would recover only through a strenuous personal endeavor, was, to the Qurʾān's audience, no longer a threat. More than once (Q 27:69; 30:42), the Qurʾān invites the listeners to roam the lands and convince themselves of the tragic ends with which the earlier peoples have met — an idea associated already by Horovitz with the *aṭlāl*-descriptions of ancient poetry as well as with the verses on the *"ubi sunt qui ante nos fuerunt"* topos (Becker, *Islamstudien*, i, 501 f.). But the Qurʾān, in contrast with the nostalgic verses of poetry, is paraenetical in orientation, conveying the message that even the most powerful peoples are annihilated when they defy the warnings of their messengers (see WARNING). It teaches the imminence, but at the same time the avoidability, of divine retaliation in this life (see CHASTISEMENT AND PUNISHMENT) that causes the destruction of one's habitat in this world. Fate can be overcome, not through heroic endeavor, but through obeying messengers (see OBEDIENCE). The absence of human presence is recompensed, not by a reassurance of previous happiness, but by a story restoring meaning, reestablishing the balance between what occurred and the suffering that was endured. Haphazard fate and all-consuming time have ceded their power to a just divine agent. Space has regained a meaningful historical dimension.

Exile and recovery of the familiar landscape: the "biblification" of pagan space

Two movements within the qurʾānic corpus mark the figuration of Mecca as a locus of salvific importance. The first presents Mecca as a calque on the biblically significant sites of the holy land and Jerusalem while the second situates Mecca as a second Jerusalem.

Mecca as a counterpart of biblical sites of revelation: the holy land and Jerusalem

It is interesting to note that early sūras, which otherwise focus on Meccan sacred space or Arabian sites of retaliation, in some instances already recall central sanctuaries of biblical geography. This applies in particular to Mount Sinai (Q 19:52; 20:80; 28:46; 95:2), the locus of the revelation received by Moses (q.v.). Through the juxtaposition of this sanctuary with Mecca, the pagan sanctuary is affirmed in its aura of a holy place honored as such in its past through a divine manifestation and thus communication of the divine will.

At a later phase, when the map of the believers has itself widened, it is no longer for the sake of Mecca that biblical loci are mentioned: a new notion of geography has arisen, relating not to experienced space but to desired space. It is the area of the holy land familiar to Judaism and Christianity that replaces the familiar local geography.

The holy land (*al-arḍ al-muqaddasa*, Q 5:21; *al-arḍ allatī bāraknā ḥawlahā/fīhā*, literally, "the land that we have blessed," Q 21:71; cf. 7:137; 17:1; 34:18) is evoked in the Qurʾān on different occasions. Particularly the middle and late Meccan periods are replete with recollections of biblical history. The earlier reminiscences of Arabian salvation history are being replaced by recollections of biblical history featuring the Children of Israel (q.v.; Banū Isrāʾīl). Local *lieux de mémoire* are substituted by geographically remote ones — a new *topographia sacra* emerges, adopted from "the others," not the genealogical, but the spiritual forebears. One of the first events recorded to have taken place in the holy land is the story of Lot (q.v.; Lūṭ) staged at the *muʾtafikāt* (Q 53:53-6; 69:9). Indeed, the whole history of the Israelites, except for the parts staged in Egypt (Miṣr) and their wandering through the desert of Sinai, is located in the holy land. The Qurʾān later relates several significant events of salvation history staged in Jerusalem, such as the annunciation of a son gifted with prophecy to the aged Zechariah (q.v.; Q 3:39; 19:7; see JOHN THE BAPTIST), the sojourn of young Mary (q.v.) in the temple in the care of Zechariah (Q 3:37), David's judgment, viewed in the Qurʾān as a divine trial (Q 38:21 f.), and finally the catastrophe of the destruction of the sanctuary by foreign conquerors, understood to be a punishment imposed on the Children of Israel (Q 17:2 f.). These qurʾānic references to Jerusalem and the holy land, though often not explicit, not only serve to complete the narrative of salvation history, but also help the listeners adopt the remote world of the memory of the others as their own spiritual past. The community, urged to go into an inner exile, yearned for a substitute for the emotionally alienated and politically hostile landscape of their origin. Through the adoption of the *qibla* towards Jerusalem dating to the last years of Muḥammad's Meccan activities, a trajectory has been constructed. Q 17:1, the sole verse which connects the holy land directly with the biography of the Prophet, is also a testimony of the establishment of the first *qibla* (q.v.; Neuwirth, The spiritual meaning): "Glorified be he who carried his servant by night from the inviolable sanctuary *(al-masjid al-ḥarām)* to the remote sanctuary *(al-masjid al-aqṣā)*, the neighborhood whereof we have blessed, in order that we might show him our signs. Verily, God is the hearer, the seer (see SEEING AND HEARING; GOD AND HIS ATTRIBUTES)."

Here, a short excursus on the *qibla* towards Jerusalem appears indispensable. Indeed, the Jerusalem sanctuary in its function as a ritual orientation — as the focus of an imaginary space becoming accessible in prayer — did not develop in the consciousness of the young Islamic community at a haphazard time. Rather, it appeared during a phase of development when, thanks to a complex process of new orientation, a remarkable widening of the young community's horizons was taking place, in terms of time as well as of space. Thus the "remote sanctuary," so suggestive in its topographical and historical setting, could become a forceful symbol. One might dare to hypothesize that the Jerusalem *qibla* came about as a gestural expression of the deeply felt experience of having gained new spiritual horizons.

Together, two essential novelties — the newly attained convergence of the qurʾānic revelations with the scriptures of the two other monotheistic religions and the simultaneous adoption of the *topographia sacra* of the earlier religions — created a new self-consciousness for the young Islamic community. This new self-awareness was no longer based primarily on the rites practiced at the Kaʿba, but on a new consciousness of being among the receivers and bearers of a scripture, and, as such, having a share in the memory of salvation history, transported by the medium of writing (see BOOK). Jan Assmann *(Das kulturelle Gedächtnis)* has coined a phrase for this type of change in orientation, the "transition of a society from ritual coherence to textual coherence." By its very gesture, the *qibla,* oriented toward Jerusalem, points to this new connection between the emerging Islamic community and the older religions. It is not surprising, then, that the qurʾānic allusions to the Meccan sanctuary and its rites as the previous guarantors of social coherence (Neuwirth, Images and metaphors) — allusions, up until that point, so numerous in the introductory sections of the Meccan sūras — were soon replaced by a stereotypical introductory evocation of the book *(al-kitāb),* now recognized as the most significant common spiritual possession. The images now appearing in the introductory sections of the sūras, the book and its requisites, unequivocally point to the awareness that a stream of tradition had come to a standstill and was now accessible through written means. It was a new form of remembrance that would soon penetrate the daily ritual practices: the strong attachment to a familiar place, which was characteristic of the worship at the Kaʿba, gave way to the perception of a new situation in a spiritual space, that reached far beyond the horizons of the inherited rites into the world and history of the others, of the Children of Israel (Banū Isrāʾīl).

Whereas in the earliest sūras there had been few places considered worth evoking except for Mecca and the deserted sites of Arabia, from this point until the emigration *(hijra)* — with the sole exception of Q 17 — one does not find any further references to Mecca in the sūras. Instead, the "blessed land" is introduced as a space in which the oppressed believer may take refuge and where most of the prophets had worked. Sūras culminate in an oft-repeated appeal to the examples reaching far back into the history of the spiritual forebears, the Children of Israel (Banū Isrāʾīl). Jerusalem is the central sanctuary of the space marked by this scripture and thus by writing. All prayers gravitate in the direction of Jerusalem as their natural destination and to Jerusalem the worshipper turns his face in prayer.

The inner exile to which allusion is already made in Q 73:10, "part from them in a pleasant manner" *(uhjurhum hajran jamīlā),* was to culminate in a territorial exile. As Cragg (*Event,* 126) has noted, "for an event so vital and formative, the Qurʾān surprisingly has little direct to say," the only explicit passage about the emigration *(hijra)* being perhaps Q 9:40-1. The move out of Mecca is, however, not definite; it presages the move against Mecca that would follow some ten years later and the spiritual recovery of the familiar space of the Meccan sanctuary before then.

Biblical sites substituted: Mecca's emergence as a second Jerusalem

When we reach the Medinan period, we find the afore-sketched trajectory from the familiar but now banned and forbidden Mecca to the "remote," imaginary sanctuary of Jerusalem being called into question.

Leaving the remote imaginary homeland — the recovery of the peninsula

It is in this period that an attempt to settle the antagonism between the local Jewish tribes and the Medinan communities is being made, and the incompatibility of the rivaling *lieux de mémoire*, the two *topographiae sacrae*, Jerusalem with the holy land on the one hand and Mecca with the Ḥijāzī landscape on the other, has become evident. Thus, places formerly carrying paradigmatic memories become loci of ambivalent events: Mount Sinai now is portrayed as the site where the Children of Israel failed to fulfill a divine command (Q 2:63-4, 93; 4:153-5; 7:171). Jerusalem does not fare very differently. The rediscovery of Mecca as the essential destination of the longing of the exiles at Medina came about barely two years after the emigration, and is documented in Q 2:142-4: "The fools from among the people will say, 'What has turned them from their former *qibla*?' Say: 'Unto God belongs the east *(al-mashriq)* and the west *(al-maghrib)*. He guides whom he will to a straight path *(ṣirāṭ mustaqīm)*.' ... We have seen the turning of your face [i.e. Muḥammad] to heaven. Now we shall make you turn to a *qibla* that is dear to you. Turn your face towards the inviolable sanctuary *(al-masjid al-ḥarām)*, and [O Muslims] wherever you are, turn your faces towards it." The spiritual return of the worshippers to the Kaʿba at Mecca heralded in these verses dislocates Jerusalem from the center. A ritual re-orientation in space (see RITUAL AND THE QURʾĀN), expressed by so dominant a gesture in worship, should not be taken as a mere religio-political step, but appears to reflect the reality of a genuine change of spiritual longing. Mecca was able to replace Jerusalem because the memory shared with the Children of Israel (Banū Isrāʾīl) by the Medinan community had been eroded to some degree by the novel experience of territorial exile, within which the Meccan central sanctuary had increased substantially in symbolic value.

Mecca had by then gone through a substantial change. It had become integrated into that particular form of memory that is transported by the vehicle of writing, which we might identify with biblical tradition — and this bestowed on it the rank of a place honored by a significant episode of salvation history. It had become the central place of the career of a biblical hero, Abraham himself. Abraham's inauguration prayer of the Kaʿba (Q 2:126 f.) has been rightfully associated with the Solomonic inauguration prayer of the temple in Jerusalem. In Abraham's prayer, the sanctuary is conceived not only as a place of pilgrimage for a particular group, but also as a sign set up for all humankind:

And when Abraham prayed, 'My lord! Make this a safe country *(baladan āminan)*'.../'Our lord! Make us submissive to you *(muslimīna laka)* and make a nation submissive to you from our seed'.../'Our lord! And raise up for them a messenger from among them who will read them your signs and teach them the book *(kitāb)* and wisdom *(al-ḥikma)* and improve them *(wa-yuzakkīhim)*.'

In this prayer, the Kaʿba appears as the monument of a new divine foundation. In view of its Abrahamic origin it has become the first monotheistic temple (cf. Q 3:96).

According to this inaugural prayer, verbal worship and the reading of scripture shall take place in this sanctuary in addition to the constitutive rites of the ancienct cult (see RECITATION OF THE QURʾĀN). The prayer reaches its fulfillment with the appearance of the prophet Muḥammad. His mission is to complete the complex structure of Islam as a religion whose cult is based equally on ritual and verbal elements. He has come to read God's signs to the community and teach them the scripture (Q 2:129, *yatlū ʿalayhim āyātika wa-yuʿallimuhumu l-kitāb*). Through this new increase in meaning, once again a vital part of the previous aura of Jerusalem is transferred to Mecca. What had been a prerogative of Jerusalem attested by the prophet Isaiah, "The law will go out from Zion and the word of the Lord from Jerusalem" (*Isa* 2:3), is finally conferred on Mecca.

The uniqueness of the rites originating in Mecca and sanctioned by the Qurʾān are perceived as temporally prior to the phenomenon of revelation through scripture, associated so closely with Jerusalem (see REVELATION AND INSPIRATION). Thus, it is only at the end of the qurʾānic development, after Mecca had been regained and its sanctuary had finally found further anchoring in Islam, that ultimate statement is found: "Surely the first house founded for people is that in Bakka, the blessed and a guidance to all beings" (*inna awwala baytin wuḍiʿa lil-nāsi la-lladhī bi-Bakkata mubārakan wa-hudan lil-ʿālamīn*, Q 3:96).

The canonical process of the Qurʾān is thus reflected not least in the changing views of space expressed in its geographical representations. At a first stage, local space replete with heroic memory or associated with the yearning for a lost paradise has been re-coded in *lieux de mémoire* recalling acts of divine mercy and generosity, as well as wrath, and mirroring human piety and obedience, but more often rebellion and obstinacy. Later, local space having become exile, had to be expanded to encompass its imaginary substitute, the *topographia sacra* of the Children of Israel (Banū Isrāʾīl). Finally, Mecca and the peninsula themselves acquired biblical associations and salvific as well as historical significance sufficient to obtain the rank of a divinely blessed topography of the new religion.

Angelika Neuwirth

Bibliography

Primary: Ibn Ḥabīb, *al-Muḥabbar*, ed. I. Lichtenstaedter, Hyderabad 1942, repr. Beirut n.d.; id., *al-Munammaq fī akhbār Quraysh*, ed. Kh.A. Fārūq, Hyderabad 1964, Beirut 1985; Labīd, *Muʿallaqa*, in A.ʿA.Ḥ. al-Zawzānī, *Sharḥ al-muʿallaqāt al-sabʿ*, ed. M.ʿA. Ḥamd Allāh, Damascus 1963.

Secondary: A. Ambros, Gestaltung und Funktionen der Biosphäre im Koran, in ZDMG 140 (1990), 290-325; J. Assmann, *Das kulturelle Gedächtnis. Schrift, Erinnerung und politische Identität in frühen Hochkulturen*, München 1997; W.W. Barthold, Der Koran und das Meer, in ZDMG 83 (1929), 37-43; C. Becker, *Islamstudien. Vom Werden und Wesen der islamischem Welt*, 2 vols., Hildesheim 1967; M.M. Bravmann, *The spiritual background of early Islam. Studies in ancient Arab concepts*, Leiden 1992; W. Caskel, *Das Schicksal in der altarabischen Poesie*, Leipzig 1926; K. Cragg, *The event of the Qurʾān. Islam in its scripture*, Oxford 1971, 1994; P. Crone, *Meccan trade and the rise of Islam*, Oxford 1987; O.A. Farrukh, *Das Bild des Frühislam in der arabischen Dichtung von der Hiǧra bis zum Tode ʿUmars I. 23 d.H./622-644 n.Chr.*, Leipzig 1937; W. Graham, "The winds to herald his mercy" and other "signs for those of certain faith." Nature as token of God's sovereignty and grace in the Qurʾān, in S. Hyun Lee, W. Proudfoot and A. Blackwell (eds.), *Faithful imagining. Essays in honor of Richard R. Niebuhr*, Atlanta 1995, 18-38; A. Grohmann, Najd, in EI², v, 864-6; A. Hamori, *The art of medieval Arabic literature*, Princeton 1974; Horovitz, KU; T. Izutsu, *God and man in the Koran. Semantics of the koranic Weltanschauung*, Tokyo 1964; H. Lammens, *La Mecque à la veille de l'hégire*, Beirut 1924; M. Lecker, Muhammad at Medina. A geographical approach, in JSAI 6 (1985), 29-62; id., *Muslims, Jews and pagans. Studies on early Islamic Medina*, Leiden 1995; id., al-Ṭāʾif, in EI², x, 116-7; J.E. Montgomery, Sundry observations on the fate of poetry in the early Islamic period, in J.R. Smart (ed.), *Tradition and modernity in Arabic language and literature*, London 1996, 49-60; G. Müller, Zum Problem des integrativen Zusammenhangs periodisch stattfindender Märkte auf der Arabischen Halbinsel im Jahrhundert vor dem Islam, in id., *Ich bin Labid und das ist mein Ziel. Zum Problem der Selbstbehauptung in der altarabischen Qaside*, Wiesbaden

1981, 141-53; A. Neuwirth, Images and metaphors in the introductory sections of the Makkan *sūras*, in Hawting and Shareef, *Approaches*, 3-26; id., The spiritual meaning of Jerusalem in Islam, in N. Rosovsky (ed.), *City of the great king. Jerusalem from David to the present*, Cambridge, MA 1996, 93-116; id. *Studien;* A. Noth, Früher Islam, in U. Haarmann (ed.), *Geschichte der arabischen Welt*, Munich 1987, 11-100; F.E. Peters, *Jerusalem and Mecca. The typology of the holy city in the Near East*, New York 1986; U. Rebstock, Das islamische Arabien bis zum Tode des Propheten (632/11h). Islamic Arabia until the death of the Prophet (632/11h), in *Tübinger Atlas des Vorderen Orients* (TAVO). No. 14, Wiesbaden 1987 (map); G. Rentz, al-Ḥidjāz, in *EI*², iii, 362-4; A. Rippin, The commerce of eschatology, in Wild, *Text*, 125-36; J. Stetkevych, *Muhammad and the golden bough. Reconstructing Arabian myth*, Bloomington, IN 1996; S. Stetkevych, *The mute immortals speak. Pre-Islamic poetry and the poetics of ritual*, Ithaca 1993; U. Thilo, *Die Ortsnamen in der altarabischen Poesie*, Wiesbaden 1958; W.M. Watt, al-Madīna, in *EI*², vi, 994-8; id., Makka, in *EI*², vi, 142-7;id., *Muhammad at Mecca*, Oxford 1953; id., *Muhammad at Medina*, Oxford 1956; J. Wellhausen, *Reste altarabischen Heidentums*, Berlin 1897², repr. 1927, 1961; A.J. Wensinck/J. Jomier, Kaʿba, in *EI*², v, 317-22.

Ghazā/Ghāzī

see EXPEDITIONS AND BATTLES

Gift-Giving

Bestowing an item without a necessary return. Two kinds of "gift-giving" occur in the Qurʾān: (1) God giving gifts *(ʿaṭāʾ)* to humans and (2) people giving, or exchanging, presents *(niḥla, hadiyya)*. That God gives *(aʿṭā)* to humans is mentioned five times in the Qurʾān. A metaphor for "bounties" and "rewards," material and moral, for good deeds (see BLESSING; GRACE; REWARD AND PUNISHMENT), the divine gift is described as "unbroken" (Q 11:108), and "not confined" (Q 17:20), and is often associated with "reckoning" (Q 38:39, Q 78:36). God also commands men to "give the women their dowries as a gift spontaneous" (*wa-ātū l-nisāʾa ṣaduqātihinna niḥlatan*, Q 4:4; see BRIDEWEALTH; MARRIAGE AND DIVORCE).

The exegetes differ in regard to the etymology and meaning of *niḥlatan*. One explanation, favored by al-Ṭabarī (d. 310/923), traces its root to the verb *intaḥala*, "to embrace a religion," the noun of which, *niḥla*, is thus a synonym of *milla, diyāna*, or *sharʿ*. The accusative *niḥlatan* therefore signifies, as a *ḥāl* clause, *farīḍatan*, "as a duty" (cf. also Q 2:236-7; 4:24), or *wājibatan*, "as an obligation," or, as a *mafʿūl lahu* clause, *diyānatan*, "in order to fulfill a religious duty" (see GRAMMAR AND THE QURʾĀN). Another explanation, held by al-Zamakhsharī (d. 538/1144) and al-Qurṭubī (d. 671/1272), is based on the verb *naḥala*, which is, according to al-Kalbī (d. 146/763) and al-Farrāʾ (d. 207/822), the same as *aʿṭā* or *wahaba*, "to give." Thus, the noun *niḥla* means *ʿaṭiyya* or *hiba*, a gift (Shawkānī, *Tafsīr*, i, 535; Zamakhsharī, *Kashshāf*, i, 459-60; Qurṭubī, *Jāmiʿ*, v, 17-8). Some exegetes note that *niḥla* denotes a gift to be given "voluntarily" *(ʿaṭiyya bi-ṭībat nafs)* without the expectation of anything being provided in return (Rāzī, *Tafsīr*, ix, 147; Ibn al-Jawzī, *Zād*, ii, 9). In this connection, the Qurʾān warns against gift-giving in the expectation of receiving more (Q 74:6). Islamic law has elaborated upon the conditions necessary for, and the problems inherent in, the giving of gifts, which touches upon the practice of almsgiving (q.v.; see Rosenthal, Hiba, 342-4; Linant de Bellefonds, Hiba, 350-1; Ṭabarī, *Tahdhīb al-āthār*, i, 3-147).

The only case that involves gift-giving in a narrative context in the Qurʾān is the Queen of Sheba's (see BILQĪS) sending a gift *(hadiyya)* to Solomon (q.v.) to test whether he was a noble "prophet" or a worldly "king" (Q 27:35-6; see PROPHETS AND PROPHETHOOD; KINGS AND RULERS). The Queen's presents are said, according to interpretations, to have consisted of bricks of gold and silver, slave boys dressed as girls and slave girls in boy's clothing, horses, and jewelry, each linked to a riddle for Solomon to solve (Ṭabarī, *Tafsīr,* ix, 515-6; Zamakhsharī, *Kashshāf,* iii, 353-4, Suyūṭī, *Durr,* v, 202-3). The qurʾānic version of the legend relates that Solomon won the Queen over not only with his magic powers, by ordering the jinn (q.v.) to move the Queen's throne, but also with his eloquence and moral stance. In refuting the Queen's envoy, Solomon declared that he was in no need of any gift from her for he was content with what God had given him: "What, would you succor me with wealth, when what God gave me is better than what he has given you? Nay, but instead you rejoice in your gift" (*hadiyyatikum,* Q 27:36). The exegetes point out that Muḥammad and all the prophets, including Solomon, both accepted and encouraged the exchange of gifts on account of their beneficial effect on human relations (Qurṭubī, *Jāmiʿ,* xiii, 132).

Li Guo

Bibliography

Primary: ʿAbd al-Ghanī b. Ismāʿīl al-Nābulusī, *Taḥqīq al-qaḍiyya fī l-farq bayna l-rishwa wa-l-hadiyya,* ed. ʿA.M. Muʿawwaḍ, Cairo 1991; Ibn al-Jawzī, *Zād,* 8 vols., Beirut 1414/1994; Qurṭubī, *Jāmiʿ,* 20 vols. in 10, Beirut 1965-7, 1996[5]; Rāzī, *Tafsīr,* 32 vols. in 16, Beirut 1990; Shawkānī, *Tafsīr,* ed. A. ʿAbd al-Salām, 5 vols., Beirut 1994; Suyūṭī, *Durr;* Ṭabarī, *Tahdhīb al-āthār. Musnad ʿUmar,* ed. Shākir, Cairo 1983; id., *Tafsīr,* 12 vols., Beirut 1992; Zamakhsharī, *Kashshāf,* 4 vols., Beirut 1995.

Secondary: D.S. El Alami, Ṣadāḳ, in *EI*[2], viii, 708 (dowry as a bridal gift); J. Lassner, *Demonizing the Queen of Sheba. Boundaries of gender and culture in post-biblical Judaism and medieval Islam,* Chicago 1993; Y. Linant de Bellefonds, Hiba, in *EI*[2], iii, 350-1 (gift as a legal term); Gh. al-Qaddūmī, *Book of gifts and rarities.* Kitāb al-hadāyā wa-l-tuḥaf, Cambridge, MA 1996, 3-25 (for the Islamic concept of gift-giving); F. Rosenthal, Hiba, in *EI*[2], iii, 342-4 (a general overview of the Islamic concept of gift-giving); B. Stowasser, *Women in the Qurʾān, traditions and interpretation,* New York/Oxford 1994, 62-6 (the Queen of Sheba's sending of gifts to Solomon).

Ginger see AGRICULTURE AND VEGETATION; FOOD AND DRINK

Glorification of God

The adoration and exaltation of God, the Arabic terms for which (derived from the root letters *s-b-ḥ*) cover a range of meanings: worship (q.v.) or prayer (i.e. Q 3:41); wonder at his ability to perform miraculaous deeds (i.e. Q 17:1); constant remembrance (q.v.) of God (*dhikr,* exemplified in Q 13:13); contrition (*tawba,* exemplified in Q 24:16; see REPENTANCE AND PENANCE); as well as a negative assertion of what God is not (see Dāmaghānī, *Wujūh,* i, 446-7 for an elaboration of these themes). *Tasbīḥ,* the qurʾānic word most often translated as glorification of God, is essentially negative: it denotes removal of all those elements from the conception of God which are unworthy of him — anthropomorphic elements, for example (see ANTHROPOMORPHISM). The infinitive *subḥān,* which comes from the same root as *tasbīḥ (s-b-ḥ)* and occurs in the Qurʾān in the interjectory constructions *subḥānahu, subḥānaka,* and *subḥāna llāhi,* brings out this meaning effectively, as in Q 2:116: "And they say, 'God has taken unto himself a son.' Far above that is he! *(subḥānahu);*" Q 3:191: "Our lord, you have not created this [universe] in vain. Far above that are you! *(subhānaka);*" and Q 37:159: "God is far above *(subḥāna llāhi)* what they attribute [to him]!" The Qurʾān thus uses *subḥān* (and other words) to purge the conception of God of all those beliefs and notions that would diminish his being, limit his power, or impute any imperfection to him.

Being negative in character, *tasbīḥ* frequently occurs in the Qurʾān in conjunction with its positive complement *ḥamd* ("grateful praise"), as in Q 25:58: *wa-sabbiḥ bi-ḥamdihi* ("And make *tasbīḥ,* together with *ḥamd* of him"), which may be glossed as: Glorify God by dissociating from him all that must be dissociated from him, and by associating with him all that ought to be associated with him.

Tasbīḥ connotes earnestness (the primary meaning of the root is swift movement); Q 79:3 refers to angels (see ANGEL) as *sābiḥāt* — those who are diligent in carrying out God's commands — and Q 21:33 speaks of the heavenly bodies as "swimming" *(yasbaḥūna)* in their orbits (also Q 36:40). The command to make *tasbīḥ* thus implies that one must glorify God with earnest devotion.

According to al-Rāghib al-Iṣfahānī (d. early fifth/eleventh cent.), *tasbīḥ,* construed as worship of God, may take the form of an utterance, an act, or an intention. He interprets the word in Q 37:143 as representing all three: *fa-law lā annahā kāna mina l-musabbiḥīna,* "Had he (Jonah [q.v.], in the belly of the fish) not been one of those who glorify God." The verse, in other words, praises Jonah for glorifying God on all three counts of speech, action and intention. In some verses, however, *tasbīḥ* has a more restricted meaning, as in Q 20:130 and 50:39-40, where it stands for the obligatory daily prayer because glorification is an essential part of that prayer. Similarly, Q 21:79 and 38:18 call David's (q.v.) hymns *tasbīḥ,* saying that mountains and birds used to sing — *(yusabbiḥna)* literally, make *tasbīḥ* — in unison with him.

According to Q 17:44, all existence glorifies God: "The seven heavens and the earth and what is in them glorify him; there is nothing but that it glorifies him, together with praise of him, but you do not understand their glorification." Commentators remark that all orders of creation — angels, jinn (q.v.), humans, animals, and inanimate phenomena — glorify God, through submission to God and his laws; that this submission may be voluntary or involuntary or both; and that the precise nature and form of this submission may not be comprehensible to all.

Mustansir Mir

Bibliography
Dāmaghānī, *Wujūh,* ed. Zafītī, i, 446-7 (where seven meanings for *subḥān/sabbaḥa* are given); al-Rāghib al-Iṣfahānī, *Mufradāt,* s.v. *f-ḍ-l.*

Glory

Height of splendor and renown. The word *jalāl* ("majesty") comes closest to being the qurʾānic term for glory. The only two occurrences of the word are in sūra 55, and in both instances it is constructed with *dhū,* "possessor, owner" (see Gimaret, *Noms divins,* 75-6; Rāzī, *Lawāmiʿ al-bayyināt fī l-asmāʾ wa-l-ṣifāt,* 270): "Your lord's countenance, possessor of majesty and honor, [alone] will survive" (Q 55:27) and "Blessed is the name of your lord, possessor of majesty and honor" (Q 55:78). The word *majd* has a similar denotation and the participle *majīd* is used in the Qurʾān for God (Q 11:73), for the throne of God (q.v.; Q 85:15) and for the Qurʾān itself (Q 50:1; 85:21). In qurʾānic usage, however, *majd* is different from *jalāl* in that while *jalāl* represents an attribute that belongs exclusively to the being of God, *majd* may be posited of other entities — hence the qualification of the divine throne and the Qurʾān as *majīd.* It may, however, be argued that the throne and scripture become *majd* only by virtue of their association with God who is *majīd.*

More important than establishing qurʾānic terms for glory is the task of clarifying the concept of glory. A clue to the concept may be found in Q 7:143, which reports God's response to the request of Moses (q.v.) to see God: "When he manifested himself to the mountain, he crushed it, and Moses fell down unconscious." The Arabic word used for "He manifested himself" is *tajallā*, which is suggestive of effulgence. In light of this verse, divine glory could be described as God's holy magnificence or majestic splendor. But the verse clearly indicates that even if this divine magnificence or splendor were to become visible, the physical eyes (q.v.) of humans in this world could not bear the sight (see SEEING AND HEARING). At the end of this world, however, it may be possible to catch a glimpse of divine glory, as suggested by Q 39:67-9, a passage of epical quality which speaks of God holding the heavens and earth in his hands on the last day (see LAST JUDGMENT; APOCALYPSE), with the earth "lit up with the light of its lord" (cf. *Isa* 6:3: "the whole earth is full of his glory").

Glory in the sense of awesome divine presence or a manifestation of that presence is indicated in Q 7:171: "And recall the time when we hung the mountain (Sinai) over them (the Israelites), as if it were a canopy, and they thought that it was about to fall on them." This verse (see also Q 2:63, 93) alludes to Exodus 19:17-8, which describes how the mountain shook when God "descended upon it in fire." According to Amīn Aḥsan Iṣlāḥī (*Tadabbur-i Qurʾān*, ad Q 2:63), God manifested his power and majesty on the mountain not in order to extract forcibly from the Israelites a commitment to follow the Torah (q.v.), but in order to remind them that God, with whom they had made a covenant (q.v.), was not a weak but a mighty being, and that his vengeance was no less great than his bounty — that it was within his power to crush them by means of a mountain if they disobeyed him. The incident, in other words, made the Israelites (see CHILDREN OF ISRAEL) aware of the close and immediate presence of God. Q 2:210 is similar: "They are waiting only for this — are they not? — that God should arrive in canopies of clouds, and his angels, too — and the matter is settled!" Neither Q 2:210 nor Q 7:171, however, can be interpreted to signify localization of divine presence (see SECHINA).

Mustansir Mir

Bibliography
Primary: Amīn Aḥsan Iṣlāḥi, *Tadabbur-i Qurʾān*, vol. 1, Lahore 1967; al-Rāghib al-Iṣfahānī, *Mufradāt*, s.v. *f-ḍ-l*; *Rāzī*, *Lawāmiʿ al-bayyināt fī l-asmāʾ wa-l-ṣifāt*, ed. Ṭ. Saʿd, Cairo 1976.
Secondary: Gimaret, *Les noms divins en islam*, Paris 1988.

Goat see ANIMAL LIFE

God and his Attributes

"Allāh," the name for God in Islam, is generally taken to mean "the God," God plainly and absolutely (Watt, The use, 245-7). The name is commonly explained linguistically as a contraction of the Arabic noun with its definite article, *al-ilāh* shortened into *Allāh* by frequency of usage in invocation. Actually, "Allāh" is not understood to be a proper name like any other, rather it is the name of the nameless God, next to whom there is no other. *Allāh* is mentioned only in the singular, no plural can be formed of the name. God, however, is not understood in Islam as an abstract absolute; rather God exists and is one: God is the only real supreme being whom all Muslims address and invoke by the name "Allāh." Faith in God is the fulcrum of Islamic monotheism and obedience (q.v.) to his will the focus of the Muslim way of life.

The principal names for God in the Qurʾān

The idea and concept of Allāh, the one and only God, are deeply rooted in the prophetic message of Muḥammad embodied in the Qurʾān. Muḥammad proclaimed the Qurʾān "in the name of Allāh" (Q 1:1; see BASMALA) and the Muslim profession of faith *(shahāda),* "there is no deity but Allāh," encapsulates the core of the qurʾānic witness to the unique God (see WITNESS TO FAITH). He is both feared by humans (see FEAR) and near to them, being both transcendent and immanent. In the Qurʾān, God is described by his "most beautiful names" *(al-asmāʾ al-ḥusnā),* traditionally enumerated as ninety-nine epithets, on which Islamic theology based its systematic expositions abour the divine essence *(dhāt)* and its attributes (*ṣifāt,* cf. D. Gimaret, *Les noms divins,* see THEOLOGY AND THE QURʾĀN). Muslims believe the Arabic Qurʾān to be the actual word of God (q.v.) through which God makes himself known to humanity. No greater self-testimony of God to himself can be found anywhere else than in the Qurʾān, in which God in his own words calls himself "Allāh," a name that appears about 2,700 times in the qurʾānic text (*Allāhu,* 980 times; *Allāha,* 592 times; *Allāhi,* 1125 times; *Allāhumma,* 5 times). Long before the time of Muḥammad, the pre-Islamic Arabs (q.v.) and the Meccans (see MECCA) in particular, worshiped a great deity and supreme provider, called Allāh (Q 13:16; 29:61; 31:25; 39:38) and invoked him in times of distress (Q 6:109; 10:22; 16:38; 29:65; 31:32; 35:42; see PRE-ISLAMIC ARABIA AND THE QURʾĀN; SOUTH ARABIA, RELIGION IN PRE-ISLAMIC). From his youth, Muḥammad was intimately familiar with this name for the supreme God since his father's name was ʿAbdallāh, "servant of Allāh." It seemed most natural to him, therefore, to employ the word "Allāh" for God in his qurʾānic proclamation, rather than to introduce a totally new name for his monotheistic concept of God. Muḥammad stripped the pre-Islamic notion of the supreme Allāh, however, of associates and companions, whom the polytheistic belief of the Arabs accepted as subordinate deities (cf. T. Fahd, *Le panthéon,* 41; see POLYTHEISM AND ATHEISM; IDOLATRY AND IDOLATERS). Prior to Islam, the Meccans asserted a kinship of Allāh with the jinn (q.v.; Q 37:158), attributed sons to Allāh (Q 6:100), regarded the local deities of al-ʿUzzā, Manāt and al-Lāt as daughters of Allāh (Q 53:19-22; 6:100; 16:57; 37:149), knew of the worship of five pre-Islamic male deities, Wadd, Suwāʿ, Yaghūth, Yaʿūq and Nasr (Q 71:23; see IDOLS AND IMAGES) and possibly associated angels (see ANGEL) with Allāh (Q 53:26-27). Muḥammad's proclamation of Allāh left no room for partners and angels or saints to fill the space between the believer and God. Rather, in the Qurʾān, humanity was made to stand directly before God, unassisted by any mediator (see INTERCESSION).

Another name for God, used parallel to Allāh in the Qurʾān mainly in the Meccan phases of Muḥammad's qurʾānic proclamation (see CHRONOLOGY AND THE QURʾĀN), is the name al-Raḥmān, cited 57 times in the qurʾānic text, as e.g. in Q 17:110, "Say, call upon Allāh or call upon al-Raḥmān; however you call upon him, to him belong the most beautiful names." Al-Raḥmān eventually lost its independence in the proclamation of Muḥammad and became subsumed under the principal name of Allāh in the final redaction of the Qurʾān. It came to be understood as an adjective modifying the word God, and meaning "the merciful," though it was not counted as one of the most beautiful names of God (cf. J. Jomier, Le nom divin, 367-381). Originally, al-Raḥmān was the name given to the God of the heavens worshiped in Yemen (q.v.) and central Arabia. Documented in an inscription from the year 505 C.E., the name appears in the old south Arabian form of Raḥmānān, with the article placed in postposition, and clearly indicates an Aramaic origin (cf. J. Rijckmans, Le christianisme, 436, 440; see EPIGRAPHY; FOREIGN VOCABULARY).

The amalgamation of the name al-Raḥmān with that of Allāh is fully achieved in the first verse of the Qurʾān, which also serves as the introductory formula to all of its sūras (see FORM AND STRUCTURE OF THE QURʾĀN), except Q 9: *"bismi llāhi l-raḥmāni l-raḥīm."* This credal formula, called the *basmala* (q.v.), appears in its full form within the qurʾānic text at the head of Solomon's (q.v.) letter to the queen of Sheba (q.v.; Q 27:30; see BILQĪS). In an abridged form it is uttered by Noah (q.v.; Q 11:41) who gives the command to embark in the ark (q.v.) with the words, "in the name of God" *(bismi llāhi)*. The formula in its full form was first used by Muḥammad, who amalgamated its component parts for a reason, linking the name of Allāh with two adjectives *(al-raḥmān* and *al-raḥīm),* both derived from the same root denoting mercy (q.v.; only the second of which, however, is a pure adjective). Arabic grammar (see GRAMMAR AND THE QURʾĀN) alone cannot decide how to differentiate the two terms and how to translate the passage. The phrase can be translated, "In the name of God, the merciful and the compassionate" or, "In the name of the merciful and compassionate God," or, and this is the crux of the issue, "In the name of Allāh, the compassionate Raḥmān." Understood from this third perspective, the *basmala* amalgamates Allāh, the supreme God of the Meccans, with al-Raḥmān, the high god of south and central Arabia, by depriving al-Raḥmān of distinct individuality and transforming the name into a mere epithet of God, leading to the traditional understanding of the formula, "In the name of God, the merciful, the compassionate" (cf. J. van Ess, Der Name Gottes, 157-60).

Aramaic origin can be demonstrated for Raḥmānān, but can it also be claimed for Allāh? The majority of scholars answer this question with skepticism (J. Blau, Arabic lexicographical miscellanies, 175-7) and explain it purely on the basis of Arabic, i.e. Allāh as a contraction of Arabic *al-ilāh* ("the deity" in the masculine form), parallel to the female deity of al-Lāt as a contraction of *al-ilāha* ("the deity" in the feminine form, cf. J. Wellhausen, *Reste,* 32-3, 217 f.; F. Buhl, *Leben,* 75, 94; A. Ambros, Zur Entstehung). It is difficult, therefore, to explain Allāh as derived from the Aramaic Alāhā (pace A. Jeffery, *For. vocab.,* 66-7), for which there is epigraphic evidence in Nabatean inscriptions, because such a suggestion accounts neither for the contraction nor for the doubling of the consonant in the Arabic "Allāh" (see ARABIC LANGUAGE). It must remain doubtful whether some secondary form of Syriac (or Hebrew) influence may have been combined with the primary Arabic usage of Allāh, a notion based on the claim that Muḥammad used this name for God in addressing both pagan Arabs and Jews or Christians in the Qurʾān (see JEWS AND JUDAISM; CHRISTIANS AND CHRISTIANITY), thus establishing common ground for the understanding of the name for God. Positing an Aramaic origin for Allāh remains highly speculatively, however, though it raises the intriguing possibility of the separate existence of two groups of pre-Islamic believers in a high god, each of them worshipping God with an Aramaic name, Raḥmānān in the Yemen and Alāhā in the Ḥijāz. Muḥammad, acquainted with both names, would then have fused the two in the introductory formula of the Qurʾān, giving Allāh pride of place and treating al-Raḥmān as if it were an adjective.

God, moreover, is invoked since pre-Islamic times by yet another name, namely *rabb,* "lord" (q.v.; cf. J. Chelhod, Note,

159-67). This term is also used several hundred times in the Qurʾān, though rather as a title for God than an actual name. In pre-Islamic north-west Semitic usage the word *rabb* means "much" or "great" and corresponds to terms such as Baʿal or Adonis (A. Jeffery, *For. vocab.*, 136-7). In what the Islamic tradition identifies as the first qurʾānic verse to have been revealed, Muḥammad is summoned to speak "in the name of your lord" (*bismi rabbika*, Q 96:1). *Rabb* is never used with the definite article in the Qurʾān, yet very often linked with a personal or possessive pronoun. A non-secular usage of *rabb* was familiar to the Meccans from pre-Islamic times since soothsayers (q.v.; *kāhin*) were given the title of *rabb* and the female deity al-Lāt was addressed as *al-rabba* (cf. H. Lammens, Le culte des bétyles, 39-101). A similar usage is demonstrated by the early qurʾānic phrase, "the lord of this house" (*rabb hādhā l-bayt*, Q 106:3; see HOUSE, DOMESTIC AND DIVINE), the house being the Kaʿba (q.v.) in Mecca. *Rabb* is rarely used in the Medinan phase of Muḥammad's qurʾānic proclamation but is most frequently employed in its Meccan phases, e.g. Q 87:1, "Extol the name of your lord the most high" (*sabbiḥi sma rabbika l-aʿlā*), or Q 79:24, "I am your lord the most high" (*anā rabbukumu l-aʿlā*, in Pharaoh's [q.v.] blasphemous utterance; see BLASPHEMY). Traditionally, *rabb* is counted among God's most beautiful names and the slave is forbidden to address his master as *rabbī*, "my lord," being commanded to use *sayyidī* instead (cf. T. Fahd, *La divination*, 107-8; see SLAVES AND SLAVERY).

The attributes of God in the Qurʾān

In Islamic theology, the attributes of God, called *ṣifāt* and kept distinct from the divine essence (*al-dhāt*), are widely discussed in scholastic discourse (cf. M. Allard, *Le problème*). This terminological usage is post-qurʾānic and cannot be traced back to the Qurʾān, which cites *ṣifāt* neither in the plural nor in the singular (*ṣifa*). In fact, the term *ṣifāt Allāh* was borrowed by Islamic theology from the classical grammarians of the Arabic language. In the Qurʾān, however, the attributes of God are consistently called God's "most beautiful names" (*al-asmāʾ al-ḥusnā*, Q 7:180; 17:110; 20:8; 59:24), a phrase that is also engraved on the eastern gate of the Dome of the Rock (see AQṢĀ MOSQUE). They are traditionally enumerated as 99 in number to which is added as the highest name (*al-ism al-aʿẓam*), the supreme name of God, Allāh. The *locus classicus* for listing the divine names in the literature of qurʾānic commentary is Q 17:110, "Call upon God, or call upon the merciful; whichsoever you call upon, to him belong the most beautiful names," and also Q 59:22-4, which includes a cluster of more than a dozen divine epithets. In their traditional enumerations, most of the beautiful names, many of which are synonyms, are listed according to euphony or similarity in linguistic patterns. In the Qurʾān, the divine names do not function as predicates of a developed theology but rather as patterned formulas of the Prophet's prayer. They are doxology not doctrine. This is in keeping with the general discourse of the Qurʾān in which God is referred to in the third person singular and speaks in the imperative or the majestic plural. Rarely, however, is God addressed by the "you" of invocational prayer (q.v.) and only in some verses is he introduced by the theophanic "I am" (cf. below; see LANGUAGE OF THE QURʾĀN).

Rather than being considered abstract attributes of God, the most beautiful divine names are regarded simply as epithets or names which describe God in the rich facets of his being. Traditionally, the name "Allāh" itself is set apart and not counted as one of the most beautiful names; rather it is taken to belong to God alone in such a way that it cannot be applied to any other thing. The majority of the divine epithets accord with linguistic patterns of the Arabic language that display a similarity of assonance and rhyme (*sajʿ*, see RHYMED PROSE), linguistic characteristics that the Qurʾān has in common with the utterances and oracles of the pre-Islamic Arab soothsayers *(kāhin)*. This linguistic similarity accounts for the frequent repetition of such divine names at the end of qurʾānic verses where they function as mnemonic devices facilitating oral recitation (see ORALITY; RECITATION OF THE QURʾĀN), especially in Medinan suras. For emphasis or pleonasm, the qurʾānic epithets of God frequently appear in pairs, either with or without the definite article, yet generally with no connecting "and" in-between, such as "the mighty, the wise", meaning "the one who is mighty and wise." Counted traditionally as ninety-nine in number (Redhouse, Most comely names; D. Gimaret, *Les noms divins*, 51-84), the traditional listings do not exhaust the actual divine epithets in the Qurʾān nor do the names necessarily appear in their qurʾānic form of quotation. Rather than enumerating the whole range and catalogue of the most beautiful names, some characteristic examples shall be chosen to demonstrate the rich and variegated nature of their usage in the Qurʾān. With each of these examples only select references will be cited to signal their, in many cases, highly repetitive occurrence.

In keeping with Muḥammad's insistence upon a strictly monotheistic understanding of Allāh, God is called in the Qurʾān "the one" (*al-wāḥid*, Q 2:163). He is God, the living (*al-ḥayy*, Q 2:255; 3:2), the self-subsisting (*al-qayyūm*, Q 2:255), the self-sufficient (*al-ghanī*, Q 2:263), the comprehensive (*al-wāsiʿ*, Q 2:247), the powerful (*al-qādīr*, Q 2:20), the glorious (*al-majīd*, Q 85:15), the strong (*al-qawī*, Q 11:66), the mighty (*al-ʿazīz*, Q 2:129), the great (*al-kabīr*, Q 22:62), the high (*al-ʿalī*, 31:30) and the exalted (*al-mutaʿālī*, Q 13:9). He is known by his epithets of the all-wise (*al-ḥakīm*, Q 2:129), the all-knowing (*al-ʿalīm*, Q 2:32), the all-hearing (*al-samīʿ*, Q 2:127), the all-seeing (*al-baṣīr*, Q 17:1). God is the overpowering restorer (*al-jabbār*, Q 59:23), the subduing dominator (*al-qahhār*, Q 12:39), the constant giver (*al-wahhāb*, Q 3:8), the good provider (*al-razzāq*, Q 51:58), and the victorious revealer (*al-fattāḥ*, Q 34:26). God is the benevolent (*al-laṭīf*, Q 67:14), the gentle (*al-ḥalīm*, Q 4:12), the generous (*al-karīm*, Q 44:49), the sagacious (*al-khabīr*, Q 6:18), the vigilant (*al-ḥafīẓ*, Q 34:21), the unshakable (*al-matīn*, Q 51:58) and the insuperable (*al-ʿaẓīm*, Q 2:255). Expressed by paired epithets in Q 57:3, God is "the first *(al-awwal)* and the last *(al-ākhir)* and the manifest *(al-ẓāhir)* and the hidden *(al-bāṭin)*." He is the reckoner (*al-ḥasīb*, Q 4:86), the watcher (*al-raqīb*, Q 4:1), the witness (*al-shahīd*, Q 3:98), the guardian (*al-wakīl*, Q 3:173), the patron (*al-walī*, Q 42:9) and the guide of those who believe (*la-hādī lladhīna āmanū*, Q 22:54).

In relation to his creatures God is named the creator (*al-khāliq*, Q 59:24), who is constantly creating (*al-khallāq*, Q 36:81; see CREATION). He is the "the creator of the heavens and the earth" (*badīʿ al-samāwāti wa l-arḍ*, Q 6:101; see HEAVEN AND SKY; EARTH), the maker (*al-bāriʾ*, Q 2:54) and the shaper (*al-muṣawwir*, Q 59:24). He gives life (q.v.) and death (Q 15:23; cf. 41:39; see DEATH AND THE DEAD), prevails over everything (*al-muqtadir*, Q 18:45) and assembles all on the day of judgment (*al-jāmiʿ*, cf. Q 3:9; 4:140; see LAST JUDGMENT; APOCALYPSE). God does not only create, sustain, rule and restore, he is also marked by antipodal epithets coined by tradition on the basis of qurʾānic statements, qualifying him as the one who honors and abases, grants and withholds, advances and defers, offers help and sends distress, because "He leads astray (q.v.) whom he wills and guides aright whom he wills" (Q 16:93; 74:31; cf.

13:27). He infuses the hearts (see HEART) of the believers with faith (q.v.) but seals with unbelief the hearts of the unbelievers (Q 4:155; see BELIEF AND UNBELIEF). Then again, God is given a plethora of names denoting his mercy and forgiveness (q.v.), in addition to being frequently called compassionate and merciful. Qualified as the kind (*al-raʾūf,* Q 2:143), the loving (*al-wadūd,* Q 85:14) and the one who answers prayers (*al-mujīb,* cf. Q 11:61), God abounds with forgiveness as the forgiving (*al-ghāfir,* Q 7:155), the oft-forgiver (*al-ghafūr,* Q 2:173) and the all-forgiving (*al-ghaffār,* Q 38:66; cf. 20:82), the pardoner (*al-ʿafuww,* cf. Q 4:43), the one "turned to" humans with favor (*al-tawwāb,* Q 2:37) and ready to acknowledge their gratitude (*al-shakūr,* cf. Q 35:30; see GRATITUDE AND INGRATITUDE).

The Qurʾān calls God "the justest of judges" (*aḥkamu l-ḥākimīn,* Q 11:45; 95:8; see JUSTICE AND INJUSTICE) and "the best of judges" (*khayru l-ḥākimīn,* Q 7:87; 10:109; 12:80) and asks, "who is fairer in judgment (q.v.) than God" (*wa-man aḥsanu mina llāhi ḥukman,* Q 5:50). It cites "God's judgment" (*ḥukmu llāhi,* Q 60:10) and contrasts it with "the judgment of pagan times" (*ḥukma l-jāhiliyya,* Q 5:50; see AGE OF IGNORANCE). God "will render judgment" *(yaḥkumu)* between humanity on the day of resurrection (q.v.; Q 4:141; 2:113; 16: 124; 22:69, cf. 22:56; 2:213; 5:50) and "judges as he desires" (Q 5:1). While a powerful reference to acting with justice is attributed to a prophetical figure, "David (q.v.), we have appointed you a successor in the earth, so judge between men in truth" (*fa-ḥkum bayna l-nāsi bi-l-ḥaqq,* Q 38:26), God alone "judges and none repels his judgment *(lā muʿaqqiba li-ḥukmihi);* he is swift at the reckoning" (Q 13:41). Close to a hundred times God is named *ḥakīm,* "wise, judicious" (cf. Q 2:32). While God is mentioned once as "bidding to justice" (*yaʾmuru bi-l-ʿadl,* 16:90), only twice, however, is "justice" attributed directly to God, when God's word is said to have been fulfilled "in veracity and justice" (*ṣidqan wa-ʿadlan,* Q 6:115) and when God is said to be "upholding justice" (*qāʾiman bi-l-qisṭ,* Q 3:18). Never, however, is God called *al-ʿādil,* "the just," in the Qurʾān. This fact may be surprising because the Qurʾān depicts God sitting in judgment over humanity on the day of judgement at the end of the world, decreeing reward or appointing punishment, granting bliss or meeting out damnation (see REWARD AND PUNISHMENT). With the absolute authority of a monarch, God passes straight to rendering a verdict, his legal decision (*ḥukm,* Q 13:41) following the model of the pre-Islamic arbiter (*ḥakam,* Q 6:114) though, unlike him, not bound by foregoing arrangements, but influenced by his good pleasure *(riḍwān)* or anger (*sakhaṭ,* cf. Q 3:162; 47:28; 3:15; 5:19).

Other divine epithets involved intricacies of interpretation, one of them illustrated above in the case of *al-raḥmān* and *al-raḥīm* in the *basmala.* Rather than denoting the abstract notion of peace (q.v.), the qurʾānic epithet *al-salām* (Q 59:23) refers to God as possessor of pure peace, giver of peace at the dawn of creation and the day of resurrection, and the one who pronounces the blessing (q.v.) of peace over creation, his house of peace (*dār al-salām,* i.e. house of God, Q 6:127; 10:25). Composite phrases such as "the possessor of majesty and generosity" (*dhū l-jalāl wa-l-ikrām,* cf. Q 55:78), "the holy king" (*al-malik al-quddūs,* Q 59:23; 62:1), "the master of the kingdom" (*mālik al-mulk,* Q 3:26) and "the master of the day of doom" (*mālik yawm al-dīn,* Q 1:4) offered enigmas to critical interpreters, while the divine name, "the real" (*al-ḥaqq,* Q 20:114; 22:6, 62; 31:30), was chosen by Ṣūfism (see ṢŪFISM AND THE QURʾĀN) as its preferred name for God. Hapax legomena such as "the benign" (*al-barr,* Q 52:28) or "the impenetrable," dense to the absolute degree, (*al-ṣamad,* Q 112:2) seem to conceal traces of pre-qur'ānic religious terminology. Although God's mercy *(raḥma)* is attested more than a hundred times in the Qur'ān, the phrase, "he inscribed mercy upon himself" *(kataba ʿalā nafsihi l-raḥmata,* Q 6:12; cf. 6:54), raised the question whether his mercy was an expression of benevolence or was linked to his forgiveness of sins (cf. Q 18:58; 39:53; 40:7; see SIN, MAJOR AND MINOR).

Some phrases in the Qur'ān, ascribing qualities of apparent imperfection to God, caused consternation to its interpreters, such as God's coming stealthily (*sanastadrijuhum,* Q 7:182; 68:44), devising (*makra llāhī,* Q 7:99; cf. 3:54; 4:142), mocking (*Allāhu yastahziʾu bihim,* Q 2:15), deriding (*sakhira llāhu minhum,* Q 9:79) and forgetting (*fa-nasiyahum,* Q 9:67; cf. *nunsihā,* Q 2:106). The phrase referring to God as a "thing" became a theological quagmire, "What thing is greatest *(ayyu shayʾin akbar)* in testimony? Say, God!" (Q 6:19; D. Gimaret, *Les noms divins,* 142-150). Other phrases squarely enunciated actual attributes of God, rather than divine names, such as, "Say, the knowledge is with God!" (Q 67:26) or, "My lord embraces all things in his knowledge" (Q 6:80; cf. 7:89; see KNOWLEDGE AND LEARNING). Similarly, the Qur'ān claimed God to have "power" (*dhū l-quwwati,* Q 51:58) though it also called him "the powerful" (*al-qawī,* Q 11:66; cf. 22:40; see POWER AND IMPOTENCE). The name qualifying God to be "loving" (*wadūd,* Q 11:90; cf. 85:14), had its unsettling counterpoint in a qur'ānic verse depicting divine love answered by human love, "he loves them and they love him" (*yuḥibbuhum wa-yuḥibbūnahu,* Q 5:54). A goodly number of other verses, however, declared stereotypically that God loves those who do good (Q 2:195; 3:134; see GOOD DEEDS), trust in God (Q 3:159; see TRUST AND PATIENCE), cleanse themselves and are repentant (Q 2:222), god-fearing (Q 3:76) or patient (Q 3:146), while he does not love corruption (q.v.; Q 2:205) or those who do evil (Q 3:57, 140; see EVIL DEEDS; GOOD AND EVIL), the aggressors (Q 2:190) or the unbelievers (Q 2:276; 3:32), etc.

The divine names of the Qur'ān may best be understood as multifarious expressions in praise (q.v.) of God rather than as doctrinal expositions concerning the nature of God. They give expression to Muḥammad's rich and multi-faceted perception of that ultimate reality which he personally experienced as the only God. This experience filled him with awe before the transcendent God, who could not be known in his very self, yet could be glorified in his names. Filled with knowledge of God as "the lord of the heavens and the earth" (Q 19:65), the Prophet also was aware of God's nearness, nearer to a person than his own "jugular vein" (Q 50:16; see ARTERY AND VEIN). This overpowering transcendence and intimate immanence of Allāh in Muḥammad's religious experience was transformed in his qur'ānic proclamation into the praise of the most beautiful names. They are landmarks of his prayer rather than tenets of his theology.

Visual imagery of God in the Qur'ān

The most beautiful names of God appear hundreds of times in the Qur'ān, while the metaphors for God figure in only a few dozen verses (see METAPHOR). The divine names attract by the frequency of their quotation, the metaphors impress by the force of their images. Three metaphors, perhaps the most famous of the Qur'ān, though often tenuous and less embellished than in ḥadīth literature (see ḤADĪTH AND THE QUR'ĀN), may be singled out to illustrate the point (D. Gimaret, *Dieu à l'image,* 123-264). In the Qur'ān God is depicted as having a face (q.v.), eyes (q.v.) and hands (q.v.), is pictured as sitting on a throne (see THRONE OF GOD) and is compared to the light (q.v.) of the heavens and the earth.

These descriptive images of God play a decisive role in the discussions on the anthropomorphic (see ANTHROPOMORPHISM) or ambiguous (q.v.) verses of the Qurʾān *(mutashābihāt)*. The locus classicus for the various ways of interpreting these ambiguous verses is found in the commentary literature on Q 3:7 (and, in dependence on it, in Q 11:1 and 39:23; see EXEGESIS OF THE QURʾĀN: CLASSICAL AND MEDIEVAL). They also figure prominently in the scholastic debate about the literal versus the allegorical interpretation of the Qurʾān in Islamic and Western scholarship. Rather than reflecting on this scholarly debate, emphasis here will be given to the vividly visual and majestic imagery these verses actually convey in the Qurʾān.

The comparison of God with the human being as "made after his image" *(ʿalā ṣūratihi)*, however, is not cited in the Qurʾān, rather it is a development of ḥadīth literature, probably in dependence on Genesis 1:27. On the contrary, the Qurʾān emphasizes that "nothing is like unto him" (*laysa ka-mithlihi shayʾun*, Q 42:11), excluding thereby any similarity between God and human beings, and that God simply "formed" *(ṣawwarnākum)* human beings, giving them beautiful forms (*fa-aḥsana ṣuwarakum*, cf. Q 7:11; 64:3). While, in his act of creation, God "composed" the human beings in the form he wished to give them (Q 82:8), God himself remained untouched by any composition. The perception that God saw his own image, i.e. his face or form *(ṣūra)*, for the first time mirrored in the waters of the primal sea is an extra-qurʾānic development of ḥadīth literature. The Qurʾān does not speak of the figure or body of God as a single or composite entity. Also, it mentions neither God's ear (see EARS), though he is "the all-hearing," (*al-samīʿ*, see SEEING AND HEARING; HEARING AND DEAFNESS), nor his mouth and tongue, though God has the preeminent quality of speech (q.v.) and commands, forbids, promises or threatens in the Qurʾān. Likewise, there is no mention of his sex (though the masculine pronoun is used consistently with reference to God in the Qurʾān; see GENDER; SEX AND SEXUALITY) nor of his nose, arm, fist, feet (q.v.), heart and beard (cf. van Ess, *TG*, iv, 396-401).

Very explicitly, however, the Qurʾān describes God as having a face (Q 2:115; 2:272; 6:52; 13:22; 18:28; see FACE OF GOD) and eyes (Q 11:37; 23:27; 52:48; 54:14) or an eye (Q 20:39) as well as possesing a hand (Q 3:73; 5:64; 48:10; 57:29), two hands (Q 5:64; 38:75) or a grasp (Q 39:67) and, somewhat obscurely, also a "side" (Q 39:56) and a "leg" (Q 68:42). Though the word *wajh*, "face," may be taken as denoting generally the self *(nafs* or *dhāt)* when related to human beings in the Qurʾān (cf. Q 2:112; 3:20; 4:125; 6:79; 10:105; 30:30, 43; 31:22; 39:24), it has a particular metaphorical impact when predicated about God. Two famous qurʾānic verses proclaim: "all that dwells upon the earth is perishing, yet still abides the face of your lord, majestic, splendid" (Q 55:26-7) and, "all things perish, except his face" (Q 28:88). Human beings are "desirous of God's face" (*ibtighāʾa wajhi llāhi*, Q 2:272; 13:22), asking for his favor, and "seek his face" (*yurīdūna wajhahu*, Q 6:52; 18:28) in their prayer (cf. J.M.S. Baljon, To seek, 263). They act for the sake of God's face, feeding the needy (see POVERTY AND THE POOR), the orphan (see ORPHANS) and the captive (see CAPTIVES) only "for the face of God" *(li-wajhi llāhi)* without any desire for recompense or gratitude (Q 76:8-9; see ALMSGIVING). Wherever human beings turn, "there is the face of God" *(fa-thamma wajhu llāhi)* to whom belong the east and the west (Q 2:115). The metaphor of the face of God, stressing both God's omnipresence and the innate desire of humans for God, finds an echo in a unique divine utterance in the Qurʾān, one that provides a parallel image for the divine presence, "We are nearer to him than the jugular vein" (Q 50:16).

The face of God, taken literally, raised the question of whether the divine countenance could be seen by human eyes in the beatific vision *(ruʾyat Allāh)*. According to the Qurʾān, God could not be seen because "the eyes attain him not" (*lā tudrikuhu l-abṣāru*, Q 6:103) and God speaks to mortals "from behind a veil" (q.v.; *min warāʾi ḥijābin*, Q 42:51). Even Mount Sinai (q.v.) crumbled to dust when God appeared in a theophany before Moses (q.v.; Q 7:143). On the other hand, Q 75:22-3 proclaimed that, on the day of judgment, "faces shall be radiant, gazing upon their lord *(ilā rabbihā nāẓiratun)*" and verses 10:26 and 50:35 intimated that "the surplus" (*ziyāda*, Q 10:26) and the "yet more" (*mazīd*, Q 50:35), promised to the upright, referred to their vison of God (cf. D. Gimaret, *La doctrine*, 329-44; van Ess, *TG*, iv, 411-15).

Interpreted in this way, it soon became necessary to make theological distinctions between the vision of God in this world and the hereafter (see ESCHATOLOGY), and its occurrence with the physical eyes *(bi-l-abṣār)* or the eyes of the heart *(bi-l-qalb)*. Moreover, the only human being capable of seeing God in the Qurʾān is none other than Muḥammad who experienced two visions of God as stated in Q 53:5-18 (cf. 81:19-25). According to early qurʾānic exegesis, which seems to be closest to the qurʾānic text, the Prophet saw God with his own eyes. Thus ḥadīth literature called Muḥammad God's beloved *(ḥabīb Allāh)*, who saw God and engaged in intimate colloquy with him, reaching nearer to God than Abraham (q.v.), God's friend *(khalīl Allāh)*, and drawing closer to God than Moses whom God had addressed on Mount Sinai *(kalīm Allāh)*. Eventually, Muḥammad's vision of God was intertwined with the legends that developed around his nocturnal journey *(isrāʾ)*, vaguely intimated by Q 17:1, and the story of his heavenly ascent *(miʿrāj)*, later developed jointly in ḥadīth literature into a major topic of his prophetic mission (see ASCENSION). The phrase that his "heart *(al-fuʾād)* lied not of what he saw" (Q 53:11) facilitated the interpretation that Muḥammad saw God with his heart, i.e. in a dream vision (see DREAMS AND SLEEP; VISIONS), and the reference that "he saw him another time by the lote-tree of the boundary" (*ʿinda sidrati l-muntahā*, Q 53:13-4; see AGRICULTURE AND VEGETATION) made it possible to speak of a veil having separated Muḥammad from his lord in this encounter. The assertions that, at the height of the Prophet's heavenly ascent, God laid his hand on Muḥammad's head or his shoulders or touched his heart are not found in the Qurʾān, rather they are gestures of prophetic initiation recorded in ḥadīth literature, not unlike the account of the angels opening Muḥammad's breast (cf. H. Birkeland, *The legend*).

In another metaphor of the Qurʾān, God's eyes are cited in the plural, rather than in the dual, which would have been required grammatically to convey bodily features unequivocally. The one passage that quotes God's eye in the singular refers to his love for the young Moses, watching over him "with divine care," i.e. literally "my eye" (*ʿalā ʿaynī*, Q 20:39). The phrase, "under our eyes" *(bi-aʿyuninā)* occurs with reference to God's care for his prophets (see PROPHETS AND PROPHETHOOD), e.g. Noah is asked to "build the ark under our eyes" (Q 11:37; 23:27; cf. 54:14), and Muḥammad is assured by God that he is "under our eyes" (Q 52:48). The phrase, *fī janbi llāhi* (Q 39:56), literally "in the side of God," expressed regret for negligence "toward" God, while the enigmatic phrase, "upon the day when the leg *(sāq)* shall be bared" (Q 68:42) left obscure what was meant by God's (?) leg or calf being revealed on the day of resurrection (cf. van Ess, *TG,* iv, 400-1).

The qurʾānic context also seems to argue for a not too literal understanding of God's hand or hands. For, "surely bounty (see GRACE; BLESSING) is in the hand of God" (*bi-yadi llāhi,* Q 3:73; 57:29; cf. 5:64; 48:10), appears as an expression for God as the source of divine favor and, "but his two hands are outspread" (*bal yadāhu mabsūṭatān,* Q 5:64) hints at divine sustenance being given freely and generously to all human beings. The expression, "God's hand is fettered" (*yadu llāhi maghlūlatun,* Q 5:64), however, sounds rather anthromorphic in the Qurʾān where it is cited as an expression uttered by the Jews who are reproached for it. The two most crucial verses implying metaphorical understanding of God's hands are Q 38:75 and 39:67. In Q 38:75 Adam (see ADAM AND EVE) is said to have been shaped by God's own two hands as Iblīs (see DEVIL) is reproached by God for not having prostrated (see BOWING AND PROSTRATION) with all the other angels "before what I created with my own hands *(limā khalaqtu bi-yadayya).*" In Q 39:67 God is depicted as holding the whole world in his hand, "the earth altogether shall be in his grasp *(qabḍatuhu)* on the day of resurrection, and the heavens shall be rolled up in his right hand *(bi-yamīnihi).*" There is no reference to the left hand of God nor any mention of the finger of God in the Qurʾān. In the works of qurʾānic exegesis, however, God was portrayed in pre-existence as holding the souls of the believers between two fingers and turning them back and forth to determine their fate and destiny (R. Gramlich, *Muḥammad al-Ġazzālīs Lehre,* 64). God's foot is not mentioned in the Qurʾān when he restrains hell's voracity (cf. Q 50:30), but ḥadīth literature places his foot *(qadam)* in hellfire to smother it (see HELL AND HELLFIRE; FIRE). When God "comes" with his angels, rank upon rank, to render judgment over humanity (Q 2:210; 6:158; 89:22), there is no mention of his footstep. Likewise, God's footprint does not appear in the Qurʾān but, within a century after Muḥammad's death, the Dome of the Rock had been built in Jerusalem and memories of God's footprint in the rock were later transformed into the one Muḥammad left behind when he ascended to heaven (cf. Q 17:1 and R. Paret, *Der Koran,* 295-6).

Jerusalem (q.v.) was also known in Muḥammad's time as the place where God sat down on a throne after completing his work of creation and where he would sit again at the end of time holding his final judgment of humanity (T. O'Shaughnessy, God's throne, 202). The Qurʾān does not refer to this geographical scenario, which can be traced in Jewish tradition (cf. Ezechiel 1:10) and is taken up in ḥadīth literature. Rather, the Qurʾān stresses the image of God sitting on a throne, the symbol of his power and presence (G. Vitestam, ʿArsh and Kursī, 369 f.). God does not move about in the Qurʾān, he is seated on his throne, ruling over creation in majesty and splendor. "Sitting back on the throne" (*istawā ʿalā l-ʿarsh,* Q 7:54; 10:3; 13:2; 20:5; 25:59; 32:4; 57:4) like a king, he neither wears a crown nor holds a scepter in the Qurʾān. The term *kursī* for "throne" appears twice in the Qurʾān, once in reference to Solomon's throne (Q 38:34; cf., however, Q 27:38, 41-2, "*arsh*") and once as God's throne encompassing heaven and earth in the famous Throne Verse (Q 2:255). The term *ʿarsh* is employed in phrases such as "lord of the throne" (*rabb al-ʿarsh,* Q 21:22; 23:86, 116; 27:26; 43:82) and "possessor of the throne" (*dhū l-ʿarsh,* Q 40:15; 85:15; cf. 17:42; 81:20). It is also used when the Qurʾān states that God's throne is carried and encircled by angels proclaiming the praise of their lord

(Q 39:75; 40:7; 69:17) and that "his throne was upon the waters" (Q 11:7). Not fatigued by his work of creation (Q 2:255; 50:38), God is seated on his throne in a relaxed fashion and, on the day of judgment, offers his elect Prophet a seat on it next to himself according to the commentary on the "laudable station" *(maqām maḥmūd),* enigmatically cited in Q 17:79. Much exegetical acumen was also devoted to questions of the throne's precise location, i.e. whether God was in the clouds before he created the throne, whether he sat above it or on it, and in which way he surpassed the throne that encompassed the heavens and the earth (van Ess, *TG,* iv, 402-11).

It is possible that the throne of God resting "upon the waters" (Q 11:7) was implicitly understood in the Qurʾān, not unlike in Jewish tradition, as made of light, perhaps appearing as a reflection of divine light in the waters of the primal sea (see WATER). More explicitly though, God himself is called, "the light of the heavens and the earth *(Allāhu nūru l-samāwāti wa l-arḍ)*" in the famous Light Verse of the Qurʾān (Q 24:35). The imagery of this verse is unique and highly complicated by the metaphor of the light, depicted as placed in a niche wherein is a lamp made of glass and resembling a glittering star kindled from a celestial tree (G. Böwering, The light verse, 115-29). Muslim interpretations of this complex imagery reached from the comparison of God with a being or substance of light to a "man of light" who could be imagined as having five senses, just as light, traditionally understood, has five colors (cf. H. Halm, *Die islamische Gnosis,* 145). This man of light, possessed of limbs representing the letters of the supreme name of God, collocated these letters in the act of creation to fashion the names of all things, whose shadows project the actual things that come into being on earth. In the Light Verse, the light is qualified as "light upon light" *(nūrun ʿalā nūrin),* a phrase recalling a formula of the Nicene Creed. In Muslim exegesis it came to be interpreted as the "light" of the believers originating from the divine light and returning into it. Other qurʾānic passages citing the term "light" referred simply to the light of God (Q 9:32; 39:69; 61:8), the light coming from God (Q 5:15; 39:22) or the light that God had sent down (Q 4:174; 7:157; 64:8), facilitating the less complicated interpretations of the light as divine guidance or of God as the all-knowing and the guide. Mystic interpreters of the Qurʾān, however, saw in the "light of light" a metaphorical reference to a kind of Muslim logos represented by either Adam or Muḥammad appearing in their light nature as the first creation in preexistence (Böwering, *Mystical,* 149-153). Metaphysically inclined exegetes saw God as the primal light and source of all being and contrasted the polarity of light and darkness (q.v.) with the world of ideas and that of the bodies. Politically inclined interpreters, however, used the Light Verse to speak of the caliph (q.v.) as "the shadow of God on earth."

Major aspects of God in the Qurʾān

The reputedly earliest passage of the Qurʾān proclaimed by Muḥammad introduces God as creator, "Recite, in the name of your lord who created" (Q 96:1). God's act of creation is an act of his will. He has created the world by the decree of his eternal will (see ETERNITY) and continues to maintain it as long as he wishes. His act of creative will is expressed in a command of his speech because God calls the things into being through his creative imperative. Creation is seen in the Qurʾān as God's permanent work, an understanding that sees creation as the ongoing existence of the world rather than as one single event at the beginning of the universe (Q 79:27-33; 80:17-42; see COSMOLOGY). God is always active conducting the affairs of the universe; he never sits still. Even on the seventh day, he rules creation from the throne of his majesty (T. Nagel, *Der Koran*, 172-84). The Qurʾān neither speaks of nothingness and chaos preceding creation nor offers a story of creation similar to that of the Book of Genesis. It includes, however, references to the creation in six days (Q 7:54 and parallels; cf. however, 41:9-12), which intimate some familiarity with the gist of the biblical story on the part of its listeners (see SCRIPTURE AND THE QURʾĀN). Creation is not a unique moment at the beginning of time (q.v.) setting history in motion (see HISTORY AND THE QURʾĀN); rather, creation is a process experienced by humans as happening at each and every moment. Creation is seen in the Qurʾān through the eyes of humans observing the world they experience around themselves rather than being viewed from its origin in God as its creator. God makes the heavens and the earth, looses the winds (see AIR AND WIND), sends down the rain, fortifies the land with the mountains, traces the rivers in its soil and places landmarks in its ground to guide humans (see GEOGRAPHY; NATURAL WORLD AND THE QURʾĀN). The animals (see ANIMAL LIFE) are created to serve humans and provide them with livestock, while the oceans yield fish and pearls (see HUNTING AND FISHING) and carry the ships (q.v.). Rain symbolizes the creative power of God in that it gives life to the land, makes grass (see GRASSES) grow and produces fruit of all sorts. God creates the human beings living in this world and after their death, in their resurrection, creates them again in the world to come. He who can make the desert sprout can also give new life to the dead.

In the Qurʾān God is called three times "the maker" (*bāriʾ*, Q 2:54 59:24), twice "the originator *(badīʿ)* of the heavens and the earth" (Q 2:117; 6:101), once "the shaper" (*muṣawwir*, Q 59:24) and about half a dozen times, "the creator" (*khāliq*, e.g. Q 13:16) who is constantly creating (*khallāq*, Q 36:81) all things, with the Arabic root *kh-l-q* being employed very frequently to describe God's creative activity in the Qurʾān. God creates "what he wishes" (*mā yashāʾ*, Q 3:47; 5:17; 24:45; 28:68; 30:54; 39:4; 42:49) and gives existence by the divine command, "'Be!,' And it is" (*kun! fa-yakūn*, Q 2:117; 3:47, 59; 6:73; 16:40; 19:35; 36:82: 40:68). God created the universe in truth and with a stated term (Q 30:8) rather than in jest (Q 44:38-9) or in vain (Q 23:115; 38:27). He created the heavens and the earth (Q 10:3) when he split the primal mass, "a mass all sewn up" *(ratqan)*, into two (Q 21:30). In six days he created the heavens and the earth (Q 7:54) and what is between them (Q 25:59) and brought all living beings out of the water (Q 21:30). From the vapors rising from the waters the seven skies were formed (Q 41:11). The vault of the heaven, which has no support (Q 13:2), was adorned with the sun (q.v.), the moon (q.v.), the stars and the constellations (Q 71:16; 78:13; 37:6; 15:16; see PLANETS AND STARS) to guide humans in the darkness of the land and the sea (Q 6:97). God created night and day (Q 21:33), succeeding each other (Q 24:44), and determined their extent and duration (Q 73:20; see DAY AND NIGHT; DAY, TIMES OF).

Following the angels as inhabitants of the earth, God created Adam, the first human being, as "successor" *(khalīfatan)* to the angels on earth (Q 2:30; the understanding of Adam as *God's* viceroy or deputy is not borne out by the qurʾānic text, cf. Q 7:69; 11:57 and R. Paret, *Der Koran*, 16). Creating Adam with his own two hands (Q 38:75), God breathed his spirit into Adam (Q 15:29; 38:72) and asked him to name the things, which the angels were unable to do (Q 2:31-2). God shaped the human figure "in the fairest stature" (*fī aḥsani taqwīm*,

Q 95:4), giving it proper proportions and erect posture, and shaping it in a balanced form. God "created you and formed you *(khalaqaka fa-sawwāka)* and balanced you *(fa-ʿadalaka)* and composed you in whatsoever form *(ṣūra)* he wished" (Q 82:7-8; cf. 18:37; 3:6). The Qurʾān mentions four stages in the creation of humans (see BIOLOGY AS THE CREATION AND STAGES OF LIFE; CLAY): God created the first human being, Adam, from dust (*min turābin*, Q 3:59), procreating human beings through the sperm, shaping them individually to their complete figure, and finally making them male and female. "(God) created you of dust, then of a sperm-drop *(min nuṭfa)*, then shaped you in the form of a man *(rajulan)*" (Q 18:37), and "then made you pairs" (Q 35:11), while other qurʾānic verses state that God created every animal of water (Q 24:45) and the jinn from a flame of fire (Q 55:15).

Two principal images are combined to depict the creation of humans: one, God created the human being of clay (*ṭīn*, Q 6:2), clinging clay (*ṭīn lāzib*, Q 37:11), an extraction of clay (*sulāla*, Q 23:12), the potter's clay (*ṣalṣāl*, Q 55:14) or stinking mud (*ḥamāʾ masnūn*, Q 15:28), and, two, of a sperm-drop *(nuṭfa)*, a drop of water (Q 25:54) or a blood-clot (*ʿalaq*, Q 96:2, *ʿalaqa*, Q 22:5; 40:67; see BLOOD AND BLOOD CLOT). Q 23:12-4 describes the process in detail, "We (God) created man of an extraction of clay, then we set him, a drop, in a receptacle secure, then we created of the drop a clot *(ʿalaqa)*, then we created of the clot a tissue *(muḍgha)*, then we created of the tissue bones, then we garmented the bones in flesh." Other depictions are added in the Qurʾān: "God caused you to spring up *(anbatakum)* from the earth" (Q 71:17); "He created you in your mothers' wombs, creation after creation" (*khalqan min baʿdi khalqin*, Q 39:6); "He it is who created of water a mortal *(basharan)*, and made him kindred of blood and marriage" (Q 25:54; see KINSHIP; MARRIAGE AND DIVORCE); "We have created you male and female, and appointeed you races and tribes" (Q 49:13; see TRIBES AND CLANS). Another image implies the creation of Adam and his mate, "He created you of a single soul *(min nafsin wāḥidatin)* and from it created its mate, and from the pair of them scattered abroad many men and women" (Q 4:1; cf. 7:189; 39:6; 6:98; 16:72; 30:21), called "children of Adam" (*banī Ādam*, Q 7:26-7, 31, 35, 172; 17:70; 36:60). In creating the human being, God also determined for him "a stated term" of life *(ajalun musammā)*. "He it is who created you of clay and then fixed a term — and a term is stated in his keeping" (Q 6:2). "From a sperm-drop! he created him and determined him *(qaddarahu)*, then he makes the way easy for him. Then he caused him to die and buried him, then when he wills he raises him again" (Q 80:19-22). "Surely we have created everything with a limit" (*bi-qadarin*, Q 54:49). He is God, "who created and formed *(fa-sawwā)* and who determined *(qaddara)* and guided" (Q 87:2-3).

The theme of God as creator was central to the earliest layers of Muḥammad's proclamation of the Qurʾān. The explicit message of God's oneness, the core of Islamic monotheism, however, increasingly became the focus as the qurʾānic proclamation progressed throughout Muḥammad's prophetic career. This uncompromising monotheism, known in ḥadīth literature and scholastic discourse by the extra-qurʾānic term, *tawḥīd*, the profession that God is one, stands in the mind of Muslims as the foremost symbol of the Islamic creed (see CREEDS). In the Qurʾān the pure profession of God's oneness is seen as innate and common to all humans. It cannot be altered because it has been rooted by God in their very nature as the primal religion on which God created all of humanity. "Set your face to the true religion, as a man of pure faith *(ḥanīfan),* God's original *(fiṭrata llāh)* upon which he originated humanity. There is no changing God's creation. That is the right religion *(al-dīnu l-qayyimu)*" (Q 30:30). The primal monotheism, called *al-ḥanīfiyya,* by its oldest name antedating the use of "Islam (q.v.)" for the religion proclaimed by Muḥammad, is documented by the wording of the qurʾānic text in the version of Ibn Masʿūd (d. 32/653; see CODICES OF THE QURʾĀN; COLLECTION OF THE QURʾĀN; READINGS OF THE QURʾĀN), "the true religion with God is *al-ḥanīfiyya*" (Q 3:19; see ḤANĪF). This innate monotheism embeds the knowledge of God in the hearts of humans and forms "the convincing argument" *(al-ḥujjatu l-bālighatu,* Q 6:149) God has made in his judgment against humans should they have compromised the oneness of God. The profession of God's oneness, "a straight path *(ṣirāṭ mustaqīm,* see PATH OR WAY) on a right religion, the creed *(milla)* of Abraham, a man of pure faith, who was no idolater" (Q 6:161), is upheld by Muḥammad who is commanded to say, "my prayer, my ritual sacrifice (q.v.), my living, my dying belong to God, the lord of all being. No associate has he" (*lā sharīka lahu,* Q 6:162-3).

God is one, the unique sovereign of the heavens and the earth and the only ruler "who has no associate *(sharīk)* in the sovereignty" (Q 17:111; 25:2) and does not share his power with anyone. This categorical denial of any partner in divine power is an expression of the explicit rejection of *shirk,* the foremost religious crime in Islam, that of associating partners with God. The phrase is directed against pre-Islamic idolatry or polytheism and, equally, against the Christian doctrine of divine sonship because Q 17:111, which is engraved in the outer hall of the Dome of the Rock, pointedly adds, "who has not taken to himself an offspring *(lam yattakhidh waladan).*" Q 25:2 repeats the phrase and Q 19:35 projects the polemics (see POLEMIC AND POLEMICAL LANGUAGE) onto Jesus (q.v.), son of Mary (q.v.), "it is not for God to take to himself an offspring" (cf. also Q 2:116). The language of the Qurʾān is multivalent in this case: it may refer to ancient Arab deities, such as the daughters of Allāh, al-Lāt, Manāt and al-ʿUzzā (Q 53:19-20; 16:57-9; 52:39), and/or to polemics against the Christian belief in the son of God because the term *walad,* "offspring," can be masculine or feminine, singular or plural, and the term *lam yattakhidh,* "has not taken," can imply adoption or generation. The categorical denial of associating partners with God is reiterated in the passage, "He has taken to himself neither a consort *(ṣāḥiba)* nor an offspring." (Q 72:3; cf. 6:101).

Most pointedly, however, the denial of *shirk* is expressed in the pithy verses of Q 112:1-4, "Say, he is God, one *(aḥad),* God, the impenetrable. He has not begotten nor has he been begotten *(lam yalid wa-lam yūlad),* and no one is equal to him." This short sūra lays great stress on rejecting the idea of generation within the concept of God and denies the Nicean creed, "begotten, not made," in the nutshell of a qurʾānic credal formula proclaiming God as one. Other phrases reinforce this strict monotheism of the Qurʾān, "Say, he is only one God" *(qul innamā huwa ilāhun wāḥidun,* Q 6:19; cf. 16:51; 14:52; 4:171), "your God is one God" *(annamā ilāhukum ilāhun wāḥidun,* Q 18:110; 21:108; 41:6; cf. 2:163; 16:22; 22:34), "no god is there but one God" *(wa-mā min ilāhin illā ilāhun wāḥidun,* Q 5:73) and, "surely your God is one" *(inna ilāhakum la-wāḥidun,* Q 37:4). The same monotheistic stress is achieved with the help of a divine name, "Glory be to him! He is God, the one, the omnipotent" (*al-wāḥidu l-qahhār*, Q 39:4; 12:39; 13:16; 40:16; 14:48) and reinforced by the statement that "God is sufficient to himself" (*anna llāha ghanī*, Q 2:267).

One set of verses stressing directly divine oneness in the sense of God's singularity, may be seen in select qur'ānic statements, when God refers to himself, "I am" *(anā)*, sometimes emphatically, "Verily, I" *(innī)*, and "Verily, I am" *(innanī anā)*. Expressions such as, "I am the one who turns toward you *(al-tawwāb)*, the compassionate" (Q 2:160) or, "I am the forgiving, the compassionate" (Q 15:49) or, "I am God, the mighty, the wise" (Q 27:9) are somewhat formulaic. Other expressions are explicit about the self reference, "there is no god but I *(lā ilāhā illā anā)*, so fear me" (Q 16:2), "there is no god but I, so serve me" (Q 20:14) or, "I am your lord *(anā rabbukum)*, so fear me" (Q 23:52), "I am your lord *(anā rabbukum)*, so serve me" (Q 21:92). Yet another passage places God emphatically at the beginning and end of human life, "He (God) said, I give life and I make to die" (Q 2:258). The intensity of self reference is increased in phrases such as, "verily, I am making" (*innī jā'ilun*, Q 2:30) or, "verily, I am creating a mortal" (*innī khāliqun basharan*, Q 15:28; 38:71). The most crucial passage proclaiming God's self assertion is Q 20:12-4, in which God addresses Moses, "Verily, I am God; there is no god but I *(innanī anā llāhu lā ilāha illā anā)*, so serve me" (Q 20:14; cf. 21:25). The qur'ānic wording, however, falls short of the full divine self-revelation expressed by the biblical, "I am who I am" (Exodus 3:14).

There are hundreds of verses in the Qur'ān which give emphasis to divine omnipotence, insist on the unimpeachable power of the divine decree, raise the question of human responsibility (see FREEDOM AND PREDESTINATION), discuss divine retribution for human action in this world, good or bad, imply the problem of predestination, open the metaphysical treatment of human freedom and offer prooftexts for the theological discussion of evil and its origin (cf. W.M. Watt, *Free will and predestination*). These issues are discussed at great length in the theological literature of Islam, their inclusive recital in this context, however, could only list a multitude of qur'ānic verses and open issues related to qur'ānic phrases that have been interpreted variously in Islamic exegetical literature. The natural environment for their discussion are works on Islamic religious thought rather than one devoted only to the Qur'ān (cf. W.M. Watt, *Formative period*). Some characteristic examples, however, may illustrate the plethora of these points. "God created you and that which you make" (Q 37:96). "Whatever good visits you, it comes from God; whatever evil visits you is of yourself" (Q 4:79). "God charges no soul save to its capacity; standing to its account is what it has earned and against its account what it has merited" (Q 2:286). "Each soul shall be recompensed for that it has earned" (Q 40:17). Upon the day of judgment, "whoever has done an atom's weight of good shall see it, and whoever has done an atom's weight of evil shall see it" (Q 99:7-8). God "leads astray whom he wishes and guides whom he wishes" (Q 14:4; 16:93; 35:8; 6:39, 125), "bestows his bounty upon whomever he wishes" (Q 57:21) and "admits whomever he wishes into his mercy" (Q 42:8). God has "laid veils on their hearts lest they understand it, and in their ears heaviness" (Q 18:57). "God has led him (i.e. man) astray out of a knowledge, and set a seal upon his hearing and his heart, and laid a covering on his eyes" (Q 45:23). Addressing

God, the Qurʾān sums up, "You exalt whom you wish and you abase whom you wish" (Q 3:26).

Gerhard Böwering

Bibliography

Primary: Ibn Isḥāq-Guillaume.
Secondary: M. Allard, *Le problème des attributs divins,* Beirut 1965; A. Ambros, Zur Entstehung der Emphase in Allāh, in *WZKM* 73 (1981), 23-32; T. Andrae, *Mohammed. The man and his faith,* New York 1936; A.J. Arberry, *The Koran interpreted,* 2 vols., London 1955; J.M.S. Baljon, To seek the face of God in Koran and ḥadīth, in *AO* 21 (1953), 254-66; Bell; id., *Commentary;* H. Birkeland, *The legend of the opening of Muḥammad's breast,* Oslo 1955; Blachère, *Introduction;* J. Blau, Arabic lexicographical miscellanies, in *JSS* 17 (1972), 173-190; G. Böwering, The light verse. Qurʾānic text and Ṣūfī interpretation, in *Oriens* 36 (2001), 113-44; id., *Mystical;* F. Buhl, *Das Leben Mohammeds,* Heidelberg 1961; J. Chelhod, Note sur l'emploi du mot rabb dans le Coran, in *Arabica* 5 (1958), 159-67; J. van Ess, Der Name Gottes im Islam, in H. von Stietencron, *Der Name Gottes,* Düsseldorf 1975, 156-175; id., *TG;* T. Fahd, *La divination arabe,* Paris 1987; id., *Le panthéon de l'Arabie centrale,* Paris 1968; D. Gimaret, *Dieu à l'image de l'homme,* Paris 1997; id., *La doctrine d'al-Ashʿarī,* Paris 1990; id., *Les noms divins en Islam,* Paris 1988; Goldziher, *Richtungen;* R. Gramlich, *Muḥammad al-Ǧazzālīs Lehre von den Stufen zur Gottesliebe,* Wiesbaden 1984; H. Halm, *Die islamische Gnosis,* Zürich 1982; Horovitz, *KU;* Jeffery, *For. vocab.;* id., *Materials;* J. Jomier, Le nom divin al-Raḥmān dans le Coran, in *Mélanges Louis Massignon,* 3 vols., Damascus 1957, ii, 361-381; H. Lammens, Le culte des bétyles et les processions religieuses, in *BIFAO* 17 (1919), 39-101; Y. Moubarac, Les noms, titres et attributs de Dieu dans le Coran et leurs corrrespondants en épigraphie sud-sémitique, in *Muséon* 68 (1955), 93-135, 325-68; Nagel; Nöldeke, *GQ;* T. O'Shaughnessy, *Creation and the teaching of the Qurʾān,* Rome 1985; T. O'Shaughnessy, God's throne and the biblical symbolism of the Qurʾān, in *Numen* 20 (1973), 202-21; Paret, *Kommentar;* id., *Mohammed und der Koran,* Stuttgart 1957; O. Pretzl, Die frühislamische Attributenlehre, in *Der Islam* (1931), 117-130; J.W. Redhouse, The most comely names, in *JRAS* 12 (1880), 1-69; J. Rijckmans, Le christianisme en Arabie du sud préislamique, in *L'Oriente cristiano nella storia della civiltà. Atti del convegno internazionale,* Rome 1964; Speyer, *Erzählungen;* G. Vitestam, ʿArsh and Kursī. An essay on the throne tradition in Islam, in E. Keck, S. Sondergaard and E. Wulff (eds.), *Living waters. Scandinavian orientalistic studies presented to Dr. Frede Lokkegaard on his seventy fifth birthday. January 27th 1990,* Copenhagen 1990, 369-78; Watt-Bell, *Introduction;* W.M. Watt, *The formative period of Islamic thought,* Edinburgh 1973; id., *Free will and predestination in early Islam,* London 1948; id., The use of the word 'Allāh' in English, in *MW* 43 (1953), 245-7; J. Wellhausen, *Reste arabischen Heidentums,* Berlin 1897; A.J. Wensinck, *Muslim creed,* Cambridge 1932.

Gog and Magog

Two peoples known to Jewish and Christian eschatology and similarly associated by the Qurʾān and Muslim tradition with events at the end of time. The coming of Gog and Magog (Ar. Yājūj and Mājūj or Yaʾjūj and Maʾjūj), according to one ḥadīth, will be one of ten principal "signs of the hour" (Muslim, *Ṣaḥīḥ [K. Fitan],* xviii, 27; Nuʿaym b. Ḥammād, *Fitan,* 404, 406); the two will be set loose upon the earth to work their evil in anticipation of the apocalyptic descent of Jesus (q.v.; see also APOCALYPSE).

Muslim tradition generally identifies Gog and Magog as two peoples descended from the biblical Japheth (*Gen* 10:2), also held to have fathered the Turks (Ṭabarī, *Taʾrīkh,* i, 2, id., *History,* ii, 11; Bayḍāwī, *Anwār,* ii, 22 f., with variants given; Ibn Kathīr, *Tafsīr,* iii, 102 [ad Q 18:94]). In taking the two names to designate entire peoples rather than individuals, Muslim tradition is consistent with post-biblical Jewish and Christian writing on the subject, which had long since modified the biblical picture (*Ezek* 38 and 39) of an individual named Gog ruling the land of Magog (cf. Gressman, *Ursprung,* 181 f.; Alexander, *Apocalyptic tradition,* 190 f.).

The names Yājūj and Mājūj appear twice in the Qurʾān, both times in apparently eschatological contexts (see ESCHATOLOGY). At Q 21:96-7, the day of judgment (see LAST JUDGMENT) will occur only after "Gog and Magog are unloosed, and they slide down out of every slope, and the true promise has drawn near." More context is supplied at Q 18:94-8, where reference to Gog and Magog is embedded in the Qurʾān's extended account of Alexander the Great (Q 18:83 f.; see ALEXANDER). There, Dhū l-Qarnayn (Alexander) agrees to build a barrier against Gog and Magog, who are to be prevented from sowing corruption in the land until "the lord's promise comes to pass." This conflation of the biblical-haggadic Gog and Magog with the Alexander legend is not unique to the Qurʾān; it is attested in the early sixth-century Syriac Christian "Legend of Alexander" and in a homiletic poem by Jacob of Sarug (d. 521 C.E.), both of which contain other suggestive parallels to Q 18:83 f. (The former is edited and translated by Budge, *History*, 255-75 [text], 144-61 [trans.]; the latter is translated at Budge, 163-200. For specific parallels to the qurʾānic passage, see Anderson, *Inclosed nations*, 28 f.; Friedlaender, *Chadhirlegende*, 51; Nöldeke, Beiträge, 32 f.)

Further details about Gog and Magog can be found in Muslim tradition. The two peoples are human or semi-human (according to one report, they are the product of Adam's sperm mixed with soil, and thus not descended from Eve; see ADAM AND EVE), and possess certain monstrous or animalistic physical qualities. They graze as wild beasts and hunt their prey as predatory animals, eating vermin such as snakes and scorpions as well as human flesh and the placentas of their wives. According to some reports, Gog and Magog are dwarfs with claws and fangs, and with enough fur to protect them against heat and cold; according to others, they are of three physical types: one as tall as cedars, a second as broad as they are tall, and a third able to use their giant ears as covering for their bodies. They are said to howl like dogs and copulate like animals. If given free reign, their numbers would soon cover the entire world, as not one among them dies before leaving a thousand others in its place; as it now stands, they constitute six-sevenths of the world. (These and other details can be found at Nuʿaym b. Ḥammād, *Fitan*, 397 f.; and Ṭabarī, *Tafsīr*, xvi, 19 f.; xvii, 88 f.)

A rough picture of Gog and Magog's role at the end of time emerges from various ḥādīths (see ḤADĪTH AND THE QURʾĀN). Imprisoned behind Alexander's gate, they continue to try to escape by tunneling under it, devouring it or climbing over it; each night, however, their progress is set back as God repairs the breaches in the wall. According to one report, Dhū l-Qarnayn set above it a stone eagle that screams an alarm each time Gog and Magog approach. The alarm summons Khiḍr (see KHAḌIR/KHIḌR) and Ilyās (see ELIJAH; DHŪ L-KIFL), who reassure the frightened people in the area, and petition God to restore the gate to its original condition (Friedlaender, *Chadhirlegende*, 149; Arabic text of ʿUmāra at 315). When the day of judgment arrives, Gog and Magog will finally be allowed to emerge into the world, devouring crops and consuming the waters of the Tigris and Euphrates, or Lake Tiberius, or all the waters of the earth. People will flee to cities and fortified places as Gog and Magog, having vanquished the inhabitants of the earth, now turn their attention to the heavens. In response to Jesus' petitions, God will send down worms to clog the nostrils and ears (or necks) of Gog and Magog. The stench of their dead will fill the earth, until God sends a cleansing rain and birds deposit the remains of Gog and Magog in the sea. Meanwhile, animals fatten themselves on the corpses (Ṭabarī, *Tafsīr*, xvi, 21; xvii, 88 f.; Tirmidhī, *Jāmiʿ*, *[K. Fitan]*, bāb 59 [no. 2240]; Nuʿaym b. Ḥammād, *Fitan*, 398; Ibn Ḥanbal, *Musnad*, ii, 510 f.). Their fate is well-deserved, as Gog and Magog had rejected Islam offered to them by the Prophet during his night journey (see ASCENSION; Ṭabarī, *Taʾrīkh,* i, 70; id., *History,* i, 237-8; Nuʿaym b. Ḥammād, *Fitan,* 404).

Neither details about Gog and Magog's physical appearance and behavior nor their precise role at the end of time, can be found in the Qurʾān itself. These are presumably the products of Muslim reflection on an older set of legends, some of which can be found in the Syriac materials already mentioned as well as in the mid-seventh-century Syriac apocalypse pseudo-Methodius (see e.g. Palmer, *Seventh century,* 239; Alexander, *Apocalyptic tradition,* 49). In any case, the gate of Alexander and the home territory of Gog and Magog piqued the Muslim imagination to the extent that the ʿAbbāsid Caliph al-Wāthiq (r. 227-232/842-847) is supposed to have sent an expedition in 842 to locate the gate. The report of the expedition leader Sallām the Interpreter, preserved by Ibn Khurradādhbih (*Masālik,* 162-70), seems largely a wonder-tale and may owe something to the Syriac "Legend of Alexander" (Nöldeke, Beiträge, 33).

Keith Lewinstein

Bibliography
Primary: Bayḍāwī, *Anwār,* 2 vols., Beirut 1988; Ibn Ḥanbal, *Musnad,* 6 vols., Cairo 1393/1978; Ibn Kathīr, *Tafsīr,* 4 vols., Medina 1413/1993; Ibn Khurradādhbih, Abū l-Qāsim ʿUbaydallāh b. ʿAlī, *al-Masālik wa-l-mamālik,* ed. M.J. de Goeje, BGA vi, repr. Leiden 1967; Kisāʾī *Qiṣaṣ;* id., *The tales of the prophets of al-Kisāʾī. Translated from the Arabic. With notes,* trans. W. Thackston, Jr., Boston 1978, 9, 18 (description of hell); 108, 334 (the children of Gog and Magog fighting against Jesus before the day of judgment); Masʿūdī, *Murūj,* para. 286, 369, 730, 910, 1419; id., *Les prairies d'or,* ed. and trans. Ch. Pellat, i, 110, 137; ii, 274, 343, 546; Muslim, *Ṣaḥīḥ (bi-sharḥ al-imām al-Nawawī),* 18 vols., Beirut n.d.; Nuʿaym b. Ḥammād, *al-Fitan,* Beirut 1418/1997; Ṭabarī, *Tafsīr,* ed. A.S. ʿAlī, 30 vols., Cairo 1954-7; repr. Beirut 1408/1988; id., *Taʾrīkh,* 10 vols., Cairo 1960-9; id., *The history of al-Ṭabarī. i. General introduction and From the creation to the flood,* trans. F. Rosenthal, Albany 1989; id. *The history of al-Ṭabarī. ii. Prophets and patriarchs,* trans. W. Brinner, Albany 1987; Tirmidhī, *Ṣaḥīḥ,* 5 vols., Beirut n.d. (repr.).
Secondary: P. Alexander, *The Byzantine apocalyptic tradition,* Berkeley 1985; A. Anderson, *Alexander's gate, Gog and Magog, and the inclosed nations,* Cambridge, MA 1932; A.W. Budge, *The history of Alexander the Great,* Cambridge 1889; *Encyclopedia Judaica,* s.v. Gog and Magog; I. Friedlaender, *Die Chadhirlegende und der Alexanderroman,* Leipzig-Berlin 1913; H. Gressman, *Der Ursprung der israelitisch-jūdischen Eschatologie,* Göttingen 1905; T. Nöldeke, Beiträge zur Geschichte des Alexanderromans, in *Denkschriften der Kais. Ak. der Wissenschaften,* vol. 38, no. 5, Vienna 1890; A. Palmer, S. Brock, R. Hoyland, *The seventh century in the west-Syriac chronicles,* Liverpool 1993; A.J. Wensinck, Yādjūdj wa-Mādjūdj, in *EI*[1], iv, 1142; C.E. Wilson, The wall of Alexander against Gog and Magog and the expedition sent out to find it by Khalīf Wāthiq in 842 A.D., in *Hirth Anniversary Volume. Asia Major,* London 1922, 575-612.

Gold

A yellow metallic element, the most precious metal used as a common medium of commercial exchange. Gold (Ar. *dhahab*) is attested eight times in the Qurʾān (Q 3:14, 91; 9:34; 18:31; 22:23; 35:33; 43:53, 71). Four verses mention gold in the context of the pleasures and luxury the believers will enjoy in paradise (q.v.; Q 18:31; 22:23; 35:33; 43:71; see REWARD AND PUNISHMENT). These verses are very similar in content. They refer to the economic value of gold and the materialistic wealth (q.v.) symbolized by jewels and clothes. In this context, gold, silver, pearls, brocade and silk (q.v.) simply denote precious materials (see METALS AND MINERALS). Thus the "bracelets of gold" (Q 18:31) can elsewhere be "bracelets of silver" (Q 76:21).

Gold, silver and silk are often mentioned together in the collections of ḥadīths and *fatwās*, as well as in the *tafsīr* literature.

Wearing gold and silk, however, is restricted to women. Abū Dāwūd (d. 275/888) and al-Nasāʾī (d. 303/915) record that ʿAlī b. Abī Ṭālib (q.v.) took silk in his right hand and gold in his left hand and said: "These two are forbidden to the men of my nation *(ummatī)*" (Ibn Bāz, *Fatāwā*, iii, 194). Men are only allowed to wear silver (Qurṭubī, *Jāmiʿ*, xii, 29). Gold and silk belong to a category of things disapproved of in this world, but explicitly allowed in paradise and even emphasized as special delights that the believers will enjoy there (cf. also the prohibition of wine; see INTOXICANTS; CUPS AND VESSELS). According to Q 43:71, golden platters in paradise contain "whatever the souls desire." In this life, however, those who drink from silver and golden vessels will feel the fire (q.v.) of hell (q.v.) in their stomachs (Muslim, *Ṣaḥīḥ*, vi, 135). Only in Q 43:53 is there an allusion to gold (specifically, bracelets of gold) as being among the insignia of earthly sovereignty and honesty. The fact that Moses (q.v.) lacks these insignia is used by Pharaoh (q.v.) to underscore his contemptibility and insincerity (Qurṭubī, *Jāmiʿ*, xv, 100).

Gold as well as silver (the two are paired in Q 3:14 and 9:34) play an important symbolic role in religions. Gold symbolizes the incorruptible and imperishable. In some religious contexts, though, it has negative connotations, as evidenced in the Abrahamic traditions (Carpenter, Gold, 68a/b). Q 9:34 points out the dangers of cheating (q.v.), greed (see AVARICE) and misbehavior caused by treasuring gold and silver for personal use, namely among rabbis and monks (see MONASTICISM AND MONKS; JEWS AND JUDAISM; CHRISTIANS AND CHRISTIANITY). Similarly, and again in the context of contrasting this world with the next, in Q 3:14 "heaped-up heaps of gold and silver" symbolize much wealth (*al-māl al-kathīr*, Ṭabarī, *Tafsīr*, vi, 249-50), which people desire, among other things, in their life on earth. Q 3:91 uses gold to delineate the difference between this- and other-worldly values: "Those who disbelieve and die in disbelief (see BELIEF AND UNBELIEF), the earth full of gold would not be accepted from any one of them were it offered as a ransom. Theirs will be a painful doom and they will have no helpers."

Despite the ambivalent attitude towards the presence of gold in this world that is found in the Qurʾān and Islamic literature, Muslim societies did find use for the material. In the *materia medica*, gold has not only been used as a remedy (eyes, heart, respiration), but also as a material for medical instruments (cauterization; cf. Leclerc, *Ibn el-Bëithar*, ii, no. 1007, 150 f.). See also MATERIAL CULTURE AND THE QURʾĀN.

Hannelore Schönig

Bibliography

Primary: ʿAbd al-ʿAzīz Ibn Bāz, Ibn al-ʿUthaymīn and Ibn Jibrīn, *Fatāwā islāmiyya*, ed. Q. al-Shammāʿī al-Rifāʿī, 3 vols., Beirut 1988; Muslim, *Ṣaḥīḥ*, 8 parts in 2 vols., Beirut [repr. of 1334]; Qurṭubī, *Jāmiʿ*, 20 vols. in 15, Cairo 1354-69/1935-50; Ṭabarī, *Tafsīr*, ed. Shākir.
Secondary: Arberry; D. Carpenter, Gold and silver, in *ER*, vi, 67-9; A.S. Ehrenkreutz, Dhahab, in *EI²*, ii, 220-1; L. Leclerc, *Traité des simples par Ibn el-Bëithar. Notices et extraits des manuscrits de la Bibliothèque Nationale et autres bibliothèques*, 3 vols., Paris 1877-83.

Goliath

Foe of the Children of Israel (q.v.) slain by David (q.v.). Goliath's name (Jālūt; this Arabic rendition of the name is possibly influenced by the Heb. word for exile, *gālūt*; cf. Vajda, Djālūt) is mentioned three times in Q 2:249-51 wherein he is portrayed as the ancient Israelites' opponent in battle. The qurʾānic account conflates the biblical story of Gideon's conflict with the Midianites (see MIDIAN) — in particular the episode wherein God instructed Gideon to select only those men who drank from the river by scooping water with their hand (*Judg* 7:1-7) — with the account of the wars of Saul (q.v.) and David against the Philistines (*I Sam* 17). The "stories of the prophets" tradition *(qiṣaṣ al-anbiyāʾ)* identifies Goliath as the king of the Amalakites; the biblical account identifies him as the champion of the Philistines (*I Sam* 17:4, 23). The *qiṣaṣ al-anbiyāʾ* tradition transforms the simple phrase, "David slew Goliath" (Q 2:151) into a tale, attributed to Wahb b. Munabbih (d. 114/732), whose origins may be found in midrashic legend. In Wahb's account, David collected the stones of his ancestors Abraham (q.v.), Isaac (q.v.), and Jacob (q.v.) and put them in his satchel. When he confronted Goliath, he reached into his satchel and the three stones became one. After he placed it in his sling and threw it at Goliath, the single stone again became three. One stone penetrated Goliath's helmet and slew him; the second vanquished his right flank; the third his left flank. Not surprisingly, the Muslim tradition views the miraculous victory of the young David's outnumbered forces over the formidable Goliath's mighty host as a foreshadowing of the battle of Badr (q.v.). In fact, one finds the passage "Many a small band has, by God's grace, vanquished a mighty army; God is with those who endure with fortitude" (Q 2:249), cited in all sorts of accounts in which the smaller armies of the righteous (however defined by the author) defeat the larger armies of their opponents (see EXPEDITIONS AND BATTLES; FIGHTING).

James E. Lindsay

Bibliography
Primary: R.G. Khoury, *Wahb ibn Munabbih,* 2 vols., Wiesbaden 1972, i, 48-56; Kisāʾī, *Qiṣaṣ,* 250-77; id., *The tales of the prophets of al-Kisāʾī,* trans. W.M. Thackston, Boston 1978, 270-300; Ṭabarī, *Taʾrīkh,* ed. De Goeje, i, 548-62.
Secondary: L. Ginzberg, *Legends of the Jews,* 7 vols., Philadelphia 1909-36, iv, 81-121; G. Vajda, Djālūt, in *EI*[2], ii, 406.

Good and Evil

Frequently paired terms that can connote moral qualities, ontological entites and categories of judgment, both human and divine. The direct opposition of an abstract good and evil as moral or ontological categories is not common in the Qurʾān, nor are there terms that are necessarily always understood as "good" or "evil," though many passages in the Qurʾān are interpreted to depend on the opposition of positive and negative intentions and consequences. Note also that unlike the biblical account, in Q 2:35 and 20:120 it is stated that it was the tree of life from which Adam and Eve (q.v.) were commanded to abstain in the garden of Eden. There is no mention of a tree of the knowledge of good and evil in the Qurʾān (see INTELLECT; KNOWLEDGE AND LEARNING).

The word normally translated as "evil," *sūʾ,* occurs forty-three times as a noun, but is not always understood by Muslim commentary on the Qurʾān as a reference to a moral or ontological category. Often the term refers to harm (Q 7:73; 11:64; 20:22; 26:156; 27:12; 28:32; 60:2), misfortune (Q 16:94; 27:62; 39:61; 40:45, 52) or God's chastisement (Q 6:157; 7:141, 167; 13:18-25; 14:6; 27:5; 39:24, 47; see CHASTISEMENT AND PUNISHMENT). Many verses refer to "evil" as the intention or consequence of actions (Q 4:110, 123; 6:54; 12:25; 13:11; 16:119; 33:17; 40:37; 47:14), though in some cases it appears that harm or misfortune can result from actions unrelated to a moral choice. Q 7:165 refers to the general prohibition against evil, and Q 9:37 seems to equate evil with unlawful actions (see LAWFUL AND UNLAWFUL). Joseph's (q.v.) renunciation of Potiphar's wife's sexual advances is described as avoiding evil deeds (q.v.) in Q 12:24 and again in Q 12:51 and Q 12:53.

Evil is also taken as a sort of entity in the accusations made against Hūd (q.v.) by his opponents in Q 11:54, and the evil that people deny in Q 16:28 seems to be the "shame" that covers them on the day of judgment (see LAST JUDGMENT) in the preceding verse, Q 16:27. Muslim exegetes often interpret qurʾānic references to Iblīs and Satan (see DEVIL) to cast him in the role of the personification of evil. Satan is cursed by God (Q 15:39) and vows to lead astray (q.v.) many of Adam's descendants (Q 7:16-7; 17:64; 38:77-85). Closely related to these various uses of the term *sūʾ* is the word *sharr*, occurring some 28 times in the Qurʾān, often translated as "bad" and used to indicate that certain ideas or actions are considered to be unfortunate.

One of the two words normally translated as "good" occurs six times as a noun *(ḥusn)* and nineteen times as an adjective *(ḥasan)*. The term usually translated as "good deeds" (q.v.; *ḥasana*) occurs twenty-six times with an additional three times in the plural *(ḥasanāt)*. Q 27:11 states that God is forgiving and merciful when a person substitutes good *(ḥusn)* for evil *(sūʾ)*, though some exegetes take this as a specific reference to the messengers of God mentioned at the end of verse 10 (Ṭabarsī, *Majmaʿ*, xix, 202). According to the *Kashshāf* of al-Zamakhsharī (d. 538/1144), the "good" mentioned in Q 27:11 is repentance from evil (see REPENTANCE AND PENANCE).

Another word often translated as "good" *(khayr)* occurs 140 times in the nominative case and thirty-seven more times in the accusative case, oftentimes used to denote a "good thing" without the object being specified. For example, in Q 28:24, Moses (q.v.) asks God to send him something good, understood by several classical commentators to refer to food and clothing needed by Moses after his long trip to Midian (q.v.; Ṭabarī, *Tafsīr*, xx, 58-9; Ibn Kathīr, *Tafsīr*, vi, 237). Q 7:188 juxtaposes the multiplication of "good" *(khayr)* and the protection from "evil" *(sūʾ)* as the result of actions directed by divine knowledge of that which is hidden (see HIDDEN AND THE HIDDEN). These usages suggest that *khayr*, which can also be used with the meaning of "better," is most appropriately opposite to those uses of *sūʾ* that denote harm and misfortune. Closely related to these usages of *khayr* is the term *ṣāliḥ*, occurring numerous times in the Qurʾān, sometimes translated as "good," but more commonly as "upright" or "righteous" in the sense of a person's character and actions being suitable to God's design.

Knowledge of good and evil

Muslim exegetes contend that thinking about the cosmos and human experience leads to acknowledging the existence of God which, in turn, leads to doing good (see GRATITUDE AND INGRATITUDE). According to the Shīʿite and Muʿtazilite exegete al-Ṭūsī (d. 460/1067; *Tibyān*, vii, 401-2), Q 23:115 makes a connection between God's purpose in creating the world and the return of this creation to God without blemish. Commenting on Q 23:115, Ibn Kathīr (d. 774/1373) writes that God created people for the express purpose of worship (q.v.; *ʿibāda*) and establishing the commands *(awāmir*, see COMMANDMENTS) of God on the earth (*Tafsīr*, v, 459).

Knowledge of God and of his intention that people do good is considered to be innate. Q 91:7-10 lists the attributes which God created as part of each person's awareness, including *taqwā* which is understood as balance and stability but also piety (q.v.) and fear (q.v.) of God. In his *Jāmiʿ* on Q 91:8, al-Qurṭubī cites several reports in which *taqwā* is portrayed as a sort of conscience, that which protects one's self from the evil consequences of one's actions. The positive result of *taqwā* is directing one's conduct to the worship of God and the establishing of his commands.

Q 7:172-3 also recounts how God revealed himself to the descendants of Adam (see ADAM AND EVE) before they were born, and how these descendants testified that they recognized God as their lord (q.v.). In his discussion of the "stories of the prophets" *(qiṣaṣ al-anbiyāʾ),* Ibn Kathīr recounts a number of related reports in which God takes Adam's descendants from his body. Some of these reports, such as those related by Ibn ʿAbbās, concern Adam's giving part of his life span to David (q.v.; Ibn Ḥanbal, *Musnad,* ed. al-Ghamrāwī, i, 197; ed. Shākir et al., iii, 42-3, no. 2270; Ibn Kathīr, *Bidāya*). Other reports, such as that transmitted by ʿUmar b. al-Khaṭṭāb and recorded by Mālik b. Anas (d. 179/796), reflect the tradition that God showed Adam how some of his descendants would end up in paradise (q.v.) but others in hell (q.v.; Mālik, *Muwaṭṭaʾ,* ii, 898-9; Ibn Ḥanbal, *Musnad,* ed. al-Ghamrāwī, i, 44-5; ed. Shākir et al., iii, 42-3, no. 2270; Ibn Kathīr, *Bidāya,* i, 8; see REWARD AND PUNISHMENT). Because of its proximity to the mention of the covenant (q.v.) with the Israelites (see CHILDREN OF ISRAEL) in Q 7:163-71, many Muslim exegetes stress that the verses of Q 7:172-3 demonstrate the existence of a covenant between God and all humanity. It is further underscored that in Q 7:173 God cautions people that they cannot now use ignorance (q.v.) as a defense of their evil deeds on the day of judgment.

In addition, the Qurʾān contains numerous accounts of the various prophets sent to different peoples in different times and places reminding them of their covenant obligation to worship God and to establish his commands on the earth (see PROPHETS AND PROPHETHOOD). Q 28:59 makes explicit that God did not destroy any peoples to whom he had not first sent a messenger (q.v.) reminding them of God and of their covenant with him (see PUNISHMENT STORIES). To some of these messengers God also revealed books which contained accounts of the laws by which people were supposed to conduct themselves. Muslim exegetes emphasize that these qurʾānic stories of prophets and their ultimate rejection by the peoples to whom they were sent underline the view of evil action as a willful act of disobedience (q.v.).

Doing evil is thus not the result of ignorance that God exists or ignorance of his commands. Because knowledge of God and of doing good is self-evident and periodically re-revealed, doing evil is a conscious decision to disobey God's commands. According to the interpretation of Q 38:27, it is those who regard the creation of the heavens and earth as being without purpose, who will, as a consequence of their actions, be cast into the fire (q.v.) of hell. On Q 2:11-2, the Muʿtazilite Ibn Kaysān (Abū Bakr al-Aṣamm, d. 200/816) remarks that even people who think they are doing good, when they deny the prophet Muḥammad and the teaching of the Qurʾān, are disobeying God (al-Qurṭubī, *Jāmiʿ,* i, 255, 1.5). Q 18:103-4 is interpreted similarly to mean that acts thought to be good but done without knowledge of God's instructions are actually fruitless and ultimately result in evil.

Consequences of good and evil

In keeping with the general association of evil with misfortune and of good with benefit, Muslim exegetes identify passages which represent this opposition in the stories of the prophets. That these stories themselves are intended as further evidence of God's instructions can be seen in the exegesis of Q 29:67-9. In his *Tafsīr,* Ibn Kathīr relates that these verses were originally addressed to the Quraysh (q.v.) as a message that it is because of God's protection, not the false gods they themselves created, nor their own efforts, that Mecca (q.v.) had remained a safe sanctuary (see POLYTHEISM AND ATHEISM; SOUTH ARABIA, RELIGION IN PRE-ISLAMIC).

Evil actions are those which are unproductive or fruitless *(bāṭil)*, whereas good actions produce sound and proper benefit *(ṣāliḥ)*. Muslim exegesis finds this juxtaposition in numerous verses which stress the ephemeral nature of earthly accomplishments. Ibn Kathīr, in his *Tafsīr* on Q 29:41, writes that those who deny the existence of God are like spiders who put their trust in their own creations, their webs made of silk and easily destroyed. Al-Ṭabarī (d. 310/923) in his *Tafsīr*, reports on the authority of Ibn ʿAbbās that the last part of Q 29:40, immediately preceding the parable of the spider (q.v.) in Q 29:41, refers to the story of Noah (q.v.) and the flood. This follows allusions in the preceding verses to the Pharaoh (q.v.), Hāmān (q.v.), Korah (q.v.), and the peoples of Lot (q.v.), Ṣāliḥ (q.v.), Hūd, and Shuʿayb (q.v.) who exalted themselves rather than God on the earth (see ARROGANCE; PRIDE).

Throughout the Qurʾān, certain characters are singled out for their attempts to achieve earthly fame in opposition to the prophets' attempts to focus attention away from this world, and directly on the worship of God. Pharaoh and Hāmān, mentioned together as persecutors of the Israelites (Q 28:6, 8, 38; 40:36) and with Korah (Q 29:39; 40:24), seem to symbolize the outright denial of God (see BELIEF AND UNBELIEF) in the attempt to exalt oneself. In Q 28:4, for example, the Pharaoh is said to have exalted himself on the earth and, again in Q 28:38, the Pharaoh and Hāmān plan to build a tower to the heavens to prove that the God of Moses is false. In Q 79:24 the Pharaoh says plainly that he is God. Many Muslim exegetes point out that Korah's fate of being swallowed by the earth (Q 28:81) is in stark contrast to his own attempts to accumulate and claim earthly wealth (q.v.).

The stories of the people of ʿĀd (q.v.) and Thamūd (q.v.) are also particularly clear in showing the contrast between earthly fame and eternal damnation. Q 89:6-13 compares the buildings of ʿĀd that were created unlike any others in the land, the buildings of Thamūd hewed out of rocks, and the city-building of the Pharaoh (see GEOGRAPHY). Q 26:128-9 accuses the people of Thamūd of using their buildings to guarantee their immortality through their fame. Yāqūt, in his *Buldān*, reports an opinion that the city of Iram Dhāt al-ʿImād (see IRAM), mentioned in Q 89:7 in connection with the ʿĀd, was built between the Ḥadramawt and Ṣanʿāʾ in imitation of paradise by one of the descendants of ʿĀd, and that God destroyed the city on account of its builder's pride. According to the exegesis of Q 46:25 in al-Rāzī's (d. 606/1210) *Tafsīr*, God left only the ruins of the dwellings of the ʿĀd after their destruction as a testament to their refusal to recognize his providence. In Ṭabarī's *Taʾrīkh*, it is reported that the wind or black birds carry away the people of ʿĀd from their houses, dropping them in the sea and leaving their houses as a sign of the artifices upon which they pinned their false hopes of immortality. The houses are left standing, but their treasury and their bodies are swept away by a noisy, roaring wind *(ṣarṣar)*. According to Nuwayrī (d. 733/1333; *Nihāya*, xiii, 73), the people of Thamūd, secure in their houses against invaders and storms, are destroyed by the sound of the "scream" *(ṣayḥa)*.

In his *Taʾrīkh*, al-Ṭabarī reports that the people of Thamūd are said to have been made invulnerable by God, and given special skills to hew their houses out of the sides of mountains. The *Sīra* of Ibn Isḥāq takes the mention of the houses of Thamūd (in Q 26:149; 29:38; 89:9) as references to the ruins located at al-Ḥijr (see HIJR), also called the "cities of Ṣāliḥ" *(madāʾin Ṣāliḥ)*, Nabataean ruins which the prophet Muḥammad passed on his way to the raid on Tabūk (Ibn Isḥāq-Guillaume, 605; see EXPEDITIONS AND BATTLES). The ruins of the people of Thamūd, according to a tradition preserved by al-Bayhaqī (d. 458/1066; *Dalāʾil*, v, 235), are called "al-Ḥijr" because of their status as a place that is interdicted or forbidden *(ḥijr)*, a monument not to the immortality but to the infamy of the people of Thamūd.

Conclusions

In contrast to the images of empty buildings and ruins, Muslim exegetes point to the qurʾānic images of fertility and life as evidence of the eventual vindication of good over evil. Noah is saved from the flood, Abraham (q.v.) from the fire, Moses from the Pharaoh, and Jesus (q.v.) from the Jews (see JEWS AND JUDAISM). According to many Muslim exegetes, the message of the Qurʾān here is that the prophet Muḥammad, and those who follow him, also will be saved. The people can choose to keep their primordial covenant with God and thus do good, or they can choose to deny God and rely on their own devices. Doing good and doing evil produce concrete results both in this world and in the next. (For further discussion of the connection between faith and good works, see FAITH. See also ETHICS AND THE QURʾĀN; OBEDIENCE.)

Brannon M. Wheeler

Bibliography

Primary: Abū Dāwūd, 4703; Bayhaqī, Abū Bakr Aḥmad b. al-Ḥusayn, *al-Asmāʾ wa-l-ṣifāt*, ed. ʿI. Ḥaydr, Beirut 1985, ii, 57; id., *Dalāʾil al-nubuwwa*, ed. ʿA. Qalʿajī, 7 vols., Beirut 1985; al-Fārisī, Abū l-Ḥāsan ʿAlī b. Balbān, *al-Iḥsān bi-tartīb Ṣaḥīḥ Ibn Ḥibbān*, ed. K.Y. al-Ḥūr, 7 vols., Beirut 1987, 6133; al-Ghazālī, Abū Ḥāmid Muḥammad, *Iḥyāʾ ʿulūm al-dīn. Bk. xix*, Cairo 1933, ii, 269-312; id., Livre de l'obligation d'ordonner le bien et d'interdire le mal, trans. L. Bercher, in *IBLA* 18 (1955), 55-91, 313-21; 20 (1957), 21-30; 21 (1958), 389-407; 23 (1960), 300-26; Ibn Ḥanbal, *Musnad* (especially i, 44-5 for more on the primordial covenant and the story of Adam's descendents being taken from his body by God); Ibn Isḥāq-Guillaume; Ibn Kathīr, *Bidāya* (the section concerning the "stories of the prophets"); id., *Tafsīr*, ed. Ghunaym; Mālik, *Muwaṭṭaʾ*; al-Nuwayrī, Abū l-ʿAbbās Aḥmad b. ʿAbd al-Wahhāb, *Nihāyat al-ʿarab fī funūn al-adab*, Cairo 1938; Suyūṭī, *Durr*, iii, 601; Ṭabarī, *Tafsīr*, Cairo 1954; id., *Taʾrīkh*; Tirmidhī, *Ṣaḥīḥ*, 3075.

Secondary: J. van Ess, *Zwischen Ḥadīth und Theologie. Studien zum Entstehen prädestiniatischer Überlieferung*, Berlin/New York 1975; I. Goldziher, *Introduction to Islamic theology and law*, trans. A. and R. Hamori, Princeton 1981; Izutsu, *Concepts*; Fazlur Rahman, *Major themes of the Qurʾān*, Minneapolis 1994[2].

Good Deeds

Meritorious acts that will accrue to an individual's benefit on the day of judgment. The term normally translated as "good deeds" *(ḥasana*, pl. *ḥasanāt)* occurs twenty-nine times in the Qurʾān. Related are two words, usually translated as "good," which occur as a noun *(ḥusn)* six times, and as an adjective *(ḥasan)* nineteen times. Another term often translated as "good deeds" *(ṣāliḥāt)* is found 63 times in the Qurʾān, but often with the sense of "good things" or actions which produce good things rather than actions which are consistent with God's will.

According to Muslim exegesis of the Qurʾān, knowledge of good and evil is given to every person. Exegesis of Q 7:172-3 recounts how all of Adam's (see ADAM AND EVE) descendants made a covenant (q.v.) with God before they were born. Q 91:7-10 and 9:8 have been interpreted to indicate that all people possess a conscience that distinguishes good from evil. Acts of worship are also equated with doing good deeds. Q 28:59 states that God has not destroyed a people (see PUNISHMENT STORIES) to whom he has not first sent one of his messengers (see MESSENGER) reminding them of God and the distinction between good and evil (q.v.). Commentary on Q 23:12 and 23:115 emphasizes that God created people for the express purpose of worshipping him. In his *Tafsīr* on these verses, Ibn Kathīr (d. 774/1373) remarks that people were created for worship *(ʿibāda)* of God and for establishing his commands *(awāmir)* on earth. In a general sense, to neglect the worship (q.v.) of God and obedience to his commands (see COMMANDMENTS) is to do evil, while to worship and follow God's commands is to do good (see OBEDIENCE). The consequence, then, of doing God's will, which includes the rituals made obligatory upon people, is being saved from punishment in hell (q.v.) and rewarded with eternal life in heaven (q.v.) on the day of judment (see LAST JUDGMENT; REWARD AND PUNISHMENT).

The required Muslim acts of worship are outlined in the Qurʾān and more fully developed in later Islamic legal codes derived from the Qurʾān and the example of the prophet Muḥammad (see ḤADĪTH AND THE QURʾĀN; SUNNA). These rituals include prayer (q.v.; Q 11:114; 17:78-9; 20:130; 30:17-8), fasting (q.v.; Q 2:184-5), almsgiving (q.v.; Q 2:43, 110, 177, 277; 4:162; 5:55), the pilgrimage (q.v.; Q 2:158, 196-203; 3:97; 5:2; 22:26-33) and, according to some schools of Muslim thought, striving in the service of God (*jihād fī sabīli llāhi*, Q 2:216, 244; 9:20; 22:78; 25:52; 26:69; 61:11; see JIHĀD). In addition to fulfilling these ritual obligations, doing good involves following the laws of God on earth, as these are expressed in the Qurʾān and the example of the prophet Muḥammad, and accumulated in what is known as the *sharīʿa* (see LAW AND THE QURʾĀN).

Good deeds also include spontaneous, non-prescribed acts that arise from addressing situations in daily life with an attitude of serving God. The result of such acts is "sound" or "proper benefit" *(ṣāliḥ)*, whereas not living with a focus on service of God produces "fruitless" or "unproductive" *(bāṭil)* results. The Qurʾān often refers to people who do good as the "upright" *(ṣāliḥūn)* who are worshippers of God (Q 21:105; 22:14). The prophet sent to the people of Thamūd (q.v.) is named Ṣāliḥ (q.v.; Q 7:73-9; 11:61-8; 26:141-59; 27:45-53), which could be translated as "the one who does good." According to Q 4:69, those with whom God is pleased include the prophets (*nabiyyūn*, see PROPHETS AND PROPHETHOOD), the righteous *(ṣiddīqūn)*, the martyrs (*shuhadāʾ*, see MARTYR), and the upright *(ṣāliḥūn)*. Q 6:85 identifies Zechariah (q.v.), John the Baptist (q.v.), Jesus (q.v.), and Elijah (q.v.) as being among the upright *(kullun mina l-ṣāliḥīn)*. See FAITH for a further discussion of the connection between belief and good deeds; see also EVIL DEEDS; ETHICS AND THE QURʾĀN.

Brannon M. Wheeler

Bibliography

Primary: Ibn Kathīr, *Tafsīr*.
Secondary: M. Fakhry, *Ethical theories in Islam*, Leiden 1991, esp. chap. 1; I. Goldziher, *Introduction to Islamic theology and law*, trans. A. and R. Hamori, Princeton 1981, especially 16-20, 41-2; Izutsu, *Concepts*; id., *The structure of the ethical terms in the Koran. A study in semantics. vol. 2 of Keio University studies in the humanities and social relations*, Tokyo 1959, esp. chap. 13; Fazlur Rahman, *Major themes of the Qurʾān*, Minneapolis 1994²; R. Roberts, *The social laws of the Qurʾān*, London 1971 (useful introduction to the non-ritual laws found in the Qurʾān).

Good News

Tidings of welcome events. In the Qurʾān, "good news" (*bushrā*, as well as various permutations of the second verbal form of the root *b-sh-r*) signifies the announcement of a birth and, by extension, other welcome occurrences. Thus, the prediction of Isaac (q.v.) and Jacob (q.v.) given to Sarah was good news (Q 11:69-74; 15:51-5; 29:31; 37:100-1, 112; 51:28) as were the announcements of John the Baptist (q.v.) to Zechariah (q.v.; Q 3:39; 19:7) and of Jesus (q.v.) to Mary (q.v.; Q 3:45). Jesus himself proclaimed the good news of the coming of Muḥammad (Q 61:6). The good news when the caravan (q.v.) found Joseph (q.v.) in the well (*yā-bushrā,* Q 12:19) is perhaps to be metaphorically related to the term's use for annunciations, as may also be the case with the messenger (q.v.) who told Jacob that his son Joseph still lived and was thus a "bearer of good news" (*bashīr,* Q 12:96). It is perhaps in an extended sense that the winds (see AIR AND WIND) bear good news *(yursilu l-riyāḥa bushran):* They go before God's mercy (q.v.), bearing clouds and rain to parched deserts (Q 7:57; 25:48; such extension does not, however, fully account for the statement at Q 30:46 that [God] sends winds as heralds of good news *[yursila l-riyāḥi mubashshirātin],* enabling ships [q.v.] to sail). The term can also be used ironically, as when the Qur'ān refers to the "good news" of the birth of a female child — addressing an audience for whom such news would not have been good at all (*bushshira,* Q 16:58-9; 43:16-7; see CHILDREN; INFANTICIDE).

In a broader signification, God has good news for those who abandon evil (see GOOD AND EVIL), who listen to the divine word and serve him (Q 39:17-8), who are pious (see PIETY) and his friends (Q 10:62-4; 19:97; see FRIENDS AND FRIENDSHIP), who believe (Q 2:25, 97, 223; 7:188; 10:2, 87; 18:2; 27:1-2; see BELIEF AND UNBELIEF; FAITH), humble themselves (Q 22:34), submit (Q 16:89, 102; see OBEDIENCE; ISLAM), do good (Q 2:25; 17:9; 18:2; 22:37; 46:12; see GOOD DEEDS) and are patient (Q 2:155; see TRUST AND PATIENCE). Unfortunately, most reject the good news and consequently neither hear nor know it (Q 34:28; 41:4; see GRATITUDE AND INGRATITUDE).

God's good news applies to both this life and the next (Q 10:62-4), banishing despair (q.v.; Q 15:55). The message of assurance and divine assistance given to the Muslims before the battle of Badr (q.v.) was *bushrā* (Q 3:126; 8:10). Preeminently, though, the good news is the promise of paradise (q.v.) for the righteous. This is the message that Muḥammad was told to convey (Q 2:25). Jesus brought good news (*mubashshiran,* Q 61:6), and Moses and Aaron were ordered to bring good news to the believers (Q 10:87). Such tidings are sent to all, but are conjoined with a warning to those who reject them (Q 17:9-10; see REWARD AND PUNISHMENT). Prophets bear these dual tidings (Q 2:213; 4:165; 6:48; 18:56; see PROPHETS AND PROPHETHOOD). So it was with Muḥammad, who, like all prophets, is both a warner (q.v.; *nadhīr*) and a bearer of good news (*bashīr,* Q 2:119; 5:19; 7:188; 10:2; 11:2; 17:105; 19:97; 25:56; 33:45; 34:28; 35:24; 48:8). The Qur'ān itself has this dual function (Q 41:1-4). In fact, it is not only a bearer of good news (Q 17:9), but *is* good news (Q 16:89, 102; 27:1-2; 46:12). Thus, in addition to the human prophets and messengers, God conveys the good news through scripture (Q 18:2) and angelic messengers (Q 2:97; 3:39, 45; 15:51-5; 29:31; 51:24-8; 69:74; cf. Q 3:126; 8:10).

On judgment day (see LAST JUDGMENT), believers will receive the good news of their admission into the gardens of paradise (Q 9:20-1; 18:2; 42:22-3; 57:12). In the eschatological context (see ESCHATOLOGY), *bushrā* (or various permutations of the second verbal form of *b-sh-r*) can ironically denote the punishment of the wicked (3:21; 4:138; 9:3, 34; 31:7; 45:8; 84:24) for whom, in the strict sense, ultimately there will be no good news (Q 25:22; compare 17:10).

Daniel C. Peterson

Bibliography
Jeffery, *For. vocab.*, 79-80; Lane; G. Widengren, *Muḥammad. The apostle of God and his ascension. (King and Saviour V)*, Uppsala 1955, 185-6 (for correction of Jeffery citation).

Gospel

In Christianity, the "good news" preached about Jesus Christ; in the Qurʾān, part of the divine message given to Jesus (q.v.). Of the twelve times the Gospel *(al-injīl)* is mentioned in the Qurʾān, in nine of them it occurs in conjunction with the mention of the Torah (q.v.; *al-tawrāt*), as a scripture sent down by God (see SCRIPTURE AND THE QURʾĀN; BOOK). Together with wisdom (q.v.; *al-ḥikma*), the Torah and the Gospel appear to comprise the 'scripture' *(al-kitāb)* that the Qurʾān says God taught to Jesus (Q 3:48; 5:110). Twice the Qurʾān says explicitly that God brought Jesus the Gospel (Q 5:46; 57:27). And once the Qurʾān instructs the 'People of the Gospel' to judge in accordance with that which God sent down to them (Q 5:47; see CHRISTIANS AND CHRISTIANITY).

In a number of passages the Qurʾān clearly presumes in its audience a prior knowledge of Gospel characters and narratives (q.v.). In some passages the Qurʾān closely parallels narratives to be found in the canonical, Christian Gospel (cf. e.g. Q 3:45-7); in others one finds some motifs familiar from the apocryphal Gospels of the Christians, or other sources of early Christian lore (cf. e.g. Q 5:110). A number of qurʾānic sayings of Jesus, and narratives about him, have no known parallels in extant Christian texts. What is more, the Qurʾān clearly teaches that the future coming of Muḥammad was written in both the Torah and the Gospel and was foretold by Jesus himself (cf. Q 7:157; 61:6).

The Arabic word *injīl* is ultimately derived from the Greek *evangelion,* but the exact philological path by which the term in its present form came into Arabic is unclear (see FOREIGN VOCABULARY). Noting that all but one of the mentions of the Gospel in the Qurʾān are in sūras traditionally designated as 'Medinan' (see CHRONOLOGY AND THE QURʾĀN), some scholars have suggested that the Ethiopic form of the word, *wangēl,* is not only philologically, but chronologically the most likely ancestor of the Arabic term.

Conceptually, in the Qurʾānic view, the Gospel is a scripture that God gave to Jesus, on the order of the Torah that God gave to Moses (q.v.), and even on the order of the Qurʾān that God gave to Muḥammad (cf. Q 9:111). Contrariwise, in the usual Christian view, the Gospel is the proclamation in the human community of the 'good news' of the salvation of all human beings that God has accomplished in Christ. Most Christians have believed that the Gospel was recorded under divine inspiration by the four evangelists in the four canonical texts: the Gospel according to Matthew, the Gospel according to Mark, the Gospel according to Luke, and the Gospel according to John, all of them written originally in Greek (see REVELATION AND INSPIRATION). Qurʾānic uses of the term *injīl,* however, are all in the singular and betray no awareness of multiple Gospels. The conceptual differences between the Christian and the Islamic views of the Gospel soon gave rise among Muslim commentators to the charge that Christian have 'distorted' *(al-taḥrīf)* the original Gospel of which the Qurʾān speaks, in the way that the Qurʾān suggests the Jews distorted the Torah (cf. Q 4:46; 5:13; see POLEMIC AND POLEMICAL LANGUAGE; JEWS AND JUDAISM). Some early Muslim writers say that the original Gospel was written in Hebrew, or in Aramaic, both of them languages in use in the Jewish community at the time of Jesus. As for the Gospel in Arabic, while one strand of

Islamic tradition credits Waraqa b. Nawfal (see INFORMANTS) with a translation of the text into Arabic, the remaining textual evidence suggests that the earliest translations were made after the rise of Islam, from Greek originals, by Christian monks in Palestine, in the late eighth century.

There is some evidence that the term Gospel was also sometimes used in the early Islamic period to indicate the whole New Testament, in the same way that the name of the Torah was used not only for the Pentateuch, but for all the books of the Jewish scriptures. While passages were liberally quoted from the Christian Gospel by some early Muslim writers, such as Ibn Qutayba (d. 276/889) and al-Yaʿqūbī (d. 292/905), among others, in general, early Muslim writers referred to Gospel characters and Gospel narratives in the forms in which they appear in the Qurʾān or in other early Islamic texts. Many sayings of Jesus current in Islamic texts have no known Christian counterparts.

A text called the *Gospel of Barnabas* has had a wide circulation in modern times. It was discovered in an Italian manuscript in Amsterdam in 1709. Since its translation into Arabic in the early 20th century, some have claimed that it preserves the original Gospel, of which the Qurʾān speaks. In fact, the *Gospel of Barnabas* has been shown to have its origins in the western Mediterranean world, probably in Spain, in the 16th century.

Sidney H. Griffith

Bibliography
M. De Epalza, Le milieu hispano-moresque de l'évangile islamisant de Barnabe, in *Islamochristiana* 8 (1982), 159-183; J.-M. Gaudeul & R. Caspar, Textes de la tradition musulmane concernant le *taḥrīf* (falsification) des écritures, in *Islamochristiana* 6 (1980), 61-104; S.H. Griffith, The Gospel in Arabic. An inquiry into its appearance in the first Abbasid century, in *OC* 69 (1985), 126-67; Jeffery, *For. vocab.;* T. Khalidi, *The Muslim Jesus. Sayings and stories in Islamic literature,* Cambridge, MA 2001; J.D. McAuliffe, The qurʾānic context of Muslim biblical scholarship, in *Islam and Christian-Muslim relations* 7 (1996), 141-58; T. Pulcini, *Exegesis as polemical discourse. Ibn Ḥazm on Jewish and Christian scriptures,* Atlanta, GA 1998; D. Sox, *The gospel of Barnabas,* London 1984; R. Stichel, Bemerkungen zum Barnabas-Evangelium, in *Byzantinoslavica* 43 (1982), 189-201; J. Carra de Vaux [G.C. Anawati], Indjīl, in *EI²*, iii, 1205-1208.

Gossip

Idle discussion of an absent party's personal affairs. Although no exact equivalent to the English "gossip" is to be found in the Qurʾān, there are several explicit condemnations of the closely related phenomenon of backbiting, that is, deliberately spreading information, whether true or false, to someone's discredit; and two further passages address, somewhat obliquely, painful incidents of destructive talk involving the Prophet's wives (see WIVES OF THE PROPHET).

Backbiting (ightiyāb, lamz, hamz, namīm)
At Q 49:11-2 the believers are enjoined to avoid expressing disrespect for one another in a number of ways — mockery (q.v.), defamation *(lā talmizū anfusakum),* the use of offensive nicknames, undue suspicion (q.v.), spying, and backbiting: "... and do not backbite *(lā yaghtab)* one another — would one of you like to eat the flesh of his dead brother (see DEATH AND THE DEAD; BROTHER AND BROTHERHOOD)? You would hate that!" Although the specific term used here for backbiting (from a root meaning "to be absent") does not recur elsewhere in the Qurʾān, the vaguer term for defamation, *lamz,* is attested. In two instances (Q 9:58, 79), concerning criticism directed at the Prophet and the believers over the distribution of alms (*ṣadaqāt,* see ALMSGIVING), it is generally understood by the

exegetes as referring to face-to-face criticism. Most of them interpret the *lumaza* in the laconic condemnation at Q 104:1 ("Woe to every *humaza lumaza!*") in the same way, contrasting such a person with the *humaza* who only defames people behind their backs; but others reverse these definitions or distinguish the two in terms of gesture (or bodily attack) versus explicit speech. The *hamazāt* of demons (*shayāṭīn,* see DEVIL) at Q 23:97 are said to be insidious whisperings; but elsewhere, in a string of epithets describing evildoers (see EVIL DEEDS) the Prophet is not to heed (Q 68:11), the commentators identify the *hammāz* as a backbiter and the immediately following *mashshā᾽ bi-namīm* ("he who walks around with harmful information") as a malicious talebearer.

Gossip and the Prophet's wives

Certainly the most notorious case of malicious gossip to which the Qur᾽ān makes reference is that of the "scandal of ʿĀ᾽isha" (*ḥadīth al-ifk,* see ʿĀ᾽ISHA BINT ABĪ BAKR), the vicious rumors that swirled around the Prophet's wife when she was accidently left behind in the desert during the return from a military engagement and was rescued by a young man. The attacks on her virtue (q.v.) were finally squelched only by a revelation (Q 24:11-20) condemning the scandalmongers and admonishing the believers to recognize a lie (q.v.; *ifk*) and a slander *(buhtān)* as such and to refrain from passing on that of which they have no knowledge (Schoeler, 119-63). Preceding this passage and linked with it (Q 24:4-5) is the stipulation of a punishment (see BOUNDARIES AND PRECEPTS; CHASTISEMENT AND PUNISHMENT) of eighty lashes for those who falsely accuse chaste women of adultery (see ADULTERY AND FORNICATION) without producing four witnesses (in legal parlance, the offense of *qadhf*). Much less clear is a reference (Q 66:1-5) to a breach of confidence on the part of one of the Prophet's wives, for which the exegetical literature provides a variety of explanatory (and mutually incompatible) accounts, but for which the Qur᾽ān, in any case, recommends repentance (see REPENTANCE AND PENANCE; VIRTUES AND VICES).

Everett K. Rowson

Bibliography

Primary: Ibn Abī l-Dunyā, *Kitāb al-Ghība wa-l-namīma,* ed. ʿA.ʿA. ʿUmar, Bombay 1988 (Qur᾽ān and *ḥadīth*); Ṭabarī, *Tafsīr,* Beirut 1984, vi, 393-4, 429-33; ix, 241-2, 265-88; xi, 389-97; xii, 147-56, 182-4, 687-8.

Secondary: G. Schoeler, *Charakter und Authentie der muslimischen Uberlieferüngen über das Leben Mohammeds,* Berlin 1996; B.F. Stowasser, *Women in the Qur᾽ān, traditions, and interpretation,* Oxford 1994, 94-7 (the Prophet's wives).

Grace

Undeserved favor or unmerited salvation. Grace has no linguistic or conceptual equivalent in the Qur᾽ān, although *faḍl* in certain contexts suggests shades of that meaning. Q 2:64, criticizing the Israelites (see CHILDREN OF ISRAEL) for breaking a covenant (q.v.) with God, says "Were it not for God's *faḍl* upon you and his mercy (q.v.), you would have been among the losers." This implies that while, strictly-speaking, the breach called for punishment (see CHASTISEMENT AND PUNISHMENT), God's *faḍl* gave the Israelites respite and another chance. It was David's (q.v.) special gift that when he sang the praises of God, mountains and birds sang with him — this was a *faḍl* from God (Q 34:10). One of Solomon's (q.v.) courtiers who possessed "knowledge of the book (q.v.)" brought him the Queen of Sheba's (q.v.; see also BILQĪS) throne before Solomon could blink his eyes — this, too, was a *faḍl* from God (Q 27:40). According to several verses, God, who possesses great *faḍl,* gives the gift of prophecy and revelation (see PROPHETS AND PROPHETHOOD; REVELATION AND INSPIRATION) to whomever he likes — thus bestowing his *faḍl* on whomever he likes (for example Q 2:90, 105; 3:74; 4:113; 57:29). In the same vein are verses that speak of the election (q.v.) of Israel (for example Q 2:47, 122). In all these verses *faḍl* represents divine bounty that is uncaused and freely given.

In the above-noted Q 2:64 (and elsewhere) *faḍl* occurs together with *raḥma,* "mercy," suggesting that while the two words belong to the same general category of divine kindness, they differ in their import. The clue to the difference may be in the literal meaning of *faḍl,* which represents excess — in this case excess, or rather superabundance, of mercy which cannot be fully explained by reference to the calculus of merit and reward or sin and punishment (see Q 4:173; 24:38; and 35:30, which seem to distinguish between deserved reward and supervenient mercy; see REWARD AND PUNISHMENT; SIN, MAJOR AND MINOR).

But even when it signifies something like unmerited favor, *faḍl* in the Qurʾān has certain distinguishing characteristics. First, it is informed by divine wisdom (q.v.). Q 6:124 says that the omniscient God "knows very well where to bestow his message" — that is, he selects the most suitable person to serve as his messenger (q.v.). Second, it is purposive: God chose the Israelites, but they were expected to be grateful for the election and show their gratitude by fulfilling the covenant God had made with them; and when they violated the terms of the covenant, they were treated with lenience, but only so that they could have another opportunity to fulfill the covenant. Divine *faḍl,* in other words, makes a certain demand on those who receive it — namely, that they show gratitude to God. It is for this reason that *faḍl* and *shukr,* "gratitude," are bracketed together in many verses, for example in Q 34:13, which calls upon the followers of David *(āl Dāwūd)* to offer gratitude (see GRATITUDE AND INGRATITUDE).

To sum up, while *faḍl* may be said to represent the qurʾānic concept of grace, it essentially means bounty and has special connotations in the qurʾānic context. In later centuries, the theme of *faḍl* would be used in the polemic against the Qadarites and Muʿtazilites (see MUʿTAZILĪS) concerning the question of human free will (cf. Ṭabarī, *Tafsīr,* i, 162-3, ad Q 1:5; Gilliot, *Elt,* 266-7; see FREEDOM AND PREDESTINATION). See also BLESSING.

Mustansir Mir

Bibliography
Primary: al-Rāghib al-Iṣfahānī, *Mufradāt,* s.v. *f-ḍ-l;* Ṭabarī, *Tafsīr,* ed. Shākir.
Secondary: Gilliot, *Elt.*

Grains see GRASSES; AGRICULTURE AND VEGETATION

Grammar and the Qurʾān

Qurʾānic language and text

Modern students of Arabic linguistics have been studying several fundamental questions about qurʾānic language and text ever since the earliest formulations of these investigations some hundred years ago (see LANGUAGE OF THE QURʾĀN; LITERARY STRUCTURES OF THE QURʾĀN). The qurʾānic text constitutes one of the three early language corpora that reflect language varieties of Arabic speakers in pre-Islamic Arabia (see ARABIC LANGUAGE). The other two corpora are poetry (usually inclusive of almost all the pre-ʿAbbāsid Islamic inventory; see POETRY AND POETS) and vestiges of the spoken dialects (q.v.). Since the recording of all three corpora has reached us through the medium of early Arab philologists, whose earliest extant writings were composed in the last quarter of the second/eighth century, none of them has escaped the scepticism of modern scholars regarding their value as authentic manifestations of the language situation of pre-Islamic Arabic.

The character of the Qurʾān's language has been investigated in comparison with the poetic idiom and the living language of the Arabs (q.v.), tribal nomads (q.v.) and town dwellers (see CITY). Vollers *(Volkssprache und Schriftsprache)* was the first to formulate a coherent hypothesis, based on the well-known diglossia of modern Arabic, which suggested that the cleavage between the poetic language and the spoken language was related to two opposed modes by which the qurʾānic text was transmitted. The first reflected the genuine living language of the two Ḥijāzī communities of Meccans and Medinese (see GEOGRAPHY; MECCA; MEDINA), the original language in which Muḥammad addressed his people (see ORALITY). The other was a later modification by Arab philologists, grounded in the grammatical standards formulated by this scholarly body on the basis of the poetic idiom that they had carefully studied. According to Vollers, a prominent element in the cleavage between these two modes of transmission was the lack of case and mood *(iʿrāb)* endings in the original text and their presence in the philologists' radical modification of it. This distinction is also fundamental in the typological classification of standard Arabic (*iʿrābi*, synthetic) and the modern (non-*iʿrābi*, analytical) dialects. It also corresponds with the linguistic situation of Arabic in the medieval Islamic world as far as the documentation of that era goes, with the somewhat debatable exception of Bedouin (q.v.) dialects during the first Islamic centuries.

Study of the history of Arabic diglossia resides currently in a distinction between old Arabic (OA) and neo-Arabic (NA) as two types of this language. A largely accepted view propagated by Nöldeke (*Beiträge*, 1-14; id., *Neue Beiträge*, 1-5), which rejects Vollers's thesis, identifies the three corpora of testimony associated with the language of pre-Islamic Arabs as OA. Its direct offspring consists of the medieval literary idiom and modern standard Arabic (MSA). Accordingly, NA developed later than the emergence of the Qurʾān and the evolution of its text. Although adherents of this view admit that some difference could have existed between the language of the Qurʾān and either the pre-Islamic poetry or the language of the townsmen of the Ḥijāz, they nevertheless argue that these differences could not have been large, considering the typological identity shared by these corpora. Some of the central arguments for the genuineness of the extant qurʾānic text as a representative of the original prophetic message and of an OA idiom will be presented in the course of our discussion below of the structure of the qurʾānic language (see also FORM AND STRUCTURE OF THE QURʾĀN).

A recent discussion of the definition of classical Arabic (CA) has attempted to draw a structural distinction between the language of these three corpora of material and that of later medieval literary production up to the fourth/eleventh century. Fischer (Die Perioden; Das Altarabische; *Grammatik*) counted some thirty items attested in the earliest corpora, which distinguish their language from that of the later stage. Accordingly, he called this distinct language layer "pre-classical Arabic." Included in his list are such morphological phenomena as verbal forms from outside the fifteen stems *(harāqa, irʿawā)*, *nisba* endings of a *yamānin* type rather than *-iyy* ending, use of the *faʿāli* pattern, relative use of a basically demonstrative *al-ulā,* an inflected cataphoric pronominal *-kum* in *dhālikum,* fifth and sixth stems without *-a-* following the characteristic *t-* (e.g. *izzayyana* < **itzayyana* = *tazayyana),* the forms *ẓalta/ ẓilta* = *ẓalilta* of the geminite verb, the energicus enclitic *-an* with the imperative (the energicus form is the imperfect or imperative plus *-an* or *-anna*), *ayyatuhā* as the vocative particle, the *-ta* in *rubbata,* use of *ʿalla* for *laʿalla,* etc., and some syntactic phenomena such as *mā al-ḥijāziyya,* occurrence of the energicus in conditional clauses, *lākin* followed by a subject rather than a verb, and imperfect verbal forms following perfect verbs. Although Ullmann (Vorklassisches Arabisch) indicated that all these phenomena are documented in later layers of standard Arabic, this search for a distinct common denominator of the corpora of the early stage of Arabic is instructive as a fresh attempt to revive the typological dimension of the study of Arabic and as an effort to be attentive to the role played by the grammarians and other philologists in the formation of the language norms of the later layer.

Outline of the grammarians' study of the Qurʾān

A group of works from the end of the second/eighth and the beginning of the third/ninth century constitutes the main body of sources about early grammarians' interest in the language of the Qurʾān. These works include Sībawayhi's (d. prob. 180/796) *Kitāb,* al-Farrāʾ's (d. 207/822) *Maʿānī l-Qurʾān,* al-Akhfash's (d. between 210 and 221/825 and 835) commentary under the same title, and Abū ʿUbayda's (d. 209/824-5) *Majāz al-Qurʾān.* Versteegh studied the few grammatical observations and a list of forty-one terms of linguistic relevance in five early *tafsīr* collections that are attributed to the exegetical effort of the middle second/eighth-century onward (that is, exegetical works attributed to Mujāhid b. Jabr [d. 104/722], Zayd b. ʿAlī [d. 122/740], Muḥammad b. al-Sāʾib al-Kalbī [d. 146/763], Muqātil b. Sulaymān [d. 150/767], Maʿmar b. Rashīd [d. 153/770], and Sufyān al-Thawrī [d. 161/778]; see Versteegh, *Grammar and exegesis,* 41-2). His conclusions about the later development of Arabic grammar, however, can hardly be supported by the evidence of the grammatically oriented sources mentioned above, which include frequent mention of yet earlier authorities who had developed grammatical thinking by their combined study of the three corpora of early Arabic. The patterns of their scholarly effort integrated a meticulous analysis of given sources and the sophistication of a grammatical theory with a rich vocabulary of linguistic terms.

We are better acquainted with the achievements of the two centers in Kūfa and Baṣra, although Ḥijāzī scholars are also mentioned in the early sources at random (cf. Talmon, An eighth century school). The growing discipline of scholarly studies in grammar was then taken over by al-Khalīl b. Aḥmad (d. ca. 170/786) and his disciple Sībawayhi, whose criticism of contemporary theory and whose innovative advanced analogical methodology soon became the leading stream of Iraqi linguistics. Sībawayhi's *al-Kitāb* has ever since stood as a source of inspiration for all generations of later grammarians. While future study of grammatically oriented qurʾānic exegesis (*tafsīr,* see EXEGESIS OF THE QURʾĀN: CLASSICAL AND MEDIEVAL) from the third/ninth century on will show the extent to which it continued to follow the patterns of pre-Khalīlian grammar, in what follows we shall concentrate on the interest of the Kūfan and Baṣran grammarians in qurʾānic grammar.

One should bear in mind, however, that the authors of the sources upon which this article will concentrate, namely Sībawayhi, al-Farrā', and the others, are far better recorded in their study of many of the topics mentioned in what follows and other observations about qur'ānic grammar than the earlier sources. Only a handful of notes exist in the early sources that indicate pre-Sībawayhian interest in phonetical matters, among them the treatment of two consecutive *hamzas* by Ibn Abī Isḥāq (d. 117/735) in Qur'ān reading (Sībawayhi, *Kitāb,* ii, 458.19; Akhfash, *Ma'ānī,* 565), such as *'a'āmantum* in Q 7:123 (other cases are mentioned by Nöldeke, *GQ,* iii, 45). Other problems of assimilation are mentioned in the sources concerning the irregular *yikhkhiṭṭifu* of a reflexive variant of *yakhṭafu* in Q 2:20 (Farrā', *Ma'ānī,* i, 18) and the shift of *s* > *ṣ* in *bi-muṣayṭirin* (Q 88:22) and *al-muṣayṭirūna* (Q 52:37; cf. Talmon, *Arabic grammar,* 265). Sībawayhi's phonetical studies, particularly his survey of the consonantal inventory in chapter 565 and the following chapters of the *Kitāb,* are closely related to Qur'ān readings.

To return now to the four foundational sources mentioned above, early morphological analysis of qur'ānic material included etymological study of the singular form of the *hapax legomena al-zabāniya* (Q 96:18; cf. Akhfash, *Ma'ānī,* 582) and *abābīl* (Q 105:3; cf. Talmon, *Arabic grammar,* 271), inquiry concerning the structure of *wayka'anna* and *wayka'annahu* (Q 28:82, Talmon, op. cit., 269), as well as the root of *yatasannah, s-n-n* or *s-n-h* (Q 2:259; id., op. cit., 267), and discussion of exceptional forms in the verbal paradigms, namely *āmarnā* (Q 17:16, *amarnā*), whose identification as a first stem verb is considered (Abū 'Ubayda, *Majāz,* i, 372). It is not evident, however, that early interest in the irregular form *mastu* of the originally geminite *masastu* (in Khalīl, *al-'Ayn;* see Talmon, *Arabic grammar,* 267 f.) is evoked by interest in the analogous morphological shift found in *ẓalta, ẓaltum* as they occur in Q 20:97 and 56:65, respectively. In general, early Arabic grammarians focused on the study of *i'rāb,* and its intricate rules and their observations were applied to qur'ānic morphology. The triptote variant of *ṭuwā/ṭuwan* at Q 79:16 (but not Q 20:12) was debated (Akhfash, *Ma'ānī,* 566); the non-nunated *mathnā* at Q 4:3 is identified by Abū 'Amr b. al-'Alā' (d. 154/771) as an "adjective" *(ṣifa)* with reference to its sense *ithnayni thnayni* (Sībawayhi, *Kitāb,* ii, 15.4). This formulation corresponds partly with the early grammarians' application of a rule of "deviation" *(ṣarf)* which relates non-nunated and diptote forms to their equivalents in the triptotic domain and a "deviation" process as the reason for a "loss" of full inflexional features.

Early sophistication in the grammatical examination of qur'ānic morphology is demonstrated (Talmon, *Arabic grammar,* 273) in the study of the pair *ḥūr 'īn,* "women of white complexion and wide open eyes," (Q 44:54; 52:20; and 56:22; see HOURIS) in which the opposite order is presented as an existing reading with the form *wa-ḥīrun 'īnun.* The shift of *ḥūr (ḥ-w-r)* to *ḥīr* is a case of attraction caused by the following *'īn ('-y-n),* and Abū Zayd al-Anṣarī (d. 214 or 215/830-1) quotes the view of "grammar experts" *(ḥudhdhāq ahl al-'arabiyya)* to this effect (Abū Zayd, *Nawādir,* 574). Next, the author resorts to Khalīl's authority for an explanation of the principle of attraction (with the sample phrase *juḥru ḍabbin kharibin,* "a ruined lair/burrow of a lizard," instead of *[...] kharibun*), and concludes with an analysis of the features of this pair of adjectives which justify identification of this occurrence as attraction.

In the early sources, syntactic study is the most extensively reported and most developed field of interest in qur'ānic grammar. It seems proper to conclude that this is the result of the general tendency among the Arab grammarians to emphasize the importance of *iʿrāb* in linguistic studies, a tendency which has endured. As a rule, qurʾānic and poetic language are understood to be one fully integrated system (*pace* Wansbrough's review of Müller's Untersuchungen, in *BSOAS* 33 [1970], 389); consequently poetic structures are taken as evidence in the analysis of issues of qurʾānic syntax. We shall give as an exemple *balā qādirīna* (Q 75:4), mentioned by Kinberg (*Lexicon of al-Farrāʾ*, 12). Al-Farrāʾ records a theorem, disseminated by anonymous grammarians, that the accusative case *(naṣb)* of the active participle results from a shift *(ṣarf)* from a finite verb form *(naqdiru)*. It is clear that this *ṣarf* principle, introduced earlier in the domain of morphology, played a major role in the theory of pre-Sībawayhian grammar. A poetic verse quoted by these grammarians as an illustration *(ḥujja)* was al-Farazdaq's (d. 110/728 or 112/730) *ʿalā qasamin lā ashtimu l-dahra musliman wa-lā khārijan min fiyya zūru kalāmi*, "swearing that I shall never curse a Muslim and will never utter a lie," in which *khārijan* is presented as an active participle shifted from the finite *yakhruju*.

Another citation is presented here as an illustration of the difference between the approach of early exegetes and grammarians in their treatment of identical structures. Q 72:18 reads *wa-anna l-masājida li-llāhi fa-lā tadʿū maʿa llāhi aḥadan* ("and the mosques are for God, so do not invoke anyone along with God"). Sībawayhi (*Kitāb*, i, 413.12) attributes to the exegetes an *ad sensum* interpretation, namely that the sentence *wa-anna*... is subordinate to an unexpressed verb "it is revealed" *(ūḥiya)*. The grammarians offer a more sophisticated analysis which is based on its identification of the *wa-anna* clause as a structure that had undergone permutation and elision of *li-* with the sense of "because" (<**fa-lā tadʿū*... *li-anna l-masājida li-llāhi*). This structure is identified also in Q 23:52. The elision of *li-* is formalized in the grammarians' jargon as *fī mawḍiʿ al-jarr*, "[the clause opened with *anna* is] in a status of a noun which follows a preposition." This passage is documented in Sībawayhi's *Kitāb* (i, 413.17) and the information about the grammarians' view is reported from al-Khalīl, but in al-Farrāʾ's commentary it is mentioned explicitly as al-Kisāʾī's (d. ca. 189/805) view (Farrāʾ, *Maʿānī*, i, 58.7, 148.8; ii, 173.9, also 238.13). It is not insignificant to note that two of the seven official readers of the ʿUthmānic Qurʾān (see CODICES OF THE QURʾĀN; COLLECTION OF THE QURʾĀN), Abū ʿAmr b. al-ʿAlāʾ and al-Kisāʾī, are recorded in early treatises of grammatical orientation as the authoritative grammarians of their days, scholars who mastered a sophisticated methodology of grammatical analysis and an advanced technical vocabulary.

It is important to mention that in the pre-Khalīlian stage of Arabic grammar, the formulation of several major syntactic categories seems to have been defined according to strict dictation of qurʾānic exegetical effort. Prominent among these is the *ibtidāʾ* category, which at that period was not defined in terms of governance grammar (and relations with *khabar/mabnī ʿalayhi*), but according to its relations with, in fact independence of, the preceding speech unit. It is especially effective in the analysis of written texts, in which boundaries of independent segments are not always clear, and case and mood marks can be crucial for the distinction of a fresh new utterance from a segment related to an antecedent.

Linguistic studies in the qurʾānic text continued intensively throughout the Middle Ages. Generally speaking, the accumulated knowledge provided by the scholars of the early centuries circulated in the later writings, with a growing tendency to improve its categorization. The study of the inimitability (q.v.) of the Qurʾān *(iʿjāz al-Qurʾān),* a branch of Arabic rhetoric (see RHETORIC OF THE QURʾĀN), provided a type of language analysis which was only partially dependent upon the principles of Arabic grammar.

In recent years there has been a growing tendency among Muslim scholars to study the language of the Qurʾān not so much in order to ceremonially follow their great medieval predecessors, but by application of some trends of literary criticism and modern fashions of western interest in language, e.g. stylistics and text analysis (see CONTEMPORARY CRITICAL PRACTICES AND THE QURʾĀN).

Sketch of modern linguistic interest in qurʾānic grammar

Elements of qurʾānic grammar were incorporated in virtually all of the main grammars of classical Arabic of the last two centuries. Fischer's chronological division mentioned above has already effected several studies in individual topics of classical Arabic. Surprisingly, the long interest in the Qurʾān expressed by western scholarship has not yielded a satisfactory description of its characteristics and peculiarities with respect to many grammatical issues. Nedjar *(Grammaire fonctionnelle)* is a unique attempt, so far, to create a comprehensive grammar of the Qurʾān, but it is far from complete. Here, we shall briefly highlight the status of qurʾānic grammar in the major systematic treatises of classical Arabic, the important work done by Nöldeke, and the issues covered by modern research in the various domains of qurʾānic grammar. We shall also consider the attitude of some prominent modern scholars regarding the contribution of the medieval Arab grammarians to the study of qurʾānic grammar.

The common tendency to discuss details of qurʾānic grammar within the general context of a presentation of CA features can be observed in Fleischer *(Kleinere Schriften),* Wright *(Grammar),* Reckendorf *(Die Syntaktische Verhältnisse; Arabische Syntax),* and Brockelmann *(Grundriß).* Ewald *(Grammatica critica)* and Nöldeke *(Zur Grammatik)* are exceptional in their more intensive attention to the peculiarities of qurʾānic grammar. Ewald (*Grammatica critica,* ii, 171 f.), for instance, reports the frequency of topicalization structures, in which the subject precedes its verbal predicate ("600 times") and notes its rarity in Arabic, in contrast to Hebrew. Peculiarities of the Qurʾān's agreement rules are discussed by Nöldeke (*Zur Grammatik,* 80, 81) regarding such cases as *jāʾakum/jāʾathum rusuluhum* (cf. Q 3:183 and 10:13, 14: 9, respectively). All these grammars state their position vis-à-vis the grammatical studies of the medieval Arab grammarians. Reservations about the adequacy of medieval explanations, however, are shared by all of them with the exception of Fleischer, about whose attitude Nöldeke expresses severe criticism in the introduction to his *Zur Grammatik.* Further, such reservations are expressed with different degrees of emphasis. In general, the Arab grammarians' theories are judged to be incompatible with the modern linguistic search for an explanation of language facts, whether this is according to the principles of the comparative study of Semitic languages or those of general linguistics. Several examples may illustrate their differences of approach to the analysis of several syntactic structures. Ewald discusses interferences in the coordination of nouns (shift from singular to plural and back to singular) in such cases as Q 40:35, *alladhīna yujādilūna... kabura maqtan* (similarly Q 5:69) and confines this phenomenon to "general sentences," mentions its frequency in Hebrew, and notes its rarity in the language of Arabic texts later than the Qurʾān. Nöldeke (*Zur Grammatik,* 33) considers the circumstantial *(ḥāl)* identification by the Arab grammarians of such accusative abstract nouns as *ṭawʿan wa-karhan* (Q 3:83) but prefers to classify them as gerunds. A series of substantives marked by the accusative in various qurʾānic verses, e.g. *farīḍatan mina llāhi* (Q 4:11, 9:60) were analyzed by the Arab grammarians as *mafʿūl muṭlaq* governed by a covert verb. Nöldeke (*Zur Grammatik,* 35) considers them adverbials and notes their limited use (eight of the nine references are qurʾānic).

Nöldeke's studies present a unique combination of linguistic analysis and consideration of Muḥammad's biography. In his *Zur Grammatik* (33) he examines the apparent irregularity of Q 104:1-2, where a structure with *kull* plus an indefinite singular noun is followed by *alladhī* (which normally follows definite nouns) and concludes that in pronouncing these words which were phrased in general terms, Muḥammad mentally associated them with a concrete rival (see OPPOSITION TO MUḤAMMAD). The scattered remarks made in this book about Muḥammad's language being inarticulate were followed by a famous essay in Nöldeke (Zur Sprache) on syntactical and stylistic peculiarities of the language of the Qurʾān. This study discusses thirty aspects of such peculiarities. Included, among others, are formulaic repetitions (cf. *hal atāka ḥadīthu...*, Zur Sprache, 8), problems resulting from the dictates of rhyme (e.g. shift of a verb form, as in *farīqan kadhdhabtum wa-farīqan taqtulūna* [Q 2:87]; Nöldeke, Zur Sprache, 9; see RHYMED PROSE), correlation of subjective and objective genitives (*huwa ahlu l-taqwā wa-ahlu l-maghfirati,* "He owns [men's] fear [q.v.] and owns mercy" [q.v.; Q 74:56]; Nöldeke, Zur Sprache, 11), repetition of identical words with distinct reference (*alladhīna qāla lahumu l-nāsu inna l-nāsa qad jamaʿū lakum* [Q 3:173] with reference to "allies" and "enemies" [q.v.] respectively; id., op. cit., 11), correlation of finite verbs and participles (*inna l-muṣṣaddiqīna wa-l-muṣṣaddiqāti wa-aqraḍū llāha qarḍan ḥasanan...* [Q 57:18]; Nöldeke, op. cit., 14), elision of the resumptive pronoun in expressions of time (*hal atā ʿalā l-insāni ḥīnun mina l-dahri lam yakun shayʾan madhkūran,* without *[lam yakun] fīhi,* [Q 76:1]; Nöldeke, op. cit., 16 f.), and use of the conjunctive *an* where the negative *allā* is expected (*wa-ḥdharhum an yaftinūka* [Q 5:49]; Nöldeke, op. cit., 19 f.). Nöldeke's thesis was that Muḥammad's pioneering position as the exponent of a new prose genre in his society was responsible for his idiosyncratic grammar and style. Given the accumulated advances in our present knowledge of pre-Islamic Arabic, it is difficult for contemporary scholars to appreciate or affirm Nöldeke's position.

Linguistic studies specific to the Qurʾān following in the pattern of the composition of the comprehensive grammars are few. Spitaler (Die Schreibung des Typus *ṣlwt*) studied the qurʾānic orthography exhibited in *ṣ-l-w-h* and its like. Diem's work on early Arabic orthography (Untersuchungen) is another key contribution to this field (see ARABIC SCRIPT; ORTHOGRAPHY OF THE QURʾĀN). No specific study treats qurʾānic phonology per se. Birkeland's studies on pause and stress in old Arabic *(Altarabische Pausalformen; Stress patterns)* are of special importance. In the field of qurʾānic morphology we have two studies of the verb by Chouémi *(Le verbe dans le Coran)* and Leemhuis *(D and H stems).* Works on qurʾānic syntax include several studies of its tense and aspect characteristics by Reuschel (Wa-kāna llāhu ʿalīman; *Aspekt und Tempus*), Nebes (ʾIn al-muḫaffafa), and Kinberg (Semi-imperfectives). Negation is another topic of intensive interest, already dealt with by Bergsträsser in 1914 *(Verneinungs- und Fragepartikeln)* and more recently by several others. On various aspects of *mafʿūl muṭlaq* there is Talmon (Syntactic category). Studies concerned with types of clauses are Tietz *(Bedingungsatz)* on conditional sentences, Correll ("Ein Esel") on relative clauses, and Goldenberg (*Allāḏī al-maṣdariyya* in Arab grammatical tradition) on the treatment of *alladhī* structures without resumptive pronouns (e.g. in Q 9:69). Syntactic features of the energetic form of the verb are described by Ambros (Syntaktische und stilistische Funktionen; also Zewi, *Syntactical study*). Several small publications concentrate on the function of specific particles: Worrell (The interrogative particle *hal*) studied *hal* and *a-*, Miquel (La particule *innamā;* La particule *ḥattā*) studied *innamā* and *ḥattā,* and Ambros *(Lākin* und *lākinna) lākin* and *lākinna*. Richter *(Der Sprachstil)* and Müller *(Untersuchungen zur Reimprosa)* are, respectively, monographs on the effect of qurʾānic style and rhyme on the Qurʾān's grammatical structure. General questions of the treatment of the Arab grammatical tradition in the Qurʾān include Sībawayhi's use of Qurʾān citations, in Beck's dissertation *(Die Koranzitate),* and *iʿrāb* errors in Burton (Linguistic errors).

A sketch of qurʾānic grammatical structure

In the absence of a comprehensive grammar of the Qurʾān the following sketch comprises a selection of orthographical and grammatical phenomena recorded mainly in the ʿUthmānic text, which are either peculiar to the Qurʾān in comparison with the other corpora of old Arabic, or considered by the present writer to be of special relevance for students of qurʾānic language. It is inescapably technical but will be of interest to those who are well-versed in the structure and semantics of classical Arabic.

Orthographic characteristics

This domain is of special importance for the study of the Qurʾān's language because it provides, according to a largely accepted scholarly view, the most reliable record of this language in the earliest days of the formation of this corpus. Brockelmann (*Grundriß,* i, 53; also 460), illustrates nicely how important the occurrence of *w, y, ā* in the noun's final position is for scholars who want to draw conclusions about the use of case endings in the "Meccan dialect." The following is mainly a synopsis of the detailed description of characteristics given by Nöldeke, *GQ,* iii:

1. Exceptions to the pausal orthography

a. Use of *t* instead of *h* for *tāʾ marbūṭa* in non-pausal state: at least forty-one times, most frequently in *niʿma* (eleven times), *raḥma,* and *imraʾa* (seven times each). Others may be interpreted as plural feminine. Four other words in which *ā* precedes: *marḍāt, al-lāt, hayhāt, dhāt*. This orthographic custom is attested mainly in the construct state *(muḍāf)*.

b. Omission of *w* (five times) and *y* (fifteen times) in word ending, e.g. *yuʾti* for *yuʾtī* (Q 4:146), *sa-nadʿu* for *sa-nadʿū* (Q 96:18). A similar omission of *alif* occurs three times in *ayyuhā* > *ayyuha* before the article.

c. Use of *n* for *tanwīn: kaʾayyin/kāʾin* > *kaʾayyin* (e.g. Q 3:146; 12:105; 22:45).

2. Merger of two particles

This occurs in *mimman, mimmā* (three times for *min mā*), *fīmā* (less frequent *fī mā*), *allan* < *an lan, ammā* (also for "or what," Q 6:143) and others. *Biʾsa mā* are separated on all but one occasion. Other peculiarities in this respect: *yā bna umma* is written *y-b-n-w-m* (Q 20:94), *mā li-(hāʾulāʾi/lladhīna kafarū,* etc.) occurs four times with separated *li-, wa-lāta ḥīna* (Q 38:3) is separated as *wa-lā taḥīn*. Also *wa-lākinnā* < *wa-lākin anā* (Q 18:38; cf. Brockelmann, *Grundriß,* i, 258 and Nöldeke, *GQ,* iii, 114, n. 1; see now Ambros, *Lākin* und *lākinna,* 22 n. 9).

3. Letters of prolongation *(matres lectionis)*

a. *Alif* in inner positions of the word is more often written than not, and almost without any regularity. The shift *a'* > *ā* resulted in such forms as *t-w-y-l* for *ta'wīl* or *'-s-t-j-r-t* for *ista'jarta* (Q 28:26).

b. *Y* is omitted when it represents *ī* following another *y* as in *al-nabiyyīna* (written *'-l-n-b-y-n; 'illiyyīna* in Q 83:18 is exceptional) and *yuḥyīkum*. Different from this orthographic convention is the massive omission of *y* in word-endings. It indicates either total elision of *ī* (cf. Q 13:9, *l-muta'āl* < *l-muta'ālī* in rhyme) or its shortening in the local dialect.

c. *W* is omitted only when it represents *ū* following another *w*, e.g. *yalwūna* is written *y-l-w-n* in Q 3:78. Also *ru'yā* > *rūyā* is written *r-y-'*, because of the shift *uy* > *ī*.

d. *H* of the pronoun *hu/hi* is shortened to *-h* in pause (for this issue, see Fischer, Die Quantität, esp. 399).

4. *Alif maqṣūra* and *ā* preceding *tā' marbūṭa*

Final *ā* is written *y* if *y* is a third radical or expressed as *y* in the inflexion. It is also written so before suffixes. It seems to reflect a pronunciation with some proximity to *e (imāla)*. The few exceptions are largely regulated and include, for example, cases in which *alif waṣl* follows, as in *ladā l-bāb* (Q 12:25) and the verb *ra'ā*, written *r-'*.

Use of *y* for *ā* preceding *tā' marbūṭa* occurs only in foreign words (see FOREIGN VOCABULARY), e.g. *tawrāh* (see TORAH). The *w* in a similar situation occurs in eight words *(ṣalāh, zakāh, ḥayāh, najāh, manāh, mishkāh, ghadāh,* and the exceptional *ribā)*. Whereas the first two follow the Aramaic orthography, the others follow them by analogy, and the last may represent a word with *w* (possible pronunciation *rabw*, see Spitaler, Die Schreibung des Typus *ṣlwt*).

5. *W* of word end

This *w* is regularly followed by *alif* (*alif al-faṣl*, "*alif* of separation"). Few exceptions exist.

6. *Hamza*

As a result of its weakening and even disappearance in word middle and end positions, the orthography of such words in the Qur'ān is modified by the following changes:

a. Omission after a vowelless consonant results sometimes in the writing of *yas'alu*, etc. as *y-s-l*, *'-l-m-w-d-h* for *al-mawūda* (< *al-maw'ūda*, Q 81:8), or the variations *l-y-k-h/'-l-'-y-k-h* for *[aṣḥāb] al-aykah* (with "*h*" here indicating *tā' marbūṭa;* cf. Q 26:176; 38:13 for the first and Q 15:78; 50:14 for the other).

b. Loss of vowelless *hamza: ri'yan* is written *r-y-'* (Q 19:74) and *t-w-y/t-w-y-h* stand for *tu'wī/tu'wīhi* (Q 33:51 and 70:13 respectively).

c. Loss of *hamza* intermediating two *-a* vowels, resulting in such orthographic forms as *l-m-l-n* for *la-amla'anna* (Q 7:18 and passim), or *'-r-y-t-m* for *a-ra'aytum* and *'-l-m-n-sh-t* for *al-munsha'ātu* (Q 55:24). The same occurs in *-i'ī* position, as in *m-t-k-y-n* for *muttaki'īna* (e.g. Q 18:31; 37:51).

d. Loss of *hamza* intermediating two different vowels. The following is a selection of forms that exemplify the intricate subcategorization of the orthographic convention in this situation: *'-w-n-b-y-k-m* for *a-unabbi'ukum* (Q 3:15), *'-n/'-'-n* variably for *a-in* with the interrogative, both exhibiting the situation following a pre-posed particle; *t-b-w-'* for *tabū'a* (Q 5:29), but also *l-t-n-w-'* for *la-tanū'u* between two vowels of the same quality (Q 28:76); change in word end orthography following case and mood vowels is typical with *-ā'* endings, such as *j-z-'-w* for *jazā'u* (Q 5:33 and passim), *t-l-q-'-y* for *[min] tilqā'i [nafsī]* (Q 10:15), though *'-w-l-y-'* with personal pronoun suffixation stands for the nominative and genitive as well; finally, sequence of *alif* plus *᾿/w/y* may indicate pronunciation of *hamza,* in a word-opening position preceded by a pre-posing particle (*l-᾿-᾿-dh-b-ḥ-n-h* for *la-adhbaḥannahu,* Q 27:21), or it may be a mere graphic peculiarity in such cases as *m-l-᾿-y-h* for *malaʾihī, b-᾿-y-y-d* for *bi-aydin* (Q 51:47) and *l-sh-᾿-y* for *li-shayʾin* (Q 18:23).

7. Omission of *n*

Its occurrence in Q 12:110 where *nunajjī* is written *n-j-y,* and, in several qurʾānic variants, two other verbs (*n-z-r* and *n-ṣ-r*), may reflect dissimilation. The form *taʾmurūnī* for *taʾmurūnanī* (also read *taʾmurūnnī,* Q 39:64) has many equivalents in poetry but not in the Qurʾān, see Nöldeke (*Zur Grammatik,* 11, n. 1).

8. Omission of *l* of the article and *alif al-waṣl*

In addition to omission of this *l-* in the relative pronouns (cf. *᾿-l-y* for *allāʾi*), it is missing in *al-layl* and *lal-dār.* Omission of *alif al-waṣl* is attested in *bi-sm* of the *basmala* (q.v.) and several other words (including *la-ttakhadhta* in Q 18:77 and *wa-sʾal*), but it is preserved in *ibn* of *ʿĪsā bnu Maryam* in all of its sixteen occurrences (see JESUS; MARY).

9. *S* > *ṣ*, *ẓ* > *ḍ*

Ṣ written instead of *s* is attested in four words, *wa-yabṣuṭu* and *baṣṭatan* (Q 2:245, 247) and *bi-muṣayṭirin* and *al-muṣayṭirūna* (Q 88:22 and 52:37). This spelling reflects assimilation of the emphatic *ṭ* as is also the case with *ṣirāṭ*. In similar fashion *ḍanīn* (Q 81:24) is said to present a shift from *ẓanīn.*

10. Regularity of pausal orthography

This regularity is largely maintained and *ā* is written in rhyming words like *al-rasūlā* (Q 33:66) and *al-sabīlā* (Q 33:67), or *-a* in *sulṭāniya* (Q 69:29), although exceptions exist.

Phonetics

1. Short vowels

a. Elision of final short vowel following liquid, such as *yanṣurukum* > *yanṣurkum* (Q 67:20) and *yushʿirukum* > *yushʿirkum* (Q 6:109; redaction of Abū ʿAmr). Nöldeke (*Zur Grammatik,* 9 f.) presents the forms *taʾmannā* (written *t-᾿-m-n-᾿;* Q 12:11), *makannī* (Q 18:95) and the reading *wa-arnā* for *wa-arinā* (Q 2:128) among others from poetry, and considers them early testimony for the gradual disappearance of *iʿrāb* (see also the discussion in Rabin, *Ancient west Arabian,* 93 n. 16).

b. Elision of unstressed short vowel as it happens in *ṣudqātihinna* < *ṣaduqātihinna* (Q 4:4) and *jumʿati* < *(yawmu) l-jumuʿati* (Q 62:9). The east Arabian, so-called Tamīmī form of Arabic, has for the first *ṣaduqa* > *ṣuduqa* > *ṣudqa,* through vowel harmony. In sound plural feminine *-āt* the eastern form omits the vowel of the preceding syllable (*fVʿlāt*), whereas the western Ḥijāzī form has it (*fVʿVlāt*), e.g. *muthlāt-mathulāt* (Q 13:6). This Ḥijāzī practice was conceived by the early philologists as *tafkhīm* (cf. Rabin, *Ancient west Arabian,* 97 f.).

2. Long vowels

a. *ā* > *ō:* Rabin argues for this shift (op. cit., 105), following all earlier scholars, for *ṣalāh* and the other words with *w* ending but Spitaler disagrees (Die Schreibung des Typus *ṣlwt;* see the section on orthography above).

b. *ī* > *i* in word end: According to the reading of several official readers, this shift is attested in a phrase like *yawma yaʾti* (Q 11:105). Al-Zamakhsharī (d. 538/1144) identifies it as a peculiarity of the dialect of Hudhayl (see Rabin, op. cit., 89).

c. *-ī* > *ø* in pause: Such are the forms *akramanī* > *akraman,* and *ahānan* (Q 89:15, 16), in the reading of the Kūfans and

Abū ʿAmr (see Rabin, op. cit., 119).

d. *āʾu > ō?* According to Rabin (op. cit., 110), this is the correct interpretation of the spelling *w-ʾ*. A more conservative view suggests *āʾu > āwu* (Nöldeke, *GQ*, iii, 47).

e. *-ā (alif maqṣūra a/y):* In the Qurʾān the two kinds of *alif maqṣūra* rhyme (e.g. *dunyā* and *abqā* in Q 20:71-3). Note also the *imāla* of *fa-nadēhu* (Q 3:39) in the reading of Ḥamza and al-Kisāʾī, (see Rabin, op. cit., 116 f.).

f. *ā > ī (imāla)*: In addition to the above, the two readers read *rāna > rīna (ryn)* in Q 83:14 (see Rabin, op. cit., 112).

3. Glottal consonants

a. *Hamza* — general: A detailed study of the orthographical evidence is provided in Rabin (*Ancient west Arabian,* 133 f.) who concludes that it is missing in most cases of qurʾānic spelling, as in *yasamu* (Q 41:49), *mashamati* (Q 56:9), *yanawna* (Q 6:26), *tajarū* (Q 23:65) and the frequent *afidatun, yasalu, malakun*. Noteworthy is *aṣḥābu laykati* (Q 38:13) with the article. *Alif* is written in *nashata* (Q 29:20; 56:62) as a single case of post-consonantal *hamza* followed by feminine ending. Rabin concludes that *hamzat bayna bayna* is the closest Ḥijāzī approximation to *hamza* and that some spellings (not specified) reflect hyper-corrections.

b. *Hamza* — *iʾu* shifts: This state occurs in verbs where the third radical is *hamza*. *Mustahziʾūna* (Q 2:14) may be rendered in the Ḥijāzī performance as either *mustahziwūna* or *mustahzūna*. Al-Akhfash, as cited in Zamakhsharī, reports *yastahziyūna*. For the third singular form in Q 2:15 Rabin suggests *yastahzī* (like **yarmiyu > yarmī;* see Rabin, *Ancient west Arabian,* 139).

c. *Hamza* — *āʾi > ay: sāʾilun > saylun* (Q 70:1) is Ibn ʿAbbās's reading according to al-Zamakhsharī. Ḥamza reads *ṭayr* for *ṭāʾir* (Q 3:49; see Rabin, op. cit., 140 and 149 n. 24).

d. *Hamza* — pausal *aʾ > ā:* The following pausal forms *al-malaʾu* (Q 7:60), *malaʾun* (Q 11:38), *al-malaʾi* (Q 2:246), and *al-malaʾa* (Q 28:20) are all spelt *m-l-ʾ* and confirm information about this Ḥijāzī pausal form (see Rabin, op. cit., 141).

e. *Hamza* — assimilation of *hamza:* Non-pausal *al-marʾi* is shifted to *al-marri* (Q 8:24) according to some readings. Similarly *juzʾun > juzzun* (Q 15:44) in the reading of the Ḥijāzī al-Zuhrī (d. 124/742). *Riʾyu > riyyu* (Q 19:74) is a Medinese reading (see Rabin, op. cit., 134 f.).

f. *wu > ʾu* is attested in *ujuhuhum* (Q 39:60; see Rabin, op. cit., 81).

g. *ʿ > ḥ:* According to the late grammarian Ibn Hishām al-Anṣārī (d. 761/1360), Ibn Masʿūd (d. 32/652; *Mughnī,* 451) read *naʿam > naḥam* four times in the Qurʾān (see Rabin, op. cit., 85).

4. Velars (post-palatal uvular)

For *q* in Qurʾān reading, see Brockelmann (*Grundriß,* i, 121).

5. Interdentals

a. *th > t:* This shift is suggested in the reading of *mukhbithīna>mukhbitīna* (Q 22:34; see Rabin, *Ancient west Arabian,* 125).

b. *ẓ/ḍ* are interchangeable (see the section on orthography above for *ẓanīn ~ ḍanīn*). This is a unique case which supports Nöldeke's argument that such cases were rare in Muḥammad's days (see Nöldeke, Das klassische Arabisch, 10 and n. 3).

c. *n* — omission of *n* in qurʾānic manuscripts (see MANUSCRIPTS OF THE QURʾĀN) occurs in the case of *nunjī, fa-nunjiya* (see the section on orthography above). Other occurrences are *li-nanẓura* (Q 10:14) and *la-nanṣuru* (Q 40:51) in which nasal pronunciation *(ghunna)* is suggested (see Rabin, *Ancient west Arabian,* 123 n. 28, 146).

It is noteworthy that Sībawayhi (Chapter 565) makes a detailed distinction between thirty-five favorite versus seven disfavored consonantal variants in the reading of the Qurʾān and poetry.

6. Stress patterns
Central questions have been discussed for decades concerning the evidence on this issue provided by qurʾānic orthography and variant readings. The earliest works on grammar and grammatical analysis of the qurʾānic language already take account of variant readings attributed to early authorities from the days of Muḥammad's Companions (see COMPANIONS OF THE PROPHET) and of the next generation. Study of such readings and their respective readers developed into an independent branch of Islamic sciences (see READINGS OF THE QURʾĀN). The assumption that the qurʾānic material supports a dichotomy of an expiratory Tamīmī versus non-expiratory Ḥijāzī stress was considered by various scholars and debated by others. Several scholars advocated its central role in the omission of unstressed vowels in open syllables and especially in word-end position and eventually in the emergence of the north Arabian language type. A useful summary of the main arguments is found in Neuwirth (*Studien zur Komposition,* 325 f.).

7. Pausal patterns
Fischer (Silbenstruktur, 54) objects to the assumption that the pausal forms reflected in the qurʾānic orthography represent with precision the spoken language, and indicates that on the basis of the pausal shift of *-an* to *-a* one would have expected the shift of *-atan* (with *tāʾ marbūṭa*) to *-atā,* whereas the qurʾānic orthography records *h (-ah).* Blau (*Pseudo-corrections,* 57 n. 14) clarifies how the orthography reflects living pronunciation, in which the accusative state of *tāʾ marbūṭa* merged with the genitive/nominative *-ah* pausal form, to prevent the anomalous contrast of *ḥasana-h* (nom./gen.) — *ḥasana-tā* (acc.), when other nouns have only *ḥasan* — *ḥasan-ā.*

Morphology

1. Personal pronouns — suffixes
-Iyya > *iyyi* and *-āya* > *-ayya: mā antum bi-muṣrikhiyyi* (Q 14:22) is a Kūfan reading reported by al-Farrāʾ. *ʿAṣāyi* (Q 20:18) is the reading of al-Ḥasan al-Baṣrī and Abū ʿAmr. The other shift is reported by the early Baṣran grammarian Ibn Abī Isḥāq for *ʿaṣayya* and for *maḥyayya* (Q 6:162). Al-Ḥasan al-Baṣrī is reported to have read *yā bushrayya* (Q 12:19). According to some readers also *hudāya* > *hudayya* (Q 2:38). Rabin (*Ancient west Arabian,* 151) concludes that *-ayya* was the west Arabian form.

2. Demonstrative pronouns
a. East-Arabian *hādhī:* The reading *hādhī l-shijrata* (Q 2:35) is interpreted by al-Bayḍāwī as Tamīmī (see Rabin, op. cit., 120).
b. *dhālika:* The Qurʾān has only *dhālika,* not *dhāka.* Accordingly al-Ushmūnī suggests Ḥijāzī versus Tamīmī identification of the two (see Rabin, op. cit., 154). *Dhālikum,* etc. with the inflected suffix in agreement with the addressee's number and gender is identified as a qurʾānic language characteristic by Brockelmann (*Grundriß,* i, 318).
c. *ūlā* vs. *ūlay:* Ibn ʿAqīl considered the first Ḥijāzī and identified *ūlā* (with *alif maqṣūra bi-ṣūrat al-yāʾ*) as Tamīmī. This observation is based on the qurʾānic changes seen in Q 2:16. Rabin (op. cit., 153), for his part, attributes to the Tamīmī the form with final *-ā,* and adopts Ibn Jinnī's attribution to Qays of the qurʾānic *ūlāʾi.*

3. Relative pronouns
For *allāʾi* < *al-ulāʾi,* see Brockelmann (*Grundriß,* i, 257).

4. The verb

a. These statistics for qur᾽ānic verb forms are based on Chouémi *(Le verbe):* 1,200 roots of verbal forms, of which fifteen are quadriliteral and the others triliteral; 801 triliteral verbs are in stem I (69%); three verbs are in stem IX and one in stem XI. Sound verbs number 629, *geminata:* 108, *hamzata:* 55, *prima w/y:* 49, *media w/y:* 152, *tertia w/y:* 131, doubly weak verbs: 61 (including one occurrence of *᾽-w-y*), $R_1R_2R_1R_2$: eight, $R_1R_2R_3R_4$: seven; from a total of 14,000 verbal occurrences of stem I (including participles; *maṣdar* forms amount to 2000), the average of passive forms is 6.3%, with similar proportions in stems II, III, and IV, 4% in stem X, 2% in stems V and VIII, none in stems VI, VII, IX, XI.

b. Verbal forms

i. Imperfect — Prefixes, *-a-* vs. *-i-* vowel: In the discussion of *nista῾īnu* (Q 1:5) al-Farrā᾽, as cited in al-Suyūṭī (*Muzhir,* beginning of *naw῾* no. 16; cf. Rabin, op. cit., 61), identifies the *-a-* as characteristic of Quraysh and Asad alone. But note that this reference does not appear in the printed addition of al-Farrā᾽'s *Ma῾ānī* (Kinberg, *Lexicon of al-Farrā᾽,* ad *lughat-*). Other readings with *-i-* include *lā tiqrabā* (Q 2:35) and *lā tirkanū* (Q 11:113). Interestingly, such forms are found only in *shawādhdh,* non-canonical readings. The form *nu῾buduhum* in Q 39:3 is presented by Vollers (*Volkssprache und Schriftsprache,* 129; see also Rabin, *Ancient west Arabian,* 61, 158). For an instructive discussion of the span of such phenomena and their minimal effect in consideration of the relations between classical Arabic and the old Arab dialects, see Nöldeke (Zur Sprache, 3).

ii. Imperfect — Prefixes, third plural feminine *y > t:* This form, which exhibits analogy with third singular feminine, is recorded in a variant reading *tatafaṭṭarna* (Q 42:5), according to Abū ῾Amr, *tanfaṭirna* (see Fleischer, *Kleinere Schriften* 99, citing al-Bayḍāwī).

iii. Imperfect — Loss of final vowel: This is attested in the case of assimilation of *n* in *ta᾽manunā > ta᾽mannā* (Q 12:11; see Brockelmann, *Grundriß,* i, 257).

iv. Imperative: *alqiyā* (Q 50:24) as a pausal form of the energicus *-an* (see Brockelmann, op. cit., 554).

5. Stems

a. Stem V — Haplology *(taqattalu < tataqattalu):* According to Rabin (*Ancient west Arabian,* 147) this reading is characteristic of Ḥijāzī readers; also *fa-timassakum < fa-tatamassa-kum* (Q 11:113; see Rabin, op. cit., 148, 158 and Brockelmann, op. cit., 257).

b. Stems V-VI — Assimilation: This phenomenon is attested in *muddaththir* (Q 74:1), though some suggest stem II, *mudaththir.*

c. Stem VIII: Rabin (op. cit., 146) identifies *muddakir* (Q 54:15 and elsewhere) as a Ḥijāzī form, while the Asadī is *idhdhakara.* This is based on al-Farrā᾽ apud al-Ṭabarī (at Q 27:56), though the express formulation of al-Farrā᾽ (*Ma῾ānī,* i, 215.11) yields the contrary, namely that in the Asadī dialect the interdental fricative assimilates with the *t* of stem VIII. This is demonstrated by *iththaghara > ittaghara,* but it stands to reason that similar assimilation of *dh > d* is also characteristic of this tribe's dialect in such conditions.

d. *Yakhaṭṭifu* (Q 2:20) with assimilation of the stem's *t* with the emphatic second radical is presented in Brockelmann (op. cit., 258) following a list of later grammarians and al-Bayḍāwī. Al-Farrā᾽ (*Ma῾ānī,* i, 215.11) gives, on the authority of an anonymous grammarian, the reading *yakhiṭṭifu* and quotes this grammarian's view that the first *i* is anaptyctic (cf. *yakhiṣṣimūna* at Q 36:49).

e. *Verba primae wāw: lā tawjal/lā tājal/tūjal* (Q 15:53). The second form exhibits a shift of *-ū᾽-iw* (see Rabin, op. cit., 158).

f. *Verba mediae wāw/yā':* There are two variations recorded for the perfect of stem I *m-w-t, mittu/muttu* (Q 19:23, 66), also in *mittum* (Q 23:35). The first reading is ʿĀṣim's (see Rabin, op. cit., 114); the passive participle *mahīl* (Q 73:14) is discussed by Rabin (op. cit., 160), where *madīn* versus *madyūn* are attributed to the Ḥijāzī versus Tamīmī varieties respectively.

g. *Verba mediae hamzatae:* The passive *sīla* (Q 2:108) is discussed by Rabin (op. cit., 138) who argues that it should not be reckoned as *uy* > *ī* but as a regular passive.

h. *Verba tertiae wāw/yā':* On *ukhfī* < *ukhfiya* (Q 32:17) and *rāḍātun* < *rāḍiyatun* (Q 88:9-12) see Rabin (op. cit., 161) who relates the last to the shift in stem I perfect pattern *baqiya* > *baqā* which existed in Yemen (q.v.) and probably in parts of the Ḥijāz. The opposite is reflected in Nāfiʿ's reading *ʿasaytum* > *ʿasītum* (Q 47:22; see Rabin, op. cit., 185). *Marḍiyyan* (Q 19:55) has a variant *marḍuwwan,* which al-Farrā' in his *Maʿānī* attributes to the Ḥijāzī dialect.

i. *Verba geminata:* Both the sound and the geminate forms of the apocopate *yartadid* (Q 2:217) and *yartadda* (Q 5:54; also 59:4 and 8:13 for *yushāqqi-yushāqiq* and 2:282 for *yuḍārra-yuḍārar*) exist in the Qur'ān. The short forms of the *faʿila* pattern *ẓalta* and *ẓaltum* (in Q 20:97 and 56:65 respectively) have always attracted scholars' interest; *faʿala* is not shortened (cf. *shaqaqnā* in Q 80:26 and *madadnā* in Q 15:19; Brockelmann, *Grundriß,* i, 247 discusses the matter together with *aḥastu/istaḥaytu*). The Arab grammarians' views are cited by Barth (Ziltu, 330 f.). *Wa-l-yumlil* < *wa-l-yumli* (Q 2:282): note that *umlī* takes, according to commentators, the sense of *umhilu* in Q 7:183; Chouémi (*Le verbe,* 4) notes their same meaning. Nöldeke (Zur Sprache, 26 n. 1) considers the Syriac *mallel* as their immediate origin.

6. Verbal nouns

a. Stem II: The Yemenite identity of the form *kidhdhāb* (Q 78:28) is given by al-Farrā' (*Maʿānī,* iii, 229) who mentions the various readers who had adopted it (against the variant *kidhāban*) and exemplifies its use in the Yemenite dialect while describing his personal experience with a Yemenite concerning this pattern (see Brockelmann, *Grundriß,* i, 346 and Nöldeke, Zur Sprache, 8, n. 4).

b. Stem IV: The rare form *iqām* (Q 21:73) is discussed in Wright (*Grammar,* i, 121a).

7. The noun

a. Patterns: *afʿal* (Nöldeke, *Zur Grammatik,* 17) indicates the wrong reading *al-asharr* in Q 54:26 for *al-ashir. Faʿāli* is not recorded in the Qur'ān, but see Vollers (*Volkssprache und Schriftsprache,* 187) on the variant *masāsi* to *(lā) misāsa* in Q 20:97.

b. Affixation: *-CCāt* > *-CVCāt: ʿawrāt* > *ʿawArāt* (Q 24:58); for *niʿimāt* (Q 31:31), see the sub-section on vowel elision above. *-Iyy:* The *nisba* suffix serves for attribution of a person to an ethnic group, e.g. *sāmiriyy* (Q 20:85, 87, 95) but also for a description of relations on a more abstract level, and the derivation of an adverbial form of it, e.g. *sikhriyyan* (Q 38:63).

c. Plural derivation — adjectival plurals: The plural adjectives of the elative *afʿal* are sound, as in *al-ardhalūna* (Q 26:111; see Wright, *Grammar,* i, 200). On the indefinite *unās* (four occurrences in the Qur'ān) versus *al-nās* (240 times), see Nöldeke (*Zur Grammatik* [1963], 15) and also Ullmann (*Untersuchengen,* 181).

8. The particles

a. Four occurrences of *(naʿam>) naʿim* in al-Kisā'ī's reading are reported by al-Suyūṭī (see Rabin, *Ancient west Arabian,* 73) who mentions a similar shift in the perfect form, namely *naʿima* > *niʿima.*

b. Al-Farrā' equates the sense of *lammā* to that of *illā* (Q 86:4). Rabin (op. cit., 163) speculates, albeit with hesitation, that its origin is from Hudhayl.
c. Uninflected *halumma* (Q 6:150) is used in addressing several persons.
d. No occurrences of *mundhu/mudh* in the Qur'ān (see Rabin, op. cit., 187).
e. *Ladun* and the two variants of *ladunī/ladunnī* (Q 18:76) are discussed by Brockelmann (*Grundriß*, 66) with reference to al-Ṭabarī's discussion of them.

Syntax

1. Preservation of *iʿrāb*
A list of cases in which the qur'ānic orthography indicates the use of *iʿrāb* is included in the comprehensive study by Diem (Untersuchungen [1981], 366; brief mention of this topic is made in the section on orthography above). Diem (op. cit., 381) concludes that the situation is undecided concerning relations of these cases to the Ḥijāzī vernacular. A strong argument made by Nöldeke (Zur Sprache, 2) is the absence of non-*iʿrāb* traces in its transmission (see Blau, *Pseudo-corrections*, 57).

2. *Iʿrāb* interference
a. The following four cases are mentioned in Nöldeke, GQ, iii, 2 f.: *wa-l-mūfūna... wa-l-ṣābirīna* (Q 2:177); *lākini l-rāsikhūna... wa-l-muqīmīna... wa-l-mu'tūna* (Q 4:162); *inna lladhīna āmanū... wa-l-ṣābi'ūna* (Q 5:69; mentioned by Reckendorf, *Syntaktische Verhältnisse*, 489); *inna hādhāni la-sāḥirāni* (Q 20:63), which Brockelmann (*Grundriß*, i, 456) considers characteristic of Rabīʿa. A summary of Arab philologists' views about these problematic occurrences is given by Burton (Linguistic errors).
b. Another case of interference is *yā jibālu awwibī maʿahu wa-l-ṭayra* (Q 34:10). Several explanations by early grammarians of the irregular *naṣb* (in *wa-l-ṭayra*) are recorded (cf. Farrā', *Maʿānī*, ii, 355 and Abū ʿUbayda, *Majāz*, at Q 34:10; also Jumaḥī's introduction to his *Ṭabaqāt al-shuʿarā'*). Most of them identify it as an object and reconsruct a covert verb *(aʿnī, sakhkhara, udʿu),* whereas Abū ʿAmr offers an alternative analysis, that this is the result of an anomaly involving a combination of *yā* plus noun identified by an article.
c. *Inna hādhāni la-sāḥirāni* (Q 20:63, see listing above): This case is extremely interesting from the cultural point of view, as it presents various attempts made by exegetes and grammarians to solve a crux in the sacred text. Among these attempts is a tradition (see ḤADĪTH AND THE QUR'ĀN) narrated on the authority of ʿĀ'isha (see ʿĀ'ISHA BINT ABĪ BAKR) to justify attempts to correct the script, an attempt to change the error, made by Abū ʿAmr, a variety of grammatical modes of analysis to secure some regularity of the structure, and scholarly testimony of peculiar dialectal forms, attributed to a certain tribe to the same effect (cf. Goldziher, *Die Richtungen*, 31 f.; see DIALECTS). Another case in which this authority is called on to solve a problem of text transmission is *yu'tūna* for *ya'tūna* in Q 23:60, with ʿĀ'isha's saying: *wa-lākinna l-hijā' ḥurrifa* (see Nöldeke, GQ, iii, 3 n. 2).
d. Tanwīn is omitted before the article in *qul huwa llāhu aḥadu llāhu l-ṣamadu* (Q 112:1-2) and *sābiqu l-nahāra* (Q 36:40; variant: *l-nahāri;* see Spitaler's additions to Nöldeke, *Zur Grammatik*, 134 [to 27/4]).
e. The verses *an takūna tijāratan* (Q 4:29)and *in kānat illā ṣayḥatan wāḥidatan* (Q 36:29) are considered by Rabin (*Ancient west Arabian*, 174) as irregular structures with *kāna* functioning as a full predicate whose agent is marked by the accusative, instead of the regular nominative.

3. Rhyming and prosodic dictation
Nöldeke (Zur Sprache, 9) notes some grammatical and stylistic interferences which result from yielding to prosodic dictation in the Qur'ān, e.g. the inaccurate expression *wa-anā maʿakum mina l-shahidīna* (Q 3:81), "and I am with you among the witnesses" while he is the only witness (see WITNESSING AND TESTIFYING), and the change of verb forms (see above); see for the recurring *kāna llāhu ʿalīman…*, Reuschel (Wa-kāna llāhu, 152; also *Aspekt und Tempus,* 100 f.), who considers the possibility of *licentia* but favors *tawkīd*. Extraction of the pronominal constituent of the verb is not always incorporated for the sake of focalization or topicalization (see below): *yā ʿibādi lā khawfun ʿalaykumu l-yawma wa-lā antum taḥzanūna* (Q 43:68); similarly syntactic nominalization can occur without formal head *(mawṣūf): in hum illā yakhruṣūna* (Q 43:20).

4. Verbal aspects and tenses
Reuschel's *Aspekt und Tempus in der Sprache des Qorans* is a comprehensive taxonomy of the verbal tense and aspect use in the Qur'ān, but it is not an attempt to sort out qur'ānic peculiarities. Structures discussed in Reuschel: *wa-mā kāna li-nafsin an tamūta illā bi-idhni llāhi,* "cannot, impossible that" (Q 3:145); *wa-mā kāna llāhu li-yuʿjizahū min shay'in,* "it is not the kind of thing that he does to…" (Q 35:44; Reuschel, *Aspekt und Tempus,* 115 f.); performative *samiʿnā wa-aṭaʿnā* (e.g. Q 2:285; Reuschel, op. cit., 130). On the expression *in kuntum fāʿilīna* (Q 12:10), see Bravmann (The phrase, 347 f.), who considers its sense an expression of "inner compulsion", without, however, studying the three other occurrences in the Qur'ān.

Kinberg (Semi-imperfectives) treats qur'ānic active participial structures and observes that some indicate "semi-imperfective present," namely, it may be bounded by a dynamic event, either at its beginning (similar to the English present perfect) or at the end (the English equivalent here is "puturate progressive"). On *arānī/arā* (lit. "I see myself") in Q 12:36 and 43 exhibiting the use of an imperfect in a narrative of one's own dream (see DREAMS AND SLEEP), see Nöldeke (*Zur Grammatik,* 67). The extensive qur'ānic use of the energicus forms (imperfect or imperative plus *-an* or *-anna*) is studied by Ambros (Syntaktische und stilistische Funktionen), where its use as a stylistic device is particularly emphasized. Zewi *(A syntactical study)* presents a meticulous classification of sentence-types with energicus, and indicates its association with indicatives, in a larger context of Semitic linguistics.

5. Nominal SP sentence
Collision of formal and notional reme (comment): The recurring *wa-mā kāna jawāba qawmihi illā an qālū…* (as in Q 7:82) exhibits what seems to be disagreement between the formal predicate marking *(naṣb)* and the notional status of *jawāb* as a subject (see Fleischer, *Kleinere Schriften,* 558 f., following al-Bayḍāwī's distinction in nominal sentences with two definite members).

6. Presentatives
The demonstrative pronouns (of both "close" and "remote" sets) are used as presentatives with the sense of "look!", "voilà" (see Bloch, *Studies in Arabic syntax,* 54 f.). The nuclear presentative plus predicate occurs in such expressions as: *yā bushrā hādhā ghulāmun* (Q 12:19); *hā'ulā'i banātī in kuntum fāʿilīna* (Q 15:71).

The following verses present an enlarged structure, with an additional finite verb or a nominal marked by accusative, which Bloch, ibid., terms the amplified structure: *hādhihi biḍāʿatunā ruddat ilaynā* (Q 12:65); *hādhā baʿlī shaykhan* (Q 11:72); *fa-tilka buyūtuhum khāwiyatan bi-mā ẓalamū* (Q 27:52; see also Nöldeke, *Zur Grammatik* [1963], 48-50).

The early Arab grammarians took great interest in this structure. A development in their conception is observable in the *Kitāb* with al-Khalīl's and Sībawayhi's identification of the accusatival nominal as circumstantial *(ḥāl)* instead of *khabar (al-maʿrifa)*, which was still conceived as such by al-Farrāʾ, for example. On the Arabic grammatical literature concerning *hāʾulāʾi banātī hunna aṭharu/aṭhara lakum* (Q 11:78) see Talmon (Problematic passage). *Hā antum hāʾulāʾi tudʿawna* (as in Q 47:38 and similar verses) are discussed by Nöldeke (op. cit., 50). Bloch (*Studies in Arabic syntax*, 74 f. and especially 80 f.) identifies them as "proclitic" with the presentative as a separate unit ("look!") and the pronoun and the verb as S plus P.

The verse *inna hādhā akhī lahu tisʿun wa-tisʿūna naʿjatan wa-lī naʿjatun wāḥidatun* (Q 38:23) includes both an affirmative *inna* (see what follows) and a presentative followed by a topicalized sentence *akhī lahu*... < *li-akhī*....

7. Function of *inna*

Bloch's (*Studies in Arabic syntax*, 102) description of classical Arabic *inna* as "[...] emphasiz[ing] the speaker's certainty... that what is said in a sentence is a fact, is true, will indeed take place," fits Goldenberg's (*Studies in Semitic linguistics*, 148 f.) model of nexal relations as corroboration of the nexal constituent. Note Bloch's observation that qurʾānic citations (Q 2:20 = 8:10, 63:1, 26:41 = 23:82, 6:19, 13:5) still exhibit this function "despite a large degree of conventionalization of its use."

The following verses have an independent pronoun in a position occupied regularly by a subject: *huwa llāhu aḥadu* (Q 112:1) and *fa-idhā hiya shākhiṣatun abṣāru lladhīna kafarū* (Q 21:97). Al-Kisāʾī, and less firmly al-Farrāʾ, consider this pronoun *ʿimād* (cf. Kinberg, *Lexicon of al-Farrāʾ*, s.v.). Occasionally instead of *inna* we find the use of *in* with the same function: *in kullun lammā jamīʿun ladaynā muḥḍarūna* (Q 36:32) and *in kullu nafsin lammā ʿalayhā ḥāfiẓun* (Q 86:4). This structure occurs also with *inna* in *wa-inna kullan lammā la-yuwaffiyannahum rabbuka aʿmālahum* (Q 11:111); similarly, *in kidta* for *innaka*... in *ta-llāhi in kidta la-turdīni* (Q 37:56).

8. Verb agreement in a verb + subject (VS) sentence

Agreement of the verb with the number of its following agent, dubbed *akalūnī l-barāghīth* in the Arab linguistic literature, is recorded in Q 5:71, 21:3 and in the reading *qad aflaḥū l-muʾminūna* in Q 23:1. Nöldeke adds *fa-aṣbaḥū fī dārihim jāthimīna lladhīna kadhdhabū Shuʿayban* (Q 7:91-2; see SHUʿAYB) and cites al-Ḥarīrī's misgivings *mā sumiʿa illā fī lugha ḍaʿīfa lam yanṭuq bihi l-Qurʾān*, but Spitaler is more equivocal about the correct attribution of the last to the list (cf. Nöldeke, *Zur Grammatik* [1963], 152). Nöldeke (op. cit., 78) adds a note about the possible development of this phenomenon which accordingly is only in its first stages in qurʾānic language. See Levin (What is meant) on the grammarians' interpretation of this structure, not in terms of number agreement. (On the possible Hudhalī origin of this variant, see DIALECTS.)

Absence of gender agreement in *kāna ʿāqibatu*... (e.g. Q 27:14) is discussed as a phenomenon discernible "in the earliest texts" in Fischer (Classical Arabic, 212). Verbs of stem II can mark agreement with a plural subject (originally an object), as in *mufattaḥatan lahumu l-abwābu* (Q 38:50).

9. Use of an impersonal verb construction

The construction exhibited by *wa-ḥushira li-Sulaymāna* (Q 27:17) in the sense of "Solomon (q.v.) collected," is better known in Aramaic (but see Ullmann, *Adminiculum*, 78 f. ex. 700-10). Reckendorf (*Arabische Syntax*, 359) explicates the structure *li-yujzā qawman* (Q 45:14). A discussion of non-inflected passives followed by an accusatival complement is found in Blau (On invariable passive forms). Nöldeke (*Zur Grammatik,* 76) mentions *la-qad taqaṭṭa'a baynahum* (Q 6:94; *baynakum* is another attested reading).

Problems concerning the negative of *ghayri l-maghḍūbi 'alayhim...* (Q 1:7; see FĀTIḤA) are discussed by the early Arab grammarians; see Farrā', *Ma'ānī,* e.g. at Q 18:99, *nufikha fī l-ṣūri* and five other occurrences, including *fīhi,* vs. *fa-idhā nufikha fī l-ṣūri nafkhatun wāḥidatun* in Q 69:13 (on which see Fleischer, *Kleinere Schriften,* 93).

Brockelmann's (*Grundriß,* ii, 119 f.) suggestion that *wa-idhā aẓlama 'alayhim* (Q 2:20) is a case in point is repeated by Blau (On invariable passive forms, 87 n. 8) but rejected by Nöldeke (cf. the margin of his private copy, located in the library of Tübingen University), who refers to the preceding *barq* "lightning" as the subject in *kullamā aḍā'a lahum mashaw fīhi.*

10. Topicalization

Topicalization, or isolation of a natural subject in a sentence's opening position, seems to be the most frequently used transposition in qur'ānic syntax, e.g. *inna lladhīna lā yu'minūna bil-ākhirati zayyannā lahum a'mālahum* (Q 27:4; see the statistics in Dahlgren, Word order). Isolation of this kind may leave its original case mark of the unmarked position as in *wa-l-samā'a banaynāhā bi-aydin* (Q 51:47) and *wa-l-arḍa madadnāhā wa-alqaynā fīhā rawāsiya* (Q 50:7); al-Farrā' restricted this structure to "continuing" sentences, conjoined to a preceding sentence (cf. Kinberg, 'Clause' and 'sentence,' 240 f.). *Ammā* is the most common particle marking topicalization, usually in combination with contrast, as in *fa-ammā lladhīna āmanū... fa-yudkhiluhum rabbuhum fī raḥmatihī... wa-ammā lladhīna kafarū...* (Q 45:30-1). Examples of contrastive clauses presented without *ammā,* especially when SV transposition seems to sufficiently mark the contrastive effect, are *wa-llāhu yaqḍī bil-ḥaqqi wa-lladhīna yad'ūna min dūnihi lā yaqḍūna bi-shay'in* (Q 40:20) and *ammā l-yatīma... fa-ammā bi-ni'mati rabbika fa-ḥaddith* (Q 93:9-11); for several readings of *ammā Thamūdan* (Q 41:17; see THAMŪD), see Rabin (*Ancient west Arabian,* 183), where, however, "extraposition" is used as a general notion covering focalization as well.

The resumptive member of the predicate portion may be related more loosely to the topicalized entity, cf. *inna lladhīna āmanū wa-'amilū l-ṣāliḥāti innā lā nuḍī'u ajra man aḥsana 'amalan* (Q 18:30); similarly Q 7:170 and elsewhere.

11. Focalization

Focalization is another extensively used syntactic transformation which serves the Qur'ān's rhetorics. The following are various modes of creation of *tawkīd:*

a. Focalization by extraposition: *iyyāka na'budu* (Q 1:5).

b. Focus on the pronoun of a predicate complex by its isolation ("pronoun reduplication"): *inna shāni'aka huwa l-abtaru* (Q 108:3); *ūlā'ika humu l-ṣādiqūna* (Q 49:15; a typical case of *ḍamīr al-faṣl* according to the grammarians' tradition); *wa-hum bil-ākhirati hum yūqinūna* (Q 27:3); and in verbal sentences: *anā ātīka bihi* (Q 27:40); *a-hum yaqsimūna raḥmata rabbika naḥnu qasamnā...* (Q 43:32); similar is the repetition in *zawjayni ithnayni* (e.g. Q 11:40); the occurrences of *(u)skun anta wa-zawjuka l-jannata* (Q 2:35; 7:19) are not cases of *tawkīd,* in spite of their description as such in the grammatical tradition, but "cases of balancing" (see Bloch, *Studies in Arabic syntax,* 1 f.).

c. Focalization of the lexical contents of the verbal complex by use of the exceptive particle *illā: mā nadrī mā l-sā'atu in naẓunnu illā ẓannan* (Q 45:32, following 45:24 *wa-mā lahum… min ʿilmin in hum illā yaẓunnūna*), on which see the general study of focalization by Goldenberg (*Studies in Semitic linguistics*, 110), where it is incorporated in a comprehensive concept of the rather independent character of the verb's constituents.

d. *Innamā* and *annamā* focalizing the member following their immediate adjacent, e.g. *innamā l-muʾminūna ikhwatun* (Q 49:10). Miquel (La particule *innamā*) offers a variety of semantic functions of the qurʾānic *innamā* based on the Arab grammarians' distinction of its restrictive *(ḥaṣr)* sense.

12. Entity terms

Kull plus singular is used not only for the partitive "every one of" but also in the sense of "all possible items of the species." See Nöldeke (*Zur Grammatik*, 82 f.) on *kullun āmana bi-llāhi* (Q 2:285), *kullun kadhdhaba* (Q 50:14), and *kullun qad ʿalima ṣalātahu* (Q 24:41) followed by a verb indicating their plurality *wa-llāhu ʿalīmun bi-mā yafʿalūna* (also Fischer, *Grammatik*, § 136, anm. 2).

13. Adjective, morphological and syntactic

a. Syntactic adjectivization, as in *yā ayyuhā lladhīna āmanū*, occurs some eighty-five times, but note the absence of qurʾānic occurrences of *(yā) ayyuhā l-muʾminūna*. The finite verb in nominal position in *mina lladhīna hādū yuḥarrifūna l-kalima* (Q 4:46) is considered by Nöldeke (Zur Sprache, 15) not to be a case of asyndetic adjectivization, but an ellipsis completed by *qawm*.

b. Agreement — irregularity: *al-samāʾu munfaṭirun* (Q 73:18); *la-ʿalla l-sāʿata qarībun* (Q 42:17); see Nöldeke (*Zur Grammatik*, 22-3) who provides his discussion with rich documentation of such cases with *faʿīl* and passive participles and mentions this active participle *munfaṭir* for the feminine *samāʾ*. Among early Arab grammarians who discussed these cases, Yūnus b. Ḥabīb al-Thaqafī (d. 182/798) is quoted (see Akhfash, *Maʿānī*, 62) saying *yudhakkaru baʿḍ al-muʾannath*, and others analogized it with *ḍāmir*. Abū ʿAmr's explanation relates it to the sense of *saqf* "roof." The inconsistency of feminine singular *ẓallat* and then plural *khāḍiʿīna* in *fa-ẓallat aʿnāquhum lahā khāḍiʿīna* (Q 26:4) is included in Nöldeke's study of cases of personification (op. cit., 81) and is related to another case of inconsistency in *yatafayyaʾu ẓilāluhu… wa-hum dākhi-rūna* (Q 16:48); al-Kisāʾī (see Farrāʾ, *Maʿānī*, ii, 277) considers the pronoun in *khāḍiʿīna* resuming human plurality of *-hum* in *aʿnāquhum* and compares this "mirror-like" structure with a similar poetic verse.

The Qurʾān is particularly abundant in cases of irregular agreement in number and gender, e.g. *wa-man yaʿṣi llāha wa-rasūlahu lahu nāra jahannama khālidīna fīhā abadan* (Q 72:23). These particular cases are studied in Nöldeke (*Zur Grammatik*, 81 f. and id., Zur Sprache, 12 f.).

c. "Indirect attribute," see Polotsky (Point in Arabic) and his criticism of Reckendorf's concept of "Attraktion" and defence of the Arab grammarians' analysis of *naʿt sababī*, as in *min hādhihi l-qaryati l-ẓālimi ahluhā* (Q 4:75) and *(ṣirāṭi…) ghayri l-maghḍūbi ʿalayhim* (Q 1:7). Nöldeke (*Zur Grammatik*, 79) treats the structure and adduces several qurʾānic and other occurrences including *mukhtalifan alwānuhu* (Q 16:13), *lil-qāsiyati qulūbuhum* (Q 39:22), *khāshiʿatan abṣāruhum* (Q 68:43) and *mufattaḥatan lahumu l-abwābu* (Q 38:50), all with singular adjectives but *khushshaʿan abṣāruhum* (Q 54:7) in the plural. A recent comprehensive study of these and similar structures is Diem *(Fa-waylun li-l-qāsiyati)*. Valuable observations are provided in Goldenberg, Two types.

14. Nominal concord

a. Inclusion of one member of a coordinative pair, known in the Arab linguistic tradition as *taghlīb*, is *buʿda l-mashriqayni*

(Q 43:38; see Sister, Metaphora, 117; Goldenberg, *Studies in Semitic linguistics*, 128). The plural *rabbu l-mashāriqi* (Q 37:5) may have resulted from attraction to the preceding *al-samāwāt*. For a discussion of *il yāsīn* (Q 37:130) as "Ilyās and his party," see Goldenberg (Allādī al-maṣdariyya, 110, n. 11 with reference to Farrā', *Ma'ānī*); also Goldziher (*Richtungen*, 18) who mentions *idrīsīn* as an alternative reading and seems to imply a possible case of *taghlīb* of either of the two figures (see IDRĪS; ELIJAH).

b. The plural noun construed with a dual pronoun in *qulūbukumā* (Q 66:4) is studied, with reference to Sībawayhi's view, in Blau (Two studies, 16 f.). For further reference to grammarians' views on this issue see Talmon (*Arabic grammar*, 225 f., 271). Other qur'ānic instances are the four occurrences of *saw'āt-uhumā/-ihimā* in Q 7:20 and elsewhere.

c. Coordination of two prepositional phrases, the first of which includes a bound pronoun, is *lladhī tasā'lūna bihi wa-l-arḥāma* (Q 4:1). Nöldeke (*Zur Grammatik*, 93; also Zur Sprache, 12, n. 1) indicates the Arab grammarians' dissatisfaction with this structure (which does not comply with their rule of *bihi wa-bi-l...*).

15. Numeralia

There is a single case of irregularity of the counted noun following a number of the 11-99 group, *ithnatay 'ashra asbāṭan* (Q 7:160) against *thnatā 'ashrata 'aynan* in the same verse; *thalātha mi'atin sinīna* (Q 18:25) does not exhibit irregularity as it stands. The "literal" use of the active part in cardinal numbers in the sense of "increasing the number up to X" is attested in *sa-yaqūlūna thalāthatun rābi'uhum kalbuhum wa-yaqūlūna khamsatun sādisuhum kalbuhum... wa-yaqūlūna sab'atun wa-thāminuhum kalbuhum* (Q 18:22; also 58:7), but *inna llāha thālithu thalāthatin* (Q 5:73) and *thāniya thnayni* (Q 9:40).

16. Verbal regimen

Transitive verbs with restricted transitivity: The verbs *safiha* and *ṣabara* of *safiha nafsahu* (Q 2:130) and *wa-ṣbir nafsaka* (Q 18:28) are recognized in the early Arab grammarians' literature as instances in which the apparent object has a different identity, i.e. instances of *mufassir*, later termed *tamyīz*. This recognition involved a description of peculiarities of these complements whose definiteness is consequently regarded as merely formal (cf. Talmon, *Arabic grammar*, 270). The syntactically problematic reading *hal tastaṭī'u rabbaka* (Q 5:112) for *hal yastaṭī'u rabbuka* and its dogmatic background is discussed in Goldziher (*Richtungen*, 23).

17. Particles, adverbials

a. *Bi-* of *bi-l-amsi* (four occurrences) is not omitted, hence there is no occurrence of *amsi* (cf. Beeston, *Arabic language*, 89).

b. The conjunctive *wa-*, following the first nominal in *fī-himā fākihatun wa-nakhlun wa-rummānun* (Q 55:68), puzzled Arab philologists and accordingly an anonymous view recorded in al-Khalīl's *Kitāb al-'Ayn* suggested its interpretation as reference to inclusion, i.e. "namely...," though this view was rejected by others (see Talmon, *Arabic grammar*, 269).

c. *Lawlā* in the sense of the cohortative *hallā* often caused misunderstanding (see Nöldeke, *Zur Grammatik*, 112 f. and Bergsträsser, *Verneinungs- und Fragepartikeln*).

d. Expressions of agreement include *balā, na'am, ajal;* disagreement and rejection are expressed by *kallā* (see Bergsträsser, op. cit., 82).

e. A comparative study of the adversative *lākin/lākinna* in Ambros *(Lākin* und *lākinna)* brings out the emphasis of added value to the latter and its frequent formulaic (stereotypical) combination, particularly with *akthar (al-nās/-hum)*.

18. Negation

a. Negation of nexal relations: *shay'an* as a verb complement in such cases as *wa-laysa bi-ḍārrihim shay'an* (Q 58:10) and some other thirty occurrences, in which this complement cannot be considered an external object, is studied in Talmon (Syntactic category) and identified there as a corroboration of nexus negation, namely the negation of relations between the person and the attribute constituents of the verb. It is considered there as a qur'ānic syntax peculiarity. Its possible relation with the negating suffix *shay/-sh* is then considered. Bergsträsser's (*Verneinungs- und Fragepartikeln,* 105 f.) classification of *shay'an*'s occurrences misses this peculiarity.

b. Redundant *lā* following negation is frequent in the Qur'ān as in *wa-mā arsalnā min qablika min rasūlin wa-lā nabiyyin* (Q 22:52; see also Q 2:105; 9:121; 42:52; 46:9; Nöldeke, *Zur Grammatik,* 90; also id., Zur Sprache, 19 f. for a detailed discussion of its occurrence after *manaʿa* etc.).

c. *(fa-) lā khawfun ʿalayhim* (Q 46:13) and elsewhere exhibits use of *-un (rafʿ)* instead of *-a* for the general negation with *lā al-nāfiya lil-jins.*

d. The negating particle *in* is probably characteristic of the Ḥijāz (see Nöldeke, Zur Sprache, 21 and for a summary see DIALECTS; also Bergsträsser, *Verneinungs- und Fragepartikeln,* 105 f.). On the use of *in* in structures of the type *in... illā...* see Rabin (*Ancient west Arabian,* 178).

e. Wehr (Funktion) first studied the difference between classical Arabic *mā/lam* and indicated the added affective value of the first.

f. *Lā* of the *laysa/mā* type is reported by al-Zamakhsharī (d. 538/1144) for the Ḥijāz, but the Qur'ān has it only coordinated (Q 31:28); and in Q 36:40 the predicate is in the nominative (cf. Rabin, op. cit., 179).

19. Affective expressions

a. *Faʿula* in an affective sense occurs in *kaburat kalimatan* (Q 18:5) and *kabura maqtan* (Q 40:35).

b. *Niʿma* (with eighteen occurrences and two others as *niʿimmā*) and *bi'sa* (with thirty-seven occurrences and three others as *bi'samā*) present in the Qur'ān a unique structure, namely without a "remote nominative," which is hardly followed in their use in other corpora of early Arabic, e.g. *niʿma l-thawābu* (Q 18:31). The structure constitutes the majority of occurrences of *niʿma* and *bi'sa* in the Qur'ān (see Beeston, Classical Arabic *niʿma*).

c. *X mā X: fa-aṣḥābu l-maymanati mā aṣḥābu l-maymanati...* in Q 56:8-9, similarly in Q 56:27; *al-qāriʿatu mā l-qāriʿatu* (Q 101:1-2) is interpreted by Arab philologists as "how happy, miserable, awful..." respectively; see also the somewhat similar *jundun mā hunālika mahzūmun mina l-aḥzābi* (Q 38:11); *huwa mā huwa* is discussed in Fleischer (*Kleinere Schriften,* 477 f.).

d. Typical interjections: *uffin lakumā* (e.g. Q 46:17); *yā ḥasratā* (Q 39:56).

20. Reported speech

A pattern represented by the verb *qāla* plus imperative plural seems to represent a lively narrative style, where the order is expected to be a cohortative "let's" in which the speaker is included: *qālat... udkhulū* (Q 27:18); *qālū anṣitū* (Q 46:29); *qālū taqāsamū bi-llāhi* (Q 27:49); *idh qālū la-Yūsufu wa-akhūhu aḥabbu ilā abīnā... qtulū Yūsufa...* (Q 12:8-9).

The speaker excludes himself from the collectivity of addressees, to whom he belongs, in *qāla qā'ilun minhum kam labithtum qālū labithnā yawman* (Q 18:19), where we would expect "how much have *we* spent...". In a way this applies to another occurrence of direct speech with *qāla qā'ilun minhum* (Q 12:10). The other occurrence of *qāla qāʾilun minhum* (Q 37:51) exhibits the same phenomenon as in Q 37:54 *qāla hal antum muṭṭaliʿūna* which is followed by his own act in the next verse *fa-ṭṭalaʿa*....

Use of *an* at the beginning of citations following verbs other than *qāla* is frequent in the Qurʾān and and is considered by Fischer (*Grammatik*, 188, n. 1) as typical of "Vorarabisch," e.g. *nūdiya an būrika*... (Q 27:8). Verbs other than *qāla* may open a citation. In the case of *wa-waṣṣā bihā Ibrāhīmu... yā baniyya* (Q 2:132) al-Farrāʾ (*Maʿānī*, ad loc.) reports that other grammarians analyzed it as a structure in which *an* is omitted whereas al-Farrāʾ himself argues that *waṣṣā* only has the sense of *qāla*.

Some sentences commencing with the verb of command *amara* and reporting the contents of the command indirectly may present an intermediary mode in which the cohortative *li-* precedes the subordinate particle *an*, as in *umirtu li-an akūna* (Q 39:12) or even dispense with it as in *wa-mā umirū illā li-yaʿbudū llāha* (Q 98:5). A case in which this mode is followed by a direct quotation is *wa-umirnā li-nuslima li-rabbi l-ʿālamīna wa-an aqīmū l-ṣalāta wa-ttaqūhu* (Q 6:71-2).

21. Nominalization, subordinate sentences in noun position

Morphological nominalization which maintains the relations of the former attributival element and the agent/recipient is shaped as a construct structure *(iḍāfa)*. Existence of both actants is attested in *qatlu awlādihim shurakāʾuhum* (Q 6:137), in which *awlād* is the recipient (killed children; see INFANTICIDE) and *shurakāʾ* is the agent, which stands in loose relation to the construct *qatl*. The reading *qatlu awlādahum shurakāʾihim* presents a stronger syntactic cohesion with the agent, yet with irregular separation by the recipient of the two constituents of the *iḍāfa* relations. This reading is reported and discussed by al-Farrāʾ (*Maʿānī*, ad Q 6:137).

Use of *an* instead of *anna* in other cases than *qāla* (see above) is considered by Fischer (*Grammatik*, 188, n. 2) characteristic of the pre-classical period of Arabic. Rabin (*Ancient west Arabian*, 172) discusses *an sa-yakūnu* (Q 73:20), and notes its relation to the preceding *ʿalima an lan tuḥṣūhu* (op. cit., 190, n. 11). Rabin (op. cit., 169) also discusses in this context *ka-an lam* for *ka-anna*... as in *fa-jaʿalnāhā ḥaṣīdan ka-an lam taghna bil-amsi* (Q 10:24) and relates *an* to *in* of the structure *in... lammā* in Q 36:32 (see also the discussion of *inna* above). For an example of an asyndetic structure with main verbs expressing a wish conjoined directly to imperfect indicative verbs without *an*, see *taʾmurūnnī aʿbudu* in Q 39:64.

22. Relative clauses

a. Asyndetic syntactic adjectivization: *al-muṣṣaddiqīna wa-l-muṣṣaddiqāti wa-aqraḍū llāha qarḍan* (Q 57:18); also *[waylun yawmaʾidhin lil-mukadhdhibīna] wa-idhā qīla lahumu rkaʿū lā yarkaʿūna* (Q 77:48); cf. Brockelmann (*Grundriß*, ii, 563) with reconstruction of the process as "Muḥammad wagt es zwar ein determiniertes Adjektiv durch einen Satz forzusetzen, aber noch nicht den Artikel auf diesen zu übertragen," referring to Nöldeke's evaluation (Zur Sprache, 14).

b. The resumptive pronoun of a locative is missing in *yawman lā tajzī* for *lā tajzī fīhi* (Q 2:48, 123. Nöldeke (op. cit., 16) considers it a case in which this pronoun behaves as if it were an object pronoun, namely *tajzīhi*. This phenomenon recurs in *fa-l-yaṣumhu* (Q 2:185) and is studied by Nöldeke (*Zur Grammatik*, 36). Early Basran and Kūfan grammarians recorded by Farrāʾ disputed the identity of the elliptic pronoun in Q 2:48.

c. Indirect relative clauses: *yā ayyuhā lladhīna āmanū* (see above under adjectives) and *yā ʿibādiya lladhīna āmanū* (Q 29:56) is discussed by Bloch (*Studies in Arabic syntax*, 28)

who suggests the notion of "encompassing generality" of believers as an explanation for its abundance. The direct relative clause should be *lladhīna āmantum*.
d. The use of *alladhī al-maṣdariyya* in Q 9:69, *wa-khuḍtum ka-lladhī khāḍū*, and the history of its linguistic treatment is studied by Goldenberg (Allāḏī al-maṣdariyya) who mentions two other verses which probably exhibit this phenomenon, namely Q 6:154 and 62:23 (cf. ibid. § 9). Reference is made to another omission of the resumptive pronoun in *niʿmataka llatī anʿamta ʿalayya* (Q 27:19).

23. Other compound sentences
a. Embedded copular structures: Nöldeke (*Zur Grammatik* [1963], 48) treats this structure, noting duplication of pronouns after *verba sintiendi* and *jaʿala* and exemplified with *in taranī anā aqalla*... (Q 18:39) and *tajidūhu ʿinda llāhi huwa khayran wa-aʿẓama ajran* (Q 73:20); Nöldeke refers to *lā yaḥsibanna lladhīna yabkhalūna bi-mā ātāhumu llāhu min faḍlihi huwa khayran lahum* (Q 3:180) as "ungeschickt."
b. *ʿAsā* structures occur thiry times in the Qurʾān. Rabin (*Ancient west Arabian*, 185) mentions two cases in which uninflected *ʿasā* has a dual or plural subject, namely in Q 2:216 and 49:11 (Ibn Masʿūd [d. 32/652] and Ubayy b. Kaʿb [d. 35/656] read the latter with inflected *ʿasā*) and two loci with inflected *hal ʿasaytum*... (Q 2:246; 47:22). Of the eight structural modes of its occurrence in classical Arabic texts (as specified by Ullmann, Vorklassisches Arabisch), only the first, namely *ʿasā* plus *an* plus subjunctive, is represented here. See also Nöldeke (Zur Sprache, 4), where the variation of inflected and uninflected *ʿasā* constitutes part of his argumentation against Vollers' thesis.
c. Exceptive member after negative *mā:* Rabin (op. cit., 181) cites the Arab grammarians' observation according to which the Ḥijāzī dialect marked the *munqaṭiʿ* (logically non-identical, of a different species) exceptive member with accusative, contrary to the Tamīmī rule which maintained agreement of this member with the noun of the main sentence. The Qurʾān exhibits what may be interpreted as the Ḥijāzī pattern in *mā lahum bihi min ʿilmin illā ttibāʿa l-ẓanni* (Q 4:157), although *ḥāl* interpretation or its like is also possible.

24. Elliptic sentences
Frequent occurrence of elliptic sentences in the Qurʾān is well noted by Nöldeke (Zur Sprache, 17) and others, especially with *idh* and *idhā* as opening new passages.

As this overview demonstrates, qurʾānic grammar poses a great challenge to modern students of the language of early Islam, especially in its historical setting. Advancement of computerized techniques of language- and text-analysis may give an added value to future research in this field (see COMPUTERS AND THE QURʾĀN).

Rafael Talmon

Bibliography
Primary: Abū ʿUbayda, *Majāz;* Abū Zayd, Saʿīd b. Aws al-Anṣārī, *al-Nawādir fī l-lugha*, ed. M.ʿA al-Q. Aḥmad, Beirut 1981; Akhfash, *Maʿānī*, Cairo, 1990; Farrāʾ, *Maʿānī;* Ibn Hishām al-Anṣārī, *Mughnī l-labīb ʿan kutub al-aʿārīb*, ed. M. al-Mubārak and M. Ḥamad Allāh, Beirut 1979[5]; Jumaḥī, *Ṭabaqāt al-shuʿarāʾ*, ed. M.M. Shākir, 2 vols., Cairo 1974; Sībawayhi, Abū Bishr ʿAmr b. ʿUthmān, *al-Kitāb*, ed. H. Derenbourg, 2 vols, Paris 1881-5; Zamakhsharī, *Kashshāf.*
Secondary: A.A. Ambros, *Lākin* und *lākinna* im Koran, in ZAL 17 (1987), 21-30; id., Syntaktische und stilistische Funktionen des Energikus im Koran, in WZKM 79 (1989), 35-56; J. Barth, Arab. *Ẓiltu* und die Verba med. gemin., in *Zeitschrift für Assyriologie und verwandte Gebiete* 24 (1910), 330-2; E. Beck, *Die Koranzitate bei Sibawaih*, unpublished Ph.D. diss., München 1939; A.F.L. Beeston, *Arabic language today*, London 1970; id., Classical Arabic *niʿma* and *biʾsa*, in BSA 3-4 (1991), 101-5 (*Proceedings of the colloquium on Arabic grammar. Budapest* 1991, ed. K. Dévényi and T. Iványi); G. Bergsträsser, *Verneinungs- und Fragepartikeln und*

Verwandtes im Kur'ān. Ein Beitrag zur historischen Grammatik des Arabischen, Leipzig 1914 (repr. 1968); H. Birkeland, *Altarabische Pausalformen,* Oslo 1940; id., *Stress patterns in Arabic,* Oslo 1954; J. Blau, On invariable passive forms in biblical Hebrew and classical Arabic, in Y. Avishur and J. Blau (eds.), *Studies in Bible and the ancient Near East presented to S.E. Loewenstamm,* Jerusalem 1978, 190-1; id., *On pseudo-corrections in some Semitic languages,* Jerusalem 1970; id., Two studies of Sībawayhi's *Kitāb,* in JSAI 12 (1989), 1-29; A. Bloch, *Studies in Arabic syntax and semantics,* Wiesbaden 1991; M.M. Bravmann, The phrase *in kuntum fā'ilīna* in *Sūrat Yusuf* v. 10, in *Der Islam* 48 (1971), 122-5 (repr. as An Arabic sentence-type expressing "inner compulsion," in id., *Studies in Semitic philology,* Leiden 1977, 347-56); C. Brockelmann, *Grundriß der vergleichenden Grammatik der semitischen Sprachen, Bde. I-II,* Berlin 1908-13; J. Burton, Linguistic errors in the Qur'ān, in JSS 33 (1988), 181-96; M. Chouémi, *Le verbe dans le Coran,* Paris 1966; C. Correll, "Ein Esel, welcher Bücher trägt...": Zum Prädikativ im Klassisch-Arabischen, in ZAL 26 (1993), 7-14; S.-O. Dahlgren, Word order and topicality in the Qur'ān, in ZAL 39 (2001), 20-35; W. Diem, *Fa-waylun li-l-qāsiyati qulūbuhum. Studien zum arabischen adjektivischen Satz,* Wiesbaden 1998; id., Untersuchungen zur frühen Geschichte der arabischen Orthographie, in *Orientalia* 48 (1979), 207-57; 49 (1980), 67-106; 50 (1981), 332-82; 52 (1983), 357-404; G.H.A. Ewald, *Grammatica critica linguae Arabicae,* 2 vols., Lipsiae 1831-3; A. Fischer, Die Quantität des Vokals des arabischen Pronominal Suffixes *hu (hi),* in C. Adler and A. Ember (eds.), *Oriental studies dedicated to Paul Haupt as director of the Oriental Seminary of the Johns Hopkins University,* Baltimore 1926, 390-402; W. Fischer, Das Altarabische in Islamischer Überlieferung: Das Klassische Arabisch, in *Grundriß der Arabischen Philologie. Band I: Sprachwissenschaft,* Wiesbaden 1982, 37-50; id., Classical Arabic, in R. Hetzron (ed.), *The Semitic languages,* London 1997, 187-219; id., *Grammatik des klassischen Arabisch,* Weisbaden 1987; id., Die Perioden des klassischen Arabisch, in *Abr-nahrain* 12 (1971-2), 15-8; id., Silbenstruktur und Vokalismus im Arabischen, in ZDMG 117 (1967), 30-77; H.L. Fleischer, *Kleinere Schriften. I,* Leipzig 1885; G. Goldenberg, *Allāḏī al-maṣdariyya* in Arab grammatical tradition, in ZAL 28 (1994), 7-35; id., The Semitic languages and the science of language, in J. Geiger (ed.), *Moises Starosta memorial lectures,* Jerusalem 1993, 99-126 (in Hebrew); id., *Studies in Semitic linguistics. Selected writings,* Jerusalem 1998; id., Two types of phrase adjectivization, in W. Arnold and H. Bobzin (eds.), *"Sprich doch mit deinem Knechten aramäisch, wir verstehen es!" Festschrift für Otto Jastrow zum 60. Geburtstag,* Wiesbaden 2002, 193-208; Goldziher, *Richtungen;* N. Kinberg, 'Clause' and 'sentence' in *Ma'anī al-Qur'ān* by al-Farrā'. A study of the term *kalām,* in BSA 3-4 (1991), 239-46; id., Figurative uses, polysemy and homonymy in systems of tense, mood and aspect, in *Lingua* 83 (1991), 319-38; id., *A lexicon of al-Farrā''s terminology in his Qur'ān commentary,* Leiden 1996; id., Semi-imperfectives and imperfectives. A case study of aspect and tense in Arabic participal clauses, in *Lingua* 83 (1992), 301-30; id., Some temporal, aspectual and modal features of the Arabic structure *la-qad* + prefix tense verb, in JAOS 108 (1988), 291-5; F. Leemhuis, *The D and H stems in koranic Arabic. A comparative study of the function and meaning of the fa''ala and 'af'ala forms in koranic usage,* Leiden 1977; A. Levin, What is meant by *'akalūnī l-barāġītu?* in JSAI 12 (1989), 40-65; A. Miquel, La particule *ḥattā* dans le Coran, in BEO 21 (1968), 411-36; id., La particule *innamā* dans le Coran, in JA 248 (1960), 483-99; F.R. Müller, *Untersuchungen zur Reimprosa im Koran,* Bonn 1969; N. Nebes, *'In al-muḫaffafa* und *al-lām al-fāriqa,* in ZAL 7 (1982), 7-22; B. Nedjar, *Grammaire fonctionnelle de l'arabe du Coran,* 4 vols., Karlsruhe 1988; Neuwirth, *Studien;* Nöldeke, GQ; id., *Zur Grammatik des classischen Arabisch* (Im Anhang: Die Handschriftlichen Ergänzungen in dem Handexemplar Theodor Nöldekes bearbeitet und mit Zusätzen versehen von Anton Spitaler), Darmstadt 1897, 1963; id., Das klassische Arabisch und die arabischen Dialekten, in id., *Beiträge zur Semitischen Sprachwissenschaft,* Straßburg 1904, 1-14 (revised version of Einige Bemerkungen über die Sprache der alten Araber, in *Zeitschrift für Assyriologie und verwandte Gebiete* 12 [1897-8], 171-87); id., Zur Sprache des Korāns: I. Der Korān und die 'Arabīja; II. Stilistische und syntaktische Eigentümlichkeiten der Sprache des Korāns; III. Willkürlich und mißverständlich gebrauchte Fremdwörter im Korān, in id., *Neue Beiträge zur Semitischen Sprachwissenschaft,* Strassburg 1910, 1-30; H.J. Polotsky, A point in Arabic syntax. The indirect attribute, in IOS 8 (1978), 159-73; Ch. Rabin, *Ancient west Arabian,* London 1951; id., The beginnings of classical Arabic, in SI 4 (1955), 19-37; H. Reckendorf, *Arabische Syntax,* Heidelberg 1921; id., *Die syntaktische Verhältnisse des Arabischen. I-II,* Leiden 1895-8; id., *Über Paronomasie in den semitischen Sprachen. Ein Beitrag zur Allgemeinen Sprachwissenschaft,* Giessen 1909; W. Reuschel, *Aspekt und Tempus in der Sprache des Qorans,* Frankfurt 1996; id., Wa-kāna llāhu 'alīman raḥīm, in *Wissenschaftlische Zeitschrift Martin Luther Universität Halle-Wittenberg* 17 (1968), 147-53; G. Richter, *Der Sprachstil des Koran. Aus dem Nachlaß herg. von Otto Spies,* Leipzig 1940; M. Sister, Metaphora und Vergleiche im Koran, in *MSOS* 2/34 (1931), 104-54; A. Spitaler, Die Schreibung des Typus *ṣlwt* im Koran. Ein Beitrag zur Erklärung der koranischen Orthographie, in *WZKM* 56 (1960), 212-26; R. Talmon, *Arabic grammar in its formative age. Kitāb al-ʿAyn and its attribution to Ḫalīl b. Aḥmad,* Leiden 1997; id., An eighth-century grammatical school in Medina. The collection and evaluation of the available material, in *BSOAS* 48 (1985), 224-36; id., A problematic passage in Sībawaihi's *Kitāb* and the authenticity of *aḫbār* about the early history of Arabic grammatical thinking, in *JAOS* 104 (1984), 691-701; id., The syntactic category *mafʿūl muṭlaq*. A study in qurʾānic syntax, in Y. Suleiman (ed.), *Arabic grammar and linguistics,* Richmond, Surrey 1999, 107-24; R. Tietz, *Bedingungsatz und Bedingungsausdruck im Koran,* Ph.D. diss., Tübingen 1963; M. Ullmann, *Adminiculum zur Grammatik des klassischen Arabisch,* Wiesbaden 1989; id., *Untersuchengen zur Rağazpoesie. Ein Beitrag zur arabischen Sprach- und Literaturwissenschaft,* Wiesbaden 1966; id., Vorklassisches Arabisch, in R. Tirani (ed.), *Studi in onore di Francesco Gabrieli nel suo ottantesimo compleanno,* 2 vols., Rome 1984, ii, 807-18; C.H.M. Versteegh, *Arabic grammar and qurʾānic exegesis in early Islam,* Leiden 1993; K. Vollers, *Volkssprache und Schriftsprache im alten Arabien,* Straßburg 1906; F. Müller, *Untersuchungen zum Reimprosa im Koran,* Bonn 1969, review by J. Wansbrough in *BSOAS* 33 (1970), 389-91; H. Wehr, Zur Funktion arabischer Negationen, in *ZDMG* 103 (1953), 27-59; W.H. Worrell, The interrogative particle *hal* in Arabic according to native sources and the Kurʾān, in *Zeitschrift für Assyriologie und verwandte Gebiete* 21 (1908), 116-50; W. Wright, *A grammar of the Arabic language,* ed. W. Robertson Smith and M.J. de Goeje, Cambridge 1896-8[3] (rev. ed.); T. Zewi, *A syntactical study of verbal forms affixed by -n(n) endings in classical Arabic, biblical Hebrew, el-Amarna Akkadian and Ugaritic,* Münster 1999.

Grapes

see FOOD AND DRINK; HOURIS; PARADISE; GARDEN

Grasses

Plants distinguished by their jointed stems, narrow and spear-shaped blades and fruits of a seedlike grain; also, the green herbage affording food for cattle and other grazing animals. The Qurʾān does not contain specific words for grass(es) as used in the modern Arabic language such as *ʿushb* and *ḥashīsh*.

The word *ḍighth* in Q 38:44, rendered in some translations as "a handful of (green or dry) grass," can also refer to a mixture of herbs or a handful of twigs from trees or shrubs; Lane conveys a gloss of the term in the same passage as "a bundle of rushes." Al-Ṭabarī (d. 310/923) understands the word to indicate a bundle of fresh wood or large grasses with which to beat somebody, although not with too much force (*Tafsīr,* xxiii, 167-9).

Another word, *ḥuṭām,* meaning something that is dry and tough, appears in Q 56:65 (and 57:20) where it can be translated as "chaff" or "straw." Both Arabic terms are embraced by the general term for "vegetation," *nabāt* (see AGRICULTURE AND VEGETATION). Despite the imprecision of these words, in one passage, Q 18:45, *nabāt* occurs together with another imprecise term, *hashīm,* meaning a plant that has become dried and broken, the entire context of which, however, clearly reveals the qurʾānic intent in its frequent references to the natural world (see NATURAL WORLD AND THE QURʾĀN). The passage reads in Pickthall's translation, "And coin for them the similitude of the life of the world as water (q.v.) which we send down from the sky (see HEAVEN), and the vegetation of the earth *(nabāt al-arḍ)* mingleth with it and then becometh dry twigs *(hashīm)* that the winds (see AIR AND WIND) scatter. Allāh is able to do all things."

A final term that is sometimes understood to refer to "grasses" is found in Q 55:6, where the *najm* (glossed variously as "grass" or "star") and the tree are both said to bow down in adoration (*yasjudān,* see BOWING AND PROSTRATION; WORSHIP).

David Waines

Bibliography
Lane; Pickthall; Ṭabarī, *Tafsīr,* Cairo 1954. For further references, see the articles AGRICULTURE AND VEGETATION; FOOD AND DRINK.

Gratitude and Ingratitude

Thankfulness or disdain in response to a kindness. A dominant feature of the concept of gratitude in the Qurʾān is its use to describe the spiritual bond binding the believer to God. Gratitude has a very broad semantic field in the Qurʾān with a strong theocentric character in the sense that gratitude is owed chiefly to God, even if that means through what God has made and the offices he has appointed. Gratitude is a spiritual and moral state of mind, spiritual in the sense of acknowledging the believer's obligation to the creator, and moral in the sense of mandating rightful conduct in relation to God and to those appointed by God (see ETHICS AND THE QURʾĀN). Ingratitude is the opposite, its fundamental defect being denial of what is rightfully owed to God. It thus twists and distorts the very basis of all moral relationships, whether those with God or with those within the human community (see COMMUNITY AND SOCIETY IN THE QURʾĀN). As the Qurʾān states it, ingratitude is a form of rebellious unbelief, of *kufr* (see BELIEF AND UNBELIEF).

The verb to thank, to be grateful *(shakara)* and its various cognates, such as *shukr* (gratitude or thanksgiving), occurs seventy-four times in the Qurʾān. Gratitude or thanksgiving is in one sense due to God alone, and, only by analogy, to others. Accordingly, worship (q.v.; *ʿibāda*) is grateful praise (q.v., *al-ḥamd*), to which only God is entitled. The roots of gratitude lie in the act of creation (q.v.) to which human beings owe their life, with sustenance of life through God's bounties and blessings (see BLESSING; GRACE) being further grounds for gratitude. The faithful person *(muʾmin),* the person of *īmān* (Q 3:147), is the grateful person *(shākir).* In Sūrat al-Raḥmān ("The Beneficent," Q 55), the Qurʾān rehearses for the believer the bounties and blessings of God with a refrain in the form of a rhetorical challenge, "which of your lord's bounties will you deny?" The word used for "denial," in the dual form, is *tukadhdhibān,* and carries the sense of falsifying, of making counterfeit the true and genuine, all because ingratitude has sealed the doors of the heart. One passage provides a graphic description of the ungrateful heart (q.v.) thus: "Then your hearts became hardened thereafter and are like stones, or even yet harder; for there are stones from which rivers come gushing, and others split, so that water issues from them, and others crash down in fear of God. And God is not heedless of the things you do" (Q 2:74).

Other metaphors are used to describe the heart of the heedless and the ungrateful. Their hearts are rusted (Q 83:14); a veil has come over their hearts; and a heaviness has fallen on their ears (q.v.), making them tone-deaf (Q 17:46; 41:5; see HEARING AND DEAFNESS). In fact, a rebellion has infected their primary organs of speech, hearing, sight, and feeling (Q 2:171; 6:25; 8:20-4; 22:46; 46:26; see SEEING AND HEARING; EYES). Nothing avails them. That situation contrasts with that of those who believe and are grateful to God: "Those who believe, their hearts being at rest in God's remembrance — in God's remembrance are at rest the hearts of those who believe..." (Q 13:28).

Ingratitude, or unbelief, like its opposite, is a matter for the exclusive attention of God. Unbelief, however, stands beyond ingratitude as the ultimate defiance of God. The Qurʾān describes unbelievers in uncompromising terms, saying God will not relent towards them: "How shall God guide a people who have disbelieved after they believed, and bore witness that the messenger (q.v.) is true, and the clear signs came to them? God guides not the people of evildoers" (Q 3:86; see EVIL DEEDS); and "surely those who disbelieve, and die disbelieving, there shall not be accepted from any of them the whole earth full of gold (q.v.), if he would ransom himself thereby; for them waits a painful chastisement, and they shall have no helpers" (Q 3:91; see REWARD AND PUNISHMENT).

The favored servants, by contrast, who are brought close to God are those who have been given thankful hearts. God is the true benefactor, the ultimate patron, and ingratitude to God therefore ranks as the ultimate act of disobedience, an act of willful rebellion against God. Accordingly the Qurʾān speaks of God's blessings as something bestowed on the grateful and ungrateful alike (*min faḍli rabbī li-yabluwanī a-ashkuru am akfuru wa-man shakara fa-innamā yashkuru li-nafsihi wa-man kafara fa-inna rabbī ghaniyyun karīmun,* Q 27:40).

Gratitude defines God's claim on the attention and devotion of believers. God is abundant in bounty, yet humanity remains ungrateful (*wa-inna rabbaka la-dhū faḍlin ʿalā l-nāsi wa-lākinna aktharahum lā yashkurūna,* Q 27:73); God has furnished people with the earthly life and the means of its enjoyment, and still ingratitude clouds the human response (Q 7:10).

Abū Ḥāmid al-Ghazālī (d. 505/1111), a theologian with considerable influence on Muslim thought and practice, devoted a detailed study to the subject. For him, remembrance of God *(dhikr)* is united with gratitude to God, as he points out in his *Kitāb al-Ṣabr wa-l-shukr* ("On patience and gratefulness," in the fourth volume of his *Iḥyāʾ ʿulūm al-dīn,* pp. 53-123). Al-Ghazālī cites the Prophet as saying that among the remembrances of God nothing is more meritorious than "thanks be to God." As such, glorification of God *(subḥān Allāh)* and "praise be to God" *(al-ḥamdu li-llāh)* signify the proper attitude of the acknowledgment of blessings from God. According to al-Ghazālī, God is the benefactor from whom gifts come without being mediated through an intermediary. Consequently, gratitude for God's blessings should rebound to God alone.

Fullness of human gratitude consists in recognizing that nature itself bears in its bosom the divine bounty and blessing, signifying that fact in its obedience to God's command. By the same token, human mediators of God's bounty remain subservient to God's power, whether or not they are conscious of it. Gratitude should not be deflected to the means God employs or to the thing God gives, for such is the gratitude of the common people when they receive food, clothing, drink and similar concessions to the appetite. Accordingly, gratitude to God is an act that God enables the faithful to perform — yet another reason for gratitude. In the final analysis, God does not need the gratitude of the faithful in order to be God. Indeed, gratitude to God is meritorious obedience to him, just as complaining is shameful disobedience, al-Ghazālī insists. A person who misuses a thing by diverting it from that for which it was created, including misuse of the organs of the body, becomes thereby ungrateful in the eyes of God. Gratitude is of the heart, hidden manifestations *(wāridāt al-qulūb),* as it were, but it must be expressed with the tongue, for God desires that of the faithful (Q 29:17; 7:206). According to Q 31:12, "Indeed, we gave Luqmān (q.v.) wisdom (q.v.): 'Give thanks to God; whosoever gives thanks gives thanks only for his own soul's good, and whosoever is ungrateful — surely God is all-sufficient, all-laudable.' "

The Qurʾān exhorts the devout, "So remember me, and I will remember you; and be thankful to me; and be you not ungrateful towards me. O all you who believe, seek you help in patience and prayer; surely God is with the patient" (Q 2:152-3; see TRUST AND PATIENCE). In the general scheme of creation, as well as in the specific conduct of human affairs, gratitude is a moral marker. No relationship with God is complete or credible without it. This is not simply because God commandeers it in the fashion of a liberationist power, but because gratitude is an attribute of divinity ("God is all-grateful *[shākirun]*, all-knowing *[ʿalīmun]*," Q 2:158). By extension, gratitude is a mark of the moral order God has ordained for human society and its furtherance, as the following verses make clear: "We have charged man, that he be kind to his parents (q.v.)... Until, when he is fully grown, and reaches forty years, he says, 'O my lord, dispose me that I may be thankful for your blessing by which you have blessed me and my father and mother, and that I may do righteousness well-pleasing to you; and make me righteous also in my seed" (Q 46:15); and "of his mercy he has appointed for you night and day, for you to repose in and seek after his bounty, that haply you will be thankful" (Q 28:73; cf. 3:190-1; see DAY AND NIGHT).

Gratitude is the criterion God will use to separate the faithful from the evil doers (Q 7:17 f., 14:7). The Qurʾān assures the faithful that at the final reckoning "God will recompense the thankful" (Q 3:144, 145). An early Meccan sūra (see CHRONOLOGY AND THE QURʾĀN) that contains the unique occurrence of one term for ingratitude, *kanūd*, alludes to the fate of the ungrateful: "Lo! man is an ingrate unto his lord *(inna l-insāna li-rabbihi la-kanūdun)*... Does he not know that when the contents of the grave are poured forth and the secrets of the breasts are made known, on that day their lord will be perfectly informed about them" (Q 100:6-11; see APOCALYPSE; LAST JUDGMENT).

The Qurʾān speaks of the prophets of God as people of gratitude, of their obedience and faithfulness as acts of thanksgiving (see PROPHETS AND PROPHETHOOD). Abraham's (q.v.) obedience (q.v.) and faithfulness were tokens of his gratitude to God (Q 16:120-1); Noah (q.v.) was a man of faith (q.v.) and gratitude (Q 17:3); Solomon (q.v.) was endowed with supernatural gifts to accomplish the ends for which God appointed him so that he would be grateful (Q 34:12-3); even the apocryphal ant (*naml*, see ANIMAL LIFE) responds in gratitude when it escapes being trampled underfoot in the path of Solomon's imperious progress (cf. Q 27:18-9); Moses (q.v.) consecrated his work of prophecy by issuing a call for gratitude to God by all who live on the earth (Q 14:5-8). Al-Ghazālī has Moses himself making supplication before God, asking how Adam (see ADAM AND EVE) showed his gratitude to God after all that God did for him. God responds by saying that Adam's knowledge *(maʿrifa)* was gratitude. Moses comments further that he is unable to express his gratitude to God except with a thanksgiving that itself is God's gift to him. In a striking passage describing David's (q.v.) anointed lineage and his appointment as prophet, the Qurʾān holds him up as a model of gratitude: "And we gave David bounty from us: 'O you mountains, echo God's praises with him, and you birds!'.... 'Labor, O house of David, in thankfulness; for few indeed are those that are thankful among my servants'" (Q 34:10 f.).

Apart from being one of God's attributes, gratitude is something in which God engages by virtue of God's beneficence (God is all-thankful *[shakūrun]*, all-clement *[ḥalīmun]*, Q 64:17). God will thank those of the faithful who strive after eternal life (Q 17:19). Upon such favored ones "shall be garments of silk and brocade (see CLOTHING); they are adorned with bracelets of silver, and their lord shall give them to drink a pure draught," and God will say to them, "Behold, this is a recompense for you, and your striving is thanked (*mashkūran,* Q 76:21 f.)."

Al-Ghazālī reflects on the implication of divine reciprocity suggested in these verses, particularly how such reciprocity can be reconciled with divine transcendence *(tanzīh)*. He comments: "It is conceivable that man may be a thankful person in respect of another man, either by praising the second person for his good treatment of him or by rewarding the second person with a greater [benefit] than he received. [Actions of this nature] spring from man's praiseworthy qualities... As far as thanking God is concerned, one can use this term only metaphorically and then only loosely. For even if man praises God, his praise is inadequate since the praise God deserves is incalculable.... However, the best way of manifesting thankfulness for the blessings of God most high is to make use of these blessings in obeying, and not disobeying [see DISOBEDIENCE], him. And even this can only happen with God's help [see FREEDOM AND PREDESTINATION] and by his making it easy for man to be a thankful person to his Lord...." (al-Ghazālī, *al-Maqṣad al-asnā,* trans. Stade, *Ninety-nine names,* 71).

Lamin Sanneh

Bibliography

Primary: al-Ghazālī, Abū Ḥāmid Muḥammad, *Gazzali's Ihya ulum-id-din. Or the revival of religious learnings,* trans. Alhaj Maulana Fazlul Karim, 5 vols., Dacca 1971; id., *Kitāb Iḥyā᾿ ʿulūm al-dīn,* bk. xxxii. *Kitāb al-Ṣabr wa-l-shukr,* Cairo 1352/1933, iv, 53-123; id., *al-Maqṣad al-asnā,* trans. and ed. R.C. Stade, *Ninety-nine names of God,* Ibadan, Nigeria 1970; Ibn Abī l-Dunyā, ʿAbdallāh b. Muḥammad, *Kitāb al-Shukr,* ed. Ṭ. al-Tantawī, Cairo 1992; al-Kharāʾiṭī, Muḥammad b. Jaʿfar, *Kitāb Faḍīlat al-shukr lillāh ʿalā niʿmatihi wa-mā yajibu mina l-shukr lil-munʿam ʿalayhi,* ed. M. al-Ḥāfiẓ, Damascus 1982.

Secondary: D. Bakker, *God and man in the Qurʾān,* Amsterdam 1965; K. Cragg, *The event of the Qurʾān. Islam in its scripture,* Oxford 1994; id., *The mind of the Qurʾān,* London 1973; J. Jomier, *Great themes of the Qurʾān,* London 1997; M.R. Waldman, The development of the concept of kufr in the Qurʾān, in *JAOS* 88 (1968), 442-55; Watt-Bell, *Introduction;* A. Wessels, *Understanding the Qurʾān,* trans. J. Bowden, London 2000.

Greed see AVARICE

Greeks see BYZANTINES

Guardianship

Care and management of the person and/or property of a person deemed incapable of managing his or her own affairs. Although the Qurʾān has no specific term for guardian and nowhere says what kind of relationship (kinship of a certain degree or otherwise) should exist between a guardian and ward, guardianship is nonetheless referred to in several verses. It is understood that (a) minors and (b) women are those who ought to be protected by male, adult guardians (see also CHILDREN; WOMEN AND THE QURʾĀN).

The Qurʾān, probably against a background of injustice and violence to which orphans (q.v.) and widows (see WIDOW) were subjected in pagan Mecca (q.v.; see also PRE-ISLAMIC ARABIA AND THE QURʾĀN), shows special solicitude for young people who have been deprived of their natural guardians. Exhortations to deeds of beneficence towards fatherless children *(yatāmā,* sing. *yatīm)* appear from the early Meccan sūras, e.g. Q 93:9 (for dating see Bell, ii, 663; see CHRONOLOGY AND THE QURʾĀN). Another, probably Meccan, verse (Q 17:34) emphasizes that the property rights of orphans should be respected, warning the guardian not to touch their property "except in a way that will improve it" (Bell, i, 265). Medinan verses from the second and third year after the emigration from Mecca to Medina (*hijra*, see EMIGRATION) deal particularly with the guardianship of children who had lost their fathers, Muḥammad's followers, in the battles of Badr (q.v.) and Uḥud (see EXPEDITIONS AND BATTLES). Q 4:5 elaborates on the obligations of guardians (*awṣiyāʾ al-yatāmā*, according to Ṭabarī, *Tafsīr*, ad loc.) appointed by God to manage the property *(jaʿala… lakum qiyāman)* of those who are "of weak intellect" *(sufahāʾ):* They are exhorted to feed and clothe them from the wealth that is entrusted to them, and they are also told to "speak to them in reputable fashion" (Bell, i, 68-9). In Q 4:2 and 4:6, guardians are warned not to misuse their wards' possessions (in these verses, the wards are specified as orphans), neither to "substitute the bad for the good" nor to "consume their property" (Bell, i, 68-9). In Q 4:6, guardians are also instructed to hand their property over to their wards in the presence of witnesses, when they will have reached the age of marriage *(balaghū l-nikāḥ)* and become able to manage their own affairs (*rushd*, see also the Medinan verses Q 4:10; 6:152).

Q 4:3 deals with the permission, given to men, to establish (limited?) polygamous unions (with their wards? with other women?, cf. Q 4:127; see MARRIAGE AND DIVORCE) in the context of their duty to treat their wards (specifically female ones?) justly. Watt (*Muhammad at Medina*, 276), accepting the traditional account that this verse was revealed shortly after the battle of Uḥud, suggests that the crux of the problem was not the large number of widows resulting from that battle but the many unmarried girls now placed under the guardianship of uncles, cousins and other kinsmen (see KINSHIP). Some of the guardians would keep their wards unmarried so as to enjoy unrestricted control over their property. According to Watt, the Qurʾān probably did not intend that the guardians should themselves marry their wards. Support for this supposition may come from Q 4:24, which continues the list begun in Q 4:23 of those women who are forbidden for a man to marry: "And *al-muḥṣanātu mina l-nisāʾi* [are forbidden to you], except those whom your right hand possesses…." The term *muḥṣanāt* may indicate "respectably housed and guarded women whether married or not" (Bell, i, 72; cf. Motzki, Wal-Muḥṣanātu, 192-218).

Even before the rise of Islam, it had become customary in Arabia for the dowry to be paid to the woman, not to her guardian (Stern, *Marriage*, 37). This is reflected in several Medinan verses (Q 4:4, 24, 25; 5:5; 60:10) which urge husbands to pass the bridal gift (*ṣaduqāt, ujūr*, see BRIDESWEALTH) directly to their brides or, according to commentaries on Q 4:4, command guardians to return to their wards dowry they had unjustly taken themselves (e.g. Ṭabarī, *Tafsīr;* Zamakhsharī, *Kashshāf;* Bayḍāwī, *Anwār*, ad loc.). That the bridal gift is the property of the wife and remains her own if the marriage is dissolved (Spies, Mahr, 79) is reflected in Q 4:20. Despite this apparent financial independence, it seems to have been the province of the male guardian to arrange the marriage of his female wards (daughters, granddaughters, and others who fell under his natural — or otherwise — guardianship): "He in whose hand is the bond of marriage" *(alladhī biyadihi ʿuqdatu l-nikāḥi*, Q 2:237; cf. Zamakhsharī, *Kashshāf*, ad loc.: *al-walī alladhī yalī ʿaqd nikāḥihinna)* is probably a reference to this facet of male guardianship of women.

Avner Giladi

Bibliography
Primary: Bayḍāwī, *Anwār;* Ṭabarī, *Tafsīr;* Zamakhsharī, *Kashshāf.*
Secondary: A. al-Azhary-Sonbol, Adoption in Islamic society. A historical survey, in E. Warnock Fernea (ed.), *Children in the Muslim Middle East,* Austin 1995, 45-67; Bell; A. Giladi, *Children of Islam. Concepts of childhood in medieval Muslim society,* London 1992; id., Ṣaghīr, in *EI²*, viii, 821-7; H. Motzki, Wal-muḥṣanātu mina n-nisāʾi illā mā malakat aimānukum (Koran 4:24) und die koranische Sexualethik, in *Der Islam* 63 (1986), 192-218; Th.J. O'Shaunessy, The qurʾānic view of youth and old age, in *ZDMG* 141 (1991), 33-51; R. Roberts, *The social laws of the Qurʾān,* London 1925; O. Spies, Mahr, in *EI²*, vi, 78-80; G. Stern, *Marriage in early Islam,* London 1939; W.M. Watt, *Muhammad at Medina,* Oxford 1956.

Guidance and Leading Astray

see FREEDOM AND PREDESTINATION; ASTRAY

H

Ḥadīth and the Qurʾān

One important genre in Arabic literature comprises the sayings attributed to the Prophet Muḥammad, descriptions of his deeds as well as accounts of events supposed to have occurred during his lifetime. This literary genre is the tradition literature, the ḥadīth, which is a term for the literature as well as for a single tradition. This article is divided into eleven sections: (1) general introduction; (2) traditions about the beginning of the divine revelations and what the Prophet is reported to have experienced while receiving them (see REVELATION AND INSPIRATION); (3) traditions dealing with the collection of the scattered qurʾānic fragments by order of the first three caliphs (see COLLECTION OF THE QURʾĀN); (4) traditions dealing with the seven variant readings (*qirāʾāt* or *aḥruf*, see READINGS OF THE QURʾĀN); (5) traditions in which the various modes of Qurʾān recitation are sorted out (see RECITATION OF THE QURʾĀN); (6) exegetical traditions in general (see EXEGESIS OF THE QURʾĀN: CLASSICAL AND MEDIEVAL); (7) traditions that clarify certain well-known qurʾānic legal prescriptions (see LAW AND THE QURʾĀN); (8) historical reports closely connected with particular qurʾānic verses (q.v.; see also OCCASIONS OF REVELATION); (9) traditions that sing the praises of certain sūras or verses; (10) special genres of ḥadīth literature closely related to the Qurʾān: "stories of the prophets" *(qiṣaṣ al-anbiyāʾ)* traditions (see PROPHETS AND PROPHETHOOD); eschatological traditions (see ESCHATOLOGY); ḥadīth *qudsī;* (11) the Shīʿī ḥadīth sources (see SHĪʿISM AND THE QURʾĀN).

(1) *General introduction*

Normally each tradition consists of (1) a list of names, beginning with the collector in whose collection the tradition found a place followed by several transmitters going back to the prophet Muḥammad or to another ancient authority, the so-called *isnād* (see further down), followed by (2) the actual text *(matn)* of the tradition. Certain collections of ḥadīths, six in all, were compiled in the latter half of the third/ninth century and became generally considered as so reliable by the Sunnī Muslim religious authorities of the day that they were canonized as it were, eventually acquiring a sanctity second only to the Qurʾān. In each of those six collections, known collectively as *al-kutub al-sitta,* i.e. "the Six Books," there is, apart from countless scattered allusions to qurʾānic verses and accompanying "occasions of revelation"

(*asbāb al-nuzūl,* the plural of *sabab al-nuzūl,* cf. sec. 8 below), as well as a host of concomitant issues, at least one special section that deals exclusively with qurʾānic matters — exegesis in the widest sense of the word. These sections contain the *tafsīr* traditions. In order of the importance of the collections, with references to the better-known editions, these sections are:
(1) *Badʾ al-waḥy* and *Faḍāʾil al-Qurʾān,* in Muḥammad b. Ismāʿīl al-Bukhārī (d. 256/870), *Ṣaḥīḥ,* ed. L. Krehl & Th.W. Juynboll, 4 vols., Leiden 1862-1908, i, 4 f.; iii, 391 f., and the edition authorized and carried out by a number of Azhar scholars and other religious dignitaries, 9 vols., Cairo 1313/1895, Maṭbaʿat Muṣṭafā al-Bābī al-Ḥalabī and reprinted many times, i, 2 f.; vi, 223 f. (al-Bukhārī's lengthy exegetical *[tafsīr]* section in iii, 193 f. = vi, 20 f., is especially important);
(2) *Bāb faḍāʾil al-Qurʾān wa-mā yataʿallaqu bihi* and *Tafsīr,* in Muslim b. al-Ḥajjāj (d. 261/875), *Ṣaḥīḥ,* ed. Muḥammad Fuʾād ʿAbd al-Bāqī, 5 vols., Cairo 1955 (reprinted many times), i, 543 f.; iv, 2312 f.;
(3) *Abwāb qirāʾat al-Qurʾān wa-taḥzībihi wa-tartīlihi, Bāb fī thawāb qirāʾat al-Qurʾān* and *Kitāb al-Ḥurūf wa l-qirāʾāt* in Abū Dāwūd Sulaymān b. al-Ashʿath al-Sijistānī (d. 275/889), *Sunan,* ed. Muḥammad Muḥyī l-Dīn ʿAbd al-Ḥamīd, 4 vols., Cairo 1354/1935 (reprinted several times), ii, 54 f., 70 f.; iv, 31 f., and Muḥammad Shams al-Ḥaqq al-ʿAẓīmābādī, *ʿAwn al-maʿbūd sharḥ sunan Abī Dāwūd,* 14 vols., Beirut 1990, iv, 186 f., 228 f.; xi, 3 f.;
(4) *Faḍāʾil* (or *Thawāb) al-Qurʾān* and *Qirāʾāt* in Muḥammad b. ʿĪsā al-Tirmidhī (d. 279/892), *al-Jāmiʿ al-ṣaḥīḥ,* ed. Aḥmad Muḥammad Shākir et al., 5 vols., Cairo 1937-65, v, 155 f., 185 f.; his *Tafsīr* section (v, 199 f.) is, like al-Bukhārī's, especially important;
(5) *Faḍāʾil al-Qurʾān, Abwāb qirāʾat al-Qurʾān* and *Tafsīr* in Aḥmad b. Shuʿayb al-Nasāʾī (d. 303/915), *Kitāb al-Sunan al-kubrā,* ed. ʿAbd al-Ghaffār Sulaymān al-Bundārī and Sayyid Kasrawī Ḥasan, 6 vols., Beirut 1991, v, 3 f., 173 f.; vi, 282 f. (n.b.: in Nasāʾī's abbreviation of this collection entitled *Sunan* or *al-Mujtabā* there are no special Qurʾān-related sections);
(6) *Bāb iftitāḥ al-qirāʾa* in Ibn Māja al-Qazwīnī (d. 273/886), *Sunan,* ed. M.F. ʿAbd al-Bāqī, 2 vols., Cairo 1952-3 (reprinted several times), i, 267 f.

Five other major pre-canonical collections of ḥadīth and related material with special sections devoted to the Qurʾān are:
(1) Mālik b. Anas (d. 179/795), *Muwaṭṭaʾ,* ed. M.F. ʿAbd al-Bāqī, 2 vols., Cairo 1951 (reprinted many times), *Kitāb al-Qurʾān,* i, 199 f.;
(2) Abū Dāwūd al-Ṭayālisī (d. 203-4/819-20), *Minḥat al-maʿbūd fī tartīb Musnad al-Ṭayālisī Abī Dāwūd,* ed. Aḥmad ʿAbd al-Raḥmān al-Bannā al-Sāʿātī Beirut 1372, ii, *al-Kitāb fī mā yataʿallaqu bi-l-Qurʾān,* 2 f.;
(3) ʿAbd al-Razzāq al-Ṣanʿānī (d. 211/826), *Muṣannaf,* ed. Ḥabīb al-Raḥmān al-Aʿẓamī, 11 vols., Beirut 1970, *Faḍāʾil al-Qurʾān,* iii, 335 f.;
(4) Abū Bakr b. Abī Shayba (d. 235/849), *Muṣannaf,* 15 vols., Hyderabad 1966-88, *Faḍāʾil al-Qurʾān,* x, 456 f.;
(5) ʿAbdallāh b. ʿAbd al-Raḥmān al-Dārimī (d. 255/869), *Sunan,* ed. Fawwāz Aḥmad Zamarlī and Khālid al-Sabʿ al-ʿAlamī, 2 vols., Cairo/Beirut 1987, *Faḍāʾil al-Qurʾān,* ii, 521 f.

Among the most important Shīʿī ḥadīth sources we find the following, each with special sections on the Qurʾān:
Muḥammad b. Yaʿqūb al-Kulaynī (d. 328/939), *al-Kāfī fī ʿilm al-dīn,* ed. ʿAlī Akbar al-Ghaffārī, 8 vols., Teheran 1381, *Faḍl al-Qurʾān,* ii, 596 f.;
Muḥammad Bāqir al-Majlisī (d. 1110/1700), *Biḥār al-anwār,* 2nd edition, ed. al-Sayyid Ibrāhīm al-Mayānjī and

Muḥammad al-Bāqir al-Bahbūdī, 104 vols., Beirut 1983, vols. lxxxix and xc, 1-145, *Kitāb al-Qurʾān*. For an appraisal of this source, see section 11 below.

Seemingly complete *isnād*s preceding longer or shorter medieval Qurʾān studies were occasionally utilized in later writings in the qurʾānic sciences (see TRADITIONAL DISCIPLINES OF QURʾĀNIC STUDY) in order to lend these prestige, but these studies are not part of ḥadīth literature per se. Thus we find, for example, a concise enumeration *(talkhīṣ)* in which passages assumed to have been revealed in Mecca (q.v.) are separated from those assumed to have been revealed in Medina (q.v.), headed by a strand ending in Mujāhid/Ibn ʿAbbās in Jamāl al-Dīn al-Suyūṭī's *Itqān* (i, 24 f.), who cites a book on abrogation (q.v.) by the grammarian al-Naḥḥās (d. 338/950, cf. *GAS*, ix, 207 f.). Throughout his massive work al-Suyūṭī (d. 911/1505) quotes other such surveys on a variety of qurʾānic subjects with the name of only one ancient authority (often Companions like Ibn ʿAbbās or Ubayy b. Kaʿb; see COMPANIONS OF THE PROPHET) prefixed as the transmitting authority. The "mysterious letters" (*fawātiḥ*, see LETTERS AND MYSTERIOUS LETTERS) with which a number of sūras begin are enumerated with a host of interpretations, each of which is again preceded by an *isnād* of sorts (cf. Suyūṭī, *Itqān*, iii, 21 f., and also Majlisī, *Biḥār*, lxxxix, 373 f.). Examples of such works on a number of qurʾānic disciplines with scattered and non-canonical *isnād*s attached to them are otherwise legion. The significance of such *isnād*s is slight on the whole, and mentioning them at all seems more a matter of habit than a purposeful attempt to substantiate historically the transmission paths of such studies.

The evolution of the ḥadīth went hand in hand with Muslim exploration and interpretation of the Qurʾān. Thus we find a variety of interpretive issues reflected in the ḥadīth: theological, ethical (see ETHICS AND THE QURʾĀN), legislative, grammatical and lexicographical exegesis (see GRAMMAR AND THE QURʾĀN), setting off the general of the Qurʾān against the specific in the ḥadīth or, on some occasions, the general in the ḥadīth against the specific of the Qurʾān, as well as providing background information on the history of the revelation *(asbāb al-nuzūl, nāsikh wa-mansūkh)*. Some of these aspects, in addition to various others, will be dealt with in sections 2-11 below.

The *isnād*s preceding accounts about the Prophet or his closest associates or anyone from the past were first instituted in the course of the final decades of the first/seventh century. From that time, people who wished to transmit something, for example a saying or anecdote which they had picked up somewhere, were required first to name their informant and the informant of that informant, and so on all the way back to the lifetime of the pivotal person of the event. This requirement led to the birth of untold numbers of *isnād* chains which, eventually, turned up in the tradition collections, heading the individual sayings and anecdotes.

*Isnād*s occurring in the canonical collections are, on the whole, accepted almost without question by the Islamic world as historically reliable authentication devices, traditional ḥadīth criticism being a highly developed discipline in the Muslim world. They are, however, rejected as such by those Western investigators of ḥadīth who opine that *isnād*s are better left alone, inasmuch as not only a good number — as is generally admitted — but, conceivably, *all* of them may be forged, and that there is no foolproof method of telling which one is sound and which one is not. In the present article the appraisal of *isnād*s is less radically skeptical. *Isnād*s heading the adduced traditions have all been scrutinized and analyzed and, as far as that seemed tenable, questions as to chronology, provenance and authorship of the traditions supported by them have been addressed. This procured satisfactory answers in some instances, but that is, unfortunately, not always the case (e.g. see sec. 6 below).

At any rate, an effort has been made in this article to adduce datable traditions with indications as to their conceivable originators. Mostly, references will be given first to the number of the *isnād* bundle as listed in the *Tuḥfa* of Yūsuf b. ʿAbd al-Raḥmān al-Mizzī (d. 742/1341; for this author, who lists in his work all canonical traditions from the Six Books and a few others in alphabetical order, according to the oldest transmitters of their respective *isnād*s, see Juynboll, Some *isnād*-analytical methods). After that, references to occurrence in one or a few important collections will be added. This will then be followed by the transmitter(s), if any, who may be held responsible for the proliferation of these traditions. In an attempt to highlight the importance of non-Arab converts to Islam *(mawālī)* in early Islam, indication is given when these transmitters belonged to that category.

Throughout this article, mention will be made of several newly-coined technical terms developed in recent *isnād*-bundle analysis, such as "common link" (= cl), "seeming common link" (= scl), "spider," "single strands" (= ss's), and the like. For the time being the following introductory excursus should suffice. For visual illustrations, one is referred to the diagrams as drawn here (Diagrams A, B and C, see p. 380) and also those in section 3 below (Diagrams D and E). (For an extensive introduction to these terms, see Juynboll, Nāfiʿ, and id., Early Islamic society.)

When all the *isnād* strands found in the collections in support of one particular, well-known tradition are put together on a sheet of paper, beginning at the bottom with the names of the oldest transmitters and working one's way upwards in time, a picture emerges which turns out to be similar to other pictures, whenever that exercise is repeated in respect to other well-known traditions. From the bottom up one finds first a single row or strand of three, four or more names (rarely two) from the Prophet or any other ancient central authority, a strand which at a given moment starts to branch out to a number of names. Where that single strand (ss) branches out first, we find a man whom we call the common link (cl), and when his alleged pupils have themselves more than one pupil we call each one of such pupils a partial common link (pcl). All these branches together constitute a so-called *isnād* bundle.

The more transmission lines there are, coming together in a certain transmitter, either reaching him or branching out from him, the greater the claim to historicity that moment of transmission, represented in what may be described as a "knot," has. Thus the transmission moments described in ss's (*fulān-fulān-fulān*, etc.), linking just one master with one pupil and then with one pupil and so on, traversing at least some two hundred years cannot lay claim to any acceptable historicity: in all likelihood they are the handiwork of the collectors in whose collections they are found. But when the transmission from a cl branches out to a number of pcls, each of whose transmissions branches out also to a number of other pcls, then these "knots" give a certain guarantee for the historical tenability of that transmission path, at least in the eyes of the rather less skeptical *isnād* analyst.

The more pcls a cl has, the more probable the authorship of the (wording of that) tradition under scrutiny is to be ascribed to

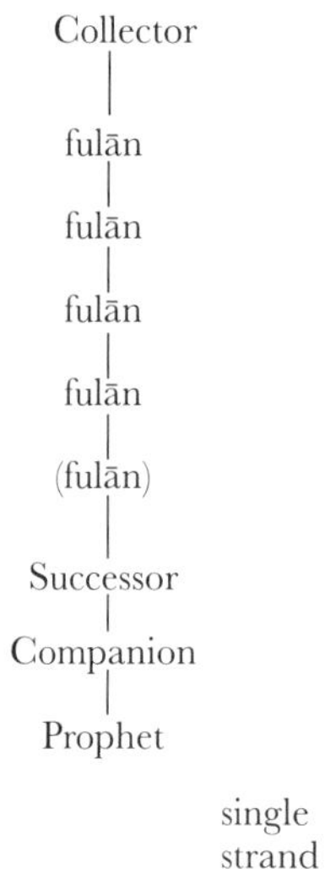

Diagram A

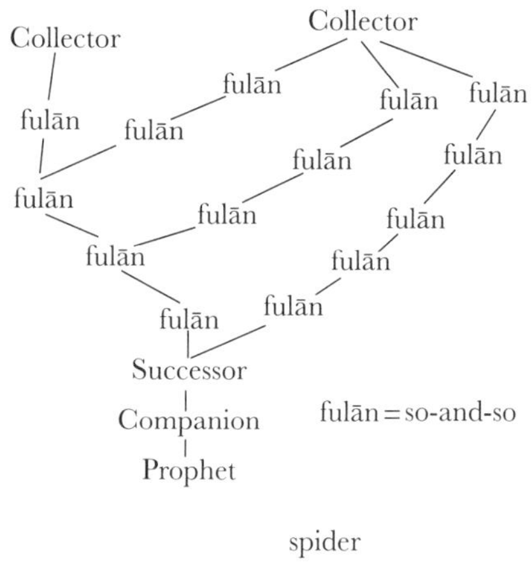

Diagram B

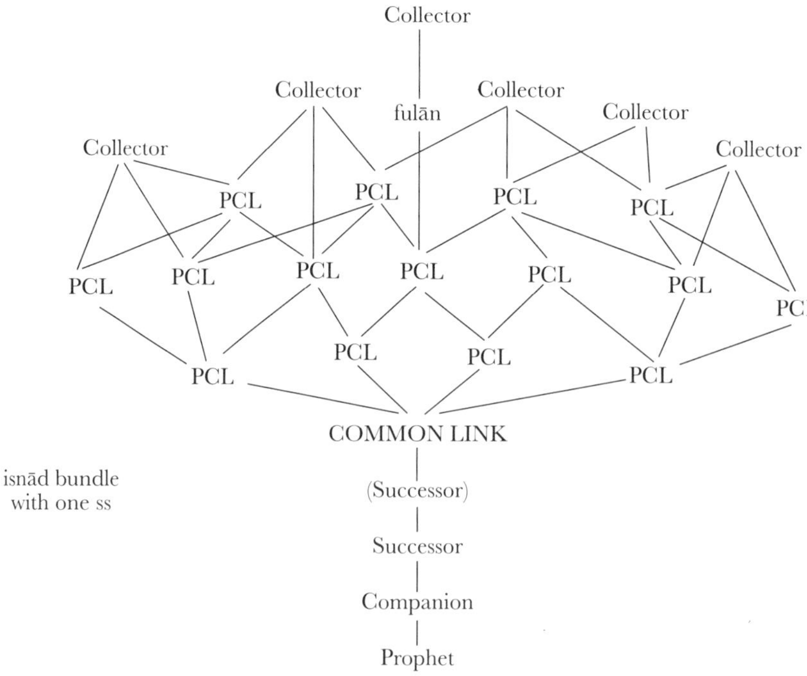

Diagram C

that cl. And that supplies at the same time answers to questions about the provenance and chronology of the tradition thus supported. In other words, a transmitter can only safely be called a cl when he has himself several pcls, and a pcl can only safely be called that, when he has himself several other, younger pcls. When the number of pcls of a cl is limited we rather speak of that cl as a seeming cl. Seeming cls may emerge in bundles which, upon scrutiny, turn out to be two or a few ss's which happen to come together in what looks like a cl, but which, for lack of pcls, is not.

Summing up, the vast majority of traditions in the Six Books are supported by *isnād* structures in the form of ss's. When, in any given tradition, several ss's seem to come together in a seeming cl, which does not have the required minimum of believable pcls, we call the *isnād* structure of that tradition a "spider." In Muslim tradition literature we find thousands upon thousands of ss's, a good many of which form into otherwise undatable spiders. Traditions supported by *isnād* bundles that deserve that qualification are rather rarer, but do seem to contain data that may point to a more or less tenable chronology, provenance and even authorship.

(2) *The beginning of the divine revelation*

The best-known tradition about the beginning of the revelation *(waḥy)* depicts how the Prophet was visited by the angel Gabriel (q.v.; Jibrīl) who gave him a short text to recite, the first divine revelation of all, five verses of Q 96: "Recite in the name of your lord...." The oldest version of the story extant in the sources may tentatively be attributed to the storyteller *(qāṣṣ)* of Mecca, ʿUbayd b. ʿUmayr (d. 68/687), officially installed in that position by the second caliph (q.v.), ʿUmar b. al-Khaṭṭāb. This version was later reworded and provided with some crucial interpolations by the Medinan/Syrian chronicler Ibn Shihāb al-Zuhrī (d. 124/742). He traced the account back to the Prophet via a ʿUrwa b. al-Zubayr/ʿĀʾisha (see ʿĀʾISHA BINT ABĪ BAKR) *isnād*. The development of the textual accretions and embellishments of the story — including an attempt of the *mawlā* Yaḥyā b. Abī Kathīr (d. between 129/747 and 132/750) to have Q 74:1-5 accepted as the first revealed verses — as well as of its multiple *isnād* strands, has been studied and provided with diagrams of the *isnād* bundles by Juynboll (Early Islamic society, 160-71) and Schoeler (*Charakter*, chap. 2; cf. also Rubin, Iqraʾ).

There are various traditions on how the Qurʾān was further revealed. Some late and undatable traditions describe how the Qurʾān was lowered in its entirety during Ramaḍān (q.v.) to the heaven (see HEAVEN AND SKY) nearest to earth (q.v.), on the "Night of the Divine Decree" (*laylat al-qadr*, see NIGHT OF POWER), whereupon it was revealed piecemeal from there to Muḥammad through the angel Gabriel (q.v.). Efforts to mark the exact night in Ramaḍān that must be identified as *laylat al-qadr* have resulted in a cluster of traditions supported by *isnād* strands, from among which various late common links are discernible. The overwhelming number of (partially conflicting) prophetic and Companion reports on the exact day in Ramaḍān leads, however, to the inevitable conclusion that the discussion was an ancient one, in all likelihood triggered by Q 97:1-3: "We have sent it (i.e. the Qurʾān) down in the Night of the Divine Decree... a night better than one thousand months (q.v.)." For some late originators of prophetic *laylat al-qadr* traditions, see Mizzī's *Tuḥfa*, iii, no. 4419 (Mālik, *Muwaṭṭaʾ*, i, 319; Muslim, *Ṣaḥīḥ*, ii, 824), in which *isnād* bundle we encounter the Baṣran transmitter Hishām b. Abī ʿAbdallāh al-Dastuwāʾī (d. 152-4/769-71) and the Medinan jurist Mālik b. Anas who are seen to occupy common link positions.

Then there are traditions in which we encounter descriptions of the physical symptoms allegedly displayed by the Prophet while he received revelations. One of the oldest of such traditions may be attributed to the Medinan (later, Kūfan) transmitter Hishām b. ʿUrwa (d. 146/763), the son of ʿUrwa b. al-Zubayr mentioned above. Here, it is related that the Prophet either heard a tinkling bell from which he had to distill the divine message or that he was approached by the angel (q.v.) in human form who delivered a spoken message. He is also depicted as perspiring profusely, even in cold weather, when a revelation was sent down upon him (cf. Mizzī, xii, no. 17152; Mālik, i, 202 f.; Muslim, iv, 1816 f.). Another early tradition, for which the Kūfan transmitter Manṣūr b. al-Muʿtamir (d. 132/750) may be held responsible, deals with the occasional forgetfulness in retaining revelations from which the Prophet is reported to have suffered. This was caused by God, it says in a later commentary, who thereby abrogated a verse's recitation. Forgetting a verse constituted, on the whole, human punishment for not having memorized it properly in the first place, in the same way one would be punished for the escape of a camel (q.v.) that had not been hobbled. Often this forgetfulness was deemed to be the result of a malicious whisper from the devil (q.v.; Mizzī, vii, no. 9295; Muslim, i, 544). Another early traditionist responsible for a similar tradition is the above-mentioned Hishām b. ʿUrwa (cf. Mizzī, xii, nos. 16807, 17046; cf. also Ibn Ḥajar, *Fatḥ*, x, 457 f.).

The revelation process was allegedly assisted by the angel Gabriel who descended from heaven once every year during Ramaḍān in order to collate with the Prophet the qurʾānic fragments that had been revealed in the course of that year, mostly in groups of no more than five verses (cf. Suyūṭī, *Itqān*, i, 124 f.). In the final year of Muḥammad's life, Gabriel is recorded to have come down to earth twice for this collation. Seemingly the earliest datable tradition in which this is reflected may be ascribed to the Kūfan *mawlā* Zakariyyāʾ b. Abī Zāʾida (d. 147-9/764-6, Mizzī, *Tuḥfa*, xii, no. 17615; Ibn Saʿd, *Ṭabaqāt*, ii 2, 40; Muslim, *Ṣaḥīḥ*, iv, 1904 f.). And there is a tradition in the same vein to be dated to the time of the Baghdādī jurist-cum-traditionist Aḥmad b. Ḥanbal (d. 241/855, cf. his *Musnad*, i, 231).

(3) *The collection of the Qurʾān*

As the early Muslim historical sources inform us, during the Prophet's life the qurʾānic fragments were noted down by several of his Companions, sometimes labeled as his "secretaries," on the available materials that could serve for that purpose. But upon his death the scattered remains could hardly be said to constitute an ordered or easily accessible redaction (see CODICES OF THE QURʾĀN). The ḥadīths in the canonical and other collections that purportedly give an account of the first caliphs' endeavors to gather up *(jamʿ)* these fragments and organize them into chapters *(taʾlīf)* in an orderly fashion do not permit hard and fast conclusions as to chronology and authorship. They can be divided into two distinct reports, the first one centering on Abū Bakr's and ʿUmar's measures (for its *isnād* bundle, see Diagram D) and the second on ʿUthmān's efforts in this respect (for its *isnād* bundle, see Diagram E).

Muḥammad's desire to keep matters open so that cases of abrogation or repeal *(naskh)* concerning certain prescriptions *(aḥkām)* could still be inserted is given as the reason why he did not already assemble the revelations in a *muṣḥaf* (q.v.), i.e. a collection of sheets (= *ṣuḥuf*, see WRITING AND WRITING MATERIALS; INSTRUMENTS), during his lifetime (cf. Ibn Ḥajar, *Fatḥ al-*

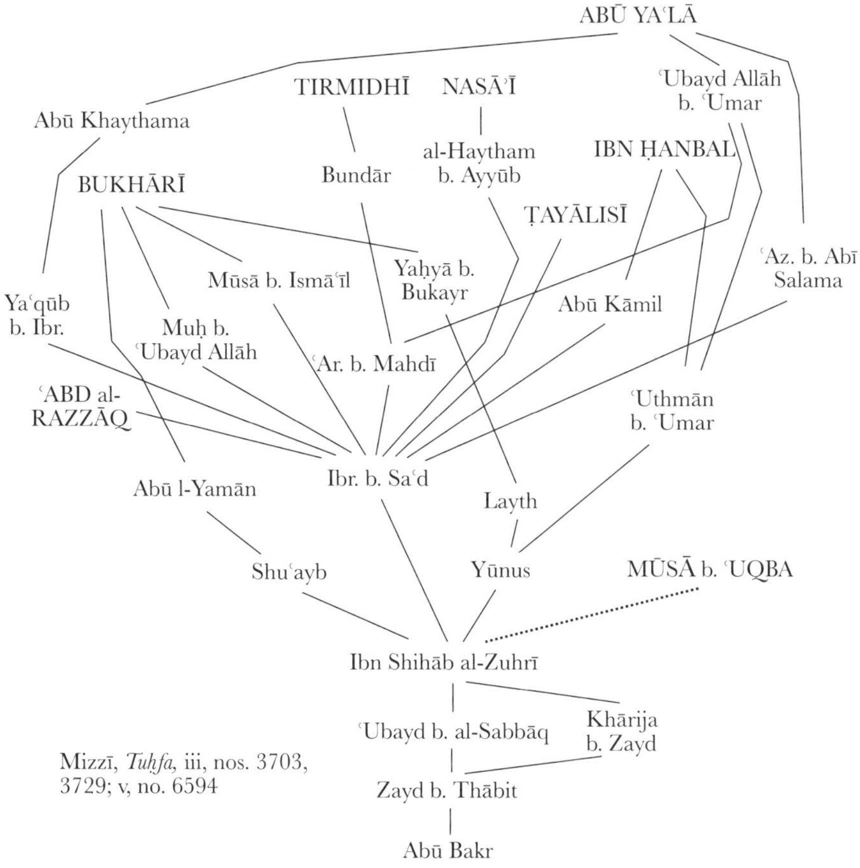

Diagram D

bārī, x, 386, ll. 8 f.). That is why the "rightly-guided caliphs" (*al-khulafāʾ al-rāshidūn*, the first four caliphs of Islam) took up the matter only after his death. Notwithstanding numerous textual variants, the background data in these two reports tally by and large with what we read in Islam's most prestigious, early historical sources, but their embellishing elements caution us that we should not take them at face value or all too literally.

Within its *isnād* bundle the first report dealing with Abū Bakr seems to show a common link: Ibn Shihāb al-Zuhrī who, with a strand down to the young Companion Zayd b. Thābit (d. between 45/665 and 55/675) via the totally obscure, and therefore probably fictitious, transmitter ʿUbayd b. al-Sabbāq, may conceivably be held responsible for the skeleton of the wording as well as for this strand, *if* that is not the handiwork of an unidentifiable transmitter higher up in the bundle who is evidently also responsible for the Khārija b. Zayd strand. As for the historicity of details, one does well to treat the report with caution.

The second report, the one concerning ʿUthmān's directives, is even more swamped by typically ahistorical or, differently put, topical, embellishments. Zuhrī is again a key figure in its *isnād* bundle but his strand down to ʿUthmān via the Baṣran Companion Anas b. Mālik (d. 91-3/710-12) is even more dubious than the one to Abū

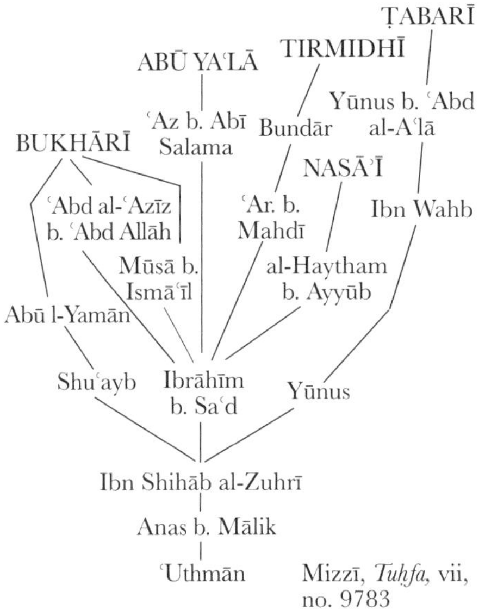

Diagram E

Bakr because of various considerations brought together in Juynboll, Shuʿba. In any case, Zuhrī cannot be held responsible for it. On the other hand, the position of his younger and distant kinsman the transmitter Ibrāhīm b. Saʿd al-Zuhrī (d. 183/799), who migrated from Medina to Baghdad, is more firmly established and, what is more significant, especially highlighted by the otherwise fierce *isnād* critic, the Baghdadi *mawlā* Yaḥyā b. Maʿīn (d. 233/847; Ibn Ḥajar, *Tahdhīb*, i, 122, 9). So it is he, and not Zuhrī, who may be held largely responsible for its wording.

The overall conclusion must be that the basic historicity of what both stories tell us remains a matter of dispute among dispassionate historians, especially in the case of the second. A reliable chronological reconstruction of the final redaction of the Qurʾān can presumably only be achieved on the basis of ancient manuscript evidence. Islam has, however, always accepted the Abū Bakr and ʿUthmān stories without question as fundamental. Schwally (in Nöldeke, GQ, ii, 18 f.) prefers to hold ʿUmar, rather than Abū Bakr, largely responsible for the first collection of the Qurʾān and in Burton's *Collection* and Wansbrough's *Qurʾānic studies* both stories are rejected out of hand on the basis of a host of different considerations. For a much less skeptical assessment of the two traditions, see Motzki, *De Koran*, 12-29.

Abū Bakr's order to have the Qurʾān organized is laid down in a report in which it is alleged that he was warned by ʿUmar that, because of the many casualties at the battle of ʿAqrabāʾ in the Yamāma (see EXPEDITIONS AND BATTLES) against the false prophet Musaylima (see MUSAYLIMA AND PSEUDO-PROPHETS), many of the memorized fragments (see ORALITY) of qurʾānic revelations might be lost for posterity. So Zayd b. Thābit was assigned to collect as many fragments preserved in peoples' memories, as well as those preserved in writing on all sorts of material, as he could find. The oldest historical source in which this report is said to have been preserved is the *Maghāzī* of Mūsā b. ʿUqba (d. 141/758; Ibn Ḥajar, *Fatḥ*, x, 390, l. 8), where a sober account is quoted from Zuhrī who, this time, dispenses with naming his authority, a highly significant omission by any standards. Except for a small fragment, that *Maghāzī* text is lost.

The second report centering on ʿUthmān is chronologically situated in the second or third year of his reign. In this report it is alleged that one of his generals had observed that his men from Iraq (q.v.) recited the Qurʾān differently than did his men from Syria. This was incentive enough for ʿUthmān, so the story tells us, to have the sheets *(ṣuḥuf)* on which Abū Bakr had recorded the fragments sorted out and copied out again, whereby the dialect of Quraysh (q.v.) was to prevail in the case of conflicting readings.

Thus the 114 sūras of the Qurʾān were supposedly collected in one *muṣḥaf*, roughly in the order of decreasing length. As

Muslim sources indicate, the last sūra to be revealed was Q 9, Sūrat al-Tawba ("Repentance") and the last verse Q 4:176, the so-called *kalāla* verse that dealt with a category of the relatives of a deceased person who are entitled to a share in the inheritance (q.v.; cf. Mizzī, *Tuḥfa,* ii, no. 1870; Muslim, *Ṣaḥīḥ,* iii, 1236). The Baṣran *mawlā* Shuʿba b. al-Ḥajjāj (d. 160/776) is the transmitter responsible for a tradition to this effect. According to a Shīʿī source the last sūra to be revealed was Q 110 (Majlisī, *Biḥār,* lxxxix, 39). An enigmatic report not contained in any of the canonical collections but listed in al-Ṭabarī (d. 310/923; *Tafsīr,* xxvi, 40), with a full *isnād* ending in Muʿāwiya b. Abī Sufyān, the first Umayyad caliph (d. 61/680), claims that the final verse of Sūrat al-Kahf ("The Cave," Q 18) was indeed the last verse sent down to Muḥammad. Another such report, for which see al-Suyūṭī (*Itqān,* i, 184 f.), relates that two more short sūras, or rather prayers, were originally thought to have been part of the Companion Ubayy b. Kaʿb's early, pre-Abū Bakr redaction, the so-called *sūrat al-khalʿ* and *sūrat al-ḥafd,* but they were eventually not added to the 114. And, finally, the existence of short sequences of rhyming prose lines *(sajʿ),* which are strongly reminiscent of early Meccan sūras (see RHYMED PROSE; FORM AND STRUCTURE OF THE QURʾĀN), complete with various, seemingly pre-Islamic oaths, and which do not deserve to be dismissed as mere pastiche (Ṭabarī, *Taʾrīkh,* i, 2484, id., *History,* xiii, 223 f.; Ibn Isḥāq, *Sīra,* iii, 343), may leave one with the impression that there were more such fragments floating about which never made it into what later came to be called the ʿUthmānic codex. Al-Suyūṭī (*Itqān,* iii, 72-5) has, furthermore, conveniently listed some assorted verses, including the famous stoning (q.v.) verse (cf. Powers, Exegetical genre, 117-38), that were, as several Companions tell us, allegedly revealed to Muḥammad, but were never incorporated in it either.

(4) *Traditions on the seven* qirāʾāt *or* aḥruf

On various occasions the Prophet is supposed to have taught his followers one particular wording of a qurʾānic fragment at one time and at other times other wordings, concluding: "… recite it in the way that is easiest for you." This course of events is reflected in a *matn* cluster in the canonical collections concerning the "seven readings" (*sabʿat aḥruf* or *sabʿ qirāʾāt;* for the variant *sabʿat aqsām,* "seven subdivisions," Majlisī, *Biḥār,* xc, 4). When ʿUmar was once reported to have voiced his anxiety as to what is truly qurʾānic and what not, the Prophet is said to have reassured him with the words: "Every phrase that is purported to be part of the Qurʾān is correct as long as forgiveness (q.v.) is not confused with chastisement (see CHASTISEMENT AND PUNISHMENT), or chastisement with forgiveness," and "Each of the seven *aḥruf* is 'sufficient and restores health' *(kāfin shāfin)*" (Ibn Ḥajar, *Fatḥ,* x, 401, 9 f.). But this is a late report, in which the flexible attitude vis-à-vis qurʾānic variant readings is presented in florid terms. It had many precursors.

The number seven for the different readings is not to be taken literally, but rather as conveying an undefined number of units under ten, as seventy is often used to convey an undefined number of tens under one hundred. As long as the inner meaning is preserved, there is no harm in variants. The first tentatively datable traditions, which deal with variant readings but do not yet center on the number seven, may be attributed to the Baṣran traditionist Shuʿba (Mizzī, *Tuḥfa,* i, no. 60; Muslim, *Ṣaḥīḥ,* i, 562 f.; and Mizzī, *Tuḥfa,* vii, no. 9591; Bukhārī, *Faḍāʾil al-Qurʾān,* 37, 3, iii, 410 = vi, 245). The number seven, mostly interpreted as representing a number of ways of placing, or deleting, variable diacritics and vowels in verbs and nouns, especially in their endings, or the metathesis of letters, whole words, or phrases, etc., is occasionally assumed, wrongly in the opinion of most medieval scholars, to point to the different dialects (q.v.) the Arabs (q.v.) spoke, when the Qurʾān was in the process of being revealed. Moreover, the number is occasionally identified with seven modes of expression: verses or phrases containing incitement (*zajr*, see EXHORTATION), command (*amr*, see COMMANDMENTS), permission (*ḥalāl*), prohibition (*ḥarām*, see LAWFUL AND UNLAWFUL), affirmed or ambiguous (q.v.) statements (*muḥkam* or *mutashābih*) and similes (*amthāl*, see METAPHOR). Perhaps the earliest datable and most comprehensive tradition based on the number seven and probably going back to a discussion that had been going on for more than half a century before his lifetime is that of Mālik b. Anas (*Muwaṭṭaʾ*, i, 201, no. 5, = Mizzī, *Tuḥfa*, viii, no. 10591; Muslim, *Ṣaḥīḥ*, i, 560). There are otherwise very few phrases in the Qurʾān that actually allow recitation in seven ways, the classic examples being: *ʿabada al-ṭāghūt* in Q 5:60 (Bayḍāwī, *Anwār*, i, 265), and *fa-lā taqul lahumā uff* in Q 17:23 (cf. ibid., i, 537).

The permission to resort to as many as seven variant readings is thought to have come forth from God's desire to facilitate (*takhfīf, tashīl*) mastery in Qurʾān recitation for those Arabs who were to embrace Islam at a later stage, especially after the emigration (q.v.; *hijra*). Following the early conquests (q.v.), in particular after the completion of the Qurʾān redaction that reportedly came to be recognized as that of ʿUthmān (see above, section 2), with the consolidation of the empire and the proliferation of Qurʾān instruction, the study of the variants began to constitute a separate qurʾānic discipline, even if some scholars hold the view that the so-called "ʿUthmān *muṣḥaf*" represents just one of the seven permissible *aḥruf*, making the other six obsolete. This seeming contradiction and accompanying harmonization attempts are set forth in detail by al-Zarkashī (*Burhān*, i, 222-7, and also Muslim, *Ṣaḥīḥ*, i, 560, note 3; for further discussion of the seven *aḥruf*, see Gilliot, *Elt*, 112-33).

(5) *On recitation*

There are traditions in which the proper ways of recitation are described, e.g. that one is not to hasten the recitation without pauses as one does while reciting poetry (see POETRY AND POETS), a recitation mode which is called *hadhdh*. Originators of such traditions are the Kūfan *mawlā* Sulaymān b. Mihrān al-Aʿmash (d. 148/765; Mizzī, *Tuḥfa*, vii, no. 9248; Muslim, *Ṣaḥīḥ*, i, 563) and Shuʿba b. al-Ḥajjāj (Mizzī, *Tuḥfa*, vii, no. 9288; Muslim, *Ṣaḥīḥ*, i, 565). Then there are traditions on the lengthening (*ishbāʿ* or *madd*) of vowel sounds while reciting with the Kūfan jurist al-Thawrī as probable originator (Mizzī, *Tuḥfa*, vi, no. 8627; Tirmidhī, *Jāmiʿ*, v, 177) and the Baṣran transmitter Jarīr b. Ḥazim (d. 175/791) as probable originator (Mizzī, *Tuḥfa*, i, no. 1145; Bukhārī, *Faḍāʾil*, iii, 406 = vi, 241). Vibrating in recitation (*tarjīʿ*) is dealt with in a tradition of Shuʿba (Mizzī, *Tuḥfa*, vii, no. 9666; Muslim, *Ṣaḥīḥ*, i, 547). This vibrating could perhaps be described as interrupting the vowel sounds with a series of glottal stops, that at least appears to be the explanation of Majd al-Dīn al-Mubārak b. al-Athīr (d. 606/1210, cf. his *Nihāya*, ii, 202).

The total number of Qurʾān verses is variously given as 6204, 6214, 6219, 6225 or 6236. That number is also thought to indicate the steps whose ascendance will bring the faithful Qurʾān reciter, practicing the solemn recitation mode of *tartīl*, ever closer to paradise (q.v.), cf. a tradition in Muḥammad Shams al-Ḥaqq al-ʿAẓīmābādī (fl.

1312/1894, cf. his *ʿAwn al-maʿbūd,* iv, 237), for which al-Thawrī may tentatively be held responsible. Furthermore, there is a well-known tradition with many details about the Prophet's prolonged night recitation (Mizzī, *Tuḥfa,* iii, no. 3351; Muslim, *Ṣaḥīḥ,* i, 536 f.) with Aʿmash as possible originator. To Shuʿba, who was eventually imitated by al-Thawrī can be attributed a tradition in which the teaching of Qurʾān recitation to others is praised (Mizzī, *Tuḥfa,* vii, no. 9813; Bukhārī, *Faḍāʾil al-Qurʾān,* 21, iii, 402 = vi, 236).

The slogan-like Prophetic tradition "Adorn the Qurʾān with your voices" (Mizzī, *Tuḥfa,* ii, no. 1775; Abū Dāwūd in *ʿAwn al-maʿbūd,* iv, 239) is supported by a complex *isnād* bundle in which the position of the early Successor and Qurʾān expert Ṭalḥa b. Muṣarrif (d. 112/730) may be construed as that of common link. In fact, his may be considered one of the earliest datable traditions in the entire canonical ḥadīth corpus. In view of his purported Qurʾān expertise he might conceivably be this tradition's originator. Moreover, the matter of Ṭalḥa's supposed authorship may be definitively settled by the long list of people mentioned in the *Ḥilya* of Abū Nuʿaym al-Iṣfahānī (d. 430/1038, cf. v, 27) who are reported to have transmitted it from him. According to the commentators, this slogan-like saying constitutes a case of inversion *(qalb),* in which the two final words are to be interpreted as if they were in reverse order, not *zayyinū l-Qurʾān bi-aṣwātikum* but *zayyinū aṣwātakum bi-l-Qurʾān,* i.e. "Adorn your voices with Qurʾān recitation."

Another very famous tradition that emphasizes the merit of recitation is the following: "A believer (see BELIEF AND UNBELIEF) who recites the Qurʾān is like a citron *(utrujj),* both its smell and taste are delicious, a believer who does not is like a date, its taste may be good but it has no smell, a hypocrite (*munāfiq,* see HYPOCRITES AND HYPOCRISY) who recites the Qurʾān is like sweet basil, its smell is good but its taste is bitter, and a hypocrite who does not recite the Qurʾān is like a colocynth which has no smell and tastes bitter" (Mizzī, *Tuḥfa,* vi, no. 8981; the Six Books, e.g. Muslim, *Ṣaḥīḥ,* i, 549). Although this tradition may convey the impression that it hails from a time later than Qatāda's (d. 117/735), he is the undeniable key figure in its *isnād* bundle. Qatāda is, moreover, also the conceivable originator of the following tradition: "He who recites the Qurʾān skillfully will find himself in the company of the honorable, godfearing scribes (obviously an allusion to Q 80:15-6: *safaratin kirāmin bararatin,* "noble and righteous scribes," identified with angels, prophets or divine messengers; see MESSENGER), and he who, to his regret, can recite the Qurʾān only haltingly will have a double reward" (Mizzī, *Tuḥfa,* xi, no. 16102; the Six Books, e.g. Muslim, *Ṣaḥīḥ,* i, 549 f.).

Reciting the Qurʾān in a singsong manner was thought to be especially meritorious. This is reflected in a relatively late tradition for which the Meccan transmitter Sufyān b. ʿUyayna (d. 198/814) can be held responsible: "God listens to nothing as he listens to a prophet singing the Qurʾān" (Mizzī, *Tuḥfa,* xi, no. 15144; Muslim, *Ṣaḥīḥ,* i, 545). The discussion on raising one's voice while reciting the Qurʾān versus muttering under one's breath seems to have been triggered directly by Q 17:110. A number of personal opinions on the issue are attributed to early first/seventh century jurists (Ibn Abī Shayba, *Muṣannaf,* ii, 440 f.). A later, more elaborate prophetic tradition has the transmitter Hushaym b. Bashīr (d. 183/799), the son of a *mawlā* from Wāsiṭ, as originator (Mizzī, *Tuḥfa,* iv, no. 5451; Muslim, *Ṣaḥīḥ,* i, 329). It had a forerunner brought into circulation by Hishām b. ʿUrwa (cf. Muslim, ibid.), in which the verse is said to pertain to private prayer (q.v.; *duʿāʾ*).

A tradition, full of narrative embellishments (cf. Ibn Ḥajar, *Fatḥ*, x, 296-8), which relates the story of how some jinn (q.v.), bombarded by shooting stars (see PLANETS AND STARS), came down from heaven to listen to Qurʾān recitation, was probably brought into circulation by the Wāsiṭī *mawlā* Abū ʿAwāna al-Waḍḍāḥ b. ʿAbdallāh (d. 175/791; Mizzī, *Tuḥfa*, iv, no. 5452; Muslim, *Ṣaḥīḥ*, i, 331 f.). This tradition harks back to an episode in Ibn Isḥāq's *Sīra* (cf. ii, 63) in which Muḥammad, on his return journey from Ṭāʾif, recites parts of the Qurʾān in the middle of the night to the amazement and delight of seven jinn who immediately committed themselves to his cause.

Prescriptions as to the minimal amount of Qurʾān recitation that is required in the various prayers *(ṣalāt)* is found in an early tradition for the skeleton of which the *mawlā* from Yamāma, Yaḥyā b. Abī Kathīr (d. 129-32/747-50), may be held responsible: in the first two prostrations (*rakʿa*s, see BOWING AND PROSTRATION) of the afternoon (q.v.; *ẓuhr)* and *ʿaṣr* recitation of Sūrat al-Fātiḥa (Q 1; see FĀTIḤA) and two sūras (variant: one) suffices, whereby performance of the first *rakʿa* of the *ẓuhr* should be drawn out, while the second may be somewhat shortened; the same rules apply to the morning *(ṣubḥ)* prayer. This tradition (see Mizzī, *Tuḥfa*, ix, no. 12108; Muslim, *Ṣaḥīḥ*, i, 333) evidences a large number of minor variants, reflecting how the issue has been the subject of an ongoing debate. The Medinan *mawlā* ʿAbd al-Malik b. ʿAbd al-ʿAzīz b. Jurayj (d. 150/767) is the common link in an *isnād* bundle supporting a tradition on the recitation requirement of the *ṣubḥ ṣalāt* (Mizzī, *Tuḥfa*, iv, no. 5313; Muslim, *Ṣaḥīḥ*, i, 336). And to Hushaym b. Bashīr can possibly be attributed a tradition which relates how the Prophet's Companions tried to compute the time to be spent in recitation during the *ẓuhr* and *ʿaṣr ṣalāt*s by measuring it against certain Qurʾān passages, such as the thirty verses of Sūrat al-Sajda ("Prostration," Q 32) for each of the first two *rakʿa*s of the *ẓuhr* and half that time for the second two *rakʿa*s of the *ẓuhr* and the first two *rakʿa*s of the *ʿaṣr*, and half that time again for each of the final two *rakʿa*s of the *ʿaṣr* (Mizzī, *Tuḥfa*, iii, no. 3974; Muslim, *Ṣaḥīḥ*, i, 334). Finally, Mālik may be credited with two traditions on the Prophet's recitation habits in the evening *(maghrib)* prayer (Mizzī, *Tuḥfa*, ii, no. 3189, xii, no. 18052, Mālik, *Muwaṭṭaʾ*, i, 78): namely Q 52 and Q 77.

(6) Tafsīr *traditions in general; Ibn ʿAbbās' role*
One of the first and at the same time most important *tafsīr* collections is that of Muḥammad b. Jarīr al-Ṭabarī (d. 310/923). Strictly speaking it is a collection of prophetic and other ancient ḥadīths that, without exception, have a bearing on a qurʾānic verse or phrase. Al-Ṭabarī's collection is available in a dependable complete edition and an incomplete one, edited by the brothers Shākir (see Bibliography). It is not only important because it presents al-Ṭabarī's considerable qurʾānic scholarship, but it also contains an array of ancient *tafsīr* collections predating his own time, collections that for the most part have otherwise not come down to us. Two major rubrics within his exegetical material are readily discernible. First of these is that of the "occasions of revelation" *(asbāb al-nuzūl)*, for which see further down. The second major rubric within *tafsīr* traditions is that of "abrogation" *(nāsikh wa-mansūkh)*. This genre of traditions grew out of the abrogation principle *(naskh):* previously revealed verses may be considered to have been abrogated by verses expressing a different ruling that came down at a later date. On the one hand, Islamic teaching in

the Qurʾān is based on the principle of *yusr*, ease, rather than *ʿusr*, hardship, leading to the alleviation of, and concessions in, several previously revealed prescripts. On the other hand, however, a hardening of a legal point of view is, for instance, discernible in Islam's increasingly outspoken disapproval of intoxicating beverages (see INTOXICANTS). *Nāsikh wa-mansūkh* collections are numerous. Apparently the earliest is the one by Abū ʿUbayd al-Qāsim b. Sallām (d. 224/838, cf. the introduction to Burton's text edition).

No survey of Muslim *tafsīr* traditions is complete without an appraisal of the most frequently quoted alleged Qurʾān expert among the Prophet's Companions, Ibn ʿAbbās (d. 68/687), a son of one of Muḥammad's uncles, who is said to have been some ten, thirteen or fifteen years old when the Prophet died. In view of his young age it should not come as a surprise that the overall number of traditions he is supposed to have actually heard from Muḥammad in person turned out to be a matter of controversy, some saying that there were no more than four, nine or ten such traditions, others suggesting larger numbers (Ibn Ḥajar, *Tahdhīb*, v, 279). He is furthermore credited with hundreds of sayings in which he is reported to have given explanations of qurʾānic passages.

Upon scrutiny of the accompanying *isnād* strands, all these — with very few exceptions, for which see below — seem to date to a relatively late time of origin, as they are at most supported by late spiders. The vast majority have only single strands as authentication (for this chronology, see the theoretical introduction found at the end of sec. 1 above and Juynboll, Nāfiʿ, and id., Early Islamic society). But this has never prevented the Islamic world, or indeed a fair number of western scholars, from regularly dubbing Ibn ʿAbbās the "father of Muslim Qurʾān exegesis." It appears that the collections of Abū Dāwūd and Nasāʾī are especially rich in these, but the four other canonical collections also contain a sizeable number. Thus we find hundreds of *tafsīr* traditions scattered in Mizzī (*Tuḥfa*, iv and v, nos. 5356-6576). A comparison of these traditions with ones dealing with the same qurʾānic passages in the older *tafsīr* collections, such as those of Mujāhid b. Jabr (d. ca. 102/720), Muqātil b. Sulaymān (d. 150/767), Sufyān al-Thawrī (d. 161/778), ʿAbd al-Razzāq (d. 211/826) and the ancient exegetical materials brought together in al-Ṭabarī's *Tafsīr*, makes clear that it is figures such as the *mawālī* Mujāhid, ʿIkrima (d. 105-7/723-5), Ḥasan al-Baṣrī (d. 110/728) and Ismāʿīl b. ʿAbd al-Raḥmān al-Suddī (d. 127/745) as well as the blind Baṣran Qurʾān expert Qatāda (d. 117/735), who are credited with personal opinions that later turn up in single strand-supported Ibn ʿAbbās traditions. These have sometimes, but not always, a slightly more elaborate exegesis, in which matters of abrogation often seem to have been settled definitively. (For more on the phenomenon that Companion-supported reports vis-à-vis Successor-supported reports can be considered to have been of later origin — one of Schacht's main hypotheses — see Juynboll, Islam's first *fuqahāʾ*, 287-90, but also Rubin, *Eye of the beholder*, 233-8.)

The overall conclusion must be that Ibn ʿAbbās' purported Qurʾān expertise constitutes, in fact, the final stage in the evolution of early Islamic exegesis, in as far as it is based upon prophetic traditions that found a place in the canonical collections. Curiously, the jurist al-Shāfiʿī (d. 204/820) is reported to have trusted no more than some one hundred *tafsīr* traditions of Ibn ʿAbbās (Suyūṭī, *Itqān*, iv, 209). Traditions that sing Ibn ʿAbbās' praises, i.e. so-called *faḍāʾil* traditions, meant to corroborate his supposed expertise, are likewise relatively late and cannot be dated more precisely than to a time in the second half of the second/eighth century at the earliest. Common links bringing such Ibn ʿAbbās *faḍāʾil* into circulation are hardly discernible in the *isnād* constellations supporting them, with the possible exception of the Baghdadi transmitter Abū l-Naḍr Hāshim b. al-Qāsim (d. 205-7/820-2; Mizzī, *Tuḥfa,* v, no. 5865; Muslim, *Ṣaḥīḥ,* iv, 1927). One thing, however, is clear: in these *faḍāʾil* God's benevolence is called upon to grant Ibn ʿAbbās juridical insight *(faqqihhu)* in the older ones, and it is only in the later ones that Qurʾān expertise is added *(wa-ʿallimhu [taʾwīl] al-Qurʾān),* an addition for which Ibn Ḥanbal may be held responsible (cf. his *Musnad,* i, 266, 269, 314 etc.).

Occasionally, we find a common link in a bundle supporting an exegetical or a background-providing remark attributed to Ibn ʿAbbās that invites dating. Seemingly the earliest such tradition that could be unearthed, pertaining to Q 4:93, has the Kūfan Manṣūr b. al-Muʿtamir (d. 132/750) as common link (Mizzī, *Tuḥfa,* iv, nos. 5624; also no. 5621; Muslim, *Ṣaḥīḥ,* iv, 2317). But its *isnād* bundle may constitute, in fact, an example of late spiders superimposed upon one another, in which the real originator is no longer visible. In any case, it is the only such Ibn ʿAbbās tradition dating to this seemingly early time. Within the output of other, later common links there are the occasional Ibn ʿAbbās/Qurʾān traditions, but they are very few in number and hardly foreshadow the veritable avalanche of such traditions with single strands and late spiders alluded to above.

A convenient survey of *tafsīr* traditions which are *expressis verbis* prophetic but without *asbāb al-nuzūl* is presented by al-Suyūṭī (cf. the end of his *Itqān,* iv, 214-57). The material, presented without complete *isnād* strands, is arranged sūra by sūra and the sources in which the traditions are found, canonical as well as post-canonical, are duly identified.

(7) *Traditions on some Qurʾān-related prescriptions*

First among these is the *sajda,* i.e. performing an extra prostration *(sajda,* pl. *sujūd)* at the recitation of certain qurʾānic passages. The practice is reported to have come into fashion before the emigration *(hijra),* when Muḥammad recited a qurʾānic passage for the first time in the open near the Kaʿba (q.v.), provoking various hostile reactions from the as yet unbelieving Meccans (see OPPOSITION TO MUḤAMMAD). What qurʾānic passages constituted actual *sajda* passages and how they became part of the ritual as determined by the legal schools of later times has given rise to one of the first extensive discussions among the earliest Muslim generations. This is clearly reflected in the dozens of reports supported by *isnād* strands ending in Companions *(= mawqūfāt),* or strands that have no Companion between the Successor and the Prophet *(= mursalāt),* and personal opinions *(aqwāl)* ascribed to the first jurists *(fuqahāʾ)* preserved in the pre-canonical collections (ʿAbd al-Razzāq, *Muṣannaf,* iii, 335-58; Ibn Abī Shayba, *Muṣannaf,* ii, 1-25). Reports supported by these three genres of strands are demonstrably earlier than those authenticated by strands ending in the Prophet (= *marfūʿāt,* cf. Juynboll, Islam's first *fuqahāʾ,* xxxix [1992], 287-90) and they became the breeding ground for a host of prophetic traditions which are found in the canonical collections, mostly — but not always — supported by an assortment of spiders and single strands.

A very early prophetic tradition prescribing that a *sajda* is to be performed when Q 17 is recited originated conceivably at the hands of the Baṣran transmitter Sulaymān b. Ṭarkhān al-Taymī (d. 143/760, cf. Mizzī, *Tuḥfa,* x, no. 14649; Muslim, *Ṣaḥīḥ,* i, 407). Special sections devoted to *sajda* prescriptions are found, for example, in Mālik (cf. *Muwaṭṭaʾ,* i, 205 f.; Bukhārī, *Faḍāʾil,* i, 273 f. = ii, 50 f.; Muslim, *Ṣaḥīḥ,* i, 405 f.). Among these traditions there are only very few supported by datable bundles which show a conceivable originator (cf. Shuʿba in Mizzī, *Tuḥfa,* vii, no. 9180; Mālik in ibid., xii, no. 14969; Sufyān b. ʿUyayna in ibid. no. 14206; and the Baṣran Yaḥyā b. Saʿīd al-Qaṭṭān [d. 198/814] in ibid., vi, no. 8144; for a survey of *sujūd*-related traditions, see Tottoli, Muslim attitudes towards prostration).

Other subjects related to law and ritual are mentioned so concisely in the Qurʾān that interpretation had to be distilled from data proliferated in ḥadīth. There are so many of these that just one well-known example should suffice here. The rules concerning the performance of the minor ritual ablution (see CLEANLINESS AND ABLUTION) when washing water is not available all go back to the *tayammum* verses, Q 4:43 and Q 5:6. In all likelihood the discussion dates to the lifetime of the Prophet, or in any case to the time when these verses became generally known, probably in the course of the first/seventh century. Traditions about *tayammum* were inserted in stories featuring ʿĀʾisha which have Hishām b. ʿUrwa as common link (Mizzī, *Tuḥfa,* xii, nos. 16802, 16990, 17060, 17205; Muslim, *Ṣaḥīḥ,* i, 279), and one which has Mālik b. Anas as common link (Mizzī, *Tuḥfa,* xii, no. 17519; Mālik, *Muwaṭṭaʾ,* i, 53 f.), and one story centering in the Companion ʿAmmār b. Yāsir (d. 37/657) with Aʿmash as common link (Mizzī, *Tuḥfa,* vii, no. 10360; Muslim, *Ṣaḥīḥ,* i, 280), and another one with Shuʿba as common link (Mizzī, *Tuḥfa,* vii, no. 10362; Muslim, *Ṣaḥīḥ,* i, 280 f.). The *tayammum* story has one feature which is also found in the ḥadīth *al-ifk* (see below in sec. 8), namely ʿĀʾisha losing her necklace. In the *tayammum* story her necklace is retrieved, too, after a while, but the circumstances forced those searching for it to perform a *ṣalāt* without a proper ritual ablution *(wuḍūʾ).* This feature was worded by Zuhrī but its historicity, if any, cannot be established with a measure of certainty.

(8) *Historical reports, in particular so-called "occasions of revelation"*

Numerous verses gave rise to more or less extensive accounts of the special circumstances leading up to, or resulting from, their respective revelation. Certain allegedly historical episodes in early Islam accompanying these instances of revelation were eventually laid down in reports, together comprising a separate literary genre within the qurʾānic sciences, the so-called "occasions of revelation" literature *(asbāb al-nuzūl).* A relatively late, major collector in this genre is ʿAlī b. Aḥmad al-Wāḥidī (d. 468/1075). One may be struck by the (quasi-) polemical tone (see POLEMIC AND POLEMICAL LANGUAGE) of a sizeable proportion of these *asbāb* traditions: a remarkably large percentage deals with situations in which Jews (see JEWS AND JUDAISM) or Christians (see CHRISTIANS AND CHRISTIANITY) are addressed, mostly in hostile terms, but that may conceivably be due to al-Wāḥidī's selection.

An *asbāb* collection consists predominantly of historical reports *(akhbār),* each headed by an *isnād* strand like any ordinary ḥadīth. Among the best-known of these reports is perhaps the one that became known as the *ḥadīth al-ifk,* the "ḥadīth of the slander," a malicious rumor launched by some men who, at one time, accused the Prophet's favorite wife (see WIVES OF THE PROPHET) ʿĀʾisha — falsely as it turned out — of having committed adultery with someone on the return journey from Muḥammad's campaign against the tribe of al-Muṣṭaliq. The affair supposedly constituted the immediate cause for the revelation of Q 24:11-5. For the skeleton of the wording of this story al-Zuhrī can on good grounds be held responsible (Mizzī, *Tuḥfa,* xi, nos. 16126, 16311; xii, nos. 16576, 17409; Bukhārī, *Ṣaḥīḥ,* iii, 103 f. = vi, 127 f.; Muslim, *Ṣaḥīḥ,* iv, 2129-37; Ibn Isḥāq, *Sīra,* iii, 310 f.). (For a study of its *isnād* strands as well as of its historicity, if any, see Juynboll, Early Islamic society, 179 f. and Schoeler, *Charakter,* chapter 3.)

The wording of the *khabar* about the Prophet's recognized miracle of splitting the moon, hinted at in the Qurʾān by the verse "The hour drew nigh and the moon (q.v.) was split" (Q 54:1) may, on the basis of *isnād* analysis and other arguments, be attributed to the Baṣran Shuʿba (Juynboll, Shuʿba b. al-Ḥajjāj, 221 f.).

An episode that reportedly was to have a particular impact on the exchanges between Muḥammad and his Meccan opponents concerns his recitation one day of Q 53:1-20, in which three ancient Arabian deities were mentioned, al-Lāt, Manāt and al-ʿUzzā. Part of his recitation highlighted their capacity to mediate with God, an additional verse which came to be regarded as having been prompted by the devil (see INTERCESSION; SATANIC VERSES). Thereupon everyone present, friend and foe, prostrated themselves, which roused Gabriel's wrath, who reproached Muḥammad for having recited a text not conveyed by himself. It was then that Q 22:52 was supposedly revealed, according to which God asserted his power to wipe from his Prophet's memory whatever the devil had implanted there. It is against this background that S. Rushdie's *The Satanic Verses* is set. The episode, concisely chronicled in al-Wāḥidī (*Asbāb,* 177) is headed by single *isnād* strands, most of which end in Successors and some in Companions, and therefore prevent us from drawing chronological inferences more precise than that they are relatively early. The observations that Muqātil, the early exegete, hints at the controversy (*Tafsīr,* iii, 133), that al-Ṭabarī (*Taʾrīkh,* i, 1192) cites Muqātil's contemporary, the Medinan (later Iraqi) *mawlā* Ibn Isḥāq, while Mujāhid leaves it unmentioned, all may point to its having originated sometime in the first half of the second/eighth century.

The nocturnal journey (*isrāʾ,* see ASCENSION), alluded to in Q 17:1, which is supposed to have formed the onset of Muḥammad's midnight ascension into the seven heavens *(miʿrāj),* is related in great detail in the canonical ḥadīth collections, but the *isnād*s that support the various accounts are either single strands or just produce undatable spiders, thus no conclusions as to authorship other than that the texts are relatively late can be drawn from the material; they probably date back, at the earliest, to the beginning of the third/ninth century (Bukhārī, *Ṣaḥīḥ,* iii, 30 f. = v, 66-9, and Muslim, *Ṣaḥīḥ,* i, 145-50).

The *ḥijāb* verse, the breeding ground of four different *asbāb al-nuzūl* reports (Ṭabarī, *Tafsīr,* xxii, 37-40) prescribes that Muḥammad's wives should answer callers at the Prophet's living quarters from behind a "partition" *(ḥijāb).* Muqātil b. Sulaymān may have had a hand in the proliferation of an early background story (*Tafsīr,* iii, 504-5), which illustrates how the Prophet, when he married Zaynab bt. al-Jaḥsh, had the *ḥijāb* verse (Q 33:53) revealed to him. During the banquet he gave, he was irritated by some guests who had overstayed their welcome. The earlier exegete Mujāhid does not yet list the story, neither does Ibn Isḥāq for that matter. We may therefore tentatively infer that the story originated during Muqātil's lifetime, if we do not want to attribute it to him directly, responsible as he was for so many "explanatory" stories *(qiṣaṣ)* which he wove through his *Tafsīr.* Soon after that, the traditionists, having taken it aboard, began to embellish it with narrative trimmings which probably originated at a much later date (e.g. Mizzī, *Tuḥfa,* i, no. 1505; Muslim, *Ṣaḥīḥ,* ii, 1050, with the Baghdadi Yaʿqūb b. Ibrāhīm b. Saʿd [d. 208/823] as common link), for there is not a single such *ḥijāb*-related tradition that is supported by an early bundle in which a common link or even a seeming common link is discernible (Muslim, *Ṣaḥīḥ,* ii, 1048-52). Another *asbāb al-nuzūl* report in this context is the one dealing with ʿUmar al-Khaṭṭāb's concern with the "unprotected" state of the women of those days (Mizzī, *Tuḥfa,* viii, no. 10409, Ibn Ḥanbal, *Musnad,* i, 23 f., with Hushaym b. Bashīr as common link). The question of whether, on the one hand, certain qurʾānic verses contained historically feasible data and thus gave rise to historically significant *asbāb* exegesis or whether, on the other hand, certain other *asbāb* traditions were brought into circulation just to embellish *tafsīr* in general, thus creating a quasi-historical background for certain other verses is discussed extensively in Rubin, *Eye of the beholder.*

(9) *Traditions with praises of particular sūras or verses*

There are sūras and verses whose recitation equals that of variously given, sizeable parts — one quarter, half, two thirds etc. — of the entire Qurʾān, and guarantees the reciter, were he to die suddenly in the midst of his recitation, a martyr's death (see MARTYR) or entrance into paradise. Shīʿī ḥadīth is even more given to hyperbole in this respect (Majlisī, *Biḥār,* lxxxix, 223-369). On the whole we find a strikingly large number of such reports molded in the form of statements ascribed to Companions and early Successors (i.e. *mawqūfāt* and *aqwāl*) in the pre-canonical collections, especially in Ibn Abī Shayba's *Muṣannaf.* This permits us to infer that popularizing the recitation of certain Qurʾān fragments was an early phenomenon that originated in the first/seventh century.

The popularity of Sūrat al-Kahf ("The Cave," Q 18) is reflected in early traditions which can be attributed to Qatāda (cf. Mizzī, *Tuḥfa,* viii, no. 10963; Muslim, *Ṣaḥīḥ,* i, 555) and his pupil Shuʿba (cf. Mizzī, *Tuḥfa,* ii, no. 1872; Muslim, *Ṣaḥīḥ,* i, 548). Sūrat al-Mulk ("Sovereignty," Q 67), a sūra of thirty verses, is valued because recitation thereof is said to engender forgiveness. Shuʿba may be held responsible for this one, too (Mizzī, *Tuḥfa,* x, no. 13550; Tirmidhī, *Jāmiʿ,* v, 164). The Kūfan *mawlā* Ismāʿīl b. Abī Khālid (d. 146/763), another famous common link, is the plausible originator of a tradition singing the praises of *al-muʿawwidhatān,* the final two sūras of the Qurʾān (Q 113 and Q 114, Mizzī, *Tuḥfa,* vii, no. 9948; Muslim, *Ṣaḥīḥ,* i, 558). There are a number of traditions in which the issue of whether or not they actually belong to the Qurʾān is differently answered. But feasible originators of these could not be identified. The issue may be old, though, for there are some *aqwāl* ascribed to the Kūfan *faqīh* ʿĀmir b. Sharāḥīl al-Shaʿbī (d. 103-10/721-8) and others that substantiate that chronology (Ibn Abī Shayba, *Muṣannaf,* x, 538 f.). It looks as if only the Companion ʿAbdallāh b. Masʿūd (d. 32/653) purportedly opposed their being included in the *muṣḥaf,* but whether or not that is historically accurate could not be ascertained.

The *muʿawwidhatān,* as well as the Fātiḥa (q.v.), were commonly recited in case of illness (see ILLNESS AND HEALTH), as some traditions assert (Mizzī, *Tuḥfa,* xii, no. 16589; Mālik, *Muwaṭṭaʾ,* ii, 942 f.; Muslim, *Ṣaḥīḥ,* iv, 1723, with Zuhrī as originator, and Mizzī, *Tuḥfa,* iii, no. 4249; Muslim, *Ṣaḥīḥ,* iv, 1727, whose author is unclear). Mālik can be considered as the proliferator of a tradition highlighting the particular merits of Sūrat al-Ikhlāṣ ("Sincerity," Q 112;

Mizzī, *Tuḥfa,* x, no. 14127; Mālik, *Muwaṭṭaʾ,* i, 208). His Iraqi contemporary Ibrāhīm b. Saʿd is possibly the author of a tradition in which the recitation of two verses of Q 2 (Sūrat al-Baqara, "The Cow") is regarded as sufficient for someone who wants to spend (part of) the night in religious devotion (Mizzī, *Tuḥfa,* vii, no. 9999 and 10000; Muslim, *Ṣaḥīḥ,* i, 555). Moreover, the controversial Syrian traditionist Baqiyya b. al-Walīd (d. 197/813) seems the common link in an *isnād* bundle (Mizzī, *Tuḥfa,* vii, no. 9888; Ibn Ḥanbal, *Musnad,* iv, 128) supporting a prophetic tradition asserting that somewhere in the *musabbiḥāt,* i.e. Q 57, Q 59, Q 61, Q 62 and Q 64, there is a verse that is more excellent than a thousand other verses. All the alleged merits of the different sūras and particular verses are conveniently brought together in Suyūṭī (*Itqān,* iv, 106-15).

Wholesale fabrication in this field was otherwise a generally recognized phenomenon. Thus the *mawlā* Abū ʿIṣma Nūḥ b. Abī Maryam (d. 173/789) was identified by early tradition critics as responsible for an *iʿrāb*-glorifying tradition, i.e. one that emphasizes the necessity of reciting the Qurʾān with full case and mood endings (Ibn ʿAdī, *Kāmil,* vii, 41) as well as one protracted tradition in which all the sūras are enumerated one by one with the recitation rewards of each (Ibn Ḥajar, *Tahdhīb,* x, 488; van Ess, *TG,* ii, 550, n. 25). Abū ʿIṣma confessed that he had brought this tradition into circulation in order to make the people concentrate more on the Qurʾān (Suyūṭī, *Itqān,* iv, 115). Motivated by the same urge, Maysara b. ʿAbd Rabbihi (fl. 150/767) is also mentioned in this respect as the originator of a similar, lengthy tradition (Ibn Ḥajar, *Lisān,* vi, 138; van Ess, *TG,* ii, 120 f.).

Finally, judging by the huge number of manuscripts of Q 36 (Sūrat Yā Sīn) and the innumerable printed versions available for very little money in talisman-like booklets throughout the Islamic world, this sūra seems to have been a particular favorite with the public. It is called the "heart *(qalb)* of the Qurʾān" whose recitation equals that of ten times (Suyūṭī, *Itqān,* iv, 110), or eleven times (Majlisī, *Biḥār,* lxxxix, 292), the whole Qurʾān. The precise origin for this popularity is hard to pin down, but it is recorded that its first partial recitation by Muḥammad allegedly coincided with one of his miracles preserved in the *Sīra:* when he (or Gabriel) sprinkled dust on the heads of his Meccan opponents, they could not see or hear him recite, and this is supposed to have prevented them from harming him (*Sīra,* ii, 127).

(10) *Other ḥadīth literature related to the Qurʾān*
Background information and stories laid down in traditions illustrating the numerous qurʾānic references to early prophets and Jewish personalities evolved into a ḥadīth-based literary genre of its own, the so-called "stories of the prophets" or *qiṣaṣ al-anbiyāʾ* literature. Although hugely popular, Muslim scholarship has always emphasized that its *isnād* structures were on the whole not to be relied upon and that the stories should be appraised for their entertainment value rather than their religio-historical contents. First and foremost among the purported ancient authorities who, from the perspective of *isnād*s, were seen to be responsible for the stories was — again — Ibn ʿAbbās. A survey of the origins of the genre is found in T. Nagel, *Qiṣaṣ al-anbiyāʾ* and in the introduction of R.G. Khoury (ed.), *Les légendes prophétiques* (see also the bibliography for studies by Kister, Gilliot and Tottoli). A striking example of how a legal decision allegedly issued by the Jewish king David (q.v.; Dāwūd) and improved upon by his son Solomon (q.v.; Sulaymān) is linked in Qurʾān exegesis (at Q 21:78) and ḥadīth lit-

erature to an ancient legal issue whose origins may well lie in pre-Islamic (*jāhiliyya,* see AGE OF IGNORANCE) usage (*ʿurf*) concerns the guarding of sowing fields against freely roaming animals and the compensation, if any, to be paid by the animals' owners for damage caused by them (cf. Ṭabarī, *Tafsīr,* xvii, 50-4; and, with al-Zuhrī as common link, Mizzī, *Tuḥfa,* ii, no. 1753; Mālik, *Muwaṭṭaʾ,* ii, 747 f.).

As soon as the many qurʾānic references to the day of resurrection (q.v.; see also LAST JUDGMENT) and what judgment the believers awaited after their death became generally known, numerous eschatological traditions were brought into circulation with details purporting to elucidate certain passages. A relatively late, major contributor to this genre who flourished in the latter half of the second/eighth century is the blind Kūfan *mawlā* Abū Muʿāwiya Muḥammad b. Khāzim (d. 195/811). But out of many such traditions a few will be mentioned here which may tentatively be assumed to be among the earliest.

The Kūfan centenarian ʿAbd al-Malik b. ʿUmayr (d. 136/754), known as the Copt, seems the originator of the oldest tradition on the *ḥawḍ,* the basin, which constitutes one of the stations the believer is to pass by on the day of resurrection where he will find the Prophet acting as water scout (*faraṭ,* Mizzī, *Tuḥfa,* ii, no. 3265; Muslim, *Ṣaḥīḥ,* iv, 1792; the tradition was taken up by Shuʿba, Mizzī, *Tuḥfa,* i, no. 148; Muslim, *Ṣaḥīḥ,* iii, 1474). The basin as such receives no mention in the Qurʾān, but the Kawthar, the river in paradise from Q 108:1 (see WATER OF PARADISE), is sometimes defined as a special basin that will be given to the Prophet (cf. also Ghazālī, *Iḥyāʾ,* iv, the *ṣifat al-ḥawḍ* paragraph). This basin and *the* basin become then occasionally confused in Muslim eschatology.

Another such station, the bridge (*ṣirāṭ*) spanning hellfire (see HELL; FIRE), is not qurʾānic either, but when asked where the people would be on the day referred to in Q 14:48, the Prophet allegedly said "on the bridge" according to a tradition proliferated by the Baṣran *mawlā* Dāwūd b. Abī Hind (d. 139-41/756-8, Mizzī, *Tuḥfa,* xii, no. 17617; Muslim, *Ṣaḥīḥ,* iv, 2150; Ṭabarī, *Tafsīr,* xiii, 252 f.). Aʿmash is the probable originator of a tradition commenting on that with which the people will be confronted on the day of grief alluded to in Q 19:39, namely death in the shape of a ram that will be slaughtered (cf. Mizzī, *Tuḥfa,* iii, no. 4002; Muslim, *Ṣaḥīḥ,* iv, 2188; Ṭabarī, *Tafsīr,* xvi, 88).

To the question about when the day of resurrection might be expected, various answers are recorded in ḥadīth. Conceivably one of the oldest is the answer the Prophet is said to have given in a tradition for which Shuʿba may be held responsible: "When I received my divine call, the hour of judgment was already as near as my two fingers here are to each other" (Mizzī, *Tuḥfa,* i, no. 1253; Muslim, *Ṣaḥīḥ,* iv, 2268 f.; Ṭabarī, *Taʾrīkh,* i, 11). In Q 4:34 it says "Men will manage the affairs of women;" this verse is incorporated in an early Shuʿba tradition on the Portents (*ashrāṭ*) of the hour (cf. Mizzī, *Tuḥfa,* i, no. 1240; Muslim, *Ṣaḥīḥ,* iv, 2056). A further description of the scene in front of God on that day is detailed in another Shuʿba tradition appended to Q 21:104 (cf. Mizzī, *Tuḥfa,* iv, no. 5622; Muslim, *Ṣaḥīḥ,* iv, 2194 f.; see APOCALYPSE).

The last tradition mentioned above is in fact partly a ḥadīth *qudsī.* This is the third separate ḥadīth genre dealt with in this section. It comprises sayings attributed by Muḥammad directly to God, sayings that were never incorporated in the book (q.v.), because the Prophet was supposed to have received these in a way fundamentally different from qurʾānic *waḥy.* Judging by the *isnād* strands the individual divine sayings are supported by — in most cases no more than single strands — it is a remarkably late genre whose earliest origins, with very few exceptions, go back to the final years of the second/eighth century. The canonical collections have preserved a fair amount of such sayings, scattered over all sorts of contexts. The one major study devoted to the genre is by W.A. Graham, *Divine word and prophetic word in early Islam* (cf. especially part two), but its list of *qudsī* sayings needs updating.

(11) *Shīʿī ḥadīth sources*
The Qurʾān-related material in the gigantic collection of Shīʿī texts, *Biḥār al-anwār* (cf. vol. lxxxix), is for the most part presented only as ḥadīths (of which several are ḥadīth *qudsī*, see sec. 10 above), but mostly supported by *isnād* strands peopled largely by Shīʿī imāms. We do find a number of Sunnī *isnād* strands being used, but then the appended texts are shortened in a way that agrees with Shīʿī tenets. Thus ʿAlī b. Abī Ṭālib's (q.v.) role as collector of the qurʾānic fragments is emphasized to the point that the merits accruing to other early Islamic authorities, such as Abū Bakr and ʿUthmān, are suppressed or left unmentioned leaving the impression that the collection of the Qurʾān (cf. sec. 3 above) is really carried through only by ʿAlī while Zayd b. Thābit's role is reduced to that of a virtual onlooker (Majlisī, *Biḥār*, lxxxix, 51, 53). Many pages later (ibid., 75 f.) the reports as found in the canonical Sunnī collections are duly mentioned.

Among the better known examples of instances where the Shīʿites accuse the Sunnites of having introduced alterations *(taḥrīfāt)* in the final redaction of the Qurʾān is the suppression of the word *aʾimma*, the plural of *imām*, and substituting for it *umma*, "community" (see Q 2:143; 3:110; cf. Majlisī, *Biḥār*, lxxxix, 60 f.; see COMMUNITY AND SOCIETY AND THE QURʾĀN; IMĀM). And Sūrat al-Aḥzāb ("The Clans," Q 33), so the Shīʿites say, was in reality even longer than Sūrat al-Baqara ("The Cow," Q 2), having been subjected to radical changes and abridgement (ibid., lxxxix, 288). The "seven readings" *(sabʿat aḥruf*, cf. sec. 4 above) are interpreted by Shīʿites also as "seven ways of issuing legal opinions (*fatwās*) by the imām" (cf. ibid., lxxxix, 49).

The *Biḥār*'s traditions are replete with the usual hyperbole, e.g. Ibn ʿAbbās is reported to have said that his Qurʾān expertise compared with that of ʿAlī was like a small pool of water compared with the sea (cf. ibid., 104 f.). On the day of judgment the Qurʾān is described as talking to God about the merits accrued by a reciter when he studies the Qurʾān while young (cf. ibid., 187 f.). Finally, we find the seemingly complete text (Majlisī, *Biḥār*, xc, 3 f.) in ḥadīth form of a *tafsīr* collection by Muḥammad b. Ibrāhīm b. Jaʿfar al-Nuʿmānī (d. 360/971) which is not even mentioned by Sezgin (cf. *GAS*, i, 543). Its main source seems to be Jaʿfar al-Ṣādiq (d. 148/765), the sixth imām of the Shīʿa. For the rest we find that Shīʿī material in general is very similar to its Sunnī counterpart.

G.H.A. Juynboll

Bibliography
Primary (for more precise bibliographical information about the canonical and some pre-canonical *ḥadīth* collections, see section 1 above): ʿAbd al-Razzāq, *Muṣannaf;* id., *Tafsīr*, Beirut 1991; Abū Dāwūd; Abū Nuʿaym al-Iṣfahānī, *Ḥilyat al-awliyāʾ*, 10 vols., Cairo 1932-8; Abū ʿUbayd, *Nāsikh;* Bayḍāwī, *Anwār;* Bukhārī, *Ṣaḥīḥ;* Dārimī, *Sunan;* al-Ghazālī, Abū Ḥāmid Muḥammad, *Iḥyāʾ ʿulūm al-dīn*, 5 vols., Beirut 1998 (arguably the most prestigious work in Islam in which virtually every section, subsection or paragraph is introduced by quotations from the Qurʾān in tandem with various relevant *ḥadīths*); Ibn Abī Shayba, Abū Bakr, *Muṣannaf*, 15 vols., Hyderabad 1966-88; Ibn ʿAdī, *al-Kāmil fī ḍuʿafāʾ al-rijāl*, ed. Y.M. Ghazzāwī, 8 vols., Beirut 1988[3]; Ibn al-

Athīr, *Nihāya;* Ibn Ḥajar, *Fatḥ al-bārī bi-sharḥ al-Bukhārī,* 17 vols., Cairo 1958; id., *Lisān al-mīzān,* 7 vols., Hyderabad 1911; id., *Tahdhīb,* Hyderabad 1907; Ibn Ḥanbal, *Musnad,* Cairo 1313/1895; Ibn Isḥāq, *Sīra,* Cairo 1955; Ibn Māja; Ibn Saʿd, *Ṭabaqāt,* Leiden 1905-40; Kulaynī, *Kāfī;* al-Majlisī, Muḥammad Bāqir, *Biḥār al-anwār,* ed. al-Sayyid Ibrāhīm al-Mayānjī & Muḥammad al-Bājir al-Bahbūdī, 104 vols., Beirut 1983²; Mālik, *Muwaṭṭaʾ;* Mizzī, Yūsuf b. ʿAbd al-Raḥmān, *Tuḥfat al-ashrāf bi-maʿrifat al-aṭrāf,* ed. ʿA. Sharaf al-Dīn, 13 vols., Bombay 1965-82; Mujāhid, *Tafsīr,* Cairo 1989; Muqātil, *Tafsīr,* Cairo 1979-89; Muslim, *Ṣaḥīḥ;* Nasāʾī, *Sunan;* Sufyān al-Thawrī, *Tafsīr;* Suyūṭī, *Itqān;* Ṭabarī, *The history of al-Ṭabarī,* 39 vols., Albany 1985-99; id., *Tafsīr,* Cairo 1954; id., *Taʾrīkh,* ed. de Goeje; al-Ṭayālisī, Abū Dāwūd, *Minḥat al-maʿbūd fī tartīb Musnad al-Ṭayālisī Abī Dāwūd,* ed. Aḥmad ʿAbd al-Raḥmān al-Bannā al-Sāʿātī, Beirut 1372; Tirmidhī, *Ṣaḥīḥ;* Wāḥidī, *Asbāb;* Zarkashī, *Burhān,* Cairo 1957-9. Secondary: M. Buitelaar and H. Motzki (eds.), *De Koran. Ontstaan, interpretatie en praktijk,* Muiderberg 1993; Burton, *Collection;* van Ess, *TG;* Gilliot, *Elt;* id., Les trois mensonges d'Abraham dans la tradition interprétante musulmane. Repères sur la naissance et le développement de l'exégèse en Islam, in *IOS* 17 (1997), 1-40; W.A. Graham, *Divine word and prophetic word in early Islam. A reconsideration of the sources with special reference to the divine saying or* ḥadīth qudsī, The Hague/Paris 1977; Hawting and Shareef, *Approaches;* G.H.A. Juynboll, Early Islamic society as reflected in its use of *isnāds*, in *Muséon* 107 (1994), 151-94; id., Nāfiʿ, the *mawlā* of Ibn ʿUmar, and his position in Muslim *ḥadīth* literature, in *Der Islam* 70 (1993), 207-44; id., Shuʿba b. al-Ḥajjāj (d. 160/776) and his position among the traditionists of Baṣra, in *Muséon* 111 (1998), 187-226; id., Some *isnād*-analytical methods illustrated on the basis of several woman-demeaning sayings from *ḥadīth* literature, in *Qanṭara* 10 (1989), 343-83; id., Some notes on Islam's first *fuqahāʾ* distilled from early *ḥadīth* literature, in *Arabica* 39 (1992), 287-314; R.G. Khoury (ed.), *Les légendes prophétiques dans l'Islam depuis le Ier jusqu'au IIIe siècle de l'Hégire. Avec édition critique du texte (Kitāb Badʾ al-ḫalq wa-qiṣaṣ al-anbiyāʾ d'après le manuscrit d'Abū Rifāʿa ʿUmāra b. Waṯīma al-Fārisī al-Fasawī),* Wiesbaden 1978; M.J. Kister, Ādam. A study of some legends in *tafsīr* and *ḥadīṯ* literature, in *IOS* 13 (1993), 113-74; H. Motzki, The collection of the Qurʾān. A reconsideration of western views in light of recent methodological developments, in *Der Islam* 78 (2001), 1-34; id. and M. Buitelaar (eds.), *De Koran. Onstaan, interpretatie en praktijk,* Muidberg 1993; T. Nagel, *Qiṣaṣ al-anbiyāʾ. Ein Beitrag zur arabischen Literaturgeschichte,* Bonn 1967; Nöldeke, *GQ;* D. Powers, The exegetical genre *nāsikh al-Qurʾān wa mansūkhuhu,* in Rippin, *Approaches,* 117-38; Rippin, *Approaches;* id., The function of *asbāb al-nuzūl* in Qurʾānic exegesis, in *BSOAS* 51 (1988), 1-20; U. Rubin, *The eye of the beholder. The life of Muḥammad as viewed by the early Muslims. A textual analysis,* Princeton 1995; id., *Iqraʾ bi-smi rabbika...!* Some notes on the interpretation of *sūrat al-ʿalaq* (vs. 1-5), in *IOS* 13 (1993), 213-30; G. Schoeler, *Charakter und Authentie der muslimischen Überlieferung über das Leben Mohammeds,* Berlin/New York 1996; Sezgin, *GAS;* R. Tottoli, Muslim attitudes towards prostration *(sujūd)*. Arabs and prostration at the beginning of Islam and in the *Qurʾān,* in *SI* 88 (1998), 5-34; id., Muslim attitudes towards prostration *(sujūd)*. II. The prominence and meaning of prostration in Muslim literature, in *Muséon* 111 (1998), 405-26; id., The *qiṣaṣ al-anbiyāʾ* of Ibn Muṭarrif al-Ṭarafī (d. 454/1062). Stories of the prophets from al-Andalus, in *Qanṭara* 19 (1998), 131-60; Wansbrough, *QS.*

Ḥafṣa

A wife of the prophet Muḥammad and a daughter of the caliph ʿUmar b. al-Khaṭṭāb. Ibn Saʿd relates that she was born in Mecca five years before Muḥammad's first revelation (ca. 605 C.E.). Her mother was Zaynab bt. Maẓʿūn. Ḥafṣa emigrated to Medina with her first husband, Khunays b. Ḥudhāfa, of the Sahm, a clan of the Quraysh (q.v.). He is believed to have died shortly after the battle of Badr (q.v.; 2/624) in which he participated (Ibn Saʿd, *Ṭabaqāt,* viii, 81), although some say that he was killed during the battle of Uḥud (Ibn Ḥajar, *Iṣāba,* vii, 582; see EXPEDITIONS AND BATTLES). Ibn Qutayba, however, reports that Khunays was Muḥammad's envoy to the Persian emperor, which indicates that he died much later (Ibn Qutayba, *Kitāb al-Maʿārif,* 59).

The Prophet is said to have married Ḥafṣa after ʿĀʾisha bint Abī Bakr (q.v.; Ibn Ḥajar, *Iṣāba,* vii, 582), two months before the battle of Uḥud (3/625; al-Balādhurī, *Ashrāf,* ii, 54). Eventually, Muḥammad divorced her, but later resumed the marriage bond (Ibn Saʿd, *Ṭabaqāt,* viii, 84). The circumstances of the divorce were read by Muslim exegetes into the interpretation of Q 66:3, in which the Prophet is said to have confided a certain matter to "one of his wives," but she is said to have failed to have kept the secret. The exegetes say it was Ḥafṣa (Balādhurī, *Ashrāf,* ii, 55-6) who disclosed the secret to ʿĀʾisha. The secret reportedly pertained to Muḥammad's intercourse with his concubine Maryam the Copt, but according to others it pertained to the future of Ḥafṣa's and ʿĀʾisha's respective fathers (i.e. ʿUmar and Abū Bakr) as caliphs (see CALIPH). Ḥafṣa's image as a disobedient wife also emerges in the story that the Prophet ordered a certain woman to teach Ḥafṣa a special charm designed to train wives not to slander and to obey their husbands (al-Zamakhsharī, *al-Fāʾiq fī gharīb al-ḥadīth,* iv, 26).

According to most versions, Ḥafṣa died in Medina at the age of 60, in Shaʿbān 45/665 during Muʿāwiya's reign (Ibn Saʿd, *Ṭabaqāt,* viii, 86). The Shīʿīs, for their part, claim that she lived until the end of ʿAlī's regime (Ibn Shahrāshūb, *Manāqib āl Abī Ṭālib,* i, 138; see ʿALĪ B. ABĪ ṬĀLIB). Ibn Qutayba, however, says she died earlier, already during Uthmān's reign *(Maʿārif,* 59).

Traditions of the Prophet as well as of her father, ʿUmar, were reported on Ḥafṣa's authority (see ḤADĪTH AND THE QURʾĀN). Her importance to the history of the Qurʾān stems from the fact that she is said to have possessed a private copy (*muṣḥaf,* q.v.) of the Qurʾān based on a version (*qirāʾa,* see READINGS OF THE QURʾĀN) which she had heard directly from the Prophet. Several Companions of the Prophet (q.v.) are said to have had such copies, but her particular one played an important role in the collection of the Qurʾān (q.v.). The copy was prepared for her by a *mawlā* (client) of her father (Ibn Abī Dāwūd, *Maṣāḥif,* 95–7). In other reports, however, this copy is said to have been prepared for another wife of Muḥammad, namely, Umm Salama (Ibn Abī Dāwūd, *Maṣāḥif,* 98). In yet other reports, Ḥafsa's copy is not her own private one, but rather an old copy already prepared during the days of Abū Bakr (q.v.), which marked the first officially organized "collection" of the Qurʾān. When Abū Bakr died the copy is said to have passed to ʿUmar, and after him, to Ḥafṣa (Ibn Abī Dāwūd, *Maṣāḥif,* 14, 15, 28). Her possession of the copy accords with reports to the effect that she was the one who inherited ʿUmar's estate (Ibn Saʿd, *Ṭabaqāt,* viii, 84). Ḥafṣa is said to have delivered this copy to ʿUthmān for the preparation of what is known as the ʿUthmānic codex of the Qurʾān. When this version was ready, her copy was returned to her. After she died, her copy was reportedly destroyed by Marwān b. al-Ḥakam, then a governor of Medina, in order to sustain the canonical status of the ʿUthmānic codex (Balādhurī, *Ashrāf,* ii, 60; Ibn Abī Dāwūd, *Maṣāḥif,* 16, 26, 27, 28, 32). See also WIVES OF THE PROPHET; WOMEN AND THE QURʾĀN.

Uri Rubin

Bibliography

al-Balādhurī, Aḥmad b. Yaḥyā, *Jummal min ansāb al-ashrāf,* ed. S. Zakkār and R. Ziriklī, 13 vols., Beirut 1996; Ibn Abī Dāwūd al-Sijistānī, *Kitāb al-Maṣāḥif,* Beirut 1985; Ibn Ḥajar, *al-Iṣāba fī maʿrifat al-ṣaḥāba,* ed. A.M. Bijāwī, 8 vols., Cairo 1970; Ibn Qutayba, *Kitāb al-Maʿārif,* ed. M. al-Ṣāwī, repr. Beirut 1970; Ibn Saʿd, *Kitāb al-Ṭabaqāt,* 8 vols., Beirut 1960; Ibn Shahrāshūb, Muḥammad b. ʿAlī, *Manāqib āl Abī Ṭālib,* 3 vols, Najaf 1956; Zamakhsharī, *al-Fāʾiq fī gharīb al-ḥadīth,* ed. ʿA. al-Bijāwī and Abū l-Faḍl Ibrāhīm, 4 vols., Cairo 1979.

Hagar see ABRAHAM

Ḥajj see PILGRIMAGE

Ḥalāl see LAWFUL AND UNLAWFUL; PROHIBITED DEGREES

Hāmān

The chief minister of Pharaoh (q.v.) who with him rejected Moses' (q.v.) call to worship the true God and to set free the children of Israel (q.v.). In the Qurʾān, there are six attestations of his name. In Q 28:6 he is mentioned alongside Pharaoh. They both have armies, and share guilt in the slaughter of the sons of the Israelites. God declares that they will be overthrown by the people they so oppress, who will then be heirs to their power and wealth (q.v.; Q 28:4-5). There is thus an irony in the fact that when Pharaoh's household took the infant Moses from the river — an infant whom Pharaoh would have slain but for the plea of his wife (Q 28:8-9) — Hāmān is singled out for mention as a member of that household.

When Moses is a young man, he kills an Egyptian, and flees to Midian (q.v.). On his return from exile, he delivers God's message to Pharaoh and Hāmān, "Send with us the children of Israel, and do not torment them" (Q 20:47). Pharaoh, having asked Moses who and what his God is, commands Hāmān to light a fire (q.v.) to bake clay for bricks (Q 28:38) in order to build a high tower he can climb to be able to see the God of Moses (Q 28:38; 40:36-7).

In Q 40:24, Korah (q.v.; Qārūn) is included with Pharaoh and Hāmān as among those in Egypt to whom Moses was sent. There is a vivid scene presenting the response of the three of them to Moses' message, "A sorcerer (see MAGIC, PROHIBITION OF)! A liar (see LIE)! … Kill the sons of those who believe along with him, and let their women live" (Q 40:24-5), and Pharaoh turns to Korah and Hāmān, saying, "Let me kill Moses, let him cry out to his lord" (Q 40:28). In Q 29:39 Hāmān, Korah and Pharaoh are named along with the peoples of Midian (Q 29:36), ʿĀd (q.v.) and Thamūd (q.v.; Q 29:38), as among those who rejected the prophets sent to them and were punished: Korah was swallowed up by the earth (Q 28:81) and Hāmān drowned with Pharaoh (Q 29:40; see PUNISHMENT STORIES; DROWNING; CHASTISEMENT AND PUNISHMENT).

There are conflicting views as to Hāmān's identity and the meaning of his name. Among them is that he is the minister of King Ahasuerus who has been shifted, anachronistically, from the Persian empire to the palace of Pharaoh (cf. Vajda, Hāmān). There is, however, no reason, other than the paradigmatic one of hostility to the Israelites (see JEWS AND JUDAISM), to make any direct connection between him and the eponymous minister of Ahasuerus referred to in Esther (3:1-6) who persuaded his ruler to issue an edict to exterminate the Jews of the Persian Empire because Mordechai refused to pay him homage. One suggestion is that Hāmān is an Arabized echo of the Egyptian Hā-Amen, the title of a high priest second only in rank to Pharaoh (Asad, *Message*, 590, n. 6). The name, however, may have become a time-honored designation for any court official hostile to the Jews and belief in the one God. His role is marginally elaborated in the "stories of the prophets" literature (*qiṣaṣ al-anbiyāʾ*, see Kisāʾī, *Tales*, 213, 226-7, 229).

Anthony Hearle Johns

Bibliography

Primary: Ibn Kathīr, *Qiṣaṣ al-anbiyāʾ*, ed. S. al-Laḥḥām, Beirut 1988; Kisāʾī, *Qiṣaṣ*, id., *The tales of the prophets of al-Kisāʾī*, trans. W.M. Thackston, Boston 1978; Ṭabarī, *The history of al-Ṭabarī. iii. The children of Israel*, trans. W.M. Brinner, Albany 1991, 53-111 and index; id., *Tafsīr;* id. *Taʾrīkh*, ed. de Goege et al., i, 468-528; Thaʿlabī, *Qiṣaṣ*, Beirut n.d.

Secondary: Horovitz, *KU*, 149; R. Tottoli, *Vita di Mosè secondo le tradizioni islamiche*, Palermo 1992, 35, 41, 48-9, 53-4; G. Vajda, Hāmān, in *EI²*, iii, 110.

Ḥamza b. ʿAbd al-Muṭṭalib

Paternal uncle of the Prophet (half-brother of the Prophet's father), as well as his foster brother (Muslim, *Ṣaḥīḥ, K. al-Riḍāʿ*, 14; Ṭabarī, *Taʾrīkh*, i, 970; id. *History*, v, 172; see FOSTERAGE). One of the great heroes of the earliest period of Islam.

Ḥamza appears to have had a close relationship with the Prophet; he accompanied him when he went to ask Khadīja's (q.v.) father for her hand and, apparently out of solidarity with his foster brother, gave Abū Jahl a serious beating when the latter had gravely abused the Prophet. On this occasion, Ḥamza announced his adherence to the new religion and became a Muslim even before ʿUmar. This act provided crucial support for the emerging community of believers.

During the battle of Badr (q.v.), Ḥamza distinguished himself, together with ʿAlī (see ʿALĪ B. ABŪ ṬĀLIB). Ḥamza, ʿAlī and ʿUbayda b. al-Ḥārith were chosen by the Prophet to fight three pagan Meccans who had initiated this conflict by issuing a challenge. They killed their opponents, although ʿUbayda later died of his wounds. According to the *Ṣaḥīḥ*s of al-Bukhārī (d. 256/870; *Les traditions*, iii, 387) and Muslim and the early commentators Sufyān al-Thawrī (d. 161/778; *Tafsīr*, ad loc.) and ʿAbd al-Razzāq (d. 211/827; *Tafsīr*, ad loc.), Q 22:19 is understood to be a reference to this event: "These are the two opposing parties who had a fight about their lord." Other early and some later commentators mention only a broader meaning (cf. Muqātil, *Tafsīr;* Farrāʾ, *Maʿānī;* Qushayrī, *Laṭāʾif;* Zamakhsharī, *Kashshāf;* Bayḍāwī, *Anwār*, ad Q 22:19). Most later commentaries favor a more expansive interpretation of this passage, as referring to Muslims and Jews (see JEWS AND JUDAISM) or the unbelievers (see BELIEF AND UNBELIEF), but, like al-Ṭabarī (d. 310/923), often mention this opening event of Badr as the occasion for its revelation (see OCCASIONS OF REVELATION). Shortly after the battle, Ḥamza, who had enjoyed drink and song at a party, killed the two camels ʿAlī had received as part of the spoils. When the Prophet and ʿAlī came to demand an account, he started to scoff at them and the Prophet turned away from him, realizing that he was drunk (Bukhārī, *Ṣaḥīḥ, K. al-Shirb*, 13 [*Les traditions*, ii, 84-6]; *K. Farḍ al-khums*, 1 [*Les traditions*, ii, 380-1]; *K. al-Maghāzī*, 12 [*Les traditions*, ii, 84-6]; Muslim, *Ṣaḥīḥ, K. al-Ashriba*, 1 and 2; Abū Dāwūd, *K. al-Imāra*, 20 [ed. al-Ḥamīd, iii, 14850, no. 2986]).

Ḥamza was killed a year later during the battle of Uḥud (see EXPEDITIONS AND BATTLES) by the Ethiopian slave Waḥshī who thereby earned his emancipation. His body was mutilated by Hind bt. ʿUtba, whose father Ḥamza had killed at Badr. She even tried to eat his liver; this is why she is referred to in later literature as the liver-eater *(ākilat al-akbād)*, and her descendants are upbraided for that. When the Prophet found Ḥamza's body he, apparently referring to his uncle's qualities as a hunter, sadly said: "If it would not grieve Ṣafiyya (Ḥamza's sister) and if it would not become a *sunna* after me, I would leave him for the bellies of lions and the stomachs of birds" (cf. Ibn Isḥāq-Guillaume, 387).

At the battle of Karbalāʾ (in 61/680), al-Ḥusayn — who himself was killed during this battle — referred to his great-uncle Ḥamza as "lord of the martyrs" (*sayyid al-shuhadāʾ*, Ṭabarī, *Taʾrīkh*, ii, 329; id., *History*, xix, 123).

Frederik Leemhuis

Bibliography
ʿAbd al-Razzāq, *Tafsīr;* Abū Dāwūd (esp. *K. Jihād,* 109); Bayḍāwī, *Anwār;* Bukhārī, *Ṣaḥīḥ* (esp. *K. al-Maghāzī,* 3, 8, 23; *Tafsīr Sūra* 22 (bāb 3); *Ṭalāq,* 11); Farrāʾ, *Maʿānī;* Ibn Ḥanbal, *Musnad,* i, 148; ii, 40, 84, 92; Ibn Isḥāq, *Sīra;* Ibn Isḥāq-Guillaume; Ibn Māja (esp. *K. al-Janāʾiz,* 53; *Jihād,* 29; *Fitan,* 34); Muqātil, *Tafsīr;* Muslim, *Ṣaḥīḥ* (esp. *K. al-Ridāʿ,* 14; *Tafsīr,* 34); Sufyān al-Thawrī, *Tafsīr;* Ṭabarī, *The history of al-Ṭabarī. v. The Sasanids, the Byzantines, the Lakhmids, and Yemen,* trans. C.E. Bosworth, Albany, NY 1999; id., *The history of al-Ṭabarī. xix. The caliphate of Yazīd b. Muʿawiyah,* trans. I.K.A. Howard, Albany, NY 1990; id., *Tafsīr;* id., *Taʾrīkh,* ed. de Goeje; Qushayrī, *Laṭāʾif;* Wāḥidī, *Asbāb,* ed. K.B. Zaghlūl, Beirut 1991, 317-8; Zamakhsharī, *Kashshāf.*

Ḥanafīs see LAW AND THE QURʾĀN

Ḥanbalīs see LAW AND THE QURʾĀN

Hand(s)

The terminal part of the arm; also, figuratively, control or agency. The hand, in both its literal and symbolic senses, is most often expressed in the Qurʾān by the Arabic *yad* (dual *yadān,* pl. *aydī*), with some 119 occurrences, found in all chronological periods of revelation (see CHRONOLOGY AND THE QURʾĀN). (The expression *bayna yaday,* "between two hands," as in Q 36:12 [cf. 36:45, *bayna aydīkum,* "between your (pl.) hands"], means "before, in front of, in the presence of.") Another term, *kaff,* is encountered only twice, with reference to one who futilely stretches out his hands to water (q.v.; Q 13:14) and to a person who wrings his hands over a great loss (Q 18:42). Other Arabic expressions refer to the right hand *(yamīn,* pl. *aymān),* which can also mean an oath (see OATHS AND PROMISES) or simply the right side. The triliteral root *y-m-n* occurs fairly frequently (some seventy times) and in all periods, which is appropriate considering its ancient positive meanings in the Arabian classification of values and acts (see ETHICS AND THE QURʾĀN). A much less frequent root, meaning "left hand, the left side" is represented by *shamāʾil* (Q 7:17; 16:48) and *shimāl* (Q 18:17, 18; 70:37 etc.), with corresponding traditional negative and ominous connotations (see LEFT HAND AND RIGHT HAND).

God is characterized metaphorically as having hands (see ANTHROPOMORPHISM), as in "All bounties are in the hand *(yad)* of God" (Q 3:73; see BLESSING; GRACE), "in whose hand *(yad)* is the dominion of everything" (Q 23:88), and "the hand *(yad)* of God is over their hands *(aydīhim)*" (Q 48:10), referring to a pledge of fealty to Muḥammad as being equivalent to pledging fealty to God. Most often, references are to hands of human beings, whether literally or symbolically. Examples are "Woe to those who write the book (q.v.) with their own hands *(bi-aydīhim),* then say: 'This is from God'" (Q 2:79; see POLEMIC AND POLEMICAL LANGUAGE); "As to the thief, male or female, cut off the hands of both *(aydiyahumā)*" (Q 5:38; see THEFT; BOUNDARIES AND PRECEPTS); the very early Meccan verse "Perish the hands *(yadā)* of Abū Lahab" (Q 111:1) carries a metaphorical meaning of what that enemy of Muḥammad had acquired in life, which would perish along with Abū Lahab himself. Q 9:29 exhorts (see EXHORTATIONS) the fighting (q.v.) of the unbelievers among the People of the Book (q.v.; see also BELIEF AND UNBELIEF; FAITH; JIHĀD) until they pay the poll tax (q.v.; *jizya*) "out of hand" (*ʿan yadin,* for discussions on this verse, see Rosenthal, Minor problems; Kister, ʿAn yadin; Cahen, Coran IX-29).

It is noteworthy that hands — and not just the left hand — sometimes have a foreboding meaning in the Qurʾān, particularly when pertaining to human agency. In Q 42:30 we read: "Whatever misfortune happens to you, is because of the things your hands have wrought *(kasabat aydīkum)*." Hands represent ability, power (see POWER AND IMPOTENCE), and will and, as such, their deeds are accountable in relation to God. In Q 38:45 Abraham (q.v.), Isaac (q.v.) and Jacob (q.v.) are characterized as possessing "power" (*al-aydī*, lit. "the hands") and "prudence/vision" (*al-abṣār*, lit. "the sight;" see SEEING AND HEARING). Part of what it means to be created according to a sound constitution (*fiṭra*, see Q 30:30) is to have "hands," whether understood literally or symbolically.

Hands themselves are not ominous but the purposes to which they are dedicated may well bring self-inflicted suffering and woe according to both natural and supernatural criteria. For example, in Q 59:2 we read of hypocrites (see HYPOCRITES AND HYPOCRISY) who miscalculate their actions and "are seized by misfortune, because of the deeds which their hands have sent forth." In Q 24:24 those who slander (see GOSSIP) chaste women (see CHASTITY; ADULTERY AND FORNICATION) will receive a severe punishment (see REWARD AND PUNISHMENT; LAST JUDGMENT) from God "on the day when their tongues, their hands *(aydīhim)*, and their feet (q.v.) will bear witness against them as to their actions." The purifying of the hands before formal prayer (q.v.; *ṣalāt*) is commanded in Q 5:6, both with respect to ablutions with water *(wuḍūʾ)* and with clean sand or earth (*tayammum;* see CLEANLINESS AND ABLUTION; RITUAL PURITY).

Frederick Mathewson Denny

Bibliography
Primary: ʿAbd al-Bāqī; ʿA.Yūsuf ʿAlī, *The holy Qurʾān*, new rev. ed., Brentwood, MD 1989.
Secondary: C. Cahen and M.M. Bravmann, Coran IX-29. Ḥatta yuʿṭū l-ğizyata ʿan yadin wahum ṣāğirūna, in *Arabica* 9 (1962), 76-9; 10 (1963), 94-5, repr. in Paret, 288-92; H.E. Kassis, *A concordance of the Qurʾān*, Berkeley 1983; M.J. Kister, ʿAn yadin (Qurʾān, IX/29). An attempt at interpretation, in *Arabica* 11 (1964), 272-8, repr. in Paret, 295-303; R. Paret (ed.), *Der Koran*, Darmstadt 1975, 283-7, 288-92, 295-303 (for the discussions of Rosenthal, Cahen and Kister of the meaning of *ʿan yadin* in Q 9:29); Penrice, *Dictionary;* F. Rosenthal, Some minor problems in the Qurʾān, in *Joshua Starr memorial volume. Studies in history and philology (Jewish social studies 5)*, New York 1953, 67-84, repr. in Paret, 283-7.

Ḥanīf

A believer who is neither a polytheist *(mushrik)* nor a Jew or a Christian (see POLYTHEISM AND ATHEISM; JEWS AND JUDAISM; CHRISTIANS AND CHRISTIANITY). The Arabic root *ḥ-n-f* initially means "to incline," so that *ḥanīf* (pl. *ḥunafāʾ*) is most probably understood in the Qurʾān as one who has abandoned the prevailing religions and has inclined to a religion of his own. It occurs once as a synonym of *muslim* (Q 3:67) and also in juxtaposition with the verb *aslama* (Q 4:125).

The qurʾānic prototype of the ideal *ḥanīf* is Abraham (q.v.; Q 3:67; 16:120), and being a *ḥanīf* signifies belonging to the "religion" *(milla)* of Abraham (Q 2:135; 3:95; 4:125; 6:161; 16:123). Abraham's disposition as a *ḥanīf* means that the Qurʾān, in accordance with the Talmud, perceives him as a natural believer, i.e. as one who has reached monotheism by means of individual insight (Q 6:75-9). In qurʾānic terminology, his *ḥanīfī* monotheism consists of inclining his face towards God who has "created *(faṭara)* the heavens and the earth" (Q 6:79). A *ḥanīfī* monotheism is therefore part of the natural constitution *(fiṭra)* with which one has been created (Q 30:30). The qurʾānic Prophet, too, is requested to become a *ḥanīf* by setting his face upright towards the true religion (Q 10:105), and the same demand is also imposed on the rest of the people (Q 22:31; 98:5).

The stress laid on the fact that a *ḥanīf* is

neither a *mushrik* nor a Jew or a Christian, underlines a polemical context in which the use of this term in the Qurʾān should be understood. Implicit here is the notion that polytheists as well as Jews and Christians have distorted the natural religion of God, which only Islam preserves. In post-qurʾānic sources, *ḥanīf* retains this polemical context and is used to bring out the particularistic aspect of Islam as a religion set apart from Judaism and Christianity. Thus the caliph ʿUmar (r. 13-23/634-44) is said to have introduced himself as *al-shaykh al-ḥanīf* to a Christian who had introduced himself as *al-shaykh al-naṣrānī* (Ibn Abī Shayba, *Muṣannaf*, iii, 199).

Inasmuch as the image of Abraham is closely associated in Islamic historical perception with the pre-Islamic history of Mecca (q.v.) and the Kaʿba (q.v.), the notion of a *ḥanīfī* monotheism was also integrated into that history. Muslim exegetes of the Qurʾān say that *ḥanīf* in the Age of Ignorance (q.v.; *jāhiliyya*) signified an Arab adhering to the religion of Abraham and that the title was also claimed by idolaters (see IDOLATERS AND IDOLATRY) who only observed certain rites of that religion, such as pilgrimage (q.v.) to Mecca and circumcision (q.v.; Abū ʿUbayda, *Majāz*, i, 58; Lane, s.v. *ḥanīf*). Among famous seekers of the Abrahamic *ḥanīfī* religion who are said to have lived in pre-Islamic Mecca are Waraqa b. Nawfal, ʿUbaydallāh b. Jaḥsh, ʿUthmān b. al-Ḥuwayrith and Zayd b. ʿAmr b. Nufayl (Ibn Isḥāq, *Sīra*, i, 237-47). In Medina, too, other *ḥunafāʾ* are said to have been active.

The historicity of the reports about the pre-Islamic *ḥunafāʾ* and the nature of their relationship with Muḥammad has become the subject of controversy among Islamicists. While some scholars of Islamic studies reject the reports as retrojection of qurʾānic concepts into pre-Islamic history, others accept all or some of the reports as authentic. Efforts have also been made to define the exact nature of the Arabian *ḥanīfiyya*, mainly according to the (somewhat enigmatic) evidence of early Arabic poetry, and with relation to Judaism and Christianity as known among the Arabs. (See ALSO PRE-ISLAMIC ARABIA AND THE QURʾĀN; SOUTH ARABIA, RELIGION IN PRE-ISLAMIC.)

The evidence of non-Islamic sources

In Jewish midrashic literature, the Hebrew root *ḥ-n-f* is associated with heretics *(minim)*, and in Syriac documents the form *ḥanpā* (pl. *ḥanpē)* denotes non-Christian "pagans." This complicates the etymological history of the qurʾānic *ḥanīf*, which nevertheless retains the sense of one who has dissociated from Judaism and Christianity. Christian apologists of the early ʿAbbāsid period retained the pagan sense of the term and applied it to Muslims in an attempt to bring out the derogatory aspect of the title *ḥanīf* by which Muslims called themselves (Griffith, The prophet, 118-9). The pagan sense of the term was also known to Muslim writers who applied the title *ḥunafāʾ* to such pagans as the Ṣābiʾūn (e.g. Masʿūdī, *Tanbīh*, 6, 90-1, 122-3, 136, 161; cf. Luxenberg, *Die Syro-aramäische Lesart*, 38-40, on Q 6:161; see SABIANS). Al-Yaʿqūbī (d. 292/905), too, describes as *ḥanīf*s pagans who worshipped the stars in Saul's (q.v.) and David's (q.v.) times (Yaʿqūbī, *Taʾrīkh*, i, 49, 50).

Uri Rubin

Bibliography

Primary: Ibn Abī Shayba, *al-Muṣannaf fī l-aḥādīth wa-l-āthār*, ed. ʿAbd al-Khāliq al-Afghānī, 15 vols., Bombay 1979-83; Ibn Isḥāq, *Sīra*, ed. al-Saqqā et al., repr. Beirut 1971; Masʿūdī, *Kitāb al-Tanbīh wa-l-ishrāf*, ed. M.J. de Goeje, Leiden 1894, repr. Beirut 1965; al-Yaʿqūbī, Aḥmad b. Abī Yaʿqūb b. Wāḍiḥ, *al-Taʾrīkh*, 2 vols., Beirut 1960.

Secondary: N.A. Faris and H.W. Glidden, The development of the meaning of the koranic *ḥanīf,* in *The Journal of the Palestine Oriental Society* 19 (1939-40), 1-13 (published in Arabic as *Taṭawwur maʿnā kalimat ḥanīf al-qurʾāniyya,* in *Abḥāth* 13 [1960], 25-42); C. Gilliot, Muḥammad, le Coran et les "contraintes de l'histoire," in Wild, *Text,* 6-19; S.H. Griffith, The prophet Muḥammad. His scripture and his message according to the Christian apologies in Arabic and Syriac from the first Abbasid century, in T. Fahd (ed.), *La vie du prophète Mahomet. Colloque de Strasbourg, Octobre* 1980, Paris 1983, 99-146; M. Lecker, *Muslims, Jews & pagans. Studies on early Islamic Medina,* Leiden 1995, 161-4; C. Luxenberg, *Die Syro-aramäische Lesart des Koran. Ein Beitrag zur Entschlüsselung der Koransprache,* Berlin 2000; Paret, *Kommentar,* 32-3 (for older, but still useful references); S. Pines, Jāhiliyya and ʿilm, in JSAI 13 (1990), 175-94; A. Rippin, RMNN and the ḥanīfs, in Wael B. Hallaq and Donald P. Little (eds.), *Islamic studies presented to Charles J. Adams,* Leiden 1991, 154-68; U. Rubin, Ḥanīfiyya and Kaʿba — an inquiry into the Arabian pre-Islamic background of Dīn Ibrāhīm, in JSAI 13 (1990), 85-112; Watt-Bell, *Introduction,* 16.

Ḥaram

see HOUSE, DOMESTIC AND DIVINE; SANCTITY AND THE SACRED

Ḥarām

see FORBIDDEN; LAWFUL AND UNLAWFUL; PROHIBITED DEGREES

Hārūn

see AARON

Hārūt and Mārūt

Two angels in Babylon who were given knowledge which, when used by humankind, causes discord on the earth. The Qurʾān mentions these two angels (*malakayn,* see ANGEL) in only one rather enigmatic verse, Q 2:102 (cf. Ibn ʿAskar, *Takmīl,* 52-3). Their names, similar in pattern to Jālūt (Goliath, q.v.) and Ṭālūt (Saul, q.v.; Q 2:247-51), have been traced etymologically by modern scholars to those of two Zoroastrian "archangels" *(amesha spenta)* Haurvatat and Ameretat, literally "integrity" and "immortality," possibly mediated into the Arabic forms by way of Aramaic. Through later elaboration by Qurʾān exegetes and authors of the "stories of the prophets" *(qiṣaṣ al-anbiyāʾ)* literature, they developed into the Islamic equivalent of fallen angels, a story genre well known in Jewish midrashic and apocryphal literature (e.g. Enoch, Jubilees), the New Testament (e.g. 2 Peter; Jude), and the writings of the Church Fathers.

Q 2:102 consists of two separate stories with magic as their unifying link (see MAGIC, PROHIBITION OF): the first defends Solomon (q.v.) from the devils' (see DEVIL) false reports about him, which were accepted as true by some people of weak faith. Solomon did not reject faith (q.v.), the demons who taught men sorcery did. Humans do not transgress by studying magic, only by using it to cause harm. Solomon, who was reputed to have possessed occult powers, is here exculpated of any wrongdoing, although according to al-Thaʿlabī's *Qiṣaṣ,* humans, tempted by demons to dig under Solomon's throne after his death, would find writings by which "he ruled over the jinn (q.v.), humans, demons, and birds." The second story tells of the angels Hārūt and Mārūt and mentions what was revealed to them in Babylon (q.v.). They taught men charms that harmed no one without God's permission. This tale was later expanded in an effort to understand and explain the meaning of the enigmatic verse because of important theological questions that it raised for Qurʾān commentators. For example, by definition, angels are sinless and faithful servants of God; although influenced by Satan in this story, their purity is preserved.

Later expansions of the story emphasize the special favor that human beings enjoy with God, relating that the angels, seeing the sinful nature of humans, spoke of them with contempt, whereupon God reproached them saying that in humankind's position they would not have done better. As an experiment, God permitted the angels to send Hārūt and Mārūt down to earth, but ordered them to abstain from idolatry (see IDOLATRY AND IDOLATERS), whoredom (see ADULTERY AND FORNICATION), murder (q.v.) and intoxication (see INTOXICANTS). Though Muslim scholars questioned whether angels could be capable of such sins, al-Thaʿlabī and others relate that on coming to earth, these two angels did indeed yield to the temptations of a beautiful woman named al-Zuhara, revealed God's ineffable name to her, enabling her thereby to ascend to heaven. For this lapse, Hārūt and Mārūt were subjected to eternal punishment: confined to a pit in Babylon, they were doomed to hang upside down and teach humankind magic. Unable to leave the heavens because she had not learned from the two angels the secret word for descent, al-Zuhara was transformed into a star bearing her name, Arabic for the planet Venus. This and other elements suggest a possibly non-Islamic origin for the story as it was later developed.

William M. Brinner

Bibliography
Primary: Ibn ʿAskar, Muḥammad b. ʿAlī al-Ghassānī, *al-Takmīl wa-l-itmām li-Kitāb al-Taʿrīf wa-l-iʿlām,* Beirut 1997; Kisāʾī, *Qiṣaṣ,* 45-6; id., *The tales of the prophets of al-Kisaʾi,* trans. W.M. Thackston, Boston 1978, 47-8; Thaʿlabī, *Qiṣaṣ,* Beirut n.d., 43-7.
Secondary: M. Ayoub, *The Qurʾān and its interpreters,* 2 vols. to date, Albany 1984-, i, 128-36 (full coverage of Islamic commentators); B. Bamberger, *Fallen angels,* Philadelphia 1952, 111-7 (popular work); M. Boyce, *Zoroastrians. Their religious beliefs and practices,* London 1979, 22-3, 71-3, 84; P.A. Eichler, *Die Dschinn, Teufel und Engel im Koran,* Inaugural Dissertation, Leipzig 1928, 115-20; A. Geiger, *Was hat Mohammed aus dem Judenthume aufgenommen,* Leipzig 1902, 107-9; B. Heller, La chute des anges Shemchazai, Ouzza et Azael, in REJ 60 (1910), 202-12; J. Horovitz, *Jewish proper names and derivatives in the Koran,* Hildesheim 1964, 20-1; id., KU, 146-8; E. Littmann, Harut und Marut, in *Festschrift Friedrich Carl Andreas zur Vollendung des siebzigsten Lebensjahres am 14 April 1916. Dargebracht von Freunden und Schülern,* Leipzig 1916, 70-87; W. Niekrens, *Die Engel und Geistervorstellungen des Korans,* Inaugural Dissertation, Rostock 1906, 37-8; D. Sidersky, *Les origines des légendes musulmanes dans le Coran et dans les vies des prophètes,* Paris 1933, 22-5; G. Vajda, Hārūt wa-Mārūt, in EI², iii, 236-7.

Harvest see AGRICULTURE AND VEGETATION

Hawā see ADAM AND EVE

Hearing and Deafness

The power or process of perceiving sound, and the inability to do so. The root *s-m-ʿ* denoting "hearing" or "listening," is, with some 185 occurrences, among the most common ones in the Qurʾān. It is found as a verb, mostly *samiʿa,* "to hear," once in the fifth verbal form, "to try to hear/listen" (*issammaʿa,* Q 37:8), a few times in the eighth form, *issamaʿa,* "to listen," and the fourth, *asmaʿa,* "to cause to hear." The verb *aḥassa* is also used in the sense "to hear" (e.g. Q 3:52; 19:98); *anṣata,* "to listen," is found twice (Q 7:204; 46:29). Other verbs meaning "to listen" such as *aṣghā* and *aṣākha* are lacking.

Among the nominal derivations of *s-m-ʿ*, by far the most frequent is *samīʿ*: all but one of its forty-three occurrences apply to God as the "hearing one," the exception being Q 11:24. It is one of God's beautiful names (see GOD AND HIS ATTRIBUTES). Later theologians and exegetes, averse to anthropomorphism (q.v.), discuss this divine "hearing" at length. In the Qurʾān, God is described as *(al-)samīʿ (al-)baṣīr,* "hearing and seeing," on ten occasions; but more usually (thirty-two times) the combination "hearing and knowing" *(samīʿ ʿalīm)* is found, which is an indication of the close relationship between audition and knowledge (see KNOWLEDGE AND LEARNING). The same link may be observed when the verb "to hear" is applied to human beings. "Hearing" may refer to the purely physical process of the perception of sounds or voices, but in the great majority of cases in the Qurʾān it implies a moral or spiritual stance, involving the acceptance of what is heard: obeying God's commands (see OBEDIENCE; DISOBEDIENCE), taking to heart his or his prophets' admonitions (see PROPHETS AND PROPHETHOOD; WARNING). The phrase "we heard and obeyed" *(samiʿnā wa-aṭaʿnā)* occurs in a number of qurʾānic passages (Q 2:285; 4:46; 5:7; 24:51; cf. 24:47), emphasizing the larger connotation of *s-m-ʿ*, which is evidenced in later Islamic thought, where "hearing and obedience" *(al-samʿ wa-l-ṭāʿa)* becomes a symbol of expressing allegiance to political authority.

That *s-m-ʿ* may have a spiritual or moral connotation is obvious in the many instances where "hearing" has no direct object, e.g. "Therein are signs for people who hear" (*li-qawmin yasmaʿūna*, Q 10:67; 30:23 etc.; the "sign" in question, the existence of the night for resting and the day for seeing [see DAY AND NIGHT], has no audile effects). It is possible, however, not only to have ears and yet not to hear (Q 7:179), but also to hear without accepting, as in Q 2:93, "We have heard and have rebelled," or to say one has heard while rejecting, "Be not like those who said: 'We have heard,' though they were not hearing" (Q 8:21).

Conversely, "deafness" (from the verbal root *ṣ-m-m*, which root is attested 15 times in the Qurʾān) means rejecting God's commands: "The worst of beasts, in God's eyes, are the deaf and the dumb who do not understand" (*al-ṣummu l-bukmu lladhīna lā yaʿqilūna*, Q 8:22; see GRATITUDE AND INGRATITUDE; BELIEF AND UNBELIEF). Just as "hearing" goes with "seeing," with both terms meaning "to understand" and "to accept," so "deafness" goes with "blindness" (e.g. Q 5:71; 11:24; 25:73; 43:40; 47:23; see VISION AND BLINDNESS). Twice the expression "deaf, dumb, blind" *(ṣummun bukmun ʿumyun)* is found (Q 2:18, 171; cf. Q 17:97 "blind, dumb, deaf," and Q 6:39 "deaf, dumb, in the darknesses"), and the "heavy" sound of the Arabic beautifully captures the sense. This deafness is often self-induced — continuing the image in the last quotation, it is said: "They put their fingers in their ears" (q.v.; Q 2:19) — but it may be the result of God's act: "We put a seal upon their hearts so that they do not hear" (Q 7:100; see HEART). But if God causes spiritual deafness, it is because the people in question deserve it: "These [viz. who turn away and cause corruption (q.v.) in the land, etc.] are they whom God has cursed (see CURSE), so he made them deaf and blinded their sight" (Q 47:23). See also SEEING AND HEARING.

Geert Jan H. van Gelder

Bibliography
Primary: Dāmaghānī, *Wujūh*, ed. al-Zafītī, i, 417 *(al-samʿ)*; Ibn al-Jawzī, *Nuzha*, 345-6 *(al-samāʿ)*; Muqātil, *Ashbāh*, 226 *(al-samīʿ)*.
Secondary: A.A. Ambros, Höre ohne zu hören zu Koran 4, 46 (48), in ZDMG 136 (1986), 15-22; D. Gimaret, *Les noms divins en Islam. Exégèse lexicographique et théologique*, Paris 1988, 262-6; T. Lohmann, Die Gleichnisreden Muhammads im Koran, in *Mitteilungen des Instituts fur Orientforschung* 12 (1966), 257-8 (on Q 2:17-8); 258-60 (on Q 2:19-20).

Heart

The organ responsible for the circulation of blood. In its singular form *(qalb)* the most common Arabic term for 'heart' appears 19 times in the Qurʾān, beginning with the second sūra and ending with the 64th. Q 33:4 represents its unique occurrence in the dual form of the noun *(qalbayn)*. As a plural *(qulūb)*, however, the term occurs well over 100 times. Textually, the first mention is Q 2:7: "God set a seal *(khatama)* on their hearts and on their hearing and a cover over their eyes." This "sealing" of the heart appears again in Q 6:46, 42:24 and 45:23 (see Ibrahim, Qurʾānic "sealing of the heart"; cf. also Q 9:98). Virtually all of the verbal forms of *khatama* are connected with this expression, except the single mention in Q 33:40 of Muḥammad as the "seal of the prophets."

Other, less frequently found qurʾānic vocabulary that convey meanings associated with the English word 'heart' include terms like *fuʾād*, *ṣadr*, *albāb* (sing. *lubb* but always found in the expression *ūlū l-albāb*, "those posssessed of understanding") and *nafs*. While all of this vocabulary appears in later theological and spiritual treatises about the nature of human beings (e.g. al-Ḥakīm al-Tirmidhī, A Ṣūfī psychological treatise), this article will concentrate chiefly on the term *qalb*. Two themes dominate the qurʾānic treatment of *qalb*, (1) the heart's association with negative emotions and behaviors and (2) the belief that God can and does act directly upon the individual heart. Underneath both emphases lies the concept that the heart is the locus of understanding (see KNOWLEDGE AND LEARNING).

Negative associations

Negative associations with the concept of heart concentrate themselves in two characteristic conjunctions: the heart as "hardened" and the heart as "diseased." In a number of passages (Q 2:74; 5:13; 6:43; 22:53; 39:22; 57:16) forms of the verb 'to be harsh or hard' *(qasā)* or 'to make hard' *(shadda)* are combined with 'hearts' in a descriptive or a prescriptive statement. For example, Q 22:53 speaks of "those whose hearts are hardened" *(wa-l-qāsiyati qulūbuhum)* and Q 57:16 *(fa-qasat qulūbuhum)* echoes this. In both cases, there is a clear connection made with evil-doers *(ẓālimūn, fāsiqūn)* and, in the latter verse, with "those who were given the book (q.v.) before," i.e. with previous recipients of divine revelation, such as the Jews and the Christians (see PEOPLE OF THE BOOK). Prescriptively, the association of heart and hardness occurs in a verse like Q 10:88 where Moses (q.v.) begs God to destroy the wealth of Pharaoh (q.v.) and his nobles and to "harden their hearts" as prelude to securing their final damnation.

Even more prevalent is the association of heart and "disease." In the numerous occurrences (Q 2:10; 5:52; 8:49; 9:125; 22:53; 24:50; 33:12, 32, 60; 47:20, 29; 74:31) of the phrase "in their hearts is a disease" or its variants, the Arabic term that can be translated 'disease' or 'sickness' — *maraḍ* — is invariable. The exegetical tradition ordinarily understands this 'sickness' to be the human failings of doubt (q.v.), disbelief or hypocrisy (Ṭabarī, *Tafsīr*, i, 120-2; xxi, 133; Ibn al-Jawzī, *Zād*, i, 31; ii, 378; v, 443; see BELIEF AND UNBELIEF; HYPOCRITES AND HYPOCRISY). In Sūrat al-Aḥzāb ("The Clans," Q 33), however, which contains the most frequent mention of this phrase, the disease or sickness is associated with a desire for illicit intercourse (see SEX AND SEXUALITY). Q 33:32, which is addressed to the wives of the prophet Muḥammad (see WIVES OF THE PROPHET), cautions them against "those in whose heart is a disease" and the commentaries make the nature of this disease explicit. Similarly, some of the early exegetes (see EXEGESIS OF THE QURʾĀN: CLASSICAL AND MEDIEVAL) draw that same signification from its mention in Q 33:60, with Ibn Zayd (i.e. ʿAbd al-Raḥmān b. Zayd b. Aslam, d. 182/798) making a direct connection between these two verses (Ṭabarī, *Tafsīr,* xxii, 47; see also Ibn al-Jawzī, *Zād,* vi, 379).

A phrase that appears twice in the Qur'ān *(qulūbunā ghulfun,* Q 2:88 and 4:155; cf. Q 41:5) can be translated as referring to the "uncircumcised heart." That expression finds parallels in biblical references (Jeremiah 9:25; Romans 2:25-9) to the uncircumcised heart as the one which fails to follow God's law. The exegetical tradition on these two qur'ānic verses has been preoccupied with the variant readings of the descriptive term, with one reading giving a sense of being enwrapped or enveloped (so that nothing can enter — 'Abd al-Razzāq, *Tafsīr,* equates Q 2:88 with Q 41:5) while the other carries the meaning of a filled container (again, into which nothing more can enter). In either case, however, the expression is understood as referring to the Jewish rejection of Muḥammad's message (cf. Ṭabarī, *Tafsīr;* Ṭūsī, *Tibyān;* Zamakhsharī, *Kashshāf;* Qurṭubī, *Jāmi',* ad loc.)

God acts upon the heart

Yet the Qur'ān also characterizes the heart in more spiritually positive terms. It is the point of loving connection between humans (Q 3:103) and the locus of piety (q.v.; *taqwā,* Q 22:32). It is associated with the remembrance of God (Q 13:28; 39:23; 57:16), and with steadfastness in faith (q.v.; Q 16:106). It is described as "sound" *(salīm,* Q 26:89; 37:84) and repentant *(munīb,* Q 50:33). The basis for such associations and descriptions lies in the dual qur'ānic claim that God knows what is in human hearts and that he acts directly upon them.

The qur'ānic references to God's action upon human hearts can be grouped, like the qur'ānic descriptions of the heart, as both positive and negative. The total number of such references is massive but examples taken from the initial sūras of the text can demonstrate the range of divine action. God "seals" the heart of the one who is headed for a painful doom (Q 2:7; 6:46; 7:100-1; 9:87; cf. Räisänen, *Divine hardening,* 13-44) or allows it to be prompted to evil (Q 2:93) or throws a veil (q.v.) over it (Q 6:25). He causes hearts to go astray (q.v.; Q 3:8; 9:127), hardens them (Q 5:13, 10:88) and frightens them (Q 8:12). Yet God can also strengthen and fortify the human heart (Q 8:11). He joins hearts in friendship (see FRIENDS AND FRIENDSHIP) and unites them (Q 3:103, 8:63), makes them forgiving (Q 3:159) and heals them (Q 9:14, 10:57).

An intriguing verse that generated substantial exegetical discussion alludes to God's placing in the hearts of Jesus' (q.v.) followers "compassion and mercy and monasticism" (Q 57:27; see MONASTICISM AND MONKS). By most readings of this phrase the word "monasticism" *(rahbāniyya)* is not conjunctive with "compassion and mercy" but begins a new sentence, an interpretation that fits more comfortably with the ambivalence toward monasticism expressed in many Muslim sources. Some commentators, such as al-Zamakhsharī (d. 538/1144), however, make it the third object of God's action upon the heart *(al-Kashshāf,* ad loc. but cf. Abū l-Futūḥ Rāzī, *Rawḥ;* Ibn al-Jawzī, *Zād;* Ibn Kathīr, *Tafsīr,* ad loc.), thereby raising interesting questions about the ways that divine and human action can be understood to intersect (McAuliffe, *Qur'ānic,* 260-84). All such references to God's action, whether negative or positive, presuppose that God has intimate knowledge of each human heart, a qur'ānic claim that is expressed explicitly in many passages, perhaps nowhere more eloquently than in the famous Throne Verse *(āyat al-kursī,* Q 2:255).

Heart as the locus of understanding

God's action, both positive and negative, on the human heart correlates directly with the qur'ānic representation of the heart as the locus of understanding (Q 6:25; 7:179;

9:87; 17:46; 18:57; 22:46; 63:3; for a succinct expression of this correlation, cf. *inna fī dhālika l-dhikrā li-man kāna lahu qalbun,* Dāmaghānī, *Wujūh,* ii, 157). In one famous scene Abraham asks God for proof that he can raise the dead, demonstrative proof "that will satisfy my heart [i.e. understanding]" (*wa-lākin li-yaṭmaʾinna qalbī,* Q 2:260). Referring to the modality of the Qurʾān's revelation, Q 2:97 tells Muḥammad that the angel Gabriel "has sent it down upon your heart" (*fa-innahu nazzalahu ʿalā qalbika;* cf. al-Jūzū, *Mafhūm,* 209-10). But the heart's capacity for recognition and comprehension of such non-verbal communication as the divine "signs" (*āyāt*) is also acknowledged (Izutsu, *God,* 136-8). While the just-cited passages use the term *qalb,* another common expression deploys alternative terminology. The phrase that can be translated as "those possessed of understanding" (*ūlū l-albāb*) occurs 16 times in the Qurʾān, with a first appearance in Q 2:179. Glossing *albāb* (sing. *lubb*) as "reason" or "intellect" (q.v.; *ʿaql*) quickly became an exegetical standard (Muqātil, *Tafsīr;* Ṭabarī, *Tafsīr,* ad loc.), with some commentators (Ṭūsī, *Tibyān,* ad loc.) explaining its larger meaning, i.e. what lies inside, such as a kernel or the choicest part of a plant. Q 3:7, a pivotal verse in the Qurʾān's self description, offers the most exegetically rich occurrence of this phrase. Here it connects closely with the preceding "those firmly-rooted in knowledge" (*al-rāsikhūn fī l-ʿilm*) and the following prayer that God "not allow our hearts to deviate" (*rabbanā lā tuzigh qulūbanā*), a connection made explicit by the classical commentators (e.g. Zamakhsharī, *Kashshāf;* Qurṭubī, *Jāmiʿ*, ad loc.; cf. Lagarde, Ambiguïté; Kinberg, Muḥkamāt; Wild, Self-referentiality; McAuliffe, Text).

Ṣūfī and other post-qurʾānic developments

The qurʾānic depiction of the heart, rather than the brain, as the locus of understanding became a central theme in the elaboration of post-qurʾānic anthropology, particularly that of medieval Ṣūfism. The notion that religious knowledge and sensitivity, i.e. conscience, are lodged in the heart grew more formalized and systematized, generating an extensive literature on spiritual formation (*ʿilm al-qulūb*). Some of the most prominent names associated with this tradition are al-Ḥasan al-Baṣrī (d. 110/728), al-Ḥusayn b. Manṣūr al-Ḥallāj (309/922), and Abū Ṭālib al-Makkī (d. 386/996). Al-Makkī's *Qūt al-qulūb* was joined by Abū Ḥāmid al-Ghazālī's (d. 505/1111) *Iḥyāʾ ʿulūm al-dīn,* and Ibn al-ʿArabī's (d. 638/1240) *al-Futūḥāt al-makkiyya* to form a group of the most famous works on this topic. The Ṣūfī tradition of qurʾānic commentary can add to these listings names like Sahl al-Tustarī (d. 283/896) and Rūzbihān al-Balqī (d. 606/1209).

Jane Dammen McAuliffe

Bibliography
Primary: ʿAbd al-Razzāq, *Tafsīr;* Abū l-Futūḥ Rāzī, *Rawḥ;* Abū Ṭālib al-Makkī, *Qūt al-qulūb,* ed. and trans. R. Gramlich, *Die Nahrung der Herzen. Abū Ṭālib al-Makkīs* Qūt al-qulūb, 4 vols., Stuttgart 1992 (see especially the analytical index for "Herz"); Dāmaghānī, *Wujūh,* ii, 157 (for the three meanings of *al-ʿaql, al-raʾy* and *al-qalb alladhī fī l-ṣadr bi-ʿaynihi);* al-Ghazālī, Abū Ḥāmid Muḥammad, *Iḥyāʾ ʿulūm al-dīn,* 5 vols., Beirut 1998; al-Ḥakīm al-Tirmidhī, Abū ʿAbd Allāh Muḥammad b. ʿAlī, *Bayān al-farq bayna l-ṣadr wa-l-qalb wa-l-fuʾād wa-l-lubb,* ed. N. Heer, Cairo 1958, repr. 1971; id., A Ṣūfī psychological treatise. A translation of the Bayān al-farq bayn al-ṣadr wa al-qalb wa al-fuʾād wa al-lubb of Abū ʿAbd Allāh Muḥammad b. ʿAlī al-Ḥakīm al-Tirmidhī, trans. N. Heer, in *MW* 51 (1961), 25-36, 163-72, 244-58; Ibn al-ʿArabī, *al-Futūḥāt al-makkiyya,* 4 vols., Beirut 1968; Ibn al-Jawzī, *Zād;* Ibn Kathīr, *Tafsīr;* Muqātil, *Tafsīr;* Qurṭubī, *Jāmiʿ;* Ṭabarī, *Tafsīr;* Ṭūsī, *Tibyān;* Zamakhsharī, *Kashshāf.*
Secondary: Y.L. Arbeitman, You gotta have heart, in A. Afsarruddin and A.H.M. Zahniser (eds.), *Humanism, culture and language in the Near East. Studies in honor of Georg Krotkoff,* Winona Lake, IN 1997, 363-368; Böwering, *Mystical,* 241-61; W.C. Chittick, *The Sufi path of knowledge.*

Ibn al-ʿArabi's metaphysics of imagination, Albany 1989, especially 106-9; H. Räisänen, *The idea of divine hardening. A comparative study of the notion of divine hardening, leading astray and inciting to evil in the Bible and the Qurʾān,* Helsinki 1976; L. Ibrahim, The qurʾānic "sealing of the heart," in *WO* 16 (1985), 126-7; T. Izutsu, *The concept of belief in Islamic theology,* Tokyo 1965, 74-5, 131-4; id., *God,* 137; id., *The structure of the ethical terms in the Koran,* Tokyo 1959, 122-6; M.ʿA. al-Jūzū, *Mafhūm al-ʿaql wa-l-qalb fī l-Qurʾān wa-l-sunna,* Beirut 1980; review by M. Dhaouadi, The concept of mind and heart in the Qurʾān and the sunna, in *IQ* 38 (1993), 291-7; L. Kinberg, *Muḥkamāt* and *mutashābihāt* (Koran 3/7). Implication of a koranic pair of terms in medieval exegesis, in *Arabica* 35 (1988), 143-72; M. Lagarde, De l'ambiguïté (mutašābih) dans le Coran. Tentatives d'explication des exégètes musulmans, in *Quaderni di studi arabi* 3 (1985), 45-62; McAuliffe, *Qurʾānic;* id., Text and textuality. Q 3:7 as a point of intersection, in I. Boullata (ed.), *Literary structures of religious meaning in the Qurʾān,* Richmond, Surrey 2000, 56-76; S. Wild, The self-referentiality of the Qurʾān. Sūra 3,7 as an exegetical challenge, in J. McAuliffe et al. (eds.), *With reverence for the word. Medieval scriptural exegesis in Judaism, Christianity and Islam* (forthcoming).

Heaven see HEAVEN AND SKY

Heaven and Sky

The expanse or firmament arching over the earth. The Arabic *al-samāʾ,* from the root *s-m-w,* denotes the upper part of anything, such as a roof, sky or heaven (Ṭabarī, *Tafsīr,* i, 151; *Lane,* iv, 1434). In the masculine it means roof or sky or heaven, in the feminine, sky or heaven. In the Qurʾān, it is attested 120 times in the singular, and 190 times in the plural *(samāwāt).* In a special usage of the term, God swears by heaven (Q 51:7; 85:1; 86:1, 11; cf. 51:23; see OATHS AND PROMISES).

Creation of heaven

As depicted by the Qurʾān, heaven and earth (q.v.) were a mass all sewn up, which God unstitched, creating every living thing from water (q.v.; Q 21:30; for the idea of creation in Islam, cf. al-Alousi, *The problem of creation;* see also CREATION). According to Q 2:29 God first created all that is on the earth and then created the seven heavens. The duration of this creation is ambiguous: although it is written that the creation of the earth *(al-arḍ)* lasted two days (Q 41:9), it is also stated that "a day in the sight of your lord is as a thousand years of your reckoning" (Q 22:47; cf. 32:5). After the creation of the earth, God turned to heaven while it was smoke *(dukhān),* and ordained seven heavens in two days (Q 41:11-2; cf. Q 2:29; 21:16; 65:12; 67:3; 71:15; for creation in six days, see Q 7:54; 11:7; 25:59; 32:4; 50:38; 57:4; cf. Speyer, *Erzählungen,* 4-17). He assigned to each heaven its proper order (Q 41:12) and then mounted *(ʾistawā)* the throne (Q 7:54; see THRONE OF GOD), directing all things (Q 10:3).

Cosmology

God then subjected the sun (q.v.) and moon (q.v.) to a divine plan, each moving to a stated term (Q 13:2; see COSMOLOGY). Although the idea of creation and of the seven heavens was evidently already familiar in its rough outline to the ancient peoples of the Near East (K. Galling, *Religion in Geschichte,* s.v. "Himmel," iii, 329-33; for a detailed discussion, see Bietenhard, *Himmlische Welt),* various qurʾānic verses prompted widespread speculation about the nature of this cosmological order. According to Q 11:7, at the beginning of creation God's throne was upon the waters, then God elevated his throne *(ʿarsh)* to the uppermost part of the seventh heaven (Q 23:86). According to Q 2:255, however, God's stool *(kursī)* contains the heavens and the earth. The throne is held by angels (see ANGEL) who sing the praise (q.v.) of God (Q 39:75; 40:7; see GLORIFICATION OF GOD). Some exegetes upheld an anthropomorphic understanding of the concept of "elevation" *(ʾistiwāʾ)* and throne or stool (Ṭabarī, *Tafsīr,* i, 149-53; iii, 7-9; Ṭabarsī, *Majmaʿ,* iii, 303; Wensinck, *Muslim creed,* 148; Daiber, *Muʿammar,* 140-2; see ANTHROPOMORPHISM). God built the heaven as an edifice (Q 2:22; 40:64) and a roof (Q 21:32) and holds it back lest it fall upon the earth (Q 22:65; cf. Ṭabarī, *Tafsīr,* xxii, 95), having raised it without visible supports (Q 13:2; 31:10; see HOUSE, DOMESTIC AND DIVINE). Some exegetes understood this verse to indicate that the heavens were supported "with pillars which man cannot see" (Ṭabarī, *Tafsīr,* xiii, 61-4; Ṭabarsī, *Majmaʿ,* xiii, 138; xxi, 48). Heaven is filled with paths (Q 51:7; for *ḥubuk,* "paths," cf. Ṭabarī, *Tafsīr,* xxvi, 117; Ṭabarsī, *Majmaʿ,* xxvi, 7) and with mighty guardians and meteors (Q 72:8). Islamic tradition believes that the distance separating one heaven from another amounts to the travel of five hundred years (Tirmidhī, *Sunan,* no. 3220; but cf. no. 3242). The lower heaven is adorned with astral constellations and planets (Q 15:16; 25:61; 37:6; 41:12; 50:6; 67:5) and with meteors meant to serve as projectiles against demons (*shayṭān,* see DEVIL) who might try to eavesdrop (Q 15: 17; 67:5; cf. Paret, *Kommentar,* 274).

The relation between the heaven(s) and earth

The lower heaven bears a direct relation to the growth of earthly flora and to subsistence and abundance on earth (see AGRICULTURE AND VEGETATION). From this lower heaven God sends rain, so that since pre-Islamic times grass (q.v.) itself has often been called *samāʾ* by the Arabs (*Lane,* iv, 1435). God also sends destruction from the lower heaven on evil nations in the form of plagues (q.v.; Q 2:59) and stones (Q 8:32; 11:82; 105:4; Ibn Zayd believes that *sijjīl* in *ḥijāra min sijjīlin* [Q 105:4; Jeffery, *For. vocab.*] is the name of the lower heaven; cf. Ṭabarī, *Tafsīr,* xii, 57). From heaven God sends revelations (see REVELATION AND INSPIRATION), a table (q.v.; i.e. a meal) to Jesus (q.v.; Q 5:112; cf. Paret, *Kommentar,* 133), and angels as messengers (see MESSENGER), exterminators of evil nations (Q 29:31; see PUNISHMENT STORIES) and combatants in battle (Q 3:124-5; Ṭabarī, *Tafsīr,* iv, 50-4; see FIGHTING; EXPEDITIONS AND BATTLES). The way from earth up to heaven, however, is blocked to humans without God's authority (Q 55:33).

Description of the heaven(s) and the location of paradise

As developed in post-qurʾānic exegesis, during his night journey to the heavens (*miʿrāj,* see ASCENSION), the prophet Muḥammad was guided by Gabriel (q.v.) through the abodes of the seven heavens where he met with the previous prophets (see PROPHETS AND PROPHETHOOD). He was shown the wonders of the heavens as well as those of paradise (q.v.) and hell (q.v.) until he reached the lote tree of the furthest boundary *(sidrat al-muntahā)* "near to which is the garden (q.v.) of the refuge" (Q 53:15) where the Prophet had a beatific vision (Q 53:1-18; cf. Ṭabarī, *Tafsīr,* xxvii, 29-35; Ṭabarsī, *Majmaʿ,* xxvii, 47; cf. Paret, *Kommentar,* 460-1; Gardet, *Dieu,* 338-40; Tuft, *Hamdard Islamicus,* 3-41). Exegetes differ as to where this lote tree is located, whether at the summit of the sixth heaven or directly beneath the throne in the seventh heaven (Ibn Ḥanbal, *Musnad,* no. 12212; Muslim, *Ṣaḥīḥ, K. al-Īmān,* no. 252; Ṭabarī, *Tafsīr,* xxvii, 29-35; Ṭabarsī, *Majmaʿ,* xxvii, 47; Horovitz, Himmelfahrt, 160-4). Paradise is believed to be in heaven near the lote tree, with *al-firdaws* (Jeffery, *For. vocab.,* 223) being the highest abode in paradise (Ṭabarī, *Tafsīr,* xvii, 30). Finally, drastic and fearful changes in the lower heaven and in the cosmological order are among the signs of the day of judgment (Q 21:104; 25:25; 44:10; 52:9; 55:37; 69:16;

70:8; 73:18; 81:11; 82:1; 84:1; see APOCALYPSE; ESCHATOLOGY; LAST JUDGMENT).

Maher Jarrar

Bibliography
Primary: Ibn Ḥanbal, *Musnad,* in *Mawsūʿat al-ḥadīth al-sharīf. Al-kutub al-tisʿa,* Sakhr CD-Rom 1991-6; Masʿūdī, *Murūj,* ed. and trans. Ch. Pellat, i, 22 (translation of paragraph 36, the description of the seven heavens); Muslim, *Ṣaḥīḥ,* in *Mawsūʿat al-ḥadīth al-sharīf. Al-kutub al-tisʿa,* Sakhr CD-Rom 1991-6; Suyūṭī, *Islamic cosmology. A study of al-Suyūṭī's al-Hayʾa as-sanīya fi-l-hayʾa as-sunnīya. With critical edition, translations and commentary,* trans. A. Heinen, Beirut/Weisbaden 1982, esp. 130-4 (throne and footstool); 138-45 (heaven and earth); Ṭabarī, *The history of al-Ṭabarī. i. General introduction and From the creation to the flood,* trans. F. Rosenthal, Albany, NY 1989, esp. 188, 205 (creation of the heavens), 206-7 (the heavens, footstool and throne), 208, 223; id., *Tafsīr,* 30 vols., Cairo 1905-11, repr. Beirut 1972; Ṭabarsī, *Majmaʿ;* Tirmidhī, *Sunan,* in *Mawsūʿat al-ḥadīth al-sharīf. Al-kutub al-tisʿa,* Sakhr CD-Rom 1991-6.
Secondary: Ḥ.E. al-Alousi, *The problem of creation in Islamic thought,* Baghdad 1965; H. Bietenhard, *Die himmlische Welt im Urchristentum und Spätjudentum,* Tübingen 1951; H. Daiber, *Das theologische-philosophische System des Muʿammar ibn ʿAbbād as-Sulamī,* Beirut 1975; K. Galling (ed.), *Die Religion in Geschichte und Gegenwart. Handwörterbuch für Theologie und Religionswissenschaft,* 7 vols., Tübingen 1957-65, s.v. "Himmel" (iii, 329-33); L. Gardet, *Dieu et la destinée de l'homme,* Paris 1967; A. Heinen, Samāʾ, in *EI²,* viii, 1014-8; J. Horovitz, Muhammeds Himmelfahrt, in *Der Islam* 9 (1919), 159-83; Jeffery, *For. vocab;* Lane; Paret, *Kommentar;* Speyer, *Erzählungen;* A.K. Tuft, The ruʾyā controversy and the interpretation of Qurʾān verse VII:143, in *Hamdard Islamicus* 6 (1983), 3-41; A.J. Wensinck, *Muslim creed. Its genesis and historical development,* Cambridge 1932.

Heavenly Book

The account of all past, present and future events, and the source of revelation to which the qurʾānic terms "mother of the book" (*umm al-kitāb,* Q 43:4), "hidden book" (*kitāb maknūn,* Q 56:78) and "guarded tablet" (*lawḥ maḥfūẓ,* Q 85:22) collectively refer. According to most interpreters, the heavenly book sits either to the right of or underneath God's throne (see THRONE OF GOD; ANTHROPOMORPHISM), above the seventh heaven (see HEAVEN AND SKY). Others hold that the heavenly book rests upon the brow of the angel Isrāfīl. Given its elevated position the heavenly book is hidden except to those pure enough to approach it; these are generally understood to be the angels (see ANGEL), who protect it against any alteration. The heavenly book's covers are said to be made of white pearls and red or green jewels, and the writing in it of light.

The heavenly book serves God in two ways. First, it is a record of everything that has happened since creation and everything that will happen until the day of resurrection (q.v.; Tirmidhī, *Ṣaḥīḥ,* vi, 325-6; Suyūṭī, *Durr,* vii, 366; Rashīd Riḍā, *Manār,* vii, 471). To the extent that the heavenly book comprehends all events, it is linked to the divine ledger of human actions which is displayed on the day of judgment (Q 17:13; 18:49; 45:28-9; 84:7-12; see LAST JUDGMENT; RECORD OF HUMAN ACTIONS).

In a second, more restricted sense, the heavenly book is the source *(aṣl)* and totality *(jumla)* of all revelations, including the Qurʾān. Some hold that the number of pages in the heavenly book is 104, others 114, divided among the revelations of Seth, Abraham (q.v.), Moses (q.v.), David (q.v.), Jesus (q.v.) and Muḥammad (for different theories about the number of pages assigned to each prophet see Bājūrī's comments on the *Sanūsiyya,* 66-7). On the "fateful night" (*laylat al-qadr,* see NIGHT OF POWER), the Qurʾān was sent in its entirety from the heavenly book above the seventh heaven down to the lowest heaven immediately above the earth (q.v.). From this staging area Gabriel (q.v.) delivered bits and pieces of it as needed during the period of Muḥammad's prophethood.

Tensions between these two conceptions

of heavenly book can be seen in two of Islam's earliest theological debates: predestination versus free will (see FREEDOM AND PREDESTINATION), and the createdness versus the uncreatedness of the Qur'ān (see CREATEDNESS OF THE QUR'ĀN). The tradition that the heavenly book in its broader sense (that is, as the written record of God's *knowledge* of all events in the history of the universe) was created before the heavens and the earth first provided support for those who first argued for predestination and against free will, and later supported the Ashʿarīs against the Muʿtazilīs (q.v.; see also THEOLOGY AND THE QUR'ĀN). The problem of theodicy was then dodged by pointing to the fact that God's foreknowledge of events in the heavenly book was not identical to his compelling humans to disobey him (Muqātil, *Tafsīr,* iv, 651; see DISOBEDIENCE; FATE; DESTINY).

The vexed question of whether the Qur'ān was created or uncreated, the focal point of Caliph al-Ma'mūn's *miḥna,* or inquisition (q.v.), during the second quarter of the third/ninth century, revolved, however, around the more restricted sense of the heavenly book as God's *speech* (q.v.; that is, as the articulation of portions of his knowledge to humanity in the form of scripture; see SCRIPTURE AND THE QUR'ĀN). In this sense, the tradition that the heavenly book was created, albeit before the heavens and the earth, supported those who first affirmed the createdness of the Qur'ān against those who denied it, and later supported the Muʿtazilīs against the Ashʿarīs (cf. Abū l-Hudhayl, Jaʿfar b. Ḥarb and Jaʿfar b. Mubashshar in Ashʿarī, *Maqālāt,* ii, 598-600). In response, those arguing for the Qur'ān's uncreatedness seemed to maintain that God's attribute of speech (see GOD AND HIS ATTRIBUTES), conceived of as co-eternal with him, underwent two processes of "inlibration:" the first from the attribute of speech to the heavenly book, and the second from the heavenly book to the Qur'ān (this is taken by Wolfson to be implied by Ashʿarī in *Ibāna,* 34). By virtue of its ultimate derivation from God's attribute of speech, therefore, the Qur'ān could still be held to be uncreated.

Early Ṣūfī commentators identified the *lawḥ maḥfūẓ* with men's hearts (*ṣudūr,* Tustarī, *Tafsīr,* 180, cited by Sulamī, *Ziyādāt,* 220; see HEART), later ones with the Muḥammadan heart (Ibn al-ʿArabī, *Tafsīr,* ii, 790; see ṢŪFISM AND THE QUR'ĀN). In more philosophical Ṣūfī texts the heavenly book plays an almost demiurgic role in the neoplatonic cosmos. While the "pen" *(qalam)* is understood to be the universal intellect *(al-ʿaql al-kullī),* that is, the first emanation from God, the *lawḥ maḥfūẓ* is seen as the second emanation, the universal soul (*al-nafs al-kulliyya,* Ibn al-ʿArabī, *Futūḥāt,* i, 209; ii, 300; x, 436). The equation of the heavenly book with the universal soul is also implied in certain Ismāʿīlī texts (e.g. Nāṣir Khusraw, *Gushāyish,* 69), with the stipulation that only the current imām (q.v.) is qualified to inspect it (Nāṣir Khusraw, *Gushāyish,* 53; see SHĪʿISM AND THE QUR'ĀN). Similar to this is the philosophers' notion that because of the strength of his imaginative faculty and his intuition, a prophet can receive an instantaneous emanation of forms and thereby envision future events (Avicenna, *De Anima,* 170-81, 248-50), a view criticized by al-Ghazālī (d. 505/1111; *Tahāfut al-falāsifa,* 156, 158-63, 167; see PROPHETS AND PROPHETHOOD; PHILOSOPHY AND THE QUR'ĀN). See also BOOK; PRESERVED TABLET.

Robert Wisnovsky

Bibliography

Primary: ʿAbd al-Jabbār, *Tanzīh,* 377; al-Ashʿarī, Abū l-Ḥasan ʿAlī b. Ismāʿīl, *al-Ibāna ʿan uṣūl al-diyāna,* Cairo 1965, 34; id., *Maqālāt al-islāmiyyīn,* ed. H. Ritter, 2 vols., Istanbul 1929-30, 598-600;

Avicenna, *De Anima (Arabic text). Being the psychological part of the* Kitāb al-Shifāʾ, ed. F. Raḥmān, Oxford 1959, 170-81, 248-5; Bājūrī, Ibrāhīm b. Muḥammad, *Ḥāshiyya ʿalā matn al-sanūsiyya,* Cairo 1856, 66-7; Bayḍāwī, *Anwār,* ii, 403, 493, 596; Bukhārī, *Ṣaḥīḥ,* iii, 326-7; Dārimī, *Sunan,* 2 vols. in 1, Beirut 1970, ii, 526-7; al-Ghazālī, Abū Ḥāmid Muḥammad, *Tahāfut al-falāsifa,* ed. and trans. M. Marmura, Provo, UT 1997, 156, 158-63, 167; Ibn al-ʿArabī, Muḥyī l-Dīn Abū ʿAbdallāh Muḥammad b. ʿAlī, *al-Futūḥāt al-Makkiyya,* ed. ʿU. Yaḥyā, Cairo 1972-, i, 48, 209; ii, 182, 300, 313-4; x, 436; id. (attr.), *Tafsīr,* 2 vols., Beirut 1968, ii, 441, 595, 790; Ibn Kathīr, *Tafsīr,* 4 vols., n.p. n.d., iv, 122, 298, 496-7; Muqātil, *Tafsīr,* iii, 789; iv, 224, 651; Nāṣir Khusraw, *Gushāyish wa-rahāyish,* ed. and trans. F. Hunzai, London 1998, 53, 69; Qummī, *Tafsīr,* Tabriz 1895, 606, 720; Rashīd Riḍā, *Manār,* 11 vols., Cairo 1931, ii, 161; vii, 471-2; Rāzī, *Tafsīr,* 8 vols., Istanbul 1891, vii, 429; viii, 101, 527-8; Sulamī, *Ẓiyādāt,* 164, 220; Suyūṭī, *Durr,* 8 vols., Beirut 1983, vii, 366; viii, 26-8, 481-2; Ṭabarī, *Tafsīr,* ed. B. Maʿrūf and ʿI. Ḥurristānī, 7 vols., Beirut 1994, vi, 508; vii, 212, 498; Tirmidhī, *Ṣaḥīḥ,* vi, 325-6; Ṭūsī, *Tibyān,* ix, 180-1, 510; x, 322; Tustarī, *Tafsīr,* ed. M. Ḥalabī, Cairo 1908, 129-30, 180; Zamakhsharī, *Kashshāf,* 4 vols., Beirut n.d., iii, 411; iv, 62, 201.
Secondary: L. Koep, *Das himmlische Buch in Antike und Christentum,* Bonn 1952; I.K. Poonawala, Ismāʿīlī *taʾwīl* of the Qurʾān, in Rippin, *Approaches,* 199-222; A.J. Wensinck/C.E. Bosworth, Lawḥ, in *EI²,* v, 698; H.A. Wolfson, *The philosophy of the kalam,* Cambridge, MA 1976, 235-303.

Hell see HELL AND HELLFIRE

Hell and Hellfire

The place or state of punishment for the wicked after death. The Qurʾān portrays a hell that tortures both body and soul. It mentions its names, something of its physical layout, just which human sinners are its fuel, and how people may save themselves from it. Sinners whose wishful thinking minimizes the scope of hell must still face the reality of it, yet when they see it, it will be too late. They will be in hell eternally but the Qurʾān remains ambiguous on whether hell is eternal in the same way that God is eternal (see ETERNITY).

The names of hell

The Qurʾān uses some ten terms to name hell and to describe it. The "proper" name of hell, Jahannam, is only the second most common of these (77 occurrences, the first at Q 2:206; cf. Heb. Ge Hinnom, possibly through Ethiopic; Jeffery, *For. vocab.,* 105-6). The most common description, the fire (q.v.; *al-nār*), refers to its best-known characteristic (some 125 occurrences, excluding non-technical uses, the first at Q 2:24). Most other terms are synonyms; thus *al-saʿīr* is "the blaze" (cf. Q 4:10), and *al-jaḥīm* is "the hot place" (Q 2:119), though in one verse (Q 37:97) the latter is not a synonym for hell but denotes the fire into which the idolaters (see IDOLATRY AND IDOLATERS) order that Abraham (q.v.) be thrown. Hell has flames, *lahab* (Q 77:31), and it punishes by combustion, *ʿadhāb al-ḥarīq* (Q 3:181). The unique term *hāwiya* (Q 101:9) is defined two verses later as "a raging fire," *nār ḥāmiya* (Q 101:11), a definition validated by an apparent Ethiopic cognate (Jeffery, *For. vocab.,* 285-6). Two other terms are defined not by what they are but by what they do. *Laẓā,* a "blaze" (Q 70:15), is known from *nār talaẓẓā* (Q 92:14); *saqar* is not defined at its first occurrence in Q 54:48 ("taste the touch of *saqar*") but Q 74:26-31 contains a functional definition: it "lets nothing remain and leaves nothing alone, turning human beings red" (*lawwāḥatun lil-bashari,* see Ṭabarsī, v, 386-9). Finally, the term *ḥuṭama* (Q 104:4) although defined in context both notionally and functionally, has elicited further interpretation from lexicographers and exegetes. "What will make you realize what *al-ḥuṭama* is? God's kindled fire, which reaches up to the hearts: it is closed in over them in long columns" (Q 104:5-9). The verbal root signifies breaking, i.e. "that which breaks in pieces," especially the shattering of something dry (Fīrūzābādī, *Qāmūs,* iv, 97). "*Al-ḥuṭama* is one of the names of the fire... I think it has been called that because it breaks up whatever is thrown into it; similarly a man who eats a lot is called *al-ḥuṭama*" (Ṭabarī, *Tafsīr,* xxx, 190). Ibn Abī Ḥātim al-Rāzī (d. 327/938-9) reported, "*Al-ḥuṭama* is one of the gates of Jahannam" (cf. Suyūṭī, *Durr,* viii, 620).

The topography of hell

The fire is spread out above and below in layers (Q 39:16), enclosed (Q 90:20), with sparks as big as forts (Q 77:32). Its fuel is human beings and stones (Q 2:24; 66:6), specifically, unbelievers (Q 3:10; see BELIEF AND UNBELIEF), the unjust (Q 72:15; see JUSTICE AND INJUSTICE), and polytheists and whatever they worship besides God (Q 21:98; see POLYTHEISM AND ATHEISM). Fakhr al-Dīn al-Rāzī (d. 606/1210; *Tafsīr,* ii, 122) interprets the "stones" as stone idols (see IDOLS AND IMAGES). With the fire comes black smoke (*yaḥmūm,* Q 56:43), three columns of shadow that do not protect against the flames (Q 77:30-1), boiling water (*ḥamīm,* Q 56:42) and the poisonous hot wind (*samūm,* Q 52:27; 56:42). People's faces are turned upside down in the fire (Q 33:66); they are dragged through it on their faces (Q 54:48), unable to keep it away from their faces or their backs (Q 21:39). Several times hell is called "an evil bed" (*biʾsa l-mihād,* Q 2:206), one with canopies (Q 7:41). The sinners wander about between hell and boiling water (Q 55:43-4).

Hell is reached by a road (*ṣirāṭ al-jaḥīm,* Q 37:23), later construed as a bridge, and by seven gates, one for each class of sinners (Q 15:44; see SIN, MAJOR AND MINOR). Heaven (see HEAVEN AND SKY; PARADISE; GARDEN) is separated from hell by a wall with a gate; inside is mercy (q.v.), and all along the outside is torment (*ʿadhāb,* Q 57:13). Yet despite that barrier and the veil between them (Q 7:46; see BARZAKH), the inhabitants of heaven and hell can see and call to each other. They compare experiences: both have found their lord's promises to be true (Q 7:44). Then "the companions of the fire cry out to the companions of the garden, 'Pour water down on us, or any nourishment God has provided you!' They reply, 'God has forbidden both of those things to the disbelievers!'" (Q 7:50). The cry for water is one of the spatially oriented descriptions that seem to confirm the usual view of heaven as an elevation and hell as a pit. The horrible tree of Zaqqūm grows up from the bottom of hell-fire (*takhruju fī aṣl al-jaḥīmi,* Q 37:64). Those who were believers in life will laugh at the unbelievers *(kuffār),* looking down from their thrones (*ʿalā l-arāʾiki yanẓurūna,* Q 83:34-5). An extended passage portrays a man who looks out from heaven and sees his old friend, a skeptic who denied the afterlife, in the middle of the fire (Q 37:51-9); the word used is *iṭṭalaʿa,* which signifies looking down from an elevation (Fīrūzābādī, *Qāmūs,* iii, 59; but cf. Q 28:38). On the other hand, the "men on *al-aʿrāf*" (Q 7:46-9), for which Q 7 (Sūrat al-Aʿrāf, "The Heights") is named, seem to look down on both the garden and the fire, as though they were side by side, although that is the same passage where the damned beg the saved to pour water on them (Q 7:50). Al-Suyūṭī (d. 911/1505; *Durr,* iii, 460-1) offers ten possible identifications of *al-aʿrāf,* including "a wall (or a mountain or a hill) between the garden and the fire," "an elevated place," "a wall with a crest like a cock's comb," "a wall with a door," and "the bridge" *(al-ṣirāṭ).*

The punishments of hell

The most common term for punishment is *ʿadhāb* (see REWARD AND PUNISHMENT). The noun occurs some 322 times, to say nothing of verbs and participles; but the word is used for earthly punishments as well, as in Solomon's (q.v.) threat to the hoopoe (Q 27:21) or Pharaoh's (q.v.) treatment of the Children of Israel (q.v.; Q 2:49). Punishment in hell is often qualified by an epithet, as in the phrase *ʿadhāb al-ḥarīq*. The Qurʾān emphasizes its magnitude and seriousness with such phrases as *ʿadhāb ʿaẓīm* (Q 2:7), *sūʾa l-ʿadhābi* (Q 2:49), and *ʿadhāb shadīd* (Q 3:4). Punishment is both physical and mental: the very common phrase *ʿadhāb alīm*, "painful punishment" (Q 2:10), refers to that part of infernal torment that affects the body, while the less common *ʿadhāb muhīn*, "humiliating punishment" (Q 3:178), refers to its effects on the mind or soul.

Physical punishment affects all the senses. It begins with the sight of hell, the vision of which is a certainty (*la-tarawunnahā ʿayna l-yaqīni*, Q 102:7). "The sinners will see the fire and recognize that they are to fall into it, and they will find no outlet" (Q 18:53): every time they try to escape, they will be forced back (Q 32:20). The fire will roast their skins and then roast them anew (Q 4:56); their garments will be of fire (Q 22:19) or of liquid pitch (Q 14:50); the treasure they stored up on earth will be heated and used to brand their foreheads, sides and backs (Q 9:35). Their faces will be black (Q 39:60); and "the fire will burn their faces, on which are grotesque grins" (Q 23:104). They will be in chains with yokes around their necks (Q 40:71). They will eat fire (Q 2:174) and drink boiling water (Q 6:70), which will also be poured on their heads, scalding their bodies inside and out (Q 22:19-20). Drinks that are not hot as melted brass (Q 18:29) will be bitter cold (Q 38:57), putrid, full of pus (Q 14:16), and, in any case, will not quench their thirst (Q 14:17; see HOT AND COLD). Food that is not fire will be the fruit of the tree Zaqqūm, like the heads of devils (Q 37:65) or "the corruption from the washing of wounds" (Q 69:36); their food will choke them (Q 73:13) but will neither nourish them nor remove their hunger (Q 88:6-7). The sounds they hear will be "sighs and sobs" (Q 11:106).

What is worse than these physical tortures is the knowledge that they will never end. "He shall have hell: in it he shall neither die nor live" (Q 20:74; cf. 14:17). "Those who disbelieve shall have the fire of hell; no final sentence shall be given them so that they might die, nor shall its punishment be lightened" (Q 35:36); nor can they claim to be wrongly condemned, for their tongues and limbs (Q 24:24), their senses and their skins (Q 41:20-3) will witness against them. "You thought that God did not know much of what you used to do! But this notion that you had has destroyed you, and now you are one of the lost!" (Q 41:22-3). The mental tortures are both individual and communal, incorporating the most painful aspects of both. The sinners will be all alone, with no intercessor (Q 6:94; see INTERCESSION) or defender (Q 10:27; see PROTECTION), or even a greeting (Q 38:59). "They shall have no share of happiness in the hereafter; God will not speak to them, or look at them on the day of resurrection, or purify them" (Q 3:77). Indeed, they will be told, "God loathes you more than you loathe yourselves" (Q 40:10).

In other verses, however, sinners are told that they will not only be in groups, they will be bound together with fetters (Q 14:49). They will curse each other (Q 7:38), and constantly argue and blame each other (Q 26:96-102). "They will argue in the fire. The weak ones will say to the haughty ones (see ARROGANCE), 'We were following you! Can you take on some of our share of the fire?' And the haughty ones will say, 'We are all in this together!...'" (Q 40:47-8). Even worse, they are able to see the inhabitants of heaven (Q 7:44-50); they are surrounded by what they used to mock (Q 45:33); and Satan himself comes to turn the knife. "God made you a true promise; I made you a promise and I broke it. I had no power over you except to call you, but you answered me; so do not blame me — blame yourselves!... I reject what you did in associating me with God..." (Q 14:22).

The tortures of hell mirror the pleasures of heaven: foul food and disgusting drinks in place of delicious food and clear drinks in crystal goblets; garments of fire instead of garments of silk (q.v.); sinful companions like themselves (Q 41:25) instead of beautiful and virtuous ones (see HOURIS); pain, humiliation and despair instead of peace and joy. A short example of the parallel rhetoric that illustrates parallel concepts (often at length) can be found in the ninth sūra: "God has promised the hypocrites (see HYPOCRITES AND HYPOCRISY), male and female, and the unbelievers the fire of hell, to remain in it forever; that is sufficient for them. And God has cursed them, and they will have a punishment of long duration" (Q 9:68). "God has promised the believers, male and female, gardens below which rivers flow, to remain in them forever, and fine dwellings in gardens of paradise. And acceptance from God is supreme: that is the great victory" (Q 9:72).

If hell is a mirror of heaven, is Satan in charge? Unlike the elaborations found in later literature, Satan's connection with the infernal regions is rather tenuous in the Qur'ān. As has been mentioned, he appears before the sinners to taunt them (Q 14:22), but the only other verse that puts him in hell indicates that it is punishment for his sins. "[Iblīs] said, 'Do you see this man whom you [God] honored over me? If you postpone [my fate] until the day of resurrection, I will take control of his descendants, except for a few.' [God] said, 'Go! And no matter who follows you, hell will be the penalty for you all — an ample penalty!' " (Q 17:62-3; see also Q 38:85). Until then, Satan will remain on the earth, making evil appear good (see GOOD AND EVIL), misleading all except God's sincere servants (Q 15:31-43; also 7:11-8), and inviting people to the fire (Q 35:6) as he invited their forefathers (Q 31:21; see DEVIL).

Pharaoh and his hosts likewise are "imāms (see IMĀM) who summon to the fire" (Q 28:41). Over it are set nineteen angels (Q 74:30-1; see ANGEL), also called *al-zabāniya:* "guardians of hell... strong and mighty angels" (Q 96:18; Jeffery, *For. vocab.* 148). The most complete description is at Q 66:6: "Over it are strong, hard-hearted angels, who do not rebel against what God has commanded them to do: they do what they are ordered."

In a number of passages, hell itself is personified. It sees those who denied it approaching from afar (Q 25:12); it invites those who turn their backs on what is right (Q 70:17). "When they are thrown into it, they hear it draw a sobbing breath as it boils up, nearly bursting with rage" (Q 67:7-8). That the word *Jahannam* is grammatically feminine is most vivid in Q 50:30: "One day we shall ask hell, 'Are you full?' and she will say, 'Are there more?' "

Who will enter hell?

All humans must face hell. "There is not one of you but that he must come to it: that is a sealed [commitment] that shall be carried out. Then we shall save the pious and leave the sinners in it on their knees" (Q 19:71-2). As al-Ghazālī (d. 505/1111; *Iḥyā'*, iv, 658) says, "You are certain of going there, but your rescue is in doubt." The list of those who will remain in hell is virtually endless. One group may be characterized by their attitudes: the disbelievers (*al-kāfirūn,* Q 2:24), particularly those who die in that state (Q 2:161-2), apostates (Q 3:86-91; see APOSTASY), hypocrites (Q 4:140), idolaters (Q 14:30; see IDOLATRY AND IDOLATERS), wastrels (*al-musrifīn,* Q 40:43), the haughty (Q 7:36), those who go against God and his messenger (q.v.; Q 9:63), those who make religion a game (Q 6:70; see GAMBLING), those who tempt and those who allow themselves to be tempted (Q 57:13), and those who die in sin, having failed to flee to where they could have been virtuous (Q 4:97). Another group has failed in specific ways: they have denied God's signs (q.v.; Q 2:39), broken the covenant (q.v.; Q 2:83-5), gone back to usury (q.v.) after God's ban (Q 2:275), deserted in battle (Q 8:16; see EXPEDITIONS AND BATTLES) or avoided it altogether (Q 9:49), been satisfied with the things of this world (Q 10:7-8; 17:18), made fun of God's messengers (Q 18:106), failed to respond to God (Q 13:18), or denied the divine origin of the Qurʾān (Q 74:16-26) or the reality of the hour of judgment (Q 25:11-4; see LAST JUDGMENT). Among those who commit particular sins are murderers (Q 4:29-30; see BLOODSHED; MURDER), including those who have killed their prophets (Q 3:21); persecutors of the believers (Q 85:10); those who consume the property of orphans (q.v.; Q 4:10) or violate inheritance (q.v.) laws (Q 4:12-4); those who claim divinity for themselves (Q 21:29); polytheists who build mosques (Q 9:17); and rumor-mongers (Q 104; see GOSSIP), especially those who slander chaste women (Q 24:23; see MODESTY; VIRTUE; CHASTITY). Hell is a certainty for some individuals: Cain (Q 5:27-32; see CAIN AND ABEL), Noah's (q.v.) and Lot's (q.v.) wives (Q 66:10; see WOMEN AND THE QURʾĀN), and the Prophet's uncle Abū Lahab and his wife (Q 111).

Is hell eternal?

Many of the damned failed while still on earth to appreciate that hell is real and that it is eternal. "They say, 'The fire will not touch us except for a countable number of days,' but they have deceived themselves with what they have made up about their religion" (Q 3:24). "We shall say to those who have sinned, 'Taste the punishment of the fire, which you used to deny!'" (Q 34:42). They think that their wealth (q.v.) will save them (Q 45:10), and they challenge the Prophet to bring on the punishment, apparently because they do not believe in it (Q 29:53-5).

On the question of whether hell is eternal, the qurʾānic verses seem clear enough: "Their punishment is that upon them is the curse of God and of his angels and of all humanity. They will be in it eternally *(khālidīna fīhā):* their punishment will not be lightened nor will they be given any delay" (Q 3:87-8). They will be given "an enduring penalty" (*ʿadhāb muqīm,* Q 5:37); they will be in the fire "eternally, as long as the heavens and the earth exist, except as your lord wills..." (Q 11:107); no limit will be set after which they might die and by dying escape hell (Q 35:36). Yet the eternality of hell set up well-known problems for theologians such as the Muʿtazilīs (q.v.), who would not compromise God's uniqueness by admitting that another eternal entity might exist. Such theological disputes generated systematic creeds (q.v.), virtually all of which contain clauses that deal with particulars of the hereafter. Thus, Aḥmad b. Ḥanbal's (d. 241/855-6) *al-Radd ʿalā l-zanādiqa wa-l-jahmiyya* (in *Aqāʾid al-salaf,* 100-3) accuses Jahm b. Ṣafwān (d. 128/745-6) of relying upon two verses, "He is the first and the last" (Q 57:3), and "Everything will be destroyed except his face" (Q 28:88; see FACE OF GOD) to prove that heaven and hell are not eternal. Ibn Ḥanbal admitted that the heavens and the earth would pass away, but only because all the people had gone to the garden or the fire, which themselves were proven by numerous verses to be eternal. Other thinkers would not admit that the eternality of garden and fire entailed the eternality of their inhabitants, rewards, and punishments. Relying upon the verse that says, "God does not forgive that anything should be associated with himself, but he forgives what is less than that" (Q 4:48), the Egyptian Ḥanafī author al-Ṭaḥāwī (d. 321/933) wrote in his *Bayān al-sunna wa-l-jamāʿa:* "If he wills [h]e punishes them in the fire in proportion to their offense in accordance with his justice. Afterwards he will withdraw them from it, in accordance with his mercy... and will send them to the garden" (cf. Elder, Ṭaḥāwī's *Bayān,* 139).

Innumerable texts elaborate upon the qurʾānic data, their order and approach varying according to the author's purpose. Al-Ghazālī's *al-Qawl fī ṣifāt jahannam wa-aḥwālihā wa-ankālihā* (in *Iḥyāʾ,* iv, 658-64) and the section on hell in Ibn Kathīr's (d. 774/1373) *Kitāb al-Nihāya* (ii, 172-358) conduct the believer through the infernal regions as (s)he will encounter them. Al-Ghazālī construes the qurʾānic names for hell as indicating separate parts of it, and he arranges them top to bottom: "*Jahannam,* then *saqar,* then *laẓā,* then *al-ḥuṭama,* then *al-saʿīr,* then *al-jaḥīm,* then *hāwiya*" (*Iḥyāʾ,* iv, 659). Among extra-qurʾānic details is his description of the final call: "Then will come the cry, 'O Adam (see ADAM AND EVE), send a contingent of your offspring to the fire!' And he will say, 'How many, O lord?' And he will say to him, 'From every thousand, 999 to the fire and one to the garden!'" (Ghazālī, *Durra,* 158). Ibn Kathīr supplements the Qurʾān with vast quantities of ḥadīth (see ḤADĪTH AND THE QURʾĀN), some of an authenticity he calls "remarkably poor" *(gharīb jiddan).* Both authors describe the tortures of hell in disgusting detail. From the poet Abū l-ʿAlāʾ al-Maʿarrī and the mystic Ibn al-ʿArabī come further masses of detail, including pictures of Iblīs as both the king of hell and its fettered prisoner, forerunners of Dante's imprisoned Lucifer, buried in ice from his chest down (Asin Palacios, *Islam and the Divine Comedy,* 58, 92, and the references therein). Finally, let us not forget the prayers of the common people, taught to them by those close to God, in this case ʿAlī Zayn al-ʿĀbidīn, "I ask thee to have mercy on this delicate skin, this slender frame which cannot endure the heat of thy sun. How then will it endure the heat of thy Fire?" (from *al-Ṣaḥīfa al-sajjādiyya,* in Padwick, *Muslim devotions,* 283).

Rosalind W. Gwynne

Bibliography

Primary: al-Fīrūzābādī, Abū l-Ṭāhir Muḥammad b. Yaqūb, *al-Qāmūs al-muḥīṭ,* ed. M.M. al-Tarkazī, 4 vols., Cairo 1306/1888-89; al-Ghazālī, Abū Ḥāmid Muḥammad, *al-Durra al-fākhira fī kashf ʿulūm al-ākhira* (together with *Sirr al-ʿālamīn*), ed. M.M. Abū l-ʿAlā, Cairo 1968; id., *Al-Ghazālī. Kitāb Dhikr al-mawt wa-mā baʿdhu. The remembrance of death and the afterlife. Book XL of The revival of the religious sciences (Iḥyāʾ ʿulūm al-dīn),* trans. T.J. Winter (with intro. and notes), Cambridge, UK 1989, 219-30 (for hell); id., *Iḥyāʾ ʿulūm al-dīn,* 4 vols., Cairo 1967; id., *La perle précieuse (ad-Dourra al-Fâkhira) de Ghazâlî. Texte arabe et traduction,* trans. L. Gautier, Geneva 1878, repr. Amsterdam 1974; Ibn Ḥanbal, al-Radd ʿalā l-zanādiqa wa-l-jahmiyya, in A.S. al-Nashshār (ed.), *ʿAqāʾid al-salaf,* Alexandria 1971; Ibn Kathīr, *Kitāb al-Nihāya,* ed. T.M. al-Zaynī, 2 vols., Cairo 1969; al-Muḥāsibī, Abū ʿAlī l-Ḥārith b. Asad, *Kitāb al-Tawahhum,* Cairo 1979; Rāzī, *Tafsīr,* Beirut 1981; Suyūṭī, *al-Budr al-safira fī umūr al-ākhira,* ed. M.Ḥ. al-Shāfiʿī, Beirut 1996, 408-72; id., *Durr,* 8 vols, Beirut 1402/1982 (repr. 1414/1993); Ṭabarī, *Tafsīr,* ed. N. al-ʿĀdilī, 30 vols. in 12, Cairo 1330/1912; Ṭabarsī, *Majmaʿ,* 5 vols., Sidon 1333/1914-5; al-Tibrīzī, Muḥammad b. ʿAbdallāh al-Khāṭib, *Mishcàt-ul-masàbih. Or a collection of the most authentic traditions regarding the actions and sayings of Muhammed. Exhibiting the origin of the manners and customs, the civil, religious and military policy of the Muslemans,* trans. A.N. Matthews, 2 vols., Calcutta 1823, ii, 634-41 (on hell and fire).

Secondary: ʿA.Y. ʿAlī (trans.), *The holy Qurʾān,* Lahore 1934 (repr. USA 1977; useful translation, occasionally used in this article); M. Asin Palacios, *Islam and the Divine Comedy,* trans. and abr. Harold Sutherland, London 1926, repr. 1968 (detailed parallels with the Qurʾan and the eschatological elaborations of Abū l-ʿAlāʾ

al-Maʿarrī, *Risālat al-ghufrān* and Ibn al-ʿArabī, *al-Futūḥāt al-makkiyya*); E.E. Elder, Al-Ṭaḥāwī's *Bayān al-sunna wa-l-jamāʿa,* in W.G. Shellabear et al. (eds.), *The Macdonald presentation volume. A tribute to Duncan Black Macdonald. Consisting of articles by former students. Presented to him on his seventieth birthday. April 9, 1933,* Princeton 1933, 129-44; S. El-Salih, *La vie futur selon le Coran,* Paris 1971; Jeffery, *For. vocab.;* T. O'Shaughnessy, The seven names for hell in the Koran, in *BSOAS* 24 (1961), 444-65; id., *Muhammad's thoughts on death. A thematic study of the qurʾānic data,* Leiden 1969; C. Padwick, *Muslim devotions,* London 1961, 1996 (repr.); S. Quṭb, *Mashāhid al-qiyāma fī l-Qurʾān,* Cairo 1947; J. Robson, Is the Moslem hell eternal? in *MW* 28 (1938), 386-96; J.B. Rüling, *Beiträge zur Eschatologie des Islam.* Inaugural-Dissertation, Leipzig 1895, esp. 27-32; J.I. Smith and Y.Y. Haddad, *The Islamic understanding of death and resurrection,* New York 1981 (fundamental; full bibliography); W.M. Watt, *Islamic creeds. A selection,* Edinburgh 1994; A.J. Wensinck, *The Muslim creed. Its genesis and historical development,* London 1932, 1965 (repr.); M. Wolff, *Muhammedanische Eschatologie (Kitab Ahwal al-qiyama). Arabisch und Deutsch,* Leipzig 1872, 147-85 of the translation (on hell).

Hereafter

see ESCHATOLOGY; RESURRECTION; PARADISE; HELL AND HELLFIRE; FIRE; LAST JUDGMENT

Heresy

Dissent from commonly accepted doctrine with a tendency towards sectarianism. Heresy, of course, only has meaning in light of orthodoxy, the elaboration of which in Islam seems to have begun as a traditionalist reaction to the politico-theological policies of the ʿAbbāsid caliph al-Maʾmūn (r. 198/813-218/833; Lewis, Observations, 43 f.; Makdisi, *Ibn ʿAqīl,* 26 f.). As the Qurʾān is the foundational text of Islam, it is difficult to locate a strict concept of heresy within the Qurʾān itself. Nevertheless, as Muḥammad is not understood to proclaim a new message, but rather is seen as the successor of previous prophets (see PROPHETS AND PROPHETHOOD), all of whom proclaimed the same message, it is possible to speak of deviations from "right belief" (see PATH OR WAY; ḤANĪF; RELIGION). The qurʾānic term that most directly conveys this concept is the fourth form of the verbal root *l-ḥ-d* (Q 7:180; 16:103; 41:40; 22:25), which connotes blasphemy (q.v.) of the names of God (Q 7:180) and disbelief in God's signs (Q 41:40) or Muḥammad's message (Q 16:103). Other qurʾānic terms that convey the concept of deviation from true belief are innovation (q.v.; *bidʿa,* Q 46:9); the first form of the verbal root *b-gh-y,* which, in a number of its attestations, implies insolence or disobedience (q.v.; cf. e.g. Q 2:90; 3:83, 99; 6:164; 10:23; see GRATITUDE AND INGRATITUDE); and the third form of the verbal root *n-f-q,* which denotes hypocrisy (see HYPOCRITES AND HYPOCRISY). But, as heresy, strictly speaking, must be defined in relation to orthodoxy (or vice-versa), it is only in the post-qurʾānic period of Islamic history that a formal concept of heresy took shape. (It is noteworthy that the Arabic term *zandaqa,* often translated as "atheism," which carries the sense of unbelief or "free thought," and which came to designate "heresy," is not attested in the Qurʾān.)

The development of the concept of heresy in Islam in its intellectual and literary expression can be seen in the transition from "books of refutation" *(kutub al-radd),* where religious doctrines (see CREEDS) are presented in contrastive format, to the progressive systematization of theological orthodoxy in the heresiographical works (i.e. literature of the *maqālāt* and the *firaq;* see THEOLOGY AND THE QURʾĀN), of which the oldest known example seems to be the work of the scholar of the Muʿtazilī school of Baghdad, Abū l-Faḍl Jaʿfar b. Ḥarb al-Hamadhānī (d. 236/850; Laoust, Hérésiographie musulmane, 160; Monnot, *Islam,*

45 f.). Already in the previous century, the Muʿtazilīs (q.v.) had become famous for their attacks against ancient religions and their strong reactions to those with sympathies for non-Islamic beliefs (see BELIEF AND UNBELIEF), especially the defenders of doctrines considered impious, such as those of dualists and especially of Manichaeans (van Ess, Ibn ar-Rīwandī, 5 f.; Stroumsa, Muslim polemics, 767-70). In the fourth-fifth/tenth-eleventh centuries, the expansion of Ashʿarism marked the decline of Muʿtazilism, and with that development, the Manichaean spiritual center, the focus of doctrinal dissent in Iraq, was transferred from Baghdad to Samarqand during the caliphate of al-Muqtadir (r. 295/908-320/932). Subsequently, the Ghaznavids and later the Seljuqs, violent defenders of the new forms of nascent orthodoxy, decisively reduced this perceived danger to Islam by rooting out subversive ideas. As a result of their orthodox rule, the need to refute doctrinal opponents was no longer pressing (see DEBATE AND DISPUTATION; POLEMIC AND POLEMICAL LANGUAGE), and heresiography henceforth definitively supplanted the literature of refutation (Ritter, Philologika, 34 f.; Colpe, *Der Manichäismus*, 191 f.). Beginning with the sixth/twelfth century, heresiography largely lost its apologetic function and became an academic science of categorization that generated various encyclopaedic works on sects and heresies, the most outstanding example of which is al-Shahrastānī's treatise (for such works, see Vajda, Le témoignage; Monnot, *Islam*, 50-79). Apologetic or polemical literature, from this point on, devoted itself almost exclusively to aspects of Sunnī-Shīʿī controversy (see SHĪʿA; SHĪʿISM AND THE QURʾĀN).

In Islam, like elsewhere, the heretic is always the other, the one who offers a different exegesis of scripture and revelation. Heresiographical terminology became fixed only over many centuries. The Khārijī (see KHĀRIJĪS) interpretation of the duty of enjoining the good (*al-amr bi-l-maʿrūf*, see ETHICS AND THE QURʾĀN; GOOD AND EVIL) provoked the reaction of Muʿtazilīs who saw them as a group of rebels *(fiʾa bāghiya)*, i.e. viewing them in terms of the qurʾānic root for rebellion or insolence towards God *(b-gh-y)*. The ascetic of Balkh, ʿAbdallāh b. al-Mubārak (d. 181/797), represented the orthodoxy of "the people of moderation" *(ahl al-ʿadl)* in opposition to the deviation of "the people of immoderation" (*ahl al-baghī*, cf. van Ess, *TG*, ii, 409; iv, 704-6; v, 207). As noted above, other qurʾānic language used to designate religious opponents or altered doctrine include hypocrisy *(n-f-q)* or blameful innovation *(b-d-ʿ)*. The Imāmī Shīʿites *(imāmiyya qaṭʿiyya)* later known as Twelver Shīʿites *(ithnā ʿashariyya)*, were identified by the non-qurʾānic term *rāfiḍa* (pl. *rawāfiḍ*, literally "those who throw back or refuse"), first by the Zaydī Shīʿites. The term may have been applied by the Zaydī Muʿtazilī Bishr b. al-Muʿtamir (d. ca. 210/825), who reacted strongly against the Imāmī Shīʿites of Kūfa since they refused to recognize (i.e. threw back) the legitimacy of the armed revolt of Zaydī. It was later adopted by non-Shīʿites as a way to disparage the Shīʿī refusal to recognize the legitimacy of the three first caliphs (Friedlaender, The heterodoxies, 137 f.). It was probably in the second/eighth century, with the spread of the famous tradition attributed to the Prophet about the seventy-two (or seventy-three) sects, only one of which would be saved, as well as the diffusion of another tradition, which seems to complement the former, saying that "my community will never agree on error *(ḍalāl)*," that the term *ḍalāla* came to designate doctrinal error in Islam (see ERROR).

In contrast to the notion of heresy per se

often associated with blameful innovation *(bidʿa,* pl. *bidaʿ),* personal and thus aimless aspiration *(hawāʾ,* pl. *ahwāʾ)* or sacrilegious doubt, erroneous doctrine or heterodox position *(shubha,* pl. *shubuhāt),* this new understanding of error *(ḍalāl* or *ḍalāla)* constituted an intermediate degree between simple error *(khaṭaʾ),* that even a Muslim in good standing can commit (see SIN, MAJOR AND MINOR), and complete infidelity (*kufr,* see Dedering, Ein Kommentar, 42 f.; Laoust, *La profession,* 40, 172). At the same time, a new term, *zandaqa,* emerged in designation of the doctrines and practices of any kind of heretic *(zindīq,* pl. *zanādiqa)* in reference to both non-Muslims (especially gnostic and gnosticizing trends) and Muslims (heterodox, free-thinkers, libertine poets, political opponents of the caliphate, etc.; see Vajda, Zindīqs; Kraemer, Heresy; Chokr, *Zandaqa*). Such groups stand in opposition to "orthodox Muslims," henceforth identified as the people of the sunna (q.v.) and the community *(ahl al-sunna wa-l-jamāʿa),* the people of consensus *(ahl al-ijmāʿ),* conventionally called Sunnites. With the consolidation of Sunnī orthodoxy in the fourth/tenth century, heresiography came to employ certain set titles or *topoi* to designate those considered, rightly or wrongly, opponents of Sunnism: *bāṭiniyya* (Shīʿīs, particularly Ismāʿīlīs), *qadariyya* (supporters of free will; see FREEDOM AND PREDESTINATION), *ibāḥiyya* (free-thinkers and other antinomian groups), *dahriyya* (philosophers and other supporters of the eternity of the universe), *tanāsukhiyya* (believers in metempsychosis) and so on (Freitag, *Seelenwanderung;* Urvoy, *Les penseurs libres*). Similarly, scholastic and rationalist Shīʿite "orthodoxy," increasingly elaborated from the second half of the fourth/tenth century in the circle of al-Shaykh al-Mufīd (d. 413/1022) in Baghdad, came to designate the heretics of its own ranks by terms like *mufawwiḍa* or *ghulāt* (gnostic and esoteric trends) and *muqallida* or *ḥashwiyya* (rigidly traditionalist trends). The notion of the commoners or masses *(al-ʿawāmm* as opposed to the elite, *al-khawāṣṣ)* or the majority *(al-akthar* as opposed to the minority, *al-aqall),* designating the non-Shīʿī Muslims, convey, for Shīʿī authors, a sense of support for erroneous doctrines (Amir-Moezzi, *Le guide divin,* especially 33 f.).

Mohammad Ali Amir-Moezzi

Bibliography

M.A. Amir-Moezzi, *Le guide divin dans le shiʿisme originel,* Paris-Lagrasse 1992; M. Chokr, *Zandaqa et zindīqs en Islam au second siècle de l'hégire,* Damascus 1993; C. Colpe, *Der Manichäismus in der arabischen Überlieferung,* Göttingen 1954; S. Dedering, Ein Kommentar der Tradition über die 73 Sekten, in *MO* 25 (1931), 38-59; J. van Ess, Ibn ar-Rāwandī or the making of an image, in *al-Abḥāth* 27 (1978-9), 5-26; id., *TG;* R. Freitag, *Seelenwanderung in der islamischen Häresie,* Berlin 1985; I. Friedlaender, The heterodoxies of the Shiʿites in the presentation of Ibn Hazm, in *JAOS* 28 (1907), 1-80 and 29 (1909), 1-183; F. Gabrieli, La *zandaqa* au Ier siècle abbasside, in *L'élaboration de l'Islam,* Paris 1961, 23-38; W.B. Hallaq, On the authoritativeness of Sunni consensus, in *IJMES* 18 (1986), 427-54; J.L. Kraemer, Heresy versus the state in medieval Islam, in S.R. Brunswick (ed.), *Studies in Judaica, Karaitica and Islamica presented to Leon Nemoy on his eightieth birthday,* Ramat Gan 1982, 167-79; H. Laoust, L'hérésiographie musulmane sous les Abbassides, in *Cahiers de civilisation médiévale* 10 (1967), 157-78; id., *La profession de foi d'Ibn Baṭṭa,* Damascus 1958; B. Lewis, Some observations on the significance of heresy in the history of Islam, in *SI* 1 (1953), 43-63; G. Makdisi, *Ibn ʿAqīl et la résurgence de l'Islam traditionaliste au Xe siècle,* Damascus 1963; C. Melchert, Sectaries in the six books. Evidence for their exclusion from the Sunni community, in *MW* 82 (1992), 287-95; G. Monnot, Les écrits musulmans sur les religions non-bibliques, in *MIDEO* 11 (1972), 4-48, repr. in id., *Islam et religions,* Paris 1986, 39-82; H. Ritter, Philologika III. Muhammedanische Häresiographen, in *Der Islam* 18 (1929), 34-55; D.J. Stewart, *Islamic legal orthodoxy. Twelver Shiʿite responses to the Sunni legal system,* Salt Lake City, UT 1999; S. Stroumsa, *Freethinkers of medieval Islam. Ibn al-Rāwandī, Abū Bakr al-Rāzī and their impact on Islamic thought,* Leiden 1999; id., From Muslim polemics to Jewish Muslim heresy. Ibn al-Rāwandī's *Kitāb al-Dāmigh,* in *JAOS* 107 (1987), 760-85; D. Urvoy, *Les penseurs libres dans l'Islam classique,* Paris 1996; G. Vajda, Le témoignage d'al-Māturīdī sur la doctrine des Manichéens, des Daysanites et des Marcionites (Note annexe: l'Aperçu sur les sectes dualistes dans *al-Mughnī fī abwāb al-tawḥīd wa-l-ʿadl* du cadi ʿAbd al-Ǧabbār), in *Arabica* 13 (1966), 1-38 and 113-28; id., Les Zindīqs en pays d'Islam au début de la période abbasside, in *RSO* 17 (1938), 173-229.

Hidden and the Hidden

Secret or mysterious matters and objects. The dialectics of "revealed" and "hidden" — of matters that can be known by all and matters that are known only to God, who at his discretion may share some of them with his elect (see ELECTION) — is an essential part of the theology of the Qurʾān (see REVELATION AND INSPIRATION). As with other theological issues dealt with in the Qurʾān, however, the view of "the hidden" reflected therein is not uniform. In qurʾānic parlance "the hidden" is usually termed *ghayb,* meaning "absence" — that is, a thing or things absent from human knowledge and concealed in God's intelligence (see KNOWLEDGE AND LEARNING; INTELLECT; IGNORANCE). Other terms used in the Qurʾān for this concept derive from the roots *b-ṭ-n, k-n-n, s-r-r,* all of which mean "to be hidden, concealed." *Ghayb,* however, is the term most commonly used, and it is often presented in the Qurʾān as God's exclusive domain: "With him are the keys of the unseen *(al-ghayb);* none knows them but he" (Q 6:59); "God will not inform you of the unseen" (Q 3:179); "None knows the unseen in the heavens and earth except God" (Q 27:65). But, side by side with God's exclusive knowledge of the hidden there is another view, expressed in other verses, suggesting that God may occasionally confer some of this hidden knowledge on his creatures. In one verse God is depicted as "knower... of the unseen, and he discloses not his unseen to anyone" (Q 72:26), yet the subsequent verse already voices a reservation: "save only to such a messenger (q.v.) as he is well-pleased with" (Q 72:27). This means that God may share his knowledge with his chosen prophets (see PROPHETS AND PROPHETHOOD). In another verse a specific prophet is understood as being party to knowledge of the hidden. God turns to Noah (q.v.) and says: "That is of the tidings of the unseen, that we reveal to you..." (Q 11:49; cf. 3:44). The crack that these verses open up is extensively exploited in post-qurʾānic literature. It is obvious, however, that the tendency prevalent in the Qurʾān is the one that endows God with exclusive knowledge of "the hidden." Furthermore, several questions associated with this topic crop up in the Qurʾān and are comprehensively developed in the writings of later commentators: What does "the hidden" include? Who among God's creatures are privileged with knowledge of "the hidden"? Are they endowed with complete knowledge, equal to God's, or does God retain certain knowledge exclusively for himself?

The Qurʾān itself hardly ever describes the domains subsumed under the concept of *ghayb.* At one point the "hour," namely, the time of resurrection (q.v.), is presented as a "hidden" thing. "The hour is coming, I would conceal it that every soul may be recompensed for its labors" (Q 20:15; see LAST JUDGMENT; APOCALYPSE; REWARD AND PUNISHMENT). Elsewhere the Qurʾān itself is presented as emerging from a "hidden book" (*kitāb maknūn,* Q 56:78), an expression commonly interpreted as referring to the *umm al-kitāb,* "the essence," literally "the mother," of the book (q.v.), namely, the heavenly archetype of the Qurʾān (see HEAVENLY BOOK). Again, the fact that, except for these few attempts to allude to the domain of "the hidden," the Qurʾān conceals more than it reveals left additional room for exegetical speculation. In their interpretation of verses Q 2:2-3 "... a guidance to the godfearing who believe in the unseen," in which "the unseen" or "the hidden" *(al-ghayb)* is presented as identical with the faith (q.v.) of the godfearing, commentators enumerate a list of tenets that are regarded as part of "the hidden." For example, in various traditions cited by al-Ṭabarī (d. 310/923) it is stated that "the unseen" in which Muslims should believe includes "heaven (q.v.) and hell (q.v.), resurrection, the day of judgment — all being hidden things *(wa-kullu hādha ghayb)*." Other traditions cited by al-Ṭabarī add to this list the belief in angels (see ANGEL) and prophets, recompense, and the revelation by God of the holy scriptures (Ṭabarī, *Tafsīr*, i, 101-2). An almost identical list of tenets is offered by Shīʿī commentators, except that they also include the belief in the coming of the redeemer (*al-mahdī*, Ṭūsī, *Tibyān*, i, 55; Ṭabarsī, *Majmaʿ*, i, 82 at Q 2:3; cf. Rāzī, *Tafsīr*, ii, 27; see SHĪʿISM AND THE QURʾĀN).

Common to things considered "hidden" is, according to some commentators, their concealment from the senses (*inna l-ghayba mā yakūnu ghāʾiban ʿan al-ḥāssati*, see e.g. Rāzī, *Tafsīr*, ii, 25). Furthermore, Fakhr al-Dīn al-Rāzī (d. 606/1210) says that these things can be divided into those that can be discovered by means of an indication *(mā dalla ʿalayhi dalīl)* from God and those that cannot be so discovered (*mā lā dalīla ʿalayhi*, ibid.). Relying on this dichotomy, claims al-Rāzī, one can remove the contradiction apparent in the verses of the Qurʾān: those claiming God's exclusive access to the world of "the hidden" refer to the areas that cannot be discovered by means of an indication from God, whereas those speaking of God sharing his knowledge of "the hidden" with some of his creatures refer to things that can be discovered in this fashion (*Tafsīr*, ii, 27).

This dichotomy was highlighted in the discussions of Qurʾān commentators, particularly the Shīʿīs, concerning Q 31:34, which lists five items the knowledge of which is reserved to God alone: knowledge of the hour (of the last judgment); knowledge of future rainfall (*wa-yunazzilu l-ghayth*, see WATER); knowledge of the gender of the infant in the mother's womb (*wa-yaʿlamu mā fī l-arḥām*, see BIRTH; BIOLOGY AS THE CREATION AND STAGES OF LIFE); knowledge of people's fate (q.v.; see also DESTINY) and knowledge of an individual's place of death (*wa-mā tadrī nafsun mādhā taksibu ghadan wa-mā tadrī nafsun bi-ayyi arḍin tamūtu*, see DEATH AND THE DEAD). Shīʿī scholars often discussed the issue of the knowledge with which the imāms (see IMĀM) were endowed — a knowledge that was occasionally believed to exceed that of the prophets. On the basis of this verse, they distinguished between two kinds of knowledge, applicable to two sorts of "hidden things." In a tradition ascribed to the Imām Muḥammad al-Bāqir (d. ca. 114/732) it is stated that "there are two forms of knowledge: the knowledge [God] taught his angels, messengers and prophets, and [the knowledge] he withheld and confided to no one *(lam yuṭliʿ ʿalayhi aḥadan)*; in this [latter form of knowledge] he brings into being what he wills (*yuḥdithu fīhi mā yashāʾu*, cf. ʿAyyāshī, *Tafsīr*, ii, 216; Qummī, *Baṣāʾir*, 111; Majlisī, *Biḥār*, 26, 102; cf. also Kohlberg, Imam and community, 30). Another text defines the higher of these two sorts of knowledge — that reserved for God alone — as "the hidden of the hidden" (*ghayb al-ghayb*, Ibn al-ʿArabī [attr.], *Tafsīr*, ii, 272).

These terminological distinctions made by Muslim scholars, both Sunnīs and Shīʿīs, are intended to overcome the contradictory evidence inherent in the theology of the Qurʾān — between the transcendental God, who is remote from his world and its creatures, and the immanent God who reveals himself at least partly to his believers (see BELIEF AND UNBELIEF; GOD AND HIS ATTRIBUTES). The Qurʾān, being a divine book, is itself an example of a hidden thing that God shares with his creatures; in the book, however, the dialectic tension between "hidden" and revealed is embodied. A qurʾānic statement such as "that is of the tidings of the unseen, that we reveal to you," (Q 3:44) referring to the miraculous birth of Jesus (q.v.), clearly indicates that the Qurʾān incorporates topics belonging to the domain of "the hidden." This is a basic assumption, on which rests the qurʾānic distinction between the inner *(bāṭin)* and external *(ẓāhir)* aspect of the divine revelation embodied in the Qurʾān.

A major qurʾānic verse upon which this dichotomy — as well as the question of who are authorized to reveal God's words in the Qurʾān — is based is Q 3:7: "It is he who sent down upon you the book, wherein are verses clear *(āyāt muḥkamāt)* that are the essence of the book and others ambiguous (q.v.; *mutashābihāt*)... and none knows its interpretation, save only God. And those firmly rooted in knowledge *(al-rāsikhūn fī l-ʿilm)* say: 'We believe in it...'" Thus the Qurʾān presents some of its verses as identical with the heavenly book, and therefore clear, while others are obscure. It should therefore come as no surprise that commentators used this verse as a basis to distinguish between "hidden" and "revealed." The clear things were identified with those "which a person has no way of knowing; things the knowledge of which God kept to himself" (*mā lam yakun li-aḥadin ilā ʿilmihi sabīlun mimmā istaʾthara llāhu bi-ʿilmihi dūna khalqihi,* Ṭabarī, *Tafsīr,* iii, 174). This list of hidden things includes, for example (in a tradition cited by al-Ṭabari, ibid.), "the time of the reappearance of Jesus son of Mary (q.v.), the time of sunrise and sunset (see DAY, TIMES OF), the hour (of the day of judgment), the end of the world and other such things unknown to anybody."

While Sunnī and Shīʿī commentators are unanimous as to the content of the hidden and revealed things to which the Qurʾān refers, the Shīʿī tradition is unique in its attitude regarding the question of who are authorized to reveal the hidden secrets of the Qurʾān. In answering this question the Shīʿīs, in particular, adopt a different reading of the syntax of the above-mentioned verse, Q 3:7. In the Shīʿī tradition, the words "those firmly rooted in knowledge" *(al-rāsikhūn fī l-ʿilm)* are associated not with the words that follow them ("And those firmly rooted in knowledge say: 'We believe in it'," *wa-l-rāsikhūna fī l-ʿilmi yaqūlūna āmannā bihi*), but with the words that precede them *(wa-mā yaʿlamu taʾwīlahu illā llāhu wa-l-rāsikhūna fī l-ʿilmi),* leading to the following understanding of the passage: "And none knows its interpretation, save only God and those firmly rooted in knowledge." These last words were, unsurprisingly, interpreted as referring to the imāms, and thus another foundation was established for the idea that the imāms are not only party to some of the hidden things but can also reveal secrets that God concealed in the Qurʾān (cf. ʿAyyāshī, *Tafsīr,* i, 162-3; Ṭūsī, *Tibyān,* iii, 399).

Thus, the prevalent tendency in the Qurʾān is the one according to which God alone knows that which is hidden and that which is revealed *(ʿālim al-ghayb wa l-shahāda).* Nevertheless, in other qurʾānic verses a more relative view is reflected — namely, that God may share his knowledge of the hidden things with the prophets and, according to the Shīʿīs, also with the imāms.

Meir M. Bar-Asher

Bibliography
Primary: ʿAyyāshī, *Tafsīr;* Ibn al-ʿArabī (attr.), *Tafsīr al-Qurʾān al-karīm,* 2 vols., Beirut 1401/1981; al-Majlisī, Muḥammad Bāqir, *Biḥār al-anwār,* 110 vols., Beirut, 1403/1983; al-Qummī, Muḥammad b. al-Ḥasan al-Ṣaffār, *Baṣāʾir al-darajāt,* Tabriz 1380/1960-1; Rāzī, *Tafsīr,* 32 vols. in 16, Beirut 1411/1990; Ṭabarī, *Tafsīr,* ed. M. al-Babī al-Ḥalabī, 30 vols. in 6, Cairo 1968; Ṭabarsī, *Majmaʿ;* Ṭūsī, *Tibyān.*
Secondary: M.M. Bar-Asher, *Scripture and exegesis in early Imāmī Shiism,* Leiden/Jerusalem 1999, 141-57; M. Gaudefroy-Demombynes, Les sens du substantif *ġayb* dans le Coran, in *Mélanges Louis Massignon,* 2 vols., Damascus 1957, ii, 245-50; E. Kohlberg, Imam and community in the pre-Ghayba period, in S.A. Arjomand (ed.), *Authority and political culture in Shiʿism,* New York 1988, 25-53, repr. in E. Kohlberg, *Belief and law in Imāmī Shīʿism,* Aldershot 1991, chap. 13.

Hides and Fleece

The skins and fur of animals. There is only one qurʾānic passage referring to hides and fleece (Q 16:80): "God has appointed for you from your tents (*buyūt,* lit. "houses") a rest, and from the skins of the cattle *(julūd al-anʿām)* he has appointed for you houses which are light for you on the day you strike them and the day you set them up, and from their wools *(aṣwāf)* and their furs *(awbār)* and their hair *(ashʿār),* furnishings and comfort for a season." (Only these animal products will be discussed in the following. Human skin, to which the Qurʾān refers in connection with hell's fire [cf. Q 4:56; 22:20; 41:20-2; see HELL; FIRE], will not be treated.)

Among the various benefits which animals yield (God has created them to be at the disposal of humankind; see ANIMAL LIFE), the qurʾānic passage just cited calls special attention to hides, wool, furs and hair of animals as examples of God's beneficence towards human beings. These materials are extremely useful for humankind, especially for bedouins (see BEDOUIN). They guaranteed a more endurable life for the Arabs (q.v.) and enabled their survival since the absence of these materials could result in great hardship. The wool of sheep, and the fur and hair of goats and camels (see CAMEL) as well as the leather produced from their skins (the production of leather was an important branch of industry in the Ḥijāz; see PRE-ISLAMIC ARABIA AND THE QURʾĀN; ECONOMICS) were utilized in various aspects of daily life, which are also cited in the Qurʾān. They were used for producing tents (see TENTS AND TENT PEGS), including their finished borders, for weapons, especially shields, and for saddles, covers and other textile products (see INSTRUMENTS; MATERIAL CULTURE AND THE QURʾĀN), as well as for clothes (see CLOTHING). Household utensils in the narrower sense of the word were also produced (e.g. hollow vessels to contain water). It is mainly camel, sheep and goat that supplied the hides, fur, wool and hair of qurʾānic parlance. As cattle were primarily bred in southern Arabia where the soil was richer, products from cattle were less prevalent in the Ḥijāz (see GEOGRAPHY). As a consequence, cowhide leather sandals, for example, were exported from the southern part of the Arabian peninsula northwards.

In general, Arabic commentators on the Qurʾān limit their remarks when discussing Q 16:80. Al-Ṭabarī (*Tafsīr,* xiv, 153) explains *buyūt* as tents made of leather *(anṭāʿ),* and *fasāṭīṭ* as tents made of hair and wool. According to al-Zamakhsharī (*Kashshāf,* ii, 422), *buyūt* are made of skin *(adam)* and leather. It is only Ibn Kathīr (*Tafsīr,* iv, 509) who explicitly attributes wool, fur and hair to specific animal species: namely, to sheep, camels and goats.

Herbert Eisenstein

Bibliography
Primary: Ibn Kathīr, *Tafsīr;* Ṭabarī, *Tafsīr,* ed. ʿAlī; Zamakhsharī, *Kashshāf,* Beirut 1979.
Secondary: A. Ambros, Gestaltung und Funktionen der Biosphäre im Koran, in ZDMG 140 (1990), 290-325; H. Eisenstein, *Einführung in die arabische Zoographie. Das tierkundliche Wissen in der arabisch-islamischen Literatur,* Berlin 1991; G. Jacob, *Altarabisches Beduinenleben nach den Quellen geschildert,* Berlin 1897.

Highway Robbery see THEFT; CHASTISEMENT AND PUNISHMENT

Ḥijāb see VEIL; BARRIER

Ḥijr

An ancient ruin in northwestern Arabia located approximately three hundred kilometers northwest of Medina (q.v.) near the modern settlement of Madāʾin Ṣāliḥ. Attested once in the Qurʾān, it is associated in qurʾānic tradition with the Thamūd (q.v.; Q 7:73-9; 15:80-4; 26:141-59), said to have been a godless people who inhabited al-Ḥijr (Q 15:80; translated "rocky tract"), carving their dwellings in the surrounding mountain cliffs. They rejected the exhortations (q.v.) of the messenger Ṣāliḥ (q.v.) who had been sent to lead them to repentance (see REPENTANCE AND PENANCE) and, as a result of their rejection, were destroyed by an earthquake (see PUNISHMENT STORIES).

The site is universally identified with Hegra, mentioned by Strabo (16.4.24), Pliny (6.32.156) and Stephanus of Byzantium (*Ethnika* 260, 11-2), which served as the southern commercial and administrative center of the Nabatean kingdom. It is situated in the middle of a plain enclosed by towering sandstone cliffs, and in antiquity sat astride the lucrative caravan route that carried south Arabian spices north to the Levant. The earliest known archaeological evidence at the site consists of seven south Arabian (Minaean) inscriptions carved on reused stone blocks, and twenty-nine Liḥyānī graffiti, all of which date broadly to the fourth and third centuries B.C.E. (see ARABIC SCRIPT; GEOGRAPHY).

In the second or early first century B.C.E., following the collapse of the Liḥyānī dynasty at nearby Dedan in the al-ʿUlā oasis, al-Ḥijr was chosen by the Nabateans as their southern base of operations. The earliest pottery for which a date can be established that was found at the site are the distinctive Nabatean painted fine wares that date to this period. Nabatean al-Ḥijr seems to have reached its zenith during the first century C.E., when as many as eighty monumental sepulchral edifices were carved in the surrounding sandstone cliffs. Units of the third Roman legion stationed at al-Ḥijr after the Roman annexation of the Nabatean kingdom in 106 C.E. attest to the town's continued strategic importance during the second and third centuries C.E. The historical record is silent about the demise of the Nabatean/Roman settlement.

In spite of its traditional association with the Thamūd, al-Ḥijr and its surroundings have produced very little archaeological evidence of their presence. Surprisingly few Thamūdic inscriptions (about forty) have been found, and only one of these, a bilingual Nabataeo-Thamūdic inscription, has been dated (267 C.E.). By the seventh century, al-Ḥijr apparently had become an abandoned ruin. According to tradition, Muḥammad, while en route to the raid at Tābūk (9/631; see EXPEDITIONS AND BATTLES), is said to have paused amidst its ruins, forbidding his army to drink from its accursed wells (see WELLS AND SPRINGS). Nevertheless, al-Ḥijr, or Madāʾin Ṣāliḥ, "the cities of Ṣāliḥ," as the site later became known, did not cease to exist entirely. In the fourth/tenth century, al-Iṣṭakhrī mentions the existence of a small village.

With the establishment of the Darb al-Ḥajj, Madā'in Ṣāliḥ became an important stop along the Syrian pilgrimage route, and with the construction of the Ḥijāz railroad, served as a refueling station.

The modern exploration of Madā'in Ṣāliḥ commenced with C.M. Doughty's visit to the site in 1877. The most complete description of its ruins remains the work published by A. Jaussen and R. Savignac in 1909. Surveys by F. Winnett and L. Reed in 1962, and P. Parr in 1968, have added further knowledge of the archaeological history of the site. Additional archaeological and epigraphic work is currently ongoing by the Department of Antiquities in Saudi Arabia. See also ARCHAEOLOGY AND THE QUR'ĀN; EPIGRAPHY AND THE QUR'ĀN.

Timothy P. Harrison

Bibliography
J. Bowsher, The frontier post of Medain Saleh, in P. Freeman and D. Kennedy (eds.), *The defense of the Roman and Byzantine east*, Oxford 1986, 19-30; C.M. Doughty, *Travels in Arabia deserta*, Cambridge 1888; J.F. Healey, The Nabataean tomb inscriptions of Meda'in Salih, in *JSS Supp.* 1 (1993); A.J. Jaussen and R. Savignac, *Mission archeologique en Arabie*, 2 vols., Paris 1909, 1914; J. McKenzie, *The architecture of Petra*, London 1990 (includes a chapter on the monuments at Madā'in Ṣāliḥ); 'A.A.Ṣ. Nāṣif, The identification of the Wādi 'l-Qurā and the ancient Islamic site of al-Mibyāt, in *Arabian studies* 5 (1979), 1-19; id., *al-'Ulā. Dirāsa fī l-turāth al-ḥaḍarī wa-l-ijtimā'ī*, Riyadh 1995; id., *al-'Ulā. An historical and archaeological survey with special reference to its irrigation system*, Riyadh 1988; A. Negev, The Nabataean necropolis at Egra, in *Revue biblique* 83 (1976), 203-36; P.J. Parr, Meda'in Saleh, in E.M. Meyers (ed.), *The Oxford encyclopedia of archaeology in the Near East*, 5 vols., Oxford 1997, iii, 446-7; id., G.L. Harding and J.E. Dayton, Preliminary survey in north west Arabia, 1968, in *Bulletin of the Institute of Archaeology, University of London* 10 (1971), 23-61; Dh. Ṭalḥī et al., Excavation at Mabiyyat. Second season 1404-1405/1984-1985, in *Aṭlāl* 10 (1986), 58-63; F.S. Vidal, Al-Ḥidjr, in *EI²*, iii, 365-6; F.V. Winnett and W.L. Reed, *Ancient records from north Arabia*, Toronto 1970; A. al-Wohaibi, *The northern Hijaz in the writings of the Arab geographers. 800-1150*, Beirut 1973.

Hijra see EMIGRATION

History and the Qur'ān

Introductory remark

This entry deals not with the Qur'ān as a source of historical information (for which see Paret, Geschichtsquelle, and, for instance, Faruqi, *Muslim historiography* or Sherif, *A guide*) nor with its influence upon world history but with its view of history as can be outlined by present-day historians and, secondarily, with its influence upon the development of later Muslim historiography. Although as a religious and metaphysical document, the Qur'ān is not meant to be a work of history, it deals to an astonishingly large extent with events of the past and is imbued with a deep sense of history in its various dimensions. Yet, all its different approaches to understanding the world are in perfect harmony with one another.

The historical terminology of the Qur'ān is mostly not the one characteristic of later Muslim historiography and, obviously, not the one that modern thought on history and historiography might wish to find in it. For instance, the word for "story" *(q-ṣ-ṣ)*, while not always employed in the sense of "history," is the very commonly used qur'ānic equivalent for it, and the same applies to other historical terms. The distinction, favored by modern historians basing themselves on research and speculative theory, between what might be accepted as historically true and correct and what might be perceived as wrong or imagined data and theories likewise does not apply. Qur'ānic statements about the past and the entire historical process were not seen as (possibly fictional) "stories" (Norris, *Qiṣaṣ* elements) and certainly not as "myths" (Beltz, *Die Mythen*) or the like, whatever we might think about them today. Even if they were chosen for the particular meanings they seem to contain, that is, for achieving a definite purpose (now often called "salvation history") and not just for presenting historical data as such, they were accepted as firmly established historical facts and seen as representing true past reality.

Our source can be only the Qur'ān itself. All the later information of ḥadīth (see ḤADĪTH AND THE QUR'ĀN) and exegetical works (*tafsīr,* see EXEGESIS OF THE QUR'ĀN: CLASSICAL AND MEDIEVAL) is indispensable for any understanding of the Qur'ān, and remains unconsciously present in the mind of everybody who studies the qur'ānic text. However, the reliability of these sources as a guide to the language and meaning of many passages of the Qur'ān remains far too uncertain to be accepted unquestioningly. In particular, the commentators' motivation for finding historical specificity in all contexts — the "historicization" of the qur'ānic text in the *tafsīr* enterprise (cf. Rippin, Tafsīr) — is more of a hindrance than a help for the historian.

The question of whether the Prophet's views of the historical process underwent changes during his lifetime does not, it seems, admit of a sufficiently well-grounded answer (for a systematic attempt to establish a chronological sequence in the Qur'ān's acquaintance with and views of biblical material, see Speyer, *Erzählungen,* 464-92 and passim). Although the information under discussion here is naturally provided in greater detail by the later revelations (see CHRONOLOGY AND THE QUR'ĀN), the underlying conceptualization of historical thought is seemingly rather uniform and consistent throughout the Qur'ān.

The historiographical climate in the Near East of the sixth and seventh centuries

The rich historical literature that existed among the Syriac-speaking Christians in the Near East was almost exclusively directed toward ecclesiastical history and the biography and martyrology of saints. Writings of this nature were certainly known to Christians in southern Arabia and, perhaps, central Arabia, but their historical details, we may guess, cannot have been of much interest to the Prophet (see ORALITY AND WRITINGS IN ARABIA; PRE-ISLAMIC ARABIA AND THE QUR'ĀN). However, their principal purpose "to demonstrate what God has done for us in his grace, and what we in our wickedness have presumed to do in opposition to him" (Brock, North Mesopotamia, 52), and to teach a moral lesson (Witakowski, *Syriac Chronicle,* 171) corresponds well to a very prominent aspect of the qur'ānic view of history (see ETHICS AND THE QUR'ĀN). Regrettably, we have no way of knowing how much if anything of this material could have been available to Muḥammad in some form or other. Likewise, the Qur'ān shows no specific acquaintance with Persian, or any other, historical literature.

The traditional Arab narratives of genealogical relationships and the storied happenings of the Arabian past and its "battle days" (*ayyām,* the word itself occurs with reference to the present but not to the past in Q 3:140), the south Arabian recollections of important, more recent events, the biblical information from the creation of the world as known and discussed by Jews (see JEWS AND JUDAISM) and Christians (see CHRISTIANS AND CHRISTIANITY) — all this constituted the stuff of history as reflected in the Qur'ān (see NARRATIVES). The problem here is not the high probability of oral transmission (see ORALITY) but the question of the possibility of circulation in some written form within the Prophet's orbit. A great reverence for anything written is obvious throughout the Qur'ān. It leaves itself open, however, to two contradictory interpretations; it may indicate either familiarity with "books" or, less likely, their virtual unavailability (see ILLITERACY). If the references to the "scrolls" *(ṣuḥuf)* of past prophets (see PROPHETS AND PROPHETHOOD) cannot be taken to indicate the actual presence of such works (see BOOK), if any existed, in their written form, the mention of "papyrus writings" *(qarāṭīs)* in such a context (Q 6:91) is quite likely to show the existence of actual books, as does the reference to "reading" and "writing" in Q 29:48; "reading" them was, of course, mainly a process of a literate person reading them aloud to his listeners (see LITERACY). Of particular significance is the repeated and much debated reference to the *asāṭīr al-awwalīn* (Q 6:25; 8:31; 16:24; 23:83; 25:5; 27:68; 46:17; 68:15; 83:13). It clearly means something like "stories of the ancients" and indicates the negative opinion held by Muḥammad's opponents of his revelations, in particular inasmuch as they dealt with past history. *Asāṭīr* corresponds exactly to Greek *historia* but is considered not to be identical with it etymologically. The word would later allow the reconstruction of a singular form *usṭūra* which, for instance, might be used in due course to translate something like Greek (heroic) myth (Aristotle, *Eth. Nicom.*, 1100a8, ed. Badawī, 74), but the pl. *asāṭīr* as used in the Qur'ān probably had no singular and is most likely to be connected with the root *s-ṭ-r* in the meaning of "to write." Thus, it could indicate an acquaintance with works of historical information, but again, no details as to the mode of such acquaintance are available to us. Later traditions explain the phrase as alluding to slander by Christians in al-Ḥīra or to Persian historical mythology circulating there, but it would be hazardous to project them into the qur'ānic passages (cf. Rosenthal, Asāṭīr al-awwalīn; see GENERATIONS).

In sum, it might be suggested with a certain degree of likelihood that particular views of history together with the historiographic material supporting them existed in some circles in the Arabian peninsula and found their reflection in the Qur'ān. This reflection was, however, of a general and commonplace nature, and possible lines of connection remain as yet concealed from us.

Past, present, and future are one in the historical process, leading to certain views on politics and society

The entire world in all its variety was created by the one creator at one particular moment (see COSMOLOGY; CREATION). It follows that oneness was the ideal state for it at all times and that to which it should always aspire. As the beginning was one, so the expected end of the world is one for everyone and everything. Whatever is and takes place in between these two definite points of created time, no matter how varied in detail, follows a set overall pattern. Thus the history of the past and of the future, including that of the present, is fundamentally uniform. No distinction between the three modes of time need be made by the observer of human history.

The ideal oneness was constantly interrupted by the tendency of the evil force of Satan (see DEVIL) to provoke splits among humanity. It proved invariably attractive to human beings and caused them to form self-contained rival groups. Thus, in the very center of events, there was always a "party of God" (*ḥizb Allāh*, Q 5:56; 58:22) and a "party of Satan" (*ḥizb al-shayṭān*, Q 58:19; cf. 35:6; see ENEMY). True and proven religious knowledge (*ʿilm, bayyināt*, see KNOWLEDGE AND LEARNING) moreover, when it asserted itself in the world, also increased the tendency to form hostile associations (Q 2:253; 42:14). In fact, God had indeed good reasons for not wishing to interfere in the divisive process and thereby accelerate the reestablishment on earth of the desirable oneness of humanity (Q 5:48;

11:118; 16:93; 42:8); under certain circumstances, even a recourse to violence (q.v.) might be necessary and beneficial (Q 2:251). The result throughout history was constant fighting between contending groups. People would kill each other and be especially hard on the prophets who were sent to them to command justice (Q 3:21; see JUSTICE AND INJUSTICE; MURDER; FIGHTING; CORRUPTION). There were always at least two groups, believers in the true religion and non-believers (see BELIEF AND UNBELIEF), who fought each other, down to the time of the Prophet. The battles they fought had varying outcomes: "those days (of battle) we alternate between people" *(wa-tilka l-ayyāmu nudāwiluhā bayna l-nāsi,* Q 3:140), but would, it was hoped, end in the victory of the true religion. This desired final outcome was not yet achieved in the Prophet's lifetime. For as there was constant fighting in the past, so there is fighting going on in the present — no matter that fighting in the sacred month is a great sin (Q 2:217; see SIN, MAJOR AND MINOR). The Prophet himself had to admit eventually that fighting would be required to the end of the world before the new religion might fully succeed in its historical task of reestablishing complete unity (Q 4:76, 84, 90). Only at the final hour (see APOCALYPSE; LAST JUDGMENT) is the contest between good and evil (q.v.) among human beings to be decided once and for all. Change can come only as an internal process with people changing themselves; external intervention by God would be of no avail in this process (Q 13:11). Meanwhile, the splintering into groups will go on, and with it the fighting and the recurring destruction of human settlements as a punishment for acting against God's plan for the world (Q 7:4, etc.; see PUNISHMENT STORIES; CHASTISEMENT AND PUNISHMENT).

These basic insights dominate all historical development. Therefore, it is not surprising that a great variety of terms are employed in the Qur'ān to refer to the inborn human urge to form groups. Some are ordinary terms for subgroups such as *farīq, ṭā'ifa, fi'a,* or *fawj* (see PARTIES AND FACTIONS). It deserves notice that the terminology for tribal subgroups so highly developed in Arabian bedouin (q.v.) society is missing and even major tribal groups *(qabīla, sha'b, 'ashīra)* are mentioned very rarely, suggesting a general sedentary/urban perspective on history (see TRIBES AND CLANS). Other terms may have entered qur'ānic Arabic in a foreign, possibly religious context, such as *ḥizb* and even *shī'a* (q.v.); while this is not fully provable, it is clearly true with respect to *milla* (Jeffery, *For. vocab.*, 108 f., 190 f., 268 f.; see FOREIGN VOCABULARY).

The most prominent term from the historical viewpoint is *umma* (pl. *umam).* The word was commonly used in the Semitic languages and no doubt existed in Arabic long before the Prophet's time but in its qur'ānic usage may have been influenced by religious notions (for a brief résumé of some of the scholarly discussion, see Humphreys, *Islamic history*, 95 f.; see COMMUNITY AND SOCIETY IN THE QUR'ĀN). It continued its long history throughout Islam to the present day, which resulted in its assuming shades of meaning not germane to the Qur'ān where (in addition to other unrelated meanings) it simply means associations of humans (or jinn [q.v.]) of any size, preferably large but also comparatively small. One *umma* may be more numerous than another (Q 16:92); the word may, for instance, indicate a minority group and, in the next verse, serve to gloss the foreign term *asbāṭ* that refers to the division of the Israelites into twelve tribes (Q 7:159 f.; see CHILDREN OF ISRAEL). While the number of *umam* actively making history was infinite, the original and desirable state was that of one and only one *umma* (Q 2:213;

5:48; 10:19; 11:118; 16:93; 21:92; 23:52; 42:8; 43:33). The prophets of the past tried in vain to reestablish the unified community *(umma wāḥida),* but it must and will be reestablished (for an authoritative third/ninth century Muslim interpretation of Q 2:213, see Gätje, *The Qur'ān,* 92-9). The destructive diverting of the flow of history caused by the permanent phenomenon in human societies of division into *umam,* especially the two irreconcilably hostile groups consisting of unbelievers and believers, must eventually come to an end. Other terms used for the human splintering process are not very different from *umma* and by and large tell the same story about such division as the driving force of history.

Associations of any kind are usually defined by some kind of ideology and characterized by highly conservative attitudes. They possess an unwillingness to change, which even divinely appointed messengers (see MESSENGER) prove unable to overcome. All of them "are glad with what they have" in the way of spiritual instruction *(kullu ḥizbin bi-mā ladayhim fariḥūna,* Q 23:53; 30:32) and are smugly content with their activities past and present (Q 6:108). Like the Meccans, they cling everywhere to their customary rituals *(mansak,* Q 22:34, 67; see MECCA; AGE OF IGNORANCE; SOUTH ARABIA, RELIGION IN PRE-ISLAMIC). Even at the very end, groups, like individuals, have their own "book" in which their deeds are recorded (Q 45:28; see HEAVENLY BOOK).

For the political organization of society, this has certain consequences. The original oneness of humanity is founded on the fact that humankind had its origin in one living being. Almost immediately after his creation, man was individuated sexually into man and woman, as, for instance, expressed in Q 4:1: "Fear your lord who created you from one soul and created from it its mate and spread out from them many men and women." Such sexual individuation, however, detracts from the historically exemplary status of human oneness as little as does the subsequent proliferation of individual human beings. The resulting formation of human clusters such as families, towns, and larger conglomerations required direction and guidance in real life (see FAMILY; CITY). From God being necessarily one, it logically followed that only one individual at a time could serve as head of kingdom and political authority (see KINGS AND RULERS; POLITICS AND THE QUR'ĀN). The Qur'ān when speaking about governance merely assumes this fact and has no occasion to be specific on this point. It was, of course, understood that the selection of a king was a grave responsibility as exemplified by the case of Saul (q.v.; Ṭalūt, Q 2:246 f.), that a good ruler would rely on the advice of select numbers of aristocrats *(naqīb, mala'),* as did Moses (q.v.; 7:155; cf. 5:12) or the Queen of Sheba (q.v.; Q 27:29; see BILQĪS), and that a tyrannical *(jabbār)* ruler would almost automatically stir up rebellious activities against him as happened to Pharaoh (q.v.) in his dealings with the Israelites. Against this background, all events in history have unfolded and taken, and then lost, their ephemeral place in the world.

Past history

a. Chronology

The various ways of calculating eras that were in use in the Near East at the time did not leave Arabia untouched, but the extent and the type of dating by years practiced in Mecca and Medina during the Prophet's lifetime are not known (see CALENDAR), although the older Arabic system of the year's division into months (q.v.) plays a prominent role and the abolition of the intercalary month *(nasī',* Q 9:37) was a far-reaching measure of lasting impact. The speed with which the *hijrī* era (see EMIGRATION) took root very soon after his death adds more probability to the likelihood that Muḥammad and his environment were familiar with the need for approximate or precise historical dates. Incidentally, negative dating by counting units like years as desirable for the recording for past events was not known then and was, in fact, not conceptually possible before modern times. The Qurʾān contains no hint as to the existence of *taʾrīkh* as the term for chronology and, eventually, history and historiography. And, above all, while basic time reckoning as made possible by the creation of the sun (q.v.) and the moon (q.v.) was seen as a very important part of the established world order (Q 10:5; 17:12; see DAY AND NIGHT; DAY, TIMES OF), exact chronology was understandably not at the heart of qurʾānic historical thought. However, the Qurʾān reveals much concern with chronological knowledge. As we would expect, this concern often finds expression in connection with inherited biblical and other information.

The six days of the creation of the world (Q 11:7; 57:4) suggested a different length for divine, as against human, time reckoning. This is echoed in the ancient equation of one divine day with 1,000 human years (Q 22:47; 32:5; cf. *Ps* 90:4; 2 *Pet* 3:8; for the continuity of the tradition in the Near East, see, in particular, *Jubilees* 4:30, trans. Charles, 41n; and Witakowski, *Syriac chronicle,* 70 f.). Such a supernatural day may also be said to equate 50,000 years for measuring the time that angels (see ANGEL) and the spirit (q.v.; see also HOLY SPIRIT) require to climb the ladder to God's majesty (Q 70:4). From subsequent world history, it was known that Noah (q.v.) achieved longevity and spent 950 years among his people (Q 29:14), which, it may be noted, corresponds to his entire lifetime according to Genesis 9:29. Joseph's (q.v.) seven-year cycles (Q 12:47 f.) figure as a chronological fact as does the Israelites' sojourn of forty years in the desert (Q 5:26), among further dates in the biography of Moses (Q 26:18; 28:27, the latter passage involving other biblical episodes). Muḥammad seems to have worried about the dearth and inaccuracy of the data available to him. This becomes particularly clear in the discussion of the history of the Seven Sleepers (see MEN OF THE CAVE) where the Prophet had to acknowledge the lack of chronological information. He worried about the uncertainty of the length of time they spent sleeping in the cave. They themselves did not know it, and the indicated precise number of 309 years is also uncertain. In the end, it must be left to God to have the correct information as to the accurate duration of their miraculous sleep (Q 18:11 f., 19, 25 f.). For the history of the future so closely integrated in Muḥammad's worldview, any dates are left, understandably and wisely, unstated (see also below under "f").

Beyond these more or less specific data, a pervasive concern with relative chronology is transparent in the persistent use of the term "before" *(qabl-, min qablu)* to express relative chronology and bring some order into the course of events with respect to the sequence in which the history of divine revelation had unrolled. It was a convenient means to set the past clearly apart from the present. It took on a formulaic character and appears sometimes where it might as well have been left unstated, as when the jinn are stated to have been created before man (Q 15:27). "Those who were before you" or "before them" distinguishes one group from the other on the temporary level and at the same time suggests the overall unity of human history; both you and those before you were created by God (Q 2:21) and received revelations (Q 2:4; see REVELATION AND INSPIRATION). The phrase is used to indicate a historical sequence where such sequence had been disregarded in the emotional fervor of the context, as when, in an enumeration of the prophets of the past, it appears that Noah is stated to have been earlier than Isaac (q.v.) and Jacob (q.v.; Q 6:84 f.), although in such enumerations the chronological sequence tends to be conspicuously disregarded (Q 50:12). It may be noted that it is always Noah who is defined according to relative time (Q 51:46; 53:52; 54:9). In connection with Abraham (q.v.), his chronological priority to the Torah (q.v.) and the Gospels (see GOSPEL) that were revealed "after his time" *(min baʿdihi)* constitutes a most important issue in the Qurʾān's developing construction of religious history (Q 3:65). "Before" — and occasionally "later" — clearly expresses the understanding of history as something unfolding over time.

The frequent reference to "the first" or "the former" *(awwalūn),* once also *al-aqdamūna* (Q 26:76), serves the same purpose. "First/former" often stands alone as, for instance, in *asāṭīr al-awwalīn,* or it may be attached to "(fore)fathers" or "generations" (*qurūn,* note the combination with "before you" in Q 10:13; 11:116, cf. also Q 20:128; 28:43). These terms also by themselves convey the idea of some event or condition in past history. The *awwalūn* had their written texts (*zubur,* Q 26:196; see PSALMS) and revealed writings (*al-ṣuḥuf al-ūlā,* Q 20:133; 87:18). They had their ways of doing things (*sunna,* Q 8:38; 15:13; 18:55; 35:43) and were gifted with preparedness *(khuluq)* for their actions (Q 26:137); this appears to be the meaning of *sunna* and *khuluq* here, although the context strongly suggests something not done by them but being done to them (Paret, *Kommentar,* 88). Most of what the *awwalūn* did was not right. They belittled their prophets (Q 15:10 f.; 43:6 f.) and were thoroughly misled in their attitudes (Q 37:71; see ASTRAY; ERROR), but the way they behaved is a thing of the past (*wa-maḍā mathalu l-awwalīna,* Q 43:8; cf. also *wa-mathalan mina lladhīna khalaw min qablikum,* Q 24:34). Whether the *awwalūn* were good or evil, very remote or comparatively near in time, the references to them serve the purpose of evoking the past as history to be noticed and remembered. Only God has no history in the human sense, as he is "the first and the last" (Q 57:3).

b. Historical memory

The physical abstraction of a particular brain function for remembering the past appears to have been unrealized in the Near East and thus one cannot expect to find it in any form in the Qurʾān. The common Semitic root *dh-k-r* which comes to mind first when dealing with the subject of memory appears in it many times, but it possesses various noticeably different meanings that do not always correspond to what is covered under "remembering." This applies not only to Arabic but also to the other Semitic languages as far back as the earliest records we possess (cf. Schottroff, *"Gedenken"*). In connection with "remembering" God's benefactions, *dh-k-r* is applied to historical events such as those that happened to Noah or the Israelites and Pharaoh (Q 2:47 f., 122; 7:69, 74); in this context, *dh-k-r* is basically remembering the past, although the hortatory implications of such remembrance are also clearly present. Giving thought and heeding is, indeed, the prime connotation of the root in the Qurʾān and also applies to the reciprocal remembrance between God and human beings (Q 2:200, 152), which is considered desirable. Where the fifth conjugation of *dh-k-r* occurs (Q 2:269; 3:7, etc.), for instance, commentators feel compelled, and with good reason, somehow to detect a combination of more than one connotation. Thus for instance, al-Ṭabarī (d. 310/923; *Tafsīr*, iii, 61, ad Q 2:269) has "being exhorted... and thus remembering." Not having the commentators' luxury of exposition by paraphrase, modern translators waver and show uncertainty in their choice of terms. Many opt for something like "take warning." Arberry offers a courageous or, perhaps, foolhardy example of sticking throughout to plain "remember," as he also does in connection with the occurrences of the noun *tadhkira* (e.g. Q 69:12). On the other hand, to give one more arbitrarily chosen example, Maḥmoud M. Ayoub (*The Qur'ān*, i, 268; ii, 20) opts for "reflect" (in Q 2:269) and "remember" (in Q 3:7).

Although no unambiguous testimony to the role of memory in the occupation with history thus appears to exist in the Qur'ān, we are justified in reaching the conclusion that the application of memory to the past was sensed to be a positive activity that was highly recommendable and constantly to be practiced. It is a great help in maintaining concern with historical events that should not be forgotten and strongly stimulates such concern. According to the sparse available evidence, however, it was not felt to be, and was not, a separate force of its own in the historical consciousness of the Qur'ān.

c. Biblical history

To assess the Qur'ān's historical understanding of information found in the Bible as well as in later Jewish or Christian elaboration, it is always necessary as a first step to identify and compare the source common to them and the Qur'ān. While Christian material would definitely derive from Christian sources, the material from the Hebrew Bible could, of course, have also been transmitted through Christian intermediaries. This question has not been fully settled to the satisfaction of all (cf. Rosenthal, in Torrey, *The Jewish foundation*, introduction) and possibly can only be decided, if at all, on a case by case basis.

The biblical information is often designated by Arabic roots in ordinary usage such as *n-b-'* (from which is derived *naba'*, "information"), which may indicate reporting on past and contemporary (Q 15:49-51) as well as future happenings (Q 22:72), or the slightly more specialized *q-ṣ-ṣ* (from whence *qiṣṣa, qaṣaṣ*, "narration,") which is also occasionally found combined with *n-b-'* (Q 7:101; 11:100, 120; 20:99). Words that in later historiography were fundamental occur very sparely. *Ḥadīth* (lit. "event," "happening") thus may refer to the "story of Moses" (Q 20:9), parallel to *naba'* of Moses (Q 28:2 f.) or Abraham (Q 26:69, cf. 51:24); the plural *aḥādīth* indicates that what happened to past nations made their history a warning example (Q 23:44; 34:19). *Khabar* (pl. *akhbār*, lit. "tidings"), where it occurs, can hardly be understood as historical information (Q 9:94; 99:4).

Significantly, the true and real character of such historical information is repeatedly stressed. As the divine revelation received by Muḥammad is described as truthful (*bi-l-ḥaqq*, Q 5:48), thus the reports on the story of the sons of Adam (see ADAM AND EVE; CAIN AND ABEL), of Jesus (q.v.), and of the Seven Sleepers are marked as "true" (*al-ḥaqq;* Q 3:62; *bi-l-ḥaqq*, 5:27; 18:13), and the creation of the heavens and the earth by a wise and knowledgeable *(khabīr)* deity is a reality (*bi-l-ḥaqq*, Q 6:73). Stories such as those of Joseph and Moses in his dealings with Pharaoh are not freely invented fiction *(ḥadīthan yuftarā)* but a lesson *('ibra)* from history for those capable of understanding and those fearful of what might happen to them in the future (Q 12:111; 79:15-26).

The Qur'ān offers a long and coherent narrative only for Joseph (in Q 12) and, to a lesser degree, the Seven Sleepers (in Q 18). Its view of the consecutive unfolding and total expanse of biblical history has to be reconstructed from numerous, mostly brief passages scattered throughout it. Speyer *(Erzählungen)* has shown how such a reconstruction can be successfully accomplished and lead to a coherent picture of the relationship of the Qur'ān with the biblical tradition: History and time begin with the creation of the world and its inhabitants living on earth as well as the majestic bodies in the heavens; Satan, the fallen angel, simultaneously introduces the element of temptation and evil that was destined to pervade the entire future course of history. The totality of these activities establishes the existence and power of an almighty God giving history a lasting metaphysical imprint. What comes thereafter and continues throughout the ages, takes place on the human level. It is perceived as a seamless lesson in ethics and moral behavior, which is exemplified by the actions of Cain and Abel; the break with the past under Noah; and the powerful influences exerted by the patriarchs, first and foremost among them Abraham whose life, among many other important events, includes the instructive happenings surrounding Lot (q.v.) and his family.

The widening stage of history is illustrated by Joseph and glorified by the events that took place under Moses. The latter's attempts to set history on its right course are marred by such spectacular aberrations of man as the worship of the golden calf (see CALF OF GOLD) and the excessive accumulation of wealth by Korah (q.v.; Qārūn), which expose the ever-present danger of materialistic corruption. The imperatives facing royal leadership become tangible in the person of David (q.v.) and, with particular force, in the rule of Solomon (q.v.). All these events, and many minor episodes concerning other figures from the Bible, are widely separated in time but held together by an unbroken chain of divine messengers as the agents chosen to attempt to straighten the course of history with their unchanging message. That message would have saved the world long ago, if it had only been accepted and not violently rejected by humanity at successive stages. The singular suggestion is once made that the procession of ever new messengers following one another in irregularly spaced succession might have been halted at some time (Q 40:34), but it was branded as totally unreal and untrue. Rather, sporadic periods without messengers (sing. *fatra,* Q 5:19) might have occurred. The divine revelation does not deal with the history of all of the messengers (Q 4:164) as only God knows it all (Q 14:9). From the times of the Hebrew Bible, however, the prophetic succession continued uninterruptedly to the time of Jesus (q.v.) whose history illustrated a higher level of religious impact upon human thought and behavior. Narratives surrounding his birth and childhood bring the figure of his mother Mary (q.v.) to prominence and presage her importance as a model for female emulation. And Christian virtue as a factor in history found another expression in the tale of the Seven Sleepers, which was cherished throughout the Near East. Miracles (see MIRACLE) were accepted as true historical occurrences throughout this long period but with the clear implication that they were the preserve of the messengerial succession that reached its final conclusion with the prophet Muḥammad.

Since this world history is viewed from the Arabian peninsula, it is not surprising that a certain tendency to center it on that region as closely as possible is discernible.

An example would be the apparent placement in Arabia of Mount al-Jūdī where Noah's ark came to rest when the flood receded (Q 11:44; see JŪDĪ); at least, there is no indication to the contrary which would locate the mountain outside of it. There also is no sense that the story of the Seven Sleepers unfolded anywhere far from Arabia. On the other hand, the role of Egypt (q.v.) as located in a rather distant part of the world is taken for granted. And the inclusion of a geographical end of the earth in journeys reported in sūra 18 under the names of Moses and the "two-horned" Dhū l-Qarnayn (who presumably can be identified with Alexander the Great; see ALEXANDER) appears to hint at an awareness of global history. It fits the Qurʾān's general picture of the way the world was created and of the oneness of humankind. The history of the past is claimed to be a global phenomenon since those remote days known through Judaism and Christianity.

d. Pre-Islamic Arabian history

The means to assess the Qurʾān's adaptation of Jewish and Christian history are available to us in the Bible but a corrective is almost entirely lacking for a critical understanding of pre-Islamic Arabian history as mirrored in the Qurʾān. Occasional references in ancient Arabic poetry (see POETRY AND POETS) can be adduced in this connection to offer some corroboration. Archaeology in central and northern Arabia is far from the point where it could furnish secure and helpful data for the elucidation of qurʾānic statements, which, however, may anyway turn out to be beyond confirmation by archaeological evidence (see ARCHAEOLOGY AND THE QURʾĀN).

Over the centuries, south Arabian high civilization, which by the time of Muḥammad also included significant contributions from Jews and Christians, had extended its influence to central Arabia. South Arabia's close ties with Ethiopia (see ABYSSINIA) just across a sea strait brought another part of the world within the ken of the Prophet's environment. While certain terms in the Qurʾān indisputably reflect these ties, historical reminiscences, as far as we can tell, are scarce. The quite detailed story of the Queen of Sheba (see Lassner, *Demonizing the queen*) did not come directly from south Arabia but is based upon the biblical tradition. The names of Sabaʾ (Q 34:15) and Tubbaʿ (q.v.; Q 44:37; 50:14) are mentioned in close connection with Solomon and other persons and events of ancient biblical times. In the case of Sabaʾ, however, flooding that resulted from (the breaking of) the dam (*sayl al-ʿarim* Q 34:16 [the latter a south Arabian word]; see AL-ʿARIM), is mentioned as the cause of a devastating catastrophe that befell the Sabaeans and there can be no doubt that this was a reference to an actual event that had taken place in the Yemen (q.v.) in recent memory. It has been suggested (Müller, Mārib) that among several similar problems with the dam, the one referred to in the Qurʾān "occurred only at the beginning of the seventh century." If correct, this would put the event in the lifetime of Muḥammad (see "d" below) and thus be something rather singular in the cycle of reported divine warnings from the past. On the other hand, the event connected with an elephant in sūra 105, can, it seems, safely be connected to sixth-century southern Arabia, but it should be noted that the text of the Qurʾān does not give any clear hint as to location or date and furnishes no explanatory details to confirm the historical context (see ABRAHA; PEOPLE OF THE ELEPHANT). Thus it is not surprising that even in this case, an attempt has been made to reinterpret it completely and divorce it from south Arabia (see De Prémare, Les éléphants).

Much more prominent are events mentioned in the Qurʾān, and no doubt viewed as historical, concerning seemingly more northern peoples and areas of the Arabian peninsula that we are not able to locate precisely. The historical reality of some of these has been doubted, sometimes even to the extent of suggesting, without convincing proof, that the names of Arabic prophets such as Ṣāliḥ (q.v.) and Hūd (q.v.) were free inventions. The historicity of the Thamūd (q.v.), however, is well attested, and assuming that the *aṣḥāb al-ḥijr* (Q 15:80) are to be equated with them, they were presumably known as located around al-Ḥijr in northern Arabia (see ḤIJR). The ʿĀd (q.v.) and "Iram (q.v.) of the columns" (Q 89:7) have so far remained historically less tangible. Many other figures that populate the qurʾānic references to Arabia (e.g. *aṣḥāb al-rass*, see PEOPLE OF THE DITCH; *aṣḥāb al-ayka*, see PEOPLE OF THE THICKET) totally escape identification. In the Qurʾān, their usual association with biblical figures would suggest a location in time of rather remote antiquity; nevertheless, they somehow give the impression of being close to Muḥammad's Arabian environment.

However great our ignorance of details, it is obvious that the qurʾānic vision of history has fully succeeded in flawlessly incorporating its post-biblical Arabian phase into the large picture of a succession of prophets and their rejection that was always accompanied by devastating occurrences. It is possible that attempts in this direction had already been made by Arabian residents belonging to earlier religious groups, but it seems more likely that this construction of an unbroken flow of history from the earliest past down to the present time as well as the place of Muḥammad was particular to the historical vision of the Qurʾān.

e. Contemporary history

Muḥammad saw himself as a crucial figure in world history and, like the biblical prophets, keenly felt his responsibility to be an observer and arbiter of his society. The Qurʾān therefore deals remarkably much with events concerning him personally and, to a very small extent, with historical happenings in more remote regions that took place in his time. Most contemporary events, however, are presented, as was appropriate in the context, in a form that, at least for us, is cryptic and makes their historical import hard to evaluate. The usefulness of these references for modern historians in reconstructing the actual biography of the Prophet is limited (see SĪRA AND THE QURʾĀN). They have been correctly described as "obscure allusions" (Sellheim, Prophet, 38) and the possibility of accurate historical evaluation is now generally approached with a skepticism that differs only in degree, as is made clear, for instance, by the works of Schoeler (Charakter und Authentie) and Rubin *(The eye of the beholder)*.

Apart from the somewhat uncertain assumption that events to the south of Mecca and Medina (q.v.) on which the Qurʾān commented were contemporary (see "c" above), a larger historical context is mentioned expressly only in sūra 30. Divine support for the nascent community of Muslims is said to be expected from the Byzantines (q.v.; al-Rūm) gaining victory after their previous defeat. The unnamed enemy can safely be identified as the Persians, but another vocalization of the Arabic text could easily yield the opposite meaning that the Byzantines' victory was followed by their later defeat. Either meaning could be fitted in the historical context as it is known to us; the greater likelihood, however, is on the side of the former alternative (Paret, *Kommentar*, 388). Be this as it may, the passage is a precious testimony to an awareness of events in the larger world outside Arabia and their integration in the Qurʾān's historical consciousness.

Beyond allusions to events, references are found to a few individuals by name such as Zayd (Q 33:37) and Muḥammad himself (Q 47:2; 48:29) or by supposedly transparent nicknames as Abū Lahab and his wife (Q 111:1, 4). The qurʾānic attestations of the names of certain localities, such as Mecca (also *Umm al-qurā* or "this place"), Medina (Yathrib), and the battle *(yawm)* at Ḥunayn (q.v.; Q 9:25 f.) are significant as giving a feel for the historical environment. Descriptions of contemporary warfare (e.g. Q 47:4, 35; see EXPEDITIONS AND BATTLES; WAR) contribute further to clarifying the situation in which contemporary events took place. Past events serve frequently as a foil for what happens among Muḥammad's contemporaries, who unfortunately used the behavior of their forefathers as an excuse for their own misdeeds (Q 7:28; cf. also 22:42 f.); and certain individuals of the past such as Abraham and Moses are held up to them as guides and examples *(imām, uswa)*, again with a conspicuous lack of success (Q 2:104; 11:17; 33:21; 60:4, 6). The proper or improper conduct exhibited by women of the past such as the wives of Noah, Lot, and Pharaoh as well as Mary, the daughter of ʿImrān (q.v.; Q 66:12), is understood as being valid for the present (see WOMEN AND THE QURʾĀN). All of it significantly illuminates the extension of past world history to the present.

f. The history of the future

The predictability of the future course of history is an urgent concern for Muḥammad. Indeed, it is the true core of his divine vocation. Full historical consciousness must take account of the future as it does of the past, although the succession of divine messengers has come to an end once and for all with the prophet Muḥammad.

There will be a day of judgment and an end to the world as hitherto known. To believe in it is equivalent to the belief in God (Q 2:8, 62; see FAITH; ESCHATOLOGY). As God created the world, he will surely bring it back (Q 21:104) after the end, the implication being that this will be in another form of incarnation and inspiritization in harmony with the known features of the afterlife. The events that will take place at the end are described colorfully and dramatically, but no date of any kind is given. The end of the world has its "definite term" *(ajal musammā)*. It may be near (Q 33:63), but only God has knowledge about when it will occur (Q 7:187; 79:42-46). A definite term, in fact, exists for everything in the world (Q 14:10; 46:3). But on the last day, the sinners do not know how long they had stayed in their graves (Q 20:102 f.; 30:55 f.; see DEATH AND THE DEAD), nor do those who were saved know with certainty the length of their stay on earth (Q 23:112 f.). The time for the condemned to spend in hell (q.v.) may be described merely as "long years" (*aḥqāb*, Q 78:23), but, in general, a root indicating long lasting or eternal sojourn (*kh-l-d*, see ETERNITY) is used to describe the final destination of human beings after resurrection (q.v.) in either paradise (q.v.) or hell (e.g. Q 2:39, 81 f.; see REWARD AND PUNISHMENT; DESTINY).

The Qurʾān's historical vision and its influence on Muslim historiography

It would seem futile to attempt establishing a connection between the techniques of Muslim historiography and the Qurʾān, and this has not been seriously considered (Cahen, L'historiographie arabe, 133, 140).

The *forms* of Muslim historical writing which largely determined its character did not have their model in the Qurʾān. Even the question of how its *view of history* might have exercised a lasting influence on later historiography and, perhaps, given it its "interpretative framework" is rarely asked (Humphreys, Qurʾānic myth, 274). The powerful historical consciousness embedded in the Qurʾān, however, continued to live on and made itself felt throughout the work of Muslim historians. Since the Qurʾān places an unmistakable emphasis on history and the historical process in describing and recommending to humans their necessary and appropriate behavior in the world, it is a fair assumption that the very fact of historiography becoming a conspicuous part of all Muslim intellectual activity had its origin or, at least, its ever-present stimulus, in the Qurʾān. Islam has been rightly deemed a historical religion and one inherently favorable to the study of history in all its aspects.

For the pre-Islamic history from the creation of the world to the time of Muḥammad the information presented in the Qurʾān inspired the contemplation of world history and offered suggestions as to how it might be pursued (Busse, Arabische Historiographie, 269) and remained basic for later historiography. It was elaborated in considerable length, and for the most part freely until more information from outside sources became available in the course of time. Universal history from the beginning to the present became a favored kind of historical writing, which at times was expanded to include the history of the future. One example, however, of Muslim historiography that goes against this trend towards the writing of universal history is the *Tajārib al-umam* of the fourth/tenth-century Miskawayh. This work deserves mention for its explicit rejection and omission of pre-Islamic history (and the Prophet's biography), a rejection which is basically incompatible with the critical spirit of the true historian (Rosenthal, *History*, 141 f.). Miskawayh's approach was evidently formed under the influence of intellectual developments that by his time had firmly established themselves in Muslim civilization but as a rule were unable to supplant the qurʾānic tradition of world history.

An unintended result of the qurʾānic view of history has derived from its original Arabia-centrism that came through rather undiluted by the wider outlook (see above under "c"). In combination with other factors, it contributed to viewing Islam and understanding its history as fundamentally unaffected by the larger world, and it tended to limit the principal concern of later historians to the history of the Muslim world. The treatment of any pre-Islamic history not within the Qurʾān's field of vision remained severely restricted. During Islamic times, non-Muslim history entered the historians' purview only to a small extent, and mainly inasmuch as it had direct bearing on the Muslim condition. However, since Islam expanded over a large part of the world, the scope of historical productivity did not fail to expand with it.

The Qurʾān taught the importance, for better or worse, of the individual as the principal human agent in history. That helped to prepare the soil for the tremendous growth of biography, one of the glories of Muslim historiography. An indispensable catalyst in this process was the desire to find an explanation for historical and autobiographical allusions and to reconstruct the biography of the Prophet as the model for all humanity and the source of the rapidly developing religion. All of this naturally required recourse to relentless interpretation of the text and an accumulation of additional material that could be accomplished only with the help of the scholarly disciplines that became known as *tafsīr* and ḥadīth. Nothing, however, contributed more and in more diverse ways to arousing a lasting interest in history than biography, and it clearly provided the earliest products of historical writing in Arabic, before further concerns took over to make biography still more essential as a subject of historiography.

The admission of miraculous happenings into the historical process may be considered a minor result of the qurʾānic view of history. That it remained sporadic and restricted to certain items, is remarkable mainly if compared to Christian historiography. Other concepts that lived on and could not be entirely discarded by later historians, for instance, were the possibility of a different time scale for remote historical events and of longevity in human beings. Longevity was suggested by Noah's life span (see above under "a"); nothing, however, is said about longevity in connection with the sage of the past named Luqmān (q.v.; Q 31:12 f.; cf. Heller and Stillman, Luḳmān). At any rate, the belief in the historical existence of extraordinarily long-lived individuals soon ceased to be of interest to historians and became more of a literary subject.

While the Qurʾān set such lines of thought and provided some basic material for the labors of future historians, without doubt the most profound impact of the qurʾānic view of history has been its stress on history as an example or lesson *(ʿibra)*, most clearly stated at the end of Q 12 "Joseph" (Sūrat Yūsuf; Q 12:111). Historical information is not only educational but it is also consummate wisdom (*muzdajarun ḥikmatun bālighatun*, Q 54:4-5); no distinction in this respect can be made between past and contemporary history (Q 59:2). The usefulness of history and the need to learn from it constitute a persistent theme of all Muslim historians. The recognition of history as an infallible guide to how human beings ought, or ought not, to behave and act justifies and legitimizes their work. They generally assume that the preoccupation with history has no other acceptable purpose and useful effect. *ʿIbar*, as the plural of *ʿibra*, may eventually appear in the titles of historical works such as al-Dhahabī's (d. 748/1348) *al-ʿIbar fī khabar man ghabar* ("The lessons of the reports of those who have passed away"), a strictly annalistic history from Muḥammad to the time of the author. Significantly, the more systematically conceived history of Ibn Khaldūn (732-808/1332-1406) bears the overarching title of *Kitāb al-ʿIbar* ("Book of lessons"). The occupation with history and historiography as providing lessons for life and actions must be reckoned among the important gifts of the Qurʾān to the intellectual development of Islam.

Franz Rosenthal

Bibliography

(Incidental sidelines on the subject can be found scattered over some of the vast historical literature dealing with early Islam, but no monographic treatment appears to exist, at least in Western scholarship [see the article by Mirza for an indication of increased contemporary Muslim interest in the topic]. The following references, including references given in the text above, are of greatly varying relevance.) Aristotle, *Ethica Nicomachea. Arabic. al-Akhlāq*, ed. ʿA. al-R. Badawī, Kuwait 1979; M.M. Ayoub, *The Qurʾān and its interpreters*, 2 vols. to date, Albany 1984-; W. Beltz, *Die Mythen des Koran*, Düsseldorf 1980; S.P. Brock, North Mesopotamia in the late seventh century, in *JSAI* 9 (1987), 51-75; H. Busse, Arabische Historiographie und Geographie, in *GAP*, ii, 264-97; C. Cahen, L'historiographie arabe. Des origines au VII s. H., in *Arabica* 33 (1986), 133-98; R.H. Charles (trans.), *The book of Jubilees*, London 1902; K. Cragg, *The event of the Qurʾān*, London 1971, 1974, 166-79 and ch. 11

("The sense of history"); A.-L. De Prémare, Les éléphants de Qādisiyya, in *Arabica* 45 (1998), 261-9; N.A. Faruqi, *Early Muslim historiography,* Delhi 1979; Horovitz, *KU;* H. Gätje, *The Qurʾān and its exegesis,* trans. A.T. Welch, London and Henley 1976; B. Heller and N.A. Stillman, Luḳmān, in *EI²,* v, 811; R.S. Humphreys, Qurʾānic myth and narrative structure in early Islamic historiography, in F.M. Clover and R.S. Humphreys (eds.), *Tradition and innovation in late antiquity,* Madison, WI 1989, 271-90; id., *Islamic history. A framework for inquiry,* Princeton 1991; Jeffery, *For. vocab.;* T. Khalidi, *Arabic historical thought in the classical period,* Cambridge 1994; J. Lassner, *Demonizing the queen of Sheba,* Chicago 1993; Kh.Z. Mirza, The qurʾānic concept of history, in *Hamdard islamicus* 13 (1990), 11-34 (a recent statement from Pakistan that indicates increasing Muslim interest in the subject); W.W. Müller, Mārib, in *EI²,* vi, 564; H.T. Norris, Qiṣaṣ elements in the Qurʾān, in *The Cambridge history of Arabic literature. i. Arabic literature to the end of the Umayyad period,* Cambridge 1983, 246-59; J. Obermann, Early Islam, in R.C. Dentan (ed.), *The idea of history in the ancient Near East,* New Haven 1955, 239-310; Paret, *Kommentar;* id., Der Koran als Geschichtsquelle, in *Der Islam* 37 (1961), 24-42; G. Parrinder, *Jesus in the Qurʾān,* New York 1965; Rippin, *Approaches;* id., Tafsīr, in *EI²,* x, 85; F. Rosenthal, *A history of Muslim historiography,* Leiden 1952, esp. 22-8; Leiden 1968², 24-30; id., The influence of the biblical tradition on Muslim historiography, in B. Lewis and P.M. Holt (eds.), *Historians of the Middle East,* London 1964, 35-45; id., Asāṭīr al-awwalīn, in *EI², Sup.,* 90 f.; U. Rubin, *The eye of the beholder. The life of Muḥammad as viewed by the early Muslims,* Princeton 1995; G. Schoeler, *Charakter und Authentie der muslimischen Überlieferung über das Leben Mohammeds,* Berlin-New York 1996; W. Schottroff, *"Gedenken" im Alten Orient und im Alten Testament,* Neukirchen-Vluyn 1967²; R. Sellheim, Prophet, Chalif and Geschichte. Die Muhammed-Biographie des Ibn Isḥāq, in *Oriens* 18-19 (1967), 33-91; Faruq Sherif, *A guide to the contents of the Qurʾān,* Reading 1995, 101-16; M. Siddiqi, *The qurʾanic concept of history,* Karachi 1965; Speyer, *Erzählungen* (Note that "Gräfenhainichen, 1931" are fictitious publication data); C.C. Torrey, *The Jewish foundation of Islam,* New York 1933, repr. New York 1967 (with intro. by F. Rosenthal); W. Witakowski, *The Syriac Chronicle of Pseudo-Dionysius of Tel-Maḥre,* Uppsala 1987.

Ḥizb Allāh/Shayṭān

see PARTIES AND FACTIONS

Holy Land

see SANCTITY AND THE SACRED; JERUSALEM

Holy Places

see SANCTITY AND THE SACRED; HOUSE, DOMESTIC AND DIVINE

Holy Spirit

An agency of divine action or communication. The Arabic phrase *rūḥ al-qudus,* as it appears in the Qurʾān, is regularly interpreted by translators to mean the 'holy spirit,' or the 'spirit of holiness.' The phrase occurs four times in the Qurʾān. In three of the four occurrences the text says that God "strengthened" *(ayyadnāhu)* Jesus (q.v.), son of Mary (q.v.), by the holy spirit (Q 2:87, 253; 5:110); in the fourth instance the holy spirit is identified as the one who has brought down the truth (q.v.) from God to his prophet (Q 16:102). This apparent personal identity of the holy spirit in the latter passage has prompted some Muslim commentators to identify the holy spirit by whom God 'strengthened' Jesus with Gabriel (q.v.), the traditional, angelic bearer of God's messages in the scriptures (see BOOK; SCRIPTURE AND THE QURʾĀN). For others the holy spirit in these passages is said to be identical with the created spirit from God, identified elsewhere in the Qurʾān as the agency by which God enlivened Adam (e.g. Q 15:29; see ADAM AND EVE), made Mary pregnant with Jesus (Q 21:91), and inspired the angels (see ANGEL) and the prophets (e.g. Q 17:85; see PROPHETS AND PROPHETHOOD). To emphasize the created nature of this gift of God's beneficence, and in an effort to avoid theological misunderstanding, some modern interpreters of the Qurʾān prefer to translate the phrase *rūḥ al-qudus* not with the usual 'holy spirit,' but with periphrastic expressions such as 'God's holy bounty,' or even 'the blessed word of God.'

Philologically the Arabic phrase *rūḥ al-qudus* is cognate with the Syriac expression *rûḥâ d-qudshâ,* used in Christian Aramaic texts as the name of the third person of the Christian Trinity (q.v.): Father, Son, and Holy Spirit (see FOREIGN VOCABULARY). On the assumption that the purpose of the revelation in the Qurʾān is at least in part to correct what it presents as the excesses in the religious claims of the earlier People of the Book (q.v.; cf. e.g. Q 4:171), and further assuming that Christian doctrines in their Syriac expression historically lay within the purview of the Qurʾān, one might see a corrective, even a polemical intent in the Qurʾān's use of the phrase *rūḥ al-qudus* in the three passages cited above in which the text says that God 'strengthened' Jesus with the holy spirit (see POLEMIC AND POLEMICAL LANGUAGE; SYRIAC AND THE QURʾĀN). Correlatively, the fourth text (Q 16:102) implicitly claims a comparable role for the holy spirit in the prophetic career of Muḥammad, i.e. to bring the truth from God to him.

In the light of these considerations, it seems particularly apt to render *rūḥ al-qudus* as 'holy spirit,' assuming that in fact the Qurʾān intends to speak in these four passages of the same Holy Spirit as the one of whom the Christians speak. In these passages, as well as in other places in the sacred text, however, the Qurʾān's intention may be seen to be at least partially corrective, and critical of the deifying language used by the earlier People of the Book in regard to the Holy Spirit.

In one particularly significant passage the Qurʾān says that Jesus, son of Mary, is himself a "spirit" (q.v.; *rūḥun*) from God (Q 4:171). According to a number of Muslim commentators this identification derives from the fact that, according to the Qurʾān's teaching, Mary became pregnant with Jesus, not by means of any human intervention, but miraculously, by reason of the fact that God 'breathed' of his spirit into her (Q 21:91). Jesus, so conceived, and as a 'spirit' from God, is nevertheless, according to the Qurʾān, like Adam, a creature (cf. Q 3:59; see CREATION). Here, too, the Qurʾān's critique of current Christian teaching is apparent.

There are at least another sixteen places in the Qurʾān where the "spirit" *(rūḥ)* is mentioned without the qualification deriving from its association with the noun "holiness" *(al-qudus),* in the sense of Holy Spirit. From a consideration of these passages one acquires a fuller understanding of the Islamic conception of God's spirit as a created agency by means of which God communicates with angels and men. In five instances the text speaks of the 'spirit' in conjunction with God's "bidding" *(amr),* suggesting that the spirit comes at God's bidding (cf. e.g. Q 17:85) upon whomever he wills of his servant creatures to bring a warning (q.v.) to humankind (cf. e.g. Q 40:15). The angels play a role in bringing down the spirit at God's bidding (cf. Q 16:2). The spirit and the angels are present together, always ready to do God's bidding (Q 70:4; 78:38), and they were there on the Night of Power (q.v.; Q 97:4). A 'spirit' from God is parallel with "his word" *(kalimatuhu)* in Jesus, son of Mary (Q 4:171; see WORD OF GOD). In the case of Muḥammad, the Qurʾān says that it was "the faithful spirit" *(al-rūḥ al-amīn)* that was bringing the revelation down onto his heart (q.v.) so that he would become one of those to bring a warning (Q 26:192-4) from God to humankind. The characterization of the spirit as 'faithful' here highlights its creaturely status in the qurʾānic view. Finally, from this same perspective, when God sent his spirit to Mary, the Qurʾān says that it appeared to her in the form of a well-formed man (Q 19:17).

Since the Qurʾān often mentions the spirit in connection with the angels, some

Muslim commentators have speculated that the spirit is itself angelic in nature; others have wondered if the spirit is not the very content of the divine revelation. A number of western, scholarly discussions of the role of the spirit in the Qurʾān call attention to the numerous verbal parallels in the discourse one can find between what is said of the spirit in the Qurʾān and what is said of the spirit of God in the Bible and in extra-biblical, Jewish and Christian literature, especially in Aramaic/Syriac texts. These references in turn call attention to the high level of intertextuallity to be discerned in what the Qurʾān says of the spirit, which consequently heighten the reader's awareness of the interreligious dimension of the Qurʾān's intention, authoritatively to critique the doctrines of the earlier communities of the People of the Book about God's spirit.

Sidney H. Griffith

Bibliography
E.E. Calverley [I.R. Netton], Nafs, in *EI*², vii, 880-4; Jeffery, *For. vocab.;* D.B. Macdonald, The development of the idea of spirit in Islam, in *MW* 22 (1932), 25-42; T. O'Shaughnessy, *The development of the meaning of spirit in the Koran.* (*Orientalia Christiana Analecta* 139), Rome 1953; F. Rahman, *Major themes of the Qurʾān,* Chicago 1980; Wensinck, *Concordance;* H. Zirker, *Der Koran. Zugänge und Lesarten,* Darmstadt 1999.

Holy War see JIHĀD; EXPEDITIONS AND BATTLES

Homosexuality

Sexual attraction towards one of the same sex. References to homosexuality in the Qurʾān are few and oblique, and have been subject to considerable controversy in the exegetical and legal traditions. The subject is most directly addressed in the context of the story of the prophet Lot (q.v.), in which the men of his people are reproached for pursuing sexual behavior with men instead of women; such acts are labeled an abomination. Some commentators have found another condemnation of homosexual activity in two difficult verses (Q 4:15-6) more usually interpreted as referring to heterosexual fornication (see ADULTERY AND FORNICATION). In addition, the youths who are described as cupbearers (see CUPS AND VESSELS) in paradise (q.v.) have occasionally been understood as providing homosexual pleasures for its male denizens.

The people of Lot

The qurʾānic accounts of the visit of God's messengers to Lot, the inhabitants' demand for (sexual) access to them, and the subsequent destruction of the city by a rain of fire (see PUNISHMENT STORIES) conform in the aggregate rather closely to the narrative in Genesis 18:16-19:29. Only once is it said explicitly that the men of the city "solicited his guests of him" (Q 54:37, *rāwadūhu ʿan ḍayfihi,* a phrase paralleling that employed at Q 12:23 for the attempted seduction of Joseph [q.v.]), but in four other passages (Q 7:81; 27:55; cf. 26:165-6; 29:29) they are accused more generally of "coming with lust *(shahwa)*" to men (or males) instead of women (or their wives), an abomination *(fāḥisha)* said to be unprecedented in the history of the world (Q 7:80; 29:28). Among the later exegetes and authors in the "stories of the prophets" genre, who augmented the story with many vivid details, there was general agreement that the sin alluded to was anal intercourse between males; but neither the Qurʾān nor a series of more explicit but poorly attested prophetic ḥadīth allowed jurisprudents to reach any consensus on either its severity or the appropriate penalty for those who committed it, determinations of the latter ranging from purely discretionary punishment *(taʿzīr)* to death (see CHASTISEMENT AND PUNISHMENT; LAW AND THE QURʾĀN).

Qurʾān 4:15-6
The first of these two verses specifies that women found guilty of "abomination" *(fāḥisha)* are to be confined in their houses until death or until God "provides a way for them"; the second verse prescribes for "two" (grammatically, either two men or a man and a woman) who commit the same offense an unspecified "chastisement" *(ādhūhumā),* unless they repent. Most exegetes believe that both verses refer to illicit heterosexual relations *(zinā)* and resolve the grammatical and logical complications in various ways; a minority view, however, first attributed to the Muʿtazilī (see MUʿTAZILĪS) exegete Abū Muslim al-Iṣfahānī (d. 322/934), would understand them as condemning, respectively, female and male homosexual relations. Mentioned only to be rejected throughout the medieval literature, this view has enjoyed more favor in modern times, notably in the works of Rashīd Riḍā (1865-1935) and Sayyid Quṭb (1906-66).

The youths of paradise
Qurʾānic descriptions of paradise refer twice to "immortal boys" (*wildān mukhalladūn,* Q 56:17; 76:19) and once to "young men" (*ghilmān,* Q 52:24) as attending the blessed as cupbearers. The exegetical literature never imputes a homosexual function to these figures, but literary works occasionally do so, mostly humorously, and some later legal texts discuss it seriously, usually drawing an analogy with the wine (see INTOXICANTS) they serve — permitted in paradise although forbidden in this world — as well as with the less ambiguous female houris (q.v.; see also SEX AND SEXUALITY; GENDER).

Everett K. Rowson

Bibliography
Primary: al-Ājurrī, Abū Bakr, *Dhamm al-liwāṭ,* ed. M. al-Sayyid Ibrāhīm, Cairo 1990; Ibn Ḥazm, *al-Muḥallā,* ed. A.M. Shākir, 11 vols., Cairo 1347-52/1927-33), xi, 380-94 (legal); Ibn al-Jawzī, *Muntaẓam,* Beirut 1992, xvi, 248 f. (on the *wildān*); al-Jāḥiẓ, Mufākharat al-jawārī wa-l-ghilmān, in id., *Rasāʾil al-Jāḥiẓ,* ed. ʿA.M. Hārūn, 4 vols. in 2, Cairo 1965, ii, 96 (on the *wildān*); Quṭb, *Ẓilāl,* Cairo 1993, i, 598-604; iii, 1314-6; iv, 1913-6; Rashīd Riḍā, *Manār,* iv, 435-40; viii, 509-22; Rāzī, *Tafsīr,* Cairo 1933, ix, 229-36; xiv, 167-71; Ṭabarī, *Tafsīr,* Beirut 1984, iv, 291-8; viii, 234; xii, 77-98; xix, 104-6; Thaʿlabī, *Qiṣaṣ,* 102-7 (on Lot).
Secondary: A. Ali (trans.), *al-Qurʾān. A contemporary translation,* Princeton 1988, 75 f. (Q 4:15-6); ʿA.Yūsuf ʿAlī (trans.), *The holy Qurʾān. Text, translation and commentary,* Washington, D.C. 1978, 183 f. (notes on Q 4:15-6); ʿA. al-Jazīrī, *Kitāb al-fiqh ʿalā l-madhāhib al-arbaʿa,* 5 vols., Beirut 1998, v, 139-46; G.H.A. Juynboll, Siḥāḳ, in *EI*², ix, 565-7; [Ch. Pellat], Liwāṭ, in *EI*², v, 776-9; E.K. Rowson, *Homosexuality in traditional Islamic culture* (forthcoming); id. and J.W. Wright (eds.), *Homoeroticism in classical Arabic literature,* New York 1997.

Honesty see VIRTUES AND VICES; LIE

Honey

Sweet viscous material produced by bees out of the nectar of flowers. Honey *(ʿasal)* appears only once in the Qurʾān (Q 47:15), in a description of paradise (q.v.) through which run rivers of the purest water (q.v.), milk (q.v.), wine (see INTOXICANTS) and honey. Additionally, in a second passage (Q 16:69, Sūrat al-Naḥl, "The Bee"), God inspired the bee to build homes in the mountains and trees and to feed on every kind of fruit, for from its belly would come a syrup of varied hues, "a cure for humankind" (see ANIMAL LIFE; FOOD AND DRINK; ILLNESS AND HEALTH).

In the ḥadīth literature (see ḤADĪTH AND THE QURʾĀN), one account from the Prophet recorded by Aḥmad b. Ḥanbal (d. 241/855), states that the celestial river of honey emerges from a sea of honey as each of the other rivers flows forth from a sea of its own kind (*Musnad,* xv, 112-3, no. 19935; see COSMOLOGY); in another account, these rivers are said to spring from a mountain of musk. Ibn Kathīr (d. 774/1372) stresses the unimaginable purity of the rivers, for the honey river does not come from the bellies of bees, nor the river of wine from grapes that must be trodden on by the feet of man. Honey also appears in an "otherworldly" context in traditions on the ascension (q.v.) of the Prophet into the seven heavens (see HEAVEN AND SKY); al-Bukhārī (d. 256/870) preserves the account from Ānas b. Mālik (d. 179/795) that Muḥammad was offered three cups, one each of milk, honey and wine and he selected the first to drink. He was then told that he had chosen the sound path for himself and his people (Bukhārī, *Ṣaḥīḥ,* iv, 33).

The allusion to honey in the second qurʾānic passage became well known in subsequent Arabic literature owing to its stated power to cure. For example, in the digest of ʿAbd al-Malik Ibn Ḥabīb (d. 238/853), which combines both prophetic and Galenic medical features, a number of cures using honey are mentioned. He cites one saying attributed to the Prophet that "there is no better remedy for people than cupping and drinking honey." Ibn Ḥabīb also includes the famous "medical" tradition in which a man seeks the Prophet's advice for his son's strong stomach pains. Three times the man attempts to give his son honey to drink without success until the Prophet observes that the problem is with the boy's stomach, not the cure, for honey is one of God's remedies (cf. Bukhārī, *Ṣaḥīḥ,* iv, 51; Ṭabarī, *Tafsīr,* xiv, 141 ad Q 16:69). Ibn Kathīr uses this tradition in his own commentary to correct the view of al-Ṭabarī (d. 310/923) that the phrase "a cure for humankind" refers to the Qurʾān; it is strictly true, concedes Ibn Kathīr, that the Qurʾān is a cure (see Q 17:82 "We reveal of the Qurʾān that which is a healing and mercy for believers") but in Q 16:69, the reference is clearly to honey (Ibn Kathīr, *Tafsīr,* iv, 501-2 ad Q 16:69). Ibn Māja cites the tradition that the Prophet once said, "You have two cures, in honey and the Qurʾān" (*Sunan,* ii, 1142, no. 3452). The same traditionist preserves the Prophet's view that no great affliction will befall anyone who takes honey three mornings every month. In al-Bukhārī's chapter on medical traditions, the dish *talbīna,* made of cereal, honey and milk, was said by the Prophet to soothe a sick person's heart (*Ṣaḥīḥ,* iv, 52); ʿĀʾisha (see ʿĀʾISHA BINT ABĪ BAKR) thought it a disagreeable food, but nevertheless useful. ʿĀʾisha is also the source of information on a Yemeni honey based beverage, *bitʿ,* which was evidently alcoholic, as the Prophet decreed that "every inebriating drink is forbidden."

In both the prophetic and Galenic divisions of the Islamic medical tradition, honey's medicinal value is fully acknowledged. The partially preserved medical work on dietetics of Muḥammad b. Aḥmad al-Tamīmī (d. late fourth/tenth century) contains an interesting section on honey and sugar, the former sweetening substance known in the Middle East from antiquity. Honey is said to have greater merits as a drug than as nourishment, is hot and dry in the second degree, and attains its best quality as spring-honey produced from absinthe or wormwood which most effectively clears obstructions in the liver and kidney (Marin and Waines, The balanced way). The later work on prophetic medicine by Ibn Qayyim al-Jawziyya

(d. 774/1372) reflects the essentials of the Galenic data with the addition of prophetic traditions and the advice that wild honey is better than domestic honey, a view based directly upon Q 16:69 (*al-Ṭibb al-nabawī,* 71-4, 286-7). In the medieval culinary tradition, honey was used in main dishes of meat and vegetable — often to offset the acidity of vinegar — in sweets together with sugar, and in well known "home remedies" such as stomachic *(jawārish),* the electuary *(maʿjūn)* and the classical oxymel or *sakanjabīn* (see also MEDICINE AND THE QURʾĀN).

David Waines

Bibliography
Primary: Bukhārī, *Ṣaḥīḥ,* ed. Krehl; Ibn Habib, Abū Marwān ʿAbd al-Malik, *Mujtasar fī l-ṭibb* (Compendio de Medicina), ed. and trans. C. Álvarez de Morales and F. Girón Irueste, Madrid 1992; Ibn Ḥanbal, *Musnad,* ed. Shākir; Ibn Kathīr, *Tafsīr,* ed. Ghunaym et al., Cairo 1971; Ibn Māja; Ibn Qayyim al-Jawziyya, *al-Ṭibb al-nabawī,* ed. al-Sayyid al-Jamīl, Beirut 1985; Ṭabarī, *Tafsīr,* ed. A.S. ʿAlī et al., Cairo 1954.
Secondary: M. Marin and D. Waines (eds.), The balanced way. Food for pleasure and health in medieval Islam, in *Manuscripts of the Middle East* 4 (1989), 123-32; ids. (eds.), *Kanz al-fawāʾid fī tanwīʿ al-mawāʾid,* Stuttgart/Beirut 1993.

Honey of Paradise see HONEY; PARADISE

Honor

Esteem due or paid to worth; manifestation of respect, or the good reputation which merits such respect. Several Arabic terms convey or assume this key qurʾānic concept. The root *ʿ-z-z* may denote the honor that ensues from the possession of power and strength; thus God is al-ʿAzīz (e.g. Q 36:5) as is Joseph's (q.v.) patron in Egypt (q.v.; Q 12:30). The root *k-r-m* may imply an honor expressed by generosity (see GIFT-GIVING; VIRTUES AND VICES), so that Q 17:70, *karramnā banī ādam,* may be translated as "We have honored Adam's (see ADAM AND EVE) progeny." God's provision *(rizq)* and reward *(ajr)* are often *karīm* (cf. Q 89:15; see BLESSING), signifying generosity and implying honor to both giver and recipient. The Qurʾān itself is *karīm* (Q 56:77) as were the dwellings of the Egyptians (*maqām karīm,* Q 44:26). The participle *mukram* is best translated as "honored," as at Q 36:27: "God has set me among the *mukramīn,*" and Q 51:24, which applies the same word to Abraham's (q.v.) guests. A third root is *w-f-y,* with the primary sense of "fulfillment," the fourth derived form of which may be rendered as "honoring" in such phrases as "he who honors his pledge" (*man awfā bi-ʿahdihi,* Q 3:76; cf. 2:40; see OATHS AND PROMISES; COVENANT; BREAKING TRUSTS AND CONTRACTS). Hebrew parallels are scarce — Arabic cognates of the root *k-b-d* (cf. *Exod* 20:12) do not connote honor — the most significant exception being *ṣ-d-q,* whose resonance of "faithfulness" and "righteousness" (cf. *ṣᵉḏāqā* in the Hebrew Bible) appears in the Qurʾān. The roots *ʿ-r-ḍ, ḥ-s-b* and *sh-r-f* have early attestations, but are not used in the Qurʾān in this sense. Finally, the concept of honoring one's parents (q.v.) is conveyed through the triliteral root *ḥ-s-n* (*iḥsān*), Q 2:83; 4:36; 6:151; 46:15) or *b-r-r* ("dutiful," Q 19:14, 32; see FAMILY; KINSHIP).

The Qurʾān's engagement with a tribal nomadic context (see TRIBES AND CLANS; NOMADS) deeply infused with honor codes is reflected in a simultaneous affirmation and interrogation of pagan Arab concepts (see PRE-ISLAMIC ARABIA AND THE QURʾĀN). Al-Aʿshā, a contemporary of the Prophet, supplied in his panegyric to the sixth-century Jewish-Arab poet al-Ṣamawʾal a catalogue of honor-virtues with clear qurʾānic parallels. The hero's father was "the most faithful of them in keeping his promise" *(awfāhum ʿahdan),* defended those to whom he had given protection (q.v.), was as generous as a rain-cloud, and would not sell his honor *(makruma)* to acquire dishonor (*ʿār,* Jones, *Early Arabic poetry,* 158, 161, 163). This honor-code is defined in terms of individual virtues which the Qurʾān partially accepts. Rejected, however, are forms of boastful extravagance (*tabdhīr;* see Izutsu, *Structure,* 69; cf. Q 17:26; see BOAST), and ritual revenge (Stetkevych, *Rithāʾ;* abolished by *qiṣāṣ* and forgiveness, Q 42:40; see BLOOD MONEY; RETALIATION). Collective, tribal honor (e.g. *Mufaḍḍaliyyāt,* 613, 636) is implicitly criticized (Q 49:13).

The Qurʾān identifies a sense of false honor as an obstacle to faith (q.v.); loyalty to ancestral ways and gods (see IDOLS AND IMAGES) is clearly figured as a sense of misplaced honor (Goldziher, *Muslim studies,* i, 18-9; see SOUTH ARABIA, RELIGION IN PRE-ISLAMIC). Q 25:60 condemns pagans who refuse to prostrate to God (see POLYTHEISM AND ATHEISM; BOWING AND PROSTRATION); the Quraysh (q.v.) elders who expected an exemption from this duty are presumably among those condemned (Tottoli, Muslim attitudes, 17, 19-20). Likewise, "*ʿizza* takes [a *munāfiq* — a hypocrite; see HYPOCRITES AND HYPOCRISY] into sin" when summoned to piety (q.v.; Q 2:206; cf. Ṭabarī, *Tafsīr,* iv, 245).

In sum, it may be said that while acknowledging some virtues, the Qurʾān effects a revolution in Arab mores by redefining honor as a heroic, self-denying loyalty to God (Q 49:13; see ISLAM) and to the believers (Q 3:140; Bravmann, *Spiritual background,* 69; see BELIEF AND UNBELIEF), rather than to the tribe (see ETHICS AND THE QURʾĀN; BROTHER AND BROTHERHOOD).

Timothy Winter

Bibliography
Primary: al-Ḍabbī, *al-Mufaḍḍaliyyāt,* ed. C. Lyall, i, Oxford 1921; Ṭabarī, *Tafsīr,* ed. Shākir.
Secondary: M.M. Bravmann, *The spiritual background of early Islam,* Leiden 1972, 39-122; R. Brunschvig, Métiers vils en Islam, in *SI* 16 (1962), 44 and passim; B. Farès, *L'honneur chez les Arabes. Étude de sociologie,* Paris 1932; Goldziher, *MS,* London 1967-72; H. Hökelekli, Irz, in *Islâm ansiklopedisi,* 2nd ed., xix, 133-4; T. Izutsu, *The structure of ethical terms in the Koran,* Tokyo 1954, 55-62, 67-9, 75-6; A. Jones, *Early Arabic poetry. ii. Selected odes,* Reading 1996; ʿA. Muḥsin, *al-Ḥimāya al-jināʾiyya lil-ʿirḍ fī l-sharīʿa al-islāmiyya wa-l-qānūn al-waḍʿī,* Cairo 1989; S.P. Stetkevych, The *rithāʾ* of Taʾabbaṭa Sharran, in *JSS* 31 (1986), 27-45; F.H. Stewart, *Honor,* Chicago and London 1994; R. Tottoli, Muslim attitudes towards prostration *(sujūd),* i, in *SI* 88 (1998), 5-34.

Hoopoe see ANIMAL LIFE

Hope

Desire or expectation of obtaining what is desired; also trust that a promise or event will come to pass. In the Qurʾān, the term is represented in Arabic by the following roots: *r-j-w* (twenty-six times), *ṭ-m-ʿ* (twelve times) and *ʾ-m-l* (two times). The sense of the term, of course, varies with the context. For example, the root *ʾ-m-l* is used both in the sense of a delusional hope in opposition to the will of God (Q 15:3) and in the sense of the hope of reward to be had from the performance of good deeds (q.v.; Q 18:46). *Ṭ-m-ʿ* is used diversely, as hope for forgiveness (q.v.; Q 26:51, 82), the desire to be admitted to paradise (q.v.; Q 7:46; 70:38; cf. Q 5:84, where the desire is to be placed among the good people, *al-qawm al-ṣāliḥīn*), as a longing for God alongside the fear (q.v.) of God (*khawfan wa-ṭamaʿan,* Q 7:56; 30:24; 32:16; this complex is most likely meant as a fear of God's punishment and longing for his reward in the life to come; cf. Q 17:57), but also as a deviant hope (e.g. the hope of slandering the wives of the Prophet [q.v.], Q 33:32).

The richest dimensions of the semantic field of hope are found in *r-j-w* in its conveyance of the deep longing of the human heart (q.v.) for God's mercy (q.v.; e.g. Q 71:13) and support in time of trial (q.v.; e.g. Q 4:104). This can also mean longing for God's reward for a life spent in pursuit of good deeds (Q 18:110; see REWARD AND PUNISHMENT) and, of course, the eschatological encounter with the living God at the end of time (Q 29:5; see ESCHATOLOGY). In all of this, one cannot underestimate the qur'ānic insistence on hope in God's mercy (Q 39:9; 2:218) and justice (e.g. Q 60:6; see JUSTICE AND INJUSTICE) at the end of time (see LAST JUDGMENT). It is in this sense that the believer's relation with God (see BELIEF AND UNBELIEF), i.e. salvation (q.v.), can be expressed as intimately linked with, if not actually dependent upon, one's hope in the almighty (Q 10:7). It is in this connection that those who demand other than what God bestows upon them, i.e. who do not accept God's ways but try to advance their own agenda, are considered bereft of hope in any final encounter with God (Q 10:15; 25:21; cf. 45:14). More specifically, there are those who believe in no final day of reckoning or resurrection (q.v.) at all (Q 25:40; 78:27). Thus, Shuʿayb (q.v.) urges the people of Midian (q.v.) to have hope, i.e. to believe, in the final day (*wa-rjū l-yawma l-ākhira,* Q 29:36). It is, then, an orientation of hope, not as a general longing for God, but as an expectation of final judgment, that determines one's moral character in this life (see ETHICS AND THE QUR'ĀN). Indeed, the connection is made explicitly at Q 35:29 between the pious life and the expectation of prosperity (*tijāra,* literally "commerce").

In sum, the qur'ānic conception of hope is very much the essence of both faith (q.v.) and the moral order. Hope means messianic aspirations, in the sense of hope in the final reign of God, but also the expectation of a daily moral order. It is in that sense that hope is used to define the character of Abraham (q.v.), the archetype of Muslim belief (see ḤANĪF): "There was indeed in them [i.e. Abraham and those who were with him] an excellent model for you to follow, for those whose hope is in God and the last day..." (Q 60:6; cf. 71:13 where it is Noah [q.v.] whose people are warned about their failure to have hope). This association of the prophetic model (see PROPHETS AND PROPHETHOOD) and hope culminates, for the Muslim believer, in the prophet Muḥammad (q.v.): "You have indeed in the messenger [q.v.] of God an excellent model for those who hope in God and the final day and who remember God" (Q 33:21).

Sheila McDonough

Bibliography
Primary: ʿAbd al-Bāqī; Ḥamza (Sidi Cheikh) Boubakeur, *Le Coran. Traduction française et commentaire,* 2 vols., Paris 1972; Dāmaghānī, *Wujūh,* i, 322-3 (for four glosses of the concept); al-Ghazālī, Abū Ḥāmid Muḥammad, *al-Ghazali's book of fear and hope,* trans. W. McKane, Leiden 1962; id., *Iḥyāʾ ʿulūm al-dīn,* Cairo 1933, iv, 123-64 (Bk. 33, *Kitāb al-Khawf wa-l-rajāʾ*), esp. 123-35; Muqātil, *Ashbāh,* 168 (for two glosses of the concept).
Secondary: G.-H. Bousquet, *Iḥyāʾ ʿouloûm ed-dîn. Ou Vivification des sciences de la foi. Analyse et index,* Paris 1955, 355-6; Izutsu, *Concepts.*

Horse see ANIMAL LIFE

Hospitality and Courtesy

Conventions of generosity, favor and respect to be observed while receiving and entertaining guests or in social relations in general. Although the Qurʾān places a great deal of stress on the need to be charitable to the poor (see POVERTY AND THE POOR; ALMSGIVING), the enormous emphasis on hospitality in Islamic culture seems to be derived from pre-Islamic Arab values (see ARABS; PRE-ISLAMIC ARABIA AND THE QURʾĀN) and draws its greatest validation in ḥadīth (see ḤADĪTH AND THE QURʾĀN), where it is seen as an integral part of faith (q.v.). The practice of courtesy is enjoined in the Qurʾān and has received full elaboration in the Ṣūfī tradition as a method of purification as well as a way of life (see ṢŪFISM AND THE QURʾĀN).

Hospitality in the Qurʾān and ḥadīth

The offering of hospitality was deeply rooted in the value structure of Arab society before Islam and continues to be important in Muslim society. The concept of "manliness" *(muruwwa),* as an emblem of one's sense of honor (q.v.) was embodied in a constellation of values that denoted the highest ethical standards of pre-Islamic Arab society and especially included lavish generosity and hospitality. The harshness of the desert environment and the serious risk of bodily harm encountered when traveling without the protection (q.v.) of one's tribe (see TRIBES AND CLANS; CLIENTS AND CLIENTAGE) were mitigated by the common courtesy of offering any traveler hospitality for at least three days. It is evident from even a cursory reading of the Qurʾān that stinginess, hoarding and ignoring the needs of the poor were considered major moral flaws (Q 69:34; 74:44; 89:18; 107:1-7; see ETHICS AND THE QURʾĀN; EVIL DEEDS; ORPHANS). The Qurʾān speaks repeatedly of the need to be generous and to give charity (where the root is *n-f-q* or *ṣ-d-q,* Q 2:215, 274, 280; 13:22; 22:35; 35:29; 57:7; 58:12; 76:8; 90:14-6), preferably in secret (Q 2:271; 4:38; see MODESTY). Finally, in the Medinan period (see CHRONOLOGY AND THE QURʾĀN) the institution of almsgiving (q.v.; *zakāt*) guaranteed some provision for the poor and wayfarers (Q 2:273; 9:60). Feeding a poor person is also offered as a means of expiation for failing to observe religious obligations (Q 2:184, 196; 5:89, 95; 58:4) and providing food for the poor became an integral part of the observance of the major Muslim feast days (see FESTIVALS AND COMMEMORATIVE DAYS), the breaking of the Ramaḍān (q.v.) fast (Bukhārī, *Ṣaḥīḥ,* 318-20; see FASTING) and the sacrifice (q.v.) during the pilgrimage (q.v.; Q 22:28).

The Qurʾān has little to say about the broader practice of hospitality — inviting and providing for the needs of guests — or the elaborate practices of courtesy for which Muslim societies are often famous. This gap is largely filled by ḥadīth and the sayings of eminent early Muslims, who extolled the offering of hospitality and the practice of courtesy, making them integral parts of the religion. When asked about "the best part of Islam," the Prophet is said to have replied, "Offering food and extending the greeting of peace *(tuṭʿim al-ṭaʿām wa-taqraʾ al-salām)* to those you know and those you do not know" (Bukhārī, *Ṣaḥīḥ,* 16, no. 12). Asked about the meaning of a "righteous pilgrimage" *(ḥajj mabrūr),* he replied, "Offering food and speaking kindly" (*iṭʿām al-ṭaʿām wa-ṭīb al-kalām;* Ghazālī, *Iḥyāʾ,* ii, 16). The Prophet is quoted as saying, "The angels do not cease to pray for blessings on any one of you as long as his table is laid out, until it is taken up" (Ghazālī, *Iḥyāʾ,* ii, 11; see ANGEL). Among the many sayings of pious early Muslims is one from the Prophet's grandson, al-Ḥasan (d. 49/669-70): "A man will have to give an account for every expenditure he makes for himself, his parents, and those in his charge, except what he spends on food for his brothers, for God is too shy to ask about that." Although the Qurʾān stipulates that God has determined the life-span of each individual, Jaʿfar b. Muḥammad assures us that God does not count the time one is at table with his "brothers," so one should prolong such gatherings (Ghazālī, *Iḥyāʾ,* ii, 11; see BROTHER AND BROTHERHOOD).

The book on eating in al-Ghazālī's (d. 505/1111) encyclopaedic work, *Iḥyāʾ ʿulūm al-dīn,* "Revival of the religious sciences" (trans. Bousquet, 109-13), contains a large number of ḥadīths and sayings *(akhbār)* that encourage hospitality and provide guidelines for all aspects of this etiquette: issuing invitations, accepting invitations, the manner of eating and ending the gathering. It is noteworthy that al-Ghazālī's work, though Ṣūfī in orientation, devotes far more space to the virtues of offering food and the etiquette of offering and receiving it, than to the virtues of fasting, a practice often associated with Ṣūfism. Indeed, al-Ghazālī says that one should not refuse an invitation to eat because one is fasting, and that one's reward for making a brother happy by accepting hospitality will be greater than the reward obtained by fasting (*Iḥyāʾ*, ii, 18). Typical among the many ḥadīths he cites are these: "There is no good in one who does not offer hospitality" (*Iḥyāʾ*, ii, 16); "among the things which expiate sins and increase in rank are offering food and praying at night while people are sleeping" (ibid.). A person should not deliberately show up at a person's house at meal time, but if he is offered food and senses that the host really does want him to eat, he should stay. If, however, he senses that the host is offering food out of a sense of obligation, despite his reluctance, the visitor should not eat (Ghazālī, *Iḥyāʾ*, ii, 12). The host obtains a spiritual reward through hospitality, and it became the practice of the early Muslims to be hospitable. Indeed, al-Ghazālī says, if the owner of the house is absent but you are sure he would be happy if you ate, go ahead and eat, for that is the way of the pious ancestors (*Iḥyāʾ*, ii, 13).

A host should not burden himself by going into debt in order to offer food to his guests (Ghazālī, *Iḥyāʾ*, ii, 14) — although in fact many do exactly that, so ingrained is the offering of hospitality in cultural mores. A hagiographic account of Shaykh Aḥmad Riḍwān of Egypt (d. 1387/1967) says: "The people knew no one equal to him in generosity in his day... He gave like one who has no fear of poverty, from all the wealth, food or clothing that God gave him" (Riḍwān, *Nafaḥāt,* 12). This reflects a description of the Prophet himself, whose generosity to even the most rude and demanding nomads (q.v.) prompted one man to urge his tribesmen to become Muslims: "For Muḥammad gives like one who has no fear of poverty" (Muslim, *Ṣaḥīḥ,* 1242, no. 5728).

There are stipulations concerning the type of person to whom hospitality should be extended. A person should invite only righteous people to share his food: "Feeding a pious man strengthens him for obedience, but feeding a depraved man strengthens him for depravity," while a ḥadīth relates that it is wicked to invite only the rich (Ghazālī, *Iḥyāʾ*, ii, 17). Conversely, acceptance of an invitation should not take into account the wealth of the host. Al-Ghazālī tells us that al-Ḥasan once greeted some people who were eating scraps in the road, and they invited him to join them. He agreed, in order not to be proud (see ARROGANCE), and later returned the courtesy by inviting them to a fine meal (ibid.). Al-Ghazālī's injunctions on eating and drinking include so many prayers and rules of etiquette that meals are literally transformed into religious rituals.

Hospitality in Ṣūfī life

Drawing upon qurʾānic concepts of God's generosity, early Ṣūfīs cultivated an attitude of absolute dependence on God and an expectation that he would provide for all their needs; in consequence, they often refrained from asking others for food. They were also deeply suspicious that food offered by others could be "doubtful," that is, obtained through possibly illicit means or paid for with money earned in a dubious fashion (see ECONOMICS). Al-Hujwīrī (d. 465/1072) and al-Ghazālī cautioned that a Ṣūfī should never accept the food of a rich man (Hujwīrī, *Kashf*, 349; Ghazālī, *Iḥyāʾ*, ii, 16-7, 18-9). Muḥammad Aḥmad Riḍwān, father of the previously-mentioned Aḥmad Riḍwān, demonstrated the continuity of this early attitude when he refused to go to the homes of government officials and declined to accept invitations to eat, cautioning that "most food these days is doubtful" (Riḍwān, *al-Nafaḥa*, 104). In contrast, the giving of hospitality became an integral part of Ṣūfī practice. Al-Hujwīrī details the regulations for residents of a Ṣūfī convent *(khanqāh)* and requirements of offering hospitality to traveling Ṣūfīs and, for the traveler, of receiving such hospitality (*Kashf*, 341-7). In the Ṣūfī gatherings of modern Egypt, centers for devotion, spiritual retreats, and hospitality, the importance of offering food to travelers is reflected in the enormous concrete tables that are sometimes built into the very floors and are able to accommodate one hundred diners at a single sitting (Hoffman, *Sufism*, 154, 259, 263).

Al-Qushayrī (d. 465/1072) tells the story of a young man who was fasting and refused to break his fast to eat with Abū Yazīd al-Bisṭāmī (d. 261/874) and two other shaykhs, although they promised him the spiritual reward of a month's or a year's fasting for the blessing of sharing this meal with them. The young man's failure to obey the desires of his spiritual superiors caused him to fall out of God's favor, become a thief, and lose his hand (Qushayrī, *Risāla*, 259, trans. Gramlich, 459-60; see CHASTISEMENT AND PUNISHMENT). This anecdote is intended to warn disciples of the dangers of disobedience to shaykhs but it also reflects the notion that food offered by a saint carries the saint's blessing *(baraka)* and should not be refused.

Hospitality is one of the most important aspects of the celebration of saints' days *(mawlid)* in modern Egypt. Many devotees of the family of the Prophet (q.v.; *ahl al-bayt*, which in Egyptian understanding includes most of the hundreds or thousands of saints buried in Egypt) set up hospitality stations *(khidma*, pl. *khidam, -āt)* in large canopied tents or simply on a cloth spread out on the sidewalk or in rented rooms in schools or other public buildings (Hoffman, *Sufism*, 111-2, 115-6). Visitors are invited to receive at least a drink and, often, a meal as well. Such gifts, called *nafḥa*, a term which means both "gift" and "fragrance," convey the *baraka* of the saint and may not be refused. Many poor people gravitate to the *mawlid* to take advantage of the charity, but the wealthy likewise eat, in order to receive the saint's *baraka*, regardless of whether one is hungry or not.

The meaning of food offering is interpreted according to the social context. When a shaykh offers food, he is offering his own *baraka*, and a blessing (q.v.) is conveyed to the person who eats it. A devoted follower of a shaykh may even wish to eat the shaykh's leftovers or drink from his cup. When a shaykh accepts an invitation to eat at someone's home, he brings *baraka* to the house when he enters, and he honors the host by partaking of his food. Hierarchy and submission are expressed not by the mere act of offering food, but by the dispensation and reception of blessing.

Courtesy and etiquette (adab)

The Qurʾān frequently enjoins the practice of courtesy: in speech — offering greetings (Q 6:54; 24:61), returning greetings with equal or greater courtesy (Q 4:86), using gentle words (Q 17:53; 35:10), returning evil with good (Q 23:96; 41:34), arguing with opponents in a pleasant manner (Q 16:125; 29:46; see DEBATE AND DISPUTATION), quiet speech (Q 31:19); modest behavior (Q 24:30-31; see MODESTY); respect for privacy (Q 24:27); kindness to parents (q.v.; Q 2:83; 4:36; 6:151; 17:23; 46:15); and, in general, observing social conventions for politeness and moral rectitude (*al-maʿrūf*, e.g. Q 3:104; see GOOD DEEDS; VIRTUES AND VICES). As important as the giving of charity is in the Qurʾān, "kind words and forgiveness (q.v.) are better than charity followed by injury" (Q 2:263).

Given the fact that many pages of ḥadīth are devoted to *adab* and most of al-Ghazālī's four-volume *Iḥyāʾ* is conceived as an elaboration on the etiquette to be observed by a pious Muslim, little more can be done here than to emphasize its importance and centrality in Muslim life. The Qurʾān describes the servants of the Merciful (see MERCY) as those who walk lightly on the earth and return the speech of the ignorant with greetings of peace (Q 25:63; see IGNORANCE). Ḥadīths concerning the importance of good manners are abundant. Among the virtues extolled here are generosity (Bukhārī, *Ṣaḥīḥ*, 1294, 1321), modesty (Bukhārī, op. cit., 19, 1309), kindness to parents (Bukhārī, op. cit., 1283-5) and to children (q.v.; Muslim, *Ṣaḥīḥ*, 1243-4), honoring one's guests (Bukhārī, *Ṣaḥīḥ*, 1312), avoiding harmful words and glances, and treating others in a manner in which one would like to be treated (Bukhārī, *Ṣaḥīḥ*, 17, no. 13). To these al-Ghazālī adds the virtue of silence and the danger of much talking. Good manners are of the very essence of faith, and much literature is devoted to elaborating on their importance.

Etiquette reached full elaboration in Ṣūfī literature. The *Kitāb al-Futuwwa* by al-Sulamī (d. 412/1021) is a Ṣūfī manual of etiquette that consists mainly of wise injunctions and short anecdotes illustrating the importance of altruism, generosity, and sensitivity to others. Relationships in the Ṣūfī orders are governed by a lofty code of ethics and a standard of courtesy that are essential to traveling the spiritual path. One must observe proper etiquette with God, with one's shaykh, with one's fellow-disciples, with the entire Muslim community, and with non-Muslims. Al-Qushayrī supplies a number of sayings emphasizing the centrality of *adab* to faith (*Risāla*, 220). Etiquette is intimately connected with morality *(akhlāq)* in Ṣūfī writings, and the Prophet's wife (see WIVES OF THE PROPHET), ʿĀʾisha (see ʿĀʾISHA BINT ABĪ BAKR), is quoted as saying, "His morals were the Qurʾān." The Qurʾān also commends Muḥammad as having an excellent character (Q 68:4) and, according to one ḥadīth, Muḥammad said, "I was sent only to perfect morality" (Malaṭāwī, *Ṣūfiyya*, i, 93-4). Shaykh Aḥmad Riḍwān said, "The people of God's presence are humble and speak softly, unlike the people of the world" (Riḍwān, *al-Nafaḥa*, 55).

Valerie J. Hoffman

Bibliography

Primary: Bukhārī, *Ṣaḥīḥ*, ed. M. Nizār Tamīm and H. Nizār Tamīm, Beirut 1416/1995; al-Ghazālī, Abū Ḥāmid Muḥammad, *Iḥyāʾ ʿouloûm ed-dîn. Ou Vivification des sciences de la foi. Analyse et index*, trans. G.-H. Bousquet, Paris 1955, 109-13; id., *Iḥyāʾ ʿulūm al-dīn*, 4 vols., Cairo 1967; id., *Über die guten Sitten beim Essen und Trinken. Das ist das 11. Buch von al-Ghazzali's Hauptwerk*, trans. H. Kindermann, Leiden 1964; al-Hujwīrī, Abū l-Ḥasan ʿAlī B. ʿUthmān, *The Kashf al-maḥjūb. The oldest Persian treatise on Sufiism*, trans. R.A. Nicholson, London 1911; Ibn Ḥajar al-Haythamī, Aḥmad b. Muḥammad, *al-Ināfa fī mā jāʾa fī l-ṣadaqa wa-l-ḍiyāfa*, ed. M.ʿA.A. ʿAṭāʾ, Beirut 1991; Ibrāhīm b. Isḥāq al-Harbī, *Ikrām al-ḍayf*, ed. ʿA.S. al-Bandarī, Beirut 1986; Muslim, *Ṣaḥīḥ*, trans. A.H. Siddiqi, 4 vols., New Delhi 1977; Qushayrī, *al-Risāla al-qushayriyya fī ʿilm al-taṣawwuf*, Cairo 1990; id., *Das Sendschreiben al-Qušayrīs über das Sufitum*, trans. R. Gramlich, Wiesbaden 1991; A. Riḍwān, *al-Nafaḥa al-rabbāniyya*, Kom Ombo 1986[3]; Sulamī, *The book of Sufi chivalry. Lessons to a son of the moment (futuwwah)*, trans. Sheikh Tosun Bayrak al-Jerrahi al-Halveti, New York 1983.

Secondary: V.J. Hoffman, *Sufism, mystics and saints in modern Egypt*, Columbia, SC 1995; I.M. Lapidus, Knowledge, virtue and action. The classical Muslim conception of *adab* and the nature of religious fulfillment, in B.D. Metcalf (ed.), *Moral conduct and authority. The place of* adab *in South Asian Islam*, Berkeley 1984; Ḥ.K. al-Malaṭāwī, *al-Ṣūfiyya fī ilhāmihim*, 2 vols., Cairo 1969.

Hostages

Persons given or kept as a pledge, as for the fulfillment of a treaty (see OATHS AND PROMISES; CONTRACTS AND ALLIANCES). Hostages and hostage-taking in the twentieth-century meaning of those words do not occur in the Qurʾān nor in Islamic law in its classical handbook form (see LAW AND THE QURʾĀN). The closest qurʾānic attestation of the concept is the triliteral root *r-h-n* (*rahīn*, Q 52:21; *rahīna*, 74:38; *rihān*, Q 2:283), whence also the modern standard Arabic word for "hostages," *rahāʾin*. But the qurʾānic usage (lit. "circumscribed") connotes personal accountability or responsibility for one's actions, not the taking of another human being as insurance for the fulfillment of a promise: "every man is a pledge *(rahīn)* for what he has earned" (Q 52:21; cf. 74:38, "every soul is a pledge for what it has earned"); "if you are on a journey and cannot find a scribe, then a contracted pledge *(rihānun maqbūḍatun)* [should suffice]" (Q 2:283). The lack of qurʾānic approval and hence the dubious legality of hostage-holding (see CAPTIVES) may have contributed to the rather limited use of this practice even by religiously inspired terrorists who otherwise would not hesitate to resort to violence (see FIGHTING; WAR; EXPEDITIONS AND BATTLES; JIHĀD).

In the contemporary period hostage taking has not been justified with arguments derived from the Qurʾān but has been seen as a practical necessity, which would make difficult or perhaps even impossible the free passage of persons, especially tourists, foreign experts and foreign diplomats. When it is impossible for tourists, experts and diplomats to travel freely in the Muslim world, this does, of course, have serious economic consequences for the countries involved. It could certainly contribute to the weakening of those governments and regimes that the religious activists see as their enemies. To defeat a weakened enemy is expected to cost less Muslim blood (see BLOODSHED). The hostages themselves have, of course, committed no crime for which they could be punished by detention, sometimes under threat of death. According to some, their seizure could, nevertheless, be justified by practical considerations because indirectly it contributes to saving Muslim blood that otherwise might have been spilled in future battles against the enemies of Islam.

Ayatollah Khomeini of Iran and the Shīʿī Lebanese leader Ḥusayn al-Musāwī have not explicitly condemned hostage-taking, and such lack of condemnation is often understood as approval. On the other hand, a number of Lebanese clerics have condemned it as not in conformity with Islamic law. Even clerics who for practical reasons were ready to see hostage-taking as unfortunate but necessary, hesitated, which must at times have embarrassed hostage-holders who professed to be willing to die and to kill for the total and precise application of the laws of Islam. Nevertheless, hostages in Lebanon in the eighties of the twentieth century were usually freed only when it served Iran's purposes, and not on religious legal grounds. Similarly, political, rather than religious, reasons have often been behind the release (or non-release) of hostages within Iran itself, as well as in the Philipines, the Yemen and other parts of the Islamic world, regardless of whether the party holding the hostages is a recognized government or an opposition group.

See also POLITICS AND THE QURʾĀN; VIOLENCE; TOLERANCE AND COMPULSION.

Johannes J.G. Jansen

Bibliography
Kh. Abou El Fadl and A. Sayeed, Hostages, in J.L. Esposito (ed.), *The Oxford encyclopaedia of the modern Islamic world,* 4 vols., Oxford 1995, ii, 134-5 (contains a short but useful bibliography); M. Kramer, *Arab awakening and Islamic revival,* New Brunswick 1996, esp. 220-5; id.,The moral logic of Hizballah, in W. Reich (ed.), *Origins of terrorism,* Cambridge 1990, 131-57; W.A. Ruwayha, *Terrorism and hostage-taking in the Middle East,* Paris 1990².

Hot and Cold

Having, or characterized by, a high or low temperature. Hot and cold are two primary qualities that have a contrastive distribution in the Qurʾān, hot being associated with pain and discomfort, cold (generally) with comfort and relief. In most of its attestations, hot is expressed by *ḥarr* and *ḥarūr*. It indicates pain in both this world and the one to come. A verse illustrating both aspects is Q 9:81. God warns those reluctant to join the expedition (see EXPEDITIONS AND BATTLES) to attack Tabūk, "They said, 'Do not set out in the [mid-summer] heat.' Reply, 'The fire (q.v.) of hell (q.v.) is a more violent heat!' Were they only to understand."

The heat of the sun (q.v.) is oppressive. God has given humankind protection against it, both by a natural phenomenon, shade *(ẓilāl),* and by the product of their own industry, the clothing (q.v.; *sarābīl*) they wear (Q 16:81). Such protection against heat is presented as an example of the richness and diversity of divine gifts: sight as opposed to blindness (see VISION AND BLINDNESS), light (q.v.) to darkness (q.v.), shade as opposed to heat *(ḥarūr),* and life (q.v.) to death (Q 35:19-22; see DEATH AND THE DEAD). In the world to come, heat in various specific forms is among the pains of hell (see REWARD AND PUNISHMENT). The damned will be burnt in a scorching (*ḥāmiya,* Q 88:4; 101:11) fire, given boiling (*āniya,* Q 88:5) water, or scalding (*ḥamīm,* Q 6:70; 10:4; and passim) water to drink, or they have to endure the searing flame of hell (*saʿīr,* Q 31:21 and passim). The gold (q.v.) and silver hoarded by the wicked will be heated *(yuḥmā)* in the fire of hell, and used to brand them (Q 9:35). Those of the left hand (see LEFT HAND AND RIGHT HAND), i.e. those against whom judgment (q.v.) has been given, are exposed to the burning Samūm wind and scalding water (Q 56:41-2), whereas those in heaven (q.v.) give thanks that they have been preserved from "the pain of the Samūm" (Q 52:27; see LAST JUDGMENT).

Cold in the general sense is attested by the word *bard* — although in every case cited coolness is the appropriate connotation of the word — and *bārid,* cooling thing. Coolness brings relief from heat and pain, and is a source of comfort. Thus in hell, there is "no cooling *(bārid)* or agreeable thing" (Q 56:44). In it "the damned shall taste boiling water and putrid fluid, but no coolness *(bard)* and no drink" (Q 78:24). When Abraham (q.v.) is thrown into the fire, God addresses the flames, "Fire, be cool *(kūnī bardan)* and peaceable to Abraham" (Q 21:69). When Job (q.v.) has been put to the test, and the time for relief has come, he is told to scuff the earth with his foot, and a spring appears, "it is cooling *(bārid),* it is drink" (Q 38:42; see WELLS AND SPRINGS; SPRINGS AND FOUNTAINS). While there are specific associations with cold that may be deadly, e.g. *ṣarṣar,* "an icy wind," such as destroyed the people of ʿĀd, (q.v.; Q 41:16; 69:6; 54:19) or unpleasant *barad,* "hail" (Q 24:43), and although clothing from the fur and skin of animals (*dif*ʾ, Q 16:5) is by implication a protection against cold and chill (see HIDES AND FLEECE), the overall message throughout the Qur'ān is that cold-coolness is desirable and brings solace, whereas hot-heat implies discomfort, and is an instrument of punishment. At this scriptural level there is no obvious association of hot and cold with the pathology of disease (see ILLNESS AND HEALTH), although there is a ḥadīth (see ḤADĪTH AND THE QUR'ĀN) that makes this connection: "Fever is vapor of hell; extinguish it with water!" (q.v.; Burgel, Secular and religious features, 57).

Anthony Hearle Johns

Bibliography
ʿAbd al-Bāqī; C. Burgel, Secular and religious features of medieval Arabic medicine, in C. Leslie (ed.), *Asian medical systems. A comparative study*, London 1976, 44-62.

Hour, The

see ESCHATOLOGY; LAST JUDGMENT; APOCALYPSE; TIME

Houris

A feminine adjective for a white skinned woman (sing. *ḥawrāʾ*, pl. *ḥūr*, Lane, ii, 666) denoting the virgins of paradise (q.v.). The singular is not attested in the Qur'ān, but the plural form *(ḥūr)* occurs four times (Q 44:54; 52:20; 55:72; 56:22), three of which appear in connection with the adjective *ʿīn* (sing. fem. *ʿaynāʾ*, masc. *aʿyan*) meaning wide-eyed with a deep black pupil (Lane, v, 2218; and cf. Künstlinger, Namen und Freuden, 629-30). In three other verses (Q 37:48-9; 38:52; 55:56) the paradise virgins are described as *qāṣirāt al-ṭarfi*, "of modest gaze" (Lane, vii, 2533). In all seven verses the paradise virgins are promised as a reward for God-fearing believers (see BELIEF AND UNBELIEF; REWARD AND PUNISHMENT) and sincere servants of God (cf. as well Q 2:25; 3:15; 4:57; 55:34-37; all Medinan sūras).

Possible origins of the idea

The possible origin of the idea of paradise virgins has been the focus of a number of studies. Berthels (Die Jungfraun, 263 f.; Jeffery, *For. vocab.*, 119) believes it is a borrowing of the Zoroastrian teaching about the *Daēnā* and the good deeds, whereas Andrae (*Mohammed*, 69 f.) suggests a direct borrowing from the Syriac Church Father, St. Ephrem (Beck, Christliche Parallel, 404 f., however, argues that Andrae has misunderstood St. Ephrem's text. See, more recently, Beck, Les houris and C. Luxenberg, *Syro-aramäische Lesart*, 221-41. The last-named work draws upon comparative philology to suggest a Syriac origin for the phrase and a meaning of "white grape," the eschatological fruit par excellence.). Some scholars propose a Pahlavi or an Aramaic origin (Jeffery, *For. vocab.*, 119 f.).

Houris in the Qur'ān

The paradise virgins are mentioned during the description of the pleasures of paradise: the believers are seated on couches lined with silk (q.v.) brocade, wearing fine garments (silk and embroidery), eating fruits and drinking wine (see INTOXICANTS; MATERIAL CULTURE AND THE QUR'ĀN). In two occasions the verb "to wed" is used — "and we shall wed them [i.e. the God-fearing believers] unto fair ones *(bi-ḥūrin ʿīnin)*" (Q 44:54, 52:20; and cf. 2:25, 3:15, 4:57). Of the paradise virgins, it is said that "neither man nor jinn (q.v.) has touched them" (Q 55:56; where *lam yaṭmith-hunna* literally means "still not deflowered"; cf. Q 56:35-8; hereto, Ṭabarī, *Tafsīr*, xxvii, 106 f.); they are like hidden pearls (Q 56:23) or hidden eggs (Q 37:49). Al-Ṭabarī (d. 310/923; *Tafsīr*, xxiii, 37) reports that Ibn

Zayd believes ostrich eggs are meant here concluding that their color is a yellowish white; other exegetes believe that pearls are intended (cf. Ibn Kathīr, *Ṣifa*, 103). The exegete Mujāhid b. Jabr (d. 104/722; Ṭabarī, *Tafsīr*, xxvii, 102; Ibn Kathīr, *Ṣifa*, 110 f.) explains the allusion to a yellowish hue by asserting that the paradise virgins are created from saffron. A tradition attributed to Ibn ʿAbbās (d. ca. 67/686) mentions that the houris are formed from four substances: musk, camphor, ambergris and saffron (Macdonald, Islamic eschatology, 353, 371). Q 55:72 describes the paradise virgins as closely guarded in pavilions (Ṭabarī, *Tafsīr*, xxvii, 92-3; Ibn Ḥabīb, *Waṣf*, 16 f.; Ibn Kathīr, *Ṣifa*, 102; cf. Macdonald, Islamic eschatology, 353-5, 371-2).

Houris in tradition

Islamic tradition has detailed quite sensuous and fanciful descriptions of the paradise virgins and of the pleasures in paradise (Ibn Ḥabīb, *Waṣf*, 16; Muḥāsibī, *Tawahhum* 139, 158 f., 166, 177; Ibn Kathīr, *Ṣifa*, 96-8, 102-17, 152-9; Ibn Qayyim, *Ḥādī*, i, 341-92; ii, 2-7; Wensinck, *Concordance*, i, 526; Ṣaleḥ, *Vie future*, 38-41; Rosenthal, Reflections). The houris are mainly reserved for the pious (see PIETY) who have abstained from the pleasures of life (see ABSTINENCE), for those who have controlled their wrath (see ANGER), and for martyrs (see MARTYR). Each believer is promised two, seventy-two, five hundred, or even eight thousand houris. Traditional sources state that the houris are forever at the age of thirty-three and will always retain their virginity; all unpleasant physical functions of the body are non-existent in paradise (see MENSTRUATION). Mystical exegetical traditions understood the paradise virgins as metaphoric symbols (Ibn ʿAṭāʾ, *Nuṣūṣ*, 154; Ibn ʿArabī, *Tafsīr*, ii, 268, 284 f., 290 f.; see ṢŪFISM AND THE QURʾĀN). Critical thinkers and rationalist exegetes have been bothered by the idea of these paradisiacal pleasures and have sought an intellectual explanation (cf. Rosenthal, Reflections, 249 f.; for the position of modern exegetes, see Ṣaleḥ, *Vie future*, 122-36; see EXEGESIS OF THE QURʾĀN: EARLY MODERN AND CONTEMPORARY). As early as the first part of the second/eighth century the promise of the paradise virgins was connected to the motivation for holy war (Jarrar, Maṣāriʿ al-ʿushshāq, 37-9): a martyr-to-be sees the houris in a vision and they invite him to their world. These traditions developed mainly within the circles of ascetic warriors and were transformed into popular narratives that share a common theme. The two facets of this theme are: death/paradise virgins or eros/death. Eros manifests itself as sexual love which strives for ultimate and permanent unification. Multiple religious traditions attest to the human longing to fulfill a desire for passionate love through reunion with "the sacred," to give these desires an eternal realization which transcends death, and allows the positive energy of eros to negate death (Jarrar, Martyrdom, 97-9, 103 f.). The motif of the paradise virgins coupled with martyrdom during holy war or jihād (q.v.) appears as well in medieval historical narratives and recurs in modern Islamic literature on jihād, especially in inspirational pamphlets, in the testimonies of martyrs and in commemorations from Iran and the Gaza Strip in Palestine (Jarrar, Martyrdom, 104-6).

Maher Jarrar

Bibliography

Primary: Ibn al-ʿArabī, Muḥyī l-Dīn, *Tafsīr*, 2 vols., Cairo 1281/1866; Ibn ʿAṭāʾ al-Adamī, *Nuṣūṣ ṣūfiyya ghayr manshūra*, ed. P. Nwyia, Beirut 1973; Ibn Ḥabīb, ʿAbd al-Malik b. Ḥabīb al-Qurṭubī, *Kitāb Waṣf al-firdaws*, Beirut 1987; Ibn Kathīr,

ʿImād al-Dīn Ismāʿīl b. ʿUmar, *Ṣifat al-janna,* ed. Y.ʿA. Budaywī, Damascus 1989; Ibn Qayyim al-Jawziyya, *Ḥādī l-arwāḥ ilā bilād al-afrāḥ,* 3 vols. in 2, Cairo 1325/1907; al-Muḥāsibī, al-Ḥārith b. Asad, *Kitāb al-Tawahhum,* ed. A. Roman, Paris 1978; Ṭabarī, *Tafsīr,* 30 vols. in 12, Cairo 1330. Secondary: T. Andrae, *Mohammed. Sein Leben und sein Glaube,* Stockholm 1917; Arberry; E. Beck, Eine christliche Parallel zu den Paradiesjungfrauen des Korans, in *Orientalia christiana periodica* 14 (1948), 398-405; id., Les houris du Coran et Ephrem le Syrien, in *MIDEO* 6 (1959-61), 405-8; E. Berthels, Die paradiesischen Jungfraun (Ḥūrīs) im Islam, in *Islamica* 1 (1925), 263-88; M. Jarrar, The martyrdom of passionate lovers. Holy war as a sacred wedding, in A. Neuwirth et al. (eds.), *Myths, historical archetypes and symbolic figures in Arabic literature. Towards a new hermeneutic approach,* Beirut 1998, 87-107; id., Maṣāriʿ al-ʿushshāq, in *al-Abḥāth* 41 (1993), 27-121; Jeffery, *For. vocab.;* D. Künstlinger, Die Namen und Freuden des kuranischen Paradieses, in *BSOAS* 6 (1930-2), 617-32; Lane; C. Luxenberg, *Die Syro-aramäische Lesart des Koran,* Berlin 2000, 225-42; J. Macdonald, Islamic eschatology. VI. Paradise, in *Islamic studies* 5 (1966), 331-83; F. Rosenthal, Reflections on love in paradise, in J.H. Marks and R.M. Good (eds.), *Love and death in the ancient Near East. Essays in honor of Marvin H. Pope,* Guilford, CT 1987, 247-54; S. Salih, *La vie future selon le Coran,* Paris 1971; Wensinck, *Concordance.*

House, Domestic and Divine

Structure for human occupation; also an edifice dedicated to God. The house *(bayt, dār, sakan, ghurfa, maʾwā, mathwā, maskin)* is a key symbol in Islam. Its semantic field extends from ordinary dwellings and kin groups (see KINSHIP; FAMILY), to palaces, mosques and shrines, regions of the world and realms in the hereafter (see ESCHATOLOGY). Drawing upon the heritage of house symbolism developed in the ancient Near Eastern civilizations and the Bible, the Qurʾān established the basic lexicon for Muslim domestic space and its meanings and it has served as a first-order instrument for transforming ordinary human dwellings into sacred places (see SANCTITY AND THE SACRED; SACRED PRECINCTS).

Domestic space in the Qurʾān

Four primary Arabic words are used to designate domestic space in the Qurʾān: *bayt* (pl. *buyūt), dār* (pl. *diyār), sakan* and *ghurfa.* There are three additional terms derived from other verbal roots: *maʾwā,* "shelter, refuge," (from *awā*), *mathwā,* "dwelling" (from *thawā*), and *maskin,* "dwelling" (from *sakana*). Together, these terms occur in the Qurʾān 164 times, mainly in the Medinan sūras, but they also occur in about one-third of the Meccan sūras (see CHRONOLOGY AND THE QURʾĀN). In addition, there are a few references to palaces *(ṣarḥ* and *qaṣr,* pl. *quṣūr).* Other terms that connote the idea of dwelling are forms of the verb *bawwaʾa,* "to provide accommodations" and *mustaqarr,* "resting place" or "dwelling." *(Manzil,* which can mean "house" in Arabic, does not occur in the Qurʾān, though its plural *[manāzil]* occurs twice to describe phases of the moon [q.v.].)

Bayt is used in fifteen instances to denote the house of God, which is described variously as "the first house," "the ancient house," "the sacred house," the "forbidden house," "the frequented house" and "my (God's) house." Only once, however, is it identified explicitly with the Kaʿba (q.v.; Q 5:97) and twice with the "sacred mosque" (Q 5:2; 8:34-5). Indeed, the Qurʾān uses the term *bayt* more frequently to designate a holy place than either the name Kaʿba or the term commonly translated as "mosque" (q.v.; *masjid*). In several important instances, it links God's house with the figure of Abraham (q.v.; Ibrāhīm). It is "the first house created for the people," containing Abraham's place (*maqām,* Q 3:96-7). It is a place that was purified and dedicated for ritual purposes, particularly pilgrimage (q.v.; *ḥajj*) rites, by Abraham and his son (see ISHMAEL; ISAAC), who petitioned God to make them his submitters *(muslimūn)* and to make their progeny into a submitting community (*umma muslima*, see Q 2:125-8). This story about the origin of the shrine and its rites probably first served as a claim by Muḥammad and his followers to the *ḥaram* area in Mecca after the emigration (q.v., *hijra*) in 622 C.E. — a claim contested by their Meccan opponents (see OPPOSITION TO MUḤAMMAD). The existence of this opposition is expressed in the Qurʾān itself, which in its polemics promises a place in hell (q.v.) for disbelievers (see BELIEF AND UNBELIEF) and those who would debar the pious from the sacred mosque area (see Q 8:34-6).

The existence of ordinary human dwellings and even their furnishings (see FURNITURE AND FURNISHINGS) is attributed to God's creative actions: "God made a dwelling place *(sakan)* for you from among your homes *(buyūt)*. He made homes for you from animal skins (see HIDES AND FLEECE; ANIMAL LIFE), so you will find them light when you travel and when you camp. [He made] furnishings and conveniences [for you] out of their wool, fur, and hair for a time... Thus does he bring his grace (q.v.) upon you to completion so that you submit" (*tuslimūn*, Q 16:80-3). On the other hand, the Qurʾān states that God abstained from creating for people luxurious houses with silver roofs *(suquf*, sing. *saqf)*, stairways *(maʿārij)*, doors *(abwāb)*, beds *(surur)* and gold (q.v.) ornaments (*zukhruf*, see ORNAMENT AND ILLUMINATION), lest everyone become too worldly and disbelieve in God (Q 43:33-5; see MATERIAL CULTURE AND THE QURʾĀN).

The qurʾānic conception of the creation of human domestic space is congruent with a wider set of discourses about the sacred histories of the ancestors and the fates of their houses (see GEOGRAPHY; FATE). In these narratives (q.v.), having houses and wealth (q.v.) is not always a sign of blessing nor is lacking them a sign of divine ire. The crux of the matter rests on people's belief and their moral comportment (see ETHICS AND THE QURʾĀN). The peoples of ʿĀd (q.v.), Thamūd (q.v.), Sheba (q.v.) and Midian (q.v.) all had houses and prospered until they rejected God and his messengers or committed evil (see MESSENGER; GOOD AND EVIL). Consequently, they were each destroyed and their houses abandoned or ruined (for example, Q 7:74-9; 27:45-52; 46:21-5; 34:15-6; 7:85-92; see PUNISHMENT STORIES). In one instance God brings the house roof *(saqf)* down upon the heads of plotters (Q 16:26). In such accounts the Qurʾān implies that a similar fate awaits unbelievers in Muḥammad's own time, a threat that became a reality for unbelieving People of the Book (q.v.) mentioned in Q 59:2-4, whom most commentators identify with the Banū Naḍīr (q.v.), a Jewish clan forced out of Medina (q.v.) in 4/626 (see JEWS AND JUDAISM; EXPEDITIONS AND BATTLES).

Believers, on the other hand, enjoy divine blessings at home, as indicated in Q 16:80-3. Situations may arise, however, when they should be prepared to give up their homes and possessions and emigrate. Emigration, too, has its rewards as stated in Q 4:100: "Whoever emigrates in God's way (see PATH OR WAY) will find many a road and open opportunity in the land. Whoever leaves his house *(bayt)*, emigrating to God and his messenger, and then death overtakes him, his reward is incumbent upon God."

There are several rules in the Qurʾān that are concerned with the houses of God, ordinary believers and the Prophet (see WIVES OF THE PROPHET). Occurring only in Medinan sūras, these rules commonly invoke distinctions between belief and disbelief and concepts of purity and impurity (q.v.), but they constitute neither a detailed architectural code nor a rabbinic system of ritual prescriptions. Rules pertaining to ritual actions conducted at God's sacred house (Q 2:125-7, 196-203; 5:2; 22:26; see RITUAL AND THE QURʾĀN) also include a prescription for pilgrimage itself: "God requires people to perform a *ḥajj* to the house if they are able to do so. If anyone disbelieves, God can do without his creations" (Q 3:97). Rules pertaining to Muslim homes in general treat matters of everyday social life as religious practices; ideas about God, right and wrong, purity, and blessing are conjoined to statements concerning visitation, eating and salutations (see Q 24:27-9, 61; see HOSPITALITY AND COURTESY; SOCIAL INTERACTIONS). Believers, for example, should obtain permission to enter a house and greet its inhabitants or they should leave if so told. This is of greater purity *(azkā)* for them. They are encouraged, however, to enter unoccupied dwellings (Q 24:27-9). These prescriptions for visitation occur together with statements about adultery (see ADULTERY AND FORNICATION), covering the body (see MODESTY) and marriage (see MARRIAGE AND DIVORCE), which suggests that Muḥammad and his followers recognized a linkage between the house, the body and sexual relations (see SEX AND SEXUALITY) — all were immured by ritual taboos, not unlike God's sacred house (see also Q 4:22). In divorce cases, the Qurʾān states that the woman shall remain in her house or where her husband resides for a prescribed period to see whether she is with child unless she is guilty of adultery. She shall neither be evicted nor leave the house during this time. These are said to be "God's limits" (*ḥudūd Allāh,* see BOUNDARIES AND PRECEPTS). Those who transgress them do wrong against themselves (Q 65:1, 6), implying an unfortunate destiny in the hereafter.

About one-third of the house terms in the Qurʾān are used to describe the abodes of the blessed and the damned in the hereafter. Paradise (q.v.) is called "the house" *(al-dār)* and also "house of residence" *(dār al-muqām),* "house of permanence" *(dār al-qarār),* "house of the god-fearing" *(dār al-muttaqīn),* "the final house" *(al-dār al-ākhira),* and "house of peace" *(dār al-salām).* That paradise is conceived to be an actual home for the blessed is conveyed by passages such as those in Q 13:20-4, which describes families living in the paradisaical gardens (see GARDEN) being visited by angels (see ANGEL), who come through their doors and bless them. Individual dwellings in paradise are referred to by terms such as "shelter" *(maʾwā),* "lofty apartment" *(ghurfa),* "dwelling" *(maskin)* and simply "house" *(bayt).* Wrongdoers, on the other hand, are consigned to hell (q.v.), which is also called "the evil house" *(sūʾ al-dār),* "the house of perdition" *(dār al-bawār)* and "the house of eternity" *(dār al-khuld).* More frequently (in twenty-nine instances), the Qurʾān uses terms for "shelter" *(maʾwā)* and "dwelling" *(mathwā)* for their abode. This is evident in verses such as Q 3:151: "We shall cast terror into the hearts (see HEART) of those who have denied God by associating partners with him.... Their shelter *(maʾwā)* shall be the fire (q.v.). How bad is the dwelling *(mathwā)* of the wrongdoers!"

Lastly, the Qurʾān preserves traces of ancient Near Eastern cosmologies, wherein the created world was conceived as a large palace (see COSMOLOGY). It is said to have a heavenly ceiling *(samk* or *saqf)* raised by God, held up by invisible pillars, beneath which stretches an earthly carpet *(bisāṭ)* upon which his creatures roam (see Q 13:2; 21:32; 71:19; 79:28; see HEAVEN AND SKY). These notions, however, are not elaborated as a mythic narrative as they are in ancient Egyptian and Mesopotamian texts.

Ḥadīth literature (see ḤADĪTH AND THE QUR'ĀN) continued to build on the foundation of many of the domestic discourses that had been set forth in the Qur'ān. It used the same Arabic terms and added *manzil* to them. Ḥadīth elaborated upon the idea of the human dwelling as a sacred enclave, provided more details on how to perform pilgrimage to the house of God in Mecca and furnished more particulars about the dwellings of the blessed in paradise. The grave itself was described in one tradition as a house *(bayt)* of exile, loneliness and maggots (Tirmidhī, *Ṣaḥīḥ,* 26) but the qur'ānic practice of using domestic terms in describing hell was discontinued.

The Qur'ān in domestic space

The Qur'ān is of central importance as an instrument used by Muslims to sanctify their homes (see EVERYDAY LIFE). Ḥadīths speak of the benefits that accrue to the dwelling and its inhabitants when particular verses, chapters or even the whole text is recited. Al-Tirmidhī (d. 279/892) relates ḥadīths stating that Satan (see DEVIL) and other malevolent beings will not approach houses where Sūrat al-Baqara (Q 2 "The Cow") and the Throne Verse (Q 2:255) are recited (Tirmidhī, *Ṣaḥīḥ, Thawāb al-Qur'ān,* 3). Al-Suyūṭī (d. 911/1505) cites a ḥadīth from Anas b. Mālik (d. 91-3/710-2) that asserts "good fortune increases in the house where the Qur'ān is recited and decreases where it is not" (*Itqān,* ii, 193). The Prophet's wife, 'Ā'isha (see 'Ā'ISHA BINT ABĪ BAKR), is reported to have said that houses where it is recited appear to the people of heaven as stars do to the people of earth (Suyūṭī, *Itqān,* i, 137). In cultural practice, passages from the Qur'ān are recited during house foundation rituals or when a new dwelling is occupied. Householders may arrange to have a complete recitation of the Qur'ān (q.v.; *khatma*) performed at home when someone dies or on other unusual occasions. In modern times, families switch on the radio to the Qur'ān station or play a cassette recording of qur'ānic recitation to make the day a propitious one or to sooth the soul of an ailing family member.

The use of qur'ānic inscriptions in Muslim homes has become perhaps as ubiquitous as it ever was in mosques (see EPIGRAPHY). The houses and palaces of medieval and Ottoman Cairo, which were until recently the best-preserved in the Muslim world, contain bands of Qur'ān inscriptions and poetry in their reception areas and great halls. The Throne Verse was the most widely used as was Sūrat al-Ikhlāṣ (Q 112, "Sincerity") and the *basmala* (q.v.). Today, even in common homes, it is not unusual to find the *basmala* or the exhortation "Enter it securely, in peace!" (Q 15:46) written over thresholds. The latter phrase affirms the symbolic relationship between the home and paradise, an idea that was used in earlier Islamic monumental architecture. Sitting room walls, where guests are received, are often decorated with individual verses or a framed poster of the entire text of the Qur'ān in miniature. A widespread practice among Muslims today is to place a finely rendered copy of the printed Qur'ān on a stand or in a velvet box for display in the guest room or living room.

The most highly developed use of the written Qur'ān in the sanctification of Muslim domestic space has emerged in Egypt and adjacent regions, where colorful murals (see ICONOCLASM) consisting of complexes of epigraphs, depictions of the Ka'ba in Mecca and the Prophet's mosque in Medina, human and animal figures, boats, trains and airplanes are painted on the houses of Muslims who have performed the *ḥajj*. This practice is attested as early as the sixteenth century. Mural epigraphs commonly include verses dealing with the *ḥajj* itself (Q 3:96-7; 22:27) but they can also be stock qurʾānic phrases concerning God and the prophet Muḥammad that have entered popular speech such as the *basmala*, praise for God (Q 1:2) and his Prophet (Q 33:56) and statements invoking divine blessing and protection (e.g. Q 2:172; 3:160; 11:56, 88; 27:40; 48:1; 49:13). Thus, the Qurʾān participates in the transformation of the Egyptian pilgrim's house into a sacred place and helps articulate his or her individual experience in terms of powerful Islamic beliefs and symbols.

Juan Eduardo Campo

Bibliography
Primary: Suyūṭī, *Itqān*, 2 vols., Beirut n.d.; Tirmidhī, *Ṣaḥīḥ*, 13 vols., Beirut, n.d.
Secondary: J.E. Campo, *The other sides of paradise. Explorations into the religious meanings of domestic space in Islam*, Columbia, SC 1991; J.-C. Garcin, and J. Revault (eds.), *L'habitat traditionnel dans les pays Musulmans autour de la Méditerranée*, 3 vols., Cairo 1988; ids. et al., *Palais et maisons du Caire*, 2 vols., Paris 1982; A.B. McCloud, This is a Muslim home. Signs of difference in the African-American row house, in B.D. Metcalf (ed.), *Making Muslim space in North America and Europe*, Berkeley 1996, 65-73; R.B. Qureshi, Transcending space. Recitation and community among South Asian Muslims in Canada, in B.D. Metcalf (ed.), *Making Muslim space in North America and Europe*, Berkeley 1996, 46-64.

Hūd

The first of the five Arabian prophets of the Qurʾān (for the other Arabian prophets, see ṢĀLIḤ; ABRAHAM; SHUʿAYB; MUḤAMMAD), from whom the eleventh sūra of the Qurʾān takes its name. His tale occurs four times in the Qurʾān, with only minor variations: Q 7:65-72, 11:50-60, 26:123-40, 46:21-6. In these narratives (q.v.), Hūd is explicitly called a messenger (q.v.; *rasūl*), whom God has sent to the people of ʿĀd (q.v.), who are portrayed as polytheists (see POLYTHEISM AND ATHEISM). Hūd persists in his faith despite his compatriots' accusations that he is a liar *(min al-kādhibīna)* and a fool (*fī safāhatin*, Q 7:66), and their refusal to forsake their idols (see IDOLS AND IMAGES) when he had no "clear proof" for his claim (Q 11:53). Hūd warns his people that if they do not heed his message, God will replace them with another people *(qawm*, Q 11:57). In Q 11:52, the people are promised bounteous rains in return for their repentance (see REPENTANCE AND PENANCE), and in Q 11:55, it is implied that the people of ʿĀd "contrived" against Hūd. God, however, rescues Hūd and those who followed him, destroying those who denied him (Q 11:58-9). In Q 46:24-5, the agent of the destruction of ʿĀd is described as a wind borne by clouds (see AIR AND WIND).

Early Islamic exegetes (see EXEGESIS OF THE QURʾĀN: CLASSICAL AND MEDIEVAL) are more forthcoming with details about ʿĀd and "many-columned Iram" (q.v.), the city associated with ʿĀd, than they are about Hūd himself. Nevertheless, the exegetes do discuss his supposed name and genealogy, and also elaborate upon the qurʾānic account of the fate of his people: in addition to a drought, they are said to have suffered from "barrenness of wombs" (Ṭabarī, *Tafsīr*, xii, 58; Ibn al-Jawzī, *Zād*, iv, 117; Qurṭubī, *Jāmiʿ*, ix, 51). (For one modern Western scholar's theory, see Horovitz, *Jewish proper names*, 29: "Perhaps the name 'Hūd' is an invention on the part of Mohammed, who, then, while looking for a name of the warner of the ʿĀd which should be in accord with names like 'Lūṭ' and 'Nūḥ,' may have made 'Hūd' out of 'Yahūd.') Both al-Thaʿlabī (d. 427/1035) and al-Kisāʾī, the unknown author of the "tales of the prophets" *(Qiṣaṣ al-anbiyāʾ)*, provide some important details about him, such as his pre-ordained birth, his early worship of one God, the content of his preaching to his fellow ʿĀdites, and even the names of some of his converts. If, as is usually assumed, such "tales of the prophets" reflect popular belief (in addition to their reliance upon exegetical material), then these narratives might indicate how most historical Muslims would have understood the allusive qurʾānic accounts about Hūd.

In al-Kisāʾī (*Tales*, 109-17), Hūd is depicted as an ardent monotheist from the very beginning, surrounded by resolute ʿĀdite polytheists. He was only rarely able to convince a few of his countrymen of his message. Ultimately, after years of such opposition, Hūd called upon God to punish the ʿĀdites for their wickedness. God responded by causing a four-year drought in ʿĀd, whereupon the king of ʿĀd — as was the custom — sent a delegation of seven notables, including a follower of Hūd named Marthad, to Mecca (q.v.) to ask God for release from their suffering (cf. Ṭabarī, *Tafsīr*, viii, 219). After a period of prolonged distraction by the hospitality of the pagan king of Mecca, the delegation made its way to the sanctuary but was refused entrance. In response to the pleas of the Muslim Marthad, God sent three clouds: one red, one white, one black. The last of these contained an angel who oversaw the "barren wind," which would be the final agent of ʿĀd's destruction. God commanded the leader of the delegation to choose one of the clouds to be sent to ʿĀd. Thinking it laden with rain, the leader chose the black cloud, which unleashed its destruction upon the land of ʿĀd and all who dwelt there, save the followers of Hūd. Al-Kisāʾī ends his account by noting that Hūd and his followers fled the destruction of ʿĀd to Yemen, where Hūd died and was buried in the Ḥaḍramawt. Al-Thaʿlabī (*Qiṣaṣ*, 60-5) adds some detail to this general account. In his (and al-Ṭabarī's; see Ṭabarī, *Taʾrīkh*, i, 231-44) version, it is a drought of three years that affects the ʿĀdites, who are described as giants and Amalekites; Hūd is in fact imprisoned by the king of Mecca at the request of his compatriots, though he escapes; and another Muslim follower of Hūd is named at Mecca: Luqmān ibn ʿĀd. Al-Thaʿlabī also provides an alternate version of the petition at Mecca involving varying requests from the ʿĀdite delegation (who boastfully request the same fate as that of their countrymen), Marthad (who requests goodness and righteousness) and Luqmān (q.v.; who requests a long life).

The tomb of Hūd has long been an important pilgrimage site in Yemen, located at the mouth of the Barhūt. The tomb and the pilgrimage practices associated with it are described in detail by medieval visitors like al-Harawī as well as modern authorities like Landberg (*Etudes*, 432-83) and Serjeant (Hūd). The prominence of the shrine in Yemen did not, however, prevent Muslims from claiming other locations for the tomb of Hūd, as in Mecca (Harawī, *Ishārāt*), Damascus (Rabaʿī, *Faḍāʾil*, 34-5) or somewhere in Palestine (Thaʿlabī, *Qiṣaṣ*; see PRE-ISLAMIC ARABIA AND THE QURʾĀN; GEOGRAPHY).

Paul M. Cobb

Bibliography

Primary: al-Harawī al-Mawṣilī, ʿAlī, *Kitāb al-Ishārāt ilā maʿrifat al-ziyārāt*, ed. J. Sourdel-Thomine, Damascus 1953; Ibn al-Jawzī, *Zād*, iv, 117; Kisāʾī, *The tales of the prophets of al-Kisāʾ*, trans. W. Thackston (with notes), Boston 1978; Qurṭubī, *Jāmiʿ*, ix, 51; al-Rabaʿī, Abū l-Ḥasan, *Kitāb Faḍāʾil al-shām wa-dimashq*, ed. S. al-Munajjid, Damascus 1950; Ṭabarī, *Tafsīr*, xii, 58; id., *Taʾrīkh*, i, 231-44; Thaʿlabī, *Qiṣaṣ*.
Secondary: J. Horovitz, *Jewish proper names and*

derivatives in the Koran, Hildesheim 1964, 28-9; id., KU, 89; C. Landberg, *Etudes sur les dialectes de l'Arabie méridionale. i. Ḥaḍramoût,* Leiden 1901; R.B. Serjeant, Hūd and other pre-Islamic prophets of Ḥaḍramawt, in *Muséon* 46 (1954), 121-79; A.J. Wensinck/Ch. Pellat, Hūd, in EI², iii, 537-8.

Ḥudaybiya

A location on the road from Jedda to Mecca (q.v.) just outside the sacred territory. Here Muḥammad stopped while attempting to perform the pilgrimage (q.v.) in 6/628 and, through the agency of ʿUthmān, negotiated a truce with the tribe of Quraysh (q.v.) which would allow the Prophet and his followers to perform the pilgrimage the following year. This truce became known as the Pact of Ḥudaybiya. For further details, see MUḤAMMAD; EXPEDITIONS AND BATTLES; TREATIES AND ALLIANCES.

Andrew Rippin

Ḥudūd see BOUNDARIES AND PRECEPTS

Hue of God see BAPTISM

Human Being see COMMUNITY AND SOCIETY IN THE QURʾĀN; ETHICS AND THE QURʾĀN; POLITICS AND THE QURʾĀN; SOCIAL INTERACTIONS; RELIGION; SOCIAL SCIENCES AND THE QURʾĀN; GENDER; FEMINISM; PATRIARCHY; FAMILY; KINSHIP; TRIBES AND CLANS; FREEDOM AND PREDESTINATION; FATE; DESTINY

Humor

That which pertains, or appeals, to the sense of the ludicrous, absurdly incongruous or comic. Humor in its relation to the qurʾānic revelation involves two major aspects: first, whether there is any humor in the Qurʾān and, if so, how it is constituted; secondly, whether the Qurʾān occurs in or forms the object of indigenous Islamic jocular literature (see LITERATURE AND THE QURʾĀN).

The issue of humor in the Qurʾān pertains to the general discussion of whether scripture can contain humor. In the Islamic case, the issue moreover implies the question of whether God has a sense of humor (see ANTHROPOMORPHISM; GOD AND HIS ATTRIBUTES). Considering God's omnipotence, any dogmatic dispute regarding his general capacity to experience and express humor appears irrelevant and, in fact, anthropomorphic imagery as attested in the ḥadīth has elaborated this trait of God's nature without clinging to strict dogmatic restraints (Gimaret, *Dieu à l'image,* 265-79; see ḤADĪTH AND THE QURʾĀN). No extensive treatment of the subject exists, but a sensitive reading of the qurʾānic text reveals passages which are not devoid of certain humorous elements. Mustansir Mir has attempted to show "that the Qurʾān does not regard humor as a contraband item" (Mir, Humor, 181). Discussing a number of instances, Mir argues that humor in the Qurʾān is used to convey a religious insight or to elucidate a theological teaching and mainly serves the purposes of characterization. The example Mir discusses in most detail is the episode of Moses (q.v.) being called to prophethood and his inability to understand the implication of this act: When God asks about his staff (see ROD), he gives a straightforward answer attempting to be exhaustive about the uses of his staff, while failing to recognize that God is about to reveal to him a miracle (q.v.; Q 20:17-21). Relying on the general definition of humor as the jocular resolution of conflicts, the contrast between the supposed and the real implied in this episode might be understood to contain humor. In a similar vein, Mir discusses a number of passages (Q 7:43; 9:127; 18:60-4, 65-82; 19:3; 20:18; 33:20; 37:91-2; 47:20; 74:18-25; 86:75-83), ultimately extracting the humorous techniques of irony, satire, anticlimax and circumlocution (see FORM AND STRUCTURE OF THE QURʾĀN; LANGUAGE OF THE QURʾĀN; RHETORIC OF THE QURʾĀN).

Given the dominant presence of the Qurʾān in the everyday life (q.v.) of the Islamic community, it is not surprising to see that it partakes in a humorous outlook on life as depicted in a large number of jocular texts (Marzolph, *Arabia ridens*, ii, 350, s.v. Koran). Stupid people are seen to "correct mistakes" in the qurʾānic text, to quote verses not verbatim but with equivalent wording or corresponding meaning as well as to suggest beautiful poetry (see POETRY AND POETS) deserving inclusion in the Qurʾān (see POLEMIC AND POLEMICAL LANGUAGE; OPPOSITION TO MUḤAMMAD). The misspelling of specific words often generates drastic humor, such as when the jester Ibn al-Jaṣṣās in an anecdote quoted in al-Ābī's *Nathr al-durr* (vii, 389) recites Q 3:192 misreading *akhzaytahu*, "you have annihilated him for good," as *akhraytahu*, understood as "you [God] make him continuously defecate." Often, qurʾānic verses are quoted in humorous contexts (such as by the stereotype *ṭufaylī*), and a number of texts expose jocular solutions to the dogmatic controversy of whether the Qurʾān should be regarded as eternal or created (*makhlūq*, see CREATEDNESS OF THE QURʾĀN). Several anecdotes are of an almost blasphemous character (see BLASPHEMY), such as the erroneous naming of Q 89 (Sūrat al-Fajr, "The Dawn") as *sūrat al-farj* (i.e. female pudendum, Tawḥīdī, *Baṣāʾir*, iv, 91) or the islamicized version of an anecdote already known from the post-classical Greek *Philogelos* (no. 9), which culminates in the punch-line that Q 112:1 should not be recited because "it killed my donkey, so it probably is even more lethal for humans!" (Ibn al-Jawzī, Ḥamqā, 147). Even the latter instances, however, aim at exposing foolish belief or behavior rather than ridiculing the revelation itself. At the same time, they document that the use of qurʾānic verse in a jocular context in medieval Islamic literature was permitted with a high degree of tolerance. See also LAUGHTER.

Ulrich Marzolph

Bibliography
Primary: al-Ābī, Abū Saʿīd Manṣūr b. al-Ḥusayn, *Nathr al-durr fī l-muḥāḍarāt*, ed. M.ʿA. Qurna et al., 7 vols., Cairo 1980-91; Ibn al-Jawzī, *Akhbār al-ḥamqā wa-l-mughaffalīn*, ed. K. al-Muẓaffar, Najaf 1966; al-Tawḥīdī, Abū Ḥayyān ʿAlī b. Muḥammad b. al-ʿAbbās, *al-Baṣāʾir wa-l-dhakhāʾir*, ed. I. Kīlānī, 4 vols. in 6, Damascus 1964-9.
Secondary: R.G. Cote, *Holy mirth. A theology of laughter*, Whitinsville 1986; D. Gimaret, *Dieu à l'image de l'homme. Les anthropomorphismes de la sunna et leur interprétation par les théologiens*, Paris 1997; M.C. Hyers, *Holy laughter. Essays on religion in the comic perspective*, New York 1969; U. Marzolph, *Arabia ridens. Die humoristische Kurzprosa der frühen adab-Literatur im internationalen Traditionsgeflecht*, 2 vols., Frankfurt am Main 1992; id., The Qurʾān and jocular literature, in *Arabica* 47 (2000), 478-87; M. Mir, Humor in the Qurʾān, in *MW* 81 (1991), 179-93; F. Rosenthal, *Humor in early Islam*, Leiden 1956; repr. Westport, CT 1976; J. Sadan, *Dirāsāt wa-nuṣūṣ adabiyya. v. al-Adab al-ʿarabī al-hāzilī wa-nawādir al-thuqalāʾ*, Tel Aviv 1983 (on humor in classical Arabic).

Ḥunayn

Name of a deep, irregular valley, one day's journey from Mecca on the road to al-Ṭāʾif, where the Muslims fought a battle in Shawwāl 8/January 630, just a few weeks after the conquest of Mecca (see EXPEDITIONS AND BATTLES). The victory of *yawm Ḥunayn*, the "battle of Ḥunayn," is pre-sented in Q 9:25-7 (cf. Ṭabarī, *Tafsīr*, xiv, 178-88, ad Q 9:25) as a reminder that victory (q.v.) can only come from God, for despite their large number, the Muslims were quickly routed by the enemy, until their panicked retreat was transformed into a successful rally by divine intervention.

Early Muslim historians agree that the battle of Ḥunayn was precipitated by the clans of Hawāzin and Thaqīf, who were associated with the city of al-Ṭāʾif, Mecca's (q.v.) chief rival for trade in the region (see TRIBES AND CLANS; ECONOMICS; GEOGRAPHY). Fearing that al-Ṭāʾif was next to be conquered by the Muslims, the clans decided to launch a pre-emptive strike against the Prophet, who marched out to meet them with 2,000 Meccans and 10,000 Helpers (*anṣār,* see EMIGRANTS AND HELPERS). Some of the Meccans who had recently submitted to Muslim rule are said to have been willing to fight to preserve the primacy of Quraysh (q.v.) rather than out of loyalty to the Prophet.

Upon arrival at the valley of Ḥunayn, the Muslims were ambushed and panic ensued. The Qurʾān, using the plural form, says, "then you turned back in retreat" (*thumma wallaytum mudbirīna,* Q 9:25). Various reports stress that the Prophet himself did not retreat, but rather, stood firm, with only a few supporters by his side. The definitive moment in the Muslim rally came when "God sent his calm (*sakīna,* see SECHINA) upon his messenger and the believers" (Q 9:26). The Prophet dismounted from his white mule and declared in concise *rajaz* (see LITERARY STRUCTURES OF THE QURʾĀN), "I am the Prophet, I do not lie; I am the son of ʿAbd al-Muṭṭalib." Surprisingly, there is relatively little explanation of the "invisible forces" which God sent to defeat the enemy, although a few reports indicate that these were angels (see ANGEL). It is also reported that the Prophet threw a handful of dust or pebbles towards the enemy, which confused or blinded their vision.

The Muslims collected an enormous booty (q.v.) when the opposing army fled: 6,000 women and children, and thousands of animals. Jurists find a legal precedent in the Prophet's order that men not touch female captives (q.v.) until they had completed a menstrual period (see MENSTRUATION) or delivered a baby (see LAW AND THE QURʾĀN). After an unsuccessful siege of al-Ṭāʾif, the Prophet turned back towards Mecca, accepted allegiance from a delegation from Hawāzin and returned all their captives. The rest of the booty was divided among the Muslim fighters, including some recent converts from Quraysh whose hearts (see HEART) the Prophet wanted "reconciled" to Islam (Q 9:60). Some of the Helpers resented these distributions, suggesting that the Prophet had inclined towards his own people. Hearing this, the Prophet declared his affinity for the Helpers in a speech that moved them to tears, then returned with them to Medina (q.v.), by-passing Mecca and leaving authority over the upcoming pilgrimage (q.v.; *ḥajj*) to a delegate.

Ingrid Mattson

Bibliography

Primary: Bukhārī, *Ṣaḥīḥ,* ed. Krehl, iii, 154-5; Ibn Isḥāq, *Sīra;* Ibn Saʿd, *Ṭabaqāt;* Muslim, *Ṣaḥīḥ;* Qurṭubī, *Jāmiʿ;* Ṭabarī, *The history of al-Ṭabarī. ix. The last years of the Prophet,* trans. I.K. Poonawala, Albany 1990, 1-20; id., *Tafsīr,* ed. Shākir; Wāqidī, *Maghāzī.*

Secondary: H. Lammens/Abd al-Hafez Kamal, Ḥunayn, in *EI*², iii, 578; W. Montgomery Watt, Hawāzin, in *EI*², iii, 285-6; J. Wellhausen, *Muhammad in Medina. Das ist Vakidis's* Kitab al-Maghazi *in verkürtzer deutscher Wiedergabe,* Berlin 1882, 354-68.

Hunting and Fishing

Pursuing and killing animals of the earth (q.v.) and water (q.v.), respectively, for the purpose of nourishment, profit and/or sport. There are only a few qurʾānic occurrences denoting hunting and fishing *(ṣayd),* all of which are found in Q 5 (Sūrat al-Māʾida, "The Repast"). The aim of the creation (q.v.) of animals by God is primarily their usefulness for humankind (see ANIMAL LIFE). As a consequence, it is principally permitted to kill and eat them or to use animal products (see HIDES AND FLEECE) if these animals and their products are clean *(ḥalāl);* indeed, they belong to the good things (*ṭayyibāt,* cf. Q 2:172; 7:157; 23:51).

Concerning hunting, the Qurʾān explicitly prohibits the killing of game when a Muslim is in a state of consecration (Q 5:95; cf. Q 5:96) and it declares game thus acquired as unacceptable (Q 5:1; see FORBIDDEN; PROHIBITED DEGREES; LAW AND THE QURʾĀN). Additionally, penalties are stipulated for intentional killing during a state of consecration: an offering must be delivered and expiation for this transgression may be the feeding of poor people or the equivalent in fasting (q.v.; Q 5:95; see ALMSGIVING; BOUNDARIES AND PRECEPTS). Only in this context does the Qurʾān speak about penalties and compensations for nonobservance of legal regulations in connection with the use of animals. The believer (see BELIEF AND UNBELIEF) is warned about encountering game while in a state of consecration; this is a severe test for humankind (cf. Q 5:94). Once a Muslim is not in a state of consecration, however, hunting is expressly permitted (Q 5:2). The Qurʾān has no further statements concerning hunting. No reference is made to hunting methods, the specific animals used to assist people in hunting, nor to the type of game pursued. The hunting of game by means of carnivorous hunting animals (the Qurʾān uses the lexeme *jawāriḥ;* in the Arabic literature of the Middle Ages, this lexeme is usually limited to designate hunting birds only) is, according to the Qurʾān, equal to ritual slaughtering (see CONSECRATION OF ANIMALS): "And if you teach any beasts of prey, training them as dogs and teaching them part of what God has taught you, then eat of what they catch on your account; make mention of the name of Allāh over it" (Q 5:4).

Contrary to game on land, aquatic animals and their consumption are permitted during a Muslim's state of consecration. Fishing is allowed (Q 5:96; cf. Q 16:14; 35:12, containing the allowance to eat food from both fresh and salt water). In spite of this general permission, the consumption of fish in the western part of the Arabian peninsula has remained an uncommon practice because fish are sparse in the interior of Arabia. Ancient Arabian poetry seldom refers to fish and, in qurʾānic times, Muslims were not yet familiar with the most common edible species of fish. In many regions of the Arab world the bias against fishing has persisted. The Qurʾān does not give prescriptions for fishing, although explicit reference is made to pearls and coral (q.v.), both animal products of the sea that are considered to be benefits from God (Q 55:22; see BLESSING). Unlike the absence of any qurʾānic mention of the individuals engaged in fishing for nourishment or profit, there is a qurʾānic reference to a pearl fisher *(ghawwāṣ):* although these pearl fishers are not humans, but devils diving for Solomon (q.v.; Q 38:37, cf. Q 21:82), this profession must have been well-known in qurʾānic times.

Herbert Eisenstein

Bibliography

Primary: M. Ibn Manglī, *Uns al-malāʾ bi-waḥsh al-falāʾ. De la chasse. Commerce des grands de ce monde avec les bêtes sauvages des déserts sans onde,* trans. and com. F. Viré, Paris 1984; F. Viré, *Le traité de l'art de volerie (Kitāb al-Bayzara). Rédigé vers 385/995 par le Grand-Fauconnier du calife fatimide al-ʿAzīz bi-llāh,* Leiden 1967 (extract of *Arabica* 12-13 [1965-6]).

Secondary: H. Eisenstein, *Einführung in die arabische Zoographie. Das tierkundliche Wissen in der arabisch-islamischen Literatur,* Berlin 1991 (especially 12-21, Koran und Recht); E. Gräf, *Jagdbeute und Schlachttier im islamischen Recht. Eine Untersuchung zur Entwicklung der islamischen Jurisprudenz,* Bonn 1959 (especially 4-66, Jagdbeute und Schlachttier im Koran); L. Mercier, *La chasse et les sports chez les Arabes,* Paris 1927; F. Viré, Sayd, in *EI²*, ix, 98-9.

Husband and Wife see FAMILY; MARRIAGE AND DIVORCE

Hypocrites and Hypocrisy

Those who feign to be what they are not; the act or practice of such people. "Hypocrites" is the word generally used to translate the qurʾānic term *munāfiqūn,* the active participle of the third form of the root *n-f-q*. Its verbal noun, *nifāq,* is usually translated as "hypocrisy," even though this does not cover the full range of meanings conveyed by the Arabic term as used in the Qurʾān. The hypocrites are considered half-hearted believers who outwardly profess Islam while their hearts (see HEART) harbor doubt or even unbelief (see BELIEF AND UNBELIEF; FAITH). Therefore, they are — at best — not fully committed to the Prophet and his community (see COMMUNITY AND SOCIETY IN THE QURʾĀN), and may deliberately harm the interests of the Muslims. The etymology of *nifāq* and *munāfiqūn* is disputed, but they are often associated with the nouns *nafaq,* which means tunnel, and *nufaqa* and *nāfiqāʾ,* i.e. the burrow of a rat or a jerboa. This connotation of hiding underground and undermining is very apt, since this is precisely what the *munāfiqūn* are accused of, especially in post-qurʾānic usage. According to Serjeant (The *Sunnah jāmiʿah,* 11 f.), however, the original meaning of the term *munāfiq* was the one obliged to pay the *nafaqa,* a kind of tax (see TAXATION) exacted from all members of the *umma* in Medina (q.v.), including the Jews, at times of war (q.v.). Those who were reluctant to pay the *nafaqa* came to be regarded as uncommitted to the cause (see PATH OR WAY), and hence as hypocrites. Apart from *nifāq,* the Qurʾān mentions another, minor, form of hypocrisy, called *riyāʾ* (or, alternatively, *riʾāʾ*), which connotes an ostentatious display of piety (q.v.; Q 2:264; 4:38; 8:47; see Deladrière, Riyāʾ).

The concepts of *nifāq* and *munāfiq(ūn),* as well as various verbal forms of *n-f-q,* are mentioned in thirty verses, viz. Q 3:167; 4:61, 88, 138, 140, 142, 145; 6:35; 8:49; 9:64, 67, 68, 73, 77, 97, 101; 29:11; 33:1, 12, 24, 48, 60, 73; 48:6; 57:13; 59:11; 63:1, 7, 8; 66:9. Q 63 is even entitled Sūrat al-Munāfiqūn. Moreover, the insincere believers are frequently discussed without explicit use of this terminology. Thus Q 2:8-20 is considered by most commentators (see EXEGESIS OF THE QURʾĀN: CLASSICAL AND MEDIEVAL; EXEGESIS OF THE QURʾĀN: EARLY MODERN AND CONTEMPORARY), e.g. al-Ṭabarī (d. 310/923), al-Ṭūṣī (d. 460/1067), al-Ṭabarsī (d. 518/1153), al-Zamakhsharī (d. 583/1144), al-Rāzī (d. 606/1210), al-Qurṭubī (d. 671/1272), Ibn Kathīr (d. 774/1373), *Jalālayn,* al-Suyūṭī (d. 911/1505), Sayyid Quṭb (d. 1966), al-Ṭabāṭabāʾī (d. 1982), to be a description of the hypocrites, though some (e.g. Muḥammad ʿAbduh) take it to refer to the Jews (see JEWS AND JUDAISM) of Medina, who were their allies. Since this is apparently the first reference to the hypocrites, many exegetes use this opportunity to expound their views on the issue and to define the phenomenon (see e.g. the lengthy exposé in Rāzī, *Tafsīr,* ad loc.). Others reserve this for their discussion of Q 63 (e.g. Ṭabāṭabāʾī, *Mīzān,* xix, 287-90).

Other apparent references to the hypocrites are Q 3:118-20, 152-8, 176-9; 8:49-55; 9:107-10. (For a complete list and discussion of these passages, see Maydānī, *Ẓāhirat al-nifāq.*) Traditionally, all passages referring to the hypocrites have been considered Medinan (see CHRONOLOGY AND THE QUR'ĀN), both by Muslim commentators and by modern scholars. Accordingly both groups identify them as the Muslim opponents of Muḥammad in Medina, those who only half-heartedly accepted him and his message, and did so for worldly gain and in order to safeguard their position in the community, which they would otherwise have lost. When their expectations were not met, they turned against Muḥammad (see OPPOSITION TO MUḤAMMAD). According to Fazlur Rahman (*Major themes*, 160-1), however, hypocrisy was a feature already present among Muḥammad's adherents in Mecca: contrary to the commonly held view, he believes that Q 22:53-4, 29:1-10, and 74:31 date from the period before the emigration (q.v.; *hijra*) from Mecca to Medina. In Rahman's view, the hypocrites of Mecca were weak and fickle-minded people who succumbed to the pressure exerted by their pagan relatives and townsmen to abandon Islam. The accepted opinion, however, is that the term hypocrites did not include Muslims from Mecca, since they were all sincere and had no wealth or power to gain from joining Muḥammad (see Ibn Kathīr, *Tafsīr*, i, 47).

The Qur'ān does not mention any names, but a long list of Muslim hypocrites and their Jewish patrons and allies may be found in the biography of the Prophet (*sīra*, Ibn Isḥāq, *Sīra*, 351-63; Ibn Isḥāq-Guillaume 242-7; see SĪRA AND THE QUR'ĀN). Here, the undisputed leader of the Medinan dissenters is identified as ʿAbdallāh b. Ubayy b. Salūl (see Watt, ʿAbd Allāh b. Ubayy), whose political ambitions were thwarted by the arrival of Muḥammad (see the account in Ibn Isḥāq, *Sīra*, 411-3; Ibn Isḥāq-Guillaume 277-9). Ibn Ubayy was not only thought to have been involved in the slanderous accusations (apparently alluded to in Q 24:23-6) that almost ruined the reputation of the Prophet's wife ʿĀ'isha (Ibn Isḥāq, *Sīra*, 731-40; Ibn Isḥāq-Guillaume 493-9; see ʿĀ'ISHA BINT ABĪ BAKR; GOSSIP; WIVES OF THE PROPHET), he also sided with the Jews of Medina and the Meccan opponents of Muḥammad. According to the *sīra* literature, Ibn Ubayy promised to come to the aid of the Jews of Naḍīr (q.v.) if Muḥammad were to confront them, but he subsequently abandoned them in their hour of need. Q 59:11-2 is taken as a reference to this (see Ibn Isḥāq, *Sīra*, 652-5; Ibn Isḥāq-Guillaume 437 f.).

The hypocrites are described in the Qur'ān as follows: they pretend to believe in God's revelations but turn to the false deities they were ordered to abjure (see IDOLS AND IMAGES). When invited by Muḥammad to accept God and his messenger (q.v.), they turn away from him with aversion. But God knows what is in their hearts. They should be opposed and admonished (Q 4:60-3). For them will be a painful doom (see REWARD AND PUNISHMENT). They seek to lead the believers astray (q.v.). They attempt to beguile God, but it is he who will beguile them. They perform their prayer (q.v.) languidly and more in order to be seen by others than to worship God. They will go to hell (q.v.), along with the unbelievers, and will be in the deepest fire (q.v.), except those of them who repent and make amends, for the repentent will be counted among the believers and will be rewarded by God (Q 4:140-6). Their true feelings become apparent when they are called upon to fight and defend the community: they make up all kinds of excuses in order to avoid participation in warfare (Q 3:166-8; see FIGHTING; EXPEDITIONS AND BATTLES). This enables God to distinguish the true believers from the lukewarm ones. They look impressive and sound sincere, but they are like decorated blocks of wood.

Although a number of verses (viz. Q 3:167; 4:143) suggest that the hypocrites occupy an intermediary position between believers and unbelievers, they are often condemned together with the declared unbelievers. The Prophet and/or the Muslims are admonished to avoid both these groups which are headed for the same punishment, or to fight them (e.g. Q 9:68, 73; 66:9). Hypocritical men and women alike are cursed by God and will eternally taste the fire of hell, since all of them are transgressors, enjoining the wrong and forbidding the right, and being stingy (Q 9:67-8; 33:73; 48:6; and cf. 57:13; see GOOD AND EVIL; ETHICS AND THE QURʾĀN). They converted only because they expected that God would enrich them (Q 9:74), but turned against Muḥammad at the first sign of adversity (Q 29:10-1). In their disappointment, they call Muḥammad's promises a delusion (Q 33:12; 8:49).

The hypocrites are sometimes called "those in whose hearts is a disease" (see ILLNESS AND HEALTH). At times these terms appear together (as in Q 33:12, 60), though often only the second epithet is mentioned; in such cases, many take the verse in question as an additional reference to the hypocrites (see *Jalālayn* on Q 2:10; 5:52; 9:125; 33:32; 47:20). The hypocrites do not believe, yet they are afraid that Muḥammad will receive a revelation (see REVELATION AND INSPIRATION) concerning them, in which their true feelings will be uncovered (Q 9:64). Although most verses featuring hypocrites appear to refer to the waverers and backsliders among the tribes of Medina, some specifically mention "the wandering Arabs (q.v.)," i.e. the Bedouin (q.v.) of the surrounding desert. Of them it is said that they are harder in disbelief and hypocrisy, and more likely to be ignorant of the limits revealed by God (Q 9:97-101).

The testimony of ḥadīth

The ḥadīth collections contain numerous traditions concerning the *munāfiqūn* that condemn them in no uncertain terms (for an inventory see Wensinck, *Concordance*, iii, 523-7; id., *Handbook*, 171; see ḤADĪTH AND THE QURʾĀN). The *Ṣaḥīḥ*s of al-Bukhārī and Muslim each contain a section on the characteristics of the hypocrites, but the most rewarding source is *Ṣifat al-munāfiq* by al-Firyābī, which contains a large collection of logia attributed to the Prophet, his Companions and the subsequent generation (see COMPANIONS OF THE PROPHET). The hypocrites are compared with sheep going astray, joining first one flock, then another. The Prophet warned that they would be the worst plague to hit his community after his death. Various frequently cited traditions describe the characteristics of the hypocrite, e.g. "when he speaks, he lies (see LIE); when he makes a contract, he deceives (see BREAKING TRUSTS AND CONTRACTS); when he promises, he fails to fulfill his promise (see OATHS AND PROMISES), and when he litigates, he is dishonest." Among the authorities quoted by al-Firyābī, al-Ḥasan al-Baṣrī takes pride of place. Al-Ḥasan is known to have held the view that the grave sinner is neither a believer nor an unbeliever but something in between, a hypocrite. The Muʿtazila (see MUʿTAZILĪS) developed this teaching of the intermediate position of the sinner, replacing the term *munāfiq* with *fāsiq*. (On the views of al-Ḥasan and his student ʿAmr b. ʿUbayd, see van Ess, *TG*, ii, 256 f., 263; v, 141 f., 148, 174.)

The status of the hypocrites in this world and the next

Even though the Qurʾān seems to be quite explicit on the fate of the hypocrites in the hellfire of the hereafter, this did not prevent (mostly sectarian) theologians from discussing this matter. After all, strictly speaking, the hypocrites are not unbelievers, since, unlike the latter, they do pronounce the witness to faith (q.v.; *shahāda*) and observe the precepts of Islam, even if this is not backed up by belief in their hearts. For this reason, some theologians were prepared to make allowances for them and to accord them the status of believers, not only in this world, but also in the afterlife (see Ashʿarī, *Maqālāt,* 141; Baghdādī, *Farq,* 9).

As for the hypocrites' status in the present world, since outwardly they behave as true Muslims, it is difficult to tell them apart from the believers and to treat them differently. As long as they keep their views to themselves and do not abandon the precepts of Islam, they are to enjoy their full rights as Muslims: they inherit from Muslims (see INHERITANCE), may marry Muslim women (see MARRIAGE AND DIVORCE), share in the booty (q.v.) captured on military campaigns, and are entitled to a Muslim funeral (see DEATH AND THE DEAD). The moment they display their true colors, however, they should be invited to repent (see REPENTANCE AND PENANCE), and failure to do so may result in the death penalty (see Qurṭubī, *Jāmiʿ,* i, 194; Ibn Kathir, *Tafsīr,* i, 48 f.; van Ess, *TG,* v, 149; see CHASTISEMENT AND PUNISHMENT).

"Hypocrites" as a pejorative term for one's opponents

Using the term hypocrite soon became a convenient way of denouncing one's opponents and discrediting them. Thus the Shīʿīs in general (see SHĪʿISM AND THE QURʾĀN), and the Ismāʿīlīs in particular, are called *munāfiqūn* by Sunnī authors, often in combination with an additional pejorative epithet, such as *zanādiqa* (heretics, freethinkers; see HERESY), *kāfirūn* (unbelievers), *mushrikūn* (polytheists; see POLYTHEISM AND ATHEISM) or *malāḥida* (heretics; e.g. Ibn Taymiyya, *Majmūʿ al-fatāwā,* xxvii, 525). All those who disagree with the *ahl al-ḥadīth,* too, are termed hypocrites. Of course every group calls its own opponents hypocrites, and the taxonomy varies between Sunnīs and Shīʿīs. Thus the Rawāfiḍ, who deny the legitimacy of the first three rightly-guided *(rāshidūn)* caliphs (see CALIPH), are called hypocrites by the Sunnīs, while they in turn apply this name to the ones who deprived ʿAlī of his rights (Van Ess, *TG,* i, 308; v, 98; see ʿALĪ B. ABĪ ṬĀLIB).

In modern times, too, various groups have been branded as *munāfiqūn,* even if they did not necessarily pretend to be Muslims. Thus the Freemasons, the Rotary Club, the Lions, the Communists and Jehovah's Witnesses — strange bedfellows, to say the least — are denounced by a modern Muslim commentator as hypocrites who are intent on destroying religion and society from within (Maydānī, *Ẓāhirat al-nifāq,* ii, 631-75). They are said to take their orders from "the Jews." Sayyid Quṭb talks about the importance of tracing the hypocrites in society so as to put a stop to their destructive activities. He, too, mentions a Jewish connection, and counts the Communists among the modern-day *munāfiqūn,* clearly indicating the politico-historical contextualizing of the word (see CONTEMPORARY CRITICAL PRACTICES AND THE QURʾĀN).

"Hypocrites" are held responsible for every disaster that has befallen the Muslim community since the death of the Prophet and that has struck at its cohesion, from the creation of sects and the incorporation of Jewish and Christian practices to the reconquest of al-Andalus. They are described as a fifth column whose purpose is to undermine Islam and Muslim society, often at the orders of some foreign power.

An example of such paranoia is the claim of an unnamed Pakistani official that the success of the Spanish Christians — aided by hypocrites — in getting rid of the Muslims of al-Andalus inspired the government of India to send a fact-finding mission to Spain in order to find out how India can deal with its Muslim neighbor (see Maydānī, *Ẓāhirat al-nifāq*, i, 21 f.).

Camilla P. Adang

Bibliography

Primary: al-Ashʿarī, Abū l-Ḥasan ʿAlī b. Ismāʿīl, *Kitāb Maqālāt al-islāmiyyīn wa-ikhtilāf al-muṣallīn*, ed. H. Ritter, Wiesbaden 1963; Baghdādī, *Farq*, Beirut 1978; Bukhārī, *Ṣaḥīḥ*, ed. ʿA.ʿA. Ibn ʿAbdallāh b. Bāz, 8 vols. and *Fihrist*, Beirut 1991; al-Firyābī, Abū Bakr Jaʿfar b. Muḥammad, *Ṣifat al-munāfiq*, ed. B. al-Badr, Kuwait 1984; Ibn al-Jawzī, *Zād*, 9 vols., Beirut 1984; Ibn Kathīr, *Tafsīr*, 4 vols., Cairo n.d.; Ibn Taymiyya, *Majmūʿ al-fatāwā*; *Jalālayn*, Beirut 1987; *Lisān al-ʿArab*, Beirut 1388/1968, x, 357-61; Muslim, *Ṣaḥīḥ Muslim bi-sharḥ al-Imām al-Nawawī*, ed. Ṣ.M. Jamīl al-ʿAṭṭār, 9 vols., Beirut 1995; Qurṭubī, *Jāmiʿ*, ed. Ṣ.M. Jamīl and ʿI. al-ʿAshā, 10 vols., Beirut 1414/1993; Quṭb, *Ẓilāl*, 8 vols., Cairo n.d.; Rashīd Riḍā, *Manār*, 12 vols., Beirut n.d.; Rāzī, *Tafsīr*, 30 vols., Tehran n.d.; Ṭabarī, *The commentary on the Qurʾān by (...) al-Ṭabarī. Being an abridged translation of* Jāmiʿ al-bayān ʿan taʾwīl āy al-Qurʾān, trans. J. Cooper (abr. with intro.), 1 vol. to date, Oxford 1987-; id., *Tafsīr*, 30 vols., Bulaq 1905-11, repr. Beirut 1972; Ṭabarsī, *Majmaʿ*, 30 vols., Beirut 1380/1961; Ṭabāṭabāʾī, *Mīzān*, 20 vols., Beirut 1393-4/1973-4; Ṭūsī, *Tibyān*, ed. A.Ḥ. Quṣayr al-ʿĀmilī, 10 vols., Beirut n.d.

Secondary: M.M. Ayoub, *The Qurʾan and its interpreters. ii. The house of ʿImrān*, Albany 1992, passim (for a discussion of the views of a number of exegetes on the relevant passages in Q 3); A. Brockett, al-Munāfiḳūn, in *EI²*, vii, 561-2 (general background); K. Cragg, *The mind of the Qurʾān. Chapters in reflection*, London 1972, 102-5 (on *nifāq* as a form of unbelief); R. Deladrière, Riyāʾ, in *EI²*, viii, 547 (general background); van Ess, *TG* (provides representative texts from various religious groups, with full bibliography); G. Hawting, *The idea of idolatry and the emergence of Islam. From polemic to history*, Cambridge 1999; Izutsu, *Concepts*, 178-83 and passim (on *nifāq* as a form of unbelief); ʿA.Ḥ. Ḥabannaka al-Maydānī, *Ẓāhirat al-nifāq wa-khabāʾith al-munāfiqīn fi-l-taʾrīkh*, 2 vols., Damascus 1993 (for a contemporary Muslim's view); Fazlur Rahman, *Major themes of the Qurʾān*, Minneapolis, Chicago 1980, 158-61 (discusses the possibility that Meccan Islam, too, had its hypocrites); R.B. Serjeant, The *sunnah jāmiʿah* pacts with the Yathrib Jews, and the *taḥrīm* of Yathrib. Analysis and translation of the documents comprised in the so-called "Constitution of Medina," in *BSOAS* 41 (1978), 1-42, repr. in U. Rubin (ed.), *The life of Muḥammad*, Aldershot 1998, 151-92 (on the possible origin of the term *munāfiq*); W.M. Watt, ʿAbd Allāh b. Ubayy, in *EI²*, i, 59 (deals with the leader of the Medinan dissenters); see Wensinck, *Concordance* (for an inventory of prophetic traditions on the hypocrites); id., *Handbook* (for an inventory of prophetic traditions on the hypocrites); id., *The Muslim creed. Its genesis and historical development*, Cambridge 1932 (discussion of theological perspectives).

I

Ibāḍīs see KHĀRIJĪS

Iblīs

The devil, mentioned by name eleven times in the Qurʾān. Given its form, the word is likely a corruption of the Greek *diabolos* used in Christian writing to denote the adversary of humans, a sense which continues in the Qurʾān. For further discussion, see DEVIL.

Andrew Rippin

Bibliography

Imām Ḥanafī Sayyid ʿAbdallāh, *Iblīs fī l-taṣawwur al-islāmī bayna l-ḥaqīqa wa-l-wahm*, Cairo 2001 (includes al-Imām Aḥmad b. Yaḥyā [al-Zaydī]'s *al-Radd ʿalā masāʾil al-mujbira*); Jeffery, *For. vocab.*, 47-8; W.S. Bodman, Stalking Iblīs. In search of an Islamic theodicy, in A. Neuwirth et al (eds.), *Myths, historical archetypes and symbolic figures in Arabic literature. Towards a new hermeneutical approach*, Beirut 1999, 247-69.

Iconoclasm

Opposition to the religious use of images. The term "iconoclasm," which literally means "image breaking," became a religious and socio-political movement in the eighth and ninth century C.E. The Byzantine empire (see BYZANTINES) under the pretext of its opposition to icons turned officially against many forms of spirituality, including the cults of saints and monasticism, for more than a century (726-843 C.E.; see MONASTICISM AND MONKS). Inasmuch as opposition to icons had been expressed long before the rise of Islam, any relationship between Byzantine iconoclasm and the Qurʾān must be seen as peripheral and coincidental, albeit cross-cultural.

On the evidence of its artistic history Islam may be called aniconic rather than iconoclastic (Grabar, Islam and iconoclasm, 51). It has opposed the creation of naturalistic-representational art, and has criticized the images themselves as irrelevant objects, unable to capture reality, and as temptations away from the requirements of a good life, rather than as evil per se (see GOOD AND EVIL). In no way does the Qurʾān argue about icons, in the doctrinal sense in which Byzantine theologians like Leontius of Neapolis (ca. 590-ca. 650 C.E.) and John of Damascus (ca. 655-ca. 749 C.E.) engaged themselves. The Qurʾān is preoccupied with the unbelief of pre-Islamic Arabs and their worship of and attachment to pagan deities and their idols (see BELIEF AND UNBELIEF; POLYTHEISM AND ATHEISM; IDOLS AND IMAGES;

IDOLATRY AND IDOLATERS; SOUTH ARABIA, RELIGION IN PRE-ISLAMIC). Deities are false gods (Q 21:52-4, 57) and idols (Q 53:19-20 regarding al-Lāt, al-ʿUzzā and Manāt; Q 71:23 regarding Wadd, Suwāʿ, Yaghūth, Yaʿūq, and Nasr [the gods of the people of Noah, q.v.]; Q 16:36 and 39:17 regarding *al-ṭāghūt,* or "false gods"). No distinction is made in the Qurʾān between a prototype and an image, a distinction made by Byzantine iconophiles in difference to the emperor Constantine V Copronymus (741-75 C.E.), who, with his fellow iconoclasts, equated the icon of Christ with Christ himself and for this they rejected his icon. Equally, if God is the one and only God, all other deities are false and idols simply represent this falsehood (Q 21:52; 25:3). Byzantine iconophiles, too, distinguished icons from idols, applying the latter only to pagan gods (cf. the definition of the second Council of Nicaea in Sahas, *Icon and logos,* 149-50). There would therefore seem to be a convergence here between iconophile and qurʾānic thought.

Deities and idols are themselves created beings (Q 25:3); thus, making and worshipping idols constitute acts of *shirk* in two ways: by worshipping (the Qurʾān makes no distinction between worship [q.v.] and veneration, Q 21:52) created things or beings, and by presuming to create them — a prerogative of God alone, "Who created the heavens and the earth in truth" (Q 6:73; see CREATION). The Qurʾān — with a most telling rhetorical question — stifles the potential claim to creativity by any artist: "Do you worship that which you have carved out... when God has created you and what you make?" (Q 37:96). Idol or image making compromises the uniqueness and unity *(tawḥīd)* of God who is "the creator, the shaper out of nothing, the fashioner" (*muṣawwir,* Q 59:24; see GOD AND HIS ATTRIBUTES). Those who worship idols become attached *(ʿākif)* and "are given up" to them (Q 7:138; 21:52; 26:71). If, indeed, there are four forces of Muslim social ethos — moralism, populism, factualism, historialism — which operate against images (Hodgson, Islām and image, 228-9), the Qurʾān seems to support all four (see COMMUNITY AND SOCIETY IN THE QURʾĀN; ETHICS AND THE QURʾĀN). The Qurʾān leads then to the rejection of "the pollution of the idols" and "any word of falsehood" (Q 22:30; see LIE). An interesting modification is the assertion that Abraham (q.v.) destroyed his kin's idols, but he left one "that haply they might have recourse to it" (Q 21:58). Similarly, an understanding of the human need for tangible manifestations may have played some role in Muḥammad's own concession to the intercession of the "daughters of Allāh" for the sake of his Meccan compatriots, implied in the so-called "satanic verses (q.v.)" of the Qurʾān (Q 53:19-20 and 22:52).

If the Qurʾān knows anything about Byzantine iconoclasm and the theological thinking that goes with it, this is nowhere immediately evident. A possible, albeit cursory, reference to the Christian devotion to icons may be found in Q 25:1-3. This is a praise to God "who... has chosen no son [a possible reference to the Christian belief in Jesus (q.v.) as the Son of God] nor has he any partner in the sovereignty... Yet they [the Christians?] choose beside him other gods who create nothing..., possess not hurt nor profit for themselves, and possess not death nor life, nor power to raise the dead" (Q 25:1-3) — a possible inference to populist Christian beliefs about the powers of icons (see CHRISTIANS AND CHRISTIANITY).

In response to the clear qurʾānic insistence that Jesus as a true prophet was not crucified (Q 4:157; see CRUCIFIXION; PROPHETS AND PROPHETHOOD), Muslims reject the cross and its veneration. In 103-4/721 Caliph Yazīd II (r. 101-5/720-4) decreed its destruction from all churches under his rule (Theophanes, i, 401-2). By coincidence or imitation and only a short while later (108-9/726) emperor Leo III the Isaurian (717-41 C.E.) issued the first decree against icons. No wonder that the ninth-century iconophile chronographer Theophanes (i, 405:1; 406:25) branded him and all other iconoclasts as "Saracene-minded." Driven by dynamic monarchic ideas, iconoclasts aimed to bring Christian practice in line with its monotheistic-Semitic background. Paulicians, Jews and Muslims appear, fictitiously or historically, as actively involved in the iconoclastic movement, particularly during the first phase (726-87 C.E.). Modern Byzantinists may be divided on the issue of degree and nature of the Islamic involvement in Byzantine iconoclasm, but they hardly deny the fact of its existence. The opposite has also been suggested (Becker, Christlische Polemik), namely that Byzantine iconoclasm influenced Muslim attitudes towards icons. Byzantine sources point to a Jewish influence on Yazīd and his followers. Evidence has shown (Schick, *Christian communities*) that his edict gave the pretext not only to Jews and Muslims, but also to iconoclast Christians in the lands conquered by the Arabs, to destroy mosaics and icons. A curious historical irony remains, however, that the "iconoclast" Muslim world early on provided a haven for the most ardent Byzantine iconophiles to fight their imperial adversaries with impunity behind the security of Muslim borders (Sahas, *John of Damascus,* 12). Muslim sources, interested mostly in matters of Byzantine-Arab border warfare (see EXPEDITIONS AND BATTLES), bypass iconoclasm as an internal and "idolatrous" affair of Byzantium.

Daniel J. Sahas

Bibliography

Primary: al-Balādhurī, *The origins of the Islamic state,* trans. P.K. Hitti, New York 1916; Ibn al-Kalbī, Hishām, *The book of idols,* trans. N.A. Fāris, Princeton 1952; *Kitāb al-ʿUyūn wa-l-ḥadāʾiq fī akhbar al-ḥaqāʾiq,* in M.J. de Goeje (ed.), *Fragmenta historicorum arabicorum. Tomus primus,* Leiden 1869; Masʿūdi, *Kitāb al-Tanbīh wa-l-ishrāf,* ed. M.J. de Goeje, 1894; id. *Le livre de l'avertissement et de la révision,* trans. B. Carra de Vaux, Paris 1896, repr. Frankfurt am Main 1986; Ṭabarī, *Taʾrīkh,* ed. M.J. de Goeje; Yaʿqūbī, *Taʾrīkh.*

Secondary: L.W. Barnard, *The Graeco-Roman and oriental background of the iconoclastic controversy,* Leiden 1974; C.H. Becker, Christlische Polemik und islamische Dogmenbildung, in *Zeitschrift für Assyriologie* 26 (1912), 191-5; K.A.C. Creswell, The lawfulness of painting in early Islam, in *Ars Islamica* 11/12 (1946), 159-66; P. Crone, Islam, Judaeo-Christianity and Byzantine iconoclasm, in *JSAI* 2 (1980), 59-95; S. Gero, *Byzantine iconoclasm during the reign of Constantine V. With particular attention to the oriental sources,* Louvain 1977; id., *Byzantine iconoclasm during the reign of Leo III. With particular attention to the oriental sources,* Louvain 1973; id., Early contacts between Byzantium and the Arab empire. A review and some reconsiderations, in M.A. Bakhit (ed.), *Proceedings of the second symposium on the history of Bilād al-Shām during the early Islamic period up to 40g A.H./640 A.D.,* vol. 1, Amman 1987, 125-32; O. Grabar, *L'iconoclasme byzantin. Dossier archéologique,* Paris 1957; id., Islam and iconoclasm, in A. Bryer and J. Herrin (eds.), *Iconoclasm,* Birmingham 1977, 45-52; id., Islamic art and Byzantium, in *Dumbarton Oaks papers* 18 (1964), 69-88; G.E. von Grunebaum, Byzantine iconoclasm and the influence of the Islamic environment, in *History of religions* 2 (1962), 1-10; J. Guttman (ed.), *The image and the world. Confrontations in Judaism, Christianity and Islam,* Missoula 1977; M.G.S. Hodgson, Islām and image, in *History of religions* 3 (1963-4), 220-60; G.R.D. King, Islam, iconoclasm, and the declaration of doctrine, in *BSOAS* 48 (1985), 267-77; D. van Reenen, The *Bilderverbot.* A new survey, in *Der Islam* 67 (1990), 27-77; D.J. Sahas, *John of Damascus on Islam. The "heresy of the Ishmaelites,"* Leiden 1972; id., *Icon and logos. Sources in eighth-century iconoclasm,* Toronto 1986; R. Schick, *The Christian communities of Palestine from Byzantine to Islamic rule. A historical and archaeological study,* Princeton 1995; A.A. Vasiliev, The iconoclastic edict of the caliph Yazid II. A.D. 721, in *Dumbarton Oaks papers* 9/10 (1956), 23-47.

Idolatry and Idolaters

Worship of a created thing as a god; those who engage in such worship. The Arabic root used most frequently in the Qurʾān in words and expressions suggestive of the idea of idolatry is *sh-r-k*. That root commonly appears in Arabic in various words connected with the idea of "sharing, participating, associating," etc., and the basic level of meaning is often appropriate, too, in qurʾānic passages. For example, the noun *shirk* seems to mean something like "partnership" or "portion" in "do they [those upon whom you call beside God] have any *shirk* in the heavens?" (Q 35:40; 46:4; see HEAVEN AND SKY). The root has come to be connected with the idea of idolatry since, from the monotheist point of view, one of the things the idolater does is to "associate" other things (supernatural beings, ideas, people, institutions, as well as natural or man-made objects) with God as objects of worship (q.v.) or sources of power. The word *shirk* is used in that sense at Q 31:13: "Do not associate anything with God *(lā tushrik bi-llāhi)* for *shirk* is a grave evil."

Words and expressions involving use of the root *sh-r-k* are relatively frequent in the Qurʾān, generally in passages directed against opponents accused of associating others with God as objects of worship and prayers. *Shirk* itself occurs five times (Q 31:13; 34:22; 35:14, 40; 46:4); *sharīk* and its plural *shurakāʾ*, usually referring to those beings which the opponents (see OPPOSITION TO MUḤAMMAD) are accused of associating with God, forty times; the fourth verbal form *ashraka* in various tenses, moods and persons, usually referring to the act of associating something with God, seventy-one times; and its active participle *mushrik*, in its singular and plural, masculine and feminine, forms, forty-nine times. In English versions of the Qurʾān, Arabic words and phrases referring to those who commit *shirk*, such as *al-mushrikūn* or *alladhīna ashrakū*, are often understood or translated as "the idolaters." However, partly because *shirk* and idolatry are not semantic equivalents, the former may frequently also be translated by other terms, particularly "polytheism" (see POLYTHEISM AND ATHEISM). The *mushrik* acts as if there were divine beings other than God and may, therefore, be viewed as a polytheist as much as an idolater.

Outside the Qurʾān *shirk* is often used in a sense partly or wholly equivalent to that of "idolatry." Modern Arabic, however, regularly uses instead words or phrases such as *ʿibādat al-aṣnām* or *al-wathaniyya*, which, building upon one or the other of the two most common Arabic words for "idol" *(ṣanam* and *wathan)*, are more parallel semantically to the English word and its equivalent in other European languages. Although both *ṣanam* and *wathan* occur in the Qurʾān, no expression based on them appears there to indicate the abstract idea of "idolatry." Another qurʾānic term that conveys the idea of something other than God being worshiped is *tamāthīl*, lit. "likenesses," as in Q 21:52, where it designates the objects of Abraham's [q.v.] father's worship (cf. Q 34:13, where the same word is used in reference to objects that the jinn [q.v.] create for Solomon [q.v.]). The word *andād* ("peers" or "equals") is also important in the way in which the charge of idolatry or polytheism is made against the *mushrikūn* in the Qurʾān (Q 2:22, 165; 14:30; 34:33; 39:8; 41:9). It often functions as a parallel to *shurakāʾ*. The opponents are attacked for setting up *andād* before or other than God *(dūna llāhi)*. Compare, for example, Q 39:8, which tells us that the opponents turn to God when they are distressed but forget him once he has responded to them and accept "equals" *(andād)* with him, with Q 29:61-5 (see below) which makes the same charge in different terms and accuses the opponents of *shirk*.

In the Qurʾān, therefore, the opponents to whom pejorative reference is made by expressions such as *al-mushrikūn* are accused of "associating" other beings with God as objects of worship and prayer. That is the essence of *shirk* in the Qurʾān: it is not that the *mushrik* is unaware of God as the creator and controller of the cosmos or that he believes that God is simply one of a number of beings with equal or equivalent powers, but rather that in his behavior and attitudes he proceeds as if other beings, supernatural or perhaps sometimes human, have powers which a true monotheist would recognize as belonging to God alone. Sometimes, for example, the *mushrikūn* are accused of expecting that beings such as angels (see ANGEL) will intercede for them with God at the last judgment (q.v.) and that their intercession (q.v.) will succeed (e.g. Q 16:86, 18:52; 41:47). In the Qurʾān it is denied that such intercession will avail unless God permits it: the reliance which the *mushrikūn* place on these mediators will in fact lead to their damnation because by relying on them they are failing to be true monotheists.

Shirk in the Qurʾān, therefore, may be understood as an equivalent of idolatry in a partial and extended sense of that latter term that, at a basic level, implies the worship of, and attribution of power to, a concrete and inanimate object. Although Muslim tradition and, following it, much modern scholarship, regard as idolaters in that more basic sense, too, the *mushrikūn* who are attacked in the Qurʾān, it is at least questionable whether that view is justified. The Qurʾān itself says little which would unambiguously justify the conclusion that the *mushrikūn* used idols (statues or other sorts of images) to represent the beings that they are accused of associating with God. It is mainly the accusation that they treat things not divine as if they were — the charge that they associate other things with God — that lies behind the translation of *mushrik* as "idolater" as far as the Qurʾān is concerned.

The charge of "idolatry" in this sense (and probably in any sense) may be an element of inter-religious polemic (see POLEMIC AND POLEMICAL LANGUAGE). Polemically, the basic meaning of idolatry has been extended to cover diverse beliefs and practices viewed as erroneous, such as, for example, the use of icons and images as devotional aids or the view that angels and saints can intercede with God on behalf of the believer. Those who have been accused of idolatry because of their acceptance of such practices and views would deny that they were idolaters and, from the viewpoint of an observer not personally involved in the polemic, may be justified in offering such a denial. What looks like idolatry to one party seems like perfectly good monotheism to the other.

In Islam the charge of *shirk* is used polemically in the same way as that of the accusation of idolatry in branches of monotheism which use European languages, it being directed at other monotheists, often other Muslims, as often as at people who could legitimately be seen as idolaters in any real sense. That polemical sense of *shirk* should be borne in mind when considering the qurʾānic usage.

It is true that the Qurʾān itself sometimes goes beyond accusing the *mushrikūn* of acting like idolaters and polytheists and implies that they were so in the literal and basic sense. That may be understood as the polemical tactic of omitting comparative particles and phrases and of using language which portrays the opponents as really worshipping a plurality of gods and as being connected with idol worship. They are accused, for instance, of associating other gods with God (e.g. Q 6:22; 10:28) and of calling upon their associates "before" or "other than" God (e.g. Q 10:66; 16:86). As for their being connected with idols, it is notable that the words used to suggest the idea of "idol" tend to be *ṭāghūt* and *jibt* rather than the common Arabic (plurals) *awthān* or *aṣnām*. In pre-Islamic monotheist usage the former pair of words had acquired connotations of idolatry by extension from more literal and basic meanings (see IDOLS AND IMAGES).

It is, however, in the traditional literature outside the Qurʾān (exegetical works *[tafsīr]* but also the traditional material on the life of the Prophet and accounts of pre-Islamic Arabia) that the *mushrikūn* of the Qurʾān have come to be portrayed more consistently as idolaters in the basic sense of the term. In the traditional material the idea, which we often receive in the Qurʾān, that the *mushrikūn* were fundamentally imperfect monotheists who allowed themselves to be misled into associating the worship of other beings with that of God, recedes. Instead they are presented much more as idolaters in a very literal and crude sense. The qurʾānic *mushrikūn* are depicted in extra-qurʾānic tradition as the Meccan and other Arab contemporaries of the Prophet whose religion consisted of worshipping idols and a multiplicity of gods. For example, Q 29:61-5 is a passage that accuses the opponents, although they will admit that God is the creator of the heavens and the earth and the source of the earth's fertility (see CREATION; COSMOLOGY), and although they will call upon God for protection (q.v.) in times of danger upon the sea, of lapsing into *shirk* in normal circumstances. It is a passage that contrasts *shirk* not really with mere monotheism *(tawḥīd)* but with true, pure monotheism *(ikhlāṣ)*. The passage does not explicitly refer to idols or to a belief in a plurality of gods as features of the opponents' religious ideas and behavior, but simply contrasts their theoretical and occasional *ikhlāṣ* with their practical and normal *shirk*.

In a gloss of this passage offered by al-Ṭabarī (d. 310/923) in his Qurʾān commentary, however, we find a much more explicit identification of the opponents as worshippers of idols and gods other than God. Adapting Q 39:3, al-Ṭabarī tells us that these opponents think that by worshipping gods other than God they can achieve a closeness and a nearness to God *(yaḥsabūna annahum li-ʿibādatihim al-āliha dūna llāhi yanālūna ʿinda llāhi zulfatan wa-qurbatan);* when travelling on the sea they do not call for help from their gods and those whom they regard as equals of God *(ālihatahum wa-andādahum);* but, once God has brought them safely back to land, they associate a partner *(sharīk)* with him in their acts of worship and pray to their gods and idols *(āliha wa-awthān)* together with him as lords (see LORD).

The *shirk* attacked in the Qurʾān is thus portrayed as a literal and explicit idolatry and polytheism *(ʿibādat al-awthān wa-l-āliha)*. That particular gloss does not tell us precisely who these polytheists and idolaters were but in others, al-Ṭabarī and other traditional scholars frequently make it clear that the Qurʾān is referring to the idolaters and polytheists among the Meccans and other Arab contemporaries of Muḥammad. An example of this type of identification, to be found in the traditional biographical literature on the life of the Prophet as well as in the *tafsīr* literature, explains an obscure practice attacked in Q 6:136. That verse tells us that the opponents divide a part of their agricultural produce between God and their "associates" *(shurakāʾ)* but when they make the division they do so unfairly, favoring the "associates" at the expense of God. In a story that is intended to elucidate the verse and which uses some of the same terminology, a report in the *Sīra* of Ibn Isḥāq tells us that it concerns the tribe of Khawlān and an idol of theirs called ʿUmyānis (the reading of the name is uncertain). When Khawlān apportioned their "tithes" between God and ʿUmyānis they would favor the idol so that if any of the share destined for the idol fell into that intended for God they would retrieve it and make sure that the idol received it; but if any intended for God fell into the portion of the idol, they would let it remain there and the idol would thus receive what was really God's. In this and similar stories the obscure qurʾānic *shurakāʾ* are identified as idols and the allusive and ambiguous qurʾānic verse is explained as referring to the Age of Ignorance (q.v.; *jāhiliyya*) as it was traditionally understood.

Traditional Islamic literature of various genres contains numerous such stories and elucidation. Sometimes they clearly relate to qurʾānic passages, sometimes they do not seem to have any relationship to a particular passage but could nevertheless be understood as exegetical in a very broad sense in that, taken as a whole, they illustrate and substantiate the traditional view that the *mushrikūn* of the Qurʾān were the idolatrous and polytheistic Arabs (q.v.) of the Ḥijāz and other parts of Arabia in the time of Muḥammad (see SOUTH ARABIA, RELIGION IN PRE-ISLAMIC). In such material *shirk* becomes equivalent to idolatry in its basic sense, not just a concept that overlaps with it and covers some of its extensions. In a report about the Prophet's destruction of idols in the vicinity of the Kaʿba (q.v.) at the time of his conquest of Mecca (q.v.), for example, we are told that Satan called out in woe, despairing that the people of that place would ever again pursue *shirk*.

Whole works came to be composed of such material illustrating and elucidating the religion of the idolatrous Arabs, the best known being the *Kitāb al-Aṣnām* "Book of Idols" attributed to Hishām b. al-Kalbī (d. 206/821). Where *shirk* in the Qurʾān can be understood as a partial equivalent of "idolatry" in some of the polemical senses of the English word, the traditional literature shows us that the *mushrikūn* were idolaters and polytheists of a crude and literal kind and thus makes *shirk* a parallel to "idolatry" in its most basic sense.

In Islam the word *shirk* has sometimes been used with reference to the religion of peoples who, from the monotheist point of view, might be regarded as idolaters in a literal sense — for instance, Hindus or adherents of African religions. More frequently, however, it has maintained the polemical tone which it has in the Qurʾān, for example when one group of Muslims accuses another of *shirk* on account of beliefs or practices which it considers incompatible with pure monotheism or when the Christian doctrine of the Trinity (q.v.) is described as *shirk* (see CHRISTIANS AND CHRISTIANITY).

Modern scholarship has generally accepted the image conveyed by the tradition of the qurʾānic *mushrikūn* as idolaters in a literal sense, and it has used the traditional material as a source of information about the religious ideas and practices which the Qurʾān was attacking. Some scholars, however, have been impressed by the difference in tone between the qurʾānic material pertaining to *shirk* and the *mushrikūn* on the one hand and that of the extra-qurʾānic material on the other, and have sought to account for it in various ways. For example, D.B. Macdonald (Allāh) wrote: "The religion of Mecca in Muḥammad's time was far from simple idolatry. It resembled much more a form of the Christian faith, in which saints and angels have come to stand between the worshippers and God." The relationship between the qurʾānic and the extra-qurʾānic material is complicated, however, by the fact that the latter, alongside its representation of the *mushrikūn* as Arab idolaters in the crude and basic sense, also presents some material which reports monotheist ideas and practices among the pre-Islamic Arabs. For example, we are told that there were individuals known as *ḥanīfs* (see ḤANĪF) who had abandoned idolatry and turned to monotheism and that even the pagan Arabs maintained certain practices (such as the *talbiya,* the repeated invocation made by pilgrims as they enter the state of ritual purity) which were fundamentally monotheistic but had been corrupted by idolatrous and polytheistic accretions. Generally, these elements of monotheism are explained in the tradition as survivals of the pure monotheism that had been brought to Arabia in the remote past by Abraham (Ibrāhīm). Over time this monotheism had been corrupted by idolatry but elements of it still survived in the time of the prophet Muḥammad, whose task it was to restore it and cleanse it of the idolatrous accretions.

Most frequently, academic scholarship has sought to harmonize all this possibly inconsistent material by applying to it evolutionary theories of religion and suggesting that in the time of Muḥammad the Arabs were evolving out of a polytheistic and idolatrous stage of religion into a monotheistic one. In this scheme the career of the Prophet and the birth of Islam are seen as the culmination of a process which had been taking place for some time.

Gerald R. Hawting

Bibliography

Primary: Ibn Isḥāq, *Sīra,* ed. al-Saqqā, i, 80-1 (for the report about ʿUmyānis); Ibn al-Kalbī, Hishām, *The book of idols,* trans. N.A. Fāris, Princeton 1952; id., *Das Götzenbuch. Kitāb al-Aṣnām des Ibn al-Kalbī,* trans. R. Klinki-Rosenberger (includes Ar. text), Leipzig 1941; id., *Les idoles de Hicham ibn al-Kalbī,* trans. W. Atallah (includes Ar. text), Paris 1969; Ṭabarī, *Tafsīr,* 30 vols., Cairo 1323-8/ 1905-12, xxi, 9 (for the commentary on Q 29:61-5); Wāqidī, *Maghāzī,* 841-2 (= al-Azraqī, *Akhbār Makka,* ed. R. Malḥas, Beirut 1969, i, 122-3; for Satan's cry at the destruction of the Meccan idols).

Secondary: C. Brockelmann, Allah und die Gützen. der Ursprung des islamischen Monotheismus, in *Archiv für Religionswissenschaft* 21 (1922), 99-121 (discussion of the traditional information about pre-Islamic Arab idolatry); T. Fahd, *Le panthéon de l'Arabie centrale à la veille de l'Hégire,* Paris 1968 (discussion of the traditional information about pre-Islamic Arab idolatry); D. Gimaret, Shirk, in *EI²*, ix, 484-6 (on *shirk* in the Qurʾān and in Muslim usage); I. Goldfeld, ʿUmyānis the idol of Khawlān, in *IOS* 3 (1977), 108-19; M. Halbertal and A. Margalit, *Idolatry,* trans. N. Goldblum, Cambridge, MA 1992 (exploration of the concept of idolatry generally); G.R. Hawting, *The idea of idolatry and the emergence of Islam. From polemic to history,* Cambridge 1999; Ibn ʿAbd al-Wahhāb, *Fī arbaʿ qawāʿid al-dīn tamīzu bayna l-muʾminīna wa-l-mushrikūn,* in id., *Majmūʿat al-tawḥīd al-najdiyya,* Mecca 1901; id., *Fī maʿnā al-ṭāghūt wa-ruʾūs anwāʿihi,* in id., *Majmūʿat al-tawḥīd al-najdiyya,* Mecca 1901; id., *Fī tafsīr kalimat al-tawḥīd,* in id., *Majmūʿat al-tawḥīd al-najdiyya,* Mecca 1901; id., *Masāʾil al-jāhiliyya,* in id., *Majmūʿat al-tawḥīd al-najdiyya,* Mecca 1901; H.E. Kassis, *A concordance of the Qurʾān,* Berkeley 1983; M. Lecker, Idol worship in pre-Islamic Medina (Yathrib), in *Muséon* 106 (1993), 331-46 (discussion of the traditional information about pre-Islamic Arab idolatry); D.B. Macdonald, Allāh, in *EI¹*, i, 302-11; H.S. Nyberg, Bemerkungen zum 'Buch der Götzenbilder' von Ibn al-Kalbī, in *Dragma. Martino P. Nilsson. A.D. IV id. jul. MCMXXXIX dedicatum,* Lund 1939, 346-66; G. Ryckmans, *Les religions arabes préislamiques,* Louvain 1951² (discussion of the traditional information about pre-Islamic Arab idolatry); E. Sirriyeh, Modern Muslim interpretations of *shirk,* in *Religion* 20 (1990), 139-59 (on *shirk* in the Qurʾān and in Muslim usage); F. Stummer, Bemerkungen zum Götzenbuch des Ibn al-Kalbī, in *ZDMG* 98 (1944), 377-94; M.I.H. Surty, *The qurʾānic concept of al-shirk (polytheism),* London 1982 (on *shirk* in the Qurʾān and in Muslim usage); J. Waardenburg, Un débat coranique contre les polythéistes, in *Ex orbe religionum. Studia Geo Widengren oblata,* 2 vols., Leiden 1972, ii, 143-54 (on *shirk* in the Qurʾān and in Muslim usage); J. Wansbrough, *The sectarian milieu,* London 1978 (for idolatry as a topic of polemic); A.T. Welch, Allah and other supernatural beings. The emergence of the qurʾānic doctrine of *tawḥīd,* in id. (guest ed.), *Journal of the American Academy of Religion. Thematic issue. Studies in Qurʾān and tafsir* 47 (1979), no. 4 S, 733-53 (on *shirk* in the Qurʾān and in Muslim usage); J. Wellhausen, *Reste arabischen Heidentum,* Berlin 1897² (discussion of the traditional information about pre-Islamic Arab idolatry); Berlin 1961³ (repr. with new intro.).

Idols and Images

Physical representations — usually of deities or supernatural powers; also, any false god. Various words in the Qurʾān are understood by the commentators (see EXEGESIS OF THE QURʾĀN: CLASSICAL AND MEDIEVAL), sometimes not unanimously, as referring to, or in some way connected with, such representations. The most obvious are two of the most common Arabic words for idols, *awthān* (sing. *wathan*) and *aṣnām* (sing. *ṣanam*), both of which occur in the Qurʾān only in their plural forms. The words *ṭāghūt* and *jibt* are often understood to refer to idols in general or to a particular idol, sometimes in other ways, and a similar uncertainty surrounds the words *nuṣub* and *anṣāb*. *Tamāthīl*, "likenesses," (pl. of *timthāl*), at one of its two occurrences seems to be similar in meaning to *aṣnām* and is often translated as "images." In addition, there are a few references to things which might be regarded as particular idols or images. The root *ṣ-w-r*, associated with the idea of shape, form and image, occurs most frequently in connection with God's fashioning of human beings (see BIOLOGY AS THE CREATION AND STAGES OF LIFE; CREATION) and not with idols or the representation of existing things.

Awthān (Q 22:30; 29:17, 25) and *aṣnām* (Q 6:74; 7:138; 14:35; 21:57; 26:71) appear nearly always in stories about past peoples, for example, in reports about Abraham's (q.v.) dealings with his father and his people. Both words clearly designate idols, and the latter is probably cognate with Hebrew *ṣelem*. Q 7:138, which concerns the Children of Israel (q.v.) after their escape from Pharaoh (q.v.), also illustrates a blurring of the distinction between idol and god: seeing that the people of the land to which they had come cleaved to their *aṣnām*, the Israelites demand of Moses (q.v.) that he make them a god *(ilāh)* like the gods of the people. There seems to be only one passage where *awthān* appears with reference to the contemporary situation addressed by the Qurʾān. Q 22:30 commands the reader or hearer to avoid "the filth of idols and the words of falsehood" (*al-rijs min al-awthān [wa-]... qawl al-zūr*, see LIE). To what, exactly, this phrase refers is not clear. Traditional commentators tend to gloss *al-rijs min al-awthān* simply as "idolatry," al-Ṭabarī (d. 310/923; *Tafsīr*, xvii, 112) supplying *ʿibādat al-awthān*. They do recognize, however, a grammatical oddity in that the phrase is not a simple genitive construction (*iḍāfa*, see GRAMMAR AND THE QURʾĀN) like the succeeding *qawl al-zūr*. The context and comparison with other similar passages may suggest an aspect of dietary regulations.

Attempts by the traditional scholars to define *wathan* and *ṣanam* more precisely and to establish a difference in significance between those two words, and between them and words such as *timthāl*, are unconvincing and frequently contradictory. *Tamāthīl* occurs at Q 21:52 and 34:13. The former is part of the story of Abraham's destruction of the idols of his people, and *tamāthīl* here seems to be an alternative for *aṣnām* and *āliha*, both of which occur elsewhere in the story (cf. Q 21:59, 57; 26:71). In Q 34:13, however, it seems to have a more positive or at least neutral significance, appearing in a list of things which were made for Solomon (q.v.) by the jinn (q.v.): "Whatever he wished of large halls, images, deep dishes, and steady cooking pots" *(mā yashāʾu min maḥārība wa-tamāthīla wa-jifānin kal-jawābi wa-qudūrin rāsiyātin)*. Outside the Qurʾān, *tamāthīl* often seems to represent three dimensional images, for example in the phrase *tamāthīl wa-ṣuwar*, where the latter noun refers to pictures or two dimensional images.

These more explicit and common words for idols and images in Arabic are rare in those qurʾānic passages which charge the contemporary opponents (see OPPOSITION TO MUḤAMMAD) labeled as *al-mushrikūn* with the sin of *shirk* (see POLYTHEISM AND ATHEISM; BELIEF AND UNBELIEF), a concept which has many points of contact with that of idolatry (see IDOLATRY AND IDOLATERS). Instead, when addressing the contemporary situation the qurʾānic polemic against "idolatry" *(shirk)* sometimes uses the less well known and more ambiguous words *ṭāghūt* and *jibt*. We are commanded to shun the *ṭāghūt* and to serve God (Q 16:36; cf. 39:17); the disbelievers are friends of the *ṭāghūt* and fight in their way (Q 2:257; 4:76); there are some who claim that what they believe has been revealed to the Prophet and to previous prophets (see PROPHETS AND PROPHETHOOD; HYPOCRITES AND HYPOCRISY) but nevertheless desire to be brought to judgment to the *ṭāghūt* (Q 4:60); and those who have received "a part of the book (q.v.)" nevertheless believe in *al-jibt wa-l-ṭāghūt* and claim to be on a more correct path than those who believe (Q 4:51; see PATH OR WAY).

Both *ṭāghūt* and *jibt* (the latter is a *hapax legomenon*, occurring only at Q 4:51 where it is found in conjunction with *ṭāghūt*) are variously understood by the traditional commentators but tend to be connected with idolatry. In addition to being explained as referring to idols generically or to a particular idol or idols, these terms are sometimes understood as places such as temples where idols are to be found. Some, on the other hand, see them as referring to such things as soothsayers (q.v.), sorcerers (see MAGIC, PROHIBITION OF) or satans (see DEVIL). It seems clear that to some extent the words and concepts were puzzling to the commentators but that the association of them with the general idea of idolatry — or with features of the Age of Ignorance (q.v.; *jāhiliyya*) connected with idolatry — was not merely speculative.

Modern scholarship has suggested and illustrated various ways in which *ṭāghūt* and *jibt* may be derived from or related to similar words used in connection with the idea of idolatry in pre-Islamic Semitic languages (see FOREIGN VOCABULARY). It seems likely, for example, that the former is related to the Aramaic *ṭʿwt*, associated with the idea of error or wandering from the right path and used in the Jerusalem Talmud and Midrash Rabba with connotations of idolatry or the worship of gods other than God. *Jibt* has been linked with Ethiopic and even Greek vocabulary used in biblical passages referring to idols, images and false gods. The qurʾānic use of these two words, therefore, seems to continue earlier monotheistic usage and significance.

Nuṣub (Q 5:3; 70:43) and *anṣāb* (Q 5:90), connected with the verb *naṣaba* (to erect, set up), are similarly explained in a variety of ways but with a tendency to be associated with idols. At Q 5:3 the phrase "what has been slaughtered on the *nuṣub*" is part of a list of types of meat which are prohibited (see FORBIDDEN; PROHIBITED DEGREES). Commentators disagree on whether *nuṣub* is a singular or a plural form, and they offer a variety of interpretations, including idol or altar of an idol. At Q 70:43 (the unbelievers, on the day of resurrection, will rush from their graves to the *nuṣub*), the same ductus is sometimes read as *naṣb* although *nuṣub* is the accepted reading. Again it is sometimes interpreted to mean idol but sometimes in a more neutral way as "an object at which one aims." At Q 5:90 the *anṣāb* are listed together with wine (see INTOXICANTS), the game of chance called *al-maysir* (see GAMBLING), and divining arrows (see FORETELLING) as "filth of the work of Satan." Some see *anṣāb* as the plural of *nuṣub* and synonymous with *aṣnām,* others attempt to distinguish between the two while still connecting *nuṣub* with idolatrous behavior.

Formations from the same root occur in several Semitic languages, with meanings such as pillar, monument, statue, image and perhaps altar. For example, the "pillar of salt" into which Lot's (q.v.) wife was changed in Genesis 19:26 is *neṣīb melaḥ* in the Hebrew, although forms with initial *m* are more common (*maṣṣēbāh, m-n-ṣ-b-t, m-ṣ-b-ʾ,* etc.). Outside the Qurʾān, in traditional accounts of pre-Islamic Arab idolatry (see SOUTH ARABIA, RELIGION IN PRE-ISLAMIC), *nuṣub* often seems to be understood as "idol" or "god." Stories tell how the Arabs would select a stone and set it up as a *nuṣub* which would be worshipped. The *anṣāb al-ḥaram,* however, are understood as stones marking the boundary of the sacred territory enclosing the Meccan sanctuary (see KAʿBA; MECCA; PRE-ISLAMIC ARABIA AND THE QURʾĀN), stones said to have been erected by Abraham.

There are a few passages which refer by name to entities that may be understood as idols, and are often so understood in the traditional literature, although they are not referred to in the Qurʾān by any of the words designating "idol." The golden calf (see CALF OF GOLD) is simply mentioned as "the calf" in the Qurʾān, although in commentary it is often identified as an idol or god. The five gods of the people of Noah (q.v.; Q 71:23; Wadd, Suwāʿ, Yaghūth, Yaʿūq and Nasr) are mentioned in the Qurʾān as "gods" while the extra-qurʾānic tradition counts them as idols. They are included in the lists provided by the tradition of idols of the Age of Ignorance *(jāhiliyya),* and information is supplied about their sites in Arabia, the tribes associated with them, and, sometimes, their forms. Names closely related to those of Wadd and Nasr are to be found in pre-Islamic epigraphy and literature while possible attestations of the other three are rarer and more questionable.

The three names al-Lāt, al-ʿUzzā and Manāt, which occur at Q 53:19-20 and widely in extra-qurʾānic tradition, notably in the different versions of the satanic verses (q.v.) story, are understood by Muslim tradition to be those of three idols or goddesses worshipped by the Meccans and other Arabs, and the traditional material provides details of their sites, the tribes associated with their cults, and stories about their destruction with the coming of Islam. The Qurʾān itself gives little if any information about them, not identifying them as idols or deities but rather insisting that they are mere names. It refers to them in a passage which is concerned with denying that God has daughters (other passages accuse the *mushrikūn* of regarding the angels [see ANGEL] as female offspring of God), refutes the idea that the angels will intercede for the opponents, and insists that it is those who do not believe in the next world who have given the angels female names. The relationship between this qurʾānic passage and the treatment of the three "idols" in the tradition is problematic. There is quite copious attestation in epigraphy and non-Muslim literature of names similar to those given in the Qurʾān and Muslim tradition. See also ICONOCLASM.

Gerald R. Hawting

Bibliography
Primary: Ibn al-Kalbī, Hishām, *The book of idols,* trans. N. Fāris, Princeton 1952; id., *Das Götzenbuch. Kitāb al-aṣnām des Ibn al-Kalbī,* trans. R. Klinke-Rosenberger, Leipzig 1941, 47, 53 (trans.) and 21, 33 (text; attempts to provide more specific definitions which would distinguish between *ṣanam, wathan,* and other words for "idol"); id., *Les idoles,* trans. W. Atallah, Paris 1969; Ṭabarī, *Tafsīr,* ed. Būlāq.

Secondary: F. Brown, S.R. Driver and C.A. Briggs, *Hebrew and English lexicon of the Old Testament,* Oxford 1907 (s.v. *n-ṣ-b*); T. Fahd, *Le panthéon de l'Arabie centrale à la veille de l'Hégire,* Paris 1968 (on the treatment of the five gods of the people of Noah and the three daughters of Allāh in Muslim tradition and for attestations of names in inscriptions and non-Muslim literature); A. Guillaume, Stroking an idol, in *BSOAS* 27 (1964), 430 (attempts to provide more specific definitions which would distinguish between *ṣanam, wathan,* and other words for "idol"); Jeffery, *For. vocab.,* s.vv. (for *ṭāghūt* and *jibt*); R. Köbert, Das koranische "ṭāġūt," in *Orientalia* 30 (1961), 415-6 (for *ṭāghūt* and *jibt*); S. Krone, *Die altarabische Gottheit al-Lāt,* Frankfurt am Main 1992 (on the treatment of the five gods of the people of Noah and the three daughters of Allāh in Muslim tradition and for attestations of names in inscriptions and non-Muslim literature); Lane, s.vv. the various words mentioned; J. Levy, *Wörterbuch über die Talmudim und Midraschim,* Berlin 1924 (s.v. *ṭ-ʿ-w-t;* for *ṭāghūt* and *jibt*); G. Ryckmans, *Les religions Arabes préislamiques,* Louvain 1951[2] (on the treatment of the five gods of the people of Noah and the three daughters of Allāh in Muslim tradition and for attestations of names in inscriptions and non-Muslim literature); J. Wellhausen, *Reste arabischen Heidentums,* Berlin 1897[2] (on the treatment of the five gods of the people of Noah and the three daughters of Allāh in Muslim tradition and for attestations of names in inscriptions and non-Muslim literature).

Idrīs

A qurʾānic prophet (see PROPHETS AND PROPHETHOOD) blessed with the virtues of piety (q.v.) and patience (see TRUST AND PATIENCE). There is no doubt that his uniqueness is the result of his ascent to a high station by the hand of God (Q 19:56-7; 21:85). Muslim tradition claims that he ascended to heaven while still alive and there he was awarded eternal life and a permanent home in the fourth heaven, although some traditions place him in the sixth heaven (see HEAVEN AND SKY). Indeed, the prophet Muḥammad meets him in heaven during his nocturnal journey (*isrāʾ,* see ASCENSION). Other traditions, however, maintain that Idrīs was put to death in heaven. Muslim commentators and modern scholars are united in the opinion that the name Idrīs originates from a language other than Arabic (see FOREIGN VOCABULARY). And, assuming that the identification of his original name would reveal more about this enigmatic figure, generations of scholars have offered many explanations about the origins of his name.

Muslim tradition has identified Idrīs with the biblical figure Enoch ben Jared, about whom it was said that "God took him" (*Gen* 5:24). At the same time, Idrīs was also identified with Hermes Trismegistus, the central character in the hermetic writings composed in the second or third century C.E., and with the planet Mercury. Yet, according to Muslim tradition, Idrīs was an antediluvian figure; God sent him to struggle with the giant children of Cain (*jabābira,* see CAIN AND ABEL) who had sinned, and his importance to humanity is that he succeeded in saving human knowledge (see KNOWLEDGE AND LEARNING) and science (see SCIENCE AND THE QURʾĀN) during the flood and transmitting it to subsequent generations. Other traditions equated him with the prophet Elijah (q.v.); but this is the result of the confusion surrounding Enoch and Elijah in the period prior to Islam because of narratives asserting that they had both ascended to heaven.

Muslim tradition claimed that Idrīs was an initiator in many areas. Most of them maintain that he was the first prophet to be given thirty tablets *(ṣuḥuf,* sing. *ṣaḥīfa),* and the first to write with a stylus *(qalam)* and on a *ṣaḥīfa* (see INSTRUMENTS). He was also the first astrologer, the first to weave cloth and the first to wear clothes (see CLOTHING); before him, people had used only animal skins for clothing (see HIDES AND FLEECE). His war against the children of Cain was the first jihād (q.v.). There are traditions that even describe his image, portraying him as a tall, fat man with a white mole.

With respect to the roles attributed to Idrīs by Muslim tradition, there is indeed a strong similarity between him and the figures with which he was identified. Hermes Trismegistus is, in effect, the incarnation of Thoth, the Egyptian god, the messenger and scribe of the gods. At the same time, some of the apocalyptic writings (see APOCALYPSE) gave Enoch eternal life in heaven based on the biblical account that God took him up to himself. During his sojourn in heaven, Enoch acquired the secrets of creation (q.v.), learned what would happen in the world in the future and the secret of the solar calendar (q.v.). He was the first to transmit heavenly knowledge to human beings. According to the Jewish book *Ben Sīrā,* Enoch was a "symbol of knowledge for all generations" (*Ben Sīrā* 44:16). Enoch's primacy also derives from his Hebrew name which means "initiation." With respect to the planet Mercury, the parallel between Hermes and Mercury is an ancient one. The Jewish Aggada identified Mercury with the sun's scribe (*BT Shabbat* 156:a). Enoch who, according to the Bible, lived to an age equal to the number of days in a solar year and who transmitted the secrets of the solar calendar to humankind, was also a scribe in the garden of Eden (*Jubilees* 4:23).

Despite the strong connection between Idrīs, Enoch, Mercury, and Hermes Trismegistus from the point of view of their common roles in human history, there is a great dissimilarity among their names. Generations of scholars have attempted to discover the origins of the name "Idrīs" both within and beyond apocryphal and hermetic literature. Casanova and Torrey maintained that the origin of the name Idrīs is from Ezra (q.v.) — which entered Islam in the Greek version of the name, Esdras — who also enjoyed a status of distinction in the apocalyptic literature. Albright claimed that Idrīs is a corruption of the last two syllables of Poimandres, the most important work of hermetic literature. Recently, Gil suggested that Idrīs is a corruption of the name Hermes, a name that reached the Arabs in the form of *hīrmīs*.

It may be possible, however, to discover the missing link between the name Idrīs and Enoch by means of the Qumran scrolls. These scrolls are based on the previously extant Enoch literature and excerpts of this apocalyptic literature in Hebrew and Aramaic were found in the twentieth century in caves in the Judean Desert. The Damascus Covenant scroll mentions a character called the "interpreter of the Torah" *(dōresh ha-Torah),* whose name describes his occupation. The "interpreter" is identified with the "legislator" *(meḥōqeq)* and this links him to Enoch of the apocalyptic literature, who brought the secrets of the heavens to human beings. The connection between Hermes, whose name means "interpretation" *(hermeneia),* and *dōresh* is clear. In the Damascus Covenant scroll, the "interpreter of the Torah" is also identified with "the star," the name used to refer to Mercury, although its full name in Hebrew is "the sun star." In view of the etymological connection between *dōresh* and Idrīs, and the similarity of their roles and those of Hermes Trismegistus and the planet Mercury, it is possible that the figure of the "interpreter of the Torah" contains the solution to the origin of the name Idrīs. Apparently, the apocalyptic literature of Enoch penetrated Islam in the era of the Prophet by means of the Manichaeans. Fragments of this literature which were discovered in the Qumran caves are the basis of Mani's *Book of giants*. After the death of Muḥammad, the Shīʿites made extensive use of the apocalyptic literature of Enoch and of Enoch himself, as well as the other antediluvian figures (see SHĪʿISM AND THE QURʾĀN). In later periods, hermetic literature was widely utilized by Muslim science. The many facets of Idrīs may thus be explained since, from the outset, Islam shaped the image of Idrīs under the influence of this earlier eclectic literature.

Yoram Erder

Bibliography

Primary: al-Bīrūnī, Abū l-Rayḥān, *al-Āthār al-bāqiya,* ed. E. Sachau, Leipzig 1878, 204-7; Ibn Abī Uṣaybiʿa, *ʿUyūn;* Kisāʾī, *Qiṣaṣ,* i, 81-5; al-Qifṭī, Abū l-Ḥasan ʿAlī b. Yūsuf, *Taʾrīkh al-ḥukamāʾ,* ed. J. Lippert, Leipzig 1903, 1-7; Thaʿlabī, *Qiṣaṣ,* 34-5.

Secondary: W.F. Albright, Review of Th. Boylan, *The hermes of Egypt,* in *Journal of the Palestine Oriental Society* 2 (1922), 190-8; P.S. Alexander, Jewish tradition in early Islam. The case of Enoch/Idrīs, in G.R. Hawting, J.A. Mojaddedi and A. Samely (eds.), *Studies in Islamic and Middle Eastern texts and traditions in memory of Norman Calder* (*JSS Supp.* 12), Oxford 2000, 11-29; P. Casanova, Idrīs et ʿOuzaïr, in *JA* 205 (1924), 356-60; Y. Erder, The origin of the name Idrīs in the Qurʾān. A study of the influence of Qumran literature on early Islam, in *JNES* 49 (1990), 339-50; M. Gil, The creed of Abū ʿAmīr, in *IOS* 12 (1982), 9-57; R. Hartmann, Zur Erklärung von Sūra 18, 59 f., in *Zeitschrift für Assyriologie und Verwandte Gebiete* 24 (1910), 307-15; Th. Noldeke, Idrīs, in *Zeitschrift für Assyriologie und Verwandte Gebiete* 17 (1903), 83-4; C.C. Torrey, *The Jewish foundation of Islam,* New York 1933, 72.

ʿIfrīt

Mentioned once in the Qurʾān as designation of a jinn (q.v.), the word *ʿifrīt* (pl. *ʿafārīt*) gave rise to numerous interpretations. In the qurʾānic version of the story about Solomon (q.v.) and the Queen of Sheba (see BILQĪS), the former asks for somebody to fetch him the Queen's throne, whereupon an *ʿifrīt* of the jinn offers to bring it even before Solomon can rise from his place (Q 27:39). The duty is not given to him, however, but to somebody who is endowed with the knowledge of the scripture (see BOOK; SCRIPTURE AND THE QURʾĀN) and still surpasses the *ʿifrīt* in swiftness (Q 27:40).

As just stated, the word *ʿifrīt* is attested only once in the Qurʾān and is not found in Arabic poetry. Instead of *ʿifrīt,* several variants are recorded, especially *ʿifriya* and *ʿifr* (Qurṭubī, *Jāmiʿ,* xiii, 203; Ālūsī, *Rūḥ,* xxi, 197). Arabic philologists in general assign the word to the root *ʿ-f-r.* They explain it to mean either "strong, powerful, effective," or "cunning, wicked, impudent, evil, rebellious" or a combination of both of these notions. Al-Zamakhsharī (d. 538/1144; *Kashshāf*) connects the word to the basic meaning of the root *ʿ-f-r,* "dust," by explaining *ʿifrīt* as "the wicked, abominable one who casts his fellow into the dust" (cf. also *Lisān al-ʿArab,* iv, 586). Western philologists speculated about a foreign origin of the word. Jeffery (*For. vocab.,* 215; see FOREIGN VOCABULARY) follows them in claiming that the word may be derived from Pahlevi *āfrītan* "create," but this etymology is highly improbable and does not correspond to the broader cultural or linguistic context of the Arabic usage of the word. Instead, Fischer (Miszellen, 871-5) established an Arabic origin to be most likely by adducing several parallel Arabic word forms, thus confirming the Arabic philologists' assignation of the word to the root *ʿ-f-r.*

The exact qurʾānic meaning of *ʿifrīt* is difficult to establish. Ideas about *ʿafārīt* in folklore may have caused the majority of translators to take *ʿifrīt* in Q 27:39 as the proper name of a specific class of the jinn and to render the passage simply as "an ʿIfrīt of the Jinn(s)" or the like. This practice stands in marked contrast to the scholarly Islamic tradition which considers *ʿifrīt* to be a descriptive adjective used in Q 27:39

to designate a special quality of the mentioned jinn. None of the classical scholarly treatises about jinn (al-Shiblī, al-Suyūṭī, al-Ḥalabī), nor even al-Damīrī's *Ḥayāt al-ḥayawān,* mentions the *ʿafārīt* as a distinct species of jinn, nor can such a notion be deduced from a famous passage in al-Jāḥiẓ (*Ḥayawān,* i, 291), where a tradition is quoted according to which a jinn will be called *ʿifrīt* if he is stronger than a jinn that is called *mārid.* Only in writings that reflect popular belief do we find this notion of *ʿifrīt* as a distinct category of jinn. So we are told in al-Ibshīhī's *Mustaṭraf* (ii, 545-7; Fr. trans. ii, 325-32) that the *ʿafārīt* form a special kind of the demons (*shayāṭīn,* see DEVIL) and are dangerous for their habit of preying upon women. This is only one example of a great range of beliefs in various kinds of demons and spirits of the dead, beliefs which are still com-mon throughout the Arab world and which have come to be called by the qurʾānic word *ʿifrīt.*

Thomas Bauer

Bibliography

Primary (of primary relevance are the commentaries and dictionaries): Ālūsī, *Rūḥ;* al-Ibshīhī, Muḥammad b. Aḥmad al-Khaṭīb, *al-Mustaṭraf fī kull fann mustaẓraf,* ed. I. Ṣālim, 3 vols., Beirut 1999 (few notes on popular belief); id., *al-Mostaṭraf,* trans. G. Rat, 2 vols, Paris 1902, ii, 325-32; al-Jāḥiẓ, *Kitāb al-Ḥayawān,* ed. ʿA.M. Hārūn, 7 vols., Beirut 1969-70; *Lisān al-ʿArab;* Qurṭubī, *Jāmiʿ;* al-Samīn al-Ḥalabī, Abū l-ʿAbbās Aḥmad b. Yūsuf, *ʿUmdat al-ḥuffāẓ fī tafsīr ashraf al-alfāẓ,* ed. M. Bāsil ʿUyūn al-Sūd, 4 vols., Beirut 1996 (esp. iii, 95-6); al-Shiblī, Abū ʿAlī Muḥammad b. Taqī al-Dīn, *Ākām al-marjān fī aḥkām al-jānn,* ed. S. al-Jumaylī, Beirut ca. 1985 (fundamental on jinn in general, few mentions of *ʿifrīt);* Zamakhsharī, *Kashshāf.*

Secondary: R. Basset, *Mille et un contes, récits et légendes arabes,* 3 vols., Paris 1924, i, 57 ("l'origine des démons," taken from Masʿūdī, *Les prairies d'or,* ed. and trans. de Meynard/de Courteille, iii, 320-1), 156; J. Chelhod, ʿIfrīt, in *EI²,* iii, 1050-1; A. Fischer, Miszellen, in ZDMG 58 (1904), 869-76 (on etymology); J. Henninger, Geisterglaube bei den vorislamischen Arabern, in id., *Arabica sacra,* Göttingen 1981, 118-69 (on the belief in demons in pre- and early Islamic as well as in modern times; comprehensive bibliography); Jeffery, *For. vocab.;* D.B. McDonald, ʿIfrīt, in *EI¹,* ii, 455 (still fundamental); A. Wieland, *Studien zur Djinn-Vorstellung im modernen Ägypten,* Würzburg 1994.

Ignorance

Lack of knowledge (see KNOWLEDGE AND LEARNING). The words ignorance, ignorant, etc., usually translate Arabic words derived from the root *j-h-l,* which appear twenty-four times in the Qurʾān. One of these words, *jāhiliyya,* is discussed in the article AGE OF IGNORANCE. The present article discusses the others and also briefly considers other roots that convey ideas related to ignorance.

The classical Arabic dictionaries define *j-h-l* mainly in contrast to *ʿ-l-m,* knowledge, but Goldziher, Izutsu and others have argued that in pre-Islamic literature *j-h-l* almost always refers to excessive and often fierce behavior rooted in pride (q.v.) and honor (q.v.). The pre-Islamic poet ʿAmr b. Kulthūm, for example, killed the king of Ḥīra when the latter's mother insulted his mother and sang, "Let no one act fiercely *(yajhalnā)* against us, for we shall be fiercer than the fierce *(fa-najhala fawqa jahli l-jāhilīna)*" (Zamakhsharī, *Kashshāf,* iii, 99). *J-h-l* here contrasts not with *ʿ-l-m,* knowledge, but with *ḥ-l-m,* the quality of self-control arising from a sense of strength. The highest virtue involved a proper balance between *jahl* and *ḥilm* and, while *ḥilm* was usually preferable, *jahl* had its place. The poet sings: "Although I be in need of *ḥilm,* of *jahl* I am at times in greater need" (Stetkevych, *Muhammad,* 8).

In the Qurʾān one can see three differences from the pre-Islamic concept of *jahl.* It loses all positive moral value and becomes an excessive and willful resistance to the truth (see BELIEF AND UNBELIEF). It is never specifically contrasted to *ḥilm* and, in fact, has no clear and consistent antonym. It comes in some cases to mean simple lack of knowledge in contrast to *ʿilm,* a usage quite rare in the earlier period. The passages that come closest to expressing the *j-h-l/ḥ-l-m* contrast are probably Q 25:63 and 28:55. In the former the servants of God are described as "those who walk the earth modestly (or humbly, *hawnan,* see MODESTY) and who, when the insolent *(jāhilūna)* address them, say 'peace.'" Al-Zamakhsharī (d. 538/1144) illustrates *jāhilūna* with the verse from ʿAmr b. Kulthūm quoted above. Many of al-Ṭabarī's (d. 310/923) sources gloss *hawn* as *ḥilm* and al-Zamakhsharī describes "peace" in Q 28:55 as "a word of *ḥilm*" (*Kashshāf,* iii, 185).

J-h-l appears as willful excess in Q 27:54-5, where Lot (q.v.; Lūṭ) asks his neighbors, "Do you commit indecency (see HOMOSEXUALITY) with your eyes open?... Indeed, you are a people given to excess *(tajhalūna).*" Likewise in the stories of Noah (q.v.; Nūḥ, Q 11:29), Hūd (q.v.; Q 46:23) and Moses (q.v. Mūsā, Q 2:67; 7:138) the root refers to a forceful resistance to the prophet's message (see PROPHETS AND PROPHETHOOD). This resistance may be maintained in the face of overwhelming evidence, as in Q 6:111: "If we sent angels (see ANGEL) to them and the dead (see DEATH AND THE DEAD) spoke... they would not have faith (q.v.), unless God willed, but most of them are given to *jahl (yajhalūna).*" In these usages, *j-h-l* seems close to *kufr* (active rejection of faith) though the roots appear together only once (Q 48:26); it is more often connected with idolatry (Q 7:138, 197-9; 39:64; 46:22-3; see IDOLATRY AND IDOLATERS) and at least once with *ẓulm* (injustice, Q 33:72; see JUSTICE AND INJUSTICE). Although often the context does not clearly dictate whether *j-h-l* means excessiveness or simple ignorance, in some places it certainly means the latter. A good example is Q 49:6: "If a corrupt person brings you news, check it, lest you harm people in ignorance *(bi-jahālatin)* and then regret it." Elsewhere such ignorance is the occasion for repentance (see REPENTANCE AND PENANCE) and (divine) forgiveness (q.v.; Q 4:17; 6:54; 16:119; possibly Q 11:46; 12:89). In these cases, as in the others, the moral concern is central (see ETHICS AND THE QURʾĀN; VIRTUES AND VICES).

Thus, from its connotations in the pre-Islamic period to those in the Qurʾān there is some degree of shift in the meaning of *j-h-l* from excessive behavior toward simple ignorance. The ḥadīth (see ḤADĪTH AND THE QURʾĀN) carry this further, since there *j-h-l* appears more often in the latter than the former meaning, at least judging by the listings in Wensinck's *Concordance.* Probably the shift in meaning was associated partly with the infrequency of *ḥ-l-m* in the Qurʾān (it appears only four times as a human characteristic), but is more likely due to the centrality of *ʿ-l-m* both in the Qurʾān and in classical Islamic culture. *J-h-l* could be seen first as causing or resulting from lack of knowledge and then as coming to refer primarily to this absence of *ʿilm.* This connection is suggested by a ḥadīth describing the signs of the last hour (see APOCALYPSE; LAST JUDGMENT): "*ʿIlm* will vanish, *jahl* will prevail, wine (see INTOXICANTS) will be drunk and people will fornicate (see ADULTERY AND FORNICATION) openly" (Bukhārī, *Ṣaḥīḥ, K. ʿIlm,* 22). The older meaning is still alive in some contexts, as is indicated by some contemporary usages of *jāhiliyya* (see AGE OF IGNORANCE).

Other roots which convey something like the idea of ignorance are *gh-f-l, n-k-r,* and *ẓ-n-n. Gh-f-l* is unawareness or negligence and may refer to innocent unawareness, as when people have not yet received a divine message (Q 6:131, 156; 7:172; 12:3; see

BOOK; MESSENGER). More often, though, it involves culpable negligence of the unseen world (Q 30:7; see HIDDEN AND THE HIDDEN), the day of judgment (Q 21:97; 50:22) or the signs (q.v.; *āyāt*) of God (Q 7:146). This may result from active denial (Q 7:146), from desires (*hawā*, Q 18:28) or from satisfaction with worldly life (Q 30:7). It may be a manifestation of *kufr* (Q 21:97) or a sign that God has sealed people's hearts (Q 16:108; see HEART). *N-k-r* conveys the idea of not knowing something and thus finding it strange and repugnant. Abraham (q.v.; Ibrāhīm), for example, finds his visitors *munkarūn*, strange and suspicious (Q 15:62; 51:25). The root most commonly appears in the form *munkar*, unrecognized and morally wrong, usually contrasted to *maʿrūf*, recognized and right (see GOOD AND EVIL). Elsewhere it connotes unheard of and terrible actions, including divine punishments. (e.g. Q 18:74; 22:44; see PUNISHMENT STORIES; CHASTISEMENT AND PUNISHMENT). In several passages it refers to the rejection of God's blessing (q.v.) or revelation (see REVELATION AND INSPIRATION), e.g. "They recognize *(yaʿrifūna)* the blessing of God, then deny it *(yunkirūnahā)* and most of them are *kāfirs*" (Q 16:83; cf. 40:81 etc.). *Ẓ-n-n* conveys the notion of guesswork as opposed to certainty. In a number of passages it refers to a correct opinion (e.g. Q 17:102; 72:12), but more often to a wrong and often ill-conceived opinion about God or God's actions. It is often contrasted with knowledge (*ʿilm*, e.g. Q 2:78; 4:157) and sometimes with truth (*ḥaqq*, Q 53:28), and is associated with idolatry (*shirk*, Q 10:36) and unbelief (*kufr*, Q 38:27), and at least once with *jāhiliyya* (Q 3:154). It characterizes those who willfully reject the truth in favor of their own opinions.

All of these terms show that, in the Qurʾān, ignorance is usually something more dynamic and dangerous than mere lack of knowledge and nearly always has moral implications which are of central concern.

William E. Shepard

Bibliography

Primary: Bukhārī, *Ṣaḥīḥ*, trans. M.M. Khan, 9 vols., Chicago 1976-9³ (rev. ed.); Fīrūzābādī, *al-Qāmūs al-muḥīṭ*, Beirut 1995; *Lisān al-ʿArab*, Beirut 1966; Ṭabarī, *Tafsīr*, Cairo 1954-68; *Tāj al-ʿarūs*, 10 vols, Cairo 1306-7; Zamakhsharī, *Kashshāf*, 4 vols., Cairo 1966.
Secondary: ʿAbd al-Bāqī; Goldziher, *MS*; R.A. Nicholson, *A literary history of the Arabs*, London 1907, repr. Cambridge 1969; Izutsu, *Concepts*; id., *God*; F. Rosenthal, *Knowledge triumphant. The concept of knowledge in Medieval Islam*, Leiden 1970; J. Stetkevych, *Muhammad and the golden bough*, Bloomington, IN 1996; Wensinck, *Concordance*; id., *al-Muʿjam al-mufahras li-alfāẓ al-ḥadīth al-nabawī*, Leiden 1936-88.

Iḥrām see PILGRIMAGE

Iʿjāz see INIMITABILITY

Ilāf

An infinitive of the Arabic root *ʾ-l-f* which has been explained in various ways by Muslim commentators of the Qurʾān as well as by modern scholars. It occurs in one qurʾānic chapter (Q 106:1-2), where it is annexed to the name Quraysh (q.v.), and is associated with the "journey of the winter and the summer" (see CARAVAN).

Most of the exegetical explanations are based on the view that *ilāf Quraysh* describes the manner in which the Meccan people of Quraysh conducted the winter and the summer journey. They revolve around the basic range of meanings of the root *ʾ-l-f*, which are "to resort habitually (to a place)," or "to become familiar (with a thing)," or "take pleasure (with a thing or a person)." Accordingly, *ilāf Quraysh* was explained as denoting the keeping of Quraysh to their journeys or their preparations for that purpose. *Ilāf (*also *īlāf* and *ilf)* was also understood in the sense of "protection," i.e. of traveling with the guarantee of safety, and eventually became one of the names for the grants of security which the leaders of Quraysh (the sons of ʿAbd Manāf) reportedly obtained from the kings of the Byzantines (q.v.), the Persians, the Abyssinians (see ABYSSINIA) and the Yemenis (see YEMEN) — a grant of security which enabled them to conduct their journeys safely. Alternatively, it was explained that the security the Quraysh enjoyed in their journeys originated in their holy status as a people of God who dwelt in the sacred territory *(ḥaram)* of Mecca, near the Kaʿba (q.v.; see GEOGRAPHY). *Ilāf* here signifies protection (q.v.) granted by God, and this notion is supported by the variant reading *īlāf*, an infinitive of the fourth form, which denotes God's habituation of Quraysh to their journeys. The perception of the term *ilāf* in the sense of divine protection goes well with the subsequent verses (Q 106:3-4) in which the Quraysh are commanded to worship "the lord of this house (see HOUSE, DOMESTIC AND DIVINE) who has fed them against hunger (see FAMINE) and secured them from fear (q.v.)." In this manner the worship (q.v.) of God emerges as a token of gratitude for the *ilāf* which God has granted Quraysh (see GRATITUDE AND INGRATITUDE). The scope of the divine benefaction (see BLESSING; GRACE) inherent in the term *ilāf* was also expanded to the position of Mecca as a center of pilgrimage (q.v.) and trade (see ECONOMICS), from which the Quraysh were said to have benefited apart from the profits made abroad during their winter and summer journeys (see PRE-ISLAMIC ARABIA AND THE QURʾĀN). Muslim exegetes (see EXEGESIS OF THE QURʾĀN: CLASSICAL AND MEDIEVAL) explained further that, thanks to Mecca's central position, the Quraysh could even afford to stay in Mecca and forego their journeys. These interpretations of *ilāf* are evidently marked by the urge to elevate Mecca to the rank of a universal center.

The preposition *li* by which *ilāf Quraysh* is preceded has been explained in accordance with the above interpretations. It has been taken to denote wonder ("wonder ye at the *ilāf* of Quraysh") or as indicating cause or purpose (see GRAMMAR AND THE QURʾĀN). In the latter sense the *li* is relevant to the notion of divine benevolence, and has been linked to the subsequent verses of the sūra ("for the *ilāf* of Quraysh... so let them worship, etc."). Since this sūra was once considered part of Q 105 "The Elephant" (Sūrat al-Fīl), the *li* — as indicating cause or purpose — has also been connected with the destruction of the People of the Elephant (q.v.; see also ABRAHA) and both chapters were taken to revolve around the idea of divine mercy (q.v.): "(God has destroyed the People of the Elephant) for the sake of the *ilāf* of Quraysh." The *li* was also explained as denoting a command and, in this case, the form *ilāf* was replaced in a variant reading (see READINGS OF THE QURʾĀN) by a verbal form: *li-yaʾlaf*, or *li-taʾlaf*. This reading probably takes verses 1 and 2 to denote: "Let the Quraysh keep to (the worship of God) just as they used to keep to the winter and summer journey." Thus, the message of the term *ilāf* has become purely religious: persistence in the worship of God.

Uri Rubin

Bibliography
H. Birkeland, *The lord guideth*, Oslo 1950, 102-23; P. Crone, *Meccan trade and the rise of Islam*, Princeton 1987; Paret, *Kommentar*, 522-3

(for older studies on the topic); U. Rubin, The *īlāf* of Quraysh. A study of *sūra* CVI, in *Arabica* 31 (1984), 165-88 (for the various Islamic interpretations).

Illegitimacy

The state of having been unlawfully conceived. Although references to adultery (see ADULTERY AND FORNICATION) with clear legal bearings are frequent in the Qurʾān (see LAW AND THE QURʾĀN), and the ability to determine the paternity of a child is a major social concern of the Qurʾān (see COMMUNITY AND SOCIETY IN THE QURʾĀN; FAMILY; KINSHIP; INHERITANCE) — as exemplified by the parameters for a woman's "waiting period" for remarriage after divorce and widowhood (see MARRIAGE AND DIVORCE; WIDOW) — there is no unequivocal reference to illegitimacy in the sense of children (q.v.) conceived out of wedlock. One qurʾānic reference is the term *zanīm* (Q 68:13), meaning "one adopted among a people to whom he does not belong, base, ignoble, mean, son of an adulteress" (cf. Lane). In the commentaries and translations of Q 68:13 the term *zanīm* is normally interpreted as "baseborn, ignoble, mean" and only rarely as "son of an adulteress."

Al-Ṭabarī (d. 310/923), in his commentary on Q 68:13 (*Tafsīr,* ad loc.), quotes a ḥadīth (see ḤADĪTH AND THE QURʾĀN) according to which the Prophet is asked about the meaning of the terms *ʿuṭull* and *zanīm* in Q 68:13. The Prophet is said to have explained *al-ʿuṭull al-zanīm* as "shameless, imprudent" *(al-fāḥish)* and as "ignoble, evil" *(al-laʾīm),* but not as an illegitimate child (see Wensinck, *Concordance,* ii, 345). The commentators also mention, however, the possible meaning "one whose father is not known and whose mother is a prostitute" (cf. Ṭabarī, *Tafsīr; Jalālayn;* Qurṭubī, *Jāmiʿ* ad Q 68:13). In any case, *zanīm* as "son of an adulteress," i.e. an illegitimate child, remains one of several possible interpretations. Even if *zanīm* refers to an illegitimate child in this verse, the term is also used disparagingly for a person of bad character with no associated legal context.

There are only a few sayings of the Prophet on illegitimacy that could have legal and theological bearings. Al-Qurṭubī (d. 671/1272; *Jāmiʿ,* on Q 68:13) quotes a ḥadīth according to which an increase in the number of illegitimate children is considered to be an omen of God's punishment (see CHASTISEMENT AND PUNISHMENT), as well as another tradition according to which the child of an adulterous union does not enter paradise (q.v.), and so forth (see also Wensinck, *Concordance,* v, 147). Al-Ṭabarī (*Tafsīr,* ad Q 68:13) gives another synonym for *zanīm,* i.e. *daʿī,* the plural form of which *(adʿiyāʾ)* also occurs once in the Qurʾān (Q 33:4-5); *daʿī* is usually interpreted as an adoptive child or a child without known parentage (cf. Lane). Owing to the lack of clear reference to illegitimacy in the Qurʾān, the subsequent legal arguments concerning an illegitimate child (normally called *walad al-zinā* or "child of adultery") do not seem to be derived directly from the Qurʾān (see Snouck Hurgronje, Rechtstoestand; id., Toelichting; Juynboll, *Handbuch,* 195 f.).

Irene Schneider

Bibliography
Primary: *Jalālayn,* ed. ʿA. Muḥammad, Cairo 1355/1936; Qurṭubī, *Jāmiʿ,* 24 vols., Beirut 1405-14/1985-93; Ṭabarī, *Tafsīr,* 15 vols., Beirut 1984.
Secondary: T. Juynboll, *Handbuch des Islamischen Gesetzes,* Leiden/Leipzig 1910; Lane; C. Snouck Hurgronje, Rechtstoestand van kinderen, buiten huwelijk geboren uit Inlandsche vrouwen, die den Mohammedaanschen godsdienst belijden, in *Het Recht in Nederlands-Indië* 69 (1897), 133-6; id., Toelichting en tweede toelichting betreffende de erkenning van natuurlijke kinderen volgens het

Mohammedaansche recht, in *Het Recht in Nederlands-Indië* 69 (1897), 285-90; 70 (1898), 87-92; Wensinck, *Concordance.*

Illiteracy

The inability to read or write any language. This inability puts a person at a disadvantage and is regarded as a defect in societies where culture transmission and human communication occurs through writing (Meagher, Illiteracy, 1766b). In considering the situation in Arabia at the time of the prophet Muḥammad (d. 632 C.E.), however, quite different categories have to be applied: the common cultural and historical property of the tribes (see TRIBES AND CLANS) — their knowledge, crystallized in Arabic poetry, genealogies, and stories of tribal battles — was retained almost exclusively in memory and transmitted orally (see ORALITY AND WRITINGS IN ARABIA). Writing and literacy (q.v.) played a minor role, even though the "art of writing" was already known among the Arabs and used, for example, by tradesmen and in cities. Yet the early Arabic sources on the history of Islam do provide some evidence that Muḥammad, especially as a statesman in Medina (q.v.), used scribes to correspond with the tribes. Likewise, though infrequently rather than constantly, he probably had them write down parts of the qurʾānic revelation (see REVELATION AND INSPIRATION) he had received. These would have been on separate pages, not yet in one single book (cf. the widespread ḥadīth, according to which the Prophet dictated, *amlā ʿalayhi,* qurʾānic verses to Zayd b. Thābit, who is well known in the Islamic tradition for the significant role he later played in the recension of the Qurʾān; Bukhārī, *Ṣaḥīḥ,* no. 2832, 4592; see also Hamidullah, *Sahifah Hammam,* 12-3; see COLLECTION OF THE QURʾĀN).

Whether or not the Prophet was able to read or write cannot be established from these historical-biographical references. The qurʾānic evidence in this respect is also equivocal and unclear. There is, on the one hand, the divine declaration in Q 29:47-8: "We have sent down to you the book (q.v.; *kitāb*)... Not before this did you recite any book, or inscribe it with your right hand, for then those who follow falsehood would have doubted." This would seem to indicate that Muḥammad did not read or write any scripture "before" he received the revelation. On the other hand, Q 25:5 points to attempts made by "unbelievers" (here polytheist Meccans; see POLYTHEISM AND ATHEISM) to discredit Muḥammad by claiming that he was not receiving a divine revelation but simply "writings of the ancients" (*asāṭīr al-awwalīn,* see GENERATIONS; HISTORY AND THE QURʾĀN) which he had written down or which he had had written down *(iktatabahā)* and which were dictated to him *(tumlā ʿalayhi)* at dawn and in the early evening (see INFORMANTS). It is notable, even if this sentence refers to the opponents of the Prophet (see OPPOSITION TO MUḤAMMAD), that the medieval commentators (see EXEGESIS OF THE QURʾĀN: CLASSICAL AND MEDIEVAL) understand *asāṭīr al-awwalīn* (which occurs nine times in the Qurʾān) to mean "writings" or "stories (taken from writings)," explaining them as "narratives that they (i.e., the ancients) used to write down in their books" (Ṭabarī, *Tafsīr*, ix, 366).

This understanding is supported by the derivation of the plural form *asāṭīr* from the Arabic singular *saṭr,* "line" (alternative plural forms *asṭur, asṭār* and *suṭūr,* cf. *Lisān al-ʿArab,* iv, 363); or the Semitic form *s-ṭ-r,* "to write" (cf. Sprenger, *Leben und Lehre,* ii, 395; Nöldeke, *GQ,* i, 16, n. 4; Fück, Das Problem, 6); but also from the singular *usṭūr,* an allegedly Ḥimyaritic loan-word, which suggests "something written" *(maktūb)* or even a "book" (cf. Suyūṭī, *Itqān,* ii, 380, no. 2466, on the authority of Ibn ʿAbbās). Some other scholars of that time explain *asāṭīr* instead as a plural of the singular *usṭūra,* "tale, story" (e.g. *Jalālayn* ad Q 25:5). *Iktataba* seems to have two meanings, "to write down" (synonymous with *istansakha,* Ibn Kathīr, *Tafsīr,* vi, 157; and with *intansakha, Jalālayn* ad Q 25:5; cf. *Lisān al-ʿArab,* i, 698; likewise Paret's translation, "die er sich aufgeschrieben hat"), but also, in a possibly secondary meaning, "to ask somebody to write down" (cf. *Lisān al-ʿArab,* i, 698). Some translations refer to the latter meaning: "[which] he has caused to be written" (Yūsuf ʿAlī), "he has got [these tales] written" (Shakir) or "he has had written down" (Arberry). The phrase *tumlā ʿalayhi* seems to be unattested in Arabic in pre-Islamic times and may have been first used in the Qurʾān (cf. *Lisān al-ʿArab,* xv, 291). Many medieval commentators explain it as "[writings or tales] were read to him" (with *tumlā* in the meaning of *tuqraʾu;* cf Ṭabarī, *Tafsīr,* ix, 366; Ibn Kathīr, *Tafsīr,* vi, 158); others add "... in order to memorize them" (*li-yaḥfaẓahā,* in *Jalālayn* ad Q 25:5; *ḥattā tuḥfaẓa,* Qurṭubī, *Jāmiʿ,* xiii, 4) or "this means that they were written down for him while he was illiterate *(ummī)*" (Rāzī, *Tafsīr,* xxiii, 51). Relying on this explanation, some modern scholars translate it as "they were dictated before him" (Yūsuf ʿAlī) or "read out to him" (Shakir), "they are recited to him" (Arberry). Nevertheless, the older philological material as evident in ḥadīth (see ḤADĪTH AND THE QURʾĀN) clearly indicates that *amlā ʿalā* at that time just meant "to dictate to a writer." The Prophet, for example, "dictated" to Zayd b. Thābit; a transmitter reports that, in the middle of the first/seventh century or even before, he wrote with his own hand a ḥadīth of the Prophet, which a Companion of the Prophet (see COMPANIONS OF THE PROPHET) had "dictated" to him (Ibn Ḥanbal, *Musnad,* no. 6478); and apparently in the year 146/763, a juridical decision was fixed in writing by *imlāʾ,* "dictation" (Dārimī, *Sunan,* ii, 62, no. 2190; see furthermore *Lisān al-ʿArab,* xv, 291). Some scholars translate accordingly "they were dictated to him" (Pickthall), "sie werden... ihm diktiert" (Paret).

In fact, it is above all the term *ummī* — a favored qurʾānic epithet for the Prophet — which plays for Muslims a key role in designating Muḥammad's (il-)literacy. Muslim consensus tends in modern times to perceive *ummī* as merely meaning "unable to read and to write," i.e. "unlettered," and it seems that this understanding of the word was popular already in the Middle Ages. As one can imagine, a rendering like this is not only significant for the comprehension of the self-understanding of the prophet Muḥammad but is of central theological importance, as well. The core meaning — as well as the actual etymology — of *ummī* is problematic. This has caused both (medieval) Muslim and non-Muslim scholars to offer a range of interpretations without, however, actually solving the problem. In western publications, the widespread comprehension of *ummī* as "illiterate" is particularly controversial. Nonetheless, there are also some attempts by contemporary Muslim scholars to alter the image of an "illiterate" Prophet of Islam by emphasizing further possible meanings of the qurʾānic *ummī* (see for example, al-Baghdādī, Ummi prophet).

In the following it will become clear that the term *ummī* must be understood in the context of two other qurʾānic expressions, *umma,* "people, nation (of the Arabs, q.v.)" (see Haarmann, Glaubensvolk, 175), though it seems that *ummī* is not a direct derivative of *umma;* and, secondly, *ummiyyūn,* the plural of *ummī.* (The more specific meaning of *umma* in the religious sense of "community [of the Muslims]," or the "not ethnically defined people of God," only became important during Muḥammad's time in Medina; for this usage, see COMMUNITY AND SOCIETY IN THE QURʾĀN.) Furthermore, in qurʾānic usage, *ummī* and *ummiyyūn* do not represent a single meaning but a spectrum of ideas covering distinct but intimately connected sub-meanings. These include such significations as anyone belonging to a people, viz. the Arabs (i.e. a people not having a scripture); anyone not having a scripture (i.e. not reading [it]); anyone not reading a scripture (i.e. not being taught or educated [by something or somebody]). This means that only the particular context can precisely determine which aspect of the semantic field is to be preferred. Finally, a philological-historical examination of the terms does not confirm the traditional interpretation of *ummī,* which focuses simply on "illiteracy." Rather, this interpretation reflects a post-qurʾānic approach that seems to have evolved in some circles of Muslim learning not before the first half of the second/eighth century (cf. Goldfeld, The illiterate prophet, 58) and that has been further shaped under the influence of Muslim apologists.

Medieval Muslim commentators on ummī

The term *ummī* occurs twice in the Qurʾān as an attribute of the Prophet, "I shall prescribe it for… those who follow the messenger (q.v.), the *ummī* Prophet, whom they find described written down with them in the Torah (q.v.) and the Gospel (q.v.)" (Q 7:157); "Believe then in God, and in his messenger, the *ummī* Prophet" (Q 7:158). Nöldeke (*GQ,* i, 158-60) considers these two verses to be possibly Medinan insertions into the otherwise Meccan sūra (see CHRONOLOGY AND THE QURʾĀN; FORM AND STRUCTURE OF THE QURʾĀN). In Medinan sūras, the plural form *ummiyyūn* occurs signifying and characterizing two different groups of people, Arabs who have not been given the book (Q 3:20, 75; 62:2) and certain Jews (i.e. "those not knowing the book," Q 2:78; see JEWS AND JUDAISM).

Medieval Muslim commentators "are of different opinions" (Ṭabarī, *Tafsīr,* iii, 316) concerning the meaning of *ummī* and its plural *ummiyyūn.* They basically present the following three explanations, of which the first is generally given priority: (a) *Ummī* is derived from *umma,* which means "people, nation (of the Arabs)." In pre-Islamic times, *umma* particularly signified or was even used synonymously for the "Arab people" (see e.g. Ṭabarī, *Tafsīr,* xxii, 88, ad Q 62:2), implying the secondary meanings of either "not being able to read or write" (i.e. "unlettered, illiterate, belonging to the common people") or "not having a holy scripture" (and so "not reading [it];" see SCRIPTURE AND THE QURʾĀN). That is to say, on the one hand, the Arabs prior to Islam, in the time of inexperience and ignorance (*jāhiliyya,* see AGE OF IGNORANCE) concerning the one God, were a people *(umma)* who "did not write nor read" (Qurṭubī, *Jāmiʿ,* vii, 299; Shawkānī, *Tafsīr,* ii, 252 — both on Q 7:157): "We are an *ummī* nation, we do not write and do not count," according to a widespread saying of the Prophet. The Arabs were "unlearned" in terms of the use of script; they were an *umma ummiyya,* a nation which was still in the original state of birth *(ʿalā aṣl wilādatihā),* who had not learned writing or reading; and so the Prophet was *ummī,* i.e. "he did not use to write, read and count" (Sijistānī, *Nuzha,* 112; Qurṭubī, *Jāmiʿ,* vii, 298). On the other hand, the Arabs were "untaught" in terms of religion, they were *mushrikūn,* "pagans, heathens (see POLYTHEIM AND ATHEISM; SOUTH ARABIA, RELIGION IN PRE-ISLAMIC)," not having a holy book (Ṭabarī, *Tafsīr,* iii, 214; *Jalālayn;* Rāzī, *Tafsīr,* vii, 227-228; also Zayd, *Tafsīr,*

106 [all four on Q 3:20]; Shawkānī, *Tafsīr,* i, 354, ad Q 3:75). Occasionally *ummī* is rendered as "illiterate" without any explanation. (b) The term is connected with *umm al-qurā* (Q 6:92; 42:7), "the mother of cities," an epithet for Mecca (q.v.) and thus indicates the "one originating from Mecca," i.e. Muḥammad (see, for instance, Qurṭubī, *Jāmiʿ,* vii, 299, ad Q 7:157). Al-Baghdādī (Ummi prophet, 40) states, "It is clear, that to say that Muḥammad being 'Ummi' means he was illiterate and not from Mecca, 'Umm-al-Qurā,' is falsity and clear blasphemy, and that those who repeat such an interpretation defy, without logical or divine proof, God's Divine Wisdom in choosing his best creation and most sublime invention to guide mankind." Generally speaking, this kind of explanation also focuses on the ethnic aspect of the question, since the inhabitants of Mecca were Arabs (see also GEOGRAPHY). (c) *Ummī* can be derived from *umm,* "mother," indicating a person "in an original state," as pure, natural and untouched as when delivered by the mother (e.g. Rāzī, *Tafsīr,* viii, 109, ad Q 3:75; Shawkānī, *Fatḥ,* ii, 252, ad Q 7:157). This would incorporate, metaphorically speaking, the meanings of "uneducated, untaught or illiterate," an understanding which seems to project onto early Islam certain Ṣūfī categories prevalent at the time of the commentators (Schimmel, *Mystical dimension,* 26, 218; see ṢŪFISM AND THE QURʾĀN).

In explaining the qurʾānic *ummī* as indicating the Prophet's illiteracy, medieval commentators maintain that the term originally included two meanings: firstly, the inability to read and write in general and, secondly, the inexperience or ignorance (q.v.) of the *kitāb* as a sacred [written] revealed text. Nevertheless, they do focus exclusively on "illiterate," possibly because Muḥammad, after he had received the qurʾānic revelation (e.g. Q 29:47) and had become the Prophet, could no longer be regarded as *ummī* in the second sense.

Once established and accepted as a tenet of the faith (q.v.), Muḥammad's illiteracy has never been understood by Muslims in a derogatory sense. In fact, it has been taken as a particularly convincing sign of the genuineness of his prophethood, one which makes him distinctive from all previous prophets. As al-Ṭabarī (d. 310/923; *Tafsīr,* vi, 83, ad Q 7:157) explains, "there is no messenger of God known to be characterized in this way — I mean by *ummī* — except our prophet Muḥammad" God had sent him as his messenger at a time when he did not write or read from a book, i.e. when he was unable to read any previously revealed scripture (Q 29:48). Muḥammad was chosen by God while in this "natural condition" in order to pass on to the Arabs and all humankind the Qurʾān, for Muslims the unadulterated and final revelation. Al-Rāzī (d. 606/1210) formulates this idea in an exemplary way:

If he [Muḥammad] had mastered writing and reading, he possibly would have been suspected of having studied the books of the ancients. Hence, he would have acquired all these branches of knowledge *(ʿulūm)* through this reading *(muṭālaʿa).* So, when he passed on this mighty Qurʾān, which includes so many fields of knowledge, without having had any learning and reading *(min ghayr taʿallum wa-lā muṭālaʿa),* this was one of the miracles *(muʿjizāt)* [of his prophethood].... God provided him with all the knowledge of the ancestors and of later generations *(ʿulūm al-awwalīn wa-l-ākhirīn),* gave him from among the branches of knowledge and truths, that which none of the human beings before him had ever achieved. In spite of this mighty power of mind and understanding, God made him [in the condition of] not having learned how to write, [a matter] which can be easily learned [even] by people with the least mind and understanding (Rāzī, *Tafsīr*, xv, 23, ad Q 7:157). [Muḥammad was] a man, who had not learned from a master *(ustādh)*, and who had not studied any book or attended any lecture of a scholar, because Mecca was not a place of scholars, and the messenger of God was not absent from Mecca for a long period of time, which would make it possible to claim that he learned [so] many sciences during that absence. God did open for him the gate of knowledge (see KNOWLEDGE AND LEARNING) and realization [of his prophethood], even though [he was unlettered]..." (ibid., xv, 29, ad Q 7:158).

Thus, the quality of the Prophet as being *ummī*, "illiterate," became a central feature of religiosity in Islam. In a manner similar to Christianity, where God reveals himself through Christ, "the word made flesh," and where the virginity of Mary is required to produce an immaculate vessel for the divine word, so God reveals himself in Islam through the word of the Qurʾān (see WORD OF GOD). And the Prophet of Islam "had to be a vessel that was unpolluted by 'intellectual' knowledge of word and script so that he could carry the trust in perfect purity" (Schimmel, *Mystical dimension*, 26-7).

Ummī *explained by Islamicists*

Non-Muslim specialists in the field also stress the derivation of *ummī* from *umma*. Although their arguments differ, they all agree in rejecting the meaning of "illiterate." One can summarize three points of view: (a) With *umma* in the sense of "people, nation [of the Arabs]," its derivatives *ummī* and *ummiyyūn* would signify somebody "belonging to the Arab *umma*, someone of Arab origin," or simply "an Arab" (e.g. Wensinck, Muhammed, 172; Nallino, *Raccolta di scritti*, 60-5). (b) On the basis of historical and etymological arguments, *ummī* is understood as meaning "untaught" (equivalent to Aramaic/Syriac *ʿālmāyā;* Hebrew *gōyīm*), "unlearned" in opposition to "learned, educated" (e.g. Geiger, *Was hat Mohammed;* Th. Khoury, *Der Koran*, ii, 30; Rubin, *Eye*, 24; Arberry translates "of the common folk," which may reflect both meanings). It is also regarded as comparable with the talmudic *ʿam hā-ʿāreṣ*, an expression used by the Jews to indicate the "people" who are ignorant of the scriptures or who are not sufficiently well-versed therein, i.e. "laymen" or "people not knowing [the scriptures]" (e.g. Fleischer, *Kleinere Schriften;* Ahrens, Christliches im Qoran). (c) Nöldeke (*GQ*, i, 14) draws attention to the fact that *ummī* and *ummiyyūn* occur in the Qurʾān always as counterparts of *ahl al-kitāb*, "the People of the Book (q.v.)," "people who possess a holy scripture, who know it, who are well-versed therein." This observation has led others to conclude that if the meaning of "untaught, uneducated" were applied in strictly religious terms, i.e. "not having received a revelation," or "not being thoroughly familiar with it," *ummī* would mean "layman" or "heathen"; see for instance Sprenger, *Leben und Lehre*, ii, 401-2; Horovitz, *KU*, 51-3; id., *Jewish proper names*, 46-7; Buhl and Schaeder, *Das Leben*, 131).

Philological, historical and theological dimensions

Muslim and western scholars alike stress the philological and historical significance of deriving *ummī* from *umma* (cf. also Lane, i, 92). According to this approach, *ummī* and *ummiyyūn* are affiliated nouns (*nisba*s) of *umma*. *Umma*, in turn, stands for any group united by a common belief, common era or common place; every individual identified by this *nisba* is part of this entity and is expected to share its general features (Ibn Qutayba, *Taʾwīl*, 74-5). *Umma* refers in this context also to "a group who summon to the good" (*ummatun yadʿūna ilā l-khayri*,

Q 3:104), which is explained as *jamāʿat al-ʿulamāʾ… ay muʿallimūn,* "a group of scholars… i.e. teachers."

Most medieval scholars base their explanations on probably accurate historical knowledge that the Arabs did not read or write, though they abstain from any further philological clarification. In fact, it is the actual meaning of *umma* as evident from the Qurʾān, and the elucidation of the word's development within the framework of the Semitic languages, which provide the following important insights.

Umma occurs frequently in the Qurʾān and it indicates four different groupings: (a) Mainly a collectivity, thus an entire community, people joined together by linguistic and/or political ties, an aggregate of tribes or parts of tribes (see especially Nallino, *Raccolta di scritti*). This is shown by the fact that prophets were sent to different *umma*s (cf. Q 6:108; 10:47; 16:36, 84, 89; all third Meccan period); some of them believed, others did not (Q 16:36). (b) That which is united by the same belief, the original *umma wāḥida* of humankind (Q 10:19, third Meccan); God could have made humankind an *umma wāḥida,* if he had wanted to do so (see Q 43:33, second Meccan period; Q 42:8, third Meccan period; Q 5:48, Medinan period); a religiously defined unit, i.e. the sum of beliefs accepted by people (Q 43:22, 23, second Meccan period, referring here to the paganism of Mecca). This can be combined with Q 21:92-3; 23:52-3 (second Meccan period), where the identity of the Islamic *umma* in contrast to the *umma*s of earlier prophets seems to be established. (c) A group of individuals who break off from a people or from all humankind (Q 3:104, 110, Medinan). (d) Other meanings are, for instance, an entity of a species or an entire genus of animals (*umam,* Q 6:38, third Meccan period); a space of time, a meaning probably connected to the duration of an *umma,* a generation of people (Q 11:8; 12:45, third Meccan period); as well as an odd reference in which the word *umma* is applied solely to Abraham (q.v.; Q 16:120, third Meccan period).

As shown throughout, the qurʾānic usage of *umma* never indicates "common folk, unlearned people" as opposed to "learned people, scholars." This observation is supported, firstly, by the qurʾānic notion that each *umma* has its messenger (*rasūl,* Q 10:47; 16:36; also 13:38; 16:63; cf. Q 35:24, all third Meccan period), and each age its sacred book (Q 13:38, end of the third Meccan period). Only the Arabs were deprived of revelation (Q 36:6; 43:20-1, second Meccan period), so God chose a messenger from among them (Q 3:164, third Meccan period). Muḥammad became the warner (q.v.) in plain Arabic speech (Q 26:194, 195, second Meccan period), to whom the "Arabic Qurʾān" was revealed (Q 20:113; 43:3, second Meccan period; Q 12:2; 39:29; 41:2; 42:5, third Meccan period; see ARABIC LANGUAGE). This is further confirmed by expressions such as *Qurʾān mubīn* (Q 15:1, second Meccan period), *kitāb mubīn* (Q 26:2; 27:1; 43:2; 44:2, second Meccan period; Q 12:1; 28:2, third Meccan period; cf. Q 5:19, Medinan period), *āyāt bayyināt* (e.g. Q 22:16; 29:49; 57:9, Meccan) and derivatives of *fuṣṣila,* "to be divided into particular sections," a term that points to the process of the revelation of the Qurʾān. The Arabs became an *umma,* a people with a sacred text in their own language in which they were obliged to believe (e.g. Q 26:198, 199, second Meccan period).

This understanding is also confirmed by the Semitic context of the word. *Umma,* and its derivative *ummī,* comes from proto-Semitic *umma* (Aramaic *ummᵉthā;* Hebrew *ummā;* see Paret, Umma; Horovitz, *Proper names,* 46-7). To signify all other peoples in contrast to the people of Israel, the Israelites used *ummōt hā-ʿōlām,* "the peoples of the world." (The phrase is not found in the Torah [q.v.], but often in the Midrash, which increasingly circulated during the third and fourth centuries C.E., a time which is important for the development of Old Arabic.) In Hebrew, *umma* signified a "nation of Gentiles," non-Jews — a notion implying "peoples who did not have a scripture and did not therefore read [it]."

According to Horovitz's citation of the Ṣafā inscription, it seems that the word *umma* found its way into Arabic at a relatively early period (see Paret, Umma; Horovitz, *Proper names*, 46-7). Presumably, the idea implied in the word was carried into Old Arabic as well. It is important to note that the Jewish designation of attributing the plural of *umma* to "other people," i.e. non-Jews, seems to have been extended in medieval Islam by Muslims to non-Muslims. This is shown by authors of the eighth/fourteenth and ninth/fifteenth centuries such as Ibn Qayyim al-Jawziyya and al-Qalqashandī who designate in this way the "opponents of Islam" who are divided into *umam*, or the "the nations of infidelity," *umam al-kufr* (cf. also Haarmann, Glaubensvolk, 178). The philological observation that in Old Arabic *ummī* as a *nisba*, at least in its plural form *ummiyyūn*, was also used to designate "non-Jews," is distinctly supported by historical information reported by Companions of the Prophet quoted in exegetical works. According to these accounts, shortly before Islam and during the lifetime of Muḥammad, Arabic speaking Jews called the Arabs *ummiyyūn*, either because "the Arabs did not have a religion" that was based on a written revealed text or because the Arabs "had given up their old [polytheist] belief for another, i.e. Islam" (see e.g. Rāzī, *Tafsīr*, viii, 108-9, ad Q 3:75).

Other quotations of early authorities confirm that the emphasis of the *umma* derivatives — *ummī* and *ummiyyūn* — was in early times primarily on the meaning of "belonging to people not having a scripture" and "belonging to a nation [of Gentiles]," though implying, in a secondary sense, "not having or not reading a revealed book." Al-Qurṭubī states that "The term *ummiyyūn* refers to all Arabs, i.e. those who did write and those who did not; [they were indicated thus] since they were not People of the Book" (*Jāmiʿ*, xviii, 91, ad Q 62:2; according to Ibn ʿAbbās). Further, "with *ummiyyūn* the Arabs are intended, i.e. both among those who used to master writing and those who did not, [they were called in this way] since they were not "People of the Book," [even though] *ummiyyūn* originally means "those who do not write and who do not read written material" (ibid., xviii, 91, ad Q 62:2). Earlier, al-Ṭabarī had made a similar assertion: "Muḥammad's people were named *ummiyyūn* since no book had been revealed to them. 'A Prophet from among the *ummiyyūn* was sent to them' means that... Muḥammad was [an?] *ummī* since he arose from among the Arabs" (*Tafsīr*, xii, 89, ad Q 62:2, on the authority of Ibn Zayd).

If these and similar explanations quoted in exegetical works are applied to the relevant qurʾānic passages, "Arabs not having a book" are therein clearly distinguished from peoples previously having received a written revelation: "And say to those who have been given the book and to the *ummiyyūn:* 'Have you surrendered?'" (Q 3:20); "... they [i.e. some Jews] say: 'There is no way over us as to the *ummiyyūn*.' They [the Jews] speak falsehood against God and knowingly" (Q 3:75); "It is he who has raised up from among the *ummiyyūn* a messenger from among them, to recite his signs to them and to purify them, and to teach them the book and the wisdom, even though before that they were in manifest error (q.v.)..." (Q 62:2). In Q 2:78 only a group of Jews is characterized by the term and the perspective has changed. Accordingly, the term emphasizes the secondary meaning of not "reading" the holy scripture: "And there are some among them [the Jews] that are *ummiyyūn* not knowing the book, but knowing only fancies and mere conjectures."

Observations like these have led Wensinck (*Muslim creed*, 6; also Muhammed, 192) to draw attention to the apostle Paul writing to the Romans: "I speak to you Gentiles, inasmuch as I am the apostle of the Gentiles" (Romans 11:13) and to distinguish Muḥammad in a similar way as "the Arabian Prophet of the Gentiles, speaking to the Gentiles to whom no Apostle had ever been sent before." It is, however, more important to note that *al-nabī al-ummī*, if understood in the way shown here, can contribute essentially to the understanding of the early history of Muḥammad's prophethood, since it stresses both the "origin" (national-Arab) and the "originality" of the Prophet of Islam — who was not influenced, taught or pre-educated by (reading) any previous sacred scripture. Thus, it is the *ummī* messenger from among the *ummiyyūn*, i.e. the Arabs not having yet a divine scripture or reading it, whom Jews and Christians find "written down with them in their Torah and in the Gospel" (Q 7:157), and who is sent to be "a warner to the world" (Q 25:1, Meccan) and the messenger of God "to all people" (Q 7:158, possibly Medinan).

Within a more general framework, one should also bear in mind that the Qurʾān expressly calls Jews and Christians *ahl al-kitāb*, "People of the Book." This term implies the notion of designating people who had previously received a divine revelation in a written form (e.g. "We gave to Moses [q.v.] the book," Q 2:87) and, by this, of distinguishing them from Muslims. On the other hand, Muḥammad "teaches" from a single universal "book," the original *kitāb* which is preserved in heaven (Q 62:2; see HEAVENLY BOOK; HEAVEN AND SKY), through admonitions (see EXHORTATIONS) in "speech (q.v.) form" and "recitation" (the literal meaning of *qurʾān*). It is this orally dominated setting forth of the divine revelation to the public (see ORALITY), which highlights the distinctiveness of Islam and its Prophet as being different from previous religions and prophets, i.e. both the complex nature of the qurʾānic characterization of Muḥammad as *ummī* and the way in which Muslims have traditionally interpreted the term. This perspective might also clarify the emphasis which has always been laid in Islam on the believers' individual experience of listening to or "reciting" the Qurʾān aloud (see RECITATION OF THE QURʾĀN).

Sebastian Günther

Bibliography

Primary: Bukhārī *Ṣaḥīḥ*, in Ibn Ḥajar al-ʿAsqalānī, *Fatḥ al-bārī*, 13 vols., Beirut 1992; Dārimī, *Sunan;* Ibn Ḥanbal, *Musnad*, Beirut 1991; Ibn Kathīr, *Tafsīr;* Ibn Qutayba, *Taʾwīl*, in *al-Qurṭayn aw kitābay mushkil al-Qurʾān wa-gharībihi*, 2 vols. in 1, Beirut n.d.; Ibn Rabban al-Ṭabarī, *Kitāb al-Dīn wa-l-dawla*, Beirut 1979 (see the chapter entitled *Fī ummiyyat al-nabī wa-anna l-kitāb alladhī anzalahu llāh ʿalayhi āyatun li-l-nubuwwa*, "On the Prophet's illiteracy and the fact that the book which God revealed to him is a sign of prophecy," esp. 98-9); id., *The book of religion and empire*, trans. A. Mingana, Manchester 1922; *Jalālayn*, Cairo n.d.; *Lisān al-ʿArab*, Beirut 1955; Qurṭubī, *Jāmiʿ*, Cairo 1967; Rāzī, *Tafsīr*, ed. ʿA. Muḥammad, 32 vols., Cairo 1938; al-Shawkānī, *Tafsīr*, 4 vols., Cairo 1964; al-Sijistānī, Abū Bakr b. ʿUzayr, *Nuzhat al-qulūb fī tafsīr gharīb al-Qurʾān al-ʿazīz*, ed. Y.ʿA. al-Marʿashlī, Beirut 1990; Suyūṭī, *Itqān*, ed. S. al-Mandūh, Beirut 1996; Ṭabarī, *Tafsīr*, 12 vols., Beirut 1992; Zayd b. ʿAlī, *Tafsīr gharīb al-Qurʾān*, ed. Ḥ.M. al-Ḥakīm, Beirut 1992.

Secondary: C. Adang, *Muslim writers on Judaism and the Hebrew Bible. From Ibn Rabban to Ibn Ḥazm*, Leiden 1996, esp. 27-30, 144-8; K. Ahrens, Christliches im Qoran, in *ZDMG* 9 (1930), 15-68, esp. 37; ʿA. Yūsuf ʿAlī, *The holy Qurʾan. Text, translation and commentary*, New York 1934[1], 1946[3]; Arberry; M. Abū ʿAlī al-Baghdādī, The ummi prophet, in *Arab review* 1 (1993), 38-40; F. Buhl and H.H. Schaeder, *Das Leben Muhammeds,* Leipzig 1930, esp. 56, 131; N. Calder, The *ummī* in early Islamic juristic literature, in *Der Islam* 67 (1990), 111-23; H. Fleischer, *Kleinere Schriften,* 2 vols, Leipzig 1841, esp. ii, 114-7; J. Fück, Das Problem des Wissens im Qurʾān (ca. 1945), in S. Günther (ed.), *Johann Fücks Voträge über den Islam,* Halle (Saale) 1999, 1-26; A. Geiger, *Judaism and Islam. Prolegomenon by M. Pearlman,* New York 1970 (trans. of *Was hat Mohammed aus dem Judenthum aufgenommen?*); id., *Was hat Mohammed aus dem Judenthum aufgenommen?* Bonn 1833, esp. 27-8; I. Goldfeld, The illiterate prophet *(nabī ummī).* An inquiry into the development of a dogma in Islamic tradition, in *Der Islam* 57 (1980), 58-67; U. Haarmann, Glaubensvolk und Nation im islamischen und lateinischen Mittelalter, in *Berlin-Brandenburgische Akademie der Wissenschaften. Berichte und Abhandlungen* 2 (1996), 161-99; M. Hamidullah (ed. and trans.), *Sahifah Hammam ibn Munabbih. The earliest extant work on the hadith,* Hyderabad 1961; J. Horovitz, *Jewish proper names and derivatives in the Koran,* Ohio 1925, repr. Hildesheim 1964, esp. 46-7; id., *KU,* esp. 51-3; A.Th. Khoury, *Der Koran. Arabisch-Deutsch. Übersetzung und wissenschaftlicher Kommentar,* Gütersloh 1990 — (for different renderings of *ummī* in western translations of the Qurʾān, see ii, 30-1); P.K. Meagher, Illiteracy, in P.K. Meagher, T.C. O'Biren, C.M. Aherene (eds.), *Encyclopedic dictionary of religion,* 3 vols., Washington 1979, ii, 1766-7; C.A. Nallino, *Raccolta di scritti editi e inediti... a cura di Maria Nallino,* Rome 1940; Nöldeke, *GQ,* esp. i, 14, 159-60; Paret, *Kommentar;* id., *Koran;* id., Ummī, in *EI¹,* iv, 1015-6; Pickthall; U. Rubin, *The eye of the beholder. The life of Muḥammad as viewed by the early Muslims,* Princeton 1995, esp. 23-30; A. Schimmel, *The mystical dimension of Islam,* Chapel Hill 1975; M.H. Shakir (trans.), The Qur'an *(al-Qurʾān al-ḥakīm),* New York 1993; A. Sprenger, *Die Leben und die Lehre des Mohammed, nach bisher grösstentheils unbenutzten Quellen bearbeitet,* 3 vols., Berlin 1869, esp. ii, 398-402 ("Konnte Muḥammad lesen?"); Watt-Bell, *Introduction,* esp. 17-8; A.J. Wensinck, Muhammed und die Propheten, in *AO* 2 (1924), 168-98, esp. 191-2; id., *The Muslim creed. Its genesis and historical development,* Cambridge 1932, esp. 6.

ʿIlliyyūn

A term occurring twice in the Qurʾān (Q 83:19 and 18) that Western scholars have considered to be derived from the Hebrew *ʿelyōn,* "the highest" (Paret, ʿIlliyyūn). Many medieval and post-medieval Muslim commentators understand the term to connote the inscribed book where the deeds of the pious are listed (see RECORD OF HUMAN ACTIONS; HEAVENLY BOOK; PRESERVED TABLET). All the early commentaries, however, appear to interpret *ʿilliyyūn* as the name of a place high in heaven (see HEAVEN AND SKY). Suggestions about the specifics of where or what it is include: paradise (q.v.), up on high, the fourth heaven, the seventh heaven, above the seventh heaven, the heaven near God, the right leg of the throne (see THRONE OF GOD), the highest place where the spirits of the believers are, (near) *sidrat al-muntahā,* "the lote tree on the boundary" (Q 53:14). In his *Tafsīr,* al-Ṭabarī (d. 310/923) concludes, as does the lexicographer al-Azharī, that the word is in the plural, because its meaning is higher than high; the book of the deeds of the pious is in the highest place, of which God alone knows the boundaries, which are not limited to the seventh heaven.

The earlier commentators (see EXEGESIS OF THE QURʾĀN: CLASSICAL AND MEDIEVAL) apparently interpret the question asked in Q 83:19: "and do you realize what *ʿilliyyūn* is?" as rhetorical or as an exclamatory remark (see RHETORIC OF THE QURʾĀN; GRAMMAR AND THE QURʾĀN). Al-Qurṭubī (d. 671/1272; *Jāmiʿ,* ad loc.) states explicitly that it is said that *kitāb marqūm,* "an inscribed book (q.v.)," of Q 83:20 is not the explanation of *ʿilliyyūn.* Most later commentators, like al-Rāzī (d. 606/1210; *Tafsīr*) and al-Zamakhsharī (d. 538/1144; *Kashshāf*), however, understand Q 83:20 to explain the previous verse, and believe *ʿilliyyūn* to be the *dīwān* in which the deeds of the pious are recorded. Al-Bayḍāwī (d. ca. 716/1316; *Anwār*) and *Jalālayn* mention both possibilities. In modern times both interpretations are found (see EXEGESIS OF THE QURʾĀN: EARLY MODERN AND

CONTEMPORARY). The early lexicographers al-Khalīl and al-Azharī define it as the plural of *ʿilliy,* the place in the seventh heaven to which the spirits of the believers are raised (see BELIEF AND UNBELIEF; RESURRECTION; SOUL). The occurrence of the term in the canonical ḥadīth (see ḤADĪTH AND THE QURʾĀN) is in accordance with the opinion of the early commentators.

In sum, it may be concluded that *ʿilliyyūn* certainly is related to the Hebrew *ʿelyon* and probably even derived from it, but the Hebrew word also may simply mean "uppermost, highest" and does not necessarily refer to heavenly realms or creatures. Nevertheless, it is interesting that at least once (Qurṭubī, *Jāmiʿ*) *ʿilliyyūn* is explained as referring to the highest assembly of angels (Q 38:69; see ANGEL).

Frederik Leemhuis

Bibliography
Primary: ʿAbd al-Razzāq, *Tafsīr;* Abū l-Layth al-Samarqandī, *Tafsīr,* ed. ʿA. Muʿawwaḍ et al.; Azharī, Abū Manṣūr Muḥammad b. Aḥmad, *Tahdhīb al-lugha,* ed. ʿA. al-Najjār and M. al-Najjār, 15 vols., Cairo 1967, iii, 187-8; Bayḍāwī, *Anwār;* Ibn Kathīr, *Tafsīr;* Ibn Wahb, ʿAbdallāh al-Qurashī, *al-Jāmiʿ. Tafsīr al-Qurʾān,* ed. M. Muranyi, Wiesbaden 1993, 264; *Jalālayn;* al-Khalīl b. Aḥmad, *Kitāb al-ʿAyn,* ed. M. al-Makhzāmī and I. al-Samarrāʾī, 8 vols., Beirut 1988, ii, 248; Māwardī, *Nukat;* Mujāhid, *Tafsīr;* Muqātil, *Tafsīr;* Qurṭubī, *Jāmiʿ;* Qushayrī, *Laṭāʾif;* Rāzī, *Tafsīr;* Sufyān al-Thawrī, *Tafsīr,* Rampur 1965, repr. Beirut 1983; Ṭabarī, *Tafsīr;* Muḥammad Sayyid al-Ṭanṭāwī, *al-Tafsīr al-wasīṭ lil-Qurʾān al-karīm,* 15 vols., Cairo 1977-86; Zamakhsharī, *Kashshāf.*
Secondary: R. Paret, ʿIlliyyūn, in *EI²,* iii, 1132-3 (with references).

Illness and Health

States of physical ailment and soundness. *Maraḍ* is sometimes used in the Qurʾān to convey the literal meaning of physical illness, while at other times, it is used in a metaphorical sense. For the literal meaning, the verbal form *mariḍa* occurs only once with the first person pronoun — the speaker is the prophet Abraham (q.v.) — as its grammatical subject (Q 26:80). This verse attracted much attention from qurʾānic commentators because its apparent meaning contradicts the dominant doctrine of God's omnipotence (see POWER AND IMPOTENCE). Although the Qurʾān teaches that everything, bad or good, happens according to God's decree and will, commentators on the Qurʾān (see EXEGESIS OF THE QURʾĀN: CLASSICAL AND MEDIEVAL) were reluctant to ascribe to God human misfortunes like illness. In addition to the aforementioned verbal form, the active participle *marīḍ* occurs five times (Q 2:184, 185, 196; 24:61; 48:17), as does its plural form *marḍā* (Q 4:43, 102; 5:6; 9:91; 73:20). The context always inclues the qurʾānic prescription to relieve sick people of certain religiously imposed constraints (i.e. fasting, q.v.), which they should otherwise observe.

The Qurʾān puts more emphasis on moral illness than on physical sickness (see ETHICS AND THE QURʾĀN). The verbal noun *maraḍ* is mentioned in the Qurʾān thirteen times referring to both disbelief (*kufr,* see BELIEF AND UNBELIEF) and hypocrisy (*nifāq,* see HYPOCRITES AND HYPOCRISY), as a disease *(maraḍ)* in the hearts (see HEART) of the disbelievers and the hypocrites. While the disease of disbelief *(kufr)* could be cured, hypocrisy *(nifāq)* is incurable because the hypocrites *(munāfiqūn)* pretend to be Muslim while they hide *kufr* in their hearts. The *munāfiqūn* are, according to the Qurʾān, born with an incurable sickness in their hearts which God has increased and they will be harshly punished in the afterlife because of their bad conduct (Q 2:10; see EVIL DEEDS). In many places, the Qurʾān refers to itself as cure *(shifāʾ)* to the diseases of the hearts: "O humankind!

There has come to you an exhortation (*maw'iẓatun*, see EXHORTATIONS) from your lord, and a cure (*shifā'un*) for what is in the hearts (*ṣudūr*). For the believers, it is guidance (*hudā*) and mercy (*raḥma*)" (Q 10:57). "But for those in whose hearts (*qulūb*) is a disease, it increases their illness" (Q 9:125). The metaphor of *maraḍ* is, indeed, "one of the most important elements in the semantic constitution of *nifā'*" (Izutsu, *Concepts*, 182). Deafness and blindness (of the heart) are two other metaphors that present, in a very vivid style, the symptoms of such a disease: "For those who do not believe [in the Qur'ān], there is deafness in their ears (q.v.) and it is blindness for them" (Q 41:44; see HEARING AND DEAFNESS; VISION AND BLINDNESS; SEEING AND HEARING).

As a result of the qur'ānic emphasis on the moral and ethical diseases, Muslim theologians and jurists have paid considerable attention to the matter of human intention (q.v.; *niyya*). Al-Bukhārī (d. 256/870) opens his *Ṣaḥīḥ* with the ḥadith, quoted in all the canonical collections, "Deeds are only judged by intention" (*innamā l-a'māl bi-l-niyyāt*). While some theologians include deeds (*af'āl*) in their definitions of faith (q.v.; *īmān*), others consider faith to be a matter of heartfelt belief (*taṣdīq*) only (cf. Ash'arī, *Maqālāt*, i, 225-34). Ṣūfism has generated a great deal of literature about the divine position of the spiritually healthy human heart; it is considered "God's throne inside man" (Ibn 'Arabī, *Tadbīrāt*, 120-32; see ṢŪFISM AND THE QUR'ĀN). Al-Ghazālī (d. 505/1111) devotes a part of his *Iḥyā'* to explaining the wonders (*'ajā'ib*) of the heart and how to clean and purify it, so that it will be ready to receive divine knowledge (see KNOWLEDGE AND LEARNING) directly from God.

Nasr Hamid Abu Zayd

Bibliography
Primary: al-Ash'arī, Abū l-Ḥasan 'Alī b. Ismā'īl, *Maqālāt al-islāmiyyīn wa-ikhtilāf al-muṣallīn*, ed. M.M. 'Abd al-Ḥamīd, Cairo 1970; al-Ghazālī, Abū Ḥāmid Muḥammad, *Iḥyā' 'ulūm al-dīn*, ed. R. al-Sayyid, Beirut 1403/1983; Ibn 'Arabī, Muḥyī l-Dīn Abū 'Abdallāh al-Ḥātimī, *al-Tadbīrāt al-ilāhiyya fī iṣlāḥ al-mamlaka al-insāniyya*, ed. H. Nyberg, Leiden 1339/1920; Ṭabarī, *Tafsīr*, 30 vols, Cairo 1388/1968.
Secondary: Izutsu, *Concepts*.

Illumination see ORNAMENT AND ILLUMINATION

Ilyās see ELIJAH

Images see IDOLS AND IMAGES

Imām

A term (pl. *a'imma*) used in the Qur'ān to mean the following: symbol, leader, model, ideal example, revelation, guide, archetype, and foremost. It appears in the Qur'ān seven times in the singular and five times in the plural form. The term *imām* has been interpreted and applied in various ways in Islamic history up to contemporary times and has been significant in shaping the politico-religious dimension of the Muslim *Weltanschauung*.

The Qur'ān's symbolic reference to the appointment of Abraham (q.v.) as an imām (leader) of humanity in Q 2:124 counsels that religious submission to the belief in the one unseen God — Islamic monotheism — is borne out of various trials (see TRIAL) in life resulting in the attainment of religious and moral integrity (see BELIEF AND UNBELIEF; ETHICS AND THE QUR'ĀN). Q 46:12 and 11:17 refer to the revelations (see REVELATION AND INSPIRATION) received by Moses (q.v.) and Muḥammad as *imām* — books (see BOOK) of religious guidance — while Q 36:12 uses the word *imām* to refer to the record of the deeds of every individual (see RECORD OF HUMAN ACTIONS), these deeds having consequences for the nature of life after death (see REWARD AND PUNISHMENT; FREEDOM AND PREDESTINATION). At the personal level, the Qurʾān urges all Muslims to pray for themselves and their families to become *imām* in faith — foremost in God-consciousness or piety (q.v.). Attainment of piety is seen as a sign of becoming an imām. The above mentioned usages of the term *imām* characterize the main features of religious experience in Islam. The following two sets of qurʾānic verses, Q 21:73; 28:5; 32:24 on the one hand and Q 9:12; 28:41 on the other, distinguish between two types of imām(s) in relation to religio-social leadership — the imāms *(aʾimma)* of guidance *(hidāya)* — religiously guided leaders who promote religious belief and righteousness, and the imāms of unbelief *(kufr)* and the fire (q.v.; *al-nār*) — immoral and unjust leaders who spread corruption (q.v.) on earth, rejecting belief in God and thereby drawing humanity to hellfire (see HELL). The Qurʾān cites the opposition of the prophets Lot (q.v.; Lūṭ) and Shuʿayb (q.v.) as representing the distinction between *aʾimma* of *kufr* and *al-nār* and *aʾimma* of *hidāya*.

Q 17:71 refers to the history of imāms among Adam's (see ADAM AND EVE) progeny. God raised prophets and righteous leaders among various groups of people who were charged with the task of conveying and upholding the message of monotheism. These figures will on the last day (see APOCALYPSE; LAST JUDGMENT) bear witness to the good deeds (q.v.) and sins (see SIN, MAJOR AND MINOR) committed by their communities in relation to the moral-theological aspects of monotheism (see also EVIL DEEDS; GOOD AND EVIL). The qurʾānic archetype of the imām as an exemplary religious-social-political leader, as presented in the narrative of the prophet Abraham (q.v.; Ibrāhīm), acquired a variety of meanings over time and has been applied eclectically by Muslims in their political and religious lives, with many sects or groups asserting the qurʾānic legitimacy of their derived politico-theological interpretations.

The Khārijīs (q.v.), the first sect of Islam, with its insistence upon the principles of human equality and the application of qurʾānic justice, called for the free election of a just and religiously steadfast Imām, to be chosen regardless of his tribal and racial background. Currently, the Ibāḍiyya of Oman and North Africa are the only surviving Khārijī sub-sect with a continuing tradition of an elected Imām. The Shīʿa (see SHĪʿISM AND THE QURʾĀN) reject the politico-religious leadership status of the first three caliphs of Islam, recognizing instead ʿAlī b. Abī Ṭālib (q.v.) as the first Imām, whose religious charisma and political leadership is transmitted genealogically. His descendants have the sole legitimate claim to the office of the imāmate. For the Shīʿa, the Imām is endowed with the inner *(bāṭinī)* meaning of the Qurʾān which was transmitted by Muḥammad to ʿAlī and Fāṭima (q.v.), his son-in-law and daughter, respectively, and from them to his blood descendants. For the Nizārī sect of the Ismāʿīlī Shīʿa, the current Aga Khan is the forty-ninth manifest/living *(ḥāḍir)* Imām. He is regarded by them as a personification of the Qurʾān. The Mustaʿlī branch of the Ismāʿīlī Shīʿa look upon their "guide" *(dāʿī muṭlaq)* as being the sole representative and religious teacher of their community since Imām al-Ṭayyib went into concealment *(ghayba)* in 524/1130. The Ithnā ʿAsharī Shīʿa, the "Twelvers," the majority of whom reside in Iran, Iraq and Lebanon, revere the twelve descendants of Fāṭima and ʿAlī up to Imām Muḥammad al-Mahdī, who went into concealment *(ghaybah)* in 260/874, as the only infallible interpreters of the Qurʾān. Since then, the Twelver Shīʿīs have looked upon their religious scholars, *mujtahid*s and *āyatullāh*s, as religious leaders in lieu of the Imām until his return. For the Khārijīs and the Shīʿīs, Imāms hold both religious and political power simultaneously. They know the inner meaning of the Qurʾān, lead the Muslim community and interpret and apply Islamic law (see LAW AND THE QURʾĀN; POLITICS AND THE QURʾĀN).

Sunnī Muslims, as proponents of the social-religious principle of the followers of the tradition of the Prophet and community (*ahl al-sunna wa-l-jamāʿa,* see SUNNA), do not believe the Imām to be divine in status. For them, the term constitutes an archetypal reference to the personalities of the prophets Abraham and Muḥammad in their capacity as model prophets and statesmen, both representing unwavering adherence to the principle of monotheism and integrated religious, moral, social, and political leadership. Sunnī Muslims confer the title "Imām" separately upon the prayer leader in the mosque, and use it as an honorific title for just political leaders and accomplished scholars of the Islamic religious sciences.

Imtiyaz Yusuf

Bibliography
Primary: Nāʿib al-Imām Rūḥullah Khumaynī, *Ḥukūmat-i Islāmī,* Teheran 1980; id., *Islam and revolution. Writings and declarations of Imam Khomeini,* trans. H. Algar, Berkeley, CA 1981; Muḥammad b. Muḥammad al-Mufīd, *Kitāb al-Irshād,* trans. I.K.A. Howard, Qom 1981; Ṭabarī, *Taʾrīkh.*
Secondary: M.A. Amir-Moezzi, *The divine guide in early Shīʿism,* Albany, NY 1994; N. Calder, The significance of the term *imām* in early Islamic jurisprudence, in *ZGAIW* I (1984), 253-64; F. Daftary (ed.), *Medieval Ismāʿīlī history and thought,* New York 1996; id., *The Ismāʿīlīs. Their history and doctrines,* New York 1990; W. Ivanov, Ismāʿīliyya, in *Shorter encyclopaedia of Islam,* Leiden 1974; S.H.M. Jafri, *Origins and early development of Shīʿa Islam,* London 1979; W. Madelung, Ismāʿīliyya, in *EI²,* iv, 198-206; M. Momen, *An introduction to Shīʿī Islam,* New Haven 1985; Fazlur Rahman, *Islamic methodology in history,* Karachi 1965; A.A. Sachedina, *The just ruler in Shīʿite Islam,* New York 1988; id., *Islamic messianism,* Albany, NY 1981; ʿAbdallāh b. Ḥumayyid al-Sālimī, *Tuḥfat al-aʿyān bi-sīrat ahl ʿUmān,* 2 vols., Kuwait 1974; W.M. Watt, *The formative period of Islamic thought,* Edinburgh 1973; J.C. Wilkinson, *The imamate tradition of Oman,* Cambridge 1987.

Īmān
see FAITH; BELIEF AND UNBELIEF

Immortality
see ESCHATOLOGY; RESURRECTION; ETERNITY; PARADISE; HELL AND HELLFIRE; FIRE; GARDEN; DEATH AND THE DEAD

Immunity

Release of or exemption from a duty. *Barāʾa,* a derivative of the Arabic root *b-r-ʾ,* is attested twice in the Qurʾān where it denotes the idea of immunity. In Q 54:43, it occurs in the sense of immunity or absolution. There, the rhetorical question arises: "Or [do you think] the sacred books (*al-zubur,* see BOOK; PSALMS) have given you immunity [from chastisement, see CHASTISEMENT AND PUNISHMENT]!" The major commentaries (see EXEGESIS OF THE QURʾĀN: CLASSICAL AND MEDIEVAL) maintain that this verse admonishes the pagans of Mecca (q.v.), reminding them that they fare no better than earlier generations (q.v.) of more prominent pagans who have perished. The reference is to the generations of Noah (q.v.), Ṣāliḥ (q.v.) and Pharaoh (q.v.; Ṭabarsī, *Majmaʿ,* vi, 78; Abū Ḥayyān, *Baḥr,* viii, 182). This is also the meaning given to the verse by Blachère (*Le Coran,* v, 1076).

Barāʾa also occurs in the opening verse of sūra 9, commonly entitled Sūrat al-Tawba ("Repentance") but also known under other names, notably, Sūrat al-Barāʾa. "A declaration of immunity from God and his messenger (q.v.), to those of the pagans with whom you have contracted mutual alliances." The interpretation of the first verse of this late Medinan sūra has given rise to some difficulties. The traditional interpretation upheld by the most authoritative commentators including al-Ṭabarī (d. 310/923), al-Ṭabarsī (d. 518/1123), al-Zamakhsharī (d. 538/1144), Ibn al-Jawzī (d. 597/1200), and al-Rāzī (d. 606/1210) explains this *barāʾa* on the basis of the subsequent verses according to which God and his Prophet will be unbound *(barīʾ)* in regard to unbelievers (see BELIEF AND UNBELIEF; POLYTHEISM AND ATHEISM; IDOLATRY AND IDOLATERS), who broke the truce they had made with the Prophet (see CONTRACTS AND ALLIANCES; BREAKING TRUSTS AND CONTRACTS). The breaking of the truce by the Prophet warranted a justification and the commentaries go to some length to explain the conditions where this is permissible (Ṭabarī, *Tafsīr*, xiv, 95-6; Rāzī, *Tafsīr*, iv, 392-4; Ibn al-Jawzī, *Zād*, iii, 388-92; see Rubin, Study, 27-32). In the context of the Qurʾān, *barāʾa* thus also means the breaking of ties, dissociation and disconnection.

Another meaning for *barāʾa* is that of excommunication. This theme was developed by several groups of Khārijīs (q.v.) who repudiated those who, according to them, did not deserve the title of Muslim; the Ajārida excluded *(barāʾa)* children from Islam until they grew and became believers, while the Azāriqa excluded the quietists and those who recognized *taqiyya* (see DISSIMULATION). In Shīʿī doctrine (see SHĪʿISM AND THE QURʾĀN), *al-wilāya* — attaching oneself to the imāms — also entails *barāʾa*, the mental dissociation from the imāms' enemies (Goldziher, *Introduction*, 181-2; see IMĀM). In legal terminology *barāʾat al-dhimma* denotes freedom from any legal obligation. In classical Muslim administration, it is a receipt given by the treasurer *(khāzin)* to the taxpayer. *Barāʾa* has also been employed to denote written documents such as a license, certificate and diploma. In Morocco, *barāʾa* was a letter addressed to the community announcing an important event or sent for the purpose of exhorting or admonishing. The night of the *barāʾa* describes a religious festival in the night of mid-Shaʿbān.

Nadia Maria El-Cheikh

Bibliography

Primary: Abū Ḥayyān, *Baḥr*, 8 vols., Riyad n.d.; Ibn al-Jawzī, *Zād*, 9 vols., Damascus 1964-5; Rāzī, *Tafsīr*, 8 vols., Cairo 1890/1308; Ṭabarī, *Tafsīr*, 16 vols., Cairo 1955; Ṭabarsī, *Majmaʿ*.
Secondary: R. Blachère, *Le Coran. Traduction nouvelle*, Paris 1949-51; I. Goldziher, *Introduction to Islamic theology*, trans. A. and R. Hamori, Princeton 1981; U. Rubin, *Barāʾa*. A study of some qurʾānic passages, in *JSAI* 5 (1984), 13-32.

Impeccability

Not being liable to sin (see SIN, MAJOR AND MINOR), immunity from fault and error (q.v.). In Islamic theology, the single Arabic term, *ʿiṣma*, connotes both impeccability and the closely related notion of infallibility (not being liable to err). It refers, in the primary instance, to the prophets (see PROPHETS AND PROPHETHOOD) and to the question of whether they are free from sin or not. Although neither the term nor the concept appear as such in the Qurʾān, the doctrine of impeccability is crucial, according to most theologians (see THEOLOGY AND THE QURʾĀN), if only to ensure that the prophets could not have been able to lie (q.v.) when they asserted the fact of God's revelation (see REVELATION AND

INSPIRATION) to them and that they transmitted its text and message perfectly.

In fact, however, the sins of the prophets are more or less freely attested in the Qurʾān and ḥadīth (see ḤADĪTH AND THE QURʾĀN), if understood literally, and the earlier Muslims apparently admitted as much. Later the Shīʿa (see SHĪʿISM AND THE QURʾĀN), in their attempt to assert the absolute authority of their imāms (see IMĀM), developed the doctrine of *ʿiṣma* and argued that the imāms were *maʿṣūm*, incapable of error and sin. One early Shīʿī theologian even claimed that the imāms had to be impeccable and infallible, despite the Prophet himself having been liable to a degree of sin as recognized and admitted by the Qurʾān. In response to any given lapse of the Prophet, God, who was in constant communication with him, could immediately initiate corrective action by means of revelation. The imāms, being only generally and not specifically guided by God, must not be capable of any error at all.

Later doctrine of the mainstream Shīʿa, however, holds that the prophets are also immune to sin and error. In a similar manner with respect to the prophets (but not the imāms), the Muʿtazila (see MUʿTAZILĪS) maintained the impeccability of the prophets. Other groups as well, including the Sunnīs, generally tend to insist that the prophets were free of sin, particularly of grave sins. Nearly all Muslims deny that any of the prophets could have ever been a polytheist or have worshipped idols (see IDOLS AND IMAGES) — a sin that, according to the Qurʾān itself, God will never forgive (see POLYTHEISM AND ATHEISM; IDOLATRY AND IDOLATERS). In regard to other lesser sins and errors, however, there are problems engendered by explicit references in the Qurʾān (e.g. Q 48:2, for Muḥammad) which, if taken literally, must mean that, previous to the advent of their respective missions, if not afterward, at least some of the prophets were guilty of sin. Thus, for the Ḥanbalīs and other literalists, such sins are a reality and are not to be dismissed. Broadly speaking, however, Muslims follow the principle that, if such texts are subject to various interpretations, then, with respect to the prophets, only the best may be ascribed to them. Sin consists in opposing God and his commandments (q.v.) and in the consequent alienation from him. Hence, any act undertaken with the deliberate intent of contravening God's law (see BOUNDARIES AND PRECEPTS; LAW AND THE QURʾĀN) constitutes a serious and possibly grave sin. But an inadvertent lapse done in a moment of forgetfulness or simple negligence does not denote sin. By means of such reasoning, it is possible to attribute the best even to Adam — a prophet (see ADAM AND EVE) — and thereby to save him from having committed an act of opposing God's explicit order (as is, however, quite apparently admitted in Q 20:121; see ASTRAY; FALL OF MAN). Clearly, then, it is critical to identify the degree of sin or possible sin in each instance and the problem is not readily solved by simply eliminating the capacity for sin from the prophets in and of themselves, since, if they are not able to sin by the very nature of their being, they will also not be deserving of reward (see REWARD AND PUNISHMENT; FREEDOM AND PREDESTINATION). Impeccability (the *ʿiṣma*) of a prophet is therefore not an inherent quality, but rather a gift or a kindness *(luṭf)* bestowed on him by God.

Perhaps the most frequently discussed case from the Qurʾān is that of Joseph (q.v.), a case which also displays a full range of the possible interpretations and nuances in respect to his ability to commit a sin and his having been saved from it. In Q 12:24, Joseph is said to have been sexually propositioned by the wife of his adopted master. The text states fairly clearly that "she coveted him and he coveted her." The verb denoting the desire of each is the same and thus, if her transgression is undeniably sinful, about which almost all authorities agree, then his must be likewise. The sin in this case is complicated by the aspect of intention (q.v.) and motive. For Joseph actually to covet her sexually may be regarded as a sin in and of itself. The verse, however, continues immediately with the phrase "if he had not seen the proof of his lord," and hence the whole passage may be construed in such a way that Joseph would have coveted her (i.e. that as a human being he was naturally susceptible to sexual desire for an attractive woman; see SEX AND SEXUALITY; ADULTERY AND FORNICATION) but that God's sign intervened, precluding any impulse in that direction and thus preventing him from committing the sin it involved. The question was, however, frequently debated and there were those who "advanced" God's intervention and those who "delayed" it. Accordingly, depending on exactly how one understands Joseph's perception of God's timely proof, it is possible to exempt him from all taint of sin or, conversely, to allow that he came close to it, some commentators even claiming that he was stopped just as he began to remove his trousers and engage in the forbidden sexual act.

What is less obvious is the implication that Joseph was not infallible with regard to his knowledge of what he should and should not do (see KNOWLEDGE AND LEARNING; IGNORANCE). If he were perfectly infallible, he would not have needed God's reminder when the situation required it. A better example of this kind of infallibility, or lack thereof, is that of Moses (q.v.) when God conversed with him (Q 7:143) and Moses said to God, "Show yourself to me so that I may observe you." Here God, of course, rebuked Moses for asking, implying rather forcefully that God cannot be seen (see SEEING AND HEARING; GOD AND HIS ATTRIBUTES; FACE OF GOD; ANTRHOPOMORPHISM). For those authorities who accept the doctrine of the impossibility of actually seeing God because he is utterly immaterial and non-corporeal, that Moses would make such a request, if the passage is to be construed literally, must indicate his lack of infallibility. Accordingly, on his own, Moses would have been quite fallible in respect to his understanding and perception of religion and religious doctrine — an interpretation that is fraught with doctrinal difficulties and is generally avoided.

Paul E. Walker

Bibliography
(In addition to the standard commentaries to the verses cited above): B. Abrahamov, Ibn Taymiya and the doctrine of ʿismah, in *Bulletin of the Henry Martyn Institute of Islamic studies* 12 (1993), 21-30; C. Gilliot, Les trois mensonges d'Abraham dans la tradition interprétante musulmane, in *IOS* 17 (1997), 37-87, esp. 68-78; W. Madelung, ʿIṣma, in *EI*², iv, 182-4 (includes bibliographical citations for a full range of primary theological sources).

Impotence

Weakness, inability to exert power. Impotence characterizes all entities in the Qurʾān except God. Countless formulas express the twin concepts of weakness of the creature *(ḍ-ʿ-f, f-q-r)* and strength *(q-d-r)* or self-sufficiency *(gh-n-y)* of the creator (see CREATION). Passages on the "stages of life" (e.g. Q 22:5; see BIOLOGY AS THE CREATION AND STAGES OF LIFE) portray the utter dependence of human beings upon God.

False gods are absolutely impotent, while the relative power of humans, jinn (q.v.) and angels (see ANGEL) depends upon harmony with God's will. False gods are idols (Q 37:95; see IDOLS AND IMAGES) or only names (Q 53:23). "O people!... Those to whom you pray besides God will never be able to create a fly, even if they all worked together on it! And if the fly took something away from them, they could not get it back!" (Q 22:73). Even when the "deity" wrongly worshiped is a prophet (see JESUS; CHRISTIANS AND CHRISTIANITY), he has no power of his own. "Say: 'Who has any power at all over God if he wished to destroy the messiah *(al-masīḥ)* the son of Mary (q.v.), and his mother, and whoever is on the earth altogether?'..." (Q 5:17).

People and nations assume that their power is real; in fact, it is illusory and, without faith (q.v.; *īmān*), their deeds are vain and their doom certain. "Do they not see how many of those before them we destroyed — generations (q.v.) whom we empowered in the earth as we have not empowered you?" (Q 6:6; see PUNISHMENT STORIES; REWARD AND PUNISHMENT). Pagan fatalism is not a true perception of human impotence but a denial of God's power (see FATE; DESTINY; TIME). "There is nothing but our life in this world. We die, and we live, and we shall never be resurrected!" (Q 23:37; see RESURRECTION). Humans judge God by their own impotence: "Does the human being not see that we created him from sperm?... Yet he compares other things to us... He says, 'Who can revive bones that have rotted?' Say, 'He will revive them who created them the first time!...'" (Q 36:77-9; see DEATH AND THE DEAD). "The Jews have said, 'God's hand is tied.' Their hands (q.v.) are tied and they are cursed for having said so! Rather, his hands are spread wide, distributing bounty (see BLESSING) as he wishes..." (Q 5:64; see JEWS AND JUDAISM). Often God emphasizes human weakness with a challenge: "Do you see the water (q.v.) that you drink? Did you bring it down from the rain-cloud or did we?" (Q 56:68-9; see COSMOLOGY). Believers may wield the power of God, as at Badr (q.v.; Q 3:123), or lose it and realize their own impotence, as at Uḥud (Q 3:152-5; see EXPEDITIONS AND BATTLES). The stories of vanished nations (see HISTORY AND THE QURʾĀN; GEOGRAPHY) prove, however, that even prophets are powerless to change some people (see PROPHETS AND PROPHETHOOD). Without divine support, Muḥammad himself might have yielded a bit to his adversaries (Q 17:74; see OPPOSITION TO MUḤAMMAD).

An enduring theological dilemma arose from efforts to reconcile human impotence with human responsibility for sin (see SIN, MAJOR AND MINOR). "As for those who refuse to believe, it is the same to them whether you warn them or do not warn them (see WARNER): they will not believe. God has sealed their hearts (see HEART) and their hearing (see EARS; HEARING AND DEAFNESS), and over their eyes (q.v.) is a veil; and they shall have a great penalty" (Q 2:6-7; see BELIEF AND UNBELIEF; SEEING AND HEARING). "God does not place a burden upon a soul greater than it can bear..." (Q 2:286). The limits on human power are most fully discussed in the works on predestination and free will, *al-qaḍāʾ wa-l-qadar* (see FREEDOM AND PREDESTINATION; ETHICS AND THE QURʾĀN).

Rosalind W. Gwynne

Bibliography
Primary: Abu Nuʿaym al-Iṣfahānī, *Ḥilyat al-awliyāʾ*, ed. M. al-Khānjī, Beirut 1387/1967, 345-53 (ʿUmar II, Letter on *qadar;* also in J. van Ess, *Anfänge muslimischer Theologie. Zwei anti-qadaritische Traktate aus dem ersten Jahrhunderten der Higra,* Wiesbaden/Beirut 1977, 43-54); al-Ḥasan al-Baṣrī, *al-Risāla fī l-qadar,* ed. H. Ritter, in *Der Islam* 21 (1933), 1-83; al-Ḥasan b. Muḥammad b. al-Ḥanafiyya, *al-Risāla fī l-radd ʿalā l-qadariyya,* in J. van Ess, *Anfänge muslimischer Theologie. Zwei anti-qadaritische Traktate aus dem ersten Jahrhunderten der Higra,* Wiesbaden/Beirut 1977, 11-37.
Secondary: W.M. Watt, *The formative period of Islamic thought,* Edinburgh 1973; id., *Free will and predestination in early Islam,* London 1949; id., *Islamic creeds. A selection,* Edinburgh 1994; A.J. Wensinck, *The Muslim creed. Its genesis and historical development,* London 1932 (repr. 1965).

ʿImrān

The father of Mary (q.v.), mother of Jesus (q.v.). ʿImrān is attested three times in the Qurʾān and Āl ʿImrān is the title of the third sūra. The name occurs incidentally in two passages of the narrative sections (see NARRATIVES) which deal with the story of Mary and her mother, passages in which "the wife of ʿImrān" (Q 3:35) and "Mary, ʿImrān's daughter" (Q 66:12) are mentioned. The third passage, from which the title of the third sūra is taken, mentions "the family of ʿImrān" (Q 3:33) which God chose — along with Adam (see ADAM AND EVE), Noah (q.v.) and the family of Abraham (q.v.) — above all beings. The dominant exegetical trend understands the expression "the family of ʿImrān" as an allusion to Mary and Jesus, to whom long passages are dedicated in the rest of the sūra. A variant interpretation is, on the other hand, adopted by one of the first exegetes, Muqātil b. Sulaymān (d. 150/767), according to whom "the family of ʿImrān" of Q 3:33 refers instead to the family of Moses (q.v.) and Aaron (q.v.; *Tafsīr*, i, 271). This difference of opinion derives from the fact that in later Muslim traditions, the same name, ʿImrān, is also attributed to the father of Moses and Aaron, the biblical ʿAmrām. The source of the confusion between these two characters and their families might be traced to the Qurʾān, where, parallelling a Christian tendency to utilize earlier biblical figures as "types" for later ones, Mary (Ar. Maryam) and Maryam, the sister of Moses, seem to coincide (cf. Q 19:28, the verse in which the mother of Jesus is addressed as the sister of Aaron).

Traditions, ḥadīths (see ḤADĪTH AND THE QURʾĀN) and "stories of the prophets" (*qiṣaṣ al-anbiyāʾ*) legends do not contain relevant material about either of the two ʿImrāns. The exegetes (see EXEGESIS OF THE QURʾĀN: CLASSICAL AND MEDIEVAL) explain that the two ʿImrāns are two different people, separated by a long period of time, one thousand and eight hundred years according to certain sources (Rāzī, *Tafsīr*, viii, 24). The father of Moses and Aaron is called ʿImrān b. Yaṣhar or ʿImrān b. Qāhith and is a figure about whom little is revealed, especially if compared to the numerous traditions that describe Moses and the other members of his family. As far as the father of Mary, called ʿImrān b. Māthān/Mātān, is concerned, it is only noted that he died before the birth of Mary.

Roberto Tottoli

Bibliography
Primary: Abū l-Layth al-Samarqandī, *Tafsīr*, Beirut 1993, i, 262; Fīrūzābādī, *Tanwīr al-miqbās min tafsīr Ibn ʿAbbās*, Cairo 1989, 37; Ibn Ḥabīb, Abū Jaʿfar Muḥammad, *Kitāb al-Muḥabbar*, ed. I. Lichtenstaedter, Hyderabad 1942, 387, 389; Ibn al-Jawzī, *Zād*, Damascus 1964-5, i, 375; Muqātil, *Tafsīr*, i, 271; Rāzī, *Tafsīr*, viii, 24; Ṭabarī, *Tafsīr*, Cairo 1968, iii, 234; id., *Taʾrīkh*, ed. de Goeje, i, 443; Wāḥidī, *Wasīṭ*, i, 430.
Secondary: Horovitz, *KU*, 128; Jeffery, *For. vocab.*, 217; Paret, *Kommentar*, Kohlhammer 1980, 65; J. Walker, *Bible characters in the Koran*, Paisley 1931, 36.

Incarnation

see ANTHROPOMORPHISM; JESUS; CHRISTIANS AND CHRISTIANITY; POLEMIC AND POLEMICAL LANGUAGE

Indifference

Apathy; lack of interest or enthusiasm. In his translation of the Qurʾān, ʿA. Yūsuf ʿAlī uses the word "indifference" only once, in Q 80:37. Of seven Arabic words potentially translatable as "indifference" (Badger, *Lexicon*), none occurs in the Qurʾān meaning precisely "indifference." The concept is, however, an important component of the qur'ānic teaching about unbelief (*kufr*, see BELIEF AND UNBELIEF). The basic meaning of *kufr* is "'to ignore knowingly the benefits… one has received,' and thence, 'to be unthankful'" (Izutsu, *Concepts*, 119-20; see IGNORANCE; GRATITUDE AND INGRATITUDE). One meaning of *kufr* then is indifference to the bounty and blessing (q.v.) of God: "If you are grateful, I will add more (favors) unto you; but if you show ingratitude *(kafartum)*, truly my punishment is terrible indeed" (Q 14:7); "Will they then believe in vain things, and be ungrateful *(yakfurūn)* for God's favors?" (Q 16:72). Whether contrasted with thankfulness or belief, *kufr* represents indifference to God's gifts (see GIFT GIVING) and favor (see GRACE).

Unbelief involves indifference to God's authority as sovereign over the day of judgment (see LAST JUDGMENT). *Taqwā*, derived from a root meaning "to guard (against)," or "to shield (from)," is the reverent awareness of the danger of unbelief and disobeying God (see FEAR; PIETY). Its opposite would be indifference to God's power (see POWER AND IMPOTENCE) and sovereignty (q.v.), leading to false security about the final judgment and the life to come (see ESCHATOLOGY). "O mankind! heed *(ittaqū)* your lord and fear a day when no father can avail aught for his son, nor a son avail aught for his father…" (Q 31:33). The people of Moses (q.v.; Mūsā) showed indifference to evidence he brought of the one God; the result was idolatry (Q 2:92; see IDOLATRY AND IDOLATERS). Others remained indifferent to the obvious testimony the ruins of civilizations provided to the destruction disobedience (q.v.) causes (Q 6:5-11; see GEOGRAPHY; PUNISHMENT STORIES). The people of ʿĀd (q.v.) reacted with indifference to the message of Hūd (q.v.): "It is the same to us whether you admonish us or… not. […] We are not the ones to receive pains and penalties" (Q 26:136-8; see REWARD AND PUNISHMENT; CHASTISEMENT AND PUNISHMENT). The worst kind of indifference is a heart (q.v.) which is veiled (Q 41:3-5; 17:45-6), sealed (Q 2:6-7; 9:93), locked (Q 47:24), rusted (Q 83:14), blind (Q 22:46), and rock-hard: "Thenceforth were your hearts hardened: they became like a rock and even worse. […] For among rocks there are some from which rivers gush forth; others when split asunder send forth water." (Q 2:74; cf. Ansari, *Qur'anic foundation*, 93).

God warns the messenger Muḥammad against grieving over such people: "It is equal to them whether you pray for their forgiveness or not; God will not forgive them" (Q 63:6; see also Q 2:6; see INTERCESSION). Indifference to the plight of such people is warranted. Shuʿayb (q.v.) acts correctly in saying to his people, "I gave you good counsel, but how shall I lament *(āsā)* over a people who refuse to believe?" (Q 7:93). Noah (q.v.; Nūḥ) had to practice enlightened indifference toward his own son (Q 11:45-7). God commanded Moses, "Lament not *(fa-lā ta'sa)* over the rebellious people" (*al-qawm al-fāsiqīn*, Q 5:26). And the prophet Muḥammad was warned that he should not sorrow (Q 3:176; 5:41), lament (Q 5:68), be overwhelmed (Q 6:35), or kill himself with mourning (Q 18:6; 26:3) over his disbelieving people.

A.H. Mathias Zahniser

Bibliography
M.F. Ansari, *The qur'anic foundation and structure of Islamic society*, 2 vols., Karachi n.d.; G.P. Badger, *An English Arabic lexicon*, London 1881; Izutsu, *Concepts*.

Infallibility

see IMPECCABILITY; ERROR; PROPHETS AND PROPHETHOOD

Infanticide

The murder of an infant. As referred to in the Qurʾān, infanticide *(waʾd)* connotes the act of burying alive, and it means the killing of an unwanted infant, usually a girl, by the simple expedient of burying her soon after birth. The termination of the life of a helpless child (see CHILDREN) is condemned in Islamic law as prohibited and inexcusable (see PROHIBITED DEGREES; LAW AND THE QURʾĀN), and in passages referring to infanticide, the Qurʾān affirms the sanctity of life.

Female infanticide was common enough among the pre-Islamic Arabs to be assigned a specific term, *waʾd* (see PRE-ISLAMIC ARABIA AND THE QURʾĀN). Two dramatic passages in the Qurʾān refer to this act: "They give daughters to God (glory be to him), but they themselves would have what they desire. When the birth of a girl is announced to one of them, his face grows dark and he is filled with inward gloom. Because of the bad news he hides himself from men: should he keep her with disgrace or bury her under the dust? How ill they judge" (Q 16:57-8); "When the infant girl, buried alive, is asked for what crime she was slain… Then each soul shall know what it has done" (Q 81:8-9, 14). Five other verses refer to infanticide (Q 6:137, 140, 151; 17:31; 60:12). Two verses, Q 6:151 and 17:31, delineate poverty (see POVERTY AND THE POOR) as a reason for infanticide, declare that God will provide for the needy families *(narzuquhum)*, and state that killing children is forbidden: "You shall not kill your children for fear of want. We will provide for them and for you. To kill them is a great sin" (Q 17:31; see SIN, MAJOR AND MINOR). Ḥadīth writings echo the qurʾānic verses in reaffirming that infanticide is a sin (see ḤADĪTH AND THE QURʾĀN).

Other cultures, notably that of Carthage, utilized infanticide for ritual purposes and often sacrificed sons. Greeks and Romans used infanticide as a form of birth control and, as in pre-Islamic Arabia, primarily disposed of infant girls. Daughters were deemed more expendable than sons for social and economic reasons (see ECONOMICS; COMMUNITY AND SOCIETY IN THE QURʾĀN). Society assigned women less social prestige than men (see SOCIAL RELATIONS; WOMEN AND THE QURʾĀN; GENDER; PATRIARCHY), and they were considered an economic drain, not an asset to families. Both parents evidently participated in infanticide, for the Qurʾān condemned not only fathers but also women for killing children (Q 60:12).

In the development of Islamic law *(fiqh)*, the prohibition against infanticide became a juridical foundation for opinions on abortion (q.v.) and contraception (see also BIRTH CONTROL). Many jurists consider abortion, the killing of the fetus while still in the womb, the equivalent of infanticide and thereby prohibit it. While most jurists judged that contraception was permissible, Ibn Ḥazm (d. 456/1064), basing his ruling on a ḥadīth to the same effect, decided that contraception *(ʿazl)* was "hidden infanticide" *(al-waʾd al-khafī)* and thereby prohibited. Al-Ghazālī (d. 505/1111) sets forth the distinctions among the three acts very clearly: "All that [that is, abstaining from marriage altogether, abstaining from intimate relations after marriage, or avoiding emission after penetration] is not the same as abortion or the burying of girls alive. These two things, in effect, constitute a crime against an already existing person, and that also has stages. The first stage of existence is that the sperm should lodge in the uterus, merge with the fluid of the woman, and become thus receptive to life; interfering with this process constitutes a crime (*jināya*, see SIN AND CRIME). If it develops into a clot (see BLOOD AND BLOOD CLOT) and a little plump of flesh then the crime becomes more serious. If the spirit (q.v.) is breathed into it and the created being takes form, then the crime [of abortion] becomes more serious still. The crime is most serious after the fetus is born alive" (*Iḥyāʾ*, ii, 47 [Bk. 12. On marriage, chap. 3, sect. 10], trans. Farah, *Marriage and sexuality*, 109-10, cited in Giladi, *Children*, 109-10; see also BIOLOGY AS THE CREATION AND STAGES OF LIFE; BIRTH). Many contemporary Muslims feel that the injunction not to kill your children for fear of want inveighs against limiting family size through contraception for financial reasons, or, on a state level, for concerns of economic development.

Some scholars consider the qurʾānic prohibition of female infanticide to be the key aspect of the prophet Muḥammad's attempts to raise the status of women. Contemporary feminist interpretation of the Qurʾān have underscored the significance of this prohibition in defining a new Islamic ethic (see FEMINISM AND THE QURʾĀN) from the perspective of this new moral vision. The passages in sūras 16 and 81 that clarified that infanticide was not tolerated provided divine confirmation for the assertion that God valued the life of a female like that of a male.

Donna Lee Bowen

Bibliography
Primary: al-Ghazālī, Abū Ḥāmid Muḥammad, *Iḥyāʾ ʿulūm al-dīn*, 4 vols., Cairo 1933; id., *Marriage and sexuality in Islam. A translation of al-Ghazālī's book on the etiquette of marriage from the* Iḥyāʾ, trans. M. Farah, Salt Lake City 1984; Ibn Ḥazm, Abū Muḥammad ʿAli b. Aḥmad al-Qurṭubī, *al-Muḥallā*, ed. Shākir, 11 vols., Cairo 1928, repr. Cairo n.d., xi, 29-32; Ibn al-Jawzī, *Aḥkām al-nisāʾ*, Beirut 1985, 99-100; Ibn Qayyim al-Jawziyya, *Tuḥfat al-mawdūd bi-aḥkām al-mawlūd*, Cairo 1977, repr. Beirut 1983, 18-9; *Lisān al-ʿArab*, 6 vols., Cairo 1981, vi, 474-5 (s.v. *w-ʾ-d*).
Secondary: A. Giladi, *Children in Islam. Concepts of childhood in medieval Muslim society*, Oxford 1992, 101-15.

Informants

According to Muḥammad's detractors, the people who provided Muḥammad with the knowledge that he said came from God. The question of whether Muḥammad relied on informants bears upon discussions surrounding the origin of the Qurʾān. Many of the qurʾānic narratives (q.v.) must not have sounded new to the Meccan opponents of Muḥammad (see OPPOSITION TO MUḤAMMAD), and they used to say, gibing at him: "'This is nothing but falsehood he has forged, and other folk have helped him to it...'. They say: 'Fairy-tales (or, probably better: writings, *asāṭīr*, pl. of *usṭura*, from *saṭara*, "to write": see Horovitz, *KU*, 69-70) of the ancients (see GENERATIONS) that he has written down, so that they are recited to him at dawn and in the evening'" (Q 25:4-5). But the classical place where the question of the informants is treated in the qurʾānic commentaries is Q 16:103: "And we know very well that they say: 'Only a mortal is teaching him.' The speech of him at whom they hint is barbarous; and this is Arabic speech (see ARABIC LANGUAGE), manifest." The other places in the Qurʾān which provide occasion for the exegetes to treat this subject are the aforementioned Q 25:4-5, as well as Q 26:195; 41:14, 44 (Gilliot, Les "informateurs," § 15-9, 23, 25).

The framework and the common features of the narratives on the informants

All the narratives addressing this issue discuss the background of these informants, and maintain that they belonged to the class of the "deprived" or "have-nots," being servants or slaves (see SERVANT; SLAVES

AND SLAVERY), non-Arabs, Jews (see JEWS AND JUDAISM) or Christians (see CHRISTIANS AND CHRISTIANITY). Some of them are said to have possessed books (see BOOK), to have read them (see LITERACY), sometimes to have read the Torah (q.v.) and/or the Gospel (q.v.). Sometimes they are said to have been blacksmiths or sword sharpeners. The Qurayshī (see QURAYSH) opponents of Muḥammad said that these informants taught him or that they taught Khadīja (q.v.), who, in turn, taught Muḥammad.

According to the renowned exegete Muqātil b. Sulaymān (d. 150/767), "There was a servant of ʿĀmir b. al-Ḥaḍramī al-Qurashī. He was a Jew, not an Arab [or spoke bad Arabic, *aʿjamī*, see ARABS], he spoke Greek [or Aramaic], and his name was Abū Fukayha Yasār. As the Qurayshīs saw the Prophet speaking with him, they said: 'Indeed, he is being taught by Abū Fukayha Yasār'" (Muqātil, *Tafsīr*, ii, 487; Gilliot, Les "informateurs," § 12). Or "[...] the Apostle used often to sit at al-Marwa at the booth of a young Christian called Jabr, slave of the Banū l-Ḥaḍramī, and they used to say: 'The one who teaches Muḥammad most of what he brings is Jabr the Christian, slave of the Banū l-Ḥaḍramī'" (Ibn Isḥāq, *Sīra*, 260; Guillaume, *Life*, 180; Gilliot, Les "informateurs," § 13). Or, "according to Ṭalḥa b. ʿAmr [al-Ḥaḍramī, d. 152/769], Khadīja used to see frequently Khayr (or Jabr?), and the Qurayshīs said that a slave of the Banū l-Ḥaḍramī taught her and that she taught Muḥammad, so the verse [i.e. Q 16:103] was revealed" (Thaʿlabī, *Kashf*, part 1, f. 260r *ult.*-260v, l. 1-2; for the entire account, see Hūd b. Muḥakkam, *Tafsīr*, ii, 201, ad Q 25:4, according to al-Ḥasan al-Baṣrī and Muḥammad b. al-Sāʾib al-Kalbī; Rāzī, *Tafsīr*, xxiv, 50-1; Ṭabarsī, *Tafsīr*, xviii, 87-8; Suhaylī, *Taʿrīf*, 173; Muir, *Life of Mahomet*, ii, 122-5).

The names of these servant/slave informants vary, but this could be due, in some cases, to copyists' mistakes. Some of these names are as follows: ʿAddās, Abū Fukayha Yasār (Nabt), Balʿām (but also Abū Maysara), Jabr (but also Khayr or Khabar), Yaʿīsh (but also ʿĀʾish), ʿĀbis, ʿAns, ʿAbbās, Yuḥannas (Suyūṭī, *Mufḥamāt*, 64, according to Qatāda: a slave of Ibn al-Ḥaḍramī; but Thaʿlabī, *Kashf*, part 2, 69v, l. 9-10, according to al-Ḥasan al-Baṣrī: ʿUbayd b. al-Ḥaḍramī al-Ḥabashī [?] the seer, which could mean an Ethiopian slave and seer of Ibn al-Ḥaḍramī; but Baghawī, *Tafsīr*, iii, 361, following Thaʿlabī, has: the seer ʿUbayd b. al-Khiḍr al-Ḥabashī), Mikhyas, Miqyas, then Yusr, but also al-Yusr or Abū l-Yusr, and finally Ibn Qammaṭa, or Ibn Qimṭa, etc. (Gilliot, Les "informateurs," § 32-52). It should be noted that most of these names are not semantically neutral but imply servitude, e.g. ʿAddās, Yasār, Yaʿīsh, Yusr (for ʿAddās, see Gilliot, Les "informateurs," 104, n. 132).

The apologetic features of these narratives

The early Islamic community and the classical sources have transformed these stories into apologetic motifs for the new predication. The Qurʾān itself does not name these informants and does not reject the existence of these men with whom the Prophet was in contact. The qurʾānic argument is based on the alleged "clarity" or "purity" of the qurʾānic Arabic (see INIMITABILITY; LANGUAGE OF THE QURʾĀN). But the Islamic tradition has developed the supposed "circumstances of the revelation (see OCCASIONS OF REVELATION)" of Q 16:103, and the other related verses (see above). So, when Muḥammad went to Ṭāʾif to seek help from the Thaqīf against his own tribe, ʿUtba and Shayba of the Banū Rabīʿa (from the Banū ʿAbd al-Shams, a tribe with close blood ties to Muḥammad; see KINSHIP; TRIBES AND

CLANS), moved by compassion for him, sent ʿAddās, their young Christian slave from Nineveh, to him with a bunch of grapes. When the Prophet said to him that Nineveh is "the town of the righteous man Jonah (q.v.), the son of Mattā [in the Bible Amittai]," continuing, "He is my brother. He was a prophet, and I am a prophet," ʿAddās "bent down before the messenger of God, kissing his head, hands, and feet" (Ṭabarī, *Taʾrīkh*, i, 1201-2; id., *History*, vi, 117; Ibn Isḥāq, *Sīra*, 280-1; Ibn Isḥāq-Guillaume, 193; Ibn al-Jawzī, *Wafāʾ*, i, 213-4; Zurqānī, *Sharḥ*, ii, 54-6; Nuwayrī, *Nihāya*, xvi, 281; Gilliot, Les "informateurs," § 32). In this instance, the process has been reversed, and the priority of Muḥammad's knowledge is emphasized: Muḥammad is not taught by the Christian slave; rather, the slave confirms, through his own knowledge, what Muḥammad already knows (from revelation; see REVELATION AND INSPIRATION; PROPHETS AND PROPHETHOOD).

Another related type of apologetic narrative is what we have called elsewhere "the topos Holy! Holy!," which is relevant not only to the hermit Baḥīrā (see below) and to Khadīja's cousin, Waraqa b. Nawfal, but also to ʿAddās (Rubin, *The eye*, 50-2, 103-12; Gilliot, Les "informateurs," § 27-31). According to al-Wāqidī (d. 207/823), Khadīja went to Waraqa to ask him about the angel Gabriel (q.v.) and he told her that he was "the great Nāmūs [Greek *nomos*] of God." Then she visited ʿAddās, who said: "Holy! Holy! How can it be that Gabriel is mentioned in that country whose inhabitants are idolaters? Gabriel is the great Nāmūs of God and he never went to anybody save a prophet" (Balādhurī, *Ansāb*, i, 111, no. 211 cited in Gilliot, Les "informateurs," § 27, 30; cf. Suhaylī, *Rawḍ*, i, 215; Sprenger, Aus Briefen, 413-4).

Some of these servants or slaves are also said to have been beaten by their masters because they praised Muḥammad or converted to Islam. This happened to Jabr, who was a Jewish (or Christian) slave of the Banū ʿAbd al-Dār. When, prior to the Prophet's emigration (q.v.) to Medina (q.v.), he heard Muḥammad reciting the chapter on Joseph (q.v.; Sūrat Yūsuf, Q 12), he recognized elements he knew from his own religion and secretly became a Muslim. When the Meccans were informed by Ibn Abī Sarḥ of Jabr's conversion, his masters tortured him in order to make him confess that he had supplied that information to Muḥammad. After the conquest of Mecca (see EXPEDITIONS AND BATTLES; MECCA), Muḥammad ransomed Jabr and emancipated him (Wāqidī, *Maghāzī*, 865-6; Gilliot, Les "informateurs," § 40. On Ibn Abī Sarḥ, linked in a "brothering" to ʿĀmir b. Luway, who is often identified with the "renegade" scribe of Muḥammad, see Ṭabarī, *Tafsīr*, xi, 533-5, no. 13555-6, ad Q 6:93; Gilliot, Les "informateurs," 88 n. 37; id., Poète ou prophète?, § 123).

The case of the hermit/monk of Buṣrā (Bostra)

The Islamic sources contain many variations on the theme of "Muḥammad's encounter with representatives of non-Islamic religions who recognize him as a future prophet" (Crone, *Meccan trade*, 219; Ibn ʿAsākir, *Taʾrīkh-sīra*, i, 335 f.). As we have seen, some of the informant slaves fall into this category, and so it is with the hermit Baḥīrā (Aram. Bekhīra, i.e. "the Elect") of Buṣrā (Bostra) in Syria (for a summary, see Trimingham, *Christianity among the Arabs*, 258 f.; Fahd, *Divination*, 82). The versions differ according to the transmitters; it is related that in his ninth, twelfth (the age of Jesus among the doctors; Luke 2: 42-9) or twenty-fifth/sixth year, Muḥammad was taken by his uncle Abū Ṭālib — in some versions accompanied by Abū Bakr and his client Bilāl — on a caravan journey, during which they encountered this monk (Ibn

Isḥāq-Guillaume, 79-81; Ibn Saʿd, *Ṭabaqāt,* i, 153-4; Ṭabarī, *Taʾrīkh,* i, 1123-5; id., *History,* vi, 43-6; Bayhaqī, *Dalāʾil,* ii, 24-8, according to Ibn Isḥāq; Abū Nuʿaym, *Dalāʾil,* 168-9; Masʿūdī, *Murūj,* no. 150 [called by the Christians Sirjis/Sirjīs; Zurqānī, *Sharḥ,* i, 362-3]; Ibn ʿAsākir, *Taʾrīkh-sīra,* i, 6-10; Ibn al-Jawzī, *Wafāʾ,* i, 131-3; Abū l-Fidāʾ, *Mukhtaṣar,* i, 172 [who does not speak of the encounter with the monk in the passages on the "second journey" with Maysara]; Nuwayrī, *Nihāya,* xvi, 90-3; Ṣāliḥī, *Subul,* ii, 140-2; Harawī, *Guide,* 43; Boulainvilliers, *Vie de Mahomed*, 202-7). Baḥīrā is also listed among those who were awaiting the coming of Muḥammad (McAuliffe, *Qurʾānic,* 106-9).

In some versions the monk is named Nasṭūr/Nasṭūrā (Ibn ʿAsākir, *Taʾrīkh-sīra,* i, 273, journey with Abū Ṭālib and Maysara; Masʿūdī, *Tanbīh,* 305; Suhaylī, *Rawḍ,* i, 211-2, saying that Nasṭūr is different from Baḥīrā and that Muḥammad was sent to Syria by Khadīja with her servant Maysara; Ḥalabī, *Sīra,* i, 216 f., "the second journey"; Nuwayrī, *Nihāya,* xvi, 95-7). Sometimes, generally in the oldest versions, the monk/hermit is nameless (Muqātil, *Tafsīr,* i, 112: the monk mentioned to Muḥammad by Salmān al-Fārisī; Ibn Saʿd, *Ṭabaqāt,* i, 153; Tirmidhī, *Sunan,* 50, *Manāqib,* v, 590-1, no. 3620; Ibn ʿAsākir, *Taʾrīkh-sīra,* i, 1-5, 344; Dhahabī, *Taʾrīkh,* 55-7, criticizing this tradition attributed to Abū Mūsā al-Ashʿarī), in an unnamed place (Ibn Saʿd, *Ṭabaqāt,* i, 120); in others, an unnamed Jewish Rabbi of Taymāʾ (Ibn Shihāb, *Maghāzī,* 40; ʿAbd al-Razzāq, *Muṣannaf,* v, 318, without declaration of prophecy; cf. Suhaylī, *Rawḍ,* i, 205-6, according to al-Zuhrī. It should be noted that this ancient recital is more sober than others).

In nearly all of the versions (for references, see Rubin, *Eye,* 50-2), Muḥammad "is recognized as a future prophet on the basis that he is an orphan, that his eyes are red, that he sits under a certain tree, or because of a combination of these" (Crone, *Meccan trade,* 219-20). It is not impossible that the journey or journeys of Muḥammad to Syria were invented so that this "miraculous event" could take place (this seems to be Crone's opinion). But here, unlike in the accounts of the slave informants, the Islamic sources do not say that the opponents of Muḥammad accused him of borrowing parts of his message from the monk; the point of these stories is to prove that the "People of the Book (q.v.)" "had known of Muhammad's coming beforehand" (Wensinck, *Muhammad and the Jews,* 39). This is the reason why Nasṭūr (named by the Christians Sergius/Sarjīs; by others Felix, the son of Jonah, nicknamed Bohaïra; see Ganier, *Vie de Mahomet,* 121-2, 127-8, this time two monks, Bohaïra and Nestor) is associated with ʿAddās in the topos "Holy! Holy" (Suhaylī, *Rawḍ,* i, 116; Sprenger, Aus Briefen, 413-4; Gilliot, Les "informateurs," § 27).

Whereas in the Muslim tradition, Baḥīrā (Nasṭūr, etc.) became one of the guarantors of Muḥammad's prophecy, he was seen in the Christian polemic against Islam, both in Arabic and in Greek, as a heretical monk who taught Muḥammad. According to ʿAbd al-Masīḥ al-Kindī, he was a Nestorian (Tartar, *Dialogue,* 107-8, Arabic text; Muir, *The apology,* 23), while, according to others, he was a Jacobite or an Arian (for the entire account, see Abel, Baḥīrā).

The informants and their role in the constitution of the Qurʾān in the Meccan period

The motif of the "informant slaves" developed among those of the exegetes of the second half of the second/eighth century who were interested in the "circumstances of revelation" and who had a good knowledge of the literature concerning the Prophet's life. These included Muḥammad

b. al-Sāʾib al-Kalbī (d. 146/763), Muqātil b. Sulaymān (d. 150/767), but also, before them, Muḥammad b. Kaʿb al-Quraẓī (d. 118/736 or 120/737; Gilliot, Les "informateurs," § 11) and Ismāʿīl b. ʿAbd al-Raḥmān al-Suddī (d. 128/745; ibid., § 10). Although this theme is less common among those exegetes interested in prophetic biography in a more narrow sense, they sometimes dealt with it, e.g. Sulaymān b. Ṭarkhān al-Taymī (d. 143/760) and Ibn Isḥāq, (d. 150/767) and, before them, by al-Zuhrī (d. 124/742; ibid., § 9, 29, 34, 57, 59). On the other hand, the topos "Holy! Holy!" and the usual accounts on ʿAddās seem to have interested them considerably.

The Qurʾān, by its mention of someone who, according to the accusations of the Qurayshīs, had instructed Muḥammad, prompted the earlier exegetes to investigate this problem. Even if, considering the multiplicity of the variants, some of the names of these "informant slaves" were quite obviously made up, there is no reason to think that the exegetes should have invented everything, given that the basic theme does not place Muḥammad in a particularly favorable light. He may have received information from these "downtrodden" who, in the light of their social position, would have been more willing to talk with him than with the Qurayshī élite. As the land of Arabia was not "a closed box" (Smith, Events in Arabia, 467), there is nothing surprising in the suggestion that Muḥammad may have had contact with people from outside of his immediate milieu (see also FOREIGN VOCABULARY). There is no reason *a priori* to doubt that Muḥammad could have spoken with slaves, or Christians or others.

It should be noted that when scraps of memories or scattered information are integrated, the knowledge is reformulated again. As for the theme of the informants, it has been reshaped within an apologetic discourse. The doors had to be "bolted" in order to assert the "absolute novelty" of the new revelation. Muḥammad had to face the accusation of being instructed by one individual (Q 16:103), or by others. The answer to the accusation was that it could not be so since the person in question spoke bad Arabic, or even a foreign language, whereas the Qurʾān was said to be revealed in "clear" or "pure" Arabic. Furthermore, written sources provided by informants could not have instructed Muḥammad because he was thought to be illiterate (see ILLITERACY). These arguments, it seems, did not impress his contemporaries and countrymen, at least in the period before they came to accept his message.

All these traditions, despite their variants, have the following points in common: the informants were foreign; they were of low birth, slaves or freed men; some of them are said to have carried on the craft of blacksmith or sword sharpener; they could read, they had "books," they read the Torah or the Gospel or both; they had contact with the Prophet. Some accounts say that he took his message from them; others say that these people had been instructed by him.

All these accounts, in spite of their differences, are steeped in an initiatory atmosphere. This is interesting to note, especially in view of the connection between reading books and the trade practiced by some of them — working with metal. The word used for this work, *qayn,* is related to Hebrew, Syriac and Ethiopic words of the same root letters referring to singing and funerary wailing *(qayn/qayna).* There is, it seems, in different cultures, a relation between the craft of the blacksmith, the occult, dance and poetry (Eliade, *Forgerons et alchimistes,* 83 f.; Lüling, Archaische Metallgewinnung, 133-48).

The initiatory atmosphere is strengthened by a tradition related by al-Ṭabarī (d. 310/923), who introduces a connection between these narratives and the theme of the seven readings (*al-aḥruf al-sabʿa,* Ṭabarī, *Tafsīr,* xiv, 179, ll. 15-21, ad Q 16:103; Gilliot, Les "informateurs," § 9). Apparently, this last account has no connection with the others. However, these accounts have to do with the "originality" of the Muḥammadan revelation. To put the Prophet in contact with followers of another religion, who, moreover, were foreigners, who knew other languages, read the holy scripture and carried on a craft near to the demiurgic function of the poet, the great enemy of the prophet of Islam (see POETS AND POETRY; SOOTHSAYERS), was also an occasion to expose the Qurʾān to criticism. And that is what happened; the commentators tried to neutralize that effect because they could not ignore the traditions which were circulating on this subject in the framework of the "circumstances of revelation." Ultimately, all these accounts are used in an apologetic view whose climax is the topos "Holy! Holy!." The same ʿAddās — it does not matter whether he is the same or another, or whether the tradition has been invented or not — whom the Qurayshīs suspected to have instructed Muḥammad, recognizes him as a prophet.

The accusations against Muḥammad have been summed up by one of his greatest opponents, al-Naḍr b. al-Ḥārith: "This Qurʾān is naught but lies that Muḥammad himself has forged.... Those who help him are ʿAddās, a slave of Ḥuwayṭib b. ʿAbd al-ʿUzza, Yasār, a servant of ʿĀmir b. al-Ḥaḍramī, and Jabr who was a Jew, and then became a Muslim. [...] This Qurʾān is only a tale *(ḥadīth)* of the ancients, like the tales of Rustam and Isfandiyār. These three are teaching Muḥammad at the dawn and in the evening" (cf. Q 25:4-5; Muqātil, *Tafsīr,* iii, 226-7; Ibn Isḥāq-Guillaume, 135-6; Ṭabarī, *Tafsīr,* xviii, 182, ad Q 25:5; Thaʿlabī, *Kashf,* part 2, f. 69v, l. 9-15; Nuwayrī, *Nihāya,* xvi, 220, 271; Gilliot, Muḥammad, 23-4, 25-6). The study of the reports about the informants leads to the conclusion that we cannot exclude the possibility that whole sections of the Meccan Qurʾān could contain elements originally established by, or within, a group of "God's seekers," in the milieu of the "deprived" or "have-nots" who possessed either biblical, post-biblical (see Luxenberg, *Die syro-aramäische Lesart des Koran*) or other information. People like Waraqa b. Nawfal and Khadīja may also have participated in that common enterprise under the direction of Muḥammad or another individual.

Claude Gilliot

Bibliography

Primary: ʿAbd al-Razzāq, *Muṣannaf;* Abū l-Fidāʾ, *al-Mukhtaṣar fī akhbār al-bashar,* ed. M. Rayyūb, Beirut 1997; Abū Nuʿaym al-Iṣfahānī, *Dalāʾil al-nubuwwa,* ed. M.R. Qalʿajī and ʿA. ʿAbbās, Beirut 1986; al-Bayhaqī, Abū Bakr Aḥmad b. al-Ḥusayn, *Dalāʾil al-nubuwwa,* ed. ʿA. Qalʿajī, 7 vols., Beirut 1985; Dhahabī, *Taʾrīkh,* ed. Tadmurī; Ḥalabī, Nūr al-Dīn Abū l-Faraj ʿAlī b. Ibrāhīm, *al-Sīra al-Ḥalabiyya,* 3 vols., Beirut n.d. (ca. 1990); al-Harawī al-Mawṣilī, ʿAlī, *Guide des lieux de pèlerinage,* trans. J. Sourdel-Thomine, Damascus 1957; Ibn ʿAsākir, *Taʾrīkh madīnat Dimashq al-Sīra al-nabawiyya,* ed. N. Ghazzāwī, 2 vols., Damascus 1984-91; Ibn al-Jawzī, *al-Wafāʾ bi-aḥwāl al-muṣṭafā,* ed. M. ʿAbd al-Wāḥid, 2 vols., Cairo 1966; Ibn Saʿd, *Ṭabaqāt;* Ibn Shihāb, *Maghāzī,* ed. S. Zakkār, Damascus 1981; Masʿūdī, *Murūj;* id., *al-Tanbīh wa-l-ishrāf. Le Livre de l'avertissement et de la révision,* trans. J. Carra de Vaux, Paris 1896; Muqātil, *Tafsīr;* al-Nuwayrī, Aḥmad b. ʿAbd al-Wahhāb, *Nihāyat al-ʿarab fī funūn al-adab,* 33 vols., Cairo 1923-98; U. Rubin, *The eye of the beholder. The life of Muḥammad as viewed by the early Muslims. A textual analysis,* Princeton, NJ 1995; Ṣāliḥī, *Subul;* Suhaylī, *al-Rawḍ al-unuf (fī tafsīr al-sīra al-nabawiyya li-Ibn Hishām),* ed. Ṭ. ʿAbd al-Raʾūf Saʿd, 4 vols., Cairo 1971; Suyūṭī, *Mufḥamāt;* Ṭabarī, *Tafsīr;* id., *Taʾrīkh;* al-Thaʿlabī, *al-Kashf wa-l-bayān ʿan tafsīr al-Qurʾān,* ms. Istanbul Ahmet III 76 (from sūra 5 to

the end); Tirmidhī, *Sunan al-Tirmidhī. Wa-huwa al-Jāmiʿ al-ṣaḥīḥ*, ed. ʿA. ʿAbd al-Laṭīf, 5 vols., Medina 1965-7; Wāqidī, *Maghāzī;* Zurqānī, *Sharḥ al-mawāhib al-laduniyya*, ed. M.ʿA. al-Khālidī, 12 vols., Beirut 1996.
Secondary: A. Abel, Baḥīrā, in *EI²*, i, 921-3; Boulainvilliers (Comte de), *La vie de Mahomed*, London 1730 (polemical); P. Crone, *Meccan trade and the rise of Islam*, Oxford 1987; M. Eliade, *Forgerons et alchimistes*, Paris 1977; T. Fahd, *La divination arabe*, Leiden 1966, Paris 1987²; J. Ganier, *La vie de Mahomet*, 3 vols., Amsterdam 1748; Cl. Gilliot, Les "informateurs" juifs et chrétiens de Muḥammad. Reprise d'un problème traité par Aloys Sprenger et Theodor Nöldeke, in *JSAI* 22 (1998), 84-126; id., Poète ou prophète? Les traditions concernant la poésie et les poètes attribuées au prophète de l'islam et aux premières générations musulmanes, in F. Sanagustin (ed.), *Paroles, signes, mythes. Mélanges offerts à J.E. Benscheikh*, Damascus 2001, 331-96; id., Muḥammad, le Coran et les "contraintes de l'histoire," in Wild, *Text*, 3-26; S.D. Goitein, Who were Mohammad's chief teachers? in *Tarbiz* 23 (1952), 146-59 (in Heb.); C. Huart, Une nouvelle source du Qorān, in *JA* (1904), 125-67; G. Lüling, Archaische Metallgewinnung und die Idee der Wiedergeburt, in id., *Sprache und archaisches Denken. Neun Aufsätze zur Geistes und Religionsgeschichte*, Erlangen 1985, 133-48; C. Luxenberg, *Die syro-aramäische Lesart des Koran. Ein Beitrag zur Entschlüsselung der Koransprache*, Berlin 2000; McAuliffe, *Qurʾānic;* W. Muir, *Life of Mahomet*, 4 vols., London 1861; repr. Osnabrück 1988; id., *The apology of al-Kindy*, London 1887; Th. Nöldeke, Hatte Muḥammad christliche Lehrer? in *ZDMG* 12 (1858), 699-708; S. Smith, Events in Arabia in the 6th century A.D., in *BSOAS* 16 (1954), 425-68; A. Sprenger, Aus Briefen an Pr. Fleischer, in *ZDMG* 7 (1853), 412-5; id., *Das Leben und die Lehre des Moḥammad*, 3 vols., Berlin 1869² (i, 81-92, 124-34: Waraqa; i, 178-204: Baḥīrā; ii, 369-70: Wie hieß der Lehrer?; ii, 390-7: *Asāṭyr alawwalyn*, d.h. die Märchen der Alten); id., Mohammad's journey to Syria and Professor Fleischer's opinion thereon, in *JAS Bengal* 21 (1852), 576-92; id., Moḥammad's Zusammenkunft mit dem Einsiedler Baḥyrā, in *ZDMG* 12 (1858), 238-49; id., Über eine Handschrift des ersten Bandes des *Kitāb Ṭabaqāt al-kabyr* vom Sekretär des Wāqidy, in *ZDMG* 3 (1849), 450-6 (453-5: Baḥīrā); G. Tartar, *Dialogue islamo-chrétien sous le calife al-Maʾmūn*, Université de Strasbourg (Thèse de 3ème cycle) 1977; J.S. Trimingham, *Christianity among the Arabs in pre-Islamic times*, London/Beirut 1979; A.J. Wensinck, *Muhammad and the Jews of Medina*, trans. W.H. Behn, Berlin 1975¹, 1982.

Ingratitude see GRATITUDE AND INGRATITUDE

Inheritance

Rules for the division of wealth (q.v.) among the heirs of a deceased Muslim man or woman.

Traditional Islamic perspective

Traditional Islamic sources indicate that the intergenerational transmission of property by means of a last will and testament *(waṣiyya)* was a common procedure prior to the rise of Islam and during the Meccan period (see PRE-ISLAMIC ARABIA AND THE QURʾĀN).

The emigration (q.v.; *hijra*) to Medina (q.v.) in 1/622 necessitated certain changes in the existing inheritance rules. By migrating to Medina, the Emigrants (*muhājirūn*, see EMIGRANTS AND HELPERS) effectively cut themselves off from their non-believing relatives in Mecca. For this reason, Muḥammad instituted a pact of brotherhood between the Emigrants and the Helpers (*anṣār*, see BROTHER AND BROTHERHOOD). According to this arrangement, Emigrants might no longer inherit from their relatives in Mecca, but they could inherit from Helpers in Medina and vice-versa (see Q 8:72). This arrangement was subsequently abrogated by Q 8:75 and Q 33:6 (see ABROGATION).

Pronouncements on inheritance, in the form of divine revelation and prophetic sunna (q.v.), were issued on numerous occasions during the Medinan period. In the early Medinan period *(fī awwal al-islām)*, six verses regulating aspects of testamentary succession were revealed to Muḥammad (for convenience, hereinafter "the bequest verses"). Q 2:180 enjoins a person contemplating death to leave a bequest for parents (q.v.) and relatives (see KINSHIP); Q 2:181 holds anyone who alters a last will and testament accountable to God; Q 2:182 encourages the reconciliation of parties who disagree about the provisions of a will; Q 2:240 permits a testator to stipulate that his widow (q.v.; see also MARRIAGE AND DIVORCE) is entitled to a maximum of one year's maintenance, on the condition that she remains in her deceased husband's home; and Q 5:106-7 establish that a last will and testament, to be valid, must be drawn up or dictated in the presence of two witnesses (see WITNESSING AND TESTIFYING). Under this regime, a person contemplating death continued to enjoy substantial freedom to determine who his or her heirs would be and how much they would inherit.

Following the battle of Uḥud in 3/625 (see EXPEDITIONS AND BATTLES), Muḥammad received a second series of revelations establishing compulsory rules for the division of property. Of several narratives circulated to explain the occasion for the revelation of these verses (*asbāb al-nuzūl,* see OCCASIONS OF REVELATION), the following is illustrative: The widow of Aws b. Thābit al-Anṣārī, who died at Uḥud, complained to the Prophet that the deceased's two paternal cousins unjustly had deprived her and her daughters of their inheritance. Muḥammad dismissed the woman "so that [he] might see what God would introduce" (Wāḥidī, *Asbāb,* 137-8). Shortly thereafter three verses were revealed: Q 4:7 affirmed the inheritance rights of both men and women ("To men a share of what parents and kindred leave and to women a share of what parents and kindred leave, whether small or large, a fixed share"; see WOMEN AND THE QURʾĀN). Q 4:11-2 specified, *inter alia,* the exact fractional shares to which daughter(s), parent(s), sibling(s), and a husband or wife are entitled:

God commands you concerning your children (q.v.): a male is entitled to the share of two females. If they are females above two, then they are entitled to two-thirds of what he leaves. If there is one, then she is entitled to half. Each one of his parents is entitled to one-sixth of what he leaves, if he has a child. But if he does not have a child, and his parents are his heirs, then his mother is entitled to one-third. If he has brothers, then his mother is entitled to one-sixth, after any legacy he bequeaths, or debt. Your fathers and your sons, you know not which of them is closer to you in usefulness. A commandment from God. God is knowing, wise (Q 4:11). You are entitled to half of what your wives leave, if they do not have a child. But if they have a child, then you are entitled to one-fourth of what they leave, after any legacy they bequeath or debt. They are entitled to one-fourth of what you leave, if you do not have a child. But if you have a child, then they are entitled to one-eighth of what you leave, after any legacy you bequeath, or debt (Q 4:12a). If a man — or a woman — dies leaving neither parent nor child *(yūrathu kalālatan),* and he [sic] has a brother or sister, each one of them is entitled to one-sixth. If they are more than that, then they are partners with respect to one-third, after any legacy that is bequeathed, or debt, without injury. A commandment from God. God is knowing, forbearing (Q 4:12b).

This legislation subsequently was supplemented by Q 4:176:

When they ask you for a decision, say: God decrees for you regarding the person who dies leaving neither parent nor child *(al-kalāla):* If a man dies without a child, and he has a sister, then she is entitled to half of what he leaves. He is her heir if she does not have a child. If they (f.) are two, then they are entitled to two-thirds of what he leaves. If they are brothers and sisters, then a male is entitled to the share of two females. God makes clear for you [lest] you go astray. God is all-knowing.

Whereas Q 4:12b awards siblings a maximum of one-third of the estate, Q 4:176 awards siblings anywhere from fifty percent of the estate to the entire estate. The apparent contradiction was harmonized by the Qurʾān commentators, who taught that the siblings mentioned in Q 4:12 are in fact uterine siblings, whereas the siblings mentioned in Q 4:176 are consanguine and/or germane siblings. The qualification of the siblings in the latter verse as consanguine and/or germane siblings is supported by a variant reading (*qirāʾa*, see READINGS OF THE QURʾĀN) attributed to Ubayy b. Kaʿb and Saʿd b. Abī Waqqāṣ (Zamakhsharī, *Kashshāf*, i, 486; Nīsābūrī, *Tafsīr*, iv, 200). In order for this explanation to work, it was important to establish that Q 4:176 was revealed subsequent to Q 4:12b; it is perhaps to this end that some commentators teach that Q 4:176 was the very last verse revealed to Muḥammad (Qurṭubī, *Jāmiʿ*, vi, 28; Bayḍāwī, *Anwār*, i, 245).

Q 4:11, 12 and 176 are traditionally referred to as "the inheritance verses" *(āyāt al-mīrāth);* together, they form the core of the *ʿilm al-farāʾiḍ* or "science of the shares," which imposes compulsory rules for the division of property. Certain redundancies in, and apparent inconsistencies between, the bequest verses and the inheritance verses were clarified by Muḥammad during the last two years of his life. It is related that, following the conquest of Mecca in 8/630, Muḥammad made a visit to the Companion (see COMPANIONS OF THE PROPHET) Saʿd b. Abī Waqqāṣ, who was sick and believed that he was about to die. When Saʿd asked the Prophet if he might bequeath his *entire* estate, Muḥammad responded, "a bequest may not exceed one-third" (*al-waṣiyya fī l-thulth*, Bukhārī, *Ṣaḥīḥ*, ii, 186; cf. Muslim, *Ṣaḥīḥ*, iii, 1250-3 [nos. 5-10]). This pronouncement strikes a balance between the compulsory and voluntary aspects of the *ʿilm al-farāʾiḍ:* a minimum of two-thirds of any estate is distributed among the heirs in accordance with the inheritance verses; a maximum of one-third may be used, at the discretion of a person contemplating death, for bequests. But might a parent or spouse receive a bequest of up to one-third of the estate *in addition to* the fractional share specified in Q 4:11-2? Apparently not, for Muḥammad is reported to have said on the occasion of his Farewell Pilgrimage (q.v.) in 10/632, "No bequest to an heir *(lā waṣiyya li-wārith),*" i.e. a person contemplating death may not leave a bequest for anyone who will receive a fractional share of the estate as specified in the inheritance verses (Ibn Hishām, *Sīra*, 970). Since the time of al-Shāfiʿī (d. 204/820), Muslim jurists have regarded this prophetic dictum as an indicator that the inheritance verses had abrogated the bequest verses (Shāfiʿī, *al-Risāla*, 69, par. 398).

The qurʾānic inheritance legislation was supplemented by additional narrative reports (*aḥādīth*, see ḤADĪTH AND THE QURʾĀN) attributed to the Prophet and his Companions, e.g. a Muslim cannot inherit from an unbeliever (see BELIEF AND UNBELIEF) and vice versa; a person who deliberately kills another may not inherit from him or her (see BLOODSHED; MURDER); a slave may not inherit from his or her master (see SLAVES AND SLAVERY); the illegitimate children of a couple whose paternity have been disputed by the procedure known as *liʿān* have no legal claim on the estates of their father and his relations (see ILLEGITIMACY); the patron and the manumitted slave inherit from one another, etc. (see CLIENTS AND CLIENTAGE).

During the first Islamic century, Muslim scholars worked out the details of the *ʿilm al-farāʾiḍ*. The earliest extant treatise on the subject is that of Sufyān al-Thawrī (d. 161/778) (Raddatz, Früislamisches Erbrecht, 26-78). The general principles of what became the Sunnī law of inheritance (see LAW AND THE QURʾĀN) are as follows: There are two classes of heirs, "sharers" *(ahl al-farāʾiḍ)* and agnates *(ʿaṣaba)*. The sharers are those persons for whom the Qurʾān specifies a fractional share of the estate (one or more daughters, a father, mother, or spouse — and, in the absence of children, one or more siblings). The agnates are persons related to the deceased exclusively through male links (see PATRIARCHY), arranged in a series of hierarchical classes, with a member of a higher class totally excluding any and all members of a lower class from entering the inheritance. Within each class, a person nearer in degree of relationship to the deceased excludes all others in a more remote degree, e.g. a son excludes a grandson. The agnates are called upon to inherit in the following order: 1. The male descendants of the deceased in the male line, a nearer excluding the more distant relatives from the succession; 2. the nearest male relative in the ascending male line with the provision that the father, but not the grandfather (and more remote ascendants) of the deceased inherits before his brothers; 3. the nearest male relative in the male line among the descendants of the father: first the full brother, then the half brother on the father's side, then the descendants of the full brother, then those of the half brother on the father's side; 4. the nearest male relative in the male line among the descendants of the grandfather; 5. The *mawlā,* i.e. the patron (or patroness), if the deceased was a freedman, and then his *ʿaṣaba*.

The division of an estate proceeds in two stages: the qualifying sharers take their qurʾānic entitlements; then the closest surviving agnate inherits whatever remains. For example, suppose that a man dies, leaving a wife, son and two brothers. The wife inherits 1/8 of the estate as a sharer. The son inherits the remaining 7/8 of the estate as the closest surviving agnate, totally excluding the brothers from the inheritance (although they might receive a bequest of up to one-third of the estate because they do not qualify as sharers, i.e. legal heirs). If, in addition to a wife, son and two brothers, the deceased also leaves a daughter, the son transforms his sister into a residuary heir *(ʿaṣaba bi-ghayrihā):* he inherits 7/12 of the estate and she inherits 7/24, after the wife takes her 1/8. In theory, the person contemplating death is powerless to affect the relative entitlement of the heirs; he or she may not, for example, stipulate that the bulk of the estate will devolve upon a son, daughter, wife or sibling.

The Imāmī Shīʿīs (see SHĪʿISM AND THE QURʾĀN), however, reject the systematic residuary entitlement of the *ʿaṣaba* as maintained by the Sunnīs. Instead of a principle of male agnatic succession, they rely on a criterion of nearness of relationship *(qarāba)* that applies equally to males and females and to both agnatic and uterine relations of the deceased. Their system gives priority in inheritance to an inner family (q.v.) consisting of the children, parents and siblings of the deceased, together with the spouse. These close relatives are regarded as the "roots" through whom are linked to the deceased the "branches" of the outer family, who stand next in priority in inheritance. No "branch" is excluded on the grounds of non-agnatic relationship to the deceased; every "root" is capable of transmitting its right of inheritance to its "branch" (Kimber, Qurʾānic law, 292, 322). The essential difference between Sunnī and Shīʿī law is expressed in a saying attributed to Jaʿfar al-Ṣādiq (d. 148/765), "The estate belongs to the nearest relation, and any [remoter] male agnate can eat dirt" (ibid., 322; also cited in Coulson, *Succession*, 108).

The *ʿilm al-farāʾiḍ* is justifiably renowned for its mathematical complexity. "Learn the laws of inheritance," Muḥammad is reported to have said, "and teach them to the people; for they are one-half of useful knowledge (see KNOWLEDGE AND LEARNING)." According to another version of this report, the Prophet said, "The laws of inheritance constitute one-half of all knowledge and are the first [discipline] to be forgotten" (Bayhaqī, *Sunan*, vi, 208-9).

Pious Muslims who devoted their attention to the text of the Qurʾān during the first century of Islam encountered a number of cases in which the application of one qurʾānic rule yielded a result that seemingly was at variance with another. Thus, Q 4:11 announces that "a male is entitled to a share of two females," a phrase which the early commentators (see EXEGESIS OF THE QURʾĀN: CLASSICAL AND MEDIEVAL) understood as a general principle applying to all males and females of the same class and degree of relationship to the deceased (e.g. sons and daughters, brothers and sisters, mothers and fathers). This principle is contradicted, however, in the case of a childless man who dies leaving his wife and both parents: Q 4:11 assigns one-third of the estate to the mother ("if he does not have a child, and his parents are his heirs, then his mother is entitled to one-third"); and Q 4:12b assigns one-fourth of the estate to the widow ("they are entitled to one-fourth of what you leave, if you do not have a child"); this leaves five-twelfths of the estate for the father, who inherits as the closest surviving agnate. Clearly, the father's share is not twice as much as the mother's. The principle is again violated — even more severely — if a childless woman dies leaving her husband and both parents: Q 4:11 again assigns one-third of the estate to the mother; Q 4:12b assigns half of the estate to the husband ("you are entitled to half of what your wives leave, if they do not have a child"); this leaves one-sixth of the estate for the father, who inherits as the closest surviving agnate. Here the mother's share (one-third) is twice as large as the father's (one-sixth), turning on its head the qurʾānic rule that a male is entitled to the share of two females.

The problem reportedly was identified by Muḥammad's Companions. With regard to the second case, Ibn Masʿūd (d. 32/652-3) is said to have exclaimed, "God never saw me give preference to a mother over a father!" (Raddatz, Früislamisches Erbrecht, 37). According to Ibn Masʿūd the case was first resolved by the second caliph (q.v.), ʿUmar b. al-Khaṭṭāb (r. 13-23/634-44), who, when asked about a childless man who died leaving a wife and both parents, replied, "The wife is entitled to one-fourth, the mother is entitled to one-third of what remains [viz. one-fourth], and the father is entitled to whatever is left [viz. one-half]" (Ibn Shuʿba, *Sunan*, iii, 12-3, pt. 1, [nos. 6-8]; Bayhaqī, *Sunan*, vi, 228, ll. 4-6). Here, ʿUmar preserves the principle that a male is entitled to the share of two females (the father inherits half, the mother one-fourth) by interpolating the qurʾānic phrase that awards a share of the estate to the mother as if it reads "one-third of *what remains*" — which it does not. But the principle was saved at the expense of the explicit wording of the qurʾānic specification that the mother in this case should inherit one-third of the estate. The solution to the case in which a woman dies leaving her husband and both parents was resolved in an analogous manner, and is attributed variously to ʿAlī (d. 40/661; see ʿALĪ B. ABĪ ṬĀLIB), al-Ḥārith al-Aʿwar (d. 64/684), and

Zayd b. Thābit (d. 45/665). But these two cases commonly are known as the *ʿumariyyatān,* roughly, the two cases solved by ʿUmar.

A different problem arose in certain cases in which a person dies leaving a particular constellation of heirs, all of whom are sharers, and yet, when their fractional shares of the estate are calculated, the resulting sum exceeds one hundred percent of the estate. Suppose, for example, that a man dies leaving two daughters, both parents, and a wife. All six persons qualify as sharers, but the sum of the shares specified in the Qurʾān (2/3 for the daughters, 1/6 for the father, 1/6 for the mother, and 1/8 for the wife) equals 27/24 of the estate. The problem reportedly was recognized and resolved during the caliphate of ʿUmar, either by ʿUmar himself, by Zayd b. Thābit, or by ʿAlī. According to one report, ʿAlī was interrupted while delivering a sermon by someone who asked him how the estate should be divided in the case of a man who died leaving his father, mother, two daughters and a wife. Without a moment's hesitation, ʿAlī responded, "The wife's one-eighth becomes one-ninth" (Ibn Shuʿba, *Sunan,* iii, 19, pt. 1 [no. 34]; Bayhaqī, *Sunan,* vi, 253, ll. 4-5). In fact, the solution was to reduce the share of each heir on a *pro rata* basis in order to bring the sum total of the shares to one. In the present case, the shares become 16/27 (for the two daughters), 4/27 (father), 4/27 (mother) and 3/27 (wife), totaling one hundred percent (27/27). Although this procedure, known as *ʿawl* or proportional reduction, solved a mathematical conundrum, it created a hermeneutic problem, for the result of reducing the share of each heir on a proportional basis is that no heir receives the exact fractional share specified in the Qurʾān. The solution was contested. Late in his life, Ibn ʿAbbās (d. 68/687-8) is reported to have remarked, "Do you think that the one who counted the innumerable sands of Arabia did not count one-half, one-half, and one-third? When both halves are gone, where is the place for the one-third?" (Bayhaqī, *Sunan,* vi, 253, ll. 7-19).

Western perspectives

Since the end of the nineteenth century, Western scholars have accepted the general outlines of the traditional Sunnī account of the formation of the *ʿilm al-farāʾiḍ.* W. Robertson Smith, W. Marçais and G.-H. Bousquet developed what has been called "the superimposition theory:" In pre-Islamic Arabia, the right to inherit was limited to the *ʿaṣaba* or male agnates. The Qurʾān modified the tribal customary law of pre-Islamic Arabia (see TRIBES AND CLANS) by superimposing upon it a new class of legal heirs, the *ahl al-farāʾiḍ,* mostly females; the *ʿaṣaba* still inherit, but now only after the claims of the qurʾānic heirs have been satisfied. These two heterogeneous elements were fused together to form the *ʿilm al-farāʾiḍ.* The dual basis of the system accounts for its mathematical complexity.

The superimposition theory has recently been challenged. In fact, the Islamic sources suggest that the Muslim community's understanding of the qurʾānic inheritance legislation was the subject of controversy during the lifetime of Muḥammad and in the years immediately following his death. At the center of this controversy stands the figure of ʿUmar b. al-Khaṭṭāb and the word *kalāla,* which occurs only twice in the Qurʾān, once in Q 4:12b and again in 4:176 (see above). The commentators traditionally explain the meaning of this word as "a person who dies leaving neither parent nor child" or as "those who inherit from the deceased, with the exception of parent and child." In his discussion of the first qurʾānic appearance of *al-kalāla,* in Q 4:12b, al-Ṭabarī (d. 310/923;

Jāmiʿ, iv, 283-6) provides a seemingly exhaustive treatment of its meaning in support of what had become the traditional understanding. Only when he comes to the second occurrence of the word *kalāla*, in Q 4:176, does al-Ṭabarī cite a series of vivid and colorful but little-known ḥadīths which point to early confusion regarding the reading *(qirāʾa)* of Q 4:12b and to a mystery surrounding the meaning of *kalāla:* On several occasions while the Prophet was still alive, ʿUmar reportedly queried him about the meaning of *kalāla* without receiving a satisfactory answer. On one occasion ʿUmar said that he would rather know the meaning of *kalāla* than possess the equivalent of the poll-tax of the fortresses of the Byzantine empire (see TAXATION). After becoming caliph, ʿUmar delivered a sermon in the mosque in Medina in which he announced his intention to issue a decree about this word and suggested that when he did, women would whisper about it in their private quarters; but he was dissuaded from fulfilling his promise by the sudden appearance of a snake, which he interpreted as a sign of divine intervention. Shortly before his own demise, ʿUmar is reported to have said, "If I live, I will issue a decree about it [viz. *kalāla*] so that no one who recites the Qurʾān will disagree about it." As he lay dying from a wound inflicted by an assassin, ʿUmar reportedly demanded that his companions bring him a document that he had written about *kalāla;* when they complied with his request, he erased the document — "And no one knew what he had written thereon" (Ṭabarī, *Tafsīr*, vi, 43-4).

These narratives, which probably were put into circulation toward the end of the first century A.H., point to early uncertainty regarding the meaning of *kalāla*. Taking these narratives as his starting-point, D. Powers (*Studies*, 21-86, 143-88) has proposed three significant departures from the traditional understanding of the qurʾānic inheritance verses. First, Q 4:12b is traditionally read, "*... wa-in kāna rajulun yūrathu kalālatan aw imraʾtun...*," and is understood as awarding a small fractional share of the estate to *uterine* siblings (see above). In place of the traditional reading, Powers has proposed: "*wa-in kāna rajulun yūrithu kalālatan aw imraʾtan...*," and he argues that the word *kalāla* originally signified a female in-law, as its Semitic cognates do. Understood in this manner, the beginning of Q 4:12b would signify, "If a man designates a daughter in-law or wife as heir." If one accepts this line of argument, then Q 4:12b can be understood as awarding a small fractional share of the estate, not to exceed one-third, to one or more siblings (of any type) who have been *disinherited* in favor of a daughter in-law or wife, i.e. a female who is not related to the deceased by ties of blood. (This provision may be compared to the *actio ad supplendam legitimam* instituted by Justinian a century prior to the revelation of the Qurʾān.) Second, Powers argues that the award of a fractional share to a surviving spouse in Q 4:12a was originally intended to apply only in the exceptional case of a wife who had received no dowery (see BRIDEWEALTH), but that the exception was transformed into a rule during the generation following the death of the Prophet in connection with a general shift in focus from *heirs* to *shares* (compare *Novella* 53.6 of Justinian's code). Third, he argues that the bequest verses remained in force throughout the lifetime of Muḥammad and for at least a quarter of a century after his death, at which time the shift in the understanding of the two halves of Q 4:12 made it appear as if the bequest verses were incompatible with the newly emerging understanding of the inheritance verses. Muslim commentators harmonized the relationship between the bequest and inheritance verses by invoking the doctrine of abrogation, ostensibly the sign of a change in the divine will, in reality the sign of changed perceptions of the meaning of the divine word.

The thesis advanced by Powers eliminates many of the mathematical complexities associated with the *ʿilm al-farāʾiḍ*. Clearly, it is the share awarded to the surviving spouse that creates all of the above-mentioned mathematical problems: in cases of *ʿawl* or over-subscription, the removal of the share awarded to the surviving spouse has the effect of reducing the total size of the shares to one hundred percent; similarly, in the *ʿumariyyatān,* the removal of the surviving spouse from the equation has the effect of restoring the respective shares of the father and mother so that they inherit in a ratio of 2:1.

Powers calls this earlier stage in the understanding of the qurʾānic inheritance legislation "the proto-Islamic law of inheritance." Proto-Islamic law appears as a more or less complete system of inheritance that was intended to replace rather than modify the tribal customary law of pre-Islamic Arabia. Certain key features of proto-Islamic law bear a striking resemblance to the inheritance rules of Near Eastern provincial law and Roman law (see above; cf. Mundy, The family, 27-33; Crone, *Roman, provincial and Islamic law*): All three of these systems allow a testator to nominate a single heir of his or her choice; in the absence of a will, simple rules of intestacy take effect.

Another revisionist approach to the qurʾānic inheritance legislation recently has been advanced by R. Kimber (Qurʾanic law). Taking as his starting-point the equivocality of the inheritance verses, Kimber proposes an alternative interpretation of the syntax and meaning of Q 4:12b. Like Powers, he regards the qurʾānic inheritance law as a complete system, but whereas Powers sees the qurʾānic legislation as a modified version of Near Eastern provincial law, and traditional Islamic sources sees it as a reform of Arabian customary law, Kimber sees it as a reform of Jewish inheritance law. He also argues that Shīʿī inheritance law is closer to the original qurʾānic system than Sunnī inheritance law. For Kimber, the bequest verses and the inheritance verses, as originally understood, were not manifestations of two separate processes (testate succession and intestacy), but a means and ends to the same process, the disposal of an estate by last will and testament in accordance with the will of God. In the bequest verses, the testator is reminded in general terms of God's requirements; in the inheritance verses, these requirements are laid down in detail. The shift in emphasis from personal obligation to divine prescription proved so successful that it became practically unnecessary for Muslims to leave a last will and testament. In order for his explanation to work, however, Kimber must decree that Q 4:176 had in fact abrogated Q 4:12b, a view which no Muslim scholar has ever advanced.

The Islamic inheritance system

During the first centuries of Islamic history, Muslims living throughout the Near East found themselves subject to the *ʿilm al-farāʾiḍ,* which, to the extent that it was applied, resulted in the progressive fragmentation of wealth and capital. It is not surprising that proprietors found numerous ways to circumvent the "science of the shares," and they received important assistance in this regard from Muslim jurists who, distinguishing between *post mortem* and *inter vivos* transactions, taught that the inheritance rules take effect only on property owned by the deceased at the moment that he or she enters his or her deathbed illness and that proprietors are free, for the most part, to dispose of their property in any way they wish prior to that moment (Yanagihashi, Doctrinal development, 326 f.). Thus a proprietor may shift assets to his desired heir or heirs by means of a gift (see GIFT-GIVING), acknowledgement of a debt (q.v.), sale or creation of a family *waqf,* on the condition that these legal actions conform to the requisite formalities. Thus, to understand how property passed from one generation to the next in Muslim societies, it is important to consider not only the *ʿilm al-farāʾiḍ,* but also the wider and more comprehensive Islamic inheritance system.

David Stephan Powers

Bibliography
Primary: Bayḍāwī, *Anwār,* Leipzig 1846-8, repr. Osnabrück 1968; al-Bayhaqī, Aḥmad, *al-Sunan al-kubrā,* 10 vols., Hyderabad 1344-57, repr. Beirut 1968; Bukhārī, *Ṣaḥīḥ,* ed. Krehl and Juynboll; Ibn Isḥāq, *Sīra,* ed. F. Wüstenfeld; Ibn Shuʿba, *Kitāb al-Sunan,* ed. Ḥ.ʿA. al-Aʿẓamī, Dabhil 1967-; Nīsābūrī, *Gharāʾib,* Cairo 1962-70; Qurṭubī, *Jāmiʿ,* Cairo 1967; al-Qushayrī, Muslim b. al-Ḥajjāj, *Ṣaḥīḥ,* ed. M.F. ʿAbd al-Bāqī, 5 vols., Cairo 1955; al-Shāfiʿī, Muḥammad b. Idrīs, *al-Risāla,* ed. M.S. Kaylānī, Cairo 1969; Ṭabarī, *Tafsīr,* 30 vols. in 12, Cairo 1954-68; Wāḥidī, *Asbāb;* Zamakhsharī, *Kashshāf,* Beirut 1947.
Secondary: E. Chaumont, Legs et succession dans le droit musulman, in J. Beaucamp et G. Dagron (eds.), *La transmission du patrimoine. Byzance et l'aire méditerranéenne,* Paris 1998, 35-51; A. Cilardo, *Diritto ereditario islamico delle scuole giuridiche sunnite (Ḥanafita, Mālikita, Šāfiʿita e Ḥanbalita) e delle scuole giuridiche Ẓaydita, Ẓāhirita e Ibāḍita,* Naples 1994; N.J. Coulson, *Succession in the Muslim family,* Cambridge 1971; P. Crone, *Roman, provincial and Islamic law. The origins of the Islamic patronate,* Cambridge 1987; C. Gilliot, Le commentaire coranique de Hūd b. Muḥakkam/Muḥkim, in *Arabica* 44 (1997), 179-233 (216-7 for inheritance for the Ibadites, on Q 4:11); R. Kimber, The qurʾanic law of inheritance, in *Islamic law and society* 5 (1998), 291-325; J.-D. Luciani, *Traité des successions musulmanes (ab intestat). Extrait du commentaire de la Rahbia par Chenchouri de la glose d'el-Badjouri et d'autres auteurs arabes,* Paris 1890; M. Mundy, The family, inheritance, and Islam. A re-examination of the sociology of *farāʾiḍ* law, in A. Al-Azmeh (ed.), *Islamic law: Social and historical contexts,* London and New York 1988, 1-123; D.S. Powers, On bequests in early Islam, in *JNES* 48 (1989), 185-200; id., Islamic inheritance law: A socio-historical approach, in C. Mallat and J. Conners (eds.), *Islamic family law and the state,* London 1990, 11-29; id., *Studies in Qurʾan and* ḥadīth. *The formation of the Islamic law of inheritance,* Berkeley 1986; id., The will of Saʿd b. Abī Waqqāṣ. A reassessment, in *SI* 58 (1983), 33-53; H.-P. Raddatz, Früislamisches Erbrecht nach dem *Kitāb al-Farāʾiḍ* des Sufyān aṯ-Ṯaurī, in *WI* 13 (1971), 26-78; E. Sachau, *Muhammadenisches Erberecht nacht der Lehre der ibaditischen Araber von Zanzibar und Nordafrika,* Berlin 1894; id., *Muhammedanisches Recht nach schafiitischer Lehre,* Stuttgart 1897; D. Santillana, *Istituzioni di diritto musulmano malichita con riguardo anche al sistema sciafiita,* 2 vols., Rome 1925-38, ii, 495-550 (Diritto ereditario); M. Teffahi, *Traité de successions musulmanes d'après le rite malékite,* Senegal 1948; H. Yanagihashi, The doctrinal development of *"maraḍ al-mawt"* in the formative period of Islamic law, in *Islamic law and society* 5 (1998), 326-58.

Inimitability

An Arabic theological and literary term for the matchless nature of the qurʾānic discourse (Ar. *iʿjāz al-Qurʾān*). Although "inimitability" *(iʿjāz)* is not attested in the Qurʾān, it has a qurʾānic cognate, the fourth form verb *aʿjazahu,* "he found him to be without strength, or power, or ability; it frustrated his power or ability" (cf. Lane); *aʿjaza* and various derived forms occur sixteen times in the Qurʾān.

Of the four times the imperfect form of the verb *(yuʿjizu)* and the twelve times the active participle *(muʿjiz)* occur in the Qurʾān, none in context refers to the question of the human capacity to produce speech like that of the Qurʾān. Q 72:12, which employs the verb twice, is representative of most of the passages: "Indeed, we thought that we should never be able to frustrate *(lan nuʿjiza)* God in the earth, nor be able to frustrate him by [taking] flight."

Several passages specifically refer to humankind being unable to frustrate or render God's will impotent (e.g. Q 8:59; 9:2, 3; see IMPOTENCE). The third form (*ʿājaza*) occurs three times in the Qurʾān, with the meaning "to contend with someone or something in order to overtake or outstrip him/it." A cognate derived form in Q 22:50-1 provides an important qurʾānic background to the later theological doctrine of *iʿjāz al-Qurʾān* with the following dialectic: "Those who believe and do deeds of righteousness (see BELIEF AND UNBELIEF; GOOD DEEDS) — theirs shall be forgiveness (q.v.) and generous provision. And those who strive against our signs to void them (*saʿaw fī āyātinā muʿājizīna*) — they shall be the inhabitants of hell" (q.v.; cf. Q 34:5, 38). The linguistic expression and religious framework of contending with God and his messenger Muḥammad by challenging divine revelation (see REVELATION AND INSPIRATION; OPPOSITION TO MUḤAMMAD) was to become an important backdrop to subsequent theological disputes about the miracle of the Qurʾān (see CREATEDNESS OF THE QURʾĀN).

If the term *aʿjaza* and its cognate forms are left aside, however, several verses in the Qurʾān are framed as occasions when Muḥammad is commanded by God to challenge his detractors among the Arabs to produce sūras like those of the Qurʾān (Q 2:23-4; 10:38; 11:13; 17:88; 52:33-4). The Qurʾān contains no verse attesting that any hearer of the word of God (q.v.) recited by the Prophet ever met the challenge, although there are reports in early sources of several attempts to do so. The Challenge Verses, as they came to be called, were taken as theological warrants for the claim that the Qurʾān was a *muʿjiz(a)*, the technical term in Islamic theology (*kalām*, see THEOLOGY AND THE QURʾĀN) for "miracle" (q.v.). The inimitable Qurʾān was understood by the theologians (*mutakallimūn*) to be a miracle that served as an earthly sign and proof (q.v.) of Muḥammad's claim to be a prophet, akin to Moses' (q.v.) division of the Red Sea and Jesus' (q.v.) raising of the dead (see PROPHETS AND PROPHETHOOD). Whether or not other miracles were necessary or even rationally possible for Muḥammad and whether or not religious functionaries besides prophets could perform miracles generated serious debates among Sunnī, Shīʿī, and Ṣūfī Muslims (see SHĪʿISM AND THE QURʾĀN; ṢŪFISM AND THE QURʾĀN).

In another sense, the Qurʾān quite clearly asserts that the recitations which constitute the Qurʾān in their most discrete form, the *āyāt* (sing. *āya*), are "signs" (q.v.) from God, that is, transcendent tokens in this world (q.v.; *al-dunyā*) of God's being and activity. The term *āya*, which also means "verse" of the Qurʾān, appears approximately 275 times in the Qurʾān, in such meaning as: "[the Jews at Sinai] disbelieved in God's signs" (*kānū yakfurūna bi-āyāti llāhi*, Q 2:61). Still another qurʾānic term that contributed to the early discourse on miracles as signs from God is the root *ʿ-j-b* and its derived forms. The tenth sūra of the Qurʾān, "Jonah" (Sūrat Yūnus), begins: "These are the signs (*āyāt*) of the wise book (q.v.). Was it a wonder (*ʿajab*) to the people that we inspired a man from among them..." (Q 10:1-2). In the theological literature on the miracle of the Qurʾān, the feminine form *ʿajība* (pl. *ʿajāʾib*) became a technical term for a particular wonder. For example, the fabled lighthouse of Alexandria, which was said to house a lens that made it possible to see the army leaving Constantinople, as well as the pyramids of Egypt, was classed as an *ʿajība*. In the *kalām* literature, an *ʿajība* generally referred to humanly produced wonders, such as strange and wonderful buildings and instruments, or the beautiful works of great poets. By contrast, the term *muʿjiz* denoted divinely commissioned miracles and was thus restricted to religious figures, some said to prophets only. The term *ʿalam* (pl. *ʿalām, ʿalāmāt*), "a sign which offers guidance, as in navigation," also appears in the Qurʾān (e.g. Q 16:16; 42:32; 55:24), and the term is also used in *kalām* literature, but usually not to refer to divine miracles.

The qurʾānic and early Muslim context

Already in the time of the Prophet, controversy over the Qurʾān developed among those who heard it, especially among the Quraysh (q.v.) tribe in Mecca, indicating that the recitation of its verses had an effect on those who heard it. Part of the evidence for this is negative, in the form of the widespread opposition that Muḥammad and the qurʾānic recitations faced. Indeed, a prevailing theme of the earlier sūras especially, is the rejection of the Prophet and his recitations. The Qurʾān reports several accusations made against Muḥammad and the Qurʾān he recited and the manner in which he recited it. Of the unbeliever, the Qurʾān says: "he has been stubborn to our revelations" (Q 74:16), for humans have turned away from the Qurʾān in pride (q.v.) and said: "This is nothing other than magic from of old; this is nothing other than speech of mortal man" (Q 74:24-5). The Qurʾān specifies the kinds of accusations hurled at the Prophet by the skeptics among the Quraysh. In a variety of passages he is tauntingly called a soothsayer (*kāhin,* see SOOTHSAYERS), a poet (*shāʿir,* see POETRY AND POETS), a madman (*majnūn,* see INSANITY); his recitations are called fabrications, tales, legends, or fables — all of which could be imitated by humans (see Boullata, Rhetorical interpretation, 140). The Qurʾān itself denies that Muḥammad is a soothsayer, madman, or poet (cf. Q 52:29-31; 69:41-2). The rebuttal by Muslim theologians and literary scholars of these accusations during the next three centuries was closely related to the development of Arabic literary theory, which took qurʾānic language as the model for the purest, most eloquent Arabic speech (see ARABIC LANGUAGE; GRAMMAR AND THE QURʾĀN; LANGUAGE OF THE QURʾĀN; LITERARY STRUCTURES OF THE QURʾĀN). The counterclaim among theologians that the Qurʾān was a unique achievement, in language that was inimitable among humans, even the most eloquent Arabs, became part of the larger framework for the discussion of *iʿjāz al-Qurʾān.*

Some support exists for the belief that qurʾānic speech was unique among the linguistic productions of seventh-century Arabs (see ORALITY AND WRITINGS IN ARABIA). In Ibn Isḥāq's (d. 151/767) biography *(sīra)* of the Prophet (as edited by Ibn Hishām [d. 218/833]), al-Walīd b. al-Mughīra, a famous opponent of the Prophet, tells his fellow opponents of Muḥammad that "... his speech is sweet, his root is a palm tree whose branches are fruitful, and everything you have said [in criticism of the Prophet's recitations] would be known to be false" (Ibn Isḥāq, *Sīra,* i, 243 f.; Ibn Isḥāq-Guillaume, 121; see ʿAbd al-Jabbār, *Mughnī,* xvi, 268-9). A similar story is told about ʿUmar b. al-Khaṭṭāb before his conversion to Islam (Ibn Isḥāq, *Sīra,* i, 294 f.; Ibn Isḥāq-Guillaume, 156). The weight of opinion among Muslim scholars in early and medieval Islam, however, was that much of the speech in the Qurʾān was like *sajʿ* (the rhymed prose speech pattern of the *kāhin,* see RHYMED PROSE), which was characterized by assonance at the end of the verses.

The theological claim that the Qurʾān could not be imitated was a calque on the poetic *muʿāraḍa,* the competitive imitation or emulation of one poet or poem (usually a *qaṣīda*) by another poet, a cultural practice going back to pre-Islamic times (see PRE-ISLAMIC ARABIA AND THE QUR'ĀN). A related concept is the *naqāʾiḍ* (polemical, repartee poems), which were offered with a stronger sense of contest and competition (Schippers, Muʿāraḍa). Insufficient textual evidence exists to ascertain how soon Muslims or non-Muslims attempted to emulate or, more negatively, to parody the Qurʾān, although the first/seventh-century false prophet, Musaylima (see MUSAYLIMA AND PSEUDO-PROPHETS), is said to have recited verses that attempted to imitate the Qurʾān. A few lines of imitation of the Qurʾān attributed to the early ʿAbbāsid Persian convert to Islam, Ibn al-Muqaffaʿ (d. ca. 139/756-7) indicate that by the second/eighth century the *muʿāraḍa* was a cultural form of honoring or challenging the qurʾānic style (van Ess, Some fragments). The linguistic association of the *muʿāraḍa* with theological discourse about the inimitability of the Qurʾān is found in major theological works of the fourth/tenth century. Abū Bakr Muḥammad b. al-Ṭayyib al-Bāqillānī (d. 403/1013), an Ashʿarī theologian, wrote a book on *iʿjāz al-Qurʾān* in which he mentions the attempts of poets to match the famous pre-Islamic *muʿallaqa* poem of Imruʾ al-Qays (d. ca. 540 C.E.) at the location of ʿUkāẓ. In comparison to any attempt to match the eloquence and style of the Qurʾān, he argues, the poetic devices of even a figure as great as an Imruʾ al-Qays are "within the orbit of human possibilities and are of a type mankind can match.... The composition of the Qurʾān, however, is a thing apart and a special process, not to be equalled, free of rivals" (quoted in von Grunebaum, *Tenth-century document*, 60).

Against this background, the Challenge Verses *(āyāt al-taḥaddī)* referred to above become the cornerstone of the doctrine of *iʿjāz al-Qurʾān*. Muḥammad challenged those who mocked the Qurʾān and who opposed him to produce speech as good as that of the Qurʾān. In Q 52:33-4, cited earlier, a series of rhetorical counterpoints are hurled at his accusers. He answers those who accuse him of fabricating the speech of the Qurʾān *(taqawwalahu)* by challenging them to bring a discourse like it *(bi-ḥadīthin mithlihi)* if they speak truly. In Q 11:13, in response to those who accused Muḥammad of forging the Qurʾān *(iftarāhu):* "Say, then bring ten sūras like it if you are truthful." Q 10:37 addresses directly the accusation that the Qurʾān is a forgery: "This Qurʾān could not have been forged apart from God, but it is a confirmation *(taṣdīq)* of what is before it and a detailing *(tafṣīl)* of the book (q.v.), wherein there is no doubt, from the lord (q.v.) of the worlds." Thereupon follows a more taunting challenge than Q 11:13 above: "Or do they say he has forged it? Say: then produce a sūra like it, and call upon whomever you can apart from God if you speak truly" (Q 10:38). Following the theme of inviting critics of the Qurʾān even to seek help in imitating the Qurʾān, the most frequently cited verse puts the challenge as follows: "Truly, if humankind and the jinn (q.v.) assembled to produce the like of this Qurʾān they could not produce the like of it, even if some of them helped others" (Q 17:88). That no one can ever match the speech of the Qurʾān, and that there are eschatological consequences (see ESCHATOLOGY) for those who try and fail is asserted in Q 2:23-4: "If you are in doubt concerning what we sent down to our servant [Muḥammad], then produce a sūra the like of it, and call upon your witnesses apart from God, if you are truthful. And if you do not [produce one] — and you never will — then fear the hell fire (q.v.), whose fuel is humans and stones, prepared for unbelievers."

Toward the end of his life, challenges to Muḥammad's religious leadership began to appear elsewhere in Arabia, beyond

Mecca. It was the period in which, according to the *Sīra* of Ibn Isḥāq, many individuals were converting to Islam and many tribes were sending delegations to pay homage to the prophet Muḥammad. As news of Muḥammad's final illness spread, many who had earlier submitted to Islam now began to apostatize (see APOSTASY) and rebel against Muḥammad's authority and the authority of his immediate successor as head of the Muslim community *(umma)*, Abū Bakr. Those who rivaled Muḥammad, and even the Qurʾān, were labeled the arch-liars *(kadhdhābūn)*. Most notable of these were Musaylima b. Ḥabīb from the tribe of Ḥanīf, Ṭulayḥa b. Khuwaylid from the tribe of Asad, and al-Aswad b. Kaʿb al-ʿAnsī. With respect to the Qurʾān and the claims made about its inimitability, Musaylima is the most interesting and the one whose claims were refuted most vehemently in the later theological literature. Margoliouth (Origin, 485) argued that Musaylima had declared himself a prophet before Muḥammad had, though others disagree with this conclusion. The dispute has some bearing on whether Musaylima in history should be regarded as an imitator of Muḥammad and the Qurʾān or as a senior rival. Whatever conclusions may be drawn on the evidence (summarized in Watt, Musaylima), Ibn Isḥāq and al-Ṭabarī (d. 310/923) record several occasions when Musaylima sought to approach Muḥammad, and indeed one occasion when he offered to rule half of Arabia leaving the other (western) half to Muḥammad, each serving as prophets of their respective areas (Ibn Isḥāq, *Sīra*, iv, 183; Ibn Isḥāq-Guillaume, 649). Groups that challenged Muḥammad's authority and scripture during his lifetime were among those who apostatized and against whom Abū Bakr was forced to send Muslim militias to stabilize a *pax islamica*. A year after the death of Muḥammad, Musaylima was killed at ʿAqrabāʾ by Muslim forces led by Khālid b. al-Walīd.

The intellectual environment of the discussion of the Qurʾān in early and medieval Islam

The earliest phase of the development of the doctrine of the inimitability of the Qurʾān is also difficult to reconstruct from extant sources. Given the challenges and opposition to the Prophet and the Qurʾān by many of his contemporaries, and the lengths to which later theologians went to emphasize the extraordinary linguistic qualities of the Qurʾān as proof of Muḥammad's prophethood, it seems quite likely that disputes about the nature of the Qurʾān as a sign of the authenticity of Muḥammad's mission took place during the first two centuries after the emigration from Mecca to Medina (*hijra*, see EMIGRATION). The earliest texts or fragments thereof that refer directly to the inimitability of the Qurʾān date, however, from the third/ninth century. Before reviewing that evidence, it will be useful to look briefly at the early intellectual and cultural environment of Islamic civilization as it conquered and was changed by the lands and religious communities it subsumed, from north Africa to central Asia.

Belief in divinely inspired prophets, raised from within and *sent* to their communities, was a common denominator of belief among the Jews, Christians, Zoroastrians, and other religious communities that were to come under Islamic rule in the first/seventh and second/eighth centuries. In this shared cultural and religious context, claims made about the validity of each community's scripture (see SCRIPTURE AND THE QURʾĀN) and the prophets who brought them became the subject of persistent controversy among Muslims, Christians, Jews and others, as well as among the sectarian groups within the Muslim community itself (see POLEMIC AND POLEMICAL LANGUAGE; DEBATE AND DISPUTATION). Numerous texts exist that record the polemics and disputes, especially between Muslims and various Christian sects, such as the Nestorians, Jacobites, and Orthodox Christians, living under Islamic rule (see e.g. Griffith, Comparative religion). In the latter part of the third/ninth century, ʿAlī b. Sahl Rabban al-Ṭabarī composed a defense of Muḥammad's prophethood, *Kitāb al-Dīn wa-l-dawla,* arguing on the basis of prophetic miracles and signs, including the Qurʾān (Martin, Basrah Muʿtazilah, 177 and n. 8, 9). Also surviving is the text of a contrived polemical exchange in the first half of the third/ninth century between a Muslim and a Christian, ʿAbdallāh b. Ismaʿīl al-Hāshimī and ʿAbd al-Masīḥ al-Kindī, who were reportedly members of the court of the caliph al-Maʾmūn (r. 198-218/813-33). Again, the Prophet and the Qurʾān were the targets of this somewhat patronizing treatise against Islam. Neither treatise, however, has yet the sophistication of the language of the *kalām* texts on *iʿjāz al-Qurʾān* that have survived from the fourth/tenth and fifth/eleventh centuries. More directly evident in theological writing in defense of *iʿjāz al-Qurʾān* are those challenges that came from Muslim intellectuals themselves. Such critics were accused of *ilḥād,* "atheism." The most frequently cited atheist *(mulḥid)* in the *kalām* literature on the Qurʾān was Ibn al-Rāwandī (d. ca. 298/910-1), a philosophical theologian *(mutakallim)* who debated and wrote against many of those Sunnī theologians of the late third/ninth century who had written in defense of *iʿjāz al-Qurʾān* (cf. Kraus/Vajda, Ibn al-Rāwandī).

Another important context for the doctrine of the inimitable Qurʾān was the interest of Muslim scholars, beginning in the late second/eighth century, in literary criticism as it related to the style and linguistic qualities of the Qurʾān. A contemporary scholar of this genre also concludes that these early works of literary criticism "did not yet amount to a theory of the inimitability of the Qurʾān" (van Gelder, *Beyond the line,* 5). Among the better known and most influential works of this genre are *Maʿānī l-Qurʾān* by al-Farrāʾ (d. 207/822), *Majāz al-Qurʾān* by Abū ʿUbayda (d. 209/824), and *Taʾwīl mushkil al-Qurʾān* by Ibn Qutayba (d. 276/889). Still another matter that has some bearing on the growing theological and literary discourse about the inimitable Qurʾān was the sharp dispute over the createdness of the Qurʾān. The Muʿtazilīs (q.v.), though not the first, were strong defenders of the view that the Qurʾān, like all that was not God, was created by God in space and time. The theological dispute over this doctrine of *khalq al-Qurʾān* intensified in 218/833 when the caliph al-Maʾmūn ordered an inquisition (q.v.; *miḥna*) against any judge or court witness who failed to proclaim his adherence to the doctrine of the created Qurʾān. Ḥanbalī traditionalists and later the Ashʿarī theologians opposed the Muʿtazilī doctrine; over the next century after al-Maʾmūn they established the Sunnī dogma of the eternity of the Qurʾān. That the dispute over *khalq al-Qurʾān* is linked to the claim that the Qurʾān was inimitable is a problem in the history of Islamic thought of considerable interest (see Bouman, *Le conflit;* Larkin, Inimitability). The third/ninth and fourth/tenth centuries, then, were a time of intense theological speculation and disputation about the Qurʾān among Muslim schools of thought *(madhāhib,* sing. *madhhab)* and between Muslims and non-Muslim confessional communities. It was in this period that the theological problem of how to establish the evidences of Muḥammad's prophethood *(tathbīt dalāʾil al-nubuwwa)* and how to establish the Qurʾān as the primary evidence of Muḥammad's prophethood developed their chief lines of argument.

Classical theories of iʿjāz al-Qurʾān

In his long, sometimes rambling, discussion of the miracles that established Muḥammad's prophethood, the Muʿtazilī theologian (al-Qāḍī) ʿAbd al-Jabbār b. Aḥmad (d. 414/1025) mentions third/ninth century *mutakallimūn* who wrote on the miracles that established the validity of Muḥammad's prophethood. From this and other sources it becomes clear that by the late third/ninth century, a new genre of literature on establishing the evidences of prophethood *(tathbīt dalāʾil al-nubuwwa)* had become popular among the *mutakallimūn* and other religious scholars. Abū l-Hudhayl (d. 227/841-2) is the earliest *mutakallim* named (ʿAbd al-Jabbār, *Tathbīt*, ii, 511). It is not yet possible to confirm on the basis of extant texts, though one may suspect, that Abū l-Hudhayl held that the Qurʾān was inimitable. His pupil and contemporary, Abū Isḥāq Ibrāhīm b. Sayyār al-Naẓẓām (d. ca. 230/845) propounded a theory that the Qurʾān *per se* was not inimitable; rather, it lay within the linguistic abilities of ordinary humans and speakers of Arabic to produce speech like that of the Qurʾān. According to Abū l-Ḥusayn al-Khayyāṭ (d. ca. 300/913), al-Naẓẓām argued that the Qurʾān was a proof *(ḥujja)* of Muḥammad's prophethood on the basis of its several passages that reported on things unseen or in the future (see HIDDEN AND THE HIDDEN). Al-Khayyāṭ says that al-Naẓẓām held the view that the linguistic qualities of the Qurʾān were not superior to ordinary human speaking abilities "in spite of Allāh's saying *(maʿa qawl Allāh):* Truly, if humankind and the jinn assembled to produce the like of this Qurʾān they could not produce the like of it, even if some of them helped others (Khayyāṭ, *Intiṣār*, 28; trans., 25; see Ashʿarī, *Maqālāt*, 225/7-13).

This argument required al-Naẓẓām to come to terms with this and the other Challenge Verses discussed above. In a later Muʿtazilī work that belongs to the theological commentary tradition of the Baṣran school of the Muʿtazila (probably late fifth/eleventh century), the following account is given of al-Naẓẓām's view: "Know that al-Naẓẓām took the position that the Qurʾān is a miracle only with respect to *ṣarfa*. The meaning of *ṣarfa* is that the Arabs were able to utter speech like that of the Qurʾān with respect to linguistic purity and eloquence *(al-faṣāḥa wa-l-balāgha)* until the Prophet was sent. When the Prophet was sent, this [characteristic] eloquence was taken away from them and they were deprived of their knowledge of it, and thus they unable to produce speech like the Qurʾān.... Subsequent writers came along and supported this school of thought, and they raised many specious arguments for it" (Br. Mus. Oriental 8613, fol. 17b [bot]-18a; see RHETORIC OF THE QURʾĀN). The theory of *ṣarfa* was rejected by al-Naẓẓām's one-time student at Baṣra, ʿAmr b. Bar al-Jāḥiẓ (d. 255/865). Half a century later, Abū Hāshim (d. 321-933), also of the Baṣran school of the Muʿtazila, and his followers during the next century, known as the Bahshamiyya, opposed the doctrine of *ṣarfa*, as well as did Abū Hāshim's contemporary and founder of the Ashʿarite school of *kalām*, Abū l-Ḥasan al-Ashʿarī, and the majority of Sunnī Muslims in the centuries to come. Nonetheless, the theory of *ṣarfa* found some acceptance in the fourth/tenth century among some of the *mutakallimūn* of the Baghdad branch of the Muʿtazila and the Imāmī Shīʿa (Martin, Basrah Muʿtazilah, 181). A lengthy account of the dispute between ʿAbd al-Jabbār with the leader of the Imāmī Shīʿa in Baghdad and a strong proponent of the theory of *ṣarfa*, al-Sharīf al-Murtaḍā (d. 436/1044), is recorded in the manuscript cited above (Br. Mus. Or. 8613, fol. 17b-28a). Some later proponents of the theory of *ṣarfa* after al-Naẓẓām also accepted theories of the Qurʾān's miraculousness that were based on its arrangement, order, and linguistic purity (see below).

Al-Jāḥiẓ is the earliest *mutakallim* and literary scholar whose writings in defense of the prophethood of Muḥammad and the superior stylistic attributes of the Qurʾān have been preserved to any degree. Among the most important of his works is the short treatise *Risāla fī ḥujaj al-nubuwwa*, "Treatise on the argument for [Muḥammad's] prophethood" and numerous short passages in his famous literary work, *Kitāb al-Ḥayawān*. Although the term *iʿjāz al-Qurʾān* does not appear in any of his works, other derived forms from the root *ʿ-j-z* do appear, such as *ʿajaza*, *ʿājiz*, and *muʿjiz* in passages that speak about the qualities of the Qurʾān (Audebert, *al-Ḫaṭṭābī*, 63 and n. 3). Regarding when *iʿjāz* became a technical term in theological and literary discussions, Bouman has concluded on reasonable grounds that it appeared after the death of Ibn Ḥanbal (d. 241/855) but before the death of the Muʿtazilī *mutakallim*, Abū ʿAbdallāh Muḥammad b. Zayd al-Wāsiṭī (d. 307/918-9), who wrote the earliest known work with *iʿjāz* in the title: *Kitāb Iʿjāz al-Qurʾān fī naẓmihi wa-taʾlīfihi* (Bouman, *Le conflit*, 52, n. 4; Audebert, *al-Ḫaṭṭābī*, 58-64). Madelung and Abrahamov report that *al-Madīḥ al-kabīr* by the Zaydī-Muʿtazilī Imām al-Qāsim b. Ibrāhīm (d. 246/860) argues in support of the Qurʾān's inimitability (*iʿjāz*, Madelung, *Der Imām*, 125; Abrahamov, *Anthropomorphism*, 19), placing the origin of the term closer to the time when al-Jāḥiẓ flourished.

Al-Naẓẓām's doctrine of the qurʾānic miracle through divine intervention *(ṣarfa)* was refuted by his illustrious pupil, al-Jāḥiẓ. As mentioned above, some passages, including the treatise on the arguments for (primarily Muḥammad's) prophethood give some insight into his counter-argument to al-Naẓẓām's doctrine of *ṣarfa*. Al-Jāḥiẓ argued that the Qurʾān was inimitable on the basis of its composition *(taʾlīf)* and its structure or arrangement of words *(naẓm)*. Al-Bāqillānī (d. 403/1013) says that al-Jāḥiẓ was not the first to write on *naẓm al-Qurʾān*, and that his book had not added anything to what the *mutakallimūn* before him had written (Bāqillānī, *Iʿjāz*, 6; see Audebert, *Al-Ḫaṭṭābī*, 58 and n. 7). By al-Bāqillānī's time a century and a half later, however, the Muʿtazilīs and Ashʿarīs were in growing disagreement over that in which the inimitability of the qurʾānic language consisted. If he was not the first to articulate a doctrine of the inimitability of the Qurʾān, al-Jāḥiẓ was undeniably influential among later Muʿtazilīs and Ashʿarīs who defended inimitability as the chief characteristic of the miracle of the Qurʾān. Although he was criticized by later Ashʿarīs for the particular understanding he gave to the concept of *naẓm al-Qurʾān*, with al-Jāḥiẓ we see the early stages of the influence of literary criticism on *kalām* argumentation as well as the shaping of the general argument among most Sunnī and some Shīʿī intellectuals for the increasingly popular belief that the Qurʾān was inimitable.

Not all *mutakallimūn* regarded al-Jāḥiẓ's notion of an inimitable Qurʾān and al-Naẓẓām's concept of divine intervention as mutually incompatible. ʿAlī b. ʿĪsā al-Rummānī (d. 384/994) was a student of Arabic grammar and a Muʿtazilī *mutakallim* of the school founded in Baghdad by Abū Bakr Aḥmad b. ʿAlī al-Ikhshīdh (d. ca.

320/932). The Ikhshīdhiyya were fiercely antagonistic toward the Bahshamiyya, the Baṣran branch of the Muʿtazila that was led by Abū Hāshim b. al-Jubbāʾī (d. 321/933; see Ibn al-Murtaḍā, *Ṭabaqāt,* 100, 107). Al-Rummānī held that there were seven manifestations of the Qurʾān's inimitability. Among these, he included aspects of the overall argument, mentioned above, such as the fact that the Arabs were challenged to produce something like the Qurʾān but did not; that the Qurʾān achieved a degree of eloquence that surpassed what was a miracle customary *(naqḍ al-ʿāda)* even for the most eloquent Arabs; and that the inimitable Qurʾān was on a par with Moses parting the Red Sea and Jesus raising the dead to life. With al-Naẓẓām, al-Rummānī also counted the divine deterrence *(ṣarfa)* and the prophets' foretelling of unseen, that is future, events. Without comment on how he reconciled its apparent contradiction with *ṣarfa,* al-Rummānī dedicated the bulk of his *al-Nukat fī iʿjāz al-Qurʾān* to arguments for the inherent inimitability of the qurʾānic language, based on an analysis of ten rhetorical figures that make up its literary eloquence (*balāgha,* Rippin and Knappert, 49-59).

The sharpest opponents of Ibn Ikhshīdh and al-Rummānī among the Muʿtazila were the Baṣran school, now known as the Bahshamiyya, which in the early fourth/tenth century moved to Baghdad. Several distinguished followers of Abū Hāshim over the next two centuries defended his theories of the inimitable Qurʾān. The surviving works of ʿAbd al-Jabbār (*Mughnī,* xv and xvi; *Sharḥ,* 563-99) and a later commentary on a work by one of his pupils, Abū Rashīd al-Nīsābūrī, entitled *Ziyādāt sharḥ al-uṣūl,* carefully lay out the doctrine of the apologetic miracle of the inimitable Qurʾān according to the Baṣran school and the arguments they had with numerous opponents among the theologians, philosophers, atheists, and non-Muslim religious intellectuals. The rationalist concern of the Baṣran Muʿtazila was to preserve the logical effect of the prophetic miracle (Moses dividing the Red Sea, Jesus raising the dead, Muḥammad reciting an inimitable scripture) as providing indubitable proof that those who produced them were indeed prophets. Thus, the doctrine of the inimitability of the Qurʾān held by the Baṣran Muʿtazila was an argument against the popular belief that Ṣūfī masters, Shīʿī imāms (see IMĀM), magicians and sorcerers could perform real miracles and thus demand a following. The Muʿtazilī *mutakallimūn* generally did not deny that such figures existed or that they claimed to perform miraculous feats; they denied that what such religious figures produced were actually miracles like *iʿjāz al-Qurʾān.*

ʿAbd al-Jabbār set forth four conditions necessary for an act to be a true miracle. First, it must come either directly or indirectly from God. Second, it must interrupt the customary course of events *(naqḍ al-ʿāda),* e.g. temporarily parting the waters of the Red Sea. Third, humans must be unable to produce such miracles with respect to genus *(jins)* or attribute *(ṣifa)* — an implicit reference to Musaylima's attempt to gain a following by producing his own Qurʾān. Finally, a miracle must belong specifically to one who claims to be a prophet (ʿAbd al-Jabbār, *Sharḥ,* 559/15 – 561/8). The case for the *iʿjāz* of the Qurʾān was made to rest on its linguistic purity *(faṣāḥa)* and eloquence *(balāgha),* which by the tenth century had become the standard concepts of the stylistic miracle of the Qurʾān.

It has already been noted that despite their sharp criticism of the Muʿtazila on other grounds, traditionalists and Ashʿarī scholars agreed with the main lines of the Muʿtazilī doctrine of the apologetic miracle of the inimitable Qurʾān. A traditionalist contemporary of al-Rummānī and ʿAbd al-Jabbār, Ḥamd b. Muḥammad al-Khaṭṭābī (d. ca. 386/996) rejected the theory of *ṣarfa*. At the same time he refuted al-Rummānī's Muʿtazilī view that the Qurʾān contained rhetorical figures whose degree of eloquence was humanly unattainable (Audebert, *al-Ḫaṭṭābī*, 107-8). Al-Khaṭṭābī's text, *Bayān iʿjāz al-Qurʾān*, has been published and shows a much greater concern with the literary aspects of *iʿjāz* than the theological arguments of the Muʿtazilīs and Ashʿarīs, although in the long run it is difficult to separate the two kinds of argumentation in this literature (see Audebert, *al-Ḫaṭṭābī*).

The Ashʿarī theologians of the late fourth/tenth and the fifth/eleventh centuries further perfected the literary rationale for the claim that the Qurʾān was inimitable. Al-Bāqillānī, already discussed above, wrote several works on prophethood and miracles that have survived, most notably *Kitāb Iʿjāz al-Qurʾān*. In this work, al-Bāqillānī presents himself as a non-specialist in Arabic literary theory who wishes to show that humans cannot attain the level of stylistic achievement of the Qurʾān. Unlike the Muʿtazila, however, al-Bāqillānī denies that the theological ground of *iʿjāz* can be established by its demonstrable linguistic superiority (von Grunebaum, *Tenth-century document*, xviii, 54-5). It was ʿAbd al-Qāhir al-Jurjānī (d. 471/1078), a scholar of Arabic literature, who set the Ashʿarī theory of the stylistic miracle of the Qurʾān on its strongest intellectual footing. Al-Jurjānī's *Dalāʾil iʿjāz al-Qurʾān* presents strong arguments against ʿAbd al-Jabbār's Muʿtazilī theory of speech *(kalām)*, thus establishing a distinct Ashʿarī theory of *iʿjāz*. Whereas al-Jāḥiẓ, al-Rummānī, al-Bāqillānī, ʿAbd al-Jabbār and others had based their theories of *iʿjāz* on the qualities of the inimitable composition *(naẓm)* of words and phrases in the Qurʾān, thus resting the case for miracle solely on style and linguistics, al-Jurjānī argued that the overall composition of the Qurʾān, its meaning as well as its wording, was the true miracle (Larkin, *Theology of meaning*).

Following the fulsome and lively discussions of *iʿjāz al-Qurʾān* by scholars like ʿAbd al-Jabbār, Abū Rashīd al-Nīsābūrī, al-Bāqillānī, and al-Jurjānī in the fourth/tenth and fifth/eleventh centuries, the theologians and literary scholars of the late medieval and early modern periods refined the earlier arguments, rather than contributing new ones. In the twentieth century, a number of Muslim scholars, such as Muḥammad ʿAbduh, Sayyid Quṭb, and ʿĀʾisha ʿAbd al-Raḥmān (Bint al-Shāṭiʾ) have attempted to define that which characterizes the stylistic superiority of the Qurʾān over other Arabic literary works of art (Boullata, Rhetorical interpretation, 148-54). Among most modern writers, the primary concern has been with Arabic stylistics and linguistics as the true basis for the inimitability of the Qurʾān. The theological dimension of the theories of *iʿjāz al-Qurʾān*, which were so intensely disputed in the medieval period, appear to be less important in contemporary writing about the Qurʾān (see CONTEMPORARY CRITICAL PRACTICES AND THE QURʾĀN; EXEGESIS OF THE QURʾĀN: CLASSICAL AND MEDIEVAL; EXEGESIS OF THE QURʾĀN: EARLY MODERN AND CONTEMPORARY).

Richard C. Martin

Bibliography

Primary: ʿAbd al-Jabbār b. Aḥmad, *Kitāb al-Mughnī fī abwāb al-tawḥīd wa-l-ʿadl*, ed. Ṭ. Ḥusayn et al., 14 (of 20) parts published to date, Cairo 1960-9; id., *Sharḥ al-uṣūl al-khamsa*, ed. ʿA. ʿUthmān, Cairo 1965; id., *Tathbīt dalāʾil al-nubuwwa*, ed. ʿA. ʿUthmān, 2 vols., Beirut 1966; al-Ashʿarī, Abū l-Ḥasan, *Kitāb Maqālāt al-islāmiyyīn*, ed. H. Ritter, Wiesbaden 1963; Bāqillānī, *Iʿjāz;* British Museum Oriental 8613, a later commentary on Abū Rashīd al-Nīsābūrī's

(d. after 424/1025) *Ziyādāt al-sharḥ;* Ibn Isḥāq (Ibn Hishām) *Sīra,* ed. Ṭ. ʿAbd al-Raʾūf, 4 vols., Beirut 1408/1987; Ibn Isḥāq-Guillaume; Ibn al-Murtaḍā, *Kitāb Ṭabaqāt al-Muʿtazila,* ed. S. Diwald Wilzer, Wiesbaden 1961; al-Jāḥiẓ, *Kitāb al-Hayawān,* ed. A.S. Hārūn, 7 vols., Cairo 1954; id., *Kitāb Ḥujaj al-nubuwwa,* in Sandūbī (ed.), *Rasāʾil al-Jāḥiẓ,* Cairo 1933; Jurjānī, *Dalāʾil,* Cairo ca. 1984; al-Khayyāṭ, Abū l-Ḥusayn, *Kitāb al-Intiṣār,* trans. A.N. Nader, Beirut 1957; Rummānī, *al-Nukat fī iʿjāz al-Qurʾān,* in M. Khalaf Allāh and M. Zaghlūl (eds.), *Thalāth rasāʾil fī iʿjāz al-Qurʾān,* Cairo 1955; Eng. trans. in A. Rippin and J. Knap pert (eds. and trans.), *Textual sources for the study of Islam,* Chicago 1990, 49-59.
Secondary: B. Abrahamov (ed. and trans), *Anthropomorphism and the interpretation of the Qurʾān in the theology of al-Qāsim ibn Ibrāhīm.* Kitāb al-Mustarshid, Leiden 1996; C.-F. Audebert, *al-Haṭṭābī et l'inimitabilité du Coran. Traduction et introduction au* Bayān iʿjāz al-Qurʾān, Damascus 1982; I.J. Boullata, The rhetorical interpretation of the Qurʾān. *Iʿjāz* and related topics, in Rippin, *Approaches,* 139-57; J. Bouman, *Le conflit autour du Coran et la solution d'al-Bāqillānī,* Amsterdam 1959; J. van Ess, Some fragments of the *Muʿāraḍat al-Qurʾān* attributed to Ibn al-Muqaffaʿ, in W. al-Qāḍī (ed.), *Studia arabica et islamica. Festschrift for Iḥsān ʿAbbās on his sixtieth birthday,* Beirut 1981, 151-63; G.J.H. van Gelder, *Beyond the line. Classical Arabic literary critics on the coherence and unity of the poem,* Leiden 1982; Gilliot, *Elt,* 73-93 (esp. 73-5: abridged translation of Ṭabarī, *Tafsīr,* ed. Shākir, i, 8-12 on inimitability); S. Griffith, Comparative religion in the apologetics of the first Christian Arabic theologians, in *Proceedings of the patristic, medieval and renaissance conference,* Villanova 1979, 63-87; G.E. von Grunebaum, *A tenth-century document of Arabic literary theory and criticism. The sections on poetry of al-Bāqillānī's* Iʿjāz al-Qurʾān. *Translated and annotated,* Chicago 1950; A.M. al-Jemaey, *al-Rummānī's* al-Nukat fī iʿjāz al-Qurʾān. *An annotated translation with introduction,* Ph.D. diss., Indiana 1987; N. Kermani, *Gott is Schön. Das Ästhetische Erleben des Koran,* Munich 1999; P. Kraus/G. Vajda, Ibn al-Rāwandī, in *EI²,* iii, 905-6; M. Larkin, The inimitability of the Qurʾān. Two perspectives, in *Religion and literature* 20 (1988), 31-47; id., *The theology of meaning. ʿAbd al-Qāhir al-Jurjānī's Theory of discourse,* New Haven 1995; W. Madelung, *Der Imām al-Qāsim ibn Ibrāhīm und die Glaubenslehre der Zaiditen,* Berlin 1965; D.S. Margoliouth, On the origin and import of the names Muslim and ḥanīf, in *JRAS* 1903, 467-93; R.C. Martin, The role of the Basrah Muʿtazilah in formulating the doctrine of the apologetic miracle, in *JNES* 39 (1980), 175-89; M. Radscheit, *Die koranische Herausforderung. Die taḥaddī-Verse im Rahmen der Polemikpassagen des Korans,* Berlin 1996; Y. Rahman, The miraculous nature of Muslim scripture. A study of ʿAbd al-Jabbār's *Iʿjāz al-Qurʾān,* in *Islamic studies* 35 (1996), 409-24; A. Schippers, Muʿāraḍa, in *EI²,* vii, 261; W.M. Watt, Musaylima, in *EI²,* vii, 664-5; Watt-Bell.

Injīl see GOSPEL

Innovation

The creation of, or belief in, something that has no precedent or support either in the texts of revelation or in juridical consensus (see REVELATION AND INSPIRATION; LAW AND THE QURʾĀN). Innovation is connoted by two Arabic terms *(bidʿa, muḥdath),* and derivatives of both roots, *b-d-ʿ* and *ḥ-d-th,* appear in the Qurʾān, but in the majority of cases they are not used in the sense of deviating from a set path or precedent. In Q 65:1, for instance, the verb *yuḥdith* is used — with God as grammatical subject — to mean "create" (probably *ex nihilo*) or "bring some new thing to pass" (see CREATION). Derivatives of *b-d-ʿ* are used in four verses, in only one of which the verb is employed in the sense of invention, namely, Q 57:27: "But monasticism *(rahbāniyya,* see MONASTICISM AND MONKS) they invented; we ordained it not for them." Its usage is largely congruent with the later definition of the term, since the context in which this statement was made was one where God sent down the prophets (see PROPHETS AND PROPHETHOOD) and books (see BOOK), including Jesus (q.v.) and the Gospel (q.v.), but monasticism had neither divine sanction nor precedent. In Q 2:117 and 6:101, God is declared as the "originator *(badīʿ)* of the heavens (see HEAVEN AND SKY) and earth (q.v.)."

In later usage, the term *bidʿa,* when it appears alone, generally has a negative connotation. To designate a laudatory innovation, it was necessary to qualify the term, usually with the adjective *ḥasana* (good). Technically, innovation came to be distinguished according to the five legal norms (*al-aḥkām al-khamsa*, see PROHIBITED DEGREES) depending on whether or not it violates a revealed text, a juridical consensus or, even, according to al-Shāfiʿī (d. 204/820), a Companion's report (*athar*, see COMPANIONS OF THE PROPHET; ḤADĪTH AND THE QURʾĀN). The first is mandatory innovation *(bidʿa wājiba)* which is incumbent upon those who are able to undertake it. The performance of a mandatory act entails reward, but its omission entails punishment. Devoting oneself to religious scholarship — which includes the study of Arabic (see ARABIC LANGUAGE) in order to understand the Qurʾān and the sunna (q.v.), the study of grammar (see GRAMMAR AND THE QURʾĀN), of ḥadīth criticism, of law, and engaging in anti-sectarian discourse — is but one example of the obligation to carry out innovation. The second is the prohibited innovation *(bidʿa muḥarrama)* which is clearly embodied in all the theological and other beliefs of the sects that diverged from the Sunnī community (see THEOLOGY AND THE QURʾĀN). Obviously, the commission of the prohibited is punishable (see CHASTISEMENT AND PUNISHMENT). The third type is the recommended innovation *(bidʿa mandūba),* such as in the construction of Ṣūfī hospices (*ribāṭ*s, see ṢŪFISM AND THE QURʾĀN) and colleges for religious education (*madrasa*s). The performance of a recommended innovation is rewarded, but its omission does not require punishment. The fourth is reprehensible innovation *(bidʿa makrūha),* such as embellishing mosques and decorating copies of the Qurʾān (see ORNAMENT AND ILLUMINATION). The reprehensible is rewarded when omitted, but is not punished when committed. The fifth and last type is permissible innovation *(bidʿa mubāḥa),* such as indulging oneself excessively in eating, in drinking or in wearing fancy clothing. Both the omission and commission of a permissible innovation are equally legitimate (see VIRTUES AND VICES).

When used negatively, *bidʿa* must be distinguished from various forms of heresy (q.v.) because the reprehensible innovator, unlike the heretic, does not intentionally aim to break ranks with the Muslim community or with the teachings of the faith (q.v.). Rather, his innovation, though deemed to be lacking any foundation in the Islamic authoritative sources, would nonetheless claim to be Islamic. This explains why in the vocabulary of Sunnism the sectarian groups were termed the "People of Innovation" or *ahl al-bidaʿ*.

Wael B. Hallaq

Bibliography
Primary: al-Qurṭubī, Muḥammad b. Waḍḍāḥ, *Kitāb al-Bidaʿ*, ed. M. Isabel Fierro, Madrid 1988; al-Shāṭibī, Abū Isḥāq Ibrāhīm, *al-Iʿtiṣām*, ed. Muḥammad Rashīd Riḍā, 2 vols., repr. Riyadh n.d.; al-Tahānawī, Muḥammad b. ʿAlī, *Kashshāf iṣṭilāḥāt al-funūn*, 2 vols., Calcutta 1862, i, 133-5; al-Ṭurṭūshī, Abū Bakr, *Kitāb al-Ḥawādith wa-l-bidaʿ*, ed. ʿAbd al-Majīd Turkī, Beirut 1990.
Secondary: ʿIzza ʿAlī ʿAṭiyya, *al-Bidʿa*, Beirut 1980; M. Fierro, The treatises against innovations *(kutub al-bidʿa)*, in *Der Islam* 69 (1992), 204-46; V. Rispler, Towards a new understanding of the term *bidʿa*, in *Der Islam* 68 (1991), 320-8; M. Talbi, Les Bidaʿ, in *SI* 12 (1960), 43-77.

Inquisition

Act or process of questioning; judicial or official questioning before a jury, often with the connotation of pursuit of heresy (q.v.) and the punishment of heretics. Two Arabic roots appear in the Qurʾān with the sense of "inquisition:" the fifth verbal form of *f-q-d* and the eighth form of *m-ḥ-n*. *Tafaqqada* is attested once, at Q 27:20, where Solomon (q.v.) searches among the birds for the hoopoe (see ANIMAL LIFE), who finally brings him news of the Queen of Sheba (q.v.; see also BILQĪS). The eighth verbal form of the root *m-ḥ-n* (whence also *miḥna*, discussed below) is attested twice (Q 49:3; 60:10) and lends itself to the title of a sūra, Q 60 (Sūrat al-Mumtaḥana, "She who is to be examined"). In both of the qurʾānic attestations, reference is made to the testing of conscience regarding faith (q.v.): in the first instance, those who lower their voices in the presence of the Prophet (see SOCIAL INTERACTIONS) are the ones whose hearts (see HEART) God has proven to righteousness *(amtaḥana llāhu qulūbahum lil-taqwā)*. The second verse, from which the name of Q 60 is derived, instructs the believers (see BELIEF AND UNBELIEF) to examine women who come to them seeking refuge. If they are found to be true believers, they are not to be returned to the unbelievers (*kuffār*, see POLYTHEISM AND ATHEISM) who, the verse continues, are not lawful (*ḥill*, see LAWFUL AND UNLAWFUL) for them. It is not, however, a sin (*junāḥ*, see SIN AND CRIME) for the believers to marry such women (see MARRIAGE AND DIVORCE; WOMEN AND THE QURʾĀN). This policy marked a modification of the truce of Ḥudaybiya, according to which the Muslims were to return all fugitives, male and female, but the polytheists were not required to give up renegades from Islam (see CONTRACTS AND ALLIANCES; EXPEDITIONS AND BATTLES). Q 60:12 contains the terms of the oath of allegiance (see OATHS AND PROMISES) that such women were to swear to Muḥammad: they were to ascribe no partner to God (see IDOLS AND IMAGES; IDOLATRY AND IDOLATERS), would not steal (see THEFT), commit adultery (see ADULTERY AND FORNICATION), kill their children (see INFANTICIDE), lie (q.v.), nor disobey Muḥammad (see DISOBEDIENCE; cf. Ibn Isḥāq-Guillaume, 509-10).

This qurʾānic connotation — of examining, and judging, the faith of the members of the Muslim community — was incorporated in the usage of the noun *miḥna* to denote the events which followed after the seventh ʿAbbāsid caliph al-Maʾmūn (r. 193-218/809-33) demanded in 218/833 that leading scholars *(ʿulamāʾ)* publicly proclaim their acquiescence in the doctrine of the createdness of the Qurʾān (q.v.). The *ʿulamāʾ* were threatened with confiscation, torture and even execution if they did not accede to the caliphal order. Though the *miḥna*, which lasted some nineteen years (218-37/833-52), was primarily conducted in the capital Baghdad, it was also enforced by caliphal representatives in a number of provinces of the Islamic empire. After al-Maʾmūn's death, the *miḥna* was continued, albeit with different degrees of rigor, by his successors al-Muʿtaṣim (r. 218-27/833-42) and especially al-Wāthiq (r. 227-32/842-7). The *miḥna* was halted by the tenth ʿAbbāsid caliph al-Mutawakkil (r. 232-47/847-61), whereupon — and till this very day — the uncreatedness or eternity of the Qurʾān came to be the majority doctrine. It should be pointed out that the *miḥna* was an exceptional episode in Islamic history and hardly resembled the duration and scale of the Christian inquisition of the Middle Ages.

Three views have been proposed to explain al-Maʾmūn's introduction of the *miḥna*. D. Sourdel *(La politique)* suggests that through the *miḥna* al-Maʾmūn sought to enforce the doctrine of the createdness of the Qurʾān as a means of uniting the two branches of Sunnī and Shīʿī Islam. A critique of this explanation rests on the current view that at the time of al-Maʾmūn both "branches" were doctrinally still evolving and, moreover, neither had an unambiguous position on the nature of the

Qurʾān. A second explanation, popular among writers of overviews of Islamic history, erroneously implies a (causal) link between the *miḥna* and the rationalist school of the Muʿtazila (see MUʿTAZILĪS) which happened to espouse the doctrine of the createdness of the Qurʾān. There were, however, other rationally-oriented movements which professed the very same view and, as J. van Ess (Ḍirār b. ʿAmr) has pointed out, al-Maʾmūn held some views which clashed with Muʿtazilī thinking. Making use of the fact that, uncharacteristically, al-Maʾmūn was quite dogmatic in demanding assent to the doctrine of the createdness of the Qurʾān by enjoining a peremptory and unequivocal yes/no answer of the men subjected to the *miḥna*, proponents of the third explanation are of the opinion that behind all this was al-Maʾmūn's resolve to have the *ʿulamāʾ* publicly acknowledge that it was not they, but the incumbent of the caliphal institution who had supreme authority on religious doctrine — of which the createdness of the Qurʾān was an example (see also POLITICS AND THE QURʾĀN; THEOLOGY AND THE QURʾĀN; TRIAL).

John A. Nawas

Bibliography
Primary: Ibn Isḥāq-Guillaume.
Secondary: P. Crone and M. Hinds, *God's Caliph. Religious authority in the first centuries of Islam*, Cambridge 1983; J. van Ess, Ḍirār b. ʿAmr und die Ǧahmīya, in *Der Islam* 43 (1967), 241-79 and 44 (1968), 1-70, 318-20; id., *TG*, iii, 446-508; M. Hinds, Miḥna, in *EI²*, vii, 2-6; I. Lapidus, The separation of state and religion in the development of early Islamic society, in *IJMES* 6 (1975), 363-85; T. Nagel, *Rechtleitung und Kalifat. Versuch über eine Grundfrage der Islamischen Geschichte*, Bonn 1975; J. Nawas, *al-Maʾmūn. Miḥna and Caliphate*, Ph.D. Diss., Catholic University Nijmegen 1992; id., A reexamination of three current explanations for al-Maʾmūn's introduction of the Miḥna, in *IJMES* 26 (1994), 615-29; id., The miḥna of 218 A.H./833 A.D. revisited. An empirical approach, in *JAOS* 116 (1996), 698-708; D. Sourdel, La politique religieuse du calife ʿabbaside al-Maʾmun, in *REI* 30 (1962), 27-48; W.M. Watt, Al-Ḥudaybiya, in *EI²*, iii, 539; M. Zaman, *Religion and politics under the early ʿAbbasids*, Leiden 1997.

Insanity

Unsoundness or derangement of mind, especially without recognition of one's illness (see ILLNESS AND HEALTH), sometimes with the connotation of possession by a demon. Sixteen passages in the Qurʾān defend prophets (see PROPHETS AND PROPHETHOOD; MESSENGER) from the accusation of being *majnūn*, "possessed by demons (see DEVIL), insane, mad." Unbelievers (see BELIEF AND UNBELIEF) of different peoples are shown in the Qurʾān to accuse a prophet of being *majnūn*, for which reason they consider his message to be a lie (q.v.). The accusation is either reported as direct speech of the unbelievers or as a refutation in the words of the respective prophet ("your prophet is not *majnūn*"). Instead of "he is (not) *majnūn*," in five cases the formulation "in him is a/no *jinna*" is used. These correlations are represented in Table A below.

All these verses were revealed in the Meccan period (see CHRONOLOGY AND THE QURʾĀN). According to Nöldeke's classification, the *majnūn*-formulation belongs to the first (sūras 51, 52, 68, 81) and second (sūras 15, 26, 37 and 44) periods, the *bihi jinna*-formulation to the second (sūra 23) and third (sūras 7 and 34) Meccan periods. Like the punishment stories (q.v.), of which some of these verses are part, they serve to affirm the veracity of the prophet's mission against the suspicions of his adversaries, who would accuse a prophet of being either a liar (see LIE), a poet

	Unbelievers about Muḥammad	The people of Noah (q.v.) about Noah	Pharaoh (q.v.) about Moses (q.v.)	All peoples about every messenger
majnūn	Q 15:6; 37:36; 44:14; 52:29; 68:2, 51; 81:22	Q 54:9	Q 26:27; 51:39	Q 51:52
bihi jinna	Q 23:70; 34:8; cf. 7:184; 34:46	Q 23:25		

Table A

(see POETRY AND POETS), a sorcerer (see MAGIC, PROHIBITION OF), a diviner (see DIVINATION; SOOTHSAYERS), or a *majnūn*. These designations occur in various combinations: sorcerer *(sāḥir)* and *majnūn* (Q 51:39, 52); sorcerer and liar *(kadhdhāb)*, or *sāḥir kadhdhāb* (Q 38:4; 40:24); poet *(shāʿir)* and *majnūn* (Q 52:29-30) or *shāʿir majnūn* (Q 37:36); diviner *(kāhin)* and *majnūn* (Q 52:29); diviner and poet (Q 69:41 f.). None of these groups can be assumed to tell the truth and they are therefore all incompatible with true prophethood, though their utterances might bear similarities to those of real prophets (see also MUSAYLIMA AND PSEUDO-PROPHETS).

The different renderings of the word *majnūn* in translations of the Qurʾān show that the main problem for its understanding is the question of whether the notion of demonic possession prevails in the word *majnūn* or if the medical notion of mental derangement is paramount. On the one hand, jinn (q.v.) figure prominently in Qurʾān, ḥadīth (see ḤADĪTH AND THE QURʾĀN) and later Islamic tradition while, on the other hand, Arabic poetry from the time of Muḥammad onward shows that the belief in an inspiring jinn had almost faded away and that the poets ascribed their poetic achievements exclusively to themselves, but never to a demon. In this context, it is important to note that Eichler (*Die Dschinn*, 23-4) has shown that the Qurʾān employs *bihi jinna* (or, negatively, *mā bihi jinna*) to denote a person subject to inspiration by jinn, and that this usage should be distinguished from *majnūn*, which signifies possession or madness. Moreover, *junūn*, "madness, insanity," was considered to be caused also by excessive emotions like love without the intervention of a demon. Even in the qurʾānic verses the notion of "possession" need not necessarily be dominant as the parallel between *sāḥir kadhdhāb* and *shāʿir majnūn* shows. Since, however, both aspects were obviously simultaneously present in early Islamic society, it is reasonable to assume that they were not considered to be contradictory. It therefore seems feasible to translate *majnūn* both as "madman, insane" as well as "possessed," though both translations do not exhaust the full meaning of the word. The word *jinna*, originally a plural noun designing a "group of jinn," has the same range of meanings and was thus considered by some commentators (cf. Ālūsī, *Rūḥ*, ix, 119) to be also a verbal noun synonymous with *junūn*.

Other expressions connected with the notion of insanity are Q 68:6 where the word *maftūn* is sometimes interpreted to mean "afflicted with madness" and Q 2:275 where the touch *(mass)* of Satan is generally held to cause insanity. The word *suʿur* in Q 54:24, 47 should be connected with *saʿīr*, "flame, fire (q.v.), hell (q.v.)," rather than considered an expression for non-demonic madness, as Dols (*Madman*, 218,

n. 38) and several lexicographers have assumed.

Thomas Bauer

Bibliography
Primary: Ālūsī, *Rūḥ*.
Secondary: R. Basset, *Mille et un contes, récits et légendes arabes*, 3 vols., Paris 1924, i, 175 (le djinn poète); M.W. Dols, *Majnūn. The madman in medieval Islamic society*, Oxford 1992; P.A. Eichler, *Die Dschinn, Teufel und Engel im Koran*, Inaugural-Dissertation, Université de Leipzig, Lucka in Thüringen 1928; J. Henninger, Geisterglaube bei den vorislamischen Arabern, in id., *Arabica sacra*, Göttingen 1981, 118-69 (on the belief in demons in pre- and early Islamic as well as in modern times; comprehensive bibliography); Izutsu, *God*, 168-77 (for a good analysis of the private or secret character of communication through verbal inspiration); F. Meier, Some aspects of inspiration by demons in Islam, in id., *Bausteine II*, Istanbul 1992, 987-95; A.T. Welch, Madjnūn, in *EI*[2], v, 1101-2; M. Zwettler, A Mantic manifesto. The sūrah of "The Poets" and the qurʾānic foundations of prophetic authority, in J. Kugel (ed.), *Poetry and prophecy. The beginnings of a literary tradition*, Ithaca 1990, 75-119.

Insolence and Obstinacy

Gross disrespect and unyielding adherence to an idea. Understanding "insolence" as an attitude or character flaw that leads to obstinate rejection may justify its joint examination with "obstinacy," which conveys the idea of stubbornness and aggression as well as arrogance (q.v.) and tyranny. This compound concept is often mentioned in the Qurʾān, always in connection with the manner in which divine providence reveals itself throughout human history (see HISTORY AND THE QURʾĀN; FATE). The Qurʾān presents tales of ancient groups of people (see GENERATIONS; GEOGRAPHY) who threw off all restraint, for they were too proud to listen to admonitions and too boastful (see BOAST) to accept the divine messages addressed to them by prophets and messengers (see PROPHETS AND PROPHETHOOD; MESSENGER). Their pride (q.v.) made them behave in an ungodly way that manifested itself in their insolence and obstinacy. Their refusal to alter their ways culminated in severe punishment (see CHASTISEMENT AND PUNISHMENT; PUNISHMENT STORIES), for which no repentance was possible (see REPENTANCE AND PENANCE).

The Qurʾān uses several terms, derived from various roots, to describe the manner in which ungodly people acted: *ʿ-n-d (ʿanīd)* to express stubbornness, *k-b-r (istakbara, takabbara, mutakabbir)* to express arrogance, *ʿ-l-y (ʿālin, ʿuluww)* to express haughtiness, *ṭ-gh-y (ṭaghā)* to express tyranny, *ʿ-ṣ-y (ʿaṣā)* to express disobedience (q.v.), *ʾ-b-y (abā)* to express refusal and *j-b-r (jabbār)* to express oppression (q.v.). Of all the expressions, *istakbara* is the most common; the verb occurs about thirty times in the Qurʾān whereas the others each appear only five times or fewer.

The following analysis focuses on three major qurʾānic tales that examine acts of insolence and obstinacy, stimulated by pride: the tale of the ancient Arab tribes ʿĀd (q.v.) and Thamūd (q.v.), who refused to listen to the messengers sent to them and were consequently destroyed; Pharaoh (q.v.), who paid dearly for his tyrannical and ungodly acts; Iblīs (see DEVIL), who was too proud to bow to Adam (see ADAM AND EVE; BOWING AND PROSTRATION) and was therefore expelled from heaven (see HEAVEN AND SKY) and became a condemned figure.

ʿĀd and Thamūd

The story of the two tribes is detailed in Q 7:65 f. It is adduced in a sequence of stories about messengers who were sent to guide their people toward godfearing conduct: Hūd (q.v.) was sent to the people of

ʿĀd, and Ṣāliḥ (q.v.) was sent to Thamūd. Both tribes rejected the call addressed to them, and by so doing brought calamities upon themselves. ʿĀd is addressed with the words "Anger and wrath from your lord have fallen upon you… We cut off the remnant of those who cried lies to our signs and were not believers" (Q 7:71-2; see BELIEF AND UNBELIEF). Those who "waxed proud" (*istakbarū,* Q 7:76) among the people of Thamūd and did not believe, "the earthquake seized them, and morning found them in their habitation fallen prostrate" (Q 7:78). In Q 41:15-8 we find: "As for ʿĀd, they waxed proud *(istakbarū)* in the earth without right, and they said 'Who is stronger than we in might?'… then we loosed against them a wind (see AIR AND WIND) clamorous in days of ill fortune, that we might let them taste the chastisement of degradation in the present life… As for Thamūd, we guided them, but they preferred blindness (see VISION AND BLINDNESS) above guidance, so the thunderbolt of the chastisement of humiliation seized them for that they were earning." Here, as well as in other verses, pride is presented as the creator of disobedience; disobedience rooted in pride causes disbelief, and the latter leads to chastisement and tribulation.

Pharaoh (Firʿawn)

Pharaoh appears in the Qurʾān as a prototype of pride and the refusal to renounce disbelief and wrongdoing. His name is mentioned over seventy times in the Qurʾān, mostly as an oppressor (*ʿālin,* Q 10:83; 44:31; cf. 23:46), the one who tortured people (as indicated by the title *dhū l-awtād,* given to him in Q 38:12; cf. 89:10) and ordered the slaughter of newborn males (Q 2:49; 7:141; 14:6; 28:4; 40:25-6). He rejected the divine message brought to him by Moses (q.v.) and Aaron (q.v.; Q 10:75-6; 17:101; 27:13; 29:39; 40:24), considered himself God and tried to build a tower to reach the sky (Q 26:29; 28:38; 40:36). God chose to harden Pharaoh's heart (q.v.), since "God sets a seal on every heart proud, arrogant" (Q 40:35). His drowning (q.v.) in the sea (Q 2:50; 8:54; 10:90) is presented as the consequence of his behavior, for which no repentance is possible: "And we brought the Children of Israel (q.v.) over the sea; and Pharaoh and his hosts followed them insolently and impetuously till, when the drowning overtook him, he said, 'I believe that there is no god but he in whom the Children of Israel believe; I am of those that surrender.' 'Now? And before you did rebel, being of those that did corruption. So today we shall deliver you with your body (i.e. dead body), that you may be a sign to those after you. Surely many are heedless of our signs.'" (Q 10:90-2). In trying to explain why Pharaoh's repentance was rejected, an argument repeated by most commentators states that Pharaoh repented only after he faced his punishment; the commentators further explain that when the threat comes true and the penalty becomes real, penitence is no longer an option. To strengthen this claim, al-Qurṭubī (d. 671/1272; *Jāmiʿ,* viii, 377) connects these verses to Q 4:18 which deals with repentance after the encounter with death (see DEATH AND THE DEAD): "But God shall not turn towards those who do evil deeds (q.v.) until, when one of them is visited by death, he says, 'Indeed now I repent'." Q 40:84-5 also deals with repentance that comes too late: "Then, when they (i.e. the unbelievers) saw our might (i.e. severe punishment), they said, 'We believe in God alone'… but their belief [when they saw our might] did not profit them…" (cf. Rāzī, *Tafsīr,* ix, 161-2, who adduces seven different explanations for Pharaoh's rejected repentance).

Iblīs

Arrogance is the vice of Iblīs: After God created Adam, he ordered all the angels (see ANGEL) to bow down before Adam. Iblīs was the only angel who refused. He believed that he was superior to humankind: "I would never bow myself before a mortal whom you have created of a clay (q.v.) of mud molded" (Q 15:33). This belief created in him an extravagant pride (Q 2:34 and 38:74 use the verb *istakbara*) that drove him to rebel against God, and ultimately brought down God's condemnation upon him. He is expelled from paradise (q.v.) and is named *rajīm*, "cursed" (Q 38:77; see CURSE). At the end of time he will be thrown into the flames of hell (q.v.; Q 26:94-5; 15:43).

Conclusion: insolence and obstinacy versus Islam

The qurʾānic analysis of the story of Iblīs, of Pharaoh and of ʿĀd and Thamūd, focuses on the edifying aspect of the stories rather than on their historical elements. The historical identification of ʿĀd and Thamūd have been examined thoroughly by R.B. Serjeant (Hūd and other pre-Islamic prophets); the identity of Pharaoh has also been the subject of research (see articles in *EI*[2]); and the nature of Iblīs is discussed in several studies, such as in F. Rahman (*Major themes*, 121-31). When dealing, however, with their common denominator, insolence and obstinacy, the identity of these figures is beside the point; they should rather be treated as a means through which the Qurʾān clarifies the correlation between ungodly behavior and arrogance.

The motif of a messenger who exhorts people to adore the one God but finds only incredulity and insolence, is found repeatedly in the Qurʾān, each time with reference to a different event, but always at once aiming at Muḥammad's own mission. Through familiar stories of the ancient past, the Qurʾān confronts the people of Quraysh (q.v.) with persuasive pieces of evidence that leave no doubt as to the fate awaiting those who will not accept the divine call sent by Muḥammad. Furthermore, while elaborating on the consequences of insolence and obstinacy, the Qurʾān delivers the basic idea of Islam, that of belief in one God and self submission to him. Pride would not allow one to keep this attitude toward the sovereign God; rather, pride encourages refusal to obey (see OBEDIENCE) and creates insolence and obstinacy. In so doing it blocks the way to God and leads the people astray (q.v.).

Leah Kinberg

Bibliography

Primary: Qurṭubī, *Jāmiʿ*; Rāzī, *Tafsīr*.

Secondary: Arberry; F. Buhl, ʿĀd, in *EI*[2], i, 169; T. Fahd and A. Rippin, Shayṭān, in *EI*[2], ix, 406-9; T. Izutsu, *Concepts;* D.B. Macdonald/H. Massé et al., Djinn, in *EI*[2], ii, 546-50; F. Rahman, *Major themes of the Qurʾān*, Chicago 1980, 121-31 (chap. 7: "Satan and evil"); R.B. Serjeant, Hūd and other pre-Islamic prophets of Ḥaḍramawt, in *Muséon* 67 (1954), 121-79; I. Shahīd, Ṣāliḥ, in *EI*[2], viii, 981-2; A.J. Wensinck/L. Gardet, Iblīs, in *EI*[2], iii, 668-9; id./Ch. Pellat, Hūd, in *EI*[2], iii, 537-8; id./G. Vajda, Firʿawn, in *EI*[2], ii, 917-8.

Inspiration see REVELATION AND INSPIRATION

Instruments

Devices used by humans to assist them with their daily routines. There is not much literature dealing with material culture in the Qurʾān (see MATERIAL CULTURE AND THE QURʾĀN). Arthur Jeffery *(For. vocab.)* and others who investigated the origins of foreign words in the Qurʾān, note that many of the cultural terms were of non-Arabic origin (see FOREIGN VOCABULARY). The borrowings for qurʾānic cultural (and religious) terminology came from other Semitic languages, such as Aramaic, Nabatean, Syriac, and Ethiopic, as well as from Persian and Greek. The studies dealing with foreign words in the Qurʾān, however, show that the identification alone of borrowings from other Semitic or from non-Semitic languages does not allow one to draw conclusions about the significance of their use in the Qurʾān. It is at least as important to know how far back the borrowing goes or if its occurrence in the Qurʾān was indeed an innovation. A panorama of the cultural environment of the Qurʾān is presented in Eleonore Haeuptner's study on material culture in the Qurʾān *(Koranische Hinweise),* which deals with the relationship between the references to material culture in the Qurʾān — not only in terms of individual words, but rather of subjects — and pre-Islamic Arab culture, as it is known from poetry and other sources such as ḥadīth and biographies (see PRE-ISLAMIC ARABIA AND THE QURʾĀN).

At least as important, perhaps, as the etymology of the material-cultural terms is the pattern of their occurrences. As in the case of vessels (see CUPS AND VESSELS), some terms for instruments or utensils in the Qurʾān occur exclusively in association with specific contexts. The word *ʿaṣā,* "staff," which is used several times, always refers to Moses' (q.v.) staff, whereas Solomon's (q.v.) staff is described as *minsaʾa* (see ROD). It is not clear, however, if the two words refer to staffs with different functions.

Other utensils, like chains and fetters, appear only in the context of punishment on the day of resurrection (q.v.; see also LAST JUDGMENT; REWARD AND PUNISHMENT). It also happens that synonyms are used together in the same context, like *aghlāl* and *salāsil* for "chains," and *mīzān* and *qisṭās* for "scale." Measuring instruments (*mīzān, qisṭās, mikyāl,* see WEIGHTS AND MEASURES) are used only metaphorically for justice (see JUSTICE AND INJUSTICE) or honesty. Writing materials *(ṣuḥuf, qirṭās, qalam, nuskha, raqq, lawḥ, midād, khātam, asfār,* and *kitāb)* are, with only a few exceptions, always associated with scripture, i.e. the Qurʾān or previous revelations and religious texts (see SCRIPTURE AND THE QURʾĀN; REVELATION AND INSPIRATION). Most words describing weapons are used in their concrete sense. In what follows, the main categories of material-culture terminology found in the Qurʾān are discussed.

Writing instruments and materials

Asfār (sing. *sifr*), "book, volume." The word is used in the parable which compares the Jews who refused the Torah (q.v.) obligations with a "donkey laden with books" (Q 62:5; see JEWS AND JUDAISM).

Khātam, "seal," is used metaphorically, referring to the Prophet *(khātam al-nabiyyīn),* the seal of the prophets (Q 33:40).

Kitāb, "book" (q.v.). Multiple occurrences which refer to the Qurʾān or other scriptures; People of the Book (q.v.; *ahl al-kitāb*) are the Christians (see CHRISTIANS AND CHRISTIANITY) and Jews who possess a holy book. The word also means a register where God keeps a record of all things (Q 6:38; 10:61; 11:6; 22:70; see HEAVENLY BOOK). *Kitāb* also denotes a "letter" (Q 24:33; 27:28).

Lawḥ, "board or plank." It is used only once in the singular form (Q 85:22) referring to the heavenly archetype of the Qurʾān (see PRESERVED TABLET). The plural form *(alwāḥ)* otherwise used has two meanings. It means at one place the planks of Noah's (q.v.) ark (q.v.; Q 54:13) and otherwise refers to Moses' tablets (Q 7:145, 150, 154; 54:13; 85:22).

Midād, "ink." Q 18:109 mentions a sea of ink as metaphor (q.v.) for God's speech (q.v.; see also WORD OF GOD).

Nuskha, "copy or exemplar." It occurs once in reference to the tablets of Moses (Q 7:154).

Qalam (pl. *aqlām*), "pen." The word is used to describe a writing utensil, probably made of reed (Q 31:27; 68:1; 96:4). Only in Q 3:44 does it refer to tubes, probably also made of reed, used by the pre-Islamic Arabs as lots for divination (q.v.; see also FORETELLING).

Qirṭās (pl. *qarāṭīs*), "parchment or papyrus." In both passages it refers to the material on which sacred texts were written down (Q 6:7, 91).

Raqq, "parchment" (Q 52:3).

Sijill, used in the Qurʾān in the sense of a scroll of parchment. The context is metaphorical: on the day of resurrection heaven (q.v.) will be rolled up like a scroll of parchment (Q 21:104; see APOCALYPSE).

Ṣuḥuf (sing. *ṣaḥīfa*), "pages of writing." The word is always used in the context of scripture (Q 20:133; 53:36; 74:52; 80:13; 87:18,19; 98:2; see also WRITING AND WRITING MATERIALS).

Measuring instruments

Kayl, a measure for volume (17 kilograms, cf. Heinz, *Islamische Masse,* 40). Together with *mīzān,* it is used metaphorically for honesty (Q 6:152; 7:85).

Mikyāl, a measuring vessel. Like *kayl,* it is used together with *mīzān,* in the metaphorical sense of justice (Q 11:84, 85).

Mīzān, "scale." The term is always used metaphorically, referring to honesty (Q 6:152; 7:85, 11:84, 85; 42:17). In Q 55:7, God sets the balance of all things, in the sense of norms not to be transgressed. In Q 57:25 God sent his apostles with the scripture and the scales of justice. The plural form *mawāzīn* occurs in the context of the day of resurrection, where the heavier scales symbolize good deeds (q.v.): "He whose scales are heavy shall dwell in bliss" (Q 21:47; 101:6).

Qaws, "bow." The word is used in the dual in Q 53:9 *(qawsayn),* not to describe the weapon it usually means but as a measuring unit of length. In older times the Arabs used bows and arrows as measuring references.

Qinṭār (pl. *qanāṭīr*), a large weight measure (100 raṭl, cf. Heinz, *Islamische Masse,* 24-7), it is used in its true sense (Q 3:75; 4:20). Al-Ṭabarī (d. 310/923) provides several hypotheses as to its exact value (*Tafsīr,* vi, 243-50 [ad Q 3:14, where the plural form is used]).

Qisṭās, "balance," like *mīzān* used metaphorically for justice (Q 17:35; 26:182).

Trade instruments

Darāhim (sing. *dirham*), a silver currency unit (see Heinz, *Islamische Masse,* 1-8; see MONEY; NUMISMATICS). Used only in the plural form in Q 12 "Joseph" (Sūrat Yūsuf), where Joseph (q.v.) is said to have been sold for a few *darāhim* (Q 12:20).

Dīnār: a gold currency unit. It is used in the context of transactions with the People of the Book (Q 3:75).

Mithqāl, a weight measure (see Heinz, *Islamische Masse,* 1-8). It is mostly used as *mithqāl dharra,* "an atom's weight," or *mithqāl khardal,* "grain of mustard seed," to mean "the least" of actions, or of good and bad deeds (Q 4:40; 10:61; 21:47; 31:16; 34:3, 22; 99:7, 8; see EVIL DEEDS; GOOD AND EVIL).

Weapons

Asliḥa (sing. *silāḥ*), "weapon." It occurs four times in the plural form in a context dealing with the precautions to be taken by the Prophet to protect himself against attacks by the unbelievers (Q 4:102; see BELIEF AND UNBELIEF; OPPOSITION TO MUḤAMMAD; EXPEDITIONS AND BATTLES).

Maqāmiʿ (sing. *miqmaʿa*), "rod," as a beating instrument. It occurs as "iron rods" *(maqāmiʿ min ḥadīd)* in the context of punishment on the day of resurrection (Q 22:21).

Nuḥās, "brass, copper, bronze," is used in the Qurʾān in the sense of molten metal, as punishment for the unbelievers in hell (q.v.; Q 55:35).

Qaws, literally "bow," but, as noted above, in the Qurʾān the term is only used as a measure unit for length (Q 53:9; see under *Measuring instruments*).

Rimāḥ (sing. *rumḥ*), "lances," used in the context of hunting (Q 5:94; see HUNTING AND FISHING).

Sābighāt (sing. *sābigha*), "coats of mail" (Q 34:11).

Sard, "chain armor." It occurs only once, in Q 34:11, a passage mentioning David's (q.v.) skill as a maker of armor. Although Arabic sources derive it from *sarada,* "to stitch," it is more likely a borrowing from the Iranian *zard.*

Other instruments

Aghlāl (sing. *ghull*), "iron chains," is used only in the plural form and refers to the punishment of the unbelievers in hell, where they shall be fastened with chains (Q 36:8; 76:4).

Ankāl (sing. *nikl*), "fetters," is used in the plural form to describe punishment in hell (q.v.; Q 73:12).

Aqfāl (sing. *qufl*), "lock," is used only once, in the plural form in Q 47:24: "Are there locks upon their hearts (see HEART)?"

ʿAṣā (pl. *ʿiṣiyy*), "staff or stick," occurs in early sūras only in references to Moses striking the rock or the sea with his staff (Q 2:60; 7:107, 117, 160; 20:18; 26:32, 45, 63; 27:10; 28:31). Its use in the plural is restricted to the futile efforts of Moses' opponents.

Aṣfād (sing. *ṣafad*), "fetters," like *ankāl,* it is used in the plural form to describe punishment in hell (Q 14:49; 38:38).

Azlām (sing. *zalam*), "arrows." The word occurs in the prohibition of using divining arrows, which were consulted to settle disputes among pre-Islamic Arabs (Q 5:3, 90).

Dusur (sing. *disār*), occurs with reference to ships made of planks *(alwāḥ)* and *dusur,* which are a kind of nail, most likely wooden pegs (Q 54:13).

Ḥabl (pl. *ḥibāl*), "rope." In the first two occurrences (Q 3:103, 112), the word is used in a metaphorical sense to mean clinging or adhering to faith (q.v.) or to God. In the other passages (Q 20:66; 26:44; 111:5), rope in its concrete sense is meant. In Q 50:16 it is used in a composed form, *ḥabl al-warīd,* meaning "the jugular vein" (see ARTERY AND VEIN).

Khayṭ, "thread," is mentioned in the context of fast-breaking (see FASTING) during the month of Ramaḍān (q.v.). Muslims are allowed to break the fast during the night, until dawn, when one can distinguish a white thread from a black one (Q 2:187; see DAY, TIMES OF; DAY AND NIGHT).

Khiyāṭ, "needle," in Q 7:40 where it is said that the evildoers shall not enter paradise (q.v.) until "a camel (q.v.) passes through the eye of a needle."

Mafātīḥ (sing. *miftāḥ*), "keys," is used only once and in the plural form in Q 6:59: "He (God) has the keys of all that is hidden" (see HIDDEN AND THE HIDDEN).

Maqālīd (sing. *miqlād*), "keys." Like *mafātīḥ,* it occurs in the plural form and is used in the same metaphorical sense for God's knowing the secrets of all things (Q 39:63; 42:12).

Masad, "rope (of palm fibers tightly twisted)." The word is used together with *ḥabl (ḥabl min masad),* to emphasize its meaning. The rope referred to is an instrument of punishment in hell, like the chains mentioned elsewhere (Q 111:5).

Minsaʾa, "staff," from *nasaʾa*, "to lead." It occurs only once referring to Solomon's staff (Q 34:14).

Miṣbāḥ (pl. *maṣābīḥ*), "lamp" (q.v.), is used metaphorically for the stars (Q 41:12; 67:5). In Q 24:35, the Light Verse *(āyat al-nūr)*, it is obviously an oil lamp since it is described as including a glass oil container.

Nuṣub, "standard," refers to the unbelievers on the day of resurrection rushing out of their graves as if to reach a banner (Q 70:43; see DEATH AND THE DEAD).

Salāsil (sing. *silsila*), "chains," occurs like *aghlāl* in the descriptions of the punishments which the unbelievers will suffer on the day of judgment (Q 40:71, 76:4). The singular form *silsila* is used once, in Q 69:32, where it refers to a seventy-cubits-long chain that will fasten the unbeliever in hell.

Sikkīn, "knife," occurs only once, in Q 12, when the female guests of Potiphar's wife wound themselves at the sight of Joseph's beauty (Q 12:31).

Sirāj, "lamp," is used as a metaphor for the sun (q.v.; Q 25:61; 71:16; 78:13). In Q 33:46, however, it symbolizes the Prophet's guidance of believers.

Ṣūr, "trumpet," is always used in connection with the day of resurrection (Q 6:73; 18:99; 20:102; 23:101; 36:51; 39:68; 50:20; 69:13; 78:18).

As this overview of the qurʾānic terminology for instruments demonstrates, such terminology occurs in a wide variety of contexts, with both concrete and metaphoric, earthly and eschatological (see ESCHATOLOGY), connotations.

Doris Behrens-Abouseif

Bibliography
Primary: *Lisān al-ʿArab;* Suyūṭī, *Durr;* Ṭabarī, *Tafsīr*, ed. Shākir; *Tāj al-ʿarūs*, Cairo 1306-7.
Secondary: ʿAbd al-Jalil Īsā, *al-Muṣḥaf al-muyassar*, Cairo 1399/1979; E. Haeuptner, *Koranische Hinweise auf die materielle Kultur der alten Araber*, PhD diss., Tübingen 1966; W. Heinz, *Islamische Masse und Gewichte*, Leiden 1970; Jeffery, *For. vocab.;* Paret; id., *Kommentar*.

Intellect

As opposed to emotion or will, the power or faculty through which humans perceive and understand the world. The concept of *ʿaql*, "intellect," is probably one of the most controversial in the history of Muslim thought. The word *ʿaql* itself does not occur in the Qurʾān. The root *ʿ-q-l*, however, appears forty-nine times and always as a verb in the first form *(ʿaqala-yaʿqilu)* meaning "to understand, to recognize." Other meanings of the verb *ʿaqala*, such as "to tie (up)," e.g. a camel, "to arrest," "to pay blood money (q.v.)" are not found. In all but three verses the verb is in the second or third person plural, usually in formulae of admonition (see EXHORTATIONS) such as *a-fa-lā taʿqilūna, wa-laʿallakum taʿqilūna* or *fī dhālika la-āyatin li-qawmin yaʿqilūna.*

The cognitive process described by *ʿaqala* is based primarily on the human's ability to perceive, to reflect and to evaluate obvious facts. This meaning of *ʿaqala* is very close to that of the word *ʿaql* in pre-Islamic poetry. But in a noticeably large number of verses *ʿaqala* is related to the senses. Quite often it also has direct associations with the senses and the heart (q.v.; *fuʾād, qalb*), which in the qurʾānic semantic is not the seat of emotions, but an organ of perception and understanding. *ʿAqala* as the process of recognition which leads to belief (see BELIEF AND UNBELIEF) is taken in the Qurʾān to include sensory perception and the understanding of the heart, and it relies in any case on the use of the senses. It does not, therefore, correspond to our modern notion of reason, which is regarded as the capacity to attain knowledge through thinking and mental reflection, being distinguished from knowledge achieved through sensual perception, i.e. sounds, smells, optical impressions or feelings.

The various manifestations of understanding in the Qurʾān, that is, all the different contexts in which the root *ʿ-q-l* makes its appearance, are part of the qurʾānic concept of *āya,* "sign." In the qurʾānic *Weltanschauung* all creation is an *āya,* i.e. a sign from God (see SIGNS). Nature (see NATURAL WORLD AND THE QURʾĀN) no less than civilization, human history (see HISTORY AND THE QURʾĀN) and divine writings (see BOOK), the pleasures of love and of food — everything that exists and takes place in the cosmos (see COSMOLOGY) and on earth (q.v.) is a revelation of God to humankind (see REVELATION AND INSPIRATION). God speaks to humankind through his signs, those that are spoken being manifested in the books of revelation, the unspoken ones through the world itself. The act of interpreting the signs is called in the Qurʾān *ʿaqala,* while the ways and means of doing so are as manifold and varied as the signs themselves. For example, in Q 30:21-4 four different kinds of expression for the recognition of signs are used in rapid succession. The expression used in the first of these four verses is *inna fī dhālika la-āyātin li-qawmin yatafakkarūna,* "There are truly signs therein for a people that thinks." In the next verse they are called signs "for those that have knowledge," then signs "for a people that listens" (*li-qawmin yasmaʿūna,* see SEEING AND HEARING; HEARING AND DEAFNESS), and finally signs "for a people that understands" *(li-qawmin yaʿqilūna).* The four expressions here are not synonymous; they indicate different ways of attaining understanding, the intellectual *(tafakkara)* and the sensual *(samiʿa),* and ultimately *ʿaqala,* which embraces the ones already described. Neither here nor elsewhere in the Qurʾān does the term *al-ʿālimūna* denote people who have acquired great knowledge or learned a great deal, but rather people who are endowed with a special religious insight, however that may be defined; *ūlū l-albāb,* as it is also called. The difference between the two conceptual areas *ʿaqala* and *ʿalima* is that only the latter can also refer to God, insofar as God is "knowing" (*ʿalīm,* see GOD AND HIS ATTRIBUTES). *ʿAqala,* on the other hand, refers to a purely human activity, namely the understanding of divine signs.

According to qurʾānic precepts the reality of God can be understood and even physically perceived by all humans, by virtue of the comprehensible arguments and clear and self-evident facts (hence the emphasis on the clarity of the signs). Unbelief (see BELIEF AND UNBELIEF) is in the first place not attributed to a lack of will but to a lack of intellectual ability and perception — the unbelievers fail to see and understand the signs "in the world at large or in themselves" (Q 41:53). God gives signs, but it is up to the individual whether he or she recognizes them and accepts their guidance — *laʿallakum taʿqilūna.* This eventuality is the reason for the apparently incongruous *laʿalla,* "perhaps," one of the most common modal expressions in the Qurʾān (see LANGUAGE OF THE QURʾĀN). It has a firm place within the qurʾānic *Weltanschauung* and by no means for stylistic reasons alone: *laʿalla,* which may (like the word *ʿasā*) have the secondary meaning "that which is desired," expresses an individual's own responsibility, i.e. the possibility that he or she will remain in darkness (q.v.).

Thus *ʿaqala* has its very special and constantly reinforced function within the relationship between God and humankind. Whereas words like *shaʿara, faqiha* or *fakkara,* which likewise belong to the area of "understanding, grasping, reflecting on," are used in other, general contexts, the activity described in the Qurʾān as *ʿaqala* relates solely to signs from God. In contrast to the concept of reason in the Enlightenment, the activity is not an end in itself; its goal is the reaction the signs are intended to elicit, namely praise (q.v.) of God (see GLORIFICATION OF GOD) and belief in him. These are the responses appropriate to humankind when confronted with God's message to all, which is made manifest through signs.

The noun *ʿaql* occurs in a somewhat different guise from its qurʾānic one in numerous ḥadīths (see ḤADĪTH AND THE QURʾĀN), particularly in some which are not regarded as canonical. There it is used in a general sense that does not refer to God's relationship to humankind (cf. the compilation of ḥadīths in Ghazālī, *Iḥyāʾ*, i, 83-9). Hence a general evaluation of intellectual understanding in Islam can only be established from post-qurʾānic sources. Although the Qurʾān's appeal to humankind's insight and its desire to — in its own words — "make clear" *(bayyana)* are indisputable, as is its description of ignorance (q.v.) as darkness and God as light (q.v.), the Qurʾān does not discuss, let alone glorify, *ʿaql* in terms of the human ability to attain all kinds of understanding through thought and reflection.

Starting from the Greek concept of *nous*, Islamic philosophy, theology and mysticism each developed their own content, meanings and connotations for the concept of *ʿaql* which were based only loosely on the *ʿaqala* of the Qurʾān (see PHILOSOPHY AND THE QURʾĀN; THEOLOGY AND THE QURʾĀN; ṢŪFISM AND THE QURʾĀN). In the aftermath of the modern renaissance *(nahḍa)* of the late nineteenth and early twentieth centuries *ʿaql* became the cornerstone of a reformist, rationalistic conception of religion. Today, reference to the intellect is commonplace among Muslim authors of almost all persuasions (see also KNOWLEDGE AND LEARNING).

Navid Kermani

Bibliography
Primary: al-Ghazālī, Abū Ḥāmid Muḥammad, *Iḥyāʾ ʿulūm al-dīn*, 5 vols. in 2, Cairo n.d., i, 83-9 (for the post-qurʾānic concept of *ʿaql*); Jurjānī, *Asrār*, 326 f.; al-Muḥāsibī, Abū ʿAlī al-Ḥārith b. Asad, *al-ʿAql wa-fahm al-Qurʾān*, Beirut 1391/1971 (with an lengthy introduction by H. al-Quwwatlī, 5-192).
Secondary: N. Abū Zayd, *al-Ittijāh al-ʿaqlī fī l-tafsīr. Dirāsa fī qaḍiyyat al-majāz fī l-Qurʾān ʿinda l-Muʿtazila*, Beirut 1983²; J. Arberry, *Revelation and reason in Islam. The Forwood lectures for* 1956. *Delivered in the University of Liverpool*, London 1957; M. Arkoun, *Pour une critique de la raison islamique*, Paris 1984, 65-99; Tj. de Boer and F. Rahman, Aḳl, in *EI²*, i, 341-2; W.C. Chittick and F. Rahman, Aql, in *Encyclopaedia iranica*, ii, 194-8; K. Cragg, *The mind of the Qurʾān. Chapters in reflection*, London 1973, 129-62 (esp. for *laʿalla*); van Ess, *TG* (s.v. *ʿaql*, Verstand in Index); C. Gilliot, Mythe et théologie. Calame et intellect, prédestination et libre arbitre, in *Arabica* 45 (1998), 151-92; Izutsu, *God*, 65 f., 133 f., 231 f.; N. Kermani, Appelliert Gott an den Verstand? Eine Randbemerkung zum koranischen Begriff *ʿaql* und seiner Paret'schen Übersetzung, in L. Edzard and C. Szyska (eds.), *Encounters of words and texts. Intercultural studies in honor of Stefan Wild*, Hildesheim/Zürich 1997, 43-66; A. von Kügelgen, *Averroes und die arabische Moderne. Ansätze zu einer Neubegründung des Rationalismus im Islam*, Leiden 1994 (s.v. Vernunft, Verstand in Index; esp. for the contemporary discussion); F. Rahman, *The philosophy of Mullā Ṣadrā*, Albany, NY 1975, 146-66, 232-46; F. Rosenthal, *Knowledge triumphant. The concept of knowledge in medieval Islam*, Leiden 1970; T. Seidensticker, *Altarabisch 'Herz' und sein Wortfeld*, Wiesbaden 1992; M. Ullmann, *Arabisch* ʿasā *"vielleicht." Syntax und Wortart*, Munich 1984.

Intention

Determination to act in a certain way. Although the closest Arabic equivalent, *niyya*, is not attested in the Qurʾān, it does exist in a very famous hadīth, albeit without the technical meaning developed later in the field of jurisprudence (*fiqh*, see LAW AND

THE QUR'ĀN). In the Qur'ān, the root *kh-l-ṣ* (*ikhlāṣ*, "sincerity"), used seventeen times in its active participial form, *mukhliṣ*, best approximates the notion of worthy and well-directed "intention." Sincerity is the foundation of all acts of worship (*ʿibāda*, cf. Q 2:139; 39:2, 11, 14) acceptable to God and of all forms of prayer (*duʿāʾ*, cf. Q 7:29; 10:22; also 29:65; 31:32; 40:14, 65; 98:5). The sincere servants of God are those whom he protects from being seduced by Iblīs (Q 15:40; 38:83; see DEVIL) or from committing sins (as he did with Joseph [q.v]; Q 12:24); they will all enjoy great happiness in the afterlife (Q 37:40, 74, 128). Sincerity of belief (see BELIEF AND UNBELIEF; HYPOCRITES AND HYPOCRISY) expresses itself in a full commitment to the performance of religious duties, which in turn makes it possible for the believer to receive God's protection (q.v.). Other qur'ānic terms, such as the fourth form of the root *r-w-d*, the fifth form of *y-m-m* and the fourth form of *ṣ-w-b* are occasionally glossed as "intention," but with a meaning apart from the religio-juridical one of *niyya*.

Taqwā, "seeking protection from God," is an essential qur'ānic term (cf. Rahman, *Major themes*, 29, 110, 127-8) that is very important in this context. Izutsu (*Concepts*, 196) explains the close relationship between "belief" and *taqwā* "in the form of an implication: if A then B." The Qur'ān clearly states that what is important is not the religious action in itself, but the internal piety (q.v.) of the hearts (*taqwā l-qulūb*, Q 22:32; see HEART). Because of its importance, piety of the heart is the basis for judging action. The Qur'ān strongly emphasizes that pretentious behavior counts for nothing because God is always watching the internal belief of everyone's heart. As all the secrets on the earth, in the heavens, and in between are well known to him, he knows what lies in people's hearts (*ʿalīmun bi-dhāti l-ṣudūri*, Q 3:119, 154; 5:7; 8:43; 11:5; 31:23; 35:38; 39:7; 42:24; 57:6; 64:4; 67:13; see HIDDEN AND THE HIDDEN; SECRETS).

The very famous ḥadīth referred to above, which is mentioned in all the canonical collections, uses the word *niyya* to convey the heartfelt intention behind religious action: "Actions are only judged on the basis of their intention. Every individual will only have [as a reward or punishment; see REWARD AND PUNISHMENT] what he has intended" (Bukhārī, *Ṣaḥīḥ*, vii, 55 [but it appears at least seven other times in the work]; cf. the first ḥadīth in Pouzet, *Une hermeneutique*, 74-89). Judging an action according to the intention behind it became the higher criterion in juridical application (cf. Wensinck, Niyya, 67). Good intention is taken into consideration by God, even if the action is not performed. Sinful intention, on the other hand, is not counted as long as the action is not performed (cf. Ṭabarī, *Tafsīr;* Ibn Kathīr, *Tafsīr*, ad Q 3:119).

Repentance *(tawba)* from sins is the way to turn back to God and to a state of right intention, the original meaning of *tawba* being to "turn back" or "return." God, in turn, returns his blessing *(yatūbu)* to the sincere penitent (see REPENTANCE AND PENANCE). This juridical definition of *tawba* is further specified to include repentance from bad thought, whether whispered by Satan *(waswasat al-shayṭān)* or emerging from desires of the soul *(waswasat al-nafs)*. Al-Ghazālī (d. 505/1111; *Iḥyāʾ [Kitāb al-tawba]*, v, 4) speaks about several aspects of repentance: attempting not to sin (see SIN, MAJOR AND MINOR), remorse for sins committed, observing good actions (see GOOD DEEDS), and the realization of one's own fallibility, and, lastly, the prophet Muḥammad's acts of abstention from amenities (which went above and beyond what is obligatory) because of his awareness of their potential to distract one from the path towards the attainment of eternal reward (see PATH OR WAY). As for Ibn ʿArabī (d. 638/1240; *al-Futūḥāt,* i, 209), the semantic structure of *tawba* is more complicated, though it is basically set forth on the same ground, that is dealing with *niyya* as a religious responsibility.

Nasr Hamid Abu Zayd

Bibliography
Primary: Bukhārī, *Ṣaḥīḥ*, Cairo 1958; al-Ghazālī, Abū Ḥāmid Muḥammad, *Iḥyāʾ ʿulūm al-dīn,* Cairo n.d.; Ibn al-ʿArabī, Muḥyī l-Dīn, *al-Futūḥāt al-makkiyya,* 4 vols., Cairo n.d., i, 209 (chap. 33); Ibn Kathīr, *Tafsīr;* Ṭabarī, *Tafsīr,* 30 vols., Cairo 1388/1968.
Secondary: Izutsu, *Concepts;* L. Pouzet, *Une herméneutique de la tradition islamique. Le commentaire des arbaʿūn al-nabawiyya de Muḥyī al-Dīn al-Nawawī (m. 676/1277),* Beirut 1982; F. Rahman, *Major themes of the Qurʾān,* Chicago 1980; A.J. Wensinck, Niyya, in *EI²*, viii, 66-7.

Intercalation see CALENDAR

Intercession

Prayer or pleading with God on behalf of someone else. In addition to the references to those gods, humans or images who will be unable to intercede with God on behalf of humankind (cf. Q 19:87; 36:23; see IDOLS AND IMAGES) and the guilty (*al-mujrimīn,* Q 74:41) who will not benefit from the assistance of any intercessors (*al-shāfiʿīn,* Q 74:48), intercession *(shafāʿa)* is mentioned in the Qurʾān with respect to angels (see ANGEL) praying for the believers and the Prophet praying for erring but repentant Muslims. It has become a cardinal belief in Islam that Muḥammad will intercede for all Muslims on the day of resurrection (q.v.; see also LAST JUDGMENT), but this belief is not well supported by the Qurʾān. Still more controversial is seeking the intercession of deceased saints by praying at their tombs (see FESTIVALS AND COMMEMORATIVE DAYS), a practice that is very common but with no obvious foundation in the Qurʾān and seen by some critics as a form of polytheism.

Intercession in the Qurʾān

Concerning Muslims who had "acknowledged their wrong-doings, mixing a good work with another that was evil" (see GOOD DEEDS; EVIL DEEDS; GOOD AND EVIL; SIN, MAJOR AND MINOR), in Q 9:102-3 the Prophet is told to "pray on their behalf *(ṣalli ʿalayhim);* truly your prayers are a source of security for them." When the Prophet prays for other people, the verb in the Qurʾān is *ṣallā,* "to pray," and the preposition is *ʿalā,* "on." But when God is the actor, this same verb and preposition are used in the sense of "to bless." For example, "He it is who blesses you (pl.), as do his angels, that he might bring you out of darkness into light" (Q 33:43) or, in a particularly famous and important passage that lies at the heart of the Muslim practice of blessing the Prophet at every mention of his name and in their daily devotions, "God and his angels bless the Prophet; you who believe, bless him and give him the greeting of peace" (Q 33:56). One may infer from the qurʾānic verse instructing Muḥammad not to pray for "hypocrites" (see HYPOCRITES AND HYPOCRISY) who had died (Q 9:84) that the practice of praying for the dead at their funerals (see DEATH AND THE DEAD) was already in place in the time of the Prophet, which is also indicated by ḥadīth. The angels also seek forgiveness (q.v.) for *(yastaghfirūna li-)* those who believe (Q 40:7) and for all those on the earth (Q 42:5). The Qurʾān alludes to Muḥammad offering to pray for the forgiveness of the hypocrites, who rebuff his offer; the Qurʾān says that no matter how much Muḥammad prayed for their forgiveness, they would never be forgiven (Q 63:5, 6; 9:80). The Qur'ān emphasizes that each person is responsible for his or her own self, and that Muḥammad is not responsible for the response of people to his message (Q 39:41).

Much more problematic is the notion of intercession *(shafāʿa)* on the day of resurrection. The Qur'ān repeatedly warns the Meccans that they will find no helper (e.g. Q 9:74, *wa-mā lahum fī l-arḍ min waliyyin wa-lā naṣīrin*) and none to hide them from God's wrath on the day of resurrection. The denial of help at the time of judgment appears to refer to the uselessness of the intercession of kin relations, patrons, wealth or idols at that time (see PRE-ISLAMIC ARABIA AND THE QUR'ĀN; CLIENTS AND CLIENTAGE; KINSHIP). The entire emphasis in the qur'ānic account of the day of resurrection is on the overwhelming power of God, king of the day of judgment, and the lack of recourse at that time for those who did not heed the warning of the prophets in this life (see WARNER; PROPHETS AND PROPHETHOOD). "Then will the weak say to those who were arrogant (see ARROGANCE), 'We followed you, can you help us against the wrath of God?' They will reply, 'If God had guided us, we would have guided you. It makes no difference whether we rage or bear patiently, there is no way for us to escape'" (Q 14:21). "Then guard yourselves against a day when one soul shall not avail another, nor shall intercession *(shafāʿa)* be accepted for it, nor shall compensation be taken from it, nor shall they be helped" (Q 2:48; cf. 2:123). Yet this apparently categorical denial of intercession appears to be mitigated in other verses: "How many angels are in the heavens whose intercession will avail nothing except after God permits it to whomever he wishes and pleases?" (Q 53:26). "On that day intercession will not benefit anyone except those for whom the Merciful has granted it" (Q 20:109; cf. 34:23); "Who is there who can intercede *(yashfaʿu)* in his presence except by his permission?" (Q 2:255); "None shall have the power of intercession but the one who has taken an oath (*ʿahd*, see OATHS AND PROMISES; COVENANT) with the merciful" (Q 19:87). These verses have been taken by Muslims to indicate that the prophet Muḥammad will have the right to intercede for his people on the day of judgment (for further discussion on the intercession of Muḥammad, see Stieglecker, *Die Glaubenslehren*, 678-83).

Faith in Muḥammad's intercession is also based on Q 17:79, "You [Muḥammad] pray in the small hours of the morning *(tahajjada)* an additional prayer *(nāfila);* perhaps your lord (q.v.) will raise you to a praiseworthy station *(maqām maḥmūd)*." A ḥadīth (Muslim, *Ṣaḥīḥ* [trans. Siddiqi], 125, no. 371) identifies this praiseworthy (or exalted) station as one which allowed the Prophet to bring out of hell all whom he wished.

Muslim belief concerning intercession on the day of judgment

Al-Ghazālī (450-505/1058-1111) wrote in *Iḥyāʾ ʿulūm al-dīn*, "Revival of the religious sciences," (iv, 653) that God will accept the intercession of the prophets and the truthful *(al-ṣiddīqūn),* indeed even of the learned *ʿulamāʾ* and the righteous *(al-ṣāliḥūn).* Everyone who has favor with God will be allowed to intercede for relatives, friends and acquaintances. The qur'ānic passage he solicits to justify this belief is Q 93:3-5, where the prophet Muḥammad is addressed: "Your lord has not forsaken you, nor is he displeased. Indeed, the hereafter will be better for you than the present. Your lord will give to you and you will be well-pleased." The pleasing gift of God to Muḥammad, according to al-Ghazālī, is the gift of intercession for his people. In one ḥadīth (Muslim, *Ṣaḥīḥ,* 135), the

Prophet raises his hands and weeps, saying, "My people *(ummatī)*, my people!" God tells Gabriel (q.v.) to inform him: "We will satisfy you concerning your people, and will not grieve you."

Sunnī Muslims came to believe that even Muslims who had committed very grave sins would enter paradise by virtue of the Prophet's intercession as long as they had an ounce of faith. "On that day," says Muḥammad in another ḥadīth, "I will be the imām (q.v.) of the prophets and their preacher and the one who intercedes *(ṣāḥib al-shafāʿa)*." This intercession, however, occurs after sinners have been punished for their sins in hellfire (see HELL; FIRE); the Prophet engages in continuous intercession until the last soul is brought into paradise (q.v.). The people will frantically seek the intercession of Adam (q.v.), Abraham (q.v.), Moses (q.v.) and Jesus (q.v.), each of whom will decline, but Muḥammad will finally be the intercessor for all people (Muslim, *Ṣaḥīḥ*, 120-32).

The teaching of the Qurʾān in some 39 verses (e.g. Q 2:162) is that punishment in hellfire is eternal. Although the people of hell plead with those in paradise to help them, they cannot because there is a veil (q.v.) between them (Q 7:46; see also BARZAKH), and there is no indication that anyone may cross from one to the other. Muslim belief, however, considerably modified this belief: just as there are seven layers in the heavens, so are there seven layers of hell (a belief suggested by the various names given to hellfire in the Qurʾān), and only unbelievers would be consigned to the lowest layers or suffer eternally. Sinning believers will be in the upper layers, from which they will be rescued by Muḥammad's intercession. Muḥammad will be "leader of humanity on the day of resurrection" (Muslim, *Ṣaḥīḥ*, 132, no. 379), the one honored with opening the gate of paradise (ibid., 132-3). He is the first to intercede, and among all the prophets he has the largest following in paradise (ibid., 133-5). Muḥammad is quoted as saying, "There is for every apostle a prayer which is granted, but every prophet showed haste in his prayer. I, however, have reserved my prayer [to be] for intercession for my people on the day of resurrection and it will be granted, God willing, for every one of them who dies without associating anything with God" (ibid., 134, no. 389). His prayer somewhat mitigates even the punishment of his unconverted uncle, Abū Ṭālib, allowing him into the upper layers of hellfire (ibid., 138-9).

On the other hand, the Khārijites (see KHĀRIJĪS) and others who believe that no one has the ability to intercede with God cite Q 11:108 as an argument against the concept of intercession (see Gilliot, Le commentaire coranique, 194-9; see FREEDOM AND PREDESTINATION).

The intercession of the saints

All over the world Muslims visit the tombs of saints, seeking the blessing of their presence. They also seek their help in earthly matters. If a woman cannot conceive, if her child is ill, if a student wishes to succeed in his or her exams or for any number of reasons, people resort to saints, the "friends" of God, whether living or dead. Saints intercede before God and are channels of blessing (q.v.; *baraka*). Egyptian Muslims believe that the Prophet's grandson and granddaughter, al-Ḥusayn and Sayyida Zaynab, and al-Shāfiʿī (150-204/767-819), eponym of one of the four schools of Sunnī jurisprudence (see LAW AND THE QURʾĀN), preside over a heavenly court that decides the outcome of earthly events. People visit their shrines in Cairo (which are assumed to be their tombs) and seek their intercession. They even write letters to al-Shāfiʿī seeking redress for injustices (ʿUways, *Min malāmiḥ*). Many modern

Muslim reformers believe that such prayers at the tombs of saints are prohibited and smack of polytheism, that the dead saint is not present or able to hear petitions or intercede with God. Ibn Taymiyya (d. 728/1328) is well-known for his campaigns against such aspects of popular religion, but such attacks became far more prominent in the twentieth century.

One contemporary Ṣūfī shaykh of Egypt, Muḥammad Zakī Ibrāhīm (b. ca. 1905), has written extensively to defend the practice of seeking the intercession of saints. He interprets the "way to God" mentioned in Q 5:35, "Fear God and seek a way *(wasīla)* to him," as the intercession of godly people, both living and dead. He says that Muslims do not pray to the saints, as critics allege, but seek a way to God by means of their eternal essence *(maʿnā)* of faith, sincerity, love and purity. He quotes a ḥadīth from the collection of al-Tirmidhī (d. ca. 270/883-4) in which the Prophet instructs a blind man to pray, "Muḥammad, I ask your intercession *(astashfiʿu bika)* with my lord to return my sight." Since Muḥammad would be absent when the man was to utter this prayer, it is Muḥammad's eternal essence, not his temporal person, that is addressed in prayer. After Muḥammad's death, people prayed for rain both in the name of Muḥammad's uncle al-ʿAbbās and at the tomb of the Prophet. The majority of Muslims, the shaykh argues, even Aḥmad b. Ḥanbal (d. 241/855), the inspiration for the legal school of Ibn Taymiyya and the Wahhābīs, major critics of saint veneration, approved of seeking a way to God through the righteous dead. Muḥammad Zakī makes a distinction between *wasīla* and mediation *(wisāṭa)*, "which no Muslim believes is necessary." "When a person out of ignorance or error or habit or tradition says, 'Sīdī so-and-so,' he really means, 'Lord of Sīdī so-and-so.' He errs only in his expression, not in his faith. To call this idolatry is ignorance and means unjustly removing the majority of Muslims from the pale of Islam." Seeking the intercession of a righteous person does not imply worship of the intercessor. The interaction of the spirits of the dead with the living is underlined by ḥadīths concerning Muḥammad's meeting with the spirits of the former prophets during his ascension (q.v.) into heaven, and by his addressing the dead polytheists who were killed at the battle of Badr (q.v.). That dead Muslims are also alive and that the dead benefit from the deeds of the living are indicated by the Qurʾān itself (Q 3:170; 59:10). Furthermore, the blessedness of praying in shrines, especially during their anniversary celebrations, may be defended by reference to the many ḥadīths that indicate the particular blessedness of praying at certain places and times (Ibrāhīm, *Qaḍāyā l-wasīla*, 5-20).

Ibn Taymiyya and the Wahhābīs prohibited erecting edifices over graves, on the basis of ḥadīths forbidding plastering tombs, sitting on them or building over them (Muslim, *Ṣaḥīḥ*, 459). But, argues shaykh Muḥammad Zakī, for seven centuries before Ibn Taymiyya there was a consensus among the Muslims concerning its permissibility. Earlier prohibitions necessary to bring an end to idolatry (see IDOLATRY AND IDOLATERS) were later overturned by the Prophet himself. A dome, he says, is nothing but a strong roof. The Prophet and the first two caliphs were buried in ʿĀʾisha's (see ʿĀʾISHA BINT ABĪ BAKR) house, which had a roof. Many domes have been built over the Prophet's tomb, and no one objected. Objections to praying at tombs may be countered by pointing out that the Prophet's tomb is right next to the mosque, and according to Islamic tradition Ishmael (q.v.; Ismāʿīl) and other people were buried beneath the walls of the

Kaʿba (q.v.). If burial next to a place of prayer were forbidden, the Prophet would not have said that prayer in that place was better than any other. Furthermore, ʿĀʾisha lived and prayed in the room in which the Prophet, Abū Bakr, and ʿUmar were buried. Mosques, he concludes, have been built near graves to grant the dead the benefit of the *baraka* of the Qurʾān recitation (see RECITATION OF THE QURʾĀN), prayer (q.v.) and *dhikr* (invocation) taking place there, and so the virtuous dead may be a good example to the living (Ibrāhīm, *Qaḍāyā l-wasīla,* 34-45).

On the efficacy of praying at saints' tombs, shaykh Muḥammad Zakī provides the example of famous Muslims. Al-Shāfiʿī allegedly prayed regularly at the tomb of Abū Ḥanīfa (d. 150/767), and his requests were answered. The help *(madad)* of the dead is stronger than that of the living. God's favor (*karāma,* a word also used for a saint's miracle) does not end with the saint's death (Ibrāhīm, *Qaḍāyā l-wasīla,* 47).

The contemporary relevance of the notion of intercession *(shafāʿa)* is captured by *Qindīl Umm Hāshim,* a novelette by Yaḥyā Ḥaqqī published in Egypt in 1944. It portrays a young man whose family venerates the Prophet's granddaughter, Sayyida Zaynab, the oil of whose lamp is reputed to heal eye diseases. After studying ophthalmology in England, the young doctor has little patience with his family's superstitions, and tries to heal his blind cousin with modern techniques, only to find that it will work solely in conjunction with oil from the saint's lamp. This story beautifully portrays popular faith in the power of the intercession of saints and the need for modern science to find a connection with the sense of authenticity that is rooted in this faith.

Valerie J. Hoffman

Bibliography
Primary: al-Ghazālī, Abu Ḥāmid Muḥammad, *Iḥyāʾ ʿulūm al-dīn,* 4 vols., Cairo 1967; Yaḥyā Ḥaqqī, *Qindīl Umm Hāshim,* Cairo 1944; id., *The saint's lamp and other stories,* trans. M.M. Badawī, Leiden 1973; Muḥammad Zakī Ibrāhīm, *Qaḍāyā l-wasīla wa-l-qubūr,* Cairo 1979; Muslim, *Ṣaḥīḥ,* trans. Abdul Siddiqi, 4 vols., New Delhi 1977 (some translations have been slightly altered); Qurṭubī, *al-Tadhkira fī aḥwāl al-mawtā wa-umūr al-ākhira,* ed. ʿI. al-Sabābitī, Cairo 1992.
Secondary: N. Abu Zahra, *The pure and powerful. Studies in contemporary Muslim society,* Reading 1997; J.P. Berkey, *Popular preaching and religious authority in the medieval Near East,* Seattle 2000; C. Gilliot, Le commentaire coranique de Hūd b. Muḥakkam/Muḥkim, in *Arabica* 44 (1997), 179-233, esp. 194-9; Goldziher, *MS,* London 1971, ii, 255-341; V.J. Hoffman, *Sufism, mystics and saints in modern Egypt,* Columbia, SC 1995; J. Johansen, *Sufism and Islamic reform in Egypt. The battle for Islamic tradition,* Oxford 1996; M.U. Memon, *Ibn Taymiyya's struggle against popular religion,* The Hague and Paris 1976; J.I. Smith, Concourse between the living and the dead in Islamic eschatological literature, in *History of religions* 19 (1980), 224-36; id. and Y.Y. Haddad, *The Islamic understanding of death and resurrection,* Albany 1981; H. Stieglecker, *Die Glaubenslehren des Islam,* 4 vols., Munich 1959-62; S. ʿUways, *Min malāmiḥ al-mujtamaʿ al-miṣrī al-muʿāṣir. Ẓāhirat irsāl al-rasāʾil ilā ḍarīḥ al-Imām al-Shāfiʿī,* Cairo 1965; M. Wolff, *Muhammedanische Eschatologie,* Leipzig 1872, 177-85 (how Muslims get out of hell).

Interest see ECONOMICS; TRADE AND COMMERCE; USURY

Intermediary see INTERCESSION

Interpolation see CHRONOLOGY AND THE QURʾĀN

Intoxicants

Substances, generally containing alcohol, the consumption of which causes a state of inebriation. Although Islamic law includes opiates, narcotics and other drugs under the category of "intoxicants," the qurʾānic terminology is limited to terms for strong drink: *sakar* (Q 16:67; cf. *sukārā*, "drunken," in Q 22:2; 4:43); *raḥīq* (the wine of the righteous in paradise, Q 83:25; but the Qurʾān emphasizes that the contents of the cups of paradise will not result in headaches or madness [*lā yunzifūna*, Q 56:19; cf. 37:47]); and the most often attestated term, *al-khamr* (lit. "wine"), mentioned six times in various contexts. Islamic jurisprudence ordinarily considers the qurʾānic usage of this term — particularly in Q 2:219 and 5:90-1 — to refer to intoxicants in general, and not solely to wine. Through the interpretative method of analogy *(qiyās)*, the word *al-khamr* is taken to mean every intoxicant *(al-muskir)*. One of the reasons why the word *al-khamr* is used as the qurʾānic *terminus technicus* for all intoxicants lies in the Qurʾān's proximity to the Semitic and, more generally, the Mediterranean cultural region where wine *(al-khamr)* was both the main intoxicant and an important element of Christian liturgy (see CHRISTIANS AND CHRISTIANITY). This can be seen in the textual evidence of the Qurʾān itself, e.g. in Q 12 "Joseph" (Sūrat Yūsuf), where it is stated that one of the two prisoners to remain alive would pour out wine for his lord to drink (Q 12:41; see JOSEPH). The context of this verse indicates that "wine" may be understood, in a cross-cultural interpretation, as the Dionysian symbol of life, for the prisoner had just dreamt that he had distilled wine from grapes (Q 12:36), the meaning of his dream being that he would survive (see DREAMS AND SLEEP). Both symbolic and literal interpretation has been offered for qurʾānic imagery such as "and rivers of wine delicious to the drinkers" in paradise (q.v.; *al-janna;* see also GARDEN), mentioned in Q 47:15. The Qurʾān speaks about the act of drinking wine and other drinks from goblets (see CUPS AND VESSELS) in paradise within an elaborated context of material culture. Divans, seats, goblets filled to the brink, "wherefrom they get no aching of the head nor any madness" (Q 56:19), bodies decorated with jewelry, the conversations of the inhabitants of paradise: all this describes a qurʾānic ideal of beauty (q.v.) and perfected existence (see also MATERIAL CULTURE AND THE QURʾĀN; FURNITURE AND FURNISHINGS; INSTRUMENTS).

Yet, while Muslim mystics (see ṢŪFISM AND THE QURʾĀN) sang songs glorifying the divine wine that does not intoxicate, Islamic theologians and jurists (see THEOLOGY AND THE QURʾĀN; LAW AND THE QURʾĀN) condemned, just as fervently, the earthly wine that does. For example, al-Zamakhsharī (d. 538/1144; *Kashhāf*, i, 261), in his identification of fermentation as that which leads to the transformation of a liquid into an intoxicating substance, extends the qurʾānic prohibition of *khamr* to include "all drinks that have an intoxicating effect" *("... wa-ʿinda akthar al-fuqahāʾ huwa ḥarām ka-l-khamr wa-kadhālika kull mā askara min kull sharāb")*. Two passages are fundamental for the qurʾānic prohibition of intoxicants *(al-khamr)*: Q 2:219 says: "They question you about strong drink and games of chance (see GAMBLING). Say: in both is great sin, and some utility for men; but the sin of them is greater than their usefulness..." and Q 5:90-1, "O you who believe! Strong drink and games of chance and idols (see IDOLS AND IMAGES) and divining arrows (see DIVINATION; FORETELLING) are only an infamy of Satan's (see DEVIL) handwork. Leave it aside in order that you may succeed. Satan seeks only to cast among you enmity and hatred by means of strong drink and games of chance, and turn you from remembrance of God and from [his] worship. Will you then have done?"

Islamic jurisprudence generally understands the qur'ānic ban of intoxicants to have developed in stages. Commentators of the Qur'ān regularly claim (cf. e.g. Zamakhsharī, *Kashshāf,* i, 260; Ṣābūnī, *Tafsīr,* i, 270) that between the revelation of Q 2:219 and Q 5:90-1, Q 4:43, which forbids performing prayer (q.v.) in a drunken state, was pronounced (see OCCASIONS OF REVELATION; CHRONOLOGY AND THE QUR'ĀN). This verse reads as follows: "O you who believe! Do not draw near to prayer when you are drunken *(sukārā),* till you know that which you utter..." Therefore, Q 5:90-1 is considered to be the conclusive and final ban of intoxicants by the Qur'ān.

The etymology of the word *al-khamr* elucidates the precise nature of intoxicants. The linguist al-Zajjāj (d. 311/923; *Lisān al-'Arab,* s.v. *kh-m-r*) defines *al-khamr* as that which covers the mind *(mā satara 'alā l-'aql).* Al-Zajjāj also adds that the cognate *khimār* means "the veil of woman," because it is something that covers a woman's head. The modern scholar Muḥammad 'Alī al-Ṣābūnī repeats this definition of *khamr (li-annahā tastur al-'aql).* The concept of "covering the mind" is understood metaphorically as the distortion of reason. Islamic legislation and jurisprudence takes this fact as fundamental in banning intoxicants, drugs and all that intoxicates the body or mind. In the books of Islamic tradition, alcohol is called "the mother of all evils" *(umm al-khabā'ith).* Islamic law, pursuant to the relevant qur'ānic verses and to various ḥadīth (e.g. *al-khamr mā khāmara al-'aql*), strictly bans every association with alcohol, drugs and intoxicants in general, such as trafficking, producing, using as medicine, deriving profit, etc.

Finally, mention should be made of the mystical commentaries of the Qur'ān, which state that the drunkenness caused by *khamr* is but one sort of drunkenness *(sukr).* These commentaries (e.g. al-Burūsāwī, *Tafsīr,* i, 341) point to the non-material forms of intoxication that can inflame the heart and soul (*sukr al-qulūb wa-l-arwāḥ,* see HEART).

Enes Karic

Bibliography

Primary: Bukhārī, *Ṣaḥīḥ,* Cairo 1958; id., *Les traditions islamiques,* trans. O. Houdas, iv, 34-40; al-Burūsāwī, Ismā'īl Ḥaqqī, *Tafsīr rūḥ al-bayān,* 10 vols., Beirut 1405/1985; Ibn Abī l-Dunyā, *Kitāb Dhamm al-muskir,* ed. M.Y. Shu'ayb, Amman 1998; *Lisān al-'Arab,* Beirut 1955-6; Y. al-Qaraḍāwī, *al-Ḥalāl wa-l-ḥarām fī l-Islām,* Beirut 1373/1973; M.'A. al-Ṣābūnī, *Tafsīr āyāt al-aḥkām,* 2 vols., Beirut 1391/1971; Shawkānī, *Tafsīr,* 5 vols., Beirut 1403/1983; Zamakhsharī, *Kashshāf,* ed. M.Ḥ. Aḥmad, 4 vols., Beirut 1407/1987.

Secondary: A.S. Fulton, Fīrūzābādī's 'wine-list,' in *BSOAS* 12 (1948), 579-85; P. Heine, Nabīdh, in *EI²*, vii, 840; id., *Weinstudien,* Wiesbaden 1982; J.D. McAuliffe, The wines of earth and paradise. Qur'ānic proscriptions and promises, in R. Savory and D. Agius (eds.), *Papers in medieval studies. vi. Logos islamikos. Studia islamica in honorem Georgii Michaelis Wickens,* Toronto 1984, 159-74; A. Rippin and J. Knappert (eds. and trans.), *Textual sources for the study of Islam,* Manchester 1986, 72-4 (from Bukhārī's *Ṣaḥīḥ*); J. Sadan, Khamr. ii. As a product, in *EI²*, iv, 997-8; id., Mashrūbāt, in *EI²*, vi, 720-3; A.J. Wensinck, Khamr, in *EI²*, iv, 994-7; id., Wine in Islam, in *MW* 18 (1928), 365-74.

Invitation

The exhortation to heed the qur'ānic message. The Qur'ān issues its basic invitation *(da'wa)* to all people: worship (q.v.) and serve the sovereign and unique God alone (Q 21:25) and practice true religion (Q 7:29; 9:33; see ISLAM; RELIGION). Invitations come through messengers (see MESSENGER) and prophets (see PROPHETS AND PROPHETHOOD) to their peoples. Muḥammad is called to "invite to the way (see PATH OR WAY) of the lord with wisdom and beautiful preaching..." (Q 16:125; also 22:67;

23:73; 28:87). Other messengers and prophets issuing invitations include Noah (q.v.; Nūḥ; Q 71:1-26; 7:59-64), Abraham (q.v.; Ibrāhīm; Q 26:69-82; 37:83-98), Moses (q.v.; Mūsā; Q 7:103-29; 10:84-6), whose call is elaborately narrated (Q 20:9-44; 79:15-9), Elijah (q.v.; Ilyās; Q 37:123-32), Ṣāliḥ (q.v.; Q 7:73-9; 11:61-8), Hūd (q.v.; Q 7:65-72; 11:50-60; 46:21-6), Shuʿayb (q.v.; Q 7:85-93; 11:84-95; 29:36-7) and Jesus (q.v.; ʿĪsā; Q 3:49-57; 61:6). Solomon (q.v.; Sulaymān) invites "a woman ruling over" Sabaʾ (Bilqīs [q.v.], the Queen of Sheba [q.v.]) to submit to true religion (Q 27:22-44).

The invitations of prophets and messengers call people out of darkness (q.v.) into the light (q.v.); rescue them from evil (see GOOD AND EVIL), sins (see SIN, MAJOR AND MINOR), and pain; stress that thankfulness (see GRATITUDE AND INGRATITUDE) and obedience (q.v.) are necessary for increase in blessing (q.v.); and warn them that disobeying God requires punishment (Jabjub, *Daʿwa,* 91-3; see DISOBEDIENCE; REWARD AND PUNISHMENT; CHASTISEMENT AND PUNISHMENT; PUNISHMENT STORIES). Noah's largely unsuccessful inviting (Q 71:1-20) of his people, extending over more than nine hundred years (Q 29:14-5), can serve as an example. He begins by awakening fear *(tarhīb):* "O people, I am your clear warner" (q.v.; Q 71:2). Then he commands them to the sole worship of God, to reverent fear (q.v.) of God, and to obedience to himself as God's prophet (Q 71:3). Awakening their desire *(targhīb),* he promises forgiveness (q.v.) of their sins and postponement of life's end (Q 71:4). After stirring up fear *(tarhīb)* again and assuring them that judgment (q.v.) cannot be delayed (Q 71:4), he urges them to ask the lord for forgiveness (Q 71:10) with an appeal rooted in God's nature: "He is oft-forgiving; he will send rain to you in abundance..." (Q 71:10-1). Finally, he appeals to the goodness of God's creation (q.v.; Q 71:13-20; cf. Jabjub, *Daʿwa,* 296-8; see COSMOLOGY).

The Qurʾān also offers invitations not issued by prophets and messengers. An unidentified man from the outer reaches of the city invites his people to follow those who are sent to them (Q 36:20). God invites all to the house of peace (Q 10:25; see HOUSE, DOMESTIC AND DIVINE) and to the garden (q.v.) of bliss and forgiveness (Q 2:221). The seductive invitations of Satan (Q 31:21; 35:6; see DEVIL), Pharaoh (q.v.) and his troops (Q 28:41) and other unbelievers (Q 2:221; 40:41-4) compete with divine invitations (see BELIEF AND UNBELIEF; ENEMIES).

Many invitations relate to the final judgment, the day of summoning (*yawm al-tanādī,* Q 40:32; see LAST JUDGMENT; APOCALYPSE). God summons some to total destruction (Q 56:41-56), some to eternal bliss (Q 17:71) and all to his praise (q.v.; Q 17:52; see REWARD AND PUNISHMENT). The caller calls *(yunādī l-munādī)* and the dead come forth (Q 50:41-2; cf. Q 30:25; see DEATH AND THE DEAD). Unbelievers (see BELIEF AND UNBELIEF) are drawn to the inviter *(al-dāʿī)* irresistibly (Q 54:6-8). God will summon *(yunādī)* idolaters to produce their deities (Q 28:62-5, 74) and the idolaters will call, but their deities will not speak up for them (Q 28:64; see IDOLS AND IMAGES; IDOLATRY AND IDOLATERS; INTERCESSION). Every nation *(umma)* will be called to appear before its book (q.v.; Q 45:28). Satan will refuse to take the blame for those who are judged deserving of painful torment (Q 14:22).

A.H. Mathias Zahniser

Bibliography

T. Arnold, *The preaching of Islam. A history of the propagation of the Muslim faith,* Westminster 1896[1]; London 1913[2]; Muḥammad b. Sīdi b. al-Ḥabīb al-Jabjūb, *al-Daʿwa ilā llāh fī sūrat Ibrāhīm,* Jedda 1985.

Iram

The name of a place or possibly a tribe. It is connected with the people of ʿĀd (q.v.) and thus, by extension, with the story of the prophet Hūd (q.v.). Iram is in fact mentioned only once in the Qurʾān, in Q 89:6-7: "Do you not see how your lord dealt with ʿĀd, [and with] Iram of the columns" *(a-lam tara kayfa faʿala rabbuka bi-ʿĀdin Irama dhāti l-ʿimādi)*. Some classical exegetes (see EXEGESIS OF THE QURʾĀN: CLASSICAL AND MEDIEVAL) interpret Iram as being in apposition to — and thus synonymous with — the people of ʿĀd. For them, Iram designates an ancient tribe, and a subdivision of ʿĀd (argued most forcefully by Ibn Khaldūn; cf. Ibn Khaldūn-Rosenthal, i, 25-8). Furthermore, for some, Iram was the progenitor of the "Nabateans," that is, Aramaeans (e.g. Ṭabarī, Taʾrīkh, i, 220). The epithet "of the columns" *(dhāti l-ʿimādi)* is in this case understood as a tribal epithet "of the tent-poles" or, more recently, "people of trust" (Ahmed Ali, *al-Qurʾān*).

The vast majority of the exegetes, however, understand Iram "of the columns" to be a place: the capital city of the land of the ʿĀdites, destroyed by God's wrath (see PUNISHMENT STORIES). The most commonly supposed location of this city is in Yemen. According to this version, an ʿĀdite king named Shaddād built a city in the desert near Aden to rival paradise (q.v.): the description of Iram's opulence varies greatly, but it is always detailed. Before Shaddād and his people could relocate to his new city, however, God destroyed him and his people for their pride (q.v.; see also ARROGANCE), along with the city of Iram. This Yemen-based narrative generated its share of adventure-stories, such as the often-retold tale of Ibn Qilāba, a wandering shepherd who is said to have discovered the lost ruins of Iram during the reign of the Umayyad caliph Muʿāwiya (d. 60/680) or that of the discovery by two intrepid explorers of Shaddād's tomb carved into a mountain overlooking the sea. Others (such as al-Rabaʿī, *Faḍāʾil*, 20) prefer to identify Iram with pre-Islamic Damascus, perhaps influenced by its association with the biblical Aram and, no doubt, its plentiful columns. Still others (such as al-Zamakhsharī, *Asās*) identify Iram with Alexandria. The strength of the tradition of identifying Iram with a place rather than a people is attested by its inclusion in the main Arabic geographical dictionaries: Abū ʿUbayd al-Bakrī, Yāqūt al-Ḥamawī and Ibn ʿAbd al-Munʿim al-Ḥimyarī (see GEOGRAPHY; HISTORY AND THE QURʾĀN).

Paul M. Cobb

Bibliography
Primary: Abū ʿUbayd al-Bakrī, *Muʿjam mā istaʿjam*, ed. M. al-Saqqā, 5 vols., Beirut n.d. (repr. of Cairo ed.), i, 140-1; Ibn ʿAbd al-Munʿim al-Ḥimyarī, *al-Rawḍ al-miʿṭār fī khabar al-aqṭār*, ed. I. ʿAbbās, Beirut 1975, 22-4; Ibn Khaldūn-Rosenthal; Masʿūdī, *Murūj*, ed. and trans. Pellat, ii, 261; al-Rabaʿī, Abū l-Ḥasan, *Kitāb Faḍāʾil al-Shām wa-Dimashq*, ed. S. al-Munajjid, Damascus 1950; Ṭabarī, *Taʾrīkh;* Thaʿlabī, *Qiṣaṣ*, 145-50; Yāqūt, *Buldān*, s.v.; Zamakhsharī, *Asās*, s.v.
Secondary: A. Ali, *al-Qurʾān*. A contemporary translation, Princeton 1984; J.E. Bencheikh, Iram ou la clameur de Dieu. Le mythe et le verset, in *REMMM* 58 (1991), 69-79; M.J. Hermosilla, Una version aljamiada de Corán. 89.6-8. Sobre Iram, la de las columnas, in *Qanṭara* 5 (1984), 33-62; A.-L. de Prémare, Le thème des peuples anéantis dans quelques textes islamiques primitifs. Une vision de l'histoire, in *REMMM* 48-49 (1988), 11-21; S. Tamari, *Iconotextual studies in mid-eastern Islamic religious architecture and urbanisation in the early Middle Ages*, Naples 1992; W.M. Watt, Iram, in *EI*², iii, 1270.

Iraq

A region extending over the southern lands of Mesopotamia including the fertile lands between the Tigris and the Euphrates rivers. Although the word Iraq does not occur in the Qurʾān (see GEOGRAPHY), a number of prophets (see PROPHETS AND PROPHETHOOD) mentioned therein are believed to have come from Iraq (i.e. Abraham, q.v.), leading some recent Western scholarship to posit Iraq as the cradle of the Qurʾān (see Wansbrough, *QS*, 49-50; and id., *Sectarian milieu* for a more fully developed version of the theory; see also SOUTH ARABIA, RELIGION IN PRE-ISLAMIC). In post-qurʾānic times, the region played a central role in the shaping of religious doctrines that profoundly influenced the different exegetical tendencies.

The Muslim conquest of Iraq began during the caliphate of ʿUmar (r. 13-23/634-44) and ended with the defeat of the Sassanians in al-Qādisiyya in 16/637 and Nihāwand in 21/642. The garrison camps of Baṣra and Kūfa were established soon thereafter. Muslim Iraq was then ruled from these two cities which rapidly evolved into major towns becoming the cultural and administrative centers of Iraq.

At a very early date, Iraq became the scene of violent clashes among the various politico-religious parties. During the caliphate of Muʿāwiya (41-60/661-80), it was the center of opposition from the Shīʿīs (see SHĪʿISM AND THE QURʾĀN) and the Khārijīs (q.v.). The Umayyad dynasty gave Syria pre-eminence over Iraq. The ʿAbbāsids replaced the Umayyads in 132/750 and established their new capital, Baghdad, in Iraq, thus acknowledging Iraq's political, economic and social importance. This new era ushered in a period of economic development and cultural and artistic efflorescence. Iraq became a major center for the elaboration of the religious sciences (see TRADITIONAL DISCIPLINES OF QURʾĀNIC STUDY), including philology (see ARABIC LANGUAGE; FOREIGN VOCABULARY; LANGUAGE OF THE QURʾĀN), grammar (see GRAMMAR AND THE QURʾĀN), qurʾānic exegesis (see EXEGESIS OF THE QURʾĀN, CLASSICAL AND MEDIEVAL), ḥadīth (see ḤADĪTH AND THE QURʾĀN) and law (see LAW AND THE QURʾĀN). A vast number of poets, historians, men of letters as well as scholars whose outstanding achievements included the fields of philosophy, medicine, mathematics and astronomy are associated with Baghdad, Baṣra and Kūfa (see PHILOSOPHY OF THE QURʾĀN; MEDICINE AND THE QURʾĀN; SCIENCE AND THE QURʾĀN). The coming of the ʿAbbāsids did not bring religious unity to Iraq. ʿAlid revolts and civil war between al-Amīn and al-Maʾmūn (194-8/810-3) brought severe disturbances to the region. Iraq also became the main center of the Muʿtazila movement (see MUTAZILĪS). The ensuing inquisition (q.v.) attempting to impose the pro-Muʿtazilī doctrine of the createdness of the Qurʾān (q.v.) added to the already existing tensions.

Al-Muʿtaṣim (r. 218-27/833-42) introduced into the capital large numbers of Turkish slaves and in 223/836 this caliph (q.v.) established a new capital up the Tigris at Sāmarrāʾ. The decay of central authority continued, exacerbated by the revolt of the Zanj (225-70/869-83) and by the repeated raids of the Qarmaṭīs. The break-up of the caliphate led to the emergence of a large number of successor states. A new era in which Iraq was controlled by the Shīʿī Buwayhid *amīrs* was ushered in 334/945 and extended until 447/1055. The fourth/tenth and fifth/eleventh centuries witnessed both the emergence of prominent Imāmī scholars and theologians and the promotion of popular Shīʿism reflected in the special veneration bestowed on the tombs of the Shīʿī imāms (see IMĀM). The arrival of the Seljuqs in 447/1055 established an essentially Sunnī regime. They encouraged the study of Islamic law and theology and formalized the institution of the *madrasa*, the

Islamic institution of higher learning. In 658/1258 the Mongol Hulagu invaded Iraq, sacked Baghdad and put to death the last ʿAbbāsid caliph. The period extending until the Ottoman conquest witnessed the political and economic decline of the province.

Nadia Maria El-Cheikh

Bibliography
J. Bottéro, *Mésopotamie. L'écriture, la raison et les dieux,* Paris 1987; F.M. Donner, *The early Islamic conquests,* Princeton 1981; J. Lassner, *The topography of Baghdad in the Middle Ages,* Detroit 1970; G. Le Strange, *The lands of the eastern caliphate,* London 1905, repr. 1966, 24-85; A. Miquel, *La géographie humaine du monde musulman jusqu'au milieu du 11ᵉ siècle,* 4 vols., Paris 1973-80; id. et al., ʿIrāḳ, in *EI²*, iii, 1250-68; M.G. Morony, *Iraq after the Muslim conquest,* Princeton 1984 (for the Islamic conquest and early Islamic period); Ch. Pellat, *Le milieu basrien et la formation de Gahiz,* Paris 1953; J. Wansbrough, *QS;* id., *The sectarian milieu. Content and composition of Islamic salvation history,* Oxford 1978.

Isaac

One of the sons of Abraham (q.v.). Isaac (Isḥāq), specifically named a prophet (Q 19:49; 37:112; see PROPHETS AND PROPHETHOOD), is mentioned by name seventeen times in sixteen qurʾānic verses. In half of these, he is included in what appears to be a litany of remembrances of ancient prophets. Such remembrances are a common qurʾānic motif in which the prophethood and message of Muḥammad are set within a context of ancient and familiar prophets and divine messages, usually but not always paralleling the scriptural traditions of Judaism and Christianity (see SCRIPTURE AND THE QURʾĀN). The most common format in which Isaac appears in this litany of the prophets is "Abraham, Ishmael (q.v.), Isaac, Jacob (q.v.) and the tribes," often followed by additional prophets and personalities known from the Bible (Q 2:136, 140; 3:84; 4:163). In other references to the Abraham clan, the order is Abraham, Isaac and Jacob. In these references, Ishmael is either mentioned a few verses later in association with other familiar prophetic personages unrelated to Abraham (Q 6:84-6; 38:45-8), or is excluded entirely (cf. Q 12:6; 19:49; 29:27).

In these formulaic lists, Isaac, like the other ancient personages mentioned, is a true prophet who has received God's communication (*mā unzila [ʿalayhi],* Q 2:136; 3:84), inspiration/revelation (*waḥy,* cf. Q 4:163; see REVELATION AND INSPIRATION) or guidance (*hady,* cf. Q 6:84). The prophets of the Abraham family are exceptional individuals, true believers who are neither Jews nor Christians (Q 2:140) but rather ancient and pre-Islamic *muslimūn* or "those who submit [entirely] to the divine will" (Q 2:133; see ḤANĪF). In fact, the polemical argument of Q 2:130-41 (see especially 134, 141) suggests that the descendants of these Abrahamic prophets have passed away, but their example may still be emulated by those who would believe and submit to God's will by following the divine message communicated through Muḥammad, the last of the great prophets. Blessed by God (Q 37:113), Isaac is a result of the divine promise to Abraham and his unnamed wife who laughed when given the good news of his impending birth (Q 11:71; cf. 15:53; 51:28; *Gen* 17:15-21). When Abraham settled some of his progeny in a barren valley near God's sacred house (see HOUSE, DOMESTIC AND DIVINE), presumably in Mecca (q.v.), he prays that they will observe the proper ritual prayers (see PRAYER) and prosper, and he thanks God for giving him Ishmael and Isaac in his old age (Q 14:37-9). Isaac, along with Abraham's other progeny, is given to Abraham for his piety (q.v.) and unswerving obedience to monotheism (Q 6:84; 19:49; 21:72; 29:27; and perhaps 37:112).

The character of Isaac is not developed in the Qurʾān and he remains a minor figure throughout, appearing almost entirely in formulaic lists or idiomatic expressions in relation to his father Abraham. This is not exceptional, for most ancient prophets in the Qurʾān are referred to as if the audience were already familiar with them and their stories. Little narrative development (see NARRATIVES) is provided, which is the case with Isaac.

The most controversial reference to Isaac is in association with the narrative of Abraham's "intended sacrifice" *(al-dhabīḥ)* in Q 37:99-113, in which Isaac is specifically mentioned but not strictly within the narrative. As a result, the qurʾānic exegetes argued over whether Isaac or Ishmael was the intended victim. At stake in this controversy was the merit understood to have accrued to the progeny of whichever son was willing to submit entirely to God's will through self-immolation. Such an act was seen as the epitome of submission (*islām*, cf. Q 37:103). The genealogical association of Jews and spiritual association of Christians with Isaac, in contrast to the common association of Arab Muslims with Ishmael, was therefore at issue. Most early Muslim exegetes understood Isaac to have been the son to whom the narrative referred. Since the early tenth century, however, most Muslims have thought that Ishmael was Abraham's intended sacrifice.

Reuven Firestone

Bibliography
Primary: Kisāʾī, *The tales of the prophets of al-Kisāʾī*, trans. W. Thackston, Boston 1978, 160-3 and index; Ṭabarī, *The history of al-Ṭabarī. ii. Prophets and patriarchs*, trans. W. Brinner, Albany, NY 1987, 48-131; id., *Taʾrīkh*, ed. de Goeje, i, 252-351; al-Ṭarafī, Abū ʿAbdallāh Muḥammad, *Storie dei profeti*, trans. R. Tottoli, Genoa 1997, 232-5.
Secondary: R. Bell, The sacrifice of Ishmael, in *Transactions of the Glasgow University Oriental Society* 10 (1940-1), 29-31; R. Firestone, Abraham's son as the intended sacrifice *(al-dhabīḥ)*, Qurʾān 37:99-113. Issues in qurʾānic exegesis, in *JSS* 89 (1989), 95-131; id., *Journeys in holy lands. The evolution of the Abraham-Ishmael legends in Islamic exegesis*, Albany, NY 1990; Y. Moubarac, *Abraham dans le Coran*, Paris 1958; J.A. Naude, Isaac typology in the Koran, in I.H. Eybers et al. (eds.), *De fructu oris sui. Essays in honour of Adrianus van Selms*, Leiden 1971, 121-9.

Isaiah

Son of Amos and a prophet who was sent to Israel. Isaiah (in Arabic, Shaʿyā or Ashaʿyāʾ) is not mentioned by name in the Qurʾān, although exegetical works (e.g. Ṭabarī, *Tafsīr*, xv, 22-3; Māwardī, *Nukat*, iii, 229) mention him in connection with Q 17:4, "We decreed for the Children of Israel (q.v.) in the book (q.v.): 'You shall do corruption (q.v.) in the earth twice, and you shall ascend exceeding high.'" Isaiah is well known in the "stories of the prophets" literature (*qiṣaṣ al-anbiyāʾ*, see PROPHETS AND PROPHETHOOD), especially for his predictions of the coming of Jesus (q.v.) and Muḥammad, but his life story was also seen as an illustration of how the acts of "corruption (q.v.)" mentioned in Q 17:4 demanded the coming of the prophet.

As told in Muslim literature, the life story of Isaiah encompasses three periods of prophecy. The account provided by al-Ṭabarī (d. 310/923) is typical. In the first period, Isaiah was recognized as a prophet during the reign of Zedekiah (or Hezekiah, as in the Bible) and he prophesied the king's death. The second period of his prophecy occurred in the time of the siege of Jerusalem by Sennacherib (Sanḥarīb). After Isaiah announced that, because of God's hearing the prayer of Zedekiah, the king's death had been postponed for fifteen years, God destroyed all of the enemy forces except Sennacherib and five scribes. After parading the commander around Jerusalem for sixty-six days, Zedekiah followed the command of God and allowed Sennacherib to return to Babylon (q.v.). So, the events became a "warning and admonition" of the strength of God. In the third period of Isaiah's prophecy, the people were leaving the ways of God in the wake of the death of the king and Isaiah warned them of their coming doom. This led to his martyrdom at the hands of his fellow Israelites. Isaiah fled when threatened and took refuge inside a tree. Satan, however, showed his enemies the fringes of his clothes and they cut down the tree, killing him in the process (see Gaster and Heller, Der Prophet; Ginzberg, *The legends*).

Isaiah's role in prophesying the coming of Muḥammad and Islam is an important element within his story. Al-Ṭabarī, for example, states plainly, "It was Isaiah who announced the advent of Jesus and Muḥammad" (*Taʾrīkh*, i, 638). Isaiah continues to play a central role in contemporary polemic, as may be seen in a book such as *Muḥammad nabī al-Islām* ("Muḥammad Prophet of Islam") by Muḥammad ʿIzzat Ismāʿīl al-Ṭahṭāwī. There, Isaiah's references to the desert (*Isa* 21:13, 40:3), to a "righteous nation" that will walk through the gates of Jerusalem (*Isa* 26:2) and to a "victor from the east" (*Isa* 41:2), etc., are all interpreted as giving biblical support to the inevitable rise (because it was a part of God's plan) of Islam.

Andrew Rippin

Bibliography
Primary: Māwardī, *Nukat;* Ṭabarī, *The history of al-Tabari. iv. The ancient kingdoms,* trans. M. Perlmann, Albany, N.Y. 1987, 36-42; id., *Tafsīr,* Cairo 1954-7; id., *Taʾrīkh,* Leiden 1879-1901; M. ʿIzzat Ismāʿīl al-Ṭahṭāwī, *Muḥammad nabī l-Islām fī l-tawrāt wa-l-injīl wa-l-qurʾān,* Cairo n.d.
Secondary: C. Adang, *Muslim writers on Judaism and the Hebrew Bible. From Ibn Rabban to Ibn Hazm,* Leiden 1996, 319-20 and Index (for Isaiah in Islamic literature in general); J.-L. Déclais, *Un récit musulman sur Isaïe,* Paris 2001; al-Fārisī, Abū Rifāʿat, *Badʾ al-khalq wa-qiṣaṣ al-anbiyāʾ,* in R.G. Khoury (ed.), *Les légendes prophétiques dans l'Islam,* Wiesbaden 1978, 237-50; M. Gaster and B. Heller, Der Prophet Jesajah und der Baum, in *Monatsschrift für die Geschichte und Wissenschaft des Judentums* 80 (1936), 35-52, 127-8; Louis Ginzberg, *The legends of the Jews,* 7 vols., Philadelphia 1909-36, iv, 279; vi, 371; Wilhelm Hoenerbach, Isaias bei Ṭabarī, in H. Junker and J. Botterweck (eds), *Alttestamentliche Studien. Friedrich Nötscher zum 60. Geburtstage gewidmet,* Bonn 1950, 98-119; S. Karoui, *Die Rezeption der Bibel in der frühislamischen Literatur am Beispiel der Hauptwerke von Ibn Qutayba (gest. 276/889),* Dissertation, Heidelberg 1997, 291 (for quotations from the Book of Isaiah in the works of Ibn Qutayba); Hava Lazarus-Yafeh, *Intertwined worlds. Medieval Islam and Bible criticism,* Princeton 1992, esp. 83-93.

Ishmael

Pre-Islamic prophet, named in the Bible as the son of Abraham (q.v.) and Hagar and the eponymous father of the Ishmaelites (a confederacy of Arab tribes; see TRIBES AND CLANS). Ishmael (Ismāʿīl) is mentioned twelve times in as many verses of the Qurʾān. In most of these, he is listed among other prophets as part of a litany of remembrances in which the pre-Islamic prophets are praised for their resolute steadfastness (see TRUST AND PATIENCE) and obedience (q.v.) to God, often in the face of adversity (see TRIAL). The subtext of these litanies is Muḥammad's position as authentic prophet *(nabī)* or messenger (q.v.; *rasūl*) in the line of authentic prophets or messengers of God (see PROPHETS AND PROPHETHOOD). Ishmael is generally listed in the following formula: "Abraham, Ishmael, Isaac (q.v.), Jacob (q.v.) and the tribes" (Q 2:136, 140; 3:84; 4:63), and in Q 2:133 as "Abraham, Ishmael and Isaac." In some lists, however, Ishmael is missing from the reference to Abraham, Isaac and Jacob (Q 6:84; 12:38; 19:49; 21:72; 29:27;

38:45) and in others he is found in association with other pre-Islamic prophets: al-Yasaʿ (Elisha?, q.v.), Jonah (q.v.) and Lot (q.v.; Q 6:86); Idrīs (q.v.) and Dhū l-Kifl (q.v.; Q 21:85); and al-Yasaʿ and Dhū l-Kifl (Q 38:48). This has led certain Western scholars to suggest, despite some evidence to the contrary, that the lists in which Ishmael is not associated with Abraham represent earlier Meccan material that recognized the prophethood of Ishmael but did not connect him with the Abraham family. Accordingly, the lists in which Ishmael is mentioned in association with the family of Abraham are considered by some to represent later Medinan material that had been more thoroughly influenced by biblical lore and tradition (see CHRONOLOGY AND THE QURʾĀN; SCRIPTURE AND THE QURʾĀN).

Little additional information can be gleaned from the few references to Ishmael outside of the lists. He is named specifically as a messenger and prophet in Q 19:54, where he is also singled out as being true to his promise *(ṣādiq al-waʿd)*. The use of this expression suggests that this verse may in fact refer to a personage other than the Ishmael known from the Bible. In the following verse he is said to have ordained worship (q.v.) and almsgiving (q.v.) for his people.

Two verses associate Ishmael and his father Abraham with the Meccan Kaʿba (q.v.). Q 2:125 and 127 form part of a larger pericope in which Abraham, known in the Hebrew Bible as a founder of sacred shrines (cf. *Gen* 12:7-8; 13:3-4; 21:33), purifies with Ishmael the location of God's great Arabian shrine, referred to in the Qurʾān as "the house" (*al-bayt*, see HOUSE, DOMESTIC AND DIVINE). Because Ishmael is associated with Abraham's raising up its foundations (Q 2:127) as well as its purification (Q 2:125), he is clearly identified with this shrine — although secondarily — with Abraham appearing overwhelmingly as the central figure. A third verse, Q 14:39, seems to connect both Ishmael and Isaac with the Kaʿba in Abraham's prayer. This verse, however, may have been placed in association with the prayer of Abraham found in Q 14:37, which does indeed refer to God's house, during the redaction process (see COLLECTION OF THE QURʾĀN) because of its thematic parallel (see FORM AND STRUCTURE OF THE QURʾĀN).

Contrary to popular belief, Ishmael is nowhere identified in the Qurʾān as Abraham's intended sacrificial victim (*al-dhabīḥ*, see Q 37:99-111; cf. *Gen* 22:1-18). No name is provided in the qurʾānic narrative itself, while Isaac is mentioned immediately thereafter (Q 37:112-3). Two schools of interpretation developed, one supportive of Isaac and the other of Ishmael as the intended sacrifice. By the early tenth century, the Ishmael school became the most popular.

Reuven Firestone

Bibliography

Primary: Masʿūdī, *Murūj*, ed. and trans. Ch. Pellat, i, 35-6; Ṭabarī, *The history of al-Ṭabarī. ii. Prophets and patriarchs*, trans. W. Brinner, Albany, NY 1987, 48-131; id., *Taʾrīkh*, ed. de Goeje, i, 253-351; al-Ṭarafī, Abū ʿAbdallāh Muḥammad, *Storie dei profeti*, trans. R. Tottoli, Genoa 1997, 232-5.

Secondary: R. Bell, The sacrifice of Ishmael, in *Transactions of the Glasgow University Oriental Society* 10 (1940-1), 29-31; N. Calder, From midrash to scripture. The sacrifice of Abraham in early Islamic tradition, in *Muséon* 101 (1988), 375-402; id., The *saʿy* and the *jabīn*. Some notes on Qurʾān 37:102-3, in *JSS* 31 (1986), 17-26; R. Dagorn, *La geste d'Ismael*, Paris 1981; R. Firestone, Abraham's son as the intended sacrifice (*al-dhabīḥ*, Qurʾān 37:99-113). Issues in qurʾānic exegesis, in *JSS* 89 (1989), 95-131; id., *Journeys in holy lands. The evolution of the Abraham-Ishmael legends in Islamic exegesis*, Albany, NY 1990; M. Hayek, *Le mystère d'Ismael*, Paris 1964; H. Lazarus-Yafeh, *Intertwined worlds. Medieval Islam and Bible criticism*, Princeton 1992, see Index; Y. Moubarac, *Abraham dans le*

Coran, Paris 1958; R. Paret, Ismāʿīl, in *EI²*, iv, 184-5; U. Rubin, *Between Bible and Qurʾān. The children of Israel and the Islamic self-image,* Princeton 1999, see Index; Speyer, *Erzählungen,* 164-6, 170-2.

Islam

The infinitive of the fourth form of the Arabic triliteral root *s-l-m* meaning "to submit," "to surrender," it also designates the monotheistic faith (q.v.) and practice observed by the followers of Muḥammad and exhorted by the Qurʾān.

Preliminary considerations

To restrict the notion of *islām* to that which emerges for the first time within the qurʾānic pronouncements, it is necessary to be clear about the problems that this limitation implies. It is misleading to gather and analyse all the verses that contain the forms *islām* or *muslim(ūn)* in an effort to arrive at an "objective" definition then deemed adequate to convey a qurʾānic Islam which can impose itself upon believers and researchers as the ultimate and obligatory referent. Particularly is this so if that definition is used to measure and to judge the changes and additions introduced over time in diverse historical and socio-cultural contexts. W.C. Smith *(Meaning and end)* already lamented the insufficiency of this exercise using the lens of a historian of religions who was interested in the identification of the origin and durable spiritual level which constitute the specific valence of each religion. Smith used this identification to distinguish the changing functions — positive and negative — assigned by the social actors to that which they universally call their religion. About twenty-five years ago, a student of Smith's explored, in a finely detailed study, the semantic shifts which the term *islām* has undergone over many centuries of exegetical amplification (J. Smith, *Historical and semantic*). This work complements the earlier investigations of Lidzbarski (Salām und islām), Künstlinger ('Islām,' 'muslim,' 'aslama' im Kurān), Ringgren *(Islam, ʿaslama and Muslim),* Robson ('Islam' as a term), Izutsu *(Ethico-religious concepts in the Qurʾān),* and W.C. Smith himself (Historical development).

Using careful philological analysis it should be possible to follow already at the qurʾānic stage the progressive elaboration of the notion of *islām* according to the chronological order of the verses in their original contexts (see CHRONOLOGY AND THE QURʾĀN; FORM AND STRUCTURE OF THE QURʾĀN). Yet in the absence of complete accord about the chronological classifications proposed for the sūras and *a fortiori* for the verses, one may not employ this perspective except for the rare cases where there are relatively reliable and coherent indices upon which to base such judgments. One knows how the collective concurrent memories were construed during the first Islamic centuries and how this mythological and ideological appropriation informed what was to become the paradigm of the earthly history and the salvation history of the Muslim community (*umma,* see COMMUNITY AND SOCIETY IN THE QURʾĀN; HISTORY AND THE QURʾĀN). This historical-mythical paradigm still operates at the beginning of the twenty-first century with an ideological force that is sustained by the modern media. The historian needs, therefore, to employ strategies of intervention in order to disentangle the mythical, ideological and historical strands in the documentation ascribed to the period of the emergence and formation of that which continues to be universally and indiscriminately termed "Islam."

It is not clear whether academic historians see anything more than the satisfaction of a scientific curiosity when they put themselves to the task of defining the distinctive traits of *islām* within the strict limits of the qurʾānic corpus (see CONTEMPORARY CRITICAL PRACTICES AND THE QURʾĀN). Against this attitude, there is that of traditionalist Muslim theologians who use the foundational text to shore up the doctrinal constructions necessary to reinforce the orthodoxy demanded of the believers (see THEOLOGY AND THE QURʾĀN; EXEGESIS OF THE QURʾĀN: CLASSICAL AND MEDIEVAL; EXEGESIS OF THE QURʾĀN: EARLY MODERN AND CONTEMPORARY). There is, however, a third position which seeks to open a new space of intelligibility within the reality of lived religion by circumventing the epistemological postulations implicit in the two preceding approaches. In the case of Islam, as in Catholic and Protestant theology, the "scientific" and the confessional perspectives are no longer adequate for defining the problematics and the themes favorable to an interactive research (cf. *Le dictionnaire de théologie*). From this third perspective, it suffices to establish that what can be called the qurʾānic stage, the instantiation of a new religion, is a complex historical process engaging simultaneously social, political (see POLITICS AND THE QURʾĀN), cultural, and normative factors. These are entangled with ritual, customs, ethics, familial structures (see FAMILY; TRIBES AND CLANS; KINSHIP), competing structures of the imagination and the collective interactive memory of such entities as Jews, Christians, Sabians (q.v.), polytheists (frequently termed "pagans"), and all cultural groups of the ancient Near East (see JEWS AND JUDAISM; CHRISTIANS AND CHRISTIANITY; POLYTHEISM AND ATHEISM; BELIEF AND UNBELIEF; PRE-ISLAMIC ARABIA AND THE QURʾĀN). All these modes and manifestations of the historical existence of such social groups in Arabia are not only present in the qurʾānic discourse but transformed. They have been sublimated, uprooted from their local conditions to constitute an "existential paradigm" of the human condition. Divested of its particularity, this qurʾānic paradigm is capable of producing and informing individual and collective existence within the most diverse cultural and historical contexts. As with the biblical discourse of the Hebrew Bible and the New Testament, the qurʾānic discourse generates the results obtained by combining mechanisms for precise linguistic articulation of the meaning with the diverse effects of changing historical situations. In both textual corpora the narrative, rhetorical, stylistic and literary processes are so complex and highly elaborated that recent methods of discourse analysis have yet to prove sufficient for the task of clarifying their interaction. These approaches — to say nothing of the classical theories of the inimitability (q.v.; *iʿjāz*) of the Qurʾān — have yet to explain adequately the genesis, the effects and the place of the Qurʾān within linguistic and semiotic usages (see SEMIOTICS AND NATURE IN THE QURʾĀN; LANGUAGE OF THE QURʾĀN).

The term "paradigm" is an appropriate designation for its qurʾānic manifestation because this manifestation became inscribed in a long history where the homologous paradigms of Judaism, Christianity, Zoroastrianism (see MAGIANS), and Manichaeism had already assumed a place within the cultural and religious space of the Mediterranean. The term "existential paradigm" is more natural and workable than that of "religion," for it frees the intellectual task from the conceptual constraint imposed by those systems of belief and nonbelief which shape in a subtle fashion, often unconsciously, the interpretation of the facts within each living religious tradition. Further, this terminology allows the inclusion within the arena of critical assessment of all the inherited systems, paradigms or models of historical action produced by modern reason in its struggle to liberate itself from the oppressive dogmatics of traditional institutional religions. To follow the developments within the qurʾānic discourse of the social and linguistic construction of the categories of "believers" and "nonbelievers," as these relate to what would be called "Islam," is to establish the historicity of the new religion. It is to do this on the basis of the first pronouncements of that which the believing tradition would theorize under the name of "Word of God" (q.v.), revealed through Muḥammad b. ʿAbdallāh, imposing himself progressively by his action and by the qurʾānic discourse, as the Prophet (*al-nabī*, see PROPHETS AND PROPHETHOOD) and messenger (q.v.; *rasūl*) of God. That is to say that the initial choice of the historical method to define Islam on strictly qurʾānic grounds is not innocent. It proceeds from a methodological and epistemological premise characteristic of modern reason and introduces a break with the axial vision, insisting that the entire qurʾānic discourse instilled the properly believing attitude in the heart (q.v.) of the first listeners. For all subsequent generations this Qurʾān-centric understanding of "Islam" creates the drama of the decision — to accept or reject the covenant of divine alliance (*mīthāq*, see CONTRACTS AND ALLIANCES) — on which would depend the realization of the entire individual existence of the Muslim person. Without having the benefit, as did western Christianity, of new possibilities for the emancipation of the human condition such as those opened by the existential paradigm constructed by modernity or by a more efficacious alternative than that presented by the traditional religions, Muslims continue to live the drama of that decision within a deadly violence where, additionally, the "unthinkable and unthought" of the two opposing paradigms are interpreted as mutually exclusive.

The theologies, the philosophies, and the still hesitant and partial problematics of the social sciences have begun to take charge of the historical drama of the human condition despite being complicated by the alternative opened by modernity: the choice is no longer simply between passing earthly existence in absolute fidelity to the debt of signification forged within the eternal covenant contracted with a living, merciful God and savior (or a wise founder like Buddha), or the radical refusal of that pact. It is not only between the fallibility of reason and the solitude of a destiny beyond the horizon of hope. Within the thought world of modernity, for many people God has become a useless hypothesis. This version of modernity insists that humans take responsibility for their destiny and substitutes an image of progress by science for the image of eternal salvation guaranteed by a loving and compassionate God.

Qurʾānic Islam

In a book issued in 1972 (*The spiritual background of early Islam. Studies in early Arab concepts*), M.M. Bravmann brought together fourteen articles which he had published between 1945 and 1971. With regard to the domain of Islamic studies, this work, as well as that cited earlier, is very representative of the epistemological attitude that governed historical writing in Europe and North America from the nineteenth century until the 1970s. The author does his utmost to rediscover the conceptual contents of the Qurʾān, namely terms like *islām*, *īmān* (see FAITH), *dīn* (see RELIGION), *dunyā* (see WORLD), *sunna* (q.v.), *sīra* (see SĪRA AND THE QURʾĀN), *ʿilm* (see KNOWLEDGE AND LEARNING), *bayʿa* (see OATHS AND

PLEDGES), etc., in the period of emerging Islam. Investigation of the etymologies of a semantically rich vocabulary is very useful as long as one does not content oneself with deceptive substrata. The danger of such research lies in the tendency to rest content with partial or fossilized meanings that are only poorly related to the living continuation of a no-longer extant language and society. This type of erudition has made progress, however, as can be illustrated with reference to the rich works of M.J. Kister and his followers on the transition from "*jāhiliyya* (see AGE OF IGNORANCE) to Islām." In this latter body of work one finds an orientation towards a social, political and cultural history that could finally make a historical-anthropological reading of the Qurʾān possible. (See also my remarks on the recent work of J. Chabbi, *Le seigneur des tribus. L'islam de Mahomet,* Paris 1997 in the article CONTEMPORARY CRITICAL PRACTICES AND THE QURʾĀN.) Aiming at such an objective is, in itself, a sign of immense progress toward a critical approach that can explain not only a nascent religion and its generative terminology but also the moment and the paradigm of human creativity in its struggle for conceptual emancipation.

Confining oneself to an examination of the occurrences of the word *islām* or *muslim* within the strict limits of the qurʾānic corpus avoids neither the fallibility of that exercise itself nor the methodological quandaries inherent in every quest for origins. This is even more the case when the mind remains focused on a definition of the religion that emerged subsequent to the qurʾānic corpus and its society and in which the paradigms forged within the anthropological scope were redefined. I have explained that the "closed official corpus" of the canonical codex (*muṣḥaf,* q.v.) poses methodological problems that are different from those linked to qurʾānic discourse at the time of its first oral enunciation (see COLLECTION OF THE QURʾĀN; CODICES OF THE QURʾĀN; ORALITY). Because it has never respected this differentiation, the philological exploitation of the "closed official corpus" concurs, though with greater care for chronological constraints, with the cognitive attitude of traditional Muslim exegesis *(tafsīr al-Qurʾān bi-l-Qurʾān).*

M.M. Bravmann, for example, assures us that the word *islām* has meant confronting death (see DEATH AND THE DEAD), sacrificing one's life for a higher goal and thus, by extension, defending one's honor (q.v.), and giving oneself unconditionally to God (see PATH OR WAY; JIHĀD). These two motivations cannot be treated on the same level but must be interrelated. More complexly, then, the term means dying for the honor *(ʿirḍ)* of the clan because the mechanical solidarity in a command group appears in the Qurʾān both as a springboard from which to substitute the attachment to the clan with the quest for God and as an obstacle to this substitution.

Q 49:14 and 17 unveil this deceptive use of a semantic equation with the confrontation of death by opposing the word *islām,* which is stigmatized as an outward, tactical and revocable adherence to the noble cause of God and his messenger, to the word *īmān,* which signifies a sincere and definitive conversion of the heart to a cause that is differentiated from that of the clan (see BELIEF AND UNBELIEF; HYPOCRITES AND HYPOCRISY). This is why the expression "he submitted his face (q.v.) to God" *(aslama wajhahu lillāhi)* recurs often as a summons to give one's self only to God. The verb "to submit" *(aslama)* occurs twenty-two times; *muslim,* pl. *muslimūn* a total of forty-two times, including one instance of the dual and two attestations of the feminine plural, *muslimāt,* to designate female "Muslims"; *islām* appears seven times. The contrast with the attestations of the various derivatives of the root letters *ʾ-m-n,* signifying "belief, faith," is striking: *īmān* (seventeen times), *āmanū* (258), *muʾminūn* (166, of which nineteen are the feminine plural, *muʾmināt*). Islam as the sacrifice of one's life is still demanded, as those who avoid going into combat are denounced according to a code of honor that opposes courage (q.v.), valiancy and the wish to die as a hero (see MARTYR) to cowardice, treason, and fleeing from battle (*qaʿada,* see WAR; EXPEDITIONS AND BATTLES; VIRTUES AND VICES).

One will note that these clear-cut definitions of *islām* and *īmān,* as well as of the conditions of the endeavor *(jihād)* for God, appear in two late sūras: in Q 49, which is classified as the 106th in the chronological order of revelation, and Q 9, classified as the 113th. The interrelation of the two concepts during the whole period of the revelation depended on the changing contexts and protagonists in Mecca (q.v.) and Medina (q.v.). In Mecca, where Muḥammad faced opposition from the polytheists, defined as those who "associated" anything with the one God *(mushrikūn),* it was necessary to stress the belief in a single God; facing the Jewish adversaries in Medina *(al-rabbāniyyūn),* however, it was important to construct a founding story for the new religious community in order to insert it into the biblical series of revelations (see SCRIPTURE AND THE QURʾĀN) that were made to Abraham (q.v.), to Moses (q.v.), and to Jesus (q.v.) son of Mary (q.v.; see also OPPOSITION TO MUḤAMMAD). It is in this Islamic re-appropriation of these great religious figures that the emerging religion takes on the dimension of a religious space for a community that has slowly become differentiated from other rival communities engaged in a mimetic combat over the control of the same symbolic capital. For the *mushrikūn,* this symbolic capital is centered on the Meccan pantheon while for Jews and Christians it is focused on the previous biblical revelations. In order to reshape the figure of Abraham, the Qurʾān uses the term *millat Ibrāhīm* rather than the word *islām,* whose signification is still in the course of construction. *Milla* refers to a group whose members necessarily share the same beliefs. This term will later be reused to designate the various confessional communities in the Ottoman Empire. In Q 3:67, Abraham is linked to the pure religion, Ḥanīfism (see ḤANĪF), that is devoid of any deviation: "Abraham was neither a Jew nor a Christian, but a *ḥanīf muslim.*" Within this context in which a corrected and redressed version (quite different from the "altered" versions of the Christians and the Jews) of the history of the "People of the Book" (q.v.; see also BOOK) is constructed, the word *muslim* cannot be translated simply as "Muslim" in the now common meaning of the word, since it does not yet have a social and doctrinal basis. Its meaning in this passage is indeed a reference to that internal submission of faith which is contracted in the alliance *(mīthāq)* with God. In the frequently cited verses "religion, in the eye of God, is Islam" (Q 3:19); or "The will to profess a religion other than Islam will not be accepted" (Q 3:85), it is necessary to preserve the original, fundamental meaning of *islām* as an internalized religious attitude that is well symbolized by the conduct of the qurʾānic Abraham. To consecrate at this stage the equivalence of the Abrahamic *islām* with that which the sciences and institutions termed Islamic would later construe, is to relegate to the "unthinkable" all of the problems associated with the passage from the human experience of the divine (*"l'expérience humaine du divin,"* title of a work of M. Meslin) to the institutionalized, ritualized, religious orthodoxy of the "managers of the sacred" *(gestionnaires du sacré).* In order to avoid this long leap within the ideological instrumentalization of the religious reality, it is preferable to speak of the religion emerging at the level of the qurʾānic discourse in its initial mode of enunciation.

There is no room here to evaluate the role of the normative pronouncements which, already in the qurʾānic discourse, engage the experience of the divine with the trajectory of ritualization, of the sacralizing institution (see RITUAL AND THE QURʾĀN). Rather, I signal the importance of analyzing the process by which, at the level of the "closed official corpus," that institutionalization comes to function as the conceptualization of Islam that is exploited by the jurists (see LAW AND THE QURʾĀN), the theolgians, the exegetes, the mystics (see ṢŪFISM AND THE QURʾĀN) and all varieties of social actors.

It is worth remembering that, at the stage of its oral enunciation, the qurʾānic discourse attaches more importance to recitations of the foundation of a new collective memory, one that is prepared to receive a system of beliefs and of non-beliefs that is both similar to and differentiated from those of competing communities, than to the doctrinal development of orthodoxy. This was done by later generations. The literary composition of these stories has exerted a decisive semantic influence on Arabic vocabulary (see ARABIC LANGUAGE; GRAMMAR AND THE QURʾĀN). In its enhanced contents the language was fortified to support the new system of values and recast as a language that bears an earthly history which is entirely inscribed within the horizon of a history of salvation (q.v.) already familiar to the People of the Book. One should also bear in mind that these founding stories, as well as the indeterminate state of the conceptual tools within the qurʾānic stage, make possible many starting points for symbolic, semantic, conceptual and, finally, existential codes. It is necessary to verify, therefore, the degree of spiritual, ethical, social, juridical and political relevance for this coding that future actors will "choose," or which will be imposed upon diverse groups who constitute themselves as "interpretive communities." This type of investigation has been neither conceived nor adopted by the historians, the exegetes or the contemporary theologians of critical modernity. One can, *a fortiori,* absolve the medieval jurists of blame for not integrating this task, which was unthinkable to them, into their claim to root *(taʾṣīl)* legal qualifications *(aḥkām)* in the Word of God, which would transform profane and contingent behavior into the categories of licit or illicit works compatible with the notion of a final judgment (see LAST JUDGMENT; GOOD DEEDS; EVIL DEEDS; LAWFUL AND UNLAWFUL; RECORD OF HUMAN ACTIONS). Now, however, there is enough of the conceptual diversity necessary for the radicalization of a critique of Islamic reason that can be undertaken within a broader and more historically, sociologically and anthropologically sensitive perspective.

M. Arkoun

Bibliography

M. Arkoun, *Lectures du Coran,* Paris 1982; id., *Pour une critique de la raison islamique,* Paris 1984; id., *Rethinking Islam. Common questions, uncommon answers,* trans. and ed. R.D. Lee, Boulder 1994; H. Berg (ed.), *Islamic origins reconsidered,* special issue of *Method and theory in the study of religion* 9 (1997); F. Bowie, *The anthropology of religion,* Oxford 2000; M.M. Bravmann, *The spiritual background of early Islam. Studies in early Arab concepts,* Leiden 1972; J. Chabbi, *Le seigneur des tribus. L'Islam de Mahomet,* Paris 1997; J. van Ess, *TG;* id., Verbal inspiration? Language and revelation in classical Islamic theology, in Wild, *Text,* 180-1; P. Gisel, *La théologie face aux sciences religieuses,* Geneva 1999; id. and P. Evrard (eds.),

La théologie en postmodernité, Geneva 1996; Graham, *Beyond;* G.R. Hawting, *The idea of idolatry and the emergence of Islam. From polemic to history,* Cambridge 1999; id. and Shareef (eds.), *Approaches;* T. Izutsu, *Ethico-religious concepts in the Qurʾān,* Montreal 1966; M.J. Kister, *Society and religion from Jahiliyya to Islam,* Brookfield, VT 1990; D. Künstlinger, 'Islām,' 'muslim,' 'aslama' im Kurān, in *Rocznik Orjentalistyczny* 11 (1935), 128-37; M. Lecker, *Muslims, Jews and pagans. Studies on early Islamic Medina,* Leiden 1995; M. Lidzbarski, Salām und islām, in *ZS* 1 (1922), 85-96; H. Ringgren, *Islam, ʿaslama and Muslim,* Uppsala 1949; Rippin, *Approaches;* id. (ed.), *The Qurʾān. Formative interpretation,* Brookfield, VT 1999; N. Robinson, *Discovering the Qurʾān. A contemporary approach to a veiled text,* London 1996; J. Robson, 'Islam' as a term, in *MW* 44 (1954), 101-9; M. Shaḥrūr, *al-Kitāb wa-l-Qurʾān,* Damascus 1990; J. Smith, *An historical and semantic study of the term 'islām' as seen in a sequence of Qurʾān commentaries,* Missoula, MT 1975; W.C. Smith, The historical development in Islam of the concept of Islam as an historical development, in B. Lewis and P.M. Holt (eds.), *Historians of the Middle East,* London 1962; id., *Meaning and end of religion,* New York 1963; C. Versteegh, *Arabic grammar and Qurʾānic exegesis in early Islam,* Leiden 1993; Wansbrough, *QS;* A.T. Welch, al-Ḳurʾān, in *EI²,* v, 400-29; Wild, *Text.*

Isma see IMPECCABILITY

Ismāʿīlīs see SHĪʿISM AND THE QURʾĀN

Isrāʾ see ASCENSION; AQṢĀ MOSQUE

Israel

Ancestor of the people of Israel (Isrāʾīl), whose name appears most frequently in the Qurʾān within the title "Children of Israel" (q.v.; Banū Isrāʾīl). Only in two places does it occur separately (Q 3:93; 19:58). The commentators identify Israel with Jacob (q.v.; Yaʿqūb), the son of Isaac (q.v.; Isḥāq).

Q 3:93, which deals with Jewish dietary restrictions (see JEWS AND JUDAISM), makes allusion to a specific event in Israel's life. It is stated here that all food was lawful (see LAWFUL AND UNLAWFUL) to the Children of Israel save what Israel forbade for himself before the Torah (q.v.) was sent down. The commentators understood the verse in a polemical context saying that it proved to the Jews of Muḥammad's time that their dietary law was not the one which all believers should follow (see FOOD AND DRINK; FORBIDDEN). The exegetes disagree, however, about the kind of food Israel forbade, and whether or not this is endorsed in the Torah of Moses (q.v.). Some say that Israel's forbidden food is not forbidden in the Torah, and that the Children of Israel only avoid it in accordance with the individual precedent of Israel. Others say that God has forbidden in the Torah the same food which Israel forbade, but only to punish the Children of Israel for their sins, as is also stated elsewhere in the Qurʾān (Q 4:160; 6:146). This means that Israel's dietary restrictions are not incumbent on the rest of the believers, i.e. the Muslims.

As for Israel's forbidden food, some say that it was the sinew of the vein, which used to hurt Israel during the nights, and he decided to abstain from it in hope that God would cure him. Others say that he abandoned for that purpose his most favorite meal, i.e. the meat and milk of camels. A less current interpretation (Ibn Abī Ḥātim al-Rāzī, *Tafsīr,* iii, no. 3819) relates that he forbade the appendage of the liver and the two kidneys and the fat that is upon them, save what is carried on the back. These were the parts that had to be burned as an offering to God. This is a verbatim representation of a biblical sacrificial rite (e.g. *Exod* 29:13, 22, etc.), combined with the qurʾānic version of Jewish dietary law (Q 6:146). The mention of the "sinew of the vein" *(ḥirq al-nasā)* points to the biblical origin of Q 3:93, which is Genesis 32:25-33. This is the story of the changing of Jacob's name to Israel following Jacob's nocturnal wrestling with the angel, during which the hollow of his thigh was touched by the angel in the sinew of the vein. For this reason the Children of Israel do not eat the sinew of the vein. Some of the Islamic traditions provide a detailed Arabic version of the story.

As for Israel's decision to forbid the food for himself, some commentators say that it was based on his own individual judgment *(ijtihād)*, which prophets are allowed to have (see PROPHETS AND PROPHETHOOD).

Uri Rubin

Bibliography
Bukhārī, *Ṣaḥīḥ*, ed. Krehl, 216-7; Ibn Abī Ḥātim al-Rāzī, Abū Muḥammad Muḥammad b. Idrīs, *Tafsīr al-Qurʾān al-ʿaẓīm*, ed. A.M. al-Ṭayyib, 10 vols., Riyadh 1997, iii, 704-6; Ṭabarī, *Tafsīr*, ed. Shākir, vii, 7-16.

Ithnā ʿAsharīs see SHĪʿISM AND THE QURʾĀN